MW01492862

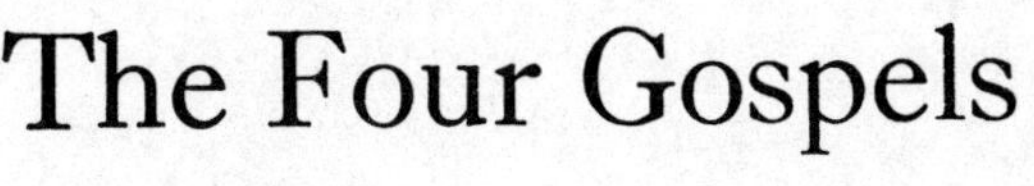

The Four Gospels

The Four Gospels

A COMMENTARY,
CRITICAL, EXPERIMENTAL
AND PRACTICAL

David Brown

THE BANNER OF TRUTH TRUST

THE BANNER OF TRUTH TRUST
3 *Murrayfield Road, Edinburgh* EH12 6EL
PO Box 621, *Carlisle, Pennsylvania* 17013, USA

*

This volume forms part of the
Jamieson, Fausset and Brown Commentary
on the whole Bible, first published 1864
First Banner of Truth Trust edition 1969
Reprinted 1976
Reprinted 1993
ISBN 0 85151 016 7

*

Printed in Great Britain
at the Bath Press, Avon

INTRODUCTION TO THE GOSPELS.

A THOROUGHLY critical Introduction to the Gospels is rather for a separate Treatise than for the Preface to such a Volume as this. Happily, if amongst the biblical works with which our language is now enriched one complete and satisfactory Treatise on this subject, adapted to the present state of research and of thought, is scarcely yet within the reach of the mere English reader, the materials for it are abundant.

In what follows we can do little more than indicate the proper line of investigation, state briefly the leading facts on the different branches of the subject, and draw the conclusions which these justify and demand.

When we enter on a critical examination of any work of ancient literature, we have first to discover its *value;* next, to ascertain its *integrity,* or the purity in which its text has come down to us; and finally, to determine its *meaning.* Applying this to the Four Gospels, our first inquiries must be *Apologetical;* our second *Critical;* our third *Exegetical.*

By the Value of any ancient book we mean both its literary and its intrinsic value: that is to say, its genuineness on the one hand, and on the other, its intrinsic worth. A work is 'genuine' when it is the production of the person it is ascribed to, or, if it be anonymous, when it belongs to the period in which it professes to have been written, and has been composed in the circumstances alleged or presumed. When it is otherwise, it is 'spurious,' or a forgery. Of this latter nature are some treatises once ascribed to Plato, for example, and several of the Apocryphal books both of the Old and New Testaments. But some spurious works may possess considerable intrinsic worth —such as the Apocryphal books of Wisdom and Ecclesiasticus (as it is called) —while there are hundreds of genuine works, in every branch of literature, which are altogether worthless. It will be necessary, therefore, to inquire into the value, in both senses, of our Four Gospels. And this inquiry must be conducted on the same general principles as an inquiry into the value of any other literary production. But before we begin, let us well understand what is at stake.

The Fourfold Gospel is the central portion of Divine Revelation. Into it, as a Reservoir, all the foregoing revelations pour their full tide, and out of it, as a Fountain, flow all subsequent revelations. In other parts of Scripture we hear Christ by the hearing of the ear; but here our eye seeth Him. Elsewhere we see Him through a glass darkly; but here, face to face. The orthodox Fathers of the Church well understood this peculiar feature of the

Gospels, and expressed it emphatically by their usages—some of them questionable, others almost childish. Nor did the heretical sects differ from them in this; the best proof of which is, that nearly all the heresies of the first four or five centuries turned upon the Person of Christ as represented in the Gospels. As to the heathen enemies of Christianity, their determined opposition was directed against the facts regarding Christ recorded in the Gospels. And it is the same still. The battle of Christianity, and with it of all Revealed Religion, must be fought on the field of the Fourfold Gospel. If its Credibility and Divine Authority cannot be made good—if we must give way to some who would despoil us of its miracles, or to others who, under the insidious name of 'the higher criticism,' would weaken its historical claims—all Christianity is undermined, and will sooner or later dissolve in our hands. But so long as the Gospels maintain their place in the enlightened convictions of the Church, as the Divine record of God manifest in the flesh, believers, reassured, will put to flight the armies of the aliens.

'I will arrange,' says *Michaelis,* who may be called the father of the modern criticism of the New Testament, whose learning and research were vast and various, and whose tendencies, certainly, were in the direction rather of scepticism than of credulity—'I will arrange under their several heads the reasons which may induce a critic to suspect a work to be spurious:—

'1. When doubts have been made from its first appearance in the world whether it proceeded from the author to whom it is ascribed. 2. When the immediate friends of the pretended author, who were able to decide upon the subject, have denied it to be his production. 3. When a long series of years has elapsed after his death, in which the book was unknown, and in which it must unavoidably have been mentioned and quoted had it really existed. 4. When the style is different from that of his other writings, or, in case no other remain, different from that which might reasonably be expected. 5. When events are recorded which happened later than the time of the pretended author. 6. When opinions are advanced which contradict those he is known to maintain in his other writings; though this latter argument *alone* leads to no positive conclusion'—for reasons which need not be here quoted.* 'Now, of all these grounds for denying a work to be genuine, not one,' adds this author, 'can be applied with justice to the New Testament.' But we must not take this upon his or any man's testimony. We must make it good for ourselves. What, then, are the facts of this case?

In one of the most important chapters of his 'Ecclesiastical History'† *Eusebius,* who wrote in the fourth century, reports the judgment of the Christian Church, from the beginning up to his time, on the books of the New Testament which claimed to be canonical. And as his testimony on such matters of fact is of the utmost weight, let us, in the first place, listen to it.‡ He divides

* Introd., vol. i. page 27. † E. H., iii. 25.

‡ We the rather call attention to this important testimony, because, from an incidental but very

all the books claiming to be canonical writings of the New Testament into three classes:

The *acknowledged* (Τὰ ὁμολογούμενα),

The *disputed* (Τὰ ἀντιλεγόμενα),

The *spurious* (Τὰ νόθα).

The first of these divisions embraces no fewer than *twenty-one* out of the *twenty-seven* books of the New Testament, or four-fifths of the whole collection. Of these twenty-one books Eusebius testifies that they had all along been received in the Christian Church, without any dispute, as canonical books of the New Testament. Of the remaining six—on what grounds, to what extent, and with what justice they were 'disputed'—we shall speak when we come to them in the Commentary. But what we wish here to mention is that, in the list of the twenty-one undisputed, always and universally acknowledged books, the first place is assigned to those which, by way of distinction from all the rest, Eusebius styles '*The Holy Quaternion of the Gospels.*' *

Important, however, as this testimony is, we cannot allow it to decide the question. What, we have still to ask, are the facts of the case? The more we investigate these, the more evident will it appear that the Genuineness of the Four Gospels is attested by a mass of evidence, external and internal, altogether unparalleled and quite overpowering. No work of classical antiquity, even the most undoubted, is half so well attested, or can lay claim, one might say, to a tithe of the evidence which the Gospels possess.

It will greatly facilitate our inquiries to bear in mind the following fact: 'It is,' to use the words of Olshausen, 'wholly a peculiar circumstance in the history of the Gospels, and one which goes a great way to sustain their genuineness, that *we nowhere find, in any writer of any part of the ancient world, any indication that only a single one of the four Gospels was in use,*

interesting fact, the testimony of any intelligent and impartial historian writing when he did was of far more value than it would have been in an earlier age. In the last of the Pagan persecutions, under Diocletian (which burst forth in the year 303), an order was issued—for the first time since Christianity had been persecuted at all—'that the Scriptures should be destroyed by fire.' This order was instigated by a bitter antagonist of the Gospel, who well knew that so long as the sacred writings of the Christians remained Christianity would continue to live, and the Church, though exterminated, would spring up afresh. What was the effect? While many preferred death to the surrender of their dearest treasures, others (who were called *traditores*), unable to face the consequences of resisting, yielded them up. But as some of the proconsuls, anxious to save the Christians, were willing to seize any books which they might resign into their hands in place of the New Testament, some gave them the writings of heretics, and those reckoned among the 'spurious' writings of the New Testament; and as the 'traditors' of the canonical books were subjected to severe ecclesiastical discipline, while these latter were subjected to none at all, the question was thus raised, *as it had never been before*—it being now a matter of life and death—'What are the Genuine Scriptures of the New Testament?' Certain it is that this whole question, by the time of Eusebius—that is, by the end of the third and beginning of the fourth century—had assumed a more scientific form than it had ever done before. Not that the conclusions then arrived at differed from the beliefs of the previous age—the reverse was the case—but that what had all along been held by the Church with little definite expression was now put with the precision which we observe in the chapter of Eusebius above referred to.

* Ἡ ἁγία τῶν εὐαγγελίων τετρακτύς.

*or ever known to exist separately. All possessed the entire collection of the four Gospels.'** Hence the current name by which they were known, as one work —'THE GOSPEL.' †

Ascending upwards to the age of the apostles, it is needless to begin so late as the age of *Councils.* It is enough here to say that in the very first General Council which was held under Constantine—that of Nicæa (A. D. 325)—though no catalogue of the books of Scripture was drawn up, because this was no subject of dispute, the Gospels were referred to on both sides of the Arian controversy, as they were by all the orthodox Fathers of that age who wrote against the Arian heresy, as of undisputed canonical and divine authority. But passing from this, the external evidence for the genuineness of the Gospels may be ranged under the four following heads:—

FIRST, The evidence of the ANCIENT VERSIONS, of which it is enough here to notice the two earliest and most venerable: The original SYRIAC (commonly called the *Peshito*) and the Old LATIN (which used to be called the *Itala*, or the *Italic*); the one prepared for the use of the Oriental portion of the Christian community; the other for the use of the Latin-speaking Christians of North Africa, and generally of the West. Whatever differences of opinion exist among critics as to the precise age of these venerable Versions of the New Testament, it is almost unanimously agreed that they both belong either to the latter half of the second century or the beginning of the third. And if so, it is obvious that the books of the New Testament which are found in those Versions must have been familiar to both the Eastern and the Western Churches, and been recognized by them, *long before those Versions were made*— which carries us back to a period not much later than the death of the Apostle John. Well, in both those earliest Versions the Four Gospels, it is almost unnecessary to say, occupy the first place.

SECOND, The evidence of individual CHRISTIAN WRITERS, both *orthodox* and *heretical.* Of the former we name the following:—

1. *Origen* (A. D. 184 or 185-253): of Egyptian birth; the greatest scholar and the first thoroughly biblical critic that the Church produced. He may be said to have spent his life in biblical inquiries; he examined MSS., observed, compared, and weighed various readings; he defended Christianity against acute enemies, and explained it to Christians themselves, and was of too independent a mind not to form his own judgment and speak out his convictions on the books of the New Testament. Well, not only did this great Father publish commentaries on the Gospels, as on other parts of Scripture, but he has in several of his extant writings given lists of the canonical Scriptures, in all of which the Four Gospels stand first among the books of the New Testament. And never does he drop a word from which it could be inferred that a doubt existed, either then or at any former period, as to the genuine and canonical character of those books.

2. *Tertullian* (as early at least as about A. D. 160-220): born at Carthage;

* 'Commentary on the Gospels' Introd. (*Clark*).

† Τὸ εὐαγγέλιον.

the most ancient of the Latin Fathers; the first great light of the African Church, and the most original, forcible, and, in his own peculiar style, the most eloquent of the Latin Fathers, until Augustin rose to eclipse all others. In the fourth of his books against the heretic Marcion—who rejected all the Gospels but that of Luke, and mutilated even that—he rests his whole case upon the notorious fact that not only Luke, entire as we have it, but the other three Gospels of Matthew, Mark, and John, had the unbroken testimony of all the churches either founded by the apostles or in ecclesiastical fellowship with them,—in other words, of the whole catholic Church; and so confident is he that an appeal on this subject to all the churches would be at once responded to, that he narrows the whole question to this one—of known and undeniable fact.* Such statements, so near the apostolic age, cannot but be felt to possess immense weight.

3. *Clement* of Alexandria (nearly contemporary with Tertullian): assistant to Pantænus, who, if not the first, was the second head of the celebrated catechetical school of Alexandria—a seminary which, though it seems to have embraced a lower department for the training of catechumens, was chiefly a school of theological teaching; and if it had not St. Mark, according to the tradition, for its founder, was at least of high antiquity. Pantænus and he seem to have taught jointly till 211, when Clement became its head—dying about two years thereafter. Only four of his writings are extant; but these are of great value, partly as illustrating the peculiar type of theological thought which reigned then at Alexandria, and partly for the facts to which they incidentally bear witness. In a fragment of one of his works,† which Eusebius has preserved,‡ he gives the tradition (says Eusebius) regarding the order of the Gospels, derived from the earliest presbyters (which we need not here repeat), and says that John, finally perceiving that all which pertained to the *body* (τὰ σωματικὰ), or the outward life of Christ, had been sufficiently recorded, being invited by his friends, and moved by the Spirit, composed a *spiritual* Gospel (πνευματικὸν εὐαγγέλιον). This testimony to the apostolic antiquity and genuineness of the Gospels is that not only of an early Presbyter but a Divinity teacher, in the highest repute over the entire Church; of one who not only taught according to what had been handed down in the Alexandrian school from the beginning, but had travelled, as he himself tells us, in Greece, Italy, and various parts of the East, studying under superior masters, and weighing the information he received from all sources. And his method of establishing the authority of the Gospels was the same with Tertullian's, asserting nothing on his own judgment—for the age of historical criticism had not then come—but sending us back to the earliest antiquity, giving no hint that there ever had been the least diversity of opinion on the subject.

4. The *Muratorian Fragment* (as it is called): an anonymous Latin fragment on the Canon of the New Testament, so called as having been discovered in the Ambrosian Library at Milan, and first published by Muratori in his 'Antiquities of Mediæval Italy' (1740), who ascribed it to Caius, a well-known Presbyter of the

* Adv. Marc. c. 2 and 5. † Entitled, Ὑποτυπώσεις ('*Outlines*'). ‡ E. H. vi. 14.

Roman Church, about the close of the second century. Though this has been disputed, it is agreed by all who have critically examined the Fragment that it belonged either to the latter part of the second, or at latest the very beginning of the third century.* If we place its composition between the years 160 or 170 and 200, we shall probably be near the truth. The Latin is that of one who hardly knew the elements of the language, and abounds in Greek idioms; confirming his connection with the Roman Church at a time when Greek, not Latin, was used at Rome. Be the writer who he may, he simply states the current view of the Church of his own day regarding the Canon of the New Testament—that is, a century or so after the death of the Apostle John. The half sentence with which the Fragment begins is unintelligible. But we gather from what immediately follows that the writer had begun to enumerate the books of the New Testament, and had just said that of the Four Gospels Matthew and Mark were the first in order; for he immediately adds that 'the third book of the Gospel† is that according to Luke. . . . The fourth of the Gospels is that of John,' &c. After describing, according to the current tradition, how John was induced to undertake this work, the Fragment proceeds to enumerate the other books of the New Testament; and after naming all the 'acknowledged' books (ὁμολογούμενα), it passes straight to the 'spurious' (νόθα), 'which cannot be received into the catholic Church, for it is not fit that gall should be mingled with honey.' ‡ While this writer simply reports the judgment of the Church in his own day—high antiquity certainly—on the books of the New Testament, he drops no hint of any difference of opinion having ever been entertained.

5. *Irenæus*—perhaps the most important witness of all, as being, until Origen appeared, the most textual and expository of the earlier Fathers. He was a disciple of Polycarp, Bishop of Smyrna, and succeeded Pothinus as Bishop of Lyons in the year 177, when that venerable man suffered martyrdom at the age of ninety or upwards. Of his works, only his Five Books 'Against Heresies' are extant, and with the exception of the first book and fragments of the others, these exist only in a Latin Version, which, however, was probably almost contemporary with the original Greek. In his third book (c. 1) occurs an important passage which, besides the Latin version of it, Eusebius has preserved to us in the original Greek. In this passage, while giving an account of each of the Gospels, this disciple of Polycarp, less than a century after the death of the Apostle John, speaks of our four Gospels (and we know them to be ours

* The late venerable Dr. Routh, who, in the second edition of his *Reliquiæ Sacræ*, has printed this Fragment, and appended to it some forty pages of valuable Latin Annotations, is of opinion that if not written soon after the middle of the second century, it must have been at least before its close. This opinion is founded on an allusion which the Fragment makes to Hermas's having 'very recently in our times (*nuperrime temporibus nostris*) written at Rome the book called "The Shepherd," during the Episcopate of his (Hermas's) brother Pius.' Now the date of Pius's Episcopate ranges from 142-157. And though *Hug* has given some ingenious reasons for assigning it a rather later date, even he ascribes it to the beginning of the third century.

† *Evangelii*, τοῦ Εὐαγγελίου.

‡ *Quæ in catholicam ecclesiam recipi non potest* (*possunt*): *fel enim cum melle misceri non congruit.*

because he quotes them so largely and verbally) as not only the genuine productions of two of the apostles and of the constant companions of two other apostles, but as the very teaching of Christ Himself; and this not as an opinion of his own, but as matter of undisputed fact. In another chapter of this same book (c. 11) occurs a grand passage, the original Greek of which has been happily recovered since the date of the early editions of the work. 'Nor,' says this Father, 'can there be more Gospels in number, nor yet fewer than these [four]. For as there are four quarters of the world which we inhabit, and four presiding spirits,* and the Church is diffused over the whole earth, and the pillar and foundation of the Church is the Gospel and the Spirit of life, on the same principle has the Church four pillars, breathing everywhere incorruption, and kindling in men new warmth. Whence it is evident that the Word, the Artificer of all things, who sitteth upon the Cherubim and keepeth all things in order, hath given us the Gospel in a four-fold kind, but informed by one Spirit.'† After giving the symbolic signification of the lion, the calf, the man, and the eagle—which made up the form of the Cherub—he continues: 'And with these harmonize the Gospels, whereon Christ sitteth' [that is, sitteth enthroned, as on the Cherubim, Ezek. i. 26—a grand idea]. After expatiating on the cherubic characteristics of each Gospel, he concludes thus: 'And these things being so, foolish and ignorant, yea, and daring, are all they [heretics] who set aside the idea (or plan) of the Gospel, bringing in either more or fewer Gospels than those we have specified; some, that they may seem to have discovered more than the truth, others, that they may set aside ‡ God's arrangements.'

Now, we make nothing of all that Irenæus says about the figures of the Cherubim; for that part of his statement is no matter of fact, but purely of speculation—ingenious, indeed, and beautiful, and like his conjecture as to "the number of the beast,"§ echoed not only by the ancient Church but by many moderns. But the fact on which Irenæus bases this speculation, which he states as a thing familiarly known and recognized in the Church—that there were not only four harmonious divinely inspired Gospels, neither more nor fewer, but this by a Divine arrangement—this is the important point. And this is stated by one between whom and the Apostle John there was but one link—Polycarp.

6. *Papias*, Bishop of Hierapolis (in Phrygia), and a disciple of John—but whether of the apostle or of a presbyter of that name, is not certain. He flourished somewhere about the year 110, 115, or 116; and he devoted himself chiefly to the collecting of every scrap of tradition which he could pick up regarding our Lord and his apostles. Some of these are silly enough, verifying the well-known opinion of Eusebius regarding him as a man of slender judgment.‖ Yet in matters of fact his testimony is not to be despised, and Eusebius himself (three chapters before) commends him in that respect. His writings are lost;

* *καθολικά, principales*:—probably ἀρχεῖα (*Stieren*).

† ἔδωκεν ἡμῖν τετράμορφον τὸ εὐαγγέλιον, ἑνὶ δὲ πνευματι συνεχόμενον. ‡ ἀθετήσωσιν.

§ "666" = λατεῖνος (Rev. xiii. 18).

‖ σφόδρα γάρ τοι σμικρὸς ὢν τὸν νοῦν. E. H. iii. 39.

but Eusebius, in whose time they were extant, tells us that he made express mention in them of the Evangelists, and how they wrote their Gospels.

Over against this *Hexapla* of express witnesses to the genuineness of the Gospels, we might place another, of those who, without expressly naming them, refer beyond all doubt to them, and are as valid, and some of them no less valuable witnesses, than the former. Ascending up from Irenæus towards the apostolic age, the latest we need quote, and the most important, is—

1. *Justin* Martyr. Though a Greek by descent, his family had settled at Flavia Neapolis, near the site of the ancient Sichem or Sychar, and there he was born (as he tells us in his first Apology, addressed at Rome to Antoninus Pius). Whether he was born so late as 103 (according to Cave), or as early as 89 (as Fabricius and Grabe judge)—some seven years before the last survivor of the apostles died—we cannot be wrong in placing his birth (with *Westcott*) about the close of the first century, or quite near the time of John's decease. His writings are all extant in the original Greek; and what renders his testimony of peculiar importance is the immense quantity of references which he makes to the facts of our Lord's life and teaching—so many and so explicit that even if the Four Gospels had perished we might construct a tolerably accurate summary of their principal contents from Justin's writings. All this, however, he draws from what he calls 'Memoirs of the Apostles,'* which, until the beginning of this century, was always understood to mean our Gospel History. The *Tübingen* critics have tried hard to show that the reference is not to it, but to shorter narratives which were in wide circulation before our Gospels appeared. But this hypothesis has been shown to rest on narrow and untenable grounds, while the positive evidence that it is our Gospels that Justin quotes from is most convincing (though there appear to have been some passages in the copies he used which are not now extant).† Here, then, we have large portions of the Gospels quoted or referred to in the works of a Christian philosopher and martyr, writing less than fifty years after the death of the Apostle John; and as this was probably about twenty years after his conversion to Christianity, and not a hint is given in any of his writings that doubts of the genuineness of the History to which he refers had been known or heard of among Christians, we are thus carried up, in a manner singularly convincing, to the very age of the apostles.

2. The anonymous and very interesting *Epistle to Diognetus:* written in a classical style of Greek, which has with good reason been assigned to the close of Trajan's reign, or about the year 117. This letter leaves no doubt that the writer of it was acquainted with the First and Fourth Gospels, and with the Epistles. We cannot doubt, therefore, that had he had occasion to refer to the other two Gospels, we should have had evidence that he knew them too.

This brings us, in our ascent towards the apostles, to the Apostolic Fathers,

* Ἀπομνημονεύματα τῶν Ἀποστόλων.

† No one has handled this subject more searchingly, candidly, and convincingly than *Westcott*, pages 126-201. If we might venture to obtrude our own judgment, founded on an examination of Justin's writings many years ago, it would be altogether in the same direction.

as they are termed, or such of the disciples and companions of the apostles as have left works behind them. Of these, the latest we name in point of time is—

3. *Polycarp,* Bishop of Smyrna, who heroically suffered martyrdom for his Lord at a great age. 'Eighty and six years have I served Christ,' said he to the Proconsul. Whether we take this to mean simply that he had been a Christian all that time—which, if he suffered under M. Antoninus, about the year 166, would make his conversion to have happened about A. D. 80—or whether we take it to refer to the duration of his services as a minister of Christ, which is not probable, it is beyond doubt that he was a disciple of the Apostle John, and may have seen other apostles and many who saw the Lord Himself; and some have thought that "the angel of the church in Smyrna," to whom our Lord directed the second of His Apocalyptic Epistles (Rev. ii. 8), was no other than this Polycarp. Well, this most venerable and apostolic bishop wrote several letters, only one of which remains—his Epistle to the Philippians—truly a precious relic, supposed by Lardner to have been written about the year 108. It contains more references to the New Testament than was customary in such early writings, though they are interwoven with his own language rather than expressly quoted; and these show beyond doubt that this Asiatic bishop, whose life and ministry were like a prolongation of the beloved disciple's, was familiar with the Gospels and the Epistles of the New Testament. Still ascending upwards, we come to—

4. *Ignatius,* Bishop of Antioch, whose ordination is placed by Eusebius in the year 69, after the death of the Apostles Peter and Paul at Rome. In this case he was doubtless acquainted with some of the apostles; and Chrysostom says he conversed familiarly with them, and was perfectly acquainted with their doctrine. He suffered martyrdom, under Trajan, about the year 107, though, according to others, a few years later. The extant writings of this bishop consist of seven Epistles, though several others, now admitted to be spurious, were ascribed to him. We have nothing to do here with the intensely interesting and much litigated question, whether the longer or the shorter Recension of these Epistles be the genuine one (by which questions of ecclesiastical antiquity are considerably affected, and which, after much learned controversy, the Syriac version of them recently discovered and edited by Dr. Cureton would seem to have set at rest in favour of the shorter). The question for us here is, What testimony does this martyr-bishop, who preceded even Polycarp, bear to the New Testament? The brief answer is, that his references to the Gospels and the Epistles of Paul are numerous and explicit,—a fact the importance of which, in one so very near the apostles themselves, cannot be over-estimated.

5. *Barnabas,* who has left an extant Greek Epistle, though part of it existed only in the Old Latin version, until quite recently, when the indefatigable *Tischendorf* discovered that it existed entire in the precious *Codex Sinaiticus,* which he brought from the convent of St. Catherine, at mount Sinai, and has now given to the world. Whether he was the very Barnabas, "the son of consolation," who was Paul's companion in missionary travel, or another of the same name—about

which even yet there is not entire unanimity among scholars—he certainly belonged to the apostolic age; and as his Epistle gives plain evidence that he was acquainted both with the Gospels and the Epistles of the New Testament, this is one more link in the chain of evidence.

We pass by *Hermas,* who has left a work entitled 'The Shepherd'*—fragments of which are also in the *Codex Sinaiticus*—and whom many have taken to be the same Hermas to whom Paul sends a salutation (Rom. xvi. 14); because there is reason to think he was a somewhat later person, though his testimony is quite as clear as the former; and we are now brought to the most ancient relic of apostolic antiquity, next to the books of the New Testament themselves. We mean the Epistle of—

6. *Clement,* Bishop of Rome. Without doubt he is the very person of whom Paul says, "With Clement also, and other my fellow-labourers, whose names are in the book of life" (Phil. iv. 3). A number of writings have been palmed upon this Clement; but all these are now rejected as spurious—even what is called his Second Epistle to the Corinthians. One Epistle to the Corinthians only is universally regarded as the genuine production of this Clement, written in the name of his own Roman church, to aid in composing the dissensions which had again sprung up in that church. Its date cannot be later than the year 90, while some think it earlier. Well, his references to the Epistles of the New Testament, as well as to the Old Testament, are numerous; and though his subject did not lead him so directly to the Gospels, the three or four passages which bore the most upon his point are quoted, and with such explicitness, as the words of the Lord Jesus, that it is quite clear he had the Gospels before him just as we have them.

Thus have we the unbroken testimony of the orthodox Fathers of the Church to the genuineness of the Gospels,—in two chains of evidence, each consisting of six links, reaching up to the apostles themselves. They are not all that might have been quoted, but they clearly prove—according to the ordinary rules of literary evidence—that those original Documents of the Christian Faith were the genuine productions of their reputed authors. But this evidence is confirmed by—

THIRD, The testimony borne by HERETICAL CHRISTIANS in their controversies with the orthodox. We can afford room here only for two of these, both within the first two centuries.

1. *Tatian:* an Assyrian convert to Christianity, who, on coming to Rome, met with Justin, and who, after the martyrdom of that Christian philosopher (about 164 to 167), continued his work at Rome with some success. Being of a restless turn, he began to introduce novelties, and returning to the East he put himself at the head of a sect called the Encratites, about the year 172. His only remaining work is an Oration against the Gentiles. But we refer merely to one exceedingly interesting fact regarding his literary activity, which is preserved by Eusebius. This Tatian, he says† 'having put together‡ a certain combination and collection of the Gospels,§ I know not how, called this the Diatessaron,‖ which is still in the hands of some.' Now, as Eusebius had

* ὁ Ποίμην. † E. H. iv. 29. ‡ συνθείς.
§ τῶν εὐαγγελίων. ‖ τὸ διὰ τεσσάρων.

just said that Tatian's sect 'made use of the Law, the Prophets, and *the Gospels*,* there can be no doubt that it is our own Four Gospels which he says Tatian wove into one continuous narrative. And that this Diatessaron, though it wanted the genealogies of Matthew and Luke, came immediately into great repute, even in the orthodox Church, is evident from two interesting facts. One, stated by Assemani (Biblioth. Orient.), is, that Ephraem the Syrian, who flourished some centuries after Tatian, issued a commentary on this Diatessaron. The other, and still more interesting fact, is, that in the diocese over which Theodoret presided, in the fifth century, this Diatessaron seems actually to have superseded the Gospels themselves in the public worship of the churches. 'I have met,' says Theodoret, 'with above two hundred of these books, which were in use in our churches,—all which I took away and laid aside in a parcel, placing in their room the Gospels of the four Evangelists.' From this it is perfectly evident, not only that the orthodox Church had the same Four Gospels that we have, little more than seventy years after the death of the Apostle John, but that the heretical sect of which Tatian was the head used the same Gospels; and when Theodoret charges his Diatessaron with leaving out the genealogies, that is only an additional evidence that in other respects it differed not from the orthodox copies.

2. *Marcion*, who preceded Tatian by about thirty years—flourishing somewhere between the years 130 and 144. From a strong antipathy to everything that seemed to savour of Judaism in Christianity, he rejected all the Gospels except Luke's, and cut down even it to suit his own ideas. The Tübingen critics, Baur † and Ritschl, ‡ made a desperate attempt —which Eichhorn had made before them—to show that Marcion's was the original Gospel from which that of Luke was derived. But the torture of internal, and the defiance of all external evidence by which alone this monstrous position was made plausible is now almost universally admitted among the scholars of Germany; and such ingenuity of negative and destructive criticism has met there with the fate which it deserved, although in this country the more critical Unitarians still entrench themselves in it. Extravagant, however, as were Marcion's claims for his own Gospel, he not only gained many followers, but impressed his own critical spirit upon them, and drew forth replies from Irenæus and Tertullian. From these, and fragments of Marcion's own statements, we find that he accused all the apostles except Paul of altering and corrupting the original Gospel. Tertullian challenged Marcion to produce a copy of the original Gospel, with historical attestation of its being handed down as such from the beginning. But he only met this challenge by alleging that as the corruption took place in apostolic times, and was perpetrated by apostles themselves, it was impossible to do so—which, as Tertullian rejoins, was only to throw the blame upon our Lord Himself for choosing such apostles. But besides this, when he begins to assign his reasons

* τοῖς εὐαγγελίοις. † 'Kritische Untersuchungen,' 1847,

‡ 'Das Evang. Marcions u. d., kanonische Evang. Lucas,' 1846.

for rejecting all but his own mutilated Gospel of Luke, we find them purely subjective or doctrinal. In other words, he rejected the rest, not because it was not historically attested, but because it taught what he was not prepared to believe. And thus Marcionism, by its unhistorical and capricious formation of an Evangelical canon of its own (we have not required to advert to the Epistolary part of it), and by its inability, when challenged, to produce such attestations as the true canon possessed, only acted as a foil to show the more clearly on what a firm historical foundation the true canon of the New Testament had all along rested.

FOURTH, If the HEATHEN AUTHORS who attempted to write down Christianity were obliged to admit the genuineness of its sacred books, they must surely be regarded as beyond question. Now there are two such, whose writings were unfortunately destroyed through the mistaken zeal of the Christian emperors, for had they survived they would have been of great service to the Christian cause. We refer to Celsus, who wrote against Christianity in the latter part of the second century, and Porphyry, who lived a century later.

1. *Porphyry* was a man of great critical sagacity, and, living in Syria, was well acquainted with the Old Testament, examined it critically, and made acute objections to the book of Daniel, for instance, on critical and philological grounds So well qualified was he to speak to the genuineness of the New Testament books, that, as Michaelis says, every real friend of Christ would gladly give the works of a pious Father to rescue his writings from the flames. 'He possessed' says this critic, 'every advantage which natural abilities or great political situation could afford for discovering whether the New Testament was a genuine work of the Apostles and Evangelists, or whether it was imposed upon the world after the decease of its pretended authors. But no trace of this suspicion is anywhere to be found, nor did it ever occur to Porphyry to suppose that it was spurious.' And again he asks, 'Is it credible, then, that so sagacious an inquirer could have failed to discover a forgery with respect to the New Testament, had a forgery existed; a discovery which would have given him the completest triumph, by striking a mortal blow at the religion which he attempted to destroy?'*

2. *Celsus's* work against Christianity, entitled 'The True Word,'† was answered by Origen in the middle of the third century; and as he speaks of the author as long since dead, he may have issued it somewhere about the year 180 or 190. Happily, Origen has quoted from it so largely that we can hardly doubt he has preserved at least its more important statements and reasonings. Though he quotes none of the New Testament books by name, no one who studies his references to it can doubt that the Gospels from which he draws his arguments are our Gospels. Indeed, he makes a merit of drawing from the Christians' own writings, and says he has no need to go beyond them, since their own weapons were enough to destroy them. He denominates the Evangelical writings 'The

* Introd. i. pages 42-44.

† Ἀληθὴς Λόγος.

Gospel,'* and refers to circumstances peculiar to each of the Gospels, showing that he had them all four before him. No testimony to the genuineness of those writings can be more satisfactory than this.

This surely is a chain of *external* evidence perfectly irrefragable. Accordingly, up to the beginning of the present century, no doubts as to the genuineness of the Four Gospels had ever arisen within the bosom of the Christian Church. Till then these had all come *from without*—from the dark regions of infidelity and scepticism. But in Germany, during the last thirty years of the last century, a spirit of rationalism had been gradually creeping over its Professors and clergy, which, like the dry rot, penetrated the whole fabric of its theology. This is not the place to write the melancholy workings and products of that spirit. But it is the place to notice one of the directions which it took, and still, in one form or another, takes. The celebrated Eichhorn, the successor of Michaelis at Göttingen, in his 'Introduction to the New Testament' (1804-1814), while admitting the Credibility of the Gospel *History*, maintained that there are no traces of our *Gospels* before the end of the second or beginning of the third century, when, out of the many different and discrepant narratives of this kind which were then in circulation, the Church deemed it necessary to select the most credible and best adapted for general use, and accordingly pitched upon four, which from that time have been acknowledged in the Church as the authentic Gospel History. Why Eichhorn fixed upon the end of the second and beginning of the third century as the time by which the Gospels must have been adopted, will be obvious after what we have stated about Irenæus's testimony to the universal reception of the Gospels in his day.

The most crushing answer to this assertion has been given by Professor Norton.† We could wish to have found room for at least the principal portion of this reply, which is very valuable for its own sake. Suffice it to say, that from the nature of the case the thing supposed is shown to be impossible; that even if it could have happened, or anything like it, there must of necessity have remained some historical traces of it; but that as there are absolutely none, it is against all the principles of historical evidence to assume and affirm it.

Other modes of destroying the credit of the Gospels have been successively and perseveringly tried in Germany, only to be first refuted and then abandoned, or to fall into neglect—such as the theory of Strauss, and that of Baur and the Tübingen school. Schleiermacher's method of handling them—which, while admitting their substantial truth, regards them as well-meaning but in many respects confused and inaccurate efforts to exhibit the Life of Jesus, and out of which it is the part of the 'higher criticism' to construct the *true* History—is more subtle, and has told to too large an extent upon many otherwise sound and able scholars.

On the score of external evidence, then, the Four Gospels stand on an immoveable foundation of continuous, unbroken, historic attestation.

* *τὸ Εὐαγγέλιον.*

† Genuineness, &c., vol. i. pages 19-35.

But mere external evidence for the Genuineness of such books as the Gospels, however unanswerable, is not all that we have a right to expect. The very nature of the case is such that we cannot rest—and, we will venture to say, ought not to rest—satisfied without *internal* evidence also. By this we mean not what are called the Internal Evidences of Christianity, or the Nature of the *Religion* itself. We shall advert to that by and by. But our present point is with the *Books* which constitute the primary Documents of our Faith; and of these we say that, after finding them attested to us from without by irrefragable evidence, we naturally, and even irresistibly, feel impelled to inquire what internal marks of genuineness they present. But here we find it impossible to separate the Genuineness of the books from the Credibility of the History; for, from the nature of the case, the vindication of the writings, as those of their reputed authors, will go far to authenticate what they relate.

Observe, then, first of all, the *language* of these narratives. It is Greek, indeed, but Jewish Greek; bearing the nearest resemblance to the Greek of the Septuagint, yet differing even from it; such Greek, in fact, as (we may say with Michaelis *) could not have been written a hundred and twenty years after Christ. For after that period there were hardly any Jewish converts to Christianity—any, at least, who became preachers or writers; and none but a Jewish convert *could* have written these narratives. Mark the style of the Greek Apostolical Fathers: not one of them writes in such a style as that of the Gospels, nor, we may safely say, could have done so.† Thus, these narratives must of necessity have been written within the three quarters of that one century which intervened between the ascension of Christ and the time when the peculiar language in which they are couched could no longer be written by any one. But that is just to say that they could only have been written in the apostolic age itself, which extended to the close of the first century.‡

Observe, next, the *style* of these productions. It is that of uneducated, yet sensible men, perfectly artless and unpolished, such as you expect from the publican on the shore of the Galilean lake, who gives his name to the First Gospel, and the fisherman on the same lake from whom the Fourth receives its name. If there be any exception, it ought to be in the Third Gospel, professing, as it does, to be from the pen of a physician, and one who, if we may judge from his other treatise—the Acts of the Apostles—must have seen something of the world. Accordingly, while the prevailing character of Luke's Gospel is that of all the rest—Jewish Greek—there are portions of it, and of the Acts also, which are written in a quite classic style.

But far more decisive of the genuineness of the Gospels are the innumerable

* Introd., i. 47.

† This remark is still more applicable to the Clementine Homilies, a romantic yet important production of the latter part of the second century, written in the name of the apostolical Clement of Rome.

‡ This is a *kind* of argument the peculiar force of which will be felt with ever-growing strength in proportion as we familiarize ourselves with the Greek of the Gospels, on the one hand, and on the other with the Greek of the Apostolic Fathers.

allusions which they incidentally make to the geography and topography of Palestine, the mixed political condition of the people, their manners and customs, religious principles, observances, and prejudices, the sects and parties into which they were divided, &c. Had these narratives been spurious productions of a later time, after Jerusalem was destroyed and the Jews dispersed, or constructed at a distance out of but a few fragments of truth, their authors would have either taken care to make as few allusions as possible of the kind we have noticed, or they would have infallibly discovered their own fraud. In fact, it is hardly possible to avoid detection in fraudulent histories which go into any degree of detail. Anachronisms are almost invariably committed, either in fact or in style; and the latter are fully more difficult to avoid than the former. Well, our Gospels, steeped as they are in all manner of allusions—every particular narrative which they contain being full of them—have supplied the severest test of their own truth. And how do they stand that test? Everything is in keeping—such a difficulty as that about the *taxing,* for example, in Luke ii., only revealing the undisputed accuracy of the rest. There is a pre-raphaelite minuteness and accuracy of detail which it is a perfect delight to trace, attesting them to all candid readers, in whose minds they are vivified afresh at every reading. Who has not been struck with those inimitable touches of character by which the Pharisees and the Sadducees, with the rivalry that subsisted between them, are depicted or chiselled to the life—not to speak of the Samaritans, differing from and disliked by both; the allusions to the different members of the Herod family, with the account of the Baptist's death, so strikingly agreeing with that of Josephus; and all that we meet with in every page of the Gospels, and which burn these incomparable narratives into the memory and imagination of every reader? Some allusions are of such a kind that their minute accuracy only appears on investigation, but which, when pointed out, are at once felt to be astonishing and beautiful. For a mass of these we must refer the reader to such writers as *Lardner, Michaelis,* and *Hug.*

There is a class of internal evidences of genuineness of a peculiar but irresistible nature,—what are called *Undesigned Coincidences* between the different Gospels. That the Four Gospels were not drawn up by one writer, nor by any number of writers acting in concert, is perfectly evident on the slightest examination of them. Remarkable as their agreement is, their differences and apparent contradictions—some of them exceedingly difficult to explain—put it beyond all doubt that they are independent productions of different pens. And yet there occur a number of coincidences, at those points where they travel over the same ground or cross each other's path, which, while manifestly undesigned, are strikingly confirmatory of the coinciding narratives. And the more trivial the circumstance about which the undesigned coincidence occurs, so much the more convincing, of course, is it as a mark of genuineness and truth in the different records.*

* One example may here be given merely to illustrate, to those to whom the remark may be new,

But there is one internal mark of genuineness in the writings, and at the same time of truth in the things written, which is beyond every other—*the Story itself* which these Documents tell. It could not by possibility have been told by any forger, designing to palm off a composition of his own as the authentic records of eye and ear-witnesses of the things related; whether we view him as inventing the whole, or only dressing up a few fragments of truth in the way which we find done in these narratives. Who could have invented such a Character and such a History as that of the Christ of these Gospels? Every one whose intellectual judgment and moral sense have not been miserably warped, must see that in order to be *written* it must first have been *real.* Nor let it be said that as many such narratives were afloat in the early Christian ages, the Four we now have may fairly be regarded as just specimens of the religiously inventive turn of that age. For while the existence of those many narratives shows beyond doubt that they all rest on the basis of a real historical Christ, the still extant remains of such productions—of the Apocryphal Gospels, we mean—are so childish, extravagant, and contradictory, as only to act as a foil to our Gospels. We shall have occasion to recur to this subject; and in the Commentary we have once and again adverted to it. Here we shall only observe, that these apocryphal fragments seem to have been providentially preserved just to show that those Four Gospels, which the Church unanimously and from the first acknowledged, were THE Gospel History, whose truth was to carry its own evidence and extinguish every rival.

Thus is the internal evidence of the Genuineness of the Four Gospels as complete and resistless as the external. Both together constitute a mass of evidence such as no other book in existence can lay claim to; and we hesitate not to say, that he who resists this evidence ought not to believe in the genuineness of any literary production of older date than the generation in which he lives.

There still, however, remain some points to be disposed of. The character of the writers is a point of much interest. If they were not wilful impostors or designing knaves—and the time has gone by when that needs to be disproved—they must be regarded as honest men; for there is no medium. It is needless to ask whether any one would fly in the face of all his known interests, and persist in doing so, with a knavish purpose—whether the Evangelists, having neither

the nature of the thing intended. In the First Gospel it is said (Matt. xxvi. 67), "Then did they spit in His face, and buffeted Him; and others smote Him with the palms of their hands, saying, *Prophesy unto us, thou Christ, Who is he that smote thee?*" Had we no other information than what is conveyed in this Gospel, or the Second, or the Fourth Gospel, we should never have been able to account for one who struck another asking the person struck to point out who did it. But in the Third Gospel the difficulty vanishes; for there (Luke xxii. 64) we read that it was after "the men that held Jesus had *blindfolded* Him" that they asked Him to point out who had smitten Him. In the present Commentary several such coincidences are pointed out (as in the remarks on Mark viii. 9, page 169). But the reader who would wish to pursue this subject, the line of which was first suggested by Paley in his 'Horæ Paulinæ,' is referred to Dr. Blunt's 'Undesigned Coincidences,' &c.—although considerable deduction must be made for some of his examples which are weak, and others which are more than doubtful.

pecuniary advantage nor literary reputation to gain by putting forth as true what they knew to be false; and belonging as they did to a party whose testimony to what they record exposed them to ridicule, reproach, loss of property, and death itself—whether they can be believed to have deliberately done that very thing, and four of them independently. But it is not needless to call attention to the peculiar character of the History itself, in so far as it bears upon such a theory. The Evangelists represent the Person whose Story they tell as brought into the world with no attractions, and born only to suffering from the first; as passing the first thirty years of a life destined to great things, in perfect obscurity, and emerging into public life only to encounter opposition from the leading spirits of the nation; as raising comparatively few constant followers, deserted about the middle of His brief career by a considerable number even of these, frequently misunderstood by the selectest band of His attendants, one of whom betrayed Him at last to His enemies, while another, to save himself from danger, swore that he knew nothing about Him; as arraigned before the highest council of the nation, and by it condemned to die, and after being treated with every species of contumely, handed over to the civil authority, which, after some feeble efforts to save Him, yielded Him up to crucifixion; as led forth to execution, nailed to a cross, and uplifted between two malefactors, with every circumstance of ignominy; as covered with the derision of all classes of the spectators, and at length dying and being buried; and, though rising again, yet appearing no more in public, but after forty days' seclusion from every eye, with the exception of occasional manifestations to His handful of adherents, leaving the world altogether for heaven; His disciples having the task committed to them of telling all this to the world, and making it the basis of a religious community over the whole earth. Is such a story, either in its substance or in its details, what a designing person would invent? Who can doubt that in the hands of a dishonest writer, the whole would have assumed a different, and in most of its particulars an opposite, complexion? We speak not of the precepts inculcated and the sins condemned, such as it is inconceivable that any writer should have put into the mouth of a Teacher whose life, as written by him, was known to be fictitious, or in the main unreal. Such transcendent morality could not by possibility have come, either more or less, from a dishonest writer. It *must* have been Reality before it became History.

But even after the thorough honesty of the Evangelists has been admitted, there are still some points to be cleared up. Had they the requisite information? Are they telling us what they had immediate access to know, or giving us information received at second or third hand, or further off? Every reader of the Gospels can answer this question. The First and Fourth of the Evangelists were two of the Twelve whom Christ selected to be constantly with Him, on purpose to be able, from their own eyes and ears, to report all that He did and said; and as for the other two, it is enough at present to say, that their narratives so perfectly agree in all main particulars with those of Matthew and John, that if the History as told by the First and Fourth be authentic, the same History as told by the Second and Third cannot consistently be rejected. Indeed, a mere glance at the narratives themselves is sufficient to show that they are given on the authority of those who saw and heard what they report. Who, for example, can doubt that the whole scene of Lazarus's sickness, death, and resurrection is recorded by an eye and ear-witness? and the resurrection of Jairus' daughter, and of the widow of Nain's son; the storms on the sea of Galilee, when Jesus and His disciples were on it, and His walking on that sea; the feeding of the five and of the four thousand:—are not all these related with a circumstantiality and an artlessness which bespeak the presence, in the Record, of parties to the scenes themselves? Still more, perhaps, is this felt in such narratives as that of the triumphal Entry into Jerusalem, the Last Supper, Gethsemane, the Betrayal, Apprehension, Trial, Crucifixion, and Burial; the scenes of the Resurrection-day, the subsequent Appearances and the eventual Ascension, in the sight of the disciples, into heaven. Each and all of these are related in a way which would defy invention, had the things never happened, or even had it been intended merely to dress up a meagre outline of fact with imaginary circumstances.

But we must look a little deeper into the History itself, or the Tale it tells. The existence of the Four Gospels, supposing the History unreal, would involve three distinct moral impossibilities. First, The conception of such a character as the Christ of the Gospels; next, the construction of the Narrative, considered as a literary task, so as to keep up the character throughout, and never let it down—to make the great Actor in all its scenes neither to say nor to do aught that is incongruous or out of keeping; finally, that not one person should do all this, nor two, nor three, but four persons, and all independently of each other, or without any collusion (as is manifest on the face of the narratives)—so as that the Story told by all four should be one and the same Story, and the success in telling it should be equal in all, while yet each narrator should have peculiarities and attractions of his own. Add to this, that one of these four astonishing writers was an untutored fisherman, another a publican, on the Galilean shore, a third the companion of another of those fishermen of Galilee; and that only one of these had any pretensions to literary culture; and that with the exception of him—if even with that exception—none of them had written a line, of a literary nature, before. When all this is considered, the moral impossibility of four such narratives coming from four such hands—not to say, if it was in the main untrue, but even if it was more or less an invention of their own—is complete and overwhelming.

Consider only for a moment what those four men have done. They have written the History of One to whom they all give the name of Jesus, because, as divinely announced, He was to be a *Saviour from sin.* Keeping this perpetually in view, they all agree in representing Him as bone of our bone, flesh of our flesh, man as we are men; yet free from all the moral imperfections by which other characters are stained; subject to every innocent infirmity of our nature, yet morally spotless. And what is particularly worthy of notice, it never appears to be their professed *object* to teach this, or teach anything at all. They are not *preaching* Histories: they tell their tale, an unvarnished tale, leaving the facts to speak for themselves. Even the Fourth Gospel, which differs from the other three in being of a *reflective* character, is so in a way which in nowise interferes with the remark just made. But the *Human* in Christ is not more manifest on every page than the *Divine*. We state this quite broadly and generally here—not requiring to do more for our immediate purpose. And what we say is, that in His claiming equality with the Father, and speaking and acting in a vast number of particulars in a way which could not fail to suggest the conviction that this, and no other, was His meaning, our Evangelists have to do with a Character altogether unique and totally unmanageable, save in the Record of a *real life*. No human ingenuity could have hidden the art, if art had had to be put in requisition at all, in the construction of such a life. At some places or other the writers would infallibly have discovered themselves. If, indeed, the story had been of a very vague and general character, we might conceive of its being passably executed. But no such History is that of the Gospels. The Evangelists carry the Person whose life they write through a multitude of the most *novel*, the most *complicated*, the most *testing* scenes conceivable—scenes such as had never before been dreamt of. They have undertaken to represent Him as so speaking, so acting—in a word, so conducting Himself throughout—that the readers of their Histories may be convinced, as they were, that this Jesus is the Son of God, and believing, may have life through His name. In doing this, need we say that they had no model whatever to guide them—no literary work, and no known example, to give them the least hint *how* to make the subject of their History speak and act so as never to be out of keeping either with real Humanity or with proper Deity.

But the strength of the case only grows upon us as we proceed. The Four Gospels only record with the pen what had been proclaimed by the lips of Christ's followers from the fiftieth day after His resurrection, without intermission, in the streets of Jerusalem, and in all the most public parts of the country where the scenes of the History are alleged to have taken place. The followers of Jesus neither waited till the whole affair was likely to be forgotten, nor went away to distant lands to be beyond the reach of detection. But they told their Tale in the very spots where it occurred, and while every circumstance was quite fresh and warm in the public mind. Even this might be conceived possible consistently with invention, provided the things related had been of so *trifling* a nature that nobody cared to sift them, or of so *private* a nature that few could be supposed privy to them, or of so *abstract and unimpassioned* a nature as to encounter no formidable prejudices and be fitted to produce no great changes. But the facts reported were of the most public and patent nature; they were of the most vivid and startling character; they were in the teeth of every existing prejudice; they were fitted to destroy the whole edifice of the existing Judaism; they were of a nature to revolutionize, so far as embraced, the religious views of all mankind. It would be ridiculous to suppose that such a Tale should stir no public interest, and be for any time let alone. If the whole thing was a falsehood, or even in its leading particulars false, it could not have lived a month. If true, and yet the Jewish community unprepared to submit to it, we may be quite sure that attempts would immediately be made to put the witnesses and preachers of it down. Such attempts we know *were* made, and that within the first day or two, but all in vain. The Story was credited, and the believers of it increased by thousands every day in Jerusalem itself. The first and most splendid triumphs of the Story of a Crucified, Risen, and Glorified Saviour were achieved in the very spots to which, and over the very people to whom, they could point as the scenes and the witnesses of the transactions which they reported—transactions the chief of which were but a few weeks old when the preachers first stood in the streets of the capital to proclaim it, and on the truth or falsehood of which the whole nation could with perfect certainty pronounce. But—to try every supposition—it is conceivable that the written Documents of our Faith, though faulty—that the character which they depict, though defective—might, if well executed on the whole, escape detection, provided they were subjected to little criticism, or criticism on narrow or false principles. But these Four Documents—*multiplied* as no writings ever were, *translated* into other tongues as no writings ever were, *commented on* as no writings ever were, *sifted* untiringly, by foes to destroy and by friends to defend them, for sixteen or seventeen centuries, as no writings ever were—must, if untrue, have been torn into ten thousand pieces long ere now, and ceased to obtain any credit or exercise any influence. But these Four Productions—which may all be read through in a few hours—live still, and sit enthroned on the faith and affection of the most cultivated portion of the human race, and most of all of those who have shown that they understand the principles and laws of evidence, and are quite competent to detect literary fraud, who have no motive whatever for maintaining the credit of any falsehood, and who, from pure conviction of the truth of this History, profound admiration of its glorious Subject, and gratitude to Him for what He hath done for them, have dedicated all their gifts to the study of this History, and their lives to the propagation of its facts among their fellow-men. Nor is it a barren faith which the Christian world reposes in this unique History. This Story of Jesus has penetrated to the core of that commanding portion of the human family which we call Christendom, has permeated its whole manifold life—its intellectual, moral, social, political, religious life—and has revolutionized and ennobled it. Paganism is dead; Judaism is dead; Mohammedanism is dead; the various intermediate speculations of restless and proud minds, if they cannot be said to be dead, constitute no substantive Religion at all, and never will nor can crystallize into anything worthy of that name, on which a living soul can repose and a dying man may build hope for a future state. Christianity alone lives. It lives not, indeed, an undisturbed life. Transcendental philosophies, rationalistic criticism, materialistic science, and political theories for the advancement of the human species, bred of materialism, are at this hour in full activity. But this History

—with the preceding and following portions of the Bible that do but minister to it—has not only stood its ground, but seen nearly every successive form of antagonism to its grave. Fresh forms of hostility succeed, because the spirit of enmity to Revelation and all divine authority, that gives them birth, still lives. But since nearly every imaginable form of hostility to Revelation has already run its course, while Biblical Christianity is only fresher and mightier than ever, we have in this a sure pledge of its undying vitality. For every new speculation in philosophy, for every new discovery in science, for every new development in the life of nations, Christianity shows itself prepared;—to grapple with and overcome it, if false and deadly; to own it, to regulate it, to ride on the top of it, if sound and salutary. It superannuates and supersedes whatever stands in its way; itself never superannuated, but eternally young. It is the vital element of modern society, and the very spirit of progress. It is the salt of the earth; it is the light of the world. It has its points of real difficulty—in criticism, in doctrine, even in form, considered as a Documentary Revelation. On all these sides it will continue to be assailed so long as enmity to whatever is Divine remains among men, and has leave to speak out. Nor will such things cease to stumble even some "who believe and know the truth." But as the efforts of its adversaries prove bootless, the hearts of its leal disciples get reassured. The difficulties remain where they were, and "that which is crooked" we find, with the wise king of Israel, "cannot be made straight." But on every side we behold shattered systems—and, alas! the wreck of noble minds who commit themselves to them. "Come and behold the works of the Lord, what desolations He hath wrought in the earth." Outside of Christianity we find no harbour of refuge for our tossed and weary souls, but here we enjoy deep and settled repose. And thus, as we survey historically the vicissitudes through which the Gospel has come, from the first day until now, is the uncorrupted heart, as by a method of exhaustion, "shut up unto the Faith," exclaiming, as it enters this haven of rest, "Lord, to whom shall we go? Thou hast the words of Eternal Life."

On the subject of *Miracles,* as a preliminary objection to the reception of the Gospel History, this is not the place to enter. One might have thought that since the days of *Hume* this objection had been sufficiently disposed of. In so far as it drew forth an astonishing amount of beautiful investigation and important illustration on the subject of human testimony, one may be pleased at the extraordinary attention which that objection attracted. At the same time we are free to confess to something akin to shame at the panic it created, the anxiety which some writers have shown in dealing with it, and the elaborateness and even metaphysical subtlety of some of the ablest replies to it—as if it involved some real difficulty. The possibility of a miracle (and the possibility of authenticating it) is, in our view, simply a question of Theism or Atheism. If there be no God, there can be no miracle, in any proper sense of the term. But if there be, 'the laws of nature' are but His own method of rule in His own physical creation.

Whether He has at any time, and in certain given cases, for ends higher than the physical creation, acted otherwise than according to these 'laws'—that men might be startled into the recognition of His own presence, and constrained to receive truths of eternal moment as an immediate message from Himself—must be purely a matter of *evidence*. And if this evidence be in its own nature convincing, and to the candid mind overwhelming, it is not to be weakened by difficulties as to the possibility of such Divine Intervention, which, explain them as men will, have their rise only in the atheistic spirit. It is a grief to us to observe these difficulties obtruded anew upon the Christian world, not by professed infidels, but by ordained ministers of the Church of Christ in our land—the victims of a wretched Naturalism, which, while clinging to the sentiment, or what they call the spirit of Christianity, is impatient of the Supernatural in every form. There seems to be a growing party, including some learned clergy, who, like an extinct school in Germany, flatter themselves that they can retain their belief in the Bible in general, and in the Gospels in particular, while they sit loose to all that is miraculous or, in the strict sense, supernatural in it. No doubt this phase of scepticism, like others, will pass away. It is an inclined plane, and we know the terminus of those who venture on it. Meanwhile, we add our testimony, in various parts of this Commentary, to that of all other thorough students of the Gospels, that they must be accepted entire, or entire rejected, as, like the Saviour's own tunic, "without seam, woven from the top throughout."

This naturally suggests the subject of *Inspiration*, on which it will be proper to say a closing word or two.

Every thoughtful reader of the Gospels must at times have asked himself how the Evangelists were able to report as they have done so much of what our Lord said and did, with all those circumstances and incidents which so much affect the sense and design of it. As mere *memory* would plainly have been inadequate to the production of such narratives, there remains but one other explanation of them. Some *prompting* from above—enabling the Evangelists to reproduce the scenes and circumstances, discourses and actions, as we have them—is irresistibly suggested to the mind as the only adequate explanation of those four unique compositions called The Gospels. Yet so little can one safely rely on mere conjecture or theory in such a case, that had we no explicit information in the narratives themselves as to the source of their proper authority, we should never have felt satisfied that we had solved the problem. But happily that information we have, and the solidity which it imparts to our faith in these Four Gospels, and by consequence in the rest of the Scripture, is complete and reassuring.

"These things have I spoken unto you," said Jesus to His disciples, in the upper room, the night before He suffered, "being yet present with you. But the Comforter, which is the Holy Ghost, Whom the Father will send in My name, He shall teach you all things, and bring all things to your remembrance, whatsoever I have said unto you."* So imperfectly did the

* John xiv. 25, 26.

apostles apprehend what Jesus said to them, that they could not be expected to remember it even as it was spoken; for nothing is harder than to recall with precision any but the briefest statement, if it be not comprehended. But while Jesus here promises to send them a Prompter from heaven, it was not to recall His teaching simply as it fell on their ears from His lips. This would have left them the same half-instructed and bewildered, weak and timid men, as before—all unfit to evangelize the world, either by their preaching or their writings. But the Spirit was to *teach* as well as *remind* them—to *reproduce the whole teaching of Christ,* not as they understood it, but *as He meant it to be understood.* Thus have we here a double promise, that through the agency of the Holy Ghost the whole teaching of Christ should stand up in the minds of His disciples, when He was gone from them, in all its *entireness,* as at first *uttered,* and in all its vast *significance,* as by Him *intended.* Before the close of this same Discourse our Lord announces an extension even of this great office of the Spirit. They were not able to take in all that he had to tell them. He had accordingly expressed much in but a seminal form, and some things He could hardly be said to have spoken at all. But when the Spirit should come, on His departure to the Father, He should "guide them into *all the truth,*" filling up whatever was wanting to their *complete apprehension of the mind of Christ.* On these great promises rests the CREDIBILITY—in the highest sense of that term—OF THE GOSPEL HISTORY, and so its DIVINE AUTHORITY.*

We have here said that the Credibility of the Gospel History, in the lofty sense guaranteed by our Lord's promise, gives it Divine Authority. We sometimes hear the Inspiration of the Gospels spoken of as if it were something distinct from the character of the History itself. But the Gospels possess no *separate* element of Inspiration—separate, that is, from their strict Historical accuracy in the lofty sense above explained. And the best proof that this accuracy is such as attaches to no human composition whatever, will be found in the Gospels themselves, which, while evincing their own Inspiration, determine also the nature of that Inspiration. Each Gospel has its own broad, indelible characteristics; yet each tells the same Tale, travelling on its own line. And not only is the History the same, but amidst not inconsiderable diversity of representation in minor details, the success of each in bringing out the One Historical Result is equal; each contributes something towards the complete conception of the Great Subject, and so may be said to be indispensable to the others; and all together—amidst partially unharmonizable diversities in subordinate features of the Narrative—constitute in four-fold perfection the True History of the Saviour of the World. Like the four seasons of the year, each is welcome and each beautiful in its turn. We read them again and again, and yet again, and never tire of them. Try this upon the most accurate and exalted history that ever came from a merely human pen. Read it twice or thrice you may; four or five times, not so likely; but oftener, never. It gets flat, stale, and unprofitable. The best do so. But these peerless Histories never do.

* See the Commentary on John xiv. 25, 26.

Millions read them and re-read them. Still they are as fresh as the first day. New wonders appear in them, and still new.. Men comment upon them, and people read with endless interest every sensible, elevated, warm commentary on them. But the text itself rises above all, and keeps above all. In our most enlarged, most heavenly frames of mind, these incomparable Documents are ever above us. And who that weighs this will not be ready to say, with the most entire conviction, that these Four Histories "came not in old time by the will of man, but holy men of God wrote them"—from personal knowledge, no doubt, and the materials they possessed, but still, in the use of that knowledge and those materials, wrote them—"as they were moved by the Holy Ghost." Yes; and while they have defied hostile criticism, and will for ever baffle all attempts to break them down, they minister alike to the rudest and the most refined, who open their souls to the reception of their testimony, light and life, daily nutriment and strength for work, joy unspeakable and full of glory;—nor will they cease to do this until that which is perfect is come, when that which is in part shall be done away.

THE GOSPEL ACCORDING TO MATTHEW.

THE *author* of this Gospel was a publican or tax-gatherer, residing at Capernaum, on the western shore of the sea of Galilee. As to his identity with the "Levi" of the Second and Third Gospels, and other particulars, see on Matt. ix. 9. Hardly anything is known of his apostolic labours. That, after preaching to his countrymen in Palestine, he went to the East, is the general testimony of antiquity; but the precise scene or scenes of his ministry cannot be determined. That he died a natural death may be concluded from the belief of the best-informed of the Fathers, that of the apostles only three, James the greater, Peter, and Paul, suffered martyrdom. That the first Gospel was written by this apostle is the testimony of all antiquity.

For the *date* of this Gospel we have only internal evidence, and that far from decisive. Accordingly, opinion is much divided. That it was the first issued of all the Gospels was universally believed. Hence, although in the order of the Gospels, those by the two apostles were placed first in the oldest MSS. of the Old Latin version, while in all the Greek MSS., with scarcely an exception, the order is the same as in our Bibles, the Gospel according to Matthew is *in every case* placed first. And as this Gospel is of all the four the one which bears the most evident marks of having been prepared and constructed with a special view to the Jews—who certainly first required a written Gospel, and would be the first to make use of it—there can be no doubt that it was issued before any of the others. That it was written before the destruction of Jerusalem is equally certain; for, when he reports our Lord's prophecy of that awful event, on coming to the warning about "the abomination of desolation" which they should "see standing in the holy place," he interposes (contrary to his invariable practice, which is to *relate* without *remark*) a call to his readers to read intelligently—"Whoso readeth, let him understand" (Matt. xxiv. 15)—a call to attend to the divine signal for flight, which could be intended only for those who lived before the event.* But how long before that event this Gospel was written is not so clear. Some internal evidences seem to imply a very early date. Since the Jewish Christians were, for five or six years, exposed to persecution from their own countrymen—until the Jews, being persecuted by the Romans, had to look to themselves—it is not likely (it is argued) that they should be left so long without some written Gospel to reassure and sustain them, and Matthew's Gospel was eminently fitted for that purpose. But the digests to which Luke refers in his Introduction (see on Luke i. 1-4, with the Remarks at the close of that Section) would be sufficient for a time, especially as the living voice of the "eye-witnesses and ministers of the word" was yet sounding abroad. Other considerations in favour of a very early date—such as the tender way in which the author seems studiously to speak of Herod Antipas, as if still reigning, and his writing of Pilate apparently as if still in power—appear to have no foundation in fact, and cannot therefore be made the ground of reasoning as to the date of this Gospel. Its Hebraic structure and hue, though they prove, as we think, that this Gospel must have been published at a period considerably anterior to the destruction of Jerusalem, are no evidence in favour of so early a date as A. D. 37 or 38—according to some of the Fathers, and, of the moderns, *Tillemont, Townson, Owen, Birks, Tregelles.* On the other hand, the date suggested by the statement of Irenæus

* Hug, page 316.

(iii. 1), that Matthew put forth his Gospel while Peter and Paul were at Rome preaching and founding the Church—or after A. D. 60—though probably the majority of critics are in favour of it, would seem rather too late, especially as the Second and Third Gospels, which were doubtless published, as well as this one, before the destruction of Jerusalem, had still to be issued. Certainly, such statements as the following, "Wherefore that field is called the field of blood *unto this day;*" "And this saying is commonly reported among the Jews *until this day*" (Matt. xxvii. 8, and xxviii. 15), bespeak a date considerably later than the events recorded. We incline, therefore, to a date intermediate between the earlier and the later dates assigned to this Gospel, without pretending to greater precision.

We have adverted to the strikingly Jewish character and colouring of this Gospel. The facts which it selects, the points to which it gives prominence, the cast of thought and phraseology—all bespeak the Jewish point of view *from* which it was written and *to* which it was directed. This has been noticed from the beginning, and is universally acknowledged. It is of the greatest consequence to the right interpretation of it; but the tendency among some even of the best of the Germans to infer, from this special design of the First Gospel, a certain laxity on the part of the Evangelist in the treatment of his facts must be guarded against.

But by far the most interesting and important point connected with this Gospel is the *language* in which it was written. It is believed by a formidable number of critics that this Gospel was originally written in what is loosely called Hebrew, but more correctly *Aramaic,* or *Syro-Chaldaic,* the native tongue of the country at the time of our Lord; and that the Greek Matthew which we now possess is a translation of that work, either by the Evangelist himself or some unknown hand. The evidence on which this opinion is grounded is wholly external. But it has been deemed conclusive by *Grotius, Michaelis,* (and his translator) *Marsh, Townson, Campbell, Olshausen, Greswell, Meyer, Ebrard, Lange, Davidson, Cureton, Tregelles, Webster and Wilkinson,* &c. The evidence referred to is the following:—

(1.) *Papias* (of whom see page ix.) is reported by Irenæus, Eusebius, &c., to have stated, in a lost work of his, that 'Matthew drew up the oracles (meaning his Gospel) in the Hebrew dialect (or tongue),* and every one interpreted them as he was able.' (2.) *Irenæus* says, 'Matthew, among the Hebrews, put forth a written Gospel in their own tongue.'† (3.) *Pantænus* is said by Eusebius (E. H. v. 10) to have gone to the Indians,‡ and there, as 'is reported,'§ to have 'found the Gospel of Matthew, which had been in the hands of some there who knew Christ before his arrival; to whom the Apostle Bartholomew is said to have preached, leaving them this writing of Matthew in Hebrew letters,|| which they kept till the time referred to.' Jerome,¶ who gives substantially the same report, adds that, 'on his return to Alexandria, Pantænus brought it with him.' (4.) *Origen* says, according to the report of Eusebius,** that 'the first Gospel was written by him who once was a publican but afterwards an apostle of Jesus Christ, Matthew, and that, having drawn it up in Hebrew letters,†† he issued it for the Jewish believers.' (5.) *Eusebius's* own statement is that 'Matthew, having first preached the Gospel to the Hebrews, when about to go to others, also

* Ἑβραΐδι διαλέκτῳ τὰ λόγια.
† τῇ ἰδίᾳ διαλέκτῳ αὐτῶν.
‡ εἰς Ἰνδούς.
§ λέγεται.
|| Ἑβραίων γράμμασι.
¶ De Viris Illustr., c. 36. 3; and in his Preface to Matthew.
** E. H. vi. 25.
†† γράμμασιν Ἑβραϊκοῖς.

delivered [to them] in writing the Gospel according to him (Matthew), in the native tongue.'* (6.) *Jerome* (later in the fourth century) says† that 'Matthew first composed a Gospel of Christ in Judæa for the benefit of the Jewish believers, in the Hebrew tongue and character. Who afterwards translated it into Greek is not sufficiently certain. Moreover, that very Hebrew Gospel is in the Library of Cæsarea, which Pamphilus the martyr collected with the greatest diligence. I myself also translated it, with permission of the Nazarenes, who make use of that volume in Berœa, a town of Syria.' And again, he speaks of the Gospel used by the Nazarenes and Ebionites, 'which we recently translated from Hebrew into Greek, and which is by most called the authentic Gospel of Matthew.'‡ (7.) *Epiphanius*, in the same fourth century, says§ regarding the Nazarenes and Ebionites, that what they call the Gospel according to the Hebrews was just the original, in the Hebrew tongue and character, of Matthew's Gospel.

This chain of testimony is certainly formidable, especially as it is unbroken, there being no external testimony to the contrary. But when closely examined, it will not, we believe, be found to bear the weight laid upon it. There is the strongest reason to suspect that most of the preceding testimonies are, after all, but one testimony—that of Papias—repeated from hand to hand. Irenæus, at least, who had the greatest regard for all that Papias wrote, as he must have seen his statement on this subject, and says nothing himself in addition to what Papias had said before him, in all probability just echoed it from him. As to Origen, the following circumstances are very suspicious: that the report comes to us only through Eusebius; that, as reported by him, Origen is not said to have ascertained it as a fact in consequence of investigations made by himself on so important a subject, but merely to have learnt it by tradition;‖ it is not said he had ever seen, or made it his business to search out, this Gospel—which, considering the energy with which he prosecuted such biblical inquiries, is somewhat surprising if he ever stated what Eusebius reports; it is not said even that he believed in the tradition, but merely that it had reached him. But more than this: in his extant commentaries on Matthew, Origen speaks of the Greek of it as if it were the only and the original Matthew, reasoning on the Greek word rendered in the Lord's Prayer "daily" (ἐπιούσιος) as one formed by the Evangelists themselves; and in several places he refers to "the Gospel according to the Hebrews" as a work known to be in existence—but only if one chose to use it for *illustration,* not as having any *authority.* This is enough of itself to throw doubt over the whole tradition. The Pantænus-story wears a very mythical air. Eusebius merely says that he was *said* to have gone to India, and there *said* to have found a Hebrew Matthew; and Jerome, who just echoes Eusebius, adds only that he was *said* to have brought it home with him to Alexandria. That he went to India (or probably southern Arabia) is likely enough. But without inquiring too critically into the Indian part of the story, if Pantænus valued it so highly as to bring it home with him, why do we hear nothing of it after that? Either, then, he brought home no such Gospel, or if he did, it was found, on further examination, too worthless to be even spoken about, much less published as Matthew's original. As to Eusebius, the probability is, that what he says was designed to express, not so much the result of his own critical judgment as what he had learnt, and the rather as elsewhere he speaks of the Greek

* πατρίῳ γλώττῃ γραφῇ.

† In his Comment on Matt. xii. 13.

‡ Vocatur a plerisque Matthæi authenticum.

§ Hær. xxx. 3.

‖ ὡς ἐν παραδόσει μαθών.

Matthew as if it were the original and only Gospel according to Matthew. Before referring to the testimony of Jerome and Epiphanius, which is more independent, let us inquire for a moment what is the value of that of Papias, on which most of the others appear to us to lean. We stay not to ask what *can* be the meaning of that strange clause, that 'every one interpreted this Hebrew Gospel of Matthew as he was able.' We accept it as a fact, that Papias did report that Matthew wrote his Gospel in Hebrew. Now, if this report had involved no exercise of *discrimination*, we should attach great weight to it; for a man of slender judgment, if honest, earnest, industrious, and successful as a collector of facts—all which even Eusebius vouches for—is entitled to deference. But it so happens that the very point now in question, so far from being a simple matter of fact, required a careful discrimination of the true from the false, the genuine from the spurious. Those Nazarenes and Ebionites were no other than the Judaizing party in the Christian Church, who were kept within its bosom so long as the apostles lived, but thereafter broke away, and became two distinct though closely allied heretical sects. That they had a Hebrew Gospel—which they confidently affirmed to be the original of the Gospel according to Matthew, which each of these sects modified according to its own ideas, and which was variously called the Gospel according to the Hebrews, according to the Twelve Apostles, and the Gospel of Peter—admits of no doubt. And as there was a total separation between them and the catholic Church, and individuals belonging to each only occasionally met, it may easily be supposed that this assertion of the Nazarenes and Ebionites regarding the original of the First Gospel would find its way into the orthodox pale, and give rise to the supposition that as the First Gospel was manifestly designed in the first instance for Jewish Christians, and of all the four was the best adapted to them, it was first drawn up in the vernacular language, and that so the Nazarene and Ebionite tradition might have some foundation in truth. We do not affirm that this was the case. But as we find Jerome and Epiphanius both expressing their belief in it, and Jerome going the length of translating this Nazarene and Ebionite Gospel into Greek, *as being the original* of Matthew's Gospel, we are not able to resist the inference that some confusion on this subject did very early get into the Church; and if it existed as early as the time of Papias, *he* at least was not the man to extricate and give us the precise truth. In a matter about which Jerome and Epiphanius write with some degree of obscurity (for so much will be allowed by the most strenuous upholders of a Hebrew original), we are not entitled to build much on anything so very brief from the pen of Papias. As to Jerome's translation of this Hebrew Gospel, different conclusions have been drawn from his way of speaking of it at different times. One thing is very suspicious. It is not now extant—indeed, he seems never to have published it; and without going into the disputes raised by his language, when we put the few fragments of it still remaining —differing considerably from the canonical Matthew—over against the fact that Jerome's version never properly saw the light, we may safely conclude that he placed no reliance upon the work, and regarded it, at most, in the light of a literary curiosity rather than a valuable instrument of interpretation, which, on his first supposition, that it was the original of Matthew's Gospel, it surely would have proved.

In a word, and leaving out of view all the suspicious things attaching to the testimonies we have adduced in favour of a Hebrew original of our First Gospel, who can readily bring himself to believe that if such Hebrew original of the Gospel according to Matthew was in existence for nearly four centuries, the orthodox Church would have allowed it to go out of their own hands almost from the first, and that this treasure was preserved exclusively among a contemptible body of Judaizing heretics, who at length melted away altogether, and their Gospel with them?

Now, how stand the facts as to our Greek Gospel? We have not a tittle of historical evidence that it is a *Translation*, either by Matthew himself or any one else. When referred to, it is invariably as the work of Matthew the publican and apostle, just as the other Gospels are ascribed to their respective authors. This Greek Gospel was from the first received by the Church as an integral part of the one Quadriform GOSPEL. And while the Fathers often advert to the two Gospels which we have from apostles, and the two which we have from men not apostles—in order to show that as that of Mark leans so entirely on Peter, and that of Luke on Paul, so these are really no less apostolical than the other two—though we attach less weight to this circumstance than they did, we cannot but think it striking that, in thus speaking, they never drop a hint that the full apostolic authority of the Greek Matthew had ever been questioned on the ground of its not being the *original*. Further, not a trace can be discovered in this Gospel itself of its being a Translation. Michaelis tried to detect, and fancied that he had succeeded in detecting, one or two such. Other Germans since, and Davidson and Cureton amongst ourselves, have made the same attempt. But the entire failure of all such attempts is now generally admitted, and candid advocates of a Hebrew original are quite ready to own that none such are to be found, and that but for external testimony no one would have imagined that the Greek was not the original. This they regard as showing how perfectly the translation has been executed. But those who know best what translating from one language into another is, will be the readiest to own that this is tantamount to giving up the question. This Gospel proclaims its own originality in a number of striking points; such as its manner of quoting from the Old Testament, and its phraseology in some peculiar cases. The length to which these observations have already extended precludes our going into detail here. But the close *verbal coincidences* of our Greek Matthew with the next two Gospels must not be quite passed over. There are but two possible ways of explaining this. Either the translator, sacrificing verbal fidelity in his Version, intentionally conformed certain parts of his author's work to the Second and Third Gospels—in which case it can hardly be called Matthew's Gospel at all—or our Greek Matthew is itself the original.

Moved by these considerations, some advocates of a Hebrew original have adopted the theory of *a double original;* the external testimony, they think, requiring us to believe in a Hebrew original, while internal evidence is decisive in favour of the originality of the Greek. This theory is espoused by *Guericke, Olshausen, Thiersch, Townson, Tregelles*, &c. But, besides that this looks too like an artificial theory, invented to solve a difficulty, it is utterly void of historical support. There is not a vestige of testimony to support it in Christian antiquity. This ought to be decisive against it.

It remains, then, that our Greek Matthew is the original of that Gospel, and that no other original ever existed. It is greatly to the credit of Dean *Alford*, that after maintaining, in the first edition of his 'Greek Testament' the theory of a Hebrew original, he thus expresses himself in the second and subsequent editions: 'On the whole, then, I find myself constrained to abandon the view maintained in my first edition, and to adopt that of a Greek original.'

One argument on the other side, on which not a little reliance has been placed, we have purposely left unnoticed till now, believing that the determination of the main question does not depend upon the point which it raises. It has been very confidently affirmed that the Greek language was not sufficiently understood by the Jews of Palestine, when Matthew published his Gospel, to make it at all probable that he would write a Gospel for their benefit in the first instance in that language. Now, as this merely alleges the improbability of a Greek original, it is enough to place against it the evidence already adduced, which is positive, in favour of the sole originality of our Greek Matthew. It is indeed a question how far the Greek language was understood in Palestine at the time referred to. But we advise the reader not to be drawn into that question as essential to the settlement of the other one. It is an element in it, no doubt, but not an essential element. There are extremes on both sides of it. The old idea, that our Lord hardly ever spoke anything but Syro-Chaldaic, is now pretty nearly exploded. Many, however, will not go the length, on the other side, of Hug* and Roberts.† For ourselves, though we believe that our Lord, in all the more public scenes of His ministry, spoke in Greek, all we think it necessary here to say is, that there is no ground to believe that Greek was so little understood in Palestine as to make it improbable that Matthew would write his Gospel exclusively in that language—so improbable as to outweigh the evidence that he did so. And when we think of the number of Digests or short narratives of the principal facts of our Lord's History, which we know from Luke (i. 1-4) were floating about for some time before he wrote his Gospel, of which he speaks by no means disrespectfully, and most of which would be in the mother tongue, we can have no doubt that the Jewish Christians and the Jews of Palestine generally would have from the first reliable written matter sufficient to supply every necessary requirement, until the publican-apostle should leisurely draw up the First of the Four Gospels in a language to them not a strange tongue, while to the rest of the world it was *the* language in which the entire Quadriform Gospel was to be for all time enshrined. The following among others hold to this view, of the sole originality of the Greek Matthew:—*Erasmus, Calvin, Beza, Lightfoot, Wetstein, Lardner, Hug, Fritzsche, Credner, de Wette, Stuart, da Costa, Fairbairn, Roberts.*

On two other questions regarding this Gospel it would have been desirable to say something had not our available space been already exhausted:—The *characteristics*, both in language and matter, by which it is distinguished from the other three; and its *relation to the Second and Third Gospels.* On the latter of these topics —whether one or more of the Evangelists made use of the materials of the other Gospels, and if so, which of the Evangelists drew from which—the opinions are just as numerous as the possibilities of the case, every conceivable way of it having one or more who plead for it. The most popular opinion until within a pretty recent period, and in this country, perhaps, the most popular still, is that the Second Evangelist availed himself more or less of the materials of the First Gospel, and the Third of the materials of both the First and Second Gospels. Here we can but state our own belief, that each of the First Three Evangelists wrote independently of both the others; while the Fourth, familiar with the First Three, wrote to supplement them, and, even where he travels along the same line, wrote quite independently of them. This judgment we express, with all deference for those who think otherwise, as the result of a pretty close study of each of the Gospels in immediate juxtaposition and comparison with the others. On

* Introduction, pages 326, &c. † Discussions, pages 25, &c.

the former of the two topics noticed, the linguistic peculiarities of each of the Gospels have been handled most closely and ably by *Credner*,* of whose results a good summary will be found in Davidson.† The other peculiarities of the Gospels have been most felicitously and beautifully brought out by *da Costa*,‡ to whom we must simply refer the reader.

THE GOSPEL ACCORDING TO MARK.

THAT the Second Gospel was written by Mark is universally agreed; though by what Mark, not so. The great majority of critics take the writer to be "John whose surname was Mark," of whom we read in the Acts, and who was "sister's son to Barnabas" (Col. iv. 10). But no reason whatever is assigned for this opinion, for which the tradition, though ancient, is not uniform; and one cannot but wonder how it is so easily taken for granted by *Wetstein*,§ *Hug*, *Meyer*, *Ebrard*, *Lange*, *Ellicott*, *Davidson*, *Tregelles*, &c. *Alford* goes the length of saying it 'has been universally believed that he was the same person with the John Mark of the Gospels.' But *Grotius* thought differently, and so did *Schleiermacher*, *Campbell*, *Burton*, and *da Costa;* and the grounds on which it is concluded that they were two different persons appear to us quite unanswerable. 'Of John, surnamed Mark,' says Campbell,‖ 'one of the first things we learn is, that he attended Paul and Barnabas in their apostolical journeys, when these two travelled together (Acts xii. 25; xiii. 5). And when afterwards there arose a dispute between them concerning him, insomuch that they separated, Mark accompanied his uncle Barnabas, and Silas attended Paul. When Paul was reconciled to Mark, which was probably soon after, we find Paul again employing Mark's assistance, recommending him, and giving him a very honourable testimony (Col. iv. 10; 2 Tim. iv. 11; Phil. 24). But we hear not a syllable of his attending Peter as his minister, or assisting him in any capacity'—although, as we shall presently see, no tradition is more ancient, more uniform, and better sustained by internal evidence, than that Mark, in his Gospel, was but 'the interpreter of Peter,' who, at the close of his first Epistle, speaks of him as 'Marcus my son' (1 Pet. v. 13), that is, without doubt, his son in the Gospel—converted to Christ through his instrumentality. And when we consider how little the Apostles Peter and Paul were together—how seldom they even met—how different were their tendencies, and how separate their spheres of labour, is there not, in the absence of all evidence of the fact, something approaching to violence in the supposition that the same Mark was the intimate associate of both? 'In brief,' adds Campbell, 'the accounts given of Paul's attendant, and those of Peter's interpreter, concur in nothing but the name, Mark or Marcus; too slight a circumstance to conclude the sameness of the person from, especially when we consider how common the name was at Rome, and how customary it was for the Jews in that age to assume some Roman name when they went thither.'

* Einleitung, u. s. w. † Introduction.

‡ 'Four Witnesses,' in which, however, there are a few things we cannot concur in.

§ Who says, 'Nihil vetat quominus simpliciter, cum *Victore* et *Theophylacto* hunc eundem Marcum intelligamus, quoties illius nomen in Actis et Epistolis reperimus.'

‖ Preface to Mark's Gospel.

Regarding the Evangelist Mark, then, as another person from Paul's companion in travel, all we know of his personal history is that he was a convert, as we have seen, of the Apostle Peter. But as to his Gospel, the tradition regarding Peter's hand in it is so ancient, so uniform, and so remarkably confirmed by internal evidence, that we must regard it as an established fact. 'Mark,' says *Papias* (according to the testimony of Eusebius) 'becoming *the interpreter of Peter,** wrote accurately, though not in order, whatever he remembered of what was either said or done by Christ; for he was neither a hearer of the Lord nor a follower of Him, but afterwards, as I said, [he was a follower] of Peter, who arranged the discourses for use, but not according to the order in which they were uttered by the Lord.' To the same effect *Irenæus:* 'Matthew published a Gospel while Peter and Paul were preaching and founding the Church at Rome; and after their departure (or decease)†, Mark, *the disciple and interpreter of Peter,*‡ he also gave forth to us in writing the things which were preached by Peter.'§ And *Clement* of Alexandria is still more specific, in a passage preserved to us by Eusebius:‖ 'Peter, having publicly preached the word at Rome, and spoken forth the Gospel by the Spirit, many of those present exhorted Mark, as *having long been a follower of his,* and remembering what he had said, to write what had been spoken; and that having prepared the Gospel, he delivered it to those who had asked him for it; which, when Peter came to the knowledge of, he neither decidedly forbade nor encouraged him.' *Eusebius's* own testimony, however, from other accounts, is rather different:¶ that Peter's hearers were so penetrated by his preaching that they gave Mark, as being *a follower of Peter,* no rest till he consented to write his Gospel, as a memorial of his oral teaching; and 'that the apostle, when he knew by the revelation of the Spirit what had been done, was delighted with the zeal of those men, and sanctioned the reading of the writing (that is, of this Gospel of Mark) in the churches.' And giving in another of his works a similar statement, he says that 'Peter, from excess of humility, did not think himself qualified to write the Gospel; but Mark, his acquaintance and pupil, is said to have recorded his relations of the actings of Jesus. And Peter testifies these things of himself; for all things that are recorded by Mark are said to be memoirs of Peter's discourses.' It is needless to go further—to *Origen,* who says Mark composed his Gospel 'as Peter guided' or 'directed him, who, in his catholic Epistle, calls him his son,' &c.; and to *Jerome,* who but echoes Eusebius.

This, certainly, is a remarkable chain of testimony; which, confirmed as it is by such striking internal evidence, may be regarded as establishing the fact that the Second Gospel was drawn up mostly from materials furnished by Peter. In *da Costa's* 'Four Witnesses' the reader will find this internal evidence detailed at length, though all the examples are not equally convincing. But if he will refer to our remarks on Mark i. 36; xi. 20-21; xiii. 3; xvi. 7; Luke xix. 32; xxii. 34, he will have evidence enough of a *Petrine* hand in this Gospel.

It remains only to advert, in a word or two, to the *readers* for whom this Gospel was, in the first instance, designed, and the *date* of it. That it was not for *Jews* but *Gentiles,* is evident from the great number of explanations of Jewish usages, opinions, and places, which to a Jew would at that time have been superfluous, but were highly needful to a Gentile. We can here but refer to ch. ii. 18; vii. 3, 4; xii. 18; xiii. 3;

* ἑρμηνευτὴς Πέτρου γενόμενος, E. H. iii. 39.
† μετὰ δὲ τὴν τουτων ἔξοδον.
‡ ὁ μαθητὴς καὶ ἑρμηνευτὴς Πέτρου.
§ Adv. Hær. iii. 1.
‖ E. H. vi. 14.
¶ E. H. ii. 15.

xiv. 12; xv. 42, for examples of these. Regarding the date of this Gospel—about which nothing certain is known—if the tradition reported by Irenæus can be relied on, that it was written at Rome, 'after the departure of Peter and Paul,' and if by that word 'departure'* we are to understand their *death,* we may date it somewhere between the years 64 and 68; but in all likelihood this is too late. It is probably nearer the truth to date it eight or ten years earlier.

THE GOSPEL ACCORDING TO LUKE.

THE writer of this Gospel is universally allowed to have been Lucas,† though he is not expressly named either in the Gospel or in the Acts. From Col. iv. 14 we learn that he was a "physician;" and by comparing that verse with verses 10, 11—in which the apostle enumerates all those of the circumcision who were then with him, but does not mention Luke, though he immediately afterwards sends a salutation from him—we gather that Luke was not a born Jew. Possibly he was a freed man (*libertinus*), as the Romans devolved the healing art on persons of this class and on their slaves, as an occupation beneath themselves. His intimate acquaintance with Jewish customs, and his facility in Hebraic Greek, seem to show that he was an early convert to the Jewish Faith; and this is curiously confirmed by Acts xxi. 27-29, where we find the Jews enraged at Paul's supposed introduction of Greeks into the temple, because they had seen "Trophimus the Ephesian" with him; and as we know that Luke was with Paul on that occasion, it would seem that they had taken him for a Jew, as they made no mention of him. On the other hand, his fluency in classical Greek confirms his Gentile origin. The time when he joined Paul's company is clearly indicated in the Acts by his changing (at ch. xvi. 10) from the third person singular ("he") to the first person plural ("we"). From that time he hardly ever left the apostle till near the period of his martyrdom (2 Tim. iv. 11). Eusebius makes him a native of Antioch. If so, he would have every advantage for cultivating the literature of Greece, and such medical knowledge as was then possessed. That he died a natural death is generally agreed among the ancients; Gregory Nazianzen alone affirming that he died a martyr.

The *time* and *place* of the publication of his Gospel are alike uncertain. But we can approximate to it. It must at any rate have been issued before the Acts, for there the 'Gospel' is expressly referred to as the same author's "former treatise" (Acts i. 1). Now the book of the Acts was not published for two whole years after Paul's arrival as a prisoner at Rome, for it concludes with a reference to this period; but probably it was published soon after that, which would appear to have been early in the year 63. Before that time, then, we have reason to believe that the Gospel of Luke was in circulation, though the majority of critics make it later. If we date it somewhere between A. D. 50 and 60, we shall probably be near the truth; but nearer it we cannot with any certainty come. Conjectures as to the place of publication are too uncertain to be mentioned here.

That it was addressed, in the first instance, to Gentile *readers,* is beyond doubt.

* ἔξοδος. † Λουκᾶς, an abbreviated form of Λουκανός, as *Silas* of *Silvanus.*

This is no more, as Davidson remarks, than was to have been expected from the companion of an 'apostle of the Gentiles,' who had witnessed marvellous changes in the condition of many heathens by the reception of the Gospel.* But the explanations in his Gospel of things known to every Jew, and which could only be intended for Gentile readers, make this quite plain—see ch. i. 26; iv. 31; viii. 26; xxi. 37; xxii. 1; xxiv. 13. A number of other minute particulars, both of things inserted and of things omitted, confirm the conclusion that it was Gentiles whom this Evangelist had in the first instance in view.

We have already adverted to the classical *style* of Greek which this Evangelist writes—just what might have been expected from an educated Greek and travelled physician. But we have also observed that along with this he shows a wonderful flexibility of style; so much so, that when he comes to relate transactions wholly Jewish, where the speakers and actors and incidents are all Jewish, he writes in such Jewish Greek as one would do who had never been out of Palestine, or mixed with any but Jews. In *da Costa's* 'Four Witnesses' will be found some traces of 'the beloved *physician*' in this Gospel. But far more striking and important are the traces in it of his intimate connection with the apostle of the Gentiles. That one who was so long and so constantly in the society of that master-mind has in such a work as this shown no traces of that connection, no stamp of that mind, is hardly to be believed. Writers of Introductions seem not to see it, and take no notice of it. But those who look into the interior of it will soon discover evidences enough in it of a *Pauline* cast of mind. Referring for a number of details to *da Costa,* we notice here only two examples. In 1 Cor. xi. 23 Paul ascribes to an express revelation from Christ Himself the account of the Institution of the Lord's Supper which he there gives. Now, if we find this account differing in small yet striking particulars from the accounts given by Matthew and Mark, but agreeing to the letter with Luke's account, it can hardly admit of a doubt that the one had it from the other; and in that case, of course, it was Luke that had it from Paul. Now Matthew and Mark both say of the Cup, "This is my blood of the New Testament;" while Paul and Luke say, in identical terms, "This cup is the New Testament in My blood." Further, Luke says, "Likewise also the cup *after supper,* saying," &c.; while Paul says, "After the same manner He took the cup *when He had supped,* saying," &c.: whereas neither Matthew nor Mark mention that this was after supper. But still more striking is another point of coincidence in this case. Matthew and Mark both say of the Bread merely this: "Take, eat; this is My body:" whereas Paul says, "Take, eat; this is My Body, *which is broken for you,*" and Luke, "This is My Body, *which is given for you.*" And while Paul adds the precious clause, "THIS DO IN REMEMBRANCE OF ME," Luke does the same, in identical terms. How can one who reflects on this resist the conviction of a Pauline stamp in this Gospel? The other proof of this to which we ask the reader's attention is in the fact that Paul, in enumerating the parties by whom Christ was seen after His resurrection, begins, singularly enough, with *Peter*—"And that He rose again the third day according to the Scriptures: and that He was seen of *Cephas,* then of the Twelve" (1 Cor. xv. 4, 5)—coupled with the remarkable fact, that Luke is the only one of the Evangelists who mentions that Christ appeared to Peter at all. When the disciples had returned from Emmaus to tell their brethren how the Lord had appeared to them in the way, and how

* Introduction, page 186.

He had made Himself known to them in the breaking of bread, they were met, as Luke relates, ere they had time to utter a word, with this wonderful piece of news, "The Lord is risen indeed, and hath appeared to *Simon*" (Luke xxiv. 34).

Other points connected with this Gospel will be adverted to in the Commentary.

THE GOSPEL ACCORDING TO JOHN.

THE author of the Fourth Gospel was the younger of the two sons of Zebedee, a fisherman on the sea of Galilee, who resided at Bethsaida, where were born Peter and Andrew his brother, and Philip also. His mother's name was Salome, who, though not without her imperfections (Matt. xx. 20, &c.), was one of those dear and honoured women who accompanied the Lord on one of His preaching circuits through Galilee, ministering to His bodily wants; who followed Him to the cross, and bought sweet spices to anoint Him after His burial, but, on bringing them to the grave, on the morning of the First Day of the week, found their loving services gloriously superseded by His resurrection ere they arrived. His father, Zebedee, appears to have been in good circumstances, owning a vessel of his own and having hired servants (Mark i. 20). Our Evangelist, whose occupation was that of a fisherman with his father, was beyond doubt a disciple of the Baptist, and one of the two who had the first interview with Jesus. He was called while engaged at his secular occupation (see on Matt. iv. 21, 22), and again on a memorable occasion (see on Luke v. 1-11), and finally chosen as one of the Twelve Apostles (see on Matt. x. 2, 4, with the Remarks at the close of that Section). He was the youngest of the Twelve—the "Benjamin," as *da Costa* calls him—and he and James his brother were named in the native tongue, by Him who knew the heart, "Boanerges," which the Evangelist Mark (iii. 17) explains to mean "Sons of thunder;" no doubt from their natural *vehemence* of character. They and Peter constituted that select triumvirate of whom we have spoken on Luke ix. 28. But the highest honour bestowed on this disciple was his being admitted to the bosom-place with his Lord at the table, as "the disciple whom Jesus loved" (John xiii. 23; xx. 2; xxi. 7, 20, 24), and to have committed to him by the dying Redeemer the care of His mother (xix. 26, 27). There can be no reasonable doubt that this distinction was due to a sympathy with His own spirit and mind on the part of John which the all-penetrating Eye of their common Master beheld in none of the rest; and although this was probably never seen either in his life or in his ministry by his fellow-apostles, it is brought wonderfully out in his writings, which, in Christ-like spirituality, heavenliness, and love, surpass, we may freely say, all the other inspired writings.

After the effusion of the Spirit on the day of Pentecost, we find him in constant but silent company with Peter, the great spokesman and actor in the infant Church until the accession of Paul. While his love to the Lord Jesus drew him spontaneously to the side of His eminent servant, and his chastened vehemence made him ready to stand courageously by him, and suffer with him, in all that his testimony to Jesus might cost him, his modest humility, as the youngest of all the apostles, made him an admiring listener and faithful supporter of his brother apostle rather than a speaker or separate actor. Ecclesiastical history is uniform in testifying that John went to Asia Minor—but it is next to certain that this could not have been till after the death both of Peter and Paul—

that he resided at Ephesus, whence, as from a centre, he superintended the churches of that region, paying them occasional visits, and that he long survived the other apostles. Whether the mother of Jesus died before this, or went with John to Ephesus, where she died and was buried, is not agreed. One or two anecdotes of his later days have been handed down by tradition, one at least bearing marks of reasonable probability. But it is not necessary to give them here. In the reign of Domitian (A. D. 81-96) he was banished to "the isle that is called Patmos" (a small rocky and then almost uninhabited island in the Ægean sea), "for the word of God and for the testimony of Jesus Christ" (Rev. i. 9). Irenæus and Eusebius say that this took place about the end of Domitian's reign.* That he was thrown into a cauldron of boiling oil, and miraculously delivered, is one of those legends which, though reported by Tertullian and Jerome, is entitled to no credit. His return from exile took place during the brief but tolerant reign of Nerva: he died at Ephesus in the reign of Trajan,† at an age above 90, according to some; according to others, 100; and even 120, according to others still. The intermediate number is generally regarded as probably the nearest to the truth.

As to the *date* of this Gospel, the arguments for its having been composed before the destruction of Jerusalem (though relied on by some superior critics) are of the slenderest nature: such as the expression in ch. v. 2, "there *is* at Jerusalem, by the sheep gate, a pool," &c.—as to which see remark on that verse; and there being no allusion to Peter's martyrdom as having occurred, according to the prediction in ch. xxi. 18—a thing too well known to require mention. That it was composed long after the destruction of Jerusalem, and after the decease of all the other apostles, is next to certain, though the precise time cannot be determined. Probably it was before his banishment, however; and if we date it between the years 90 and 94, we shall probably be pretty near the truth.

As to the *readers* for whom it was more immediately designed, that they were Gentiles we might naturally presume from the lateness of the date; but the multitude of explanations of things familiar to every Jew puts this beyond all question.

No doubt was ever thrown upon the genuineness and authenticity of this Gospel till about the close of the last century, nor were these embodied in any formal attack upon it till *Bretschneider*, in 1820, issued his famous treatise,‡ the conclusions of which he afterwards was candid enough to admit had been satisfactorily disproved. To advert to these would be as painful as unnecessary; consisting as they mostly do of assertions regarding the Discourses of our Lord recorded in this Gospel which are revolting to every spiritual mind. The Tübingen school did their best, on their peculiar mode of reasoning, to galvanize into fresh life this theory of the post-Joannean date of the Fourth Gospel; and some Unitarian critics in this country still cling to it. But to use the striking language of *van Osterzee* regarding similar speculations on the Third Gospel, 'Behold, the feet of them that shall carry it out dead are already at the door' (Acts v. 9). Is there one mind of the least elevation of spiritual discernment that does not see in this Gospel marks of historical truth and a surpassing glory such as none of the other Gospels possess, brightly as they too attest their own verity; and who will not be ready to say that if not historically true, and true *just as it stands*, it never could have been by mortal man composed or conceived?

Of the peculiarities of this Gospel we note here only two. The one is its *reflective*

* Eus. E. H. iii. 18. † Eus. E. H. iii. 23.

‡ Probabilia de Evangelii et Epistolarum Joannis Apostoli Indole et Origine.

character. While the others are purely *narrative*, the Fourth Evangelist 'pauses, as it were, at every turn,' as *da Costa* says, 'at one time to give a reason, at another to fix the attention, to deduce consequences, or make applications, or to give utterance to the language of praise.'* See ch. ii. 20, 21; ii. 23-25; iv. 1, 2; vii. 37-39; xi. 12, 13; xi. 49-52; xxi. 18, 19, 22, 23. The other peculiarity of this Gospel is its *supplementary* character. By this, in the present instance, we mean something more than the studiousness with which he omits many most important particulars in our Lord's history, for no conceivable reason but that they were already familiar as household words to all his readers, through the three preceding Gospels, and his substituting in place of these an immense quantity of the richest matter not found in the other Gospels. We refer here more particularly to the *nature* of the additions which distinguish this Gospel; particularly the notices of the different passovers which occurred during our Lord's public ministry, and the record of His teaching at Jerusalem, without which it is not too much to say that we could have had but a most imperfect conception either of the duration of His ministry or of the plan of it. But another feature of these additions is quite as noticeable and not less important. 'We find,' to use again the words of *da Costa*, slightly abridged, 'only six of our Lord's miracles recorded in this Gospel, but these are all of the most remarkable kind, and surpass the rest in depth, specialty of application, and fulness of meaning. Of these six we find only one in the other three Gospels—the multiplication of the loaves. That miracle chiefly, it would seem, on account of the important instructions of which it furnished the occasion (ch. vi.), is here recorded anew. The five other tokens of Divine power are distinguished from among the many recorded in the three other Gospels, by their furnishing a still higher display of power and command over the ordinary laws and course of nature. Thus we find recorded here the first of all the miracles that Jesus wrought—the changing of water into wine (ch. ii.), the cure of the nobleman's son *at a distance* (ch. iv.); of the numerous cures of the lame and the paralytic by the word of Jesus, only one—of the man impotent for *thirty and eight years* (ch. v.); of the many cures of the blind, one only—of the man *born blind* (ch. ix.); the restoration of Lazarus, not from a death-bed, like Jairus' daughter, nor from a bier, like the widow of Nain's son, but *from the grave*, and after lying there four days, and there sinking into corruption (ch. xi.); and lastly, after His resurrection, the miraculous draught of fishes on the sea of Tiberias, (ch. xxi.) But these are all recorded chiefly to give occasion for the record of those astonishing Discourses and Conversations, alike with friends and with foes, with His disciples and with the multitude, which they drew forth.'†

Other illustrations of the peculiarities of this Gospel will occur, and other points connected with it be adverted to, in the course of the Commentary.

* 'Four Witnesses,' page 234. † 'Four Witnesses,' pages 238, 239.

SOURCES OF AUTHORITY FOR THE TEXT OF THE GOSPELS.

THESE are ancient MANUSCRIPTS of the text; ancient VERSIONS of the text; and CITATIONS from the text, or the Versions of it, in the works of the ancient ecclesiastical writers. Of these three sources, the *Manuscripts* of the text itself are, of course, of primary authority; the *Versions* come next, but only in so far as we may gather from them what they included or excluded from the text, and what readings of the text they recognized; and the *Citations*, so far as they discover to us the text which the writers acknowledged.

The Manuscripts of the Gospels now known to exist, in whole or in part, amount to nearly a *Thousand*—which can be said of no other ancient work whatever. These are divided into two classes: *Uncial* Manuscripts, or those written in what we call capital letters; and *Cursive* Manuscripts, or those written in what are called small or running hand. The former are, of course, of older date than the latter. Uncial characters continued to be employed in the manuscripts of the New Testament from the fourth down to about the tenth century; cursive letters came into use in the tenth century, or perhaps a little earlier, and continued till the invention of printing. In the present Commentary, *Uncial* Manuscripts are denoted by the large capitals—MSS.; *Cursive*, by the small capitals—MSS.

On the palæographic principles on which the age and general value of New Testament manuscripts are approximately determined there is now a pretty general agreement among those who have devoted special attention to this interesting subject; the best proof of which is, that in the results arrived at there is scarcely any difference, and in the few cases where a difference exists it hardly exceeds half a century. Of course, high probability is all that can be attained, except where the date is expressly given, which it hardly ever is, and in none of the older manuscripts.

No known manuscript contains the New Testament entire, except the recently discovered, and now published, *Codex Sinaiticus;* and it is important to know what portions are wanting in any manuscript, lest the want of reference to it in a statement of evidence for or against a particular reading should be thought to decide, when it does not, how that manuscript read in such a case.

The Uncial MSS. are denoted by the capital letters of the Roman Alphabet, with a few additions from the Greek and Hebrew alphabets; the Cursive MSS., by numbers, and, in the case of some recently collated, by small letters.

For a full description of these and the ancient Versions, we must refer the reader to *Tregelles's* Volume of Horne's 'Introduction to the Scriptures,' and *Scrivener's* 'Introduction to the Criticism of the New Testament.' A shorter account of them will be found in *Tischendorf's* 'Synopsis Evangelica.'

The oldest MSS. which are comparatively entire are the five following :—

Name.	*Probable Date.*	*Where Deposited.*
ℵ—CODEX SINAITICUS,	4th century,	Imperial Library of St. Petersburg.*
B—CODEX VATICANUS,	4th century,	Vatican Library, Rome.†

* The romantic history of the discovery of this precious treasure is given by the discoverer himself, and all its peculiarities are carefully described in the Prolegomena to the New Testament part of it, newly published under his editorial care, in splendid royal quarto, entitled NOVUM 'TESTAMENTUM SINAITICUM' . . . Ex Codice Sinaitico . . . AEN. FRID. CONST. TISCHENDORF. Lips., 1863. The most remarkable fact regarding this MS., in connection with its great antiquity, is its being *entire*.

† This MS., in the original hand, *goes no further than* Heb. ix. 14 (καθα) : all the rest is in a

{ A—CODEX ALEXANDRINUS, ...5th century,...British Museum, London. *
{ C—CODEX EPHRAEMI (*rescriptus*), ...5th century,...Imperial Library, Paris. †
D—CODEX BEZÆ (or CANTABRIGIENSIS), 6th century,...Cambridge Library. ‡

The following are a few Fragments of MSS. which, from their antiquity—being all of date *prior to the seventh century*—are of greater value than those of later date :—

N—CODEX PURPUREUS; end of 6th or beginning of 7th century: Twelve Leaves of the Gospels—of which four are in the British Museum (J of *Tischendorf*); six in the Vatican Library (T of *Tischendorf*); and two in the Imperial Library of Vienna (N of *Tischendorf*).

Z—CODEX DUBLINENSIS (*rescriptus*); 6th century: Dublin University Library, containing the greater part of the First Gospel.

{T
{T^s—CODEX BORGIANUS; 5th century: Propaganda Library, Rome. A few leaves of the Third and Fourth Gospels in Greek and Thebaic (or Sahidic). T^s (*Fragmentum Woideanum*) appears to be part of the same MS.

{P—CODEX GUELPHERBYTANUS A} 6th century. These are two palimpsests or rescripts (over
{Q—————————— B} which other works have been written), in the Ducal Library of Wolfenbüttel.

R—CODEX NITRIANUS; 6th century: British Museum. A considerable part of the Third Gospel.

FRAGMENTA TISCHENDORFIANA; mostly of 5th century: a number of very short fragments.

Of the later Uncials the following three are regarded by *Tregelles* as of not much inferior value to the five oldest §:—

L—CODEX REGIUS; about 8th century: Imperial Library, Paris.
X—CODEX MONACENSIS; end of 9th or beginning of 10th century: University Library, Munich.
Δ—CODEX SANGALLENSIS; 9th century: Monastic Library, St. Gall.

The following, though of somewhat less value, are, along with any of the oldest class, important links in a chain of evidence :—

E—CODEX BASILEENSIS; 8th century: Basle Library.
F—CODEX BOREELI; 9th or 10th century: Utrecht Library.
{ G—CODEX SEIDELII A} 9th or 10th century: { A is in the British Museum;
{ H—————— B} { B in the Hamburg Library.
K—CODEX CYPRIUS; 9th century: Imperial Library, Paris.
M—CODEX CAMPIANUS; end of 9th, or beginning of 10th century: Imperial Library, Paris.
S—CODEX VATICANUS (No. 354 ||); A. D. 949 ¶: Vatican Library, Rome.

very late hand, and useless, therefore, for critical purposes. It has at length been published, with permission of the Papal authorities, but so uncritically that, even as re-edited, we cannot always be sure what belongs exclusively to the first hand, and what is by a second hand, which about the 8th century retouched it.

* This MS. *commences in the middle of* Matt. xxv. 6; and wants part of three chapters in John, ch. vi. 50—viii. 52. It was published, in letters resembling the original characters, in 1786.

† So called from a Greek version of some of the works of Ephraem the Syrian having been (according to the barbarous practice of the middle ages) written over it. Though the original writing has been by chemical processes recovered, it is a pity that so valuable a MS. has so many gaps—so many indeed, and in so many places, that it is impossible to enumerate them here. They will be found enumerated in *Tischendorf, Tregelles*, and *Scrivener*.

‡ This MS. receives its name from its having been presented by *Beza* to the *Cambridge* University. It contains only the Gospels and Acts, though the Catholic Epistles at least were once in it. It is a Græco-Latin MS., the Greek being on the left page, the Latin on the right. Its very singular character has occasioned much discussion and diversity of opinion.

§ In consequence, chiefly, of their agreeing so frequently with B, where B differs from A. But as A in such cases has generally all, or nearly all, the other MSS. on its side, this is equivalent to such a preference for B, with its few supporters, over A, with its many, as only a fuller collation than has yet been made will warrant.

|| The No. of this MS. in the Vatican Library is given, to distinguish it from B, which is called Cod. Vat., No. 1209.

¶ This date is given in the MS. itself.

U—CODEX NANIANUS; 9th or 10th century: Library of St. Mark's, Venice.
V—CODEX MOSQUENSIS; 9th century: Library of Holy Synod, Moscow.

A few Fragments of this later class will complete these lists of Uncials:—

Ξ—CODEX ZACYNTHIUS; 8th or 9th century: Library of British and Foreign Bible Society—Edited by *Tregelles*.
O—FRAGMENTUM MOSQUENSE: Library of Holy Synod, Moscow.
{Wa—Two Leaves of Luke; 8th century: Imperial Library, Paris.
{Wb—————— John; do. Tübingen.
{Wc—Three Leaves of Mark and Luke; do. St. Gall.
Y—CODEX BARBERINI; 8th century: Barberini Library, Rome.

Of the many hundreds of extant Cursive Manuscripts only a very few are as yet *known* to possess much critical value. Of these we name only the following, with the *numbers* by which they are distinguished:—

1. *Codex Basileensis;* 10th century: Basle Library. It closely resembles B, L, and others of that class.
2. *Codex Colbertinus;* 11th century: Imperial Library, Paris. It resembles B, D, L, more than any other of the Cursives.
3. *Codex Leicestrensis;* 14th century: Town Council Library of Leicester. Its text is very remarkable.

Of the ancient Versions of the New Testament the following are the most important for critical purposes:—

1. The SYRIAC VERSIONS. Of these the three principal are,—
   (1). The *Peshito* Syriac (as it is called); probably the oldest Version of the New Testament. It may be regarded as belonging to the *second century*, (see p. vi.)
   (2). The *Curetonian* Syriac; discovered by Dr. Cureton amongst the Syriac treasures of the British Museum, and edited by him in 1858: a version of great antiquity, though later, in all probability, than the Peshito.
   (3.) The *Philoxenian* or *Harclean* Syriac: a version originally made for *Philoxenus*, Bishop of Mabug (or Hierapolis), near the beginning of the 6th century, and about a century afterwards critically revised by Thomas of *Harkel*, who rendered the original with excessive literality, which, however, gives it, in the opinion of *Tregelles*, greater critical value than either of the other Syriac versions.
   (4). The *Jerusalem* Syriac; of which but one MS. is known to exist: it is in a very peculiar dialect, more Chaldee than Syriac; and from its resemblance to the dialect of the *Jerusalem* Targum, has its distinctive name. Whether it belongs to the 5th or 6th century is not agreed. But many of its readings resemble those of B and D. *It is the only Syriac book which contains John* vii. 53—viii. 11 (The Woman taken in Adultery).

It is needless to refer to what is called the *Karkaphensian,* of which very little is known, save that it closely resembles the Peshito; and a fragment nearly resembling the Jerusalem Syriac, which *Tischendorf*, who assigns it to the 5th century, brought from the East to St. Petersburg.

2. The LATIN VERSIONS. Of these there are two, or rather but one and a revision of it.
   (1.) The *Old Latin.* Critics are now generally agreed that instead of there being many, there was but one such Version, and that this venerable Version was made in North Africa for the use of the Latin-speaking Christians; and though opinions differ as to the exact date, the probability is that it belongs to the *second century*, and if not older, or as old, cannot be of much later date than the Peshito.

   Of this Version upwards of twenty Manuscripts are extant, denoted by the small Italic letters *a*, *b*, *c*, &c.

(2.) *Jerome's Revision* of the same, or the *Vulgate;* executed at the request of Damasus, Bishop of Rome, on account of the confounding variety of readings, many of them manifest corruptions, which had crept into the current copies of the Old Latin. The Gospels were published A. D. 384, and the rest afterwards. This work took some three centuries entirely to supersede the Old, when it got the name of *Vulgata.* The Clementine Vulgate, alone recognized in the Church of Rome, differs to a considerable extent from the same Version as left by Jerome, of which, happily, we have some valuable Manuscripts—the best of which is the *Codex Amiatinus,* in the Laurentian Library at Florence, executed, there is reason to believe, in the *sixth century.* The high value of the true Vulgate for critical purposes, not only above the Old Latin, but intrinsically, is now generally recognized.

3. The EGYPTIAN VERSIONS. Of these there are two; the one designed for the Christians of *Upper,* the other for those of *Lower* Egypt.

(1.) The *Memphitic* Version, or that used by the Christians of Lower Egypt, whose capital was *Memphis.* It used to be called the Coptic, when no other was known to exist; but as that did not designate the region to which it belonged, but rather the Upper region, it is now better named as above. It belongs, at least portions of it, probably to the *fifth century.*

(2.) The *Thebaic* Version, or that used by the Christians of Upper Egypt, of which *Thebes* was the capital. Fragments only of this Version now exist; but there is every reason to believe that it is more ancient than the Memphitic, as the Christians of Upper Egypt, early in the *fourth century* appear to have been acquainted with the New Testament, though even the clergy were ignorant of Greek and knew only their own tongue.

4. The GOTHIC VERSION, made about the middle of the fourth century. The *Codex Argenteus,* containing Fragments of the Gospels, discovered in the 17th century, and now in the University Library at Upsala in Sweden, is a precious treasure, whose date is the *fifth,* or early in the *sixth* century. This and other Fragments, since discovered, have been published more than once.

5. The ARMENIAN VERSION of the *fifth* century.

It is needless to come further down for critical purposes.

To give a list of the ancient ecclesiastical writers whose *citations* from the New Testament are of chief importance for critical purposes would hardly be desirable here. Those who have opportunity may consult the works to which we have referred for an account of the MSS. and Versions; and a little familiarity with the references in critical editions of the New Testament will soon give all the information that is needed by the general student.

The three critical editions of the Greek Testament to which continual reference is made in the Commentary, for the settlement of the Text, are the following:—

1. NOVUM TESTAMENTUM GRÆCE ET LATINE: CAROLUS LACHMANNUS Recensuit, *Philip. Buttmannus* Ph. T. Græcæ Lectionis Auctoritates apposuit, 1842-1850.
2. NOVUM TESTAMENTUM GRÆCE: Ad Antiquos Testes denuo Recensuit, Apparatum Criticum omni studio perfectum Apposuit, Commentationem Isagogicam Protexuit ÆNOTH. FRID. CONST. TISCHENDORF. *Editio Septima,* 1859.
3. THE GREEK NEW TESTAMENT: SAM. PRID. TREGELLES, LL.D. Part I., Matthew and Mark, 1857. Part II., Luke and John, 1860.

WORKS QUOTED OR REFERRED TO IN THIS VOLUME.

ALEXANDER (Joseph Addison, D.D.)—The Gospel according to Matthew Explained, 1861.

——————— The Gospel according to St. Mark Explained, 1859.

ALFORD (Henry, D.D.)—The Greek Testament, with a Critically Revised Text, &c., and a Critical and Exegetical Commentary. Third Edition. Vol. i., 1856.

BAUR (Dr. F. Chr.)—Kritische Untersuchungen ü die Kanononischen Evangelien, 1847.

BENGELII (Joh. Alb.)—Gnomon Novi Testamenti. Tom. i. Ed Tertia, 1835.

BEZA (Theod.)—Novum Testamentum. Interpretatio et Annotationes, 1698.

BIRKS (Rev. T. R.)—Horæ Evangelicæ, &c., 1852.

BLOOMFIELD (S. T., D.D.)—The Greek Testament, with English Notes, Critical, Philological, and Explanatory. Eighth Edition. Vol. i., 1850.

BLUNT (J. J., B.D.)—Undesigned Coincidences in the Writings of the Old and New Testaments, an Argument for their Veracity. Fourth Edition, 1853.

CALVINI (Joan.) in Nov. Test. Commentarii, Vol. i. ii. In Harmoniam ex Matth., Marc, et Luca, Compositam. Ed. Tholuck, 1833.

——————— Vol. iii. In Evangelium Joannis, 1833.

CAMPBELL (George, D.D.)—The Four Gospels, Translated from the Greek, with Preliminary Dissertations and Notes. 3 Vols , 1821.

Da COSTA (Dr. Isaac)—The Four Witnesses. Being a Harmony of the Gospels on a New Principle. Translated by D. D. Scott, Esq., 1851.

DAVIDSON (Dr. Sam.)—Introduction to the New Testament. Vol i., The Four Gospels. 1848.

EBRARD (Dr. J. H. A.)—Wissenchaftliche Kritik der Evangelischen Geschichte, 2te Auflage, 1850.

ELLICOTT (Bp. C. J.)—Historical Lectures on the Life of our Lord Jesus Christ. First Edition, 1860.

EUSEBIUS (Pamph.)—Historiæ Ecclesiasticæ, Gr. 3 Vols., 8vo, 1827—1840.

FAIRBAIRN (Patrick, D.D.)—Hermeneutical Manual, &c. 1858.

FRITZSCHE (C. F. A.)—Evangelium Matthæi recens. et cum Commentariis Perpetuis ed. 1826.

——————— Evangelium Marci, &c., 1830.

GROTII (Hug.)—Annotationes in Libros Evangeliorum, 1641.

GRESWELL (Edw., B.D.)—Dissertations upon the Principles and Arrangement of an Harmony of the Gospels. Second Edition. 4 Vols., 1837.

HALL (Bp. Joseph)—Contemplations on the Historical Passages of the Old and New Testaments. 3 Vols., 1749. The Gospels. Vol. iii.

HUG.—Introduction to the New Testament. Translated by Fosdick, &c., 1836.

LANGE (Dr. J. P.)—Theolog. Homil. Bibelwerk: Matt.—Johannes, 1857—1859. 3 Vols. The Same, Translated as far as Luke. (*Clark.*) The Gospels of St. Matthew and St. Mark, from the German of Dr. J. P. Lange. 3 Vols. The Gospel of St. Luke, from the German of Dr. J. J. Van Osterzee. 2 Vols. Das Evang. nach Joannes, von Dr. J. P. Lange, 1860.

LAMPE (F. A.) Commentarius . . . Evangelii sec. Joannem, 3 Vol. 4to, 1727.

LARDNER (Nath., D. D.)—Works, 10 Vols., 1838: especially The Credibility of the Gospel History.

LIGHTFOOT (John, D.D.)—Works, Vol. xi., Hebrew and Talmudical Exercitations upon the Gospels of St. Matthew and St. Mark; and Vol. xii., Hebrew and Talmudical Exercitations upon the Gospels of St. Luke and St. John. 1823.

LÜCKE (Dr. Fr.)—Commentar über das Evangelium des Johannes. Dritte Auflage, 1840—1843.

LUTHARDT (Chr. E.)—Das Joanneische Evangelium, u. s. w., 1852, 1853.

MALDONATI (Joan.)—Commentarii in Quatuor Evangelistas. 2 Tom, 1853, 1854.

MEYER (Dr. H. A. W.)—Kritisch Exegetischer Kommentar über das Neue Testament. Matth., 1853; Marcus u. Lukas, 1855; Johann. 1852.

MICHAELIS (J. D.)—Introduction to the New Testament, Translated by Bishop Herbert Marsh. Fourth Edition. 6 Vols., 1823.

MIDDLETON (Bishop T. F.)—The Doctrine of the Greek Article applied to the Criticism and Illustration of the New Testament. Edited by Rose, 1841.

NEANDER (Dr. Aug.)—The Life of Jesus Christ, &c. Translated by M'Lintock and Blumenthal, 1851.
NORTON (Prof. Andrew)—The Evidences of the Genuineness of the Gospels. 2 Vols. Second Edition, 1847.
OLSHAUSEN (Dr. Herm.)—Biblical Commentary on the Gospels, from the German. (*Clark.*) 4 Vols.
RITSCHL (Dr. A.)—Evangelium Marcions u. das Kanonische Evangelium des Lukas, 1846.
ROBERTS (Rev. A.)—Discussions on the Gospels, 1862.
ROBINSON (Dr. Edw.)—Biblical Researches in Palestine, &c. Second Edition. 3 Vols., 1851.
——— Harmony of the Four Gospels in Greek, with Explanatory Notes, 1845. The same in English, edited for the Tract Society (by Rev. Dr. Davies).
ROUTH (Dr. M. J.)—Reliquiæ Sacræ, &c. Ed. Altera. 4 Vols., 1846.
SCHLEIERMACHER (Dr. Fr.)—Critical Essay on the Gospel of St. Luke, with Critical Introduction by the Translator, 1825.
SCRIVENER (Rev. F. H.)—Plain Introduction to the Criticism of the New Testament, 1861.
——— Supplement to the Authorized English Version of the New Testament, &c., 1845.
STANLEY (A. P.)—Sinai and Palestine, &c. First Edition, 1856.
STIER (Dr. Rud.)—The Words of the Lord Jesus. 8 Vols. Translated. (*Clark.*)
THOLUCK (Dr. Aug.)—Commentary on the Sermon on the Mount. Translated from the Fourth German Edition. (*Clark.*) 1860.
——— Commentary on the Gospel of St. John. Translated from the last German Edition. (*Clark.*) 1860.
TISCHENDORF (Dr. Fr. Const.)—Synopsis Evangelica, &c., 1854.
TRENCH (Rich. Chen.)—Notes on the Parables of our Lord. Sixth Edition, 1855.
——— Notes on the Miracles of our Lord. Fifth Edition, 1856.
——— Synonyms of the New Testament, &c. First Edition, 1854.
WEBSTER (W. F.) AND WILKINSON (W. F.)—The Greek Testament, with Notes, Grammatical and Exegetical. Vol. i., 1855.
WESTCOTT (Brooke Foss)—General Survey of the History of the Canon of the New Testament during the First Four Centuries, 1855.
De WETTE (Dr. N. M. L.)—Kurtzgefasstes Exegetisches Handbuch zum Neuen Testament, Matth., 1845; Lukas und Markus, 1846; Johann., 1852.
WIESELER (K.)—Chronologische Synopse der vier Evangelien, 1843.
WINER (Dr. G. B.) Grammar of the New Testament Diction. Translated from the Sixth German Edition. (*Clark.*) 2 Vols., 1859.
The Works of the principal Greek and Latin Fathers.

N.B.—In references to the Psalms, the verses are given, for the convenience of ordinary readers, as in our English version, where it differs from the Hebrew.

THE GOSPEL ACCORDING TO

ST. MATTHEW.

1 THE book of the [a]generation of Jesus Christ, [b]the son of David, [c]the
son of Abraham.
2 Abraham begat Isaac; and Isaac begat Jacob; and Jacob begat Judas
3 and his brethren; and Judas begat Phares and Zara of Thamar; and
4 [d]Phares begat Esrom; and Esrom begat Aram; and Aram begat Amina-
5 dab; and Aminadab begat [e]Naasson; and Naasson begat Salmon; and
Salmon begat Booz of [f]Rachab; and Booz begat Obed of Ruth; and
6 Obed begat Jesse; and [g]Jesse begat David the king;
And David [h]the king begat Solomon of her *that had been the wife* of
7 Urias; and [i]Solomon begat Roboam; and Roboam begat Abia; and Abia
8 begat Asa; and Asa begat Josaphat; and Josaphat begat Joram; and

A. M. 4000.

CHAP. 1.
[a] Luke 3. 23.
[b] Ps. 132. 11. Isa. 11. 1. Acts 2. 30.
[c] Gal. 3. 16.
[d] Ruth 4. 18.
[e] Num. 1. 7.
[f] Jos. 6. 22. Heb. 11. 31.
[g] 1 Sam. 16. 1.
[h] 2 Sam. 12. 24.
[i] 1 Chr. 3. 10.

CHAP. I. Verses 1-17.—GENEALOGY OF CHRIST. (=Luke iii. 23-38.)

1. The book of the generation—an expression purely Jewish; meaning, 'Table of the genealogy.' In Gen. v. 1 the same expression occurs in this sense [ספר תולדת, which the LXX. translate by our phrase here—βίβλος γενέσεως]. We have here, then, the title, not of this whole Gospel of Matthew, but only of the first seventeen verses. **of Jesus Christ.** For the meaning of these glorious words, see on *v.* 21 and on *v.* 16. "Jesus," the name given to our Lord at His circumcision (Luke ii. 21), was that by which He was familiarly known while on earth. The word "Christ"—though applied to Him as a proper name by the angel who announced His birth to the shepherds (Luke ii. 11), and once or twice used in this sense by our Lord Himself (ch. xxiii. 8, 10; Mark ix. 41)—only began to be so used by others about the very close of His earthly career (ch. xxvi. 68; xxvii. 17). The full form, "Jesus Christ," though once used by Himself in His Intercessory Prayer (John xvii. 3), was never used by others till after His ascension and the formation of churches in His name. Its use, then. in the opening words of this Gospel (and in *v.* 17, 18) is in the style of the late period when our Evangelist wrote, rather than of the events he was going to record. **the son of David, the son of Abraham.** As Abraham was the *first* from whose family it was predicted that Messiah should spring (Gen. xxii. 18), so David was the *last.* To a Jewish reader, accordingly, these behoved to be the two great starting-points of any true genealogy of the promised Messiah; and thus this opening verse, as it stamps the first Gospel as one peculiarly Jewish, would at once tend to conciliate the writer's people. From the nearest of those two fathers came that familiar name of the promised Messiah, "the son of David" (Luke xx. 41), which was applied to Jesus, either in devout acknowledgment of His rightful claim to it (ch. ix. 27; xx. 31), or in the way of insinuating inquiry whether such were the case (see on John iv. 29; ch. xii. 23).

2. Abraham begat Isaac; and Isaac begat Jacob; and Jacob begat Judas and his brethren. Only the fourth son of Jacob is here named, as it was from his loins that Messiah was to spring (Gen. xlix. 10). **3. And Judas begat Phares and Zara of Thamar; and Phares begat Esrom; and Esrom begat Aram; 4. And Aram begat Aminadab; and Aminadab begat Naasson; and Naasson begat Salmon; 5. And Salmon begat Booz of Rachab; and Booz begat Obed of Ruth; and Obed begat Jesse; 6. And Jesse begat David the king; and David the king begat Solomon of her of Urias.** [The words, "that had been the wife," introduced by our translators, only weaken the delicate brevity of our Evangelist—ἐκ τῆς τοῦ Οὐρίου]. Four women are here introduced: two of them Gentiles by birth—*Rahab* and *Ruth;* and three of them with a blot at their names in the Old Testament—*Thamar*, *Rahab*, and *Bath-sheba.* This feature in the present genealogy—herein differing from that given by Luke—comes well from him who styles himself in his list of the Twelve, what none of the other lists do, "Matthew *the publican;*" as if thereby to hold forth, at the very outset, the unsearchable riches of that grace which could not only fetch in "them that are afar off," but reach down even to "publicans and harlots," and raise them to "sit with the princes of his people." David is here twice emphatically styled "David the king" (for the MS. authority against the repetition is insufficient), as not only the first of that royal line from which Messiah was to descend, but the one king of all that line from which the throne that Messiah was to occupy took its name—"the throne of David." The angel Gabriel, in announcing Him to His virgin-mother, calls it "the throne of David His father," sinking all the intermediate kings of that line, as having no importance save as links to connect the first and the last king of Israel as father and son. It will be observed that Rahab is here represented as the great-great-grandmother of David (see Ruth iv. 20-22; and 1 Chr. ii. 11-15)—a thing not beyond possibility indeed, but extremely improbable, there being about four centuries between them. There can hardly be a doubt that one or two intermediate links are omitted. (See on *v.* 17, and Remarks 1. and 2. at the end of this section.)

7. And Solomon begat Roboam; and Roboam begat Abia; and Abia begat Asa; 8. And Asa begat Josaphat; and Josaphat begat Joram; and Joram begat Ozias (or Uzziah). Three kings are here omitted—*Ahaziah*, *Joash*, and *Amaziah* (1 Chr. iii. 11, 12). Some omissions behoved to be made, to compress the whole into three fourteens (*v.* 17). The reason why these, rather than other names, are omitted must be sought in *religious* considerations—either in the connection of those kings with the house of Ahab (as *Lightfoot*, *Ebrard*, and *Alford* view it); in their slender right to be regarded as true links in the

9 Joram begat Ozias; and Ozias begat Joatham; and Joatham begat Achaz;
10 and Achaz begat Ezekias; and [j] Ezekias begat Manasses; and Manasses
11 begat Amon; and Amon begat Josias; and [1] Josias begat Jechonias and
his brethren, about the time they were [k] carried away to Babylon:
12 And after they were brought to Babylon, Jechonias begat Salathiel;
13 and Salathiel begat [l] Zorobabel; and Zorobabel begat Abiud; and Abiud
14 begat Eliakim; and Eliakim begat Azor; and Azor begat Sadoc; and
15 Sadoc begat Achim; and Achim begat Eliud; and Eliud begat Eleazar;
16 and Eleazar begat Matthan; and Matthan begat Jacob; and Jacob begat
Joseph the husband of Mary, of whom was born [m] Jesus who is called Christ.
17 So all the generations from Abraham to David *are* fourteen generations;

A. M. 4000.

j 2 Ki. 20. 21.
1 Some read, Josias begat Jakim, and Jakim begat Jechonias.
k 2 Ki. 25. 11. Jer. 27. 20.
l Ezra 3. 2. Hag. 1. 1.
m Gen. 3. 15. Isa. 9. 6.

theocratic chain (as *Lange* takes it); or in some similar disqualification. **9. And Ozias begat Joatham; and Joatham begat Achaz; and Achaz begat Ezekias; 10. And Ezekias begat Manasses; and Manasses begat Amon; and Amon begat Josias; 11. And Josias begat Jechonias and his brethren.** Jechoniah was Josiah's grandson, being the son of Jehoiakim, Josiah's second son (1 Chr. iii. 15); but Jehoiakim might well be sunk in such a catalogue, being a mere puppet in the hands of the king of Egypt (2 Chr. xxxvi. 4). The "brethren" of Jechonias here evidently mean his uncles—the chief of whom, Mattaniah or Zedekiah, who came to the throne (2 Kin. xxiv. 17), is, in 2 Chr. xxxvi. 10, called "his brother," as well as here. **about the time they were carried away to Babylon** [ἐπὶ τῆς μετοικεσίας]—literally, 'of their migration,' for the Jews avoided the word 'captivity' [αἰχμαλωσία] as too bitter a recollection, and our Evangelist studiously respects the national feeling.

12. And after they were brought to ('after the migration of') **Babylon, Jechonias begat Salathiel.** So 1 Chr. iii. 17. Nor does this contradict Jer. xxii. 30, "Thus saith the Lord, Write ye this man (Coniah, or Jechoniah) childless;" for what follows explains in what sense this was meant—"for no man of his seed shall prosper, sitting upon the throne of David." He *was* to have seed, but no *reigning* child. **and Salathiel** (or Shealtiel) **begat Zorobabel.** So Ezra iii. 2; Neh. xii. 1; Hag. i. 1. But it would appear from 1 Chr. iii. 19 that Zerubbabel was Salathiel's grandson, being the son of Pedaiah, whose name, for some reason unknown, is omitted. **13-15. And Zorobabel begat Abiud, &c.** None of these names are found in the Old Testament; but they were doubtless taken from the public or family registers, which the Jews carefully kept, and their accuracy was never challenged. **16. And Jacob begat Joseph, the husband of Mary, of whom was born Jesus.** From this it is clear that the genealogy here given is not that of Mary, but of Joseph; nor has this ever been questioned. And yet it is here studiously proclaimed that Joseph was not the natural, but only the legal father of our Lord. His birth of a virgin was known only to a few; but the acknowledged descent of his legal father from David secured that the descent of Jesus Himself from David should never be questioned. See on *v.* 20. **who is called Christ** [Χριστός]—from the Hebrew [מָשִׁיחַ], both signifying 'anointed.' It is applied in the Old Testament to the *kings* (1 Sam. xxiv. 6, 10); to the *priests* (Lev. iv. 5, 16, &c.); and to the *prophets* (1 Kin. xix. 16)—these all being anointed with oil, the symbol of the needful spiritual gifts, to consecrate them to their respective offices; and it was applied, in its most sublime and comprehensive sense, to the promised Deliverer, inasmuch as He was to be consecrated to an office embracing all three by the immeasurable anointing of the Holy Ghost (Isa. lxi. 1; compare Joh. iii. 34). **17. So all the generations from Abraham to David are fourteen generations; and from David until the carrying away** (or migration) **into Babylon are fourteen generations; and from the carrying away into** ('the migration of') **Babylon unto Christ are fourteen generations.** That is, the whole may be conveniently divided into three fourteens, each embracing one marked era, and each ending with a notable event, in the Israelitish annals. Such artificial aids to memory were familiar to the Jews, and much larger gaps than those here are found in some of the Old Testament genealogies. In Ezra vii. 1-5 no fewer than six generations of the priesthood are omitted, as will appear by comparing it with 1 Chr. vi. 3-15. It will be observed that the last of the three divisions of fourteen appears to contain only thirteen distinct names, including Jesus as the last. *Lange* thinks that this was meant as a tacit hint that *Mary* was to be supplied, as the thirteenth link of this last chain, as it is impossible to conceive that the Evangelist could have made any mistake in the matter. But there is a simpler way of accounting for it. As the Evangelist himself (*v.* 17) reckons David twice—as the last of the first fourteen and the first of the second—so, if we reckon the second fourteen to end with Josiah, who was coeval with the "carrying away into captivity" (*v.* 11), and the third to begin with Jechoniah, it will be found that this last division, as well as the other two, embraces fourteen names, including that of our Lord.

Remarks. — 1. When superficial readers ask what can be the use of those long, dry catalogues of names which fill whole chapters of the Old Testament, they may be referred to this and the corresponding genealogy in Luke for one very sufficient answer. They enable us, in some measure, to trace the golden thread which connects our Lord with David, Abraham, and Adam, according to the flesh, and so make good one of His claims to the Messiahship. The links in the chain of those two genealogies which we *can* test by the corresponding tables of the Old Testament serve to verify those which must be received on their own sole authority. And that this is thoroughly reliable is manifest, both because these catalogues would not have been published at a time when, if inaccurate, they could easily have been refuted by reference to the well-known family and public registers; and because there is not a particle of evidence that they were ever questioned, much less invalidated. 2. That there should be difficulty in these genealogies is not surprising, considering, first, the want of sufficient materials of comparison; second, the double or triple names given to the same persons; third, the intermediate names omitted; fourth, the name of *sons* given to

and from David until the carrying away into Babylon *are* fourteen
generations; and from the carrying away into Babylon unto Christ *are*
fourteen generations.
18 Now the [n]birth of Jesus Christ was on this wise: When as his
mother Mary was espoused to Joseph, before they came together, she was
19 found with child of the Holy Ghost. Then Joseph her husband, being a
just *man*, and not willing [o]to make her a public example, was minded to
20 put her away privily. But while he thought on these things, behold, the
angel of the Lord appeared unto him in a dream, saying, Joseph, thou son
of David, fear not to take unto thee Mary thy wife; [p]for that which is
21 [2]conceived in her is of the Holy Ghost. And she shall bring forth a son,
and thou shalt call his name [3]Jesus; for [q]he shall save his people from
22 their sins. (Now all this was done, that [r]it might be fulfilled which was
23 spoken of the Lord by the prophet, saying, Behold, [s]a virgin shall be

A. M. 4000.

n Luke 1. 27. Gal. 4. 4. Heb. 10. 5.
o Deut. 24. 1.
p Luke 1. 35.
2 begotten.
3 That is, Saviour.
q Gen. 49. 10. Jer. 33. 16. Dan. 9. 24. Acts 5. 31. Heb. 7. 25. 1 John 3. 5. Rev. 1. 5.
r Heb. 6. 18.
s Isa. 7. 14.

---

those who were only in the direct line of descent, and of *brothers* to those who were only collaterally related; and, finally, the Levirate law, by which one is called the son, not of his actual, but of his Levirate father (see Deut. xxv. 5, 6; Luke xx. 28). From these causes great perplexity and much discussion have arisen, nor is it possible to solve every difficulty. So much, however, is clear as to make it "evident that our Lord sprang out of Juda" (Heb. vii. 14), and was "the Seed of the woman" "who should bruise the Serpent's head." (For a beautiful remark of *Olshausen's* on this whole subject, see on Luke's genealogy, ch. iii., at the close.) To a Jewish Christian how delightful it must have been, and to any unprejudiced Jew how conciliatory, to find themselves, in the very first section of this Gospel, so entirely at home, and to see even the more external lines of their ancient economy converging upon Jesus of Nazareth as its proper goal; but this only to pave the way for the exhibition of that same Jesus, in the sequel of this Gospel, in a still deeper relation to the old economy—as the very "Travail of its soul, its Satisfaction!"

18-25.—Birth of Christ.

18. Now the birth of Jesus Christ [*Tischendorf* and *Tregelles* read 'the birth of Christ;' a very ancient reading, but otherwise most insufficiently attested.] **was on this wise**, or 'thus:' **When as his mother Mary was espoused** [μνηστευθείσης] —rather, 'betrothed'—**to Joseph, before they came together, she was found** (or discovered to be) **with child of the Holy Ghost.** It was, of course, the fact only that was discovered: the explanation of the fact here given is the Evangelist's own. That the Holy Ghost is a living, conscious Person is plainly implied here, and is elsewhere clearly taught (Acts v. 3, 4, &c.); and that, in the unity of the Godhead, He is distinct both from the Father and the Son, is taught with equal distinctness (Matt. xxviii. 19; 2 Cor. xiii. 14). On the Miraculous Conception of our Lord, see on Luke i. 35. **19. Then Joseph her husband:** compare ver. 20, "Mary, thy wife." Betrothal was, in Jewish law, valid marriage. In giving Mary up, therefore, Joseph had to take legal steps to effect the separation. **being a just man, and not willing to make her a public example**—or 'to expose her' (see Deut. xxii. 23, 24)—**was minded to put her away privily** ('privately')—by giving her the required writing of divorcement (Deut. xxiv. 1), in presence only of two or three witnesses, and without cause assigned, instead of having her before a magistrate. That some communication had passed between him and his betrothed, directly or indirectly, on the subject, after she returned from her three months' visit to Elizabeth, can hardly be doubted. Nor does the purpose to divorce her necessarily imply disbelief, on Joseph's part, of the explanation given him. Even supposing him to have yielded to it some reverential assent—and the Evangelist seems to convey as much, by ascribing the proposal to screen her to the *justice* of his character—he might think it altogether unsuitable and incongruous in such circumstances to follow out the marriage. **20. But while he thought on these things.** Who would not feel for him after receiving such intelligence, and before receiving any light from above? As he brooded over the matter alone, in the stillness of the night, his domestic prospects darkened and his happiness blasted for life, his mind slowly making itself up to the painful step, yet planning how to do it in the way least offensive—at the last extremity the Lord Himself interposes. **behold, the angel of the Lord appeared to him in a dream, saying, Joseph, son of David.** This style of address was doubtless advisedly chosen to remind him of what all the families of David's line so eagerly coveted, and thus it would prepare him for the marvellous announcement which was to follow. **fear not to take unto thee Mary thy wife:** *q. d.*, 'Though a dark cloud now overhangs this relationship, it is unsullied still.' **for that which is conceived** ['begotten,' γεννηθὲν] **in her is of the Holy Ghost. 21. And she shall bring forth a son.** Observe, it is not said, 'she shall bear *thee* a son,' as was said to Zacharias of his wife Elizabeth (Luke i. 13). **and thou** (as his legal father) **shalt call his name JESUS** [Ἰησοῦν]—from the Hebrew יְהוֹשֻׁעַ, *Jehoshua*, Num. xiii. 16; or, as after the captivity it was contracted, יֵשׁוּעַ, *Jeshua*, Neh. vii. 7]; meaning 'Jehovah the Saviour;' in Greek Jesus—to the awakened and anxious sinner sweetest and most fragrant of all names, expressing so melodiously and briefly His whole saving office and work! **for he shall save** [αὐτὸς γὰρ σώσει]. The "He" is here emphatic—'He it is that shall save:' He personally, and by personal acts (as *Webster and Wilkinson* express it). **his people**—the lost sheep of the house of Israel, in the first instance; for they were the only people He then had. But, on the breaking down of the middle wall of partition, the saved people embraced the "redeemed unto God by His blood out of every kindred and people and tongue and nation." **from their sins**—in the most comprehensive sense of salvation from sin (Rev. i. 5; Eph. v. 25-27.) **22. Now all this was done, that it might be fulfilled which was spoken of the Lord by the prophet** (Isa. vii. 14), **saying, 23. Behold, a virgin**—it should be 'the virgin' [ἡ

with child, and shall bring forth a son, and [4]they shall call his name
24 Emmanuel, which, being interpreted, is, [t]God with us.) Then Joseph,
being raised from sleep, did as the angel of the Lord had bidden him,
25 and took unto him his wife; and knew her not till she had brought forth
[u]her first-born son: and he called his name JESUS.

2 NOW when [a]Jesus was born in Bethlehem of Judea, in the days of
Herod the king, behold, there came wise men [b]from the east to Jerusalem,
2 saying, [c]Where is he that is born King of the Jews? for we have seen [d]his
3 star in the east, and are come to worship him. When Herod the king had

A. M. 4000.

[4] Or, his name shall be called.
[t] Isa. 9. 6.
[u] Ex. 13. 2.

CHAP. 2.
[a] Dan. 9. 24.
[b] 1 Ki. 4. 30.
[c] Luke 2. 11.
[d] Num. 24. 17.

παρθένος, exactly as in the Hebrew, הָעַלְמָה]; meaning that particular virgin destined to this unparalleled distinction. **shall be with child, and shall bring forth a son, and they shall call his name Emmanuel** [עִמָּנוּ אֵל, *nobiscum-Deus*], **which, being interpreted, is, God with us.** Not that He was to have this for a proper name (like "Jesus"), but that He should come to be known *in this character*, as God manifested in the flesh, and the living bond of holy and most intimate fellowship between God and men from henceforth and for ever. **24. Then Joseph, being raised from sleep** (and all his difficulties now removed), **did as the angel of the Lord had bidden him, and took unto him his wife.** With what deep and reverential joy would this now be done on his part; and what balm would this minister to his betrothed one, who had till now lain under suspicions of all others the most trying to a chaste and holy woman—suspicions, too, arising from what, though to her an honour unparalleled, was to all around her wholly unknown! **25. And knew her not till she had brought forth her first-born son.** [τὸν πρωτότοκον. *Lachmann*, *Tischendorf*, and *Tregelles*, on certainly ancient, but, as we think, insufficient authority, exclude τὸν πρωτότοκον from the text here, though inserting it in Luke ii. 7, where it is undisputed. Here they read simply υἱοῦ—'till she had brought forth a son.'] **and he called his name JESUS.** The word "till" does not necessarily imply that they lived on a different footing afterwards (as will be evident from the use of the same word in 1 Sam. xv. 35; 2 Sam. vi. 23; Matt. xii. 20); nor does the word "first-born" decide the much disputed question, whether Mary had any children to Joseph after the birth of Christ; for, as *Lightfoot* says, 'The law, in speaking of the first-born, regarded not whether any were born *after* or no, but only that none were born before.' (See on ch. xiii. 55, 56.)

Remarks.—1. Was ever faith more tried than the Virgin's, when for no fault of hers, but in consequence of an act of God Himself, her conjugal relation to Joseph was allowed to be all but snapped asunder by a legal divorce? Yet how glorious was the reward with which her constancy and patience were at length crowned! And is not this one of the great laws of God's procedure towards his believing people? Abraham was allowed to do all but sacrifice Isaac (Gen. xxii.); the last year of the predicted Babylonish captivity had arrived ere any signs of deliverance appeared (Dan. ix. 1, 2); the massacre of all the Jews in Persia had all but taken place (Esth. vii. viii.); Peter, under Herod Agrippa, was all but brought forth for execution (Acts xii.); Paul was all but assassinated by a band of Jewish enemies (Acts xxiii.); Luther all but fell a sacrifice to the machinations of his enemies (1521); and so in cases innumerable since,—of all which it may be said, as in the song of Moses, "The Lord shall judge His people, and repent Himself for His servants, *when He seeth that their power is gone*" (Deut. xxxii. 36). 2. What divine wisdom was there in the arrangement by which our Lord was born of a betrothed virgin, thus effectually providing against the reproach of illegitimacy, and securing for His Infancy an honourable protection! "This also cometh forth from the Lord of hosts, who is wonderful in counsel and excellent in working" (Isa. xxviii. 29).

CHAP. II. 1-12.—VISIT OF THE MAGI TO JERUSALEM AND BETHLEHEM.

The Wise Men reach Jerusalem—The Sanhedrim, on Herod's demand, pronounce Bethlehem to be Messiah's predicted Birth-place (1-6). **1. Now when Jesus was born in Bethlehem of Judea**—so called to distinguish it from another Bethlehem in the tribe of Zebulun, near the sea of Galilee (Jos. xix. 15): called also *Beth-lehem-judah*, as being in that tribe (Jud. xvii. 7); and *Ephrath* (Gen. xxxv. 16); and combining both, *Beth-lehem Ephratah* (Mic. v. 2). It lay about six miles south-west of Jerusalem. But how came Joseph and Mary to remove thither from Nazareth, the place of their residence? Not of their own accord, and certainly not with the view of fulfilling the prophecy regarding Messiah's birth-place; nay, they stayed at Nazareth till it was almost too late for Mary to travel with safety; nor would they have stirred from it at all, had not an order which left them no choice forced them to the appointed place. A high hand was in all these movements. (See on Luke ii. 1-6.) **in the days of Herod the king**—styled the Great; son of Antipater, an *Edomite*, made king by the Romans. Thus was "the sceptre departing from Judah" (Gen. xlix. 10), a sign that Messiah was now at hand. As Herod is known to have died in the year of Rome 750, in the fourth year before the commencement of our Christian era, the birth of Christ must be dated four years before the date usually assigned to it, even if He was born within the year of Herod's death, as it is next to certain that he was. **there came wise men** [μάγοι] lit., 'Magi' or 'Magians;' probably of the learned class who cultivated astrology and kindred sciences. Balaam's prophecy (Num. xxiv. 17), and perhaps Daniel's (ch. ix. 24, &c.), might have come down to them by tradition; but nothing definite is known of them. **from the east**—but whether from Arabia, Persia, or Mesopotamia is uncertain. **to Jerusalem**—as the Jewish metropolis. **2. Saying, Where is he that is born King of the Jews?** From this it would seem they were not themselves Jews. (Compare the language of the Roman governor, John xviii. 33, and of the Roman soldiers, ch. xxvii. 29, with the very different language of the Jews themselves, ch. xxvii. 42, &c.) The Roman historians, *Suetonius* and *Tacitus*, bear witness to an expectation, prevalent in the East, that out of Judea should arise a sovereign of the world. **for we have seen his star in the east.** Much has been written on the subject of this star; but from all that is here said it is perhaps safest to regard it as simply a

4 heard *these things,* he was troubled, and all Jerusalem with him. And
when he had gathered all [e]the chief priests and [f]scribes of the people
5 together, [g]he demanded of them where Christ should be born. And
they said unto him, In Bethlehem of Judea: for thus it is written by the
6 prophet, And [h]thou, Bethlehem, *in* the land of Juda, art not the least
among the princes of Juda: for out of thee shall come a Governor, [i]that
7 shall [1]rule my people Israel. Then Herod, when he had privily called
the wise men, enquired of them diligently what time the star appeared.
8 And he sent them to Bethlehem, and said, Go and search diligently for
the young child; and when ye have found *him,* bring me word again,
9 that I may come and worship him also. When they had heard the king,

A. M. 4000.

[e] Ps. 2. 1.
[f] 2 Chr. 34. 13. Ezra 7. 6, 11, 12.
[g] Mal. 2. 7. John 3. 10.
[h] Mic. 5. 2. John 7. 42.
[i] Rev. 2. 27. Gen. 49. 10. Nu. 24. 19.
1 Or, feed. Isa. 40. 11.

luminous meteor, which appeared under special laws and for a special purpose. **and are come to worship him**—'to do Him homage,' as the word [προσκυνῆσαι] signifies; the nature of that homage depending on the circumstances of the case. That not civil but religious homage is meant here is plain from the whole strain of the narrative, and particularly *v.* 11. Doubtless these simple strangers expected all Jerusalem to be full of its new-born King, and the time, place, and circumstances of His birth to be familiar to every one. Little would they think that the first announcement of His birth would come from themselves, and still less could they anticipate the startling, instead of transporting, effect which it would produce—else they would probably have sought their information regarding His birth-place in some other quarter. But God overruled it to draw forth a noble testimony to the predicted birth-place of Messiah from the highest ecclesiastical authority in the nation. **3. When Herod the king heard these things, he was troubled**—viewing this as a danger to his own throne: perhaps his guilty conscience also suggested other grounds of fear. **and all Jerusalem with him**—from a dread of revolutionary commotions, and perhaps also of Herod's rage. **4. And when he had gathered all the chief priests and scribes of the people together.** The class of the "*chief priests*" included the high priest for the time being, together with all who had previously filled this office; for though the then head of the Aaronic family was the only rightful high priest, the Romans removed them at pleasure, to make way for creatures of their own. In this class probably were included also the heads of the four-and-twenty courses of the priests. The "*scribes*" were at first merely transcribers of the law and synagogue-readers; afterwards interpreters of the law, both civil and religious, and so both lawyers and divines. The first of these classes, a proportion of the second, and "*the elders*"—that is, as *Lightfoot* thinks, 'those elders of the laity that were not of the Levitical tribe,' constituted the supreme council of the nation, called the *Sanhedrim,* the members of which, at their full complement, were seventy-two. That this was the council which Herod now convened is most probable, from the solemnity of the occasion; for though the elders are not mentioned we find a similar omission where all three were certainly meant (cf. ch. xxvi. 59; xxvii. 1). As *Meyer* says, it was all the theologians of the nation whom Herod convened, because it was a theological response that he wanted. **he demanded of them**—as the authorized interpreters of Scripture—**where Christ** [ὁ Χριστὸς]—'the Messiah'—**should be born**—according to prophecy. **5. And they said unto him, In Bethlehem of Judea**—a prompt and involuntary testimony from the highest tribunal; which yet at length condemned Him to die. **for thus it is written by the prophet** (Mic. v. 2), **6. And thou, Bethlehem,** [in] **the land of Juda**—the "in" being familiarly left out, as we say, 'London, Middlesex'—**art not the least among the princes of Juda: for out of thee shall come a Governor, &c.** This quotation, though differing verbally, agrees substantially with the Hebrew and LXX. For says the prophet, "Though thou be little, yet out of thee shall come the Ruler"—this honour more than compensating for its natural insignificance; while our Evangelist, by a lively turn, makes him say, "Thou art *not the least:* for out of thee shall come a Governor"—this distinction lifting it from the lowest to the highest rank. The "thousands of Juda," in the prophet, mean the subordinate divisions of the tribe: our Evangelist, instead of these, merely names the "princes" or heads of these families, including the districts which they occupied. **that shall rule** [ποιμανεῖ]—or 'feed,' as in the margin—**my people Israel.** In the Old Testament, kings are, by a beautiful figure, styled "shepherds" (Ezek. xxxiv. &c.) The classical writers use the same figure. The pastoral rule of Jehovah and Messiah over His people is a representation pervading all Scripture, and rich in import. (See Ps. xxiii.; Isa. xl. 11; Ezek. xxxvii. 24; John x. 11; Rev. vii. 17). That this prophecy of Micah referred to the Messiah, was admitted by the ancient Rabbins.

The Wise Men, despatched to Bethlehem by Herod to see the Babe, and bring him word, make a Religious Offering to the Infant King, but, divinely warned, return home by another way (7-12). **7. Then Herod, when he had privily called the wise men.** Herod has so far succeeded in his murderous design: he has tracked the spot where lies his victim, an unconscious babe. But he has another point to fix—the date of His birth—without which he might still miss his mark. The one he had got from the Sanhedrim: the other he will have from the sages; but secretly, lest his object should be suspected and defeated. So he **enquired of them diligently** [ἠκρίβωσε]—rather, 'precisely'—**what time the star appeared**—presuming that this would be the best clue to the age of the child. The unsuspecting strangers tell him all. And now he thinks he is succeeding to a wish, and shall speedily clutch his victim; for at so early an age as they indicate, He would not likely have been removed from the place of his birth. Yet he is wary. He sends them as messengers from himself, and bids them come to *him,* that he may follow their pious example. **8. And he sent them to Bethlehem, and said, Go and search diligently** [ἀκριβῶς ἐξετάσατε]—'search out carefully'—**for the young child; and when ye have found him, bring me word again, that I may come and worship him also.** The cunning and bloody hypocrite! Yet this royal mandate would meantime serve as a safe-conduct to the strangers. **9. When they had heard the king, they departed.** But where were ye, O Jewish ecclesiastics, ye chief priests and

they departed; and, lo, the star, which they saw in the east, went before
10 them, till it came and stood over where the young child was. When
11 they saw the star, they rejoiced with exceeding great joy. And when
they were come into the house, they saw the young child with Mary his
mother, and fell down and [j] worshipped him: and when they had opened
their treasures, they [2] presented unto him gifts; gold, and frankincense,
12 and myrrh. And being warned of God [k] in a dream that they should
not return to Herod, they departed into their own country another way.

A. M. 4000.

j Ps. 2. 12. Ps. 95. 6. John 5. 23. Acts 10. 26. Rev. 19. 10.

2 Or, offered. Ps. 22. 29. Ps. 72. 10.

k ch. 1. 20.

scribes of the people? Ye could tell Herod where Christ should be born, and could hear of these strangers from the far East that the Desire of all nations had actually come: but I do not see you trooping to Bethlehem—I find these devout strangers journeying thither all alone. Yet God ordered this too, lest the news should be blabbed, and reach the tyrant's ears, ere the Babe could be placed beyond his reach. Thus are the very errors and crimes and cold indifference of men all overruled. **and, lo, the star, which they saw in the east**—implying apparently that it had disappeared in the interval—**went before them, and stood over where the young child was.** Surely this could hardly be but by a luminous meteor, and not very high. **10. When they saw the star, they rejoiced with exceeding great joy** [ἐχάρησαν χαρὰν μεγάλην σφόδρα]. The language is very strong, expressing exuberant transport. **11. And when they were come into the house**—not the stable; for as soon as Bethlehem was emptied of its strangers, they would have no difficulty in finding a dwelling-house. **they saw.** The received text has "found" [εὗρον]; but here our translators rightly depart from it, for it has no authority. **the young child with Mary his mother.** The blessed Babe is naturally mentioned first, then the mother; but Joseph, though doubtless present, is not noticed, as being but the head of the house. **and fell down and worshipped him.** Clearly this was no civil homage to a petty Jewish king, whom these star-guided strangers came so far, and enquired so eagerly, and rejoiced with such exceeding joy to pay, but a lofty spiritual homage. The next clause confirms this. **and when they had opened their treasures, they presented**—rather, 'offered'—**unto him gifts** [προσήνεγκαν αὐτῷ δῶρα]. This expression, used frequently in the Old Testament of the oblations presented to God, is in the New Testament employed seven times, and always in a *religious* sense of *offerings to God.* Beyond doubt, therefore, we are to understand the presentation of these gifts by the Magi as *a religious offering.* **gold, frankincense, and myrrh.** Visits were seldom paid to sovereigns without a present (1 Ki. x. 2, &c.): compare Ps. lxxii. 10, 11, 15; Isa. lx. 3, 6. "Frankincense" was an aromatic used in sacrificial offerings; "myrrh" was used in perfuming ointments. These, with the gold which they presented, seem to show that the offerers were persons in affluent circumstances. That the gold was presented to the infant King in token of His royalty; the frankincense in token of His divinity, and the myrrh, of his sufferings; or that they were designed to express His divine and human natures; or that the prophetical, priestly, and kingly offices of Christ are to be seen in these gifts; or that they were the offerings of three individuals respectively, each of them kings, the very names of whom tradition has handed down;—all these are, at the best, precarious suppositions. But that the feelings of these devout givers are to be seen in the richness of their gifts, and that the gold, at least, would be highly serviceable to the parents of the blessed Babe in their unexpected journey to Egypt and stay there—thus much at least admits of no dispute. **12. And being warned of God in a dream that they should not return to Herod, they departed** [ἀνεχώρησαν]—or 'withdrew'—**to their own country another way.** What a surprise would this vision be to the sages, just as they were preparing to carry the glad news of what they had seen to the *pious* king! But the Lord knew the bloody old tyrant better than to let him see their face again.

Remarks.—1. As in the first chapter of this Gospel Christ's genealogy and His birth of the Virgin show that salvation is of the *Jews*, so the visit of these eastern Magi, in the second chapter, exhibits the interest of the *Gentile* world in Christ. And as the genealogical tree of the first chapter is bright on the Jewish side, while the Gentile side is pitch-dark, so in the second chapter the picture is reversed — the Gentile world presenting the bright, while unbelieving Israel presents the dark side, as *Lange* well observes. 2. How differently was the birth of Christ regarded by different parties! While the shepherds, Simeon and Anna, with as many as waited for the consolation of Israel, hailed it with joy, and these eastern sages, attracted from afar, hied them to Jerusalem to do homage to the new-born King, the cruel tyrant that sat upon the throne of Israel, the temporizing and turbulent priesthood, and the fickle, frivolous multitude, were only startled and troubled at the announcement. Thus is it in every age, as old Simeon said, that "the thoughts of many hearts might be revealed" (Luke ii. 35). 3. We have here a striking illustration of the important distinction between the civil and the ecclesiastical functions, and of the signal services which each may render to the other. While the religious liberties of the Church are under the protection of the civil power, it will be the wisdom of the State, instead of intermeddling with ecclesiastical functions, to refer questions affecting religion to those who are its proper representatives, as Herod did in this case. 4. What a commentary is furnished by this narrative on such sayings as these: "Many shall come from the east and west, and shall sit down with Abraham, and Isaac, and Jacob, in the kingdom of heaven; but the children of the kingdom shall be cast out;" "The last shall be first, and the first last;" "I am found of them that sought me not;" but "I have stretched out my hands all day long to a disobedient and gainsaying people" (Matt. viii. 11, 12; xx. 16; Rom. xi. 20, 21). Here, in the city of divine solemnities, the seat of a divinely instituted worship, we see unbelief and religious indifference reigning not only among the chosen people, but among the consecrated ecclesiastics; while from distant heathenism come devout and eager enquirers after the new-born King of Israel. Yea, here we see persons directing others to Christ who show no readiness to enquire after Him themselves. 5. How gloriously does God serve Himself, not only of those who themselves have no such intention, but of those whose only intention is to thwart His purposes! The Word had been made flesh, but in poverty rather than riches—meanness than ma-

13 And when they were departed, behold, the angel of the Lord appeareth to Joseph in a dream, saying, Arise, and take the young child and his
mother, and flee into Egypt, and be thou there until I bring thee word:
14 for Herod will seek the young child to destroy him. When he arose, he
took the young child and his mother by night, and departed into Egypt;
15 and was there until the death of Herod: that it might be fulfilled which
was spoken of the Lord by the prophet, saying, Out [l] of Egypt have I
called my son.

A. M. 4000.

Gen. 20. 6, 7. Gen. 27. 19. Gen. 31. 24. Job 33. 15. Dan. 2. 19.
l Ex. 4. 22. Num. 24. 8. Hos. 2. 15. Hos. 11. 1.

jesty. It was fitting, then, that some public seal should be set upon Him. Accordingly, as His birth-place had been explicitly foretold by the ancient prophets, He will have this proclaimed by lips all unconscious of what they were attesting, lips beyond all suspicion—by the greatest and most august assembly of the Church's rulers—that His Son, in being born at Bethlehem, had come into the world at the right place. And whereas Herod's purpose in convening this grave synod and despatching the sages to Bethlehem, was dark and murderous—only to scent out his victim—he was herein but God's puny instrument for obtaining a glorious testimony in behalf of His Son, and procuring Him the homage of these honourable representatives of the heathen world. 6. See here the importance of the written Word, and of an intelligent acquaintance and familiarity with it; but yet how compatible this is with a total absence of the spirit and life of it; or, as *Lange* quaintly expresses it, 'the value of lifeless Bible learning, and the worthlessness of the lifeless Bible-learned.' 7. How glorious is that faith which triumphs over all visible appearances! To the expectations of these eastern visitors "the house" at Bethlehem would be not a little disappointing. Yet "when they saw the child"—differing in nothing to the outward eye from any other babe—"they fell down and worshipped Him." That Babe was reverend and majestic in their eyes. 'This baseness (as *Bishop Hall* says) hath bred wonder, not contempt: they well knew the star could not lie.' Even so in every age, the more unaided by visible probabilities, and the more it triumphs over all that to sense would seem irrational, the nobler faith is. 8. How beautiful is natural knowledge when it leads, as in these sages, to Christ! But what sadder spectacle is there than towering attainments in science and philosophy, accumulating, as we have seen in our own day, to extreme old age, and attracting the homage of the world, yet conjoined with blank irreligion, and going out at length in atheistic silence as to all that is supernatural! 9. How grand is the providence which concealed both from the sages and from the parents of our Lord all suspicion of Herod's designs, until the divine purposes in this visit were all attained! The Magi, on reaching the capital, are allowed to visit the king in his palace; and on a *religious* mission from the king himself they hie them to Bethlehem. Haunted by no suspicions of foul play, they have free scope for their joy at the star, and for their rapture at the sight of the child. And they are about to return to Herod ere they get the warning to return by another way. Thus on their part, and to the very last, all is unalloyed satisfaction. Joseph and Mary, too, left in the same blessed ignorance, are free to wonder and exult at the visit of the Magi—possibly also to anticipate an introduction to Herod, and honour at his court. But this stage reached, the veil is lifted, and the king is revealed to both parties as a murderer in disguise. Both are warned off without delay, and not a moment is lost. While the wise men withdraw to their own country by another way, the same "night" Joseph and Mary, with the blessed Babe, are off to Egypt. "O the depth of the riches both of the wisdom and knowledge of God! how unsearchable are His judgments and His ways past finding out! For of Him, and through Him, and to Him, are all things: to Whom be glory for ever. Amen." (Rom. xi. 33, 36.)

13-25.—The Flight into Egypt—The Massacre at Bethlehem—The Return of Joseph and Mary with the Babe, after Herod's Death, and their Settlement at Nazareth. (= Luke ii. 39.)

The Flight into Egypt. (13-15.) **13. And when they were departed, behold, the angel of the Lord appeareth to Joseph in a dream, saying, Arise, and take the young child and his mother.** Observe this form of expression, repeated in the next verse—another indirect hint that Joseph was no more than the Child's *guardian.* Indeed, personally considered, Joseph has no spiritual significance, and very little place at all, in the Gospel history. **and flee into Egypt**—which, being near, as *Alford* says, and a Roman province independent of Herod, and much inhabited by Jews, was an easy and convenient refuge. Ah! blessed Saviour, on what a chequered career hast Thou entered here below! At Thy birth there was no room for Thee in the inn; and now all Judea is too hot for Thee. How soon has the sword begun to pierce through the Virgin's soul! (Luke ii. 35.) How early does she taste the reception which this mysterious Child of her's is to meet with in the world! And whither is He sent? To "the house of bondage"? Well, it once was that. But Egypt was a house of refuge before it was a house of bondage, and now it has but returned to its first use. **and be thou there until I bring thee word: for Herod will seek the young child to destroy him.** The word [μέλλει] implies that the action was already in progress, though incomplete. Herod's murderous purpose was formed ere the Magi set out for Bethlehem. **14. When he arose, he took the young child and his mother by night**—doubtless the same night—**and departed into Egypt; 15. And was there until the death of Herod**—which took place not very long after this of a horrible disease; the details of which will be found in *Josephus* (Antt. xvii. 6. 1, 5, 7, 8), **that it might be fulfilled which was spoken of the Lord by the prophet, saying** (Hos. xi. 1), **Out of Egypt have I called my son.** Our Evangelist here quotes directly from the Hebrew, warily departing from the LXX., which renders the words, 'From Egypt have I recalled his children' [τὰ τέκνα αὐτοῦ], meaning Israel's children. The prophet is reminding his people how dear Israel was to God in the days of his youth; how Moses was bidden say to Pharaoh, "Thus saith the Lord, Israel is my *son*, my first-born: and I say unto thee, Let *my* son go, that he may serve me: and if thou refuse to let him go, behold, I will slay *thy* son, even thy first-born" (Ex. iv. 22, 23); how, when Pharaoh refused, God, having slain all *his* first-born, "called his own son out of Egypt," by a stroke of high-handed power

16 Then Herod, when he saw that he was mocked of the wise men, was
exceeding wroth, and sent forth, and slew all the children that were in
Bethlehem, and in all the coasts thereof, from two years old and under,
according to the time which he had diligently enquired of the wise men.
17 Then was fulfilled that which was spoken by [m] Jeremy the prophet, saying,
18 In Rama was there a voice heard, lamentation, and weeping, and great
mourning, Rachel weeping *for* her children, and would not be comforted,
because they are not.
19 But when [n] Herod was dead, behold, an [o] angel of the Lord appeareth in
20 a dream to Joseph in Egypt, saying, [p] Arise, and take the young child and

A. M. 4000.
[m] Jer. 31. 15.
[n] Ps. 76. 10. Isa. 51. 12. Dan. 8. 25; 11. 45.
[o] ch. 5. 13; 1. 20. Ps. 139. 7. Jer. 30. 10. Ez. 11. 16.
[p] Pro. 3. 5, 6.

and love. Viewing the words in this light, even if our Evangelist had not applied them to the recall from Egypt of God's own beloved, Only-begotten Son, the application would have been irresistibly made by all who have learnt to pierce beneath the surface to the deeper relations which Christ bears to His people, and both to God; and who are accustomed to trace the analogy of God's treatment of each respectively.

16. Then Herod, &c. As Deborah sang of the mother of Sisera, "She looked out at a window, and cried through the lattice, Why is his chariot so long in coming? why tarry the wheels of his chariots? Have they not sped?" so Herod wonders that his messengers, with pious zeal, are not hastening with the news that all is ready to receive him as a worshipper. What can be keeping them? Have they missed their way? Has any disaster befallen them? At length his patience is exhausted. He makes his enquiries, and finds they are already far beyond his reach on their way home. **when he saw that he was mocked** [ἐνεπαίχθη]—'was trifled with'—**of the wise men.** No, Herod, thou art not mocked of the wise men, but of a Higher than they. He that sitteth in the heavens doth laugh at thee; the Lord hath thee in derision. He disappointeth the devices of the crafty, so that their hands cannot perform their enterprise. He taketh the wise in their own craftiness, and the counsel of the froward is carried headlong. (Ps. ii. 4; Job v. 12, 13.) That blessed Babe shall die indeed, but not by thy hand. As He afterwards told that son of thine—as cunning and as unscrupulous as thyself—when the Pharisees warned Him to depart, for *Herod would seek to kill Him*—"Go ye, and tell that *fox*, Behold, I cast out devils, and I do cures to-day and to-morrow, and the third day I shall be perfected. Nevertheless I must walk to-day, and to-morrow, and the day following: for it cannot be that a prophet perish out of Jerusalem" (Luke xiii. 32, 33). Bitter satire! **was exceeding wroth.** To be made a fool of is what none like, and proud kings cannot stand. Herod burns with rage, and is like a wild bull in a net. So he **sent forth** a band of hired murderers, **and slew all the** [male] **children** [πάντας τοὺς παῖδας] **that were in Bethlehem, and in all the coasts**, or 'environs,' **thereof, from two years old and under, according to the time which he had diligently**—'carefully'—**enquired of the wise men.** In this ferocious step Herod was like himself—as crafty as cruel. He takes a large sweep, not to miss his mark. He thinks this will surely embrace his victim. And so it had, if He had been there. But He is gone. Heaven and earth shall sooner pass away than thou shalt have that Babe into thy hands. Therefore, Herod, thou must be content to want Him; to fill up the cup of thy bitter mortifications, already full enough—until thou die not less of a broken heart than of a loathsome and excruciating disease. Why, ask sceptics and sceptical critics, is not this massacre, if it really occurred, recorded by *Josephus*, who is minute enough in detailing the cruelties of Herod? To this the answer is not difficult. If we consider how small a town Bethlehem was, it is not likely there would be many male children in it from two years old and under; and when we think of the number of fouler atrocities which Josephus has recorded of him, it is unreasonable to make anything of his silence on this. **17. Then was fulfilled that which was spoken by Jeremy the prophet, saying** (Jer. xxxi. 15—from which the quotation differs but verbally), **18. In Rama was there a voice heard, lamentation, and weeping, and great mourning, Rachel weeping for her children, and would not be comforted, because they are not.** These words, as they stand in Jeremiah, undoubtedly relate to the Babylonish captivity. Rachel, the mother of Joseph and Benjamin, was buried in the neighbourhood of Bethlehem (Gen. xxxv. 19), where her sepulchre is still shown. She is figuratively represented as rising from the tomb and uttering a double lament for the loss of her children—first, by a bitter captivity, and now by a bloody death. And a foul deed it was. O ye mothers of Bethlehem, methinks I hear you asking why your innocent babes should be the ram caught in the thicket, whilst Isaac escapes. I cannot tell you; but one thing I know, that ye shall, some of you, live to see a day when that Babe of Bethlehem shall be Himself the Ram, caught in another sort of thicket, in order that your babes may escape a worse doom than they now endure. And if these babes of yours be now in glory, through the dear might of that blessed Babe, will they not deem it their honour that the tyrant's rage was exhausted upon themselves instead of their Infant Lord? (See *Keble's* exquisite Hymn, entitled, "The Holy Innocents," on the appropriate words, "These were redeemed from among men, being the *first-fruits* unto God and to the Lamb," Rev. xiv. 4.)

19. But when Herod was dead—Miserable Herod! Thou thoughtest thyself safe from a dreaded Rival; but it was He only that was safe from thee; and thou hast not long enjoyed even this fancied security. See on v. 15. **behold, an angel of the Lord.** Our translators, somewhat capriciously, render the same expression [ἄγγελος Κυρίου] "*the* angel of the Lord," ch. i. 20; ii. 13; and "*an* angel of the Lord," as here. As the same angel appears to have been employed on all these high occasions—and most likely he to whom in Luke is given the name of "Gabriel," ch. i. 19, 26—perhaps it should, in every instance except the first, be rendered "*the* angel." **appeareth in a dream to Joseph in Egypt, 20. Saying, Arise, and take the young child and his mother, and go into the land of Israel**—not to the land of Judea, for he was afterward expressly warned not to settle there, nor to Galilee, for he only went thither when he found it unsafe to settle in Judea, but to "the land of Israel," in its most general sense; meaning the Holy Land at large—the particular province being not as yet indicated.

his mother, and go into the land of Israel: for they are dead which
21 sought the young child's life. And he arose, and took the young child
22 and his mother, and came into the land of Israel. But when he heard
that Archelaus did reign in Judea in the room of his father Herod, he
was afraid to go thither: notwithstanding, being warned of God in a
23 dream, he turned aside [q]into the parts of Galilee: and he came and
dwelt in a city [r]called Nazareth: that it might be fulfilled [s]which was
spoken by the prophets, He shall be called a [3]Nazarene.

A. M. 4000.
[q] ch. 3. 13. Luke 2. 39.
[r] John 1. 45.
[s] Jud. 13. 5.
[3] That is, Branch, or, Separated one. Num. 6. 2.

So Joseph and the Virgin had, like Abraham, to "go out, not knowing whither they went," till they should receive further direction. **for they are dead which sought the young child's life**—a common expression in most languages where only one is meant, who here is Herod. But the words are taken from the strikingly analogous case in Ex. iv. 19, which probably suggested the plural here; and where the command is given to Moses to return *to* Egypt for the same reason that the Greater than Moses was now ordered to be brought back *from* it—the death of him who sought his life. Herod died in the seventieth year of his age, and thirty-seventh of his reign. **21. And he arose, and took the young child and his mother, and came into the land of Israel**—intending, as is plain from what follows, to return to Bethlehem of Judea, there, no doubt, to rear the Infant King, as at His own royal city, until the time should come when they would expect Him to occupy Jerusalem, "the city of the Great King." **22. But when he heard that Archelaus did reign in Judea in the room of his father Herod.** Archelaus succeeded to Judea, Samaria, and Idumea; but Augustus refused him the title of *king* till it should be seen how he conducted himself; giving him only the title of *Ethnarch* (*Joseph.* Antt. xvii., 11, 4). Above this, however, he never rose. The people, indeed, recognized him as his father's successor; and so it is here said that he "*reigned* in the room of his father Herod." But, after ten years' defiance of the Jewish law and cruel tyranny, the people lodged heavy complaints against him, and the emperor banished him to Vienne in Gaul, reducing Judea again to a Roman province. Then "the sceptre" clean "departed from Judah." **he was afraid to go thither**—and no wonder, for the reason just mentioned. **notwithstanding**—or more simply, 'but'—**being warned of God in a dream, he turned aside** [ἀνεχώρησεν]—'withdrew'—**into the parts of Galilee**, or the Galilean parts. The whole country west of the Jordan was at this time, as is well known, divided into three provinces—GALILEE being the northern, JUDEA the southern, and SAMARIA the central province. The province of Galilee was under the jurisdiction of Herod Antipas, the brother of Archelaus, his father having left him that and Perea, on the east side of the Jordan, as his share of the kingdom, with the title of *tetrarch*, which Augustus confirmed. Though crafty and licentious, according to *Josephus*—precisely what the Gospel History shows him to be (see on Mark vi. 14-30, and on Luke xiii. 31-35)—he was of a less cruel disposition than Archelaus; and Nazareth being a good way off from the seat of government, and considerably secluded, it was safer to settle there. **23. And he came and dwelt in a city called Nazareth**—a small town in Lower Galilee, lying in the territory of the tribe of Zebulon, and about equally distant from the Mediterranean sea on the west and the sea of Galilee on the east. 'The town of Nazareth (says *Dr. Robinson*) lies upon the western side of a narrow oblong basin, extending, from S.S.W. to N.N.E., perhaps about twenty minutes in length by eight or ten in breadth. The houses stand on the lower part of the slope of the western hill, which rises steep and high above them, and is crowned by a Wely, or saint's tomb, called Neby Isma'îl. After breakfast I walked out alone to the top of this western hill above Nazareth. Here, quite unexpectedly, a glorious prospect opened on the view. The air was perfectly clear and serene; and I shall never forget the impression I received as the enchanting panorama burst suddenly upon me. There lay the magnificent plain of Esdraelon, or at least all its western part; on the left was seen the round top of Tabor over the intervening hills, with portions of the little Hermon and Gilboa, and the opposite mountains of Samaria, from Jenin westwards to the lower hills extending towards Carmel. Then came the long line of Carmel itself. In the west lay the Mediterranean gleaming in the morning sun. Below, on the north, was spread out another of the beautiful plains of northern Palestine, called el-Bŭttauf. Farther towards the right is a sea of hills and mountains; backward lay the higher ones beyond the lake of Tiberias; and in the north-east lay the majestic Hermon with its icy crown. I remained for some hours upon this spot, lost in the contemplation of the wide prospect, and of the events connected with the scenes around. In the village below the Saviour of the world had passed His childhood. He must often have visited the fountain near which we had pitched our tent; His feet must frequently have wandered over the adjacent hills; and His eyes, doubtless, have gazed upon the splendid prospect from this very spot. Here the Prince of peace looked down upon the plain where the din of battles so often had rolled, and the garments of the warrior been dyed in blood; and He looked out, too, upon that sea over which the swift ships were to bear the tidings of His salvation to nations and to continents then unknown. How has the moral aspect of things been changed! Battles and bloodshed have indeed not ceased to desolate this unhappy country, and gross darkness now covers the people; but from this region a light went forth which has enlightened the world and unveiled new climes; and now the rays of that light begin to be reflected back from distant isles and continents, to illuminate anew the darkened land where it first sprung up.' *N. B.* If, from Luke ii. 39, one would conclude that the parents of Jesus brought Him straight back to Nazareth after His presentation in the temple—as if there had been no visit of the Magi, no flight to Egypt, no stay there, and no purpose on returning to settle again at Bethlehem—one might, from our Evangelist's way of speaking here, equally conclude that the parents of our Lord had never been at Nazareth until now. Did we know exactly the sources from which the matter of each of the Gospels was drawn up, or the mode in which these were used, this apparent discrepancy would probably disappear at once. In neither case is there any inaccuracy. At the same time it is difficult, with these facts before us, to conceive that

3 IN those days came [a] John the Baptist, preaching [b] in the wilder-
2 ness of Judea, and saying, Repent ye: for [c] the kingdom of heaven is at
3 hand. For this is he that was spoken of by the prophet Esaias, saying,

A. D. 26.

[a] Mal. 3. 1.
[b] Jos. 14. 10.
[c] Dan. 2. 44.

either of these two Evangelists wrote his Gospel with the other's before him—though many think this a precarious inference. **that it might be fulfilled which was spoken by the prophets, He shall be called a Nazarene** [Ναζωραῖος]—better, perhaps, 'Nazarene.' The best explanation of the origin of this name appears to be that which traces it to the word *netzer* [נֵצֶר], in Isa. xi. 1—the small '*twig*,' '*sprout*,' or '*sucker*,' which the prophet there says "shall come forth from the stem (or rather 'stump') of Jesse, the branch which should fructify [יִפְרֶה] from his roots." The little town of Nazareth —mentioned neither in the Old Testament nor in *Josephus*—was probably so called from its insignificance—a weak twig in contrast to a stately tree; and a special contempt seemed to rest upon it—"Can any good thing come out of Nazareth?" (John i. 46)—over and above the general contempt in which all Galilee was held, from the number of Gentiles that settled in the upper territories of it, and, in the estimation of the Jews, debased it. Thus, in the providential arrangement by which our Lord was brought up at the insignificant and opprobrious town called *Nazareth*, there was involved, first, a local humiliation; next, an allusion to Isaiah's prediction of His lowly, twig-like upspringing from the branchless, dried-up stump of Jesse; and yet further, a standing memorial of that humiliation which "the prophets," in a number of the most striking predictions, had attached to the Messiah.

Remarks.—1. In the sleepless watch which the providence of God kept over His Son when a helpless Babe, and the ministry of angels so busily employed in directing all His movements, we see a lively picture of what over-canopies and secures and directs that Church which is His body. "No man ever yet hated his own flesh; but nourisheth and cherisheth it, even as the Lord the Church: for we are members of His body, of His flesh, and of His bones" (Eph. v. 29, 30). 2. Didst Thou spend all but thirty years, blessed Jesus, in the obscurity of a place whose very name afterwards brought opprobrium upon Thee? And should not this reconcile us to like humiliation for Thy sake; and all the more, as we are sure that like as Thou didst thereafter emerge into glorious manifestation, so do Thy servants shine out of obscurity, and make even the world to see that God is with them of a truth, and that at length, "if we suffer with Him, we shall also reign with Him."

CHAP. III. 1-12.—PREACHING AND MINISTRY OF JOHN. (= Mark i. 1-8; Luke iii. 1-18.) For the proper introduction to this section, we must go to—

Luke iii. 1, 2. Here, as *Bengel* well observes, the curtain of the New Testament is, as it were, drawn up, and the greatest of all epochs of the Church commences. Even our Lord's own age is determined by it (*v.* 23). No such elaborate chronological precision is to be found elsewhere in the New Testament, and it comes fitly from him who claims it as the peculiar recommendation of his Gospel, that 'he had traced down all things with precision from the very first' (ch. i. 3). Here evidently commences his proper narrative. *V.* 1. "Now in the fifteenth year of the reign of Tiberius Cæsar"—not the fifteenth from his full accession on the death of Augustus, but from the period when he was associated with him in the government of the empire, three years earlier, about the end of the year of Rome 779, or about four years before the usual reckoning. "Pontius Pilate being governor of Judea." His proper title was *Procurator*, but with more than the usual powers of that office. After holding it for about ten years, he was summoned to Rome to answer to charges brought against him; but ere he arrived Tiberius died (A.D. 35), and soon after miserable Pilate committed suicide. "and Herod being tetrarch of Galilee (see on Mark vi. 14), and his brother Philip"—a very different and very superior Philip to the one whose name was *Herod Philip*, and whose wife, Herodias, went to live with Herod Antipas (see on Mark vi. 17)—"tetrarch of Iturea"—lying to the north-east of Palestine, and so called from *Itur* or *Jetur*, Ishmael's son (1 Chr. i. 31), and anciently belonging to the half-tribe of Manasseh. "and of the region of Trachonitis"—lying farther to the north-east, between Iturea and Damascus; a rocky district infested by robbers, and committed by Augustus to Herod the Great to keep in order. "and Lysanias the tetrarch of Abilene"—still more to the north-east; so called, says *Robinson*, from *Abila*, eighteen miles from Damascus. *V.* 2. "Annas and Caiaphas being the high priests." The former, though deposed, retained much of his influence, and, probably, as *Sagan* or deputy, exercised much of the power of the high priesthood along with Caiaphas his son-in-law (John xviii. 13; Acts iv. 6). In David's time both Zadok and Abiathar acted as high priests (2 Sam. xv. 35), and it seems to have been the fixed practice to have two (2 Ki. xxv. 18). "the word of God came unto John the son of Zacharias in the wilderness." Such a way of speaking is never once used when speaking of Jesus, because He was himself *The Living Word;* whereas to all merely creature-messengers of God, the word they spake was a foreign element. See on John iii. 31, and *Remark* 5 at the close of that Section. We are now prepared for the opening words of Matthew.

1. In those days—of Christ's secluded life at Nazareth, where the last chapter left Him. **came John the Baptist, preaching**—about six months before his Master. **in the wilderness of Judea**—the desert valley of the Jordan, thinly peopled and bare in pasture, a little north of Jerusalem. **2. And saying, Repent ye.** Though the word [μετανοεῖτε] strictly denotes a *change of mind*, it has respect here, and wherever it is used in connection with salvation, primarily to that *sense of sin* which leads the sinner to flee from the wrath to come, to look for relief only from above, and eagerly to fall in with the provided remedy. (See on Acts xx. 21.) **for the kingdom of heaven is at hand.** This sublime phrase [ἡ βασιλεία τῶν οὐρανῶν = מַלְכוּת הַשָּׁמַיִם], used in none of the other Gospels, occurs in this peculiarly Jewish Gospel nearly thirty times; and being suggested by Daniel's grand vision of the Son of Man coming in the clouds of heaven to the Ancient of days, to receive His Investiture in a world-wide kingdom (Dan. vii. 13, 14), it was fitted at once both to meet the national expectations and to turn them into the right channel. A kingdom for which *repentance* was the proper preparation behoved to be essentially spiritual. Deliverance from sin, the great blessing of Christ's kingdom (ch. i. 21), can be valued by those only to whom sin is a burden (ch. ix. 12). John's great work, accordingly, was

[d]The voice of one crying in the wilderness, [e]Prepare ye the way of the
4 Lord, make his paths straight. And [f]the same John [g]had his raiment
of camel's hair, and a leathern girdle about his loins; and his meat
was [h]locusts and wild [i]honey.
5 Then went out to him Jerusalem, and all Judea, and all the region round
6 about Jordan, and [j]were baptized of him in Jordan, confessing their sins.
7 But when he saw many of the Pharisees and Sadducees come to his baptism, he said unto them, O generation of vipers, who hath warned you to
8 flee from [k]the wrath to come? Bring forth therefore fruits meet for

A. D. 26.

d Isa. 40. 3. Luke 3. 4.
e Luke 1. 76.
f Mark 1. 6.
g 2 Ki. 1. 8. Zech. 13. 4.
h Lev. 11. 22.
i 1 Sam. 14. 25.
j Acts 19. 4.
k Rom. 5. 9. 1 Thes. 1. 10.

to awaken this feeling, and hold out the hope of a speedy and precious remedy. **3. For this is he that was spoken of by the prophet Esaias, saying** (ch. xi. 3), **The voice of one crying in the wilderness** (see on John i. 23, and on Luke iii. 2)—the scene of his ministry corresponding to its rough nature. **Prepare ye the way of the Lord, make his paths straight.** This prediction is quoted in all the four Gospels, showing that it was regarded as a great outstanding one, and the predicted forerunner as the connecting link between the old and the new economies. Like the great ones of the earth, the Prince of peace was to have His immediate approach proclaimed and His way prepared; and the call here—taking it generally—is a call to put out of the way whatever would obstruct His progress and hinder His complete triumph, whether those hindrances were public or personal, outward or inward. In Luke (iii. 5, 6) the quotation is thus continued: "Every valley shall be filled, and every mountain and hill shall be brought low; and the crooked shall be made straight, and the rough ways shall be made smooth; and all flesh shall see the salvation of God." Levelling and smoothing are here the obvious figures whose sense is conveyed in the first words of the proclamation—"*Prepare ye the way of the Lord.*" The idea is, that every obstruction shall be so removed as to reveal to the whole world the Salvation of God in Him whose name is the "Saviour." (Compare Ps. xcviii. 3; Isa. xi. 10; xlix. 6; lii. 10; Luke ii. 31, 32; Acts xiii. 47.) **4. And the same John had his raiment of camel's hair**—that is, woven of it—**and a leathern girdle about his loins**—the prophetic dress of Elijah (2 Ki. i. 8; and see Zech. xiii. 4). **and his meat was locusts**—the great well-known eastern locust, a food of the poor (Lev. xi. 22). **and wild honey**—made by wild bees (1 Sam. xiv. 25, 26). This dress and diet, with the shrill cry in the wilderness, would recall the stern days of Elijah.

5. Then went out to him Jerusalem, and all Judea, and all the region round about Jordan. From the metropolitan centre to the extremities of the Judean province the cry of this great preacher of repentance and herald of the approaching Messiah brought trooping penitents and eager expectants. **6. And were baptized of him in Jordan, confessing**—probably confessing aloud [ἐξομολογούμενοι]—**their sins.** This baptism was at once a public seal of their felt need of deliverance from sin, of their expectation of the coming Deliverer, and of their readiness to welcome Him when He appeared. The baptism itself startled, and was intended to startle them. They were familiar enough with the *baptism of proselytes* from heathenism; but this *baptism of Jews* themselves was quite new and strange to them. **7. But when he saw many of the Pharisees and Sadducees come to his baptism** (on these sects, and what they represented, see *Remark* 2. at the close of this Section), **he said unto them**—astonished at such a spectacle—**O generation of vipers** [Γεννήματα ἐχιδνῶν]—'Viper-brood;' expressing the deadly influence of both sects alike upon the community. Mutually and entirely antagonistic as were their religious principles and spirit, the stern prophet charges both alike with being the poisoners of the nation's religious principles. In ch. xii. 34, and xxiii. 33, this strong language of the Baptist is anew applied by the faithful and true Witness to the Pharisees specifically—the only party that had zeal enough actively to diffuse this poison. **who hath warned you** [ὑπέδειξεν]—'given you the hint,' as the idea is—**to flee from the wrath to come?**—'What can have brought *you* hither?' John more than suspected it was not so much their own spiritual anxieties as the popularity of his movement that had drawn them thither. What an expression is this, "The wrath to come!" [ἡ μέλλουσα ὀργή.] God's "wrath," in Scripture, is His righteous displeasure against sin, and consequently against all in whose skirts sin is found, arising out of the essential and eternal opposition of His nature to all moral evil. This is called "the *coming* wrath," not as being wholly future—see remark on the verb [μέλλω], on ch. ii. 13—for as a merited sentence it lies on the sinner already, and its effects, both inward and outward, are to some extent experienced even now—but because the impenitent sinner will not, until "the judgment of the great day," be concluded under it, will not have sentence publicly and irrevocably passed upon him, will not have it discharged upon him and experience its effects without mixture and without hope. In this view of it, it is a wrath *wholly* to come—as is implied in the noticeably different form of the expression employed by the apostle in 1 Thes. i. 10 [ἡ ὀργὴ ἡ ἐρχομένη]. Not that even true penitents came to John's baptism with all these views of "the wrath to come." But what he says is, that this was the *real import of the step* itself, and so much is implied in the use of the aorist [φυγεῖν]. In this view of it, how striking is the word he employs to express that step—*fleeing* from it—as of one who, beholding a tide of fiery wrath rolling rapidly towards him, sees in instant flight his only escape! **8. Bring forth therefore fruits** [καρποὺς]—but the true reading clearly is 'fruit' [καρπόν]—**meet for repentance**—that is, such fruit as *befits* a true penitent. John, not being gifted with a knowledge of the human heart, like a true minister of righteousness and lover of souls, here directs them how to evidence and carry out their repentance, supposing it genuine; and in the following verses warns them of their danger in case it were not. **9. And think not to say within yourselves, We have Abraham to our father**—that pillow on which the nation so fatally reposed, that rock on which at length it split. (John viii. 33, 39, 53, &c.) **for I say unto you, that God is able of these stones to raise up children unto Abraham**—*q. d.*, 'Flatter not yourselves with the fond delusion that God stands in need of you, to make good his promise of a seed to Abraham; for I tell you that, though you were all to perish, God is as able to raise up a seed to Abraham out of those stones as He was to take Abraham himself out of the rock whence he was hewn, out of the

9 repentance: and think not to say within yourselves, We [l]have Abraham
to *our* father: for I say unto you, that God is able of these stones to
10 raise up children unto Abraham. And now also the ax is laid unto the
root of the trees: [m]therefore every tree which bringeth not forth good
11 fruit is hewn down, and cast into the fire. I [n]indeed baptize you with
water unto repentance: but he that cometh after me is mightier than I,
whose shoes I am not worthy to bear: [o]he shall baptize you with the

A. D. 26.

[l] John 8. 33. Acts 13. 26.
[m] ch. 7. 19. John 15. 6.
[n] Mark 1. 8. Luke 3. 16.
[o] Isa. 4. 4. Mal. 3. 2.

hole of the pit whence he was digged' (Isa li. 1.) Though the stern speaker may have pointed as he spake to the pebbles of the bare clay hills that lay around (so *Stanley's* "Sinai and Palestine"), it was clearly the calling of the *Gentiles*—at that time stone-dead in their sins, and quite as unconscious of it—into the room of unbelieving and disinherited Israel that he meant thus to indicate. (See ch. xxi. 43; Rom. xi. 20, 30.) **10. And now also** [Ἤδη δὲ καὶ]—'And even already'—**the ax is laid unto** [κεῖται]—'lieth at'—**the root of the trees**—as it were ready to strike; an expressive figure of impending judgment, only to be averted in the way next described. **therefore every tree which bringeth not forth good fruit is hewn down, and cast into the fire.** Language so personal and individual as this can scarcely be understood of any national judgment like the approaching destruction of Jerusalem, with the breaking up of the Jewish polity and the extrusion of the chosen people from their peculiar privileges which followed it; though this would serve as the dark shadow, cast before, of a more terrible retribution to come. The "fire," which in another verse is called "unquenchable," can be no other than that future "torment" of the impenitent, whose "smoke ascendeth up for ever and ever," and which by the Judge Himself is styled "everlasting punishment" (Matt. xxv. 46). What a strength, too, of just indignation is in that word "cast" or "flung into the fire!" [βάλλεται].

The Third Gospel here adds the following important particulars, Luke iii. 10-16: *V.* 10. "And the people"—rather, 'the multitudes' [οἱ ὄχλοι]—"asked him, saying, What shall we do then?"—that is, to show the sincerity of our repentance. *V.* 11. "He answereth and saith unto them, He that hath two coats, let him impart to him that hath none; and he that hath meat"—'provisions,' 'victuals' [βρώματα]—"let him do likewise." This is directed against the reigning avarice and selfishness. (Compare the corresponding precepts of the Sermon on the Mount, ch. v. 40-42.) *V.* 12. "Then came also the publicans to be baptized, and said unto him, Master," or 'Teacher' [Διδάσκαλε], "what shall we do?"—in what special way is the genuineness of our repentance to be manifested? *V.* 13. "And he said unto them, Exact no more than that which is appointed you." This is directed against that extortion which made the publicans a by-word. (See on ch. v. 46; and on Luke xv. 1.) *V.* 14. "And the soldiers"—rather, 'And soldiers' [στρατευόμενοι]—the word means 'soldiers on active duty'—"likewise demanded (or asked) of him, saying, And what shall we do? And he said unto them, Do violence to," or 'Intimidate' [διασείσητε], "no man." The word signifies to 'shake thoroughly,' and refers probably to the extorting of money or other property. "neither accuse any falsely"—by acting as informers vexatiously on frivolous or false pretexts—"and be content with your wages," or 'rations' [τοῖς ὀψωνίοις ὑμῶν]. We may take this, say *Webster and Wilkinson*, as a warning against mutiny, which the officers attempted to suppress by largesses and donations. And thus the "fruits" which would evidence their repentance were just resistance to the reigning sins—particularly of the *class* to which the penitent belonged—and the manifestation of an opposite spirit. *V.* 15. "And as the people were in expectation"—in a state of excitement, looking for something new—"and all men mused in their hearts of John, whether he were the Christ, or not" [μήποτε αὐτὸς εἴη ὁ Χριστός]—rather, 'whether he himself might be the Christ.' The structure of this clause implies that they could hardly think it, but yet could not help asking themselves whether it might not be; showing both how successful he had been in awakening the expectation of Messiah's immediate appearing, and the high estimation, and even reverence, which his own character commanded. *V.* 16. "John answered"—either to that deputation from Jerusalem, of which we read in John i. 19, &c., or on some other occasion, to remove impressions derogatory to his blessed Master, which he knew to be taking hold of the popular mind—"saying unto them all"—in solemn protestation: (We now return to the First Gospel.)

11. I indeed baptize you with water unto repentance (see on *v.* 6): **but he that cometh after me is mightier than I.** In Mark and Luke this is more emphatic—"But there cometh the Mightier than I" [ἔρχεται δὲ ὁ ἰσχυρότερός μου]. **whose shoes,** or 'sandals' [ὑποδήματα], **I am not worthy to bear.** The sandals were tied and untied, and borne about by the meanest servants. **he shall baptize you** [Αὐτὸς]—the emphatic "He;" 'He it is,' to the exclusion of all others 'that shall baptize you.' **with the Holy Ghost.** 'So far from entertaining such a thought as laying claim to the honours of Messiahship, the meanest services I can render to that "Mightier than I that is coming after me" are too high an honour for me; I am but the servant, but the Master is coming; I administer but the outward symbol of purification; His it is, as His sole prerogative, to dispense the inward reality.' Beautiful spirit, distinguishing this servant of Christ throughout! **and with fire.** To take this as a distinct baptism from that of the Spirit—a baptism of the impenitent with hell-fire—is exceedingly unnatural. Yet this was the view of *Origen* among the Fathers; and among moderns, of *Neander*, *Meyer*, *de Wette*, and *Lange*. Nor is it much better to refer it to the fire of the great day, by which the earth and the works that are therein shall be burned up. Clearly, as we think, it is but the *fiery* character of the Spirit's operations upon the soul—searching, consuming, refining, sublimating—as nearly all good interpreters understand the words. And thus, in two successive clauses, the two most familiar emblems—*water* and *fire*—are employed to set forth the same purifying operations of the Holy Ghost upon the soul. **12. Whose** [winnowing] **fan is in his hand**—ready for use. This is no other than the preaching of the Gospel, even now beginning, the effect of which would be to separate the solid from the spiritually worthless, as wheat, by the winnowing fan, from the chaff. (Compare the similar representation in Mal. iii. 1-3.) **and he will throughly purge** [διακαθαριεῖ] **his** [threshing] **floor**—that is, the visible Church. **and gather his wheat**—His true-hearted saints; so called for their solid worth (cf. Amos ix. 9; Luke xxii. 31). **into the garner**—"the kingdom of their

12 Holy Ghost, and *with* fire: whose [p] fan *is* in his hand, and he will
throughly purge his floor, and gather his wheat into the garner; but he
will [q] burn up the chaff with unquenchable fire.

A. D. 26.
[p] Mal. 3. 3.
[q] Mal. 4. 1. ch. 13. 30.

Father," as this "garner" or "barn" [ἀποθήκη] is beautifully explained by our Lord in the parable of the Wheat and the Tares (ch. xiii. 30, 43). **but he will burn up the chaff**—empty, worthless professors of religion, void of all solid religious principle and character (see Ps. i. 4). **with unquenchable fire.** Singular is the strength of this apparent contradiction of figures:—to be burnt up, but with a fire that is unquenchable; the one expressing the *utter destruction* of all that constitutes one's true life, the other the *continued consciousness of existence* in that awful condition.

Luke adds the following important particulars, iii. 18-20: *V.* 18. "And many other things in his exhortation preached he unto the people," showing that we have here but an abstract of his teaching. Besides what we read in John i. 29, 33, 34; iii. 27-36; the incidental allusion to His having taught His disciples to pray (Luke xi. 1)—of which not a word is said elsewhere—shows how varied His teaching was. *V.* 19. "But Herod the tetrarch, being reproved by him for Herodias his brother Philip's wife, and for all the evils which Herod had done." In this last clause we have an important fact, here only mentioned, showing how *thorough-going* was the fidelity of the Baptist to his royal hearer, and how strong must have been the workings of conscience in that slave of passion when, notwithstanding such plainness, he "did many things, and heard John gladly" (Mark vi. 20). *V.* 20. "Added yet this above all, that he shut up John in prison." This imprisonment of John, however, did not take place for some time after this; and it is here recorded merely because the Evangelist did not intend to recur to his history till he had occasion to relate the message which he sent to Christ from his prison at Machærus (Luke vii. 18, &c.).

Remarks.—1. If the view we have given of the import of John's ministry be correct, it has its counterpart in the divine procedure towards each individual believer. In the transition of the Church from Moses to Christ—from the Law to the Gospel—the ministry of the forerunner was expressly provided, in order to bear in upon the national conscience the sense of sin, and shut it up to the coming Deliverer. The dispensation even of the Law itself was introduced, we are told, for the same purpose—merely as a transition-stage from Adam to Christ. "The Law *entered*," says the apostle—'entered incidentally' or 'parenthetically' [παρεισῆλθεν]—"that the offence might abound" (see on Rom. v. 20). The promulgation of the Law was no primary or essential feature of the divine plan. It "was added" [προσετέθη] (Gal. iii. 19) for a subordinate purpose—the more fully to reveal the evil that had been done by Adam, and the need and glory of the remedy by Christ. Thus, as in every age God has provided special means for making the need of salvation, and the value of His Son as a Saviour, felt on a wide scale by the obtuse conscience, so in the history of every believer it will be found that the cordial reception of Christ, as all his salvation and all his desire, has been preceded by some *forerunning* dispensation of mercy; in some cases lengthened and slow, in others brief and rapid—in some operating perceptibly enough, in others all unconsciously—but in every case real and necessary, as "a schoolmaster, to bring us unto Christ." 2. The Pharisees and Sadducees were not *sects*, in the modern sense of that term—holding no ecclesiastical fellowship with each other—but rather *schools* or *parties*, antagonistic both in principle and feeling. The Pharisees were the zealots of outward, literal, legal Judaism—not, however, as represented in Scripture, but as interpreted, or rather perverted, by the traditions which had from age to age grown up around it, penetrated to its core, and eaten into its life. The Sadducees, occupying sceptical or rationalistic ground, were, of course, anti-traditional; but they went much further, limiting their canon of Scripture—in effect if not professedly—to the Pentateuch, and explaining away almost everything supernatural even in it. The Essenes were a sect, it would appear, in the modern sense of the term; and so, not coming across the Evangelical territory, the Gospels are silent regarding them. Their religious system appears to have been a compound of Oriental, Alexandrian, and Jewish elements, while a peculiar ritualism in practice and asceticism in spirit kept them very much by themselves. In these religious divisions of the Jews at this time, we have but the representatives for the time being of abiding and outstanding forms of religious thought—of that traditionary *formalism*, that sceptical *rationalism*, and that separative *mysticism*, which, with various modifications in kind and degree, divide among themselves the unwholesome thinking and feeling of Christendom at this day. And just as then, so still, the medicine which will alone heal the Church visible, and make it "white and ruddy" with spiritual health and vigour, lies in those three notes of the Baptist's teaching—"Flee from the wrath to come;" "Behold the Lamb of God which taketh away the sin of the world;" "He shall baptize you with the Holy Ghost and with fire!" 3. In times of religious awakening, the most unpromising classes are sometimes found making a religious profession. But, whatever just suspicions this may awaken, where the change is not very marked, let not the preacher repel any who even seem to be turning to the Lord, but, like the Baptist, temper his faithful warnings with encouragements and directions. 4. How sharp is the contrast here drawn between all mere human agency in the salvation of men and that of the Master of whom John here speaks. When John, the greatest of all the prophets, says of his own agency, "I indeed baptize you with water unto repentance," he manifestly means not only that this was all he could do towards their salvation, but that it was all *outside* work; he could not work repentance in them, nor deposit in their hearts one grain of true grace. When, therefore, he adds, "He that cometh after me is mightier than I; He shall baptize you with the Holy Ghost, and with fire," beyond doubt he means to teach not only that Christ could do what he could not, but that it was His sole prerogative to do it—as "the Mightier than he" (Mark i. 7; Luke iii. 16)—imparting the inner element, of which water-baptism was but the outward sign, and giving it a glorious, fiery efficacy in the heart. No wonder that at the thought of this difference John should say, "Whose shoes' latchet I am not worthy to bear"—language very offensive if we could suppose it meant of any mere *creature*, however gifted and honoured of God, but most fit and proper regarding *Emmanuel*, "God with us." 5. As the saving operations of the Holy Ghost are here first mentioned in the New Testament, so His precise relation to Christ in the economy of

13 Then cometh Jesus [r]from Galilee to Jordan unto John, to be baptized of
14 him. But John forbade him, saying, I have need to be baptized of thee,
15 and comest thou to me? And Jesus answering said unto him, Suffer *it to*
be so now: for thus it becometh us to [s]fulfil all righteousness. Then he
16 suffered him. And [t]Jesus, when he was baptized, went up straightway

A. D. 26.

[r] ch. 2. 22.
[s] Dan. 9. 24.
[t] Mark 1. 10.
Luke 3. 21.

salvation is here distinctly taught—that He is *Christ's Agent*, carrying into effect *in* men all that He did *for* men. 6. The vengeance here denounced against impenitence under all this spiritual culture best exhibits the guilt of it—"Every tree, therefore, which bringeth not forth good fruit is hewn down, and cast into the fire." "Be instructed, then, O Jerusalem, lest my soul depart from thee."

13-17.—BAPTISM OF CHRIST, AND DESCENT OF THE SPIRIT UPON HIM IMMEDIATELY THEREAFTER. (= Mark i. 9-11; Luke iii. 21, 22; John i. 31-34.)

Baptism of Christ (13-15). **13. Then cometh Jesus from Galilee to Jordan unto John, to be baptized of him.** Moses rashly anticipated the Divine call to deliver his people, and for this was fain to flee the house of bondage, and wait in obscurity for forty years more (Ex. ii. 11, &c.). Not so this Greater than Moses. All but thirty years had He now spent in privacy at Nazareth, gradually ripening for His public work, and calmly awaiting the time appointed of the Father. Now it had arrived; and this movement from Galilee to Jordan is the step, doubtless, of deepest interest to all heaven since that first one which brought Him into the world. Luke (iii. 21) has this important addition—"Now *when all the people were baptized*, it came to pass, that Jesus being baptized," &c.—implying that Jesus waited till all other applicants for baptism that day had been disposed of, ere He stepped forward, that He might not seem to be merely one of the crowd. Thus, as He rode into Jerusalem upon an ass "whereon yet never man sat" (Luke xix. 30), and lay in a sepulchre "wherein was never man yet laid" (John xix. 41), so in His baptism too He would be "separate from sinners." **14. But John forbade him** [διεκώλυεν]—rather, 'was [in the act of] hindering him,' or 'attempting to hinder him'—**saying, I have need to be baptized of thee, and comest thou to me?** (How John came to recognize Him, when he says he knew Him not, see on John i. 31-34.) The emphasis of this most remarkable speech lies all in the pronouns ['Εγὼ ὑπὸ σοῦ . . . καὶ σὺ . . . πρός με]: 'What! Shall the Master come for baptism to the servant—the sinless Saviour to a sinner?' That thus much is in the Baptist's words will be clearly seen if it be observed that he evidently regarded Jesus as *Himself needing no purification*, but rather *qualified to impart it to those who did.* And do not all his other testimonies to Christ fully bear out this sense of the words? But it were a pity if, in the glory of this testimony to Christ, we should miss the beautiful spirit in which it was borne—'Lord, must *I* baptize *Thee?* Can I bring myself to do such a thing?'—reminding us of Peter's exclamation at the supper-table, "Lord, dost Thou wash my feet?" while it has nothing of the false humility and presumption which dictated Peter's next speech, "Thou shalt never wash my feet" (John xiii. 6, 8). **15. And Jesus answering said unto him, Suffer it to be so now** [Ἄφες ἄρτι]—'Let it pass for the present' (*Webster and Wilkinson*); *q. d.*, 'Thou recoilest, and no wonder, for the seeming incongruity is startling; but in the present case do as thou art bidden.' **for thus it becometh us**—"*us*," not in the sense of 'me and thee,' or 'men in general,' but as in John iii. 11. **to fulfil all righteousness** [πᾶσαν δικαιοσύνην]. If this be rendered, with *Scrivener*, 'every ordinance,' or, with *Campbell*, 'every institution,' the meaning is obvious enough; and the same sense is brought out by "all righteousness," or compliance with everything enjoined, baptism included. Indeed, if this be the meaning, our version perhaps best brings out the force of the opening word "Thus" [οὕτως]. But we incline to think that our Lord meant more than this. The import of Circumcision and of Baptism seems to be radically the same. And if our remarks on the circumcision of our Lord (on Luke ii. 21-24) are well founded, He would seem to have said, 'Thus do I impledge myself to the whole righteousness of the Law—thus symbolically do enter on and engage to fulfil it all.' Let the thoughtful reader weigh this. **Then he suffered him**—with true humility, yielding to higher authority than his own impressions of propriety.

Descent of the Spirit upon the Baptized Redeemer (16, 17). **16. And Jesus, when he was baptized, went up straightway out of** [ἀπὸ]—rather, 'from'—**the water.** Mark has "out of the water" [ἐκ]. **and**—adds Luke (iii. 21), "while He was praying;" a grand piece of information. Can there be a doubt about the burden of that prayer; a prayer sent up, probably, while yet in the water—His blessed head suffused with the baptismal element; a prayer continued likely as He stepped out of the stream, and again stood upon the dry ground? The work before Him, the needed and expected Spirit to rest upon Him for it, and the glory He would then put upon the Father that sent Him—would not these fill His breast, and find silent vent in such form as this?—'Lo, I come; I delight to do thy will, O God. Father, glorify thy name. Show me a token for good. Let the Spirit of the Lord God come upon me, and I will preach the Gospel to the poor, and heal the broken-hearted, and send forth judgment unto victory.' Whilst He was yet speaking—**lo, the heavens were opened.** Mark says, sublimely, "He saw the heavens cleaving" [σχιζομένους]. **and he saw the Spirit of God descending**—that is, He only, with the exception of His honoured servant, as He tells us Himself, John 1. 32-34; the by-standers apparently seeing nothing. **like a dove, and lighting upon him.** Luke says, "in a bodily shape" (iii. 22); that is, the blessed Spirit, assuming the corporeal form of a dove, descended thus upon His sacred head. But why in this form? The Scripture use of this emblem will be our best guide here. "My dove, *my undefiled* is one," says the Song (vi. 9). This is chaste purity. Again, "Be ye *harmless* as doves," says Christ Himself (Matt. x. 16). This is the same thing, in the form of inoffensiveness towards men. "A conscience void of offence toward God and toward men" (Acts xxiv. 16) expresses both. Further, when we read in the Song (ii. 14), "O my dove, that art in the *clefts* of the rock, in the *secret places* of the stairs (see Isa. lx. 8), let me see thy countenance, let me hear thy voice; for sweet is thy voice, and thy countenance is comely"—it is shrinking modesty, meekness, gentleness, that is thus charmingly depicted. In a word—not to allude to the historical emblem of the dove that flew back to the ark, bearing in its

out of the water: and, lo, the heavens were opened unto him, and he saw
17 [u]the Spirit of God descending like a dove, and lighting upon him: and
[v]lo a voice from heaven, saying, This [w]is my beloved Son, in whom I am
well pleased.

4 THEN was [a]Jesus led up of [b]the Spirit into the wilderness to be

A. D. 26.

[u] Isa. 11. 2.
[v] John 12. 28.
[w] Ps. 2. 7.

[a] Mark 1. 12.
[b] 1 Ki. 18. 12.

mouth the olive leaf of *peace* (Gen. viii. 11)—when we read (Ps. lxviii. 13), "Ye shall be as the wings of a dove covered with silver, and her feathers with yellow gold," it is *beauteousness* that is thus held forth. And was not such that "Holy, harmless, undefiled One," the "Separate from sinners?" "Thou art fairer than the children of men; grace is poured into Thy lips; therefore God hath blessed Thee for ever!" But the fourth Gospel gives us one more piece of information here, on the authority of one who saw and testified of it: "John bare record, saying, I saw the Spirit descending from heaven like a dove, and IT ABODE UPON HIM" [καὶ ἔμεινεν ἐπ' αὐτόν]. And lest we should think that this was an accidental thing, he adds that this last particular was expressly given him as part of the sign by which he was to recognize and identify Him as the Son of God: "And I knew Him not: but He that sent me to baptize with water, the same said unto me, Upon whom thou shalt see the Spirit descending AND REMAINING ON HIM [καὶ μένον ἐπ' αὐτὸν], the same is He which baptizeth with the Holy Ghost. And I saw, and bare record that this is the Son of God" (John i. 32-34). And when with this we compare the predicted descent of the Spirit upon Messiah (Isa. xi. 2), "And *the Spirit of the Lord shall rest upon him*" [וְנָחָה, ἀναπαύσεται], we cannot doubt that it was this permanent and perfect resting of the Holy Ghost upon the Son of God—now and henceforward in His *official* capacity—that was here visibly manifested. **17. And lo a voice from heaven, saying, This is**—Mark and Luke give it in the direct form, "Thou art"—**my beloved Son, in whom I am well pleased** [εὐδόκησα]. The verb is put in the aorist to express absolute complacency, once and for ever felt towards Him. The English here, at least to modern ears, is scarcely strong enough. 'I delight' comes the nearest, perhaps, to that ineffable *complacency* which is manifestly intended; and this is the rather to be preferred, as it would immediately carry the thoughts back to that august Messianic prophecy to which the voice from heaven plainly alluded (Isa. xlii. 1), "Behold my Servant, whom I uphold; mine Elect, IN WHOM MY SOUL DELIGHTETH" [רָצְתָה]. Nor are the words which follow to be overlooked, "I have put my Spirit upon Him; He shall bring forth judgment to the Gentiles." (The LXX. pervert this, as they do most of the Messianic predictions, interpolating the word "Jacob," and applying it to the Jews.) Was this voice heard by the by-standers? From Matthew's form of it, one might suppose it so designed; but it would appear that it was not, and probably John only heard and saw anything peculiar about that great baptism. Accordingly, the words "Hear ye Him" are not added, as at the Transfiguration.

Remarks.—1. Here we have three of the most astonishing things which eye could behold and ear hear. *First*, We have Jesus formally entered and articled to His Father, contracted and engaged, going voluntarily under the yoke, and by a public deed sealed over to obedience. *Next*, We have Him consecrated and anointed with the Holy Ghost above measure (John iii. 34); and thus thoroughly furnished, divinely equipped for the work given Him to do. *Thirdly*, We have Him divinely attested by Him who knew Him best and cannot lie; and thus publicly inaugurated, formally installed in all the authority of His mediatorial office, as the Son of God in the flesh, and the Object of His Father's absolute complacency. 2. That the Holy Ghost, whose supernatural agency formed the human nature of Christ, and sanctified it from the womb, was a stranger to the breast of Jesus until now that He descended upon Him at His baptism, is not for a moment to be conceived. The whole analogy of Scripture, on the work of the Spirit and of sanctification, leads to the conclusion that as He "grew in favour with God and man," from infancy to youth, and from youth to manhood, His moral beauty, His spiritual loveliness, His faultless excellence, was enstamped and developed from stage to stage by the gentle yet efficacious energy of the Holy Ghost; though only at His full maturity was He capable of all that fulness which He then received. To use the words of *Olshausen*, 'Even the pure offspring of the Spirit needed the anointing of the Spirit; and it was only when His human nature had grown strong enough for the support of the fulness of the Spirit that it remained stationary, and fully endowed with power from above.' Knowing, therefore, as we do, that at His baptism He passed out of private into public life, we can have no doubt that the descent of the Spirit upon Christ at His baptism was for *official* purposes. But in this we include His whole public work—life, character, spirit, carriage, actings, endurances, everything that constituted and manifested Him to be the pure, inoffensive, gentle, beauteous "DOVE"—all this was of the Spirit of the Lord that "*rested*"—that "*abode*"—upon Him. How well may the Church now sing, "God, thy God, hath anointed Thee with the oil of gladness above thy fellows. All thy garments smell of myrrh, and aloes, and cassia, out of the ivory palaces, whereby they have made Thee glad!" (Ps. xlv. 7, 8.) 3. Here, in the baptism of our blessed Head, we find ourselves in the presence at once of THE FATHER, THE SON, and THE HOLY GHOST, into whose adorable name we are baptized (ch. xxviii. 19). The early Fathers of the Church were struck with this, and often advert to it. 'Go to Jordan,' said *Augustin* to the heretic Marcion, 'and thou shalt see the Trinity' [*I ad Jordanem et videbis Trinitatem*]. Nor is it to be overlooked, as *Lange* remarks, that as it is at Christ's own baptism that we have the first distinct revelation of the doctrine of the Trinity, so it is at the institution of baptism for His Church that this doctrine brightens into full glory.

CHAP. IV. 1-11.—TEMPTATION OF CHRIST. (=Mark i. 12, 13; Luke iv. 1-13.)

1. Then [Τότε]—an indefinite note of sequence. But Mark's word (i. 12) fixes what we should have presumed was meant, that it was "immediately" [εὐθὺς] after His baptism; and with this agrees the statement of Luke (iv. 1). **was Jesus led up** [ἀνήχθη]—*i. e.*, from the low Jordan valley to some more elevated spot. **of the Spirit**—that blessed Spirit immediately before spoken of as descending upon Him at His baptism, and abiding upon Him. Luke, connecting these two scenes, as if the one were but the sequel of the other, says, "Jesus, being full of the Holy Ghost, returned from Jordan, and was led," &c. Mark's expression has a startling sharpness about it—"Immediately the Spirit driveth

2 [c]tempted of the devil. And when he had [d]fasted forty days and forty
nights, he was afterward an hungered.
3 And when the tempter came to him, he said, If thou be the Son of God,
4 command that these stones be made bread. But he answered and said, [e]It

A. D. 27.

[c] Heb. 4. 15.
[d] Ex. 34. 28.
[e] Eph. 6. 17.

Him" [ἐκβάλλει], 'putteth,' or 'hurrieth, Him forth,' or 'impelleth Him.' (See the same word in Mark i. 43; v. 40; Matt. ix. 25; xiii. 52; John x. 4.) The thought thus strongly expressed is the mighty constraining impulse of the Spirit under which He went; while Matthew's more gentle expression, "was led up," intimates how purely voluntary on His own part this action was. **into the wilderness**—probably the wild Judean desert. The particular spot which tradition has fixed upon has hence got the name of *Quarantana* or *Quarantaria*, from the forty days,—'an almost perpendicular wall of rock twelve or fifteen hundred feet above the plain.' —*Robinson's* Palestine. The supposition of those who incline to place the Temptation amongst the mountains of Moab is, we think, very improbable. **to be tempted** [πειρασθῆναι]. The Greek word [πειράζειν] means simply to *try* or make proof of; and when ascribed to God in His dealings with men, it means, and can mean no more than this. Thus, Gen. xxii. 1, "It came to pass that God did tempt Abraham," or put his faith to a severe proof. (See Deut. viii. 2.) But for the most part in Scripture the word is used in a bad sense, and means to entice, solicit, or provoke to sin. Hence the name here given to the wicked one—"the tempter" (*v.* 3). Accordingly, "to be tempted" here is to be understood both ways. The Spirit conducted Him into the wilderness simply to have His faith *tried;* but as the agent in this trial was to be the wicked one, whose whole object would be to seduce Him from His allegiance to God, it was a *temptation* in the bad sense of the term. The unworthy inference which some would draw from this is energetically repelled by an apostle (Jas. i. 13-17). **of the devil.** The word [διάβολος] signifies a slanderer—one who casts imputations upon another. Hence that other name given him (Rev. xii. 10), "The accuser of the brethren, who accuseth them before our God day and night." Mark (i. 13) says, "He was forty days tempted of *Satan*" [שָׂטָן], a word signifying an *adversary*, one who lies in wait for, or sets himself in opposition to another. These and other names of the same fallen spirit point to different features in his character or operations. What was the high design of this? First, as we judge, to give our Lord a taste of what lay before Him in the work He had undertaken; next, to make trial of the glorious furniture for it which He had just received; further, to give Him encouragement, by the victory now to be won, to go forward spoiling principalities and powers, until at length He should make a show of them openly, triumphing over them in His Cross; that the tempter, too, might get a taste, at the very outset, of the new kind of material in *Man* which he would find he had here to deal with; finally, that He might acquire experimental ability "to succour them that are tempted" (Heb. ii. 18). The temptation evidently embraced two stages: the one continuing throughout the forty days' fast; the other, at the conclusion of that period. FIRST STAGE: **2. And when he had fasted forty days and forty nights.** Luke says, "When they were quite ended [συντελεσθεισῶν]. **he was afterward** [ὕστερον] **an hungered**—evidently implying that the sensation of hunger was unfelt during all the forty days; coming on only at their close. So it was apparently with Moses (Ex. xxxiv. 28) and Elijah (1 Ki. xix. 8) for the same period. (The ὕστερον in Luke iv. 2 has scarcely sufficient authority, and was probably introduced from Matthew.) A supernatural power of endurance was of course imparted to the body; but this probably operated through a natural law—the absorption of the Redeemer's spirit in the dread conflict with the tempter. (See on Acts ix. 9.) Had we only this Gospel, we should suppose the temptation did not begin till after this. But it is clear, from Mark's statement that "He was in the wilderness forty days tempted of Satan," and Luke's "being forty days tempted of the devil," that there was a forty days' temptation *before* the three specific temptations afterwards recorded. And this is what we have called the First Stage. What the precise nature and object of the forty days' temptation was is not recorded. But two things seem plain enough. First, the tempter had utterly failed of his object, else it had not been renewed; and the terms in which he opens his second attack imply as much. But further, the tempter's whole object during the forty days evidently was to get Him to distrust the heavenly testimony borne to Him at His baptism as THE SON OF GOD—to persuade Him to regard it as but a splendid illusion—and, generally, to dislodge from His breast the consciousness of His Sonship. With what plausibility the events of His previous history from the beginning would be urged upon Him in support of this temptation it is easy to imagine. And it makes much in support of this view of the forty days' temptation, that the particulars of it are not recorded; for how the details of such a purely internal struggle could be recorded it is hard to see. If this be correct, how naturally does the SECOND STAGE of the temptation open! In Mark's brief notice of the temptation there is one expressive particular not given either by Matthew or by Luke—that "He was with the wild beasts," no doubt to add terror to solitude, and aggravate the horrors of the whole scene.

3. And when the tempter came to him. Evidently we have here a new scene. **he said, If thou be the Son of God, command that these stones be made bread** [ἄρτοι]—rather, 'loaves,' answering to "stones" in the plural; whereas Luke, having said, "Command this stone," in the singular, adds, "that it be made bread" [ἄρτος], in the singular. The sensation of hunger, unfelt during all the forty days, seems now to have come on in all its keenness—no doubt to open a door to the tempter, of which he is not slow to avail himself: *q. d.*, 'Thou still clingest to that vainglorious confidence, that thou art the Son of God, carried away by those illusory scenes at the Jordan. Thou wast born in a stable—but thou art the Son of God! hurried off to Egypt for fear of Herod's wrath—but thou art the Son of God! a carpenter's roof supplied thee with a home, and in the obscurity of a despicable town of Galilee thou hast spent thirty years—yet still thou art the Son of God; and a voice from heaven, it seems, proclaimed it in thine ears at the Jordan! Be it so; but after *that*, surely thy days of obscurity and trial should have an end. Why linger for weeks in this desert, wandering among the wild beasts and craggy rocks, unhonoured, unattended, unpitied, ready to starve for want of the necessaries of life? Is this befitting "the Son of God?" At the bidding of

is written, Man [f]shall not live by bread alone, but by every word that
proceedeth out of the mouth of God.
5 Then the devil taketh him up [g]into the holy city, and setteth him
6 on a pinnacle of the temple, and saith unto him, If thou be the Son of
God, cast thyself down: for it is written, He [h]shall give his angels charge
concerning thee; and in *their* hands they shall bear thee up, lest at any
7 time thou dash thy foot against a stone. Jesus said unto him, It is
written again, Thou [i]shalt not tempt the Lord thy God.
8 Again, the devil taketh him up into an exceeding high mountain, and

A. D. 27.

[f] Deut. 8. 3.
[g] Neh. 11. 1. Isa. 48. 2; 52. 1.
[h] Ps. 91. 11. Heb. 1. 14.
[i] Ex. 17. 2, 7. Num. 14.22. Deut. 6. 16. Mal. 3. 15.

"the Son of God" sure those stones shall all be turned into loaves, and in a moment present an abundant repast?' **4. But he answered and said, It is written** (Deut. viii. 3), **Man shall not live by bread alone**—more emphatically, as in the Greek, 'Not by bread alone shall man live'—**but by every word that proceedeth out of the mouth of God.** Of all passages in Old Testament scripture, none could have been pitched upon more apposite, perhaps not one so apposite, to our Lord's purpose. "The Lord led thee (said Moses to Israel, at the close of their journeyings) these forty years in the wilderness, to humble thee, and to prove thee, to know what was in thine heart, whether thou wouldest keep his commandments, or no. And he humbled thee, and suffered thee to hunger, and fed thee with manna, which thou knewest not, neither did thy fathers know; that he might make thee know that man doth not live by bread only," &c. 'Now, if Israel spent, not forty days, but forty years in a waste, howling wilderness, where there were no means of human subsistence, not starving, but divinely provided for, on purpose to prove to every age that human support depends not upon bread, but upon God's unfailing word of promise and pledge of all needful providential care, am I, distrusting this word of God, and despairing of relief, to take the law into my own hand? True, the Son of God is able enough to turn stones into bread: but what the Son of God is able to do is not the present question, but what is *Man's duty* under want of the necessaries of life. And as Israel's condition in the wilderness did not justify their unbelieving murmurings and frequent desperation, so neither would mine warrant the exercise of the power of the Son of God in snatching despairingly at unwarranted relief. As man, therefore, I will await divine supply, nothing doubting that at the fitting time it will arrive.' The *second* temptation in this Gospel is in Luke's the *third*. That Matthew's order is the right one will appear, we think, pretty clearly in the sequel.

5. Then the devil taketh him up [παραλαμβάνει]—rather, 'conducteth him'—**into the holy city**—so called (as in Isa. xlviii. 2; Neh. xi. 1) from its being "the city of the Great King," the seat of the temple, the metropolis of all Jewish worship. **and setteth him on a pinnacle** [τὸ πτερύγιον]—rather, 'the pinnacle'—**of the temple**—a certain well-known projection. Whether this refer to the highest summit of the temple [the κορυφή], which bristled with golden spikes (*Joseph.* Antt. v. 5, 6); or whether it refer to another peak, on Herod's royal portico, overhanging the ravine of Kedron, at the valley of Hinnom—an immense tower built on the very edge of this precipice, from the top of which dizzy height Josephus says one could not look to the bottom (*Antt.* xv. 11, 5)—is not certain; but the latter is probably meant. **6. And saith unto him, If thou be the Son of God.** As this temptation starts with the same point as the first—our Lord's determination not to be disputed out of His Sonship—it seems to us clear that the one came directly after the other; and as the remaining temptation shows that the hope of carrying that point was abandoned, and all was staked upon a desperate venture, we think that remaining temptation is thus shown to be the last; as will appear still more when we come to it. **cast thyself down** ("from hence," Luke iv. 9): **for it is written** (Ps. xci. 11, 12). 'But what is this I see?' exclaims stately *Bishop Hall*, 'Satan himself with a Bible under his arm and a text in his mouth!' Doubtless the tempter, having felt the power of God's word in the former temptation, was eager to try the effect of it from his own mouth (2 Cor. xi. 14). **He shall give his angels charge concerning thee; and in**—rather, 'on' [ἐπὶ]—**their hands they shall bear thee up, lest at any time thou dash thy foot against a stone.** The quotation is precisely as it stands in the Hebrew and LXX., save that after the first clause the words, "to keep thee in all thy ways," is here omitted. Not a few good expositors have thought that this omission was intentional, to conceal the fact that this would *not* have been one of "His ways," that is, of duty. But as our Lord's reply makes no allusion to this, but seizes on the great principle involved in the promise quoted; so when we look at the promise itself, it is plain that the sense of it is precisely the same whether the clause in question be inserted or not. **7. Jesus said unto him, It is written again** (Deut. vi. 16)—*q. d.*, 'True, it is so written, and on that promise I implicitly rely; but in using it there is another scripture which must not be forgotten, **Thou shalt not tempt the Lord thy God.** Preservation in danger is divinely pledged: shall I then *create* danger, either to put the promised security sceptically to the proof, or wantonly to demand a display of it? That were to "tempt the Lord my God," which, being expressly forbidden, would forfeit the right to expect preservation.'

8. Again, the devil taketh him up—'conducteth him,' as before—**into**, or 'unto,' **an exceeding high mountain, and showeth him all the kingdoms of the world, and the glory of them.** Luke (iv. 5) adds the important clause, "in a moment of time;" a clause which seems to furnish a key to the true meaning. That a scene was presented to our Lord's natural eye seems plainly expressed. But to limit this to the most extensive scene which the natural eye could take in, is to give a sense to the expression, "all the kingdoms of the world," quite violent. It remains, then, to gather from the expression, "in a moment of time"—which manifestly is intended to intimate some supernatural operation—that it was permitted to the tempter to extend preternaturally for a moment our Lord's range of vision, and throw a "glory" or glitter over the scene of vision; a thing not inconsistent with the analogy of other scriptural statements regarding the permitted operations of the wicked one. In this case, the "exceeding height" of the "mountain" from which this sight was beheld would favour the effect intended to be produced. **9. And saith unto him, All these things will I give thee**—"and the glory of them," adds Luke. But

9 showeth him all the kingdoms of the world, and the glory of them; and
saith unto him, All these things will I give thee, if thou wilt fall down
10 and worship me. Then saith Jesus unto him, Get thee hence, Satan: for
it is written, [j]Thou shalt worship the Lord thy God, and him only shalt

A. D. 27.

j Deut. 6. 13; 10. 20. Jos. 24. 14. 1 Sam. 7. 3.

Matthew having already said that this was "showed Him," did not need to repeat it here. Luke (iv. 6) adds these other very important clauses, here omitted—"for that is," or 'has been,' "delivered unto me, and to whomsoever I will I give it." Was this wholly false? That were not like Satan's usual policy, which is to insinuate his lies under cover of some truth. What truth, then, is there here? We answer, Is not Satan thrice called by our Lord Himself, "the prince of this world?" (John xii. 31; xiv. 30; xvi. 11;) does not the apostle call him "the God of this world?" (2 Cor. iv. 4;) and still further, is it not said that Christ came to destroy by His death "him that *hath the power of death*, that is, the devil?" (Heb. ii. 14.) No doubt these passages only express men's voluntary subjection to the rule of the wicked one while they live, and his power to surround death to them, when it comes, with all the terrors of the wages of sin. But as this is a real and terrible sway, so all Scripture represents men as righteously sold under it. In this sense he speaks what is not devoid of truth, when he says, "All this is delivered unto me." But how does he deliver this "to whomsoever he will?" As employing whomsoever he pleases of his willing subjects in keeping men under his power. In this case his offer to our Lord was that of a *deputed* supremacy commensurate with his own, though as *his gift* and for *his ends*. **if thou wilt fall down and worship me.** This was the sole, but monstrous condition. No Scripture, it will be observed, is quoted now, because none could be found to support so blasphemous a claim. In fact, he has ceased now to present his temptations under the mask of piety, and stands out unblushingly as the rival of God Himself in his claims on the homage of men. Despairing of success as an angel of light, he throws off all disguise, and with a splendid bribe solicits divine honour. This again shows that we are now at the last of the temptations, and that Matthew's order is the true one. **10. Then saith Jesus unto him, Get thee hence, Satan.** (The evidence for the *insertion* here of the words ὀπίσω μου—'behind me,'—and the *omission* of them in Luke iv. 8, is nearly equal; but perhaps the received text in both places has slightly the better support.) Since the tempter has now thrown off the mask, and stands forth in his true character, our Lord no longer deals with him as a pretended friend and pious counsellor, but calls him by his right name—His knowledge of which from the outset He had carefully concealed till now—and orders him off. This is the final and conclusive evidence, as we think, that Matthew's must be the right order of the temptations. For who can well conceive of the tempter's returning to the assault after this, in the pious character again, and hoping still to dislodge the consciousness of His Sonship; while our Lord must in that case be supposed to quote Scripture to one He had called the Devil to his face—thus throwing His pearls before worse than swine? **for it is written** (Deut. vi. 13): Thus does our Lord part with Satan on the rock of Scripture, **Thou shalt worship.** In the Hebrew and LXX. it is, "Thou shalt *fear;*" but as the sense is the same, so "worship" is here used to show emphatically that what the tempter claimed was precisely what God had forbidden. **the Lord thy God, and him only shalt thou serve.** The word "serve" [λατρεύσεις], in the second clause, is one never used by the LXX. of any but *religious* service; and in this sense exclusively is it used in the New Testament, as we find it here. Once more the word "only," in the second clause—not expressed in the Hebrew and LXX.—is here added to bring out emphatically the *negative* and *prohibitory* feature of the command. (See Gal. iii. 10 for a similar supplement of the word "all," in a quotation from Deut. xxvii. 26.) **11. Then the devil leaveth him.** Luke says, "And when the devil had exhausted"—or, 'quite ended' [συντελέσας], as in Luke iv. 2—"every [mode of] temptation [πάντα πειρασμὸν], he departed from him till a season" [ἄχρι καιροῦ]. The definite "season" here indicated is expressly referred to by our Lord in John xiv. 30, and Luke xxii. 52, 53. **and, behold, angels came and ministered unto him**—or supplied Him with food, as the same expression means in Mark i. 31, and Luke viii. 3. Thus did angels to Elijah (1 Ki. xix. 5-8). Excellent critics think that they ministered, not food only, but supernatural support and cheer also. But this would be the natural *effect* rather than the direct *object* of the visit, which was plainly what we have expressed. And after having refused to claim the *illegitimate* ministration of angels in His behalf, O with what deep joy would He accept their services when sent, unasked, at the close of all this Temptation, direct from Him whom He had so gloriously honoured! What "angels' food" would this repast be to Him; and as He partook of it, might not a Voice from heaven be heard again, by any who could read the Father's mind, 'Said I not well, This is my beloved Son, in whom I am well pleased!'

Remarks.—1. After such an exalted scene as that of the Baptism, the Descent of the Spirit, and the Voice from heaven, and before entering on His public ministry, this long period of solitude would doubtless be to Jesus a precious interval for calmly pondering His whole past history, and deliberately weighing the momentous future that lay before Him. So would Moses feel his forty years' seclusion in Midian, far from the glitter and pomp of an Egyptian court, and before entering on the eventful career which awaited him on his return. So would Elijah, after the grandeur of the Carmel scene, feel his forty days' solitary journey to Horeb, the mount of God. So would the beloved disciple feel his Patmos exile, after a long apostolic life, short and uneventful though his after career was. So, doubtless, Luther felt his ten months' retreat in the castle of Wartburg to be, after four years of exciting and incessant warfare with the Romish perverters of the Gospel, and before entering afresh on a career which has changed the whole face of European Christendom. And so will such periods, whether longer or shorter, ever be felt by God's faithful people, when in His providence they are called to pass through them. 2. Sharp temptations, as they often follow seasons of high communion, so are they often preparatives for the highest work. 3. What a contrast does Christ here present to Adam! Adam was tempted in a paradise, and yet fell: Christ was tempted in a wilderness, and yet stood. Adam, in a state of innocence, was surrounded by the beasts of the field, all tame and submissive to their lord: Christ, in a fallen world, had the wild beasts raging around him, and only supernaturally restrained. In Adam we see man easily and quickly falling, without a

11 thou serve. Then the devil [k]leaveth him; and, behold, [l]angels came and
ministered unto him.

A. D. 27.

k Jas. 4. 7.
l Heb. 1. 14.

single incentive to evil save the tempter's insinuations: in Christ we see man standing encircled by all that is terrific, and harassed by long-continued, varied, and most subtle attacks from the tempter. 4. Deep is the disquietude which many Christians suffer from finding themselves subject to internal temptations to sin, both continuous and vehement. It staggers them to find that, without any external solicitations, they are tempted so frequently, and at times so violently, that as by a tempest they are ready to be carried away, and in a moment make shipwreck of faith and of a good conscience. Surely, they think, this can only be accounted for but by some depth and virulence of corruption never reached by the grace of God, and inconsistent with that delight in the law of God after the inward man which is characteristic of His children. But here we see, in the holy One of God, an example of solicitations to sin purely internal, for aught that we can perceive, continued throughout the long period of forty days. The *source* of them, it is true, was all external to the Redeemer's soul—they were from the devil solely—but the sphere of them was wholly internal; and it is impossible to doubt that, in order to their being temptations at all, there must have been permitted a vivid presentation by the tempter, to the mind of Jesus, of all that was adverse to His claims—so vivid, indeed, as to make entire and continued resistance a fruit of pure faith. And though probably no temptation of any strength and duration passes over the spirit of a Christian without finding some echo, however faint, and leaving some stain, however slight, the Example here presented should satisfy us that it is neither the duration nor the violence of our temptations—though they come as "fiery darts" (Eph. vi. 16) thick as hail—that tells the state of the heart before God, but *how they are met.* 5. It has long been a prevalent opinion that the three temptations here recorded were addressed to what the beloved disciple calls (1 John ii. 16) "the lust of the flesh (the first one), the lust of the eyes (Luke's second one), and the pride of life" (Luke's third one). Others also, as *Ellicott*, think they were addressed respectively to that three-fold division of our nature (1 Thes. v. 23)—the "body, soul, and spirit," in the same order. Whether this does not presuppose Luke's order of the temptations to be the right one, contrary to what we have endeavoured to show, we need not enquire. But too much should not be made of such things. One thing is certain, that after so long trying our Lord *internally* without success, and then proceeding to solicit Him from *without*, the tempter would leave no avenue to desire, either bodily or mental, unassailed; and so we may rest assured that He "was *in all points* tempted like as we are." The first temptation was to *distrust the providential care of God*—on the double plea that 'it had not come to the rescue in time of need,' and that 'He had the remedy in His own hands, and so need not be at a moment's loss.' This is repelled, not by denying His power to relieve Himself, but by holding up the sinfulness of distrusting God, which that would imply, and the duty, even in the most straitened circumstances, of unshaken confidence in God's word of promise, which is man's true life. O what a word is this for the multitudes of God's children who at times are at their wit's end for the things that are needful for the body—things easily to be had, could they but dare to snatch at them unlawfully, but which seem divinely withheld from them at the very time when they appear most indispensable! The second temptation was to just the opposite of distrust (and this may further show that it *was* the second)—to *presumption* or a *wanton appeal to promised safety*, by creating the danger against which that safety is divinely pledged. And O how many err here! adventuring themselves where they have no warrant to expect protection, and there, exercising a misplaced confidence, are left to suffer the consequences of their presumption. The last temptation is addressed to the principle of *ambition*, which makes us accessible to the lust of possessions, grandeur, and power. These, to a boundless extent, and in all their glitter, are held forth to Jesus as His own, on one single condition—that He will do homage for them to another than God; which was but another way of saying, 'if thou wilt transfer thine allegiance from God to the devil.' It is just the case, then, which our Lord Himself afterwards put to His disciples, "What shall it profit a man if he should gain the whole world, and lose his own soul? Or what shall a man give in exchange for his soul?" And how many are there, naming the name of Christ, who, when, not the whole world, but a very fractional part of it, lies open before them as even likely to become theirs, on the single condition of selling their conscience to what they know to be sinful, give way, and incur the dreadful penalty; instead of resolutely saying, with Joseph, "How can I do this great wickedness, and sin against God," or, with a Greater than Joseph here, "Get thee behind me, Satan, for it is written, Thou shalt worship the Lord thy God, and Him only shalt thou serve." We thus see, however, that within the limits of this temptation-scene—however it be arranged and viewed—all the forms of human temptation were, in *principle*, experienced by "the Man Christ Jesus," and accordingly that "He was tempted in all points like as we are, yet without sin." 6. That the second stage of the Temptation was purely internal as well as the first—which is the theory of some otherwise sound critics, especially of Germany—is at variance with the obvious meaning of the text; creates greater difficulties than those it is intended to remove; is suggested by a spirit of subjective criticism which would explain away other external facts of the Evangelical History as well as this; and is rejected by nearly all orthodox interpreters, as well as repudiated by the simple-minded reader of the narrative. 7. What a testimony to the *divine authority of the Old Testament* have we here! Three quotations are made from it by our Lord—two of them from "the law," and one from "the Psalms"—all introduced by the simple formula, "*It is written*," as divinely settling the question of human duty in the cases referred to; while elsewhere, in quoting from the remaining division of the Old Testament—"the Prophets"—the same formula is employed by our Lord, "*It is written*," (Matt. xxi. 13, &c.) Nor will the theory of 'accommodation to the current views of the time'—as if that would justify an erroneous interpretation of the Old Testament to serve a present purpose—be of any service here. For here our Lord is not contending with the Jews, nor even in their presence, but with the foul tempter alone. Let any one take the trouble to collect and arrange our Lord's quotations from the Old Testament, and indirect references to it, and he will be constrained to admit either that the Old Testament is of divine authority, as a record of

12 Now [m]when Jesus had heard that John was [1]cast into prison, he
13 departed into Galilee; and leaving Nazareth, he came and dwelt in
Capernaum, which is upon the sea coast, in the borders of Zabulon and

A. D. 31.

[m] Luke 3. 20.
[1] Or, delivered up.

truth and directory of duty, because the Faithful and True Witness so regarded it, or if it be not, that Christ Himself was not above the erroneous views of the time and the people to which He belonged, and in regard to the true character of the Old Testament was simply mistaken: a conclusion which some in our day who call themselves Christians have not shrunk from insinuating. 8. See how one may most effectually resist the devil. "The whole armour of God" is indeed to be used; but particularly "the sword of the Spirit, which is the Word of God"—so called because it is the Spirit that gives that Word living power, as God's own testimony, in the heart. As His divine and authoritative directory in duty against all the assaults of the tempter, Jesus wielded that sword of the Spirit with resistless power. To this secret of successful resistance the beloved disciple alludes when he says, "I have written unto you, young men, because ye are strong, and the Word of God abideth in you, and ye have overcome the wicked one" (1 John ii. 14). But 9. This presupposes, not only that the Scriptures are not impiously and cruelly withheld from the tempted children of God, but that they "search" them, and "meditate in them day and night." We have seen how remarkably apposite as well as ready was our Lord's use of Scripture; but this must have arisen from His constant study of it and experimental application of it to His own uses, both in the daily occupations of His previous life, and in the view of all that lay before Him. Nor will the tempted children of God find the Scriptures to be the ready sword of the Spirit in the hour of assault otherwise than their Lord did; but thus "resist the devil, and he will flee from you" (Jas. iv. 7): "Whom resist *stedfast in the faith*, knowing that the same afflictions are accomplished in your brethren that are in the world" (1 Pet. v. 9). 10. Let not God's dear children suffer themselves to be despoiled, by the tempter, of the sense of that high relationship. It is their strength as well as joy, not less really, though on a vastly lower scale, than it was their Lord's. 11. What can be more glorious, to those who see in Christ the only begotten of the Father, than the sense which Christ had, during all this temptation, of His standing, as *Man*, under the very same law of duty as His "brethren!" When tempted to supply His wants as man, by putting forth His power as the Son of God, He refused, because it was written that "MAN doth not live by bread only, but by every word of God," Again, when tempted to cast Himself down from the pinnacle of the temple, because the saints—even as many as "made the most High their habitation"—were under the charge of God's angels, He declined, because it was written, "Thou (meaning God's people, whether collectively or individually) shalt not tempt the Lord thy God." 'I therefore refuse to tempt the Lord *my* God.' Finally, when solicited, by a splendid bribe, to fall down and worship the tempter, He indignantly ordered him off with that scripture, "Thou shalt worship the Lord thy God, and Him only shalt thou serve." Evidently, Christ read that command as *addressed to Himself* as man; and on the rock of adoring subjection to the Lord as His God He is found standing at the close of this whole Temptation-scene. How identical with our entire tempted life does our Lord thus show His own to be! And what vividness and force does this give to the assurance that "in that He Himself hath suffered, being tempted, He is able also to succour them that are tempted!" (Heb. ii. 18.) This way of viewing our Lord's victory over the tempter is far more natural and satisfactory than the quaint conceit of the Fathers, that our Lord, 'by His divinity, caught the tempter on the hook of His humanity.' Not but that there is a truth couched under it. But it is too much in the line of a vicious separation, in His actions, of the one nature from the other, in which they indulged, and is apt to make His human life and obedience appear fantastic and unreal. His personal divinity secured to Him that operation of the Spirit in virtue of which He was born the Holy Thing, and that continued action of the Spirit in virtue of which His holy humanity was gradually developed into the maturity and beauty of holy manhood; but when the Spirit descended upon Him at His baptism, it was for His whole official work; and in this, the very first scene of it, and one so precious, He overcame throughout as man, through the power of the Holy Ghost—His Godhead being the security that He should not and could not fail. 12. Henceforth there is no mention of Satan making any formal assault upon our Lord until the night before He suffered. Nor did he come then, as he did now, to try directly to seduce Him from His fidelity to God; but in the way of compassing His death, and by the hands of those whose part it was, if He were the Son of God, to acknowledge His claims. Once before, indeed, He said to Peter, "Get thee behind me, Satan" (Matt. xvi. 22, 23)—as if He had descried the tempter again stealthily approaching Him in the person of Peter, to make Him shrink from dying. And again, when the Greeks expressed their wish to see Him, He spoke mysteriously of His hour having come, and had a kind of agony by anticipation; but after it was over, He exclaimed, "Now is the judgment of this world; now shall the prince of this world be cast out" (John xii. 20-31)—as if, in the momentary struggle with the horrors of His final "hour," He had descried the tempter holding up this as his master-stroke for at length accomplishing His overthrow, but at the same time got a glimpse of the glorious victory over Satan which this final stroke of his policy was to prove. These, however, were but tentative approaches of the adversary. After the last supper, and ere they had risen from the table, our Lord said, "Henceforth [ἔτι] I will not talk much with you: for the *prince of this world cometh, and hath nothing in me*" (John xiv. 30); as if the moment of his "coming" were just at hand. At length, when in the garden they drew near to take Him, He said, "When I was daily with you in the temple, ye stretched forth no hands against me: *but this is* your hour, and *the power of darkness*" (Luke xxii. 52, 53). The tempter had "departed from Him till a season," and this at length is it. Not but that he was in everything that tried our Lord's stedfastness from first to last. But his formal and outstanding efforts against our Lord were at the *outset* and at the *close* of His career, and, as we have seen, of a very different nature the one from the other. Blessed Saviour, look upon our tempted condition here below; and what time the enemy cometh in upon us like a flood, by Thy good Spirit help us to tread in Thy footsteps: so shall we be more than conquerors through Him that loved us!

12-25.—CHRIST BEGINS HIS GALILEAN MINISTRY

14 Nephthalim: that it might be fulfilled which was spoken by Esaias the
15 prophet, saying, The [n]land of Zabulon, and the land of Nephthalim, *by* the

A. D. 31.

[n] Isa. 9. 1, 2.

—Calling of Peter and Andrew, James and John—His First Galilean Circuit. (= Mark i. 14-20, 35-39; Luke iv. 14, 15.)

There is here a notable gap in the History, which but for the fourth Gospel we should never have discovered. From the former Gospels we should have been apt to draw three inferences, which from the fourth one we know to be erroneous: First, that our Lord awaited the close of John's ministry, by his arrest and imprisonment, before beginning His own; next, that there was but a brief interval between the baptism of our Lord and the imprisonment of John; and further, that our Lord not only opened His work in Galilee, but never ministered out of it, and never visited Jerusalem at all nor kept a Passover till He went thither to become "our Passover, sacrificed for us." The fourth Gospel alone gives the true succession of events; not only recording those important openings of our Lord's public work which preceded the Baptist's imprisonment—extending to the end of the third chapter—but so specifying the Passovers which occurred during our Lord's ministry as to enable us to line off, with a large measure of certainty, the events of the first three Gospels according to the successive Passovers which they embraced. *Eusebius*, the ecclesiastical historian, who, early in the fourth century, gave much attention to this subject, in noticing these features of the Evangelical Records, says (iii. 24) that John wrote his Gospel at the entreaty of those who knew the important materials he possessed, and filled up what is wanting in the first three Gospels. Why it was reserved for the fourth Gospel, published at so late a period, to supply such important particulars in the Life of Christ, it is not easy to conjecture with any probability. It may be, that though not unacquainted with the general facts, they were not furnished with reliable details. But one thing may be affirmed with tolerable certainty, that as our Lord's teaching at Jerusalem was of a depth and grandeur scarcely so well adapted to the prevailing character of the first three Gospels, but altogether congenial to the fourth; and as the bare mention of the successive Passovers, without any account of the transactions and discourses they gave rise to, would have served little purpose in the first three Gospels, there may have been no way of preserving the unity and consistency of each Gospel, so as to furnish by means of them all the precious information we get from them, save by the plan on which they are actually constructed.

Entry into Galilee (12-17). **12. Now when Jesus had heard that John was cast into prison** [παρεδόθη]—more simply, 'was delivered up;' as recorded in ch. xiv. 3-5; Mark vi. 17-20; Luke iii. 19, 20—**he departed**—rather, 'withdrew' [ἀνεχώρησεν]—**into Galilee**—as recorded, in its proper place, in John iv. 1-3. **13. And leaving** [καταλιπὼν] **Nazareth.** The prevalent opinion is, that this refers to a *first* visit to Nazareth after His baptism, whose details are given by Luke (iv. 16, &c.); a *second* visit being that detailed by our Evangelist (ch. xiii. 54-58), and by Mark (ch. vi. 1-6). But to us there seem all but insuperable difficulties in the supposition of two visits to Nazareth after His baptism; and on the grounds stated on Luke iv. 16, &c., we think that the *one only visit* to Nazareth is that recorded by Matthew (xiii.), Mark (vi.), and Luke (iv.) But how, in that case, are we to take the word "*leaving* Nazareth" here? We answer, just as the same word is used in Acts xxi. 3, "Now when we had sighted [ἀναφάναντες] Cyprus, and *left* it [καταλιπόντες] on the left, we sailed unto Syria," &c.—that is, without entering Cyprus at all, but merely 'sighting' it, as the nautical phrase is, they steered south-east of it, leaving it on the north-west. So here, what we understand the Evangelist to say is, that Jesus, on His return to Galilee, did not, as might have been expected, make Nazareth the place of His stated residence, but "leaving (or passing by) Nazareth," **he came and dwelt in Capernaum, which is upon the sea coast** [K. τὴν παραθαλασσίαν]—'maritime Capernaum,' on the north-west shore of the sea of Galilee; but the precise spot is unknown. (See on ch. xi. 23.) Our Lord seems to have chosen it for several reasons. Four or five of the Twelve lived there; it had a considerable and mixed population, securing some freedom from that intense bigotry which even to this day characterizes all places where Jews in large numbers dwell nearly alone; it was centrical, so that not only on the approach of the annual festivals did large numbers pass through it or near it, but on any occasion multitudes could easily be collected about it; and for crossing and recrossing the lake, which our Lord had so often occasion to do, no place could be more convenient. But one other high reason for the choice of Capernaum remains to be mentioned, the only one specified by our Evangelist. **in the borders of Zabulon and Nephthalim**—the one lying to the west of the sea of Galilee, the other to the north of it; but the precise boundaries cannot now be traced out. **14. That it might be fulfilled which was spoken by Esaias the prophet** (ch. ix. 1, 2, or, as in *Heb.*, ch. viii. 23, and ix. 1), **saying, 15. The land of Zabulon, and the land of Nephthalim,** [by] **the way of the sea**—the coast skirting the sea of Galilee westward—**beyond Jordan**—a phrase commonly meaning eastward of Jordan; but here and in several places it means westward of the Jordan. The word [πέραν] seems to have got the general meaning of 'the other side;' the nature of the case determining which side that was. **Galilee of the Gentiles**—so called from its position, which made it 'the frontier' between the Holy Land and the external world. While Ephraim and Judah, as *Stanley* says, were separated from the world by the Jordan-valley on one side and the hostile Philistines on another, the northern tribes were in the direct highway of all the invaders from the north, in unbroken communication with the promiscuous races who have always occupied the heights of Lebanon, and in close and peaceful alliance with the most commercial nation of the ancient world—the Phœnicians. Twenty of the cities of Galilee were actually annexed by Solomon to the adjacent kingdom of Tyre, and formed, with their territory, the "boundary" or "offscouring" ("Gebul" or "Cabul") of the two dominions—at a later time still known by the general name of "the boundaries ("coasts" or "borders") of Tyre and Sidon." In the first great transportation of the Jewish population, Naphthali and Galilee suffered the same fate as the trans-Jordanic tribes before Ephraim or Judah had been molested (2 Ki. xv. 29). In the time of the Christian era this original disadvantage of their position was still felt; the speech of the Galileans "bewrayed them" by its uncouth pronunciation (Matt. xxvi. 73); and their distance from the seats of government and civilization at Jeru-

16 way of the sea, beyond Jordan, Galilee of the Gentiles: the [o]people which
sat in darkness saw great light; and to them which sat in the region and
17 shadow of death light is sprung up. From [p]that time Jesus began to
preach, and to say, [q]Repent: for the kingdom of heaven is at hand.
18 And [r]Jesus, walking by the sea of Galilee, saw two brethren, Simon
[s]called Peter, and Andrew his brother, casting a net into the sea: for
19 they were fishers. And he saith unto them, Follow me, and [t]I will make
20 you fishers of men. And [u]they straightway left *their* nets, and followed
21 him. And [v]going on from thence, he saw other two brethren, James *the*
son of Zebedee, and John his brother, in a ship with Zebedee their father,
22 mending their nets; and he called them. And they immediately left
the ship and their father, and followed him.

A. D. 31.

[o] Isa. 42. 7. Luke 2. 32.
[p] Mark 1. 14.
[q] ch. 10. 7.
[r] Mark 1. 16.
[s] Matt. 16.18. John 1. 42.
[t] Ezek. 47.10. Luke 5. 10.
[u] ch. 10.37,38. Mark 10.28. Luke 18.28. Gal. 1. 16.
[v] Mark 1. 19. Luke 5. 10.

salem and Cæsarea gave them their character for turbulence or independence, according as it was viewed by their friends or their enemies. **16. The people which sat in darkness saw great light; and to them which sat in the region and shadow of death light is sprung up.** [This is rendered pretty closely from the Hebrew—not at all from the LXX., as usual, which here goes quite aside from the original.] The prophetic strain to which these words belong commences with Isa. vii., to which ch. vi. is introductory, and goes down to the end of ch. xii., which hymns the spirit of that whole strain of prophecy. It belongs to the reign of Ahaz, and turns upon the combined efforts of the two neighbouring kingdoms of Syria and Israel to crush Judah. In these critical circumstances Judah and her king were, by their ungodliness, provoking the Lord to sell them into the hands of their enemies. What, then, is the burden of this prophetic strain, on to the passage here quoted? First, Judah shall not, cannot perish, because IMMANUEL, the Virgin's Son, is to come forth from his loins. Next, One of the invaders shall soon perish, and the kingdom of neither be enlarged. Further, While the Lord will be the Sanctuary of such as confide in these promises and await their fulfilment, He will drive to confusion, darkness, and despair the vast multitude of the nation who despised His oracles, and, in their anxiety and distress, betook themselves to the lying oracles of the heathen. This carries us down to the end of the eighth chapter. At the opening of the ninth chapter a sudden light is seen breaking in upon one particular part of the country, the part which was to suffer most in these wars and devastations —"the land of Zebulun, and the land of Naphtali, the way of the sea, beyond Jordan, Galilee of the Gentiles." The rest of the prophecy stretches over both the Assyrian and the Chaldean captivities, and terminates in the glorious Messianic prophecy of ch. xi., and the choral hymn of ch. xii. Well, this is the point seized on by our Evangelist. By Messiah's taking up His abode in those very regions of Galilee, and shedding His glorious light upon them, this prediction, he says, of the evangelical prophet was now fulfilled; and if it was not thus fulfilled, we may confidently affirm it was not fulfilled in any age of the Jewish economy, and has received no fulfilment at all. Even the most rationalistic critics have difficulty in explaining it in any other way. **17. From that time Jesus began to preach, and to say, Repent: for the kingdom of heaven is at hand.** Thus did our Lord not only take up the strain, but give forth the identical summons of His honoured forerunner. Our Lord sometimes speaks of the new kingdom as already come—in His own Person and ministry; but the *economy* of it was only "at hand" [ἤγγικεν] until the blood of the cross was shed, and the Spirit on the day of Pentecost opened the fountain for sin and for uncleanness to the world at large.

Calling of Peter and Andrew, James and John (18-22). **18. And Jesus, walking.** (The word "Jesus" here appears not to belong to the text, but to have been introduced from those portions of it which were transcribed to be used as Church Lessons; where it was naturally introduced as a connecting word at the commencement of a Lesson.) **by the sea of Galilee, saw two brethren, Simon called Peter**—for the reason mentioned in ch. xvi. 18—**and Andrew his brother, casting a net into the sea: for they were fishers. 19. And he saith unto them, Follow me**—rather, as the same expression is rendered in Mark, "Come ye after me" [Δεῦτε ὀπίσω μου]—**and I will make you fishers of men** —raising them from a lower to a higher *fishing*, as David was from a lower to a higher *feeding* (Ps. lxxviii. 70-72). **20. And they straightway left their nets, and followed him. 21. And going on from thence, he saw other two brethren, James the son of Zebedee, and John his brother, in a ship** [ἐν τῷ πλοίῳ]—rather, 'in the ship,' their fishing boat—**with Zebedee their father, mending their nets; and he called them. 22. And they immediately left the ship and their father.** Mark adds an important clause: "They left their father Zebedee in the ship with the *hired servants;*" showing that the family were in easy circumstances. **and followed him.** Two harmonistic questions here arise. *First*, Was this the same calling with that recorded in John i. 35-42? Clearly not. For, 1. That call was given while Jesus was yet in Judea: this, after His return to Galilee. 2. Here, Christ calls Andrew: there, Andrew solicits an interview with Christ. 3. Here, Andrew and Peter are called together: there, Andrew having been called, with an unnamed disciple, who was clearly the beloved disciple (see on John i. 40), goes and fetches Peter his brother to Christ, who then calls him. 4. Here, John is called along with James his brother: there, John is called along with Andrew, after having at their own request had an interview with Jesus; no mention being made of James, whose call, if it then took place, would not likely have been passed over by his own brother. Thus far nearly all are agreed. But on the *next* question opinion is divided—Was this the same calling as that recorded in Luke v. 1-11? Many able critics think so. But the following considerations are to us decisive against it. First, Here, the four are called separately, in pairs: in Luke, all together. Next, In Luke, after a glorious miracle: here, the one pair are casting their net, the other are mending theirs. Further, Here, our Lord had made no public appearance in Galilee,

23 And Jesus went about all Galilee, teaching [w]in their synagogues, and
preaching the gospel of the kingdom, and healing all manner of sickness
24 and all manner of disease among the people. And his [x]fame went
throughout all Syria: and they brought unto him all sick people that
were taken with divers diseases and torments, and those which were
possessed with devils, and those which were lunatic, and those that had
25 the palsy; and he healed them. And there followed him [y]great multitudes of people from Galilee, and *from* Decapolis, and *from* Jerusalem,
and *from* Judea, and *from* beyond Jordan.

A. D. 31.

[w] ch. 9. 35. Mark 1. 21, 39. Luke 4. 15.
[x] Isa. 52. 13. Mark 1. 28. Luke 4. 14.
[y] Gen. 49. 10. Isa. 55. 5. ch. 19. 2. Mark 3. 7.

and so had gathered none around Him; He is walking solitarily by the shores of the lake when He accosts the two pairs of fishermen: in Luke, "the multitude [τὸν ὄχλον] are lying upon Him [ἐπικεῖσθαι αὐτῷ], and hearing the word of God, as He stands by the lake of Gennesaret"—a state of things implying a somewhat advanced stage of His early ministry, and some popular enthusiasm. Regarding these successive callings, see on Luke v. i.

First Galilean Circuit (23-25). **23. And Jesus went about all Galilee, teaching in their synagogues.** These were houses of local worship. It cannot be proved that they existed before the Babylonish captivity; but as they began to be erected soon after it, probably the idea was suggested by the religious inconveniences to which the captives had been subjected. In our Lord's time, the rule was to have one wherever ten learned men, or professed students of the law, resided; and they extended to Syria, Asia Minor, Greece, and most places of the dispersion. The larger towns had several, and in Jerusalem the number approached 500. In point of officers and mode of worship, the Christian congregations were modelled after the synagogue. **and preaching the gospel**—'proclaiming the glad tidings' **of the kingdom, and healing all manner of sickness** [πᾶσαν νόσον]—'every disease'—**and all manner of disease** [πᾶσαν μαλακίαν]—'every complaint.' The word means any incipient malady causing 'softness.' **among the people. 24. And his fame went throughout all Syria**—reaching first to that part of it adjacent to Galilee, called Syrophenicia (Mark vii. 26), and thence extending far and wide. **and they brought unto him all sick people** [τοὺς κακῶς ἔχοντας]—' all that were ailing' or 'unwell.' [those] **that were taken**—for this is a distinct class, not an explanation of the "unwell" class, as our translators understood it: **with divers diseases and torments**—that is, acute disorders; **and those which were possessed with devils** [δαιμονιζομένους]—'that were demonized' or 'possessed with demons.' On this subject, see Remark 4 below. **and those which were lunatic** [σεληνιαζομένους]—'moon-struck'—**and those that had the palsy** [παραλυτικούς]—'paralytics,' a word not naturalized when our version was made—**and he healed them.** These healings were at once His credentials and illustrations of "the glad tidings" which He proclaimed. After reading this account of our Lord's first preaching tour, can we wonder at what follows? **25. And there followed him great multitudes of people from Galilee, and from Decapolis**—a region lying to the east of the Jordan, so called as containing ten cities, founded and chiefly inhabited by Greek settlers. **and from Jerusalem, and from beyond Jordan**—meaning from Perea. Thus not only was all Palestine upheaved, but all the adjacent regions. But the more immediate object for which this is here mentioned is, to give the reader some idea both of the vast concourse and of the varied complexion of eager attendants upon the great Preacher, to whom the astonishing Discourse of the next three chapters was addressed. On the importance which our Lord Himself attached to this first preaching circuit, and the preparation which He made for it, see on Mark i. 35-39.

Remarks.—1. When, in the prophetic strain regarding Emmanuel, we read that a great light was to irradiate certain specified parts of Palestine—the most disturbed and devastated in the early wars of the Jews, and in after times the most mixed and the least esteemed—and when, in the Gospel History, we find our Lord taking up His stated abode in those very regions, as every way the most suited to His purposes, while at the same time it furnished the bright fulfilment of Isaiah's prophecy—can we refrain from exclaiming, "This also must have come forth from the Lord of hosts, who is wonderful in counsel, and excellent in working"? 2. What marvellous power over the hearts of men must Jesus have possessed, when, on the utterance of those few now familiar words, "Follow Me"—"Come ye after Me," men instantly obeyed, leaving all behind them! But is His power to captivate men's hearts, with a word or two from the lips of His servants, less now that He "has ascended on high, and led captivity captive, and received gifts for men, yea for the rebellious also, that the Lord God might dwell among them"? 3. Did the Prince of preachers not only "teach in the synagogues," the regular places of public worship, but under the open canopy of heaven proclaim the glad tidings to the crowds that gathered around Him, whom no synagogue would have held, and not a few of whom would probably never have heard Him in a synagogue? And shall those who profess to be the followers of Christ account all open-air preaching disorderly and fanatical, or at least regard it as irregular, unnecessary, and inexpedient in a Christian country and a settled state of the Church? When the apostle says to Timothy, "Preach the word; be instant in season, *out of season*" [εὐκαίρως, ἀκαίρως, 2 Tim. iv. 2], does he not enjoin it at what are called *canonical* hours and at uncanonical too? And is not the same principle applicable to what may be called canonical places? These are good, but every other place where crowds can be collected to hear the glad tidings is good also; especially if such would not likely be reached in any other way, and if the uncanonical, abnormal way of it should be fitted, at any particular period, to arrest the attention of those who, in the regular places of worship, have become listless and indifferent to eternal things. 4. It is remarkable, as *Campbell* observes in an acute Dissertation, vi. 1., that in the New Testament men are never said to be possessed with the *devil* or with devils [διάβολος], but always with a *demon* or demons [δαίμων, but much more frequently δαιμόνιον], or to be *demonized* [δαιμονίζεσθαι]. On the other hand, the ordinary operations of the wicked one—even in their most extreme and malignant forms—are invariably ascribed to the "*devil*"

5 AND seeing the multitudes, [a]he went up into a mountain: and when
2 he was set, his disciples came unto him: and he opened his mouth, and
taught them, saying,

A. D. 31.

[a] Mark 3. 13. Luke 6. 12.

himself or to "*Satan.*" Thus Satan "filled the heart" of Ananias (Acts v. 3); men are said to be "taken captive by the devil [διαβόλου] at his will" (2 Tim. ii. 26); unregenerate men are the children of the devil (1 John iii. 10); Satan entered into Judas (John xiii. 27); and he is called by our Lord Himself (John vi. 70) "a devil" [διάβολος]. It is impossible that a distinction so invariably observed throughout the New Testament should be without a meaning; but, whatever it be, it is lost to the English reader, as our translators have in both cases used the term "devil." It is true that we have our Lord's own authority for viewing this whole mysterious agency of *demons* as belonging to the kingdom of *Satan* (ch. xii. 24-29), and set in motion, as truly as his own more immediate operations on the souls of men, for his destructive ends. But some notable features in his general policy are undoubtedly intended by the marked distinction of terms observed in the New Testament. One thing comes out of it clearly enough—that these possessions were something totally different from the ordinary operations of the devil on the souls of men; otherwise the distinction would be unintelligible. And that they are not to be confounded with any mere bodily disease—as lunacy or epilepsy—is evident, both from their being expressly distinguished from all such in this very passage, and from the personal intelligence, intentions, and actions ascribed to them in the New Testament. Deeply mysterious is such agency; and one cannot but enquire what may have been the reason why such amazing activity and virulence were allowed it during our Lord's sojourn upon earth. The answer to this, at least, is not difficult. For if all his miracles were designed to illustrate the *character* of His mission; and if "For this purpose the Son of God was manifested, that He might destroy the works of the devil" (1 John iii. 8), there can be no doubt that it was to make this destruction all the more manifest and illustrious that the enemy was allowed such terrific swing at that period. And thus might we imagine it said to the great Enemy from above, with respect to that mighty power allowed him at this time—"Even for this same purpose have I raised thee up, that I might show my power in thee, and that my name might be declared throughout all the earth" (Rom. ix. 17). On the *impurity* so often ascribed to evil spirits in the Gospels, it is impossible to enter here; but perhaps it may be intended to express, not so much anything in human sensuality peculiarly diabolical, as the general vileness or loathsomeness of the character in which these evil spirits revel. But the whole subject is one of difficulty. 5. But the illustrative design of our Lord's miracles takes wider range than this. His miraculous cures were all of a purely beneficent nature, rolling away one or other of the varied evils brought in by the fall, and in no instance inflicting any. And when we find Himself saying, "The Son of Man is not come to destroy men's lives, but to *save* them" (Luke ix. 56), does He not teach us to behold in all His miraculous cures a faint manifestation of THE HEALING SAVIOUR, in the highest sense of that office? [Compare Exod. xv. 26, "Jehovah that healeth thee"—יְהוָה רֹפְאֶךָ.] 6. *Lange* justly notices here an important difference between the ministry of John and that of our Lord; the one being stationary, the other moving from place to place—the *diffusive* character of the Gospel thus peering forth at the very outset in the movements of the Great Preacher. And we may add, that the glorious ordinance of preaching could not have been more illustriously inaugurated.

CHAP. V—VII. SERMON ON THE MOUNT.

When surrounded by multitudes of eager listeners, of every class and from all quarters, and solemnly seated on a mountain on purpose to teach them for the first time the great leading principles of His kingdom, why, it may be asked, did our Lord not discourse to them in such strains as these:—"God so loved the world, that He gave His only begotten Son, that whosoever believeth in Him should not perish, but have everlasting life;" "Come unto me, all ye that labour and are heavy laden, and I will give you rest," &c.? While the absence of such sayings from this His first great Discourse startles some to whom they are all-precious, it emboldens others to think that evangelical Christians make too much of them, if not entirely misconceive them. But since the Jewish mind had been long systematically perverted on the subject of human *duty*, and consequently of *sin* by the breach of it, and under such teaching had grown obtuse, unspiritual, and self-satisfied, it was the dictate of wisdom first to lay broad and deep the foundations of all revealed truth and duty, and hold forth the great principles of true and acceptable righteousness, in sharp contrast with the false teaching to which the people were in bondage. At the same time this Discourse is by no means so exclusively ethical as many suppose. On the contrary, though avoiding all evangelical *details*, at so early a stage of His public teaching, our Lord holds forth, from beginning to end of this Discourse, the great *principles* of evangelical and spiritual religion; and it will be found to breathe a spirit entirely in harmony with the subsequent portions of the New Testament.

That this is the *same Discourse* with that in Luke vi. 17 to 49—only reported more fully by Matthew, and less fully, as well as with considerable variation, by Luke—is the opinion of many very able critics (of the Greek commentators; of *Calvin*, *Grotius*, *Maldonatus*—who stands almost alone among Romish commentators; and of most moderns, as *Tholuck*, *Meyer*, *De Wette*, *Tischendorf*, *Stier*, *Wieseler*, *Robinson*). The prevailing opinion of these critics is, that Luke's is the original form of the Discourse, to which Matthew has added a number of sayings, uttered on other occasions, in order to give at one view the great outlines of our Lord's ethical teaching. But that they are *two distinct Discourses*—the one delivered about the close of His first missionary tour, and the other after a second such tour and the solemn choice of the Twelve—is the judgment of others who have given much attention to such matters (of most Romish commentators, including *Erasmus*; and among the moderns, of *Lange*, *Greswell*, *Birks*, *Webster and Wilkinson*. The question is left undecided by *Alford*). *Augustin's* opinion—that they were both delivered on one occasion, Matthew's on the mountain, and to the disciples; Luke's in the plain, and to the promiscuous multitude—is so clumsy and artificial as hardly to deserve notice. To us the weight of argument appears to lie with those who think them two separate Discourses. It seems hard to conceive that Matthew should have put

3 Blessed [b]*are* the poor in spirit: for theirs is the kingdom of heaven.
4 5 Blessed [c]*are* they that mourn: for they shall be comforted. Blessed

A. D. 31.

b Ps. 51. 17.
c 2 Cor. 1. 7.

this Discourse before his own calling, if it was not uttered till long after, and was spoken in his own hearing as one of the newly-chosen Twelve. Add to this, that Matthew introduces his Discourse amidst very definite markings of time, which fix it to our Lord's first preaching tour; while that of Luke, which is expressly said to have been delivered immediately after the choice of the Twelve, could not have been spoken till long after the time noted by Matthew. It is hard, too, to see how either Discourse can well be regarded as the expansion or contraction of the other. And as it is beyond dispute that our Lord repeated some of His weightier sayings in different forms, and with varied applications, it ought not to surprise us that, after the lapse of perhaps a year—when, having spent a whole night on the hill in prayer to God, and set the Twelve apart, He found Himself surrounded by crowds of people, few of whom probably had heard the Sermon on the Mount, and fewer still remembered much of it—He should go over again its principal points, with just as much sameness as to show their enduring gravity, but at the same time with that difference which shows His exhaustless fertility as the great Prophet of the Church.

CHAP. V. 1-16.—THE BEATITUDES, AND THEIR BEARING UPON THE WORLD.

1. And seeing the multitudes—those mentioned in ch. iv. 25—**he went up into a mountain** [εἰς τὸ ὄρος]—one of the dozen mountains which *Robinson* says there are in the vicinity of the sea of Galilee, any one of them answering about equally well to the occasion. So charming is the whole landscape that the descriptions of it, from *Josephus* downwards (*J. W.*, iv. 10, 8), are apt to be thought a little coloured. **and when he was set**—'had sat' or 'seated Himself' [καθίσαντος αὐτοῦ]—**his disciples came unto him**—already a large circle, more or less attracted and subdued by His preaching and miracles, in addition to the smaller band of devoted adherents. Though the latter only answered to the subjects of His kingdom, described in this Discourse, there were drawn from time to time into this inner circle souls from the outer one, who, by the power of His matchless word, were constrained to forsake their all for the Lord Jesus. **2. And he opened his mouth**—a solemn way of arousing the reader's attention, and preparing him for something weighty (Job iii. 1; Acts viii. 35; x. 34)—**and taught them, saying, 3. Blessed, &c.** Of the two words which our translators render "blessed," the one here used [μακάριοι] points more to what is *inward*, and so might be rendered "happy," in a lofty sense; while the other [εὐλογημένοι] denotes rather what comes to us *from without* (as Matt. xxv. 34). But the distinction is not always nicely carried out. One Hebrew word [אַשְׁרֵי] expresses both.

On these precious Beatitudes, observe that though eight in number, there are here but *seven* distinct features of character. The eighth one—the "persecuted for righteousness' sake"—denotes merely the possessors of the seven preceding features, on account of which it is that they are persecuted (2 Tim. iii. 12). Accordingly, instead of any distinct promise to this class, we have merely a repetition of the first promise. This has been noticed by several critics, who by the *sevenfold* character thus set forth have rightly observed that a *complete* character is meant to be depicted, and by the *sevenfold* blessedness attached to it, a *perfect* blessedness is intended. Observe, again, that the language in which these beatitudes are couched is purposely fetched from the Old Testament, to show that the new kingdom is but the old in a new form; while the characters described are but the varied forms of that *spirituality* which was the essence of real religion all along, but had well-nigh disappeared under corrupt teaching. Further, the things here promised, far from being mere arbitrary rewards, will be found in each case to grow out of the characters to which they are attached, and in their completed form are but the appropriate coronation of them. Once more, as "the kingdom of heaven," which is the first and the last thing here promised, has two stages—a present and a future, an initial and a consummate stage—so the fulfilment of each of these promises has two stages—a present and a future, a partial and a perfect stage.

3. Blessed are the poor in spirit. All familiar with Old Testament phraseology know how frequently God's true people are styled "the poor" [עֲנִיִּם]—the 'oppressed,' 'afflicted,' 'miserable'—"the needy" [אֶבְיוֹנִים], or both together (as in Ps. xl. 17; Isa. xli. 17). The explanation of this lies in the fact that it is generally "the poor of this world" who are "rich in faith" (Jas. ii. 5; cf. 2 Cor. vi. 10, and Rev. ii. 9); while it is often "the ungodly" who "prosper in the world" (Ps. lxxiii. 12). Accordingly, in Luke (vi. 20, 21), it seems to be this class—the literally "poor" and "hungry"—that are specially addressed. But since God's people are in so many places styled "the poor" and "the needy," with no evident reference to their temporal circumstances (as in Ps. lxviii. 10; lxix. 29-33; cxxxii. 15; Isa. lxi. 1; lxvi. 2), it is plainly a *frame of mind* which those terms are meant to express. Accordingly, our translators sometimes render such words "the humble" (Ps. x. 12, 17), "the meek" (Ps. xxii. 26), "the lowly" (Prov. iii. 34), as having no reference to outward circumstances. But here the explanatory words, "in spirit" [τῷ πνεύματι], fix the sense to 'those who in their deepest consciousness realize their entire need' (cf. the *Gr.* of Luke x. 21; John xi. 33; xiii. 21; Acts xx. 22; Rom. xii. 11; 1 Cor. v. 3; Phil. iii). This self-emptying conviction, that 'before God we are void of everything,' lies at the foundation of all spiritual excellence, according to the teaching of Scripture. Without it we are inaccessible to the riches of Christ: with it we are in the fitting state for receiving all spiritual supplies (Rev. iii. 17, 18; Matt. ix. 12, 13). **for theirs is the kingdom of heaven.** [Our translators rightly disregard the plural—τῶν οὐρανῶν—here, as it is merely a literal rendering of הַשָּׁמַיִם, which has no singular.] See on ch. iii. 2. The poor in spirit not only shall have—they already have—the kingdom. The very sense of their poverty is begun riches. While others "walk in a vain show" [בְּצֶלֶם]—'in a shadow,' 'an image'—in an unreal world, taking a false view of themselves and all around them—the poor in spirit are rich in the knowledge of their real case. Having courage to look this in the face, and own it guilelessly, they feel strong in the assurance that "unto the upright there ariseth light in the darkness" (Ps. cxii. 4); and soon it breaks forth as the morning. God wants nothing from us as the price of His saving gifts; we have but to feel our universal destitution, and cast ourselves upon His compassion

6 [d] *are* the meek: for [e] they shall inherit the earth. Blessed *are* they
which do hunger and thirst after righteousness: [f] for they shall be
filled.

A. D. 31.
[d] Ps. 37. 11.
[e] Rom. 4. 13.
[f] Isa. 65. 13.

(Job xxxiii. 27, 28; 1 John i. 9). So the poor in spirit are enriched with the fulness of Christ, which is the kingdom in substance; and when He shall say to them from His great white throne, "Come, ye blessed of my Father, inherit the kingdom *prepared* for you," He will invite them merely to the full enjoyment of an already possessed inheritance. **4. Blessed are they that mourn: for they shall be comforted.** [*Lachmann*, *Tischendorf*, and *Tregelles* place this verse after *v.* 5, but on evidence decidedly inferior, in our judgment, to that for the received order. And certainly the order of the *ideas* is in favour of the common arrangement; while in Isa. lxi. 1, and Luke iv. 18, the "mourners" come immediately after the "poor."] This "mourning" must not be taken loosely for that feeling which is wrung from men under pressure of the ills of life, nor yet strictly for sorrow on account of committed sins. Evidently it is that entire feeling which the sense of our spiritual poverty begets; and so the second beatitude is but the complement of the first. The one is the intellectual, the other the emotional aspect of the same thing. It is poverty of spirit that says, "I am undone;" and it is the mourning which this causes that makes it break forth in the form of a lamentation—"Woe is me, for I am undone." Hence this class are termed "mourners *in Zion*," or, as we might express it, religious mourners, in sharp contrast with all other sorts (Isa. lxi. 1-3; lxvi. 2). Religion, according to the Bible, is neither a set of intellectual convictions nor a bundle of emotional feelings, but a compound of both, the former giving birth to the latter. Thus closely do the first two beatitudes cohere. The mourners shall be "comforted." Even now they get beauty for ashes, the oil of joy for mourning, the garment of praise for the spirit of heaviness. Sowing in tears, they reap even here in joy. Still all present comfort, even the best, is partial, interrupted, short-lived. But the days of our mourning shall soon be ended, and then God shall wipe away all tears from our eyes. Then, in the fullest sense, shall the mourners be "comforted." **5. Blessed are the meek: for they shall inherit the earth.** This promise to the meek is but a repetition of Ps. xxxvii. 11; only the word which our Evangelist renders "the meek," [*οἱ πραεῖς*] after the LXX. is the same which we have found so often translated "the poor" [עֲנָוִים], showing how closely allied these two features of character are. It is impossible, indeed, that "the poor in spirit" and "the mourners" in Zion should not at the same time be "meek;" that is to say, persons of a lowly and gentle carriage. How fitting, at least, it is that they should be so, may be seen by the following touching appeal: "Put them in mind to be subject to principalities and powers, to obey magistrates, to be ready to every good work, to speak evil of no man, to be no brawlers, *but gentle, showing all meekness unto all men:* FOR WE OURSELVES WERE ONCE [*ποτὲ*] FOOLISH, disobedient, deceived, serving divers lusts and pleasures. . . . But after that the kindness and love of God our Saviour toward man appeared, . . . according to His mercy He saved us," &c. (Titus iii. 1-7.) But He who had no such affecting reasons for manifesting this beautiful carriage, said, nevertheless, of Himself, "Take My yoke upon you, and learn of Me; for I am meek and lowly in heart: and ye shall find rest unto your souls" (Matt. xi. 29); and the apostle besought one of the churches by "the meekness and gentleness of Christ" (2 Cor. x. 1). In what esteem this is held by Him who seeth not as man seeth, we may learn from 1 Pet. iii. 4, where the true adorning is said to be that of "a meek and quiet spirit, which in the sight of God is of great price." Towards men this disposition is the opposite of high-mindedness, and a quarrelsome and revengeful spirit; it "rather takes wrong, and suffers itself to be defrauded" (1 Cor. vi. 7); it "avenges not itself, but rather gives place unto wrath" (Rom. xii. 19); like the meek One, "when reviled, it reviles not again; when it suffers, it threatens not; but commits itself to Him that judgeth righteously" (1 Pet. ii. 19-22). "The earth" [*τὴν γῆν* = הָאָרֶץ or אֶרֶץ] which the meek are to inherit might be rendered "the land"—bringing out the more immediate reference to Canaan as the promised land, the secure possession of which was to the Old Testament saints the evidence and manifestation of God's favour resting on them, and the ideal of all true and abiding blessedness. Even in the Psalm from which these words are taken the promise to the meek is not held forth as an arbitrary reward, but as having a kind of natural fulfilment. When they delight themselves in the Lord, He gives them the desires of their heart: When they commit their way to Him, He brings it to pass; bringing forth their righteousness as the light, and their judgment as the noon-day: The little that they have, even when despoiled of their rights, is better than the riches of many wicked, &c. (Ps. xxxvii.) All things, in short, are theirs—in the possession of that favour which is life, and of those rights which belong to them as the children of God—whether the world, or life, or death, or things present, or things to come; all are theirs (1 Cor. iii. 21, 22); and at length, overcoming, they "inherit all things" (Rev. xxi. 7). Thus are the meek the only rightful occupants of a foot of ground or a crust of bread here, and heirs of all coming things. **6. Blessed are they which do hunger and thirst after righteousness** [*τὴν δικαιοσύνην* = צְדָקָה]: **for they shall be filled** [*χορτασθήσονται*]—'shall be saturated.' 'From this verse,' says *Tholuck*, 'the reference to the Old Testament background ceases.' Surprising! On the contrary, none of these beatitudes is more manifestly dug out of the rich mine of the Old Testament. Indeed, how could any one who found in the Old Testament "the poor in spirit," and "the mourners in Zion," doubt that he would also find those same characters also *craving* that righteousness which they feel and mourn their want of? But what is the precise meaning of "righteousness" here? Lutheran expositors, and some of our own, seem to have a hankering after that more restricted sense of the term in which it is used with reference to the sinner's justification before God. (See Jer. xxiii. 6; Isa. xlv. 24; Rom. iv. 6; 2 Cor. v. 21.) But, in so comprehensive a saying as this, it is clearly to be taken—as in *v.* 10 also—in a much wider sense, as denoting that spiritual and entire conformity to the law of God, under the want of which the saints groan, and the possession of which constitutes the only true saintship. The Old Testament dwells much on this righteousness, as that which alone God regards with approbation (Ps. xi. 7;

7 8 Blessed *are* the merciful: [g]for they shall obtain mercy. Blessed
9 [h]*are* the pure in heart: for [i]they shall see God. Blessed *are* [j]the
peacemakers: for they shall be called the children of God.

[g] Ps. 41. 1.
[h] Heb. 12. 14.
[i] 1 Cor. 13. 12.
Heb. 12. 14.

xxiii. 3; cvi. 3; Pro. xii. 28; xvi. 31; Isa. lxiv. 5, &c.) As hunger and thirst are the keenest of our appetites, our Lord, by employing this figure here, plainly means 'those whose deepest cravings are after spiritual blessings.' And in the Old Testament we find this craving variously expressed:—"Hearken unto me, ye that follow after righteousness, ye that seek the Lord" (Isa. li. 1); "I have waited for thy salvation, O Lord," exclaimed dying Jacob (Gen. xlix. 18); "My soul," says the sweet Psalmist, "breaketh for the longing that it hath unto thy judgments at all times" (Ps. cxix. 20); and in similar breathings does he give vent to his deepest longings in that and other Psalms. Well, our Lord just takes up here this blessed frame of mind, representing it as the surest pledge of the coveted supplies, as it is the best preparative, and indeed itself the beginning of them. "They shall be saturated," He says; they shall not only have what they so highly value and long to possess, but they shall have their fill of it. Not here, however. Even in the Old Testament this was well understood. "Deliver me," says the Psalmist, in language which, beyond all doubt, stretches beyond the present scene, "from men of the world, which have their portion in this life: As for me, I shall behold thy face in righteousness: I shall be satisfied, when I awake, with thy likeness" (Ps. xvii. 13-15).

The foregoing beatitudes—the first four—represent the saints rather as *conscious of their need of salvation*, and acting suitably to that character, than as possessed of it. The next three are of a different kind—representing the saints as *having now found salvation*, and conducting themselves accordingly.

7. Blessed are the merciful [ἐλεήμονες = חֲסִידִים]: **for they shall obtain mercy.** Beautiful is the connection between this and the preceding beatitude. The one has a natural tendency to beget the other. As for the words, they seem directly fetched from Ps. xviii. 25, "With the merciful thou wilt show thyself merciful." Not that our mercifulness comes absolutely first. On the contrary, our Lord Himself expressly teaches us that God's method is to awaken in us compassion towards our fellow-men by His own exercise of it, in so stupendous a way and measure, towards ourselves. In the parable of the unmerciful debtor, the servant to whom his lord forgave ten thousand talents was naturally expected to exercise the small measure of the same compassion required for forgiving his fellow-servant's debt of a hundred pence; and it is only when, instead of this, he relentlessly imprisoned him till he should pay it up, that his lord's indignation was roused, and he who was designed for a vessel of mercy is treated as a vessel of wrath (Matt. xviii. 23-35; and see ch. v. 23, 24; vi. 15; Jas. ii. 13). 'According to the view given in Scripture,' says *Trench* most justly, 'the Christian stands in a middle point, between a mercy received and a mercy yet needed. Sometimes the first is urged upon him as an argument for showing mercy—"forgiving one another, as Christ forgave you" (Col. iii. 13; Eph. iv. 32); sometimes the last—"Blessed are the merciful: for they shall obtain mercy;" "Forgive, and ye shall be forgiven" (Luke vi. 37; Jas. v. 9). And thus, while he is ever to look back on the mercy received as the source and motive of the mercy which he shows, he also looks forward to the mercy which he yet needs, and which he is assured that the merciful—according to what *Bengel* beautifully calls the *benigna talio* (the gracious requital) of the kingdom of God—shall receive, as a new provocation to its abundant exercise.' The foretastes and beginnings of this judicial recompense are richly experienced here below: its perfection is reserved for that day when, from His great white throne, the King shall say, "Come, ye blessed of my Father, inherit the kingdom prepared for you from the foundation of the world; for I was an hungered, and thirsty, and a stranger, and naked, and sick, and in prison, and ye ministered unto me." Yes, thus He acted towards us while on earth, even laying down His life for us; and He will not, He cannot disown, in the merciful, the image of Himself. **8. Blessed are the pure in heart** [οἱ καθαροὶ τῇ καρδίᾳ = בָּרִים לֵבָב, Ps. xxiv. 4; lxxiii. 1]: **for they shall see God.** Here, too, we are on Old Testament ground. There the difference between outward and inward purity, and the acceptableness of the latter only in the sight of God, is everywhere taught. Nor is the 'vision of God' strange to the Old Testament; and though it was an understood thing that this was not possible in the present life (Exod. xxxiii. 20; and cf. Job xix. 26, 27; Isa. vi. 5), yet spiritually it was known and felt to be the privilege of the saints even here, (Gen. v. 24; vi. 9; xvii. 1; xlviii. 15; Ps. xxvii. 4; xxxvi. 9; lxiii. 2; Isa. xxxviii. 3, 11, &c.) But O, with what grand simplicity, brevity, and power is this great fundamental truth here expressed! And in what striking contrast would such teaching appear to that which was then current, in which exclusive attention was paid to ceremonial purification and external morality? This heart-purity begins in a "heart sprinkled from an evil conscience," or a "conscience purged from dead works" (Heb. x. 22; ix. 14; and see Acts xv. 9); and this also is taught in the Old Testament (Ps. xxxii. 1, 2; cf. Rom. iv. 5-8; and Isa. vi. 5-8). The conscience thus purged—the heart thus sprinkled—there is light within wherewith to see God. "If we say that we have fellowship with Him, and walk in darkness, we lie, and do not the truth: but if we walk in the light, as He is in the light, we have fellowship one with the other" [μετ' ἀλλήλων]—He with us and we with Him—"and the blood of Jesus Christ His Son cleanseth us"—us who have this fellowship, and who, without such continual cleansing, would soon lose it again—"from all sin" (1 John i. 6, 7). "Whosoever sinneth hath not seen Him, neither known Him" (1 John iii. 6); "He that doeth evil hath not seen God" (3 John 11). The inward vision thus clarified, and the whole inner man in sympathy with God, each looks upon the other with complacency and joy, and we are "changed into the same image from glory to glory." But the full and beatific vision of God is reserved for that time to which the Psalmist stretches his views—"As for me, I shall behold Thy face in righteousness: I shall be satisfied, when I awake, with Thy likeness" (Ps. xvii. 15). Then shall His servants serve Him: and they shall see His face; and His name shall be in their foreheads (Rev. xxii. 3, 4). They shall see Him as He is (1 John iii. 2). But, says the apostle, expressing the converse of this beatitude—"Follow holiness, without which no man shall see the Lord" (Heb.

10 Blessed [k] *are* they which are persecuted for righteousness' sake: for
11 theirs is the kingdom of heaven. Blessed are ye when *men* shall
revile you, and persecute *you*, and shall say all manner of evil against
12 you [1] falsely, for my sake. Rejoice, and be exceeding glad; for great
is your reward in heaven: for so persecuted they the prophets which
were before you.

A. D. 31.

k Mark 10. 30. Luke 6. 22, 23. 2 Cor. 4. 17. 2 Tim. 2. 12. 1 Pet. 3. 14.

1 lying.

xii. 14). **9. Blessed are the peacemakers** [εἰρηνοποιοί = יֹעֲצֵי שָׁלוֹם, Pro. xii. 20]—who not only study peace, but diffuse it—**for they shall be called the children**—'shall be called sons'—**of God** [υἱοὶ Θεοῦ]. Of all these beatitudes this is the only one which could hardly be expected to find its definite ground in the Old Testament; for that most glorious character of God, the likeness of which appears in the peacemakers, had yet to be revealed. His glorious name, indeed—as "The Lord, the Lord God, merciful and gracious, long-suffering, and abundant in goodness and truth, forgiving iniquity and transgression and sin"—had been proclaimed in a very imposing manner (Exod. xxxiv. 6), and manifested in action with affecting frequency and variety in the long course of the ancient economy. And we have undeniable evidence that the saints of that economy felt its transforming and ennobling influence on their own character. But it was not till Christ "made peace by the blood of the cross" that God could manifest Himself as "the God of peace, that brought again from the dead our Lord Jesus, that great Shepherd of the sheep, through the blood of the everlasting covenant" (Heb. xiii. 20)—could reveal Himself as "in Christ reconciling the world unto Himself, not imputing their trespasses unto them," and hold Himself forth in the astonishing attitude of beseeching men to be "reconciled to Himself" (2 Cor. v. 19, 20). When this reconciliation actually takes place, and one has "peace with God through our Lord Jesus Christ"—even "the peace of God which passeth all understanding"—the peace-receivers become transformed into peace-diffusers. God is thus seen reflected in them; and by the family likeness these peacemakers are recognized as the children of God.

In now coming to the eighth, or supplementary beatitude, it will be seen that all that the saints are *in themselves* has been already described, in seven features of character; that number indicating *completeness* of delineation. The last feature, accordingly, is a passive one, representing the treatment that the characters already described may expect from the world. He who shall one day fix the destiny of all men here pronounces certain characters "blessed;" but He ends by forewarning them that the world's estimation and treatment of them will be the reverse of His. **10. Blessed are they which are persecuted for righteousness' sake, &c.** How entirely this final beatitude has its ground in the Old Testament, is evident from the concluding words, where the encouragement held out to endure such persecutions consists in its being but a continuation of what was experienced by the Old Testament servants of God. But how, it may be asked, could such beautiful features of character provoke persecution? To this the following answers should suffice: "Every one that doeth evil hateth the light, neither cometh to the light, lest his deeds should be reproved." "The world cannot hate you; but me it hateth, because I testify of it, that the works thereof are evil." "If ye were of the world, the world would love his own: but because ye are not of the world, but I have chosen you out of the world, therefore the world hateth you." "There is yet one man (said wicked Ahab to good Jehoshaphat), by whom we may enquire of the Lord: but I hate him; for he never prophesied good unto me, but always evil" (John iii. 20; vii. 7; xv. 19; 2 Chr. xviii. 7). But more particularly, the seven characters here described are all in the teeth of the spirit of the world, insomuch that such hearers of this Discourse as breathed that spirit must have been startled, and had their whole system of thought and action rudely dashed. Poverty of spirit runs counter to the pride of men's heart; a pensive disposition, in the view of one's universal deficiences before God, is ill relished by the callous, indifferent, laughing, self-satisfied world; a meek and quiet spirit, taking wrong, is regarded as pusillanimous, and rasps against the proud, resentful spirit of the world; that craving after spiritual blessings rebukes but too unpleasantly the lust of the flesh, the lust of the eye, and the pride of life; so does a merciful spirit the hardheartedness of the world; purity of heart contrasts painfully with painted hypocrisy; and the peacemaker cannot easily be endured by the contentious, quarrelsome world. Thus does "righteousness" come to be "persecuted." But blessed are they who, in spite of this, dare to be righteous. **for theirs is the kingdom of heaven.** As this was the reward promised to the poor in spirit—the leading one of these seven beatitudes—of course it is the proper portion of such as are persecuted for exemplifying them. **11. Blessed are ye when men shall revile you**—or abuse you to your face, in opposition to backbiting. (See Mark xv. 32.) **and persecute you, and shall say all manner of evil against you falsely** [*Tischendorf*—on quite insufficient evidence, we think—omits this last word ψευδόμενοι: *Tregelles*, however, retains it. Even though it had not been expressed, it would of course have been implied.] **for my sake.** Observe this. He had before said, "for righteousness' sake." Here He identifies Himself and His cause with that of righteousness, binding up the cause of righteousness in the world with the reception of Himself. Would Moses, or David, or Isaiah, or Paul have so expressed themselves? Never. Doubtless they suffered for righteousness' sake. But to have called this "their sake," would, as every one feels, have been very unbecoming. Whereas He that speaks, being Righteousness incarnate (see Mark i. 24; Acts iii. 14; Rev. iii. 7), when He so speaks, speaks only like Himself. **12. Rejoice, and be exceeding glad**—'exult' [ἀγαλλιᾶσθε]. In the corresponding passage of Luke (vi. 22, 23), where every indignity trying to flesh and blood is held forth as the probable lot of such as were faithful to Him, the word is even stronger than here, "leap" [σκιρτήσατε], as if He would have their inward transport to overpower and absorb the sense of all these affronts and sufferings; nor will anything else do it. **for great is your reward in heaven: for so persecuted they the prophets which were before you:**—*q. d.*, 'You do but serve yourselves heirs to their character and sufferings, and the reward will be common.'

13-16. We have here the practical application

13 Ye are the salt of the earth: but if the salt have lost his savour,
wherewith shall it be salted? it is thenceforth good for nothing, but to
14 be cast out, and to be trodden under foot of men. Ye [l]are the light of
15 the world. A city that is set on an hill cannot be hid. Neither do men
light a candle, and put it under a [2]bushel, but on a candlestick; and it
16 giveth light unto all that are in the house. Let your light so shine before

A. D. 31.

[l] Pro. 4. 18. Phil. 2. 15.

[2] modius. It contained nearly a peck.

of the foregoing principles to those disciples who sat listening to them, and to their successors in all time. Our Lord, though he began by pronouncing certain *characters* to be blessed—without express reference to any of His hearers—does not close the beatitudes without intimating that such characters were in existence, and that already they were before Him. Accordingly, from characters He comes to *persons* possessing them, saying, "Blessed are ye when men shall revile you," &c. And now, continuing this mode of direct personal address, He startles those humble, unknown men by pronouncing them the exalted benefactors of their whole species. **13. Ye are the salt of the earth**—to preserve it from corruption, to season its insipidity, to freshen and sweeten it. The value of salt for these purposes is abundantly referred to by classical writers as well as in Scripture; and hence its symbolical significance in the religious offerings as well of those without as of those within the pale of revealed religion. In Scripture, mankind, under the unrestrained workings of their own evil nature, are represented as entirely corrupt. Thus, before the flood (Gen. vi. 11, 12); after the flood (Gen. viii. 21); in the days of David (Ps. xiv. 2, 3); in the days of Isaiah (Isa. i. 5, 6); and in the days of Paul (Eph. ii. 1-3; see also Job xiv. 4; xv. 15, 16; John iii. 6; compared with Rom. viii. 8; Titus iii. 2, 3). The remedy for this, says our Lord here, is the active presence of His disciples among their fellows. The character and principles of Christians, brought into close contact with it, are designed to arrest the festering corruption of humanity and season its insipidity. But how, it may be asked, are Christians to do this office for their fellow-men, if their righteousness only exasperate them, and recoil, in every form of persecution, upon themselves? The answer is, That is but the first and partial effect of their Christianity upon the world: though the great proportion would dislike and reject the truth, a small but noble band would receive and hold it fast; and in the struggle that would ensue, one and another even of the opposing party would come over to His ranks, and at length the Gospel would carry all before it. **but if the salt have lost his savour** [μωρανθῇ]—'become unsavoury' or 'insipid;' losing its saline or salting property. The meaning is, If that Christianity on which the health of the world depends, does in any age, region, or individual, exist only in *name*, or if it contain not those *saving elements* for want of which the world languishes, **wherewith shall it be salted?**—how shall the salting qualities be restored to it? (Cf. Mark ix. 50.) Whether salt ever does lose its saline property—about which there is a difference of opinion—is a question of no moment here. The point of the case lies in the supposition—that *if it should lose it*, the consequence would be as here described. So with Christians. The question is not, Can, or do, the saints ever totally lose that grace which makes them a blessing to their fellow-men? But, What is to be the issue of that Christianity which is found wanting in those elements which can alone stay the corruption and season the tastelessness of an all-pervading carnality? The restoration or non-restoration of *grace*, or true living Christianity, to those who have lost it, has, in our judgment, nothing at all to do here. The question is not, If a man lose his grace, how shall *that grace* be restored to him? but, Since living Christianity is the only "salt of the earth," if men lose that, *what else* can supply its place? What follows is the appalling answer to this question. **it is thenceforth good for nothing, but to be cast out**—a figurative expression of indignant exclusion from the kingdom of God (cf. ch. viii. 12; xxii. 13; John vi. 37; ix. 34). **and to be trodden under foot of men**—expressive of contempt and scorn. It is not the mere want of a certain character, but the want of it in those whose *profession* and *appearance* were fitted to beget expectation of finding it. **14. Ye are the light of the world** [τὸ φῶς τοῦ κόσμου]. This being the distinctive title which our Lord appropriates to Himself (John viii. 12; ix. 5; and see John i. 4, 9; iii. 19; xii. 35, 36)—a title expressly said to be unsuitable even to the highest of all the prophets (John i. 8)—it must be applied here by our Lord to His disciples only as they shine with His light upon the world, in virtue of His Spirit dwelling in them, and the same mind being in them which was also in Christ Jesus. Nor are Christians anywhere else so called. Nay, as if to avoid the august title which the Master has appropriated to Himself, Christians are said to "shine"—not as "lights," as our translators render it, but—"as *luminaries* [φωστῆρες] in the world" (Phil. ii. 15); and the Baptist is said to have been "the burning and shining"—not "light," as in our translation, but—"*lamp*" [λύχνος] of his day (John v. 35). Let it be observed, too, that while the two figures of salt and sunlight both express the same function of Christians—their blessed influence on their fellow-men—they each set this forth under a different aspect. Salt operates *internally*, in the mass with which it comes in contact; the sunlight operates *externally*, irradiating all that it reaches. Hence Christians are warily styled "the salt of the *earth*"—with reference to the masses of mankind with whom they are expected to mix; but "the light of the *world*"—with reference to the vast and variegated surface which feels its fructifying and gladdening radiance. The same distinction is observable in the second pair of those seven parables which our Lord spoke from the Galilean lake—that of the "mustard seed," which grew to be a great overshadowing tree, answering to the sunlight which invests the world, and that of the "leaven," which a woman took and, like the salt, *hid* in three measures of meal, till the whole was leavened (ch. xiii. 31-33). **A city that is set on an hill cannot be hid**—nor can it be supposed to have been so built except to be seen by many eyes. **15. Neither do men light a candle**—or 'lamp' [λύχνον]—**and put it under a bushel**—a dry measure—**but on a candlestick**—rather, 'under the bushel, but on the lamp-stand' [ὑπὸ τὸν μόδιον, ἀλλ' ἐπὶ τὴν λυχνίαν]. The article is inserted in both cases to express the familiarity of every one with those household utensils. **and it giveth light** [λάμπει]—'shineth'—**unto all that are in the house. 16. Let your light so shine before men, that they may see your good works, and glorify your**

men, that [m] they may see your good works, and glorify [n] your Father which
is in heaven.
17 Think [o] not that I am come to destroy the Law, or the Prophets: I am
18 not come to destroy, but to fulfil. For verily I say unto you, [p] Till heaven
and earth pass, one jot or one tittle shall in no wise pass from the law,

A. D. 31.

[m] 1 Pet. 2. 12.
[n] John 15. 8. 1 Cor. 14. 25.
[o] Dan. 9. 24.
[p] Luke 16. 17.

Father which is in heaven. As nobody lights a lamp only to cover it up, but places it so conspicuously as to give light to all who need light, so Christians, being the light of the world, instead of hiding their light, are so to hold it forth before men that they may see what a life the disciples of Christ lead, and seeing this, may glorify their Father for so redeeming, transforming, and ennobling earth's sinful children, and opening to themselves the way to like redemption and transformation.

Remarks.—1. All-precious though the doctrines of the Gospel be, since the proper appreciation and cordial reception of them depends upon a previous preparation of the heart—especially, on the soul's being thoroughly emptied of its own fancied excellences, and made painfully alive to its spiritual necessities—it will be the wisdom of all Christian preachers to imitate the Great Preacher here, in laying first the foundation of this frame. 2. The theology of the Old Testament, when stripped of its accidents and reduced to its essence, is one with that of the New: it is spiritual; it is evangelical. 3. The earthly and the heavenly stages of the kingdom of God are essentially one; the former preparing the way for the latter, and opening naturally into it, as the commencing and consummating stages of the same condition. Thus the connection between them, far from being arbitrary, is inherent. 4. How entirely contrary to the spirit and design of Christianity is that monkish seclusion from society and ascetic solitude which, attractive though it be to a morbid spirituality, is just to do the very thing which our Lord here represents as against the nature of the Christian calling, and rendering observance of His injunctions here impossible. If even a lamp is not lighted to be put under a bushel, but placed conspicuously for the very purpose of giving light to all within reach of its rays, how much less is the sun placed in the heavens in order that men on the earth may walk in darkness? Even so, says our Lord, instead of hiding the light of your Christianity from the dark world around you, bring it out into the view of men, on purpose to let them see it. Much more plainly does this come out in the other figure. As salt must come into actual contact with what is to be seasoned by it, so must Christians, instead of standing at a distance from their fellows, come into contact with them, on purpose to communicate to them their own qualities. Nor does our Lord think it necessary to guard against confounding this with the spirit of religious ostentation, of which He treats sufficiently in the following chapter; for what follows is quite enough to prevent any such perversion of His language: "that they may see your good works, and glorify your Father which is in heaven"—not 'see how much superior you are to them,' but 'see what an astonishing change He can work by the Gospel upon men of every class.' Thus, God is deprived of the testimony He expects from His redeemed and transformed people, when, instead of manifesting before their fellows what He hath wrought for their souls, they shut themselves up—whether systematically or otherwise—or habitually retire within themselves. But, 5. Not by the preaching or publication of mere *truths*, are Christians to bear down the opposition and effect the conversion of their fellow-men. Not thus is their light to "shine before men." But it is so to shine that men "may *see their good works*, and (so) glorify their Father which is in heaven." In other words, while it is Christianity which is to carry all before it, it is not the Christianity of books, nor even of mere preaching—much less of an empty profession—but the Christianity of *life*. "YE (whom I have been pronouncing blessed, as possessors of a blessed character) are the light of the world." Yes: It is humility, not as preached, but as practised; it is contrition, not as depicted, not as inculcated, but as exemplified; it is meekness manifested; it is spiritual aspiration, not as enjoined, but as beheld in men on whose whole carriage may be seen written *Excelsior;* it is mercy embodied; it is heart-purity in flesh and blood; it is peace incarnate. This many-sided manifestation of a divine life in men, mixing with their fellows, and of like passions with their fellows, is the divinely ordained specific for arresting the progress of human corruption, diffusing health and sweetness through it, and irradiating it with the fructifying and gladdening beams of heavenly light.

17-48.—IDENTITY OF THESE PRINCIPLES WITH THOSE OF THE ANCIENT ECONOMY, IN CONTRAST WITH THE REIGNING TRADITIONAL TEACHING.

Exposition of Principles (17-20). **17. Think not that I am come**—'that I came' [ἦλθον] **to destroy the Law, or the Prophets**—that is, 'the authority and principles of the Old Testament.' (On the phrase, see ch. vii. 12; xxii. 40; Luke xvi. 16; Acts xiii. 15.) This general way of taking the phrase is much better than understanding "the Law" and "the Prophets" separately, and enquiring, as many good critics do, in what sense our Lord could be supposed to meditate the subversion of each. To the various classes of His hearers, who might view such supposed abrogation of the Law and the Prophets with very different feelings, our Lord's announcement would, in effect, be such as this—'Ye who "tremble at the word of the Lord," *fear* not that I am going to sweep the foundations from under your feet: Ye restless and revolutionary spirits, *hope* not that I am going to head any revolutionary movement: And ye who hypocritically affect great reverence for the Law and the Prophets, *pretend* not to find anything in my teaching derogatory to God's living oracles.' **I am not come to destroy, but to fulfil.** 'Not to subvert, abrogate, or annul, but to establish the Law and the Prophets—to unfold them, to embody them in living form, and to enshrine them in the reverence, affection, and character of men, am I come.' **18. For verily I say unto you** ['Αμὴν = אָמֵן—λέγω ὑμῖν]. Here, for the first time, does that august expression occur in our Lord's recorded teaching, with which we have grown so familiar as hardly to reflect on its full import. It is the expression, manifestly, of *supreme legislative authority;* and as the subject in connection with which it is uttered is the Moral Law, no higher claim to an authority *strictly divine* could be advanced. For when we observe how jealously Jehovah asserts it as His exclusive prerogative to give law to men

19 till all be fulfilled. Whosoever [q]therefore shall break one of these least
commandments, and shall teach men so, he shall be called the least in
the kingdom of heaven: but whosoever shall do and teach *them*, the same
20 shall be called great in the kingdom of heaven. For I say unto you,
That except your righteousness shall exceed [r]*the righteousness* of the
scribes and Pharisees, ye shall in no case enter into the kingdom of
heaven.
21 Ye have heard that it was said [3]by them of old time, [s]Thou shalt not

A. D. 31.
q Jas. 2. 10. Gal. 3. 10.
r Rom. 10. 3. 2 Cor. 5. 17. Phil. 3. 9.
3 Or, to them.
s Ex. 20. 13. 2Sam. 20. 18. Job 8. 8.

(Lev. xviii. 1-5; xix. 37; xxvi. 1-4, 13-16, &c.), such language as this of our Lord will appear totally unsuitable, and indeed abhorrent, from any creature-lips. When the Baptist's words—"I say unto you" (ch. iii. 9)—are compared with those of his Master here, the difference of the two cases will be at once apparent. **Till heaven and earth pass.** Though even the Old Testament announces the ultimate "perdition of the heavens and the earth," in contrast with the immutability of Jehovah (Ps. cii. 24-27), the prevalent representation of the heavens and the earth in Scripture, when employed as a popular figure, is that of their *stability* (Ps. cxix. 89-91; Eccl. i. 4; Jer. xxxiii. 25, 26). It is the enduring stability, then, of the great truths and principles, moral and spiritual, of the Old Testament Revelation which our Lord thus expresses. **one jot** [ἰῶτα]—the smallest of the Hebrew letters—**or one tittle** [κεραία]—one of those little strokes by which alone some of the Hebrew letters are distinguished from others like them—**shall in no wise pass from the law, till all be fulfilled.** The meaning is, that 'not so much as the smallest loss of authority or vitality shall ever come over the law.' The expression, "till all be fulfilled," is much the same in meaning as 'it *shall* be had in undiminished and enduring honour, from its greatest to its least requirements.' Again, this general way of viewing our Lord's words here seems far preferable to that *doctrinal* understanding of them which would require us to determine the different kinds of "fulfilment" which the *moral* and the *ceremonial* parts of it were to have. **19. Whosoever therefore shall break** [λύσῃ]—rather, 'dissolve,' 'annul,' or 'make invalid'—**one of these least commandments**—an expression equivalent to 'one of the least of these commandments'—**and shall teach men so**—referring to the Pharisees and their teaching, as is plain from the next verse, but of course embracing all similar schools and teaching in the Christian Church—**he shall be called the least in the kingdom of heaven.** As the thing spoken of is not the practical breaking, or disobeying, of the law, but annulling, or enervating its obligation by a vicious system of interpretation, and teaching others to do the same; so the thing threatened is not exclusion from heaven, and still less the lowest place in it, but a degraded and contemptuous position in the present stage of the kingdom of God. In other words, 'they shall be reduced, by the retributive providence that overtakes them, to the same condition of dishonour to which, by their system and their teaching, they have brought down those eternal principles of God's law.' **but whosoever shall do and teach them**—whose principles and teaching go to exalt the authority and honour of God's law, in its lowest as well as highest requirements—**the same shall be called great in the kingdom of heaven**—'shall, by that providence which watches over the honour of God's moral administration, be raised to the same position of authority and honour to which they exalt the law.' **20. For I say unto you, That except your righteousness shall exceed the righteousness of the scribes and Pharisees.** For the characteristics of the Pharisaic school, see on ch. iii. 1-12, Remark 2. But the superiority to the Pharisaic righteousness here required is plainly in *kind*, not *degree;* for all Scripture teaches that entrance into God's kingdom, whether in its present or future stage, depends, not on the degree of our excellence in anything, but solely on our having the character itself which God demands. Our righteousness, then—if it is to contrast with the *outward* and *formal* righteousness of the scribes and Pharisees—must be *inward, vital, spiritual.* Some, indeed, of the scribes and Pharisees themselves might have the very righteousness here demanded; but our Lord is speaking, not of persons, but of the *system* they represented and taught. **ye shall in no case enter into the kingdom of heaven.** If this refer, as in the preceding verse, rather to the earthly stage of this kingdom, the meaning is, that without a righteousness exceeding that of the Pharisees, we cannot be members of it at all, save in name. This was no new doctrine (Rom. ii. 28, 29; ix. 6; Phil. iii. 3). But our Lord's teaching here stretches beyond the present scene, to that everlasting stage of the kingdom, where without "purity of heart" none "shall see God."

The spirituality of the true righteousness, in contrast with that of the Scribes and Pharisees, illustrated from the Sixth Commandment (21-26). **21. Ye have heard that it was said by them of old time** [ἐῤῥήθη—a better authorized form than ἐῤῥέθη—τοῖς ἀρχαίοις]—or, as in the margin, 'to them of old time.' Which of these translations is the right one has been much controverted. Either of them is grammatically defensible, though the latter—"*to* the ancients"—is more consistent with New Testament usage (see the *Greek* of Rom. ix. 12, 26; Rev. vi. 11; ix. 4); and most critics decide in favour of it. But it is not a question of Greek only. Nearly all who would translate "to the ancients" take the speaker of the words quoted to be *Moses in the law;* "the ancients" to be *the people* to whom Moses gave the law; and the intention of our Lord here to be to contrast His own teaching, more or less, with that of Moses; either as opposed to it—as some go the length of affirming—or at least as modifying, enlarging, elevating it. But who can reasonably imagine such a thing, just after the most solemn and emphatic proclamation of the perpetuity of the law, and the honour and glory in which it was to be held under the new economy? To us it seems as plain as possible that our Lord's one object is to contrast the traditional perversions of the law with the true sense of it as expounded by Himself. A few of those who assent to this still think that "to the ancients" is the only legitimate translation of the words; understanding that our Lord is reporting what had been said to the ancients, not by Moses, but by the perverters of his law. We do not object to this; but we incline to think (with *Beza*, and after him with *Fritzsche*, *Olshausen*, *Stier*, and *Bloomfield*) that "by the ancients" must have been what our Lord meant

22 kill; and whosoever shall kill shall be in danger of the judgment: but
I say unto you, That [t]whosoever is angry with his brother without a
cause shall be in danger of the judgment: and whosoever shall say to his
brother, [4]Raca! shall be in danger of the council: but whosoever shall
23 say, Thou [5]fool! shall be in danger of hell fire. Therefore, if thou bring
thy gift to the altar, and there rememberest that thy brother hath ought
24 against thee; leave [u]there thy gift before the altar, and go thy way;
first be reconciled to thy brother, and then come and offer thy gift.

A. D. 31.

[t] 1 John 3. 15.
[4] That is, vain fellow.
[5] Or, graceless wretch. John 8. 44. Acts 13. 10.
[u] Job 42. 8.

here, referring to the corrupt teachers rather than the perverted people. **Thou shalt not kill**:—*q. d.*, 'This being all that the law requires, whosoever has imbrued his hands in his brother's blood, but he only, is guilty of a breach of this commandment;' **and whosoever shall kill shall be in danger of**—'liable to' [ἔνοχος] **the judgment**—that is, of the sentence of those inferior courts of judicature which were established in all the principal towns, in compliance with Deut. xvi. 16. Thus was this commandment reduced, from a holy law of the heart-searching God, to a mere criminal statute, taking cognizance only of outward actions, such as that which we read in Exod. xxi. 12; Lev. xxiv. 17. **22. But I say unto you.** Mark the authoritative tone in which—as Himself the Lawgiver and Judge—Christ now gives the true sense, and explains the deep reach, of the commandment. **That whosoever is angry with his brother without a cause** [εἰκῇ. Most recent critical editors either wholly exclude, or place within brackets, as of doubtful authority, the word εἰκῇ. External authority, however, preponderates in its favour. On the internal evidence opinions differ; some thinking it got in to soften the apparent harshness of the precept, while others think it was left out of some MSS. and early versions from jealousy at anything which looked like an attempt to dilute the strength of our Lord's teaching. But however we decide as to the *text*, we must restrict our *interpretation* to 'causeless anger.'] **shall be in danger of the judgment: and whosoever shall say to his brother, Raca!** [Ρακὰ = רֵיקָא, 'brainless'] **shall be in danger of the council** [τῷ συνεδρίῳ]: **but whosoever shall say, Thou fool!** [Μωρὲ = נָבָל] **shall be in danger of hell fire** [εἰς τὴν γέενναν—a word formed from גֵּי הִנֹּם, or 'valley of Hinnom']. It is unreasonable to deny, as *Alexander* does, that three degrees of punishment are here meant to be expressed, and to say that it is but a threefold expression of one and the same thing. But Romish expositors greatly err in taking the first two—"the judgment" and "the council"—to refer to degrees of *temporal* punishment with which lesser sins were to be visited under the Gospel, and only the last—"hell fire"—to refer to the future life. All three clearly refer to *divine retribution*, and that alone, for breaches of this commandment; though this is expressed by an *allusion* to Jewish tribunals. The "judgment," as already explained, was the lowest of these; the "council," or 'Sanhedrim'—which sat at Jerusalem—was the highest; while the word used for "hell fire" contains an allusion to the "valley of the son of Hinnom" (Josh. xviii. 16). In this valley the Jews, when steeped in idolatry, went the length of burning their children to Moloch "on the high places of Tophet" [תֹּפֶת, Jer. vii. 31]—in consequence of which good Josiah defiled it, to prevent the repetition of such abominations (2 Ki. xxiii. 10); and from that time forward, if we may believe the Jewish writers, a fire was kept burning in it to consume the carrion, and all kinds of impurities, that collected about the capital. Certain it is, that while the final punishment of the wicked is described in the Old Testament by allusions to this valley of Tophet or Hinnom (Isa. xxx. 33; lxvi. 24), our Lord Himself describes the same by merely quoting these terrific descriptions of the evangelical prophet (Mark ix. 43-48). What precise degrees of unholy feeling towards our brother are indicated by the words "Raca" and "fool" it would be as useless as it is vain to enquire. Every age and every country has its modes of expressing such things; and, no doubt, our Lord seized on the then current phraseology of unholy disrespect and contempt, merely to express and condemn the different degrees of such feeling when brought out in words, as He had immediately before condemned the feeling itself. In fact, so little are we to make of mere *words*, apart from the feeling which they express, that as *anger* is expressly said to have been borne by our Lord towards His enemies, though mixed with "grief for the hardness of their hearts" (Mark iii. 5), and as the apostle teaches us that there is an anger which is not sinful (Eph. iv. 26); so in the Epistle of James (ii. 20) we find the words, "O vain" or 'empty' man [ὦ ἄνθρωπε κενέ]; and our Lord Himself applies the very word "fools" [μωροὶ] twice in one breath to the blind guides of the people (ch. xxiii. 17, 19)—although, in both cases, it is to *false reasoners* rather than persons that such words are applied. The spirit, then, of the whole statement may be thus given—'For ages ye have been taught that the sixth commandment, for example, is broken only by the murderer, to pass sentence upon whom is the proper business of the recognized tribunals: but I say unto you that it is broken even by causeless anger, which is but hatred in the bud, as hatred is incipient murder (1 John iii. 15); and if by the feelings, much more by those *words* in which all ill feeling, from the slightest to the most envenomed, are wont to be cast upon a brother: and just as there are gradations in human courts of judicature, and in the sentences which they pronounce according to the degrees of criminality, so will the judicial treatment of all the breakers of this commandment at the divine tribunal be according to their real criminality before the heart-searching Judge.' O what holy teaching is this! **23. Therefore**—to apply the foregoing, and show its paramount importance—**if thou bring thy gift to the altar, and there rememberest that thy brother hath aught**—of just complaint **against thee; 24. Leave there thy gift before the altar, and go thy way; first be reconciled to thy brother** [διαλλάγηθι τῷ ἀδελφῷ]. The meaning evidently is—not, 'dismiss from thine own breast all ill-feeling,' but, 'get thy brother to dismiss from his mind all grudge against thee.' **and then come and offer thy gift.** 'The picture,' says *Tholuck*, 'is drawn from life. It transports us to the moment when the Israelite, having brought his sacrifice to the court of the Israelites, awaited the instant when the priest would approach to receive it at his hands.

25 Agree [v]with thine adversary quickly, whiles [w]thou art in the way with
him; lest at any time the adversary deliver thee to the judge, and the
26 judge deliver thee to the officer, and thou be cast into prison. Verily I
say unto thee, Thou [x]shalt by no means come out thence, till thou hast
paid the uttermost farthing.
27 Ye have heard that it was said by them of old time, Thou shalt not
28 commit adultery: but I say unto you, That whosoever looketh [y]on a
woman to lust after her hath committed adultery with her already in his

A. D. 31.

v Job 22. 21. Pro. 25. 8. Heb. 3. 7.
w Ps. 32. 6. Isa. 55. 6.
x 2 Thes. 1. 9.
y Gen. 34. 2. Pro. 6. 25. Eph. 5. 5.

He waits with his gift at the rails which separate the place where he stands from the court of the priests, into which his offering will presently be taken, there to be slain by the priest, and by him presented upon the altar of sacrifice.' It is at this solemn moment, when about to cast himself upon divine mercy, and seek in his offering a seal of divine forgiveness, that the offerer is supposed, all at once, to remember that some brother has a just cause of complaint against him through breach of this commandment in one or other of the ways just indicated. What then? Is he to say, As soon as I have offered this gift I will go straight to my brother, and make it up with him? Nay; but before another step is taken—even before the offering is presented—this reconciliation is to be sought, though the gift have to be left unoffered before the altar. The converse of the truth here taught is very strikingly expressed in Mark xi. 25, 26. "And *when ye stand praying* (in the very act), forgive, if ye have aught (of just complaint) against any; that your Father also which is in heaven may forgive you your trespasses. But if ye do not forgive, neither will your Father which is in heaven forgive you." Hence the beautiful practice of the early Church, to see that all differences amongst brethren and sisters in Christ were made up, in the spirit of love, before going to the Holy Communion; and the Church of England has a rubrical direction to this effect in her Communion service. Certainly, if this be the highest act of worship on earth, such reconciliation—though obligatory on all other occasions of worship—must be peculiarly so then. **25. Agree with thine adversary** [ἀντιδίκῳ]—thine opponent in a matter cognizable by law, **quickly, whiles thou art in the way with him**—"to the magistrate," as in Luke xii. 58; **lest at any time** [μήποτε]—here, rather, 'lest at all,' or simply 'lest' **the adversary deliver thee to the judge, and the judge**—having pronounced thee in the wrong, **deliver thee to the officer**—the official whose business it is to see the sentence carried into effect, **and thou be cast into prison. 26. Verily I say unto thee, Thou shalt by no means come out thence, till thou hast paid the uttermost farthing** [κοδράντην = *quadrantem*]; a fractional Roman coin, to which our "farthing" answers sufficiently well. That our Lord meant here merely to give a piece of prudential advice to his hearers, to keep out of the hands of the law and its officials by settling all disputes with one another privately, is not for a moment to be supposed, though there are critics of a school low enough to suggest this. The concluding words—"Verily I say unto thee, Thou shalt by no means come out," &c.—manifestly show that though the *language* is drawn from human disputes and legal procedure, He is dealing with a higher than any human quarrel, a higher than any human tribunal, a higher than any human and temporal sentence. In this view of the words—in which nearly all critics worthy of the name agree—the spirit of them may be thus expressed:—'In expounding the sixth commandment, I have spoken of offences between man and man; reminding you that the offender has another party to deal with besides him whom he has wronged on earth, and assuring you that all worship offered to the Searcher of hearts by one who knows that a brother has just cause of complaint against him, and yet takes no steps to remove it, is vain: But I cannot pass from this subject without reminding you of One whose cause of complaint against you is far more deadly than any that man can have against man; and since with that Adversary you are already on the way to judgment, it will be your wisdom to make up the quarrel without delay, lest sentence of condemnation be pronounced upon you, and then will execution straightway follow, from the effects of which you shall never escape as long as any remnant of the offence remains unexpiated.' It will be observed that as the *principle* on which we are to "agree" with this "Adversary" is not here specified, and the precise *nature* of the retribution that is to light upon the despisers of this warning is not to be gathered from the mere use of the word "prison;" so, the *remedilessness* of the punishment is not in so many words expressed, and still less is its actual *cessation* taught. The language on all these points is designedly general; but it may safely be said that the *unending duration* of future punishment—elsewhere so clearly and awfully expressed by our Lord Himself, as in verses 29 and 30, and Mark ix. 43, 48—is the only doctrine with which His language here quite naturally and fully accords. (Compare ch. xviii. 30, 34.)

The same subject illustrated from the Seventh Commandment (27-32). **27. Ye have heard that it was said.** The words [τοῖς ἀρχαίοις] "by," or "to them of old time," in this verse are insufficiently supported, and probably were not in the original text. **Thou shalt not commit adultery.** Interpreting this seventh, as they did the sixth commandment, the traditional perverters of the law restricted the breach of it to *acts* of criminal intercourse between, or with, married persons exclusively. Our Lord now dissipates such delusions. **28. But I say unto you, That whosoever looketh on a woman to lust after her** [πρὸς τὸ]—with the intent to do so, as the same expression is used in ch. vi. 1; or, with the full consent of his will, to feed thereby his unholy desires. **hath committed adultery with her already in his heart.** We are not to suppose, from the word here used—"adultery"—that our Lord means to restrict the breach of this commandment to married persons, or to criminal intercourse with such. The expressions, "*whosoever* looketh," and "looketh upon a *woman*," seem clearly to extend the range of this commandment to all forms of impurity, and the counsels which follow—as they most certainly were intended for all, whether married or unmarried—seem to confirm this. As in dealing with the sixth commandment our Lord first expounds it, and then in the four following verses applies His exposition, so here, He first expounds the seventh commandment, and then in

29 heart. And [z]if thy right eye [6]offend thee, pluck it out, and cast *it* from
thee: for it is profitable for thee that one of thy members should perish,
30 and not *that* thy whole body should be cast into hell. And if thy right
hand offend thee, cut it off, and cast *it* from thee: for it is profitable for
thee that one of thy members should perish, and not *that* thy whole body
should be cast into hell.
31 It hath been said, [a]Whosoever shall put away his wife, let him give
32 her a writing of divorcement: but I say unto you, That [b]whosoever
shall put away his wife, saving for the cause of fornication, causeth her
to commit adultery: and whosoever shall marry her that is divorced
committeth adultery.
33 Again, ye have heard that it hath been said [7]by them of old time,
[c]Thou shalt not forswear thyself, but [d]shalt perform unto the Lord thine
34 oaths: but I say unto you, [e]Swear not at all: neither by heaven; for it

A. D. 31.

[z] Mark 9. 43.
[6] Or, do cause thee to offend. Ps. 119. 37.
[a] Deut. 24. 1. Jer. 3. 1. Mark 10. 2.
[b] Rom. 7. 3. 1 Cor. 7. 10.
[7] to the ancients.
[c] Ex. 20. 7. Lev. 19. 12. Num. 30. 2.
[d] Deut. 23. 23.
[e] Jas. 5. 12.

the four following verses applies His exposition. **29. And if thy right eye**—the readier and the dearer of the two, **offend thee** [σκανδαλίζει σε]—be [a σκανδάληθρον] a 'trap-spring,' or, as in the New Testament, be 'an occasion of stumbling' to thee, **pluck it out, and cast it from thee**—implying a certain indignant promptitude, heedless of whatever cost to feeling the act may involve. Of course, it is not *the eye simply* of which our Lord speaks—as if execution were to be done upon the bodily organ—though there have been fanatical ascetics who have both advocated and practised this, showing a very low apprehension of spiritual things—but *the offending eye*, or the eye considered as the occasion of sin; and consequently, only the *sinful exercise* of the organ which is meant. For as one might put out his eyes without in the least quenching the lust to which they ministered, so, "if thine eye be single, thy whole body shall be full of light," and, when directed by a holy mind, becomes an "instrument of righteousness unto God." At the same time, just as by cutting off a hand, or plucking out an eye, the *power* of acting and of seeing would be destroyed, our Lord certainly means that we are to *strike at the root* of such unholy dispositions, as well as cut off the occasions which tend to stimulate them. **for it is profitable for thee that one of thy members should perish, and not that thy whole body should be cast into hell.** He who despises the warning to "cast from him," with indignant promptitude, an offending member, will find his whole body "cast," with a retributive promptitude of indignation, "into hell." Sharp language this, from the lips of Love incarnate! **30. And if thy right hand**—the organ of *action*, to which the eye excites, **offend thee, cut it off, and cast it from thee: for it is profitable, &c.** See on *v.* 29. The repetition, in identical terms, of such stern truths and awful lessons seems characteristic of our Lord's manner of teaching. Compare Mark ix. 43-48.

31. It hath been said. This shortened form was perhaps intentional, to mark a transition from the commandments of the Decalogue to a civil enactment on the subject of Divorce, quoted from Deut. xxiv. 1. The law of Divorce—according to its strictness or laxity—has so intimate a bearing upon purity in the married life, that nothing could be more natural than to pass from the seventh commandment to the loose views on that subject then current. **Whosoever shall put away his wife, let him give her a writing of divorcement**—a legal check upon reckless and tyrannical separation. The one legitimate ground of divorce allowed by the enactment just quoted was "some uncleanness" [עֶרְוַת דָּבָר, ἄσχημον πρᾶγμα]—in other words, conjugal infidelity. But while one school of interpreters (that of Shammai) explained this quite correctly, as prohibiting divorce in every case save that of adultery, another school (that of Hillel) stretched the expression so far as to include everything in the wife offensive or disagreeable to the husband—a view of the law too well fitted to minister to caprice and depraved inclination not to find extensive favour. And, indeed, to this day the Jews allow divorces on the most frivolous pretexts. It was to meet this that our Lord uttered what follows: **32. But I say unto you, That whosoever shall put away his wife, saving for the cause of fornication, causeth her to commit adultery**—that is, drives her into it, in case she marries again; **and whosoever shall marry her that is divorced**—for anything short of conjugal infidelity, **committeth adultery**—for if the commandment is broken by the one party, it must be by the other also. But see on chap. xix. 4-9. Whether the innocent party, after a just divorce, may lawfully marry again, is not treated of here. The Church of Rome says, No; but the Greek and Protestant Churches allow it.

Same subject illustrated from the Third Commandment (33-37). **33. Again, ye have heard that it hath been said by them of old time, Thou shalt not forswear thyself.** These are not the precise words of Exod. xx. 7; but they express all that it was currently understood to condemn, namely, false swearing (Lev. xix. 12, &c.) This is plain from what follows. **But I say unto you, Swear not at all.** That this was meant to condemn swearing of every kind and on every occasion—as the Society of Friends and some other ultra-moralists allege—is not for a moment to be thought. For even Jehovah is said once and again to have sworn by Himself; and our Lord certainly answered upon oath to a question put to Him by the high priest; and the apostle several times, and in the most solemn language, takes God to witness that He spoke and wrote the truth; and it is inconceivable that our Lord should here have quoted the precept about not forswearing ourselves but performing to the Lord our oaths, only to give a precept of His own directly in the teeth of it. Evidently, it is 'swearing in common intercourse and on frivolous occasions' that is here meant. Frivolous oaths were indeed severely condemned in the teaching of the times. But so narrow was the circle of them that a man might swear, says *Lightfoot*, a hundred thousand times and yet not be guilty of vain swearing. Hardly anything was regarded as an oath if only the name of God were not in it; just as among ourselves, as *Trench* well

35 is [f]God's throne: nor by the earth; for it is his footstool: neither by
36 Jerusalem; for it is the city of the great King. Neither shalt thou swear
37 by thy head, because thou canst not make one hair white or black. But
[g]let your communication be, Yea, yea; Nay, nay: for whatsoever is more
than these cometh of evil.
38 Ye have heard that it hath been said, An [h]eye for an eye, and a tooth
39 for a tooth: but I say unto you, [i]That ye resist not evil; [j]but whosoever
40 shall smite thee on thy right cheek, turn to him the other also. And if
any man will sue thee at the law, and take away thy coat, let him have
41 *thy* cloak also. And whosoever [k]shall compel thee to go a mile, go with
42 him twain. Give to him that asketh thee, and from [l]him that would
borrow of thee turn not thou away.

A. D. 31.

f Isa. 66. 1.
g 1 Cor. 1. 17-20. Col. 4. 6. Jas. 5. 12.
h Lev. 24. 20.
i Pro. 20. 22. Rom. 12. 17. 1 Cor. 6. 7. 1 Thes. 5. 15. 1 Pet. 3. 9.
j Isa. 50. 6.
k Mark 15. 21.
l Deut. 15. 8.

remarks, a certain lingering reverence for the name of God leads to cutting off portions of His name, or uttering sounds nearly resembling it, or substituting the name of some heathen deity, in profane exclamations or asseverations. Against all this our Lord now speaks decisively; teaching His audience that every oath carries an appeal to God, whether named or not. **neither by heaven; for it is God's throne: 35. Nor by the earth; for it is his footstool** (quoting Isa. lxvi. 1): **neither by Jerusalem; for it is the city of the great King** (quoting Ps. xlviii. 2). **36. Neither shalt thou swear by thy head, because thou canst not make one hair white or black.** In the other oaths specified, God's name was profaned quite as really as if His name had been uttered, because it was instantly *suggested* by the mention of His "throne," His "footstool," His "city." But in swearing by our own *head* and the like, the objection lies in their being 'beyond our control,' and therefore profanely assumed to have a stability which they have not. **37. But let your communication**—'your word' [λόγος], in ordinary intercourse, **be, Yea, yea; Nay, nay**:—'Let a simple *Yes* and *No* suffice, in affirming the truth or the untruth of anything. (See Jas. v. 12, and 2 Cor. i. 17, 18.) **for whatsoever is more than these cometh of evil** [ἐκ τοῦ πονηροῦ]—not 'of the evil One;' though an equally correct rendering of the words, and one which some expositors prefer. It is true that all evil in our world is originally of the devil, that it forms a kingdom at the head of which he sits, and that, in every manifestation of it he has an active part. But any reference to this here seems unnatural [cf. τῷ πονηρῷ, *v.* 39], and the allusion to this passage in the Epistle of James (v. 12) seems to show that this is not the sense of it—"Let your yea be yea; and your nay, nay; *lest ye fall into condemnation.*" The untruthfulness of our corrupt nature shows itself not only in the tendency to deviate from the strict truth, but in the disposition to suspect others of doing the same; and as this is not diminished, but rather aggravated, by the habit of confirming what we say by an oath, we thus run the risk of having all reverence for God's holy name, and even for strict truth, destroyed in our hearts, and so "fall into condemnation." The practice of going beyond Yes and No, in affirmations and denials—as if our word for it were not enough, and we expected others to question it—springs from that vicious root of untruthfulness which is only aggravated by the very effort to clear ourselves of the suspicion of it. And just as swearing to the truth of what we say begets the disposition it is designed to remove, so the love and reign of truth in the breasts of Christ's disciples reveals itself so plainly even to those who themselves cannot be trusted, that their simple Yes and No come soon to be more relied on than the most solemn asseverations of others. Thus does the grace of our Lord Jesus Christ, like a tree cast into the bitter waters of human corruption, heal and sweeten them.

Same Subject—Retaliation (38-42). We have here the converse of the preceding lessons. They were *negative:* these are *positive.* **38. Ye have heard that it hath been said** (Exod. xxi. 23-25; Lev. xxiv. 19, 20; Deut. xix. 21), **An eye for an eye, and a tooth for a tooth**—that is, whatever penalty was regarded as a proper equivalent for these. This law of retribution—designed to take vengeance out of the hands of private persons, and commit it to the magistrate—was abused in the opposite way to the commandments of the Decalogue. While they were reduced to the level of civil enactments, this judicial regulation was held to be a warrant for taking redress into their own hands, contrary to the injunctions of the Old Testament itself (Prov. xx. 22; xxiv. 29). **39. But I say unto you, That ye resist not evil; but whosoever shall smite thee on thy right cheek, turn to him the other also.** Our Lord's own meek, yet dignified bearing, when smitten rudely on the cheek (John xviii. 22, 23), and *not* literally presenting the other, is the best comment on these words. It is the preparedness, after one indignity, not to invite but to submit meekly to another, without retaliation, which this strong language is meant to convey. **40. And if any man will sue thee at the law, and take away thy coat** [χιτῶνα]—the inner garment; in pledge for a debt (Exod. xxii. 26, 27)—**let him have thy cloak also** [ἱμάτιον]—the outer and more costly garment. This overcoat was not allowed to be retained over-night as a pledge from the poor, because they used it for a bed-covering. **41. And whosoever shall compel thee to go a mile, go with him twain**—an allusion, probably, to the practice of the Romans and some eastern nations, who, when Government-despatches had to be forwarded, obliged the people not only to furnish horses and carriages, but to give personal attendance, often at great inconvenience, when required. But the thing here demanded is a readiness to submit to unreasonable demands of whatever kind, rather than raise quarrels, with all the evils resulting from them. What follows is a beautiful extension of this precept. **42. Give to him that asketh thee.** The sense of *unreasonable* asking is here implied (cf. Luke vi. 30). **and from him that would borrow of thee turn not thou away.** Though the word [δανείζομαι in Med.] signifies classically 'to have money lent to one on security,' or 'with interest,' yet as this was not the original sense of the word, and as usury was forbidden among the Jews (Exod. xxii. 25, &c.), it is doubtless simple borrowing which our Lord here means, as indeed the whole strain of the exhortation implies. This shows that such counsels as "Owe no man anything" (Rom. xiii. 8) are not to be taken absolutely; else the Scripture commen-

43 Ye have heard that it hath been said, Thou [m]shalt love thy neighbour,
44 [n]and hate thine enemy: but I say unto you, [o]Love your enemies, bless
them that curse you, do good to them that hate you, and pray [p]for them
45 which despitefully use you, and persecute you; that ye may be the
children of your Father which is in heaven: for he maketh his sun to
rise on the evil and on the good, and sendeth rain on the just and on the
46 unjust. For [q]if ye love them which love you, what reward have ye? do
47 not even the publicans the same? And if ye salute your brethren only,

A. D. 31.

[m] Lev. 19. 18.
[n] Deut. 23. 6.
[o] Pro. 25. 21. Rom. 12. 14.
[p] Luke 23. 34. Acts 7. 60. 1 Cor. 4. 12. 1 Pet. 2. 23.
[q] Luke 6. 32.

dations of the righteous for "lending" to his necessitous brother (Ps. xxxvii. 26; cxii. 5; Luke vi. 37) would have no application. **turn not thou away**—a graphic expression of unfeeling refusal to relieve a brother in extremity.

Same Subject—Love to Enemies (43-48). **43. Ye have heard that it hath been said** (Lev. xix. 18), **Thou shalt love thy neighbour.** To this the corrupt teachers added, **and hate thine enemy**—as if the one were a legitimate inference from the other, instead of being a detestable gloss, as *Bengel* indignantly calls it. *Lightfoot* quotes some of the cursed maxims inculcated by those traditionists regarding the proper treatment of all Gentiles. No wonder that the Romans charged the Jews with hatred of the human race. **44. But I say unto you, Love your enemies.** The word [ἀγαπᾶν] here used denotes *moral* love, as distinguished from the other word [φιλεῖν], which expresses *personal* affection. Usually, the former denotes 'complacency in the character' of the person loved; but here it denotes the benignant, compassionate outgoing of desire for another's good. [**bless them that curse you, do good to them that hate you**], **and pray for them which despitefully use you, and persecute you.** [The two bracketed clauses are omitted here by recent editors, who think them borrowed from Luke vi. 27, 28; but the evidence on both sides is pretty equally balanced.] The best commentary on these matchless counsels is the bright example of Him who gave them. (See 1 Pet. ii. 21-24; and cf. Rom. xii. 20, 21; 1 Cor. iv. 12; 1 Pet. iii. 9.) But though such precepts were never before expressed—perhaps not even conceived—with such breadth, precision, and sharpness as here, our Lord is here only the incomparable Interpreter of a law in force from the beginning; and this is the only satisfactory view of the entire strain of this Discourse. **45. That ye may be the children**—'that ye may be sons' [υἱοὶ]—**of your Father which is in heaven.** The meaning is, 'that ye may show yourselves to be such by *resembling* Him (cf. v. 9 and Eph. v. 1). **for he maketh his sun**—'your Father's sun.' Well might *Bengel* exclaim, 'Magnificent appellation!'—**to rise on the evil and on the good, and sendeth rain on the just and on the unjust**—rather [without the article], 'on evil and good, and on just and unjust.' When we find God's own procedure held up for imitation in the law, and much more in the prophets (Lev. xix. 2; xx. 26; and cf. 1 Pet. i. 15, 16), we may see that the principle of this surprising verse was nothing new: but the form of it certainly is that of One who spake as never man spake. **46. For if ye love them which love you, what reward have ye? do not even the publicans the same?** [τὸ αὐτό. The reading οὕτως has perhaps slightly the better support.] The publicans, as collectors of taxes due to the Roman government, were even on this account obnoxious to the Jews, who sat uneasy under a foreign yoke, and disliked whatever brought this unpleasantly before them. But the extortion practised by this class made them hateful to the community, who in their current speech ranked them with "harlots." Nor does our Lord scruple to speak of them as others did, which we may be sure He never would if it had been calumnious. The meaning, then, is, 'In loving those who love you, there is no evidence of superior principle: the worst of men will do this: even a publican will go that length.' **47. And if ye salute your brethren only**—of the same nation and religion with yourselves—**what do ye more [than others]?** [τί περισσόν]—'what do ye uncommon' or 'extraordinary?' that is, wherein do ye *excel?* **do not even the publicans so?** The true reading here appears to be, 'Do not even the heathens the same?' [ἐθνικοί.] Cf. ch. xviii. 17, where the excommunicated person is said to be "as an heathen man and a publican." **48. Be ye therefore** [Ἔσεσθε οὖν]—rather, 'Ye shall therefore be,' or 'Ye are therefore to be,' as My disciples and in My kingdom—**perfect** [τέλειοι], or 'complete.' Manifestly, our Lord here speaks, not of *degrees* of excellence, but of the *kind* of excellence which was to distinguish His disciples and characterize His kingdom. When therefore He adds, **even as your Father which is in heaven is perfect,** He refers to that full-orbed glorious completeness which is in the great Divine Model, "their Father which is in heaven." ['Your heavenly Father'—οὐράνιος—is here the preferable reading.]

Remarks.—1. In the light of this Section what shall we think of those low views of the Old Testament which have long been current in Germany, even among the most distinguished theologians and critics, and which from them have passed over to this country and across the Atlantic; poisoning some otherwise well affected to evangelical truth, and introducing a principle of laxity into their whole Biblical system? Not to speak of our Lord's solemn asseverations of the enduring authority of "the Law and the Prophets," and the honour in which they were to be held in His kingdom: who can read with intelligence, impartiality, and reverential docility, the illustrations which our Lord here gives of the spirituality and breadth of the ancient law, in opposition to the detestable perversions of it under which His hearers had grown up, without perceiving that instead of supplanting or even modifying it—which some excellent critics have too hastily conceded—the highest position towards the ancient law which our Lord here assumes, is that of its supreme and authoritative Interpreter? It is only the glorious comprehensiveness, the pure spirituality, the self-evidencing truth, and the heavenly radiance of His interpretations of the law—transcending, it is true, everything which we read in the Old Testament—that has deceived many into the notion that we have here a more or less *new code of morals;* a thing as contrary to a sound exposition of this Section as derogatory to the honour of God's ancient law. And if this is not to be endured, much less the Romish notion that all our Lord's teachings here are but 'evangelical counsels' (*consilia evangelica*), or counsels of perfection—not obligatory upon any, but the more meritorious in those who can work them-

48 what do ye more *than others?* do not even the publicans so? Be [r]ye
therefore perfect, even [s]as your Father which is in heaven is perfect.

A. D. 31.
[r] Gen. 17. 1.
[s] Eph. 5. 1.

selves up to them. 2. After reading such spiritual and searching expositions of the law, with what force is the apostolic inference borne in upon the awakened conscience, "Therefore by the deeds of the law there shall no flesh be justified in His sight: for by the law is the knowledge of sin"! (Rom. iii. 20.) The whole doctrinal system, indeed, of the Epistle to the Romans is seminally contained in the Gospels; but this truth in particular is written here as with a sunbeam. And yet, there are those who take refuge, from the pretended severity of the Pauline doctrine, in the Sermon on the Mount—as if it were of a milder type. We have ourselves heard the Jews chanting in the synagogue the praises of the law, while rejecting Him who alone can deliver them from the curse of it; but what better are those called Christians who turn away from the Pauline doctrine of Justification to that teaching from the Mount which, but for this Pauline doctrine the awakened conscience cannot abide—a teaching which, but for salvation by free grace, makes us feel ourselves standing under a very different Mount from that of the Beatitudes, beneath whose thunderings, and lightnings, and earthquakes, and voices the people exclaimed, "Let not God speak with us, lest we die" (Exod. xx. 19). Now this, without doubt, was what our Lord in the first instance sought to produce by so constructing His Sermon on the Mount. Accordingly, 3. Who that weighs the faint exposition we have given of the holy teaching of this Section, can fail to see the wisdom with which our Lord selected this line of thought for the first formal proclamation of the principles of His kingdom, rather than anything more definite regarding the "Lamb of God" which was to "take away the sin of the world"? While this would have been of little avail to such a motley assemblage, "alive without the law" and "at ease in Zion," nothing could be better fitted to dash vain expectations from Him of support to the reigning ideas; to rouse to anxious thought as many as were prepared to give Him even a respectful hearing; and to humble to the dust the thoroughly awakened, and create in them longings after further light and solid rest to their troubled souls. 4. When will Christians strive in earnest, as one man, to carry out the law of love, in respect of 'causeless anger,' here laid down? That little of it is to be seen at present is but too manifest; but that, if resolutely and habitually exemplified, it would astonish and impress the world around them more than all other arguments in favour of Christianity, who can doubt? O brother—sister—in Christ, blush, first of all, that thy Lord hath spoken to thee from the Mount so much in vain, and hath hitherto gotten so little testimony from thee. Then, on thy knees, pledge thyself to Him anew, and in strength divine make it thy daily business, whether in the quiet walks of domestic intercourse, or in the busy haunts of a more public calling, to exemplify the law of love here expounded. Nor, if thou hast broken it, despair or rest contented; but quickly repair, at any cost to feeling, the wrong thou hast hastily done to a brother, whether by unwarrantable anger in thy heart, or by unmerited and unbecoming rudeness of speech. Failing this, every act of worship offered to the Searcher of hearts will be vain (Ps. lxvi. 18), and should rather be interrupted till thou hast come to one with thy brother, than performed with a guilty conscience. (See Job xlii. 8.) 5. In vain do Romanists plead for the sacrifice of the mass, and some Protestants for "altars" in the Christian Church, from the "gifts brought to the altar," to which our Lord alludes in this Section. Spoken to Jews while the temple service was in full force, such language was altogether natural; it was most intelligible; it was life-like. But how far such things would or would not remain under an economy which was to supersede the Jewish, must be decided, not by such phraseology occurring here, but by other considerations altogether. 6. When we see how naturally our Lord rose, in His teaching, from disputes between man and man to the great controversy between man and God (*v.* 25, 26), it should be our study to imitate such spirituality—even in ordinary intercourse, but much more in teaching—and to make the immediate settlement of the great question of *peace with God* the paramount subject of all we say and teach on eternal things. 7. The sense in which our Lord here uses the phrase "*be reconciled*" [διαλλάγηθι, *v.* 24], is to be carefully noted, as the expression has been laid hold of to subvert the proper doctrine of the Atonement. It has been confidently affirmed that God is nowhere said to be reconciled to us—as if any change were needed, or possible, in the Unchangeable One towards men—but always we are said to be reconciled to God. In proof of this we are referred to 2 Cor. v. 18-20—"All things are of God, who hath reconciled *us to Himself* by Jesus Christ. God was in Christ, reconciling *the world unto Himself* . . . Now then . . . we pray you, in Christ's stead, be *ye reconciled to God.*" But since our Lord, in this Sermon on the Mount, when He requires the offending party to '*be reconciled to his offended brother*,' plainly means—not that the offender is to get rid of the cause of offence in his own breast, or to banish all doubts of his brother's willingness to forgive him—but that he is to take steps towards obtaining his brother's forgiveness, or getting his brother's just displeasure against himself removed; so in the words quoted from the Epistle to the Corinthians, the world's reconciliation to God by Jesus Christ, as a thing already accomplished—which is the great fact that the Gospel ministry is appointed to publish—cannot possibly mean any change which has come over the world's views of God: it can only mean the altered view of the world which God takes in consequence of Christ's death; or, to speak more properly, a new relation in which He stands to it *as reconciled through that death;* and it is when we "set to our seal that this is true," that we "are reconciled to God," for it must take effect on both sides. 8. If we would avoid sin we must cut off the occasions of it. This obvious rule solves a great many casuistical questions, as to how far Christians may warrantably go to this place and that, or join in this amusement and that. It is not enough to show that there is no express divine prohibition of them. If what the eyes see, and the hands handle, is found to suck one into the vortex of sin, it is no more to be indulged at such expense than if we should pluck them out, and cut them off, and cast them from us. A hard saying this, some will say. But a harder still, our Lord would answer, if I tell you those eyes and hands will otherwise drag you down to hell. No soft, silken teaching is this; and yet it is the teaching of Him to whom some affect to retreat as that of 'the meek and lowly Jesus,' from what they deem the harsh notes of the apostle of the Gentiles. To such one would be disposed to say, "Jesus I know, and Paul I know, but who are ye?" (Acts

6 TAKE heed that ye do not your [1] alms before men, to be seen of them;
otherwise ye have no reward [2] of your Father which is in heaven.
2 Therefore, [a] when thou doest *thine* alms, [3] do not sound a trumpet
before thee, as the hypocrites do in the synagogues and in the streets,
that they may have glory of men. Verily I say unto you, They have
3 their reward. But when thou doest alms, let not thy left hand know
4 what thy right hand doeth; that thine alms may be in secret: and thy
Father which seeth in secret himself shall reward thee openly.

A. D. 31.

[1] Or, righteousness.
[2] Or, with.
[a] Rom. 12. 8.
[3] Or, cause not a trumpet to be sounded.

xix. 15). 9. What sanctity is stamped upon the married life by our Lord's teaching here, especially when taken in connection with His teaching on the subject of purity in general! (*vv.* 28-32). 10. By cutting off all swearing in ordinary intercourse, with what sacredness is lawful swearing invested; especially when the presence of God, as the Avenger of falsehood, is seen to be invoked even when not expressly named! 11. Were simple truth to be so reverend in the eyes, and dear to the heart of every genuine disciple of Christ, that all around them were constrained to regard their "Yes" and "No" as far more to be trusted than the most solemn asseverations of others, what a testimony would thus be borne to Him to whom they owe their all! And why should it not be universally so? But, 12. What shall we say to the concluding expositions of this Section? To what a God-like height—not only of forbearance with those who wrong us, and submission to unreasonable demands, but of well-doing to the uttermost in return for ill-doing of the worst—does Jesus teach His disciples to rise! They are not to deem it enough to be as good as others, or up to the current standard, or 'neighbour-like.' As "the light of the world" and "the salt of the earth," their walk is to be a model for others, as their Heavenly Father Himself is to be their Model. (See Col. iii. 14; 1 John iv. 16.) Does any ingenuous disciple ask, But how is this to be attained and carried out? Let him hear the answer from the same blessed lips, "I say unto you, Ask, and it shall be given you; seek, and ye shall find; knock, and it shall be opened unto you: for if ye, being evil, know how to give good gifts unto your children, how much more shall your heavenly Father give the Holy Spirit to them that ask Him?" (Luke xi. 9, 13). And if we do but think that it was when we were *enemies* that we ourselves were reconciled to God by the death of His Son (Rom. v. 10), can we choose but extend that love to any enemies, even the greatest, that we may have among our fellow-men?

CHAP. VI. SERMON ON THE MOUNT—*continued.*

1-18.—FURTHER ILLUSTRATION OF THE RIGHTEOUSNESS OF THE KINGDOM—ITS UNOSTENTATIOUSNESS.

General Caution against Ostentation in Religious Duties (1). **1. Take heed that ye do not your alms** [ἐλεημοσύνην]. But the true reading seems clearly to be 'your righteousness' [δικαιοσύνην]. The external authority for both readings is pretty nearly equal; but internal evidence is decidedly in favour of 'righteousness.' The subject of the second verse being 'almsgiving,' that word—so like the other in Greek—might easily be substituted for it by the copyist: whereas the opposite would not be so likely. But it is still more in favour of "righteousness," that if we so read the first verse, it then becomes a general heading for this whole Section of the Discourse, inculcating unostentatiousness in *all* deeds of righteousness —Almsgiving, Prayer, and Fasting being, in that case, but selected examples of this righteousness; whereas, if we read "Do not your *alms*," &c., this first verse will have no reference but to that one point. By "righteousness," in this case, we are to understand that same righteousness of the kingdom of heaven, whose leading features—in opposition to traditional perversions of it—it is the great object of this Discourse to open up; that righteousness of which the Lord says, "Except your righteousness shall exceed the righteousness of the Scribes and Pharisees, ye shall in no case enter into the kingdom of heaven" (ch. v. 20). To "*do*" this righteousness, was an old and well understood expression. Thus, "Blessed is he that doeth righteousness [עֹשֵׂה צְדָקָה, ποιοῦντες δικαιοσύνην] at all times" (Ps. cvi. 3). It refers to the *actings* of righteousness in the life—the outgoings of the gracious nature—of which our Lord afterwards said to His disciples," "Herein is my Father glorified, that ye bear much fruit: so shall ye be my disciples" (John xv. 8). **before men, to be seen of them** [πρὸς τὸ θεαθῆναι αὐτοῖς]—'with the view' or 'intention of being beheld of them.' See the same expression in ch. v. 28. True, He had required them to let their light so shine before men that they might see their good works, and glorify their Father which is in heaven (ch. v. 16). But this is quite consistent with not making a display of our righteousness for self-glorification. In fact, the doing of the former necessarily implies our *not* doing the latter. **otherwise ye have no reward of your Father which is in heaven.** When all duty is done to God—as primarily enjoining and finally judging of it—He will take care that it be duly recognized; but when done purely for ostentation, God cannot own it, nor is His judgment of it even thought of —God accepts only what is done to Himself. So much for the general principle. Now follow three illustrations of it.

Almsgiving (2-4). **2. Therefore, when thou doest thine alms, do not sound a trumpet before thee.** The expression is to be taken figuratively for *blazoning* it. Hence our expression to 'trumpet.' **as the hypocrites do.** This word [ὑποκριτὴς]—of such frequent occurrence in Scripture, signifying primarily 'one who acts a part'—denotes one who either *pretends* to be what he is not (as here), or *dissembles* what he really is (as in Luke xii. 1, 2). **in the synagogues and in the streets**—the places of religious and of secular resort—**that they may have glory of men. Verily I say unto you.** In such august expressions, it is the Lawgiver and Judge Himself that we hear speaking to us. **They have their reward.** All they wanted was human applause, and they have it—and with it, all they will ever get. **3. But when thou doest alms, let not thy left hand know what thy right hand doeth.** 'So far from making a display of it, dwell not on it even in thine own thoughts, lest it minister to spiritual pride.' **4. That thine alms may be in secret, and thy Father which seeth in secret [Himself] shall reward thee openly.** The word "Himself" [αὐτὸς] appears to be an unauthorized addition to the text, which the sense no doubt suggested. See 1 Tim. v. 25; Rom. ii. 16; 1 Cor. iv. 5.

5 And when thou [b]prayest, thou shalt not be as the hypocrites *are:* for
they love to pray standing in the synagogues and in the corners of the
streets, that they may be seen of men. Verily I say unto you, They
6 have their reward. But thou, when thou prayest, enter into thy closet,
and when thou hast shut thy door, pray to thy Father which is in secret;
7 and thy Father [c]which seeth in secret shall reward thee openly. But
when ye pray, [d]use not vain repetitions, as the heathen *do:* [e]for they
8 think that they shall be heard for their much speaking. Be not ye
therefore like unto them: for your [f]Father knoweth what things ye

A. D. 31.

b Jer. 29. 12. Luke 18. 1. John 16. 24.
c Jer. 17. 10.
d Eccl. 5. 2. Dan. 9. 18, 19. ch. 26.39,42, 44.
e 1 Ki. 18. 26.
f Ps. 139. 2.

Prayer (5, 6). **5. And when thou prayest** [προσεύχῃ], **thou shalt**—or, according to the preferable reading, 'when ye pray [προσεύχησθε] ye shall' **not be as the hypocrites are: for they love to pray standing in the synagogues and in the corners of the streets** (see on *v.* 2), **that they may be seen of men. Verily I say unto you, They have, &c.** The *standing* posture in prayer was the ancient practice, alike in the Jewish and in the early Christian Church, as is well known to the learned. But of course this conspicuous posture opened the way for the ostentatious. **6. But thou, when thou prayest, enter into thy closet** [ταμεῖον, a 'store-house'—here, a 'place of retirement'], **and when thou hast shut thy door, pray to thy Father which is in secret; and thy Father which seeth in secret shall reward thee openly.** Of course it is not the simple publicity of prayer which is here condemned. It may be offered in any circumstances, however open, if not prompted by the spirit of ostentation, but dictated by the great ends of prayer itself. It is the *retiring* character of true prayer which is here taught.

Supplementary Directions, and Model-Prayer (7-15). **7. But when ye pray, use not vain repetitions** [μὴ βαττολογήσητε]. 'Babble not' would be a better rendering, both for the form of the word—which in both languages is intended to imitate the sound—and for the sense, which expresses not so much the repetition of the same words as a senseless multiplication of them; as appears from what follows. **as the heathen do: for they think that they shall be heard for their much speaking.** This method of heathen devotion is still observed by Hindu and Mohammedan devotees. With the Jews, says *Lightfoot*, it was a maxim, that 'Every one who multiplies prayer is heard.' In the Church of Rome, not only is it carried to a shameless extent, but, as *Tholuck* justly observes, the very Prayer which our Lord gave as an antidote to vain repetitions is the most abused to this superstitious end; the number of times it is repeated counting for so much more merit. Is not this just that characteristic feature of heathen devotion which our Lord here condemns? But praying much, and using at times the same words, is *not* here condemned, and has the example of our Lord Himself in its favour. **8. Be not ye therefore like unto them: for your Father knoweth what things ye have need of before ye ask him**—and so needs not to be *informed* of our wants, any more than to be *roused* to attend to them by our incessant speaking. What a view of God is here given, in sharp contrast with the gods of the heathen! But let it be carefully noted that it is not as *the general Father of Mankind* that our Lord says, "Your Father" knoweth what ye need before ye ask it; for it is not men, as such, that He is addressing in this Discourse, but His own disciples—the poor in spirit, the mourners, the meek, hungry and thirsty souls, the merciful, the pure in heart, the peacemakers, who allow themselves to have all manner of evil said against them for the Son of Man's sake—in short, the new-born children of God, who, making their Father's interests their own, are here assured that their Father, in return, makes their interests His, and needs neither to be told nor to be reminded of their wants. Yet He will have His children pray to Him, and links all His promised supplies to their petitions for them; thus encouraging us to draw near and keep near to Him, to talk and walk with Him, to open our every case to Him, and assure ourselves that thus asking we shall receive—thus seeking we shall find—thus knocking it shall be opened to us. **9. After this manner** [Οὕτως]—more simply, 'Thus,' **therefore pray ye.** The "ye" [ὑμεῖς] is emphatic here, in contrast with the heathen prayers. That this matchless prayer was given not only as a *model*, but as a *form*, might be concluded from its very nature. Did it consist only of hints or directions for prayer, it could only be used as a directory; but seeing it is an actual prayer—designed, indeed, to show how much real prayer could be compressed into the fewest words, but still, as a prayer, only the more incomparable for that—it is strange that there should be a doubt whether we ought to pray that very prayer. Surely the words with which it is introduced, in the second utterance and varied form of it which we have in Luke xi. 2, ought to set this at rest: "When ye pray, *say* [λέγετε], Our Father." Nevertheless, since the second form of it varies considerably from the first, and since no example of its actual use, or express quotation of its phraseology, occurs in the sequel of the New Testament, we are to guard against a superstitious use of it. How early this began to appear in the Church-services, and to what an extent it was afterwards carried, is known to every one versed in Church History. Nor has the spirit which bred this abuse quite departed from some branches of the Protestant Church, though the opposite and equally condemnable extreme is to be found in other branches of it.

Model-Prayer (9-13). According to the Latin fathers and the Lutheran Church, the petitions of the Lord's Prayer are *seven* in number; according to the Greek fathers, the Reformed Church, and the Westminster divines, they are only *six;* the two last being regarded—we think, less correctly—as one. The first three petitions have to do exclusively with GOD: "*Thy* name be hallowed"—"*Thy* kingdom come"—"*Thy* will be done." And they occur in a *descending* scale—from Himself down to the manifestation of Himself in His kingdom; and from His kingdom to the entire subjection of its subjects, or the complete doing of His will. The remaining four petitions have to do with OURSELVES: "Give *us* our bread"—"Forgive *us* our debts"—"Lead *us* not into temptation"—"Deliver *us* from evil." But these latter petitions occur in an *ascending* scale—from the bodily wants of every day up to our final deliverance from all evil.

Invocation: **Our Father which art in heaven.** In the former clause we express His nearness to

9 have need of before ye ask him. After this manner therefore pray ye:
10 [g]Our Father which art in heaven, [h]Hallowed be thy name. Thy
11 kingdom come. Thy will be done in earth, [i]as *it is* in heaven. Give

A. D. 31.

g Luke 11. 2.
h Isa. 6. 3.
i Ps. 103. 20.

us; in the latter, His distance from us. (See Eccl. v. 2; Isa. lxvi. 1.) Holy, loving familiarity suggests the one; awful reverence the other. In calling Him "Father," we express a relationship we have all known and felt surrounding us even from our infancy; but in calling Him our Father "who art in heaven," we contrast Him with the fathers we all have here below, and so raise our souls to that "heaven" where He dwells, and that Majesty and Glory which are there as in their proper home. These first words of the Lord's Prayer—this Invocation with which it opens—what a brightness and warmth does it throw over the whole prayer, and into what a serene region does it introduce the praying believer, the child of God, as he thus approaches Him! It is true that the paternal relationship of God to His people is by no means strange to the Old Testament. (See Deut. xxxii. 6; Ps. ciii. 13; Isa. lxiii. 16; Jer. iii. 4, 19; Mal. i. 6; ii. 10.) But these are only glimpses—the "back parts" (Exod. xxxiii. 23), if we may so say, in comparison with the "open face" of our Father revealed in Jesus. (See on 2 Cor. iii. 18.) Nor is it too much to say, that the view which our Lord gives, throughout this His very first lengthened discourse, of "our Father in heaven," beggars all that was ever taught, even in God's own Word, or conceived before by His saints, on this subject.

First Petition: **Hallowed be** [ἁγιασθήτω]—that is, 'Be held in reverence'—*regarded* and *treated* as holy. **thy name.** God's name means 'Himself as revealed and manifested.' Everywhere in Scripture God defines and marks off the faith and love and reverence and obedience He will have from men by the disclosures which He makes to them of what He is; both to shut out false conceptions of Him, and to make all their devotion take the shape and hue of His own teaching. Too much attention cannot be paid to this.

Second Petition: **10. Thy kingdom come.** The kingdom of God is that moral and spiritual kingdom which the God of grace is setting up in this fallen world, whose subjects consist of as many as have been brought into hearty subjection to His gracious sceptre, and of which His Son Jesus is the glorious Head. In the inward reality of it, this kingdom existed ever since there were men who "walked with God" (Gen. v. 24), and "waited for His salvation" (Gen. xlix. 18); who were "continually with Him, holden by His right hand" (Ps. lxxiii. 23), and who, even in the valley of the shadow of death, feared no evil, when He was with them (Ps. xxiii. 4). When Messiah Himself appeared, it was, as a visible kingdom, "at hand." His death laid the deep foundations of it—His ascension on high, "leading captivity captive and receiving gifts for men, yea, for the rebellious, that the Lord God might dwell among them," and the Pentecostal effusion of the Spirit, by which those gifts for men descended upon the rebellious, and the Lord God was beheld, in the persons of thousands upon thousands "dwelling" among men—was a glorious "coming" of this kingdom. But it is still to come, and this petition, "Thy kingdom come," must not cease to ascend so long as one subject of it remains to be brought in. But does not this prayer stretch further forward—to "the glory to be revealed," or that stage of the kingdom called "the everlasting kingdom of our Lord and Saviour Jesus Christ"? (2 Pet. i. 11). Not directly, perhaps, since the petition that follows this—"Thy will be done in earth, as it is in heaven"—would then bring us back to this present state of imperfection. Still, the mind refuses to be so bounded by stages and degrees, and in the act of praying "Thy kingdom come," it irresistibly stretches the wings of its faith, and longing, and joyous expectation out to the final and glorious consummation of the kingdom of God.

Third Petition: **Thy will be done in earth, as it is in heaven**—or, as the same words are rendered in Luke, 'as in heaven, so upon earth'—as *cheerfully*, as *constantly*, as *perfectly*. But some will ask, Will this ever be? We answer, If the "new heavens and new earth" are to be just our present material system purified by fire and transfigured, of course it will. But we incline to think that the aspiration which we are taught in this beautiful petition to breathe forth has no direct reference to any such *organic* fulfilment, and is only the spontaneous and resistless longing of the renewed soul—put into words—to see the whole inhabited earth in entire conformity to the will of God. It asks not if ever it shall be—or if ever it can be—in order to pray this prayer. It *must* have its holy yearnings breathed forth, and this is just the bold yet simple expression of them. Nor is the Old Testament without prayers which come very near to this, (Ps. vii. 9; lxvii.; lxxii. 19; &c.)

Fourth Petition: **11. Give us this day our daily bread.** The compound word here rendered "daily" [ἐπιούσιος] occurs nowhere else, either in classical or sacred Greek, and so must be interpreted by the analogy of its component parts. But on this critics are divided. To those who would understand it to mean, "Give us this day the bread of to-morrow"—as if the sense thus slid into that of Luke, "Give us *day by day*" (as *Bengel*, *Meyer*, &c.)—it may be answered that the sense thus brought out is scarcely intelligible, if not something less; that the expression "bread of to-morrow" is not at all the same as bread "from day to day," and that, so understood, it would seem to contradict *v.* 34. The great majority of the best critics [taking the word to be compounded of οὐσία, '*substance*,' or 'being'] understand by it the '*staff* of *life*,' 'the bread of *subsistence*;' and so the sense will be, 'Give us this day the bread which this day's necessities require.' In this case, the rendering of our authorized version (after the *Vulgate*, *Luther*, and some of the best modern critics)—"our daily bread"—is, in sense, accurate enough. (See Prov. xxx. 8.) Among commentators, there was early shown an inclination to understand this as a prayer for the heavenly bread, or spiritual nourishment; and in this they have been followed by many superior expositors, even down to our own times. But as this is quite unnatural, so it deprives the Christian of one of the sweetest of his privileges—to cast his bodily wants, in this short prayer, by one simple petition, upon his heavenly Father. No doubt the spiritual mind will, from "the meat that perisheth," naturally rise in thought to "that meat which endureth to everlasting life." But let it be enough that the petition about bodily wants irresistibly *suggests* a higher petition; and let us not rob ourselves—out of a morbid spirituality—of our one petition in this prayer for that bodily provision which the immediate sequel of this discourse shows that our heavenly Father has so much at heart. In limiting our petitions, however, to provision *for the*

12 us this day our [j]daily bread. And forgive us our debts, as we
13 forgive our debtors. And [k]lead us not into temptation, but deliver

A. D. 31.
j Job 23. 12.
k 1 Cor. 10.13.

day, what a spirit of child-like dependence does the Lord both demand and beget!

Fifth Petition: **12. And forgive us our debts.** A vitally important view of sin this—as an offence against God demanding reparation to His dishonoured claims upon our absolute subjection. As the debtor in the creditor's hands, so is the sinner in the hands of God. This idea of sin had indeed come up before in this Discourse—in the warning to agree with our adversary quickly, in case of sentence being passed upon us, adjudging us to payment of the last farthing, and to imprisonment till then (ch. v. 25, 26). And it comes up once and again in our Lord's subsequent teaching—as in the parable of the Creditor and his two debtors (Luke vii. 41, &c.), and in the parable of the Unmerciful debtor, (ch. xviii. 23, &c.) But by embodying it in this brief Model of acceptable prayer, and as the first of three petitions more or less bearing upon sin, our Lord teaches us, in the most emphatic manner conceivable, to regard this view of sin as the primary and fundamental one. Answering to this is the "forgiveness" which it directs us to seek—not the removal from our own hearts of the stain of sin, nor yet the removal of our just dread of God's anger, or of unworthy suspicions of His love, which is all that some tell us we have to care about —but the removal from God's own mind of His displeasure against us on account of sin, or, to retain the figure, the wiping or crossing out from His "book of remembrance" of all entries against us on this account. **as we forgive our debtors**—the same view of sin as before; only now transferred to the region of offences given and received between man and man. After what has been said on ch. v. 7, it will not be thought that our Lord here teaches that our exercise of forgiveness towards our offending fellow-men absolutely precedes and is the proper ground of God's forgiveness of us. His whole teaching, indeed—as of all Scripture—is the reverse of this. But as no one can reasonably imagine himself to be the object of Divine forgiveness who is deliberately and habitually unforgiving towards his fellow-men, so it is a beautiful provision to make our right to ask and expect daily forgiveness of our daily shortcomings, and our final absolution and acquittal at the great day of admission into the kingdom, dependent upon our consciousness of a forgiving disposition towards our fellows, and our preparedness to protest before the Searcher of hearts that we do actually forgive them. (See Mark xi. 25, 26.) God sees His own image reflected in His forgiving children; but to ask God for what we ourselves refuse to men, is to insult Him. So much stress does our Lord put upon this, that immediately after the close of this Prayer, it is the one point in it which He comes back upon (*vv.* 14, 15), for the purpose of solemnly assuring us that the Divine procedure in this matter of forgiveness will be exactly what our own is.

Sixth Petition: **13. And lead us not into temptation.** He who honestly seeks, and has the assurance of, forgiveness for past sin, will strive to avoid committing it for the future. But conscious that "when we would do good evil is present with us," we are taught to offer this sixth petition, which comes naturally close upon the preceding, and flows, indeed, instinctively from it in the hearts of all earnest Christians. There is some difficulty in the form of the petition, as it is certain that God does bring His people—as He did Abraham, and Christ Himself—into circumstances both fitted and designed to try them, or test the strength of their faith. Some meet this by regarding the petition as simply an humble expression of self-distrust and instinctive shrinking from danger; but this seems too weak. Others take it as a prayer against yielding to temptation, and so equivalent to a prayer for 'support and deliverance when we are tempted;' but this seems to go beyond the precise thing intended. We incline to take it as a prayer against being *drawn* or sucked, *of our own will*, into temptation, to which the word here used [εἰσενέγκῃς] seems to lend some countenance—'Introduce us not.' This view, while it does not put into our mouths a prayer against being tempted—which is more than the Divine procedure would seem to warrant—does not, on the other hand, change the sense of the petition into one for support *under* temptation, which the words will hardly bear; but it gives us a subject for prayer, in regard to temptation, most *definite*, and of all others most *needful*. It was precisely this which Peter needed to ask, but did not ask, when—of his own accord, and in spite of difficulties—he pressed for entrance into the palace-hall of the high priest, and where, once sucked into the scene and atmosphere of temptation, he fell so foully. And if so, does it not seem pretty clear that this was exactly what our Lord meant His disciples to pray against when he said in the garden—"Watch and pray, that ye *enter not into* temptation" [ἵνα μὴ εἰσέλθητε εἰς πειρασμόν]? (ch. xxvi. 41).

Seventh Petition: **But deliver us from evil.** We can see no good reason for regarding this as but the second half of the sixth petition. With far better ground might the second and third petitions be regarded as one. The "but" [ἀλλὰ] connecting the two petitions is an insufficient reason for regarding them as one, though enough to show that the one thought naturally follows close upon the other. As the expression "from evil" [ἀπὸ τοῦ πονηροῦ] may be equally well rendered 'from the evil one,' a number of superior critics think the devil is intended, especially from its following close upon the subject of "temptation." But the comprehensive character of these brief petitions, and the place which this one occupies, as that on which all our desires die away, seems to us against so contracted a view of it. Nor can there be a reasonable doubt that the apostle, in some of the last sentences which he penned before he was brought forth to suffer for his Lord, alludes to this very petition in the language of calm assurance—"And the Lord shall deliver me from every evil work (compare the Greek of the two passages), and will preserve me unto his heavenly kingdom" (2 Tim. iv. 18). This final petition, then, is only rightly grasped when regarded as a prayer for deliverance from all evil of whatever kind—not only from sin, but from all its consequences—fully and finally. Fitly, then, are our prayers ended with this. For what can we desire which this does not carry with it? [**For thine is the kingdom, and the power, and the glory, for ever. Amen.**—If any reliance is to be placed on external evidence, this doxology, we think, can hardly be considered part of the original text. It is wanting in all the most ancient MSS.; it is wanting in the *Old Latin* version and in the *Vulgate:* the former mounting up to about the middle of the second century, and the latter being a revision of it in the fourth century by *Jerome*, a most reverential and conservative as well as able and impartial critic. As might be expected from this,

[l]us from evil: For thine is the kingdom, and the power, and the glory,
14 for ever. Amen. For [m]if ye forgive men their trespasses, your hea-
15 venly Father will also forgive you: but [n]if ye forgive not men their
trespasses, neither will your Father forgive your trespasses.
16 Moreover, [o]when ye fast, be not, as the hypocrites, of a sad countenance: for they disfigure their faces, that they may appear unto men to
17 fast. Verily I say unto you, They have their reward. But thou, when
18 thou fastest, anoint thine head, and wash thy face; that thou appear
not unto men to fast, but unto thy Father which is in secret: and thy
Father, which seeth in secret, shall reward thee openly.

A. D. 31.
l John 17. 15.
m Mark 11. 25. Eph. 4. 32. Col. 3. 13.
n ch. 18. 35. Jas. 2. 13.
o 2 Sam. 12. 16. Neh. 1. 4. Esth. 4. 16. Ps. 35. 13. Ps. 69. 10. Isa. 58. 5.

it is passed by in silence by the earliest Latin fathers; but even the Greek commentators, when expounding this Prayer, pass by the doxology. On the other hand, it is found in a majority of MSS., though not the oldest; it is found in all the Syriac versions, even the Peshito—dating probably as early as the second century—although this version wants the "Amen," which the doxology, if genuine, could hardly have wanted; it is found in the *Sahidic* or *Thebaic* version made for the Christians of Upper Egypt, possibly as early as the Old Latin; and it is found in perhaps most of the later versions. On a review of the evidence, the strong probability, we think, is that it was no part of the original text. Not that our Lord could be supposed to direct that this or any prayer should close thus abruptly. But as, ever since David's exuberant doxology in 1 Chr. xxix. 11, the Jewish prayers had become rich in such doxologies (as may be seen in all their Liturgies), perhaps our Lord designedly left this model of prayer to be concluded more or less fully as circumstances might direct. This would account for the fact, that this doxology is variously given even in those MSS. and versions that have it, while some which omit it have the "Amen." On the whole, while we may in this way account for its finding its way into the venerable Peshito-Syriac and Old Latin versions, perhaps from the margins of some MSS., though not in the original text, it is very hard to conceive how it should have been allowed to drop out of all the most ancient MSS. if it was originally in the sacred text.]

14. For if ye forgive men, &c.: 15. But if ye forgive not, &c. See on *v.* 12.

Fasting (16-18). Having concluded His supplementary directions on the subject of Prayer with this divine Pattern, our Lord now returns to the subject of *Unostentatiousness* in our deeds of righteousness, in order to give one more illustration of it, in the matter of Fasting. **16. Moreover, when ye fast**—referring, probably, to private and voluntary fasting, which was to be regulated by each individual for himself; though in spirit it would apply to any fast. **be not, as the hypocrites, of a sad countenance: for they disfigure their faces**—[ἀφανίζουσιν]—lit., 'make unseen;' very well rendered "disfigure." They went about with a slovenly appearance, and ashes sprinkled on their head. **that they may appear unto men to fast.** It was not the *deed*, but *reputation* for the deed which they sought; and with this view those hypocrites multiplied their fasts. And are the exhausting fasts of the Church of Rome, and of Romanizing Protestants, free from this taint? **Verily I say unto you, They have their reward. 17. But thou, when thou fastest, anoint thine head, and wash thy face**—as the Jews did, except when mourning (Dan. x. 3); so that the meaning is, 'Appear as usual'—appear so as to attract no notice. **18. That thou appear not unto men to fast, but unto thy Father which is in secret: and thy Father, which seeth in secret, shall reward thee [openly]** [ἐν τῷ φανερῷ]. The "openly" seems evidently a later addition to the text of this verse from *vv.* 4, 7, though of course the idea is implied.

Remarks.—1. We have here one of many proofs that the whole teaching of the Epistles of the New Testament is seminally contained in the Gospels. When the apostle bids servants obey their masters, "not with eye-service, as men-pleasers; but *in singleness of heart, fearing God*" (Col. iii. 22), what is this but the great precept of this Section, to "do our righteousness"—whatsoever we do in word or deed—*to the Lord alone?* Not that we are to be indifferent to men's observations on our conduct—quite the reverse—for servants are exhorted so to carry themselves towards their masters as to "please them well in all things" (Tit. ii. 9). But just as the supreme authority for all duty, and the final judgment on all we do in respect of it, lies with God, so in simple obedience to Him must all duty be done, and to His judicial procedure upon it must all be referred. 2. As nothing is more hateful to God, and beneath the true dignity of His children, than an ostentatious way of performing any duty—while a retiring spirit, and an absorbing desire to please God in all we do, is as beautiful in itself as it is in the Divine eye—so at the great day this will be signally manifested, when "they that despise Him shall be lightly esteemed," and as "having had their reward," shall be "sent empty away;" whereas "them that honour Him He will honour" by "rewarding them openly." 3. What power and warmth is there in the brevity of those prayers which are offered by God's dear children to a Father who wants no information from them, and no stimulus to attend to them, though with equal love and wisdom He has linked all His supplies to their confiding petitions! What "babbling" would this spirit effectually disperse, and what a glorious contrast would it present, not only to the prayers of "the heathen," but to the heathenish prayers which one too often hears from professedly Christian lips! 4. Surely it is not for nothing that the first three Petitions in the Model-Prayer have respect to GOD; and that not till we have exhausted the uttermost desires of the gracious soul for His glory are we directed to seek anything for OURSELVES. This was very early observed by the devout students of this Prayer, and has been often, but cannot be too often, pointed out. The inference is obvious, but weighty—that God must have the first place, as in our prayers, so in the desires of our heart (Ps. lxxiii. 25, 26). 5. Are not the fountains of the *missionary spirit* opened by the first three Petitions of this incomparable Prayer; and must not its living waters spring up into everlasting life within us the oftener we pour them forth from the bottom of our hearts? Can he who says daily, "Hallowed be Thy name," hear that name "continually every day blasphemed," without trying to "come to the help of the Lord against the mighty"? Can he who ceases not to say, "Thy

19 Lay [p]not up for yourselves treasures upon earth, where moth and rust
20 doth corrupt, and where thieves break through and steal: but [q]lay up
for yourselves treasures in heaven, where neither moth nor rust doth
21 corrupt, and where thieves do not break through nor steal: for where
22 your treasure is, there will your heart be also. The [r]light of the body is
the eye: if therefore thine eye be single, thy whole body shall be full of

A. D. 31.

[p] Pro. 23. 4. 1 Tim. 6. 17. Heb. 13. 5.
[q] 1 Tim. 6. 19. 1 Pet. 1. 4.
[r] Luke 11. 34.

kingdom come; Thy will be done in earth, as it is in heaven," know that the kingdom of God's enemy embraces, even in this nineteenth century of the Christian era, a majority of the earth's population, and that even where God's kingdom is set visibly up, and where it is had in greatest honour, His will is yet far, O how far! from being done as it is in heaven—and not feel his spirit stirred within him, remembering that to His own disciples did the Master, ere he took His flight for glory, commit the evangelization of the world, and that the curse of Meroz (Jud. v. 23) rests upon those who come not to the help of the Lord, to the help of the Lord against the mighty? 6. Dear to all the children of God should be the fourth petition of this matchless prayer—in its proper literal sense—because it teaches them that this body, which God thus cares for, is of value in His esteem: because, if they be needy, it gives them "cords of a man, and bands of love," to draw them to the fountain of plenty, and calms their anxious spirits with the assurance that the needed supply will not be withheld; and if they be not needy, but blessed with plenty, it teaches them consideration and compassion for those whose case is the reverse, and identifies them with such—constraining them to feel that for the gift, and the continuance of their abundance, they are as dependent upon their Father in heaven as are the poorest of their brethren for their scanty means. 7. By directing God's children to say daily, "Forgive us our debts," our Lord rebukes not only those perfectionists who say that as believers "they have no sin" (1 John i. 8), but those who, without going this length, deem it so the privilege of believers to *have* forgiveness, that to *ask* it is unbelief. Were this really the case, who that knows the plagues of his own heart would not think it a pity, and would not irresistibly break through the restraint, for the very privilege of crying, "Forgive us our debts"? But that it is not the case, this petition plainly shows. It is true that "he that is washed needeth not save to wash his feet, but is clean every whit;" but it is just this exceptive "washing of the feet," the felt need of which daily makes it such a necessity and such a privilege to say daily, "Forgive us our debts." (See on John xiii. 10.) 8. O how much hypocrisy is there in multitudes of worshippers, who protest before the Searcher of hearts that they "forgive their debtors!" And if we have just so much forgiveness of God as we ourselves extend to men, may not this be at least one explanation of the inability of some real Christians to attain to the joy of God's salvation? 9. How strange it is that any real Christians, after saying, "Lead us not into temptation," should deliberately adventure themselves into scenes which not only they ought to know are trying to Christian principle, but from which they themselves have already suffered! It is not enough that what is transacted is not intrinsically sinful. Whatever is found by experience to wound the conscience, or even greatly endanger its purity, ought to be eschewed by all who cry daily from the heart, "Lead us not into temptation." 10. How precious is the closing petition of this Model-Prayer—"But deliver us from evil"! lifting the soul into a region of superiority to evil, even while yet in the midst of it, encouraging it to stretch the neck of its expectation beyond it all, and assuring it, as its believing aspirations are dying away, that the time is drawing nigh when it shall bid an eternal adieu to the last remnant and memorial of it.

19-34.—Concluding Illustrations of the Righteousness of the Kingdom—Heavenly-mindedness and Filial Confidence.

19. Lay not up for yourselves—or hoard not—**treasures upon earth, where moth** [σής = סָס]—a 'clothes-moth.' Eastern treasures, consisting partly in costly dresses stored up (Job xxvii. 16), were liable to be consumed by moths (Job xiii. 28; Isa. l. 9; li. 8). In Jas. v. 2 there is an evident reference to our Lord's words here. **and rust** [βρῶσις]—any 'eating into' or 'consuming;' here, probably, 'wear-and-tear.' **doth corrupt** [ἀφανίζει]—'cause to disappear.' By this reference to moth and rust our Lord would teach how *perishable* are such earthly treasures. **and where thieves break through and steal.** Treasures these, how *precarious!* **20. But lay up for yourselves treasures in heaven.** The language in Luke (xii. 33) is very bold—"Sell that ye have, and give alms; provide yourselves bags which wax not old, a treasure in the heavens that faileth not," &c. **where neither moth nor rust doth corrupt, and where thieves do not break through nor steal.** Treasures these, *imperishable* and *unassailable!* (Compare Col. iii. 2.) **21. For where your treasure is**—that which ye value most, **there will your heart be also.** ['Thy treasure—thy heart' is probably the true reading here: 'your,' in Luke xii. 34, from which it seems to have come in here.] Obvious though this maxim be, by what multitudes who profess to bow to the teaching of Christ is it practically disregarded! 'What a man loves,' says *Luther*, quoted by *Tholuck*, 'that is his God. For he carries it in his heart, he goes about with it night and day, he sleeps and wakes with it; be it what it may—wealth or pelf, pleasure or renown.' But because "laying up" is not in itself sinful, nay, in some cases enjoined (2 Cor. xii. 14), and honest industry and sagacious enterprise are usually rewarded with prosperity, many flatter themselves that all is right between them and God while their closest attention, anxiety, zeal, and time are exhausted upon these earthly pursuits. To put this right, our Lord adds what follows, in which there is profound practical wisdom. **22. The light**—rather, 'The lamp' [λύχνος]—**of the body is the eye: if therefore thine eye be single** [ἁπλοῦς]—'simple,' 'clear.' As applied to the outward eye, this means general soundness; particularly, not looking two ways. Here, as also in classical Greek, it is used figuratively to denote the simplicity of the mind's eye, singleness of purpose, looking right at its object, as opposed to having two ends in view. (See Pro. iv. 25-27.) **thy whole body shall be full of light** [φωτεινὸν]—'illuminated.' As with the bodily vision, the man who looks with a good, sound eye walks in light, seeing every object clear; so a simple and persistent purpose to serve and please God in everything will make the whole character consistent and bright. **23. But if thine eye be evil** [πονηρὸς]—'distem-

23 light. But if thine eye be evil, thy whole body shall be full of darkness.
If therefore the light that is in thee be darkness, [s]how great *is* that dark-
24 ness! No [t]man can serve two masters: for either he will hate the one,
and love the other; or else he will hold to the one, and despise the other.
25 [u]Ye cannot serve God and mammon. Therefore I say unto you, [4]Take
no thought for your life, what ye shall eat, or what ye shall drink; nor
yet for your body, what ye shall put on. Is not the life more than meat,
26 and the body than raiment? Behold [v]the fowls of the air: for they sow
not, neither do they reap, nor gather into barns; yet your heavenly
27 Father feedeth them. Are ye not much better than they? Which of you,

A. D. 31.

s Rom. 1. 21. 2 Cor. 4. 4.
t Luke 16. 13.
u Gal. 1. 10. 1 Tim. 6. 17.
4 Be not anxiously careful. Ps. 55. 22. Phil. 4. 6.
v Job 38. 41. Ps. 147. 9.

pered,' or, as we should say, If we have got a *bad* eye [cf. Prov. xxiii. 6, "an evil eye," רַע עַיִן]. **thy whole body shall be full of darkness** [σκοτεινὸν]—'darkened.' As a vitiated eye, or an eye that looks not straight and full at its object, sees nothing as it is, so a mind and heart divided between heaven and earth is all dark. **If therefore the light that is in thee** [not λύχνος now, but φῶς, 'light'] **be darkness, how great is that darkness!** As the conscience is the regulative faculty, and a man's inward purpose, scope, aim in life, determines his character—if these be not simple and heavenward, but distorted and double, what must all the other faculties and principles of our nature be which take their direction and character from these, and what must the whole man and the whole life be, but a mass of darkness? In Luke (xi. 36) the converse of this statement very strikingly expresses what pure, beautiful, broad perceptions the *clarity of the inward eye* imparts: "If thy whole body therefore be full of light, having no part dark, the whole shall be full of light, as the bright shining of a candle doth give thee light." But now for the application of this. **24. No man can serve** [δουλεύειν]. The word means to 'belong wholly and be entirely under command to,' **two masters: for either he will hate the one, and love the other; or else he will hold to the one, and despise the other.** Even if the two masters be of one character and have but one object, the servant must *take law* from one or other: though he may do what is agreeable to both, he cannot, in the nature of the thing, be *servant* to more than one. Much less if, as in the present case, their interests are quite different, and even conflicting. In this case, if our affections be in the service of the one—if we "love the one"—we must of necessity "hate the other;" if we determine resolutely to "hold to the one," we must at the same time disregard, and, if he insist on his claims upon us, even "despise the other." **Ye cannot serve God and mammon.** The word "mamon"—better written with one *m*—is a foreign one, whose precise derivation cannot certainly be determined, though the most probable one gives it the sense of 'what one trusts in.' Here, there can be no doubt it is used for *riches*, considered as an idol-master, or god of the heart. The service of this god and the true God together is here, with a kind of indignant curtness, pronounced impossible. But since the teaching of the preceding verses might seem to endanger our falling short of what is requisite for the present life, and so being left destitute, our Lord now comes to speak to that point. **25. Therefore I say unto you, Take no thought** [μὴ μεριμνᾶτε]—'Be not solicitous.' The English word "thought," when our version was made, expressed this idea of 'solicitude,' 'anxious concern'—as may be seen in any old English classic; and in the same sense it is used in 1 Sam. ix, 5, &c. But this sense of the word has now nearly gone out, and so the mere English reader is apt to be perplexed. *Thought* or forethought, for temporal things—in the sense of reflection, consideration—is required alike by Scripture and common sense. It is that anxious solicitude, that carking care, which springs from unbelieving doubts and misgivings, which alone is here condemned. (See Phil. iv. 6.) **for your life, what ye shall eat, or what ye shall drink; nor yet for your body, what ye shall put on.** In Luke (xii. 29) our Lord adds, 'neither be ye unsettled' [μετεωρίζεσθε]—not "of doubtful mind," as in our version. When "careful (or 'full of care') about nothing," but committing all in prayer and supplication with thanksgiving unto God, the apostle assures us that "the peace of God, which passeth all understanding, shall keep our hearts and minds [νοήματα] in Christ Jesus" (Phil. iv. 6, 7); that is, shall guard both our feelings and our thoughts from undue agitation, and keep them in a holy calm. But when we commit our whole temporal condition to the wit of our own minds, we get into that "unsettled" state against which our Lord exhorts His disciples. **Is not the life more than meat**—or 'food' [τροφῆς], **and the body than raiment?** If God, then, give and keep up the greater—the life, the body—will He withhold the less, food to sustain life and raiment to clothe the body? **26. Behold the fowls of the air**—in *v.* 28, 'observe well' [καταμάθετε], and in Luke xii. 24, "consider" [κατανοήσατε]—so as to learn wisdom from them. **for they sow not, neither do they reap, nor gather into barns; yet your heavenly Father feedeth them. Are ye not much better than they?**—nobler in yourselves and dearer to God. The argument here is from the greater to the less; but how rich in detail! The brute creation—void of reason—are incapable of sowing, reaping, and storing; yet your heavenly Father suffers them not helplessly to perish, but sustains them without any of those processes: Will He see, then, His own children using all the means which reason dictates for procuring the things needful for the body—looking up to Himself at every step—and yet leave them to starve? **27. Which of you, by taking thought** ('anxious solicitude'), **can add one cubit unto his stature** [ἡλικίαν]? "Stature" can hardly be the thing intended here: first, because the subject is the *prolongation of life*, by the supply of its necessaries of food and clothing; and next, because no one would dream of adding a cubit—or a foot and a half—to his stature, while in the corresponding passage in Luke (xii. 25, 26), the thing intended is represented as "that thing which is *least*." But if we take the word in its primary sense of '*age*' (for 'stature' is but a secondary sense) the idea will be this, 'Which of you, however anxiously you vex yourselves about it, can add so much as a step to the length of your life's journey?' To compare the length of life to measures of this nature is not

28 by taking thought, can add one cubit unto his stature? And why take
ye thought for raiment? Consider the lilies of the field, how they grow:
29 they toil not, neither do they spin: and yet I say unto you, That even
30 Solomon in all his glory was not arrayed like one of these. Wherefore, if
God so clothe the grass of the field, which to-day is, and to-morrow is
cast into the oven, *shall he* not much more *clothe* you, O ye of little faith?
31 Therefore take no thought, saying, What shall we eat? or, What shall
32 we drink? or, Wherewithal shall we be clothed? (For after all these
things do the Gentiles seek:) for [w]your heavenly Father knoweth that ye
33 have need of all these things. But [x]seek ye first the kingdom of God,
and his righteousness; [y]and all these things shall be added unto you.
34 Take therefore no [5]thought for the morrow: for the morrow shall take
thought for the things of itself. Sufficient unto the day *is* the evil
thereof.

A. D. 31.

w Ps. 23. 1. Phil. 4. 19.
x 1 Ki. 3. 13. Ps. 34. 9. Ps. 37. 25. Mark 10.30. Luke 12. 31. Rom. 8. 32. 1 Tim. 4. 8.
y Ps. 34. 9, 10. ch. 19. 29. Mark 10.30. Luke 18.29, 30. Rom. 8. 32.
5 anxious thought.

foreign to the language of Scripture, (cf. Ps. xxxix. 5; 2 Tim. iv. 7, &c.) So understood, the meaning is clear and the connection natural. In this the best critics now agree. **28. And why take ye thought for raiment? Consider** ('observe well') **the lilies of the field, how they grow: they toil not**—as men, planting and preparing the flax, **neither do they spin**—as women: **29. And yet I say unto you, That even Solomon in all his glory was not arrayed like one of these.** What incomparable teaching!—best left in its own transparent clearness and rich simplicity. **30. Wherefore, if God so clothe the grass**—the 'herbage' [χόρτον]—**of the field, which to-day is, and to-morrow is cast into the oven**—wild flowers cut with the grass, withering by the heat, and used for fuel. (See Jas. i. 11.) **shall he not much more clothe you, O ye of little faith?** The argument here is something fresh. 'Gorgeous as is the array of the flowers that deck the fields, surpassing all artificial human grandeur, it is for but a brief moment; you are ravished with it to-day, and to-morrow it is gone; your own hands have seized and cast it into the oven: Shall, then, God's children, so dear to Him, and instinct with a life that cannot die, be left naked?' He does not say, Shall they not be more beauteously arrayed? but, Shall He not much more *clothe* them? that being all He will have them regard as secured to them (cf. Heb. xiii. 5). The expression, 'Little-faithed ones' [ὀλιγόπιστοι], which our Lord applies once and again to His disciples (ch. viii. 26; xiv. 31; xvi. 8), can hardly be regarded as rebuking any actual manifestations of unbelief at that early period, and before such an audience. It is His way of gently chiding the *spirit* of unbelief, so natural even to the best, who are surrounded by a world of sense, and of kindling a generous desire to shake it off. **31. Therefore take no thought** ('solicitude'), **saying, What shall we eat? or, What shall we drink? or, Wherewithal shall we be clothed? 32. (For after all these things do the Gentiles seek)** [ἐπιζητεῖ]—rather, 'pursue.' Knowing nothing definitely beyond the present life to kindle their aspirations and engage their supreme attention, the heathen naturally pursue present objects as their chief, their only good. To what an elevation above these does Jesus here lift His disciples! **for your heavenly Father knoweth that ye have need of all these things.** How precious this word! Food and raiment are pronounced *needful* to God's children; and He who could say, "No man knoweth the Father but the Son, and he to whomsoever the Son will reveal Him" (ch. xi. 27), says with an authority which none but Himself could claim, "Your heavenly Father *knoweth* that ye have need of all these things." Will not that suffice you, O ye needy ones of the household of faith? **33. But seek ye first the kingdom of God, and his righteousness; and all these things shall be added unto you.** This is the great summing up. Strictly speaking, it has to do only with the subject of the present Section—the right state of the heart with reference to heavenly and earthly things; but being couched in the form of a brief general directory, it is so comprehensive in its grasp as to embrace the whole subject of this Discourse. And, as if to make this the more evident, the two key-notes of this great Sermon seem purposely struck in it—"the KINGDOM" and "the RIGHTEOUSNESS" of the kingdom—as the grand objects, in the supreme pursuit of which all things needful for the present life will be added to us. The precise sense of every word in this golden verse should be carefully weighed. "*The kingdom of God*" is the primary subject of the Sermon on the Mount—that kingdom which the God of heaven is erecting in this fallen world, within which are all the spiritually recovered and inwardly subject portion of the family of Adam, under Messiah as its divine Head and King. "*The righteousness thereof*" is the character of all such, so amply described and variously illustrated in the foregoing portions of this Discourse. The "*seeking*" of these is the making them the object of supreme choice and pursuit; and the seeking of them "*first*" is the seeking of them before and above all else. The "*all these things*" which shall in that case be added to us are just the "all these things" which the last words of the preceding verse assured us "our heavenly Father knoweth that we have need of;" that is, all we require for the present life. And when our Lord says they shall be "*added*," it is implied, as a matter of course, that the seekers of the kingdom and its righteousness shall have these as their proper and primary portion; the rest being their gracious reward for *not* seeking them. (See an illustration of the principle of this in 2 Chr. i. 11, 12.) What follows is but a reduction of this great general direction into a practical and ready form for daily use. **34. Take therefore no thought** ('anxious care') **for the morrow: for the morrow shall take thought for the things of itself** (or, according to other authorities, 'for itself')—shall have its own causes of anxiety. **Sufficient unto the day is the evil thereof.** An admirable practical maxim, and better rendered in our version than in almost any other, not excepting the preceding English ones. Every day brings its own cares; and to anticipate is only to double them.

Remarks.—1. Worldly-mindedness is as insidious as it is destructive to spirituality in the Christian.

7 JUDGE [a]not, that ye be not judged. For with what judgment ye
2 judge, ye shall be judged: [b]and with what measure ye mete, it shall be
3 measured to you again. And [c]why beholdest thou the mote that is in
thy brother's eye, but considerest not the beam that is in thine own eye?
4 Or how wilt thou say to thy brother, Let me pull out the mote out of
5 thine eye; and, behold, a beam *is* in thine own eye? Thou hypocrite,

A. D. 31.

CHAP. 7.
[a] Rom. 2. 1.
Rom. 14. 3.
Jas. 4. 11.
[b] Mark 4. 24.
Luke 6. 38.
[c] Luke 6. 41.

The innocence of secular occupations is the plea on which inordinate attention to them is permitted to steal away the heart. And thus it is that the care of this world, and the deceitfulness of riches, and the pleasures of this life—silently but surely—choke the word, and no fruit is brought to perfection (see on Mark iv. 7). 2. What vanity and folly might be written over the life of many persons in high repute for religion; made up as it is of a long struggle to solve an impossible problem—how to serve two masters! But this is not the worst of their case. For, 3. This dividedness of heart vitiates and darkens their whole inner man; making them strangers to that glorious light which irradiates the path of the just, whose one aim in life is to serve and glorify their Father who is in heaven. 4. Since the whole animal and vegetable creation—so liberally fed and so gorgeously clad—is silently, perpetually, and charmingly preaching to the children of God the duty of confidence in their Father who is in heaven, what a noble field of devout study do these kingdoms of nature open up to us; and what a monstrous misuse of this study is made by those who study themselves into an Atheistic Naturalism, which not only makes the laws of nature their sole object of pursuit, but drearily rests in them as the ultimate account of all physical things! 5. In this Discourse we find our Lord telling us what "the heathen" do, that He may teach us how differently He expected His own disciples to do. The heathen "babble" their prayers, and the heathen pursue this present world as their all. But if so, O how many heathen are there in the visible Christian Church; and what a heathenish formality in devotion and secularity in the business of life do too many of the children of God suffer to invade and to mar the spirituality, and liberty, and joy, and strength of their Christian life! 6. As honesty is the best policy, so spirituality of mind in the prosecution of the business of life is the true secret of all real temporal prosperity. "The blessing of the Lord it maketh rich; and he addeth no sorrow with it" (Prov. x. 22)—not, He addeth no sorrow with the blessing; but none with the riches—whereas unblest riches are full of sorrow. 7. Let it never be forgotten that what our Lord here condemns is not *attention* to business, nor any amount or range of *thought* on the subject of it which may be necessary for its most successful prosecution; but only such attention to it as is due exclusively to heavenly things, and cannot possibly be given to both; and such *anxiety* of mind about the means of life as springs from distrust of God, and corrodes the heart, while it does not in the least advance the object we have in view. Nor is riches spoken against here, but only the setting of the heart upon them, which the poor may do and the rich not. (See Ps. lxii. 10; 1 Tim. vi. 17-19.)

CHAP. VII. SERMON ON THE MOUNT—*concluded.*

1-12.—MISCELLANEOUS SUPPLEMENTARY COUNSELS. That these verses are entirely supplementary is the simplest and most natural view of them. All attempts to make out any evident connection with the immediately preceding context are, in our judgment, forced. But, though supplementary, these counsels are far from being of subordinate importance. On the contrary, they involve some of the most delicate and vital duties of the Christian life. In the vivid form in which they are here presented, perhaps they could not have been introduced with the same effect under any of the foregoing heads; but they spring out of the same great principles, and are but other forms and manifestations of the same evangelical "righteousness."

Censorious Judgment (1-5). **1. Judge not, that ye be not judged.** To "judge" here [κρίνειν] does not exactly mean to pronounce condemnatory judgment [κατακρίνειν]; nor does it refer to simple judging at all, whether favourable or the reverse. The context makes it clear that the thing here condemned is that disposition to look unfavourably on the character and actions of others, which leads invariably to the pronouncing of rash, unjust, and unlovely judgments upon them. No doubt it is the judgments so pronounced which are here spoken of; but what our Lord aims at is the spirit out of which they spring. Provided we eschew this unlovely spirit, we are not only warranted to sit in judgment upon a brother's character and actions, but, in the exercise of a necessary discrimination, are often constrained to do so for our own guidance. It is the violation of the law of love involved in the exercise of a censorious disposition which alone is here condemned. And the argument against it—"that ye be not judged"—confirms this: 'that your own character and actions be not pronounced upon with the like severity;' that is, at the great day. **2. For with what judgment ye judge, ye shall be judged: and with what measure ye mete**—whatever standard of judgment ye apply to others, **it shall be measured to you [again]** [ἀντιμετρηθήσεται. The ἀντὶ—'again,' or 'in return'—which belongs to the corresponding passage in Luke vi. 38, has hardly any support here; though of course it is implied.] This proverbial maxim is used by our Lord in other connections—as in Mark iv. 24, and with a slightly different application in Luke vi. 38—as a great principle in the divine administration. Untender judgment of others will be judicially returned upon ourselves, in the day when God shall judge the secrets of men by Jesus Christ. But, as in many other cases under the divine administration, such harsh judgment gets self-punished even here. For people shrink from contact with those who systematically deal out harsh judgment upon others—naturally concluding that they themselves may be the next victims—and feel impelled in self-defence, when exposed to it, to roll back upon the assailant his own censures. **3. And why beholdest thou the mote** [κάρφος]—'splinter;' here very well rendered "mote," denoting any small fault. **that is in thy brother's eye, but considerest not the beam** [δοκὸν] **that is in thine own eye?**—denoting the much greater fault which we overlook in ourselves. **4. Or how wilt thou say to thy brother, Let me pull out the mote out of thine eye; and, behold, a beam is in thine own eye? 5. Thou hypocrite** [Ὑποκριτὰ]—'Hypocrite!' **first cast out the beam out of thine own eye; and then shalt thou see clearly to cast out the mote out of**

first cast out the beam out of thine own eye; and then shalt thou see
clearly to cast out the mote out of thy brother's eye.
6 Give [d]not that which is holy unto the dogs, neither cast ye your pearls
before swine, lest they trample them under their feet, and turn again and
rend you.
7 Ask, [e]and it shall be given you; seek, and ye shall find; knock, and
8 it shall be opened unto you: for [f]every one that asketh receiveth;
and he that seeketh findeth; and to him that knocketh it shall be
9 opened. Or what man is there of you, whom if his son ask bread, will
10 he give him a stone? or if he ask a fish, will he give him a serpent?
11 If ye then, being evil, know how to give good gifts unto your children,
how much [g]more shall your Father which is in heaven give good things
to them that ask him!
12 Therefore all things [h]whatsoever ye would that men should do to you,
do ye even so to them: for [i]this is the Law and the Prophets.

A. D. 31.

[d] Pro. 9. 7, 8. Pro. 23. 9. Acts 13. 45.
[e] ch. 21. 22. Mark 11. 24. John 15. 7. Jas. 1. 5, 6. 1 John 3. 22.
[f] Pro. 8. 17. Jer. 29. 12. Jon. 2. 2. Jon. 3. 8-10.
[g] Isa. 49. 15. Rom. 8. 32.
[h] Luke 6. 31.
[i] Lev. 19. 18. Rom. 13. 8. Gal. 5. 14. 1 Tim. 1. 5.

thy brother's eye. Our Lord uses a most hyperbolical, but not unfamiliar figure, to express the monstrous inconsistency of this conduct. The "hypocrisy" which, not without indignation, He charges it with, consists in the pretence of a zealous and compassionate charity, which cannot possibly be real in one who suffers worse faults to lie uncorrected in himself. He only is fit to be a reprover of others who jealously and severely judges himself. Such persons will not only be slow to undertake the office of censor on their neighbours, but, when constrained in faithfulness to deal with them, will make it evident that they do it with *reluctance* and not satisfaction, with *moderation* and not exaggeration, with *love* and not harshness.

Prostitution of Holy Things (6). The opposite extreme to that of censoriousness is here condemned—want of discrimination of character. **6. Give not that which is holy unto the dogs**—savage or snarling haters of truth and righteousness. **neither cast ye your pearls before swine**—the impure or coarse, who are incapable of appreciating the priceless jewels of Christianity. In the East dogs are wilder and more gregarious, and, feeding on carrion and garbage, are coarser and fiercer than the same animals in the West. Dogs and swine, besides being ceremonially unclean, were peculiarly repulsive to the Jews, and indeed to the ancients generally. **lest they trample them under their feet**—as swine do—**and turn again and rend you**—as dogs do. Religion is brought into contempt, and its professors insulted, when it is forced upon those who cannot value it and will not have it. But while the indiscriminately zealous have need of this caution, let us be on our guard against too readily setting our neighbours down as dogs and swine, and excusing ourselves from endeavouring to do them good on this poor plea.

Prayer (7-11). Enough, one might think, had been said on this subject in ch. vi. 5-15. But the difficulty of the foregoing duties seems to have recalled the subject, and this gives it quite a new turn. 'How shall we ever be able to carry out such precepts as these, of tender, holy, yet discriminating love?' might the humble disciple enquire. 'Go to God with it,' is our Lord's reply; but He expresses this with a fulness which leaves nothing to be desired, urging now not only confidence, but importunity in prayer. **7. Ask, and it shall be given you; seek, and ye shall find; knock, and it shall be opened unto you.** Though there seems evidently a climax here, expressive of more and more importunity, yet each of these terms used presents what we desire of God in a different light. We *ask* for what we *wish;* we *seek* for what we *miss;* we *knock* for that from which we feel ourselves *shut out.* Answering to this threefold representation is the triple assurance of success to our believing efforts. 'But ah!' might some humble disciple say, 'I cannot persuade myself that *I* have any interest with God.' To meet this, our Lord repeats the triple assurance he had just given, but in such a form as to silence every such complaint. **8. For every one that asketh receiveth; and he that seeketh findeth; and to him that knocketh it shall be opened.** Of course, it is presumed that he asks aright—that is, in faith—and with an honest purpose to make use of what he receives. "If any of you lack wisdom, let him ask of God. But let him ask in faith, nothing wavering (undecided whether to be altogether on the Lord's side). For he that wavereth is like a wave of the sea driven with the wind and tossed. For *let not that man think that he shall receive any thing of the Lord*" (Jas. i. 5-7). Hence, "Ye ask, and receive not, because ye ask amiss, that ye may consume it upon your lusts" (Jas. iv. 3). **9. Or what man is there of you, whom if his son ask bread** [ἄρτον]—'a loaf,' **will he give him a stone?**—round and smooth like such a loaf or cake as was much in use, but only to mock him. **10. Or if he ask a fish, will he give him a serpent?**—like it, indeed, but only to sting him. **11. If ye then, being evil, know how to give good gifts unto your children, how much more shall your Father which is in heaven give good things to them that ask him!** Bad as our fallen nature is, the *father* in us is not extinguished. What a heart, then, must the Father of all fathers have towards His pleading children! In the corresponding passage in Luke (see on xi. 13), instead of "good things," our Lord asks whether He will not much more give *the Holy Spirit* to them that ask Him. At this early stage of His ministry, and before such an audience, He seems to avoid such sharp doctrinal teaching as was more accordant with His plan at the riper stage indicated in Luke, and in addressing His own disciples exclusively.

Golden Rule (12). **12. Therefore**—to say all in one word—**all things whatsoever ye would that men should do to you, do ye even so** [οὕτως]—the same thing and in the same way, **to them: for this is the Law and the Prophets.** 'This is the substance of all relative duty; all Scripture in a nutshell.' Incomparable summary! How well called "the royal law"! (Jas. ii. 8; cf. Rom. xiii. 9). It is true that similar maxims are found floating in the writings of the cultivated Greeks and Romans, and naturally enough in the Rabbinical

13 Enter [j]ye in at the strait gate: [k]for wide *is* the gate, and broad *is* the
way, that leadeth to destruction, and many there be which go in thereat:
14 [1]because strait *is* the gate, and narrow *is* the way, which leadeth unto
life, and few there be that find it.

A. D. 31.
j Luke 9. 23. Luke 13. 24.
k 1 John 5. 19.
1 Or, how.

writings. But so expressed as it is here—in immediate connection with, and as the sum of *such* duties as had been just enjoined, and such principles as had been before taught—it is to be found nowhere else. And the best commentary upon this fact is, that never till our Lord came down thus to teach did men effectually and widely exemplify it in their practice. The precise sense of the maxim is best referred to common sense. It is not, of course, what—in our wayward, capricious, grasping moods—we should *wish* that men would do to us, that we are to hold ourselves bound to do to them; but only what—in the exercise of an impartial judgment, and putting ourselves in their place—we consider it reasonable that they should do to us, that we are to do to them.

Remarks.—1. How grievous is it to think to what an extent, in spite of our Lord's injunctions and warnings here, censoriousness prevails, not only amongst the mass of professing Christians, but even among the undoubted children of God! Of two or more motives by which any action or course may have been prompted, and only one of which is wrong, how readily do many Christians—in a spirit the reverse of love—fasten upon the wrong one, without any evidence, but merely on presumption! And even after they have discovered themselves to have wronged their neighbour—perhaps a brother or sister in Christ—by imputing to them motives to which they find they were strangers, instead of grieving over such want of love (Prov. x. 12; 1 Pet. iv. 8), and guarding against it for the future, are they not as ready again to do the same thing? We speak not of such snarling dispositions as seem incapable of looking upon any person or action but unfavourably—of which one meets with unhappy specimens in some whom one would fain include among the sincere disciples of Christ. But we refer to a too prevalent tendency in many who are above this. Let such think whether, at the great day, they would like to have their own harsh measure meted out to themselves; let them remember to what a small extent one is able to enter into the circumstances of another; let them consider whether in any given case, they are called on to pronounce a judgment at all; and if they think they are, let it be with reluctance and regret that an unfavourable judgment is pronounced; and let full weight be given to extenuating circumstances. As the law of love demands all this, so shall we find, at the great day, that we have our own merciful measure meted out to ourselves. But after all, 2. Self-knowledge will be the best preservative against a censorious disposition. He who knows how often his own motives would be misunderstood, if judged in every case from first appearances, will not be ready to judge thus of his neighbour's; nor will he who is conscious of his own uprightness, even when he has been betrayed into something wrong, be ready to put the worst construction even upon what cannot be defended. And as the censorious get self-punished even here, so a considerate, kind, charitable way of looking at the character and actions of others is rewarded with general respect, esteem, and confidence. 3. Christian zeal must be tempered with discretion. No love to the souls of men can oblige a Christian to thrust divine truth upon ears that will not listen to it, that will but loathe it, and are only irritated to keener hatred by efforts made to force it on them. (See Prov. ix. 7, 8; xiv. 7; xxiii. 9, &c.) And yet how few are there so virulent that love cannot approach them and persevering love cannot subdue them! Discernment of character is indeed indispensable for hopefully giving "that which is holy" to those who are strangers to it, and offering safely our "pearls" to the needy. But He who said to obstinate and scornful Jerusalem, "How often would I have gathered thy children, and ye would not"—He who has, even for ages, "stretched out His hands all day long to a disobedient and gainsaying people!"—will not have us too readily to despair of our fellow-men, and cease from endeavouring to win them to the truth. And surely, when we remember what forbearance we ourselves have needed and experienced, and how hopeless some of us once were, we should not be over-hasty in turning even from the obstinate opponents of truth and righteousness as "dogs" and "swine," whom to meddle with is equally bootless and perilous. 4. Delicate and difficult as are the duties enjoined in this Section, demanding a high tone and involving habitual self-command, the disciple of Christ has an unfailing resource in his Father which is in heaven, to whom there is free access by prayer for all, and no believing application is made in vain. 5. Had the *universal depravity* of our nature not been an understood and acknowledged truth, it is difficult to see how our Lord could have expressed Himself as He does in the 11th verse of this chapter, nor can the full force of His reasoning be felt on any other principle. For this is it: 'The natural affection of human parents towards their children has to struggle through the *evil* which every child of Adam brings with him into the world, and carries about with him to his dying day; and yet, in spite of this, what parent is there whose heart does not yearn over his own child, or is able to resist his reasonable pleadings? But your heavenly Father has no evil in His nature to struggle with; and has a heart towards His children, compared with which the affections of all the parents that ever did, do, or shall exist, though they were blended into one mighty affection, is not even as a drop to the ocean: How much more, then, will He give good gifts to His pleading children!' What an argument this for faith to plead upon!

13-29.—Conclusion and Effect of the Sermon on the Mount. We have here the application of the whole preceding Discourse.

Conclusion of the Sermon on the Mount (13-27). "The righteousness of the kingdom," so amply described, both in principle and in detail, would be seen to involve *self-sacrifice* at every step. Multitudes would never face this. But it must be faced, else the consequences will be fatal. This would divide all within the sound of these truths into two classes: the many, who will follow the path of ease and self-indulgence—end where it might; and the few, who, bent on eternal safety above everything else, take the way that leads to it—at whatever cost. This gives occasion to the two opening verses of this application. **13. Enter ye in at the strait gate**—as if hardly wide enough to admit one at all. This expresses the difficulty of the first right step in religion, involving, as it does, a triumph over all our natural inclinations. Hence the still stronger expression in Luke (xiii. 24), "Strive [ἀγωνίζεσθε] to enter in at the strait gate." **for wide is the gate**—easily

15 Beware [l]of false prophets, [m]which come to you in sheep's clothing, but
16 inwardly they are [n]ravening wolves. Ye shall know them by their fruits.
17 [o]Do men gather grapes of thorns, or figs of thistles? Even so [p]every
good tree bringeth forth good fruit; but a corrupt tree bringeth forth
18 evil fruit. A good tree cannot bring forth evil fruit, neither *can* a cor-
19 rupt tree bring forth good fruit. Every tree that bringeth not forth good
20 fruit is hewn down, and cast into the fire. Wherefore by their fruits ye
shall know them.
21 Not every one that saith unto me, [q]Lord, Lord, shall enter into the
kingdom of heaven; but he that doeth the will of my Father which is in
22 heaven. Many will say to me in that day, Lord, Lord, have we [r]not
prophesied in thy name? and in thy name have cast out devils? and in

A. D. 31.

[l] Deut. 13. 3. Jer. 23. 16. Rom. 16. 17.
[m] Mic. 3. 5. 2 Tim. 3. 5.
[n] Acts 20. 29.
[o] Luke 6. 43.
[p] Jer. 11. 19.
[q] Hos. 8. 2. Acts 19. 13. Rom. 2. 13. Jas. 1. 22.
[r] Num. 24. 4. John 11. 51. 1 Cor. 13. 2.

entered—**and broad is the way**—easily trodden—**that leadeth to destruction, and**—thus lured—**many there be which go in thereat: 14. Because strait is the gate, and narrow is the way, which leadeth unto life**—in other words, the whole course is as difficult as the first step; **and** (so it comes to pass that) **few there be that find it.** The recommendation of the broad way is the ease with which it is trodden and the abundance of company to be found in it. It is sailing with a fair wind and a favourable tide. The natural inclinations are not crossed, and fears of the issue, if not easily hushed, are in the long run effectually subdued. The one disadvantage of this course is its end—it "leadeth to destruction." The great Teacher says it, and says it as "One having authority." To the supposed injustice or harshness of this He never once adverts. He leaves it to be inferred that such a course righteously, naturally, necessarily so ends. But whether men see this or no, here He lays down the law of the kingdom, and leaves it with us. As to the other way, the disadvantage of it lies in its narrowness and solitude. Its very first step involves a revolution in our whole purposes and plans for life, and a surrender of all that is dear to natural inclination, while all that follows is but a repetition of the first great act of self-sacrifice. No wonder, then, that few find and few are found in it. But it has one advantage—it "leadeth unto life." Some critics take "the gate" here, not for the first, but the last step in religion; since gates seldom open into roads, but roads usually terminate in a gate, leading straight to a mansion. But as this would make our Lord's words to have a very inverted and unnatural form as they stand, it is better, with the majority of critics, to view them as we have done. [The reading in *v.* 14, of Τί for Ὅτι—'How strait!'—preferred by *Tregelles*—is, we think, with *Tischendorf*, to be disapproved.]

But since such teaching would be as unpopular as the way itself, our Lord next forewarns His hearers that preachers of smooth things—the true heirs and representatives of the false prophets of old—would be rife enough in the new kingdom. **15. Beware** [Προσέχετε δὲ]—'But beware' **of false prophets**—that is, of teachers coming as authorized expounders of the mind of God and guides to heaven. (See Acts xx. 29, 30; 2 Pet. ii. 1, 2.) **which come to you in sheep's clothing**—with a bland, gentle, plausible exterior; persuading you that the gate is not strait nor the way narrow, and that to teach so is illiberal and bigoted—precisely what the old prophets did (Ezek. xiii. 1-10, 22). **but inwardly they are ravening wolves**—bent on devouring the flock for their own ends (2 Cor. xi. 2, 3, 13-15). **16. Ye shall know them by their fruits**—not their doctrines—as many of the elder interpreters and some later ones explain it—for that corresponds to the tree itself; but the practical effect of their teaching, which is the proper fruit of the tree. **Do men gather grapes of thorns** [ἀκανθῶν]—any kind of prickly plant, **or figs of thistles?** [τριβόλων]—a three-pronged variety. The general sense is obvious—Every tree bears its own fruit. **17. Even so every good tree bringeth forth good fruit; but a corrupt tree bringeth forth evil fruit. 18. A good tree cannot bring forth evil fruit, neither can a corrupt tree bring forth good fruit.** Obvious as is the truth here expressed in different forms—that the heart determines and is the only proper interpreter of the actions of our life—no one who knows how the Church of Rome makes a merit of actions, quite apart from the motives that prompt them, and how the same tendency manifests itself from time to time even among Protestant Christians, can think it too obvious to be insisted on by the teachers of divine truth. Here follows a wholesome digression. **19. Every tree that bringeth not forth good fruit is hewn down, and cast into the fire.** See on ch. iii. 10. **20. Wherefore by their fruits ye shall know them:**—*q. d.*, 'But the point I now press is not so much the end of such, as the means of detecting them; and this, as already said, is their fruits.' The hypocrisy of teachers now leads to a solemn warning against religious hypocrisy in general.

21. Not every one that saith unto me, Lord, Lord—the reduplication of the title "Lord" denoting zeal in according it to Christ (see Mark xiv. 45). Yet our Lord claims and expects this of all His disciples, as when He washed their feet, "Ye call me Master and Lord: and ye say well; for so I am" (John xiii. 13). **shall enter into the kingdom of heaven; but he that doeth the will of my Father which is in heaven**—that will which it had been the great object of this Discourse to set forth. Yet our Lord says warily, not 'the will of *your* Father,' but "of *My* Father;" thus claiming a relationship to His Father with which His disciples might not intermeddle, and which He never lets down. And He so speaks here, to give authority to His asseverations. But now He rises higher still—not formally *announcing* Himself as the Judge, but intimating what men will say to Him, and He to them, *when* He sits as their final judge. **22. Many will say to me in that day** [ביום ההוא]. What day? It is emphatically unnamed. But it is the day to which He had just referred, when men shall "enter" or not enter "into the kingdom of heaven." (See a similar way of speaking of "that day" in 2 Tim. i. 12; iv. 8). **Lord, Lord.** The reiteration denotes surprise. 'What, Lord? How is this? Are *we* to be disowned?' **have we not prophesied**—or 'publicly taught.' As one of the special gifts of the Spirit in the early Church, it has the sense of 'inspired and authoritative teaching,'

23 thy name done many wonderful works? And then will I profess unto
them, I never knew you: [s]depart from me, ye that work iniquity.
24 Therefore, [t]whosoever heareth these sayings of mine, and doeth them,
25 I will liken him unto a wise man, which built his house upon a rock: and
[u]the rain descended, and the floods came, and the winds blew, and beat
upon that house; and [v]it fell not: for it was founded upon a rock.
26 And every one that heareth these sayings of mine, and doeth them not,
shall be likened unto a foolish man, which built his house upon the sand:
27 and the rain descended, and the floods came, and the winds blew, and
beat upon that house; and it fell: [w]and great was the fall of it.
28 And it came to pass, when Jesus had ended these sayings, [x]the people
29 were astonished at his doctrine: for [y]he taught them as *one* having
authority, and not as the scribes.

A. D. 31.
[s] Ps. 5. 5. Ps. 6. 8. ch. 25. 41.
[t] Luke 6. 47.
[u] Acts 14. 22. 2 Tim. 3. 12.
[v] 2 Tim. 2. 19. 1 Pet. 1. 5.
[w] Heb. 10. 31. 2 Pet. 2. 20.
[x] ch. 13. 54. Mark 1. 22. Mark 6. 2. Luke 4. 32.
[y] Isa. 50. 4. John 7. 46.

and is ranked next to the apostleship. (See 1 Cor. xii. 28; Eph. iv. 11.) In this sense it is used here, as appears from what follows. **in thy name?**—or, 'to thy name,' and so in the two following clauses [τῷ σῷ ὀνόματι, only here and in Mark ix. 38]—'having reference to Thy name as the sole power in which we did it.' **and in thy name have cast out devils? and in thy name done many wonderful works?**—or 'miracles' [δυνάμεις]. These are selected as three examples of the highest services rendered to the Christian cause, and through the power of Christ's own name, invoked for that purpose; Himself, too, responding to the call. And the threefold repetition of the question, each time in the same form, expresses in the liveliest manner the astonishment of the speakers at the view now taken of them. **23. And then will I profess unto them,** [ὁμολογήσω]—or, 'openly proclaim'—tearing off the mask—**I never knew you.** What they claimed—intimacy with Christ—is just what He repudiates, and with a certain scornful dignity. 'Our acquaintance was not broken off—there never was any.' **depart from me** (cf. ch. xxv. 41). The connection here gives these words an awful significance. They claimed intimacy with Christ, and in the corresponding passage, Luke xiii. 26, are represented as having gone out and in with Him on familiar terms. 'So much the worse for you,' He replies: 'I bore with that long enough; but now—begone!' **ye that work iniquity**—not 'that *wrought* iniquity;' for they are represented as fresh from the scenes and acts of it as they stand before the Judge. (See on the almost identical, but even more vivid and awful, description of the scene in Luke xiii. 24-27.) That the apostle alludes to these very words in 2 Tim. ii. 19, there can hardly be any doubt—"Nevertheless the foundation of God standeth sure, having this seal, The Lord *knoweth* them that are His. And, let every one that nameth the *name* of Christ depart from *iniquity.*"

24. Therefore—to bring this Discourse to a close, **whosoever heareth these sayings of mine, and doeth them.** See Jas. i. 22, which seems a plain allusion to these words; also Luke xi. 28; Rom. ii. 13; 1 John iii. 7. **I will liken him unto a wise man** [ἀνδρὶ φρονίμῳ]—a shrewd, prudent, provident man, **which built his house upon a rock**—the rock of true discipleship, or genuine subjection to Christ. **25. And the rain**—from above—**descended, and the floods**—from below—**came** [ποταμοὶ], **and the winds**—sweeping across—**blew, and**—thus from every direction—**beat upon that house; and it fell not: for it was founded upon a rock.** See 1 John ii. 17. **26. And every one that heareth these sayings of mine**—in the attitude of discipleship, **and doeth them not, shall be likened unto a foolish man, which built his house upon the sand**—denoting a loose foundation—that of an empty profession and mere external services. **27. And the rain descended, and the floods came, and the winds blew, and beat upon** [προσέκοψαν]—or 'struck against' **that house; and it fell: and great was the fall of it**—terrible the ruin! How lively must this imagery have been to an audience accustomed to the fierceness of an Eastern tempest, and the suddenness and completeness with which it sweeps everything unsteady before it!

Effect of the Sermon on the Mount (28-29). **28. And it came to pass, when Jesus had ended these sayings, the people were astonished at his doctrine**—rather, 'His teaching' [διδαχῇ], for the reference is to the manner of it quite as much as to the matter, or rather more so. **29. For he taught them as [one] having authority.** The word "one," which our translators have here inserted, only weakens the statement. **and not as the scribes.** The consciousness of divine authority, as Lawgiver, Expounder, and Judge, so beamed through His teaching, that the scribes' teaching could not but appear drivelling in such a light.

Remarks.—1. Let the disciples of Christ beware of obliterating the distinction between the "broad" and the "narrow" way; and neither be carried away by the plausibilities of that 'liberal' school of preachers and writers whose aim is to refine away the distinguishing peculiarities of the two classes, nor be ashamed of the fidelity which holds them up in bold, clear, sharp outline. It is easy to run down the latter class as narrow bigots, and cry up the former as sensible and large-minded. But He, Whom none claiming the Christian name dare call narrow or harsh, concludes this incomparable Discourse with the assurance that there are but two great courses—the one ending in "life," the other in "destruction;" that the easy one is the fatal, the difficult the only safe way; and that true wisdom lies in eschewing the former and making choice of the latter. Genuine, out-and-out discipleship yields its devout assent to this, and casts in its lot with all that teach it, however despised; stopping its ears to the preachers of smooth things, charm they never so wisely. 2. While corrupt teaching is followed, sooner or later, by corresponding practice, the *immediate* effects are often, to all appearance, the reverse. There is often a simplicity, an earnestness, an absorption in the objects at which they aim, in preachers who are conscious that they have peculiar ideas to lodge in the minds of their hearers; and there are other subtle elements in the popularity of some, who, by widening the strait gate and broadening the narrow way, win to religious

8 WHEN he was come down from the mountain, great multitudes followed him.
2 And, [a]behold, there came a leper and worshipped him, saying, Lord,
3 if thou wilt, thou canst make me clean. And Jesus put forth *his* hand,
and touched him, saying, I will; be thou clean. And immediately his

A. D. 31.

CHAP. 8.

[a] Mark 1. 40. Luke 5. 12. 2 Ki. 5. 1. 2 Chr. 26. 19.

thought and earnestness not a few who otherwise would in all probability have remained strangers to both. But when we see clearly the character of such teaching, let us never doubt what its ultimate issue must be, and, in spite of all present appearances, and in answer to all charges of bigotry, let us be ready, with our Master, to exclaim, "Do men gather grapes of thorns, or figs of thistles?" 3. The light in which our Lord presents Himself in the closing words of this Discourse has a grandeur, on supposition of His proper personal Divinity, which must commend itself to every devout, reflecting mind; whereas, if we regard Him as a mere creature, they are so dishonouring to God as to be repulsive in the last degree to all who are jealous for His glory. The dialogue form in which the appeals at the great day are said to be made to Him, and rejected by Him—though expressive, it may be, of nothing more than the principles and feelings of both parties towards each other, which will then be brought out—places our Lord Himself in a light wholly incompatible with anything which Scripture warrants a *creature* to assume. Not only does it exhibit Him as the Judge, but it represents all moral and religious duties as terminating in *Him*, and the blissful or blighted future of men as turning upon their doing or not doing all to Him. In perfect, yet awful accordance with this is the sentence—"DEPART FROM ME"—as if separation from HIM were death and hell. If the Speaker were a mere creature, no language can express the mingled absurdity and profanity of such assumptions; but if He was the Word, who at the beginning was with God and was God, and if thus rich He for our sakes only became poor, then all that He says here is worthy of Himself, and shines in its own lustre. See Remark 2 at the close of the corresponding Section (Luke xiii. 23-30). 4. While most persons within the pale of the Christian Church are ready to admit that, not professed, but proved subjection to the Father of our Lord Jesus Christ—not lip, but life service—will avail "in that day," it is not so readily admitted and felt that services such as "prophesying in Christ's name, and in His name casting out devils, and in His name doing many miracles"—or, what in later ages correspond to these, eloquent and successful preaching—even to the deliverance of souls from the thraldom of sin and Satan; learned contributions to theological literature; great exertions for the diffusion of Christianity and the vindication of religious liberty; and princely donations for either or both of these—may all be rendered in honour of Christ, while the heart is not subjected to Him, and the life is a contradiction to His precepts. What need, then, have we to tremble at the closing words of this great Discourse; and, "Let every one that nameth the name of Christ depart from iniquity"! See Remark 1 at the close of the corresponding Section (Luke xiii. 23-30). 5. Is there not something awful in the astonishment and dismay with which the inconsistent disciples of the Lord Jesus are here represented as receiving their sentence at the great day? What a light does it throw upon the extent to which men may be the victims of self-deception, and the awful inveteracy of it—as if nothing would open their eyes but the Judge's own sentence: "I never knew you: depart from me"! Well may one, on rising from the study of this solemn close to the Sermon on the Mount, exclaim with Bunyan, in the closing words of his immortal 'Pilgrim,' 'THEN I SAW THAT THERE WAS A WAY TO HELL EVEN FROM THE GATES OF HEAVEN.'

CHAP. VIII. 1-4.—HEALING OF A LEPER. (= Mark i. 40-45; Luke v. 12-16.)

The time of this miracle seems too definitely fixed here to admit of our placing it where it stands in Mark and Luke, in whose Gospels no such precise note of time is given.

1. [And] When he was come down from the mountain, great multitudes followed him. 2. And, behold, there came a leper—"a man full of leprosy," says Luke, v. 12. Much has been written on this disease of leprosy, but certain points remain still doubtful. All that needs be said here is, that it was a cutaneous disease, of a loathsome, diffusive, and, there is reason to believe, when thoroughly pronounced, incurable character; that though in its distinctive features it is still found in several countries—as Arabia, Egypt, and South Africa—it prevailed, in the form of what is called white leprosy, to an unusual extent, and from a very early period, among the Hebrews; and that it thus furnished to the whole nation a familiar and affecting symbol of SIN, considered as (1) *loathsome*, (2) *spreading*, (3) *incurable*. And while the ceremonial ordinances for detection and cleansing prescribed in this case by the law of Moses (Lev. xiii., xiv.) held forth a coming remedy "for sin and for uncleanness" (Ps. li. 7; 2 Ki. v. 1, 7, 10, 13, 14), the numerous cases of leprosy with which our Lord came in contact, and the glorious cures of them which He wrought, were a fitting manifestation of the work which He came to accomplish. In this view, it deserves to be noticed that the first of our Lord's miracles of healing recorded by Matthew is this cure of a leper. **and worshipped him**—in what sense we shall presently see. Mark says (i. 40), he came, "beseeching and kneeling to Him," and Luke says (v. 12), "he fell on his face." **saying, Lord, if thou wilt, thou canst make me clean.** As this is the only cure of leprosy recorded by all the three first Evangelists, it was probably the first case of the kind; and if so, this leper's faith in the power of Christ must have been formed in him by what he had heard of His other cures. And how striking a faith is it! He does not say he *believed* Him able, but with a brevity expressive of a confidence that knew no doubt, he says simply, "Thou canst" [δύνασαι]. But of Christ's willingness to heal him he was not so sure. It needed more knowledge of Jesus than he could be supposed to have to assure him of that. But one thing he was sure of, that He had but to "will" it. This shows with what "worship" of Christ this leper fell on his face before him. Clear theological knowledge of the Person of Christ was not then possessed even by those who were most with Him and nearest to Him. Much less could full insight into all that we know of the Only begotten of the Father be expected of this leper. But he who at that moment felt and owned that to heal an incurable disease needed but the *fiat* of the Person who

4 leprosy was cleansed. And Jesus saith unto him, [b]See thou tell no man;
but go thy way, show thyself to the priest, and offer the gift that
[c]Moses commanded, for a testimony unto them.
5 And [d]when Jesus was entered into Capernaum, there came unto him
6 a centurion, beseeching him, and saying, Lord, my servant lieth at
7 home sick of the palsy, grievously tormented. And Jesus saith unto him,
8 I will come and heal him. The centurion answered and said, Lord, I [e]am
not worthy that thou shouldest come under my roof: but [f]speak the word
9 only, and my servant shall be healed. For I am a man under authority,
having soldiers under me: and I say to this *man*, Go, and he goeth; and
to another, Come, and he cometh; and to my servant, Do this, and he
10 doeth *it*. When Jesus heard *it*, he marvelled, and said to them that followed, Verily I say unto you, I have not found so great faith, no, not in
11 Israel. And I say unto you, That [g]many shall come from the east and
west, and shall sit down with Abraham, and Isaac, and Jacob, in the

A. D. 31.

[b] ch. 9. 30. Mark 5. 43.
[c] Lev. 14. 3. Luke 5. 14.
[d] Luke 7. 1.
[e] Luke 15. 19.
[f] Ps. 33. 9. Ps. 107. 20.
[g] Gen. 12. 3. Isa. 2. 2, 3. Isa. 11. 10. Mal. 1. 11. Luke 13. 29. Acts 10. 45. Acts 11. 18. Acts 14. 27. Rom. 15. 9. Eph. 3. 6.

stood before him, had assuredly that very faith in the germ which now casts its crown before Him that loved us, and would at any time die for His blessed name. **3. And Jesus** [or 'He,' according to another reading]—"moved with compassion," says Mark (i. 41); a precious addition, **put forth his hand, and touched him.** Such a touch occasioned ceremonial defilement (Lev. v. 3); even as the leper's coming near enough for contact was against the Levitical regulations (Lev. xiii. 46). But as the man's faith told him there would be no case for such regulations if the cure he hoped to experience should be accomplished, so He who had healing in His wings transcended all such statutes. **saying, I will; be thou clean** [Θέλω, καθαρίσθητι]. How majestic those two words! By not assuring the man of His *power* to heal him, He delightfully sets His seal to the man's previous confession of that power; and by assuring him of the one thing of which he had any doubt, and for which he waited—His *will* to do it—He makes a claim as divine as the cure which immediately followed it. **And immediately his leprosy was cleansed.** Mark, more emphatic, says (i. 42), "And as soon as He had spoken, immediately the leprosy departed from him, and he was cleansed"—as perfectly as instantaneously. What a contrast this to modern pretended cures! **4. And Jesus** ("straitly charged him, and forthwith sent him away," Mark i. 43, and) **saith unto him, See thou tell no man.** A hard condition this would seem to a grateful heart, whose natural language, in such a case, is, "Come, hear, all ye that fear God, and I will declare what He hath done for my soul" (Ps. lxvi. 16). We shall presently see the reason for it. **but go thy way, show thyself to the priest, and offer the gift that Moses commanded** (Lev. xiv.), **for a testimony unto them**—a palpable witness that the Great Healer had indeed come, and that "God had visited His people." What the sequel was, our Evangelist says not; but Mark thus gives it (i. 45): "But he went out, and began to publish it much, and to blaze abroad the matter, insomuch that Jesus could no more openly enter into the city, but was without in desert places: and they came to Him from every quarter." Thus—by an over-zealous, though most natural and not very culpable, infringement of the injunction to keep the matter quiet—was our Lord, to some extent, thwarted in His movements. As His whole course was sublimely noiseless (ch. xii. 19), so we find Him repeatedly taking steps to prevent matters coming prematurely to a crisis with Him. (But see on Mark v. 19, 20.) "And He withdrew Himself," adds Luke (v. 16), "into the wilderness, and prayed;" retreating from the popular excitement into the secret place of the Most High, and thus coming forth as dew upon the mown grass, and as showers that water the earth (Ps. lxxii. 6). And this is the secret both of strength and of sweetness in the servants and followers of Christ in every age.

Remarks.—1. It is, at least, a pleasing thought, that this first healed leper was none other than he who within a few days of his Lord's death, under the familiar name of "Simon the leper," made Him a supper at Bethany in his own house. (See on Mark xiv. 3.) And if so, is it not refreshing to think that he who so early experienced the healing power and grace of Jesus, and abode true and grateful to Him throughout, should have had the privilege of ministering to him at His loved retreat of Bethany when the hour of His last sufferings was so near at hand? 2. How gloriously is the absolute authority of Christ to heal or not, just as He "will," both owned by this leper and claimed by Himself! And as the cure instantaneously followed the expression of that will, how bright is the attestation of Heaven thus given to the Personal Divinity of the Lord Jesus! (Compare Ps. xxxiii. 9; Gen. i. 3, &c.) 3. Would those who groan under the leprosy of sin obtain a glorious cure? Let them but honour the power of Christ as did this poor leper, adding to this a confidence in His "will" which the leper could not be expected to reach; and they will not be disappointed. 4. Our own sense of propriety is never to be carried out in opposition to commanded duty. The strange command of Christ would seem to this healed leper to be more honoured in the breach than in the observance. In blazing abroad his cure, he would seem to himself to be simply obeying a resistless and holy impulse; and but for the injunction, in this particular case, to do the very opposite, he would have acted most laudably. But after receiving a command to keep silence, the part of duty was not to judge of it, but to obey it. As he was no competent judge of the reasons which dictated the command, so he ought to have "brought into captivity every thought to the *obedience* of Christ;" and thus should we act in every such case. 5. Healed lepers, not now required to keep silence, let the love of Christ constrain you to sing forth the honour of His name, and make His praise glorious: so will the sense of it habitually retain its freshness and warmth.

5-13.—HEALING OF THE CENTURION'S SERVANT. (= Luke vii. 1-10.) This incident belongs to a later stage. For the exposition, see on Luke vii. 1-10.

12 kingdom of heaven: but [h]the children of the kingdom [i]shall be cast
out into outer darkness: there shall be weeping and gnashing of teeth.
13 And Jesus said unto the centurion, Go thy way; and as thou hast
believed, *so* be it done unto thee. And his servant was healed in the
self-same hour.
14 And [j]when Jesus was come into Peter's house, he saw [k]his wife's mother
15 laid, and sick of a fever. And he touched her hand, and the fever left
her: and she arose, and ministered unto them.
16 When [l]the even was come, they brought unto him many that were
possessed with devils: and he cast out the spirits with *his* word, and
17 healed all that were sick: that it might be fulfilled which was spoken by
Esaias the prophet, saying, Himself [m]took our infirmities, and bare *our*
sicknesses.
18 Now when Jesus saw great multitudes about him, he gave command-
19 ment to depart unto the other side. And [n]a certain scribe came, and said
20 unto him, Master, I will follow thee whithersoever thou goest. And
Jesus saith unto him, The foxes have holes, and the birds of the air *have*
21 nests; but [o]the Son of man hath not where to lay *his* head. And [p]an-
other of his disciples said unto him, Lord, [q]suffer me first to go and bury
22 my father. But Jesus said unto him, Follow me; and let [r]the dead bury
their dead.

A. D. 31.

[h] ch. 21. 43.
[i] ch. 13. 42. ch. 22. 13. ch. 24. 51. ch. 25. 30. Luke 13.28. 2 Pet. 2. 17. Jude 13.
[j] Mark 1. 29. Luke 4. 38.
[k] 1 Cor. 9. 5.
[l] Mark 1. 32. Luke 4. 40.
[m] Isa. 53. 4. 1 Pet. 2. 24.
[n] Luke 9. 57.
[o] Ps. 22. 6. Ps. 40. 17. Ps. 69. 29. Luke 2. 7, 12. Luke 8. 3. John 1. 10, 11.
[p] Luke 9. 59.
[q] 1 Ki. 19. 20.
[r] Eph. 2. 1.

14-17.—HEALING OF PETER'S MOTHER-IN-LAW, AND MANY OTHERS. (=Mark i. 29-34; Luke iv. 38-41.) For the exposition, see on Mark i. 29-34.

18-22.—INCIDENTS ILLUSTRATIVE OF DISCIPLESHIP. (= Luke ix. 57-62.)

The incidents here are two: in the corresponding passage of Luke they are three. Here they are introduced before the mission of the Twelve; in Luke, when our Lord was making preparation for His final journey to Jerusalem. But to conclude from this, as some good critics do, as *Bengel*, *Ellicott*, &c., that one of these incidents at least occurred twice—which led to the mention of the others at the two different times—is too artificial. Taking them, then, as one set of occurrences, the question arises, Whether are they recorded by Matthew or by Luke in their proper place? *Neander*, *Schleiermacher*, and *Olshausen* adhere to Luke's order; while *Meyer*, *de Wette*, and *Lange* prefer that of Matthew. Probably the first incident is here in its right place. But as the command, in the second incident, to preach the kingdom of God, would scarcely have been given at so early a period, it is likely that it and the third incident have their true place in Luke. Taking these three incidents, then, up here, we have—

I. *The Rash or Precipitate Disciple* (19, 20). **19. And a certain scribe came, and said unto him, Master, I will follow thee whithersoever thou goest. 20. And Jesus saith unto him, The foxes have holes, and the birds of the air have nests; but the Son of man hath not where to lay his head.** Few as there were of the scribes who attached themselves to Jesus, it would appear, from his calling Him 'Teacher' [Διδάσκαλε], that this one was a "disciple" in that looser sense of the word in which it is applied to the crowds who flocked after Him, with more or less conviction that His claims were well founded. But from the answer which he received we are led to infer that there was more of transient emotion—of temporary impulse—than of intelligent principle in the speech. The preaching of Christ had riveted and charmed him; his heart had swelled; his enthusiasm had been kindled; and in this state of mind he will go anywhere with Him, and feels impelled to tell Him so. 'Wilt thou?' replies the Lord Jesus, 'Knowest thou Whom thou art pledging thyself to follow, and whither haply He may lead thee? No warm home, no downy pillow has He for thee: He has them not for Himself. The foxes are not without their holes, nor do the birds of the air want their nests; but the Son of man has to depend on the hospitality of others, and borrow the pillow whereon He lays His head.' How affecting is this reply! And yet He rejects not this man's offer, nor refuses him the liberty to follow Him. Only He will have him know what he is doing, and 'count the cost.' He will have him weigh well the real nature and the strength of his attachment, whether it be such as will abide in the day of trial. If so, he will be right welcome, for Christ puts none away. But it seems too plain that in this case that had not been done. And so we have called this The Rash or Precipitate Disciple.

II. *The Procrastinating or Entangled Disciple* (21, 22). As this is more fully given in Luke, we must take both together. "And He said unto another of his disciples, Follow me. But he said," **Lord, suffer me first to go and bury my father. But Jesus said unto him, Follow me; and let the dead bury their dead**—or, as more definitely in Luke, "Let the dead bury their dead: but go thou and preach the kingdom of God." This disciple did not, like the former, volunteer his services, but is called by the Lord Jesus, not only to follow, but to preach Him. And he is quite willing; only he is not ready just yet. "Lord, I *will;* but"—'There is a difficulty in the way just now; but that once removed, I am Thine.' What now is this difficulty? Was his father actually dead—lying a corpse—having only to be buried? Impossible. As it was the practice, as noticed on Luke vii. 12, to bury on the day of death, it is not very likely that this disciple would have been here at all if his father had just breathed his last; nor would the Lord, if He was there, have hindered him discharging the last duties of a son to a father. No doubt it was the common case of a son having a frail or aged father, not likely to live long, whose head he thinks it his duty to see under the ground ere he goes abroad. 'This aged father of mine will soon be removed; and if I

23 And when he was entered into a ship, his disciples followed him.
24 And, [s]behold, there arose a great tempest in the sea, insomuch that the
25 ship was covered with the waves: but he was asleep. And his disciples
26 came to *him*, and awoke him, saying, Lord, save us: we perish. And he
saith unto them, Why [t]are ye fearful, O ye of little faith? Then [u]he
arose, and rebuked the winds and the sea; and there was a great calm.
27 But the men marvelled, saying, What manner of man is this, that even
the winds and the sea obey him!

A. D. 31.

[s] Mark 4. 37. Luke 8. 23.
[t] Phil. 4. 6.
[u] Job 38. 8-11. Ps. 65. 7. Ps. 89. 9. Ps. 93. 4. Ps. 104. 3. Ps. 107. 29.

might but delay till I see him decently interred, I should then be free to preach the kingdom of God wherever duty might call me.' This view of the case will explain the curt reply, "Let the dead bury their dead: but go thou and preach the kingdom of God." Like all the other paradoxical sayings of our Lord, the key to it is the different senses—a higher and a lower—in which the same word "dead" is used: 'There are two kingdoms of God in existence upon earth; the kingdom of nature, and the kingdom of grace: To the one kingdom all the children of this world, even the most ungodly, are fully alive; to the other, only the children of light: The reigning irreligion consists not in indifference to the common humanities of social life, but to things spiritual and eternal: Fear not, therefore, that your father will in your absence be neglected, and that when he breathes his last there will not be relatives and friends ready enough to do to him the last offices of kindness. Your wish to discharge these yourself is natural, and to be allowed to do it a privilege not lightly to be foregone. But the Kingdom of God lies now all neglected and needy: Its more exalted character few discern; to its paramount claims few are alive; and to "preach" it fewer still are qualified and called: But thou art: The Lord therefore hath need of thee: Leave, then, those claims of nature, high though they be, to those who are dead to the still higher claims of the kingdom of grace, which God is now erecting upon earth—Let the dead bury their dead: but go thou and preach the Kingdom of God.' And so have we here the genuine, but Procrastinating or Entangled Disciple. The next case is recorded only by Luke:

III. *The Irresolute or Wavering Disciple* (Luke ix. 61, 62). 61. "And another also said, Lord, I will follow thee; but let me first go bid them farewell which are at home at my house. 62. And Jesus said unto him, No man, having put his hand to the plough, and looking back, is fit for the kingdom of God." But for the very different replies given, we should hardly have discerned the difference between this and the second case: the one man called, indeed, and the other volunteering, as did the first; but both seemingly alike willing, and only having a difficulty in their way just at that moment. But, by help of what is said respectively to each, we perceive the great difference between the two cases. From the warning given against "looking back," it is evident that this man's discipleship was not yet *thorough*, his separation from the world not entire. It is not a case of *going* back, but of *looking* back; and as there is here a manifest reference to the case of "Lot's wife" (Gen. xix. 26; and see on Luke xvii. 32), we see that it is not *actual return* to the world that we have here to deal with, but a *reluctance to break with it.* The figure of putting one's hand to the plough and looking back is an exceedingly vivid one, and to an agricultural people most impressive. As ploughing requires an eye intent on the furrow to be made, and is marred the instant one turns about, so will they come short of salvation who prosecute the work of God with a distracted attention, a divided heart. The reference may be chiefly to ministers; but the application at least is general. As the image seems plainly to have been suggested by the case of Elijah and Elisha, a difficulty may be raised, requiring a moment's attention. When Elijah cast his mantle about Elisha—which the youth quite understood to mean appointing him his successor, he was ploughing with twelve yoke of oxen, the last pair held by himself. Leaving his oxen, he ran after the prophet, and said, "Let me, I pray thee, kiss my father and my mother, and [then] I will follow thee." Was this said *in the same spirit* with the same speech uttered by our disciple? Let us see. "And Elijah said unto him, Go back again: for what have I done to thee." Commentators take this to mean that Elijah had really done nothing to hinder him from going on with all his ordinary duties. But to us it seems clear that Elijah's intention was to try what manner of spirit the youth was of:—'Kiss thy father and mother? And why not? By all means, go home and stay with them; for what have I done to thee? I did but throw a mantle about thee; but what of that?' If this was his meaning, Elisha thoroughly apprehended and nobly met it. "He returned back from him, and took a yoke of oxen, and slew them, and boiled their flesh with the instruments of the oxen [the wood of his ploughing implements], and gave unto the people, and they did eat: then he arose, and went after Elijah, and ministered unto him" (1 Ki. xix. 19-21). We know not if even his father and mother had time to be called to this hasty feast. But this much is plain, that, though in affluent circumstances, he gave up his lower calling, with all its prospects, for the higher, and at that time perilous office to which he was called. What now is the bearing of these two cases? Did Elisha do wrong in bidding them farewell with whom he was associated in his earthly calling? Or, if not, would this disciple have done wrong if he had done the same thing, and in the same spirit, with Elisha? Clearly not. Elisha's doing it proved that he could *with safety* do it; and our Lord's warning is not against bidding them farewell which were at home at his house, but against the probable *fatal consequences* of that step; lest the embraces of earthly relationship should prove too strong for him, and he should never return to follow Christ. Accordingly, we have called this the Irresolute or Wavering Disciple.

Remarks.—1. Rash or precipitate discipleship is scarcely to be looked for in times of spiritual death in lethargic conditions of the Church. The man who said he would follow Christ wherever He went had doubtless had his enthusiasm kindled, as we have said, by Christ's matchless preaching, though possibly also by the sight of His miracles. Even so an earnest, warm, rousing ministry, or a season of unusual awakening, stirring the most thoughtless, calls forth the enthusiasm of not a few, particularly among the young and ardent, who resolve—perhaps with tears of joy—that

28 And [v]when he was come to the other side, into the country of the
Gergesenes, there met him two possessed with devils, coming out of the
29 tombs, exceeding fierce, so that no man might pass by that way. And,
behold, they cried out, saying, What [w]have we to do with thee, Jesus,
thou Son of God? art thou come hither to torment us before the time?
30 And there was a good way off from them an herd of many [x]swine feeding.
31 So the devils [y]besought him, saying, If thou cast us out, suffer us to go
32 away into the herd of swine. And he said unto them, Go. And when
they were come out, they went into the herd of swine: and, behold, the
whole herd of swine ran violently down a steep place into the sea, and
33 perished in the waters. And they that kept them fled, and went their
ways into the city, and told every thing, and what was befallen to the
34 possessed of the devils. And, behold, the whole city came out to meet
Jesus: and when they saw him, they [z]besought *him* that he would depart
out of their coasts.

9 AND he entered into a ship, and passed over, [a]and came into his own
2 city. And, [b]behold, they brought to him a man sick of the palsy,
lying on a bed: [c]and Jesus, seeing their faith, said unto the sick of the
3 palsy, Son, be of good cheer; [d]thy sins be forgiven thee. And, behold,
certain of the scribes said within themselves, This *man* blasphemeth.

A. D. 31.

[v] Mark 5. 1.
[w] 2 Sam. 16. 10. 2 Sam. 19. 22. Joel 3. 4. Mark 1. 24. Mark 5. 7. Luke 4. 34. 2 Pet. 2. 4.
[x] Deut. 14. 8.
[y] Phil. 2. 10.
[z] Deut. 5. 25. 1 Ki. 17. 18. Luke 5. 8. Acts 16. 39.

CHAP. 9.
[a] ch. 4. 13.
[b] Mark 2. 3. Luke 5. 8.
[c] ch. 8. 10.
[d] Ps. 32, 1. 2. Luke 5. 20. Rom. 4. 6-8. Rom. 5. 11. Eph. 1. 7.

they will henceforth abandon the world and follow Christ. "Yet have they not root in themselves, but endure *for a while;* for when tribulation or persecution ariseth because of the word, presently they are stumbled." They want depth of solid conviction. Their spiritual necessities and danger have never led them to flee from the wrath to come. Their faith in Christ, then, and joy in the Gospel being but superficial, it gives way in the day of trial. The thing which such require is to 'count the cost;' and while rejoicing to see men, in a time of general awakening, drinking in the truth, melted under it, and giving in their accession to Christ, let them see to it that they "break up their fallow ground, and sow not among thorns." 2. How many real disciples are not ready disciples. The Lord hath need of them, and they are heartily desirous of serving Him—"*but.*" They will do this and that—*but:* they will go hither or thither when called to do so—*but.* There is a difficulty in the way just now. As soon as that is out of the way they are ready. But what if the work required of them can only be done just now—cannot stand still till their difficulty is removed? What if, ere that is out of the way, their disposition to go has evaporated, or, if still there, has no field—"help having come from another quarter"? Young ministers are wanted as missionaries abroad, and young, ardent, female disciples, who are wanted as helps meet for them, both hesitate. 'But for those aged parents, I would gladly go; but till their head is beneath the ground I am not free.' By that time, however, they are neither so in love with the work, nor is the field open to them. While the harvest is so plenteous and the labourers so few, let those who hear the Macedonian cry, "Come over and help us," beware of allowing secular obstacles, however formidable, to arrest the impulse to obey the summons. Beyond all doubt it is owing to this, among other things, that the commission, "Go, make disciples of all nations," remains still to so vast an extent unexecuted—eighteen centuries since it was given forth. 3. The best illustration of the danger of "looking back," after having "put our hand to the plough," is the case of those converts from Hinduism, whose parents, when apprised of their intention to be baptized, travel to the mission-house, and plead, with tears and threats, that they will not take a step so fatal. Failing by this means to shake their resolution, they at length submit to their hard fate; only requesting that before they undergo the rite which is to sever them for ever from home, they will pay them one parting visit—to "bid them farewell which are at home at their house." It seems but reasonable. To refuse it looks like gratuitously wounding parental feeling. 'Well, I will go; but my heart is with you, my spiritual fathers, and soon I will rejoin you.' He goes—*but never returns.* How many promising converts have thus been lost to Christianity, to the anguish of dear missionaries, travailing in birth till Christ be formed in the heathen, and to their own undoing! And though some have, after again conforming to heathenism, been filled with such remorse, that, like Peter when he denied his Lord, they have gone out and wept bitterly, and, after severe and protracted struggles, have returned to be more resolute followers of Christ than ever, what seas of trouble does this "looking back" cost them! and how very few are such cases compared to the many that "make shipwreck of faith and of a good conscience"! "Let him that thinketh he standeth take heed lest he fall."

23-27.—JESUS, CROSSING THE SEA OF GALILEE, MIRACULOUSLY STILLS A TEMPEST. (= Mark iv. 35-41.; Luke viii. 22-25.) For the exposition, see on Mark iv. 35-41.

28-34.—JESUS HEALS THE GERGESENE DEMONIACS. (= Mark v. 1-20; Luke viii. 26-39.) For the exposition, see on Mark v. 1-20.

CHAP. IX. 1-8.—HEALING OF A PARALYTIC. (= Mark ii. 1-12; Luke v. 17-26.) This incident appears to follow next in order of time to the cure of the leper (ch. viii. 1-4). For the exposition, see on Mark ii. 1-12.

9-13.—MATTHEW'S CALL AND FEAST. (=Mark ii. 14-17; Luke v. 27-32.)

The Call of Matthew (9). **9. And as Jesus passed forth from thence**—that is, from the scene of the paralytic's cure in Capernaum, towards the shore of the sea of Galilee, on which that town lay. Mark, as usual, pictures the scene more in detail, thus (ii. 13): "And He went forth again by the sea-side; and all the multitude resorted unto Him, and He taught them" [ἐδίδασκεν αὐτούς]—or, 'kept teaching them.' "And as he passed

4 And Jesus, [e]knowing their thoughts, said, Wherefore think ye evil in
5 your hearts? For whether is easier to say, *Thy* sins be forgiven thee; or
6 to say, Arise, and walk? But that ye may know that [f]the Son of man
hath power on earth to forgive sins, (then saith he to the sick of the
7 palsy,) Arise, take up thy bed, and go unto thine house. And he arose,
8 and departed to his house. But when the multitudes saw *it,* they marvelled, and glorified God, which had given such power unto men.
9 And [g]as Jesus passed forth from thence, he saw a man, named
Matthew, sitting at the receipt of custom: and he saith unto him, Follow me. And he arose, and followed him.
10 And [h]it came to pass, as Jesus sat at meat in the house, behold, many
11 publicans and sinners came and sat down with him and his disciples. And
when the Pharisees saw *it,* they said unto his disciples, Why eateth your
12 Master with [i]publicans and [j]sinners? But when Jesus heard *that,* he said
unto them, They that be whole need not a physician, but they that are sick.
13 But go ye and learn what *that* meaneth, I [k]will have mercy, and not sacrifice: for I am not come to call the righteous, [l]but sinners to repentance.

A. D. 31.

e Ps. 139. 2. ch. 12. 25. Mark 12.15.
f Luke 5. 21. Acts 5. 31. 2 Cor. 2. 10.
g Mark 2. 14. Luke 5. 27.
h Mark 2. 15. Luke 5. 29.
i Luke 5. 30. Luke 15. 2. Luke 19. 7. Gal. 2. 5.
j Gal. 2. 15. Eph. 2. 12.
k Pro. 21. 3. Hos. 6. 6. Mic. 6. 6.
l 1 Tim. 1.15. 1 John 3. 5.

by," **he saw a man, named Matthew**—the writer of this precious Gospel, who here, with singular modesty and brevity, relates the story of his own calling. In Mark and Luke he is called *Levi* [Λευεί, or, according to the preferable reading, Λευείν], which seems to have been his family name. In their lists of the twelve apostles, however, Mark and Luke give him the name of Matthew, which seems to have been the name by which he was known as a disciple. While he himself sinks his family name, he is careful not to sink his occupation, the obnoxious associations with which he would place over against the grace that called him from it, and made him an apostle. (See on ch. x. 3.) Mark alone tells us (ii. 14) that he was "the son of Alpheus"—the same, probably, with the father of James the less. From this and other considerations it is pretty certain that he must at least have heard of our Lord before this meeting. Unnecessary doubts, even from an early period, have been raised about the identity of Levi and Matthew. No English jury, with the evidence before them which we have in the Gospels, would hesitate in giving in a unanimous verdict of identity. **sitting at the receipt of custom**—as a publican, which Luke (v. 27) calls him. It means the place of receipt, the toll-house or booth in which the collector sat. Being in this case by the sea-side, it might be the ferry-tax, for the transit of persons and goods across the lake, which he collected. (See on ch. v. 46.) **and he saith unto him, Follow me.** Witching words these, from the lips of Him who never employed them without giving them resistless efficacy in the hearts of those they were spoken to. **And he** "left all" (Luke v. 28), **arose and followed him.**

The Feast (10-13). **10. And it came to pass, as Jesus sat at meat in the house.** The modesty of our Evangelist signally appears here. Luke says (*v.* 29) that "Levi made Him *a great feast,*" or 'reception' [δοχὴν μεγάλην], while Matthew merely says, "He sat at meat;" and Mark and Luke say that it was in Levi's "own house," while Matthew merely says, "He sat at meat *in the house.*" Whether this feast was made now, or not till afterwards, is a point of some importance in the order of events, and not agreed among harmonists The probability is that it did not take place till a considerable time afterwards. For Matthew, who ought surely to know what took place while his Lord was speaking at his own table, tells us that the visit of Jairus, the ruler of the synagogue, occurred at that moment (*v.* 18). But we know from Mark and Luke that this visit of Jairus did not take place till after our Lord's return, at a later period, from the country of the Gadarenes. (See Mark v. 21, &c., and Luke viii. 40, &c.) We conclude, therefore, that the feast was not made in the novelty of his discipleship, but after Matthew had had time to be somewhat established in the faith; when, returning to Capernaum, his compassion for old friends, of his own calling and character, led him to gather them together that they might have an opportunity of hearing the gracious words which proceeded out of His Master's mouth, if haply they might experience a like change. **behold, many publicans and sinners**—Luke says, "a great company" (v. 29), **came and sat down with him and his disciples.** In all such cases the word rendered 'sat' is 'reclined,' in allusion to the ancient mode of lying on couches at meals. **11. And when the Pharisees**—"and scribes," add Mark and Luke. **saw it, they** "murmured" or 'muttered,' says Luke (v. 30), and **said unto his disciples**—not venturing to put their question to Jesus Himself. **Why eateth your Master with publicans and sinners?** (See on Luke xv. 2.) **12. But when Jesus heard [that], he said unto them**—to the Pharisees and scribes; addressing Himself to them, though they had shrunk from addressing Him. **They that be whole need not a physician, but they that are sick**—*q.d.*, 'Ye deem yourselves whole; My mission, therefore, is not to you: The physician's business is with the sick; therefore eat I with publicans and sinners.' O, what myriads of broken hearts, of sin-sick souls, have been bound up by this matchless saying! **13. But go ye and learn what that meaneth** (Hos. vi. 6), **I will have mercy, and not sacrifice**—that is, the one rather than the other. "Sacrifice," the chief part of the ceremonial law, is here put for a religion of literal adherence to mere rules; while "Mercy" expresses such compassion for the fallen as seeks to lift them up. The duty of keeping aloof from the polluted, in the sense of "having no fellowship with the unfruitful works of darkness," is obvious enough; but to understand this as prohibiting such intercourse with them as is necessary to their recovery, is to abuse it. This was what these pharisaical religionists did, and this is what our Lord here exposes. **for I am not come to call the righteous, but sinners [to repentance].** The words enclosed in brackets are of doubtful authority here, and more than doubtful authority in Mark ii. 17; but in Luke v. 32 they are undisputed. We have here just the former statement

14 Then came to him the disciples of John, saying, [m]Why do we and the
15 Pharisees fast oft, but thy disciples fast not? And Jesus said unto them,
Can [n]the children of the bride-chamber mourn, as long as the bridegroom
is with them? but the days will come, when the bridegroom shall be
16 taken from them, and [o]then shall they fast. No man putteth a piece
of [1]new cloth unto an old garment; for that which is put in to fill it up
17 taketh from the garment, and the rent is made worse. Neither do men
put new wine into old bottles; else the bottles break, and the wine
runneth out, and the bottles perish: but they put new wine into new
bottles, and both are preserved.
18 While [p]he spake these things unto them, behold, there came a certain
ruler, and worshipped him, saying, My daughter is even now dead: but
19 come and lay thy hand upon her, and she shall live. And Jesus arose,
and followed him, and *so did* his disciples.
20 And, [q]behold, a woman, which was diseased with an issue of blood
twelve years, came behind *him*, and touched the hem of his garment:
21 For she said within herself, If I may but touch his garment, I shall be
22 whole. But Jesus turned him about; and when he saw her, he said,
Daughter, be of good comfort; [r]thy faith hath made thee whole. And
the woman was made whole from that hour.
23 And [s]when Jesus came into the ruler's house, and saw [t]the minstrels
24 and the people making a noise, he said unto them, [u]Give place; for the
25 maid is not dead, but sleepeth. And they laughed him to scorn. But
when the people were put forth, he went in, and took her by the hand,
26 and the maid arose. And [2]the fame hereof went abroad into all that
land.
27 And when Jesus departed thence, two blind men followed him, crying,

A. D. 31.

m Mark 2. 18. Luke 5. 33. Luke 18. 12.
n Luke 24. 13. John 3. 29. John 16. 6. Acts 1. 10.
o Acts 13. 2. Acts 14. 23. 1 Cor. 7. 5.
1 Or, raw, or, unwrought cloth.
p Mark 5. 22. Luke 8. 41.
q Lev. 15. 25. Mark 5. 25. Luke 8. 43.
r Mark 10. 52. Luke 7. 50. Luke 8. 48. Luke 17. 19. Luke 18. 42. Acts 14. 9. Heb. 4. 2.
s Mark 5. 38. Luke 8. 51.
t 2 Chr. 35. 25.
u 1 Ki. 17. 18-24. Acts. 9. 40. Acts 20. 10.
2 Or, this fame. Isa. 52. 13.

stripped of its figure. "The righteous" are the whole; "sinners," the sick. When Christ "called" the latter, as He did Matthew, and probably some of those publicans and sinners whom he had invited to meet with Him, it was to heal them of their spiritual maladies, or save their souls: "The righteous," like those miserable, self-satisfied Pharisees, "He sent empty away."

Remarks.—1. How glorious is the grace which not only saves the chief of sinners, but places one of a proverbially sunken class among "the princes of His people"! (See on ch. i. 3, 5, 6.) 2. How delightful is it to trace the deep humility with which this disciple ever after carried himself—whether in the Genealogy which he gives of His Master, to which reference has just been made; or in avoiding, in the record of his own calling, what was to his own credit; or in noting, in his catalogue of the Twelve, as none of the other New Testament writers do, the justly branded class out of which he had been called. (See on ch. x. 3.) 3. But let us not fail to observe the compassion with which he sought to fetch in his old associates to the circle of the saved, "that they also might have fellowship with him" in the love of Jesus. There is no more certain evidence of genuine repentance and true discipleship than this. (See Ps li. 12, 13; Luke xxii. 32, second clause.) 4. How grievously do they err, and pervert the simple, who represent the object of Christ's mission to have been merely to furnish a code of sound morality, or establish spirituality of worship, or certify the doctrine of the resurrection, or the like. He came to heal the sick soul, to raise the sunken, to save sinners; to bring back to God the vilest prodigals, and beautify them with salvation. Such as want Him not for this He passes by; they are not His patients, and they get nothing from Him. They may laud the purity and loftiness of His teaching and example; but they are strangers to Him as "the Balm in Gilead and the Physician there."

14-17.—DISCOURSE ON FASTING. (= Mark ii. 18-22; Luke v. 33-39.) As this Discourse is recorded by all the three first Evangelists immediately after their account of Matthew's Call and Feast, there can be no doubt that it was delivered on that occasion. For the exposition of this important Discourse, see on Luke v. 33-39, where it is given most fully.

18-26.—THE WOMAN WITH THE ISSUE OF BLOOD HEALED.—THE DAUGHTER OF JAIRUS RAISED TO LIFE (= Luke viii. 40-56; Mark v. 21-43.) For the exposition, see on Mark v. 21-43.

27-34.—TWO BLIND MEN, AND A DUMB DEMONIAC, HEALED. These two miracles are recorded by Matthew alone.

Two Blind Men Healed (27-31). **27. And when Jesus departed thence, two blind men followed him**—hearing, doubtless, as in a later case is expressed, "that Jesus passed by" (ch. xx. 30), **crying, and saying, Thou Son of David, have mercy on us.** It is remarkable that in the only other recorded case in which the blind applied to Jesus for their sight, and obtained it, they addressed Him, over and over again, by this one Messianic title, so well known—"Son of David" (ch. xx. 30). Can there be a doubt that their faith fastened on such great Messianic promises as this, "Then the eyes of the blind shall be opened"? &c. (Isa. xxxv. 5); and if so, this appeal to Him, as the Consolation of Israel, to do His predicted office, would fall with great weight upon the ears of Jesus. **28. And when he was come into the house.** To try their faith and patience, He seems to have made them no answer. But **the blind men came to Him**—which, no doubt, was what He desired, **and Jesus saith unto them, Believe ye that I**

28 and saying, [v]*Thou* son of David, have mercy on us. And when he was
come into the house, the blind men came to him: and Jesus saith unto
them, Believe ye that I am able to do this? They said unto him, Yea,
29 Lord. Then touched he their eyes, saying, According to your faith be it
30 unto you. And [w]their eyes were opened: and Jesus straitly charged
31 them, saying, [x]See *that* no man know *it*. But [y]they, when they were
departed, spread abroad his fame in all that country.
32 As [z]they went out, behold, they brought to him a dumb man pos-
33 sessed with a devil. And when the devil was cast out, the dumb spake:
34 and the multitudes marvelled, saying, It was never so seen in Israel. But
the Pharisees said, He casteth out devils through the prince of the devils.
35 And [a]Jesus went about all the cities and villages, teaching in their
synagogues, and preaching the gospel of the kingdom, and healing
every sickness and every disease, among the people.

A. D. 31.

v ch. 15. 22. ch. 20. 30. Mark 9. 22. Mark 10. 47. Luke 17. 13. Luke 18. 38. John 7. 42.
w Ps. 146. 8. John 9. 7, 26.
x Luke 5. 14.
y Mark 7. 36.
z ch. 12. 22. Mark 9. 17. Luke 11. 14.
a Mark 6. 6. Luke 13. 22.

am able to do this? They said unto him, Yea, Lord. Doubtless our Lord's design was not only to put their faith to the test by this question, but to deepen it, to raise their expectation of a cure, and so prepare them to receive it; and the cordial acknowledgment, so touchingly simple, which they immediately made to Him of His power to heal them, shows how entirely that object was gained. **29. Then touched he their eyes, saying, According to your faith be it unto you**—not, Receive a cure *proportioned* to your faith, but, Receive this cure as *granted to* your faith. Thus would they carry about with them, in their restored vision, a gracious seal of the faith which drew it from their compassionate Lord. **30. And their eyes were opened: and Jesus straitly charged them.** The expression is very strong [ἐνεβριμήσατο αὐτοῖς], denoting great earnestness. **31. But they, when they were departed, spread abroad his fame in all that country.** (See on ch. viii. 4, and Remark 4 on that Section.)

A Dumb Demoniac Healed (32-34). **32. As they went out, behold, they brought to him a dumb man possessed with a devil** [δαιμονιζόμενον]—'demonized.' The dumbness was not natural, but was the effect of the possession. **33. And when the devil**—or 'demon'—**was cast out, the dumb spake.** The particulars in this case are not given; the object being simply to record the instantaneous restoration of the natural faculties, on the removal of the malignant oppression of them, the form which the popular astonishment took, and the very different effect of it upon another class. **and the multitudes marvelled, saying, It was never so seen in Israel**—referring, probably, not to this case only, but to all those miraculous displays of healing power which seemed to promise a new era in the history of Israel. Probably they meant by this language to indicate, as far as they thought it safe to do so, their inclination to regard Him as the promised Messiah. **34. But the Pharisees said, He casteth out devils through the prince of the devils**—'the demons through the prince of the demons.' This seems to be the first muttering of a theory of such miracles which soon became a fixed mode of calumniating them—a theory which would be ridiculous if it were not melancholy, as an outburst of the darkest malignity. (See on ch. xii. 24, &c.)

Remarks.—1. So manifestly were these bodily cures designed to set forth analogous operations of grace on the soul, that in the case of opening the eyes of the blind, our Lord, before performing it, in one notable instance, expressly announced the higher design of it, saying, "As long as I am in the world, I am the light of the world" (John ix. 5). Nor would it have been possible beforehand to tell with certainty whether the predictions of such glorious miracles (for example, in Isa. xxxv. 5, 6; xlii. 7)—as inaugurating and distinguishing the Messianic economy—were designed to be understood literally, or spiritually, or both. Hence, we are to regard all such incidents as are here recorded as having higher aspects and bearings than any that terminate on the body; and on the same principle, the honour which our Lord here put upon the faith and patience of these blind men may surely be reckoned on by all who sigh to be "turned by Him from darkness to light, and from the power of Satan unto God." 2. How differently are the same operations and events regarded by the unsophisticated and the prejudiced! 'More light,' is the cry of many besides these prejudiced Pharisees. But what they want is more simplicity and godly sincerity, the stifling of which leaves the soul a prey to the darkest passions.

35—X. 5.—Third Galilean Circuit—Mission of the Twelve Apostles. As the Mission of the Twelve supposes the previous Choice of them—of which our Evangelist gives no account, and which did not take place till a later stage of our Lord's public life—it is introduced here out of its proper place, which is after what is recorded in Luke vi. 12-19.

Third Galilean Circuit (35)—and probably the last. **35. And Jesus went about all the cities and villages, teaching in their synagogues, and preaching the gospel of the kingdom, and healing every sickness and every disease, [among the people].** The bracketed words are of more than doubtful authority here, and were probably introduced from ch. iv. 23. The language here is so identical with that used in describing the first circuit (ch. iv. 23), that we may presume the work done on both occasions was much the same. It was just a further preparation of the soil, and a fresh sowing of the precious seed. (See on ch. iv. 23.) To these fruitful journeyings of the Redeemer, "with healing in His wings," Peter no doubt alludes, when, in his address to the household of Cornelius, he spoke of "How God anointed Jesus of Nazareth with the Holy Ghost and with power: who *went about* doing good [διῆλθεν εὐεργετῶν], and healing all that were oppressed of the devil: for God was with Him" (Acts x. 38).

Jesus, Compassionating the Multitudes, Asks Prayer for Help (36-38). He had now returned from His preaching and healing circuit, and the result, as at the close of the first one, was the gathering of a vast and motley multitude around Him. After a whole night spent in prayer, He had called His more immediate disciples, and

36 But when he saw the multitudes, he was moved with compassion on
them, because they [3]fainted, and were scattered abroad, as sheep having
37 no shepherd. Then saith he unto his disciples, [b]The harvest truly *is*
38 plenteous, but the labourers *are* few; pray [c]ye therefore the Lord of the
harvest, that he will send forth labourers into his harvest.
10 AND [a]when he had called unto *him* his twelve disciples, he gave
them power [1]*against* unclean spirits, to cast them out, and to heal all
manner of sickness, and all manner of disease.
2 Now the names of the twelve apostles are these; The first, Simon,
[b]who is called Peter, and Andrew his brother; James *the son* of Zebedee,
3 and John his brother; Philip, and Bartholomew; Thomas, and Matthew
the publican; James *the son* of Alpheus, and Lebbeus, whose surname
4 was [2]Thaddeus; Simon [c]the Canaanite, and Judas [d]Iscariot, who also
betrayed him.

A. D. 31.

[3] Or, were tired and lay down.
[b] Luke 10. 2. John 4. 35.
[c] Acts 13. 2. Acts 20. 28. 1 Cor. 12.28.

CHAP. 10.

[a] Mark 3. 13. Mark 6. 7.
[1] Or, over.
[b] John 1. 42.
[2] Or, Judas. Jude 1.
[c] Acts 1. 13.
[d] John 13.26.

from them had solemnly chosen the Twelve; then, coming down from the mountain, on which this was transacted, to the multitudes that waited for Him below, He had addressed to them—as we take it—that Discourse which bears so strong a resemblance to the Sermon on the Mount that many critics take it to be the same. (See on Luke vi. 12-49; and on Matt. v., Introductory Remarks.) Soon after this, it should seem, the multitudes still hanging on Him, Jesus is touched with their wretched and helpless condition, and acts as is now to be described.

36. But when he saw the multitudes, he was moved with compassion on them, because they fainted [ἦσαν ἐκλελυμμένοι]. This reading, however, has hardly any authority at all. The true reading doubtless is, 'were harassed' [ἦσαν ἐσκυλμένοι], **and were scattered abroad** [ἐῤῥιμμένοι]—rather, 'lying about,' 'abandoned,' or 'neglected' —**as sheep having no shepherd**—their pitiable condition as wearied and couching under bodily fatigue, a vast disorganized mass, being but a faint picture of their wretchedness as the victims of Pharisaic guidance; their souls uncared for, yet drawn after and hanging upon Him. This moved the Redeemer's compassion. **37. Then saith he unto his disciples, The harvest truly is plenteous.** His eye doubtless rested immediately on the Jewish field, but this he saw widening into the vast field of "the world" (ch. xiii. 38), teeming with souls having to be gathered to Him. **but the labourers**—men divinely qualified and called to gather them in—**are few; 38. Pray ye therefore the Lord of the harvest**—the great Lord and Proprietor of all. Compare John xv. 1—"I am the true Vine, and my Father is the Husbandman." **that he will send forth labourers into his harvest.** The word [ἐκβάλῃ] properly means 'thrust forth;' but this emphatic sense disappears in some places, as in *v.* 25, and John x. 4—"When He *putteth forth* His own sheep." (See on ch. iv. 1.)

CHAP. X. 1-5.—*Mission of the Twelve Apostles.* (= Mark vi. 7-13; Luke ix. 1-6.)

The last three verses of ch. ix. form the proper introduction to the Mission of the Twelve; as is evident from the remarkable fact that the Mission of the Seventy was prefaced by the very same words. (See on Luke x. 2.) **1. And when he had called unto him his twelve disciples, he gave them power** [ἐξουσίαν]. The word signifies both 'power,' and 'authority' or 'right.' Even if it were not evident that here both ideas are included, we find both words expressly used in the parallel passage of Luke (ix. 1)—"He gave them power and authority" [δύναμιν καὶ ἐξουσίαν]—in other words, He both *qualified* and *authorized* them—**against**—or 'over'—**unclean spirits, to cast them out, and to heal all manner of sickness, and all manner of disease.**

2. Now the names of the twelve apostles are these. The other Evangelists enumerate the Twelve in immediate connection with their appointment (Mark iii. 13-19; Luke vi. 13-16). But our Evangelist, not intending to record the appointment, but only the Mission of the Twelve, gives their names here. And as in the Acts (i. 13) we have a list of the Eleven who met daily in the upper room with the other disciples after their Master's ascension until the day of Pentecost, we have four catalogues in all for comparison. **The first, Simon, who is called Peter** (see on John i. 42), **and Andrew his brother; James the son of Zebedee, and John his brother**—named after James, as the younger of the two. **3. Philip, and Bartholomew.** That this person is the same with "Nathanael of Cana in Galilee," is justly concluded for the three following reasons: First, because Bartholomew [=בַּר תַּלְמַי, or 'son of Ptolomy'] is not so properly a name as a family surname; next, because not only in this list, but in Mark's and Luke's, he follows the name of "Philip," who was the instrument of bringing Nathanael first to Jesus (John i. 45); and again, when our Lord, after His resurrection, appeared at the sea of Tiberias, "Nathanael of Cana in Galilee" is mentioned along with six others, all of them apostles, as being present (John xxi. 2). **Matthew the publican.** In none of the four lists of the Twelve is this apostle so branded but in his own one, as if he would have all to know how deep a debtor he had been to his Lord. (See on ch. i. 3, 5, 6; and ix. 9, and Remark 2 on that Section.) **James the son of Alpheus** [=חַלְפַי]—the same person apparently who is called *Cleopas* or *Clopas* (Luke xxiv. 18; John xix. 25); and as he was the husband of Mary, sister to the Virgin, James the less must have been our Lord's cousin. **and Lebbeus, whose surname was Thaddeus**—the same, without doubt, as "Judas the brother of James," mentioned in both the lists of Luke (vi. 16; Acts i. 13), while no one of the name of Lebbeus or Thaddeus is so. It is he who in John (xiv. 22) is sweetly called "Judas, not Iscariot." That he was the author of the Catholic Epistle of "Jude," and not "the Lord's brother" (ch. xiii. 55), unless these be the same, is most likely. **4. Simon the Canaanite**; rather 'Kananite' [Καναvίτης], but better still, 'the Zealot' [Ζηλωτής], as he is called in Luke vi. 15, where the original term should not have been retained as in our version ("Simon, called Zelotes"), but rendered 'Simon, called the Zelot.' The word "Kananite" is just the Aramaic, or Syro-Chaldaic, term for 'Zealot' [Heb.

5 These twelve Jesus sent forth, and commanded them, saying, Go not
into the way of the Gentiles, and into *any* city of [e]the Samaritans enter

A. D. 31.

[e] 2 Ki. 17. 24.

קַנָּא, 'jealous' or 'zealous'—Chald. קַנְאָן]. Probably before his acquaintance with Jesus, he belonged to the sect of the Zealots, who bound themselves, as a sort of voluntary ecclesiastical police, to see that the law was not broken with impunity. **and Judas Iscariot**—that is, Judas of Kerioth, a town of Judah (Josh. xv. 25); so called to distinguish him from "Judas the brother of James" (Luke vi. 16). **who also betrayed him**—a note of infamy attached to his name in all the catalogues of the Twelve.

Remarks.—1. As the reapers of every harvest are appointed by the proprietor of the field, so the labourers whom God will own in "His harvest" are of His own appointing, and to be sought of Him by prayer (ch. ix. 38). Even the Lord Jesus spent a whole night in prayer to God before selecting the Twelve Apostles (Luke vi. 12, 13). But just as in that case the Redeemer followed up His prayer by action, so must we. If to take action for providing preachers without asking them from God be the spirit of naturalism, to cry to God for preachers and do nothing to provide them, is mere fanaticism; but to do both, with full assurance that each is indispensable for its own purposes, and necessary to make the other available—this is to tread in the very footsteps of Christ. In every age and every land the nature of the steps requisite on our part to procure and prepare the proper labourers will vary; but our action in this matter is not superseded by divine interpositions. The Lord indeed will not bind Himself to employ none on whom no human preparation has been bestowed; and facts prove that to disown the labours of all on whom the stamp of an organized Church has not been affixed, would be to fight against God. But to make such exceptional cases determine the Church's line of procedure, in so solemn a matter as the Gospel ministry, would be short-sighted and ruinous. On the other hand, as the tendency of all churches is to depend upon its own measures for providing qualified preachers of the everlasting Gospel, it will be our true wisdom to drink in the spirit of the Master's teaching here—that the Lord appoints His own labourers, and for this thing must be entreated of us to do it for us; remembering that whatever be the gifts which men bring to the work of the ministry, and whatever their external success in it, unless they be of God's own selecting and appointing, they have no right to be there, and are liable at the last to hear from the lips of the Lord of the harvest those awful words, "I never knew you." 2. Did the Redeemer, as He beheld the multitudes harassed and abandoned, like shepherdless sheep, have compassion upon them, and go out in thought to the vastness of the harvest to be gathered in and the fewness of the labourers to do it; and did He call the attention of His disciples to this affecting state of things, that they might enter into His own mind about it, and, like Himself, carry the matter to God for relief? Then, what a model-attitude for ourselves is here held up before us! Were the churches, and all the true followers of Christ, to direct their eye steadily upon the spiritually wretched and necessitous condition of the world, till their eye affected their heart, and the cry of faith went up from it to God, to send forth labourers into His harvest, how speedily would the answer come, and in how rich a form! Nor would it be confined to the direct object of their prayer. For He, whose own very attitude in the days of His flesh would thus be reflected by His believing people, would set the seal of His complacency upon them in a thousand ways—drying up the fountains of dissension and separation and weakness amongst themselves, and drawing them into love and concord and strength, to the astonishment of a surrounding world. Blessed Jesus, shall not this consummation be realized at length? "My soul breaketh for the longing that it hath at all times" to see this great sight, which we cannot doubt will be fulfilled in its season. On the choice of the apostles, we observe, 3. That the number *Twelve* was fixed on to correspond with the number of the tribes of Israel, as is evident from ch. xix. 28; as the number of *Seventy*, to go on a subsequent mission (Luke x. 1), had certainly a reference to the seventy elders of Israel, on whom the Spirit of the Lord was made to rest, that they might bear along with Moses the burden of administration (Num. xi. 16, 17, 25). 4. The relationship existing among those Twelve is one of the most remarkable facts. There were no fewer than three pairs of brothers among them: Andrew and Peter; James and John; James the less and Judas, or Lebbæus, or Simon the Zealot—not to speak of the peculiar tie which bound Bartholomew, or Nathanael, to Philip, and the common tie that bound them all together as disciples—probably the most devoted and advanced—of John the Baptist, and as drawn mostly from the same locality. Reasons for all this may easily be imagined; but we here leave the fact to speak for itself. 5. Our Evangelist enumerates the Twelve in couples, with evident allusion to their being sent on this mission "by two and two" (Mark vi. 7). 6. In all the first three lists the names are arranged in three quaternions, or divisions of four each. Nor can it be doubted that this has reference to some distribution of them by the Lord Himself; for in all of them *Philip* stands first in the second quaternion—as in the third, *James the son of Alpheus.* 7. The first quaternion evidently stood highest in order. Peter and James and John, who constituted a sacred trio in some of the leading events of our Lord's public life, were at the head of all; Andrew being associated with them, to make up the first quaternion, not only as being Peter's brother, but as having been the first to "bring him to Jesus" (John i. 41, 42). In the lists of Matthew and Luke he stands next after Peter, from connection with him; while in the other two lists the sacred trio stand first, the name of Andrew completing that quaternion. 8. When our Evangelist says, "The *first*, Simon"—without assigning a number to any of the rest—while in the other three lists his name stands first, as it does here, the evident design is to hold forth his prominence amongst the Twelve: not as having any authority above the rest—for not a vestige of this appears in the New Testament—but as marking the use which His Lord made of him above any of the rest; for which his qualifications, in spite of failings, stand out on almost every page of the Gospel History, and in the earlier portion of the Acts of the Apostles. 9. With the exception of the four first names, the rest are almost unknown in the New Testament; and the slight variety with which they are arranged in the several lists shows the little prominence with which they were regarded for the purposes of this History. 10. In all the catalogues the

6 ye not: but [f] go rather to the [g] lost sheep of the house of Israel.
7 And [h] as ye go, preach, saying, The kingdom of heaven is at hand.
8 Heal the sick, cleanse the lepers, raise the dead, cast out devils: freely ye
9 have received, freely give. [3] Provide neither gold, nor silver, nor brass in
10 your purses, nor scrip for *your* journey, neither two coats, neither shoes,
11 nor yet [4] staves; [i] for the workman is worthy of his meat. And into
whatsoever city or town ye shall enter, enquire who in it is worthy;
12 and there abide till ye go thence. And when ye come into an house,
13 salute it. And if the house be worthy, let your peace come upon it:

A. D. 31.
f Acts 13. 46.
g Isa. 53. 6. Rom. 11. 1.
h Luke 9. 2.
3 Or, Get. 1 Sam. 9. 7.
4 a staff.
i Luke 10. 7. 1 Cor. 9. 7. 1 Tim. 5. 18.

name of *Judas* not only stands last, but "*traitor*" is added to it as a brand of abhorrence; and so revolting were the associations connected with his name, that the beloved disciple, in recording a deeply interesting question put at the last supper by Judas to his Lord, hastens to explain, in a sweet parenthesis, that it was "*not* Iscariot" that he meant (John xiv. 22). 11. How terrific is the warning which the case of Judas holds forth to the ministers of Christ, not to trust in any gifts, any offices, any services, any success, as sure evidence of divine acceptance, apart from that "holiness without which no man shall see the Lord"!

5-42.—THE TWELVE RECEIVE THEIR INSTRUCTIONS. This Directory divides itself into three distinct parts. The *first* part—extending from *vv.* 5 to 15—contains directions for the brief and temporary mission on which they were now going forth, with respect to the places they were to go to, the works they were to do, the message they were to bear, and the manner in which they were to conduct themselves. The *second* part—extending from *vv.* 16 to 23—contains directions of no such limited and temporary nature, but opens out into the permanent exercise of the Gospel ministry. The *third* part—extending from *vv.* 24 to 42—is of wider application still, reaching not only to the ministry of the Gospel in every age, but to the service of Christ in the widest sense. *It is a strong confirmation of this threefold division, that each part closes with the words*, "VERILY I SAY UNTO YOU" (*vv.* 15, 23, 42).

Directions for the Present Mission (5-15). 5. **These twelve Jesus sent forth, and commanded them, saying, Go not into the way of the Gentiles, and into any city of the Samaritans enter ye not.** The Samaritans were Gentiles by blood; but being the descendants of those whom the king of Assyria had transported from the East to supply the place of the ten tribes carried captive, they had adopted the religion of the Jews, though with admixtures of their own; and, as the nearest neighbours of the Jews, they occupied a place intermediate between them and the Gentiles. Accordingly, when this prohibition was to be taken off, on the effusion of the Spirit at Pentecost, the apostles were told that they should be Christ's witnesses first "in Jerusalem, and in all Judea," then "in Samaria," and lastly, "unto the uttermost part of the earth" (Acts i. 8). 6. **But go rather to the lost sheep of the house of Israel.** Until Christ's death, which broke down the middle wall of partition (Eph. ii. 14), the Gospel commission was to the Jews only, who, though the visible people of God, were "lost sheep," not merely in the sense in which all sinners are (Isa. liii. 6; 1 Pet. ii. 25; with Luke xix. 10), but as abandoned and left to wander from the right way by faithless shepherds, (Jer. l. 6, 17; Ezek. xxxiv. 2-6, &c.) 7. **And as ye go, preach, saying, The kingdom of heaven is at hand.** (See on ch. iii. 2.) 8. **Heal the sick, cleanse the lepers, [raise the dead,] cast out devils.** [The bracketed clause—"raise the dead"—is wanting in so many MSS. and ancient versions that *Tischendorf* and others omit it altogether, as having found its way into this verse from ch. xi. 5. *Griesbach*, *Lachmann*, and *Tregelles* insert it, putting it before the words "cleanse the lepers," which, if it be genuine, is its right place. But it seems very improbable that our Lord imparted at so early a period this highest of all forms of supernatural power.] Here we have the first communication of supernatural power by Christ Himself to his followers—thus anticipating the gifts of Pentecost. And right royally does he dispense it. **freely ye have received, freely give.** Divine saying, divinely said! (cf. Deut. xv. 10, 11; Acts iii. 6)—an apple of gold in a setting of silver (Prov. xxv. 11). It reminds us of that other golden saying of our Lord, rescued from oblivion by Paul, "It is more blessed to give than to receive" (Acts xx. 35). Who can estimate what the world owes to such sayings, and with what beautiful foliage and rich fruit such seeds have covered, and will yet cover, this earth! 9. **Provide neither gold, nor silver, nor brass in** [εἰς]—'for' **your purses** [ζώνας]—lit., 'your belts,' in which they kept their money. 10. **Nor scrip for your journey**—the wallet used by travellers for holding provisions—**neither two coats** [χιτῶνας]—or tunics, worn next the skin. The meaning is, Take no change of dress, no additional articles. **neither shoes**—that is, change of them—**nor yet staves.** The received text here has 'a staff' [ῥάβδον], but our version follows another reading [ῥάβδους], 'staves,' which is found in the received text of Luke (ix. 3). The true reading, however, evidently is 'a staff'—meaning, that they were not to procure even thus much expressly for this missionary journey, but to go with what they had. No doubt it was the misunderstanding of this that gave rise to the reading "staves" in so many MSS. Even if this reading were genuine, it could not mean 'more than one;' for who, as *Alford* well asks, would think of taking a spare staff? **for the workman is worthy of his meat** [τροφῆς]—his 'food' or 'maintenance;' a principle which, being universally recognized in secular affairs, is here authoritatively applied to the services of the Lord's workmen, and by Paul repeatedly and touchingly employed in his appeals to the churches (Rom. xv. 27; 1 Cor. ix. 11; Gal. vi. 6), and once as "Scripture" (1 Tim. v. 18). 11. **And into whatsoever city or town** [πόλιν ἢ κώμην]—'town or village' **ye enter** [carefully] **enquire** [ἐξετάσατε] **who in it is worthy**—or 'meet' to entertain such messengers; not in point of rank, of course, but of congenial disposition. **and there abide till ye go thence**—not shifting about, as if discontented, but returning the welcome given them with a courteous, contented, accommodating disposition. 12. **And when ye come into an house**—or 'the house' [τὴν οἰκίαν], but it means not the worthy house, but the house ye first enter, to try if it be worthy. **salute it**—show it the usual civilities. 13. **And if the house be worthy**—

14 but if it be not worthy, let your peace return to you. And whosoever
shall not receive you, nor hear your words, when ye depart out of that
15 house or city, [j]shake off the dust of your feet. Verily I say unto you,
It shall be more tolerable for the land of Sodom and Gomorrha in the
day of judgment, than for that city.
16 Behold, I send you forth as sheep in the midst of wolves: [k]be ye there-
17 fore wise as serpents, and [5]harmless as doves. But beware of men; for
they will deliver you up to the councils, and [l]they will scourge you in
18 their synagogues: and [m]ye shall be brought before governors and kings
19 for my sake, for a testimony against them and the Gentiles. But when
they deliver you up, take no thought how or what ye shall speak: for [n]it
20 shall be given you in that same hour what ye shall speak. For [o]it is not
ye that speak, but the Spirit of your Father which speaketh in you.
21 And [p]the brother shall deliver up the brother to death, and the father
the child: and the children shall rise up against *their* parents, and cause
22 them to be put to death. And ye shall be hated of all *men* for my name's

A. D. 31.

j Neh. 5. 13. Acts 13. 51. Acts 18. 6. Acts 20. 26, 27.
k Gen. 3. 1. Luke 21. 15. Rom. 16. 19. Eph. 5. 15.
5 Or, simple. 1 Cor. 14. 20.
l Acts 5. 40.
m Acts 12. 1. Acts 24. 10.
n Ex. 4. 12. Jer. 1. 7.
o 2 Sam. 23. 2. Acts 4. 8. Acts 6. 10.
p Mic. 7. 6.

showing this by giving you a welcome—**let your peace come upon it.** This is best explained by the injunction to the Seventy, "And into whatsoever house ye enter, first say, Peace be to this house" (Luke x. 5). This was the ancient salutation of the East, and it prevails to this day. But from the lips of Christ and his messengers, it means something far higher, both in the gift and the giving of it, than in the current salutation. (See on John xiv. 27.) **but if it be not worthy, let your peace return to you.** If your peace finds a shut instead of an open door in the heart of any household, take it back to yourselves, who know how to value it, and it will taste the sweeter to you for having been offered, even though rejected. **14. And whosoever shall not receive you, nor hear your words, when ye depart out of that house or city**—for possibly a whole town might not furnish one "worthy", **shake off the dust of your feet**—"for a testimony against them," as Mark and Luke add. By this symbolical action they vividly shook themselves from all *connection* with such, and all *responsibility* for the guilt of rejecting them and their message. Such symbolical actions were common in ancient times, even among others than the Jews, as strikingly appears in Pilate (ch. xxvii. 24). And even to this day it prevails in the East. **15. Verily I say unto you, It shall be more tolerable**—more bearable, **for Sodom and Gomorrha in the day of judgment, than for that city.** Those cities of the plain, which were given to the flames for their loathsome impurities, shall be treated as less criminal, we are here taught, than those places which, though morally respectable, reject the Gospel message and affront those that bear it.

Directions for the Future and Permanent Exercise of the Christian Ministry (16-23). **16. Behold, I send you forth.** The "I" here [Ἐγὼ] is emphatic, holding up Himself as the Fountain of the Gospel ministry, as He is also the Great Burden of it. **as sheep**—defenceless, **in the midst of wolves**—ready to make a prey of you (John x. 12). To be left exposed, as sheep to wolves, would have been startling enough; but that the sheep should be *sent* among the wolves would sound strange indeed. No wonder this announcement begins with the exclamation, "Behold." **be ye therefore wise as serpents, and harmless as doves.** Wonderful combination this! Alone, the wisdom of the serpent is mere cunning, and the harmlessness of the dove little better than weakness: but in combination, the wisdom of the serpent would save them from unnecessary exposure to danger; the harmlessness of the dove, from sinful expedients to escape it. In the apostolic age of Christianity, how harmoniously were these qualities displayed! Instead of the fanatical thirst for martyrdom, to which a later age gave birth, there was a manly combination of unflinching zeal and calm discretion, before which nothing was able to stand. **17. But beware of men; for they will deliver you up to the councils** [συνέδρια]—the local courts, used here for civil magistrates in general. **and they will scourge you in their synagogues.** By this is meant persecution at the hands of the ecclesiastics. **18. And ye shall be brought before governors**—or provincial rulers, **and kings**—the highest tribunals—**for my sake, for a testimony against them** [αὐτοῖς]—rather, 'to them,' in order to bear testimony to the truth and its glorious effects—**and** [to] **the Gentiles**—a hint that their message would not long be confined to the lost sheep of the house of Israel. The Acts of the Apostles are the best commentary on these warnings. **19. But when they deliver you up, take no thought**—'be not solicitous' or 'anxious' [μὴ μεριμνήσητε]. (See on ch. vi. 25.) **how or what ye shall speak**—that is, either in what *manner* ye shall make your defence, or of what *matter* it shall consist—**for it shall be given you in that same hour what ye shall speak.** (See Exod. iv. 12; Jer. i. 7.) **20. For it is not ye that speak, but the Spirit of your Father which speaketh in you.** How remarkably this has been verified, the whole history of persecution thrillingly proclaims—from the Acts of the Apostles to the latest martyrology. **21. And the brother shall deliver up the brother to death, and the father the child: and the children shall rise up against their parents, and cause them to be put to death**—for example, by lodging informations against them with the authorities. The deep and virulent hostility of the old nature and life to the new—as of Belial to Christ—was to issue in awful wrenches of the dearest ties; and the disciples, in the prospect of their cause and themselves being launched upon society, are here prepared for the worst. **22. And ye shall be hated of all men for my name's sake.** The universality of this hatred would make it evident to them, that since it would not be owing to any temporary excitement, local virulence, or personal prejudice, on the part of their enemies, so no amount of discretion on their part, consistent with entire fidelity to the truth, would avail to stifle that enmity—though it might soften its violence, and in some cases avert the outward

23 sake: [q] but he that endureth to the end shall be saved. But [r] when they persecute you in this city, flee ye into another: for verily I say unto you, Ye
shall not [6] have gone over the cities of Israel, till [s] the Son of man be come.
24 The disciple is not above *his* master, nor the servant above his
25 lord. It is enough for the disciple that he be as his master, and
the servant as his lord. If they have called the master of the house
[7] Beelzebub, how much more *shall they call* them of his household?
26 Fear them not therefore: for there is nothing covered, that shall not be
27 revealed; and hid, that shall not be known. What I tell you in darkness, *that* speak ye in light: and what ye hear in the ear, *that* preach
28 ye upon the house-tops. And [t] fear not them which kill the body, but
are not able to kill the soul: but rather fear him which is able to destroy
29 both soul and body in hell. Are not two sparrows sold for a [8] farthing?

A. D. 31.

[q] Dan. 12. 12. Gal. 6. 9.
[r] Acts 14. 6.
[6] Or, end, or, finish.
[s] ch. 16. 28. Acts 2. 1.
[7] Beelzebul.
[t] Isa. 8. 12. 1 Pet. 3. 14.
[8] Halfpenny farthing, the tenth part of the Roman penny.

manifestations of it. **but he that endureth to the end shall be saved**—a great saying, repeated, in connection with similar warnings, in the prophecy of the destruction of Jerusalem (ch. xxiv. 13); and often reiterated by the apostle as a warning against "drawing back unto perdition." (Heb. iii. 6, 13; vi. 4-6; x. 23, 26-29, 38, 39; &c.) As "drawing back unto perdition" is merely the palpable evidence of the want of "root" from the first in the Christian profession (Luke viii. 13), so "enduring to the end" is just the proper evidence of its reality and solidity. **23. But when they persecute you in this city, flee ye into another** [εἰς τὴν ἄλλην]—'into the other.' This, though applicable to all time, and exemplified by our Lord Himself once and again, had special reference to the brief opportunities which Israel was to have of "knowing the time of his visitation." **for verily I say unto you**—what will startle you, but at the same time show you the solemnity of your mission, and the need of economizing the time for it—**Ye shall not have gone over** [οὐ μὴ τελέσητε]—'Ye shall in nowise have completed' **the cities of Israel, till the Son of man be come.** To understand this—as *Lange* and others do—in the first instance, of Christ's own peregrinations, as if He had said, 'Waste not your time upon hostile places, for I myself will be after you ere your work be over'—seems almost trifling. "The coming of the Son of man" has a fixed doctrinal sense, here referring immediately to the crisis of Israel's history as the visible kingdom of God, when Christ was to come and judge it; when "the wrath would come upon it to the uttermost;" and when, on the ruins of Jerusalem and the old economy, He would establish His own kingdom. This, in the uniform language of Scripture, is more immediately "the coming of the Son of man," "the day of vengeance of our God" (ch. xvi. 28; xxiv. 27, 34; with Heb. x. 25; Jas. v. 7-9)—but only as being such a lively anticipation of His Second Coming for vengeance and deliverance. So understood, it is parallel with ch. xxiv. 14 (on which see).

Directions for the Service of Christ in its widest sense (24-42). **24. The disciple is not above his master** [διδάσκαλον]—'teacher,' **nor the servant above his lord**—another maxim which our Lord repeats in various connections (Luke vi. 40; John xiii. 16; xv. 20). **25. It is enough for the disciple that he be as his Master, and the servant as his Lord. If they have called the master of the house Beelzebub.** All the Greek MSS. write "Beelzebul," which undoubtedly is the right form of this word. The other reading came in no doubt from the Old Testament "Baalzebub," the god of Ekron (2 Ki. i. 2), which it was designed to express. As all idolatry was regarded as devil-worship (Lev. xvii. 7; Deut. xxxii. 17; Ps. cvi. 37; 1 Cor. x. 20), so there seems to have been something peculiarly Satanic about the worship of this hateful god, which caused his name to be a synonym of Satan. Though we nowhere read that our Lord was actually called "Beelzebul," He was charged with being in league with Satan under that hateful name (ch. xii. 24, 26), and more than once Himself was charged with "having a devil" or "demon" (Mark iii. 30; John vii. 20; viii. 48). Here it is used to denote the most opprobrious language which could be applied by one to another. **how much more [shall they call] them of his household?** [οἰκιακοὺς]—'the inmates.' Three relations in which Christ stands to His people are here mentioned: He is their Teacher—they His disciples; He is their Lord—they His servants; He is the Master of the household—they its inmates. In all these relations, He says here, He and they are so bound up together that they cannot look to fare better than He, and should think it enough if they are no worse. **26. Fear them not therefore: for there is nothing covered, that shall not be revealed; and hid, that shall not be known**:—*q. d.*, 'There is no use, and no need, of concealing anything; right and wrong, truth and error, are about to come into open and deadly collision; and the day is coming when all hidden things shall be disclosed, everything seen as it is, and every one have his due' (1 Cor. iv. 5). **27. What I tell you in darkness**—in the privacy of a teaching for which men are not yet ripe—**that speak ye in the light**—for when ye go forth all will be ready—**and what ye hear in the ear, that preach ye upon the house-tops**:—Give free and fearless utterance to all that I have taught you while yet with you. *Objection:* But this may cost us our life? *Answer:* It may, but there their power ends: **28. And fear not them which kill the body, but are not able to kill the soul.** In Luke xii. 4, "and after that have no more that they can do." **but rather fear him**—in Luke this is peculiarly solemn, "I will forewarn you whom ye shall fear," even Him **which is able to destroy both soul and body in hell.** A decisive proof this that there is a hell for the body as well as the soul in the eternal world; in other words, that the torment that awaits the lost will have elements of suffering adapted to the *material* as well as the spiritual part of our nature, both of which, we are assured, will exist for ever. In the corresponding warning contained in Luke, Jesus calls His disciples "My friends," as if He had felt that such sufferings constituted a bond of peculiar tenderness between Him and them. **29. Are not two sparrows sold for a farthing?** In Luke (xii. 6) it is "Five sparrows for two

30 and one of them shall not fall on the ground without your Father. But
31 [u]the very hairs of your head are all numbered. Fear ye not therefore,
32 ye are of more value than many sparrows. Whosoever [v]therefore shall
confess me before men, [w]him will I confess also before my Father which
33 is in heaven. But [x]whosoever shall deny me before men, him will I
34 also deny before my Father which is in heaven. Think not that I am
come to send peace on earth: I came not to send peace, but a sword.
35 For I am come to set a man at variance [y]against his father, and the
daughter against her mother, and the daughter-in-law against her
36 mother-in-law. And a man's foes *shall be* they of his own household.
37 He that loveth father or mother more than me, is not worthy of me; and
38 he that loveth son or daughter more than me, is not worthy of me. And
he that taketh not his cross, and followeth after me, is not worthy of me.
39 He [z]that findeth his life shall lose it: and he that loseth his life for my
40 sake shall find it. He that receiveth you, receiveth me; and he that
41 receiveth me, receiveth him that sent me. He [a]that receiveth a prophet
in the name of a prophet shall receive a prophet's reward; and he that
receiveth a righteous man in the name of a righteous man shall receive

A. D. 31.

[u] Acts 27. 34.
[v] Ps. 119. 46. Rom. 10. 9. 1 Tim. 6. 12, 13. Rev. 2. 13.
[w] 1 Sam. 2. 30. ch. 25. 34. Rev. 3. 5.
[x] ch. 26. 70-75. Mark 8. 38. Luke 9. 26. Luke 12. 9. 2 Tim. 2. 12.
[y] Mic. 7. 6. ch. 24. 10. Mark 13. 12.
[z] ch 16. 25. Luke 17. 33. John 12. 25. Rev. 2. 10.
[a] 1 Ki. 17. 10. 2 Ki. 4. 8.

farthings;" so that, if the purchaser took two farthings' worth, he got one in addition—of such small value were they. **and one of them shall not fall on the ground**—exhausted or killed—**without your Father**—"Not one of them is forgotten before God," as it is in Luke. **30. But the very hairs of your head are all numbered.** See Luke xxi. 18, (and compare for the language 1 Sam. xiv. 45; Acts xxvii. 34). **31. Fear ye not therefore, ye are of more value than many sparrows.** Was ever language of such simplicity felt to carry such weight as this does? But here lies much of the charm and power of our Lord's teaching. **32. Whosoever therefore shall confess me before men**—"despising the shame", **him will I confess also before my Father which is in heaven**—I will not be ashamed of him, but will own him before the most august of all assemblies. **33. But whosoever shall deny me before men, him will I also deny before my Father which is in heaven**—before that same assembly: 'He shall have from Me his own treatment of Me on the earth.' But see on ch. xvi. 27. **34. Think not that I am come to send peace on earth: I came not to send peace, but a sword**—strife, discord, conflict; deadly opposition between eternally hostile principles, penetrating into and rending asunder the dearest ties. **35. For I am come to set a man at variance against his father, and the daughter against her mother, and the daughter-in-law against her mother-in-law.** See on Luke xii. 51-53. **36. And a man's foes shall be they of his own household.** This saying, which is quoted, as is the whole verse, from Mic. vii. 6, is but an extension of the Psalmist's complaint, Ps. xli. 9; lv. 12-14, which had its most affecting illustration in the treason of Judas against our Lord Himself (John xiii. 18; Matt. xxvi. 48-50). Hence would arise the necessity of a choice between Christ and the nearest relations, which would put them to the severest test. **37. He that loveth father or mother more than me, is not worthy of me; and he that loveth son or daughter more than me, is not worthy of me.** Compare Deut. xxxiii. 9. As the preference of the one would, in the case supposed, necessitate the abandonment of the other, our Lord here, with a sublime, yet awful self-respect, asserts His own claims to supreme affection. **38. And he that taketh not his cross, and followeth after me, is not worthy of me**—a saying which our Lord once and again emphatically reiterates (ch. xvi. 24; Luke ix. 23; xiv. 27). We have become so accustomed to this expression—"taking up one's cross"—in the sense of 'being prepared for trials in general for Christ's sake,' that we are apt to lose sight of its primary and proper sense here—'a preparedness to go forth even to crucifixion,' as when our Lord had to bear His own cross on His way to Calvary—a saying the more remarkable as our Lord had not as yet given a hint that He would die this death, nor was crucifixion a Jewish mode of capital punishment. **39. He that findeth his life shall lose it: and he that loseth his life for my sake shall find it**—another of those pregnant sayings which our Lord so often reiterates (ch. xvi. 25; Luke xvii. 33; John xii. 25). The pith of such paradoxical maxims depends on the double sense attached to the word "life"—a lower and a higher, the natural and the spiritual, the temporal and eternal. An entire sacrifice of the lower, with all its relationships and interests—or, which is the same thing, a willingness to make it—is indispensable to the preservation of the higher life; and he who cannot bring himself to surrender the one for the sake of the other shall eventually lose both. **40. He that receiveth**—or 'entertaineth' **you, receiveth me; and he that receiveth me, receiveth him that sent me.** As the treatment which an ambassador receives is understood and regarded as expressing the light in which he that sends him is viewed, so, says our Lord here, 'Your authority is mine, as mine is my Father's.' **41. He that receiveth a prophet**—one divinely commissioned to deliver a message from heaven. Predicting future events was no necessary part of a prophet's office, especially as the word is used in the New Testament. **in the name of a prophet**—for his office' sake and love to his Master. (See 2 Kings iv. 9, 10.) **shall receive a prophet's reward.** What an encouragement to those who are *not* prophets! (See 3 John 5-8.) **and he that receiveth a righteous man in the name of a righteous man**—from sympathy with his character and esteem for himself as such, **shall receive a righteous man's reward**—for he must himself have the seed of righteousness who has any real sympathy with it and complacency in him who possesses it. **42. And whosoever shall give to drink unto one of these little ones.** Beautiful epithet! originally taken from Zech. xiii. 7. The reference is to their

42 a righteous man's reward. And [b]whosoever shall give to drink unto
one of these little ones a cup of cold *water* only in the name of a disciple,
verily I say unto you, [c]he shall in no wise lose his reward.
11 AND it came to pass, when Jesus had made an end of commanding his
twelve disciples, he departed thence, to teach and to preach in their
cities.

A. D. 31.

[b] ch. 25. 40. Mark 9. 42. Heb. 6. 10.

[c] Prov. 24. 14. Luke 6. 35.

lowliness in spirit, their littleness in the eyes of an undiscerning world, while high in Heaven's esteem. **a cup of cold water only**—meaning, the smallest service, **in the name of a disciple**—or, as it is in Mark (ix. 41), because ye are Christ's [Χριστοῦ ἐστέ]: from love to Me, and to him from his connection with Me, **verily I say unto you, he shall in no wise lose his reward.** There is here a descending climax—"a prophet," "a righteous man," "a little one;" signifying that however low we come down in our services to those that are Christ's, all that is done for His sake, and that bears the stamp of love to His blessed name, shall be divinely appreciated and owned and rewarded.

Remarks.—1. It is a manifest abuse of the directions here given for this first, hasty and temporary, mission (*vv.* 5-15), to take them as a general Directory for the missionaries of Christ in all time and under all circumstances. The cessation of those miraculous credentials with which the Twelve were furnished for this present Mission, might surely convince Christian men that the directions for such a mission were not intended to be literally followed by the missionaries of the Cross in all time. Even our Lord Himself did not act on the strict letter of these directions, having for needful uses, as *Luther* (in *Stier*) quaintly says—"money, bag, and bread-baskets too." It is true that one or two servants of Christ, in the course of an age, are found, who, in a spirit of entire self-abnegation, consecrate themselves to works of Christian philanthropy without wealth or other ordinary resources, and yet not only obtain enough to maintain them in their work, but the means of extending it beyond all anticipation, and that for a long series of years, or even a life-time. But the interest and admiration which such cases draw forth throughout the Christian world shows them to be exceptional illustrations of answer to prayer, and childlike confidence in working the work of God, rather than the normal character of the work of His kingdom. At the same time, the servants of Christ will do well to imbibe the *spirit* of these first directions—in simplicity of purpose and superiority to fastidious concern about their personal comfort; in energy also, and alacrity in prosecuting their work: taking as their motto that golden maxim, "Freely ye have received, freely give;" yet "not casting their pearls before swine," but acting on the principle that the rejection of their message is an affront put upon their Master, rather than themselves. 2. Though the vast change which the Gospel has produced upon Christendom is apt to make men think that our Lord's statements, here and elsewhere, of the universal hatred with which Christians would be regarded, have become inapplicable, we are never to forget that the hostility He speaks of is a hostility of *unchangeable principles;* and that although the unfaithfulness and timidity of Christians, on the one hand, may so compromise or keep in the background those principles which the world hates, or on the other hand, the world itself may from various causes be restrained from manifesting that hatred, yet, whenever and wherever the light and the darkness, Christ and Belial, are brought face to face in vivid juxtaposition, there will the eternal and irreconcileable opposition of the one to the other appear. 3. How vastly greater would be the influence of Christians upon the world around them if they were more studious to combine the wisdom of the serpent with the harmlessness of the dove! We have Christians and Christian ministers who pride themselves upon their knowledge of the world, and the shrewdness with which they conduct themselves in it; while the simplicity of the dove is almost entirely in abeyance. Even the world can discern this, and, discerning it, despise those who to all appearance are no better than others, and yet pretend to be so. But on the other hand, there are Christians and Christian ministers who have the harmlessness of the dove, but being totally void of the wisdom of the serpent, carry no weight, and even expose themselves and their cause to the contempt of the world. O that the followers of the Lamb would lay this to heart! 4. What weighty inducements to suffer unflinchingly for the Gospel's sake are here provided! Such as do so are no worse off than their Master, and may rest assured of His sympathy and support, in a furnace which in His own case was heated seven times. And what though their life should be taken from them for Jesus' sake? The power of their enemies ceases there; whereas He whose wrath they incur by selling their conscience to save life is able to cast both soul and body into hell-fire. (See on Mark ix. 43-48.) God's suffering children are unspeakably dear to Him; their every trial in His service is full before Him; and their courage in confessing the name of Jesus will be rewarded by the confession of their name amidst the solemnities and the splendours of the great day: whereas a faithless denial of Christ here will be followed by the indignant and open denial of such by the Judge from His great white throne. 5. When Jesus here demands of His followers a love beyond all that is found in the tenderest relations of life, and pronounces all who withhold this to be unworthy of Him, He makes a claim which, on the part of any mere creature, would be wicked and intolerable, and in Him who honoured the Father as no other on earth ever did, is not to be imagined, if He had not been "the Fellow of the Lord of Hosts." 6. It is an abuse of the duty of *disinterestedness* in religion to condemn all reference to our own future safety and blessedness as a motive of action. For what have we here, as the conclusion of this lofty Directory, but an encouragement to entertain His servants, and welcome His people, and do offices of kindness, however small, to the humblest of His disciples, by the emphatic assurance that not the lowest of such offices shall go unrewarded? And shall not Christians be stimulated to lay themselves thus out for Him to whom they owe their all?

CHAP. XI. 1-19.—THE IMPRISONED BAPTIST'S MESSAGE TO HIS MASTER—THE REPLY, AND DISCOURSE, ON THE DEPARTURE OF THE MESSENGERS, REGARDING JOHN AND HIS MISSION. (=Luke vii. 18-35.)

1. And it came to pass, when Jesus had made an end of commanding his—rather, 'the' **twelve disciples, he departed thence to teach and to preach in their cities.** This was scarcely a fourth

2 Now [a]when John had heard [b]in the prison the works of Christ, he sent
3 two of his disciples, and said unto him, Art thou [c]he that should come,
4 or do we look for another? Jesus answered and said unto them, Go and
5 show John again those things which ye do hear and see: the [d]blind receive their sight, and the lame walk, the lepers are cleansed, and the
deaf hear, the dead are raised up, and the [e]poor have the Gospel preached
6 to them. And blessed is *he*, whosoever shall not be [f]offended in me.
7 And [g]as they departed, Jesus began to say unto the multitudes concerning John, What went ye out into the wilderness to see? A reed
8 shaken with the wind? But what went ye out for to see? A man clothed
in soft raiment? Behold, they that wear soft *clothing* are in kings'
9 houses. But what went ye out for to see? A prophet? yea, I say unto
10 you, [h]and more than a prophet. For this is *he*, of whom it is written,
[i]Behold, I send my messenger before thy face, which shall prepare thy
11 way before thee. Verily I say unto you, Among them that are born of
women there hath not risen a greater than John the Baptist; notwithstanding he that is least in the kingdom of heaven is greater than he.
12 And [j]from the days of John the Baptist until now the kingdom of
13 heaven [1]suffereth violence, and the violent take it by force. For [k]all
14 the Prophets and the Law prophesied until John. And if ye will receive
15 *it*, this is [l]Elias, which was for to come. He [m]that hath ears to hear,
16 let him hear. But [n]whereunto shall I liken this generation? It is like
17 unto children sitting in the markets, and calling unto their fellows, and
saying, We have piped unto you, and ye have not danced; we have
18 mourned unto you, and ye have not lamented. For John came neither
19 eating nor drinking, and they say, He hath a devil. The Son of man
came eating and drinking, and they say, Behold a man gluttonous, and
a wine-bibber, [o]a friend of publicans and sinners. [p]But Wisdom is justified of her children.
20 Then [q]began he to upbraid the cities wherein most of his mighty works
21 were done, because they repented not: Woe unto thee, Chorazin! woe
unto thee, Bethsaida! for if the mighty works which were done in you
had been done in Tyre and Sidon, they would have repented long ago

A. D. 31.

a Luke 7. 18.
b ch. 14. 3.
c Gen. 49. 10. Num. 24. 17. Dan. 9. 24. Mal. 3. 1-3.
d Isa. 29. 18. Isa 35. 4. Isa. 42. 7.
e Ps. 22. 26. Isa. 61. 1. Luke 4. 18. Jas. 2. 5.
f Isa. 8. 14. ch. 13. 57. ch. 24. 10. ch 26. 31. Rom. 9. 32. 1 Cor. 1. 23. 1 Cor. 2. 14. Gal. 5. 11. 1 Pet. 2. 8.
g Luke 7. 24.
h Luke 1. 76.
i Mal. 3. 1. Mark 1. 2.
j Luke 16. 16.
1 Or, is gotten by force, and they that thrust men.
k Mal. 4. 6.
l Mal. 4. 5. ch. 17. 12. Luke 1. 17. John 1. 23.
m Rev. 2. 7.
n Luke 7. 31.
o ch. 9. 10.
p Phil. 2. 15.
q Luke 10. 13.

circuit—if we may judge from the less formal way in which it is expressed—but, perhaps, a set of visits paid to certain places, either not reached at all, or too rapidly passed through before, in order to fill up the time till the return of the Twelve. As to their labours, nothing is said of them by our Evangelist. But Luke (ix. 6) says, "They departed, and went through the towns" [κώμας], or 'villages,' "preaching the Gospel, and healing everywhere." Mark (vi. 12, 13), as usual, is more explicit: "And they went out, and preached that men should repent. And they cast out many devils (or 'demons'), and anointed with oil many that were sick, and healed them." Though this "anointing with oil" was not mentioned in our Lord's instructions—at least in any of the records of them—we know it to have been practised long after this in the apostolic Church (see Jas. v. 14, and compare Mark vi. 12, 13)—not *medicinally*, but as a sign of the healing virtue which was communicated by their hands, and a symbol of something still more precious. It was *unction*, indeed, but, as *Bengel* remarks, it was something very different from what Romanists call *extreme* unction. He adds, what is very probable, that they do not appear to have carried the oil about with them, but, as the Jews used oil as a medicine, to have employed it just as they found it with the sick, in their own higher way.

2. Now when John had heard in the prison. For the account of this imprisonment, see on Mark vi. 17-20. **the works of Christ, he sent, &c.** On the whole passage, see on Luke vii. 18-35.

20-30.—Outburst of Feeling, suggested to the Mind of Jesus by the Result of His Labours in Galilee.

The connection of this with what goes before it, and the similarity of its tone, makes it evident, we think, that it was delivered on the same occasion, and that it is but a new and more comprehensive series of reflections in the same strain. **20. Then began he to upbraid the cities wherein most of his mighty works were done, because they repented not: 21. Woe unto thee, Chorazin!**—not elsewhere mentioned, but it must have lain near Capernaum. **woe unto thee, Bethsaida!** [בֵּית and צַיָּדָה, 'hunting' or 'fishing-house'—'a fishing station']—on the western side of the sea of Galilee, and to the north of Capernaum; the birth-place of three of the apostles—the brothers Andrew and Peter, and Philip. These two cities appear to be singled out to denote the whole region in which they lay—a region favoured with the Redeemer's presence, teaching, and works above every other. **for if the mighty works** [*αἱ δυνάμεις*]—'the miracles' **which were done in you had been done in Tyre and Sidon**—ancient and celebrated commercial cities, on the north-eastern shores of the Mediterranean sea, lying north of Palestine, and the latter the northernmost. As their wealth and prosperity engendered

22 [r]in sackcloth and ashes. But I say unto you, It shall be more tolerable
23 for Tyre and Sidon at the day of judgment, than for you. And thou,
Capernaum, [s]which art exalted unto heaven, shalt be brought down to
hell: for if the mighty works, which have been done in thee, had been
24 done in Sodom, it would have remained until this day. But I say unto
you, That it shall be more tolerable for the land of Sodom in the
day of judgment, than for thee.
25 At that time Jesus answered and said, I thank thee, O Father, Lord of
heaven and earth, because [t]thou hast hid these things from the wise and
26 prudent, and hast revealed them unto babes. Even so, Father; for so it
27 seemed good in thy sight. All [u]things are delivered unto me of my
Father: and no man knoweth the Son, but the Father; [v]neither knoweth
any man the Father, save the Son, and *he* to whomsoever the Son will

A. D. 31.

[r] Job 13. 6. Jon. 3. 8.
[s] Isa. 14 13. Lam. 2. 1.
[t] Ps. 8. 2. 1 Cor. 1. 27. 1 Cor. 2.7,8. 2 Cor. 3. 14.
[u] ch. 28. 18. Luke 10. 22. John 3. 35. 1 Cor. 15.27. Eph. 1. 21.
[v] John 1. 18. John 6. 46. John 10. 15.

luxury and its concomitant evils—irreligion and moral degeneracy—their overthrow was repeatedly foretold in ancient prophecy, and once and again fulfilled by victorious enemies. Yet they were rebuilt, and at this time were in a flourishing condition. **they would have repented long ago in sackcloth and ashes.** Remarkable language, showing that they had done less violence to conscience, and so, in God's sight, were less criminal than the region here spoken of. **22. But I say unto you, It shall be more tolerable**—more 'endurable,' **for Tyre and Sidon at the day of judgment, than for you. 23. And thou, Capernaum** (see on ch. iv. 13), **which art exalted unto heaven.** Not even of Chorazin and Bethsaida is this said. For since at Capernaum Jesus had His stated abode during the whole period of His public life which He spent in Galilee, it was *the most favoured spot upon earth*, the most exalted in privilege. **shalt be brought down to hell: for if the mighty works, which have been done in thee, had been done in Sodom**—destroyed for its pollutions, **it would have remained until this day**—having done no such violence to conscience, and so incurred unspeakably less guilt. **24. But I say unto you, That it shall be more tolerable for the land of Sodom in the day of judgment, than for thee.** 'It has been indeed,' says *Dr. Stanley*, 'more tolerable, in one sense, in the day of its earthly judgment, for the land of Sodom than for Capernaum: for the name, and perhaps even the remains, of Sodom are still to be found on the shores of the Dead Sea; whilst that of Capernaum has, on the Lake of Gennesareth, been utterly lost.' But the judgment of which our Lord here speaks is still future; a judgment not on material cities, but their responsible inhabitants—a judgment final and irretrievable.

25. At that time Jesus answered and said. We are not to understand by this, that the previous discourse had been concluded; and that this is a record only of something said about the same period. For the connection is most close, and the word "answered"—which, when there is no one to answer, refers to something just before said, or rising in the mind of the speaker in consequence of something said—confirms this. What Jesus here "answered" evidently was the melancholy results of His ministry, lamented over in the foregoing verses. It is as if He had said, 'Yes; but there is a brighter side of the picture: even in those who have rejected the message of eternal life, it is the pride of their own hearts only which has blinded them, and the glory of the truth does but the more appear in their inability to receive it: Nor have all rejected it even here; souls thirsting for salvation have drawn water with joy from the wells of salvation; the weary have found rest; the hungry have been filled with good things, while the rich have been sent empty away.' **I thank thee** ['Εξομολογοῦμαί σοι]—rather, 'I assent to thee.' But this is not strong enough. The idea of '*full*' or 'cordial' concurrence is conveyed by the preposition ['Εξ]. The thing expressed is adoring acquiescence, holy satisfaction with that law of the divine procedure about to be mentioned. And as, when He afterwards uttered the same words, He "exulted in spirit" (see on Luke x. 21), probably He did the same now, though not recorded. **O Father, Lord of heaven and earth.** He so styles His Father here, to signify that from Him of right emanate all such high arrangements. **because thou hast hid these things**—the knowledge of these saving truths—**from the wise and prudent** [σοφῶν καὶ συνετῶν]. The former of these terms points to the men who pride themselves upon their speculative or philosophical attainments; the latter to the men of worldly shrewdness—the clever, the sharp-witted, the men of affairs. The distinction is a natural one, and was well understood. (See 1 Cor. i. 19; &c.) But why had the Father hid from such the things that belonged to their peace, and why did Jesus so emphatically set His seal to this arrangement? Because it is not for the offending and revolted to speak or to speculate, but to listen to Him from whom we have broken loose, that we may learn whether there be any recovery for us at all; and if there be, on what principles—of what nature—to what ends. To bring our own "wisdom and prudence" to such questions is impertinent and presumptuous; and if the truth regarding them, or the glory of it, be "hid" from us, it is but a fitting retribution, to which all the right-minded will set their seal along with Jesus. But, Thou **hast revealed them unto babes**—to babe-like men; men of unassuming docility, men who, conscious that they know nothing, and have no right to sit in judgment on the things that belong to their peace, determine simply to "hear what God the Lord will speak." Such are well called "babes." (See Heb. v. 13; 1 Cor. xiii. 11; xiv. 20; &c.) **26. Even so, Father; for so it seemed good** [εὐδοκία]—the emphatic and chosen term for expressing any object of divine complacency; whether Christ Himself (see on ch. iii. 17) or God's gracious eternal arrangements (see on Phil. ii. 13)—**in thy sight.** This is just a sublime echo of the foregoing words; as if Jesus, when He uttered them, had paused to reflect on it, and as if the glory of it—not so much in the light of its own reasonableness as of God's absolute will that so it should be—had filled His soul. **27. All things are delivered unto me of my Father.** He does not say, They are *revealed*—as to one who knew them not, and

28 reveal *him*. Come unto me, all *ye* that labour and are heavy laden, and
29 I will give you rest. Take my yoke upon you, [w]and learn of me;
for I am meek and [x]lowly in heart: and [y]ye shall find rest unto your
30 souls. For [z]my yoke *is* easy, and my burden is light.

A. D. 31.

[w] 1 John 2. 6.
[x] Zech. 9. 9.
[y] Jer. 6. 16.
[z] 1 John 5. 3.

was an entire stranger to them save as they were discovered to him—but, They are 'delivered over' [παρεδόθη], or 'committed,' to me of my Father; meaning the whole administration of the kingdom of grace. So in John iii. 35, "The Father loveth the Son, and hath given all things into His hand" (see on that verse). But though the "all things" in both these passages refer properly to the kingdom of grace, they of course include all things necessary to the full execution of that trust—that is, *unlimited* power. (So ch. xxviii. 18; John xvii. 2; Eph. i. 22.) **and no man knoweth the Son, but the Father; neither knoweth any man the Father, save the Son, and he to whomsoever the Son will**—or 'willeth' [βούληται] to **reveal him.** What a saying is this, that 'the Father and the Son are mutually and exclusively known to each other!' A higher claim to equality with the Father cannot be conceived. Either, then, we have here one of the most revolting assumptions ever uttered, or the proper Divinity of Christ should to Christians be beyond dispute. 'But alas for me!' may some burdened soul, sighing for relief, here exclaim. If it be thus with us, what can any poor creature do but lie down in passive despair, unless he could dare to hope that *he* may be one of the favoured class 'to whom the Son is willing to reveal the Father'? But nay. This testimony to the sovereignty of that gracious "will," on which alone men's salvation depends, is designed but to reveal the source and enhance the glory of it when once imparted—not to paralyze or shut the soul up in despair. Hear, accordingly, what follows: **28. Come unto me, all ye that labour and are heavy laden, and I will give you rest.** Incomparable, ravishing sounds these—if ever such were heard in this weary, groaning world! What gentleness, what sweetness is there in the very style of the invitation —'Hither to Me' [Δεῦτε πρός Με]: and in the words, 'All ye that toil and are burdened' [οἱ κοπιῶντες καὶ πεφορτισμένοι], the universal wretchedness of man is depicted, on both its sides—the *active* and the *passive* forms of it. **29. Take my yoke upon you**—the yoke of subjection to Jesus—**and learn of me; for I am meek and lowly in heart: and ye shall find rest unto your souls.** As Christ's willingness to empty Himself to the uttermost of His Father's requirements was the spring of ineffable repose to His own spirit, so in the same track does He invite all to follow Him, with the assurance of the same experience. **30. For my yoke is easy, and my burden is light.** Matchless paradox, even amongst the paradoxically couched maxims in which our Lord delights! That rest which the soul experiences, when once safe under Christ's wing, makes all yokes easy, all burdens light.

Remarks.—1. Perhaps in no Section of this wonderful History is the veil so fully lifted from the Redeemer's soul, and His inmost thoughts and deepest emotions more affectingly disclosed, than here. When we think how much more profound and acute must have been His sensibilities than any other's—from the unsullied purity of His nature and the vast reach of His perceptions—we may understand, in some degree, what "a Man of sorrows" He must have been, and how "acquainted with grief"—to see His Person slighted, His errand misapprehended, and His message rejected, in the very region on which He bestowed the most of His presence and the richest of His labours. Even in ancient prophecy we find Him exclaiming, "I have laboured in vain, I have spent My strength for nought and in vain;" and falling back upon this affecting consolation, that there was One that knew Him, and was the Judge of His doings:—"Yet surely my judgment is with the Lord, and my work with my God" (Isa. xlix. 4). But, as we turn to the bright side of the picture, who can fathom the depth of that exultant complacency with which His eye rested upon those "babes" into whose souls streamed the light of God's salvation, and with which He set His seal to that law of the divine procedure in virtue of which this was done, while from the self-sufficient it was hidden! And after thus seeming to wrap Himself and His Father up from all human penetration, save of some favoured class, what ineffable joy must it have been to His heart to disabuse the anxious of such a thought, by giving forth that most wonderful of all invitations, "Come unto Me!" &c. These are some of the lights and shadows of the Redeemer's life on earth; and what a reality do they impart to the Evangelical Narrative—what resistless attraction, what heavenly sanctity! 2. Let those who, under the richest ministrations of the word of life, "repent not," but live on unrenewed in the spirit of their minds, remember the doom of the cities of Galilee—executed in part, but in its most dread elements yet to come—and rest assured that at the judgment-day the degree of guilt will be estimated, not by the flagrancy of outward transgression, but by the degree of violence habitually offered to the voice of conscience—the extent to which light is quenched and conviction stifled. (See on Luke xii. 47, 48.) Ah! blighted Chorazin, Bethsaida, Capernaum—who, and more particularly what pastor, can wander over that region somewhere in which ye once basked in the very sunshine of Heaven's light, as no other spots on earth ever did, and not enter thrillingly into the poet's soliloquy,—

"These days are past—Bethsaida, where?
Chorazin, where art thou?
His tent the wild Arab pitches there,
The wild reed shades thy brow.

"Tell me, ye mouldering fragments, tell,
Was the Saviour's city here?
Lifted to heaven, has it sunk to hell,
With none to shed a tear?

"Ah! would my flock from thee might learn
How days of grace will flee;
How all an offered Christ who spurn
Shall mourn at last like thee."—M'CHEYNE.

3. If it be true that "no man knoweth the Son but the Father," how unreasonable is it to measure the statements of Scripture regarding the Person and work of Christ by the limited standard of human apprehension—rejecting, modifying, or explaining away whatever we are unable fully to comprehend, even though clearly expressed in the oracles of God! Nay, in the light of what our Lord here says of it, are not the difficulties just what might have been expected? 4. Let those who set the sovereignty of divine grace in opposition to the freedom and responsibility of the human will —rejecting now the one and now the other, as if they were irreconcileable—take the rebuke

12 AT that time [a]Jesus went on the sabbath day through the corn; and
his disciples were an hungered, and began to pluck the ears of corn, and
2 to eat. But when the Pharisees saw *it*, they said unto him, Behold, thy
3 disciples do that which is not lawful to do upon the sabbath day. But
he said unto them, Have ye not read [b]what David did, when he was an
4 hungered, and they that were with him; how he entered into the house

A. D. 31.

CHAP. 12.
[a] Deut. 23. 25. Mark 2. 23. Luke 6. 1.
[b] Ex. 25. 30. 1 Sam. 21. 6.

which our Lord here gives them. For while nowhere is there a more explicit declaration than here of the one doctrine—That the saving knowledge of the Father depends absolutely on the sovereign "will" of the Son to impart it; yet nowhere is there a brighter utterance of the other also—That this knowledge, and the rest it brings, is open to all who will come to Christ for it, and that all who sigh for rest unto their souls are freely invited, and will be cordially welcomed, under Christ's wing. 5. But Whose voice do I hear in this incomparable Invitation? Moses was the divinely commissioned lawgiver of Israel, but I do not find him speaking so; nor did the chiefest of the apostles presume to speak so. But that is saying little. For no human lips ever ventured to come within any measurable approach to such language. We could fancy one saying—We might say it and have said it ourselves—'Come, and I will show you where rest is to be found.' But here the words are, "COME UNTO ME, AND I WILL GIVE YOU REST." To give repose even to one weary, burdened soul—much more to all of every age and every land—what mortal ever undertook this? what creature is able to do it? But here is One who undertakes it, and is conscious that He has power to do it. It is the voice of my Beloved. It is not the syren voice of the Tempter, coming to steal away our hearts from the living God—it *would* be that, if the spokesman were a creature—but it is the Only begotten of the Father, full of grace and truth; and in calling so lovingly, "Come hither to ME," He is but wooing us back to that blessed Bosom of the Father, that original and proper home of the heart, from which it is our misery that we were ever estranged. 6. As the source of all unrest is estrangement from God, so the secret of true and abiding repose is that of the prodigal, who, when at length he came to say, "I will arise and go to my Father," straightway "arose and went." But as Jesus is the way, and the truth, and the life of this return, so in *subjection to Jesus*—as Himself was in absolute subjection to His Father—is the heart's true rest. When "the love of Christ constrains us to live not unto ourselves, but unto Him who died for us, and rose again;" when we enter into His meekness and lowliness of heart who "made Himself of no reputation," and "pleased not Himself" in anything, but His Father in everything—then, and only then, shall we find rest unto our souls. Whereas those who chafe with restless discontent and ambition and self-seeking are "like the troubled sea when it cannot rest, whose waters cast up mire and dirt." 7. Although the Fathers of the Church were not wrong in calling the Fourth Gospel, 'the *spiritual* Gospel [τὸ πνευματικὸν], in contradistinction to the First Three, which they called 'the corporeal' ones [τὰ σωματικὰ]—striving thus to express the immensely higher platform of vision to which the Fourth lifts us—yet is it the same glorious Object who is held in all the Four; and while the Fourth enshrines some of its most divine and spiritual teachings in a framework of exquisitely concrete historical fact, the First Three rise at times—as Matthew here, and Luke in the corresponding passage (x. 21, 22)—into a region of pure Joannean thought; insomuch that on reading the last six verses of this Section, we seem to be reading out of the 'spiritual' Gospel. In fact, it is all corporeal and all spiritual; only, the one side was committed peculiarly to the First Three Evangelists, "by the same Spirit;" the other, to the Fourth Evangelist, "by the same Spirit"—"but all these worketh that one and the self-same Spirit, dividing to every man severally as He will."

CHAP. XII. 1-8.—PLUCKING CORN-EARS ON THE SABBATH DAY. (= Mark ii. 23-28; Luke vi. 1-5.)

The season of the year when this occurred is determined by the event itself. Ripe corn-ears are only found in the fields just before harvest. The barley harvest seems clearly intended here, at the close of our March and beginning of our April. It coincided with the Passover-season, as the wheat harvest with Pentecost. But in Luke (vi. 1) we have a still more definite note of time, if we could be certain of the meaning of the peculiar term which he employs to express it. "It came to pass (he says) on the sabbath, which was the *first-second*" [σαββάτῳ δευτεροπρώτῳ]—for that is the proper rendering of the word, and not "the second sabbath after the first," as in our version. Of the various conjectures what this may mean, that of *Scaliger* is the most approved, and, as we think, the freest from difficulty, namely, 'the first sabbath after the second day of the Passover;' that is, the first of the seven sabbaths which were to be reckoned from the second day of the Passover, which was itself a sabbath, until the next feast, the feast of Pentecost (Lev. xxiii. 15, 16; Deut. xvi. 9, 10). In this case, the day meant by the Evangelist is the first of those seven sabbaths intervening between Passover and Pentecost. And if we are right in regarding the "feast" mentioned in John v. 1 as a *Passover*, and consequently the second during our Lord's public ministry (see on that passage), this plucking of the ears of corn must have occurred immediately after the scene and the Discourse recorded in John v., which, doubtless, would induce our Lord to hasten His departure for the north, to avoid the wrath of the Pharisees, which He had kindled at Jerusalem. Here, accordingly, we find Him in the fields—on His way probably to Galilee. **1. At that time Jesus went on the sabbath day through the corn**—"the corn fields" (Mark ii. 23; Luke vi. 1). **and his disciples were an hungered**—not as one may be before his regular meals; but evidently from shortness of provisions; for Jesus defends their plucking the corn-ears and eating them on the plea of *necessity*. **and began to pluck the ears of corn, and to eat**—"rubbing them in their hands" (Luke vi. 1). **2. But when the Pharisees saw it, they said unto him, Behold, thy disciples do that which is not lawful to do upon the sabbath day.** The act itself was expressly permitted (Deut. xxiii. 25). But as being "servile work," which was prohibited on the sabbath day, it was regarded as sinful. **3. But he said unto them, Have ye not read**—or as Mark has it, "Have ye never read"—**what David did** (1 Sam. xxi. 1-6), **when he was an hungered, and they that were with him; 4. How he entered into**

of God, and did eat [c]the showbread, which was not lawful for him to eat,
5 neither for them which were with him, [d]but only for the priests? Or
have ye not read in the [e]Law, how that on the sabbath days the priests
6 in the temple profane the sabbath, and are blameless? But I say unto
7 you, That in this place is *one* [f]greater than the temple. But if ye had
known what *this* meaneth, I [g]will have mercy, and not sacrifice, ye would
8 not have condemned the guiltless. For the [h]Son of man is Lord even
of the sabbath day.
9 And [i]when he was departed thence, he went into their synagogue:
10 And, behold, there was a man which had *his* hand withered. And they
asked him, saying, [j]Is it lawful to heal on the sabbath days? that they

A. D. 31.
c Ex. 25. 30. Lev. 24. 5.
d Ex. 29. 32. Lev. 8. 31.
e Num. 28. 9. John 7. 22.
f 2 Chr. 6. 18. Hag. 2. 7, 9.
g Hos. 6. 6.
h Dan. 7. 13.
i Mark 3. 1.
j Luke 13. 14. Luke 14. 3.

the house of God, and did eat the showbread, which was not lawful for him to eat, neither for them which were with him, but only for the priests? No example could be more apposite than this. The man after God's own heart, of whom the Jews ever boasted, when suffering in God's cause and straitened for provisions, asked and obtained from the high priest what, according to the law, it was illegal for any one save the priests to touch. Mark (ii. 26) says this occurred "in the days of Abiathar the high priest." But this means not during his high priesthood—for it was under that of his father Ahimelech—but simply, in his time. Ahimelech was soon succeeded by Abiathar, whose connection with David, and prominence during his reign, may account for his name, rather than his father's, being here introduced. Yet there is not a little confusion in what is said of these priests in different parts of the Old Testament. Thus he is called both the son and the father of Ahimelech (1 Sam. xxii. 20; 2 Sam. viii. 17); and Ahimelech is called Ahiah (1 Sam. xiv. 3), and Abimelech (1 Chr. xviii. 16). **5. Or have ye not read in the Law, how that on the sabbath days the priests in the temple profane the sabbath**—by doing "servile work,"—**and are blameless?** The double offerings required on the sabbath day (Num. xxviii. 9) could not be presented, and the new-baked showbread (Lev. xxiv. 5; 1 Chr. ix. 32) could not be prepared and presented every sabbath morning, without a good deal of servile work on the part of the priests; not to speak of circumcision, which, when the child's eighth day happened to fall on a sabbath, had to be performed by the priests on that day. (See on John vii. 22, 23.) **6. But I say unto you, That in this place is one greater** [μείζων] **than the temple**—or rather, according to the reading which is best supported [μεῖζον], 'something greater.' The argument stands thus: 'The ordinary rules for the observance of the sabbath give way before the requirements of the temple; but there are rights here before which the temple itself must give way.' Thus indirectly, but not the less decidedly, does our Lord put in His own claims to consideration in this question—claims to be presently put in even more nakedly. **7. But if ye had known what [this] meaneth, I will have mercy, and not sacrifice,** (Hos. vi. 6; Mic. vi. 6-8, &c.) See on ch. ix. 13. **ye would not have condemned the guiltless:**—*q. d.*, 'Had ye understood the great principle of all religion, which the Scripture everywhere recognizes—that ceremonial observances must give way before moral duties, and particularly the necessities of nature—ye would have refrained from these captious complaints against men who in this matter are blameless.' But our Lord added a specific application of this great principle to the law of the sabbath, preserved only in Mark: "And he said unto them, the sabbath was made for man, and not man for the sabbath" (Mark ii. 27). A glorious and far-reaching maxim, alike for the permanent establishment of the sabbath and the true freedom of its observance. **8. For the Son of man is Lord [even] of the sabbath day.** [The bracketed word "even"—καὶ—should not be in the text, as the overwhelming weight of authority against it shows.] In what sense now is the Son of man Lord of the sabbath day? Not surely to abolish it—that surely were a strange lordship, especially just after saying that it was made or instituted [ἐγένετο] for MAN—but to *own* it, to *interpret* it, to *preside over* it, and to *ennoble* it, by merging it in "the Lord's Day" (Rev. i. 10), breathing into it an air of liberty and love necessarily unknown before, and thus making it the nearest resemblance to the eternal sabbatism.

Remarks.—1. How affecting are the glimpses, of which this is one, which the Gospel History furnishes of the straitened circumstances into which once and again our Lord found Himself in the discharge of His public work! Doubtless, He whose is every beast of the forest, and the cattle upon a thousand hills, could have easily and simply supplied Him, or sent "twelve legions of angels" to minister to Him. But He did not; partly, that we might know how "poor He who was rich for our sakes became, that we through His poverty might be rich," and partly, no doubt, to give Him an experimental taste of His people's and His servants' straits, and thus assure them of His sympathy with them, and ability to succour them. 2. How valuable is an intelligent and ready familiarity with Scripture, when beset by the temptations of Satan (see on ch. iv. 3, &c.) and the cavils of captious men! 3. How miserable a thing is a slavish adherence to the letter of Scripture, which usually the closer it is occasions only a wider departure from its spirit! 4. How can the teaching of this Section be made to agree with the theory of the temporary and local character of the sabbath-law, and its abrogation under the Gospel? (See on Rom. xiv. 6.)

9-21. THE HEALING OF A WITHERED HAND ON THE SABBATH DAY, AND RETIREMENT OF JESUS TO AVOID DANGER. (=Mark iii. 1-12; Luke vi. 6-11.)

Healing of a Withered Hand (9-14). **9. And when he was departed thence**—but "on another sabbath" (Luke vi. 6), **he went into their synagogue**—"and taught." He had now, no doubt, arrived in Galilee; but this, it would appear, did not occur at Capernaum, for after it was over He "withdrew Himself," it is said, "*to the sea*" (Mark iii. 7), whereas Capernaum was *at* the sea. **10. And, behold, there was a man which had his hand withered**—disabled by paralysis (as 1 Kings xiii. 4). It was his right hand, as Luke graphically notes. **And they asked him, saying, Is it lawful to heal on the sabbath days? that they might accuse him.** Matthew and Luke say

11 might accuse him. And he said unto them, What man shall there be
among you that shall have one sheep, and [k]if it fall into a pit on the
12 sabbath day, will he not lay hold on it, and lift *it* out? How much then
is a man better than a sheep? Wherefore it is lawful to do well on the
13 sabbath days. Then saith he to the man, Stretch forth thine hand.
And he stretched *it* forth; and it was restored whole, like as the other.
14 Then [l]the Pharisees went out, and [1]held a council against him, how
they might destroy him.
15 But when Jesus [m]knew *it*, [n]he withdrew himself from thence: and
16 great multitudes followed him, and he healed them all; and charged
17 them that they should not make him known: that [o]it might be fulfilled
18 which was spoken by Esaias the prophet, saying, Behold [p]my servant,
whom I have chosen; my beloved, in whom my soul is well pleased: I
will put [q]my Spirit upon him, and he shall show judgment to the Gen-
19 tiles. He shall not strive, nor cry; neither shall any man hear his voice
20 in the streets. A [r]bruised reed shall he not break, and smoking flax

A. D. 31.
[k] Ex. 23. 4. Deut. 22. 4.
[l] Mark 3. 6. Luke 6. 11. John 5. 18. John 10. 39. John 11. 53.
[1] Or, took counsel.
[m] Heb. 4. 13. Ps. 139. 2.
[n] Mark 3. 7.
[o] Num. 23.19. Isa. 49. 5, 6. Isa. 52. 13.
[p] Isa. 42. 1. ch. 3. 16.
[q] Isa. 61. 1. ch. 11. 28.
[r] Isa. 40. 11.

they "watched Him whether He would heal on the sabbath day." They were now come the length of dogging His steps, to collect materials for a charge of impiety against Him. It is probable that it was to their *thoughts* rather than their words that Jesus addressed Himself in what follows. **11. And he said unto them, What man shall there be among you that shall have one sheep, and if it fall into a pit on the sabbath day, will he not lay hold on it, and lift it out? 12. How much then is a man better than a sheep?** Resistless appeal! "A righteous man regardeth the life of his beast" (Prov. xii. 10), and would instinctively rescue it from death or suffering on the sabbath day; how much more his nobler fellow-man. But the reasoning, as given in the other two Gospels, is singularly striking: "But He knew their thoughts, and said to the man which had the withered hand, Rise up, and stand forth in the midst. And he arose and stood forth. Then said Jesus unto them, I will ask you one thing; Is it lawful on the sabbath days to do good, or to do evil? to save life or to destroy it?" (Luke vi. 8, 9) or as in Mark (iii. 4) "to kill?" He thus shuts them up to this startling alternative: 'Not to do good, when it is in the power of our hand to do it, is to do evil; not to save life, when we can, is to kill'—and must the letter of the sabbath-rest be kept at this expense? This unexpected thrust shut their mouths. By this great ethical principle our Lord, we see, held Himself bound, as Man. But here we must turn to Mark, whose graphic details make the second Gospel so exceedingly precious. "When He had looked round about on them with anger, being grieved for the hardness of their hearts, He saith unto the man" (Mark iii. 5). This is one of the very few passages in the Gospel History which reveal our Lord's *feelings.* How holy this anger was, appears from the "grief" which mingled with it at "the hardness of their hearts." **13. Then saith he to the man, Stretch forth thine hand. And he stretched it forth**—the power to obey going forth with the word of command. **and it was restored whole, like as the other.** The poor man, having faith in this wonderful Healer—which no doubt the whole scene would singularly help to strengthen—disregarded the proud and venomous Pharisees, and thus gloriously put them to shame. **14. Then the Pharisees went out, and held a council against him, how they might destroy him.** This is the first explicit mention of their murderous designs against our Lord. Luke (vi. 11) says "they were filled with madness, and communed one with another what they might do to Jesus." But their doubt was not, *whether* to get rid of Him, but *how* to compass it. Mark (iii. 6), as usual, is more definite: "The Pharisees went forth, and straightway took counsel with the Herodians against Him, how they might destroy Him." These Herodians were supporters of Herod's dynasty, created by Cæsar—a political rather than religious party. The Pharisees regarded them as untrue to their religion and country. But here we see them combining together against Christ, as a common enemy. So on a subsequent occasion, Matt. xxii. 15, 16.

Jesus Retires to Avoid Danger (15-21). **15. But when Jesus knew it, he withdrew himself from thence**—whither, our Evangelist says not; but Mark (iii. 7) says "it was *to the sea*"—to some distance, no doubt, from the scene of the miracle, the madness, and the plotting just recorded. **and great multitudes followed him, and he healed them all.** Mark gives the following interesting details: "A great multitude from Galilee followed Him, and from Judea, and from Jerusalem, and from Idumea, and from beyond Jordan; and they about Tyre and Sidon, a great multitude, when they had heard what great things he did, came unto Him. And he spake to His disciples, that a small ship"—or 'wherry' [πλοιάριον]—"should wait on Him because of the multitude, lest they should throng Him. For He had healed many; insomuch that they pressed upon Him for to touch Him, as many as had plagues. And unclean spirits, when they saw Him, fell down before Him, and cried, saying, Thou art the Son of God. And He straitly charged them that they should not make Him known" (Mark iii. 7-12). How glorious this extorted homage to the Son of God! But as this was not the time, so neither were they the fitting preachers, as *Bengel* says. (See on Mark i. 25, and cf. Jas. ii. 19.) Coming back now to our Evangelist: after saying "He healed them all," he continues, **16. And charged them**—the healed—**that they should not make him known.** (See on ch. viii. 4.) **17. That it might be fulfilled which was spoken by Esaias the prophet, saying** (Isa. xlii. 1), **18. Behold my servant, whom I have chosen; my beloved, in whom my soul is well pleased: I will put my Spirit upon him, and he shall show judgment to the Gentiles. 19. He shall not strive, nor cry; neither shall any man hear his voice in the streets. 20. A bruised reed shall he not break, and smoking flax shall he not quench, till he send forth judgment unto victory**—"unto truth," says the

21 shall he not quench, till he send forth judgment unto victory. And in
his name shall the Gentiles trust.
22 Then [s]was brought unto him one possessed with a devil, blind and
dumb: and he healed him, insomuch that the blind and dumb both
23 spake and saw. And all the people were amazed, and said, Is not this

A. D. 31.

[s] ch. 9. 32. Mark 3. 11. Mark 9. 17. Luke 11. 14.

Hebrew original, and the LXX. also. But our Evangelist merely seizes the spirit, instead of the letter of the prediction in this point. The grandeur and completeness of Messiah's victories would prove, it seems, not more wonderful than the unobtrusive noiselessness with which they were to be achieved. And whereas one rough touch will break a bruised reed, and quench the flickering, smoking flax, His it should be, with matchless tenderness, love, and skill, to lift up the meek, to strengthen the weak hands and confirm the feeble knees, to comfort all that mourn, to say to them that are of a fearful heart, Be strong, fear not. **21. And in his name shall the Gentiles trust.** Part of His present audience were Gentiles —from Tyre and Sidon--first-fruits of the great Gentile harvest, contemplated in the prophecy.

Remarks.—1. Did Christians habitually act on the great principle by which our Lord held Himself bound—that to neglect any opportunity of doing good is to do evil—what a different face would the Church, and society, and even the world at large, soon put on! And shall not we who write, and we who read or hear these things, strive prayerfully for ourselves to act upon it? 2. What a picture of finely-balanced sensibilities have we in the emotions of "anger" and "grief" which the conduct of the Pharisees on this occasion kindled in the bosom of Jesus! It is possible, we see, to "be angry and sin not" (Eph. iv. 26); but first, the anger must not be causeless (see on ch. v. 22); and next, even though just, nay, though demanded by the occasion, as in the present case, that anger is never sinless, unless when "grief" for what kindles the "anger" mingles with and tempers it. 3. In the remarkable command, to stretch forth a withered hand, we have an illustration of such seemingly unreasonable calls as these: "Prophesy upon these bones, and say unto them, O ye dry bones, hear the word of the Lord" (Ezek. xxxvii. 4); "Incline your ear, and come unto me: hear, and your soul shall live" (Isa. lv. 3); "Awake thou that sleepest, and arise from the dead, and Christ shall give thee light" (Eph. v. 14). To ask dry bones to hear and live, and call upon the dead to listen and live, and demand from the impotent an exercise of power—there is apparent mockery in all this. Yet as the dry bones, in the vision, when prophesied to as commanded, did hear and obey; and the withered hand found power to extend itself—even so, it is no vain thing to say to the dead in sin, "Hear, and your soul shall live." Your "wise and prudent" (see on ch. xi. 25), will demonstrate to you, that one or other of these things must be false:—'either they are *not* dead, or, if they be, they can't hear; and if they hear, you need not add "and your soul shall live," for they are alive already.' But if the narrative of this Section be not a fable, all such reasoning is false; and as long as the Gospel History lives, this narrative will stand out at once as a directory and as a glorious encouragement, to preach to the dead in sin as the divinely appointed means of summoning them into life. 4. Determined prejudice against the truth is only irritated by additional evidence. Of this the whole conduct of the Pharisees towards our Lord forms one varied, vivid, and affecting illustration. 5. If the enemies of the truth, notwithstanding their mutual jealousies and discords, find it easy to unite and co-operate against the truth which they feel a common interest in crushing, how shameful is it that Christians should allow their petty differences to prevent combined action for the advancement of their common Christianity! 6. The predicted noiselessness of Messiah's footsteps, and the gentleness of His dealings with feeble and tender souls, opens up a great general principle of moral and spiritual strength. This was grandly illustrated to Elijah. Standing on Mount Horeb, the Lord passed by, while a great and strong wind rent the mountains, and brake in pieces the rocks before him; but the Lord was not in the *wind:* and after the wind an earthquake; but the Lord was not in the *earthquake:* and after the earthquake a fire; but the Lord was not in the *fire:* and after the fire, *a still small voice:* And it was so, when Elijah heard it, that he wrapped his face in his mantle (1 Ki. xix. 11-13). Yes, in that still small voice the prophet felt the immediate presence of God, as he had not done in the wind, nor in the earthquake, nor in the fire. True power is quiet. Even "a *soft* answer turneth away wrath" (Prov. xv. 1); and how grand—though all noiseless and imperceptible—is the growth of the animal and vegetable world! Let the servants of Christ, then, not estimate the value of the work done in His service by the sound of their movements and the noise of the machinery, but by the steady silent purpose and the persistent activity with which they prosecute the work given them to do.

22-37.—A Blind and Dumb Demoniac Healed, and Reply to the Malignant Explanation put upon it. (=Mark iii. 20-30; Luke xi. 14-23.)

The precise time of this Section is uncertain. Judging from the statements with which Mark introduces it, we should conclude that it was when our Lord's popularity was approaching its zenith, and so, before the feeding of the five thousand. But, on the other hand, the advanced state of the charges brought against our Lord, and the plainness of His warnings and denunciations in reply, seem to favour the later period at which Luke introduces it. "And the multitude," says Mark (iii. 20, 21), "cometh together again," referring back to the immense gathering which Mark had before recorded (ch. ii. 2)—"so that they could not so much as eat bread. And when His friends" [οἱ παρ' αὐτοῦ]—or rather, 'relatives,' as appears from verse 31, and see on ch. xii. 46—"heard of it, they went out to lay hold on Him: for they said, He is beside Himself" [ἐξέστη]. Compare 2 Cor. v. 13, "For whether we be beside ourselves [ἐξέστημεν], it is *to God.*"

22. Then was brought unto him one possessed with a devil—or 'a demonized person' [δαιμονιζόμενος]—**blind and dumb: and he healed him, insomuch that the blind and dumb both spake and saw. 23. And all the people were amazed, and said, Is not this the son of David?** [Μήτι οὗτός ἐστιν ὁ υἱὸς Δαβίδ?] The form of the interrogative requires this to be rendered, 'Is this the Son of David?' And as questions put in this form (in Greek) suppose doubt, and expect rather a negative answer, the meaning is, 'Can it possibly be?'—the people thus indicating their secret impression that this *must* be He; yet saving them-

24 [t]the son of David? But [u]when the Pharisees heard *it*, they said, This
fellow doth not cast out devils, but by [2]Beelzebub the prince of the devils.
25 And Jesus [v]knew their thoughts, and said unto them, Every kingdom
divided against itself is brought to desolation; and every city or house
26 divided against itself shall not stand: and if Satan cast out Satan, he
27 is divided against himself; how shall then his kingdom stand? And
if I by Beelzebub cast out devils, by whom do your children cast
28 *them* out? therefore they shall be your judges. But if I cast out
devils by the Spirit of God, then [w]the kingdom of God is come unto
29 you. Or [x]else how can one enter into a strong man's house, and
spoil his goods, except he first bind the strong man? and then he
30 will spoil his house. He that is not with me is against me; and
31 he that gathereth not with me scattereth abroad. Wherefore I say
unto you, [y]All manner of sin and blasphemy shall be forgiven unto men:
[z]but the blasphemy *against* the *Holy* Ghost shall not be forgiven unto
32 men. And whosoever [a]speaketh a word against the Son of man, [b]it shall
be forgiven him: but whosoever speaketh against the Holy Ghost, it
shall not be forgiven him, neither in this world, neither in the *world* to

A. D. 31.
t Rom. 9. 5.
u Mark 3. 22.
2 Beelzebul.
v ch. 9. 4. John 2. 25. Rev. 2. 23.
w Dan. 2. 44. Dan. 7. 14. Luke 1. 33. Luke 11. 20. Luke 17. 20. Heb. 12. 28.
x Isa. 49. 24.
y Mark 3. 28. Luke 12. 10. Heb. 10. 26. 1 John 5. 16.
z Acts 7. 51. Heb. 6. 4.
a ch. 11. 19. ch. 13. 55. John 7. 12.
b 1 Tim. 1. 13.

selves from the wrath of the ecclesiastics, which a direct assertion of it would have brought upon them. (See on a similar question in John iv. 29; and on the phrase, "Son of David," on ch. ix. 27.) **24. But when the Pharisees heard it.** Mark (iii. 22) says "the scribes which came down from Jerusalem;" so that this had been a hostile party of the ecclesiastics, who had come all the way from Jerusalem to collect materials for a charge against Him. (See on *v.* 14.) **they said, This fellow** [Οὗτος]—an expression of contempt—**doth not cast out devils, but by Beelzebub**—rather, Beelzebul (see on ch. x. 25)—**the prince of the devils.** Two things are here implied—first, that the bitterest enemies of our Lord were unable to deny the reality of His miracles; and next, that they believed in an *organized infernal kingdom of evil*, under one chief. This belief would be of small consequence, had not our Lord set His seal to it; but this He immediately does. Stung by the unsophisticated testimony of "all the people," they had no way of holding out against His claims, but by the desperate shift of ascribing His miracles to Satan.

25. And Jesus knew their thoughts—"called them" (Mark iii. 23), **and said unto them, Every kingdom divided against itself is brought to desolation; and every city or house**—that is, household—**divided against itself shall not stand: 26. And if Satan cast out Satan, he is divided against himself; how shall then his kingdom stand?** The argument here is irresistible: 'No organized society can stand—whether kingdom, city, or household—when turned against itself; such intestine war is suicidal: But the works I do are destructive of Satan's kingdom: That I should be in league with Satan, therefore, is incredible and absurd.' **27. And if I by Beelzebub cast out devils, by whom do your children**—'your sons' [υἱοὶ] meaning here, the 'disciples' or pupils of the Pharisees, who were so termed after the familiar language of the Old Testament in speaking of the sons of the prophets. (1 Ki. xx. 35; 2 Ki. ii. 3, &c.) Our Lord here seems to admit that such works were wrought by them; in which case the Pharisees stood self-condemned, as expressed in Luke (xi. 19), "Therefore shall they be your judges." **28. But if I cast out devils by the Spirit of God.** In Luke (xi. 20) it is, "with (or 'by') the finger of God." This latter expression is just a figurative way of representing the *power* of God, while the former tells us the *living Personal Agent* made use of by the Lord Jesus in every exercise of that power. **then**—"no doubt" (Luke xi. 20)—**the kingdom of God is come unto you** [ἐφ' ὑμᾶς]—rather 'upon you,' as the same expression is rendered in Luke:—*q. d.*, 'If this expulsion of Satan is, and can be, by no other than the Spirit of God, then is his Destroyer already in the midst of you, and that kingdom which is destined to supplant his, is already rising on its ruins,' **29. Or else how can one enter into a**—or rather, 'the'—**strong man's house, and spoil his goods, except he first bind the strong man? and then he will spoil his house. 30. He that is not with me is against me; and he that gathereth not with me scattereth abroad.** On this important parable, in connection with the corresponding one, *vv.* 43-45, see on Luke xi. 21-26. **31. Wherefore I say unto you, All manner of sin and blasphemy shall be forgiven unto men.** The word "blasphemy" [βλασφημία] properly signifies 'detraction' or 'slander.' In the New Testament it is applied, as it is here, to vituperation directed against God as well as against men; and in this sense it is to be understood as an aggravated form of sin. Well, says our Lord, all sin—whether in its ordinary or its more aggravated forms—shall find forgiveness with God. Accordingly, in Mark (iii. 28) the language is still stronger: "All sins shall be forgiven unto the sons of men, and blasphemies wherewith soever they shall blaspheme." There is no sin whatever, it seems, of which it may be said, 'That is not a pardonable sin.' This glorious assurance is not to be limited by what follows; but, on the contrary, what follows is to be explained by this. **but the blasphemy against the Holy Ghost shall not be forgiven unto men. 32. And whosoever speaketh a word against the Son of man, it shall be forgiven him: but whosoever speaketh against the Holy Ghost, it shall not be forgiven him, neither in this world, neither in the world to come.** In Mark the language is awfully strong, "hath never forgiveness, but is in danger of eternal damnation" [κρίσεως]—or rather, according to what appears to be the preferable, though very unusual reading, 'in danger of eternal guilt' [ἁμαρτήματος]—a guilt which he will underlie for ever. Mark has the important addition (*v.* 30), "Because they said, He hath an unclean spirit." (See on ch. x. 25). What, then, is this sin against the Holy Ghost—the unpardonable sin? One thing is clear: Its

33 come. Either make the tree good, and [c]his fruit good; or else make the
tree corrupt, and his fruit corrupt: for the tree is known by *his* fruit.
34 O [d]generation of vipers, how can ye, being evil, speak good things? [e]for
35 out of the abundance of the heart the mouth speaketh. A good man,
out of the good treasure of the heart, bringeth forth good things:
and an evil man, out of the evil treasure, bringeth forth evil things.
36 But I say unto you, That every [f]idle word that men shall speak, they
37 shall give account thereof in the day of judgment. For by thy words
thou shalt be justified, and by thy words thou shalt be condemned.

A. D. 31.
[c] ch. 7. 17. Luke 6. 43.
[d] ch. 3. 7. ch. 23. 33. Luke 3. 7. John 8. 44. 1 John 3. 10.
[e] Luke 6. 45.
[f] Eccl. 12. 14. Eph. 5. 4. Rev. 20. 12.

unpardonableness cannot arise from anything in the nature of the sin itself; for that would be a naked contradiction to the emphatic declaration of verse 31st, that all manner of sin is pardonable. And what is this but the fundamental truth of the Gospel? (See Acts xiii. 38, 39; Rom. iii. 22, 24; 1 John i. 7; &c.) Then, again, when it is said (*v.* 32), that to speak against or blaspheme the Son of man is pardonable, but the blasphemy against the Holy Ghost is not pardonable, it is not to be conceived that this arises from any greater sanctity in the one blessed Person than the other. These remarks so narrow the question, that the true sense of our Lord's words seem to disclose themselves at once. It is a contrast between slandering "the Son of man" *in His veiled condition and unfinished work*—which might be done "ignorantly, in unbelief" (1 Tim. i. 13), and slandering the same blessed Person after the blaze of glory which *the Holy Ghost* was soon to throw around His claims, and in the full knowledge of all that. This would be to slander Him with eyes open, or to do it "presumptuously." To blaspheme Christ in the former condition—when even the apostles stumbled at many things—left them still open to conviction on fuller light; but to blaspheme Him in the latter condition would be to hate the light the clearer it became, and resolutely to shut it out; which, of course, precludes salvation. (See on Heb. x. 26-29.) The Pharisees had not as yet done this; but in charging Jesus with being in league with hell they were displaying beforehand a malignant determination to shut their eyes to all evidence, and so, *bordering upon*, and *in spirit* committing the unpardonable sin. **33. Either make the tree good, &c. 34. O generation of vipers** (see on ch. iii. 7), **how can ye, being evil, speak good things? for out of the abundance of the heart the mouth speaketh**—a principle obvious enough, yet of deepest significance and vast application. In Luke vi. 45 we find it uttered as part of the Discourse delivered after the choice of the apostles. **35. A good man, out of the good treasure of the heart, bringeth** [ἐκβάλλει]—'or putteth' **forth good things: and an evil man, out of the evil treasure, bringeth**—or 'putteth' **forth evil things.** The word 'putteth' indicates the spontaneousness of what comes from the heart; for it is out of the *abundance* of the heart that the mouth speaketh. We have here a new application of a former saying (see on ch. vii. 16-20). Here, the sentiment is, 'There are but two kingdoms, interests, parties—with the proper workings of each: If I promote the one, I cannot belong to the other; but they that set themselves in wilful opposition to the kingdom of light openly proclaim to what other kingdom they belong. As for you, in what ye have now uttered ye have but revealed the venomous malignity of your hearts.' **36. But I say unto you, That every idle word that men shall speak, they shall give account thereof in the day of judgment.** They might say, 'It was nothing; we meant no evil; we merely threw out a supposition, as one way of accounting for the miracle we witnessed; if it will not stand, let it go; why make so much of it, and bear down with such severity for it?' Jesus replies, 'It was not nothing, and at the great day will not be treated as nothing: Words, as the index of the heart, however idle they may seem, will be taken account of, whether good or bad, in estimating character in the day of judgment.'

Remarks.—1. Instead of wondering that our Lord should have been thought "beside Himself," by those who were totally unable to sympathize with, or even to comprehend, His exalted views, His compassionate feelings, His gracious errand, and the preciousness of the time allotted for the execution of it, this is precisely what we might have expected from those who "judged after the flesh." Nor is it any wonder, if those who tread the most in His steps are similarly misunderstood and misrepresented. (See on 2 Cor. v. 13.) 2. When we see the vast organized unseen kingdom of evil, though full of contradiction and division within itself, so tremendously harmonious in its opposition to truth and righteousness, what a consolation is it to know that "for this purpose the Son of God was manifested, that he might destroy the works of the devil" (1 John iii. 8), subvert his kingdom, and utterly bruise the serpent's head (Gen. iii. 15)! 3. Let scoffers at Christianity tremble. For, if they tread under foot the Son of God, and do despite unto the Spirit of grace, "there remaineth no more sacrifice for sins," and nothing more to be done by the Spirit of grace (Heb. x. 26-29); and having poured contempt upon the uttermost provisions of Heaven for their restoration to eternal life, they shut themselves up by their own act and deed, and, with their eyes open, to irremediable ruin. But 4. How distressing is it, on the other hand, to find tender consciences making themselves miserable with the apprehension that the guilt of the unpardonable sin lies upon them? If this arise, as in many cases it does, from a morbid state of the nervous system, acting on a religious temperament, the remedy lies beyond the limits of this Exposition. But if it be the fruit of inaccurate conceptions of Bible teaching, surely a dispassionate consideration of verses 31, 32 of the present Section, as above expounded, ought to dissipate such apprehensions. And if the language of 1 John v. 16, 17, should seem still to present some difficulty (see on those verses)—let not the plain sense of the great catholic statements of Scripture be stripped of their value by the supposed meaning of some isolated and obscure passage; but, in spite of all such obscurities, let the trembling sinner assure himself of this, that "*all* manner of sin and blasphemy shall be forgiven unto men," and that "the blood of Jesus Christ, God's Son, cleanseth from *all* sin."

38-50.—A SIGN DEMANDED, AND THE REPLY—HIS MOTHER AND BRETHREN SEEK TO SPEAK WITH HIM, AND THE ANSWER. (= Luke xi. 16, 24-36; Mark iii. 31-35; Luke viii. 19-21.)

A Sign demanded, and the Reply (38-45). The

38 Then [g]certain of the scribes and of the Pharisees answered, saying,
39 Master, we would see a sign from thee. But he answered and said unto
them, An evil and [h]adulterous generation seeketh after a sign; and there
40 shall no sign be given to it, but the sign of the prophet Jonas: For
[i]as Jonas was three days and three nights in the whale's belly, so
shall the Son of man be three days and three nights in the heart
41 of the earth. The [j]men of Nineve shall rise in judgment with this
generation, and [k]shall condemn it: [l]because they repented at the preach-
42 ing of Jonas; and, behold, [m]a greater than Jonas *is* here. The [n]queen
of the south shall rise up in the judgment with this generation, and shall
condemn it: for she came from the uttermost parts of the earth to hear
the wisdom of Solomon; and, behold, a [o]greater than Solomon *is* here.
43 When [p]the unclean spirit is gone out of a man, [q]he walketh through dry
44 places, seeking rest, and findeth none. Then he saith, I will return into
my house from whence I came out; and when he is come, he findeth *it*
45 empty, swept, and garnished. Then [r]goeth he, and taketh with himself
seven other spirits more wicked than himself, and they enter in and
dwell there: and [s]the last *state* of that man is worse than the first.
Even so shall it be also unto this wicked generation.

A. D. 31.

[g] ch. 16. 1. Mark 8. 11. Luke 11. 16. John 2. 18. 1 Cor. 1. 22.
[h] Isa. 57. 3. Mark 8. 38. John 4. 48.
[i] Jon. 1. 17.
[j] Luke 11. 32.
[k] Jer. 3. 11. Ezek. 16. 51.
[l] Jon. 3. 5.
[m] Isa. 9. 6. Rom. 9. 5.
[n] 1 Ki. 10. 1. 2 Chr. 9. 1.
[o] Col. 2. 2, 3.
[p] Luke 11. 24.
[q] Job 1. 7. 1 Pet. 5. 8.
[r] Isa. 66. 3, 4.
[s] Heb. 6. 4. Heb. 10. 26.

occasion of this Section was manifestly the same with that of the preceding. **38. Then certain of the scribes and of the Pharisees answered, saying, Master** [Διδάσκαλε]—'Teacher,' equivalent to 'Rabbi'—**we would see a sign from thee**—"a sign from heaven" (Luke xi. 16); something of an immediate and decisive nature, to show, not that his miracles were *real*—that they seemed willing to concede—but that they were from above, not from beneath. These were not the same class with those who charged Him with being in league with Satan (as we see from Luke xi. 15, 16); but as the spirit of both was similar, the tone of severe rebuke is continued. **39. But he answered and said unto them**—"when the people were gathered thick together" (Luke xi. 29), **An evil and adulterous generation.** This latter expression is best explained by Jer. iii. 20, "Surely as a wife treacherously departeth from her husband, so have ye dealt treacherously with me, O house of Israel, saith the Lord." For this was the relationship in which He stood to the covenant people—"I am married unto you" (Jer. iii. 14). **seeketh after a sign.** In the eye of Jesus this class were but the spokesmen of their generation, the exponents of the reigning spirit of unbelief. **and there shall no sign be given to it, but the sign of the prophet Jonas: 40. For as Jonas was**—"a sign unto the Ninevites, so shall also the Son of man be to this generation" (Luke xi. 30). For as Jonas was **three days and three nights in the whale's belly** (Jon. i. 17), **so shall the Son of man be three days and three nights in the heart of the earth.** This was the second public announcement of His resurrection three days after His death. (For the first, see John ii. 19.) Jonah's case was analogous to this, as being a signal judgment of God; reversed in three days; and followed by a glorious mission to the Gentiles. The expression "in the heart of the earth," suggested by the expression of Jonah with respect to the sea (ii. 3, in LXX.), means simply the grave, but this considered as the most emphatic expression of real and total entombment. The period during which He was to lie in the grave is here expressed in round numbers, according to the Jewish way of speaking, which was to regard any part of a day, however small, included within a period of days, as a full day. (See 1 Sam. xxx. 12, 13; Esth. iv. 16; v. 1; Matt. xxvii. 63, 64; &c.) **41. The men of Nineve shall rise in judgment with this generation, and shall condemn it: because they repented at the preaching of Jonas; and, behold, a greater than Jonas is here.** The Ninevites, though heathens, repented at a man's preaching; while they, God's covenant people, repented not at the preaching of the Son of God—whose supreme dignity is rather implied here than expressed. **42. The queen of the south shall rise up in the judgment with this generation, and shall condemn it: for she came from the uttermost parts of the earth to hear the wisdom of Solomon; and, behold, a greater than Solomon is here.** The queen of Sheba—a tract in Arabia, near the shores of the Red Sea—came from a remote country, "south" of Judea, to hear the wisdom of a mere man, though a gifted one, and was transported with wonder at what she saw and heard (1 Ki. x. 1-9). They, when a Greater than Solomon had come *to them*, despised and rejected, slighted and slandered Him.

43-45. When the unclean spirit is gone out of a man, &c. On this important parable, in connection with the corresponding one—*v.* 29—see on Luke xi. 21-26.

A charming little incident, given only in Luke xi. 27, 28, seems to have its proper place here. "And it came to pass, as He spake these things, a certain woman of the company" [ἐκ τοῦ ὄχλου]—'out of the crowd,' "lifted up her voice and said unto Him, Blessed is the womb that bare thee, and the paps which Thou hast sucked." With true womanly feeling, she envies the mother of such a wonderful Teacher. And a higher and better than she had said as much before her (see on Luke i. 28). 42. How does our Lord, then, treat it? He is far from condemning it. He only holds up as "blessed rather" another class: "But he said, Yea rather, blessed are they that hear the word of God, and keep it"—in other words, the humblest real saint of God. How utterly alien is this sentiment from the teaching of the Church of Rome, which would doubtless excommunicate any one of its members that dared to talk in such a strain!

His Mother and Brethren Seek to Speak with Him, and the Answer (46-50). **46. While he yet talked to the people, behold, his mother and his brethren** (see on ch. xiii. 55, 56) **stood without, desiring to speak with him**—"and could not come

46 While he yet talked to the people, behold, [t]*his* mother and [u]his
47 brethren stood without, desiring to speak with him. Then one said unto
him, Behold, thy mother and thy brethren stand without, desiring to
48 speak with thee. But he answered and said unto him that told him,
49 Who is my mother? and who are my brethren? And he stretched forth
his hand toward his disciples, and said, Behold my mother and my
50 brethren! For [v]whosoever shall do the will of my Father which is in
heaven, the same is my brother, and sister, and mother.

13 THE same day went Jesus out of the house, [a]and sat by the sea-side.
2 And [b]great multitudes were gathered together unto him, so that [c]he
went into a ship, and sat; and the whole multitude stood on the shore.
3 And he spake many things unto them in parables, saying,
4 Behold, a sower went forth to sow: and when he sowed, some *seeds* fell
5 by the way-side, and the fowls came and devoured them up: some fell

A. D. 31.

t Mark 3. 31. Luke 8. 19.
u Mark 6. 3. John 2. 12. John 7. 3,5. Acts 1. 14. 1 Cor. 9. 5. Gal. 1. 19.
v John 15. 14. Gal. 5. 6. Gal. 6. 15. Col. 3. 11. Heb. 2. 11.

CHAP. 13.
a Mark 4. 1.
b Luke 8, 4.
c Luke 5. 3.

at Him for the press" (Luke viii. 19). For what purpose these came, we learn from Mark iii. 20, 21. In His zeal and ardour He seemed indifferent both to food and repose, and "they went to lay hold of Him" as one "beside himself." Mark says graphically, "And the multitude sat about Him" [περὶ αὐτόν]—or 'around Him.' **47. Then one said unto him, Behold, thy mother and thy brethren stand without, desiring to speak with thee. 48. But he answered and said unto him that told him, Who is my mother? and who are my brethren?** Absorbed in the awful warnings He was pouring forth, He felt this to be an unseasonable interruption, fitted to dissipate the impression made upon the large audience—such an interruption as duty to the nearest relatives did not require Him to give way to. But instead of a direct rebuke, He seizes on the incident to convey a sublime lesson, expressed in a style of inimitable condescension. **49. And he stretched forth his hand toward his disciples.** How graphic is this! It is the language evidently of an eye-witness. **and said, Behold my mother and my brethren! 50. For whosoever shall do the will of my Father which is in heaven, the same is my brother, and sister, and mother**:—*q. d.*, 'There stand here the members of a family transcending and surviving this of earth: Filial subjection to the will of my Father in heaven is the indissoluble bond of union between Me and all its members; and whosoever enters this hallowed circle becomes to Me brother, and sister, and mother!'

Remarks.—1. What strange revelations will the day of judgment make, particularly as to the relative character of some of the most, and some of the least, favoured of the human family! (*vv.* 41-42.) Verily "the last shall be first, and the first last." 2. When the demands of even the nearest and dearest relatives, urging on us only that attention to our personal interests or comforts which in other circumstances would be natural and proper, are seen to interfere with some present work of God, let the spirit of our Lord's example here be our guiding principle, rather than the suggestions of nature. 3. How glorious is the thought that there is a family even upon earth of which the Son of God holds Himself a part; a family, the loving bond and reigning principle of which is subjection to the Father of our Lord Jesus Christ, and so embracing high and low, rude and refined, bond and free, of every kindred and every age that have tasted that the Lord is gracious; a family whose members can at once understand each other and take sweetest counsel together, though meeting for the first time from the ends of the earth—while with their nearest relatives, who are but the children of this world, they have no sympathy in such things; a family which death cannot break up, but only transfer to their Father's house! Did Christians but habitually realize and act upon this, as did their blessed Master, what would be the effect upon the Church and upon the world?

CHAP. XIII. 1-52.—JESUS TEACHES BY PARABLES. (= Mark iv. 1-34; Luke viii. 4-18; xiii. 18-20.)

Introduction (1-3). **1. The same day went Jesus out of the house, and sat by the sea-[side]. 2. And great multitudes were gathered together unto him, so that he went into a ship**—the article in the received text wants authority—**and sat; and the whole multitude stood on the shore.** How graphic this picture—no doubt from the pen of an eye-witness, himself impressed with the scene! It was "the same day" on which the foregoing solemn discourse was delivered, when His kindred thought Him "beside Himself" for His indifference to food and repose—that same day, retiring to the sea-shore of Galilee, and there seating Himself, perhaps for coolness and rest, the crowds again flock around Him, and He is fain to push off from them, in the boat usually kept in readiness for Him; yet only to begin, without waiting to rest, a new course of teaching by parables to the eager multitudes that lined the shore. To the parables of our Lord there is nothing in all language to be compared, for simplicity, grace, fulness, and variety of spiritual teaching. They are adapted to all classes and stages of advancement, being understood by each according to the measure of his spiritual capacity. **3. And he spake many things unto them in parables, saying, &c.**

These parables are SEVEN in number; and it is not a little remarkable that while this is the *sacred number*, the first FOUR of them were spoken to the mixed multitude, while the remaining THREE were spoken to the Twelve in private—these divisions, *four* and *three*, being themselves notable in the symbolical arithmetic of Scripture. Another thing remarkable in the structure of these parables is, that while the first of the Seven—that of the Sower—is of the nature of an Introduction to the whole, the remaining Six consist of *three pairs*—the Second and Seventh, the Third and Fourth, and the Fifth and Sixth, corresponding to each other; each pair setting forth the same general truths, but with a certain diversity of aspect. All this can hardly be accidental.

First Parable: THE SOWER (3-9, 18-23). This Parable may be entitled, THE EFFECT OF THE WORD DEPENDENT ON THE STATE OF THE HEART. For the exposition of this parable, see on Mark iv. 1-9, 14-20.

upon [d]stony places, where they had not much earth; and forthwith they
6 sprung up, because they had no deepness of earth: and when the sun was
up, they were scorched; and because they had no [e]root, they withered
7 away: and some fell among thorns; and the thorns sprung up and
8 choked them: but other fell into good ground, and brought forth fruit,
9 some [f]an hundred-fold, some sixty-fold, some thirty-fold. Who [g]hath
ears to hear, let him hear.
10 And the disciples came, and said unto him, Why speakest thou unto
11 them in parables? He answered and said unto them, Because [h]it is
given unto you to know the mysteries of the kingdom of heaven, but to
12 them it is not given. For [i]whosoever hath, to him shall be given, and
he shall have more abundance; but whosoever hath not, from him shall
13 be taken away even that he hath. Therefore speak I to them in
parables: because they seeing, see not; and hearing, they hear not;
14 neither do they understand. And in them is fulfilled the prophecy of
Esaias, which saith, [j]By hearing ye shall hear, and shall not understand;
15 and seeing ye shall see, and shall not perceive: for this people's heart
is waxed gross, and *their* ears [k]are dull of hearing, and their eyes they
have closed; lest at any time they should see with *their* eyes, and hear
with *their* ears, and should understand with *their* heart, and should be
16 converted, and I should heal them. But [l]blessed *are* your eyes, for they

A. D. 31.

d Ezek. 11.19.
e Col. 2. 7.
f Gen. 26. 12.
g Mark 4. 9.
h ch. 11. 25. ch. 16. 17. Mark 4. 11. 1 Cor. 2. 10. 1 John 2.27. Col. 1. 26.
i Mark 4. 25. Luke 8. 18. Luke 19. 26.
j Isa. 6. 9. Ezek. 12. 2. Mark 4. 12. Luke 8. 10. John 12. 40. Acts 28. 26, 27. Rom. 11. 8. 2 Cor. 3. 14.
k Heb. 5. 11.
l ch. 16. 17. Luke 10. 23, 24. John 20. 29.

Reason for Teaching in Parables (10-17). **10. And the disciples came, and said unto him**—"they that were with Him, when they were alone" (Mark iv. 10)—**Why speakest thou unto them in parables?** Though before this He had couched some things in the parabolic form, for more vivid illustration, it would appear that He now, for the first time, formally employed this method of teaching. **11. He answered and said unto them, Because it is given unto you to know the mysteries of the kingdom of heaven.** The word "mysteries" [μυστήρια] in Scripture is not used in its classical sense—of 'religious secrets,' nor yet of 'things incomprehensible, or in their own nature difficult to be understood'—but in the sense of 'things of purely divine revelation,' and, usually, 'things darkly announced under the ancient economy, and during all that period darkly understood, but fully published under the Gospel' (1 Cor. ii. 6-10; Eph. iii. 3-6, 8, 9). "The mysteries of the kingdom of heaven," then, mean those glorious Gospel truths which at that time only the more advanced disciples could appreciate, and they but partially. **but to them it is not given.** (See on ch. xi. 25.) Parables serve the double purpose of *revealing* and *concealing;* presenting 'the mysteries of the kingdom' to those who know and relish them, though in never so small a degree, in a new and attractive light; but to those who are insensible to spiritual things yielding only, as so many tales, some temporary entertainment. **12. For whosoever hath**—that is, keeps; as a thing which he values, **to him shall be given, and he shall have more abundance**—he will be rewarded by an increase of what he so much prizes; **but whosoever hath not**—who lets this go or lie unused, as a thing on which he sets no value—**from him shall be taken away even that he hath**—or as it is in Luke (viii. 18), "what he seemeth to have" [ὃ δοκεῖ ἔχειν], or 'thinketh he hath.' This is a principle of immense importance, and, like other weighty sayings, appears to have been uttered by our Lord on more than one occasion, and in different connections. (See on ch. xxv. 9.) As a great ethical principle, we see it in operation everywhere, under the general law of *habit;* in virtue of which moral principles become stronger by exercise, while by disuse, or the exercise of their contraries, they wax weaker, and at length expire. The same principle reigns in the intellectual world, and even in the animal—if not in the vegetable also—as the facts of physiology sufficiently prove. Here, however, it is viewed as a divine ordination, as a judicial retribution in continual operation under the divine administration. **13. Therefore speak I to them in parables**—which our Lord, be it observed, did not begin to do till His miracles were malignantly ascribed to Satan. **because they seeing, see not.** They "saw," for the light shone on them as never light shone before; but they "saw not," for they closed their eyes. **and hearing, they hear not; neither do they understand.** They "heard," for He taught them who "spake as never man spake;" but they "heard not," for they took nothing in, apprehending not the soul-penetrating, life-giving words addressed to them. In Mark and Luke, what is here expressed as a human fact is represented as the fulfilment of a divine purpose—"that seeing they may see, and not perceive," &c. The explanation of this lies in the statement of the foregoing verse—that, by a fixed law of the divine administration, the duty men voluntarily refuse to do, and in point of fact do not do, they at length become morally incapable of doing. **14. And in them is fulfilled** [ἀναπληροῦται]—rather, 'is fulfilling,' or is receiving its fulfilment—**the prophecy of Esaias, which saith** (Isa. vi. 9, 10—here quoted according to the LXX.), **By hearing ye shall hear, and shall not understand, &c. 15. For this people's heart is waxed gross . . . and their eyes they have closed; lest at any time they should see . . . and hear . . . and should understand . . . and should be converted, and I should heal them.** They were thus judicially sealed up under the darkness and obduracy which they deliberately preferred to the light and healing which Jesus brought nigh to them. **16. But blessed are your eyes, for they see; and your ears, for they hear:**—*q. d.*, 'Happy ye, whose eyes and ears, voluntarily and gladly opened, are drinking in the light divine.' **17. For verily I say unto you, That many prophets and righteous**

17 see; and your ears, for they hear. For verily I say unto you, [m]That
many prophets and righteous *men* have desired to see *those things* which
ye see, and have not seen *them;* and to hear *those things* which ye hear,
and have not heard *them.*
18 Hear [n]ye therefore the parable of the sower. When any one hear-
19 eth the word of the kingdom, and understandeth *it* not, then cometh
[o]the wicked *one,* and catcheth away that which was sown in his heart.
20 This is he which received seed by the way-side. But he that received
the seed into stony places, the same is he that heareth the word, and
21 anon [p]with joy receiveth it: yet hath he not root in himself, but
dureth for a while; for when tribulation or persecution ariseth because
22 of the word, by and by [q]he is offended. He [r]also that received seed
[s]among the thorns is he that heareth the word; and the care of this
world, and the deceitfulness of riches, choke the word, and he becometh
23 unfruitful. But he that received seed into the good ground is he that
heareth the word, and understandeth *it;* which also beareth fruit, and
bringeth forth, some an hundred-fold, some sixty, some thirty.
24 Another parable put he forth unto them, saying, The kingdom of
25 heaven is likened unto a man which sowed good seed in his field: but
while men slept, [t]his enemy came and sowed tares among the wheat, and
26 went his way. But when the blade was sprung up, and brought forth
27 fruit, then appeared the tares also. So the servants of the householder
came and said unto him, Sir, didst not thou sow good seed in thy field?
28 from whence then hath it tares? He said unto them, An enemy hath
done this. The servants said unto him, Wilt thou then that we go and
29 gather them up? But he said, Nay; lest, while ye gather up the tares,
30 ye root up also the wheat with them. Let both grow together until the
harvest: and in the time of harvest I will say to the reapers, Gather ye
together first the tares, and bind them in bundles to burn them; but
[u]gather the wheat into my barn.
31 Another parable put he forth unto them, saying, [v]The kingdom of
heaven is like to a grain of mustard seed, which a man took, and sowed
32 in his field: which indeed is the least of all seeds; but when it is
grown, it is the greatest among herbs, and becometh a tree, so that the
birds of the air come and lodge in the branches thereof.
33 Another [w]parable spake he unto them; The kingdom of heaven is
like unto leaven, which a woman took and hid in three [1]measures of
meal, till the whole was leavened.
34 All these things spake Jesus unto the multitude in parables; and
35 without a parable spake he not unto them: that it might be fulfilled
which was spoken by the prophet, saying, [x]I will open my mouth in
parables; [y]I will utter things which have been kept secret from the
foundation of the world.

A. D. 31.

[m] Luke 10. 24. John 8. 56. Eph. 3. 5. Heb. 11. 13. 1 Pet. 1. 10.
[n] Mark 4. 14. Luke 8. 11.
[o] Mark 4. 15. Luke 8. 12. 2 Cor. 2. 11.
[p] Isa. 58. 2. Ezek. 33. 31. Mark 4. 16. John 5. 35. Acts 8. 13.
[q] ch. 11. 6. 2 Tim. 1. 15.
[r] ch. 19. 23. Mark 10. 23. Luke 18. 24. 1 Tim. 6. 9. 2 Tim. 4. 10.
[s] Jer. 4. 3.
[t] Luke 10. 19. 2 Cor. 11. 13-15. 1 Pet. 5. 8.
[u] ch. 3. 12. ch. 24. 31. Luke 3. 17. 1 Thes. 4. 17. 2 Thes. 2. 1.
[v] Isa. 2. 2, 3. Mic. 4. 1. Mark 4. 30. Luke 13. 18. 2 Pet. 3. 18.
[w] Luke 13. 20.
[1] The word in the Greek is a measure containing about a peck and a half, wanting a little more than a pint.
[x] Ps. 78. 2.
[y] Ps. 49. 4. Am. 3. 7. Rom. 16. 25. 1 Cor. 2. 7. Eph. 3. 9. Col. 1. 26.

men have desired [ἐπεθύμησαν]—rather, 'coveted,' **to see those things which ye see, and have not seen them; and to hear those things which ye hear, and have not heard them.** Not only were the disciples blessed above the blinded just spoken of, but favoured above the most honoured and the best that lived under the old economy, who had but glimpses of the things of the new kingdom, just sufficient to kindle in them desires not to be fulfilled to any in their day. In Luke x. 23, 24, where the same saying is repeated on the return of the Seventy—the words, instead of "many prophets and righteous men," are "many prophets *and kings;*" for several of the Old Testament saints were kings.

Second and Seventh Parables, or *First Pair:* THE WHEAT AND THE TARES, and THE GOOD AND BAD FISH (24-30; 36-43; and 47-50). The subject of both these Parables—which teach the same truth, with a slight diversity of aspect—is

THE **MIXED CHARACTER** OF THE KINGDOM IN ITS PRESENT STATE, AND THE **FINAL ABSOLUTE SEPARATION** OF THE TWO CLASSES.

The Tares and the Wheat (24-30, 36-43). **24. Another parable put he forth unto them, saying, The kingdom of heaven is likened unto a man which sowed good seed in his field.** Happily for us, these exquisite parables are, with like charming simplicity and clearness, expounded to us by the Great Preacher Himself. Accordingly, we pass to *vv.* 36-38. **Then Jesus sent the multitude away, and went into the house: and his disciples came unto him, saying, Declare unto us the parable of the tares of the field. He answered and**

36 Then Jesus sent the multitude away, and went into the house: and
his disciples came unto him, saying, Declare unto us the parable of the
37 tares of the field. He answered and said unto them, He that [z]soweth
38 the good seed is the Son of man; the [a]field is the world; the good seed
are the children of the kingdom; but the tares are [b]the children of the
39 wicked *one;* the enemy that sowed them is the devil; [c]the harvest is
40 the end of the world; and the reapers are the angels. As therefore the
tares are gathered and burned in the fire; so shall it be in the end of
41 this world. The Son of man shall send forth his angels, [d]and they shall
gather out of his kingdom all [2]things that offend, and them which do
42 iniquity, and [e]shall cast them into a furnace of fire: there shall be
43 wailing and gnashing of teeth. Then [f]shall the righteous shine forth as

A. D. 31.

[z] Isa. 61. 1.
[a] ch. 24. 14. Luke 24. 47.
[b] Gen. 3. 13. Acts 13. 10.
[c] Joel 3. 13. Rev. 14. 15.
[d] 2 Pet. 2. 1,2.
[2] Or, scandals.
[e] Rev. 19. 20. Rev. 20. 10.
[f] Dan. 12. 3. 1 Cor. 15.42.

said unto them, He that soweth the good seed is the Son of man (see on John i. 52); **the field is the world; the good seed are the children of the kingdom.** In the parable of the Sower, "the seed is the word of God" (Luke viii. 11). But here that word has been received into the heart, and has converted him that received it into a new creature, a "child of the kingdom," according to that saying of James (i. 18), "Of His own will begat He us with the word of truth, that we should be a kind of first-fruits of His creatures." It is worthy of notice that this vast field of the world is here said to be *Christ's own*—"His field," says the parable. (See Ps. ii. 8.) **25. But while men slept, his enemy came and sowed tares among the wheat, and went his way. 38. The tares are the children of the wicked one.** As this sowing could only be "while men slept," no blame seems intended, and certainly none is charged upon "the servants:" it is probably just the dress of the parable. **39. The enemy that sowed them is the devil**—emphatically "*His* enemy" (*v.* 25). See Gen. iii. 15; 1 John iii. 8. By "tares" [ζιζάνια] is meant, not what in our husbandry is so called, but some noxious plant, probably *darnel.* "The tares are the children of the wicked one;" and by their being sown "among the wheat" is meant their being deposited within the territory of the visible Church. As they resemble the children of the kingdom, so they are produced, it seems, by a similar process of "sowing"—the seeds of evil being scattered and lodging in the soil of those hearts upon which falls the seed of the word. The enemy, after sowing his "tares," "went his way"—his dark work soon done, but taking time to develop its true character. **26. But when the blade was sprung up, and brought forth fruit, then appeared the tares also**—the growth in both cases running parallel, as antagonistic principles are seen to do. **27. So the servants of the householder came**—that is, Christ's ministers—**and said unto him, Sir, didst not thou sow good seed in thy field? from whence then hath it tares?** This well expresses the surprise, disappointment, and anxiety of Christ's faithful servants and people, at the discovery of "false brethren" among the members of the Church. **28. He said unto them, An enemy hath done this.** Kind words these from a good Husbandman, honourably clearing His faithful servants of the wrong done to His field. **The servants said unto him, Wilt thou then that we go and gather them up?** Compare with this the question of James and John (Luke ix. 54), "Lord, wilt thou that we command fire to come down from heaven and consume" those Samaritans? In this kind of zeal there is usually a large mixture of carnal heat. (See Jas. i. 20.) **29. But he said, Nay**—'It will be done in due time, but not now, nor is it your business.' **lest, while ye gather up the tares, ye root up also the wheat with them.** Nothing could more clearly or forcibly teach the difficulty of distinguishing the two classes, and the high probability that in the attempt to do so these will be confounded. **30, 39. Let both grow together**—that is, in the visible Church—**until the harvest**—till the one have ripened for full salvation, the other for destruction. **The harvest is the end of the world** [συντελεία τοῦ αἰῶνος]—the period of Christ's second coming, and of the judicial separation of the righteous and the wicked. Till then, no attempt is to be made to effect such separation. But to stretch this so far as to justify allowing openly scandalous persons to remain in the communion of the Church, is to wrest the teaching of this parable to other than its proper design, and go in the teeth of apostolic injunctions (1 Cor. v). **and in the time of harvest I will say to the reapers. And the reapers are the angels.** But whose angels are they? "The Son of man shall send forth HIS angels" (*v.* 41). Compare 1 Pet. iii. 22—"Who is gone into heaven, and is on the right hand of God; angels and authorities and powers being made subject unto Him." **Gather ye together first the tares, and bind them in bundles to burn them**—"in the fire" (*v.* 40)—**but gather the wheat into my barn.** Christ, as the Judge, will separate the two classes (as in ch. xxv. 32). It will be observed that the tares are burned *before* the wheat is housed; in the exposition of the parable (*vv.* 41, 43) the same order is observed; and the same in ch. xxv. 46—as if, in some literal sense, "with thine eyes shalt thou behold and see the reward of the wicked" (Ps. xci. 8). **41. The Son of man shall send forth his angels, and they shall gather out of his kingdom**—to which they never really belonged. They usurped their place and name and outward privileges; but "the ungodly shall not stand in the judgment, nor sinners [abide] in the congregation of the righteous" (Ps. i. 5). **all things that offend** [πάντα τὰ σκάνδαλα]—all those who have proved a stumbling-block to others, **and them which do iniquity.** The former class, as the worst, are mentioned first. **42. And shall cast them into a furnace**—rather, 'the furnace' **of fire: there shall be wailing and gnashing of teeth.** What terrific strength of language—the "casting" or "flinging" expressive of indignation, abhorrence, contempt (cf. Ps. ix. 17; Dan. xii. 2); "the furnace of fire" denoting the fierceness of the torment; the "wailing" signifying the anguish this causes; while the "gnashing of teeth" is a graphic way of expressing the despair in which its remedilessness issues (see on ch. viii. 12)! **43. Then shall the righteous shine forth as the sun in the kingdom of their Father**—as if they had been under a cloud during their present association with ungodly pretenders to their character, and claimants of their privileges, and obstructors

the sun in the kingdom of their Father. Who hath ears to hear, let him
hear.
44 Again, the kingdom of heaven is like unto treasure hid in a field; the
which when a man hath found, he hideth, and for joy thereof goeth and
[g]selleth all that he hath, and [h]buyeth that field.
45 Again, the kingdom of heaven is like unto a merchant-man seeking
46 goodly pearls: who, when he had found [i]one pearl of great price, went
and sold all that he had, and bought it.

A. D. 31.

[g] ch. 19. 27. Phil. 3. 7.
[h] Pro. 23. 23. Isa. 55. 1. ch. 25. 9. Rev. 3. 18.
[i] Pro. 2. 4. Pro. 3. 14. Pro. 8. 10.

of their course. **Who hath ears to hear, let him hear.** (See on Mark iv. 9.)

The Good and Bad Fish (47-50). The object of this brief parable is the same with that of the Tares and Wheat. But as its details are fewer, so its teaching is less rich and varied. **47. Again, the kingdom of heaven is like unto a net, that was cast into the sea, and gathered of every kind.** The word here rendered "net" [σαγήνη] signifies, a large *drag-net*, which draws everything after it, suffering nothing to escape, as distinguished from 'a *casting-net*' [ἀμφίβληστρον, and δίκτυον], Mark i. 16, 18. The far-reaching efficacy of the Gospel is thus denoted. This Gospel net "gathered of every kind," meaning every variety of character. **48. Which, when it was full, they drew to shore**—for the separation will not be made till the number of the elect is accomplished—**and sat down**—expressing the deliberateness with which the judicial separation will at length be made—**and gathered the good into vessels, but cast the bad away** [τὰ δὲ σαπρὰ]—lit., 'the rotten,' but here meaning, 'the foul' or 'worthless' fish; corresponding to the "tares" of the other parable. **49. So shall it be at the end of the world: the angels shall come forth, and sever the wicked from among the just, 50. And shall cast them into the furnace of fire: there shall be wailing and gnashing of teeth.** See on verse 42. We have said that each of these two parables holds forth the same truth under a slight diversity of aspect. What is that diversity? First, the *bad*, in the former parable, are represented as vile seed sown amongst the wheat by the enemy of souls; in the latter, as foul fish drawn forth out of the great sea of human beings by the Gospel net itself. Both are important truths—that the Gospel draws within its pale, and into the communion of the visible Church, multitudes who are Christians only in name; and that the injury thus done to the Church on earth is to be traced to the wicked one. But further, while the former parable gives chief prominence to the present mixture of good and bad, in the latter, the prominence is given to the future separation of the two classes.

Remarks.—1. These two parables teach clearly the vanity of expecting a perfectly pure Church in the present state, or before Christ comes. In the latter parable, it is the Gospel net itself that gathers the bad as well as the good; and as it is by this tie that they get and keep their connection with the Church, we cannot expect so to cast that net as to draw in the good only. But, on the other hand, as the presence of tares among the wheat, in the former parable, is ascribed to the enemy of the Church and her Lord, it follows that, in so far as we *encourage* the entrance of such into the communion of the Church, we do the devil's work. Thus does this parable give as little encouragement to *laxity* as to a utopian *purism* in church-discipline. 2. When the servants, in the former parable, ask liberty to pull up the tares, that the growth of the wheat may not suffer from their presence, and that liberty is denied them, does not this rebuke *intolerance* in religion, on pretence of purging out heresy? 3. How grand is the view here given by the Great Preacher of His own majesty, as *Bengel* remarks! The field of the world into which the seed of the kingdom is cast is "*His field*" (*v.* 24); the angels who do the work of separation at the end of the world are "*His angels;*" and as it is "the Son of man that sends them forth," so in "gathering out of *His kingdom* all things that offend, and them which do iniquity," they do but obey His commands (*vv.* 30, 41.) 4. The Scripture nowhere holds out the expectation of a Millennium in which there will be none but regenerate men on the earth, in flesh and blood—or, in the language of our parable, in which the earth will be one field of wheat without any tares. It would seem to follow that there are but two great stages of Humanity under the Gospel: the present *mixed* state, and the future, final, absolutely *unmixed* condition; the Millennial era being, in that case, but a continuation of the present condition—vastly superior, indeed, and with much less mixture than we now see, but—not *essentially* differing from it, and so, having no place in this parable at all. The proper place of the Millennium, in these parables, is in the next pair. 5. Do those who talk so much of "the meekness and gentleness of Christ," as if that were the one feature of His character, set their seal to the sharp lines of His teaching in these two parables—on the subject of the tares as "the children of the wicked one," and "the enemy that sows them" being "the devil;" as to the "furnace of fire" prepared for them, the "casting" or "flinging" of them into the furnace, which that gentle Lamb of God shall demand of His angels, and the "wailing and gnashing of teeth" in which this will end? O, if men but knew it, it is just the gentleness of the Lamb which explains the eventual "wrath of the Lamb."

Third and Fourth Parables, or *Second Pair:* THE MUSTARD SEED and THE LEAVEN (31-33). The subject of both these parables, as of the first pair, is the same, but under a slight diversity of aspect: namely,

THE **GROWTH OF THE KINGDOM,** FROM THE SMALLEST BEGINNINGS TO ULTIMATE UNIVERSALITY.

The Mustard Seed (31, 32). **31. Another parable put he forth unto them, saying, The kingdom of heaven is like to a grain of mustard seed, which a man took, and sowed in his field: 32. Which indeed is the least of all seeds**—not absolutely, but popularly and proverbially, as in Luke xvii. 6, "If ye had faith as a grain of mustard seed," that is, 'never so little faith.' **but when it is grown, it is the greatest among herbs**—not absolutely, but in relation to the small size of the seed, and in warm latitudes proverbially great. **and becometh a tree, so that the birds of the air come and lodge in the branches thereof.** This is added, no doubt, to express the *amplitude* of the tree. But as this seed has a hot, fiery vigour, gives out its best virtues when bruised, and is grateful to the taste of birds, which are accordingly attracted to

47 Again, the kingdom of heaven is like unto a net, that was cast into
48 the sea, and gathered of every kind: which, when it was full, they
drew to shore, and sat down, and gathered the good into vessels, but cast
49 the bad away. So shall it be at the end of the world: the angels shall
50 come forth, and [j] sever the wicked from among the just, and shall cast
them into the furnace of fire: there shall be wailing and gnashing of
teeth.

A. D. 31.

j Mal. 3. 18. ch. 22. 12-14. ch. 25. 5-12. ch. 25. 33. 2 Thes. 1. 7-10. Rev. 20. 12-15.

its branches both for shelter and food, is it straining the parable, asks *Trench*, to suppose that, besides the wonderful *growth* of His kingdom, our Lord selected this seed to illustrate further the *shelter*, *repose*, and *blessedness* it is destined to afford to the nations of the world?

The Leaven (33). **33. Another parable spake he unto them; The kingdom of heaven is like unto leaven, which a woman took and hid in three measures of meal, till the whole was leavened.** This parable, while it teaches the same general truth as the foregoing one, holds forth, perhaps, rather the *inward* growth of the kingdom, while "the Mustard Seed" seems to point chiefly to the *outward*. It being a woman's work to knead, it seems a refinement to say that "the woman" here represents *the Church*, as the instrument of depositing the leaven. Nor does it yield much satisfaction to understand the "three measures of meal" of that threefold division of our nature into "spirit, soul, and body," alluded to in 1 Thes. v. 23, or of the threefold partition of the world among the three sons of Noah (Gen. x. 32), as some do. It yields more real satisfaction to see in this brief parable just the *all-penetrating* and *assimilating* quality of the Gospel, by virtue of which it will yet mould all institutions and tribes of men, and exhibit over the whole earth one "Kingdom of our Lord and of His Christ." (See on Rev. xi. 15.)

34. All these things spake Jesus unto the multitude in parables; and without a parable spake he not unto them—that is, on this occasion; refraining not only from all naked discourse, but even from all interpretation of these parables to the mixed multitude. **35. That it might be fulfilled which was spoken by the prophet, saying** (Ps. lxxviii. 2, nearly as in LXX.), **I will open my mouth in parables; I will utter things which have been kept secret from the foundation of the world.** Though the Psalm seems to contain only a summary of Israelitish *history*, the Psalmist himself calls it "a parable," and "dark sayings from of old" [מִנִּי־קֶדֶם, ἀπ' ἀρχῆς]—as containing, *underneath the history*, truths for all time, not fully brought to light till the Gospel-day.

Remarks.—1. Those who maintain that the Millennial era will be organically different from the present Gospel dispensation, and denounce as unscriptural the notion that the one will be but the universal triumph of the other, will find it hard to interpret the parables of the Mustard Seed and the Leaven on any other principle. The gradual growth of the Christian tree until the world be overshadowed by its wide-spreading branches—the silent operation of the Gospel on the mass of mankind, until the whole be leavened —these are representations of what the Gospel is designed to do, which it will be hard to reconcile to the belief that the world is not to be Christianized before Christ's Second Coming; that Christendom is to wax worse and worse, and be at its worst condition, when He comes; and that not till after He appears the second time, without sin, unto salvation, will the Millennium commence and a universal Christianity be seen upon the earth. That those gigantic superstitions, and spiritual tyrannies, and hideous corruptions, which have for ages supplanted and well-nigh crushed out a pure Christianity in some of the fairest portions of Christendom, will not disappear without a struggle, and that in this sense the blessed Millennial era will be ushered in *convulsively*, we may well believe, and Scripture prophecy is abundant and clear in such details. But in the light of such grand divisions as are presented to us in the parables of the Tares and Wheat and of the Good Fish and Bad—between the present mixed and the future unmixed condition of Humanity, all such minor divisions disappear; and the representations of the parables of the Mustard Seed and the Leaven are seen to stretch from the commencement of the Christian era, *unbroken*, into and through and on to the termination of the Millennial era. But 2. It were a pity if these parables were used merely for adjusting our views of the kingdom of Christ. They cheer the servants of Christ, when planting the standard of the Cross on new ground, with the assurance of ultimate triumph; when exposed to crushing persecution, with assurances of final victory; and when gaining little ground on the heathen world, while old forms of corrupted Christianity seem never to yield, with the certainty that the time tc favour Zion is coming, even the set time, and the kingdom and dominion, and the greatness of the kingdom under the whole heaven shall be given unto the saints of the Most High, and the kingdoms of this world shall become the Kingdom of our Lord and of His Christ.

Fifth and Sixth Parables, or *Third Pair:* THE HIDDEN TREASURE and THE PEARL OF GREAT PRICE (44-46). The subject of this last Pair, as of the two former, is the same, but also under a slight diversity of aspect: namely,

THE **PRICELESS VALUE** OF THE BLESSINGS OF THE KINGDOM. And while the one parable represents the Kingdom as *found without seeking*, the other holds forth the Kingdom as *sought and found*.

The Hidden Treasure (44-46). **44. Again, the kingdom of heaven is like unto treasure hid in a field**—no uncommon thing in unsettled and half-civilized countries, even now as well as in ancient times, when there was no other way of securing it from the rapacity of neighbours or marauders. (Jer. xli. 8; Job iii. 21; Prov. ii. 4.) **the which when a man hath found**—that is, unexpectedly found—**he hideth, and for joy thereof**—on perceiving what a treasure he had lighted on, passing the worth of all he possessed, **goeth and selleth all that he hath, and buyeth that field**—in which case, by Jewish law, the treasure would become his own.

The Pearl of Great Price (45, 46). **45. Again, the kingdom of heaven is like unto a merchant-man, seeking goodly pearls: 46. Who, when he had found one pearl of great price, went and sold all that he had, and bought it.** The one pearl of great price, instead of being found by accident, as in the former case, is found by one whose *business* it is to seek for such, and who finds

51 Jesus saith unto them, Have ye understood all these things? They
52 say unto him, Yea, Lord. Then said he unto them, Therefore every
scribe *which is* instructed unto the kingdom of heaven, is like unto a
man *that is* an householder which bringeth forth out of his treasure
[k]*things* new and old.
53 And it came to pass, *that,* when Jesus had finished these parables, he
54 departed thence. And [l]when he was come into his own country, he
taught them in their synagogue, insomuch that they were astonished,
and said, Whence hath this *man* this wisdom, and *these* mighty works?
55 Is [m]not this the carpenter's son? is not his mother called Mary? and [n]his
56 brethren, [o]James, and Joses, and Simon, and Judas? and his sisters, are

A. D. 31.

k Song 7. 13.
l Deut. 18. 15. ch. 2. 23. Mark 6. 1. Luke 4. 16. John 1. 11.
m Isa. 49. 7. Isa. 53. 2, 3. Mark 6. 3. Luke 3. 23. John 6. 42.
n ch. 12. 46.
o Mark 15. 40.

it just in the way of *searching* for such treasures. But in both cases the surpassing value of the treasure is alike recognized, and in both all is parted with for it.

51. Jesus saith unto them—that is, to the Twelve. He had spoken the first *four* in the hearing of the mixed multitude: the last *three* He reserved till, on the dismissal of the mixed audience, He and the Twelve were alone, (*v.* 36, &c.) **Have ye understood all these things? They say unto him, Yea, Lord. 52. Then said he unto them, Therefore**—or as we should say, Well, then, **every scribe**—or Christian teacher; here so called from that well-known class among the Jews. (See ch. xxiii. 34.) **which is instructed unto the kingdom of heaven**—himself taught in the mysteries of the Gospel which he has to teach to others, **is like unto a man that is an householder which bringeth forth**—'turneth' or 'dealeth out' [ἐκβάλλει]—**out of his treasure**—his store of divine truth, **things new and old**—old truths in ever new forms, aspects, applications, and with ever new illustrations.

Remarks.—1. The truths taught in the third pair of these parables—the Hidden Treasure and the Pearl of Great Price—are these: that the blessings of Christ's kingdom are of incomparable value; that they only truly deem them so who are prepared to part with all for them; and that while some find Christ without seeking Him, others find Him as the result of long and anxious search. Of the *former* sort, Messiah Himself says, "I was found of them that sought me not; I was made manifest unto them that asked not after me." (Isa. lxv. i.; Rom. x. 20.) Such was the woman of Samaria (John iv.); such was Matthew the publican (ch. ix. 9); such was Zaccheus the publican (Luke xix. 1-10); such was the thief on the cross (Luke xxiii. 39-43); such was the man born blind (John ix.); and such was Saul of Tarsus, (Acts ix.) Of the *latter* sort it is said, "Ye shall seek me, and find me, when ye shall search for me with all your heart" (Jer. xxix. 13). Such was Nathanael (John i. 45-49), and many others of whom we read in the New Testament. Of the former sort were nearly all who were called from among the Gentiles, as are the fruits of missions still in heathen lands: of the latter sort were probably most of John's disciples who went from him to His Master, and generally, "all who in Jerusalem looked for Redemption" and "waited for the Consolation of Israel" (Luke ii. 25, 38); and to them must be added all now in Christian lands reared in the knowledge of Christ, taught to seek Him early, yet often long of finding Him. 2. Those who find Christ without seeking Him have usually the liveliest joy—the joy of a blessed surprise; while those who find Him after long and anxious search have usually the deepest apprehensions of His value. It will be observed that the "joy" of discovery is only in the former parable—as if to express, not the *value* set upon the treasure, but the *unexpectedness* of it. On this principle, there was "more joy" over the unexpected return of the Prodigal Son than over the son who had been with his father all his days. (Luke xv.) Yet not less, but more profound is the sense of Christ's preciousness, when found after lengthened and weary search, which has deepened the sense of wretchedness without Him and the craving of the soul after Him.

53-58.—How Jesus was Regarded by His Relatives. (= Mark vi. 1-6; Luke iv. 16-30.)

53. And it came to pass, that, when Jesus had finished these parables, he departed thence. 54. And when he was come into his own country—that is, *Nazareth;* as is plain from Mark vi. 1. See on John iv. 43, where also the same phrase occurs. This, according to the majority of Harmonists, was the *second* of *two* visits which our Lord paid to Nazareth during His public ministry; but in our view it was His *first* and *only* visit to it. See on ch. iv. 13; and for the reasons, see on Luke iv. 16-30. **he taught them in their synagogue, insomuch that they were astonished, and said, Whence hath this man this wisdom, and these mighty works?** —'these miracles' [δυνάμεις]. These surely are not like the questions of people who had asked precisely the same questions before, who from astonishment had proceeded to rage, and in their rage had hurried Him out of the synagogue, and away to the brow of the hill whereon their city was built, to thrust Him down headlong, and who had been foiled even in that object by His passing through the midst of them, and going His way. But see on Luke iv. 16, &c. **55. Is not this the carpenter's son?** In Mark (vi. 3) the question is, "Is not this the carpenter?" In all likelihood, our Lord, during His stay under the roof of His earthly parents, wrought along with His legal father. **is not his mother called Mary?**—'Do we not know all about His parentage? Has He not grown up in the midst of us? Are not all His relatives our own townsfolk? Whence, then, such wisdom and such miracles?' These particulars of our Lord's *human* history constitute the most valuable testimony, first, to His true and real humanity—for they prove that during all His first thirty years His townsmen had discovered nothing about Him different from other men; secondly, to the divine character of His mission—for these Nazarenes proclaim both the unparalleled character of His teaching and the reality and glory of His miracles, as transcending human ability; and thirdly, to His wonderful humility and self-denial—in that when He was such as they now saw Him to be, He yet never gave any indications of it for thirty years, because "His hour was not yet come." **and his brethren, James, and Joses, and Simon, and Judas? 56. And his sisters, are they not all with us? Whence then**

they not all with us? Whence then hath this *man* all these things?
57 And they [p] were offended in him. But Jesus said unto them, [q] A prophet
is not without honour, save in his own country, and in his own house.
58 And [r] he did not many mighty works there, because of their unbelief.
14 AT that time [a] Herod the tetrarch heard of the fame of Jesus, and
2 said unto his servants, This is John the Baptist: he is risen from the dead;
and therefore mighty works [1] do show forth themselves in him.
3 For [b] Herod had laid hold on John, and bound him, and put *him* in
4 prison for Herodias' sake, his brother Philip's wife. For John said unto
5 him, [c] It is not lawful for thee to have her. And when he would have
put him to death, he feared the multitude, [d] because they counted him
6 as a prophet. But when Herod's [e] birthday was kept, the daughter of
7 Herodias danced [2] before them, and pleased Herod. Whereupon he pro-
8 mised with an oath to give her whatsoever she would ask. And she,
being before instructed of her mother, said, Give me here John Bap-
9 tist's head in a charger. And the king was sorry: [f] nevertheless, for
the oath's sake, and them which sat with him at meat, he commanded
10 *it* to be given *her*. And he sent, and beheaded John in the prison.
11 And his head was brought in a charger, and given to the damsel: and
12 she brought *it* to her mother. And his disciples came, and took up the
body, and buried it, and went and told Jesus.
13 When [g] Jesus heard *of it*, he departed thence by ship into a desert

A. D. 31.

[p] Ps. 22. 6. ch. 11. 6.
[q] Luke 4. 24. John 4. 44.
[r] Heb. 3. 19. Heb. 4. 2.

CHAP. 14.
[a] Mark 6. 14. Luke 9. 7.
[1] Or, are wrought by him.
[b] Pro. 10. 17. Pro. 15. 10.
[c] Lev. 18. 16. Lev. 20. 21.
[d] ch. 21. 26. Luke 20. 6.
[e] Gen. 40. 20.
[2] in the midst.
[f] Titus 1. 16.
[g] ch. 10. 23. ch. 12. 15. Mark 6. 32. Luke 9. 10. John 6. 1, 2.

hath this [man] all these things? An exceedingly difficult question here arises—What were these "brethren" and "sisters" to Jesus? Were they, *First*, His full brothers and sisters? or, *Secondly*, Were they his step-brothers and step-sisters, children of Joseph by a former marriage? or, *Thirdly*, Were they His cousins, according to a common way of speaking among the Jews respecting persons of collateral descent? On this subject an immense deal has been written; nor are opinions yet by any means agreed. For the second opinion there is no ground but a vague tradition, arising probably from the wish for some such explanation. The first opinion undoubtedly suits the text best in all the places where the parties are certainly referred to (ch. xii. 46, and its parallels, Mark iii. 31, and Luke viii. 19; our present passage, and its parallel, Mark vi. 3; John ii. 12; vii. 3, 5, 10; Acts i. 14). But, in addition to other objections, many of the best interpreters, thinking it in the last degree improbable that our Lord, when hanging on the cross, would have committed His mother to John if He had had full brothers of His own then alive, prefer the third opinion; although, on the other hand, it is not to be doubted that our Lord might have good reasons for entrusting the guardianship of His doubly widowed mother to the beloved disciple in preference even to full brothers of His own. Thus dubiously we prefer to leave this vexed question, encompassed as it is with difficulties. As to the names here mentioned, the *first* of them, "JAMES," is afterwards called "the Lord's brother" (see on Gal. i. 19), but is perhaps not to be confounded with "James the son of Alpheus," one of the Twelve, though many think their identity beyond dispute. This question also is one of considerable difficulty, and not without importance; since the James who occupies so prominent a place in the Church of Jerusalem, in the latter part of the Acts, was apparently the apostle, but is by many regarded as "the Lord's brother," while others think their identity best suits all the statements. The *second* of those here named, "JOSES" (or Joseph), who must not be confounded with "Joseph called Barsabas, who was surnamed Justus" (Acts i. 23); and the *third* here named, "SIMON," is not to be confounded with Simon the Kananite or Zealot (see on ch. x. 4). These three are nowhere else mentioned in the New Testament. The *fourth* and last-named, "JUDAS," can hardly be identical with the apostle of that name—though the brothers of both were of the name of "James"—nor (unless the two be identical, was this Judas) with the author of the catholic Epistle so called. **57. And they were offended in him. But Jesus said unto them, A prophet is not without honour, save in his own country, and in his own house. 58. And he did not many mighty works there, because of their unbelief**—"save that He laid His hands on a few sick folk, and healed them" (Mark vi. 5). See on Luke iv. 16-30, and Remarks at the close of that Section.

CHAP. XIV. 1-12.—HEROD THINKS JESUS A RESURRECTION OF THE MURDERED BAPTIST—ACCOUNT OF HIS IMPRISONMENT AND DEATH. (= Mark vi. 14-29; Luke ix. 7-9.)

The time of this alarm of Herod Antipas appears to have been during the mission of the Twelve, and shortly after the Baptist—who had lain in prison for probably more than a year—had been cruelly put to death.

Herod's Theory of the Works of Christ (1, 2). **1. At that time Herod the tetrarch**—Herod Antipas, one of the three sons of Herod the Great, and own brother of Archelaus (ch. ii. 22), who ruled as *Ethnarch* over Galilee and Perea. **heard of the fame of Jesus**—"for His name was spread abroad" (Mark vi. 14). **2. And said unto his servants**—his counsellors or court-ministers, **This is John the Baptist: he is risen from the dead; and therefore mighty works do show forth themselves in him.** The murdered prophet haunted his guilty breast like a spectre, and seemed to him alive again and clothed with unearthly powers in the person of Jesus.

Account of the Baptist's Imprisonment and Death (3-12). For the exposition of this portion, see on Mark vi. 17-29.

12-21.—HEARING OF THE BAPTIST'S DEATH, JESUS CROSSES THE LAKE WITH THE TWELVE, AND MIRACULOUSLY FEEDS FIVE THOUSAND.

place apart: and when the people had heard *thereof*, they followed him
on foot out of the cities.
14 And Jesus went forth, and saw a great multitude, and [h]was moved
with compassion toward them, and he healed their sick.
15 And when it was evening, his disciples came to him, saying, This is a
desert place, and the time is now past; send the multitude away, that
16 they may go into the villages, and buy themselves victuals. But Jesus
17 said unto them, They need not depart; [i]give ye them to eat. And they
18 say unto him, We have here but five loaves, and two fishes. He said,
19 Bring them hither to me. And he commanded the multitude to sit
down on the grass, and took the five loaves, and the two fishes, and,
looking up to heaven, [j]he blessed, and brake, and gave the loaves to *his*
20 disciples, and the disciples to the multitude. And they did all eat, and
were filled: and they took up of the fragments that remained twelve
21 baskets full. And they that had eaten were about five thousand men,
besides women and children.
22 And straightway Jesus constrained his disciples to get into a ship, and
to go before him unto the other side, while he sent the multitudes away.
23 And [k]when he had sent the multitudes away, he went up into a mountain apart to pray: [l]and when the evening was come, he was there alone.
24 But the ship was now in the midst of the sea, tossed with waves: for the
25 wind was contrary. And in the fourth watch of the night Jesus went
26 unto them, walking on the sea. And when the disciples saw him [m]walking on the sea, they were troubled, saying, It is a spirit: and they cried
27 out for fear. But straightway Jesus spake unto them, saying, Be of
28 good cheer: it is I; be not afraid. And Peter answered him and said,
29 Lord, if it be thou, bid me come unto thee on the water. And he said,
Come. And when Peter was come down out of the ship, he walked on
30 the water, to go to Jesus. But when he saw the wind [3]boisterous,
he was afraid; and, beginning to sink, he cried, saying, Lord, save me!
31 And immediately Jesus stretched forth *his* hand, and caught him,
and said unto him, O thou of little faith, wherefore [n]didst thou
32 doubt? And when they were come into the ship, the [o]wind ceased.
33 Then they that were in the ship came and worshipped him, saying, Of a
truth thou [p]art the Son of God.
34 And [q]when they were gone over, they came into the land of Gennesaret.
35 And when the men of that place had knowledge of him, they sent out
into all that country round about, and brought unto him all that were
36 diseased; and besought him that they might only touch the hem of his
garment: and [r]as many as touched were made perfectly whole.

15 THEN [a]came to Jesus scribes and Pharisees, which were of Jerusalem,
2 saying, Why [b]do thy disciples transgress [c]the tradition of the elders? for

A. D. 31.

[h] ch. 9. 36. Heb. 2. 17. Heb. 4. 15. Heb. 5. 2.
[i] 2 Ki. 4. 42, 43. Luke 3. 11. John 13. 29. 2 Cor. 8. 2,3.
[j] ch. 15 36. ch. 26. 26. Mark 8. 6. Luke 22. 19. John 6. 11, 23. Acts 27. 35.
[k] ch. 6. 6. ch. 26. 36. Mark 6. 46. Luke 6. 12. Acts 6. 4.
[l] John 6. 16.
[m] Job 7. 19. Job 9. 8. Ps. 39. 13. Ps. 73. 19. Isa. 43. 16. Lam. 3. 3,8.
[3] Or, strong.
[n] ch. 8. 26. ch. 16. 8. Jas. 1. 6.
[o] Ps. 107. 29. Mark 4. 41. Mark 6. 5. John 6. 21.
[p] Ps. 2. 7. Mark 1. 1. ch. 16. 16. ch. 26. 63. Luke 4. 41. John 1. 49. John 6. 69. John 11. 27.
[q] Mark 6. 53.
[r] ch. 9. 20. Mark 3. 10. Luke 6. 19. Acts 19, 12.

CHAP. 15.
[a] Mark 7. 1.
[b] Mark 7. 5.
[c] Gal. 1. 14. Col. 2. 8.

(= Mark vi. 30-44; Luke ix. 10-17; John vi. 1-14.) For the exposition of this Section—one of the very few where all the four Evangelists run parallel—see on Mark vi. 30-44.

22-36.—JESUS CROSSES TO THE WESTERN SIDE OF THE LAKE WALKING ON THE SEA—INCIDENTS ON LANDING. (= Mark vi. 45; John vi. 15-24.) For the exposition, see on John vi. 15-24.

CHAP. XV. 1-20.—DISCOURSE ON CEREMONIAL POLLUTION. (= Mark vii. 1-23.)

The time of this Section was after that Passover which was nigh at hand when our Lord fed the five thousand (John vi. 4)—the third Passover, as we take it, since His public ministry began, but which He did not keep at Jerusalem for the reason mentioned in John vii. 1.

1. Then came to Jesus scribes and Pharisees, which were of [ἀπὸ]—or 'from' **Jerusalem.** Mark says they "came from" it; a deputation probably sent from the capital expressly to watch Him. As He had not come to them at the last Passover, which they had reckoned on, they now come to Him. "And," says Mark, "when they saw some of His disciples eat bread with defiled, that is to say, with unwashen, hands"—hands not ceremonially cleansed by washing—"they found fault. For the Pharisees, and all the Jews, except they wash their hands oft" [πυγμῇ]—lit., 'in' or 'with the fist;' that is, probably, washing the one hand by the use of the other—though some understand it, with our version, in the sense of 'diligently,' 'sedulously'—"eat not, holding the tradition of the elders;" acting religiously according to the custom handed down to them. "And when they come from the market" [Καὶ ἀπὸ ἀγορᾶς]—'And after market;' after any common business, or attending a court of justice, where the Jews, as *Webster and Wil-*

3 they wash not their hands when they eat bread. But he answered and
said unto them, Why do ye also transgress the commandment of God by
4 your tradition? For God commanded, saying, [d]Honour thy father and
mother: and, [e]He that curseth father or mother, let him die the death.
5 But ye say, Whosoever shall say to *his* father or *his* mother, [f]*It is* a gift,
6 by whatsoever thou mightest be profited by me; and honour not his
father or his mother, *he shall be free*. Thus have ye made the com-
7 mandment of God of none effect by your tradition. *Ye* [g]hypocrites,
8 well did Esaias prophesy of you, saying, This [h]people draweth nigh unto
me with their mouth, and honoureth me with *their* lips; but their heart
9 is far from me. But in vain they do worship me, [i]teaching *for* doctrines
the commandments of men.
10 And [j]he called the multitude, and said unto them, Hear, and under-
11 stand: not [k]that which goeth into the mouth defileth a man; but that
which cometh out of the mouth, this defileth a man.
12 Then came his disciples, and said unto him, Knowest thou that the
13 Pharisees were offended, after they heard this saying? But he answered
and said, [l]Every plant, which my heavenly Father hath not planted,

A. D. 32.

d Ex. 20. 12. Lev. 19. 3. Deut. 5. 16. Pro. 23. 22.
e Ex. 21. 17. Lev. 20. 9. Deut. 27. 16. Pro. 20. 20. Pro. 30. 17.
f Mark 7. 11.
g Mark 7. 6.
h Isa. 29. 13. Ezek. 33 31.
i Isa. 29. 13. Col. 2. 18. Titus 1. 14.
j Mark 7. 14.
k Acts 10. 15. Rom. 14. 14. 1 Tim. 4. 4. Titus 1. 15.
l John 15. 2. 1 Cor. 3. 12.

---

kinson remark, after their subjection to the Romans, were especially exposed to intercourse and contact with heathens —"except they wash, they eat not. And many other things there be, which they have received to hold, as the washing of cups and pots, brazen vessels and tables" [κλινῶν]—rather 'couches,' such as were used at meals, which probably were merely *sprinkled* for ceremonial purposes. "Then the Pharisees and scribes asked Him," **saying, 2. Why do thy disciples transgress the tradition of the elders? for they wash not their hands when they eat bread. 3. But he answered and said unto them, Why do ye also transgress the commandment of God by your tradition?** The charge is retorted with startling power: 'The tradition they transgress is but *man's*, and is itself the occasion of heavy transgression, undermining the authority of *God's law*.' **4. For God commanded, saying** (Exod. xx. 12; &c.), **Honour thy father and mother: and** (Exod. xxi. 17; &c.), **He that curseth father or mother, let him die the death. 5. But ye say, Whosoever shall say to his father or his mother, It is a gift** [Δῶρον]—or simply, 'A gift!' In Mark it is, "Corban!" [קָרְבָּן]—that is, 'An oblation!' meaning, any unbloody offering or gift dedicated to sacred uses. **by whatsoever thou mightest be profited by me; 6. And honour not his father or his mother, [he shall be free].**—*q. d.*, 'It is true, father—mother—that by giving to thee this, which I now present, thou mightest be profited by me; but I have gifted it to pious uses, and therefore, at whatever cost to thee, I am not now at liberty to alienate any portion of it.' "And," it is added in Mark, "ye suffer him no more to do aught for his father or his mother." To dedicate property to God is indeed lawful and laudable, but not at the expense of filial duty. **Thus have ye made the commandment of God of none effect** [ἠκυρώσατε]—'cancelled' or 'nullified' it—**by your tradition. 7. Ye hypocrites, well did Esaias prophesy of you, saying** (Isa. xxix. 13), **8. This people draweth nigh unto me with their mouth, and honoureth me with their lips; but their heart is far from me. 9. But in vain they do worship me, teaching for doctrines the commandments of men.** By putting the commandments of men on a level with the divine requirements, *their whole worship was rendered vain*—a principle of deep moment in the service of God. "For," it is added in Mark vii. 8, "laying aside the commandment of God, ye hold the tradition of men, as the washing of pots and cups; and many other such like things ye do." [*Tregelles* brackets all the words after "men" in this verse as of doubtful authority; but we see no ground for this: *Tischendorf* inserts the whole as in the received text.] The drivelling nature of their multitudinous observances is here pointedly exposed, in contrast with the manly observance of "the commandment of God;" and when our Lord says, "Many other such like things ye do," it is implied that He had but given a specimen of the hideous treatment which the divine law received, and the grasping disposition which, under the mask of piety, was manifested by the ecclesiastics of that day. **10. And he called the multitude, and said unto them.** The foregoing dialogue, though in the people's hearing, was between Jesus and the pharisaic cavillers, whose object was to disparage Him with the people. But Jesus, having put them down, turns to the multitude, who at this time were prepared to drink in everything He said, and with admirable plainness, strength, and brevity lays down the great principle of real pollution, by which a world of bondage and uneasiness of conscience would be dissipated in a moment, and the sense of sin be reserved for deviations from the holy and eternal law of God. **Hear and understand: 11. Not that which goeth into the mouth defileth a man; but that which cometh out of the mouth, this defileth a man.** This is expressed even more emphatically in Mark (vii. 15, 16), and it is there added, "If any man have ears to hear, let him hear." [*Tregelles* brackets this little verse here, as wanting in some good MSS.; but *Tischendorf*, we think rightly, gives it as in the received text.] As in ch. xiii. 9, this so oft-repeated saying seems designed to call attention to the *fundamental* and *universal* character of the truth it refers to. **12. Then came his disciples, and said unto him, Knowest thou that the Pharisees were offended, after they heard this saying?** They had given vent to their irritation, and perhaps threats, not to our Lord Himself, from whom they seem to have slunk away, but to some of the disciples, who report it to their Master. **13. But he answered and said, Every plant, which my heavenly Father hath not planted, shall be rooted up.** 'They are offended, are they? Heed it not: their corrupt teaching is already doomed; the Garden of the Lord upon earth, too

14 shall be rooted up. Let [m]them alone: [n]they be blind leaders of the
blind. And if the blind lead the blind, both shall fall into the
15 ditch. Then [o]answered Peter and said unto him, Declare unto us this
16 parable. And Jesus said, [p]Are ye also yet without understanding?
17 Do not ye yet understand, that [q]whatsoever entereth in at the mouth
18 goeth into the belly, and is cast out into the draught? But [r]those
things which proceed out of the mouth come forth from the heart; and
19 they defile the man. For [s]out of the heart proceed evil thoughts,
20 murders, adulteries, fornications, thefts, false witness, blasphemies: these
are *the things* which defile a man: but to eat with unwashen hands
defileth not a man.
21 Then Jesus went thence, and departed into the coasts of Tyre and
22 Sidon. And, behold, a woman of Canaan came out of the same coasts,
and cried unto him, saying, Have mercy on me, O Lord, *thou* son of
23 David; my daughter is grievously vexed with a devil. But he answered

A. D. 32.

[m] Hos. 4. 14, 17.
[n] Isa. 9. 16. Mal. 2. 8. ch. 23. 16. Luke 6. 39.
[o] Mark 7. 17.
[p] ch. 16. 9. Mark 7. 18.
[q] 1 Cor. 6. 13.
[r] Pro. 6. 12. ch. 12. 34. Jas. 3. 6.
[s] Gen. 6. 5. Gen. 8. 21. Pro. 6. 14. Jer. 17. 9. Mark 7. 21.

long cumbered with their presence, shall yet be purged of them and their accursed system; yea, and whatsoever is not of the planting of My heavenly Father, the great Husbandman (John xv. 1), shall share the same fate.' **14. Let them alone: they be blind leaders of the blind. And if the blind lead the blind, both shall fall into the ditch.** Striking expression of the ruinous effects of erroneous teaching! **15. Then answered Peter and said unto him**—"when He was entered into the house from the people," says Mark—**Declare unto us this parable. 16. And Jesus said, Are ye also yet without understanding?** Slowness of spiritual apprehension in His genuine disciples grieves the Saviour: from others He expects no better (ch. xiii. 11). **17, 18. Do not ye yet understand, that whatsoever entereth in at the mouth, &c.** Familiar though these sayings have now become, what freedom from bondage to outward things do they proclaim, on the one hand, and on the other, how searching is the truth which they express—that nothing which enters from without can really defile us; and that only the evil that is in the heart, that is allowed to stir there, to rise up in thought and affection, and to flow forth in voluntary action, really defiles a man! **19. For out of the heart proceed evil thoughts** [διαλογισμοὶ πονηροὶ]—'evil reasonings;' referring here more immediately to those corrupt reasonings which had stealthily introduced and gradually reared up that hideous fabric of tradition which at length practically nullified the unchangeable principles of the moral law. But the statement is far broader than this, namely, that the first shape which the evil that is in the heart takes, when it begins actively to stir, is that of 'considerations' or 'reasonings' on certain suggested actions. **murders, adulteries, fornications, thefts, false witness, blasphemies** [βλασφημίαι]—'detractions,' whether directed against God or man: here the reference seems to be to the latter. Mark adds, "covetousnesses" [πλεονεξίαι]—or desires after more; "wickednesses" [πονηρίαι]—here meaning, perhaps, 'malignities' of various form; "deceit, lasciviousness" [ἀσέλγεια]—meaning, 'excess' or 'enormity' of any kind, though by later writers restricted to lewdness; "an evil eye"—meaning, all looks or glances of envy, jealousy, or ill-will towards a neighbour; "pride, foolishness" [ἀφροσύνη]—in the Old Testament sense of "folly;" that is, criminal senselessness, the folly of the *heart*. How appalling is this black catalogue! **20. These are the things which defile a man: but to eat with unwashen hands defileth not a man.** Thus does our Lord sum up this whole searching Discourse.

Remarks.—1. There is a *principle* at the bottom of such traditional practices as are here exposed, without the knowledge of which we cannot rightly improve the teaching of our Lord on the subject. Be it observed, then, that the practices here referred to, though based only on "the tradition of the elders," might seem, even to conscientious Israelites, in the highest degree laudable. It was a ceremonial economy they lived under; and as one principal design of this economy was to *teach the difference between clean and unclean by external symbols*, it was natural to think that *the more vividly and variously* they could bring this before their own minds, the more would they be falling in with the spirit and following out the design of that economy. Such are the plausibilities by which most of the symbolical features of the Romish ritual are defended. Nor is it merely as acts of will-worship, without divine warrant, that they are to be condemned, but as tending to *weaken the sense of divine authority for what* IS *commanded by mixing it up with what is purely human*, though originally introduced with the best intentions. Examples of this deep principle will readily occur—such as the effect, everywhere seen, of observing a multitude of saints' days in weakening the sense of the paramount claims of "the Lord's Day." 2. When we read here of the detestable pretexts under which those Jewish ecclesiastics suffered no more their deluded followers, when once they had them committed to some rash pledge, "to do aught for their father or mother," who can help thinking of the clergy of the Church of Rome, who have served themselves heirs to the worst features of Rabbinical Judaism? 3. If it be true that to multiply human devices for strengthening the force of religious principles in the life tends to draw the attention so far off from the divine law enjoining duty, and to rivet it upon the human device for securing obedience to it, may it not be worthy of the consideration of Christians whether, when sin is committed in spite of these devices, the breach of their own pledges is not apt to trouble them more than that of the divine law, which they were designed to fortify? But we would not press this too far; and there certainly are cases where evil habits, when inveterate, require restraints which in other cases are superfluous. It is to the former only that we refer. 4. If nothing outward can *defile*, it is obvious that nothing purely outward can *sanctify*—as the Church of Rome teaches that *Sacraments*, for example, do of themselves ['*ex opere operato*']. "God is a Spirit, and they that worship Him must worship Him in spirit and in truth."

21-28.—THE WOMAN OF CANAAN AND HER

her not a word. And his disciples came and besought him, saying, Send
24 her away; for she crieth after us. But he answered and said, [t]I am not
25 sent but unto the lost sheep of the house of Israel. Then came she and
26 worshipped him, saying, Lord, help me! But he answered and said, It
27 is not meet to take the children's bread, and to cast *it* to [u]dogs. And
she said, Truth, Lord: yet the dogs eat of the crumbs which fall from
28 their master's table. Then Jesus answered and said unto her, O woman,
great *is* thy faith: be it unto thee even as thou wilt. And her daughter
was made whole from that very hour.

29 And [v]Jesus departed from thence, and came nigh [w]unto the sea of
30 Galilee; and went up into a mountain, and sat down there. And [x]great
multitudes came unto him, having with them *those that were* lame,
blind, dumb, maimed, and many others, and cast them down at Jesus'
31 feet; and he healed them: insomuch that the multitude wondered,
when they saw the dumb to speak, the maimed to be whole, the lame to
walk, and the blind to see: and they glorified the God of Israel.

32 Then [y]Jesus called his disciples *unto him*, and said, I [z]have compassion
on the multitude, because they continue with me now three days, and
have nothing to eat: and I will not send them away fasting, lest they
33 faint in the way. And [a]his disciples say unto him, Whence should we
have so much bread in the wilderness as to fill so great a multitude?
34 And Jesus saith unto them, How many loaves have ye? And they said,
35 Seven, and a few little fishes. And he commanded the multitude to sit
36 down on the ground. And [b]he took the seven loaves and the fishes, and
[c]gave thanks, and brake *them*, and gave to his disciples, and the disciples
37 to the multitude. And they did all eat, and were filled: and they took
38 up of the broken *meat* that was left seven baskets full. And they that
did eat were four thousand men, besides women and children.

39 And [d]he sent away the multitude, and took ship, and came into the
coasts of Magdala.

16 THE [a]Pharisees also with the Sadducees came, and tempting desired
2 him that he would show them a sign from heaven. He answered and
said unto them, When it is evening, ye say, *It will be* fair weather; for
3 the sky is red: and in the morning, *It will be* foul weather to-day; for
the sky is red and lowring. O *ye* hypocrites, ye can discern the face of
4 the sky; but can ye not *discern* the [b]signs of the times? A [c]wicked and
adulterous generation seeketh after a sign; and there shall no sign be
given unto it, but the sign of the prophet Jonas. And he left them,
and departed.

5 And [d]when his disciples were come to the other side, they had for-
6 gotten to take bread. Then Jesus said unto them, [e]Take heed and
7 beware of the leaven of the Pharisees and of the Sadducees. And
they reasoned among themselves, saying, *It is* because we have taken
8 no bread. *Which* when Jesus perceived, he said unto them, O ye of
little faith, why reason ye among yourselves, because ye have brought
9 no bread? Do [f]ye not yet understand, neither remember the five loaves
10 of the five thousand, and how many baskets ye took up? Neither [g]the
seven loaves of the four thousand, and how many baskets ye took up?
11 How is it that ye do not understand that I spake *it* not to you concerning
bread, that ye should beware of the leaven of the Pharisees and of the
12 Sadducees? Then understood they how that he bade *them* not beware

A. D. 32.

t Isa. 53. 6. ch. 10. 5, 6. Acts 3. 25, 26. Acts 13. 46. Rom. 15. 8.
u ch. 7. 6. Eph. 2. 12. Phil. 3. 2.
v Mark 7 31
w ch. 4 18 John 6. 1, 23. Mark 1. 16.
x Isa. 35. 5, 6. ch. 11. 5. Luke 7. 22.
y Mark 8. 1.
z Ps. 86. 15. Ps. 103. 13. Ps. 111. 4. Mark 1. 41. Heb. 2. 17. Heb. 4. 15. Heb. 5. 2.
a Num. 11. 21, 22. 2 Ki. 4. 43.
b ch. 14. 19.
c Deut. 8. 10. 1 Sam. 9. 13. Ps. 104. 28. Luke 22. 19.
d Mark 8. 10.

CHAP. 16.

a ch. 12. 38. Mark 8. 11. Luke 11. 16. Luke 12. 54-56. 1 Cor. 1. 22.
b Gen. 49. 10. Isa. 7. 14. Isa. 11. 1. Isa. 42. 1. Ezek. 21. 27. Dan. 9. 24. Mic. 5. 2. Hag. 2. 7. Mal. 3. 1.
c ch. 12. 39.
d ch. 15. 39. Mark 8. 14.
e ch. 7. 15. ch. 24. 4. Luke 12. 1. Rom. 16. 17, 18. Eph. 5. 6. Col. 2. 8. Phil. 3. 2. 2 Pet. 3. 17.
f ch. 14. 17. ch. 15. 16, 17. John 6. 9. Rev. 2. 23.
g ch. 15. 34.

DAUGHTER. For the exposition, see on Mark vii. 24-30.

29-39.—MIRACLES OF HEALING—FOUR THOUSAND MIRACULOUSLY FED. For the exposition, see on Mark vii. 31—viii. 10.

CHAP. XVI. 1-12.—A SIGN FROM HEAVEN SOUGHT AND REFUSED—CAUTION AGAINST THE LEAVEN OF THE PHARISEES AND SADDUCEES. For the exposition, see on Mark viii. 11-21.

13-28.—PETER'S NOBLE CONFESSION OF CHRIST, AND THE BENEDICTION PRONOUNCED UPON HIM—CHRIST'S FIRST EXPLICIT ANNOUNCEMENT OF HIS

of the leaven of bread, but of the doctrine of the Pharisees and of the
Sadducees.
13 When Jesus came into the coasts of Cesarea Philippi, he asked his
14 disciples, saying, [h]Whom do men say that I the Son of man am? And
they said, [i]Some *say that thou art* John the Baptist; some, [j]Elias; and
15 others, Jeremias, or one of the prophets. He saith unto them, But
16 whom say ye that I am? And Simon Peter answered and said, Thou
17 [k]art the Christ, the Son of the living God. And Jesus answered and said
unto him, Blessed art thou, Simon Bar-jona: [l]for flesh and blood hath

A. D. 32.

h Dan. 7. 13. Mark 8. 27. Luke 9. 18.
i ch. 14. 2. Luke 9. 7, 8, 9.
j Mal. 4. 5.
k Ps. 2. 7. ch. 14. 33.
l Eph. 2. 8.

APPROACHING SUFFERINGS, DEATH, AND RESURRECTION—HIS REBUKE OF PETER AND WARNING TO ALL THE TWELVE. (=Mark viii. 27; ix. 1; Luke ix. 18-27.) The time of this Section—which is beyond doubt, and will presently be mentioned—is of immense importance, and throws a touching interest around the incidents which it records.

Peter's Confession and the Benediction pronounced upon him (13-20). **13. When Jesus came into the coasts** [τὰ μέρη]—'the parts;' that is, the territory or region: In Mark (viii. 27) it is "the towns" or 'villages' [κώμας]. **of Cesarea Philippi.** It lay at the foot of mount Lebanon, near the sources of the Jordan, in the territory of Dan, and at the north-east extremity of Palestine. It was originally called *Panium* (from a cavern in its neighbourhood dedicated to the god *Pan*) and *Paneas.* Philip, the tetrarch, the only good son of Herod the Great, in whose dominions Paneas lay, having beautified and enlarged it, changed its name to *Cesarea*, in honour of the Roman emperor, and added *Philippi* after his own name, to distinguish it from the other Cesarea (Acts x. 1) on the north-east coast of the Mediterranean sea. (*Joseph.* Antt. xv. 10, 3; xviii. 2, 1.) This quiet and distant retreat Jesus appears to have sought, with the view of talking over with the Twelve the fruit of His past labours, and breaking to them for the first time the sad intelligence of His approaching death. **he asked his disciples**—"by the way," says Mark (viii. 27), and "as He was alone praying," says Luke (ix. 18)—**saying, Whom**—or more grammatically, "Who" **do men say that I the Son of man am?** [or, 'that the Son of man is'—recent editors omitting here the με of Mark and Luke; though the evidence seems pretty nearly balanced]—*q. d.*, 'What are the views generally entertained of Me, the Son of man, after going up and down among them so long?' He had now closed the first great stage of His ministry, and was just entering on the last dark one. His spirit, burdened, sought relief in retirement, not only from the multitude, but even for a season from the Twelve. He retreated into "the secret place of the Most High," pouring out His soul "in supplications and prayers, with strong crying and tears" (Heb. v. 7). On rejoining His disciples, and as they were pursuing their quiet journey, He asked them this question. **14. And they said, Some say that thou art John the Baptist**—risen from the dead. So that Herod Antipas was not singular in his surmise (ch. xiv. 1, 2). **some, Elias**—cf. Mark vi. 15. **and others, Jeremias.** Was this theory suggested by a supposed resemblance between the "Man of Sorrows" and 'the weeping prophet?' **or one of the prophets**—or, as Luke (ix. 8) expresses it, "that one of the old prophets is risen again." In another report of the popular opinions which Mark (vi. 15) gives us, it is thus expressed, "That it is a prophet, [or] as one of the prophets" [the word "or"—ἢ—is wanting in authority]:—in other words, That he was a prophetical person, resembling those of old. **15. He saith unto them, But whom**—rather, "Who" **say ye that I am?** He had never put this question before, but the crisis He was reaching made it fitting that He should now have it from them. We may suppose this to be one of those moments of which the prophet says, in His name, "Then I said, I have laboured in vain; I have spent my strength for nought, and in vain" (Isa. xlix. 4): Lo, these three years I come seeking fruit on this fig tree; and what is it? As the result of all, I am taken for John the Baptist, for Elias, for Jeremias, for one of the prophets. Yet some there are that have beheld My glory, the glory as of the Only begotten of the Father, and I shall hear their voice, for it is sweet. **16. And Simon Peter answered and said, Thou art the Christ, the Son of the living God.** He does not say, 'Scribes and Pharisees, rulers and people, are all perplexed; and shall we, unlettered fishermen, presume to decide?' But feeling the light of his Master's glory shining in his soul, he breaks forth—not in a tame, prosaic acknowledgment, '*I believe that thou art,*' &c.—but in the language of adoration—such as one uses in worship, "THOU ART THE CHRIST, THE SON OF THE LIVING GOD!" He first owns Him the promised *Messiah* (see on ch. i. 16); then he rises higher, echoing the voice from heaven—"This is my beloved Son, in whom I am well pleased;" and in the important addition—"Son of the LIVING GOD,"—he recognizes the essential and eternal life of God as in this His Son—though doubtless without that distinct perception afterwards vouchsafed. **17. And Jesus answered and said unto him, Blessed art thou.** Though it is not to be doubted that Peter, in this noble testimony to Christ, only expressed the conviction of all the Twelve, yet since he alone seems to have had clear enough apprehensions to put that conviction in proper and suitable words, and courage enough to speak them out, and readiness enough to do this at the right time—so he only, of all the Twelve, seems to have met the present want, and communicated to the saddened soul of the Redeemer at the critical moment that balm which was needed to cheer and refresh it. Nor is Jesus above giving indication of the deep satisfaction which this speech yielded Him, and hastening to respond to it by a signal acknowledgment of Peter in return. **Simon Bar-jona** [בַּר יוֹנָה]—or, 'son of Jona' (John i. 42) or Jonas (John xxi. 15). This name, denoting his humble fleshly extraction, seems to have been purposely here mentioned, to contrast the more vividly with the spiritual elevation to which divine illumination had raised him. **for flesh and blood hath not revealed it unto thee**—'This is not the fruit of human teaching.' **but my Father which is in heaven.** In speaking of God, Jesus, it is to be observed, never calls Him, "Our Father" (see on John xx. 17), but either "*your* Father"—when He would encourage His timid believing ones with the assurance that He was theirs, and teach themselves to call Him so—or, as here, "My Father," to signify some peculiar action or aspect

18 not revealed *it* unto thee, but [m]my Father which is in heaven. And I
say also unto thee, That [n]thou art Peter, and [o]upon this rock I will
build my church; and [p]the gates of hell shall not prevail against it.
19 And [q]I will give unto thee the keys of the kingdom of heaven: and
whatsoever thou shalt bind on earth shall be bound in heaven; and
20 whatsoever thou shalt loose on earth shall be loosed in heaven. Then
charged he his disciples that they should tell no man that he was Jesus
the Christ.
21 From that time forth began Jesus to show unto his disciples, how that
he must go unto Jerusalem, and suffer many things of the elders and
chief priests and scribes, and be killed, and be raised again the third day.
22 Then Peter took him, and began to rebuke him, saying, [1]Be it far from
23 thee, Lord: this shall not be unto thee. But he turned, and said unto
Peter, Get thee behind me, Satan: [r]thou art an offence unto me; for
thou savourest not the things that be of God, but those that be of men.

A. D. 32.

[m] 1 Cor. 2. 10. Gal. 1. 16.
[n] John 1. 42.
[o] Isa. 28. 16. 1 Cor. 3. 11. Eph. 2. 20. Rev. 21. 14.
[p] Isa. 54. 17.
[q] John 20. 23.
[1] Pity thyself.
[r] Gen. 3. 1-6, 17. ch. 4. 10. Mark 8. 33. Luke 4. 8. Rom. 8. 7. 2 Cor. 11. 14, 15.

of Him as "the God and Father of our Lord Jesus Christ." **18. And I say also unto thee** [Κἀγὼ δὲ σοὶ λέγω]:—*q. d.*, 'As thou hast borne such testimony to Me, even so in return do I to thee;' **That thou art Peter.** At his first calling, this new name was announced to him as an honour *afterwards* to be conferred on him (John i. 43). Now he gets it, with an explanation of what it was meant to convey. **and upon this rock.** As "Peter" and "Rock" are one word in the dialect familiarly spoken by our Lord—the Aramaic or Syro-Chaldaic, which was the mother tongue of the country--this exalted *play upon the word* [כֵּיפָא] Κηφᾶς, John i. 43] can be fully seen only in languages which have one word for both. Even in the Greek it is imperfectly represented [σὺ εἶ Πέτρος, καὶ ἐπὶ ταύτῃ τῇ πέτρᾳ]. In French, as *Webster and Wilkinson* remark, it is perfect, *Pierre—pierre.* **I will build my church**—not on the man Simon Bar-jona; but on him as the heaven-taught Confessor of such a faith. "My Church," says our Lord, calling the Church HIS OWN; a magnificent expression, remarks *Bengel*, regarding Himself—nowhere else occurring in the Gospels. See on ch. xiii. 24-30, 36-43, Remark 3. **and the gates of hell** [ᾅδου]—'of Hades,' or, the unseen world; meaning, the gates of Death: in other words, 'It shall never perish.' Some explain it of 'the assaults of the powers of darkness;' but though that expresses a glorious truth, probably the former is the sense here. **19. And I will give unto thee the keys of the kingdom of heaven**—the kingdom of God about to be set up on earth—**and whatsoever thou shalt bind on earth shall be bound in heaven; and whatsoever thou shalt loose on earth shall be loosed in heaven.** Whatever this mean, it was soon expressly *extended to all the apostles* (ch. xviii. 18); so that the claim of supreme authority in the Church, made for Peter by the Church of Rome, and then arrogated to themselves by the Popes as the legitimate successors of St. Peter, is baseless and impudent. As first in confessing Christ, Peter got this commission before the rest; and with these "keys," on the day of Pentecost, he first "opened the door of faith" to the *Jews*, and then, in the person of Cornelius, he was honoured to do the same to the *Gentiles.* Hence, in the lists of the apostles, Peter is always first named. See on ch. xviii. 18. One thing is clear, that not in all the New Testament is there the vestige of any authority either claimed or exercised by Peter, or conceded to him, above the rest of the apostles—a thing conclusive against the Romish claims in behalf of that apostle. See on ch. x. 1-5, Remark 8. **20. Then charged he his disciples that they should tell no man that he was Jesus the Christ.** Now that He had been so explicit, they might naturally think the time come for giving it out openly; but here they are told it had not.

Announcement of His approaching Death, and Rebuke of Peter (21-28). The occasion here is evidently the same. **21. From that time forth began Jesus to show unto his disciples**—that is, with an *explicitness and frequency* He had never observed before, **how that he must go unto Jerusalem, and suffer many things** ("and be rejected," Matt. and Mark) **of the elders and chief priests and scribes**—not as before, merely by not receiving Him, but by formal deeds—**and be killed, and be raised again the third day.** Mark (viii. 32) adds, that "He spake that saying openly" [παῤῥησίᾳ]—'explicitly,' or 'without disguise.' **22. Then Peter took him** [aside], apart from the rest; presuming on the distinction just conferred on him; showing how *unexpected* and *distasteful* to them all was the announcement. **and began to rebuke him**—affectionately, yet with a certain generous indignation, to chide him. **saying, Be it far from thee, Lord: this shall not be unto thee**—*i. e.*, 'If I can help it;' the same spirit that prompted him in the garden to draw the sword in His behalf (John xviii. 10). **23. But he turned, and said**—in the hearing of the rest; for Mark (viii. 33) expressly says, "When He had turned about and looked on His disciples, He rebuked Peter;" perceiving that he had but boldly uttered what others felt, and that the check was needed by them also. **Get thee behind me, Satan**—the same words as He had addressed to the Tempter (Luke iv. 8); for He felt in it a Satanic lure, a whisper from hell, to move Him from His purpose to suffer. So He shook off the Serpent, then coiling around Him, and "felt no harm" (Acts xxviii. 5). How quickly has the "rock" turned to a devil! The fruit of divine teaching the Lord delighted to honour in Peter; but the mouthpiece of hell, which he had in a moment of forgetfulness become, the Lord shook off with horror. **thou art an offence** [σκάνδαλον]—'a stumbling-block' **unto me**: 'Thou playest the Tempter, casting a stumbling-block in my way to the Cross. Could it succeed, where wert thou? and how should the Serpent's head be bruised?' **for thou savourest not** [οὐ φρονεῖς]—'thou thinkest not'—**the things that be of God, but those that be of men.** 'Thou art carried away by human views of the way of setting up Messiah's kingdom, quite contrary to those of God.' This was kindly said, not to take off the sharp edge of the

24 Then [s]said Jesus unto his disciples, If any *man* will come after me, let
25 him deny himself, and take up his cross, and follow me. For whosoever
will save his life shall lose it: and whosoever will lose his life for my
26 sake shall find it. For what is a man profited, if he shall gain the
whole world, and lose his own soul? or [t]what shall a man give in
27 exchange for his soul? For the Son of man shall come in the glory of
his Father [u]with his angels; [v]and then he shall reward every man
28 according to his works. Verily I say unto you, There be some standing
here which shall not taste of death, till they see the Son of man coming
in his [w]kingdom.

A. D. 32.

[s] Acts 14. 22. 1 Thes. 3. 3. 2 Tim. 3. 12.
[t] Ps. 49. 7, 8.
[u] Dan. 7. 10. Zech. 14. 5. Jude 14.
[v] Jer. 17. 10. Rom. 2. 6. 2 Cor. 5. 10. 1 Pet. 1. 17.
[w] Mark 9. 1.

rebuke, but to explain and justify it, as it was evident Peter knew not what was in the bosom of his rash speech. **24. Then said Jesus unto his disciples.** Mark (viii. 34) says, "When He had called the people unto Him, with His disciples also, He said unto them"—turning the rebuke of one into a warning to all. **If any man will come after me, let him deny himself, and take up his cross, and follow me. 25. For whosoever will save** [θέλῃ σῶσαι]—'is minded to save,' or bent on saving, **his life shall lose it: and whosoever will lose his life for my sake shall find it.** See on ch. x. 38, 39. 'A suffering and dying Messiah liketh you ill; but what if His servants shall meet the same fate? They may not; but who follows Me must be prepared for the worst.' **26. For what is a man profited, if he shall gain the whole world, and lose** [ζημιωθῇ]—or 'forfeit' **his own soul? or what shall a man give in exchange for his soul?** Instead of these weighty words, which we find in Mark also, it is thus expressed in Luke: "If he gain the whole world, and lose himself, or be cast away" [ἑαυτὸν δὲ ἀπολέσας ἢ ζημιωθείς], or better, 'If he gain the whole world, and destroy or forfeit himself.' How awful is the stake as here set forth! If a man makes the present world—in its various forms of riches, honours, pleasures, and such like—the object of supreme pursuit, be it that he gains the world; yet along with it he forfeits his own soul. Not that any ever did, or ever will gain the whole world—a very small portion of it, indeed, falls to the lot of the most successful of the world's votaries—but to make the extravagant concession, that by giving himself entirely up to it, a man gains the whole world; yet, setting over against this gain the forfeiture of his soul—necessarily following the surrender of his whole heart to the world—what is he profited? But, if not the whole world, yet possibly something else may be conceived as an equivalent for the soul. Well, what is it?—"Or what shall a man give in exchange for his soul?" Thus, in language the weightiest, because the simplest, does our Lord shut up His hearers, and all who shall read these words to the end of the world, to the priceless value to every man of his own soul. In Mark and Luke the following words are added: "Whosoever therefore shall be ashamed of Me and of My words"—'shall be ashamed of belonging to Me, and ashamed of My Gospel,' "in this adulterous and sinful generation" (see on ch. xii. 39), "of him shall the Son of man be ashamed when He cometh in the glory of His Father, with the holy angels" (Mark viii. 38; Luke ix. 26). He will render back to that man his own treatment, disowning him before the most august of all assemblies, and putting him to "*shame* and everlasting *contempt*" (Dan. xii. 2). 'O shame,' exclaims *Bengel*, 'to be put to shame before God, Christ, and angels!' The sense of *shame* is founded on our love of *reputation*, which causes instinctive aversion to what is fitted to lower it, and was given us as a preservative from all that is properly *shameful*. To be *lost to shame*, is to be nearly past hope. (Zeph. iii. 5; Jer. vi. 15; iii. 3.) But when Christ and "His words" are unpopular, the same instinctive desire to *stand well with others* begets that temptation to be ashamed of Him which only the 'expulsive power' of a higher affection can effectually counteract. **27. For the Son of man shall come in the glory of his Father with his angels**—in the splendour of His Father's authority and with all His angelic ministers, ready to execute His pleasure; **and then he shall reward, &c. 28. Verily I say unto you, There be some standing here** [τινες τῶν ὧδε ἑστηκότων]—'some of those standing here,' **which shall not taste of death, till they see the Son of man coming in his kingdom**—or, as in Mark (ix. 1), "till they see the kingdom of God come with power;" or, as in Luke (ix. 27), more simply still, "till they see the kingdom of God." The reference, beyond doubt, is to the firm establishment and victorious progress, in the life-time of some then present, of that new Kingdom of Christ, which was destined to work the greatest of all changes on this earth, and be the grand pledge of His final coming in glory.

Remarks.—1. The distraction and indecision of the public mind on the great vital questions of Religion will be no excuse for the want of definite convictions on the part either of the educated or the illiterate on such momentous matters. On the contrary, it is just when such distraction and indecision are greatest that the Lord Jesus expects firm conviction and decision on the part of His true friends, and values it most. 2. The testimony here borne, in our Lord's commendation of Peter, to the reality of an inward divine teaching, distinct from the outward communication of divine truth, is very precious. For Peter had enjoyed the outward teaching of the Son of God Himself. But since many others had done this to no saving effect, the Lord expressly ascribes the difference between Peter and them to supernatural illumination. 3. When the Lord has any eminent work to do in His kingdom, He always finds the fitting instruments to do it; and yet, how different, usually, from those He might have been expected to select! Who would have thought that a humble Galilean fisherman would be chosen, and found qualified, to do what at that time was the highest work for Christ, to lay the foundations of the Church—opening the door of faith to the Jews first, and thereafter to the Gentiles? But this is God's way—to choose the foolish things of the world to confound the wise, and the weak things of the world to confound the mighty, and base things of the world, and things which are despised, yea, and things which are not, to bring to nought the things that are: that no flesh should glory in His presence (1 Cor. i. 27-29). 4. In the words of commendation and reward here addressed to Peter we have a striking example of the extremes to be avoided in the interpretation of

17 AND [a]after six days Jesus taketh Peter, James, and John his brother,
2 and bringeth them up into an high mountain apart, and was transfigured
before them; and his face did shine as the sun, and his raiment was
3 white as the light. And, behold, there appeared unto them Moses [b]and
4 Elias talking with him. Then answered Peter, and said unto Jesus,
Lord, it is good for us to be here: if thou wilt, let us make here three
5 tabernacles; one for thee, and one for Moses, and one for Elias. While
[c]he yet spake, behold, a bright cloud overshadowed them: and behold
a voice out of the cloud, which said, [d]This is my beloved Son, [e]in
6 whom I am well pleased; [f]hear ye him. And [g]when the disciples
7 heard *it*, they fell on their face, and were sore afraid. And Jesus came
8 and touched them, and said, Arise, and be not afraid. And when they
9 had lifted up their eyes, they saw no man, save Jesus only.
9 And as they came down from the mountain, Jesus charged them,
saying, Tell the vision to no man, until the Son of man be risen again
10 from the dead. And his disciples asked him, saying, Why [h]then say
11 the scribes that Elias must first come? And Jesus answered and said
12 unto them, Elias truly shall first come, and restore [i]all things. But [j]I
say unto you, That Elias is come already, and they knew him not, but
have [k]done unto him whatsoever they listed. Likewise shall also the
13 Son of man suffer of them. Then the disciples understood that he
spake unto them of John the Baptist.
14 And [l]when they were come to the multitude, there came to him a
15 *certain* man, kneeling down to him, and saying, Lord, have mercy on my

A. D. 32.

CHAP. 17.
a Mark 9. 2. Luke 9. 28.
b Rom. 3. 21.
c 2 Pet. 1. 17.
d ch. 3. 17. Mark 1. 11. Luke 3. 22. Luke 9. 35. John 3. 16, 35. John 5. 20.
e Isa. 42. 1.
f Deut. 18. 15. Acts 3. 22. Heb. 12. 25.
g 2 Pet. 1. 18.
h Mal. 4. 5. ch. 11. 14. ch. 27. 47-49. Mark 9. 11. John 1. 21, 25.
i Mal. 4. 6. Luke 1. 16. Acts 3. 21.
j Mark 9. 12.
k ch. 14. 3.
l Mark 9. 14. Luke 9. 37.

Scripture. While Romanists and Romanizers build upon this a distinction in favour of Peter, in which none else, even of the Twelve, were destined to share, able Protestants have gone to the opposite extreme, of denying that our Lord, in speaking of "that rock on which He was to build His Church," had any reference to Peter at all; and take the rock to mean either the Speaker Himself, or at least the fundamental truth regarding Him which Peter had just uttered—that He was "the Christ, the Son of the living God." But as in that case the manifest play upon the word "rock," which the name of Peter was designed to express, would be lost, so we do not lose the truth for which these Protestant interpreters contend by admitting that Peter himself is intended in this announcement, provided it be understood that it was not as the man "Simon, son of Jonas," that anything was to be built upon Peter, but on Peter as the man of most distinguished faith in Jesus as the Christ, the Son of the living God. Thus, while the plain sense of the passage is preserved, the truth expressed is according to Scripture. 5. How hard is it even for eminent Christians to stand high commendation without forgetting themselves! (See on Luke xxii. 31, &c.; and see 2 Cor. xii. 7.) Peter, it is to be feared, must have been carried somewhat off his feet by the encomium pronounced upon him—even though his superiority was expressly ascribed to Grace—ere he could have been betrayed into the presumption of taking his Master to task. 6. How deeply instructive is the sharp distinction which Christ here draws between the things that be of God and those that be of men, and how severe the rebuke administered to Peter for judging of the one by the standard of the other! If the things of God be hid from "the wise and prudent" (see on ch. xi. 25), can we wonder that when God's own children make use of the world's wisdom and prudence to measure His ways, they should misjudge and run against them? And yet, so plausible is this worldly wisdom, that when, having fallen into unspiritual conceptions of the things of God, Christians throw stumbling-blocks before those servants of Christ who are more devoted than themselves, they fancy they are only checking a too fiery zeal, and arresting proceedings which are injudicious and hurtful; while our Lord here teaches us that they are but tools of Satan! 7. Let the example of Jesus, in not only resenting and repelling all such suggestions as tended to arrest His onward career, but even when they came from His most eminent disciple, tracing them with horror to their proper source in the dark Enemy of man's salvation, stand out before us as our perfect Model in all such cases. 8. In times of severe persecution, and in prospect of suffering in any shape for the sake of the Gospel, it will be our wisdom, and be found a tower of strength, calmly to weigh both issues—the gain and the loss of each course. And to be prepared for the worst, it will be well to put the best of the world's gain over against the worst of Christ's service. Put the gain of the whole world against only one loss—the loss of the soul—and the loss of everything in this world, friends, goods, liberty, life itself, against only one gain—the gain of the soul. Then let us ask ourselves, in the sight of conscience and God, and an eternity of bliss or woe, With which side lies the advantage? And to make the answer to this question the more certain and the more impressive, let us habitually summon up before us the scene here presented to us by Him who is to be Himself the Judge—the great assize, the parties at the bar, the open acknowledgment and acquittal of the one, the disavowal and condemnation of the other, and the eternal issues. So shall we feel ourselves driven out of the denial of that blessed Name, and shut up and shut in to Christ and the fearless confession of His truth and grace, come what may.

CHAP. XVII. 1-13.—JESUS IS TRANSFIGURED—CONVERSATION ABOUT ELIAS. (=Mark ix. 2-13; Luke ix. 28-36.) For the exposition, see on Luke ix. 28-36.

14-23.—HEALING OF A DEMONIAC BOY—SECOND

son: for he is lunatic, and sore vexed: for ofttimes he falleth into the
16 fire, and oft into the water. And I brought him to thy disciples, and
17 they could not cure him. Then Jesus answered and said, O faithless
and perverse generation, how long shall I be with you! how long shall I
18 suffer you! Bring him hither to me. And Jesus rebuked the devil;
and he departed out of him: and the child was cured from that very
19 hour. Then came the disciples to Jesus apart, and said, Why could
20 not we cast him out? And Jesus said unto them, Because of your
unbelief: for verily I say unto you, If [m]ye have faith as a grain of
mustard seed, ye shall say unto this mountain, Remove hence to yonder
place; and it shall remove; and nothing shall be impossible unto you.
21 Howbeit this kind goeth not out but by prayer and fasting.
22 And [n]while they abode in Galilee, Jesus said unto them, The Son of
23 man shall be betrayed into the hands of men; and [o]they shall kill him,
and the third day he shall be raised again. And they were exceeding
sorry.
24 And when they were come to Capernaum, they that received [1]tribute
25 *money* came to Peter, and said, Doth not your master pay tribute? He
saith, Yes. And when he was come into the house, Jesus prevented
him, saying, What thinkest thou, Simon? of whom do the kings of the
earth take custom or tribute? of their own children, or of strangers?

A. D. 32.

[m] ch. 21. 21. Mark 11. 23. Luke 17. 6. 1 Cor. 12. 9. 1 Cor. 13. 2.

[n] ch. 16. 21. ch. 20. 17. Mark 8. 31. Mark 9. 30, 31. Mark 10. 33. Luke 9. 22. Luke 18. 31. Luke 24. 6, 7.

[o] Ps. 22. 15, 22. Isa. 53. 7, 10-12. Dan. 9. 26. Mark 9. 33. 1 Cor. 15. 3, 4.

[1] didrachma, in value fifteen-pence. Ex. 30. 13. Ex. 38. 26.

EXPLICIT ANNOUNCEMENT BY OUR LORD OF HIS APPROACHING DEATH AND RESURRECTION. (= Mark ix. 14-32; Luke ix. 37-45.) The time of this Section is sufficiently denoted by the events which all the narratives show to have immediately preceded it—the first explicit announcement of His death, and the transfiguration—both being between his third and his fourth and last Passover,

Healing of the Demoniac and Lunatic Boy (14-21). For the exposition of this portion, see on Mark ix. 14-32.

Second Announcement of His Death (22, 23). **22. And while they abode in Galilee, Jesus said unto them.** Mark (ix. 30), as usual, is very precise here: "And they departed thence"—that is, from the scene of the last miracle—"and passed through Galilee; and He would not that any man should know it." So this was not a preaching, but a private journey through Galilee. Indeed, His public ministry in Galilee was now all but concluded. Though He sent out the Seventy after this to preach and heal, Himself was little more in public there, and He was soon to bid it a final adieu. Till this hour arrived He was chiefly occupied with the Twelve, preparing them for the coming events. **The Son of man shall be betrayed into the hands of men; 23. And they shall kill him, and the third day he shall be raised again. And they were exceeding sorry.** Though the shock would not be so great as at the first announcement (ch. xvi. 21, 22), their "sorrow" would not be the less, but probably the greater, the deeper the intelligence went down into their hearts, and a new wave dashing upon them by this repetition of the heavy tidings. Accordingly, Luke (ix. 43, 44), connecting it with the scene of the miracle just recorded, and the teaching which arose out of it—or possibly with all His recent teaching—says our Lord forewarned the Twelve that they would soon stand in need of all that teaching: "But while they wondered every one at all things which Jesus did, He said unto His disciples, Let these sayings sink down into your ears; for the Son of Man shall be delivered, &c.:" 'Be not carried off your feet by the grandeur you have lately seen in Me, but remember what I have told you, and now tell you again, that that Sun in whose beams ye now rejoice is soon to set in midnight gloom.' Remarkable is the antithesis in those words of our Lord, preserved in all the three Narratives—"The Son of *man* shall be betrayed into the hands of *men*." He adds (*v.* 45) that "they understood not this saying, and it was hid from them, that they perceived it not"—for the plainest statements, when they encounter long-continued and obstinate prejudices, are seen through a distorting and dulling medium—"and were afraid to ask Him;" deterred partly by the air of lofty sadness with which doubtless these sayings were uttered, and on which they would be reluctant to break in, and partly by the fear of laying themselves open to rebuke for their shallowness and timidity. How artless is all this!

For Remarks on this Section, see on Mark ix. 14-32. at the close of that Section.

24-27.—THE TRIBUTE MONEY.

The time of this Section is evidently in immediate succession to that of the preceding one. The brief but most pregnant incident which it records is given by our Evangelist alone—for whom, no doubt, it would have a peculiar interest, from its relation to his own town and his own familiar lake. **24. And when they were come to Capernaum, they that received tribute money** [τὰ δίδραχμα]—'the double drachma;' a sum equal to two Attic drachmas, and corresponding to the Jewish "half-shekel," payable, towards the maintenance of the Temple and its services, by every male Jew of twenty years old and upwards. For the origin of this annual tax, see Exod. xxx. 13, 14; 2 Chr. xxiv. 6, 9. Thus, it will be observed, it was not a civil, but *an ecclesiastical tax*. The tax mentioned in the next verse was a civil one. The whole teaching of this very remarkable scene depends upon this distinction. **came to Peter**—at whose house Jesus probably resided while at Capernaum. This explains several things in the narrative. **and said, Doth not your master pay tribute?** The question seems to imply that the payment of this tax was *voluntary*, but *expected;* or what, in modern phrase, would be called a 'voluntary assessment.' **25. He**

26 Peter saith unto him, Of strangers. Jesus saith unto him, Then are the
27 children free. Notwithstanding, lest we [p]should offend them, go thou
to the sea, and cast an hook, and take up the fish that first cometh
up; and when thou hast opened his mouth, thou shalt find [2]a piece
of money: that take, and give unto them for me and thee.
18 AT [a]the same time came the disciples unto Jesus, saying, Who is
2 the greatest in the kingdom of heaven? And Jesus called a little child
3 unto him, and set him in the midst of them, and said, Verily I say
unto you, [b]Except ye be converted, and become as little children, ye
4 shall not enter into the kingdom of heaven. Whosoever [c]therefore shall
humble himself as this little child, the same is greatest in the kingdom
5 of heaven. And [d]whoso shall receive one such little child in my name
6 receiveth me. But whoso shall offend one of these little ones which
believe in me, it were better for him that a millstone were hanged about
his neck, and *that* he were drowned in the depth of the sea.
7 Woe unto the world because of offences! for [e]it must needs be that

A. D. 32.

p Mark 12.17. 1 Cor. 10.32.
2 Or, a stater. It is in value 2s. 6d. after 5s. the ounce.

CHAP. 18.
a Mark 9. 33. Luke 9. 46.
b Ps. 131. 2. Mark 10.14. Luke 18. 16.
c Ps. 57. 15. Ps. 66. 2.
d ch. 10. 42.
e Luke 17. 1. 1 Cor.11.19.

saith, Yes—*q. d.*, 'To be sure He does;' as if eager to remove even the suspicion of the contrary. If Peter knew—as surely he did—that there was at this time no money in the bag, this reply must be regarded as a great act of faith in his Master. **And when he was come into the house**—Peter's, **Jesus prevented him** [προέφθασεν αὐτὸν]—'anticipated him;' according to the old sense of the word "prevent," **saying, What thinkest thou, Simon?**—using his family name for familiarity, **of whom do the kings of the earth take custom** [τέλη]—meaning custom on goods exported or imported—**or tribute?** [κῆνσον, from the Latin word *census*]—meaning the poll-tax, payable to the Romans by every one whose name was in the 'census.' This, therefore, it will be observed, was strictly *a civil tax.* **of their own children, or of strangers** [ἀλλοτρίων]? This cannot mean 'foreigners,' from whom sovereigns certainly do not raise taxes, but 'those who are not of their own family,' that is, their subjects. **26. Peter saith unto him, Of strangers**—or, 'Of those not their children.' **Jesus saith unto him, Then are the children free.** By "the children" our Lord cannot here mean Himself and the Twelve together, in some loose sense of their near relationship to God as their common Father. For besides that our Lord never once mixes Himself up with His disciples in speaking of their relation to God, but ever studiously keeps His relation and theirs apart (see, for example, on the last words of this chapter)—this would be to teach the right of believers to exemption from the dues required for sacred services, in the teeth of all that Paul teaches and that He Himself indicates throughout. He can refer here, then, only to Himself; using the word "children" evidently in order to express the general principle observed by sovereigns, who do not draw taxes from their own children, and thus convey the truth respecting His own exemption the more strikingly:—*q. d.*, 'If the sovereign's own family be exempt, you know the inference in My case;' or to express it more nakedly than Jesus thought needful and fitting: 'This is a tax for upholding My Father's House: As His Son, then, that tax is not due by Me—I AM FREE.' **27. Notwithstanding, lest we should offend**—or 'stumble'—**them**—all ignorant as they are of My relation to the Lord of the Temple, and should misconstrue a claim to exemption into indifference to His honour who dwells in it, **go thou to the sea**—Capernaum, it will be remembered, lay on the sea of Galilee, **and cast an hook, and take up the fish that first cometh up; and when thou hast opened his mouth, thou shalt find a piece of money** [στατῆρα]—'a stater.' So it should have been rendered, and not indefinitely, as in our version; for the coin was an Attic silver coin, equal to two of the fore-mentioned "didrachms" of half-a-shekel's value, and so, was the exact sum required for both. Accordingly, the Lord adds, **that take, and give unto them for me and thee** [ἀντὶ ἐμοῦ καὶ σοῦ]—lit., 'instead of Me and thee;' perhaps because the payment was a *redemption of the person* paid for (Exod. xxx. 12)—in which view Jesus certainly was "free." If the house was Peter's, this will account for payment being provided on this occasion, not for all the Twelve, but only for him and His Lord. Observe, our Lord does not say "for us," but "for Me and thee;" thus distinguishing the Exempted One and His non-exempted disciple. (See on John xx. 17.)

Remarks.—1. A stronger claim to essential Divinity than our Lord in this scene at Capernaum advances—as "own Son" of the Lord of the Temple—cannot well be conceived. Either, therefore, the teaching of the Lord Jesus was systematically subversive of the prerogatives of Him who will not give His glory to another, or He was the Fellow of the Lord of hosts. But the former cannot be true, attested as Jesus was in every imaginable way by His Father in heaven: His claim, then, to supreme personal Divinity, ought with Christians to be beyond dispute, and is so with all who deserve the name—who would die sooner than surrender it, and with whose loftiest joys and hopes it is inseparably bound up. 2. What manifold wonders are there in the one miracle of this Section! The exact sum required was found in a fish's mouth; Jesus showed that He knew this; this very fish came to the spot where Peter's hook was to be cast, and at the very time when it was cast; that fish took that hook, retained it till drawn to land, and there yielded up the needed coin! And yet, 3. Amidst such wealth of divine resources—lo, the Lord's whole means of temporal subsistence at this time appear to have been exhausted! "Ye know the grace of our Lord Jesus Christ"—but *do ye know it*, O my readers?—"that though He was rich, yet for your sakes He became poor, that ye through his poverty might be rich!" (2 Cor. viii. 9).

CHAP. XVIII. 1-9.—STRIFE AMONG THE TWELVE WHO SHOULD BE GREATEST IN THE KINGDOM OF HEAVEN, WITH RELATIVE TEACHING. (= Mark ix. 33-50; Luke ix. 46-50.) For the exposition, see on Mark ix. 33-50.

10-35.—FURTHER TEACHING ON THE SAME

offences come; but [f]woe to that man by whom the offence cometh!
8 Wherefore [g]if thy hand or thy foot offend thee, cut them off, and cast
them from thee: it is better for thee to enter into life halt or maimed,
rather than having two hands or two feet to be cast into everlasting fire.
9 And if thine eye offend thee, pluck it out, and cast *it* from thee: it is
better for thee to enter into life with one eye, rather than having two
eyes to be cast into hell fire.
10 Take heed that ye despise not one of these little ones; for I say unto
you, That in heaven [h]their angels do always [i]behold the face of my
11 Father which is in heaven. For the Son of man is come to save that
12 which was lost. How [j]think ye? If a man have an hundred sheep,
and one of them be gone astray, doth he not leave the ninety and nine,
and goeth into the mountains, and seeketh that which is gone astray?
13 And if so be that he find it, verily I say unto you, He rejoiceth more of
14 that *sheep*, than of the ninety and nine which went not astray. Even so
it is not the will of your Father which is in heaven, that one of these
little ones should perish.
15 Moreover, [k]if thy brother shall trespass against thee, go and tell him
his fault between thee and him alone: if he shall hear thee, [l]thou hast
16 gained thy brother. But if he will not hear *thee, then* take with thee
one or two more, that in [m]the mouth of two or three witnesses every
17 word may be established. And if he shall neglect to hear them, tell *it*
unto [n]the church: but if he neglect to hear the church, let him be unto
thee as an [o]heathen man and a publican.
18 Verily I say unto you, [p]Whatsoever ye shall bind on earth shall be

A. D. 32.
f ch. 26. 24.
g Deut. 13. 6. ch. 5. 29, 30. ch. 14. 3, 4. Mark 9. 43. Luke 14. 26. Luke 18. 22.
h Ps. 34. 7. Zech. 13. 7. Heb. 1. 14.
i Esth. 1. 14. Luke 1. 19.
j Luke 15. 4.
k Lev. 19. 17. Luke 17. 3.
l Jas. 5. 20. 1 Pet. 3. 1.
m Num. 35. 30. Deut. 17. 6. Deut. 19. 15. 1 Ki. 21. 13. John 8. 17. 2 Cor. 13. 1. Heb. 10. 28. 1 John 5. 7, 8. Rev. 11. 3.
n 1 Tim. 5. 20.
o Rom. 16. 17. 1 Cor. 5. 9. 2 John 10.
p John 20. 23.

SUBJECT, INCLUDING THE PARABLE OF THE UNMERCIFUL DEBTOR.

Same Subject (10-20). **10. Take heed that ye despise**—'stumble'—**not one of these little ones; for I say unto you, That in heaven their angels do always behold the face of my Father which is in heaven.** A difficult verse; but perhaps the following may be more than an illustration:—Among men, those who nurse and rear the royal children, however humble in themselves, are allowed free entrance with their charge, and a degree of familiarity which even the highest state-ministers dare not assume. Probably our Lord means that, in virtue of their charge over His disciples (Heb. i. 13; John i. 51), the angels have *errands* to the throne, a *welcome* there, and *a dear familiarity* in dealing with "His Father which is in heaven," which on their own matters they could not assume (See on John v. 1-47, Remark 1, at the close of that Section.) **11. For the Son of man is come to save that which was**—or 'is'—**lost.** A golden saying, once and again repeated in different forms. Here the connection seems to be, 'Since the whole object and errand of the Son of Man into the world is to save the lost, take heed lest, by causing 'offences, ye lose the saved.' That this is the idea intended we may gather from verse 14. **12, 13. How think ye? If a man have an hundred sheep, and one of them be gone astray, &c.** This is another of those pregnant sayings which our Lord uttered more than once. See on the delightful parable of the lost sheep in Luke xv. 4-7. Only the object *there* is to show what the good Shepherd will do, when even one of His sheep is lost, to *find* it; *here* the object is to show, when found, how reluctant He is to *lose* it. Accordingly, it is added, *v.* **14. Even so it is not the will of your Father which is in heaven, that one of these little ones should perish.** How, then, can He but visit for those "offences" which endanger the souls of these little ones!

15. Moreover, if thy brother shall trespass against thee, go and tell him his fault between thee and him alone: if he shall hear thee, thou hast gained thy brother. 16. But if he will not hear thee, then take with thee one or two more, that in the mouth of two or three witnesses every word may be established. (Deut. xvii. 6; xix. 15.) **17. And if he shall neglect to hear them, tell it unto the church: but if he neglect to hear the church, let him be unto thee as an heathen man and a publican.** Probably our Lord has reference still to the late dispute, Who should be the greatest? After the rebuke—so gentle and captivating, yet so dignified and divine—under which they would doubtless be smarting, perhaps each would be saying, It was not *I* that began it, it was not I that threw out unworthy and irritating insinuations against my brethren. Be it so, says our Lord; but as such things will often arise, I will direct you how to proceed. *First*, Neither harbour a grudge against your offending brother, nor break forth upon him in presence of the unbelieving, but take him aside, show him his fault, and if he own and make reparation for it, you have done more service to him than even justice to yourself. *Next*, If this fail, take two or three to witness how just your complaint is, and how brotherly your spirit in dealing with him. *Again*, If this fail, bring him before the church or congregation to which both belong. *Lastly*, If even this fail, regard him as no longer a brother Christian, but as one "without"—as the Jews did Gentiles and Publicans.

18. Verily I say unto you, Whatsoever ye shall bind on earth shall be bound in heaven; and whatsoever ye shall loose on earth shall be loosed in heaven. Here, what had been granted but a short time before to Peter only (see on ch. xvi. 16) is plainly extended to all the Twelve; so that whatever it means, it means nothing peculiar to Peter, far less to his pretended successors at Rome. It has to do with admission to and rejection from the membership of the Church. But see on John

bound in heaven; and whatsoever ye shall loose on earth shall be loosed
19 in heaven. Again [q]I say unto you, That if two of you shall agree on
earth as touching any thing that they shall ask, [r]it shall be done for
20 them of my Father which is in heaven. For where two or three are
gathered together in my name, [s]there am I in the midst of them.
21 Then came Peter to him, and said, Lord, how oft shall my brother sin
22 against me, and I forgive him? [t]till seven times? Jesus saith unto him,
I say not unto thee, Until seven times; [u]but, Until seventy times seven.
23 Therefore is the kingdom of heaven likened unto a certain king, which
24 would take account of his servants. And when he had begun to reckon,
25 one was brought unto him, which owed him ten thousand [1]talents: but
forasmuch as he had not to pay, his lord commanded him [v]to be sold,
and his wife and children, and all that he had, and payment to be made.
26 The servant therefore fell down, and [2]worshipped him, saying, Lord, have

A. D. 32.

q ch. 5. 24.
r Jas. 5. 16.
s Ezek. 48. 35.
t Luke 17. 4.
u Col. 3. 13.
1 A talent is 750 ounces of silver, which after five shillings the ounce is 187*l* 10s.
v 2 Ki. 4. 1.
2 Or, besought him.

xx. 23. **19. Again I say unto you, That if two of you shall agree on earth as touching any thing that they shall ask, it shall be done for them of my Father which is in heaven. 20. For where two or three are gathered together in** [or 'unto'—εἰς] **my name, there am I in the midst of them.** On this passage—so full of sublime encouragement to Christian union in action and in prayer—observe, first, the connection in which it stands. Our Lord had been speaking of church-meetings, before which the obstinate perversity of a brother was, in the last resort, to be brought, and whose decision was to be final—such honour does the Lord of the Church put upon its lawful assemblies. But not these assemblies only does He deign to countenance and honour. For even two uniting to bring any matter before Him shall find that they are not alone, for My Father is with them, says Jesus. Next, observe the *premium here put upon union in prayer*. As this cannot exist with fewer than two, so by letting it down so low as that number, He gives the utmost conceivable encouragement to union in this exercise. But what kind of union? Not an agreement merely to pray in concert, but to pray *for some definite thing*. "As touching anything which they shall ask," says our Lord—anything they shall agree to ask in concert. At the same time, it is plain He had certain things at that moment in His eye, as most fitting and needful subjects for such concerted prayer. The Twelve had been "falling out by the way" about the miserable question of precedence in their Master's kingdom, and this, as it stirred their corruptions, had given rise—or at least was in danger of giving rise—to "offences" perilous to their souls. The Lord Himself had been directing them how to deal with one another about such matters. "But now shows He unto them a more excellent way." Let them bring all such matters—yea, and everything whatsoever by which either their own loving relationship to each other, or the good of His kingdom at large, might be affected—to their Father in heaven; and if they be but agreed in petitioning Him about that thing, it shall be done for them of His Father which is in heaven. But further, it is not merely union in prayer for the same thing—for that might be with very jarring ideas of the thing to be desired—but it is to symphonious prayer [as the word signifies—συμφωνήσωσιν], to prayer by kindred spirits, members of one family, servants of one Lord, constrained by the same love, fighting under one banner, cheered by assurances of the same victory; a living and loving union, whose voice in the Divine ear is as the sound of many waters. Accordingly, what they ask "*on earth*" is done for them, says Jesus, "of my Father which is *in heaven*." Not for nothing does He say, "of MY FATHER"—not "YOUR FATHER;" as is evident from what follows: "For where two or three are gathered together *unto my name*"—the "My" is emphatic [εἰς τὸ ἐμὸν ὄνομα] "*there am I* in the midst of them." As His name would prove a spell to draw together many clusters of His dear disciples, so if there should be but two or three, that will attract Himself down into the midst of them; and related as He is to both the parties, the petitioners and the Petitioned—to the one on earth by the tie of His assumed flesh, and to the other in heaven by the tie of His eternal Spirit—their symphonious prayers on earth would thrill upwards through Him to heaven, be carried by Him into the holiest of all, and so reach the Throne. Thus will He be the living Conductor of the prayer upward and the answer downward.

Parable of the Unmerciful Debtor (21-35). **21. Then came Peter to him, and said, Lord, how oft shall my brother sin against me, and I forgive him?** In the recent dispute, Peter had probably been an object of special envy, and his forwardness in continually answering for all the rest would likely be cast up to him—and if so, probably by Judas—notwithstanding his Master's commendations. And as such insinuations were perhaps made once and again, he wished to know how often and how long he was to stand it. **till seven times?** This being the sacred and complete number, perhaps his meaning was, Is there to be a limit at which the needful forbearance will be *full?* **22. Jesus saith unto him, I say not unto thee, Until seven times; but, Until seventy times seven**—that is, so long as it shall be needed and sought: you are never to come to the point of refusing forgiveness sincerely asked. (See on Luke xvii. 3, 4.) **23. Therefore**—'with reference to this matter,' **is the kingdom of heaven likened unto a certain king, which would take account of his servants**—or, would scrutinize the accounts of his revenue-collectors. **24. And when he had begun to reckon, one was brought unto him, which owed him ten thousand talents.** If *Attic* talents are here meant, 10,000 of them would amount to above *a million and a half* sterling; if Jewish talents, to a much larger sum. **25. But forasmuch as he had not to pay, his lord commanded him to be sold, and his wife and children, and all that he had, and payment to be made.** (See 2 Ki. iv. 1; Neh. v. 8; Lev. xxv. 39.) **26. The servant therefore fell down, and worshipped him**—or did humble obeisance to him, **saying, Lord, have patience with me, and I will pay thee all.** This was just an acknowledgment of the justice of the claim made against

27 patience with me, and I will pay thee all. Then the lord of that servant
was moved with compassion, and loosed him, and forgave him the debt.
28 But the same servant went out, and found one of his fellow-servants,
which owed him an hundred [3] pence; and he laid hands on him, and took
29 *him* by the throat, saying, Pay me that thou owest. And his fellow-
servant fell down at his feet, and besought him, saying, Have patience
30 with me, and I will pay thee all. And he would not; but went and cast
31 him into prison, till he should pay the debt. So when his fellow-servants saw what was done, they were very sorry, and came and told unto
32 their lord all that was done. Then his lord, after that he had called him,
said unto him, O thou wicked servant, I forgave thee all that debt,
33 because thou desiredst me: shouldest [w] not thou also have had compassion
34 on thy fellow-servant, even as I had pity on thee? And his lord was
wroth, and delivered him to the tormentors, till he should pay all that
35 was due unto him. So [x] likewise shall my heavenly Father do also unto
you, if ye from your hearts forgive not every one his brother their
trespasses.

A. D. 32.

[3] The Roman penny is the eighth part of an ounce, which after five shillings the ounce is sevenpence halfpenny. ch. 20. 2.

[w] Eph. 4. 32. Eph. 5. 2. Col. 3. 13.

[x] Pro. 21. 13. ch 6. 12. Mark 11. 26. Jas. 2. 13.

him, and a piteous imploration of mercy. **27. Then the lord of that servant was moved with compassion, and loosed him, and forgave him the debt.** Payment being hopeless, the Master is, first, moved with compassion; next, liberates his debtor from prison; and then cancels the debt freely. **28. But the same servant went out, and found one of his fellow-servants.** Mark the difference here. The first case is that of master and servant; in this case, both are on a footing of equality. (See *v.* 33, below.) **which owed him an hundred pence.** If Jewish money is intended, this debt was to the other less than *one to a million.* **and he laid hands on him, and took him by the throat** [κρατήσας αὐτὸν ἔπνιγε]—'he seized and throttled him,' **saying, Pay me that thou owest.** Mark the mercilessness even of the tone. **29. And his fellow-servant fell down at his feet, and besought him, saying, Have patience with me, and I will pay thee all.** The same attitude, and the same words which drew compassion from his master are here employed towards himself by his fellow-servant. **30. And he would not; but went and cast him into prison, till he should pay the debt. 31. So when his fellow-servants saw what was done, they were very sorry, and came and told unto their lord all that was done.** Jesus here vividly conveys the intolerable injustice and impudence which even the servants saw in this act, on the part of one so recently laid under the heaviest obligations to their common master. **32. Then his lord, after that he had called him, said unto him, O thou wicked servant, I forgave thee all that debt, because thou desiredst me: 33. Shouldest not thou also have had compassion on thy fellow-servant, even as I had pity on thee?** Before bringing down his vengeance upon him, he calmly points out to him how shamefully unreasonable and heartless his conduct was; which would give the punishment inflicted on him a double sting. **34. And his lord was wroth, and delivered him to the tormentors** [βασανισταῖς]—more than *jailers;* denoting the severity of the treatment which he thought such a case demanded. **till he should pay all that was due unto him. 35. So likewise** [Οὕτως καὶ]—in this *spirit,* or on this principle, **shall my heavenly Father do also unto you, if ye from your hearts forgive not every one his brother their trespasses.**

Remarks.—1. When we think how Jesus here speaks of God's "little ones"—how dear, He tells us, even one of them is to His Father, and what perdition to them lies in the bosom of those "offences" which are apt to spring up amongst them—how incredible would it appear, if we did not see it with our eyes, that Christians should think so little of falling out on the merest trifles, and insist so rancorously on their own point in every argument! See on Mark ix. 33-50, and Remark 1 there; and compare Rom. xiv. 13-17, where our Lord's teaching on this subject seems to have been in the apostle's eye. Ours rather be the Good Shepherd's jealous care to recover His sheep when lost, and keep them when found! 2. How delightful is the truth—here and elsewhere taught in Scripture—that God's dear children are committed by Him, during their sojourn here, to the guardianship of angels! Whatever may be the meaning of the remarkable expression, "*their angels*"—whether it be designed to teach us that each child of God is under the special care of one particular angel, a doctrine in which, notwithstanding Romish abuses, we can see nothing unscriptural; or whether it mean no more than simply 'the angelic guardians of believers'—the information communicated here only, that they do always behold the face of Christ's Father in heaven, is surely designed to teach us how dear to God and how high in His favour each of them is, when even their guardians have uninterrupted and familiar access to their Father on their account. Children of God, brighten up, when ye hear this. But O, have a care how ye think and speak and act, under such high guardianship! 3. How much unlovely feeling among Christians would disappear under the treatment here enjoined! Many misunderstandings melt away under a quiet brotherly expostulation with the offending party: failing this, the affectionate and faithful dealings of two or three more—still in private—might be expected to have more weight: and if even an appeal, in the last resort, to the body of Christians to which both belonged, should fail to bring an offending party to reason, the matter would but require to end there, and Christian fellowship with the refractory member henceforth to cease. 4. The opening and shutting of the doors of Christian fellowship—in other words, Church Discipline—is an ordinance of the Church's Living Head, whose sanction is pledged to the faithful exercise of it, in accordance with His word. 5. What sublime encouragement to concerted prayer among Christians, for definite objects, have we in this Section. And should not Christians prove their Lord now herewith, if He will not open to them the windows of heaven, and

19 AND it came to pass, [a]*that* when Jesus had finished these sayings, he
departed from Galilee, and came into the coasts of Judea beyond Jordan;
2 and [b]great multitudes followed him; and he healed them there.
3 The Pharisees also came unto him, tempting him, and saying unto
4 him, Is it lawful for a man to put away his wife for every cause? And
he answered and said unto them, Have ye not read, [c]that he which made
5 *them* at the beginning made them male and female, and said, [d]For this
cause shall a man leave father and mother, and shall cleave to his wife:
6 and [e]they twain shall be one flesh? Wherefore they are no more twain,
but one flesh. What therefore God hath joined together, let not man
put asunder.
7 They say unto him, [f]Why did Moses then command to give a writing
8 of divorcement, and to put her away? He saith unto them, Moses
because of the hardness of your hearts suffered you to put away your

A. D. 32.

CHAP. 19.
[a] Mark 10. 1. John 10. 40.
[b] ch. 12. 15. ch. 15. 20. Mark 6. 55.
[c] Gen. 1. 27. Gen. 5. 2. Mal. 2. 15.
[d] Gen. 2. 24. Mark 10. 5, 9. Eph. 5. 31.
[e] 1 Cor. 6. 16. 1 Cor. 7. 2.
[f] Deut. 24. 1. ch. 5. 31.

pour them out a blessing that there shall not be room enough to receive it? 6. When we read our Lord's injunctions here to stretch our forbearance with brethren to the utmost, can we but blush to think how little it is done, especially in the light of that other saying of His—"Ye are my friends, if ye do whatsoever I command you"? (John xv. 14). Let us hear the apostle. "Put on therefore, as the elect of God, holy and beloved, bowels of mercies, kindness, humbleness of mind, meekness, long-suffering; forbearing one another, and forgiving one another, if any man have a quarrel against any: even as Christ forgave you, so also do ye. And above all these things put on charity, which is the bond of perfectness. And let the peace of God rule in your hearts, to the which also ye are called in one body; and be ye thankful" (Col. iii. 12-15). 7. Let the grand evangelical principle on which turns the beautiful parable of the Unmerciful Debtor be written as in letters of gold and hung up before every Christian eye—that *God's forgiveness of our vast debts to Him precedes our forgiveness of the petty debts we owe to one another;* that this is that which *begets in us the forgiving disposition;* and that it *furnishes us with the grand model of forgiving Mercy which we have to copy.* 8. When our Lord represents the king in the parable as cancelling the free pardon of the relentless debtor, and again shutting him up in prison till he should pay all that he owed; and when He then says, "So shall My heavenly Father do also unto you, if ye from your hearts forgive not every one his brother their trespasses"—we must not understand Him to teach that such literal reversals of pardon do actually take place in God's treatment of His pardoned children—for that, we take it, is but the dress of the parable—but simply, that *on this principle* God will deal, in the matter of forgiveness, with unforgiving men; and so, we have here just a repetition—in the form of a parable—of the truth expressed in ch. vi. 15, and elsewhere, that "if we forgive not men their trespasses, neither will our heavenly Father forgive our trespasses."

CHAP. XIX. 1-12.—FINAL DEPARTURE FROM GALILEE—DIVORCE. (=Mark x. 1-12; Luke ix. 51.)

Farewell to Galilee. **1. And it came to pass, that when Jesus had finished these sayings, he departed from Galilee.** This marks a very solemn period in our Lord's public ministry. So slightly is it touched here, and in the corresponding passage of Mark (x. 1), that few readers probably note it as the Redeemer's *Farewell to Galilee,* which however it was. See on the sublime statement of Luke (ix. 51), which relates to the same transition-stage in the progress of our Lord's work. **and came into the coasts**—or 'boundaries'—**of Judea beyond Jordan**—that is, to the further, or east side of the Jordan, into Perea, the dominions of Herod Antipas. But though one might conclude from our Evangelist that our Lord went straight from the one region to the other, we know from the other Gospels that a considerable time elapsed between the departure from the one and the arrival at the other, during which many of the most important events in our Lord's public life occurred—probably a large part of what is recorded in Luke ix. 51, onwards to ch. xviii. 15, and part of John vii. 2—xi. 54. **2. And great multitudes followed him; and he healed them there.** Mark says further (x. 1), that "as He was wont, He taught them there." What we now have on the subject of Divorce is some of that teaching.

Divorce (3-12). **3. The Pharisees also came unto him, tempting him, and saying unto him, Is it lawful for a man to put away his wife for every cause?** Two rival schools (as we saw on ch. v. 31) were divided on this question—a delicate one, as *de Wette* pertinently remarks, in the dominions of Herod Antipas. **4. And he answered and said unto them, Have ye not read, that he which made them at the beginning made them male and female**—or better, perhaps, 'He that made them made them from the beginning a male and a female.' **5. And said, For this cause**—to follow out this divine appointment, **shall a man leave father and mother, and shall cleave to his wife: and they twain shall be one flesh? 6. Wherefore they are no more twain, but one flesh. What therefore God hath joined together, let not man put asunder.** Jesus here sends them back to the original constitution of man as one pair, a male and a female; to their marriage, as such, by divine appointment; and to the purpose of God, expressed by the sacred historian, that in all time one man and one woman should by marriage become one flesh—so to continue as long as both are in the flesh. This being *God's* constitution, let not *man* break it up by causeless divorces.

7. They say unto him, Why did Moses then command to give a writing of divorcement, and to put her away? 8. He saith unto them, Moses—as a civil lawgiver, **because of** [πρὸς τὴν]—or 'having respect to' **the hardness of your hearts**—looking to your low moral state, and your inability to endure the strictness of the original law, **suffered you to put away your wives**—tolerated a relaxation of the strictness of the marriage bond—not as approving of it, but to prevent still greater evils. **but from the beginning it was not so.** This is repeated, in order to impress upon His audience the temporary and purely civil character of this Mosaic relaxation. **9. And I say**

9 wives: but [g]from the beginning it was not so. And [h]I say unto you,
Whosoever shall put away his wife, except *it be* for fornication, and shall
marry another, committeth adultery; and whoso marrieth her which is
put away doth commit adultery.
10 His disciples say unto him, [i]If the case of the man be so with *his* wife,
11 it is not good to marry. But he said unto them, [j]All *men* cannot receive
12 this saying, save *they* to whom it is given. For there are some eunuchs,
which were so born from *their* mother's womb; and there are some
eunuchs, which were made eunuchs of men; and [k]there be eunuchs,
which have made themselves eunuchs for the kingdom of heaven's sake.
He that is able to receive *it*, let him receive *it*.
13 Then [l]were there brought unto him little children, that he should put
14 *his* hands on them, and pray: and the disciples rebuked them. But
Jesus said, Suffer little children, and forbid them not, to come unto me;
15 for of [m]such is the kingdom of heaven. And he laid *his* hands on them,
and departed thence.
16 And, behold, one came and said unto him, [n]Good Master, what [o]good
17 thing shall I do, that I may have eternal life? And he said unto him,
Why callest thou me good? *there is* none good but one, *that is*, God:
18 but if thou wilt enter into life, keep the commandments. He saith unto
him, Which? Jesus said, Thou [p]shalt do no murder, Thou shalt not commit adultery, Thou shalt not steal, Thou shalt not bear false witness,
19 Honour [q]thy father and *thy* mother; and, [r]Thou shalt love thy neighbour
20 as thyself. The young man saith unto him, All these things have I kept
21 from my youth up: what lack I yet? Jesus said unto him, If thou wilt
be perfect, [s]go *and* sell that thou hast, and give to the poor, and thou
22 shalt have treasure in heaven; and come *and* follow me. But when the
young man heard that saying, he went away sorrowful: for he had great
possessions.
23 Then said Jesus unto his disciples, Verily I say unto you, That [t]a rich
24 man shall hardly enter into the kingdom of heaven. And again I say

A. D. 33.

g Jer. 6. 16.
h ch. 5. 32. Mark 10. 11. Luke 16. 18. 1 Cor. 7. 10, 11.
i Gen. 2. 18. Pro. 5. 15-19. Pro. 21. 19. 1 Cor. 7. 1, 2, 8. 1 Tim. 4. 3. 1 Tim. 5. 11-15.
j 1 Cor. 7. 2, 7, 9, 17.
k 1 Cor. 7. 32, 34. 1 Cor. 9. 5, 15.
l Mark 10. 13. Luke 18. 15.
m ch. 18. 3. 1 Pet. 2. 1, 2.
n Luke 10. 25.
o Rom. 9. 31.
p Exod. 20. 13. Deut. 5. 17.
q ch. 15. 4.
r Lev. 19. 18. Rom. 13. 9. Gal. 5. 14. Jas. 2. 8.
s Luke 12. 33. Luke 16. 9. Acts 2. 45. Acts 4. 34. 1 Tim. 6, 18.
t 1 Cor. 1. 26. 1 Tim. 6. 9.

unto you, Whosoever shall put away his wife, except, &c.; and whoso marrieth her which is put away doth commit adultery. See on ch. v. 32. [*Tregelles* brackets this last clause, as of doubtful authority—but without sufficient reason, as we think. *Tischendorf* inserts it, as in the received text.]

10. His disciples say unto him, If the case of the man be so with his wife, it is not good to marry:—*q. d.*, 'In this view of marriage, surely it must prove a snare rather than a blessing, and had better be avoided altogether.' **11. But he said unto them, All men cannot receive this saying, save they to whom it is given:**—*q. d.*, 'That the unmarried state is better, is a saying not for every one, and indeed only for such as it is divinely intended for.' But who are these? they would naturally ask; and this our Lord proceeds to tell them in three particulars. **12. For there are some eunuchs, which were so born from their mother's womb**—persons constitutionally either incapable of or indisposed to marriage; **and there are some eunuchs, which were made eunuchs of men**—persons rendered incapable by others; **and there be eunuchs, which have made themselves eunuchs for the kingdom of heaven's sake**—persons who, to do God's work better, deliberately choose this state. Such was Paul (1 Cor. vii. 7). **He that is able to receive it, let him receive it**—'He who feels this to be his proper vocation, let him embrace it;' which, of course, is as much as to say—'he only.' Thus, all is left free in this matter.

Remarks.—1. If the sanctity of the marriage-tie, as the fountain of all social well-being, is to be upheld among men, it must be by basing it on the original divine institution of it; nor will those relaxations of it which corrupt ingenuity introduces and defends be effectually checked but by reverting, as our Lord here does, to the great primary character and design of it as established at the beginning. 2. Let those who reverence the authority of Christ mark the divine authority which He ascribes to the Old Testament in general, and to the books of Moses in particular, in the settlement of all questions of divine truth and human duty (*vv.* 4, 5); nor let us fail to observe the important distinction which He draws between things commanded and things permitted—between things tolerated for a time, and regulated by civil enactment, to keep the barriers of social morality from being quite broken down, and the enduring sanctities of the great moral law (*vv.* 8, 9). 3. When our Lord holds forth the single life as designed for and suited to certain specific classes, let Christians understand that, while their own plan and condition of life should be regulated by higher considerations than mere inclination or personal advantage, they are not to lay down rules for others, but let each decide for himself, as to his own Master he standeth or falleth. For he that in these things serveth Christ is acceptable to God and approved of men.

13-15.—Little Children Brought to Christ. (= Mark x. 13-16; Luke xviii. 15-17.) For the exposition, see on Luke xviii. 15-17.

16-30.—The Rich Young Ruler. (= Mark x. 17-31; Luke xviii. 18-30.) For the exposition, see on Luke xviii. 18-30.

unto you, It is easier for a camel to go through the eye of a needle, than
25 for a rich man to enter into the kingdom of God. When his disciples
heard *it*, they were exceedingly amazed, saying, Who then can be saved?
26 But Jesus beheld *them*, and said unto them, With men this is impossible;
but with [u] God all things are possible.
27 Then [v] answered Peter and said unto him, Behold, [w] we have forsaken
28 all, and followed thee; what shall we have therefore? And Jesus said
unto them, Verily I say unto you, That ye which have followed me, in
[x] the regeneration, when the Son of man shall sit in the throne of his
glory, [y] ye also shall sit upon twelve thrones, judging the twelve tribes of
29 Israel. And every one that hath forsaken houses, or brethren, or sisters,
or father, or mother, or wife, or children, or lands, for my name's sake,
30 shall receive an hundredfold, and shall inherit everlasting life. But [z] many
that are first shall be last; and the last *shall be* first.

20 FOR the kingdom of heaven is like unto a man *that is* an householder,
which went out early in the morning to hire labourers into his vineyard.
2 And when he had agreed with the labourers for a [1] penny a day, he sent
3 them into his vineyard. And he went out about the third hour, and saw
4 others standing idle in the market-place, and said unto them, Go ye
also into the vineyard, and whatsoever is right I will give you. And
5 they went their way. Again he went out about the sixth and ninth hour,
6 and did likewise. And about the eleventh hour he went out, and found
others standing idle, and saith unto them, Why stand ye here all the day
7 idle? They say unto him, Because no man hath hired us. He saith unto
them, Go ye also into the vineyard; and whatsoever is right, *that* shall
8 ye receive. So when [a] even was come, the lord of the vineyard saith unto
his steward, Call the labourers, and give them *their* hire, beginning from
9 the last unto the first. And when they came that *were hired* about the
10 eleventh hour, they received every man a penny. But when the first

A. D. 33.

[u] Gen. 18. 14. Job 42. 2. Jer. 32. 17. Zech. 8. 6. Mark 10. 27.
[v] Mark 10. 28.
[w] Deut. 33. 9. ch. 4. 20. ch. 9. 9. Mark 1. 17-20. Mark 2. 14. Luke 5. 11. Luke 14. 33. Luke 18. 28.
[x] 2 Cor. 5. 17.
[y] Luke 22. 28. 1 Cor. 6. 2, 3. Rev. 2. 26.
[z] ch. 20. 16. Mark 10. 31.

CHAP. 20.
[1] The Roman penny is the eighth part of an ounce, which after five shillings the ounce is sevenpence halfpenny.
[a] Acts 17. 31. 1 Thes. 4. 16.

CHAP. XX. 1-16.—PARABLE OF THE LABOURERS IN THE VINEYARD.

This parable, recorded only by Matthew, is closely connected with the end of ch. xix., being spoken with reference to Peter's question, How it should fare with those who, like himself, had left all for Christ? It is designed to show that while *they* would be richly rewarded, a certain equity would still be observed towards *later* converts and workmen in His service. **1. For the kingdom of heaven is like unto a man that is an householder, which went out early in the morning to hire labourers into his vineyard.** The figure of a Vineyard, to represent the rearing of souls for heaven, the culture required and provided for that purpose, and the care and pains which God takes in that whole matter, is familiar to every reader of the Bible. (Ps. lxxx. 8-16; Isa. v. 1-7; Jer. ii. 21; Luke xx. 9-16; John xv. 1-8.) At vintage-time, as *Webster and Wilkinson* remark, labour was scarce, and masters were obliged to be early in the market to secure it. Perhaps the pressing nature of the work of the Gospel, and the comparative paucity of labourers, may be incidentally suggested, ch. ix. 37, 38. The "labourers," as in ch. ix. 38, are first, the *official* servants of the Church, but after them and along with them *all* the servants of Christ, whom he has laid under the weightiest obligation to work in His service. **2. And when he had agreed with the labourers for a penny** [δηναρίου]—a usual day's hire (the amount of which will be found in the margin of our Bibles), **he sent them into his vineyard. 3. And he went out about the third hour**—about nine o'clock, or after a fourth of the working day had expired: the day of twelve hours was reckoned from six to six. **and saw others standing idle** [ἀργοὺς]—'unemployed—**in the market-place, 4. And said unto them, Go ye also into the vineyard; and whatsoever is right** [δίκαιον]—'just,' 'equitable,' in proportion to their time—**I will give you. And they went their way. 5. Again he went out about the sixth and ninth hour**—about noon, and about three o'clock afternoon—**and did likewise**—hiring and sending into his vineyard fresh labourers each time. **6. And about the eleventh hour**—but one hour before the close of the working day; a most unusual hour both for offering and engaging—**and found others standing idle, and saith, Why stand ye here all the day idle? 7. They say unto him, Because no man hath hired us. He saith unto them, Go ye also into the vineyard; and whatsoever is right, that shall ye receive.** Of course they had not been there, or not been disposed to offer themselves at the proper time; but as they were now willing, and the day was not over, and "yet there was room," they also are engaged, and on similar terms with all the rest. **8. So when even was come**—that is, the reckoning-time between masters and labourers (see Deut. xxiv. 15); pointing to the day of final account—**the lord of the vineyard saith unto his steward**—answering to Christ Himself, represented "as a Son over His own house" (Heb. iii. 6; see Matt. xi. 27; John iii. 35; v. 27), **Call the labourers, and give them their hire, beginning from the last unto the first.** Remarkable direction this—'last hired, first paid.' **9. And when they came that were hired about the eleventh hour, they received every man a penny**—a full day's wages. **10. But when the first came, they supposed that they should have received more.** This is that calculating,

came, they supposed that they should have received more; and they like-
11 wise received every man a penny. And when they had received *it*, they
12 murmured against the goodman of the house, saying, These last [2]have
wrought *but* one hour, and thou hast made them equal unto us, which
13 have borne the burden and heat of the day. But he answered one of
them, and said, Friend, I do thee no wrong: didst not thou agree with
14 me for a penny? Take *that* thine *is*, and go thy way: I will give unto
15 this last even as unto thee. Is [b]it not lawful for me to do what I will
16 with mine own? [c]Is thine eye evil, because I am good? So [d]the last
shall be first, and the first last: [e]for many be called, but few chosen.

A. D. 33.

[2] Or, have continued one hour only.
[b] Rom. 9. 21.
[c] Deut. 15. 9. Pro. 23. 6. Jon. 4. 1. ch. 6. 23.
[d] ch. 19. 30.
[e] ch. 22. 14. Luke 14. 24.

mercenary spirit which had peeped out—though perhaps very slightly—in Peter's question (ch. xix. 27), and which this parable was designed once for all to put down among the servants of Christ. **11. And when they had received it, they murmured against the goodman of the house** [οἰκοδεσπότου]—rather, 'the householder,' the word being the same as in verse 1. **12. Saying, These last have wrought [but] one hour, and thou hast made them equal unto us, which have borne the burden and heat**—'the burning heat' [καύσωνα] **of the day**—who have wrought not only longer but during a more trying period of the day. **13. But he answered one of them**—doubtless the spokesman of the complaining party—**and said, Friend, I do thee no wrong: didst not thou agree with me for a penny? 14. Take that thine is, and go thy way: I will give unto this last even as unto thee. 15. Is it not lawful for me to do what I will with mine own? Is thine eye evil, because I am good?**—*q. d.*, 'You appeal to *justice*, and by that your mouth is shut; for the sum you agreed for is paid you: Your case being disposed of, with the terms I make with other labourers you have nothing to do; and to grudge the benevolence shown to others, when by your own admission you have been honourably dealt with, is both unworthy envy of your neighbour, and discontent with the goodness that engaged and rewarded you in his service at all.' **16. So the last shall be first, and the first last:**—*q. d.*, 'Take heed lest by indulging the spirit of these "murmurers" at the "penny" given to the last hired, ye miss your own penny, though first in the vineyard; while the consciousness of having come in so late may inspire these last with such a humble frame, and such admiration of the grace that has hired and rewarded them at all, as will put them into the foremost place in the end.' **for many be called, but few chosen.** This is another of our Lord's terse and pregnant sayings, more than once uttered in different connections. (See ch. xix. 30; xxii. 14.) The "calling" of which the New Testament almost invariably speaks is what divines call *effectual* calling, carrying with it a supernatural operation on the will to secure its consent. But that cannot be the meaning of it here; the "called" being emphatically distinguished from the "chosen." It can only mean here the 'invited.' And so the sense is, Many receive the invitations of the Gospel whom God has never "chosen to salvation through sanctification of the Spirit and belief of the truth" (2 Thes. ii. 13). But what, it may be asked, has this to do with the subject of our parable? Probably this—to teach us that men who have wrought in Christ's service all their days may, by the spirit which they manifest at the last, make it too evident that, as between God and their own souls, they never were chosen workmen at all.

Taking the parable thus, the difficulties which have divided so many commentators seem to melt away, and its general teaching may be expressed in the following

Remarks.—1. True Christianity is a life of active service rendered to Christ, whose love, as soon as one has tasted that the Lord is gracious, constrains him to live not unto himself, but unto Him that died for him and rose again. 2. Though we might well deem it a privilege to work for Christ without fee or reward, yet is our Father pleased to attach rewards—not of merit, of course, but of pure grace, as all rewards to those who once were sinners must be—to faithful working in His vineyard. 3. Although the Lord may surely "do what He will with His own," and so His rewards must be regarded as all flowing from His own sovereign will, yet there is a certain equity stamped upon them in relation to each other. That true attachment to Christ, and that fidelity in His service which is common to all chosen labourers in His vineyard—this is acknowledged by a reward common to all alike; and only those services in which Christians differ from each other in self-sacrificing devotedness are distinguished by special rewards corresponding with their character. And thus, while aspiring to those special rewards to distinguished Christians which are promised at the close of ch. xix., we are never to forget that there are gracious rewards common to all the true servants of Christ. 4. How unreasonable and ungrateful are those who, not contented with being called into the service of Christ—itself a high privilege—and graciously rewarded for all they do, envy their fellow-servants, and reflect upon their common Master, for seeming to do to others more than is consistent with justice to themselves. Such was the spirit of the elder brother in the parable of the Prodigal Son (Luke xv). Those men who appeal to God's justice will find their mouth closed in the day that He deals with them. 5. Let those who, conscious of having come in *late*, are afraid lest neither themselves nor their offers of service should be accepted at all, be encouraged by the assurance which this parable holds forth, that as long as the working-day of life and the present state of the kingdom of grace lasts, so long will the great Householder be found looking out for fresh labourers in His vineyard, and so long will He be ready to receive the offers and engage the services of all that are prepared to yield themselves to Him. 6. What strange revelations will the day of final reckoning make—discovering some that came latest in, and were least accounted of, amongst the first in the ranks of heaven; and some that were earliest in, and stood the highest in Christian estimation, among the last and lowest in the ranks of heaven; and some not amongst them at all who were of greatest note in the Church below! "Nevertheless, the foundation of God standeth sure, having this seal, The Lord knoweth them that are His; and, Let every one that nameth the name of Christ depart from iniquity" (2 Tim. ii. 19).

17 And [f]Jesus going up to Jerusalem took the twelve disciples apart in
18 the way, and said unto them, behold, [g]we go up to Jerusalem; and the
Son of man shall be betrayed unto the chief priests and unto the scribes,
19 and they shall condemn him to death, and [h]shall deliver him to the
Gentiles to mock, and to scourge, and to crucify *him:* and the third day
he shall rise again.
20 Then [i]came to him [j]the mother of Zebedee's [k]children with her sons,
21 worshipping *him*, and desiring a certain thing of him. And he said unto
her, What wilt thou? She saith unto him, Grant that these my two sons
[l]may sit, the one on thy right hand, and the other on the left, in thy
22 kingdom. But Jesus answered and said, Ye know not what ye ask. Are
ye able to drink of the [m]cup that I shall drink of, and to be baptized
with [n]the baptism that I am baptized with? They say unto him, We are
23 able. And he saith unto them, [o]Ye shall drink indeed of my cup, and
be baptized with the baptism that I am baptized with: but to sit on my
right hand, and on my left, is not mine to [p]give, but *it shall be given to*
them for whom it is prepared of my Father.
24 And [q]when the ten heard *it*, they were moved with indignation against
25 the two brethren. But Jesus called them *unto him*, and said, Ye know
that the princes of the Gentiles exercise dominion over them, and they
26 that are great exercise authority upon them. But [r]it shall not be so
among you: but whosoever [s]will be great among you, let him be your
27 minister; and [t]whosoever will be chief among you, let him be your
28 servant: even [u]as the Son of man came not to be ministered unto, [v]but
to minister, and to [w]give his life a ransom [x]for many.
29 And [y]as they departed from Jericho, a great multitude followed him.
30 And, behold, [z]two blind men sitting by the way-side, when they heard
that Jesus passed by, cried out, saying, Have mercy on us, O Lord, *thou*
31 son of David! And the multitude rebuked them, because they should
hold their peace: but they cried the more, saying, Have mercy on us, O
32 Lord, *thou* son of David! And Jesus stood still, and called them, and
33 said, What will ye that I shall do unto you? They say unto him, Lord,
34 that our eyes may be opened. So Jesus had [a]compassion *on them*, and
touched their eyes; and immediately their eyes received sight, and they
followed him.

21 AND [a]when they drew nigh unto Jerusalem, and were come to Beth-
2 phage, unto [b]the mount of Olives, then sent Jesus two disciples, saying
unto them, Go into the village over against you, and straightway ye shall
find an ass tied, and a colt with her: loose *them*, and bring *them* unto me.
3 And if any *man* say ought unto you, ye shall say, The [c]Lord hath [d]need
4 of them; and straightway he will send them. (All this was done, that
5 it might be fulfilled which was spoken by the prophet, saying, Tell [e]ye
the daughter of Sion, Behold, thy King cometh unto thee, meek, and
6 sitting upon an ass, and a colt the foal of an ass.) And [f]the disciples
7 went, and did as Jesus commanded them, and brought the ass, and the
8 colt, and put [g]on them their clothes, and they set *him* thereon. And a
very great multitude spread their garments in the way; [h]others cut down
9 branches from the trees, and strawed *them* in the way. And the multitudes that went before, and that followed, cried, saying, [i]Hosanna to the

A. D. 33.

[f] John 12. 12.
[g] ch. 16. 21.
[h] ch. 27. 2. John 18. 28. Acts 3. 13.
[i] Mark 10. 35.
[j] ch. 27. 56. Mark 15. 40.
[k] ch. 4. 21.
[l] ch. 19. 28. Jas. 4. 3.
[m] ch. 26. 39. Mark 14. 36. John 18. 11.
[n] Luke 12. 50.
[o] Acts 12. 2. Rom. 8. 17. 2 Cor. 1. 7. Rev. 1. 9.
[p] ch. 25. 34.
[q] Luke 22. 24.
[r] 1 Pet. 5. 3.
[s] ch. 23. 11. Mark 9. 35. Mark 10. 43.
[t] ch. 18. 4.
[u] John 13. 4. Phil. 2. 7.
[v] Luke 22. 27. John 13. 14.
[w] Isa. 53. 10. Dan. 9. 24. John 11. 51. 1 Tim. 2. 6. Tit. 2. 14. 1 Pet. 1. 19.
[x] ch. 26. 28. Rom. 5. 15. Heb. 9. 28.
[y] Mark 10. 46. Luke 18. 35.
[z] ch. 9. 27.
[a] Ps. 145. 8. Heb. 4. 15.

CHAP. 21.

[a] Mark 11. 1. Luke 19. 29.
[b] Zec. 14. 4.
[c] Ps. 24. 1.
[d] 2 Cor. 8. 9.
[e] 1 Ki. 1. 33. Isa. 62. 11. Zec. 9. 9.
[f] Mark 11. 4.
[g] 2 Ki. 9. 13.
[h] Lev. 23. 40. John 12. 13.
[i] Ps. 118. 25. ch. 22. 42. Mark 12. 35-37. Luke 18. 38. Rom. 1. 3.

But that is not all the teaching of this parable; for, as *Olshausen* finely says, the parables are like many-sided precious stones, cut so as to cast their lustre in more than one direction.

17-28.—THIRD EXPLICIT ANNOUNCEMENT OF HIS APPROACHING SUFFERINGS, DEATH, AND RESURRECTION—THE AMBITIOUS REQUEST OF JAMES AND JOHN, AND THE REPLY. (= Mark x. 32-45; Luke xviii. 31-34.) For the exposition, see on Mark x. 32-45.

29-34.—TWO BLIND MEN HEALED. (= Mark x. 46-52; Luke xviii. 35-43.) For the exposition, see on Luke xviii. 35-43.

CHAP. XXI. 1-9.—CHRIST'S TRIUMPHAL ENTRY INTO JERUSALEM ON THE FIRST DAY OF THE WEEK. (= Mark xi. 1-11; Luke xix. 29-40; John

A. D. 33.

son of David! [j]Blessed *is* he that cometh in the name of the Lord!
Hosanna in the highest!
10 And [k]when he was come into Jerusalem, all the city was moved, saying,
11 Who is this? And the multitude said, This is Jesus the [l]prophet of
Nazareth of Galilee.
12 And [m]Jesus went into the temple of God, and cast out all them that
sold and bought in the temple, and overthrew the tables of the [n]money-
13 changers, and the seats of them that sold doves, and said unto them, It
is written, [o]My house shall be called the house of prayer; but [p]ye have
14 made it a den of thieves. And [q]the blind and the lame came to him in
15 the temple; and he healed them. And when the chief priests and scribes
saw the wonderful things that he did, and the children crying in the
temple, and saying, Hosanna to [r]the son of David; they were sore dis-
16 pleased, and said unto him, Hearest thou what these say? And Jesus
saith unto them, Yea; have ye never read, [s]Out of the mouth of babes
17 and sucklings thou hast perfected praise? And he left them, and went
out of the city into [t]Bethany; and he lodged there.
18 Now in the morning, as he returned into the city, he hungered.
19 And when he saw [1]a fig tree in the way, he came to it, and found
nothing thereon, but leaves only, and said unto it, Let no fruit grow
on thee henceforward for ever. And presently the fig tree withered away.
20 And when the disciples saw *it*, they marvelled, saying, How soon is
21 the fig tree withered away! Jesus answered and said unto them, Verily
I say unto you, [u]If ye have faith, and [v]doubt not, ye shall not only
do this *which is done* to the fig tree, [w]but also if ye shall say unto this
mountain, Be thou removed, and be thou cast into the sea; it shall be
22 done. And [x]all things, whatsoever ye shall ask in prayer, believing, ye
shall receive.
23 And [y]when he was come into the temple, the chief priests and the
elders of the people came unto him as he was teaching, and [z]said, By
what authority doest thou these things? and who gave thee this au-
24 thority? And [a]Jesus answered and said unto them, I also will ask you
one thing, which if ye tell me, I in like wise will tell you by what author-
25 ity I do these things. The baptism of John, whence was it? from
heaven, or of men? And they reasoned with themselves, saying, If we
shall say, From heaven; he will say unto us, Why did ye not then be-
26 lieve him? But if we shall say, Of men; we fear the people; [b]for all

[j] ch. 23. 39.
[k] Mark 11.15. Luke 19. 45. John 12. 13.
[l] John 6. 14.
[m] Mal. 3. 1, 2. Mark 11. 11. John 2. 15.
[n] Deut. 14. 25.
[o] Isa. 56. 7.
[p] Jer. 7. 11. Mark 11.17. Luke 19.46.
[q] Isa. 35. 5. ch. 9. 35. ch. 11. 4, 5. Acts 3. 1-9. Acts 10. 38.
[r] Isa. 11. 1. ch. 22. 42. John 7. 42.
[s] Ps. 8. 2. ch. 11. 25.
[t] Mark 11.11. John 11. 18.
[1] one fig tree.
[u] ch. 17. 20. Luke 17. 6.
[v] Jas. 1. 6.
[w] 1 Cor. 13. 2.
[x] ch. 7. 7. Mark 11.24. Luke 11. 9. Jas. 5. 16. 1 John 3.22. 1 John 5.14.
[y] Luke 20.21.
[z] Ex. 2. 14. Acts 4. 7. Acts 7. 27.
[a] Job 5. 13.
[b] ch. 14. 5. Luke 20. 6. Mark 6. 20. John 5. 35. John 10. 41, 42.

---

xii. 12-19.) For the exposition of this majestic scene—recorded, as will be seen, by all the Evangelists—see on Luke xix. 29-40.

10-22.—STIR ABOUT HIM IN THE CITY—SECOND CLEANSING OF THE TEMPLE, AND MIRACLES THERE—GLORIOUS VINDICATION OF THE CHILDREN'S TESTIMONY—THE BARREN FIG TREE CURSED, WITH LESSONS FROM IT. (= Mark xi. 11-26; Luke xix. 45-48.) For the exposition, see Luke xix. after *v.* 44; and on Mark xi. 12-26.

23-46.—THE AUTHORITY OF JESUS QUESTIONED, AND THE REPLY—THE PARABLES OF THE TWO SONS, AND OF THE WICKED HUSBANDMEN. (= Mark xi. 27—xii. 12; Luke xx. 1-19.)

Now commences, as *Alford* remarks, that series of parables and discourses of our Lord with His enemies, in which He develops, more completely than ever before, His hostility to their hypocrisy and iniquity: and so they are stirred up to compass His death.

The Authority of Jesus Questioned, and the Reply (23-27). **23. And when he was come into the temple, the chief priests and the elders of the people came unto him as he was teaching, and said, By what authority doest thou these things?**—referring particularly to the expulsion of the buyers and sellers from the temple. **and who gave thee this authority? 24. And Jesus answered and said unto them, I also will ask you one thing, which if ye tell me, I in like wise will tell you by what authority I do these things. 25. The baptism of John**—meaning, his whole mission and ministry, of which baptism was the proper character, **whence was it? from heaven, or of men?** What wisdom there was in this way of meeting their question, will best appear by their reply. **And they reasoned with themselves, saying, If we shall say, From heaven; he will say unto us, Why did ye not then believe him?**—'Why did ye not believe the testimony which he bore to Me, as the promised and expected Messiah?' for that was the burden of his whole testimony. **26. But if we shall say, Of men; we fear the people** [τὸν ὄχλον]—rather the multitude. In Luke (xx. 6) it is, "all the people will stone us" [καταλιθάσει]—'stone us to death.' **for all hold John as a prophet.** Crooked, cringing hypocrites! No wonder Jesus gave you no answer. **27. And they answered Jesus, and said, We cannot tell.** Evidently their difficulty was, how to

27 hold John as a prophet. And they answered Jesus, and said, We cannot tell. And he said unto them, Neither tell I you by what authority
I do these things.
28 But what think ye? A *certain* man had two sons; and he came to
29 the first, and said, Son, go work to-day in my vineyard. He answered
30 and said, I will not: but afterward [c]he repented, and went. And he
came to the second, and said likewise. And he answered and said, I *go,*
31 sir; and went not. Whether of them twain did the will of *his* father?
They say unto him, The first. Jesus saith unto them, Verily I say unto
you, That the publicans and the harlots go into the kingdom of God be-
32 fore you. For [d]John came unto you in the way of righteousness, and ye
believed him not: but [e]the publicans and the harlots believed him: and
ye, when ye had seen *it,* repented not afterward, that ye might believe
him.
33 Hear another parable: There was a certain householder, [f]which
planted a vineyard, and hedged it round about, and digged a winepress
in it, and built a tower, and let it out to husbandmen, and [g]went into a
34 far country: and when the time of the fruit drew near, he sent his
servants to the husbandmen, [h]that they might receive the fruits of it.

A. D. 33.

[c] ch. 3. 2. 2 Chr. 33. 19. Isa. 1. 16. Isa. 55. 6, 7. Ezek. 18. 28. Dan. 4. 34-37. Jonah 3. 2. Luke 15. 18. Acts 26. 20. Eph. 2. 1-10.
[d] Isa. 35. 8. Jer. 6. 16. ch. 3. 1. Luke 3. 8-13.
[e] Luke 3. 12.
[f] Ps. 80. 9. Song 8. 11. Isa. 5. 1. Jer. 2. 21. Mark 12. 1. Luke 20. 9.
[g] ch. 25. 14.
[h] Song 8. 11.

answer, so as neither to shake their determination to reject the claims of Christ nor damage their reputation with the people. For the truth itself they cared nothing whatever. **And he said unto them, Neither tell I you by what authority I do these things.** What composure and dignity of wisdom does our Lord here display, as He turns their question upon themselves, and, while revealing His knowledge of their hypocrisy, closes their mouths! Taking advantage of the surprise, silence, and awe, produced by this reply, our Lord followed it immediately up by the two following parables.

Parable of the Two Sons (28-32). **28. But what think ye? A certain man had two sons; and he came to the first, and said, Son, go work to-day in my vineyard**—for true religion is a practical thing, a "bringing forth fruit unto God." **29. He answered and said, I will not.** *Trench* notices the rudeness of this answer, and the total absence of any attempt to excuse such disobedience, both characteristic; representing careless, reckless sinners, resisting God to His face. **but afterward he repented, and went. 30. And he came to the second, and said likewise. And he answered and said, I [go], sir** [Ἐγὼ κύριε]—'I, sir.' The emphatic "I," here, denotes the self-righteous complacency which says, "God, I thank thee that *I* am not as other men" (Luke xviii. 11). **and went not.** *He* did not "afterward repent" and refuse to go; for there was here no *intention* to go. It is the class that "say and do not" (ch. xxiii. 3)—a falseness more abominable to God, says *Stier*, than any "I will not." **31. Whether of them twain did the will of his Father? They say unto him, The first.** [Instead of ὁ πρῶτος, "the first," *Tregelles* reads ὁ ὕστερος, 'the latter,' contrary not only to the manifest sense of the parable, but to the decided preponderance, as we think, of MS. authority. *Tischendorf* adheres to the received text.] Now comes the application. **Jesus saith unto them, Verily I say unto you, That the publicans and the harlots go**—or 'are going;' even now entering, while ye hold back. **into the kingdom of God before you.** The publicans and the harlots were the first son, who, when told to work in the Lord's vineyard, said, I will not; but afterwards repented and went. Their early life was a flat and flagrant refusal to do what they were commanded; it was one continued rebellion against the authority of God. "The chief priests and the elders of the people," with whom our Lord was now speaking, were the second son, who said, I go, Sir, but went not. They were early called, and all their life long professed obedience to God, but never rendered it; their life was one of continued disobedience. **32. For John came unto you in the way of righteousness**—that is, 'calling you to repentance;' as Noah is styled "a preacher of righteousness" (2 Pet. ii. 5), when like the Baptist he warned the old world to "flee from the wrath to come." **and ye believed him not.** "They did not reject him;" nay, they "were willing for a season to rejoice in his light" (John v. 35): but they would not receive his testimony to Jesus. **but the publicans and the harlots believed him.** Of the publicans this is twice expressly recorded, Luke iii. 12; vii. 29. Of the harlots, then, the same may be taken for granted, though the fact is not expressly recorded. These outcasts gladly believed the testimony of John to the coming Saviour, and so hastened to Jesus when He came. See Luke vii. 37; xv. 1, &c. **and ye, when ye had seen it, repented not afterward, that ye might believe him.** Instead of being "provoked to jealousy" by their example, ye have seen them flocking to the Saviour and getting to heaven, unmoved.

Parable of the Wicked Husbandmen (33-46). **33. Hear another parable: There was a certain householder, which planted a vineyard.** See on Luke xiii. 6. **and hedged it round about, and digged a winepress in it, and built a tower.** These details are taken, as is the basis of the parable itself, from that beautiful parable of Isa. v. 1-7, in order to fix down the application and sustain it by Old Testament authority. **and let it out to husbandmen.** These are just the ordinary spiritual guides of the people, under whose care and culture the fruits of righteousness are expected to spring up. **and went into a far country**—"for a long time" (Luke xx. 9), leaving the vineyard to the laws of the spiritual husbandry during the whole time of the Jewish economy. On this phraseology, see on Mark iv. 26. **34. And when the time of the fruit drew near, he sent his servants to the husbandmen,** By these "servants" are meant the prophets and other extraordinary messengers, raised up from time to time. See on ch. xxiii. 37. **that they might receive**

35 And [i]the husbandmen took his servants, and beat one, and killed
36 another, and stoned another. Again, he sent other servants more than
37 the first; and they did unto them likewise. But last of all [j]he sent unto
38 them his son, saying, They will reverence my son. But when the husbandmen saw the son, they said among themselves, [k]This is the heir;
39 [l]come, let us kill him, and let us seize on his inheritance. And [m]they
40 caught him, and cast *him* out of the vineyard, and slew *him*. When the
Lord therefore of the vineyard cometh, what will he do unto those hus-
41 bandmen? They [n]say unto him, [o]He will miserably destroy those
wicked men, [p]and will let out *his* vineyard unto other husbandmen,
42 which shall render him the fruits in their seasons. Jesus saith unto them,
[q]Did ye never read in the Scriptures, The stone which the builders rejected, the same is become the head of the corner: this is the Lord's
43 doing, and it is [r]marvellous in our eyes? Therefore say I unto you,
[s]The kingdom of God shall be taken from you, and given to a nation
44 bringing forth the fruits thereof. And whosoever [t]shall fall on this stone
shall be broken: but on whomsoever it shall fall, [u]it will grind him to
powder.

A. D. 33.

[i] 2 Chr. 24. 21. 2 Chr. 36. 16.
[j] Gal. 4. 4.
[k] Ps. 2. 8.
[l] Ps. 2. 2. John 11. 53. Acts 4. 27.
[m] Acts 2. 23.
[n] Luke 20. 16.
[o] Deut. 4. 26.
[p] Acts 13. 46. Rom. 9. 1.
[q] Ps. 118. 22. Isa. 28. 16. Mark 12. 10. Acts 4. 11.
[r] 1 Tim. 3. 16.
[s] ch. 8. 12.
[t] Isa. 8. 14. Zec. 12. 3.
[u] Isa. 60. 12. Dan. 2. 44.

the fruits of it. See again on Luke xiii. 6. **35. And the husbandmen took his servants, and beat one**—see Jer. xxxvii. 15; xxxviii. 6. **and killed another**—see Jer. xxvi. 20-23. **and stoned another**—see 2 Chr. xxiv. 21. Compare with this whole verse ch. xxiii. 37, where our Lord reiterates these charges in the most melting strain. **36. Again, he sent other servants more than the first; and they did unto them likewise**—see 2 Kings xvii. 13; 2 Chr. xxxvi. 15, 16; Neh. ix. 26. **37. But last of all he sent unto them his son, saying, They will reverence my son.** In Mark (xii. 6) this is most touchingly expressed: "Having yet therefore one son, His well-beloved, He sent Him also last unto them, saying, They will reverence my son." Luke's version of it too (xx. 13) is striking: "Then said the lord of the vineyard, What shall I do? I will send my beloved son: it may be they will reverence Him when they see Him." Who does not see that our Lord here severs Himself, by the sharpest line of demarcation, from all merely *human* messengers, and claims for Himself *Sonship* in its loftiest sense? (Compare Heb. iii. 3-6.) The expression, "*It may be* they will reverence my son," is designed to teach the almost unimaginable guilt of *not* reverentially welcoming God's Son. **38. But when the husbandmen saw the son, they said among themselves**—compare Gen. xxxvii. 18-20; John xi. 47-53, **This is the heir.** Sublime expression this of the great truth, that God's inheritance was destined for, and in due time is to come into the possession of, His own Son *in our nature* (Heb. i. 2). **come, let us kill him, and let us seize on his inheritance**—that so, from mere *servants*, we may become *lords*. This is the deep aim of the depraved heart; this is emphatically "the root of all evil." **39. And they caught him, and cast him out of the vineyard**—compare Heb. xiii. 11-13 ("without the gate—without the camp"); 1 Ki. xxi. 13; John xix. 17, **and slew him. 40. When the lord therefore of the vineyard cometh.** This represents 'the settling time,' which, in the case of the Jewish ecclesiastics, was that judicial trial of the nation and its leaders which issued in the destruction of their whole state. **what will he do unto those husbandmen? 41. They say unto him, He will miserably destroy those wicked men** [κακοὺς κακῶς]—an emphatic alliteration not easily conveyed in English: 'He will badly destroy those bad men.' or 'miserably destroy those miserable men,' is something like it. **and will let out his vineyard unto other husbandmen, which shall render him the fruits in their seasons.** If this answer was given by the Pharisees, to whom our Lord addressed the parable, they thus unwittingly pronounced their own condemnation; as did David to Nathan the prophet (2 Sam. xii. 5-7), and Simon the Pharisee to our Lord, (Luke vii. 43, &c.) But if it was given, as the two other Evangelists agree in representing it, by our Lord Himself, and the explicitness of the answer would seem to favour that supposition, then we can better explain the exclamation of the Pharisees which followed it, in Luke's report—"And when they heard it, they said, God forbid"—His whole meaning now bursting upon them. **42. Jesus saith unto them, Did ye never read in the Scriptures** (Ps. cxviii. 22, 23), **The stone which the builders rejected, the same is become the head of the corner: this is the Lord's doing, and it is marvellous in our eyes?** A bright Messianic prophecy, which reappears in various forms (Isa. xxviii. 16, &c.), and was made glorious use of by Peter before the Sanhedrim (Acts iv. 11). He recurs to it in his first Epistle (1 Pet. ii. 4-6). **43. Therefore say I unto you, The kingdom of God**—God's visible Kingdom, or Church, upon earth, which up to this time stood in the seed of Abraham, **shall be taken from you, and given to a nation bringing forth the fruits thereof**—that is, the great Evangelical community of the faithful, which, after the extrusion of the Jewish nation, would consist chiefly of Gentiles, until "all Israel should be saved" (Rom. xi. 25, 26). This vastly important statement is given by Matthew only. **44. And whosoever shall fall on this stone shall be broken: but on whomsoever it shall fall, it will grind him to powder.** The Kingdom of God is here a Temple, in the erection of which *a certain stone*, rejected as unsuitable by the spiritual builders, is, by the great Lord of the House, made the key-stone of the whole. On that Stone the builders were now "falling" and being "broken" (Isa. viii. 15). They were sustaining great spiritual hurt; but soon that Stone should "fall upon *them*" and "grind them to powder" (Dan. ii. 34, 35; Zec. xii. 3)—in their *corporate* capacity, in the tremendous destruction of Jerusalem, but *personally*, as unbelievers, in a more awful sense still.

45. And when the chief priests and Pharisees had heard his parables—referring to that of the

45 And when the chief priests and Pharisees had heard his parables, they
46 perceived that he spake of them. But when they sought to lay hands on
him, they feared the multitude, because they [v] took him for a prophet.
22 AND Jesus answered [a] and spake unto them again by parables, and
2 said, The kingdom of heaven is like unto a certain king, which made a

A. D. 33.

[v] Luke 7. 16.

CHAP. 22.

[a] Luke 14.16. Rev. 19. 7,9.

Two Sons and this one of the Wicked Husbandmen, **they perceived that he spake of them. 46. But when they sought to lay hands on him**—which Luke (xx. 19) says they did "the same hour," hardly able to restrain their rage, **they feared the multitude**—rather 'the multitudes' [τοὺς ὄχλους], **because they took him for a prophet**—just as they feared to say John's baptism was of men, because the masses took him for a prophet (*v.* 26.) Miserable creatures! So, for this time, "they left Him and went their way" (Mark xii. 12).

Remarks.—1. Though argument be thrown away upon those who are resolved not to believe, the wisdom that can silence them and thus obtain a hearing for weighty truths and solemn warnings, is truly enviable. In this our Lord was incomparable, and He hath herein, as in all else, left us an example that we should follow His steps. 2. The self-righteousness of the Pharisees, which scornfully rejected the salvation of the Gospel, and the conscious unworthiness of the publicans and sinners, which thankfully embraced it, reappear from age to age as types of character. Wherever the Gospel is faithfully preached and earnestly pressed, the self-satisfied religious professors show the old reluctance to receive it on the same footing with the profligate; while these great sinners, conscious that they deeply need it, and cannot dare to hope for it on the footing of merit, gladly hail it as a message of free grace. 3. A purely democratic form of the Church seems inconsistent with the representations of our Lord in this Section—in which official men are supposed, to whom the Great Proprietor of the vineyard "lets it out," and to whom He will naturally look that they should render Him of its fruits. And though the language of parables is not to be stretched beyond the lessons which they may naturally be supposed intended to teach, it is difficult to make anything out of the parable of the Wicked Husbandmen—at least as regards the Christian Church—on anything short of the above view. 4. Though our Lord—to meet the charge of setting Himself up against God, by the loftiness of His claims—represents Himself invariably as the Father's commissioned Servant in every step of His work; yet, in relation to other servants and messengers of God, He is careful so to sever Himself from them all, that there may be no danger of His being confounded with them—holding Himself forth as the Son, Only and Well-beloved (Mark xii. 6), in the sense of a *relationship of nature* not to be mistaken, a relationship manifestly implying proper Personal Divinity. 5. The disinheriting of Israel after the flesh, and the substitution or surrogation of the Gentiles in their place, must not be misunderstood. As Gentiles were not absolutely excluded from the Church of God under the Jewish economy, so neither are Jews now shut out from the Church of Christ. All that we are taught is, that as it was the purpose of God to constitute the seed of Abraham of old to be His visible people, so now, for their unfaithfulness to the great trust committed to them, it has been transferred to the Gentiles, from amongst whom, accordingly, God is now taking out a people for His name. When, therefore, we are assured that the time is coming when "all Israel shall be saved" (Rom. xi. 26), that cannot mean merely that they will drop into the Christian Church individually from time to time—for that they have been doing all along, and have never ceased to do—but that they shall be *nationally* re-engrafted into their own olive tree, not now to the exclusion of the Gentiles, but to constitute along with them one universal Church of God upon earth. (See on Rom. xi. 22-24, 26, 28.) 6. "If some of the branches be broken off, and thou," O Gentile, "being a wild olive tree, wert graffed in among them, and with them partakest of the root and fatness of the olive tree; boast not against the branches. Thou wilt say, The branches were broken off, that I might be graffed in. Well; because of unbelief they were broken off, and thou standest by faith. Be not highminded, but fear: for if God spared not the natural branches, take heed lest He also spare not thee. Behold therefore the goodness and severity of God: on them which fell, severity; but toward thee, goodness, if thou continue in His goodness: otherwise thou also shalt be cut off" (Rom. xi. 17, 19-22). Nor is this a mere threatening *in case* of Gentile unbelief; for Scripture prophecy too clearly intimates, that at that great crisis in the history of Christendom when "all Israel shall be saved," a vast portion of the Gentile Church shall be found equally unfaithful to the trust committed to them with Israel of old, and will be judged accordingly. "Wherefore, let him that thinketh he standeth take heed lest he fall."

CHAP. XXII. 1-14.—PARABLE OF THE MARRIAGE OF THE KING'S SON.

This is a different parable from that of the Great Supper, in Luke xiv. 15, &c., and is recorded by Matthew alone. **1. And Jesus answered and spake unto them again by parables, and said, 2. The kingdom of heaven is like unto a certain king, which made a marriage for his son.** 'In this parable,' as *Trench* admirably remarks, 'we see how the Lord is revealing Himself in ever clearer light as the central Person of the kingdom, giving here a far plainer hint than in the last parable of the nobility of His descent. There He was indeed the Son, the only and beloved one (Mark xii. 6), of the Householder; but here His race is royal, and He appears as Himself at once the King and the King's Son. (Ps. lxxii. 1.) The last was a parable of the Old Testament history; and Christ is rather the last and greatest of the line of its prophets and teachers than the Founder of a new kingdom. In that, God appears *demanding* something *from* men; in this, a parable of grace, God appears more as *giving* something *to* them. Thus, as often, the two complete each other; this taking up the matter where the other left it.' The "marriage" of Jehovah to His people Israel was familiar to Jewish ears; and in Ps. xlv. this marriage is seen consummated in the Person of Messiah 'THE KING,' Himself addressed as 'GOD' and yet as anointed by 'HIS GOD' with the oil of gladness above His fellows.' These apparent contradictories (see on Luke xx. 41-44) are resolved in this parable; and Jesus, in claiming to be this King's Son, *serves Himself Heir to all that the prophets and sweet singers of Israel held forth as to Jehovah's ineffably near and endearing union to His*

3 marriage for his son, and sent forth his servants to call them that were
4 bidden to the wedding: and they would not come. Again, he sent forth
other servants, saying, Tell them which are bidden, Behold, I have prepared my dinner: [b]my oxen and *my* fatlings *are* killed, and all things
5 *are* ready: come unto the marriage. But they [c]made light of *it*, and
6 went their ways, one to his farm, another to his merchandise: and [d]the
remnant took his servants, and entreated *them* spitefully, and slew *them*.
7 But when the king heard *thereof*, he was wroth: and he sent forth [e]his
8 armies, and destroyed those murderers, and burned up their city. Then
saith he to his servants, The wedding is ready, but they which were
9 bidden were not [f]worthy. Go ye therefore into the highways, and as
10 many as ye shall find, bid to the marriage. So those servants went out
into the highways, and [g]gathered together all as many as they found,
11 both bad and good: and the wedding was furnished with guests. And
when the king came in to see the guests, he saw there a man [h]which had

A. D. 33.

[b] Pro. 9. 2.
[c] Ps. 81. 11.
[d] 1 Thes. 2. 14, 15.
[e] Isa. 10. 5-7. Jer. 51. 20-23. Dan. 9. 26. Luke 19. 27.
[f] ch. 10. 11. Luke 20. 35. Acts 13. 46.
[g] ch. 13. 38.
[h] 2 Cor. 5. 3. Eph. 4. 24. Col. 3. 10, 12. Rev. 3. 4. Rev. 16. 15. Rev. 19. 8.

people. But observe carefully, that THE BRIDE does not come into view in this parable; its design being to teach certain truths under the figure of *guests* at a wedding *feast*, and the want of a wedding *garment*, which would not have harmonized with the introduction of the Bride. **3. And sent forth his servants**—representing all preachers of the Gospel, **to call them that were bidden**—here meaning the Jews, who were "bidden," from the first choice of them onwards through every summons addressed to them by the prophets to hold themselves in readiness for the appearing of their King. **to the wedding**—or the marriage festivities, when the preparations were all concluded. **and they would not come**—as the issue of the whole ministry of the Baptist, our Lord Himself, and His apostles thereafter, too sadly showed. **4. Again, he sent forth other servants, saying, Tell them which are bidden, Behold, I have prepared my dinner: my oxen and my fatlings are killed, and all things are ready: come unto the marriage.** This points to those Gospel calls *after* Christ's death, resurrection, ascension, and effusion of the Spirit, to which the parable could not directly allude, but when only it could be said, with strict propriety, "that all things were ready." Compare 1 Cor. v. 7, 8, "Christ our passover is sacrificed for us; therefore, let us keep the feast:" also John vi. 51, "I am the living bread which came down from heaven: if any man eat of this bread, he shall live for ever: and the bread which I will give is my flesh, which I will give for the life of the world." **5. But they made light of it, and went their ways, one to his farm, another to his merchandise: 6. And the remnant took his servants, and entreated them spitefully** [ὕβρισαν]—'insulted them,' **and slew them.** These are two different classes of unbelievers; the one simply *indifferent;* the other absolutely *hostile*—the one, contemptuous *scorners;* the other, bitter *persecutors.* **7. But when the king**—the Great God, who is the Father of our Lord Jesus Christ, **heard thereof.** [*Tregelles*, with not sufficient warrant, as we think, omits the word ἀκούσας. *Tischendorf* retains it.] **he was wroth**—at the affront put both on His Son, and on Himself who had deigned to invite them. **and he sent forth his armies.** The *Romans* are here styled God's armies, just as the Assyrian is styled "the rod of His anger" (Isa. x. 5), as being the executors of His judicial vengeance. **and destroyed those murderers**—and in what vast numbers did they do it! **and burned up their city.** Ah! Jerusalem, once "the city of the Great King" (Ps. xlviii. 2), and even up almost to this time (ch. v. 35); but now it is "*their* city"—just as our Lord, a day or two after this, said of the temple, where God had so long dwelt, "Behold *your* house is left unto you desolate" (ch. xxiii. 38)! Compare Luke xix. 43, 44. **8. Then saith he to his servants, The wedding is ready, but they which were bidden were not worthy**—for how should those be deemed worthy to sit down at His table who had affronted Him by their treatment of His gracious invitation? **9. Go ye therefore into the highways**—the great outlets and thoroughfares, whether of town or country, where human beings are to be found, **and as many as ye shall find bid to the marriage**—that is, just as they are. **10. So those servants went out into the highways, and gathered together all as many as they found, both bad and good**—that is, without making any distinction between open sinners and the morally correct. The Gospel call fetched in Jews, Samaritans, and outlying heathen alike. Thus far the parable answers to that of 'the Great Supper,' Luke xiv. 16, &c. But the distinguishing feature of our parable is what follows: **11. And when the king came in to see the guests.** Solemn expression this, of that *omniscient inspection of every professed disciple of the Lord Jesus* from age to age, in virtue of which his true character will hereafter be judicially proclaimed! **he saw there a man.** This shows that it is the judgment of *individuals* which is intended in this latter part of the parable: the first part represents rather *national* judgment. **which had not on a wedding garment.** The language here is drawn from the following remarkable passage in Zeph. i. 7, 8:—"Hold thy peace at the presence of the Lord God; for the day of the Lord is at hand: for the Lord hath prepared a sacrifice, He hath bid His guests. And it shall come to pass in the day of the Lord's sacrifice, that I will punish the princes, and the king's children, and all such as are clothed with strange apparel." The custom in the East of presenting festival garments (See Gen. xlv. 22; 2 Ki. v. 22), even though not clearly proved, is certainly presupposed here. It undoubtedly means something which they bring not of their own—for how could they have any such dress who were gathered in from the highways indiscriminately?—but which they *receive* as their appropriate dress. And what can that be but what is meant by "putting on the Lord Jesus" as "THE LORD OUR RIGHTEOUSNESS"? (See Ps. xlv. 13, 14.) Nor could such language be strange to those in whose ears had so long resounded those words of prophetic joy: "I will greatly rejoice in the Lord, my soul shall be

12 not on a wedding garment: and he saith unto him, Friend, how camest
thou in hither not having a wedding garment? And he [i]was speechless.
13 Then said the king to the servants, Bind him hand and foot, and take
him away, and cast *him* [j]into outer darkness; there shall be weeping and
14 gnashing of teeth. For [k]many are called, but few *are* chosen.
15 Then [l]went the Pharisees, and took counsel how they might entangle
16 him in *his* talk. And they sent out unto him their disciples with the
Herodians, saying, Master, we know that thou art true, and teachest the
way of God in truth, neither carest thou for any *man;* for thou regardest
17 not the person of men. Tell us therefore, What thinkest thou? Is it
18 lawful to give tribute unto Cesar, or not? But Jesus perceived their
19 wickedness, and said, Why tempt ye me, *ye* hypocrites? Show me the
20 tribute money. And they brought unto him a [1]penny. And he saith
21 unto them, Whose *is* this image and [2]superscription? They say unto
him, Cesar's. Then saith he unto them, [m]Render therefore unto Cesar
the things which are Cesar's; and unto God the things that are God's.
22 When they had heard *these words,* they [n]marvelled, and left him, and
went their way.
23 The [o]same day came to him the Sadducees, [p]which say that there is
24 no resurrection, and asked him, saying, Master, [q]Moses said, If a man
die, having no children, his brother shall marry his wife, and raise up

A. D. 33.

i Rom. 3. 19.
j ch. 8. 12.
k ch. 20. 16.
l Mark 12. 13. Luke 20. 20.
1 In value seven-pence half-penny. ch. 20. 2.
2 Or, inscription.
m ch. 17. 25. Luke 23. 2. Rom. 13. 7.
n Job 5. 13.
o ch. 3. 7. ch. 16. 6. Mark 12. 18. Luke 20. 27. Acts 4. 1. Acts 5. 17.
p Acts 23. 8. 1 Cor. 15. 12. 2 Tim. 2. 17.
q Gen. 38. 8. Deut. 25. 5.

joyful in my God; for He hath clothed me with the garments of salvation, He hath covered me with the robe of righteousness, as a bridegroom decketh himself with ornaments, and as a bride adorneth herself with her jewels" (Isa. lxi. 10). **12. And he saith unto him, Friend, how camest thou in hither not having a wedding garment? And he was speechless**—being self-condemned. **13. Then said the king to the servants**—the angelic ministers of divine vengeance (as in ch. xiii. 41). **Bind him hand and foot**—putting it out of his power to resist, **and take him away, and cast him into outer darkness;** [εἰς τὸ σκότος τὸ ἐξώτερον]. So ch. viii. 12; xxv. 30. The expression is emphatic—'The darkness which is outside.' To be '*outside*' at all—or, in the language of Rev. xxii. 15, to be '*without*' the heavenly city [ἔξω], excluded from its joyous nuptials and gladsome festivities—is sad enough of itself, without anything else. But to find themselves not only excluded from the brightness and glory and joy and felicity of the kingdom above, but thrust into a region of "darkness," with all its horrors, this is the dismal retribution here announced, that awaits the unworthy at the great day. **[there]** [ἐκεῖ]—in that region and condition, **shall be weeping and gnashing of teeth.** See on ch. xiii. 42. **14. For many are called, but few are chosen.** So ch. xix. 30. See on ch. xx. 16.

Remarks.—1. What claim to supreme Divinity brighter and more precious than our Lord here advances can be conceived? Observe the succession of ideas, as unfolded in the Old Testament, and how Jesus places Himself in the centre of them. First, all the gracious relations which Jehovah is represented as sustaining to His people culminate in the intimate and endearing one of a marriage-union (Jer. iii. 14; Hos. ii. 16; &c). But next, when the nuptial-song of this high union is sung, in the Forty-fifth Psalm, we find it to celebrate a union, not directly and immediately between *Jehovah* and the Church, but between *Messiah* and the Church; yet a Messiah who, while anointed *of God* with the oil of gladness above His fellows, is addressed in the Psalm as *Himself God:* so that it is just Jehovah in the Person of Messiah "the King" who in that nuptial-song is celebrated as taking the Church to be His Bride. But this is not all; for in other predictions this Divine Messiah is expressly called the *Son of God* (Ps. ii. 7, 12; compare Prov. xxx. 4; Dan. iii. 25). Such being the representations of the Old Testament, what does Jesus here but serve Himself Heir to them, holding Himself forth as Himself *the King's Son* of Old Testament prophecy, as the Anointed King in whose Person Jehovah was to marry His people to Himself, and whose nuptials are celebrated in the lofty Messianic Psalm to which we have adverted? 2. As in the parable of the Great Supper (Luke xiv.), so here, it is not those who have all along basked in the sunshine of religious privileges who are the readiest to embrace the Gospel call, but the very opposite classes. And is it not so still? 3. The terrible destruction which fell upon Jerusalem, and the breaking up and dispersion and wretchedness of the nation which ensued, and continues to this hour—what a warning are they of that vengeance of God which awaits the despisers of His Son! 4. Though sinners are invited to Christ as they are, and salvation is "without money and without price," we are "accepted" only "in the Beloved" (Eph. i. 6); if there be "no condemnation," it is "to them that are *in Christ Jesus*" (Rom. viii. 1). These are they that have "put on the Lord Jesus" (Rom. xiii. 14; Gal. iii. 27). This is to have the wedding garment. 5. Though we may deceive not only others but ourselves, there is an Eye which comes in expressly to see the guests; the one thing He looks for is that wedding garment; and amongst myriads of persons, all professing to be His, He can discern even one who is not. 6. No moral or religious excellences will compensate for the absence of this wedding garment. If we have not put on the Lord Jesus, if we are not "in Christ Jesus," our doom is sealed; and what a doom—to be cast indignantly and without the power of resistance into outer darkness, where there shall be weeping and gnashing of teeth! Oh! do men really believe that this doom awaits those who, however exemplary in other respects, venture to present themselves before God *out of Christ?*

15-40.—Entangling Questions about Tribute, the Resurrection, and the Great Com-

25 seed unto his brother. Now there were with us seven brethren: and the
first, when he had married a wife, deceased, and, having no issue, left his
26 wife unto his brother: likewise the second also, and the third, unto the
27, [3]seventh. And last of all the woman died also. Therefore in the
28 resurrection whose wife shall she be of the seven? for they all had her.
29 Jesus answered and said unto them, Ye do err, [r]not knowing the
30 Scriptures, nor the power of God. For in the resurrection they neither
marry, nor are given in marriage, but [s]are as the angels of God in heaven.
31 But as touching the resurrection of the dead, have ye not read that
32 which was spoken unto you by God, saying, I [t]am the God of Abraham,
and the God of Isaac, and the God of Jacob? God is not the God of
33 the dead, but of the living. And when the multitude heard *this*, they
[u]were astonished at his doctrine.

34 But when the Pharisees had heard that he had put the Sadducees to
35 silence, they were gathered together. Then one of them, *which was* [v]a
36 lawyer, asked *him a question*, tempting him, and saying, Master, which
37 *is* the great commandment in the law? Jesus said unto him, [w]Thou
shalt love the Lord thy God with all thy heart, and with all thy soul,
38 and with all thy mind. This is the first and great commandment.
39 And the second *is* like unto it, [x]Thou shalt love thy neighbour as thyself.
40 On [y]these two commandments hang all the Law and the Prophets.

41 While [z]the Pharisees were gathered together, Jesus asked them,
42 saying, What think ye of Christ? whose son is he? They say unto him,
43 *The son* of David. He saith unto them, How then doth David [a]in spirit
44 call him Lord, saying, The [b]LORD said unto my Lord, Sit thou on my
45 right hand, till I make thine enemies thy footstool? If David then call
46 him Lord, how is he his son? And [c]no man was able to answer him a
word; neither durst any *man* from that day forth ask him any more
questions.

23 THEN spake Jesus to the multitude, and to his disciples, saying, [a]The
2, scribes and the Pharisees sit in Moses' seat: all therefore whatsoever
3 they bid you observe, *that* observe and do; but do not ye after their
4 works: for [b]they say, and do not. For [c]they bind heavy burdens
and grievous to be borne, and lay *them* on men's shoulders; but they
5 *themselves* will not move them with one of their fingers. But [d]all their

A. D. 33.

[3] seven.
[r] John 20. 9.
[s] Ps. 103. 20. Zec. 3. 7. ch. 13. 43. 1 Cor. 7. 29. 1 John 3. 2.
[t] Ex. 3. 6, 16. Mark 12. 26. Luke 20. 37. Acts 7. 32. Heb. 11. 16.
[u] ch. 7. 28.
[v] Luke 10. 25.
[w] Deut. 6. 5. Deut. 10. 12. Deut. 30. 6. Pro. 23. 26.
[x] Lev. 19. 18. ch. 19. 19. Mark 12. 31. Rom. 13. 9. Gal. 5. 14. Jas. 2. 8.
[y] ch. 7. 12. 1 Tim. 1. 5.
[z] Mark 12. 35. Luke 20. 41.
[a] 2 Sam. 23. 2. Acts 2. 30. 2 Pet. 1. 21.
[b] Ps. 110. 1. Acts 2. 34. 1 Cor. 15. 25. Heb. 1. 13. Heb. 10. 12.
[c] Luke 14. 6.

CHAP. 23.
[a] Neh. 8. 4, 8. Mal. 2. 7.
[b] Rom. 2. 19.
[c] Luke 11. 46. Acts 15. 10. Gal. 6. 13.
[d] ch. 6. 1, 2.

MANDMENT, WITH THE REPLIES. (= Mark xii. 13-34; Luke xx. 20-40.) For the exposition, see on Mark xii. 13-34.

41-46.—CHRIST BAFFLES THE PHARISEES BY A QUESTION ABOUT DAVID AND MESSIAH. (= Mark xii. 35-37; Luke xx. 41-44.) For the exposition, see on Mark xii. 35-37.

CHAP. XXIII. 1-39.—DENUNCIATION OF THE SCRIBES AND PHARISEES—LAMENTATION OVER JERUSALEM, AND FAREWELL TO THE TEMPLE. (= Mark xii. 38-40; Luke xx. 45-47.) For this long and terrible discourse we are indebted, with the exception of a few verses in Mark and Luke, to Matthew alone. But as it is only an extended repetition of denunciations uttered not long before at the table of a Pharisee, and recorded by Luke (xi. 37-54), we may take both together in the exposition.

Denunciation of the Scribes and Pharisees (1-36). The first twelve verses were addressed more immediately to the disciples, the rest to the scribes and Pharisees.

1. Then spake Jesus to the multitude [ὄχλοις]—'to the multitudes,' **and to his disciples, 2. Saying, The scribes and the Pharisees sit.** The Jewish teachers *stood* to read, but *sat* to expound the Scriptures, as will be seen by comparing Luke iv. 16 with *v.* 20. **in Moses' seat**—that is, as interpreters of the law given by Moses. **3. All therefore**—that is, all which, as *sitting in that seat* and teaching *out of that law*, **they bid you observe, that observe and do.** The word "therefore" is thus, it will be seen, of great importance, as limiting those injunctions which He would have them obey to what they fetched from the law itself. In requiring implicit obedience to such injunctions, He would have them to recognize the authority with which they taught over and above the obligation of the law itself—an important principle truly; but He who denounced the traditions of such teachers (ch. xv. 3) cannot have meant here to throw His shield over these. It is remarked by *Webster and Wilkinson* that the warning to *beware* of the scribes is given by Mark and Luke without any qualification; the charge to *respect* and *obey* them being reported by Matthew alone, indicating for whom this Gospel was especially written, and the writer's desire to conciliate the Jews. **4. For they bind heavy burdens and grievous to be borne, and lay them on men's shoulders; but they themselves will not move them**—"touch them not" (Luke xi. 46), **with one of their fingers**—referring not so much to the irksomeness of the legal rites, though they were irksome enough (Acts xv. 10), as to the heartless rigour with which they were enforced,

works they do for to be seen of men: [e]they make broad their phylac-
6 teries, and enlarge the borders of their garments, and [f]love the uppermost
7 rooms at feasts, and the chief seats in the synagogues, and greetings in
8 the markets, and to be called of men, Rabbi, Rabbi. But [g]be not ye
called Rabbi: for one is your Master, *even* Christ; and all ye are brethren.
9 And call no *man* your father upon the earth: [h]for one is your Father,
10 which is in heaven. Neither be ye called masters: for one is your Master,
11 *even* Christ. But [i]he that is greatest among you shall be your servant.
12 And [j]whosoever shall exalt himself shall be abased; and he that shall
humble himself shall be exalted.
13 But [k]woe unto you, scribes and Pharisees, hypocrites! for ye shut up
the kingdom of heaven against men: for ye neither go in *yourselves*,
14 neither suffer ye them that are entering to go in. Woe unto you, scribes
and Pharisees, hypocrites! [l]for ye devour widows' houses, and for a pretence make long prayer: therefore ye shall receive the greater damnation.
15 Woe unto you, scribes and Pharisees, hypocrites! for ye compass sea and
land to make one proselyte; and when he is made, ye make him two-
16 fold more the child of hell than yourselves. Woe unto you, [m]*ye* blind
guides, which say, [n]Whosoever shall swear by the temple, it is nothing;
but whosoever shall swear by the gold of the temple, he is a debtor!
17 *Ye* fools, and blind! for whether is greater, the gold, [o]or the temple that

A. D. 33.

[e] Num. 15. 38. Deut. 22. 12.
[f] Mark 12. 38. Luke 20. 46.
[g] Jas. 3. 1.
[h] Mal. 1. 6. Rom. 8. 14-17.
[i] ch. 20. 26.
[j] Job 22. 29. Pro. 15. 33. Pro. 29. 23. Dan. 4. 37. Luke 14. 11. Luke 18. 14. Jas. 4. 6. 1 Pet. 5. 5.
[k] Luke 11. 52.
[l] Ezek. 22. 25. Mark 12. 40. Luke 20. 47. 2 Tim. 3. 6. Titus 1. 11.
[m] Isa. 56. 10. ch. 15. 14.
[n] ch. 5. 33.
[o] Ex. 30. 29.

and by men of shameless inconsistency. **5. But all their works they do for to be seen of men.** Whatever good they do, or zeal they show, has but one motive—human applause. **they make broad their phylacteries**—strips of parchment with Scripture-texts on them, worn on the fore-head, arm, and side, in time of prayer. **and enlarge the borders of their garments**—fringes of their upper garments (Num. xv. 37-40). **6. And love the uppermost rooms.** The word "room" is now obsolete in the sense here intended. It should be 'the uppermost place' [πρωτοκλισίαν], that is, the place of highest honour. **at feasts, and the chief seats in the synagogues.** See on Luke xiv. 7, 8. **7. And greetings in the markets, and to be called of men, Rabbi, Rabbi.** It is the *spirit* rather than the *letter* of this that must be pressed; though the violation of the letter, springing from spiritual pride, has done incalculable evil in the Church ot Christ. The reiteration of the word "Rabbi" shows how it tickled the ear and fed the spiritual pride of those ecclesiastics. [*Tregelles* improperly, as we think, omits the repetition, but *Tischendorf* does not.] **8. But be not ye called Rabbi: for one is your Master** [Καθηγητὴς]—'your Guide, your Teacher,' **even Christ; and all ye are brethren. 9. And call no man your father upon the earth: for one is your Father, which is in heaven. 10. Neither be ye called masters: for one is your Master, even Christ.** To construe these injunctions into a condemnation of every title by which church rulers may be distinguished from the flock which they rule, is virtually to condemn that rule itself; and accordingly the same persons do both—but against the whole strain of the New Testament and sound Christian judgment. But when we have guarded ourselves against these extremes, let us see to it that we retain the full spirit of this warning against that itch for ecclesiastical superiority which has been the bane and the scandal of Christ's ministers in every age. (On the use of the word "Christ" here, see on ch. i. 1.) **11. But he that is greatest among you shall be your servant.** This plainly means, 'shall show that he is so by becoming your servant;' as in ch. xx. 27, compared with Mark x. 44. **12. And whosoever shall exalt himself shall be abased; and he that shall humble himself shall be exalted.** See on Luke xviii. 14.

What follows was addressed more immediately to the scribes and Pharisees. **13. But woe unto you, scribes and Pharisees, hypocrites! for ye shut up the kingdom of heaven against men: for ye neither go in [yourselves], neither suffer ye them that are entering to go in.** Here they are charged with *shutting heaven* against men: in Luke xi. 52, they are charged with what was worse, *taking away the key*—"the key of knowledge"—which means, not the key to open knowledge, but knowledge as the only key to open heaven. A right knowledge of God's revealed word is eternal life, as our Lord says (John xvii. 3, and v. 39); but this they took away from the people, substituting for it their wretched traditions. **14. Woe unto you, scribes and Pharisees, hypocrites! for ye devour widows' houses, and for a pretence make long prayer: therefore ye shall receive the greater damnation.** Taking advantage of the helpless condition and confiding character of "widows," they contrived to obtain possession of their property, while by their "long prayers" they made them believe they were raised far above "filthy lucre." So much "the greater damnation" awaits them. What a life-like description of the Romish clergy, the true successors of those scribes! **15. Woe unto you, scribes and Pharisees, hypocrites! for ye compass sea and land to make one proselyte**—from heathenism. We have evidence of this in *Josephus*. **and when he is made, ye make him two-fold more the child of hell than yourselves**—condemned, for the hypocrisy he would learn to practice, both by the religion he left and that he embraced. **16. Woe unto you, ye blind guides.** Striking expression this of the ruinous effects of erroneous teaching. Our Lord, here and in some following verses, condemns the subtle distinctions they made as to the sanctity of oaths, distinctions invented only to promote their own avaricious purposes. **which say, Whosoever shall swear by the temple, it is nothing**—he has incurred no debt, **but whosoever shall swear by the gold of the temple**—meaning not the gold that adorned the temple itself, but the *Corban*, set apart for sacred uses (see on ch. xv. 5),

18 sanctifieth the gold? And, Whosoever shall swear by the altar, it is
nothing; but whosoever sweareth by the gift that is upon it, he is [1]guilty.
19 *Ye* fools, and blind! for whether *is* greater, the gift, or [p]the altar that
20 sanctifieth the gift? Whoso therefore shall swear by the altar, sweareth
21 by it, and by all things thereon. And whoso shall swear by the temple,
22 sweareth by it, and by [q]him that dwelleth therein. And he that shall
swear by heaven, sweareth by [r]the throne of God, and by him that
sitteth thereon.
23 Woe unto you, scribes and Pharisees, hypocrites! [s]for ye pay tithe of
mint and [2]anise and cummin, and [t]have omitted the weightier *matters*
of the law, judgment, mercy, and faith: these ought ye to have done,
24 and not to leave the other undone. *Ye* blind guides, which strain at a
25 gnat, and swallow a camel. Woe unto you, scribes and Pharisees, hypocrites! [u]for ye make clean the outside of the cup and of the platter, but
26 within they are full of extortion and excess. *Thou* blind Pharisee,
cleanse first that *which* [v]*is* within the cup and platter, that the outside
of them may be clean also.
27 Woe unto you, scribes and Pharisees, hypocrites! [w]for ye are like unto
whited sepulchres, which indeed appear beautiful outward, but are within

A. D. 33.
[1] Or, debtor, or, bound.
[p] Ex. 29. 37.
[q] 1 Ki. 8. 13. 2 Chr. 6. 2. Ps. 26. 8. Ps. 132. 14.
[r] ch. 5. 34. Ps. 11. 4. Acts 7. 49.
[s] Luke 11.42.
[2] anethon, dill.
[t] 1 Sam. 15. 22. Hos. 6. 6. Mic. 6. 8.
[u] Mark 7. 4. Luke 11. 39.
[v] Isa. 55. 7. Jer. 4. 14. Ezek. 18. 31. Luke 6. 45. Titus 1. 15.
[w] Acts 23. 3.

he is a debtor!—that is, it is no longer his own, even though the necessities of a parent might require it. We know who the successors of these men are. **17. Ye fools, and blind! for whether is greater, the gold, or the temple that sanctifieth the gold? 18. And, Whosoever shall swear by the altar, it is nothing; but whosoever sweareth by the gift that is upon it, he is guilty** [ὀφείλει]. It should have been rendered, "he is a debtor," as in *v.* 16. **19. Ye fools, and blind! for whether is greater, the gift, or the altar that sanctifieth the gift?** (See Exod. xxix. 37.) **20-22. Whoso therefore shall swear by the altar, . . . And . . . by the temple, . . . And . . . by heaven, &c.** See on Matt. v. 33-37.

23. Woe unto you, scribes and Pharisees, hypocrites! for ye pay tithe of mint and anise—rather 'dill,' as in margin [ἄνηθον], **and cummin.** In Luke (xi. 42) it is "and rue, and all manner of herbs." They grounded this practice on Lev. xxvii. 30, which they interpreted rigidly. Our Lord purposely names the most trifling products of the earth, as examples of what they punctiliously exacted the tenth of. **and have omitted the weightier matters of the law, judgment, mercy, and faith.** In Luke (xi. 42) it is, "judgment, mercy, and the love of God"—the expression being probably varied by our Lord Himself on the two different occasions. In both His reference is to Mic. vi. 6-8, where the prophet makes all acceptable religion to consist of three elements—"doing justly, loving mercy, and walking humbly with our God;" which third element pre-supposes and comprehends both the "faith" of Matthew and the "love" of Luke. See on Mark xii. 29, 32, 33. The same tendency to merge greater duties in less besets even the children of God; but *it is the characteristic of hypocrites.* **these ought ye to have done, and not to leave the other undone.** There is no need for one set of duties to jostle out another; but it is to be carefully noted that of the *greater* duties our Lord says, "Ye ought to have done" them, while of the *lesser* He merely says, "Ye ought not to leave them undone." **24. Ye blind guides, which strain at a gnat.** The proper rendering—as in the older English translations, and perhaps our own as it came from the translators' hands—evidently is, 'strain out.' It was the custom, says *Trench,* of the stricter Jews to strain their wine, vinegar, and other potables through linen or gauze, lest unawares they should drink down some little unclean insect therein, and thus transgress (Lev. xi. 20, 23, 41, 42)—just as the Budhists do now in Ceylon and Hindostan—and to this custom of theirs our Lord here refers. **and swallow a camel**—the largest animal the Jews knew, as the "gnat" was the smallest: both were by the law *unclean.* **25. Woe unto you, scribes and Pharisees, hypocrites! for ye make clean the outside of the cup and of the platter, but within they are full of extortion** [ἁρπαγῆς]. In Luke (xi. 39) the same word is rendered "ravening," that is, 'rapacity.' **and excess. 26. Thou blind Pharisee, cleanse first that which is within the cup and platter, that the outside of them may be clean also.** In Luke (xi. 40) it is, "Ye fools, did not he that made that which is without make that which is within also?"—'He to whom belongs the outer life, and of right demands its subjection to Himself, is the inner man less His?' A remarkable example this of our Lord's power of drawing the most striking illustrations of great truths from the most familiar objects and incidents in life. To these words, recorded by Luke, He adds the following, involving a principle of immense value: "But rather give alms of such things as ye have, and behold, all things are clean unto you" (Luke xi. 41). As the greed of these hypocrites was one of the most prominent features of their character (Luke xvi. 14), our Lord bids them exemplify the opposite character, and then their *outside,* ruled by this, would be beautiful in the eye of God, and their meals would be eaten with clean hands, though never so fouled with the business of this worky world. (See Eccl. ix. 7).

27. Woe unto you, scribes and Pharisees, hypocrites! for ye are like whited (or 'white-washed') **sepulchres** (cf. Acts xxiii. 3). The process of white-washing the sepulchres, as *Lightfoot* says, was performed on a certain day every year, not for ceremonial cleansing, but, as the following words seem rather to imply, to beautify them. **which indeed appear beautiful outward, but are within full of dead men's bones, and of all uncleanness.** What a powerful way of conveying the charge, that with all their fair show their hearts were full of corruption! (Cf. Ps. v. 9; Rom. iii. 13.) But our Lord, stripping off the figure, next holds up their iniquity in naked colours: **28. Even so ye also outwardly appear**

28 full of dead *men's* bones, and of all uncleanness. Even so ye also outwardly appear righteous unto men, but within ye are full of hypocrisy
29 and iniquity. Woe unto you, scribes and Pharisees, hypocrites! because
ye build the tombs of the prophets, and garnish the sepulchres of the
30 righteous, and say, If we had been in the days of our fathers, we would
31 not have been partakers with them in the blood of the prophets. Wherefore ye be witnesses unto yourselves, that [x]ye are the children of them
32 which killed the prophets. Fill [y]ye up then the measure of your fathers.
33 *Ye* serpents, *ye* [z]generation of vipers, how can ye escape the damnation
34 of hell? Wherefore, [a]behold, I send unto you prophets, and wise men,
and scribes: and *some* [b]of them ye shall kill and crucify; and [c]*some* of
them shall ye scourge in your synagogues, and persecute *them* from city
35 to city: that [d]upon you may come all the righteous blood shed upon the
earth, [e]from the blood of righteous Abel unto the blood of Zacharias son
36 of Barachias, whom ye slew between the temple and the altar. Verily I
say unto you, All these things shall come upon this generation.
37 O Jerusalem, Jerusalem, *thou* that killest the prophets, and stonest
them which are sent unto thee, how often would I [f]have gathered thy
children together, even as a hen gathereth her chickens under *her* wings

A. D. 33.

[x] Acts 7. 51. 1 Thes. 2. 15.
[y] Gen. 15. 16. Num. 32. 14. Zec. 5. 6-11. 1 Thes. 2. 16.
[z] ch. 3. 7. ch. 12. 34. Luke 3. 7.
[a] ch. 21. 34. Luke 11. 49. Acts 11. 27. Acts 13. 1. Acts 15. 32. Rev. 11. 10.
[b] Acts 5. 40. Acts 7. 58. Acts 22. 19.
[c] 2 Cor. 11. 24.
[d] Rev. 18. 24.
[e] Gen. 4. 8. 1 John 3. 12.
[f] Deut. 32. 11.

righteous unto men, but within ye are full of hypocrisy and iniquity. 29-31. Woe unto you, . . . hypocrites! ye build the tombs of the prophets, . . . And say, If we had been in the days of our fathers, we would not, &c. Wherefore ye be witnesses unto yourselves, that ye are the children of them which killed the prophets—that is, 'ye be witnesses that ye have inherited, and voluntarily served yourselves heirs to, the truth-hating, prophet-killing, spirit of your fathers.' Out of pretended respect and honour, they repaired and beautified the sepulchres of the prophets, and with whining hypocrisy said, "If we had been in their days, how differently should we have treated these prophets?" while all the time they were witnesses to themselves that they were the children of them that killed the prophets, convicting themselves daily of as exact a resemblance in spirit and character to the very classes over whose deeds they pretended to mourn, as child to parent. In Luke xi. 44 our Lord gives another turn to this figure of a grave: "Ye are as graves which appear not, and the men that walk over them are not aware of them." As one might unconsciously walk over a grave concealed from view, and thus contract ceremonial defilement, so the plausible exterior of the Pharisees kept people from perceiving the pollution they contracted from coming in contact with such corrupt characters. **32. Fill ye up then the measure of your fathers. 33. Ye serpents, ye generation of vipers, how can ye escape the damnation of hell?** In thus, at the end of His ministry, recalling the words of the Baptist at the outset of his, our Lord would seem to intimate that the only difference between their condemnation now and then was, that now they were ripe for their doom, which they were not then. **34. Wherefore, behold, I send unto you prophets, and wise men, and scribes** ['Εγὼ ἀποστέλλω]. The *I* here is emphatic: 'I am sending,' that is, 'am about to send.' In Luke xi. 49, the variation is remarkable: "Therefore also, said the wisdom of God, I will send them," &c. What precisely is meant by "the wisdom of God" here, is somewhat difficult to determine. To us it appears to be simply an announcement of a purpose of the Divine Wisdom, in the high style of ancient prophecy, to send a last set of messengers whom the people would reject, and rejecting, would fill up the cup of their iniquity. But, whereas in Luke it is 'I, the Wisdom of God, will send them,' in Matthew it is 'I, Jesus, am sending them;' language only befitting the one Sender of all the prophets, the Lord God of Israel now in the flesh. They are evidently Evangelical messengers, but called by the familiar Jewish names of "prophets, wise men, and scribes," whose counterparts were the inspired and gifted servants of the Lord Jesus; for in Luke (xi. 49) it is "prophets and apostles." **And some of them ye shall kill and crucify; and some scourge, . . . and persecute . . . 35. That upon you may come all the righteous blood shed upon the earth, from the blood of righteous Abel unto the blood of Zacharias son of Barachias, whom ye slew between the temple and the altar.** As there is no record of any fresh murder answering to this description, probably the allusion is not to any recent murder, but to 2 Chr. xxiv. 20-22, as the *last recorded* and most suitable case for illustration. And as Zacharias' last words were, "The Lord *require it*," so they are here warned that of that generation it should be *required*. **36. Verily I say unto you, All these things shall come upon this generation.** As it was only in the last generation of them that "the iniquity of the Amorites was full" (Gen. xv. 16), and then the abominations of ages were at once completely and awfully avenged, so the iniquity of Israel was allowed to accumulate from age to age till in that generation it came to the full, and the whole collected vengeance of Heaven broke at once over its devoted head. In the first French Revolution the same awful principle was exemplified, and *Christendom has not done with it yet.*

Lamentation over Jerusalem, and Farewell to the Temple (37-39). **37. O Jerusalem, Jerusalem, thou that killest the prophets, and stonest them which are sent unto thee, how often would I have gathered thy children together, even as a hen gathereth her chickens under her wings, and ye would not!** How ineffably grand and melting is this apostrophe! It is the very heart of God pouring itself forth through human flesh and speech. It is this incarnation of the innermost life and love of Deity, pleading with men, bleeding for them, and ascending only to open His arms to them and win them back by the power of this Story of matchless love, that has conquered the world, that will yet "draw all men unto Him," and beautify and ennoble Humanity

38 and ye would not! Behold, your house is left unto you desolate.
39 For I say unto you, [g]Ye shall not see me henceforth, till ye shall say,
[h]Blessed *is* he that cometh in the name of the Lord.

A. D. 33.

[g] Pro. 1. 26.
[h] Ps. 118. 26.

itself! "Jerusalem" here does not mean the mere city or its inhabitants; nor is it to be viewed merely as the metropolis of the *nation*, but as the *centre of their religious life*,—"the city of their solemnities, whither the tribes went up, to give thanks unto the name of the Lord;" and at this moment it was full of them. It is the whole family of God, then, which is here apostrophized, by a name dear to every Jew, recalling to him all that was distinctive and precious in his religion. The intense feeling that sought vent in this utterance comes out first in the redoubling of the opening word—"Jerusalem, Jerusalem!" but, next, in the picture of it which He draws—"that killest the prophets, and stonest them which are sent unto thee!"—not content with spurning God's messages of mercy, that canst not suffer even the messengers to live! (See 2 Chr. xxxvi. 15, 16; Neh. ix. 26; Matt. v. 12; xxi. 35-39; xxiii. 29-32; Acts vii. 51-54, 57-59.) When He adds, "How often would I have gathered thee!" He refers surely to something beyond the six or seven times that He visited and taught in Jerusalem while on earth. No doubt it points to "the prophets," whom they "killed," to "them that were sent unto her," whom they "stoned;" for, says Peter, it was "the Spirit of Christ which was in them that did testify beforehand the sufferings of Christ and the following glories" [τὰς μετὰ ταῦτα δόξας, 1 Pet. i. 11]. He it was that "sent unto them all His servants the prophets, rising early and sending them, saying, Oh, do not this abominable thing that I hate!" (Jer. xliv. 4). In His divine and eternal nature, as *Olshausen* says, He was the Prophet of the prophets. But whom would He have gathered so often? "Thee," truth-hating, mercy-spurning, prophet-killing Jerusalem—how often would I have gathered *Thee!* Compare with this that affecting clause in the great ministerial commission, "that repentance and remission of sins should be preached in His name among all nations, *beginning at Jerusalem!*" (Luke xxiv. 47). What encouragement to the heart-broken at their own long-continued and obstinate rebellion! But we have not yet got at the whole heart of this outburst. I would have gathered thee, He says, "even as a hen gathereth her chickens under her wings." Was ever imagery so homely invested with such grace and such sublimity as this, at our Lord's touch? And yet how exquisite the figure itself—of protection, rest, warmth, and all manner of conscious well-being in those poor, defenceless, dependent little creatures, as they creep under and feel themselves overshadowed by the capacious and kindly wing of the mother-bird! If, wandering beyond hearing of her peculiar call, they are overtaken by a storm or attacked by an enemy, what can they do but in the one case droop and die, and in the other submit to be torn in pieces? But if they can reach in time their place of safety, under the mother's wing, in vain will any enemy try to drag them thence. For rising into strength, kindling into fury, and forgetting herself entirely in her young, she will let the last drop of her blood be shed out and perish in defence of her precious charge, rather than yield them to an enemy's talons. How significant all this of what Jesus is and does for men! Under His great Mediatorial wing would He have "gathered" Israel. For the figure, see Deut. xxxii. 10-12; Ruth ii. 12; Ps. xvii. 8; xxxvi. 7; lxi. 4; lxiii. 7; xci. 4; Isa. xxxi. 5; Mal. iv. 2. The ancient rabbins had a beautiful expression for proselytes from the heathen—that they had 'come under the wings of the Shechinah.' For this last word, see on *v.* 38. But what was the result of all this tender and mighty love? The answer is, "And ye would not." (See Neh. ix. 26; Ps. lxxxi. 11, 13; Isa. vi. 9, 10; xxviii. 12; xxx. 8, 9, 15; xlix. 4; liii. 1; with John xii. 37-40.) O mysterious word! mysterious the resistance of such patient Love—mysterious the liberty of self-undoing! The awful dignity of the *will*, as here expressed, might make the ears to tingle. **38. Behold, your house**—the Temple, beyond all doubt; but *their* house now, not *the Lord's*. See on ch. xxii. 7. **is left unto you desolate** [ἔρημος]—'deserted;' that is, of its Divine Inhabitant. But who is that? Hear the next words: **39. For I say unto you**—and these were *His last words* to the impenitent nation: see opening remarks on Mark xiii.—**Ye shall not see me henceforth.** What? Does Jesus mean that He was Himself the Lord of the temple, and that it became "deserted" when HE finally left it? It is even so. Now is thy fate sealed, O Jerusalem, for the glory is departed from thee! That glory, once visible in the holy of holies, over the mercy-seat, when on the day of atonement the blood of typical expiation was sprinkled on it and in front of it—called by the Jews the *Shechinah*, or the *Dwelling* [שְׁכִינָה], as being the visible pavilion of Jehovah—that glory, which Isaiah (ch. vi.) saw in vision, the beloved disciple says was *the glory of Christ* (John xii. 41). Though it was never visible in the second temple, Haggai foretold that "*the glory of that latter house should be greater than of the former*" (ch. ii. 9), because "the Lord whom they sought was suddenly to come to His temple" (Mal. iii. 1), not in a mere bright cloud, but enshrined in living Humanity! Yet brief as well as "sudden" was the manifestation to be; for the words He was now uttering were to be HIS VERY LAST within its precincts. **till ye shall say, Blessed is he that cometh in the name of the Lord**: that is, till those "Hosannas to the Son of David" with which the multitude had welcomed Him into the city—instead of "sore displeasing the chief priests and scribes" (ch. xxi. 15)—should break forth from the whole nation, as their glad acclaim to their once pierced but now acknowledged Messiah. That such a time will come is clear from Zec. xii. 10; Rom. xi. 26; 2 Cor. iii. 15, 16, &c. In what sense they shall then "see Him," may be gathered from Zec. ii. 10-13; Ezek. xxxvii. 23-28; xxxix. 28, 29, &c.

Remarks.—1. Though the proceedings of church rulers have no intrinsic validity against the truth of God, they have a divine sanction, and as such are to be reverenced, when their sole object is to maintain, unfold, and enforce the word of God (*vv.* 2, 3). 2. Humility and brotherly love, and that supreme attachment to CHRIST which will beget and strengthen both these, are the glory and stability of the Christian ministry; but when the ministers of religion, seeking the fleece rather than the flock, abandon themselves to pride and self-seeking, they not only reveal their own hypocrisy, but bring their office into contempt. What sad illustrations of this does history furnish! If the Jewish ecclesiastics are faithfully, and not too darkly, depicted in this Section, what language would adequately describe their Romish successors, who, with far clearer light, have exceeded them in every detestable feature of their charac-

24 AND [a]Jesus went out, and departed from the temple: and his dis-
2 ciples came to *him*, for to show him the buildings of the temple. And
Jesus said unto them, See ye not all these things? Verily I say unto
you, There [b]shall not be left here one stone upon another, that shall not
be thrown down.
3 And as he sat upon the mount of Olives, the disciples came unto
him privately, saying, [c]Tell us, when shall these things be? and what

A. D. 33.

CHAP. 24.
[a] Mark 13. 1. Luke 21. 5.
[b] 1 Ki. 9. 7. Jer. 5. 10. Jer. 26. 18. Mic. 3. 12.
[c] 1 Thes. 5. 1.

ter? 3. As "evil men and seducers wax worse and worse, deceiving and being deceived" (2 Tim. iii. 13), and treasure up unto themselves wrath against the day of wrath (Rom. ii. 5); so over and above the partial retribution which often overtakes them individually, there are outstanding accounts left to be settled with them as a class, which accumulate from time to time—sometimes for ages—and are at length, "in the day of visitation," awfully brought up against them and settled, by an exercise of collective and crushing vengeance (*vv.* 31-36). This terrific but righteous law of the divine administration has been illustrated at different times on a scale of no little magnitude; but perhaps its most appalling illustration is yet to come (see Dan. vii. 9-14; 2 Thes. ii. 7-12; Rev. xi. 15-18; xvii. 14; xviii. 5-8, 24). 4. What a combination of withering denunciation and weeping lamentation do we find here—as if the intensity of the Redeemer's holy emotions, in their most vivid contrast, had only found full vent at this last visit to Jerusalem, and in this *His last public address to the impenitent nation!* And if the verses which conclude this chapter were indeed His last words to them, as it is evident they were (see opening remarks on Mark xiii.), how worthy were they of Him, and of the awful occasion, and how pregnant with warning to every such favoured region:—

JERUSALEM.

Jerusalem! Jerusalem! enthroned once on high,
Thou favour'd home of God on earth, thou heaven below the sky!
Now brought to bondage with thy sons, a curse and grief to see,
Jerusalem! Jerusalem! our tears shall flow for thee.

Oh! hadst thou known thy day of grace, and flock'd beneath the wing
Of Him who called thee lovingly, thine own anointed King,
Then had the tribes of all the world gone up thy pomp to see,
And glory dwelt within thy gates, and all thy sons been free!

"And who art thou that mournest me?" replied the ruin gray,
"And fear'st not rather that thyself may prove a castaway?
I am a dried and abject branch,—my place is given to thee;
But woe to ev'ry barren graft of thy wild olive tree!

"Our day of grace is sunk in night, our time of mercy spent,
For heavy was my children's crime, and strange their punishment;
Yet gaze not idly on our fall, but, sinner, warned be,—
Who spared not His chosen seed may send His wrath on thee!

"Our day of grace is sunk in night, thy noon is in its prime;
Oh, turn and seek thy Saviour's face in this accepted time!
So, Gentile, may Jerusalem a lesson prove to thee,
And in the New Jerusalem thy home for ever be!"—HEBER.

5. Ye that are ready to despair of salvation, when ye think of your obstinate and long-continued rebellion against light and love, truth and grace—yea, bloody persecutors, '*Jerusalem-sinners*'—come hither, and suffer me to plead with you. Listen once more to the Friend of sinners. "O Jerusalem, Jerusalem," says He, "that killest the prophets, and stonest them that are sent unto thee, how often would I have gathered thee!" And would He not have gathered them even then, whilst He was yet speaking? Verily He would, "*but they would not.*" That was all the hindrance: there was none, none at all, in Him. If thou, then, art of their mind, there is indeed no help, no hope, for thee; but if thou only *wilt* be made whole—

'Jesus ready stands to save thee,
Full of pity, love, and power:
He is able,
He is willing, ask no more.'

6. The doctrine of Scripture regarding man's *will* embraces the following points:—First, that whether men are to be saved or lost hinges entirely upon their own will. "Whosoever *will* [ὁ θέλων], let him take the water of life freely" (Rev. xxii. 17). "I would have gathered you, and ye *would* not" [οὐκ ἠθελήσατε]. This great truth must not be qualified or explained away. Next, the will of man is utterly indisposed and disabled from yielding itself to Christ. "No man can come to Me, except the Father which hath sent Me draw him" (John vi. 44). And hence, finally, when the will is effectually gained, and salvation thus obtained, it is in consequence of a divine operation upon it. "It is God that worketh in you, both to *will* and to do" of His good pleasure (Phil. ii. 13). Nor is this to be modified or attenuated in the least. The result of all is, that when a soul is undone, it is self-destroyed; but when surrendered to Christ and saved, it is purely of grace (Hos. xiii. 9). That self-surrender to Christ which secures its salvation is as purely voluntary as the rejection of Him which is fatal to unbelievers; but never is this done till God "worketh in us to will" it. How this is effected, consistently with the entire freedom of the human will, we shall never know—here below, at least. But it is a pitiful thing for men, who see the same principle of divine operation on the free will of man in the ordinary administration of the world, to pitch the one of these against the other in the matter of salvation: Pelagians and Semi-pelagians, of different name, denying the *grace* which alone ever gains the consent of man's will to salvation in Christ Jesus; and ultra-Calvinists, denying the entire freedom of that *will* which in one class rejects Christ and is undone, and in another embraces Him and lives for ever. With what awful dignity and responsibility is the human will invested by these words of Christ, "I would have gathered you, but—ye would not;" and by those other words of the same Lips, now glorified and enthroned, "Behold, I stand at the door, and knock: if any man hear my voice, and *open the door*, I will come in to him, and will sup with him, and he with Me"! (Rev. iii. 20). But when we have opened our willing hearts to this glorious and full-handed Saviour, our resistless language is, "By the grace of God I am what I am" (1 Cor. xv. 10). 7. What a day will that be when those whom Christ solicited so long in vain "shall look on Him whom they have pierced, and mourn for Him as one mourneth for his only son, and be in bitterness for Him as one that is in bitterness for his first-born!" What acclamations of "Hosanna to the Son of David" will those be that come from the lips of Abraham's seed that once cried, "Crucify Him, crucify Him"! No wonder that the apostle asks, "What shall the receiving of them be but life from the dead?" (Rom. xi. 15). The Lord hasten it in its time.

CHAP. XXIV. 1-51.—CHRIST'S PROPHECY OF THE DESTRUCTION OF JERUSALEM, AND WARN-

4 *shall be* the sign of thy coming, and of the end of the world? And
Jesus answered and said unto them, Take [d]heed that no man deceive
5 you. For [e]many shall come in my name, saying, I am Christ; and shall
6 deceive many. And ye shall hear of wars and rumours of wars: see
that ye be not troubled: for all *these things* must come to pass, but the
7 end is not yet. For [f]nation shall rise against nation, and kingdom
against kingdom: and there shall be famines, and pestilences, and
8 earthquakes, in divers places. All these *are* the beginning of sorrows.
9 Then [g]shall they deliver you up to be afflicted, and shall kill you: and
10 ye shall be hated of all nations for my name's sake. And then shall
many [h]be offended, and shall betray one another, and shall hate one
11 another. And [i]many false prophets shall rise, and [j]shall deceive many.
12 And because iniquity shall abound, the love of many shall wax cold.
13 But [k]he that shall endure unto the end, the same shall be saved.
14 And this gospel of the kingdom [l]shall be preached in all the world for a
witness unto all nations; and then shall the end come.
15 When ye therefore shall see the abomination of desolation, spoken of
by Daniel [m]the prophet, stand in the holy place, ([n]whoso readeth, let
16 him understand,) then let them which be in Judea flee into the moun-
17 tains: let him which is on the house-top not come down to take any
18 thing out of his house: neither let him which is in the field return back
19 to take his clothes. And woe unto them that are with child, and to
20 them that give suck, in those days! But pray ye that your flight be not
21 in the winter, neither on the sabbath day: for [o]then shall be great tribulation, such as was not since the beginning of the world to this time,
22 no, nor ever shall be. And except those days should be shortened, there
should no flesh be saved: [p]but for the elect's sake those days shall be
23 shortened. Then if any man shall say unto you, Lo, here *is* Christ, or
24 there; believe *it* not. For [q]there shall arise false Christs, and false prophets, and shall show great signs and wonders; insomuch that, [r]if *it were*
25 possible, they shall deceive the very elect. Behold, I have told you
26 before. Wherefore, if they shall say unto you, Behold, he is in the
desert; go not forth: behold, *he is* in the secret chambers; believe *it* not.
27 For as the lightning cometh out of the east, and shineth even unto the
28 west; so shall also the coming of the Son of man be. For [s]wheresoever
the carcase is, there will the eagles be gathered together.
29 Immediately [t]after the tribulation of those days [u]shall the sun be
darkened, and the moon shall not give her light, and the stars shall fall
30 from heaven, and the powers of the heavens shall be shaken: and [v]then
shall appear the sign of the Son of man in heaven: [w]and then shall all
the tribes of the earth mourn, [x]and they shall see the Son of man coming
31 in the clouds of heaven with power and great glory. And [y]he shall send
his angels [1]with a great sound of a trumpet, and they shall gather
together his elect from the four winds, from one end of heaven to the
other.
32 Now learn [z]a parable of the fig tree: When his branch is yet tender,
33 and putteth forth leaves, ye know that summer *is* nigh: so likewise ye,
when ye shall see all these things, know that [2]it is near, *even* at the
34 doors. Verily I say unto you, [a]This generation shall not pass, till all
35 these things be fulfilled. Heaven [b]and earth shall pass away, but my
words shall not pass away.
36 But [c]of that day and hour knoweth no *man*, no, not the angels of
37 heaven, [d]but my Father only. But as the days of Noe *were*, so shall

A. D. 33.

d Eph. 5. 6. 2 Thes. 2. 3. 1 John 4. 1.
e Jer. 14. 14. Jer. 23. 21. John 5. 43.
f Isa. 19. 2. Hag. 2. 22. Zec. 14. 13.
g Acts 4. 2, 3. Acts 7. 59. Acts 12. 1.
h 2 Tim. 1. 15.
i Acts 20. 29. 2 Cor. 11. 13. 2 Pet. 2. 1.
j 1 Tim. 4. 1.
k Heb. 3. 6.
l Rom. 10. 18.
m Dan. 9. 27. Dan. 12. 11.
n Dan. 9. 23.
o Dan. 12. 1. Joel 1. 2. Joel 2. 2.
p Isa. 65. 8, 9. Zec. 14. 2, 3.
q Deut. 13. 1. 2 Thes. 2. 9. Rev. 13. 13.
r Rom. 8. 28. 2 Tim. 2. 19. 1 Pet. 1. 5.
s Job 39. 30.
t Dan. 7. 11.
u Isa. 13. 10. Ezek. 32. 7. Acts 2. 20. Rev. 6. 12.
v Dan. 7. 13.
w Zec. 12. 12.
x Rev. 1. 7.
y 1 Cor. 15. 52. 1 Thes. 4. 16.
1 Or, with a trumpet, and a great voice.
z Luke 21. 29.
2 Or, he.
Jas. 5. 9.
a ch. 16. 28. ch. 23. 36.
b Ps. 102. 26, 27. Isa. 34. 4. Isa. 51. 6. Jer. 31. 35. ch. 5. 18. Mark 13. 31. Luke 21. 33. Heb. 1. 11. 2 Pet. 3. 7-12. Rev. 6. 14.
c Acts 1. 7. 1 Thes. 5. 2. 2 Pet. 3. 10.
d Zec. 14. 7.

INGS SUGGESTED BY IT TO PREPARE FOR HIS SECOND COMING. (= Mark xiii. 1-37; Luke xxi. 5-36.) For the exposition of this wonderful Prophecy, which will be best apprehended by taking all the records of it together, see on Mark xiii. 1-37.

38 also the coming of the Son of man be. For [e]as in the days that were
before the flood they were eating and drinking, marrying and giving in
39 marriage, until the day that Noe entered into the ark, and knew not
until the flood came, and took them all away; so shall also the coming
40 of the Son of man be. Then shall two be in the field; the one shall be
41 taken, and the other left. Two *women shall be* grinding at the mill; the
one shall be taken, and the other left.
42 Watch therefore; for ye know not what hour your Lord doth come.
43 But [f]know this, that if the goodman of the house had known in what
watch the thief would come, he would have watched, and would not
44 have suffered his house to be broken up. Therefore be ye also ready:
45 for in such an hour as ye think not the Son of man cometh. Who [g]then
is a faithful and wise servant, whom his lord hath made ruler over his
46 household, to give them meat in due season? Blessed [h]*is* that servant
47 whom his lord when he cometh shall find so doing. Verily I say unto
48 you, That he shall make him ruler over all his goods. But and if that
49 evil servant shall say in his heart, My lord delayeth his coming; and
shall begin to smite *his* fellow-servants, and to eat and drink with the
50 drunken; the lord of that servant shall come in a day when he looketh
51 not for *him*, and in an hour that he is not aware of, and shall [3]cut him
asunder, and appoint *him* [i]his portion with the hypocrites: there shall
be weeping and gnashing of teeth.

25 THEN shall the kingdom of heaven be likened unto ten virgins, which
2 took their lamps, and went forth to meet [a]the bridegroom. And [b]five
3 of them were wise, and five *were* foolish. They that *were* foolish took their
4 lamps, and took [c]no oil with them: but the wise took oil in their vessels

A. D. 33.

e Gen. 6. 3. Gen. 7. 1. Luke 17. 26. 1 Pet. 3. 20.
f Mark 13. 33, 36. 1 Thes. 5. 6. Rev. 3. 3. Rev. 16. 15.
g 1 Cor. 4. 2. Heb. 3. 5.
h ch. 25. 34. 1 Tim. 4. 7, 8. Rev. 16. 15.
3 Or, cut him off.
i Ps. 11. 6. ch. 25. 30. Luke 12. 46.

CHAP. 25.
a John 3. 29. Eph. 5. 29. Rev. 19. 7. Rev. 21. 2, 9.
b ch. 13. 47. ch. 22. 10.
c Isa. 29. 13. Ezra 33. 30-32. 2 Tim. 3. 5. Titus 1. 16.

CHAP. XXV. 1-13.—PARABLE OF THE TEN VIRGINS. This and the following parable are in Matthew alone.

1. Then—at the time referred to at the close of the preceding chapter, the time of the Lord's Second Coming to reward His faithful servants and take vengeance on the faithless. *Then* **shall the kingdom of heaven be likened unto ten virgins, which took their lamps, and went forth to meet the bridegroom.** This supplies a key to the parable, whose object is, in the main, the same as that of the last parable—to illustrate *the vigilant and expectant attitude of faith*, in respect of which believers are described as "they that look for Him" (Heb. ix. 28), and "love His appearing" (2 Tim. iv. 8). In the last parable it was that of servants waiting for their absent Lord; in this it is that of virgin-attendants on a Bride, whose duty it was to go forth at night with lamps, and be ready on the appearance of the Bridegroom to conduct the Bride to his house, and go in with him to the marriage. This entire and beautiful change of figure brings out the lesson of the former parable in quite a new light. But let it be observed that, just as in the parable of the Marriage Supper, so in this—the *Bride* does not come into view at all in this parable; the *Virgins* and the *Bridegroom* holding forth all the intended instruction: nor could believers be represented both as Bride and Bridal Attendants without incongruity. **2. And five of them were wise, and five were foolish.** They are not distinguished into good and bad, as *Trench* observes, but into "wise" and "foolish"—just as in Matt. vii. 25-27, those who reared their house for eternity are distinguished into "wise" and "foolish builders;" because in both cases a certain degree of good will towards the truth is assumed. To make anything of the equal number of both classes would, we think, be precarious, save to warn us how large a portion of those who, up to the last, so nearly resemble those that love Christ's appearing will be disowned by Him when He comes. **3. They that were foolish took their lamps, and took no oil with them: 4. But the wise took oil in their vessels with their lamps.** What are these "lamps" and this "oil?" Many answers have been given. But since the foolish as well as the wise took their lamps and went forth with them to meet the bridegroom, these lighted lamps, and this advance a certain way in company with the wise, must denote that Christian profession which is common to all who bear the Christian name; while the insufficiency of this without something else, of which they never possessed themselves, shows that "the foolish" mean those who, with all that is common to them with real Christians, *lack the essential preparation for meeting Christ.* Then, since the wisdom of "the wise" consisted in their taking with their lamps a supply of oil in their vessels, keeping their lamps burning till the Bridegroom came, and so fitting them to go in with Him to the marriage—this supply of oil must mean that *inward reality of grace* which alone will stand when He appeareth whose eyes are as a flame of fire. But this is too general; for it cannot be for nothing that this inward grace is here set forth by the familiar symbol of *oil*, by which *the Spirit of all grace* is so constantly represented in Scripture. Beyond all doubt, this was what was symbolized by that precious anointing oil with which Aaron and his sons were consecrated to the priestly office (Exod. xxx. 23-25, 30); by "the oil of gladness above His fellows" with which Messiah was to be anointed (Ps. xlv. 7; Heb. i. 9), even as it is expressly said, that "God giveth not the Spirit by measure unto Him" (John iii. 34); and by the bowl full of golden oil, in Zechariah's vision, which, receiving its supplies from the two olive-trees on either side of it, poured it through seven golden pipes into the golden lamp-stand, to keep it continually burning bright (Zec. iv.)—for

5 with their lamps. While the bridegroom tarried, [d]they all slumbered
6 and slept. And at midnight [e]there was a cry made, Behold, the bride-
7 groom cometh; go ye out to meet him. Then all those virgins arose,
8 and trimmed their [f]lamps. And the foolish said unto the wise, Give
9 us of your oil; for our lamps are [1]gone out. But the wise answered,
saying, *Not so;* lest there be not enough for us and you: but go ye rather
10 to them that sell, and buy for yourselves. And while they went to buy,
the bridegroom came; and they that were ready went in with him to

A. D. 33.

d 1 Thes. 5. 6.
e ch 24. 31. 1 Thes. 4.16. 2 Thes. 1. 7-10. Jude 14. 15.
f Luke 12.35.
1 Or, going out.

the prophet is expressly told that it was to proclaim the great truth, "Not by might, nor by power, but by MY SPIRIT, saith the Lord of hosts [shall this temple be built]. Who art thou, O great mountain [of opposition to this issue]? Before Zerubbabel thou shalt become a plain [or, be swept out of the way], and he shall bring forth the head-stone [of the temple], with shoutings [crying], GRACE, GRACE unto it." This supply of oil, then, representing that inward grace which distinguishes the wise, must denote, more particularly, that "supply of the Spirit of Jesus Christ," which, as it is the source of the new spiritual life at the first, is the secret of its *enduring* character. Everything *short of this* may be possessed by "the foolish;" while it is the possession of this that makes "the wise" to be "ready" when the Bridegroom appears, and fit to "go in with Him to the marriage." Just so in the parable of the Sower, the stony ground hearers, "having no deepness of earth" and "no root in themselves," though they spring up and get even into ear, never ripen, while they in the good ground bear the precious grain. **5. While the bridegroom tarried.** So in ch. xxiv. 48, "My Lord delayeth His coming;" and so Peter says sublimely of the ascended Saviour, "Whom the heaven must receive until the times of restitution of all things" (Acts iii. 21, and compare Luke xix. 11, 12). Christ "tarries," among other reasons, to try the faith and patience of His people. **they all slumbered and slept**—the wise as well as the foolish. The word "slumbered" [ἐνύσταξαν] signifies, simply, 'nodded,' or, 'became drowsy;' while the word "slept" [ἐκάθευδον] is the usual word for 'lying down to sleep:' denoting two stages of spiritual declension—first, that half-involuntary lethargy or drowsiness which is apt to steal over one who falls into inactivity; and then a conscious, deliberate yielding to it, after a little vain resistance. Such was the state alike of the wise and the foolish virgins, even till the cry of the Bridegroom's approach awoke them. So likewise in the parable of the Importunate Widow: "When the Son of man cometh, shall He find faith on the earth?" (Luke xviii. 8). **6. And at midnight**—that is, the time when the Bridegroom will be least expected; for "the day of the Lord so cometh as a thief in the night" (1 Thes. v. 2), **there was a cry made, Behold, the bridegroom cometh; go ye out to meet him**—that is, 'Be ready to welcome Him.' **7. Then all those virgins arose, and trimmed their lamps**—the foolish virgins as well as the wise. How very long do both parties seem the same—almost to the moment of decision! Looking at the mere form of the parable, it is evident that the folly of "the foolish" consisted not in having no oil at all; for they must have had oil enough in their lamps to keep them burning up to this moment: their folly consisted in not making provision against its *exhaustion*, by taking with their lamp an *oil-vessel* wherewith to replenish their lamp from time to time, and so have it burning until the bridegroom should come. Are we, then—with some even superior expositors—to conclude that the foolish virgins must represent true Christians as well as the wise, since only true Christians have the Spirit; and that the difference between the two classes consists only in the one having the necessary watchfulness which the other wants? Certainly not. Since the parable was designed to hold forth the prepared and the unprepared to meet Christ at His coming, and how the unprepared might, up to the very last, be confounded with the prepared—the structure of the parable behoved to accommodate itself to this, by making the lamps of the foolish to burn, as well as those of the wise, up to a certain point of time, and only then to discover their inability to burn on for want of a fresh supply of oil. But this is evidently just a *structural device;* and the real difference between the two classes who profess to love the Lord's appearing is a *radical* one—the possession by the one class of *an enduring principle of spiritual life*, and the want of it by the other. **8. And the foolish said unto the wise, Give us of your oil; for our lamps are gone out** [σβέννυνται]—rather, as in the margin, 'are going out;' for oil will not light an extinguished lamp, though it will keep a burning one from going out. Ah! now at length they have discovered not only their own folly, but the wisdom of the other class, and they do homage to it. They did not perhaps despise them before, but they thought them righteous overmuch; now they are forced, with bitter mortification, to wish they were like them. **9. But the wise answered, [Not so]; lest there be not enough for us and you.** The words "Not so," it will be seen, are not in the original, where the reply is very elliptical [Μήποτε οὐκ ἀρκέσῃ ἡμῖν καὶ ὑμῖν]—'In case there be not enough for us and you.' A truly wise answer this. 'And what, then, if we shall share it with you? Why, both will be undone.' **but go ye rather to them that sell, and buy for yourselves.** Here again it would be straining the parable beyond its legitimate design to make it teach that men may get salvation even after they are supposed and required to have it already gotten. It is merely a friendly way of reminding them of the proper way of obtaining the needed and precious article, with a certain reflection on them for having it now to seek. Also, when the parable speaks of "selling" and "buying" that valuable article, it means simply, 'Go, get it in the only legitimate way.' And yet the word "buy" is significant; for we are elsewhere bidden "buy wine and milk without money and without price," and "buy of Christ gold tried in the fire," &c. (Isa. lv. 1; Rev. iii. 18). Now, since what we pay the demanded price for becomes thereby *our own property*, the salvation which we thus take gratuitously at God's hands, being bought in His own sense of that word, becomes ours thereby in inalienable possession. (Compare, for the language, Prov. xxiii. 23; Matt. xiii. 44.) **10. And while they went to buy, the bridegroom came; and they that were ready went in with him to the marriage: and the door was shut.** They are sensible of their past folly; they have taken good advice: they are in the act of getting

11 the marriage: and the [g]door was shut. Afterward came also the other
12 virgins, saying, [h]Lord, Lord, open to us. But he answered and said,
13 Verily I say unto you, [i]I know you not. Watch [j]therefore; for ye know
neither the day nor the hour wherein the Son of man cometh.

A. D. 33.

[g] Luke 13. 25.
[h] ch. 7. 21.
[i] Ps. 5. 5.
[j] ch. 24. 42.

what alone they lacked: a very little more, and they also are ready. But the Bridegroom comes; the ready are admitted; "the door is shut," and they are undone. How graphic and appalling this picture of one *almost saved—but lost!* **11. Afterward came also the other virgins, saying, Lord, Lord, open to us.** In ch. vii. 22 this reiteration of the name was an exclamation rather of surprise: here it is a piteous cry of urgency, bordering on despair. Ah! now at length their eyes are wide open, and they realize all the consequences of their past folly. **12. But he answered and said, Verily I say unto you, I know you not.** The attempt to establish a difference between "I know you not" here, and "I never knew you" in ch. vii. 23—as if this were gentler, and so implied a milder fate, reserved for "the foolish" of this parable—is to be resisted, though advocated by such critics as *Olshausen*, *Stier*, and *Alford*. Besides being inconsistent with the general tenor of such language, and particularly the solemn moral of the whole (*v.* 13), it is a *kind* of criticism which tampers with some of the most awful warnings regarding the future. If it be asked why unworthy guests were admitted to the marriage of the King's Son, in a former parable, and the foolish virgins are excluded in this one, we may answer, in the admirable words of *Gerhard*, quoted by *Trench*, that those festivities are celebrated in this life, in the Church militant; these at the last day, in the Church triumphant: to those, even they are admitted who are not adorned with the wedding-garment; but to these, only they to whom it is granted to be arrayed in fine linen clean and white, which is the righteousness of saints (Rev. xix. 8): to those, men are called by the trumpet of the Gospel; to these by the trumpet of the Archangel: to those, who enters may go out from them, or be cast out; who is once introduced to these never goes out, nor is cast out, from them any more: wherefore it is said, "The door is shut." **13. Watch therefore; for ye know neither the day nor the hour [wherein the Son of man cometh.]** This, the moral or practical lesson of the whole parable, needs no comment. [The evidence against the genuineness, in this verse, of the words enclosed in brackets is decisive. They seem to have been first copied, exactly as they stand in ch. xxiv. 44, into what are called *Lectionaries*, or portions of Scripture transcribed to be read as Church Lessons—in all of which these words are found—in order to avoid the apparent abruptness with which the verse otherwise closes, and then to have found their way into a tolerable number of MSS. and versions. But the abruptness is more apparent than real; and the event itself being supposed, the uncertainty ascribed simply to "the day and the hour" has something striking and emphatic in it.]

Remarks.—1. So essential a feature of the Christian character, according to the New Testament, is looking for Christ's Second Appearing, that both real and apparent disciples are here described as "going forth to meet Him." And so everywhere. It is "to them that *look for Him*" that "He will appear the second time, without sin, unto salvation" (Heb. ix. 28); it is to "them that *love His appearing*" that "He will give a crown of righteousness at that day" (2 Tim. iv. 8); to His servants, His parting word, on "going to the far country," is, "Occupy *till I come*" (Luke xix. 13); communicants at His table, "as often as they eat this bread and drink this cup, do show forth the Lord's death *till He come*" (1 Cor. xi. 26); and when the Thessalonians turned to God from idols, it was, on the one hand, "to serve the living God, and," on the other, "to *wait for His Son from heaven*" (1 Thess. i. 9, 10). No expectation of the Latter-Day glory—no, nor preparedness to die, ought to take the place, or is fitted to produce the effects, of this love of Christ's appearing and waiting for Him from heaven, which lifts the soul into its highest attitude and dress for heaven, carrying every other scriptural expectation along with it. But 2. It should be carefully observed that it was not the want of expectation that the bridegroom would come that constituted the folly of "the foolish," but their not having any provision for meeting him in case he should tarry. The burning lamp represents the state of readiness. But whereas the lamps of the foolish, though burning at the first, went out ere the bridegroom came, this is to signify that the class intended are such as have no real preparedness to meet Christ at all. On the other hand, lively expectation of Christ's coming, up to the time of His arrival, is so far from being the distinguishing mark of the wise, that even these wise virgins, as well as the foolish, first sank into a lethargic state, and then yielded themselves up to sleep. Were they shut out, then? Nay. At the time of deepest sleep, a warning cry was kindly sent them, loud enough to rouse the foolish and the wise alike; both now set themselves to meet the bridegroom; and then did it become manifest that the wisdom of the wise and the folly of the foolish lay, not in the one *expecting the coming* which the other did not, but in the one having from the very outset a *provision for meeting* the bridegroom, *however long he might tarry*, while the provision of the other was but temporary, and so failed in the time of need. We make these observations because those who expect the Second Coming of Christ *before* the Millennium have made a use of this parable, against such as think this expectation unscriptural, which appears to us to distort its proper teaching. The love of their Lord's appearing is certainly not confined to those who take the former of these views; and perhaps they might do well to consider whether it be not possible to substitute this expectation for that enduring principle of spiritual life in Christ Jesus which is the grand and never-wanting preparation for meeting Him, however long He may tarry. But we deprecate controversy here among the loving expectants of a common Lord. Our sole object is to get at the actual teaching of our blessed Master, and gently to brush away what we think has been obtruded upon it. 3. How appalling it is to think of the nearness to final salvation and heaven's fruition in the presence of Christ to which some may attain, and yet miss it! But see on ch. vii. 13-29, Remark 5, at the close of that Section. 4. The way to secure ourselves against being found *wrong at the last* is to get *right at the first.* The wisdom of the wise virgins lay in their taking along with their lamps, from the time they first went forth to meet the bridegroom, *a supply of oil* that should keep their lamps burning however long he might tarry: the foolish virgins, by their not doing so, showed that they *began with inadequate preparation against the future.*

14 For [k]*the kingdom of heaven is* [l]as a man travelling into a far country,
15 *who* called his own servants, and delivered unto them his goods. And
unto one he gave five [2]talents, to another two, and to another one; [m]to
every man according to his several ability; and straightway took his
16 journey. Then he that had received the five talents went and [n]traded
17 with the same, and made *them* other five talents. And likewise he that
18 *had received* two, he also gained other two. But he that had received
19 one went and digged in the earth, and [o]hid his lord's money. After a
long time the lord of those servants cometh, and reckoneth with them.
20 And so he that had received five talents came and brought other five
talents, saying, Lord, thou deliveredst unto me five talents: behold, I

A. D. 33.

k Luke 19. 12.
l ch. 21. 33. Mark 13. 34. Luke 19. 12, 13.
2 A talent is 187*l*. 10*s*.
m Rom. 12. 6. 1 Cor. 12. 7. Eph. 4. 11.
n Pro. 3. 14. 1 Pet. 4. 10.
o Phil. 2. 21.

They never were right, and the issue only brought out what was their radical mistake all along. 5. Nothing will avail for meeting Christ in peace but that unction from the Holy One, of which it is said, "If any man have not the Spirit of Christ, he is none of His" (Rom. viii. 9): "But the anointing which ye have received of Him abideth in you, and ye need not that any man teach you: but as the same anointing teacheth you all things, and is truth, and is no lie, and even as it hath taught you, ye shall abide in Him" (1 John ii. 27). 6. We have here a lively illustration of the great truth, that what is *saving* cannot be imparted by one man to another (*v.* 9). "The just shall live by his (own) faith" (Hab. ii. 4). "If thou be wise," says the wisest of men, "thou shalt be wise for thyself; but if thou scornest, thou alone shalt bear it" (Pro. ix. 12). "Let every man prove his own work, and then shall he have rejoicing in himself, and not in another: for every man shall bear his own burden" (Gal. vi. 4, 5). 7. Though such as love their Lord's appearing—when through His long tarrying they have sunk into a lethargic state, and even surrendered themselves to sleep—may have only to "trim their lamps" when the cry of His coming is heard, there being a supply of oil within them sufficient to brighten them up, it is a sad and shameful thing they should have this to do. As these slumbers are dishonouring to the heavenly Bridegroom, so they are the bane of the soul, paralyzing it for all good. "Therefore, let us not sleep, as do others, but let us watch and be sober; putting on the breast-plate of faith and hope, and for an helmet the hope of salvation." And as for others, when they shall be saying, Peace and safety, then sudden destruction shall come upon them, as travail upon a woman with child, and they shall not escape.

14-30.—Parable of the Talents. This parable, while closely resembling it, is yet a different one from that of The Pounds, in Luke xix. 11-27; though *Calvin*, *Olshausen*, *Meyer*, &c., identify them—but not *de Wette* and *Neander*. For the difference between the two parables, see the opening remarks on that of The Pounds. While—as *Trench* observes with his usual felicity—'the virgins were represented as *waiting* for their Lord, we have the servants *working* for Him: there the *inward spiritual life* of the faithful was described; here his *external activity*. It is not, therefore, without good reason that they appear in their actual order—that of the Virgins first, and of the Talents following—since it is the sole condition of a profitable outward activity for the Kingdom of God, that the life of God be diligently maintained within the heart.'

14. For [the kingdom of heaven is] as a man. The ellipsis is better supplied by our translators in the corresponding passage of Mark (xiii. 34), "[For the Son of man is] as a man," &c., **travelling into a far country** [ἀποδημῶν]—or more simply, 'going abroad.' The idea of long "tarrying" is certainly implied here, since it is expressed in *v.* 19. **who called his own servants, and delivered unto them his goods.** Between master and slaves this was not uncommon in ancient times. Christ's "servants" here mean all who, by their Christian profession, stand in the relation to Him of entire subjection. His "goods" mean all their gifts and endowments, whether original or acquired, natural or spiritual. As all that slaves have belongs to their master, so Christ has a claim to everything which belongs to His people, everything which may be turned to good, and He demands its appropriation to His service; or, viewing it otherwise, they first offer it up to Him, as being "not their own, but bought with a price" (1 Cor. vi. 19, 20), and He "delivers it to them" again to be put to use in His service. **15. And unto one he gave five talents, to another two, and to another one.** While the *proportion of gifts* is different in each, the same *fidelity* is required of all, and equally rewarded. And thus there is perfect equity. **to every man according to his several ability**—his natural capacity as enlisted in Christ's service, and his opportunities in providence for employing the gifts bestowed on him. **and straightway took his journey.** Compare ch. xxi. 33, where the same departure is ascribed to God, after setting up the ancient economy. In both cases, it denotes the leaving of men to the action of all those spiritual laws and influences of Heaven under which they have been graciously placed for their own salvation and the advancement of their Lord's kingdom. **16. Then he that had received the five talents went and traded with the same** [εἰργάσατο]—expressive of the activity which he put forth, and the labour he bestowed. **and made them other five talents. 17. And likewise he that had received two** [τὰ δύο]—rather, 'the two'—**he also gained other two**—each doubling what he received, and therefore *both equally faithful*. **18. But he that had received one went and digged in the earth, and hid his lord's money**—not misspending, but simply making no use of it. Nay, his action seems that of one anxious that the gift should not be misused or lost, but ready to be returned, just as he got it. **19. After a long time the lord of those servants cometh and reckoneth with them.** That any one—within the life-time of the apostles at least—with such words before them, should think that Jesus had given any reason to expect His Second Appearing within that period, would seem strange, did we not know the tendency of enthusiastic, ill-regulated love of His appearing ever to take this turn. **20. And so he that had received five talents came and brought other five talents, saying, Lord, thou deliveredst unto me five talents: behold, I have gained besides them five talents more.** How beautifully does this illustrate what the beloved disciple says of "boldness in the

21 have gained besides them five talents more. His lord said unto him,
Well done, *thou* good and faithful servant: thou hast been faithful over
a few things, [p]I will make thee ruler over many things: enter thou into
22 [q]the joy of thy lord. He also that had received two talents came and
said, Lord, thou deliveredst unto me two talents: behold, I have gained
23 two other talents besides them. His lord said unto him, Well done,
good and faithful servant: thou hast been faithful over a few things, I
will make thee ruler over many things: enter thou into the joy of thy
24 lord. Then he which had received the one talent came and said, Lord, I
knew thee that thou art an hard man, reaping where thou hast not sown,
25 and gathering where thou hast not strawed: and I was afraid, and went
26 and hid thy talent in the earth: lo, *there* thou hast *that is* thine. His
lord answered and said unto him, *Thou* wicked and slothful servant,
thou knewest that I reap where I sowed not, and gather where I have
27 not strawed; thou oughtest therefore to have put my money to the
exchangers, and *then* at my coming I should have received mine own
28 with usury. Take therefore the talent from him, and give *it* unto him
29 which hath ten talents. For [r]unto every one that hath shall be given,
and he shall have abundance: but from him that hath not shall be taken
30 away even that which he hath. And cast ye the unprofitable servant
into outer darkness: there shall be weeping and gnashing of teeth.

A. D. 33.

[p] ch. 10. 40, 42. ch. 24. 47. ch. 25. 34, 40. Mark 8. 35. Mark 13. 13. Luke 12. 44. Luke 22. 29, 30. John 12. 25. 2 Tim. 4. 7, 8. Rev. 2. 10, 26-28. Rev. 3. 21. Rev. 21. 7.

[q] Acts 2. 28. Heb. 12. 2. 2 Tim. 2. 12. 1 Pet. 1. 8.

[r] Luke 8. 18. John 15. 2. 1 Cor. 15. 10. 2 Cor. 6. 1.

day of judgment," and his desire that "when He shall appear we may have confidence, and not be ashamed before Him at His coming"! (1 John iv. 17; ii. 28). **21. His lord said unto him, Well done** [Εὖ]—a single word, not of bare satisfaction, but of warm and delighted commendation. And from what Lips! **good and faithful servant: thou hast been faithful over a few things, I will make thee ruler over many things: enter thou into the joy of thy lord. 22. He also that had received two talents came and said, Lord, thou deliveredst unto me two talents: behold, I have gained two other talents besides them. 23. His lord said unto him, Well done, good and faithful servant: thou hast been faithful over a few things, I will make thee ruler over many things.** *Both are commended in the same terms, and the reward of both is precisely the same.* (See on *v.* 15.) Observe also the contrasts: 'Thou hast been faithful as a *servant;* now be a *ruler*—thou hast been *entrusted* with a *few* things; now have *dominion* over *many* things.' **enter thou into the joy of thy lord**—thy Lord's own joy. (See John xv. 11; Heb. xii. 2.) **24. Then he which had received the one talent came and said, Lord, I knew thee that thou art an hard**—or 'harsh,' **man** [σκληρός]. The word in Luke (xix. 21) is "austere" [αὐστηρός]. **reaping where thou hast not sown, and gathering where thou hast not strawed.** The sense is obvious: 'I knew thou wast one whom it was impossible to serve, one whom nothing would please; exacting what was impracticable, and dissatisfied with what was attainable.' Thus do men secretly think of God as a hard Master, and virtually throw on Him the blame of their fruitlessness. **25. And I was afraid**—of making matters worse by meddling with it at all. **and went and hid thy talent in the earth.** This depicts the conduct of all those who shut up their gifts from the active service of Christ, without actually prostituting them to unworthy uses. Fitly, therefore, may it, at least, comprehend those, to whom *Trench* refers, who, in the early Church, pleaded that they had enough to do with their own souls, and were afraid of losing them in trying to save others; and so, instead of being the salt of the earth, thought rather of keeping their own saltness, by withdrawing sometimes into caves and wildernesses, from all those active ministries of love by which they might have served their brethren. **lo, there thou hast that is thine. 26. His lord answered and said unto him, Thou wicked and slothful servant.** "Wicked" or "bad" [Πονηρὲ] means 'false-hearted,' as opposed to the others, who are emphatically styled "*good* servants." The addition of "slothful" [ὀκνηρὲ] is to mark the precise nature of his wickedness: it consisted, it seems, not in his doing anything *against*, but simply nothing *for* his master. **Thou knewest that I reap where I sowed not, and gather where I have not strawed.** He takes the servant's own account of his demands, as expressing graphically enough, not the "*hardness*" which he had basely imputed to him, but simply his demand of '*a profitable return for the gift entrusted.*' **27. thou oughtest therefore to have put my money to the exchangers** [τοῖς τραπεζίταις]—or, 'the bankers,' **and then at my coming I should have received mine own with usury** [τόκῳ]—or 'interest.' **28. Take therefore the talent from him, and give it unto him which hath ten talents. 29. For unto every one that hath shall be given, &c.** See on ch. xiii. 12. **30. And cast ye**—'cast ye out' [ἐκβάλλετε, but the true reading is ἐκβάλετε]. **the unprofitable servant** [ἀχρεῖον]—'the useless servant,' that does his Master no service, **into outer darkness**—'the darkness which is outside.' On this expression see on ch. xxii. 13. **there shall be weeping and gnashing of teeth.** See on ch. xiii. 42.

Remarks.—1. Christ's voice in this parable is not, as in the former one, '*Wait* for your Lord'—'Love His appearing'—but, as in that of the Pounds (Luke xix. 13), "*Occupy* till I come." Blessed is that servant whom His Lord, when He cometh, shall find—not *watching*, as in the former parable—but *working*. 2. How interesting is the view here given of the relation in which every Christian stands to Christ. Not only are they all "servants of Jesus Christ," but all that distinguishes each of them from all the rest—in natural capacity and in acquirements, in providential position, influence, means, and opportunities—all

31 When [s]the Son of man shall come in his glory, and all the holy angels
32 with him, then shall he sit upon the throne of his glory: and [t]before him
shall be gathered all nations: and [u]he shall separate them one from
33 another, as a shepherd divideth *his* sheep from the goats: and he shall
set the sheep on his right hand, but the goats on the left.
34 Then shall the King say unto them on his right hand, Come, ye blessed
of my Father, [v]inherit the kingdom [w]prepared for you from the founda-

A. D. 33.
[s] Zec. 14. 5. Acts 1. 11.
[t] Rom. 14. 10. 2 Cor. 5. 10.
[u] Ezek. 20 38. ch. 13. 49.
[v] Rom. 8. 17.
[w] 1 Cor. 2. 9.

are Christ's; rendered up to Him by them first, with their body and their spirit, which are His by purchase (1 Cor. vi. 19, 20), and then given back by Him to them to be employed in His service. Hence that diversity in the proportion of talents which this parable represents the Master as committing respectively to each of His servants. But 3. Since it is neither the *amount* nor the *nature* of the work done which this parable represents as rewarded, but the *fidelity* shown in the doing of it, the possessor of two talents has an equal reward—proportionably to what was committed to him—with the possessor of five. And thus it is that the most exalted in intellectual gifts, or wealth, or opportunity—though consecrating all these in beautiful fidelity to Christ—may be found occupying no higher position in the kingdom above than the lowest in all these respects, who have shown equal fidelity to the common Master. And thus may we use the language of an apostle in a wider sense than that more immediately intended—"Let the brother of low degree rejoice in that he is exalted, but the rich in that he is made low; because as the flower of the grass he shall pass away" (Jas. i. 9, 10). 4. To be "cast out" at the great day, it is not necessary that we prostitute our powers to a life of positive wickedness: it is enough that our Christianity be merely negative, that we do nothing for Christ, that we are found to have been *unprofitable*, or *useless* servants of the Lord Jesus. But, ah! is it indeed so? Then what numbers are there within the Christian pale whose doom this seals—their life perfectly unexceptionable, and their frame apparently devout, yet negative Christians, and nothing more! But is not the principle on which such shall be condemned most reasonable? If Jesus has a *people* upon earth whom He deigns to call His "mothers and sisters and brothers," and those who claim the Christian name know them not and treat them with cold indifference; if He has a *cause* upon earth which is dear to Him, requiring the services of all His people, and such persons ignore it, and never lend a helping-hand to it—how should they expect Him to recognize and reward them at the great day? But there is something more than righteous disavowal and rejection here. There is "indignation and wrath, tribulation and anguish," in the treatment here awarded to the profitless servant. "Cast ye—thrust ye—fling ye out the useless servant into outer darkness; there shall be weeping and gnashing of teeth." 5. The truth expressed in the taking of the talent from the unprofitable servant and giving it to him that had the ten talents—if we are to view it, as it would seem we should, with reference to the *future* state—is somewhat difficult to conceive. But as it is just as difficult to conceive of it in relation even to the present state, perhaps nothing more is meant by it than this, that while the useless servants shall be *judicially incapacitated* from ever rendering that service to Christ which once they might have done, the faithful servants of the Lord Jesus shall richly "supply their lack of service."

31-46. THE LAST JUDGMENT. The close connection between this sublime scene—peculiar to Matthew—and the two preceding parables is too obvious to need pointing out.

31. When the Son of man shall come in his glory—His *personal* glory, **and all the holy angels with him.** See Deut. xxxiii. 2; Dan. vii. 9, 10; Jude 14; with Heb. i. 6; 1 Pet. iii. 22. [*Lachmann, Tischendorf*, and *Tregelles* omit the word ἅγιοι—"holy"—but, as we read the authorities, it is to be retained as genuine.] **then shall he sit upon the throne of his glory**—the glory of His *judicial authority.* **32. And before him shall be gathered all nations** [πάντα τὰ ἔθνη]—or, 'all the nations.' That this should be understood to mean the *heathen nations*, or all *except* believers in Christ, will seem amazing to any simple reader. Yet this is the exposition of *Olshausen, Stier, Keil, Alford* (though latterly with some diffidence), and of a number, though not all, of those who hold that Christ will come the Second Time before the Millennium, and that the saints will be caught up to meet Him in the air before His Appearing. Their chief argument is, the impossibility of any that ever knew the Lord Jesus wondering, at the Judgment Day, that they should be thought to have done—or left undone—anything "unto Christ." To that we shall advert when we come to it. But here we may just say, that if this scene do not describe a personal, public, final judgment on men, according to the treatment they have given to Christ—and consequently men within the Christian pale—we shall have to consider again whether our Lord's teaching on the greatest themes of human interest does indeed possess that incomparable simplicity and transparency of meaning which, by universal consent, has been ascribed to it. If it be said, But how can this be the General Judgment, if only those within the Christian pale be embraced by it?—we answer, What is here described, as it certainly does not meet the case of all the family of Adam, is of course *so far* not general. But we have no right to conclude that the whole "Judgment of the great day" will be limited to the points of view here presented. Other explanations will come up in the course of our exposition and following Remarks. **and he shall separate them**—now for the first time; the two classes having been mingled all along up to this awful moment—**as a shepherd divideth his sheep from the goats** (see Ezek. xxxiv. 17.) **33. And he shall set the sheep on his right hand**—the side of honour (1 Ki. ii. 19; Ps. xlv. 9; cx. 1, &c.)—**but the goats on the left**—the side consequently of dishonour.

34. Then shall the King. Magnificent title, here for the first and only time, save in parabolical language, given to Himself by the Lord Jesus, and that on the eve of his deepest humiliation! It is to intimate that in then addressing the heirs of the kingdom *He will put on all His regal majesty.* **say unto them on his right hand, Come** [Δεῦτε]—the same sweet word with which He had so long invited all the weary and heavy laden to come unto Him for rest. Now it is addressed exclusively to such as *have* come and found

35 tion of the world: for [x]I was an hungered, and ye gave me meat: I was
thirsty, and ye gave me drink: [y]I was a stranger, and ye took me in:
36 naked, [z]and ye clothed me: I was sick, and ye visited me: [a]I was in
37 prison, and ye came unto me. Then shall the righteous answer him,
saying, Lord, when saw we thee an hungered, and fed *thee?* or thirsty, and
38 gave *thee* drink? When saw we thee a stranger, and took *thee* in? or
39 naked, and clothed *thee?* Or when saw we thee sick, or in prison, and
40 came unto thee? And the King shall answer and say unto them, Verily
I say unto you, [b]Inasmuch as ye have done *it* unto one of the least of
these my brethren, ye have done *it* unto me.
41 Then shall he say also unto them on the left hand, [c]Depart from me,
ye cursed, into [d]everlasting fire, prepared for [e]the devil and his angels:

A. D. 33.

[x] Isa. 58. 7. Ezek. 18. 7. 2 Tim. 1. 16. Jas. 1. 27.
[y] Heb. 13. 2. 3 John 5.
[z] Jas. 2. 15.
[a] 2 Tim. 1. 16.
[b] Pro. 14. 31. Pro. 19. 17. Heb. 6. 10.
[c] Ps. 6. 8.
[d] ch. 13. 40.
[e] 2 Pet. 2. 4. Jude 6.

rest. It is still "Come," and to "rest" too; but to rest in a higher style, and in another region. **ye blessed of my Father, inherit the kingdom prepared for you from the foundation of the world.** The whole story of this their blessedness is given by the apostle, in words which seem but an expansion of these: "Blessed be the God and Father of our Lord Jesus Christ, who hath blessed us with all spiritual blessings in heavenly places in Christ; according as He hath chosen us in Him before the foundation of the world, that we should be holy and without blame before Him in love." They were chosen from everlasting to the possession and enjoyment of all spiritual blessings in Christ, and so chosen in order to be holy and blameless in love. This is the holy love whose practical manifestations the King is about to recount in detail; and thus we see that their whole life of love to Christ is the fruit of an eternal purpose of love to them in Christ. **35. For I was an hungered, and ye gave me meat: . . . thirsty, and ye gave me drink: . . . a stranger, and ye took me in: 36. Naked, and ye clothed me: . . . sick, and ye visited me: . . . prison, and ye came unto me. 37-39. Then shall the righteous answer him, saying, Lord, when saw we thee an hungered, and fed thee? &c. 40. And the King shall answer and say unto them, Verily I say unto you, Inasmuch as ye have done it unto one of the least of these my brethren, ye have done it unto me.** Astonishing dialogue this between the King, from the Throne of His glory, and His wondering people! "I was an hungered, and ye gave Me meat," &c.—'Not we,' they reply, 'We never did that, Lord: We were born out of due time, and enjoyed not the privilege of ministering unto Thee.' 'But ye did it to these My brethren, now beside you, when cast upon your love.' 'Truth, Lord, but was that doing it to Thee? Thy name was indeed dear to us, and we thought it an honour too great to suffer shame for it. When among the destitute and distressed we discerned any of the household of faith, we will not deny that our hearts leapt within us at the discovery, and when their knock came to our dwelling, "our bowels were moved," as though "our Beloved Himself had put in His hand by the hole of the door." Sweet was the fellowship we had with them, as if we had "entertained angels unawares;" all difference between giver and receiver somehow melted away under the beams of that love of Thine which knit us together; nay rather, as they left us with gratitude for our poor givings, we seemed the debtors—not they. But, Lord, were we all that time in company with Thee?' 'Yes, that scene was all with Me,' replies the King—'Me in the disguise of My poor ones. The door shut against Me by others was opened by you'—"Ye took Me in." Apprehended and imprisoned by the enemies of the truth, ye whom the truth had made free sought Me out diligently and found Me; visiting Me in My lonely cell at the risk of your own lives, and cheering My solitude: ye gave Me a coat, for I shivered; and then I felt warm. With cups of cold water ye moistened My parched lips; when famished with hunger ye supplied Me with crusts, and My spirit revived—"YE DID IT UNTO ME." What thoughts crowd upon us as we listen to such a description of the scenes of the Last Judgment! And in the light of this view of the heavenly Dialogue, how bald and wretched, not to say unscriptural, is that view of it to which we referred at the outset, which makes it a Dialogue between Christ and *heathens* who never heard of His name, and of course never felt any stirrings of His love in their hearts! To us it seems a poor, superficial objection to the *Christian* view of this scene, that Christians could never be supposed to ask such questions as the "blessed of Christ's Father" are made to ask here. If there were any difficulty in explaining this, the difficulty of the other view is such as to make *it*, at least, insufferable. But there is no real difficulty. The surprise expressed is not at their being told that they acted from love to Christ, but that *Christ Himself* was the *Personal Object* of all their deeds:—that they found *Him* hungry, and supplied Him with food; that they brought water to *Him*, and slaked His thirst; that seeing *Him* naked and shivering, they put warm clothing upon Him, paid *Him* visits when lying in prison for the truth, and sat by *His* bedside when laid down with sickness. This, this is the astonishing interpretation which Jesus says "the King" will give to them of their own actions here below. And will any Christian reply, 'How could this astonish them? Does not every Christian know that He does these very things, when He does them at all, just as they are here represented? Nay, rather, is it conceivable that they should *not* be astonished, and almost doubt their own ears, to hear such an account of their own actions upon earth from the lips of the Judge? And remember, that Judge has come in His glory, and now sits upon the Throne of His glory, and all the holy angels are with Him; and that it is from those glorified Lips that the words come forth, 'Ye did all this unto ME.' O can we imagine such a word addressed to *ourselves*, and then fancy ourselves replying, 'Of course we did—To whom else did we anything? It must be others than we that are addressed, who never knew, in all their good deeds, what they were about'? Rather, can we imagine ourselves not overpowered with astonishment, and scarcely able to credit the testimony borne to us by the King?

41. Then shall he say also unto them on the

42 for I was an hungered, and ye gave me no meat: I was thirsty, and ye
43 gave me no drink: I was a stranger, and ye took me not in: naked, and
44 ye clothed me not: sick, and in prison, and ye visited me not. Then shall
they also answer him, saying, Lord, when saw we thee an hungered, or
athirst, or a stranger, or naked, or sick, or in prison, and did not minister
45 unto thee? Then shall he answer them, saying, Verily I say unto you,
[f]Inasmuch as ye did *it* not to one of the least of these, ye did *it* not to
46 me. And [g]these shall go away into everlasting punishment: but the
righteous into life [h]eternal.

A. D. 33.

f Pro. 14. 31. Pro. 17. 5. Zec. 2. 8. Acts 9. 5.
g Dan. 12. 2. John 5. 29. Rom. 2. 7. Rev. 20. 10, 15.
h Rev. 3. 21. Rev. 7. 15.

left hand, Depart from me, ye cursed, into everlasting fire, prepared for the devil and his angels: 42, 43. For I was an hungered, and ye gave me no meat, &c. 44. Then shall they also answer him, saying, Lord, when saw we thee an hungered, &c., and did not minister unto thee? 45. Then shall he answer them, saying, Verily I say unto you, Inasmuch as ye did it not to one of the least of these, ye did it not to me. 'As for you on the left hand, ye did nothing for Me. I came to you also, but ye knew Me not; ye had neither warm affections nor kind deeds to bestow upon Me: I was as one despised in your eyes.' 'In *our* eyes, Lord? We never saw Thee before, and never, sure, behaved we so to Thee.' 'But thus ye treated these little ones that believe in Me and now stand on My right hand. In the disguise of these poor members of Mine I came soliciting your pity, but ye shut up your bowels of compassion from Me: I asked relief, but ye had none to give Me. Take back therefore your own coldness, your own contemptuous distance: Ye bid Me away from your presence, and now I bid you from Mine—*Depart from Me, ye cursed!*' **46. And these shall go away**—these "cursed" ones. Sentence, it should seem, was first *pronounced*—in the hearing of the wicked—upon the *righteous*, who thereupon sit as assessors in the judgment upon the wicked (1 Cor. vi. 2); but sentence is first *executed*, it should seem, upon the *wicked*, in the sight of the righteous—whose glory will thus not be beheld by the wicked, while *their* descent into "their own place" will be witnessed by the righteous, as *Bengel* notes. **into everlasting punishment** [κόλασιν αἰώνιον]—or, as in *v.* 41, "everlasting fire, prepared for the devil and his angels." Compare ch. xiii. 42; 2 Thes. i. 9, &c. This is said to be "prepared for the devil and his angels," because they were "first in transgression." But both have one doom, because one unholy character. See on Mark i. 21-39, Remark 1. **but the righteous into life eternal** [ζωὴν αἰώνιον]—'life everlasting.' The word in both clauses, being in the original the same, should have been the same in the translation also. Thus the decisions of this awful day will be final, irreversible, unending. "The Lord grant," to both the writer and his readers, "that they may find mercy of the Lord in THAT DAY!" (2 Tim. i. 18).

Remarks.—1. What claims does "the Son of Man" here put forward for Himself! He is to come in His own glory; all the holy angels are to come with Him; He is to take his seat on the Throne, and that the Throne of His own glory; all nations are to be gathered before Him; the awful separation of the two great classes is to be His doing; the word of *decision* on both—"Ye blessed!" "Ye cursed!" and the word of *command* to the one, "Come!" to the other, "Depart!"—'To the Kingdom!' 'To the flames!'—all this is to be His doing. But most astonishing of all, *The blissful or blighted eternity of each one of both classes is suspended upon his treatment of Him*—is made to turn upon those mysterious ministrations from age to age to the Lord of glory, disguised in the persons of those who love His Name: 'Ye did thus and thus unto Me—Come, ye blessed! Ye did it not to Me—Depart, ye cursed!' In that "ME" lies an emphasis, the strength of which only the scene itself and its everlasting issues will disclose. Verily, "GOD IS JUDGE HIMSELF" (Ps. l. 6); but it is *God in flesh*, God in One who is "not ashamed to call us BRETHREN." 2. What a *practical* character is here stamped upon Christ's service! It is not, 'Ye had it in your hearts,' but 'Ye DID it with your hands.' It is the love of Christ in the heart rushing to the eyes, ears, hands, feet—going in search of Him, hastening to embrace and to cherish Him, as He wanders through this bleak and cheerless world in His persecuted *cause* and needy *people.* O what has this done, and what will it yet do, to bless and to beautify this fallen world! Lo! He casts His entire cause in the earth upon the love of His people. His own poverty was to have an end, but His Church in its poverty was to take His place. His Personal conflict "finished," that of His *cause* was then only to begin. *The whole Story of His necessities and endurances from the world was to be repeated in the Church*, which was to "fill up *that which was behind of the afflictions* of Christ" (Col. i 24). And what condescension is there in identifying Himself with "THE LEAST of His brethren," holding Himself to be the Person to whom anything whatever is done that is done to the humblest and the meanest of them. Nor let it be overlooked, as *Webster and Wilkinson* beautifully remark, that the assistance to the sick and imprisoned here is not *healing* and *release*, which only few could render, but just that which all could bestow—*visitation, sympathy, attention.* (See Exod. ii. 11; 1 Ki. xvii. 10-15; Jer. xxx. 7-13; Acts xvi. 15; 2 Tim. i. 16-18; 3 John 5-8.) 3. Here also, as in the former parable, we are taught that a life of positive wickedness is not necessary to rejection at the great day. It is enough that, according to the former parable, we do nothing for Christ; and according to the present one, that we recognize Him not in His cause and people, and do not to them as would be due to Himself, if Personally present, suffering and dependent. And will not this set the eyes and ears of those who love Him astir to seek Him out, and catch His tones—in the thin disguises in which He still deigns to walk amongst us—and make us tremble at the thought of turning Him away from our door, or passing Him by on the other side? Perhaps JAMES MONTGOMERY'S charming comment on this scene may help us here:—

A poor wayfaring man of grief
Hath often crossed me in my way,
Who asked so humbly for relief
That I could never answer, "Nay:"
I had not power to ask his name,
Whither he went or whence he came,
Yet was there something in his eye
That won my love, I knew not why.

26 AND it came to pass, when Jesus had finished all these sayings, he
2 said unto his disciples, ye [a]know that after two days is *the feast of* the
passover, and the Son of man is betrayed to be crucified.
3 Then [b]assembled together the chief priests, and the scribes, and the
elders of the people, unto the palace of the high priest, who was called
4 Caiaphas, and consulted that they might take Jesus by subtilty, and
5 kill *him*. But they said, Not on the feast *day*, lest there be an uproar
among the people.
6 Now [c]when Jesus was in [d]Bethany, in the house of Simon the leper,
7 there came unto him a woman having an alabaster box of very precious
8 ointment, and poured *it* on his head, as he sat *at meat*. But [e]when his
disciples saw *it*, they had indignation, saying, To what purpose *is* this
9 waste? For this ointment might have been sold for much, and given to
10 the poor. When Jesus understood *it*, he said unto them, Why trouble
11 ye the woman? for she hath wrought a good work upon me. For [f]ye
12 have the poor always with you; but [g]me ye have not always. For in
that she hath poured this ointment on my body, she did *it* for my
13 burial. Verily I say unto you, [h]Wheresoever this gospel shall be
preached in the whole world, *there* shall also this, that this woman hath
done, be told for a memorial of her.
14 Then [i]one of the twelve, called Judas [j]Iscariot, went unto the chief
15 priests, and said *unto them*, [k]What will ye give me, and I will deliver
him unto you? And they covenanted with him for thirty pieces of
16 silver. And from that time he sought opportunity to betray him.
17 Now [l]the first *day* of the *feast of* unleavened bread the disciples came
to Jesus, saying unto him, Where wilt thou that we prepare for thee to
18 eat the passover? And he said, Go into the city to such a man, and say
unto him, The Master saith, My time is at hand; I will keep the passover
19 at thy house with my disciples. And the disciples did as Jesus had
appointed them; and they made ready the passover.
20 Now when the even was come, he sat down with the twelve.
21 And as they did eat, he said, Verily I say unto you, That one of you
22 shall betray me. And they were exceeding sorrowful, and began every
23 one of them to say unto him, Lord, is it I? And he answered and said,
[m]He that dippeth *his* hand with me in the dish, the same shall betray

A. D. 33.

CHAP. 26.
a Mark 14. 1. Luke 22. 1. John 13. 1.
b Ps. 2. 2. John 11. 47. Acts 4. 25.
c Mark 14. 3. John 11. 1, 2. John 12. 3.
d ch. 21. 17.
e John 12. 4.
f Deut. 15. 11. Pro. 22. 2. Mark 14. 7. John 12. 8.
g ch. 18. 20. John 8. 21. John 13. 33. John 14. 19. John 16. 5, 28. John 17. 11. Acts 3. 21. Acts 19. 11.
h Mark 13. 10. Luke 24. 47. Rom. 1. 8. Rom. 10. 18. Col. 1. 6, 23. 1 Tim. 2. 6.
i Mark 14. 10. Luke 22. 3. John 13. 2.
j ch. 10. 4.
k Zec. 11. 12. ch. 27. 3.
l Ex. 12. 6. Lev. 23. 5, 6.
m Ps. 41. 9. Luke 22. 21. John 13. 18.

"HUNGRY, AND YE FED ME."

Once, when my scanty meal was spread,
He entered;—not a word he spake;—
Just perishing for want of bread;
I gave him all; he blest it, brake,
And ate,—but gave me part again
Mine was an angel's portion then,
For while I fed with eager haste
That crust was manna to my taste.

"THIRSTY, AND YE GAVE ME DRINK."

I spied him where a fountain burst
Clear from the rock; his strength was gone;
The heedless water mocked his thirst,
He heard it, saw it hurrying on:
I ran to raise the sufferer up;
Thrice from the stream he drained my cup,
Dipt, and returned it running o'er:
I drank, and never thirsted more.

"A STRANGER, AND YE TOOK ME IN."

'Twas night; the floods were out; it blew
A winter hurricane aloof;
I heard his voice abroad, and flew
To bid him welcome to my roof.

"NAKED, AND YE CLOTHED ME."

I warm'd, I cloth'd, I cheer'd my guest;
Laid him on my own couch to rest;
Then made the hearth my bed, and seem'd
In Eden's garden while I dream'd.

"SICK, AND YE VISITED ME."

Stript, wounded, beaten, nigh to death,
I found him by the highway-side;
Revived his spirit, and supplied
Wine, oil, refreshment: he was heal'd.
I had myself a wound conceal'd,
But from that hour forgot the smart,
And peace bound up my broken heart.

"IN PRISON, AND YE CAME UNTO ME."

In prison I saw him next, condemn'd
To meet a traitor's doom at morn;
The tide of lying tongues I stemm'd,
And honour'd him 'midst shame and scorn:
My friendship's utmost zeal to try,
He ask'd if I for Him would die:
The flesh was weak, my blood ran chill,
But the free spirit cried, "I will."

Then in a moment to my view
The stranger darted from disguise
The tokens in his hands I knew,
My Saviour stood before mine eyes:
He spake, and my poor name He nam'd;
"Of Me thou hast not been asham'd
These deeds shall thy memorial be;
Fear not, thou didst them unto Me."

4. If the concluding words of this chapter, expressly intended to teach the duration of future bliss and future woe—personal and conscious—do not proclaim them to be both alike unending, what words, supposing our Lord *meant* to teach this, could possibly do it? And shall we venture—on the strength of our own notions of what is just or worthy of God—to tamper with His teaching of Whom the Father hath said, "This is My Beloved Son, in Whom I am well pleased: HEAR HIM"?

CHAP. XXVI. 1-16.—CHRIST'S FINAL ANNOUNCEMENT OF HIS DEATH, AS NOW WITHIN TWO DAYS, AND THE SIMULTANEOUS CONSPIRACY

24 me. The Son of man goeth [n]as it is written of him: but [o]woe unto that
man by whom the Son of man is betrayed! it had been good for that
25 man if he had not been born. Then Judas, which betrayed him, answered
and said, Master, is it I? He said unto him, Thou hast said.
26 And as they were eating, [p]Jesus took bread, and [1]blessed *it*, and brake
it, and gave *it* to the disciples, and said, Take, eat; this [q]is my body.
27 And he took the cup, and gave thanks, and gave *it* to them, saying,
28 Drink ye all of it; for [r]this is my blood [s]of the new testament, which is
29 shed [t]for many for the remission of sins. But I say unto you, I will not
drink henceforth of this fruit of the vine, [u]until that day when I drink it
new with you in my Father's kingdom.
30 And [v]when they had sung an [2]hymn, they went out into the mount
31 of Olives. Then saith Jesus unto them, [w]All ye shall [x]be offended
because of me this night: for it is written, [y]I will smite the Shepherd,
32 and the sheep of the flock shall be scattered abroad. But after I am
33 risen again, [z]I will go before you into Galilee. Peter answered and said
unto him, Though all *men* shall be offended because of thee, *yet* will I
34 never be offended. Jesus said unto him, [a]Verily I say unto thee, That
35 this night, before the cock crow, thou shalt deny me thrice. Peter said
unto him, Though I should die with thee, yet will I not deny thee.
Likewise also said all the disciples.
36 Then [b]cometh Jesus with them unto a place called Gethsemane, and
37 saith unto the disciples, Sit ye here, while I go and pray yonder. And
he took with him Peter and [c]the two sons of Zebedee, and began to be
38 sorrowful and very heavy. Then saith he unto them, [d]My soul is
exceeding sorrowful, even unto death: tarry ye here, and [e]watch with
39 me. And he went a little farther, and fell on his face, and [f]prayed,
saying, [g]O my Father, if it be possible, [h]let this cup pass from me:
40 nevertheless [i]not as I will, but as thou *wilt*. And he cometh unto the
disciples, and findeth them asleep, and saith unto Peter, What! could ye
41 not watch with me one hour? Watch [j]and pray, that ye enter not into
42 temptation: the spirit indeed *is* willing, but the flesh *is* weak. He went
away again the second time, and prayed, saying, O my Father, if this
cup may not pass away from me, except I drink it, thy will be done.
43 And he came and found them asleep again: for their eyes were heavy.
44 And he left them, and went away again, and prayed the third time,
45 saying the same words. Then cometh he to his disciples, and saith unto
them, Sleep on now, and take *your* rest: behold, the hour is at hand,
46 and the Son of man is betrayed into the hands of sinners. Rise, let us
be going: behold, he is at hand that doth betray me.
47 And [k]while he yet spake, lo, Judas, one of the twelve, came, and with
him a great multitude with swords and staves, from the chief priests and
48 elders of the people. Now he that betrayed him gave them a sign, say-
49 ing, Whomsoever I shall kiss, that same is he: hold him fast. And
forthwith he came to Jesus, and said, Hail, Master! [l]and kissed him.
50 And Jesus said unto him, [3]Friend, wherefore art thou come? Then came
51 they, and laid hands on Jesus, and took him. And, behold, [m]one of

A. D. 33.
[n] Gen. 3. 15. Ps. 22. 1. Isa. 53. 1. Dan. 9. 26. Acts 26. 22. 1 Cor. 15. 3.
[o] John 17.12.
[p] 1 Cor. 11.23.
[1] Many Greek copies have, gave thanks. Mark 6. 41.
[q] Or, represents. 1 Cor. 10. 4. 1 Cor. 10.16.
[r] Ex. 24. 8. Lev. 17. 11.
[s] Jer. 31. 31.
[t] Rom. 5. 15. Heb 9. 22.
[u] Acts 10. 41.
[v] Mark 14.26.
[2] Or, psalm.
[w] John 16. 32.
[x] ch. 11. 6.
[y] Zec. 13. 7.
[z] ch. 28. 7. Mark 16. 7.
[a] Luke 22.34. John 13. 38.
[b] John 18. 1.
[c] ch. 4. 21.
[d] John 12. 27.
[e] 1 Pet. 5. 8.
[f] Mark 14.36. Luke 22.42. Heb. 5. 7.
[g] John 12. 27.
[h] ch. 20. 22. John 18. 11.
[i] 2Sam. 15.26. John 5. 30. John 6. 38. Phil. 2. 8.
[j] Mark 13.33. Mark 14.38. Luke 22. 40. 1 Cor. 16.13.
[k] Mark 14. 43. Luke 22.47. John 18. 3. Acts 1. 16.
[l] 2 Sam. 20. 9.
[3] Companion. Ps 41. 9. Ps. 55. 13.
[m] John 18.10.

OF THE JEWISH AUTHORITIES TO COMPASS IT—THE ANOINTING AT BETHANY—JUDAS AGREES WITH THE CHIEF PRIESTS TO BETRAY HIS LORD. (= Mark xiv. 1-11; Luke xxii. 1-6; John xii. 1-11.) For the exposition, see on Mark xiv. 1-11.

17-30.—PREPARATION FOR AND LAST CELEBRATION OF THE PASSOVER, ANNOUNCEMENT OF THE TRAITOR, AND INSTITUTION OF THE SUPPER. (= Mark xiv. 12-26; Luke xxii. 7-23; John xiii. 1-3, 10, 11, 18-30.) For the exposition, see on Luke xxii. 7-23.

31-35.—THE DESERTION OF JESUS BY HIS DISCIPLES, AND THE FALL OF PETER FORETOLD. (= Mark xiv. 27-31; Luke xxii. 31-46; John xiii. 36-38.) For the exposition, see on Luke xxii. 31-38.

36-46.—THE AGONY IN THE GARDEN. (= Mark xiv. 32-42; Luke xxii. 39-46.) For the exposition, see on Luke xxii. 39-46.

47-56.—BETRAYAL AND APPREHENSION OF JESUS—FLIGHT OF HIS DISCIPLES. (= Mark xiv. 43-52; Luke xxii. 47-54; John xviii. 1-12.) For the exposition, see on John xviii. 1-12.

them which were with Jesus stretched out *his* hand, and drew his sword,
52 and struck a servant of the high priest, and smote off his ear. Then
said Jesus unto him, [n]Put up again thy sword into his place: [o]for all
53 they that take the sword shall perish with the sword. Thinkest thou that
I cannot now pray to my Father, and he shall presently give me [p]more
54 than twelve legions of angels? But how then shall [q]the Scriptures be
fulfilled, that thus it must be?
55 In that same hour said Jesus to the multitudes, Are ye come out as
against a thief with swords and staves for to take me? I sat daily with
56 you teaching in the temple, and ye laid no hold on me. But all this was
done, that the [r]scriptures of the prophets might be fulfilled. Then [s]all
the disciples forsook him, and fled.
57 And [t]they that had laid hold on Jesus led *him* away to Caiaphas the
58 high priest, where the scribes and the elders were assembled. But Peter
followed him afar off unto the high priest's palace, and went in, and sat
59 with the servants, to see the end. Now the chief priests, and elders, and
all the council, sought false witness against Jesus, to put him to death;
60 but found none: yea, though [u]many false witnesses came, *yet* found they
61 none. At the last came [v]two false witnesses, and said, This *fellow* said,
[w]I am able to destroy the temple of God, and to build it in three days.
62 And the high priest arose, and said unto him, Answerest thou nothing?
63 what *is it which* these witness against thee? But [x]Jesus held his peace.
And the high priest answered and said unto him, [y]I adjure thee by the
living God, that thou tell us whether thou be the Christ, the Son of God.
64 Jesus saith unto him, Thou hast said: nevertheless, I say unto you,
[z]Hereafter shall ye see the Son of man [a]sitting on the right hand of
65 power, and coming in the clouds of heaven. Then the high priest [b]rent
his clothes, saying, He hath spoken blasphemy; what further need have
66 we of witnesses? behold, now ye have heard his blasphemy. What think
67 ye? They answered and said, [c]He is guilty of death. Then [d]did they
spit in his face, and buffeted him; and [e]others smote *him* with [4]the
68 palms of their hands, saying, [f]Prophesy unto us, thou Christ, Who is he
that smote thee?
69 Now Peter sat without in the palace: and a damsel came unto him,
70 saying, Thou also wast with Jesus of Galilee. But he denied before
71 *them* all, saying, I know not what thou sayest. And when he was gone
out into the porch, another *maid* saw him, and said unto them that
72 were there, This *fellow* was also with Jesus of Nazareth. And again he
73 denied with an oath, I do not know the man. And after a while came
unto *him* they that stood by, and said to Peter, Surely thou also art *one*
74 of them; for thy speech bewrayeth thee. Then began he to curse and to
swear, *saying*, I know not the man. And immediately the cock crew.
75 And Peter remembered the word of Jesus, which said unto him, Before
the cock crow, thou shalt deny me thrice. And he went out, and [g]wept
bitterly.
27 WHEN the morning was come, [a]all the chief priests and elders of
2 the people took counsel against Jesus to put him to death: and when
they had bound him, they led *him* away, and [b]delivered him to Pontius
Pilate the governor.
3 Then [c]Judas, which had betrayed him, when he saw that he was

A. D. 33.

[n] 1 Cor. 4. 12.
[o] Gen 9. 6. Rev. 13. 10.
[p] 2 Ki. 6. 17. Ps. 91. 11. Dan. 7. 10.
[q] Isa. 53. 7. Dan. 9. 26.
[r] Lam. 4. 20.
[s] John 18. 15.
[t] Mark 14. 53. Luke 22. 54.
[u] 1 Ki. 21. 10. Ps. 27. 12.
[v] Deut. 19. 15.
[w] ch. 27. 40. John 2. 19.
[x] Isa. 53. 7. ch. 27. 12.
[y] Lev. 5. 1. 1 Sam. 14. 24.
[z] Ps. 110. 1. Dan. 7. 13. John 1. 51. Rom. 14 10. 1 Thes. 4. 16. Rev. 1. 7.
[a] Ps. 110. 1. Acts 7. 55.
[b] 2 Ki. 18. 37. 2 Ki. 19. 1.
[c] Lev. 24. 16. John 19. 7.
[d] Isa. 50. 6. Isa. 53. 3. ch. 27. 30. Mark 14. 65. Luke 18. 32.
[e] Mic. 5. 1. Luke 22. 63.
[4] Or, rods.
[f] Mark 14. 65.
[g] 2 Sam. 12. 13. Zec. 12. 10. Rom. 7. 18-20. 1 Cor. 4. 7. 2 Cor. 7. 10. Gal. 6. 1.

CHAP. 27.
[a] Ps. 2. 2. Mark 15. 1. Luke 22. 66. Luke 23. 1. John 18. 28.
[b] ch. 20. 19. Acts 3. 13. 1 Thes. 2. 14.
[c] Job 20. 5. ch. 26. 14. Mark 14. 10, 11, 43-46. Luke 22. 2-6, 47, 48. 2 Cor. 7. 10.

57-75.—JESUS ARRAIGNED BEFORE THE SANHEDRIM, CONDEMNED TO DIE, AND SHAMEFULLY ENTREATED—THE FALL OF PETER. (= Mark xiv. 53-72; Luke xxii. 54-71; John xviii. 13-18, 24-27.) For the exposition, see on Mark xiv. 53-72.

CHAP. XXVII. 1-10.—JESUS LED AWAY TO PILATE—REMORSE AND SUICIDE OF JUDAS. (= Mark xv. 1; Luke xxiii. 1; John xviii. 28.)

Jesus Led Away to Pilate (1-2). For the exposition of this portion, see on John xviii. 28, &c.

Remorse and Suicide of Judas (3-10). This portion is peculiar to Matthew. On the progress of guilt in the traitor, see on Mark xiv. 1-11, Remark 8; and on John xiii. 21-30.

3. Then Judas, which had betrayed him, when he saw that he was condemned. The condemna-

condemned, repented himself, and brought again the thirty pieces of
4 silver to the chief priests and elders, saying, I have sinned in that I have
betrayed the innocent blood. And they said, What *is that* to us? see
5 thou *to that.* And he cast down the pieces of silver in the temple, [d]and
6 departed, and went and hanged himself. And the chief priests took the
silver pieces, and said, It is not lawful for to put them into the treasury,
7 because it is the price of blood. And they took counsel, and bought
8 with them the potter's field, to bury strangers in. Wherefore that field
9 was called, The field of blood, unto this day. Then was fulfilled that
which was spoken by Jeremy the prophet, saying, [e]And they took the
thirty pieces of silver, the price of him that was valued, [1]whom they of
10 the children of Israel did value, and gave them for the potter's field,
as the Lord appointed me.

A. D. 33.

d 1 Sam. 31. 4, 5. 2Sam.17.23. Job. 2. 9. Job. 7. 15. Ps. 55, 23. Acts 1. 18.

e Zec. 11. 12, 13. ch. 26. 15.

1 Or, whom they bought of the children of Israel.

tion, even though not unexpected, might well fill him with horror. But perhaps this unhappy man expected that, while he got the bribe, the Lord would miraculously escape, as He had once and again done before, out of His enemies' power; and if so, his remorse would come upon him with all the greater keenness. **repented himself**—but, as the issue too sadly showed, it was "the sorrow of the world, which worketh death" (2 Cor. vii. 10). **and brought again the thirty pieces of silver to the chief priests and elders.** A remarkable illustration of the power of an awakened conscience. A short time before, the promise of this sordid pelf was temptation enough to his covetous heart to outweigh the most overwhelming obligations of duty and love; now, the possession of it so lashes him that he cannot use it, cannot even keep it! **4. Saying, I have sinned in that I have betrayed the innocent blood.** What a testimony this to Jesus! Judas had been with Him in all circumstances for three years; his post, as treasurer to Him and the Twelve (John xii. 6), gave him peculiar opportunity of watching the spirit, disposition, and habits of his Master; while his covetous nature and thievish practices would incline him to dark and suspicious, rather than frank and generous, interpretations of all that He said and did. If, then, he could have fastened on one questionable feature in all that he had so long witnessed, we may be sure that no such speech as this would ever have escaped his lips, nor would he have been so stung with remorse as not to be able to keep the money and survive his crime. **And they said, What is that to us? see thou to that**:—'Guilty or innocent is nothing to us: We have him now—begone!' Was ever speech more hellish uttered? **5. And he cast down the pieces of silver.** The sarcastic, diabolical reply which he had got, in place of the sympathy which perhaps he expected, would deepen his remorse into an agony. **in the temple** [ἐν τῷ ναῷ]—the temple proper, commonly called 'the sanctuary,' or 'the holy place,' into which only the priests might enter. How is this to be explained? Perhaps he flung the money in after them. But thus were fulfilled the words of the prophet—"I cast them to the potter in the house of the Lord" (Zec. xi. 13). **and departed, and went and hanged himself.** See, for the details, on Acts i. 18. **6. And the chief priests took the silver pieces, and said, It is not lawful for to put them into the treasury** [κορβανᾶν]—'the *Corban*,' or chest containing the money dedicated to sacred purposes (see on ch. xv. 5)—**because it is the price of blood.** How scrupulous now! But those punctilious scruples made them unconsciously fulfil the Scripture. **7. And they took counsel, and bought with them the potter's field, to bury strangers in.** **8. Wherefore that field was called, The field of blood, unto this day. 9. Then was fulfilled that which was spoken by Jeremy the prophet, saying** (Zec. xi. 12, 13), **And they took the thirty pieces of silver, the price of him that was valued, whom they of the children of Israel did value, 10. And gave them for the potter's field, as the Lord appointed me.** Never was a complicated prophecy, otherwise hopelessly dark, more marvellously fulfilled. Various conjectures have been formed to account for Matthew's ascribing to Jeremiah a prophecy found in the book of Zechariah. But since with this book he was plainly familiar, having quoted one of its most remarkable prophecies of Christ but a few chapters before (ch. xxi. 4, 5), the question is one more of critical interest than real importance. Perhaps the true explanation is the following, from *Lightfoot*:—'Jeremiah of old had the first place among the prophets, and hereby he comes to be mentioned above all the rest in ch. xvi. 14; because he stood first in the volume of the prophets (as he proves from the learned *David Kimchi*) therefore he is first named. When, therefore, Matthew produceth a text of Zechariah under the name of Jeremy, he only cites the words of the volume of the prophets under his name who stood first in the volume of the prophets. Of which sort is that also of our Saviour (Luke xxiv. 44), "All things must be fulfilled which are written of me in the Law, and the Prophets, and the Psalms," or the Book of Hagiographa, in which the Psalms were placed first.'

Remarks.—1. The mastery acquired by the passions is, probably in every case, gradual. In the case of Judas—the most appalling on record—it must have been very gradual; otherwise it is incredible that he should have been such a constant and promising follower of our Lord as to be admitted by Him into the number of the Twelve, and that he should not only have been allowed to remain within that sacred circle to the last, but have remained undiscovered in his true character to the Eleven till after he had sold his Master, and even within an hour of his consummated treason. What a lesson does this read to the self-confident, to resist the beginnings of sinful indulgence! 2. The love of money, when it becomes the ruling passion, blinds—as does every other passion—the mind of its victim, which is only to be opened by some unexpected and disappointing event. 3. The true character of repentance is determined neither by its sincerity nor by its bitterness, but by the *views* under which it is wrought. Judas and Peter repented, it should seem, with equal sincerity and equal pungency, of what they had done. But the one "went and hanged himself;" the other "went out and wept bitterly." Whence this difference? The one, under the sense of his guilt, had nothing

11 And Jesus stood before the governor: and [f]the governor asked him,
saying, Art thou the King of the Jews? And Jesus said unto him, [g]Thou
12 sayest. And when he was accused of the chief priests and elders, [h]he
13 answered nothing. Then said Pilate unto him, [i]Hearest thou not how
14 many things they witness against thee? And he answered him to never
a word; insomuch that the governor marvelled greatly.
15 Now [j]at *that* feast the governor was wont to release unto the people a
16 prisoner, whom they would. And they had then a notable prisoner,
17 called Barabbas. Therefore, when they were gathered together, Pilate
said unto them, Whom will ye that I release unto you? Barabbas, or
18 Jesus which is called Christ? For he knew that for [k]envy they had
delivered him.
19 When he was set down on the judgment seat, his wife sent unto him,
saying, Have thou nothing to do with that just man: for I have suffered
many things this day in [l]a dream because of him.
20 But [m]the chief priests and elders persuaded the multitude that they
21 should ask Barabbas, and destroy Jesus. The governor answered and
said unto them, Whether of the twain will ye that I release unto you?
22 They said, Barabbas. Pilate saith unto them, What shall I do then with
Jesus which is called Christ? *They* all say unto him, Let him be cruci-
23 fied. And the governor said, Why, what evil hath he done? But they
24 cried out the more, saying, Let him be crucified. When Pilate saw that
he could prevail nothing, but *that* rather a tumult was made, he [n]took
water, and washed *his* hands before the multitude, saying, I am innocent
25 of the blood of this just person: see ye *to it.* Then answered all the
26 people, and said, [o]His blood *be* on us, and on our children. Then
released he Barabbas unto them: and when [p]he had scourged Jesus,
he delivered *him* to be crucified.
27 Then the soldiers of the governor took Jesus into the [2]common hall,
28 and gathered unto him the whole band *of soldiers.* And they stripped
29 him, and [q]put on him a scarlet robe. And [r]when they had platted a
crown of thorns, they put *it* upon his head, and a reed in his right hand:
and they bowed the knee before him, and mocked him, saying, Hail,
30 King of the Jews! And [s]they spit upon him, and took the reed, and

A. D. 33.
f Mark 15. 2. Luke 23. 3. John 18. 33.
g John 18.37. 1 Tim. 6.13.
h Isa. 53. 7. ch. 26. 63. John 19. 9. 1 Pet 2. 23.
i ch. 26. 62. John 19. 10.
j Mark 15. 6. Luke 23. 17. John 18. 39.
k Acts 7. 9.
l Job 33. 15.
m Mark 15. 11. Luke 23. 18. John 18. 40. Acts 3. 14.
n Deut. 21. 6.
o Deut. 19. 10. Jos. 2. 19. 1 Ki. 2. 32. 2 Sam. 1.16.
p Isa. 53. 5. Mark 15.15. John 19. 1.
2 Or, governor's house.
q Luke 23. 11.
r Ps. 35. 15,16. Ps. 69. 19. Isa. 49. 7. Isa. 53. 3. Jer. 20. 7. Heb. 12.2.3.
s Job 30. 10. Isa. 50. 6. Isa. 52. 14. Mark 15.19. Luke 18.32, 33.

to fall back upon; and deeming pardon for such a wretch utterly hopeless, and unable to live without it, he hasted to terminate with his own hand a life of insupportable misery. The other, having done a deed which might well have made him incapable of ever again looking his Lord in the face, nevertheless turned toward Him his guilty eyes, when, lo! the Eye of his wounded Lord, glancing from the hall of judgment full down upon himself, with a grief and a tenderness that told their own tale, shot right into his heart, and brought from it a flood of penitential tears! In the one case we have natural principles working themselves out to deadly effect; in the other, we see grace working repentance unto salvation, not to be repented of. 4. What a vivid illustration have we here of the reality of supernatural illumination and the divine truth of the Scriptures, as also of the consistency of the divine arrangements with the liberty of the human will in executing them! Here we have a prophet, five centuries before the birth of Christ, personating Messiah, in bidding the Jewish authorities give him his price, if they thought good, and if not, to forbear; whereupon they weigh him for his price the exact sum agreed upon between Judas and the chief priests for the sale of his Lord—thirty pieces of silver. Then, the Lord bids him cast this to the *potter;* adding, with sublime satire, "A goodly price that I was prized at of them!" Whereupon he takes the 'thirty pieces of silver, and casts them to the potter in the house of the Lord' (Zec. xi. 12, 13). Now, each of these acts was so unessential to the main business, that they might have been quite different from what they were, without in the least affecting it. Our Lord might have been identified and apprehended without being betrayed by one of His apostles; for the plan was first suggested to the authorities by Judas offering, for a consideration, to do it. And when agreed to, the sum offered and accepted might have been more or less than that actually agreed on. But so it was, that of their own accord they bargained with Judas for precisely the predicted thirty pieces of silver. Nor was this all. For, as the consciences of those holy hypocrites would have been hurt by putting the price of blood into the treasury, and therefore it must be put to some pious use, they resolve to buy with it "the *potter's* field" as a burial-ground for strangers—thus again unconsciously, and with marvellous minuteness, fulfilling a prediction five centuries old, and so setting a double seal on the Messiahship of Jesus!

11-26.—Jesus again before Pilate—He seeks to Release Him, but at length delivers Him to be Crucified. (= Mark xv. 1-15; Luke xxiii. 1-25; John xviii 28-40.) For the exposition, see on Luke xxiii. 1-25, and on John xviii. 28-40.

27-33.—Jesus, Scornfully and Cruelly Entreated of the Soldiers, is Led away to be

31 [t]smote him on the head. And after that they had mocked him, they
took the robe off from him, and put his own raiment on him, [u]and led
him away to crucify *him*.
32 And [v]as they came out, [w]they found a man of Cyrene, Simon by name:
33 him they compelled to bear his cross. And when they were come unto
34 a place called Golgotha, that is to say, A place of a skull, they [x]gave
him vinegar to drink mingled with gall: and when he had tasted *thereof*,
35 he would not drink. And they crucified him, and parted his garments, casting lots: that it might be fulfilled which was spoken by
the prophet, They [y]parted my garments among them, and upon my
36 vesture did they cast lots. And sitting down they watched him there;
37 and set up over his head his accusation written, THIS IS JESUS THE
38 KING OF THE JEWS. Then [z]were there two thieves crucified with
him; one on the right hand, and another on the left.
39, And [a]they that passed by reviled him, wagging their heads, and
40 saying, [b]Thou that destroyest the temple, and buildest *it* in three days,
save thyself. If thou be the Son of God, come down from the cross.
41 Likewise also the chief priests, mocking *him*, with the scribes and elders,
42 said, He saved others; himself he cannot save. If he be the King of
Israel, let him now come down from the cross, and we will believe him.
43 He [c]trusted in God; let him deliver him now, if he will have him: for
44 he said, I am the Son of God. The [d]thieves also, which were crucified
with him, cast the same in his teeth.
45 Now [e]from the sixth hour there was darkness over all the land unto
46 the ninth hour. And about the ninth hour [f]Jesus cried with a loud
voice, saying, Eli! Eli! lama sabachthani? that is to say, [g]My God! My
47 God! why hast thou forsaken me? Some of them that stood there, when
48 they heard *that*, said, This *man* calleth for Elias. And straightway one
of them ran, and took a sponge, [h]and filled *it* with vinegar, and put *it* on
49 a reed, and gave him to drink. The rest said, Let be, let us see whether
Elias will come to save him.
50 Jesus, when he had cried again with a loud voice, yielded up the
ghost.
51 And, behold, [i]the veil of the temple was rent in twain from the top

A. D. 33.
t Mic. 5. 1. Mark 15.19. Luke 22.63.
u Isa. 53. 7. ch. 20. 19. ch 21. 39. John 19. 16, 17.
v Num. 15.35. 1 Ki. 21. 13. Acts 7. 58. Heb. 13. 12.
w Mark 15.21.
x Ps. 22. 18. Ps. 69. 21. Mark 15.23. John 19. 28 30.
y Ps. 22. 18.
z Isa. 53. 12. Mark 15.27. Luke 23.32. John 19.18.
a Ps. 22. 7. Ps. 109. 25.
b ch. 26. 61. John 2. 19.
c Ps. 22. 8.
d Luke 23.39.
e Isa. 50. 3. Amos 8. 9.
f Heb. 5. 7.
g Ps. 22. 1.
h Ps. 69. 21. John 19. 29.
i Ex. 26. 31. 2 Chr. 3. 14. Mark 15.38. Luke 23. 45. Eph. 2. 14, 18. Heb. 6. 19. Heb. 10. 19, 20.

CRUCIFIED. (= Mark xv. 16-22; Luke xxiii. 26-31; John xix. 2, 17.) For the exposition, see on Mark xv. 16-22.

34-50.—CRUCIFIXION AND DEATH OF THE LORD JESUS. (= Mark xv. 25-37; Luke xxiii. 33-46; John xix. 18-30.) For the exposition, see on John xix. 18-30.

51-66.—SIGNS AND CIRCUMSTANCES FOLLOWING THE DEATH OF THE LORD JESUS—HE IS TAKEN DOWN FROM THE CROSS, AND BURIED—THE SEPULCHRE IS GUARDED. (= Mark xv. 38-47; Luke xxiii. 47-56; John xix. 31-42.)

The Veil Rent (51). **51. And, behold, the veil of the temple was rent in twain from the top to the bottom.** This was the thick and gorgeously wrought veil which was hung between the "holy place" and the "holiest of all," shutting out all access to the presence of God as manifested "from above the mercyseat and from between the cherubim:"—"the Holy Ghost this signifying, that the way into the holiest of all was *not yet* made manifest" (Heb. ix. 8). Into this holiest of all none might enter, not even the high priest, save once a year, on the great day of atonement, and then only with the blood of atonement in his hands, which he sprinkled "upon and before the mercyseat seven times" (Lev. xvi. 14)—to signify that *access for sinners to a holy God is only through atoning blood.* But as they had only the blood of bulls and of goats, which could not take away sins (Heb. x. 4), during all the long ages that preceded the death of Christ, the thick veil remained; the blood of bulls and of goats continued to be shed and sprinkled; and once a year access to God through an atoning sacrifice was vouchsafed—*in a picture*, or rather, was *dramatically represented*, in those symbolical actions—nothing more. But *now*, the one atoning Sacrifice being provided in the precious bl od of Christ, access to this holy God could no longer be denied; and so the moment the Victim expired on the altar, that thick veil which for so many ages had been the dread symbol of *separation between God and guilty men* was, without a hand touching it, mysteriously "rent in twain from top to bottom:"—"the Holy Ghost this signifying, that the way into the holiest of all was NOW made manifest!" How emphatic the statement, "*from top to bottom;*" as if to say, Come boldly now to the Throne of Grace; *the veil is clean gone;* the Mercyseat stands open to the gaze of sinners, and the way to it is sprinkled with the blood of Him—"who through the eternal Spirit hath offered Himself without spot to God"! Before, it was death *to go in*, now it is *death to stay out.* See more on this glorious subject on Heb. x. 19-22.

An Earthquake—The Rocks Rent—The Graves Opened, that the Saints which slept in them might Come Forth after their Lord's Resurrection (51-53). **51. and the earth did quake.** From what follows

52 to the bottom; and [j]the earth did quake, and the rocks rent; and the
graves were opened; [k]and many bodies of the saints which slept arose,
53 And came out of the graves after his resurrection, and went into the holy
city, and appeared unto many.
54 Now [l]when the centurion, and they that were with him watching
Jesus, saw the earthquake, and those things that were done, they feared
greatly, saying, Truly this was the Son of God.
55 And many women were there beholding afar off, [m]which followed
56 Jesus from Galilee, ministering unto him: among [n]which was Mary
Magdalene, and Mary the mother of James and Joses, and the mother
of Zebedee's children.
57 When [o]the even was come, there came a rich man of Arimathea, named
58 Joseph, who also himself was Jesus' disciple: he went to Pilate, and
begged the body of Jesus. Then Pilate commanded the body to be
59 delivered. And when Joseph had taken the body, he wrapped it in a
60 clean linen cloth, and [p]laid it in his own new tomb, which he had hewn
out in the rock: and he rolled a great stone to the door of the sepulchre,

A. D. 33.

j Ex. 19. 18. Ps. 18. 7. Mic. 1. 3, 4. Nah. 1. 5. Hab. 3. 10.
k Ps. 68. 20. Dan. 12. 2. 1 Cor. 11. 30. 1 Cor. 15 57.
l Ex. 20. 18, 19. Deut. 22. 31. Mark 15. 39. Luke 23. 47.
m Luke 8. 2. Luke 23. 27, 28, 48, 49.
n Mark 15. 40.
o Mark 15. 42. Luke 23. 50. John 19. 38.
p Isa. 53. 9.

it would seem that this earthquake was local, having for its object the rending of the rocks and the opening of the graves. **and the rocks rent** ('were rent')—the physical creation thus sublimely proclaiming, at the bidding of its Maker, the *concussion* which at that moment was taking place in the moral world at the most critical moment of its history. Extraordinary rents and fissures have been observed in the rocks near this spot. **52. And the graves were opened; and many bodies of the saints which slept arose, 53. And came out of the graves after his resurrection.** These sleeping saints (see on 1 Thes. iv. 14) were Old Testament believers, who—according to the usual punctuation in our version—were quickened into resurrection-life at the moment of their Lord's death, but lay in their graves till His resurrection, when they came forth. But it is far more natural, as we think, and consonant with other scriptures, to understand that only the graves were opened, probably by the earthquake, at our Lord's death, and this only in preparation for the subsequent exit of those who slept in them, when the Spirit of life should enter into them from their risen Lord, and along with Him they should come forth, trophies of His victory over the grave. Thus, in the opening of the graves at the moment of the Redeemer's expiring, there was a glorious symbolical proclamation that the Death which had just taken place had "swallowed up death in victory;" and whereas the saints that slept in them were awakened only by their risen Lord, to accompany Him out of the tomb, it was fitting that "the Prince of Life" "should be *the First* that should rise from the dead" (Acts xxvi. 23; 1 Cor. xv. 20, 23; Col. i. 18; Rev. i. 5). **and went into the holy city**—that city where He, in virtue of whose resurrection they were now alive, had been condemned, **and appeared unto many**—that there might be undeniable evidence of their own resurrection first, and through it of their Lord's. Thus, while it was not deemed fitting that He Himself should appear again in Jerusalem, save to the disciples, provision was made that the fact of His resurrection should be left in no doubt. It must be observed, however, that the resurrection of these sleeping saints was not like those of the widow of Nain's son, of Jairus' daughter, of Lazarus, and of the man who "revived and stood upon his feet," on his dead body touching the bones of Elisha (2 Ki. xiii. 21)—which were mere temporary recallings of the departed spirit to the *mortal* body, to be followed by a final departure of it "till the trumpet shall sound." But this was a resurrection *once for all, to life everlasting;* and so there is no room to doubt that they went to glory with their Lord, as bright trophies of His victory over death.

The Centurion's Testimony (54). **54. Now when the centurion**—the military superintendent of the execution, **and they that were with him watching Jesus, saw the earthquake**—or felt it and witnessed its effects, **and those things that were done**—reflecting upon the entire transaction, **they feared greatly**—convinced of the presence of a Divine Hand, **saying, Truly this was the Son of God.** There cannot be a reasonable doubt that this expression was used in the Jewish sense, and that it points to the claim which Jesus made to be the Son of God, and on which His condemnation expressly turned. The meaning, then, clearly is, that He must have been what He professed to be; in other words, that He was no impostor. There was no medium between those two. See, on the similar testimony of the penitent thief—"This man hath done nothing amiss"—on Luke xxiii. 41.

The Galilean Women (55, 56). **55. And many women were there beholding afar off, which followed Jesus** [ἠκολούθησαν]. The sense here would be better brought out by the use of the pluperfect, 'which had followed Jesus,' **from Galilee, ministering unto him.** As these dear women had ministered to Him during His glorious missionary tours *in* Galilee (see on Luke viii. 1-3), so from this statement it should seem that they accompanied Him and ministered to His wants *from* Galilee on His final journey to Jerusalem. **56. Among which was Mary Magdalene** (see on Luke viii. 2), **and Mary the mother of James and Joses**—the wife of Cleophas, or rather Clopas, and sister of the Virgin (John xix. 25). See on ch. xiii. 55, 56. **and the mother of Zebedee's children**—that is, Salome: compare Mark xv. 40. All this about the women is mentioned for the sake of what is afterwards to be related of their purchasing spices to anoint their Lord's body.

The Taking Down from the Cross and the Burial (57-60). For the exposition of this portion, see on John xix. 38-42.

The Women mark the Sacred Spot, that they might recognize it on coming thither to Anoint the Body (61). **61. And there was Mary Magdalene, and the other Mary**—"the mother of James and Joses," mentioned before (*v.* 56), **sitting over against the sepulchre.** See on Mark xvi. 1.

61 and departed. And there was Mary Magdalene, and the other Mary,
sitting over against the sepulchre.
62 Now the next day, that followed the day of the preparation, the chief
63 priests and Pharisees came together unto Pilate, saying, Sir, we remember that [q]that deceiver said, while he was yet alive, After [r]three days
64 I will rise again. Command therefore that the sepulchre be made sure
until the third day, lest his disciples come by night, and steal him away,
and say unto the people, He is risen from the dead: so the last error
65 shall be worse than the first. Pilate said unto them, Ye have a watch:
66 go your way, make *it* as sure as ye can. So they went, and made the
sepulchre sure, [s]sealing the stone, and setting a watch.

A. D. 33.

q Ps. 2. 1-6. Acts 4. 27, 28. 2 Cor. 6. 8.
r ch. 16. 21. ch. 17. 23. ch. 20. 19. ch. 26. 61. Mark 8. 31. Mark 10.34. Luke 9. 22. Luke 18. 33.
s Dan. 6. 17.

The Sepulchre Guarded (62-66). **62. Now the next day, that followed the day of the preparation**—that is, after six o'clock of our *Saturday* evening. The crucifixion took place on the *Friday*, and all was not over till shortly before sunset, when the Jewish Sabbath commenced; and "that sabbath day was an high day" (John xix. 31), being the first day of the feast of Unleavened Bread. That day being over at six on Saturday evening, they hastened to take their measures. **the chief priests and Pharisees came together unto Pilate, 63. Saying, Sir, we remember that that deceiver**—Never, remarks *Bengel*, will you find the heads of the people calling Jesus by His own name. And yet here there is betrayed a certain uneasiness, which one almost fancies they only tried to stifle in their own minds, as well as crush in Pilate's, in case he should have any lurking suspicion that he had done wrong in yielding to them. **said, while he was yet alive.** Important testimony this, from the lips of His bitterest enemies, to *the reality of Christ's death;* the cornerstone of the whole Christian religion. **After three days**—which, according to the customary Jewish way of reckoning, need signify no more than 'after the commencement of the third day.' **I will rise again** [ἐγείρομαι]—'I rise,' in the present tense, thus reporting not only the *fact* that this prediction of His had reached their ears, but that they understood Him to look forward *confidently* to its occurring on the very day named. **64. Command therefore that the sepulchre be made sure**—by a Roman guard, **until the third day**—after which, if He still lay in the grave, the imposture of His claims would be manifest to all. **lest his disciples come by night, and steal him away, and say unto the people, He is risen from the dead.** [The word νυκτὸς, 'by night,' appears by the authorities not to belong to the genuine text here, and was probably introduced from ch, xxviii. 13.] Did they really fear this? **so the last error shall be worse than the first**—the imposture of His pretended resurrection worse than that of His pretended Messiahship. **65. Pilate said unto them, Ye have a watch.** The guards had already acted under orders of the Sanhedrim, with Pilate's consent; but probably they were not clear about employing them as a night-watch without Pilate's express authority. **go your way, make it as sure as ye can** [ὡς οἴδατε]—'as ye know how,' or in the way ye deem securest. Though there may be no irony in this speech, it evidently insinuated that *if* the event should be contrary to their wish, it would not be for want of sufficient human appliances to prevent it. **66. So they went, and made the sepulchre sure, sealing the stone**—which Mark (xvi. 4) says was "very great," **and setting a watch**—to guard it. What more could man do? But while they are trying to prevent the resurrection of the Prince of Life, God makes use of their precautions for His own ends. Their stone-covered, seal-secured sepulchre shall preserve the sleeping dust of the Son of God free from all indignities, in undisturbed, sublime repose; while their watch shall be His guard of honour until the angels shall come to take their place!

Remarks.—1. How grandly was the true nature of Christ's death proclaimed by the rending of the veil at the moment when it took place! He was "by wicked hands," indeed, "crucified and slain." He died, it is true, a glorious example of suffering "for righteousness' sake." Yet not these, nor any other explanations of His death, however correct in themselves, furnish the true key to the divine intent of it. But if the temple and its services were the centre and soul of the Church's instituted worship under the ancient economy; if that portion of the temple which was the holiest of all, and the symbol of God's dwelling place among men, was shut to every Israelite by a thick veil through which it was death to pass, and was accessible to His high-priestly representative only on that one day of the year when he carried within the veil *the blood of atonement*, and sprinkled it upon and before that mercyseat which represented the Throne of God; if on that one occasion, and *upon that one action*, in all the year, Jehovah manifested Himself in visible glory, as a God graciously present with sinful men, and accepting the persons and services of sinful worshippers—thus symbolically proclaiming that without the shedding of blood there was no remission, and without remission, no access to God, and no acceptable worship—while yet it was manifest that the only blood which ever was shed upon the Jewish altar, and sprinkled upon the mercyseat had no atoning virtue in it at all, and so could not, and never did take away sin; and finally, if after all this teaching of the ancient economy up to the moment of Christ's death, as to the *necessity* and yet the *absence* of atoning blood, it came to pass that at the moment when Christ died—without a hand touching it—the thick veil of the Temple was rent in twain *from the top to the bottom*, and so the holiest was thrown open: who can fail to see that this was done by a Divine Hand, in order to teach, even by the naked eye, that the true atoning Victim had now been slain, and that, having put away sin by the sacrifice of Himself—having finished the transgression, and made an end of sins, and made reconciliation for iniquity, and brought in everlasting righteousness, and sealed up the vision and prophecy, He had anointed the holy of holies (Dan. ix. 24), in order that not the high priest only, but every believer, not once a year, but at all times, might have boldness to enter by the blood of Jesus, by the new and living way which He hath consecrated for us through the veil, that is to say, His own flesh" (Heb. x. 19, 20). Nor is it possible to give any tolerable explanation of this rending of

28 IN the [a]end of the sabbath, as it began to dawn toward the first *day*
of the week, came Mary Magdalene [b]and the other Mary to see the
2 sepulchre. And, behold, there [1]was a great earthquake: for [c]the angel
of the Lord descended from heaven, and came and rolled back the stone

A. D. 33.
a Mark 16. 1.
b ch. 27. 56.
1 had been.
c Mark 16. 5.

the veil at Christ's death, if its sacrificial, atoning character be denied or explained away. To talk of its signifying the breaking down of the wall of partition between Jew and Gentile, as some do, is altogether wide of the mark. For the veil was intended to shut out, not Gentiles, but *Jews themselves*, from the presence of God; and the liberty to pass through it once, but once only, with atoning blood, both showed what alone would remove that veil for any worshipper, and the absence of that one thing so long as the veil remained. And thus the great doctrine of the sacrificial design and atoning efficacy of the death of Christ was proclaimed in the most expressive symbolical language at the moment when it took place. 2. Do Christians sufficiently recognize *the fact*, that sin is "put away" as a ground of exclusion from the favour of God; so that the most guilty on the face of the earth, believing this, has "boldness to enter in by the blood of Jesus" to *perfect reconciliation*. As no worshipper was holy enough to have right to go within that veil which shut out the guilty under the law, so no worshipper is sinful enough to be shut out from the holiest of all who will enter it by the blood of Jesus. As all were shut out alike under the law, so all are alike free to enter under the Gospel. This is that *present* salvation which Christ's servants are honoured to preach to every sinner, the faith of which sets the conscience free, and overcomes the world; but want of the clear apprehension of which keeps multitudes of sincere Christians all their lifetime subject to bondage. 3. What a grand testimony did the rending of the rocks and the opening of the graves at the moment of Christ's death bear to the subserviency of all nature to the purposes of Redemption! As when He walked the earth all nature was at His bidding, so now at His Death—which was the reconciliation of Heaven, the life of the dead, the knell of the kingdom of darkness, and Paradise regained—Nature felt the deed, and heaved sympathetic. 4. How beautifully does the resurrection of those sleeping saints of the Old Testament, by virtue of Christ's resurrection—that they might grace with their presence His exit from the tomb—proclaim the unity of the Church of the redeemed under every economy, and the fact that, whether they lived before or live after Christ, it is 'because He lives that they live also!' 5. How remarkable is it to find a heathen officer—who probably knew little or nothing of Christ save the charge on which He was condemned to die, that "He made Himself the Son of God"—unable to resist the evidence which the scenes of Calvary furnished of His innocence, and consequently of the truth of His claims, little as he would understand what they were; while those who had been trained to the study of the Scriptures, and had been favoured with overpowering evidence of the claims of Jesus to be the Hope of Israel, were His bloody murderers! 6. How precious to Christians should be those testimonies to the reality of Christ's death which even His enemies unconsciously bore, since on this depends the reality of His resurrection, and on both of these hang all that is dear to God's children! So little did they doubt of His death, that their only fear—whether real or pretended—was that His disciples would come and steal away His dead body, and pretend that He had risen from the dead. Then, having got what they wanted from Pilate—full power to see to the sealing of the stone and the placing of a military guard to watch it till the third day—they thus themselves unconsciously attested the reality of the resurrection which, on the morning of the third day took place, when, in spite of all their precautions, the sepulchre was found empty, and the grave-clothes lying disposed in grand orderliness, as they had been laid calmly aside when no longer needed! 7. Have we not here one of the most striking commentaries imaginable on those words of the Psalmist, "Surely the wrath of man shall praise thee: the remainder of wrath shalt thou restrain"? (Ps. lxxvi. 10). For as the death of Christ, which the wrath of man procured, was infinitely to the praise of God, and the "remainder of that wrath" might have extended to the infliction of indignities even upon the dead body, had it been exposed, it pleased God to put it into the heart of Pilate to give the body for interment into the hands of Jesus' friends, and so to "restrain the remainder" of His enemies' wrath that they themselves sealed up the grave and set the military guard over it—thus securing its sacred repose till the appointed hour of release. O the depth of the riches, both of the wisdom and knowledge of God! How unsearchable are His judgments, and His ways past finding out! 8. How sweet should be the grave to Christ's sleeping saints! Might we not hear Him saying to them beforehand, "Fear not to go down into Egypt; for I will go down with you, and I will surely bring you up again"? And indeed He has gone down, and lain in as cold, and dark, and narrow, and repulsive a bed as any of you, O believers, will ever be called to lie down in; and has He not sweetened the clods of the valley—or haply, the great deep—as a perfumed bed for you to lie down in?

CHAP. XXVIII. 1-15.—GLORIOUS ANGELIC ANNOUNCEMENT ON THE FIRST DAY OF THE WEEK, THAT CHRIST IS RISEN—HIS APPEARANCE TO THE WOMEN—THE GUARDS BRIBED TO GIVE A FALSE ACCOUNT OF THE RESURRECTION. (= Mark xvi. 1-8; Luke xxiv. 1-8; John xx. i.)

The Resurrection Announced to the Women (1-8). **1. In the end of the sabbath, as it began to dawn** [ὀψὲ δὲ σαββάτων, ἐπιφωσκούσῃ]—'After the Sabbath, as it grew toward daylight.' **toward the first day of the week.** Luke (xxiv. 1) has it, "very early in the morning" [ὄρθρου βαθέος, but the true reading is βαθέως]—properly, 'at the first appearance of day-break;' and corresponding with this, John (xx. 1) says, "when it was yet dark." See on Mark xvi. 2. Not an hour, it would seem, was lost by those dear lovers of the Lord Jesus. **came Mary Magdalene and the other Mary**—"the mother of James and Joses" (see on ch. xxvii. 56, 61), **to see the sepulchre**—with a view to the anointing of the body, for which they had made all their preparations. See on Mark xvi. 1. **2. And, behold, there was**—that is, there had been, before the arrival of the women, **a great earthquake: for the angel of the Lord descended from heaven, and came and rolled back the stone from the door, and sat upon it.** And this was the state of things when the women drew near. Some judicious critics think all this was transacted while the women were approaching; but the view we have given, which is the prevalent

3 from the door, and sat upon it. His [d]countenance was like lightning,
4 and his raiment white as snow: and for fear of him the keepers did
5 shake, and became as dead *men*. And the angel answered and said unto
the women, [e]Fear not ye; for I know that ye seek Jesus, which was
6 crucified. He is not here; for he is risen, [f]as he said. Come, see the
7 place where the Lord lay: and go quickly, and tell his disciples that he
is risen from the dead; and, behold, he [g]goeth before you into Galilee;
8 there shall ye see him: lo, I have told you. And they departed quickly
from the sepulchre with fear and great joy, and did run to bring his
disciples word.
9 And as they went to tell his disciples, behold, [h]Jesus met them, saying,
All hail! And they came and held him by the feet, and worshipped
10 him. Then said Jesus unto them, Be not afraid: go tell [i]my brethren
that they go into Galilee, and there shall they see me.
11 Now when they were going, behold, some of the watch came into the
city, and showed unto the chief priests all the things that were done.
12 And when they were assembled with the elders, and had taken counsel,
13 they gave large money unto the soldiers, saying, Say ye, His disciples
14 came by night, and stole him *away* while we slept. And if this come to

A. D. 33.

[d] Dan. 10. 6. ch. 17. 2. Rev. 10. 1. Rev. 18. 1.
[e] Isa. 35. 4. Dan. 10. 12. Mark 16. 6. Luke 1. 12. Heb. 1. 14. Rev. 1. 17.
[f] ch. 12. 40. ch. 16. 21. ch. 17. 23. ch. 20. 19. Mark 8. 31.
[g] ch. 26. 32. Mark 16. 7.
[h] Mark 16. 9. John 20. 14. Rev. 1. 17, 18.
[i] Rom. 8. 29. Heb. 2. 11.

one, seems the more natural. All this august preparation—recorded by Matthew alone—bespoke the grandeur of the exit which was to follow. The angel sat upon the huge stone, to overawe, with the lightning-lustre that darted from him, the Roman guard, and do honour to his rising Lord. **3. His countenance** [ἰδέα]—or, 'appearance,' **was like lightning, and his raiment white as snow**—the one expressing the *glory*, the other the *purity* of the celestial abode from which he came. **4. And for fear of him the keepers did shake, and became as dead men.** Is the sepulchre "sure" now, O ye chief priests? He that sitteth in the heavens doth laugh at you. **5. And the angel answered and said unto the women, Fear not ye** [Μὴ φοβεῖσθε ὑμεῖς]. The "ye" here is emphatic, to contrast their case with that of the guards. 'Let those puny creatures, sent to keep the Living One among the dead, for fear of Me shake and become as dead men (*v.* 4); but ye that have come hither on another errand, fear not ye.' **for I know that ye seek Jesus, which was crucified** [τὸν ἐσταυρωμένον]—'Jesus the Crucified.' **6. He is not here; for he is risen, as he said.** See on Luke xxiv. 5-7. **Come** [Δεῦτε], as in ch. xi. 28, **see the place where the Lord lay.** Charming invitation! 'Come, see the spot where the Lord of glory lay: now it is an empty grave: He lies not, but He *lay* there. Come, feast your eyes on it!' But see on John xx. 12; and Remarks below. **7. And go quickly, and tell his disciples.** For a precious addition to this, see on Mark xvi. 7. **that he is risen from the dead; and, behold, he goeth before you into Galilee**—to which those women belonged (ch. xxvii. 55). **there shall ye see him.** This must refer to those more public manifestations of Himself to large numbers of disciples at once, which He vouchsafed only in Galilee; for individually He was seen of some of those very women almost immediately after this (*v.* 9, 10). **lo, I have told you.** Behold, ye have this word from the world of light! **8. And they departed quickly.** Mark (xvi. 8) says "they fled" **from the sepulchre with fear and great joy.** How natural this combination of feelings! See on a similar statement of Mark xvi. 11. **and did run to bring his disciples word.** "Neither said they anything to any man [by the way]; for they were afraid" (Mark xvi. 8).

Appearance to the Women (9, 10). This appearance is recorded only by Matthew. **9. And as they went to tell his disciples, behold, Jesus met them, saying, All hail!** [Χαίρετε]—the usual salute, but from the lips of Jesus bearing a higher signification. **And they came and held him by the feet.** How truly womanly! **and worshipped him. 10. Then said Jesus unto them, Be not afraid.** What dear associations would these familiar words—now uttered in a higher style, but by the same Lips—bring rushing back to their recollection! **go tell my brethren that they go into Galilee, and there shall they see me.** The brethren here meant must have been His brethren after the flesh (ch. xiii. 55); for His brethren in the higher sense (see on John xx. 17) had several meetings with Him at Jerusalem *before* he went to Galilee, which they would have missed if they had been the persons ordered to Galilee to meet Him.

The Guards Bribed (11-15). The whole of this important portion is peculiar to Matthew. **11. Now when they were going**—while the women were on their way to deliver to His brethren the message of their risen Lord, **behold, some of the watch came into the city, and showed unto the chief priests all the things that were done.** Simple, unsophisticated soldiers! How could ye imagine that such a tale as ye had to tell would not at once commend itself to your sacred employers? Had they doubted this for a moment, would they have ventured to go near them, knowing it was death to a Roman soldier to be proved asleep when on guard? and of course that was the only other explanation of the case. **12. And when they were assembled with the elders.** But Joseph at least was absent; Gamaliel probably also; and perhaps others. **and had taken counsel, they gave large money unto the soldiers.** It would need a good deal; but the whole case of the Jewish authorities was now at stake. With what contempt must these soldiers have regarded the Jewish ecclesiastics! **13. Saying, Say ye, His disciples came by night, and stole him away while we slept**—which, as we have observed, was a capital offence for soldiers on guard. **14. And if this come to the governor's ears** [ἐὰν ἀκουσθῇ τοῦτο ἐπὶ τοῦ ἡγεμόνος]—rather, 'If this come before the governor;' that is, not in the way of mere report, but for judicial investigation. **we will persuade him, and secure you** [ἡμεῖς πείσομεν αὐτὸν, καὶ ὑμᾶς ἀμερίμνους ποιήσομεν]. The "we" and the "you" are emphatic here—'We

15 the governor's ears, we will persuade him, and secure you. So they took
the money, and did as they were taught: and this saying is commonly
reported among the Jews until this day.
16 Then the [j]eleven disciples went away into Galilee, into a mountain

A. D. 33.

[j] Mark 16.14. John 6. 70. Acts 1. 13. 1 Cor. 15. 5.

shall [take care to] persuade him and keep you from trouble,' or 'save you harmless.' The grammatical form of this clause [ἐὰν ἀκουσθῇ . . πείσομεν] implies that the thing supposed was expected to happen. The meaning then is, 'If this come before the governor—as it likely will—we shall see to it that,' &c. The "persuasion" of Pilate meant, doubtless, quieting him by a bribe, which we know otherwise he was by no means above taking (like Felix afterwards, Acts xxiv. 26). **15. So they took the money, and did as they were taught**—thus consenting to brand themselves with infamy—**and this saying is commonly reported among the Jews until this day**—to the date of the publication of this Gospel. The wonder is that so clumsy and incredible a story lasted so long. But those who are resolved *not* to come to the light will catch at straws. *Justin Martyr*, who flourished about A.D. 170, says, in his 'Dialogue with Trypho the Jew,' that the Jews dispersed the story by means of special messengers sent to every country.

Remarks.—1. If the Crucifixion and Burial of the Son of God were the most stupendous manifestations of self-sacrifice, His Resurrection was no less grand a vindication of His character and claims — rolling away the reproach of the Cross, revealing His Personal dignity, and putting the crown upon His whole claims. (See Rom. i. 4). As His own Self bare our sins in His own body on the tree (1 Pet. ii. 24), and so was "made a curse for us" (Gal. iii. 13), His resurrection was a public proclamation that He had now made an end of sin, and brought in everlasting righteousness (Dan. ix. 24). And how august was this proclamation! While His enemies were watching the hours, in hope that the third day might see Him still in the tomb, and His loving disciples were almost in despair of ever beholding Him again, lo! the ground heaves sublime, an angel, bright as lightning and clad in raiment of snowy white, descends from heaven, rolls the huge sealed stone from the door of the sepulchre, and takes his seat upon it as a guard of honour from heaven; while the keepers for fear of him are shaking and crouching as dead men. *What then took place, none of the Four sacred Narrators has dared to describe*, or rather, none of them knew. All that we need to know they do record—that when the women arrived, the grave was empty, and speedily Jesus Himself stood before them in resurrection-life and love! What a glorious Gospel-voice issues from these facts! O, if even the guiltiest sinner on the face of the earth would but draw near, might he not hear a voice saying to him, "He is not here; for He has risen, as He said. Come, see the place where the Lord lay;" and as he looks into this open grave, shall he not hear the Risen One Himself whispering to him, "Peace be unto thee," and as He says this "showing him His hands and His side," in evidence of the price paid for the remission of sins? 3. How delightful a subject of contemplation is the ministry of angels, especially in connection with Christ Himself, and most of all in connection with this scene of His resurrection; where we not only find them hovering around the Person of Jesus, as their own adored Lord, but showing the liveliest interest in every detail, and the tenderest care for the disciples of their Lord! And what is this but a specimen of what they feel and do towards "the heirs of salvation" of every quality, every age, every clime? 4. If anything were needed to complete the proof of the reality of Christ's resurrection, it would be the silliness of the explanation which the guards were bribed to give of it. That a whole guard should go to sleep on their watch at all, was not very likely; that they should do it in a case like this, where there was such anxiety on the part of the authorities that the grave should remain undisturbed, was in the last degree improbable; but—even if it could be supposed that so many disciples should come to the grave as would suffice to break the seal, roll back the huge stone, and carry off the body—that the guards should all sleep soundly enough and long enough to admit of all this tedious and noisy work being gone through at their very side without being awoke, and done too so leisurely, that the very grave clothes—which would naturally have been kept upon the body, if only to aid them in bearing the heavy burden—should be found carefully folded and orderly disposed within the tomb:—all this *will not believe* even by credulity itself, and could not have been credited even at the first, though it might suit those who were determined to resist the Redeemer's claims to pretend that they believed it. And the best proof that it was not believed is, that within a few weeks of this time, and in the very place where the imposture of a pretended resurrection—if it really was such—could most easily have been detected, thousands upon thousands, many of whom had been implicated in His death, came trooping into the ranks of the risen Saviour, resting their whole salvation upon the belief of His Resurrection. Now, therefore, is Christ risen from the dead, and become the First-Fruits of His sleeping people! 5. Let believers take the full comfort of that blessed assurance, that "as Jesus died and rose again, even so them also which sleep in Jesus will God bring with Him" (1 Thes. iv. 14). "But each [ἕκαστος] in his own order, Christ the first-fruits, afterwards they that are Christ's at His coming" (1 Cor. xv. 23). 6. The Resurrection of Christ—as it brought resurrection-life not only to believers in their persons, but to the cause of truth and righteousness in the earth—should animate the Church, in its seasons of deepest depression, with assurances of resurrection, and encourage it to sing such "songs in the night" as these: "*After two days will He revive us; in the third day He will raise us up, and we shall live in His sight.*" "*I shall not die, but live, and declare the works of the Lord*" (Hos. vi. 2; Ps. cxviii. 17).

16-20.—JESUS MEETS WITH THE DISCIPLES ON A MOUNTAIN IN GALILEE, AND GIVES FORTH THE GREAT COMMISSION. **16. Then the eleven disciples went away into Galilee**—but certainly not before the second week after the resurrection, and probably somewhat later. **into a mountain** [τὸ ὄρος], **where Jesus had appointed them.** It should have been rendered 'the mountain,' meaning some certain mountain which He had named to them—probably the night before He suffered, when He said, "After I am risen, I will go before you into Galilee" (ch. xxvi. 32; Mark xiv. 28). What it was can only be conjectured; but of the two between which opinions are divided—the Mount of the Beatitudes or Mount Tabor—the former is

17 where Jesus had appointed them. And when they saw him, they
worshipped him: but some doubted.
18 And Jesus came and spake unto them, saying, [k]All power is given unto

A. D. 33.
k Dan. 7. 13. Rev. 19. 16.

much the more probable, from its nearness to the sea of Tiberias, where last before this the Narrative tells us that He met and dined with seven of them. (John xxi. 1, &c.) That the interview here recorded was the same with that referred to in one place only—1 Cor. xv. 6—when "He was seen of above five hundred brethren at once; of whom the greater part remained unto that day, though some were fallen asleep," is now the opinion of the ablest students of the Evangelical History. Nothing can account for such a number as five hundred assembling at one spot but the expectation of some promised manifestation of their risen Lord; and the promise before His resurrection, twice repeated after it, best explains this immense gathering. **17. And when they saw him, they worshipped him: but some doubted**—certainly none of "the Eleven," after what took place at previous interviews in Jerusalem. But if the five hundred were now present, we may well believe this of some of them.

18. And Jesus came and spake unto them, saying, All power is given unto me in heaven and in earth. 19. Go ye therefore, and teach all nations [μαθητεύσατε]—rather, 'make disciples of all nations;' for "teaching," in the more usual sense of that word, comes in afterwards, and is expressed by a different term. **baptizing them in the name** [εἰς τὸ ὄνομα]. It should be, 'into the name:' as in 1 Cor. x. 2, "And were all baptized unto (or rather '*into*') Moses" [εἰς τὸν Μωσῆν]; and Gal. iii. 27, "For as many of you as have been baptized *into* Christ" [εἰς Χριστόν]. **of the Father, and of the Son, and of the Holy Ghost; 20. Teaching them** [Διδάσκοντες]. This is teaching in the more usual sense of the term; or instructing the converted and baptized disciples. **to observe all things whatsoever I have commanded you: and, lo, I.** The "*I*" [Ἐγώ] here is emphatic. It is enough that *I* **am with you alway** [πάσας τὰς ἡμέρας]—'all the days;' that is, till making converts, baptizing, and building them up by Christian instruction, shall be no more. **even unto the end of the world** [αἰῶνος]. **Amen.** [On the difference between the words αἰών and κόσμος, see on Heb. i. 2.] This glorious Commission embraces two primary departments, the *Missionary* and the *Pastoral*, with two sublime and comprehensive *Encouragements* to undertake and go through with them.

First, The MISSIONARY department (*v.* 18): "Go, make disciples of all nations." In the corresponding passage of Mark (xvi. 15) it is, "Go ye into all the world, and preach the Gospel to every creature." The only difference is, that in this passage the *sphere*, in its world-wide compass and its universality of *objects*, is more fully and definitely expressed; while in the former the great *aim* and certain *result* is delightfully expressed in the command to "make disciples of all nations." 'Go, conquer the world for Me; carry the glad tidings into all lands and to every ear, and deem not this work at an end till all nations shall have embraced the Gospel and enrolled themselves My disciples.' Now, Was all this meant to be done by the Eleven men nearest to Him of the multitude then crowding around the risen Redeemer? Impossible. Was it to be done even in their lifetime? Surely not. In that little band Jesus virtually addressed Himself to all who, in every age, should take up from them the same work. Before the eyes of the Church's risen Head were spread out, in those Eleven men, all His servants of every age; and one and all of them received His commission at that moment. Well, what next? Set the seal of visible discipleship upon the converts, by "baptizing them into the name," that is, into the whole fulness of the grace "of the Father, and of the Son, and of the Holy Ghost," as belonging to them who believe. (See on 2 Cor. xiii. 14.) This done, the Missionary department of your work, which in its own nature is temporary, must merge in another, which is permanent. This is,

Second, The PASTORAL department (*v.* 20): "Teach them"—teach these baptized members of the Church visible—"to observe all things whatsoever I have commanded you," My apostles, during the three years ye have been with Me.

What must have been the feelings which such a Commission awakened! 'WE conquer the world for Thee, Lord, who have scarce conquered our own misgivings—we, fishermen of Galilee, with no letters, no means, no influence over the humblest creature? Nay, Lord, do not mock us.' 'I mock you not, nor send you a warfare on your own charges. For'—Here we are brought to

Third, The ENCOURAGEMENTS to undertake and go through with this work. These are two; one in the van, the other in the rear of the Commission itself.

First Encouragement: "All power in *heaven*"—the whole power of Heaven's love and wisdom and strength, "and all power in *earth*"—power over all persons, all passions, all principles, all movements—to bend them to this one high object, the evangelization of the world: All this "is *given unto Me*," as the risen Lord of all, to be *by Me placed at your command*—"Go ye therefore." But there remains a

Second Encouragement—which will be best taken up in the Remarks below—"And lo! I am with you all the days"—not only to perpetuity, but without one day's interruption, "even to the end of the world." The "Amen" is of doubtful genuineness in this place. If, however, it belongs to the text it is the Evangelist's own closing word.

Remarks.—1. In this Great Commission we have the permanent institution of the Gospel Ministry, in both its departments, the Missionary and the Pastoral—the one for fetching in, the other for building up—together with Baptism, the link of connection and point of transition from the one to the other. The Missionary department, it is true, merges in every case in the Pastoral, as soon as the converts are baptized into visible discipleship; yet since the servants of Christ are commanded to "go into all the world, and preach the Gospel to every creature," it follows that so long as there is an inhabited spot unreached, or a human being outside the pale of visible discipleship, so long will the Missionary department of the Christian ministry abide in the Church as a divine institution. As for the Pastoral office, it is manifest that as the children of believers will require to be trained in the truth, and the members of the Church to be taught, not only to know, but to observe, all that Christ commanded, there can be no cessation of it so long as the Church itself continues in the flesh, or before Christ comes in glory. 2. But we have here also something for the Church's private members as well as for its ministers. Are they to deem themselves exempt from all concern in this matter? Nay, is it not certain that just as all ministers are to trace their commission to this Great

19 me in heaven and in earth. Go ye therefore, and [2]teach all nations,
baptizing them in the name of the Father, and of the Son, and of the Holy

A. D. 33.

[2] Or, make disciples.

Commission, so the whole Church, from age to age, should regard itself as here virtually addressed in its own sphere, and summoned forth to *co-operate* with its ministers, to *aid* its ministers, to *encourage* its ministers in the doing of this missionary and pastoral work to the world's end? 3. We must have a care not unduly to narrow that direction regarding the Pastoral instruction of the disciples —"Teach them to observe all things whatsoever I have commanded you," the Twelve. For some talk of Christ as the only Lawgiver of Christians, to the exclusion of the Old Testament, as authoritative for Christians; while some would exclude, in this sense, all the New Testament save the Evangelical Records of our Lord's own teaching. But does not our Lord Himself set His seal on the Old Testament Scriptures at large as the Word of God and the Record of eternal life? And what are all the subsequent portions of the New Testament but the development of Christ's own teaching by those on whom, for that very end, He set the seal of His own authority? Thus may our Lord be said virtually to have referred His servants to the entire Scripture as their body of instructions. Still it may be asked, Is there nothing peculiar in all those things whatsoever Christ commanded the Twelve, that He should refer the pastors of the flock for their instructions in every age specifically to that as their grand repository? Undoubtedly there is; for as all that preceded Christ pointed forward to Him, and all that follows His teaching refers back to it, so His personal teaching is the incarnation and vitalization, the maturity and perfection of all divine teaching, to which all else in Scripture is to be referred, and in the light of which all else is to be studied and apprehended. 4. What an all-comprehensive encouragement to the continued discharge of even the most difficult and trying duties embraced in this Commission is found in the closing words of it! Thus:—

'Feel ye your utter incompetency to undertake the work? Lo! *I am with you*, to furnish you for it; for all power in heaven and in earth is Mine. Fear ye for the safety of the cause, amidst the indifference and the hatred of a world that crucified your Lord? Be of good cheer: *I am with you*, who have overcome the world. Dare ye not to hope that the world will fall before you? It is Mine by promise—the heathen for My inheritance, the uttermost parts of the earth for My possession; and to conquer and to keep it by your agency, all power in heaven and in earth is given unto Me and by Me made over to you.

'Dread ye the exhaustion of My patience or power, amidst oft-recurring seasons of difficulty, despondency and danger, and the dreary length of time it will take to bring all nations to the obedience of faith, and to build them up unto life eternal? Lo! I am with you *always*, to whom *all* power in heaven and in earth is given for your behoof.'

'Truth, Lord'—perhaps ye will still say—'this pledge to be with us to perpetuity is indeed cheering; but may there not be *intervals of withdrawal*, to be followed, no doubt, by seasons of certain return, but enough, in the meantime, to fill us with anxiety, on whose shoulders Thou art laying the whole weight of Thy cause in the earth?' 'Nay, have ye not marked those words of Mine, "Lo! I am with you," not only to perpetuity, but "*all the days*"—without any break—"even unto the end of the world."' What more could they, or the servants of Christ in any age, desire or imagine of encouragement to fulfil this blessed Commission? 5. Is it necessary to ask any intelligent reader whether such a Commission could have issued from the lips of one who knew himself to be a mere creature? Would "all power in heaven and in earth" be *given away to* a creature, by Him who will not give His glory to another? or if this were conceivable, could it be *lodged in* a creature, or *wielded by* a creature? And whereas it is here said to be *given* to Christ, that is only in conformity with the whole economy of Redemption and the uniform language of the New Testament, which represents the Son as sent and furnished by the Father, in order to bring men back, as prodigal children, to their Father's love. But while the Son thus honours the Father, the Father requires, in return, "that all men should honour the Son even as they honour the Father." 6. If there is one inference from the language of this Great Commission more obvious than another, it is this, that Jesus would have Himself regarded by His servants in every age as *sole Master in His own House.* Are they to make disciples of all nations? It is disciples *to Him.* Are they to set the seal of visible discipleship upon them? It is to bind them over only the more effectually *to Him.* Are they to teach the converts thus made and thus sealed? It is to observe all things whatsoever HE has *commanded* them. Want they support and encouragement in all the branches of this work? They are to derive it from this twofold consideration, that all the resources of heaven and earth are, for their benefit, given *unto Him*, and that *He is with them* alway, even unto the end of the world. Thus are they to transact, each with the other—no other third party coming in between them. Hence, whatever understanding or arrangement they may deem it lawful and expedient to come to with the civil powers in matters ecclesiastical, they are to stipulate for perfect *freedom to carry out all their Master's requirements;* nor dare they abridge themselves of one iota of this liberty for any temporal consideration whatever. 7. We have here the secret of the Church's poverty during long ages of its past history, and of the world's present condition, to so appalling an extent estranged from the Christian pale. The Church has neglected the Missionary, and corrupted the Pastoral, department of its great Commission. For long ages the missionary energy of the Church had either ceased, or expended itself chiefly on efforts to extend the ghostly authority of Papal Rome; and when at the Reformation-period it sprang forth in such glorious rejuvenescence, instead of sending forth its healing waters into the vast deserts of heathenism, making the wilderness and the solitary place to rejoice, it kept them pent up within its own narrow boundaries till they stank and bred the pestilence of rancorous controversy and deadly heresy and every evil. And then did the Pastoral work languish, thousands upon thousands fell away from all observance of Christian ordinances, and within the bosom of Christendom infidelity and irreligion spread apace, while real Christianity came to a very low ebb. Nor could aught else be expected of such unfaithfulness to the Church's Head. Neglecting either branch of this great Commission, neither the *Power* nor the *Presence* promised dare be expected. But going forth in faith to both alike, the conquest of the world to Christ—as it might have been achieved long ago, but for the Church's unbelief, selfishness, apathy, corruption, division—so it will be achieved,

20 Ghost; teaching them to observe all things whatsoever I have commanded you: and, lo, [l]I am with you alway, *even* unto the end of the world. Amen.

A. D. 33.

[l] Acts 18. 19. Rev. 22. 21.

when, through the Spirit poured upon it from on high, it shall become "fair as the moon, clear as the sun, and terrible as an army with banners" (Song vi. 10). 8. In concluding this First Portion of our Fourfold Gospel, who that has followed our humble efforts to display a little of its riches does not feel it to be as treasure hid in a field, the which, when a man hath found, he hideth, and for joy thereof goeth and selleth all that he hath and buyeth that field? The good Lord lodge its contents in the hearts both of the writer and his readers!

THE GOSPEL ACCORDING TO

ST. MARK.

---

1 THE beginning of the gospel of Jesus Christ, [a]the Son of God;
2 as it is written in the Prophets, [b]Behold, I send my messenger before
3 thy face, which shall prepare thy way before thee. The [c]voice of one
crying in the wilderness, Prepare ye the way of the Lord, make his paths
4 straight. John did baptize in the wilderness, and preach the baptism of
5 repentance [1]for the remission of sins. And there went out unto him all
the land of Judea, and they of Jerusalem, and were all baptized of him
6 in the river of Jordan, confessing their sins. And John was clothed with
camel's hair, and with a girdle of a skin about his loins; and he did eat
7 [d]locusts and wild honey; and preached, saying, [e]There cometh one
mightier than I after me, the latchet of whose shoes I am not worthy to
8 stoop down and unloose. I [f]indeed have baptized you with water; but
he shall baptize you [g]with the Holy Ghost.
9 And [h]it came to pass in those days, that Jesus came from Nazareth
10 of Galilee, and was baptized of John in Jordan. And [i]straightway coming up out of the water, he saw the heavens [2]opened, and the Spirit like
11 a dove descending upon him: and there came a voice from heaven, *saying,* [j]Thou art my beloved Son, in whom I am well pleased.
12 And [k]immediately the Spirit driveth him into the wilderness.

A. D. 26. ending.

CHAP. 1.
[a] Ps. 2. 7. Luke 1. 35. John 1. 34. Rom. 8. 3. 1 John 4. 15.
[b] Mal. 3. 1.
[c] Isa. 40. 3. Luke 3. 4. John 1. 15, 23.
[1] Or, unto.
[d] Lev. 11. 22.
[e] Acts 13. 25.
[f] Acts 11. 16. Acts 19. 4.
[g] Isa. 44. 3.
[h] Matt. 3. 13.
[i] John 1. 32.
[2] Or, cloven, or, rent.
[j] Ps. 2. 7.
[k] Matt. 4. 1.

CHAP. I. 1-8.—THE PREACHING AND BAPTISM OF JOHN. (= Matt. iii. 1-12; Luke iii. 1-18.)

1. The beginning of the gospel of Jesus Christ, the Son of God. By the "Gospel" of Jesus Christ here is evidently meant the blessed Story which our Evangelist is about to tell of His Life, Ministry, Death, Resurrection and Glorification, and of the begun Gathering of Believers in His Name. The abruptness with which he announces his subject, and the energetic brevity with which, passing by all preceding events, he hastens over the ministry of John and records the Baptism and Temptation of Jesus—as if impatient to come to the Public Life of the Lord of glory—have often been noticed as characteristic of this Gospel; a Gospel whose direct, practical power and singularly vivid setting impart to it a preciousness peculiar to itself. What strikes every one is, that though the briefest of all the Gospels, this is in some of the principal scenes of our Lord's history the fullest. But what is not so obvious is, that wherever the finer and subtler feelings of humanity, or the deeper and more peculiar hues of our Lord's character were brought out, these, though they should be lightly passed over by all the other Evangelists, are sure to be found here, and in touches of such quiet delicacy and power, that though scarce observed by the cursory reader, they leave indelible impressions upon all the thoughtful, and furnish a key to much that is in the other Gospels.

These few opening words of the Second Gospel are enough to show, that though it was the purpose of this Evangelist to record chiefly the outward and palpable facts of our Lord's public life, he recognized in Him, in common with the Fourth Evangelist, the glory of the Only begotten of the Father. **2. As it is written in the Prophets** (Mal. iii. 1; and Isa. xl. 3), **Behold, I send my messenger before thy face, which shall prepare thy way before thee. 3. The voice of one crying in the wilderness, Prepare ye the way of the Lord, make his paths straight.** The second of these quotations is given by Matthew and Luke in the same connection, but they reserve the former quotation till they have occasion to return to the Baptist, after his imprisonment (Matt. xi. 10; Luke vii. 27). [Instead of the words, "as it is written in the Prophets," there is weighty evidence in favour of the following reading: 'As it is written in Isaiah the prophet.' This reading is adopted by all the latest critical editors. If it be the true one, it is to be explained thus—that of the two quotations, the one from Malachi is but a later development of the great primary one in Isaiah, from which the whole prophetical matter here quoted takes its name. But the received text is quoted by *Irenæus*, before the end of the second century, and the evidence in its favour is greater in *amount*, if not in weight. The chief objection to it is, that if this was the true reading, it is difficult to see how the other one could have got in at all; whereas, if it be not the true reading, it is very easy to see how it found its way into the text, as it removes the startling difficulty of a prophecy beginning with the words of Malachi being ascribed to Isaiah.] For the exposition, see on Matt. iii. 1-6, 11.

9-11.—BAPTISM OF CHRIST, AND DESCENT OF THE SPIRIT UPON HIM IMMEDIATELY THEREAFTER. (=Matt. iii. 13-17; Luke iii. 21, 22.) For the exposition, see on Matt. iii. 13-17.

12, 13.—TEMPTATION OF CHRIST. (= Matt. iv. 1-11; Luke iv. 1-13.) For the exposition, see on Matt. iv. 1-11.

13 And he was there in the wilderness forty days, tempted of Satan; and
was with the wild beasts; [l]and the angels ministered unto him.
14 Now after that John was put in prison, Jesus came into Galilee,
15 [m]preaching the gospel of the kingdom of God, and saying, [n]The time is
fulfilled, and the kingdom of God is at hand: repent ye, and believe the
Gospel.
16 Now [o]as he walked by the sea of Galilee, he saw Simon, and Andrew
17 his brother casting a net into the sea: for they were fishers. And Jesus
said unto them, Come ye after me, and I will make you to become fishers
18 of men. And straightway [p]they forsook their nets, and followed him.
19 And [q]when he had gone a little farther thence, he saw James the *son* of
Zebedee, and John his brother, who also were in the ship mending their
20 nets. And straightway he called them: and they left their father
Zebedee in the ship with the hired servants, and went after him.
21 And [r]they went into Capernaum; and straightway on the sabbath day
22 he entered into the synagogue, and taught. And [s]they were astonished
at his doctrine: for he taught them as one that had authority, and not
23 as the scribes. And [t]there was in their synagogue a man with an unclean
24 spirit; and he cried out, saying, Let *us* alone; [u]what have we to do
with thee, thou Jesus of Nazareth? art thou come to destroy us? I know
25 thee who thou art, the [v]Holy One of God. And Jesus rebuked him,
26 saying, Hold thy peace, and come out of him. And when the unclean
spirit [w]had torn him, and cried with a loud voice, he came out of him.

A. D. 31.
[l] Matt. 4. 11. 1 Tim. 3. 16.
[m] Matt. 4. 23.
[n] Ps. 110. 3. Dan. 2. 44. Dan. 9. 25. Gal. 4. 4. Eph. 1. 10.
[o] Matt. 4. 18. Luke 5. 4. John 1. 35-44.
[p] Matt. 19. 27. Luke 5. 11.
[q] Matt. 4. 21.
[r] Matt. 4. 13. Luke 4. 31.
[s] Matt. 7. 28.
[t] Luke 4. 33.
[u] Matt. 8. 29. ch 5. 7. Luke 4. 34. Luke 8. 28. John 2. 4.
[v] Ps. 16. 10. Luke 4. 34. Acts 2. 31. Jas. 2. 19.
[w] ch. 9. 20.

14-20.—CHRIST BEGINS HIS GALILEAN MINISTRY—CALLING OF SIMON AND ANDREW, JAMES AND JOHN. See on Matt. iv. 12-22.

21-39.—HEALING OF A DEMONIAC IN THE SYNAGOGUE OF CAPERNAUM, AND THEREAFTER OF SIMON'S MOTHER-IN-LAW AND MANY OTHERS—JESUS, NEXT DAY, IS FOUND IN A SOLITARY PLACE AT MORNING PRAYERS, AND IS ENTREATED TO RETURN, BUT DECLINES, AND GOES FORTH ON HIS FIRST MISSIONARY CIRCUIT. (= Luke iv. 31-44; Matt. viii. 14-17; iv. 23-25.)

21. And they went into Capernaum—see on Matt. iv. 13—**and straightway on the sabbath day he entered into the synagogue, and taught** [τοῖς σάββασιν]. This should have been rendered, 'straightway on the sabbaths He entered into the synagogue and taught,' or 'continued to teach.' The meaning is, that as He began this practice on the very first Sabbath after coming to settle at Capernaum, so He continued it regularly thereafter. **22. And they were astonished at his doctrine**—or 'teaching' [διδαχῇ]—referring quite as much to the manner as the matter of it. **for he taught them as one that had authority, and not as the scribes.** See on Matt. vii. 28, 29. **23. And there was in their synagogue a man with** (lit., 'in') **an unclean spirit**—that is, so entirely under demoniacal power that his personality was sunk for the time in that of the spirit. The frequency with which this character of 'impurity' is ascribed to evil spirits—some twenty times in the Gospels—is not to be overlooked. For more on this subject, see on Matt. iv. 12-25, Remark 4. **and he cried out, 24. Saying, Let** [**us**] **alone**—or rather, perhaps, 'ah!' expressive of mingled *astonishment* and *terror*. [The exclamation Ἔα is probably not here the imperative of the verb ἐᾶν, to 'permit'—as the *Vulgate* in Luke iv. 34, *Luther*, and our own version take it, or, at least, had ceased to be so regarded—but an interjection=אֲהָהּ, Jud. vi. 22, &c.] **what have we to do with thee** [Τί ἡμῖν καὶ σοί=מַה־לִּי וָלָךְ]—an expression of frequent occurrence in the Old Testament, (1 Ki. xvii. 18; 2 Ki. iii. 13; 2 Chr. xxxv. 21, &c.) It denotes '*entire separation of interests*:'—*q. d.*, 'Thou and we have nothing in common: we want not Thee; what wouldst thou with us?' For the analogous application of it by our Lord to His mother, see on John ii. 4. [**thou**] **Jesus of Nazareth?**—'Jesus, Nazarene!' an epithet originally given to express contempt, but soon adopted as the current designation by those who held our Lord in honour (Luke xviii. 37; Mark xvi. 6; Acts ii. 22)—**art thou come to destroy us?** In the case of the Gadarene demoniac the question was, "Art thou come hither to torment us before the time?" (Matt. viii. 29). Themselves tormentors and destroyers of their victims, they discern in Jesus their own destined Tormentor and Destroyer, anticipating and dreading what they know and feel to be awaiting them! Conscious, too, that their power was but permitted and temporary, and perceiving in Him, perhaps, the Woman's Seed that was to bruise the head and destroy the works of the devil, they regard His approach to them on this occasion as a signal to let go their grasp of this miserable victim. **I know thee who thou art, the Holy One of God.** This and other even more glorious testimonies to our Lord were given, as we know, with no good will, but in hope that by the acceptance of them He might appear to the people to be in league with evil spirits—a calumny which His enemies were ready enough to throw out against Him. But a Wiser than either was here, who invariably rejected and silenced the testimonies that came to Him from beneath, and thus was able to rebut the imputations of His enemies against Him (Matt. xii. 24-30). The expression, "Holy One of God," seems evidently taken from that Messianic Psalm (xvi. 10), in which He is styled "Thine Holy One" [τὸν ὅσιόν σου, חֲסִידְךָ—in קרי]. **25. And Jesus rebuked him, saying, Hold thy peace, and come out of him.** A glorious word of command. *Bengel* remarks that it was only the testimony borne to Himself which our Lord meant to silence. That he should afterwards cry out for fear or rage (*v.* 26) He would right willingly permit. **26. And when the unclean**

27 And they were all amazed, insomuch that they questioned among themselves, saying, What thing is this? what new doctrine *is* this? for with
authority commandeth he even the unclean spirits, and they do obey
28 him. And immediately his fame spread abroad throughout all the
region round about Galilee.
29 And [x]forthwith, when they were come out of the synagogue, they
entered into the house of Simon and Andrew, with James and John.
30 But Simon's wife's mother lay sick of a fever, and anon they tell him of
31 her. And he came and took her by the hand, and lifted her up; and
[y]immediately the fever left her, and she ministered unto them.
32 And [z]at even, when the sun did set, they brought unto him all that
33 were diseased, and them that were possessed with devils. And all the
34 city was gathered together at the door. And he healed many that were
sick of divers diseases, and cast out many devils; and [a]suffered not the
devils [3]to speak, because they knew him.
35 And [b]in the morning, rising up a great while before day, he went out,

A. D. 31.

[x] Matt. 8. 14. Luke 4 38.
[y] Ps. 103. 3.
[z] Luke 4. 40.
[a] Matt. 8. 16. ch. 3, 12. Luke 4. 41. Acts 16. 17, 18.
[3] Or, to say that they knew him.
[b] Ps. 5. 3. Ps. 109. 4. ch. 6. 46. Luke 4. 42. John 4. 34. Eph. 6. 18. Heb. 5. 7.

spirit had torn him. Luke (iv. 35) says, "When he had thrown him in the midst." Malignant cruelty—just showing what he *would* have done, if permitted to go further: it was a last fling! **and cried with a loud voice**—the voice of enforced submission and despair—**he came out of him.** Luke (iv. 35) adds, "and hurt him not." Thus impotent were the malignity and rage of the impure spirit when under the restraint of "the Stronger than the strong one armed" (Luke xi. 21, 22). **27. And they were all amazed, insomuch that they questioned among themselves, saying, What thing is this? what new doctrine** ('teaching') **is this? for with authority commandeth he even the unclean spirits, and they do obey him.** The audience, rightly apprehending that the miracle was wrought to illustrate the teaching and display the character and glory of the Teacher, begin by asking what novel kind of teaching this could be, which was so marvellously attested. [The various reading which the latest editors prefer here—τί ἐστιν τοῦτο; διδαχὴ καινὴ κατ' ἐξουσίαν καὶ τοῖς πνεύμασιν . . . αὐτῷ; κ. τ. λ.—has too slender support, we think, and is harsh.] **28. And immediately his fame spread abroad throughout all the region round about Galilee** [ὅλην τὴν περίχωρον τῆς Γ.]—rather, 'the whole region of Galilee;' though some, as *Meyer* and *Ellicott*, explain it of the country surrounding Galilee.

29. And forthwith, when they were come out of the synagogue—so also in Luke iv. 38, **they entered into the house of Simon and Andrew, with James and John.** The mention of these four—which is peculiar to Mark—is the first of those traces of Peter's hand in this Gospel, of which we shall come to many more. (See Introduction.) The house being his, and the disease and cure so nearly affecting himself, it is interesting to observe this minute specification of the number and names of the witnesses; interesting also as the first occasion on which the sacred triumvirate of Peter and James and John are selected from amongst the rest, to be a threefold cord of testimony to certain events in their Lord's life (see on ch. v. 37)—Andrew being present on this occasion, as the occurrence took place in his own house. **30. But Simon's wife's mother lay sick of a fever,** Luke, as was natural in "the beloved *physician*" (Col. iv. 14), describes it professionally; calling it a "great fever" [πυρετῷ μεγάλῳ], and thus distinguishing it from that lighter kind which the Greek physicians were wont to call "small fevers," as *Galen*, quoted by *Wetstein*, tells us. **and anon**—or 'immediately' **they tell him of her**—naturally hoping that His compassion and power towards one of His own disciples would not be less signally displayed than towards the demonized stranger in the synagogue. **31. And he came and took her by the hand**—rather, 'And advancing, He took her,' &c.—[προσελθὼν κ. τ. λ]. The beloved physician again is very specific: "And He stood over her" [ἐπιστὰς ἐπάνω αὐτῆς, Luke iv. 39]. **and lifted her up.** This act of condescension, much felt doubtless by Peter, is recorded only by Mark. **and immediately the fever left her, and she ministered unto them**—preparing their Sabbath-meal; in token both of the perfectness and immediateness of the cure, and of her gratitude to the glorious Healer.

32. And at even, when the sun did set—so Matt. viii. 16. Luke (iv. 40) says it was setting [δύνοντος]. **they brought unto him all that were diseased, and them that were possessed with devils**—'the demonized.' From Luke xiii. 14 we see how unlawful they would have deemed it to bring their sick to Jesus for a cure during the Sabbath hours. They waited, therefore, till these were over, and then brought them in crowds. Our Lord afterwards took repeated occasion to teach the people by example, even at the risk of His own life, how superstitious a straining of the Sabbath-rest this was. **33. And all the city was gathered together at the door**—of Peter's house; that is, the sick and those who brought them, and the wondering spectators. This bespeaks the presence of an eye-witness, and is one of those lively specimens of word-painting so frequent in this Gospel. **34. And he healed many that were sick of divers diseases, and cast out many devils.** In Matt. viii. 16 it is said, "He cast out the spirits with His word;" or rather, 'with a word' [λόγῳ]—a word of command. **and suffered not the devils to speak, because they knew him.** Evidently they *would* have spoken, if permitted, proclaiming His Messiahship in such terms as in the synagogue; but once in one day, and that testimony immediately silenced, was enough. See on *v.* 24. After this account of His miracles of healing, we have in Matt. viii. 17 this pregnant quotation, "That it might be fulfilled which was spoken by Esaias the prophet, saying (liii. 4), Himself took our infirmities, and bare our sicknesses." On this pregnant quotation, see Remark 2 below.

35. And in the morning—that is, of the day after this remarkable Sabbath; or, *on the First day of the week.* His choosing this day to inaugurate

36 and departed into a solitary place, and [c]there prayed. And Simon and
37 they that were with him followed after him. And when they had found
38 him, they said unto him, All *men* seek for thee. And he said unto them,
[d]Let us go into the next towns, that I may preach there also: for [e]there-
39 fore came I forth. And [f]he preached in their synagogues throughout all
Galilee, and [g]cast out devils.

A. D. 31.

c Heb. 5. 7.
d Luke 4. 43.
e Isa. 61. 1. John 16. 28.
f Matt. 4. 23.
g Gen. 3. 15.

a new and glorious stage of His public work, should be noted by the reader. **rising up a great while before day** [πρωῒ ἔννυχον or ἔννυχα λίαν]—'while it was yet night,' or long before day-break, **he went out**—from Peter's house, where He slept, all unperceived, **and departed into a solitary place, and there prayed** [προσηύχετο]—or, 'continued in prayer.' He was about to begin His first preaching and healing Circuit; and as on similar solemn occasions (Luke v. 16; vi. 12; ix. 18, 28, 29; Mark vi. 46), He spends some time in special prayer, doubtless with a view to it. What would one not give to have been, during the stillness of those grey morning-hours, within hearing—not of His "strong crying and tears," for He had scarce arrived at the stage for that—but of His calm, exalted anticipations of the work which lay immediately before Him, and the outpourings of His soul about it into the bosom of Him that sent Him! 'The Spirit of the Lord God is upon Me, because the Lord hath anointed Me to preach the Gospel to the poor; and I am going to heal the broken-hearted, to preach deliverance to the captives, and recovering of sight to the blind, to set at liberty them that are bruised, to preach the acceptable year of the Lord. Now, Lord, let it be seen that grace is poured into These lips, and that God hath blessed Me for ever: Here am I, send Me: I must work the works of Him that sent Me while it is day; and, lo, I come! I delight to do Thy will, O My God: yea, Thy law is within My heart.' He had doubtless enjoyed some uninterrupted hours of such communings with His heavenly Father ere His friends from Capernaum arrived in search of Him. As for them, they doubtless expected, after such a day of miracles, that the next day would witness similar manifestations. When morning came, Peter, loath to break in upon the repose of his glorious Guest, would await His appearance beyond the usual hour; but at length, wondering at the stillness, and gently coming to see where the Lord lay, he finds it—like the sepulchre afterwards—empty! Speedily a party is made up to go in search of Him, Peter naturally leading the way. **36. And Simon and they that were with him followed after him** [κατεδίωξαν]—rather, 'pressed after Him.' Luke (iv. 42) says, "The multitudes sought after Him" [οἱ ὄχλοι ἐπεζήτουν αὐτόν]: but this would be a party from the town. Mark, having his information from Peter himself, speaks only of what related directly to him. "They that were with him" would probably be Andrew his brother, James and John, with a few other choice brethren. **37. And when they had found him**—evidently after some search. [The reading adopted here by *Tischendorf* and *Tregelles*—καὶ εὗρον αὐτὸν καὶ λέγουσιν, 'And they found Him and said'—seems to us without sufficient evidence.] **they said unto him, All men seek for thee.** By this time, "the multitudes" who, according to Luke, "sought after Him"—and who, on going to Peter's house, and there learning that Peter and a few more were gone in search of Him, had set out on the same errand—would have arrived, and "came unto Him and stayed Him, that He should not depart from them" (Luke iv. 42); all now urging His return to their impatient townsmen. **38. And he said unto them, Let us go**—or, according to another reading, 'Let us go elsewhere' [though the word ἀλλαχοῦ, added by *Tischendorf* and *Tregelles*, has scarcely sufficient authority]. **into the next towns** [εἰς τὰς ἐχομένας κωμοπόλεις]—rather, 'unto the neighbouring village-towns;' meaning those places intermediate between towns and villages, with which the western side of the sea of Galilee was studded. **that I may preach there also: for therefore came I forth**—not from Capernaum, as *De Wette* miserably interprets, nor from His privacy in the desert place, as *Meyer*, no better; but from the Father. Compare John xvi. 28, "I came forth from the Father, and am come into the world," &c.—another proof, by the way, that the lofty phraseology of the Fourth Gospel was not unknown to the authors of the others, though their design and point of view are different. The language in which our Lord's reply is given by Luke (iv. 43) expresses the high necessity under which, in this as in every other step of His work, He acted—"I must preach the kingdom of God to other cities also; for therefore" [εἰς τοῦτο]—or, 'to this end'—"am I sent." An act of self-denial it doubtless was, to resist such pleadings to return to Capernaum. But there were overmastering considerations on the other side.

Remarks.—1. How terrific is the consciousness in evil spirits, when brought into the presence of Christ, of a total opposition of feelings and separation of interests between them and Him! But how grand is their sense of impotence and subjection, and the expression of this, which His presence wrings out from them! Knowing full well that He and they cannot dwell together, they expect, on His approach to them, a summons to quit, and, haunted by their guilty fears, they wonder if the judgment of the great day be coming on them before its time. How analogous is this to the feelings of the wicked and ungodly among men—opening up glimpses of that dreadful oneness in fundamental character between the two parties, which explains the final sentence, "Depart from Me, ye cursed, into everlasting fire, *prepared for the devil and his angels*"! (Matt. xxv. 41). 2. The remarkable words which the first Evangelist quotes from Isa. liii. 4—"HIMSELF TOOK OUR INFIRMITIES AND BARE OUR SICKNESSES"—involve two difficulties, the patient study of which, however, will be rewarded by deeper conceptions of the work of Christ. First, the prediction is applied, in 1 Pet. ii. 24, to Christ's "bearing our *sins* in His own body on the tree," whereas here it is applied to the removal of *bodily maladies*. Again, the Evangelist seems to view the diseases which our Lord cured as only transferred from the patients to Himself. But both difficulties find their explanation in that profound and comprehensive view of our Lord's redeeming work which a careful study of Scripture reveals. When He took our nature upon Him and made it His own, He identified Himself with its sin and curse, that He might roll them away on the cross (2 Cor. v. 21), and felt all the maladies and ills that sin had inflicted on humanity as His own; His great *conscience* drinking in the sense of that sin of which Himself knew none, and His mighty *heart* feeling all the ills He saw

40 And [h]there came a leper to him, beseeching him, and kneeling down
to him, and saying unto him, If thou wilt, thou canst [i]make me clean.
41 And Jesus, [j]moved with compassion, put forth *his* hand, and touched
42 him, and saith unto him, I will; be thou clean. And as soon as he had
spoken, immediately the leprosy departed from him, and he was
43 cleansed. And he straitly charged him, and forthwith sent him away;
44 And saith unto him, See thou say nothing to any man: but go thy way,
show thyself to the priest, and offer for thy cleansing those things [k]which
45 Moses commanded, for a testimony unto them. But [l]he went out, and
began to publish *it* much, and to blaze abroad the matter, insomuch that
Jesus could no more openly enter into the city, but was without in desert
places: [m]and they came to him from every quarter.
2 AND again [a]he entered into Capernaum after *some* days; and it was
2 noised that he was in the house. And straightway many were gathered
together, insomuch that there was no room to receive *them*, no, not so
3 much as about the door: and he [b]preached the word unto them. And
they come unto him, bringing one sick of the palsy, which was borne of
4 four. And when they could not come nigh unto him for the press, they

A. D. 31.

[h] Matt. 8. 2. Luke 5. 12.
[i] Gen. 18. 14. Jer. 32. 17.
[j] Heb. 2. 17. Heb. 4. 15.
[k] Lev. 14. 3, 4, 10. Luke 5. 14.
[l] Luke 5. 15.
[m] ch. 2. 13.

CHAP. 2.

[a] Matt. 9. 1. Luke 5. 18.
[b] Isa. 61. 1. Matt. 5. 2. ch. 6. 34. Luke 8. 1. Acts 8. 25. Rom. 10. 8. Eph. 2. 17. Heb. 2. 3.

around Him as attaching to Himself. And as we have already seen that His whole ministry of healing, as respects the body, was but a visible exhibition and illustration of His mission "to destroy the works of the devil," so the eye which rightly apprehends the visible miracle, piercing downwards, will discover the deeper and more spiritual aspect of it as a portion of the Redeemer's work, and see the sin-bearing Lamb of God Himself, the Bearer, in this sense, of every ill of sinful humanity that He cured. But the subject is fitter for devout thought than adequate expression. 3. Did Jesus, ere He started on His first missionary tour, "rising up a great while before it was day," steal away unperceived even by those under whose roof He slept, and hieing Him to a solitary spot, there spend the morning hours in still communion with His Father, no doubt about the work that lay before Him? And will not His servants learn of Him not only to sanctify their whole work by prayer, but to set apart special seasons of communion with God before entering on its greater stages, or any important step of it, and for this end to withdraw as much as possible into undisturbed solitude? 4. When we find our Lord, from the very outset of His ministry, acting on that great principle enunciated by Himself, "I must work the works of Him that sent me while it is day: the night cometh when no man can work" (John ix. 4); and actuated by this principle, disregarding the demands of wearied nature and the solicitations of friends, what an example is thus furnished to His ministers in every age, of self-denial and devotion to their work! Oh, if the Lord of the harvest would but thrust forth *such* labourers into his harvest, what work might we not see done! 5. What an affecting contrast does Capernaum here present to its final condition! Ravished with the wonderful works and the matchless teaching of Him who had taken up His abode amongst them, they are loath to part with Him; and while the Gadarenes prayed Him to depart out of their coasts, they are fain to stay Him, that He should not depart from them. And if our Lord declined to settle in Nazareth, and even to do there the mighty works which He did at Capernaum, because of the disrespect with which He was regarded in the place where He had been brought up, how grateful to His feelings would be this early welcome at Capernaum! But, alas! in them was fulfilled that great law of the divine kingdom, "Many that are first shall be last." What a warning is this to similarly favoured spots!

40-45.—HEALING OF A LEPER. (=Matt. viii. 1-4; Luke v. 12-16.) For the exposition, see on Matt. viii. 1-4.

CHAP. II. 1-12.—HEALING OF A PARALYTIC. (= Matt. ix. 1-8; Luke v. 17-26.) This incident, as remarked on Matt. ix. 1, appears to follow next in order of time after the cure of the Leper (ch. i. 40-45).

1. And again he entered into Capernaum—"His own city" (Matt. ix. 1), **and it was noised that he was in the house**—no doubt of Simon Peter (ch. i. 29). **2. And straightway many were gathered together, insomuch that there was no room to receive them, no, not so much as about the door.** This is one of Mark's graphic touches. No doubt in this case, as the scene occurred at his informant's own door, these details are the vivid recollections of that honoured disciple. **and he preached the word unto them**—that is, in-doors; but in the hearing, doubtless, of the multitude that pressed around. Had He gone forth, as He naturally would, the paralytic's faith would have had no such opportunity to display itself. Luke (v. 17) furnishes an additional and very important incident in the scene—as follows: "And it came to pass on a certain day, as He was teaching, that there were Pharisees and doctors of the law sitting by, which were come out of every town," or 'village' [κώμης]," of Galilee, and Judea, and Jerusalem." This was the highest testimony yet borne to our Lord's growing influence, and the necessity increasingly felt by the ecclesiastics throughout the country of coming to some definite judgment regarding Him. "And the power of the Lord was [present] to heal them" [ἦν εἰς τὸ ἰᾶσθαι αὐτούς]—or, 'was [efficacious] to heal them,' that is, the sick that were brought before Him. So that the miracle that is now to be described was only the most glorious and worthy to be recorded of many then performed; and what made it so was doubtless the faith which was manifested in connection with it, and the proclamation of the forgiveness of the patient's sins that immediately preceded it. **3. And they come unto him**—that is, towards the house where He was, **bringing one sick of the palsy**—"lying on a bed" (Matt. ix. 2), **which was borne of four**—a graphic particular of Mark only. **4. And when they could not come nigh unto him for the press**—or, as in Luke,

uncovered the roof where he was: and when they had broken *it* up, they
5 let down the bed wherein the sick of the palsy lay. When Jesus [c]saw
their faith, he said unto the sick of the palsy, [d]Son, thy sins be forgiven
6 thee. But there were certain of the scribes sitting there, and reasoning
7 in their hearts, Why doth this *man* thus speak blasphemies? [e]who can
8 forgive sins but God only? And immediately [f]when Jesus perceived in
his spirit that they so reasoned within themselves, he said unto them,
9 Why reason ye these things in your hearts? Whether [g]is it easier to say
to the sick of the palsy, *Thy* sins be forgiven thee; or to say, Arise, and
10 take up thy bed, and walk? But that ye may know that [h]the Son of
man hath power on earth to forgive sins, (he saith to the sick of the
11 palsy,) I say unto thee, Arise, and take up thy bed, and go thy way into
12 thine house. And [i]immediately he arose, took up the bed, and went
forth before them all; insomuch that they were all amazed, and glorified
God, saying, We never saw it on this fashion.

A. D. 31.

c Gen. 22. 12. Heb. 4. 13.
d Ps. 103. 3. Isa. 53. 11.
e Job 14. 4. Ps. 130. 4. Isa. 43. 25. Rom. 8. 33.
f 1 Sam. 16.7. 1 Chr. 29.17. Ps 7. 9. Ps. 139. 1. Jer. 17. 10. Matt. 9. 4. Heb. 4. 13.
g Matt. 9. 5.
h Isa. 53. 11. Dan. 7. 13.
i Ps. 33. 9.

"when they could not find by what way they might bring him in because of the multitude," **they** "went upon the house-top"—the flat or terrace-roof, universal in eastern houses—and **uncovered the roof where he was: and when they had broken it up, they let down the bed** [κράββατον]—or portable couch, **wherein the sick of the palsy lay.** Luke says, they "let him down through the tiling with his couch into the midst before Jesus." Their whole object was to *bring the patient into the presence of Jesus;* and this not being possible in the ordinary way, for the multitude that surrounded Him, they took the very unusual method here described of accomplishing their object, and succeeded. Several explanations have been given of the way in which this was done; but unless we knew the precise plan of the house, and the part of it from which Jesus taught—which may have been a quadrangle or open court, within the buildings of which Peter's house was one, or a gallery covered by a verandah—it is impossible to determine precisely how the thing was done. One thing, however, is clear, that we have both the accounts from an eye-witness. **5. When Jesus saw their faith.** It is remarkable that all the three narratives call it "*their* faith" which Jesus saw. That the patient himself had faith, we know from the proclamation of his forgiveness, which Jesus made before all; and we should have been apt to conclude that his four friends bore him to Jesus merely out of benevolent compliance with the urgent entreaties of the poor sufferer. But here we learn, not only that his bearers had the same faith with himself, but that Jesus marked it as a faith which was not to be defeated—a faith victorious over all difficulties. This was the faith for which He was ever on the watch, and which He never saw without marking, and, in those who needed anything from Him, richly rewarding. **he said unto the sick of the palsy, Son,** "be of good cheer" (Matt. ix. 2), **thy sins be forgiven thee** [ἀφέωνται σοὶ αἱ ἁμαρτίαι]. By the word "be," our translators perhaps meant "are," as in Luke (v. 20). For it is not a command to his sins to depart, but an authoritative proclamation of the man's pardoned state as a believer. And yet, as the Pharisees understood our Lord to be *dispensing* pardon by this saying, and Jesus not only acknowledges that they were right, but founds His whole argument upon the correctness of it, we must regard the saying as a royal proclamation of the man's forgiveness by Him to whom it belonged to dispense it; nor could such a style of address be justified on any lower supposition. (See on Luke vii. 41, &c.) **6. But there were certain of the scribes**—"and the Pharisees" (Luke v. 21), **sitting there**—those Jewish ecclesiastics who, as Luke told us, "were come out of every village of Galilee, and Judea, and Jerusalem," to make their observations upon this wonderful Person, in anything but a teachable spirit, though as yet their venomous and murderous feeling had not showed itself; **and reasoning in their hearts, 7. Why doth this man thus speak blasphemies? who can forgive sins but God only?** In this second question they expressed a great truth. (See Isa. xliii. 25; Mic. vii. 18; Exod. xxxiv. 6, 7, &c.) Nor was their first question altogether unnatural, though in our Lord's sole case it was unfounded. That a man, to all appearance like one of themselves, should claim authority and power to forgive sins, they could not, on the first blush of it, but regard as in the last degree startling; nor were they entitled even to weigh such a claim, as worthy of a hearing, save on supposition of resistless evidence afforded by Him in support of the claim. Accordingly, our Lord deals with them as men entitled to such evidence, and supplies it; at the same time chiding them for rashness, in drawing harsh conclusions regarding Himself. **8. And immediately when Jesus perceived in his spirit that they so reasoned within themselves, he said unto them, Why reason ye these things**—or, as in Matthew, "Wherefore think ye evil" **in your hearts? 9. Whether is it easier to say to the sick of the palsy, Thy sins be** (or 'are') **forgiven thee; or to say, Arise, and take up thy bed, and walk?** 'Is it easier to command away disease than to bid away sin? If, then, I do the one, which you can see, know thus that I have done the other, which you cannot see.' **10. But that ye may know that the Son of man hath power on earth to forgive sins**—'that forgiving power dwells in the Person of this Man, and is exercised by Him while on this earth and going out and in with you'—**(he saith to the sick of the palsy,) 11. I say unto thee, Arise, and take up thy bed, and go thy way into thine house.** This taking up the portable couch, and walking home with it, was designed to prove the completeness of the cure. **12. And immediately he arose, took up the bed.** 'Sweet saying!' says *Bengel:* 'The bed had borne the man: now the man bore the bed.' **and went forth before them all**—proclaiming by that act to the multitude, whose wondering eyes would follow Him as He pressed through them, that He who could work such a glorious miracle of healing, must indeed "have power on earth to forgive sins." **insomuch that they were all amazed, and glorified God, saying, We never saw it on this**

13 And [j]he went forth again by the sea-side; and all the multitude
14 resorted unto him, and he taught them. And [k]as he passed by, he
saw Levi the *son* of Alpheus sitting [1]at the receipt of custom, and said
15 unto him, Follow me. And he arose and followed him. And [l]it came
to pass, that, as Jesus sat at meat in his house, many publicans and
sinners sat also together with Jesus and his disciples: for there were
16 many, and they followed him. And when [m]the scribes and Pharisees
saw him eat with publicans and sinners, they said unto his disciples,
How is it that he eateth and drinketh with publicans and sinners?
17 When Jesus heard *it,* he saith unto them, [n]They that are whole have
no need of the physician, but they that are sick: I came not to call
the righteous, but sinners to repentance.
18 And [o]the disciples of John and of the Pharisees used to fast: and
they come and say unto him, Why do the disciples of John and of the
19 Pharisees fast, but thy disciples fast not? And Jesus said unto them,
Can the children of [p]the bride-chamber fast while the bridegroom is
with them? as long as they have [q]the bridegroom with them, they
20 cannot fast. But the days will come, when the bridegroom shall be
21 taken away from them, and then shall they fast in those days. No
man also seweth a piece of [2]new cloth on an old garment; else the new
piece that filled it up taketh away from the old, and the rent is made
22 worse. And no man putteth new wine into old bottles; else the new
wine doth burst the bottles, and the wine is spilled, and the bottles will
be marred: but new wine must be put into new bottles.
23 And [r]it came to pass, that he went through the corn fields on the
sabbath day; and his disciples began, as they went, [s]to pluck the ears of
24 corn. And the Pharisees said unto him, Behold, why do they on the
25 sabbath day that which is not lawful? And he said unto them, Have ye
never read [t]what David did, when he had need, and was an hungered,
26 he, and they that were with him? How he went into the house of God
in the days of Abiathar the high priest, and did eat the showbread,
[u]which is not lawful to eat but for the priests, and gave also to them
27 which were with him? And he said unto them, The sabbath was made
28 for man, and not man for the sabbath: therefore [v]the Son of man is Lord
also of the sabbath.

3 AND [a]he entered again into the synagogue; and there was a man
2 there which had a withered hand. And they watched him, whether he
3 would heal him on the sabbath day; that they might accuse him. And

A. D. 31.

[j] Matt. 9. 9.
[k] Luke 5. 27.
[1] Or, at the place where the custom was received.
[l] Matt. 9. 10.
[m] Isa. 65. 5.
[n] Matt. 9. 12, 13. Matt. 18. 11. Luke 5. 31, 32. Luke 15. 7, 29. Luke 16 15. Luke 19. 10. 1 Tim. 1. 15.
[o] Matt. 9. 14. Luke 5 33.
[p] Song 1. 4.
[q] Ps. 45. Isa. 54. 5. Matt 22. 2. John 3. 29. 2 Cor. 11. 2. Eph. 5. 25, 32. Rev. 19. 7. Rev. 21. 1.
[2] Or, raw, or, unwrought.
[r] Matt. 12. 1. Luke 6. 1.
[s] Deut. 23. 25.
[t] 1 Sam. 21. 6.
[u] Ex. 25. 30. Ex. 29. 32, 33.
[v] Matt. 12. 8. Eph. 1. 20, 21. 1 Pet. 3. 22.

CHAP. 3.
[a] Matt. 12. 9. Luke 6. 6.

fashion [οὕτως]—'never saw it thus,' or, as we say, 'never saw the like.' In Luke (v. 26) it is, "We have seen strange (or 'unexpected') things [παράδοξα] to-day"—referring both to the miracles wrought and the forgiveness of sins pronounced by Human Lips. In Matthew (ix. 8) it is, "They marvelled, and glorified God, which had given such power unto men." At forgiving power they wondered not, but that a man, to all appearance like one of themselves, should possess it!

Remarks.—1. Was it not a blessed deed those four did, to bring a patient to the Great Physician? But may not this be done many ways still? And how encouraging is the notice which Jesus took, not only of the patient's, but of his bearers' faith! 2. What a lesson does the extraordinary determination of these believing bearers of the paralytic teach us, to let no obstacles stand in the way of our reaching Jesus, either for ourselves or for those dear to us! 3. How does the supreme Divinity of the Lord Jesus shine forth here, in the authority and power to forgive sins, even as the Son of Man upon earth, which He first put forth and then demonstrated that He possessed! and the half-suppressed horror which filled those ecclesiastics who were spectators of the scene, as they heard from Human Lips what it was the sole prerogative of God to utter, when we connect with it the evidence which Jesus gave them of the justice of His claim, only crowns the proof which this scene furnishes of the Divine glory of Christ. 4. If even on earth, or in the depth of His humiliation, the Son of Man had power to forgive sins, shall we doubt His "ability to save to the uttermost," now that He is set down at the right hand of the Majesty on high?

13-17.—LEVI'S (OR MATTHEW'S) CALL AND FEAST. (= Matt. ix. 9-13; Luke v. 27-32.) For the exposition, see on Matt. ix. 9-13.

18-22.—DISCOURSE ON FASTING. (= Matt. ix. 14-17; Luke v. 33-39.) For the exposition, see on Luke v. 33-39.

23-28.—PLUCKING CORN-EARS ON THE SABBATH DAY. (= Matt. xii. 1-8; Luke vi. 1-5.) For the exposition, see on Matt. xii. 1-8.

CHAP. III. 1-12.—THE HEALING OF A WITHERED HAND ON THE SABBATH DAY, AND RETIREMENT OF JESUS TO AVOID DANGER. (= Matt. xii.

4 he saith unto the man which had the withered hand, [1]Stand forth. And
he saith unto them, Is it lawful to do good on the sabbath days, or to do
5 evil? to save life, or to kill? But they held their peace. And when he
had looked round about on them with [b]anger, being grieved for the
[2]hardness of their hearts, he saith unto the man, Stretch forth thine
hand. And he stretched *it* out: and his hand was restored whole as the
6 other. And [c]the Pharisees went forth, and straightway took counsel
with [d]the Herodians against him, how they might destroy him.
7 But Jesus withdrew himself with his disciples to the sea: and a great
8 multitude from Galilee followed him, [e]and from Judea, and from Jerusalem, and from Idumea, and *from* beyond Jordan; and they about Tyre
and Sidon, a great multitude, when they had heard what great things
9 he did, came unto him. And he spake to his disciples, that a small
ship should wait on him because of the multitude, lest they should
10 throng him: for he had healed many; insomuch that they [3]pressed upon
11 him for to touch him, as many as had plagues. And [f]unclean spirits,
when they saw him, fell down before him, and cried, saying, [g]Thou art
12 the Son of God. And [h]he straitly charged them that they should not
make him known.
13 And [i]he goeth up into a mountain, and calleth *unto him* whom he
14 would: and they came unto him. And he ordained twelve, that they
15 should be with him, and that he might send them forth to preach, and
16 to have power to heal sicknesses, and to cast out devils. And Simon [j]he
17 surnamed Peter; and James the *son* of Zebedee, and John the brother of
James; (and he surnamed them Boanerges, which is, [k]The sons of
18 thunder;) and Andrew, and Philip, and Bartholomew, and Matthew, and
Thomas, and James the *son* of Alpheus, and [l]Thaddeus, and Simon the
19 Canaanite, and Judas Iscariot, which also betrayed him. And they went
[4]into an house.
20 And the multitude cometh together again, [m]so that they could not so
21 much as eat bread. And when his [5]friends heard *of it*, they went out to
22 lay hold on him: for they said, He is beside himself. And the scribes
which came down from Jerusalem said, [n]He hath Beelzebub, and by the
23 prince of the devils casteth he out devils. And [o]he called them *unto*
him, and said unto them in parables, How can Satan cast out Satan?
24 And if a kingdom be divided against itself, that kingdom cannot
25 stand. And if a house be divided against itself, that house cannot stand.
26 And if Satan rise up against himself, and be divided, he cannot stand,
27 but hath an end. No [p]man can enter into a strong man's house, and
spoil his goods, except he will first bind the strong man; and then
28 he will spoil his house. Verily [q]I say unto you, All sins shall be
forgiven unto the sons of men, and blasphemies wherewith soever they
29 shall blaspheme; but he that shall blaspheme against the Holy Ghost
30 hath [r]never forgiveness, but is in danger of eternal damnation: because
they said, He hath an unclean spirit.
31 There [s]came then his brethren and his mother, and, standing without,
32 sent unto him, calling him. And the multitude sat about him; and
they said unto him, Behold, [t]thy mother and thy brethren without seek
33 for thee. And he answered them, saying, Who is my mother, or my
34 brethren? And he looked round about on them which sat about him,
35 and said, [u]Behold my mother and my brethren! For whosoever shall
do the will of God, the same is my brother, and my sister, and mother.

A. D. 31.

1 Arise, stand forth in the midst. Dan. 6. 10. Phil. 1. 14.
b Ps. 69. 9. Ps. 119. 139.
2 Or, blindness.
c Matt 12.14.
d Matt. 22.16.
e Luke 6. 17.
3 Or, rushed.
f ch. 1. 23. Luke 4. 41.
g Acts 16. 17. Matt. 14.33. ch. 1. 1.
h ch. 1. 25,34. Matt. 12.16.
i Matt. 10. 1. Luke 6. 12. Luke 9. 1.
j John 1. 42.
k Isa. 58. 1.
l Jude 1.
4 Or, home.
m ch. 6. 31.
5 Or, kinsmen. John 7. 5. John 10. 20.
n Matt. 9. 34. Matt. 10.25. Luke 11. 15. John 7. 20. John 8. 48, 52. John 10. 22.
o Matt. 12.25. Luke 11. 17-23.
p Isa. 49. 24. Matt. 12.29.
q Matt. 12.31. Luke 12.10. Heb. 6. 4-8. Heb. 10. 26-31. 1 John 5.16.
r Matt. 25.46. ch. 12. 40. Acts 7. 51. 2 Thes. 1. 9. Heb. 6. 4. Jude 7. 13.
s Matt. 12.46. Luke 8. 19.
t Matt. 13.55. ch. 6. 3. John 7. 3.
u Deut. 33. 9. Song 4.9,10. Matt. 25.40-45. Rom. 8. 29. Heb. 2. 11.

9-21; Luke vi. 6-11.) For the exposition, see on Matt. xii. 9-21.

13-19.—The Twelve Apostles Chosen. For the exposition, see on Luke vi. 12-19.

20-30.—Jesus is Charged with Madness and Demoniacal Possession—His Reply. (=Matt. xii. 22-37; Luke xi. 14-26.) For the exposition, see on Matt. xii. 22-37, and on Luke xi. 21-26.

31-35.—His Mother and Brethren seek to Speak with Him, and the Reply. (=Matt.

4 AND [a]he began again to teach by the sea-side: and there was gathered
unto him a great multitude, so that he entered into a ship, and sat in
2 the sea; and the whole multitude was by the sea on the land. And
he taught them many things by parables, and said unto them
3 in his doctrine, [b]Hearken; Behold, there went out a sower to sow:
4 and it came to pass, as he sowed, some fell by the way-side, and the fowls
5 of the air came and devoured it up. And some fell on stony ground,
where it had not much earth; and immediately it sprang up, because it
6 had no depth of earth: but when the sun was up, it was scorched; and
7 because it had no root, it withered away. And some [c]fell among thorns,
8 and the thorns grew up, and choked it, and it yielded no fruit. And
other fell on good ground, and did yield fruit that sprang up and
increased; and brought forth, some thirty, and some sixty, and some an
9 hundred. And he said unto them, He that hath ears to hear, let him
hear.

A. D. 31.

CHAP. 4.
[a] Matt. 13. 1. ch. 2. 13. Luke 8. 4.
[b] Deut. 4. 1. Ps. 34. 11. Ps. 45. 10. Pro. 7. 24. Pro. 8. 32. Isa. 55. 1. Acts 2. 14. Jas. 2. 5.
[c] Gen. 3. 18. Jer. 4. 3. Luke 8. 7. John 15. 5. 1 Tim. 6. 9. Col. 1. 6.

xii. 46-50; Luke viii. 19-21.) For the exposition, see on Matt. xii. 46-50.

CHAP. IV. 1-29.—PARABLE OF THE SOWER—REASON FOR TEACHING IN PARABLES—PARABLES OF THE SEED GROWING WE KNOW NOT HOW, AND OF THE MUSTARD SEED. (= Matt. xiii. 1-23, 31, 32; Luke viii. 4-18.)

1. And he began again to teach by the sea-side: and there was gathered unto him a great multitude—or, according to another well-supported reading, 'a mighty,' or 'immense multitude' [ὄχλος πλεῖστος], **so that he entered into a ship** [εἰς τὸ πλοῖον]—rather, 'into the ship,' meaning the one mentioned in ch. iii. 9. (See on Matt. xii. 15.) **and sat in the sea; and the whole multitude was by the sea on the land**—crowded on the sea-shore to listen to Him. See on Matt. xiii. 1, 2. **2. And he taught them many things by parables, and said unto them in his doctrine** [διδαχῇ]—or 'teaching.'

Parable of the Sower (3-9, 13-20). After this parable is recorded, the Evangelist says, *v.* **10. And when he was alone, they that were about him with the twelve**—probably those who followed Him most closely and were firmest in discipleship, next to the Twelve. **asked of him the parable.** The reply would seem to intimate that this parable of the Sower was of that fundamental, comprehensive, and introductory character which we have assigned to it (see on Matt. xiii. 1). **13. And he said unto them, Know ye not this parable? and how then will ye know all parables?** Probably this was said not so much in the spirit of rebuke, as to call their attention to the exposition of it which He was about to give, and so train them to the right apprehension of His future parables. As in the parables which we have endeavoured to explain in Matt. xiii., we shall take this parable and the Lord's own exposition of the different parts of it together.

The SOWER, the SEED, and the SOIL. **3. Hearken; Behold, there went out a sower to sow.** What means this? **14. The sower soweth the word**—or, as in Luke (viii. 11), "Now the parable is this: The seed is *the word of God.*" But who is "the sower?" This is not expressed here, because if "the word of God" be the seed, every scatterer of that precious seed must be regarded as a sower. It is true that in the parable of the Tares it is said, "He that soweth the good seed is the Son of Man," as "He that soweth the tares is the devil"(Matt. xiii. 37, 38). But these are only the great unseen parties, struggling in this world for the possession of man. Each of these has his agents among men themselves; and Christ's agents in the sowing of the good seed are the *preachers* of the word. Thus, as in all the cases about to be described, the Sower is the same, and the seed is the same, while the result is entirely different, the whole difference must lie in the *soils*, which mean the *different states of the human heart.* And so, the great general lesson held forth in this parable of the Sower is, That however faithful the preacher, and how pure soever his message, *the effect of the preaching of the word depends upon the state of the hearer's heart.* Now follow the cases.

First Case: THE WAY-SIDE. **4. And it came to pass, as he sowed, some fell by the way-side**—by the side of the hard path through the field, where the soil was not broken up: **and the fowls [of the air] came and devoured it up** [τοῦ οὐρανοῦ is wanting in support]. Not only could the seed not get beneath the surface, but "it was trodden down" (Luke viii. 5), and afterwards picked up and devoured by the fowls. What means this? **15. And these are they by the way-side, where the word is sown; but, when they have heard, Satan cometh immediately, and taketh away the word that was sown in their hearts**—or, more fully, Matt. xiii. 19, "When any one heareth the word of the kingdom, and understandeth it not, then cometh the wicked one, and catcheth away that which was sown in his heart." The great truth here taught is, that *Hearts all unbroken and hard are no fit soil for saving truth.* They apprehend it not (Matt. xiii. 19), as God's means of restoring them to Himself; it penetrates not, makes no impression, but lies loosely on the surface of the heart, till the wicked one—afraid of losing a victim by his "believing to salvation," Luke viii. 12)—finds some frivolous subject by whose greater attractions to draw off the attention, and straightway it is gone. Of how many hearers of the word is this the graphic but painful history!

Second Case: THE STONY, or rather, ROCKY GROUND. **5. And some fell on stony ground, where it had not much earth** [τὸ πετρῶδες]—'the rocky ground;' in Matthew (xiii. 5), 'the rocky places' [τὰ πετρώδη]; in Luke, 'the rock' [τὴν πέτραν]. The thing intended is, not ground with stones in it, which would not prevent the roots striking downward, but ground where a quite thin surface of earth covers a rock. What means this? **16. And these are they likewise which are sown on stony ground; who, when they have heard the word, immediately receive it with gladness; 17. And have no root in themselves, and so endure but for a time: afterward, when affliction or persecution ariseth for the word's sake, immediately they are offended.** "Immediately" the seed in such case "springs

N

10 And [d]when he was alone, they that were about him with the twelve
11 asked of him the parable. And he said unto them, Unto you it is given
to know [e]the mystery of the kingdom of God: but unto [f]them that are
12 without, all *these* things are done in parables: that [g]seeing they may see,
and not perceive; and hearing they may hear, and not understand; lest
at any time they should be converted, and *their* sins should be forgiven
13 them. And he said unto them, Know ye not this parable? and
14 how then will ye know all parables? The [h]sower soweth the word.
15 And these are they by the way-side, where the word is sown; but, when
they have heard, [i]Satan cometh immediately, and taketh away the word
16 that was sown in their hearts. And these are they likewise which are
sown on stony ground; who, when they have heard the word, immediately
17 receive it with gladness; and have [j]no root in themselves, and so endure
but for a time: afterward, when affliction or persecution ariseth for the
18 word's sake, immediately they are offended. And these are they which
19 are sown among thorns; such as hear the word, and the cares of this

A. D. 31.

[d] Pro. 2. 1. Pro. 4. 7. Pro. 13. 20. Matt. 13.10. Luke 8. 9.
[e] 1 Cor. 2. 10.
[f] 1 Cor. 1. 18. 1 Cor. 5. 12.
[g] Isa. 6. 9. Isa. 44. 18. Jer. 5. 21. Matt. 13.14.
[h] Matt. 13.19. Eph. 3. 8. 1 Pet. 1. 23, 25.
[i] 2 Cor. 2. 11. 2 Cor. 4. 4. 1 Pet. 5. 8.
[j] Job 27. 10

up"—all the quicker from the shallowness of the soil—"because it has no depth of earth." But the sun, beating on it, as quickly scorches and withers it up, "because it has no root" (*v.* 6), and "lacks moisture" (Luke viii. 6). The great truth here taught is that *Hearts superficially impressed are apt to receive the truth with readiness, and even with joy* (Luke viii. 13); *but the* heat of tribulation or persecution because of the word, or *the trials which their new profession brings upon them quickly dries up their relish for the truth, and withers all the hasty promise of fruit which they showed.* Such disappointing issues of a faithful and awakening ministry—alas, how frequent are they!

Third Case: THE THORNY GROUND. **7. And some fell among thorns, and the thorns grew up, and choked it, and it yielded no fruit.** This case is that of ground not thoroughly cleaned of the thistles, &c.; which, rising above the good seed, "choke" or "smother" it, excluding light and air, and drawing away the moisture and richness of the soil. Hence it "becomes unfruitful" (Matt. xiii. 22); it grows, but its growth is checked, and it never ripens. The evil here is neither a hard nor a shallow soil—there is *softness* enough, and *depth* enough; but it is the existence in it of what draws all the moisture and richness of the soil away to itself, and so *starves the plant.* What now are these "thorns?" **18. And these are they which are sown among thorns; such as hear the word, 19. And the cares of this world, and the deceitfulness of riches, and the lusts of other things entering in**—or "the pleasures of this life" (Luke viii. 14), **choke the word, and it becometh unfruitful.** First, "The cares of this world"—anxious, unrelaxing attention to the business of this present life; second, "The deceitfulness of riches"—of those riches which are the fruit of this worldly "care;" third, "The pleasures of this life," or "the lusts of other things entering in"—the enjoyments, in themselves it may be innocent, which worldly prosperity enables one to indulge. These "*choke*" or "*smother*" the word; drawing off so much of one's attention, absorbing so much of one's interest, and using up so much of one's time, that only the dregs of these remain for spiritual things, and a fagged, hurried, and heartless formalism is at length all the religion of such persons. What a vivid picture is this of the mournful condition of many, especially in great commercial countries, who once promised much fruit! "They bring no fruit *to perfection*" (Luke viii. 14); indicating how much *growth* there may be, in the early stages of such a case, and *promise* of fruit—which after all never *ripens.*

Fourth Case: THE GOOD GROUND. **8. And other fell on good ground, and did yield fruit that sprang up and increased; and brought forth, some thirty, and some sixty, and some an hundred.** The goodness of this last soil consists in its qualities being precisely the reverse of the other three soils: from its softness and tenderness, receiving and cherishing the seed; from its depth, allowing it to take firm root, and not quickly losing its moisture; and from its cleanness, giving its whole vigour and sap to the plant. In such a soil the seed "brings forth fruit," in all different degrees of profusion, according to the measure in which the soil possesses those qualities. So **20. And these are they which are sown on good ground; such as hear the word, and receive it, and bring forth fruit, some thirty-fold, some sixty, and some an hundred.** A heart soft and tender, stirred to its depths on the great things of eternity, and jealously guarded from worldly engrossments, such only is the "*honest and good heart*" (Luke viii. 15), which "*keeps*" [κατέχουσι]—that is, "*retains*" the seed of the word, and bears fruit just in proportion as it is such a heart. Such "bring forth fruit with *patience*" (*v.* 15), or continuance, 'enduring to the end;' in contrast with those in whom the word is "choked" and brings no fruit *to perfection.* The "thirty-fold" is designed to express the *lowest* degree of fruitfulness; the "hundred-fold" the *highest;* and the "sixty-fold" the *intermediate* degrees of fruitfulness. As 'a hundred-fold,' though not unexampled (Gen. xxvi. 12), is a rare return in the natural husbandry, so the highest degrees of spiritual fruitfulness are too seldom witnessed. The closing words of this introductory parable seem designed to call attention to the *fundamental* and *universal* character of it. **9. And he said unto them, He that hath ears to hear, let him hear.**

Reason for Teaching in Parables (11, 12). **11, 12. And he said unto them, Unto you it is given to know the mystery of the kingdom of God: but unto them, &c.** See on Matt. xiii. 10-17. **21. And he said unto them, Is a candle**—or 'lamp,' [ὁ λύχνος]—**brought to be put under a bushel, or under a bed? and not to be set on a candlestick?**—"that they which enter in may see the light" (Luke viii. 16). See on Matt. v. 15, of which this is nearly a repetition. **22. For there is nothing hid, which shall not be manifested;**

world, [k]and the deceitfulness of riches, and the lusts of other things
20 entering in, choke the word, and it becometh unfruitful. And these are
they which are sown on good [l]ground; such as hear the word, and receive
it, and bring forth fruit, some thirty-fold, some sixty, and some an
hundred.
21 And [m]he said unto them, Is a candle brought to be put under a
22 [1]bushel, or under a bed? and not to be set on a candlestick? For [n]there
is nothing hid, which shall not be manifested; neither was any thing kept
23 secret, but that it should come abroad. If [o]any man have ears to hear,
24 let him hear. And he saith unto them, [p]Take heed what ye hear: [q]with
what measure ye mete, it shall be measured to you; and unto you that
25 hear shall more be given. For [r]he that hath, to him shall be given; and
he that hath not, from him shall be taken even that which he hath.
26 And he said, [s]So is the kingdom of God, as if a man should cast seed
27 into the ground; and should sleep, and rise night and day, and the seed
28 should spring and grow up, he knoweth not how. For the earth bringeth
forth fruit of himself; first the blade, then the ear, after that the full
29 corn in the ear. But when the fruit is [2]brought forth, immediately [t]he
putteth in the sickle, because the harvest is come.
30 And he said, [u]Whereunto shall we liken the kingdom of God? or with
31 what comparison shall we compare it? *It is* like a grain of mustard seed,
which, when it is sown in the earth, is less than all the seeds that be in
32 the earth: but when it is sown, it [v]groweth up, and becometh greater
than all herbs, and shooteth out great branches; so that the fowls of the
air may lodge under the shadow of it.
33 And [w]with many such parables spake he the word unto them, as they
34 were able to hear *it.* But without a parable spake he not unto them:
and when they were alone, he expounded all things to his disciples.

A. D. 31.

[k] Ps. 52. 7. Pro. 23. 5. Eccl. 5. 13.
[l] Rom. 7. 4. 2 Cor. 5. 17. 2 Pet. 1. 4.
[m] Matt. 5. 15. Luke 8. 16. Luke 11.33.
[1] The word in the original signifieth a less measure, as Matt. 5. 15.
[n] Matt. 10.26.
[o] Matt. 11.15.
[p] 1 John 4. 1.
[q] Matt. 7. 2.
[r] Matt. 13.12.
[s] Matt. 13.24.
[2] Or, ripe. Eph. 4. 13.
[t] Rev. 14. 15.
[u] Matt. 13.31. Luke 13.18. Acts 2. 41. Acts 4. 4. Acts 5. 14. Acts 19. 20.
[v] Mal. 1. 11. Rev. 11. 15.
[w] Matt. 13.34. John 16.12.

neither was any thing kept secret, but that it should come abroad. See on Matt. x. 26, 27; but the connection there and here is slightly different. Here the idea seems to be this:—'I have privately expounded to you these great truths, but only that ye may proclaim them publicly; and if ye will not, others will. For these are not designed for secrecy. They are imparted to be diffused abroad, and they shall be so; yea, a time is coming when the most hidden things shall be brought to light.' **23. If any man have ears to hear, let him hear.** This for the second time on the same subject (see on *v.* 9). **24. And he saith unto them, Take heed what ye hear** [τί]. In Luke (viii. 18) it is, "Take heed how ye hear" [πῶς]. The one implies the other, but both precepts are very weighty. **with what measure ye mete, it shall be measured to you.** See on Matt. vii. 2. **and unto you that hear**—that is, thankfully, teachably, profitably, **shall more be given. 25. For he that hath, to him shall be given; and he that hath not, from him shall be taken even that which he hath**—or "seemeth to have," or 'thinketh he hath' [ὃ δοκεῖ ἔχειν]. See on Matt. xiii. 12. This "having" and "thinking he hath" are not different; for when it hangs loosely upon him, and is not appropriated to its proper ends and uses, it both *is* and *is not* his.

Parable of the Seed Growing We Know Not How (26-29). This beautiful parable is peculiar to Mark. Its design is to teach the *Imperceptible Growth* of the word sown in the heart, from its earliest stage of development to the ripest fruits of practical righteousness. **26. And he said, So is the kingdom of God, as if a man should cast seed into the ground; 27. And should sleep, and rise night and day**—go about his other ordinary occupations, leaving it to the well-known laws of vegetation under the genial influences of heaven. This is the sense of "the earth bringing forth fruit *of herself,*" in the next verse. **and the seed should spring and grow up, he knoweth not how. 28. For the earth bringeth forth fruit of herself; first the blade, then the ear, after that the full corn in the ear.** Beautiful allusion to the succession of similar stages, though not definitely-marked periods, in the Christian life, and generally in the kingdom of God. **29. But when the fruit is brought forth**—to maturity, **immediately he putteth in the sickle, because the harvest is come.** This charmingly points to the transition from the earthly to the heavenly condition of the Christian and the Church.

Parable of the Mustard Seed (30-32). For the exposition of this Portion, see on Matt. xiii. 31, 32.

33. And with many such parables spake he the word unto them, as they were able to hear it. Had this been said in the corresponding passage of Matthew, we should have concluded that what that Evangelist recorded was but a specimen of other parables spoken on the same occasion. But Matthew (xiii. 34) says, "All *these* things spake Jesus unto the multitude in parables;" and as Mark records only some of the parables which Matthew gives, we are warranted to infer that the "many such parables" alluded to here mean no more than the full complement of them which we find in Matthew. **34. But without a parable spake he not unto them.** See on Matt. xiii. 34. **and when they were alone, he expounded all things to his disciples.** See on *v.* 22.

Remarks.—1. In the parable of the Sower, we have an illustration of the principle that our Lord's parables illustrate only certain features of a subject, and that though others *may* be added as accessory and subsidiary, no conclusions are to

35 And [x]the same day, when the even was come, he saith unto them,
36 Let us pass over unto the other side. And when they had sent away

A. D. 31.

[x] Isa. 42. 4.

be drawn as to those features of the subject which are not in the parable at all. (See on Matt. xxii. 2, &c., xxv. 1, where, though the subject in both is a *marriage*, the *Bride* appears in neither.) Thus, the one point in this parable is the *diversity of the soils*, as affecting the result of the sowing. To make this the clearer, the *sower* and the *seed* are here supposed to be the same in all. But were one to infer from this that the preacher and his doctrine are of no importance, or of less moment than the state of the heart on which the word lights, he would fall into that spurious style of interpretation which has misled not a few. 2. Perhaps our Lord's own ministry furnishes the most striking illustration of this Parable of the Sower. Look first at Chorazin, Bethsaida, Capernaum, Jerusalem—what a hard *Way-side* did they present to the precious seed that fell upon it—yielding, with few exceptions, not only no fruit, but not so much as one green blade! Turn next to him who said to Him, "Lord, I will follow thee whithersoever thou goest," and the crowds that followed Him with wonder and heard Him with joy, and cast in their lot with Him—until the uncompromising severity of His teaching, or the privations and the obloquy they had to suffer, or the prospect of a deadly conflict with the world, stumbled them, and then they went back, and walked no more with Him: this was the *Rocky Ground*. As for the *Thorny Ground*—not hard, like the wayside; nor shallow, like the rocky ground; but soft enough and deep enough; in which, therefore the good seed sprang up, and promised fruit, and *would have ripened* but for the thorns which were allowed to spring up and choke the plant—this kind of hearers had scarcely time to develop themselves ere the Lord Himself was taken from them. But *Judas*—in so far as he bade so fair as a disciple as to be taken into the number of the Twelve, and went forth with the rest of the apostles on their preaching-tour, and in every other thing acted so faithfully to all appearance as to inspire no suspicion of his false-heartedness up to the very night of his treason—perhaps he may be taken as one of a class which, but for one or more predominant sins, cherished till they become resistless, *would have borne fruit* unto life eternal. Of honest and good hearts there were but too few to cheer the heart of the Great Sower. But the Eleven certainly were such, and "as many as received Him, to whom He gave power to become sons of God;" and them He deigned to call "His brother, and sister, and mother." As to the varying fruitfulness of these, Peter and John might perhaps be taken as examples of the "some who brought forth an hundred-fold;" Andrew, and Nathanael (or Bartholomew), and Matthew, and Thomas, and it may be others, sixty-fold; and the rest thirty. But from age to age these diversified characters are developed; and some more in one, some in another. There are periods of such spiritual death in the Church, that its whole territory presents to the spiritual eye the aspect of one vast Way-side, with but here and there, at wide distances, a green spot. There are periods of intense religious excitement, in which, as if all were Rocky ground, the sower's heart is gladdened by the quick up-springing of an immense breadth of beautiful green "blade," as if the Latter Day of universal turning to the Lord were about to dawn; and a goodly portion of it comes into "ear;" but of "the full corn in the ear," scarce any is there to reward the reaper's toil. And there are periods of high orthodox belief, fair religious profession, and universally proper outward Christianity, in which the all-engrossing pursuit of wealth in the walks of untiring industry, and the carnal indulgences to which outward prosperity ministers, starve the soul and suffer no spiritual fruit to come "to perfection." These are the Thorny-ground periods. Of Good-ground periods have there been any? In a partial sense there certainly have; but on any great scale it is rather to be expected in the Times of Refreshing which are coming upon the earth, than referred to as an experienced fact. Perhaps every congregation furnishes some of all these classes; but would to God we could see more of the last! 3. What encouragement may not be fetched from the parable of the *imperceptible growth* of the good seed! It is slow; it is gradual; it is unseen—alike in the natural and the spiritual kingdom. Hence the wisdom of early sowing, and long patience, and cheerful expectancy. 4. Illustrative preaching has here the highest example. Not more attractive than instructive is this style of preaching; and the parables of our Lord are incomparable models of both. If there be such a thing in perfection as "apples of gold in a framework of silver," these are they. It is true that to excel in this style requires an original capacity, with which every preacher is not gifted. But the systematic observation of nature and of human life, with continual reference to spiritual things, will do a good deal to aid the most unapt, while luxuriant fancies, which are apt to overpower with their illustrations the thing illustrated, have quite as much need of pruning. For both classes of mind the careful study of that grand simplicity and freedom, and freshness and elegance, and whatever else there be, which combine to render our Lord's parables indescribably perfect, both in the truths they convey and the mode of conveying them, would be a fruitful exercise. 5. The command to take heed *what* we hear is to be taken as a hint supplementary to the parable of the Sower, and is just on that account the more worthy of attention. For since the quality of the seed sown had nothing to do with the design of that parable—it being supposed in all the cases to be good seed—a supplementary caution to look well to "what" we hear, as well as "how," must have been intended to teach us that, in point of fact, the doctrine taught requires as much attention as the right frame of mind in listening to it. For in respect of both, "the word which we hear, the same shall judge us at the last day."

35—V. 20.—Jesus, Crossing the Sea of Galilee, miraculously Stills a Tempest—He Cures the Demoniac of Gadara. (= Matt. viii. 23-34; Luke viii. 22-39.)

The time of this Section is very definitely marked by our Evangelist, and by him alone, in the opening words.

Jesus Stills a Tempest on the Sea of Galilee (35-41). **35. And the same day**—on which He spoke the memorable parables of the preceding Section, and of Matt. xiii., **when the even was come.** See on ch. vi. 35. This must have been the earlier evening—what we should call the afternoon—since after all that passed on the other side, when He returned to the west side, the people were waiting for Him in great numbers (*v.* 21; Luke viii. 40). **he saith unto them, Let us pass over unto the other side**—to the east side of the Lake, to grapple

the multitude, they took him even as he was in the ship. And there
37 were also with him other little ships. And there arose a great storm of
38 wind, and the waves beat into the ship, so that it was now full. And he
was in the hinder part of the ship, asleep on a pillow: and they awake
39 him, and say unto him, Master, carest thou not that we perish? And
he arose, and [y]rebuked the wind, and said unto the sea, Peace, be still.
40 And the wind ceased, and there was a great calm. And he said unto
41 them, Why are ye so fearful? how is it that ye have no faith? And
they [z]feared exceedingly, and said one to another, What manner of man
is this, that even the wind and the sea obey him?

5 AND [a]they came over unto the other side of the sea, into the country
2 of the Gadarenes. And when he was come out of the ship, immediately

A. D. 31.

[y] Job 28. 11. Job 38. 11. Ps. 29. 10. Ps. 65. 5, 7. Ps. 89. 9. Ps. 93. 4. Ps. 107. 23-29. Ps. 135. 5, 6. Nah. 1. 4.

[z] Ps. 33. 8, 9.

CHAP. 5.

[a] Matt. 8. 28. Luke 8. 26.

---

with a desperate case of possession, and set the captive free, and to give the Gadarenes an opportunity of hearing the message of salvation, amid the wonder which that marvellous cure was fitted to awaken and the awe which the subsequent events could not but strike into them. **36. And when they had sent away the multitude, they took him even as he was in the ship**—that is, without any preparation, and without so much as leaving the vessel, out of which He had been all day teaching. **And there were also with him other little ships**—with passengers, probably, wishing to accompany Him. **37. And there arose a great storm of wind** [λαῖλαψ ἀνέμου]—'a tempest of wind.' To such sudden squalls the sea of Galilee is very liable from its position, in a deep basin, skirted on the east by lofty mountain-ranges, while on the west the hills are intersected by narrow gorges through which the wind sweeps across the lake, and raises its waters with great rapidity into a storm. **and the waves beat into the ship** [ἐπέβαλλεν εἰς τὸ πλοῖον]—'kept beating' or 'pitching on the ship,' **so that it was now full** [ὥστε αὐτὸ ἤδη γεμίζεσθαι]—rather, 'so that it was already filling.' In Matt. (viii. 24), "insomuch that the ship was covered with the waves;" but this is too strong. It should be, 'so that the ship was getting covered by the waves' [ὥστε τὸ πλοῖον καλύπτεσθαι]. So we must translate the word used in Luke (viii. 23)—not as in our version—"And there came down a storm on the lake, and they were filled [with water]"—but 'they were getting filled' [συνεπληροῦντο], that is, those who sailed; meaning, of course, that their ship was so. **38. And he was in the hinder**—or stern, **part of the ship, asleep on a pillow** [ἐπὶ τὸ προσκεφάλαιον]—either a place in the vessel made to receive the head, or a cushion for the head to rest on. It was evening; and after the fatigues of a busy day of teaching under the hot sun, having nothing to do while crossing the lake, He sinks into a deep sleep, which even this tempest raging around and tossing the little vessel did not disturb. **and they awake him, and say unto him, Master** [Διδάσκαλε]—or 'Teacher.' In Luke (viii. 24) this is doubled—in token of their life-and-death-earnestness—"Master, Master" ['Επιστάτα, 'Επιστάτα]. **carest thou not that we perish?** Unbelief and fear made them sadly forget their place, to speak so. Luke has it, "Lord, save us, we perish." When those accustomed to fish upon that deep thus spake, the danger must have been imminent. They say nothing of what would become of *Him*, if they perished; nor think whether, if He could not perish, it was likely He would let this happen to them: but they hardly knew what they said. **39. And he arose, and rebuked the wind**—"and the raging of the water" (Luke viii. 24), **and said unto the sea, Peace, be still**—two sublime words of command, from a Master to His servants, the elements [Σιώπα, πεφίμωσο]. **And the wind ceased, and there was a great calm.** The sudden hushing of the wind would not at once have calmed the sea, whose commotion would have settled only after a considerable time. But the word of command was given to both elements at once. **40. And he said unto them, Why are ye so fearful?** There is a natural apprehension under danger; but there was unbelief in their fear. It is worthy of notice how considerately the Lord defers this rebuke till He had first removed the danger, in the midst of which they would not have been in a state to listen to anything. **how is it that ye have no faith?**—next to none, or none in present exercise. In Luke it is, "Why are ye fearful, O ye of little faith?" *Faith* they had, for they applied to Christ for relief; but *little*, for they were afraid, though Christ was in the ship. Faith dispels fear, but only in proportion to its strength. **41. And they feared exceedingly**—were struck with deep awe, **and said one to another, What manner of man is this, that even the wind and the sea obey him?**—'What is this? Israel has all along been singing of JEHOVAH, "Thou rulest the raging of the sea: when the waves thereof arise, Thou stillest them"! "The Lord on high is mightier than the noise of many waters, yea, than the mighty waves of the sea"! (Ps. lxxxix. 9; xciii. 4). But, lo, in this very boat of ours is One of our own flesh and blood, who with His word of command hath done the same! Exhausted with the fatigues of the day, He was but a moment ago in a deep sleep, undisturbed by the howling tempest, and we had to awake Him with the cry of our terror; but rising at our call, His majesty was felt by the raging elements, for they were instantly hushed—"WHAT MANNER OF MAN IS THIS?"'

CHAP. V. *Glorious Cure of the Gadarene Demoniac* (1-20). **1. And they came over unto the other side of the sea, into the country of the Gadarenes.** [*Lachmann*, *Tischendorf*, and *Tregelles* read here and in the corresponding passage of Luke (viii. 26) "Gerasenes"—Γερασηνῶν—on ancient, but not, as we think, sufficient authority to displace the received reading. In Matthew (viii. 28) the received reading, "Gergesenes," would seem the true one, and not "Gerasenes" with *Lachmann*, nor "Gadarenes" with *Tischendorf* and *Tregelles*. While the MS. evidence for it is satisfactory, some recent geographical discoveries seem to favour it. *Gadara* perhaps denoted the general locality. *Josephus* (Antt. xvii. 11. 4) speaks of it as the chief city of Perea, and a Greek city. It or its suburbs lay on the southern shore of the lake on the east side. Possibly the reading "Gergesenes," which seems a corrupted form of "Gadarenes," originated in that tract of country being still called after the "Girgashites" of ancient Canaan.] **2.**

3 there met him out of the tombs a man with an unclean spirit, who had
his dwelling among the tombs; and no man could bind him, no, not
4 with chains: because that he had been often bound with fetters and
chains, and the chains had been plucked asunder by him, and the
5 fetters broken in pieces: neither could any *man* tame him. And always,
night and day, he was in the mountains, and in the tombs, crying, and
6 cutting himself with stones. But when he saw Jesus afar off, he ran and
7 [b]worshipped him, and cried with a loud voice, and said, What have I to
do with thee, Jesus, *thou* Son of the most high God? I adjure thee by
8 God, that thou torment me not. (For he said unto him, Come out of
9 the man, *thou* unclean spirit.) And he asked him, What *is* thy name?
10 And he answered, saying, My name *is* Legion: for we are many. And
he besought him much that he would not send them away out of the
11 country. Now there was there, nigh unto the mountains, a great herd
12 of [c]swine feeding. And all the devils besought him, saying, Send us
13 into the swine, that we may enter into them. And forthwith Jesus
[d]gave them leave. And the unclean spirits went out, and entered into

A. D. 31.

[b] Ps. 66. 3. Acts 16. 17. Phil. 2. 10, 11. Jas. 2. 19.
[c] Lev. 11. 7. Deut. 14. 8. Isa. 65. 4. Isa. 65. 3. Matt. 8. 30. Luke 8. 32.
[d] 1 Ki. 22. 22. Job 1. 12. Job 2. 6. Job 12. 16 Matt. 28. 18. Luke 4. 36. Eph. 1. 20, 23. Col. 2. 10. Heb. 2. 8.

And when he was come out of the ship, immediately (see *v.* 6) **there met him a man with an unclean spirit**—"which had devils (or 'demons') long time" (Luke viii. 27). In Matthew (viii. 28), "there met Him two men possessed with devils." Though there be no discrepancy between these two statements—more than between two witnesses, one of whom testifies to something done by one person, while the other affirms that there were two—it is difficult to see how the principal details here given could apply to more than one case. **3. Who had his dwelling among the tombs.** Luke says, "He ware no clothes, neither abode in any house." These tombs were hewn out of the rocky caves of the locality, and served for shelters and lurking-places (Luke viii. 26). **and no man could bind him, no, not with chains: 4. Because that he had been often bound with fetters and chains, and the chains had been plucked asunder by him, and the fetters broken in pieces.** Luke says (viii. 29) that "often times it (the unclean spirit) had caught him;" and after mentioning how they had vainly tried to bind him with chains and fetters, because "he brake the bands," he adds, "and was driven of the devil (or 'demon') into the wilderness." The dark tyrant-power by which he was held clothed him with superhuman strength, and made him scorn restraint. Matthew (viii. 28) says he was "exceeding fierce, so that no man might pass by that way." He was the terror of the whole locality. **5. And always, night and day, he was in the mountains, and in the tombs, crying, and cutting himself with stones.** Terrible as he was to others, he himself endured untold misery, which sought relief in tears and self-inflicted torture. **6. But when he saw Jesus afar off, he ran and worshipped him**—not with the spontaneous alacrity which says to Jesus, "Draw me, we will *run* after thee," but inwardly compelled, with terrific rapidity, before the Judge, to receive sentence of expulsion. **7. And cried with a loud voice, What have I to do with thee, Jesus, Son of the most high God? I adjure thee by God, that thou torment me not**—or, as in Matt. viii. 29, "Art thou come to torment us before the time?" See on ch. i. 24. Behold the *tormentor* anticipating, dreading, and entreating exemption from *torment!* In Christ they discern their destined Tormentor; the time, they know, is fixed, and they feel as if it were come already! (Jas. ii. 19). **8. (For he said unto him**—that is, before the unclean spirit cried out, **Come out of the man, unclean spirit!)** Ordinarily, obedience to a command of this nature was immediate. But here, a certain delay is permitted, the more signally to manifest the power of Christ and accomplish his purposes. **9. And he asked him, What is thy name?** The object of this question was to extort an acknowledgment of the virulence of demoniacal power by which this victim was enthralled. **And he answered, saying, My name is Legion: for we are many**—or, as in Luke, "because many devils (or 'demons') were entered into him." A legion, in the Roman army, amounted, at its full complement, to six thousand; but here the word is used, as such words with us, and even this one, for an indefinitely large number—large enough however to rush, as soon as permission was given, into two thousand swine and destroy them. **10. And he besought him much that he would not send them away out of the country.** The entreaty, it will be observed, was made by *one spirit*, but in behalf of *many*—"*he* besought Him not to send *them*," &c.—just as in the former verse, "*he* answered *we* are many." But what do they mean by entreating so earnestly not to be ordered out of the country? Their next petition (*v.* 12) will make that clear enough. **11. Now there was there, nigh unto the mountains** [πρὸς τὰ ὄρη]—rather, 'to the mountain' [πρὸς τῷ ὄρει], according to what is clearly the true reading. In Matt. viii. 30 they are said to have been "a good way off." But these expressions, far from being inconsistent, only confirm, by their precision, the minute accuracy of the narrative. **a great herd of swine feeding.** There can hardly be any doubt that the owners of these were Jews, since to them our Lord had now come to proffer His services. This will explain what follows. **12. And all the devils besought him, saying**—"if thou cast us out" (Matt. viii. 31), **Send us into the swine, that we may enter into them.** Had they spoken out all their mind, perhaps this would have been it: 'If we must quit our hold of this man, suffer us to continue our work of mischief in another form, that by entering these swine and thus destroying the people's property, we may steel their hearts against Thee!' **13. And forthwith Jesus gave them leave.** In Matthew this is given with majestic brevity—"Go!" The owners, if Jews, drove an illegal trade; if heathens, they insulted the national religion: in either case the permission was just. **And the unclean spirits went out** (of the man), **and entered into the swine: and the herd ran violently**—or 'rushed' [ὥρμησεν] **down a steep place**—'down the hanging cliff' [κατὰ

the swine: and the herd ran violently down a steep place into the sea,
14 (they were about two thousand,) and were choked in the sea. And
they that fed the swine fled, and told *it* in the city, and in the country.
15 And they went out to see what it was that was done. And they come
to Jesus, and see him that was possessed with the devil, and had the
legion, sitting, and clothed, and [e]in his right mind: and they were afraid.
16 And they that saw *it* told them how it befell to him that was possessed
17 with the devil, and *also* concerning the swine. And [f]they began to pray
18 him to depart out of their coasts. And when he was come into the
ship, he [g]that had been possessed with the devil prayed him that he
19 might be with him. Howbeit Jesus suffered him not, but saith unto
him, Go home to thy friends, and tell them how great things the

A. D. 31.

[e] Rom. 16. 20. 1 John 3. 8.
[f] Gen. 26. 16. Deut. 5. 25. 1 Ki. 17. 18. Job 21. 14. Matt. 8. 34. ch. 1. 24. Acts 16. 39. 1 Cor. 2. 14.
[g] Ps. 116. 12. Luke 8. 38. Luke 17. 15, 17.

τοῦ κρημνοῦ], **into the sea (they were about two thousand.)** The number of them is given by our graphic Evangelist alone. **and were choked in the sea**—or "perished in the waters" (Matt. viii. 32). **14. And they that fed the swine fled, and told it**—"told everything, and what was befallen to the possessed of the devils" (Matt. viii. 33), **in the city, and in the country. And they went out to see what it was that was done.** Thus had they the evidence both of the herdsmen and of their own senses to the reality of both miracles. **15. And they come to Jesus.** Matthew (viii. 34) says, "Behold, the whole city came out to meet Jesus." **and see him that was possessed with the devil**—'the demonized person' [τὸν δαιμονιζόμενον], **and had the legion, sitting**—"at the feet of Jesus," adds Luke (viii. 35); in contrast with his former *wild* and *wandering* habits, **and clothed.** As our Evangelist had not told us that he "ware no clothes," the meaning of this statement could only have been conjectured but for "the beloved physician" (Luke viii. 27), who supplies the missing piece of information here. This is a striking case of what are called *Undesigned Coincidences* amongst the different Evangelists; one of them taking a thing for granted, as familiarly known at the time, but which we should never have known but for one or more of the others, and without the knowledge of which some of their statements would be unintelligible. The clothing which the poor man would feel the want of, the moment his consciousness returned to him, was doubtless supplied to him by some of the Twelve. **and in his right mind**—but now, O in what a lofty sense! (Compare an analogous, though a different kind of case, Dan. iv. 34-37.) **and they were afraid.** Had this been *awe* only, it had been natural enough; but other feelings, alas! of a darker kind, soon showed themselves. **16. And they that saw it told them how it befell to him that was possessed with the devil** ('the demonized person') **and also concerning the swine.** Thus had they the double testimony of the herdsmen and their own senses. **17. And they began to pray him to depart out of their coasts.** Was it the owners only of the valuable property now lost to them that did this? Alas, no! For Luke (viii. 37) says, "Then the whole multitude of the country of the Gadarenes round about besought Him to depart from them; for they were taken [or 'seized'—συνείχοντο] with great fear." The evil spirits had thus, alas! their object. Irritated, the people could not suffer His presence; yet awe-struck, they dared not order Him off: so they entreat Him to withdraw, and—He takes them at their word. **18. And when he was come into the ship, he that had been possessed with the devil** ['he that had been demonized'—the word is not now δαιμονιζόμενος, but δαιμονισθεὶς] **prayed him that he might be with him**—the grateful heart, fresh from the hands of demons, clinging to its wondrous Benefactor. How exquisitely natural! **19. Howbeit Jesus suffered him not, but saith unto him, Go home to thy friends, and tell them how great things the Lord hath done for thee, and hath had compassion on thee.** To be a missionary for Christ, in the region where he was so well known and so long dreaded, was a far nobler calling than to follow Him where nobody had ever heard of Him, and where other trophies not less illustrious could be raised by the same power and grace. **20. And he departed, and began to publish**—not only among his friends, to whom Jesus more immediately sent him, but **in Decapolis**—so called, as being a region of ten cities. (See on Matt. iv. 25.) **how great things Jesus had done for him: and all men did marvel.** Throughout that considerable region did this monument of mercy proclaim his new-found Lord; and some, it is to be hoped, did more than "marvel."

Remarks—1. Nowhere, perhaps, in all the Gospel History does the true Humanity and proper Divinity of the one Lord Jesus Christ come out in sharper, brighter, and, if we might so say, more pre-raphaelite outline than in this Section. Behold here the Prince of preachers. He has finished those glorious parables which He spoke from His boat to the multitudes that lined the shore. The people are dismissed; but though early evening has come, He rests not, but bids the Twelve put out to sea, as He has work to do on the other side. They push off, accordingly, for the eastern side; but have not gone very far when one of those storms to which the lake is subject, but of more than usual violence, arises; and the fishermen, who knew well the element they were on, expecting that their little wherry would upset and send them to the bottom, hasten to their Master. As for Him, the fatigues of the day have come upon Him; and having other occupation awaiting Him at Gadara, He has retired to the stern-end of the vessel, to give Himself up, during the passage across, to balmy sleep. So deep is that sleep, that neither howling winds nor dashing waves break in upon it; and in this profound repose the disciples find Him, when in their extremity they come to Him for help. What a picture of innocent Humanity! Why did they disturb Him? Why were they so fearful? Was it possible that *He* should perish? or—"with Christ in the vessel"—could they? How was it that they had no faith? They were but training. Their faith as yet was but as a grain of mustard seed. But He shall do a thing now that will help it forward. He wakens up at their call; and He who but a moment before was in profound unconsciousness, under the care of His Father, looks around Him and just

20 Lord hath done for thee, and hath had compassion on thee. And he
departed, and [h]began to publish in Decapolis how great things Jesus
had done for him: and all *men* did marvel.

A. D. 31.

[h] Ex. 15. 2. Isa. 63. 7.

gives the word of command, and the raging elements are hushed into an immediate calm. This sleeping and waking Man, it seems, is the Lord of nature. It feels its Maker's presence, it hears His voice, it bows instant submission! The men marvel, but He does not. He is walking amongst His own works, and in commanding them He is breathing His proper element. 'What aileth you?' He exclaims, with sublime placidity amidst their perturbation: 'Have I been so long time with you, and yet ye have not known Me? I have stilled this tempest with a word: Doth that amaze you? Ye shall see greater things than these.' And now they are at the eastern side. But who is that who, descrying Him from a distance as He steps ashore, runs to Him, as if eager to embrace Him? It is a poor victim of Demoniacal malignity. The case is one of unusual virulence and protracted suffering. But the hour of deliverance has at length arrived. Demons, in frightful number, yet all marshalled obediently under one master-spirit, combine to inflict upon their victim all the evil he seems capable of suffering, in mind and in body. But the Lord of devils, stepping forth from that boat, has summoned them to His presence, and in their human victim they stand before Him. Ere they are made to quit their hold, they are forced to tell their number, and while uttering a reluctant testimony to the glory of their destined Tormentor whom they see before them, they are constrained to avow that they have not a spark of sympathy with Him, and utter forth their dread of Him, as if the day of their final doom had come. But with all this—the malignity of their nature nothing abated—they ask permission, if they must quit the higher victim, to take possession of victims of another kind, thereby to gain the same end on even a larger scale and to more fatal purpose. What a spectacle is this! That legion of spirits that were able to defy all the power of men to restrain and to tame their victim, behold them now crouching before one Man, who had never been in that region before, trembling as in the presence of their Judge, conscious that His word, whatever it be, must be law to them, and meekly petitioning, as servants of a master, to be allowed to enter a lower class of victims on letting go their long-secure prey! But the majesty of that word "Go!"—what conscious power over the whole kingdom of darkness does it display! Then their instant obedience, the perfect liberation of the poor demoniac, and the rage and rout with which they rushed upon the creatures they had selected to destroy—all at the word of this Man, newly arrived on the shores of Gadara! But this display of power and majesty Divine was crowned and irradiated by the grace which brought the grateful captive, now set free, to the feet of his Deliverer. What a spectacle was that, on which the eye of all heaven might have rested with wonder—the wild creature, "driven of the devil into the wilderness," whom no man could tame, "sitting at the feet of Jesus;" the man who walked naked, and was not ashamed—like our first parents in Paradise, but, ah! for how different a reason—now "clothed;" the frightful maniac, now "in his right mind," and in an attitude of mute admiration and gratitude and love, at his great Deliverer's feet! Blessed Saviour—fairer than the children of men, yet Thyself the Son of Man—we worship Thee, and yet are not afraid to come near unto Thee: we fall down before Thee, yet we embrace Thee. The Word is God, but the Word has been made flesh and dwells, and will for ever dwell, among us; and of Thy fulness have all we received, who have tasted that Thou art gracious, and grace for grace! 2. Observe the complicated evil which the powers of darkness inflicted on their victim. They deprived him of the exercise of his rational powers; they so lashed his spirit that he could not suffer even a garment upon his body, but went naked, and could not endure the sight of living men and social comfort, but dwelt among the tombs, as if the sepulchral gloom had a mysterious congeniality with the wretchedness of his spirit; they allowed him not a moment's repose even there, for "*always, night and day*, he was in the mountains and in the tombs, crying"—his ceaseless misery venting itself in wild wailing cries; nay, so intolerable was his mental torture, that he "kept cutting himself with stones!"—the *natural* explanation of which seems to be, that one in this state is fain to draw off his feelings from the *mind*, when its anguish grows unendurable, by trying to make the *body*, thus lacerated and smarting, to bear its own share. One other feature of the evil, thus diabolically inflicted, is very significant—"No man could tame him; for he had been often bound with fetters and chains, and the chains had been plucked asunder by him, and the fetters broken in pieces!" And now, suppose ye that this man was a sinner above all sinners, because he suffered such things? Nay (see Luke xiii. 2, 3); but thus was it designed that on the theatre of the *body* we should see affectingly exhibited what the powers of darkness are, when uncontrolled, and what men have to expect from them when once given into their hand! Human *reason* they cannot abide, for it is a light shining full upon their own darkness. Human *liberty*, which is one with *law*, in its highest state—"the perfect *law* of *liberty*"—this they hate, substituting for it a wild anarchy, that can submit to no rational control. Human *peace* they cannot endure, for they have lost their own—"There is no peace to the wicked." For the same reason, human *comfort*, in any the least and lowest of its forms, they will never leave, if they can take it away. And over the howlings and self-inflicted tortures of their maddened victims they sing the dance of death, saying to all their complaints and appeals for sympathy, with the chief priests to Judas, "What is that to us? see thou to that!" 3. Is it so? Then, O the blessedness of being delivered from the power of darkness, and "translated into the Kingdom of God's dear Son"! (Col. i. 13). Till then we are as helpless captives of "the rulers of the darkness of this world, the spirit that now worketh in the children of disobedience," as was this poor demoniac before Jesus came to him. The strong man armed guardeth his palace, and his goods are in peace, until the Stronger than he doth come upon him, and taketh from him all his armour, dividing his spoil (Luke xi. 21, 22). It is a deadly struggle between Heaven and Hell for the possession of man. Only, since Demoniacal possession deprives its victims of their personal consciousness, rational considerations are not in the least instrumental to their deliverance, which must come by a sheer act of divine power; whereas the *soul* is rescued from the tyranny of Satan by the eyes of the understanding being divinely opened to see its wretched condition and descry the remedy, and the heart being drawn

21 And [i]when Jesus was passed over again by ship unto the other side,
22 much people gathered unto him: and he was nigh unto the sea. And,
[j]behold, there cometh one of the rulers of the synagogue, Jairus by name;
23 and when he saw him, he fell at his feet, and besought him greatly, saying,
My little daughter lieth at the point of death: *I pray thee,* come and
24 lay thy hands on her, that she may be healed; and she shall live. And
Jesus went with him; and much people followed him, and thronged
him.
25 And a certain woman, [k]which had an issue of blood twelve years,
26 and had suffered many things of many physicians, and had spent all that
27 she had, and [l]was nothing bettered, but rather grew worse, when she had

A. D. 31.
i Gen. 49. 10. Matt. 9. 1. Luke 8. 37.
j Matt. 9. 18. Luke 8. 40. Luke 13. 14. Acts 13. 15. Acts 18. 8, 17.
k Lev. 15. 25. Matt. 9. 20. Luke 8. 43.
l Ps. 108. 12.

willingly to embrace it. "The God of this world hath blinded the minds of them that believe not, lest the light of the glorious Gospel of Christ, who is the image of God, should shine unto them. But God, who commanded the light to shine out of darkness, shines in our hearts, to give the light of the knowledge of the glory of God in the face of Jesus Christ" (2 Cor. iv. 4, 6). Thus are we, in our deliverance from the power of Satan and of sin, sweetly voluntary, while the deliverance itself is as truly divine as when Jesus uttered His majestic "Go" to the demons of darkness and the demoniac was freed. 4. In this grateful soul's petition to be with Jesus, we see the clinging feeling of all Christ's freed-men towards Himself; while in his departure, when Jesus suggested something better, and in his itineracy through Decapolis with the story of his deliverance, himself a living story of the grace and power of the Lord Jesus, we may read these words:—*The liberated believer a missionary for Christ!* 5. As Christ took those wretched Gadarenes at their word, when they besought Him to depart out of their coasts, so it is to be feared He still does to not a few who, when He comes to them in mercy, bid Him away. Will not awakened sinners dread this, and welcome Him whilst it is called To-day?

21-43.—The Daughter of Jairus Raised to Life—The Woman with an Issue of Blood Healed. (= Matt. ix. 18-26; Luke viii. 41-56.) The occasion of this scene will appear presently.

Jairus' Daughter (21-24). **21. And when Jesus was passed over again by ship unto the other side**—from the Gadarene side of the lake, where He had parted with the healed demoniac, to the west side, at Capernaum—**much people gathered unto him**—who "gladly received Him; for they were all waiting for Him" (Luke viii. 40). The abundant teaching of that day (ch. iv. 1, &c., and Matt. xiii.) had only whetted the people's appetite; and disappointed, as would seem, that He had left them in the evening to cross the lake, they remain hanging about the beach, having got a hint, probably through some of His disciples, that He would be back the same evening. Perhaps they witnessed at a distance the sudden calming of the tempest. The tide of our Lord's popularity was now fast rising. **and he was nigh unto the sea. 22. And, behold, there cometh one of the rulers of the synagogue**—of which class there were but few who believed in Jesus (John vii. 48). One would suppose from this that the ruler had been with the multitude on the shore, anxiously awaiting the return of Jesus, and immediately on His arrival had accosted Him as here related. But Matthew (ix. 18) tells us that the ruler came to Him while He was in the act of speaking at his own table on the subject of fasting; and as we must suppose that this converted publican ought to know what took place on that memorable occasion when he made a feast to his Lord, we conclude that here the right order is indicated by the First Evangelist alone. **Jairus by name** [Ἰάειρος]—or 'Jaeirus.' It is the same name as *Jair,* in the Old Testament (Num. xxxii. 41; Jud. x. 3; Esth. ii. 5). **and when he saw him, he fell at his feet**—in Matthew (ix. 18), "worshipped Him." The meaning is the same in both. **23. And besought him greatly, saying, My little daughter** [θυγάτριον]. Luke (viii. 42) says, "He had one only daughter, about twelve years of age." According to a well-known rabbin, quoted by *Lightfoot,* a daughter, till she had completed her twelfth year, was called 'little,' or 'a little maid;' after that, 'a young woman.' **lieth at the point of death.** Matthew gives it thus: "My daughter is even now dead" [ἄρτι ἐτελεύτησεν]—'has just expired.' The news of her death reached the father after the cure of the woman with the issue of blood; but Matthew's brief account gives only the *result,* as in the case of the centurion's servant, (Matt. viii. 5, &c.) **come and lay thy hands on her, that she may be healed; and she shall live** [ζήσεται]—or, 'that she may be healed and live' [ζήσῃ], according to a fully preferable reading. In one of the class to which this man belonged, so steeped in prejudice, such faith would imply more than in others.

The Woman with an Issue of Blood Healed (24-34). **24. And Jesus went with him; and much people followed him, and thronged him** [συνέθλιβον]. The word in Luke is stronger [συνέπνιγον]—'choked,' 'stifled Him.' **25. And a certain woman, which had an issue of blood twelve years, 26. And had suffered many things of many physicians** [πολλὰ παθοῦσα]. The expression perhaps does not necessarily refer to the suffering she endured under medical treatment, but to the much varied treatment which she underwent. **and had spent all that she had, and was nothing bettered, but rather grew worse.** Pitiable case, and affectingly aggravated; emblem of our natural state as fallen creatures (Ezek. xvi. 5, 6), and illustrating the worse than vanity of all human remedies for spiritual maladies (Hos. v. 13). The higher design of all our Lord's miracles of healing irresistibly suggests this way of viewing the present case, the propriety of which will still more appear as we proceed. **27. When she had heard of Jesus, came.** This was the right experiment at last. What had she "heard of Jesus"? No doubt it was His marvellous cures she had heard of; and the hearing of these, in connection with her bitter experience of the vanity of applying to any other, had been blessed to the kindling in her soul of a firm confidence that He who had so willingly wrought such cures on others was able and would not refuse to heal her also. **in the press behind**—shrinking, yet seeking, **and touched his garment.** According to the ceremonial law, the touch of any one having the disease which this woman had would have defiled the person touched. Some think that the

28 heard of Jesus, came in the press behind, and [m]touched his garment. For
29 she said, If I may touch but his clothes, I shall be whole. And [n]straight-
way the fountain of her blood was dried up; and she felt in *her* body that
30 she was healed of that plague. And Jesus, immediately knowing in
himself that [o]virtue had gone out of him, turned him about in the press,
31 and said, Who touched my clothes? And his disciples said unto him,
Thou seest the multitude thronging thee, and sayest thou, Who touched
32 me? And he looked round about to see her that had done this thing.
33 But the woman, fearing and trembling, knowing what was done in her,
34 came and fell down before him, and told him all the truth. And he said
unto her, Daughter, [p]thy faith hath made thee whole; go in peace, and
be whole of thy plague.
35 While [q]he yet spake, there came from the ruler of the synagogue's
house certain which said, Thy daughter is dead: why troublest thou the
36 Master any further? As soon as Jesus heard the word that was spoken,
he saith unto the ruler of the synagogue, [r]Be not afraid, only believe.
37 And he suffered no man to follow him, save Peter, and James, and John
38 the brother of James. And he cometh to the house of the ruler of the
synagogue, and seeth the tumult, and them that wept and wailed greatly.

A. D. 31.
m ch. 3. 10. Acts 5. 15. Acts 19. 12.
n Ex. 15. 26. Luke 6. 19. Luke 8. 46.
o Luke 6. 19. Luke 8. 46.
p Matt. 9. 22. ch. 10. 52. Luke 7. 50. Luke 8. 48. Luke 17.19. Luke 18. 42. Acts 14. 9.
q Luke 8. 49.
r 2 Chr. 20. 20. Ps. 103. 13. Matt. 9. 28, 29. Matt. 17. 20. Luke 8. 50. John 11. 25, 40.

recollection of this may account for her stealthily approaching Him in the crowd behind, and touching but the hem of His garment. But there was an instinct in the faith which brought her to Jesus, which taught her, that if that touch could set her free from the defiling disease itself, it was impossible to communicate defilement to Him, and that this wondrous Healer must be above such laws. **28. For she said**—"within herself" (Matt. ix. 21), **If I may touch but his clothes, I shall be whole**—that is, if I may but *come in contact* with this glorious Healer *at all*. Remarkable faith this! **29. And straightway the fountain of her blood was dried up.** Not only was "her issue of blood stanched" (Luke viii. 44), but the cause of it was thoroughly removed, insomuch that by her bodily sensations she immediately knew herself perfectly cured. **and she felt in her body that she was healed of that plague. 30. And Jesus, immediately knowing in himself that virtue**—or 'efficacy' [δύναμιν]—**had gone out of him.** He was conscious of the forth-going of His healing power, which was not—as in prophets and apostles—something *foreign to Himself* and imparted merely, but what He had *dwelling within Him* as "His own fulness." **turned him about in the press**—'or crowd' [ἐν τῷ ὄχλῳ]—**and said, Who touched my clothes? 31. And his disciples said unto him.** Luke says (viii. 45), "When all denied, Peter and they that were with Him, said, Master" ['Επιστάτα], **Thou seest the multitude thronging thee, and sayest thou, Who touched me?** 'Askest thou, Lord, who touched Thee? Rather ask who touched Thee *not* in such a throng.' "And Jesus said, Somebody hath touched me"—'a certain person hath touched Me ["Ηψατό μου τίς], "for I perceive that virtue is gone out of Me" (Luke viii. 46). Yes, the multitude "*thronged* and *pressed* Him"—they *jostled against* Him, but all *involuntarily;* they were merely *carried along;* but one, one only—"a certain person—TOUCHED HIM," with the conscious, voluntary, dependent touch of faith, reaching forth its hand expressly to have contact with Him. This and this only Jesus acknowledges and seeks out. Even so, as *Augustin* long ago said, *multitudes still come similarly close to Christ in the means of grace, but all to no purpose, being only sucked into the crowd.* The voluntary, living contact of faith is that electric conductor which alone draws virtue out of Him.

32. And he looked round about to see her that had done this thing—not for the purpose of summoning forth a culprit, but, as we shall presently see, to obtain from the healed one a testimony to what He had done for her. **33. But the woman, fearing and trembling, knowing what was done in her**—alarmed, as a humble, shrinking female would naturally be, at the necessity of so public an exposure of herself, yet conscious that she had a tale to tell which would speak for her. **came and fell down before him, and told him all the truth.** In Luke (viii. 47) it is, "When the woman saw that she was not hid, she came trembling, and falling down before Him, she declared unto Him before all the people for what cause she had touched Him, and how she was healed immediately." This, though it tried the modesty of the believing woman, was just what Christ wanted in dragging her forth, her public testimony to the facts of her case—the disease with her abortive efforts at a cure, and the instantaneous and perfect relief which her touching the Great Healer had brought her. **34. And he said unto her, Daughter**—"be of good comfort" (Luke viii. 48), **thy faith hath made thee whole; go in peace, and be whole of thy plague.** Though healed as soon as she believed, it seemed to her a stolen cure—she feared to acknowledge it. Jesus therefore sets His royal seal upon it. But what a glorious dismissal from the lips of Him who is "our Peace" is that, "Go in peace!"

Jairus' Daughter Raised to Life (35-43). **35. While he yet spake, there came from the ruler of the synagogue's house certain which said, Thy daughter is dead: why troublest thou the Master**—'the Teacher' [τὸν Διδάσκαλον]—**any further? 36. As soon as Jesus heard the word that was spoken, he saith unto the ruler of the synagogue, Be not afraid, only believe.** Jesus knowing how the heart of the agonized father would sink at the tidings, and the reflections at the *delay* which would be apt to rise in his mind, hastens to reassure him, and in His accustomed style; "Be not afraid, only believe"—words of unchanging preciousness and power! How vividly do such incidents bring out Christ's knowledge of the human heart and tender sympathy! (Heb. iv. 15). **37. And he suffered no man to follow him, save Peter, and James, and John the brother of James.** See on ch. i. 29. **38. And he cometh**—rather 'they

39 And when he was come in, he saith unto them, Why make ye this ado,
40 and weep? the damsel is not dead, but [s]sleepeth. And they laughed
him to scorn. [t]But when he had put them all out, he taketh the father
and the mother of the damsel, and them that were with him, and entereth
41 in where the damsel was lying. And he took the damsel by the hand,
and said unto her, Talitha cumi; which is, being interpreted, Damsel, I
42 say unto thee, arise. And [u]straightway the damsel arose, and walked;
for she was *of the age* of twelve years. And they were astonished with a
43 great astonishment. And [v]he charged them straitly that no man should
know it; and commanded that something should be given her to eat.

A. D. 31.

s John 11.11. Acts 20. 10. 1 Cor. 11. 30. 1 Thes. 4. 14. 1 Thes. 5. 10.
t Acts 9. 40.
u Ps. 33. 9.
v Matt. 12. 16. Matt. 17. 9. ch. 3. 12. Luke 5. 14.

come' [ἔρχονται has much better support than ἔρχεται]—**to the house of the ruler of the synagogue, and seeth the tumult, and them that wept and wailed greatly**—"the minstrels and the people making a noise" (Matt. ix. 23)—lamenting for the dead. (See 2 Chr. xxxv. 25; Jer. ix. 20; Am. v. 16.) **39. And when he was come in, he saith unto them, Why make ye this ado, and weep? the damsel is not dead, but sleepeth**—so brief her state of death as to be more like a short sleep. **40. And they laughed him to scorn** [κατεγέλων αὐτοῦ]—rather, simply, 'laughed at Him'—"knowing that she was dead" (Luke viii. 53); an important testimony this to the reality of her death. **But when he had put them all out.** The word is strong [ἐκβαλὼν]—'when he had put,' or 'turned them all out;' meaning all those who were making this noise, and any others that may have been there from sympathy, that only those might be present who were most nearly concerned, and those whom He had Himself brought as witnesses of the great act about to be done. **he taketh the father and the mother of the damsel, and them that were with him** (Peter, and James, and John), **and entereth in where the damsel was lying. 41. And he took the damsel by the hand**—as He did Peter's mother-in-law (ch. i. 31)—**and said unto her, Talitha cumi.** The words are Aramaic, or Syro-Chaldaic, the then language of Palestine. Mark loves to give such wonderful words just as they were spoken. See ch. vii. 34; xiv. 36. ['Cūm' is evidently the true reading, being the popular form of the other, to which it has been corrected as the more accurate form = טְלִיתָא קוּמִי]. **42. And straightway the damsel** [τὸ κοράσιον]. The word here is different from that in *vv.* 39, 40, 41 [τὸ παιδίον], and signifies 'young maiden,' or 'little girl.' **arose, and walked**—a vivid touch evidently from an eye-witness—**for she was of the age of twelve years. And they were astonished with a great astonishment** [ἐξέστησαν ἐκστάσει μεγάλῃ]. The language here is the strongest. **43. And he charged them straitly**—or strictly, **that no man should know it.** The only reason we can assign for this is His desire not to let the public feeling regarding Him come too precipitately to a crisis. **and commanded that something should be given her to eat**—in token of perfect restoration.

Remarks.—1. Burdened soul, wearied and wasted with an inward malady which has baffled every human specific, and forced thee to say from bitter experience of those who have recommended change of air and scene, business, pleasure, travel, and the like—'Miserable comforters are ye all, forgers of lies, physicians of no value!' hast thou not "heard of Jesus"—what miracles of healing, what wonders of transformation He has wrought in some of the most obstinate and hopeless cases; opening blind eyes, casting out devils, cleansing lepers, making the lame man to leap as an hart, and the tongue of the dumb to sing? Bring thy case to Him at last, and doubt not His power to bring thee a perfect cure who said to such as Thou, "They that be whole need not a physician: I came not to call the righteous, but sinners." But thou art afraid to show thyself, lest they who knew thy reckless life should say of thee jeeringly, Is Saul also among the prophets? Come, then, in the press behind, and do but touch Him, and thou shalt instantly feel the virtue that has gone out of Him. It needeth not a close embrace, or vehement handling, or much ado. It is *living contact*, the simple *touch of faith*, that fetches out the healing virtue. And it will tell its own tale. Thou shalt know the difference between Christ and all other healers; and when Jesus calls for thy testimony to His power and grace, thou shalt have something to say, thou shalt have a tale to tell, which will glorify His name and be His desired reward; thou shalt be fain to say, "Come, all ye that fear God, and I will declare what He hath done for my soul." 2. Dumb debtors to healing mercy, be rebuked by the narrative of the Lord's procedure towards this healed woman. He suffered her not, as doubtless she would have preferred, to depart in silence, to pour out her secret thanksgivings, or at some private meeting to testify her love to Jesus. He would have her, in spite of her shrinking modesty, to come forward before all and declare what she had done and how she had sped. Thus, in her own way, was she a preacher of Christ. And such witness will He have from all His saved ones. "If thou shalt *confess with thy mouth* the Lord Jesus, and believe in thine heart that God hath raised Him from the dead, thou shalt be saved." 3. Amidst the multitudes who crowd—with no spiritual desires and to no saving purpose—around the Saviour, in the services of His house and the profession of His name, He discerns the timid, tremulous touch of faith in even one believing soul, and is conscious of the healing virtue which that touch has drawn resistlessly forth from Him. What encouragement this to such as fear that their worthless feelings and poor exercises will have no interest for Him; and what a warning to those who, without wanting anything from Him, suffer themselves to be sucked into the current of those who follow Him and crowd about Him—not to set any store by this, as if it would draw more of Christ's regard towards them at the great day than if they had never heard of His name. (See on Luke xiii. 26, 27.) For see how, taking no notice of all that thronged Him and pressed upon Him on this occasion, He exclaimed of this humble, believing woman, "Some *one* hath touched Me." 4. If the Lord Jesus was so tender and considerate of human feelings as to anticipate this believing ruler's regret that by being so slow of coming to him his darling child had been allowed to die—bidding him, "Fear not, only believe"—just as He had before quelled the storm ere He rebuked the unbelief of His disciples in the view of it (see on *v.* 24)—we may rest well assured that on the right hand of the Majesty in the heavens

6 AND [a]he went out from thence, and came into his own country; and
2 his disciples follow him. And when the sabbath day was come, he began
to teach in the synagogue: and many hearing *him* were astonished,
saying, [b]From whence hath this *man* these things? and what wisdom *is*
this which is given unto him, that even such mighty works are wrought
3 by his hands? Is [c]not this the carpenter, the son of Mary, [d]the brother
of James, and Joses, and of Juda, and Simon? and are not his sisters
4 here with us? And they [e]were offended at him. But Jesus said unto
them, [f]A prophet is not without honour, but in his own country, and
5 among his own kin, and in his own house. And [g]he could there do no
mighty work, save that he laid his hands upon a few sick folk, and healed
6 *them.* And [h]he marvelled because of their unbelief. [i]And he went
round about the villages, teaching.
7 And [j]he called *unto him* the twelve, and began to send them forth by
8 two and two; and gave them power over unclean spirits; and commanded
them that they should take nothing for *their* journey, save a staff only;
9 no scrip, no bread, no [1]money in *their* purse: but [k]*be* shod with sandals;
10 and not put on two coats. And [l]he said unto them, In what place soever
11 ye enter into an house, there abide till ye depart from that place. And
[m]whosoever shall not receive you, nor hear you, when ye depart thence,
shake [n]off the dust under your feet for a testimony against them. [o]Verily
I say unto you, It shall be more tolerable for Sodom [2]and Gomorrha in
12 the day of judgment, than for that city. And they went out, and
13 preached that men should repent. And they cast out many devils, [p]and
anointed with oil many that were sick, and healed *them.*
14 And [q]king Herod heard *of him;* (for his name was spread abroad:) and
he said, That John the Baptist was risen from the dead, and therefore
15 mighty works do show forth themselves in him. Others [r]said, That it is
Elias. And others said, That it is a prophet, or as one of the prophets.
16 But [s]when Herod heard *thereof,* he said, It is John, whom I beheaded:
he is risen from the dead.
17 For Herod himself had sent forth and laid hold upon John, and

A. D. 31.

CHAP. 6.
[a] Matt. 13.54.
[b] John 6. 42.
[c] Isa. 53. 2, 3.
[d] Matt. 12.46.
[e] Matt. 11. 6.
[f] Matt. 13.57.
[g] Gen. 19. 22.
[h] Isa. 59. 1, 2, 16.
[i] Matt. 9. 35.
[j] Matt. 10. 1.
[1] The word signifieth a piece of brass money, in value somewhat less than a farthing, Matt. 10. 9; but here it is taken in general for money. Luke 9. 3.
[k] Acts 12. 8.
[l] Matt. 10.11. Luke 9. 4.
[m] Matt. 10.14. Luke 10.10.
[n] Acts 13. 51.
[o] Heb. 10. 31.
[2] or.
[p] Jas. 5. 14.
[q] Matt. 14. 1. Luke 9. 7.
[r] Matt 16.14. ch. 8. 28.
[s] Luke 3. 19.

"we have not an High Priest which cannot be touched with the feeling of our infirmities," and that still, as in the days of His flesh, "He will not break the bruised reed." 5. Of the three resuscitations to life, recorded in the Gospel History, it is worthy of notice that one was *newly dead*—Jairus' daughter; another, *on his way to the grave*—the widow of Nain's son; and the third—Lazarus—was *dead four days*, was in his grave, insomuch that his sister said, "By this time he stinketh:" as if to teach us that it matters not how long we have lain in the state of death—whether three or four score years in spiritual death, or thousands of years in death temporal—the Spirit of life in Christ Jesus is as able to quicken us at one stage as at another. "Said I not unto thee, that, if thou wouldest believe, thou shouldest see the glory of God? I am the Resurrection and the Life: he that believeth in Me, though he were dead, yet shall he live: and he that liveth and believeth in Me shall never die." 6. Though when the classical writers (euphemistically) liken death to a sleep, we may please ourselves with the hope that the gleams of a future state were never quite extinguished in the heathen mind, it is only in the light of this incomparable Gospel History, interpreted by the teaching of the Pentecostal Gift, that faith hears Jesus saying of every dead believer of the one sex, "The damsel is not dead, but sleepeth," and of the other, "Our friend Lazarus sleepeth; but I go, that I may awake him out of sleep."

CHAP. VI. 1-6.—CHRIST REJECTED AT NAZARETH. (= Matt. xiii. 54-58; Luke iv. 16-30.) For the exposition, see on Luke iv. 16-30.

7-13.—MISSION OF THE TWELVE APOSTLES. (= Matt. x. 1, 5-15; Luke ix. 1-6.) For the exposition, see on Matt. x. 1, 5-15.

14-29.—HEROD THINKS JESUS A RESURRECTION OF THE MURDERED BAPTIST—ACCOUNT OF HIS DEATH. (= Matt. xiv. 1-12; Luke ix. 7-9.)

Herod's View of Christ (14-16). **14. And king Herod**—that is, Herod Antipas, one of the three sons of Herod the Great, and own brother of Archelaus (Matt. ii. 22), who ruled as *Ethnarch* over Galilee and Perea. **heard of him; (for his name was spread abroad:) and he said**—"unto his servants" (Matt. xiv. 2), his councillors or court-ministers, **That John the Baptist was risen from the dead, and therefore mighty works do show forth themselves in him.** The murdered prophet haunted his guilty breast like a spectre, and seemed to him alive again and clothed with unearthly powers, in the person of Jesus. **15. Others said, That it is Elias. And others, That it is a prophet, or as one of the prophets.** See on Matt. xvi. 14. **16. But when Herod heard thereof, he said, It is John, whom I beheaded: he is risen from the dead.** [αὐτὸς]—'Himself has risen;' as if the innocence and sanctity of his faithful reprover had not suffered that he should lie long dead.

Account of the Baptist's Imprisonment and Death (17-29). **17. For Herod himself had sent forth, and laid hold upon John, and bound him**

bound him in prison for Herodias' sake, his brother Philip's wife;
18 for he had married her. For John had said unto Herod, [t] It is not
19 lawful for thee to have thy brother's wife. Therefore Herodias had
[3] a quarrel against him, and would have killed him; but she could not:
20 for Herod [u] feared John, knowing that he was a just man and an holy,
and [4] observed him; and when he heard him, he did many things,
21 and heard him gladly. And [v] when a convenient day was come, that
Herod, [w] on his birth day, made a supper to his lords, high captains, and
22 chief *estates* of Galilee; and when [x] the daughter of the said Herodias
came in, and danced, and pleased Herod and them that sat with him,
the king said unto the damsel, Ask of me whatsoever thou wilt, and I
23 will give *it* thee. And he sware unto her, [y] Whatsoever thou shalt ask
24 of me, I will give *it* thee, unto the half of my kingdom. And she went
forth, and said unto her mother, What shall I ask? And she said, The
25 [z] head of John the Baptist. And she came in straightway with haste
unto the king, and asked, saying, I will that thou give me by and by in
26 a charger the head of John the Baptist. And the king was exceeding
sorry; *yet* for his oath's sake, and for their sakes which sat with him, he
27 would not reject her. And immediately the king sent [5] an executioner,

A. D. 32.

[t] Lev. 18. 16. Lev. 20. 21. 2 Sam. 12.7. Dan. 5. 22, 23. Eph. 5. 11. 2 Tim. 4. 2. Heb. 13. 4.
[3] Or, an inward grudge.
[u] Matt. 14. 5. Matt. 21.26.
[4] Or, kept him, or, saved him.
[v] Matt. 14. 6.
[w] Gen. 40. 20.
[x] Esth. 1. 11, 12.
[y] Esth. 5. 3,6.
[z] Pro. 12. 10.
[5] Or, one of his guard.

in prison—in the castle of Machærus, near the southern extremity of Herod's dominions, and adjoining the Dead Sea. (*Joseph.* Antt. xviii. 5, 2). **for Herodias' sake.** She was the grand-daughter of Herod the Great. **his brother Philip's wife**—and therefore the niece of both brothers. This Philip, however, was not the tetrarch of that name mentioned in Luke iii. 1 (see there), but one whose distinctive name was 'Herod Philip,' another son of Herod the Great, who was disinherited by his father. Herod Antipas's own wife was the daughter of Aretas, king of Arabia; but he prevailed on Herodias, his half-brother Philip's wife, to forsake her husband and live with him, on condition, says *Josephus* (Antt. xviii. 5, 1), that he should put away his own wife. This involved him afterwards in war with Aretas, who totally defeated him and destroyed his army, from the effects of which he was never able to recover himself. **18. For John had said unto Herod, It is not lawful for thee to have thy brother's wife.** Noble fidelity! It was not lawful, because Herod's wife and Herodias' husband were both living; and further, because the parties were within the forbidden degrees of consanguinity (see Lev. xx. 21); Herodias being the daughter of Aristobulus, the brother of both Herod and Philip (*Joseph.* xviii. 5, 4). **19. Therefore Herodias had a quarrel against him** [ἐνεῖχεν αὐτῷ]—rather, as in the margin, 'had a grudge against him.' Probably she was too proud to speak to him: still less would she quarrel with him. **and would have killed him; but she could not: 20 For Herod feared John**—but, as *Bengel* notes, John feared not Herod. **knowing that he was a just man and an holy.** Compare the case of Elijah with Ahab, after the murder of Naboth (1 Ki. xxi. 20). **and observed him** [συνετήρει αὐτὸν]—rather, as in the margin, 'kept' or 'saved him:' that is, from the wicked designs of Herodias, who had been watching for some pretext to get Herod entangled and committed to despatch him. **and when he heard him, he did many things**—many good things under the influence of the Baptist on his conscience; **and heard him gladly**—a striking statement this, for which we are indebted to our graphic Evangelist alone; illustrating the working of contrary principles in the slaves of passion. But this only shows how far Herodias must have wrought upon him, as Jezebel upon Ahab, that he should at length agree to what his awakened conscience kept him long from executing. **21. And when a convenient day** (for the purposes of Herodias) **was come, that Herod** [γενομένης ἡμέρας εὐκαίρου, ὅτε]—rather, 'A convenient day being come, when Herod,' **on his birth day, made a supper to his lords, high captains, and chief [estates] of Galilee.** This graphic minuteness of detail adds much to the interest of the tragic narrative. **22. And when the daughter of the said Herodias**—that is, her daughter by her proper husband, Herod Philip: Her name was Salome, (*Joseph.* Ib.) **came in, and danced, and pleased Herod and them that sat with him, the king said unto the damsel** [κορασίῳ]—'the girl.' (See on ch. v. 42.) **Ask of me whatsoever thou wilt, and I will give it thee. 23. And he**—the king, so called, but only by courtesy (see on *v.* 14)—**sware unto her, Whatsoever thou shalt ask of me, unto the half of my kingdom.** Those in whom passion and luxury have destroyed self-command will in a capricious moment say and do what in their cool moments they bitterly regret. **24. And she went forth, and said unto her mother, What shall I ask? And she said, The head of John the Baptist.** Abandoned women are more shameless and heartless than men. The Baptist's fidelity marred the pleasures of Herodias, and this was too good an opportunity of getting rid of him to let slip. **25. And she came in straightway with haste unto the king, and asked, saying, I will that thou give me by and by** [ἐξ αὐτῆς]—rather, 'at once,' **in a charger**—or large flat 'trencher' [πίνακι]—**the head of John the Baptist. 26. And the king was exceeding sorry.** With his feelings regarding John, and the truths which so told upon his conscience from that preacher's lips, and after so often and carefully saving him from his paramour's rage, it must have been very galling to find himself at length entrapped by his own rash folly. **yet for his oath's sake.** See how men of no principle, but troublesome conscience, will stick at breaking a rash oath, while yielding to the commission of the worst crimes! **and for their sakes which sat with him**—under the influence of that false shame, which could not brook being thought to be troubled with religious or moral scruples. To how many has this proved a fatal snare! **he would not reject her. 27. And immediately the king sent an executioner** [σπεκουλάτωρα—the true

and commanded his head to be brought: and he went and beheaded him
28 in the prison, and brought his head in a charger, and gave it to the
29 damsel: and the damsel gave it to her mother. And when his disciples
heard *of it*, they came and [a]took up his corpse, and laid it in a tomb.

A. D. 32.

[a] Matt. 14.12. Matt. 27.57-60. Acts 8. 2.

reading is evidently σπεκουλάτορα]—one of the guards in attendance. The word is Roman, denoting one of the Imperial guard. **and commanded his head to be brought: and he went and beheaded him in the prison**—after, it would seem, more than twelve months' imprisonment. Blessed martyr! Dark and cheerless was the end reserved for thee; but now thou hast thy Master's benediction, "Blessed is he whosoever shall not be offended in Me" (Matt. xi. 6), and hast found the life thou gavest away (Matt. x. 39). But where are they in whose skirts is found thy blood? **28. And brought his head in a charger, and gave it to the damsel: and the damsel gave it to her mother.** Herodias did not shed the blood of the stern reprover; she only got it done, and then gloated over it, as it streamed from the trunkless head. The striking analogy to this in the Church of Rome will be noticed in Remark 3, below. **29. And when his disciples heard of it**—that is, the Baptist's own disciples, **they came and took up his corpse, and laid it in a tomb**—"and went and told Jesus" (Matt. xiv. 12). If these disciples had, up to this time, stood apart from Him, as adherents of John (Matt. xi. 2), perhaps they now came to Jesus, not without some secret reflection on Him for His seeming neglect of their master; but perhaps, too, as orphans, to cast in their lot henceforth with the Lord's disciples. How Jesus felt, or what He said, on receiving this intelligence, is not recorded; but He of whom it was said, as He stood by the grave of His friend Lazarus, "Jesus wept," was not likely to receive such intelligence without deep emotion. And one reason why He might not be unwilling that a small body of John's disciples should cling to him to the last, might be to provide some attached friends who should do for his precious body, on a small scale, what was afterwards to be done for His own.

Remarks—1. The truth of the Gospel History is strikingly illustrated in this Section. Had the Life of Christ which it contains been a literary invention, instead of a historical reality, the last thing probably which the writers would have thought of would have been to terminate the life of His honoured forerunner in the way here recorded. When we read it, we at once feel that, to be written, it must have been real. But we turn to the Jewish historian, and in his Antiquities of his nation we find precisely the same account of the Baptist's character, his fidelity to Herod, and his death, which is here given—with just this difference, that *Josephus*, as might be expected, presents rather the public bearings of this event, while our Evangelists treat it solely with reference to the Baptist's connection with his blessed Master. Thus each throws light upon the other. 2. When men in power connect themselves, whether by marriage or otherwise, with unprincipled women, they usually become their tools, and are not unfrequently dragged by them to ruin. Illustrations of this are furnished by history, from the days of that accursed Jezebel, who first drew Ahab into the commission of treason against the God of Israel and the murder of his own subjects, and then hurried him to destruction; and of Herodias, who was the means of imbruing the hands of Herod Antipas in the blood of the saintly Baptist, and was the occasion of that war which proved so fatal to him, down to pretty modern times. And might not the working of the same passions to similar issues be seen in the history of less exalted persons, if only it were written? A warning this, surely, against such unhallowed unions. 3. When we read of Herodias, how she shed, not with her own hand nor by her own immediate order, the blood of this faithful witness for the truth, but only got it done by the secular arm, and how she then gloated over it—we can hardly help thinking that, when the harlot-Church was depicted by the apocalyptic seer, as a "woman drunken with the blood of the saints, and with the blood of the martyrs of Jesus" (Rev. xvii. 6), this bloody adulteress, Herodias, must have sat for her picture. For the apocalyptic woman does not herself shed the blood of saints or martyrs, nor order them to be slain; it is "the beast"—the secular power of apostate Christendom—that makes war against the saints, the faithful witnesses for the truth, and overcomes them, and kills them (Rev. xi. 7; xiii. 7). But yet the "woman" rides this beast, seen as a scarlet-coloured, or bloody, beast (Rev. xvii. 6); the secular power acting according to her dictates, in ridding her of those hateful witnesses against her abominations as a horse obeys his rider; while she herself is represented as drunken with their blood—revelling in her freedom from their withering rebukes. Can so vivid and deep an analogy be quite accidental? 4. Fidelity in testifying against sin, though sometimes rewarded here, is not unfrequently allowed to be borne at the cost of temporal interests, liberty, and even life itself. How easily could He who healed the sick, cleansed the lepers, opened blind eyes, and raised even the dead to life, have interposed for the rescue of His true-hearted servant from the rage of Herodias, that he should not have been deprived of his liberty, and at least that his precious life should be spared! But He did not do it. Instead of this He suffered His public career to be closed by arrest and imprisonment; and after lying long in prison, and without any light as to his prospects—in answer to a deputation which he sent expressly from his prison—He allowed him to seal his testimony with his blood in that gloomy cell, with none to comfort him, and none to witness the deed but the bloody executioner, as if to proclaim to his servants in all time what He had bidden the messengers say to himself, "Blessed is he whosoever shall not be offended in Me." How noble was the answer of the three Hebrew youths to King Nebuchadnezzar, when he threatened them with the burning fiery furnace if they would not fall down and worship the golden image which he had set up—"If it be so, our God whom we serve is able to deliver us from the burning fiery furnace; and he will deliver us out of thine hand, O king. *But if not*, be it known unto thee, O king, that we will not serve thy gods," &c. (Dan. iii. 17, 18). They had full confidence that deliverance would be vouchsafed for the honour of Jehovah's name. But they might in that be mistaken; He might not see it fit to interpose; and "*if not*," then they were prepared to burn for Him: but, deliverance or none, they were resolved not to sin. And that is the spirit in which all Christ's servants should take up their

30 And [b]the apostles gathered themselves together unto Jesus, and told
him all things, both what they had done, and what they had taught.
31 And [c]he said unto them, Come ye yourselves apart into a desert place,
and rest a while: for [d]there were many coming and going, and they had
32 no leisure so much as to eat. And they departed into a desert place by
ship privately.
33 And the people saw them departing, and many knew him, and ran
afoot thither out of all cities, and outwent them, and came together
34 unto him. And [e]Jesus, when he came out, saw much people, and was
moved with compassion toward them, because they were as sheep not
having a shepherd: and [f]he began to teach them many things.
35 And [g]when the day was now far spent, his disciples came unto him,
36 and said, This is a desert place, and now the time *is* far passed: send

A. D. 32.

b Luke 9. 10.
c Matt. 14.13. John 6. 1.
d ch. 3. 20.
e Ps. 86. 15. Ps 111. 4. Ps. 145. 8. Matt. 9. 36. Matt. 14.14. Heb. 4. 15. Heb. 5. 2.
f Isa. 54. 13. Isa. 61. 1. Luke 9. 11.
g Matt. 14.15. Luke 9. 12.

cross; prepared to be nailed to it, if necessary, which it may or may not be—they cannot tell—rather than prove faithless to the Lord Jesus.

30-56.—THE TWELVE, ON THEIR RETURN, HAVING REPORTED THE SUCCESS OF THEIR MISSION, JESUS CROSSES THE SEA OF GALILEE WITH THEM, TEACHES THE PEOPLE, AND MIRACULOUSLY FEEDS THEM TO THE NUMBER OF FIVE THOUSAND—HE SENDS HIS DISCIPLES BY SHIP AGAIN TO THE WESTERN SIDE, WHILE HIMSELF RETURNS AFTERWARDS WALKING ON THE SEA—INCIDENTS ON LANDING. (=Matt. xiv. 13-36; Luke ix. 10-17; John vi. 1-24.)

Here, for the first time, all the four streams of sacred text run parallel. The occasion, and all the circumstances of this grand Section are thus brought before us with a vividness quite remarkable.

Five Thousand Miraculously Fed (30-44). **30. And the apostles gathered themselves together** —probably at Capernaum, on returning from their mission (*vv.* 7-13)—**and told him all things, both what they had done, and what they had taught. 31. And he said, Come ye yourselves apart into a desert place, and rest a while: for there were many coming and going, and they had no leisure so much as to eat.** Observe the various reasons He had for crossing to the other side. First, Matthew (xiv. 13) says, that "when Jesus heard" of the murder of His faithful forerunner—from those attached disciples of his who had taken up his body and laid it in a sepulchre (see on *v.* 29)—"He departed by ship into a desert place apart;" either to avoid some apprehended consequences to Himself, arising from the Baptist's death (Matt. x. 23), or more probably to be able to indulge in those feelings which that affecting event had doubtless awakened, and to which the bustle of the multitude around Him was very unfavourable. Next, since He must have heard the report of the Twelve with the deepest interest, and probably with something of the emotion which He experienced on the return of the Seventy (see on Luke x. 17-22), He sought privacy for undisturbed reflection on this begun preaching and progress of His kingdom. Once more, He was wearied with the multitude of "comers and goers"—depriving Him even of leisure enough to take His food—and wanted *rest:* "Come ye yourselves apart into a desert place, and rest a while," &c. Under the combined influence of all these considerations, our Lord sought this change. **32. And they departed into a desert place by ship privately**—"over the sea of Galilee, which is the sea of Tiberias," says John (vi. 1), the only one of the Evangelists who so fully describes it; the others having written when their readers were supposed to know something of it, while the last wrote for those at a greater distance of time and place. This "desert place" is more definitely described by Luke (ix. 10) as "belonging to the city called Bethsaida." This must not be confounded with the town so called on the western side of the lake (see on Matt. xi. 21). This town lay on its north-eastern side, near where the Jordan empties itself into it; in Gaulonitis, out of the dominions of Herod Antipas, and within the dominions of Philip the Tetrarch (Luke iii. 1), who raised it from a village to a city, and called it *Julias*, in honour of Julia, the daughter of Augustus (*Joseph.* Antt. xviii. 2, 1).

33. And the people—'the multitudes' [οἱ ὄχλοι] **saw them departing, and many knew him.** The true reading would seem to be: 'And many saw them departing, and knew or recognized [them]'—[Καὶ εἶδον αὐτοὺς ὑπάγοντας καὶ ἐπέγνωσαν πολλοί]. **and ran afoot** [πεζῇ]. Here, perhaps, it should be rendered 'by land'—running round by the head of the lake, and taking one of the fords of the river, so as to meet Jesus, who was crossing with the Twelve by ship. **thither out of all cities, and outwent them**—got before them, **and came together unto him.** How exceedingly graphic is this! every touch of it betokening the presence of an eye-witness. John (vi. 3) says, that "Jesus went up into a mountain"—somewhere in that hilly range, the green table-land which skirts the eastern side of the lake. **34. And Jesus, when he came out** of the ship [ἐξελθών]—'having gone on shore.' **saw much people**—'a great multitude' [πολὺν ὄχλον], **and was moved with compassion toward them, because they were as sheep not having a shepherd: and he began to teach them many things.** At the sight of the multitudes who had followed Him by land and even got before Him, He was so moved, as was His wont in such cases, with compassion, because they were like shepherdless sheep, as to forego both privacy and rest that He might minister to them. Here we have an important piece of information from the Fourth Evangelist (John vi. 4), "And the passover, a feast of the Jews, was nigh"—rather, 'Now the passover, the feast of the Jews [ἡ ἑορτή], was nigh.' This accounts for the multitudes that now crowded around Him. They were on their way to keep that festival at Jerusalem. But Jesus did not go up to this festival, as John expressly tells us (ch. vii. 1)—remaining in Galilee, because the ruling Jews sought to kill Him.

35. And when the day was now far spent—"began to wear away" or 'decline,' says Luke (ix. 12), [κλίνειν]. Matthew (xiv. 15) says, "when it was evening;" and yet he mentions a later evening of the same day (*v.* 23). This earlier evening began at three o'clock P.M.; the later began at sunset. **his disciples came unto him, and said, This is a desert place, and now the time is far passed:**

them away, that they may go into the country round about, and into
the villages, and buy themselves bread: for they have nothing to eat.
37 He answered and said unto them, Give ye them to eat. And they say
unto him, [h]Shall we go and buy two hundred [6]pennyworth of bread, and
38 give them to eat? He saith unto them, How many loaves have ye? go
39 and see. And when they knew, they say, [i]Five, and two fishes. And
he commanded them to make all sit down [7]by companies upon the
40 green grass. And they sat down in ranks, by hundreds, and by fifties.
41 And when he had taken the five loaves and the two fishes, he looked up to
heaven, and [j]blessed, and brake the loaves, and gave *them* to his disciples
42 to set before them; and the two fishes divided he among them all. And
43 they did all eat, and were filled. And they took up twelve baskets full of
44 the fragments, and of the fishes. And they that did eat of the loaves
were about five thousand men.
45 And [k]straightway he constrained his disciples to get into the ship, and
to go to the other side before [8]unto Bethsaida, while he sent away the

A. D. 32.

[h] Num. 11. 13, 22.
[6] The Roman penny is sevenpence halfpenny. Matt. 18 28.
[i] Matt. 14. 17. Matt. 15. 34.
[7] banquets, banquets. 1 Cor. 14. 40.
[j] 1 Sam. 9. 13. Matt. 26. 26.
[k] Matt. 14. 22. John 6. 17.
[8] Or, over against Bethsaida.

36. Send them away, that they may go into the country round about, and into the villages, and buy themselves bread: for they have nothing to eat. John tells us (vi. 5, 6) that "Jesus said to Philip, Whence shall we buy bread, that these may eat? (And this He said to prove him: for He Himself knew what He would do.)" The subject may have been introduced by some remark of the disciples; but the precise order and form of what was said by each can hardly be gathered with precision, nor is it of any importance. **37. He answered and said unto them,** "They need not depart" (Matt. xiv. 16), **Give ye them to eat**—doubtless said to prepare them for what was to follow. **And they say unto him, Shall we go and buy two hundred pennyworth of bread, and give them to eat?** "Philip answered Him, Two hundred pennyworth of bread is not sufficient for them, that every one of them may take a little" (John vi. 7). **38. He saith unto them, How many loaves have ye? go and see. And when they knew, they say, Five, and two fishes.** John is more precise and full. "One of his disciples, Andrew, Simon Peter's brother, saith unto Him, There is a lad here which hath five barley loaves and two small fishes: but what are they among so many?" (John vi. 8, 9). Probably this was the whole stock of provisions then at the command of the disciples—no more than enough for one meal to them—and entrusted for the time to this lad. "He said, Bring them hither to me" (Matt. xiv. 18). **39. And he commanded them to make all sit down by companies upon the green grass** [ἐπὶ τῷ χλωρῷ χόρτῳ]—or 'green hay;' the rank grass of those bushy wastes. For, as John (vi. 10) notes, "there was much grass [χόρτος] in the place." **40. And they sat down in ranks, by hundreds, and by fifties.** Doubtless this was to show at a glance the number fed, and to enable all to witness in an orderly manner this glorious miracle. **41. And when he had taken the five loaves and the two fishes, he looked up to heaven.** Thus would the most distant of them see distinctly what He was doing. **and blessed** [εὐλόγησε]. John says, "And when He had given thanks" [εὐχαριστήσας]. The sense is the same. This thanksgiving for the meat, and benediction of it as the food of thousands, was the crisis of the miracle. **and brake the loaves, and gave them to his disciples to set before them**—thus virtually holding forth these men as His future ministers. **and the two fishes divided he among them all. 42. And they did all eat, and were filled.** All the four Evangelists mention this; and John (vi. 11) adds, "and likewise of the fishes, as much as they would"—to show that vast as was the multitude, and scanty the provisions, the meal to each and all of them was a plentiful one. "When they were filled, He said unto His disciples, Gather up the fragments that remain, that nothing be lost" (John vi. 12). This was designed to bring out the whole extent of the miracle. **43. And they took up twelve baskets full of the fragments, and of the fishes.** "Therefore (says John vi. 13), they gathered them together, and filled twelve baskets with the fragments of the five barley loaves, which remained over and above unto them that had eaten." The article here rendered "baskets" [κόφινοι] in all the four narratives was part of the luggage taken by Jews on a journey—to carry, it is said, both their provisions and hay to sleep on, that they might not have to depend on Gentiles, and so run the risk of ceremonial pollution. In this we have a striking corroboration of the truth of the four narratives. Internal evidence renders it clear, we think, that the first three Evangelists wrote independently of each other, though the fourth must have seen all the others. But here, each of the first three Evangelists uses the same word to express the apparently insignificant circumstance, that the baskets employed to gather up the fragments were of the kind which even the Roman satirist, *Juvenal*, knew by the name of *cophĭnus;* while in both the narratives of the feeding of the Four Thousand the baskets used are expressly said to have been of the kind called *spuris.* (See on ch. viii. 19, 20.) **44. And they that did eat of the loaves were [about] five thousand men**—"besides women and children" (Matt. xiv. 21). Of these, however, there would probably not be many; as only the males were obliged to go to the approaching festival. [The word "about"—ὡσεὶ—should be omitted here, as quite void of authority; but in the other three Gospels it certainly belongs to the genuine text.]

Jesus Re-crosses to the Western side of the Lake, Walking on the Sea (45-56). One very important particular given by John alone (vi. 15) introduces this portion: "When Jesus therefore perceived that they would take Him by force, to make Him a king, He departed again into a mountain Himself alone." **45. And straightway he constrained his disciples to get into the ship, and to go to the other side before**—Him—**unto Bethsaida**—Bethsaida of Galilee (John xii. 21). John says they "went over the sea towards Capernaum"—the wind, probably,

46 people. And when he had sent them away, [l]he departed into a mountain
to pray.
47 And when even was come, the ship was in the midst of the sea, and
48 he alone on the land. And he saw them toiling in rowing; for the wind
was contrary unto them: and about the fourth watch of the night he
cometh unto them, walking upon the sea, and would have passed by
49 them. But when they saw him walking upon the sea, they supposed it
50 had been a spirit, and cried out: for they all saw him, and were troubled.
And immediately he talked with them, and saith unto them, [m]Be of good
cheer: it is I; be not afraid.

A. D. 32.

l ch. 1. 35. Matt. 6. 6. Matt. 14.23. Luke 6. 12. John 6. 15. 1 Pet. 2. 21.

m Ps. 23. 4. Isa. 43. 2. Matt. 14.27. Luke 20.19. Luke 24.38. John 6. 19.

occasioning this slight deviation from the direction of Bethsaida. **while he sent away the people** [τόν ὄχλον]—'the multitude.' His object in this was to put an end to the misdirected excitement in His favour (John vi. 15), into which the disciples themselves may have been somewhat drawn. The word "constrained" [ἠνάγκασεν] implies reluctance on their part, perhaps from unwillingness to part with their Master and embark at night, leaving Him alone on the mountain. **46. And when he had sent them away, he departed into a mountain to pray**—thus at length getting that privacy and rest which He had vainly sought during the earlier part of the day; opportunity also to pour out His soul in connection with the extraordinary excitement in His favour that evening—which appears to have marked the zenith of His reputation, for it began to decline the very next day; and a place whence He might watch the disciples on the lake, pray for them in their extremity, and observe the right time for coming to them, in a new manifestation of His glory, on the sea.

47. And when even was come—the later evening (see on *v.* 35). It had come even when the disciples embarked (Matt. xiv. 23; John vi. 16). **the ship was in the midst of the sea, and he alone on the land.** John says (vi. 17), "It was now dark, and Jesus was not come to them." Perhaps they made no great effort to push across at first, having a lingering hope that their Master would yet join them, and so allowed the darkness to come on. "And the sea arose (adds the beloved disciple, vi. 18), by reason of a great wind that blew." **48. And he saw them toiling in rowing; for the wind was contrary unto them**—putting forth all their strength to buffet the waves and bear on against a head-wind, but to little effect. He "saw" this from His mountain-top, and through the darkness of the night, for His heart was all with them: yet would He not go to their relief till His own time came. **and about the fourth watch of the night.** The Jews, who used to divide the night into three watches, latterly adopted the Roman division into four watches, as here. So that, at the rate of three hours to each, the fourth watch, reckoning from six P.M., would be three o'clock in the morning. "So when they had rowed about five and twenty or thirty furlongs" (John vi. 19)—rather more than half-way across. The lake is about seven miles broad at its widest part. So that in eight or nine hours they had only made some three and a-half miles. By this time, therefore, they must have been in a state of exhaustion and despondency bordering on despair; and now at length, having tried them long enough, **he cometh unto them, walking upon the sea**—"and drawing nigh unto the ship" (John vi. 19), **and would have passed by them**—but only in the sense of Luke xxiv. 28; Gen. xxxii. 26: compare Gen. xviii. 3, 5; xlii. 7. **49. But when they saw him walking upon the sea, they supposed it had been a spirit, and cried out**—"for fear" (Matt. xiv. 26). He would appear to them at first like a dark moving speck upon the waters; then as a human figure; but in the dark tempestuous sky, and not dreaming that it could be their Lord, they take it for a spirit. Compare Luke xxiv. 37. **50. For they all saw him, and were troubled. And immediately he talked with them, and saith unto them, Be of good cheer: It is I; be not afraid.** There is something in these two little words—given by Matthew, Mark, and John—"'Tis I" ['Εγώ εἰμι—'I AM'], which from the mouth that spake it and the circumstances in which it was uttered, passes the power of language to express. Here were they in the midst of a raging sea, their little bark the sport of the elements, and with just enough of light to descry an object on the waters which only aggravated their fears. But Jesus deems it enough to dispel all apprehension to let them know that *He was there.* From other lips that "I am" would have merely meant that the person speaking was such a one and not another person. That, surely, would have done little to calm the fears of men expecting every minute, it may be, to go to the bottom. But spoken by One who at that moment was "treading upon the waves of the sea," and was about to hush the raging elements with His word, what was it but the Voice which cried of old in the ears of Israel, even from the days of Moses, "I AM;" "I, EVEN I, AM HE!" Compare John xviii. 5, 6; viii. 58. Now, that word is "made flesh, and dwells among us," uttering itself from beside us in dear familiar tones—"It is the Voice of my Beloved!" How far was this apprehended by these frightened disciples? There was one, we know, in the boat who outstripped all the rest in susceptibility to such sublime appeals. It was not the deep-toned writer of the Fourth Gospel, who, though he lived to soar beyond all the apostles, was as yet too young for prominence, and all unripe. It was Simon-Barjonas.

Here follows a very remarkable and instructive episode, recorded by Matthew alone:—

Peter ventures to Walk upon the Sea (Matt. xiv. 28-32). 28. "And Peter answered Him, and said, Lord, If it be Thou [εἰ Σὺ εἶ—'If Thou art'—responding to his Lord's "I am"], bid me come unto thee on the water;" not '*let* me,' but 'give me the word of *command*' [κέλευσόν με πρός Σε ἐλθεῖν ἐπὶ τὰ ὕδατα]—'command,' or 'order me to come unto Thee upon the waters.' 29. "And He said, Come." Sublime word, issuing from One conscious of power over the raging element, to bid it serve both Himself and whomsoever else He pleased! "And when Peter was come down out of the ship, he walked upon the water"—'waters' [ὕδατα]—"to come to Jesus." 'It was a bold spirit,' says *Bp. Hall*, 'that could wish it; more bold that could act it—not fearing either the softness or the roughness of that uncouth passage.' 30. "But when he saw the wind boisterous, he was afraid; and

51 And he went up unto them into the ship; and the wind ceased: and
they were sore amazed in themselves beyond measure, and wondered.
52 For [n] they considered not *the miracle* of the loaves: for their [o] heart
was hardened.
53 And [p] when they had passed over, they came into the land of Genne-
54 saret, and drew to the shore. And when they were come out of the ship,
55 straightway they knew him, and ran through that whole region round
about, and began to carry about in beds those that were sick, where they

A. D. 32.

[n] ch. 8. 17. Luke 24.25.
[o] Jer. 17. 9. ch. 3. 5. ch. 16. 14. Rom. 8. 7.
[p] Matt. 14.34. Luke 5. 1. John 6. 24.

beginning to sink, he cried, saying, Lord, save me." The wind was as boisterous before, but Peter "*saw*" it not; seeing only the power of Christ, in the lively exercise of faith. Now he "*sees*" the fury of the elements, and immediately the power of Christ to bear him up fades before his view, and this makes him "afraid"—as how could he be otherwise, without any *felt* power to keep him up? He then "begins to sink;" and finally, conscious that his experiment had failed, he casts himself, in a sort of desperate confidence, upon his "Lord" for deliverance! 31. "And immediately Jesus stretched forth His hand, and caught him, and said unto him, O thou of little faith, wherefore didst thou doubt?" *This rebuke was not administered while Peter was sinking, nor till Christ had him by the hand;* first re-invigorating his faith and then with it enabling him again to walk upon the crested wave. Bootless else had been this loving reproof, which owns the *faith* that had ventured on the deep upon the bare word of Christ, but asks why that *distrust* which so quickly marred it? 32. "And when they were come into the ship (Jesus and Peter), the wind ceased."

51. And he went up unto them into the ship. John (vi. 21) says, "Then they willingly received him into the ship" [Ἤθελον οὖν λαβεῖν αὐτὸν]—or rather, 'Then were they willing to receive Him' (with reference to their previous terror); but implying also a glad welcome, their first fears now converted into wonder and delight. "And immediately," adds the beloved disciple, "they were at the land whither they went" [εἰς ἣν ὑπῆγον], or 'were bound.' This additional miracle, for as such it is manifestly related, is recorded by the Fourth Evangelist alone. As the storm was suddenly calmed, so the little bark—propelled by the secret power of the Lord of nature now sailing in it—glided through the now unruffled waters, and, while they were wrapt in wonder at what had happened, not heeding their rapid motion, *was found* at port, to their still further surprise.

"Then are they glad, because at rest
And quiet now they be;
So to the haven He them brings
Which they desired to see."

Matthew (xiv. 33) says, "Then they that were in the ship came (that is, ere they got to land) and worshipped him, saying, Of a truth Thou art the Son of God." But our Evangelist is wonderfully striking. **and the wind ceased: and they were sore amazed in themselves beyond measure, and wondered.** The Evangelist seems hardly to find language strong enough to express their astonishment. [*Tregelles*, on too slight authority, omits altogether the clause, καὶ ἐθαύμαζον—"and wondered"—and brackets the phrase, ἐκ περισσοῦ—"beyond measure,"as of doubtful genuineness; but *Tischendorf* does neither.] **52. For they considered not the miracle of the loaves: for their heart was hardened.** What a singular statement! The meaning seems to be that if they had but "considered (or reflected upon) the miracle of the loaves," wrought but a few hours before, they would have *wondered at nothing* which He might do within the whole circle of power and grace.

Incidents on Landing (53-56). The details here are given with a rich vividness quite peculiar to this charming Gospel. **53. And when they had passed over, they came into the land of Gennesaret**—from which the lake sometimes takes its name, stretching along its western shore. Capernaum was their landing-place (John vi. 24, 25). **and drew to the shore** [προσωρμίσθησαν]—a nautical phrase, nowhere else used in the New Testament. **54. And when they were come out of the ship, straightway they knew him**—"immediately they recognized Him;" that is, the people did. **55. And ran through that whole region round about, and began to carry about in beds those that were sick, where they heard he was.** At this period of our Lord's ministry the popular enthusiasm in His favour was at its height. **56. And whithersoever he entered, into villages, or cities, or country, they laid the sick in the streets, and besought him that they might touch if it were but the border of his garment**—having heard, no doubt, of what the woman with the issue of blood experienced on doing so (ch. v. 25-29), and perhaps of other unrecorded cases of the same nature. **and as many as touched** [him]—or 'it'—the border of His garment, **were made whole.** All this they *continued* to do and to experience while our Lord was in that region [as is implied in the imperfect tenses here employed—εἰσεπορεύετο, ἐτίθουν, παρεκάλουν, ἐσώζοντο]. The *time* corresponds to that mentioned (John vii. 1), when He "walked in Galilee," instead of appearing in Jerusalem at the Passover, "because the Jews," that is, *the rulers*, "sought to kill Him"—while *the people* sought to enthrone Him!

Remarks.—1. What devout and thoughtful reader can have followed the graphic details of this wonderful Section without hearing the tread of Divinity in the footstep and voice, and beholding it in the hands and eyes of that warm, living, tender Humanity whose movements are here recorded? While yet on the western side of the lake, the Twelve return to Him and report the success of their missionary tour. Almost simultaneously with this, tidings reach Him of the foul murder and decent burial of His loving and faithful forerunner. He would fain get alone with the Twelve, after such moving events, but cannot, for the crowds that kept moving about Him. So He bids the Twelve put across to the eastern side, to "rest a while." But the people, dismayed at the sight of His departure, and having no boats, run round by the head of the lake, hastily cross the river, and observing the direction in which His boat made for the land, were there before Him. He pities them as shepherdless sheep, and instead of putting them away, preaches to them, until the decline of the day warns Him to think of the meat that perisheth as now needful for them. The Twelve were for dispersing them in search of victuals, but He bids them supply them with these themselves. But how can they? Let them see what they can

56 heard he was. And whithersoever he entered, into villages, or cities, or
country, they laid the sick in the streets, and besought him that they
[q] might touch if it were but the border of his garment: and as many as
touched [9] him were made whole.

A. D. 32.

q Matt 9. 20. Luke 8. 44. Acts 5. 15.

9 Or, it.

muster. The exact quantity in hand is given with precision by all the four Evangelists. The barley loaves—they are five; and the small fishes, two. But what will these do? They will suffice. Direction is given to make the vast multitude sit down on the rank green grass in orderly form, by hundreds and by fifties. It is done, and He stands forth, we might conceive, within an outer semicircle of thirty hundreds, and an inner semicircle of forty fifties; the women and children by themselves, it may be in groups, still nearer the glorious Provider. All eyes are now fastened upon Him as He took up the five loaves and the two fishes, and looking up to heaven, blessed them as Heaven's bountiful provision for that whole multitude, and then gave them to the Twelve to distribute amongst them. Who can imagine the wonder that would sit upon every countenance, as the thought shot across them, How is this handful to feed even one of the fifties, not to speak of the hundreds? But as they found it passed by the Twelve from rank to rank unexhausted, and the last man, and woman, and child of them fed to the full, and the *leavings*, both of the loaves and of the fishes, greatly more than the whole provision at the first—the baskets filled with these being twelve, and the number fed five thousand, besides women and children—what must they have thought, if they thought at all? It is true, we have faint precursors of this glorious miracle in the doings of *Elijah* (1 Ki. xvii. 14-16), and still more of *Elisha* (2 Ki. iv. 1-7, 42-44); but besides the inferiority of the things done, those prophets acted ever as *servants*, saying, "Thus saith the Lord," when they announced the miracles they were to perform; whereas, the one feature which most struck all who came in contact with Jesus was the air of *Personal authority* with which He ever taught and wrought His miracles, thus standing confessed before the devout and penetrating eye as the *Incarnate Lord of Nature:*

"Here may we sit and dream
Over the heavenly theme,
Till to our soul the former days return;
Till on the grassy bed
Where thousands once He fed,
The world's incarnate Maker we discern."—KEBLE

But the scene changes. The transported multitude, in a frenzy of enthusiasm, are consulting together how they are to hasten His Installation in the regal rights of "the King of Israel," which they now plainly saw Him to be. (What a testimony, by the way, is this to the reality of the miracle—the testimony of five thousand participants of the fruit of the miracle!) They have taken no action, but "knowing their thoughts," He quickly disperses them; and retiring for the night to a solitary mountain-top, overlooking the sea, He there pours out His great soul in prayer, watching at the same time the gathering tempest and the weary struggle of the disciples—whom He made to put out reluctantly to sea without Him—with the contrary wind and the beating waves; until, after some eight hours' trial of them in these perilous circumstances, He rises, descends to the sea, and walks to them, cresting the roaring billows; and when the sight of His dim figure only aggravates their terror and makes them cry out for fear, He bids them be calm and confident, *for it was He*—Himself as unmoved as on dry land and under a serene sky. This reassures them; insomuch that Peter thinks even he would be safe upon the great deep if only JESUS would order him to come to Him upon it. He does it; and for a moment—as he looks to HIM only—the watery element, obedient to its Lord, bears him up. But looking to the angry roar of the wind, as it whisked up the sea, he is ready to be swallowed up, and cries for help to the mighty Lord of the deep, who gives him His hand and steps with him into the ship, when at His presence the storm immediately ceases, and ere they have time to pour forth their astonishment they are in port. The thing which is so amazing here is scarcely so much the absolute *command* which Jesus shows over the elements of nature in all their rage, as *His own perfect ease*, whether in riding upon them or keeping His poor disciple from being swallowed up of them, and gently chiding him for having any fear of the elements so long as HE was with him. Not all the chanting of the Old Testament over Jehovah's power to "raise the stormy wind which lifteth up the waves," and then to "make the storm a calm, so that the waves thereof are still" (Ps. cvii. 25-29, &c.) makes such an impression upon the mind, as the concrete manifestation of it in this sublime narrative. In the one, we hear of Him by the hearing of the ear; in the other, our eye seeth Him. It is like the difference between shadow and substance. Indeed, the one may be regarded as the incarnation of the other. 2. Since all Christ's miracles had a deeper significance than that which appears on the surface of them, we cannot doubt that the multiplication of the loaves, which was one of the most stupendous, has its profound meaning also. We may say, indeed, that as this multitude had made such exertions and sacrifices to be with Jesus and drink in His wonderful teaching, and were not sent empty away, but got more than they expected—even the meat that perisheth, when they seemed to look only for that which endureth to everlasting life—so if we "seek first the kingdom of God and His righteousness, all these things will be added unto us." But this and similar lessons hardly reach the depth of this subject, much less exhaust it. As the Lord Jesus multiplied on this occasion the meat that perisheth, so is the meat that endureth to everlasting life capable of indefinite multiplication. Look at the Scriptures at large; look at the glorious Gospel History; look at this one stupendous Section of it. In bulk, how little is it—like the five barley loaves and the two small fishes it tells of. But what thousands upon thousands has it fed, and will it feed, in every age, in every land of Christendom, to the world's end! And is this true only of inspired Scripture? There, we may say, it is Christ Himself that ministers the bread of life. But just as Elijah and Elisha did something of the same kind—though on a small scale, and with a humble acknowledgment that they were but *servants*, or instruments in the hand of the Lord—so have the ministers of the Lord Jesus been privileged, from a little portion of "the oracles of God," to feed the souls of thousands, and that so richly as to leave baskets of fragments unconsumed. Nor can the writer refrain from testifying to all who read these lines, what a feast of fat things he has found daily for himself as he passed from Section to Section of this wonderful History, exhilarating him amidst the considerable labour which this work involves; nor can he wish anything better for his readers than

7 THEN [a]came together unto him the Pharisees, and certain of the
2 scribes, which came from Jerusalem. And when they saw some of his
disciples eat bread with [1]defiled (that is to say, with unwashen) hands,
3 they found fault. (For the Pharisees, and all the Jews, except they wash
4 *their* hands [2]oft, eat not, holding the tradition of the elders. And *when*
they come from the market, except they wash, they eat not. And many
other things there be which they have received to hold, *as* the washing of
5 cups, and [3]pots, brasen vessels, and of [4]tables.) Then [b]the Pharisees
and scribes asked him, Why walk not thy disciples according to the
6 tradition of the elders, but eat bread with unwashen hands? He answered
and said unto them, Well hath Esaias prophesied of you hypocrites, as it
is written, [c]This people honoureth me with *their* lips, but their heart is
7 far from me. Howbeit in vain do they worship me, teaching *for* doctrines
8 the commandments of men. For, laying aside the commandment of God,
ye hold the tradition of men, *as* the washing of pots and cups: and many
9 other such like things ye do. And he said unto them, Full well ye
[5]reject the commandment of God, that ye may keep your own tradition.
10 For Moses said, [d]Honour thy father and thy mother; and, [e]Whoso
11 curseth father or mother, let him die the death: but ye say, If a man
shall say to his father or mother, *It is* [f]Corban, (that is to say, a gift,)
12 by whatsoever thou mightest be profited by me; *he shall be free.* And
13 ye suffer him no more to do ought for his father or his mother; making

A. D. 32.

CHAP. 7.
[a] Matt. 15. 1.
[1] Or, common.
[2] with the fist, or, diligently. Theophylact, up to the elbow.
[3] Sextarius is about a pint and a half.
[4] Or, beds.
[b] Matt. 15. 2.
[c] Isa. 29. 13. Matt. 15. 8.
[5] Or, frustrate.
[d] Ex. 20. 12. Deut. 5. 16.
[e] Ex. 21. 17. Lev. 20. 9. Pro. 20. 20.
[f] Matt. 15. 5. Matt. 23. 18. 1 Tim. 5. 8.

that they also may have fellowship with him, for truly his fellowship in this bread of life has been with the Father and with His Son Jesus Christ. 3. In these poor disciples, after this day of wonders, we have a picture of the blindness of the best of us ofttimes to the divine purposes and our own mercies. How reluctant were they to put out to sea without their Master; but had He not stayed behind, they had missed—and along with them the Church in all time had missed—the one manifestation of His glory which He saw fit to give in that majestic form, of walking upon the sea, and that too when the waves thereof roared by reason of a mighty wind. Doubtless, when they urged Him to come with them, if He would not let them spend the night with Him on the eastern side, He would assure them that He was *coming after them.* But how little would they dream of what He meant! Anxiously and often would they look back, to see if they could descry any other wherry by which He might have set sail at a later hour; and when, after eight hours' beating against the storm, they found themselves, ere the morning light dawned on them, alone and helpless in the midst of the sea, how would they say one to another, 'O that we had not parted from Him! Would that He were here! When that storm arose as we crossed with Him to the country of the Gadarenes, though He was fast asleep in the stern-end of the ship, how quickly, on our awaking Him, did He hush the winds and calm the sea, even with one word of command; but now, alas, we are alone!' At length they descry a dark object. What can it be? It draws nearer and nearer them; their fears arise; now it is near enough to convince them that it is a living form, in quest of *them.* And what can a living, moving form upon the waters be but a spectre? and what can a spectre want with them? At length, as it approaches them, they shriek out for fear. And yet this is their Beloved, and this is their Friend—so eagerly longed for, but at length despaired of! Thus do we often miscall our chiefest mercies; not only thinking them distant when they are near, but thinking the best the worst. Yes, Jesus was with them all the while, though they knew it not. His heart followed them with His eye, as the storm gathered; though in body far away, in spirit He was with them, giving command to the furious elements to be to them as was the burning fiery furnace to the Hebrew youths when they were in it, and the lions when Daniel was in their den—to do them no hurt. He pitied them as He "saw them toiling in rowing," but for their own sake He would not come to them till the right time. But O what words were those with which He calmed their fears—"Be of good cheer: it is I; be not afraid"! The re-assuring word was that central one "*I*" ['Εγώ]; and after what they had seen of His glory but a few hours before, in addition to all their past experience, what a fulness of relief would be to them wrapt up in that one little word "*I!*" And what else need even we, tossed, and O how often! upon a tempestuous sea—at one time of doubts and fears, at another, of difficulties and wants, at another, of sorrows and sufferings—"toiling in rowing" to beat our way out of them: What need we, to stay our souls when all these waves and billows are going over us, and to cheer us with songs in the night, but to hear that Voice so loving, so divine, "Be of good cheer: IT IS I; be not afraid"! 4. When sure of a divine warrant, what may not faith venture on, and so long as our eye is directed to a present Saviour, what dangers may we not surmount? But when, like Peter, we direct our eye to the raging element, and "see the wind boisterous," fear takes the place of faith; and beginning to sink, our only safety lies in casting our critical case upon Him whose are all the elements of nature and providence and grace. Happy then are we, if we can feel that warm fleshly Hand which caught sinking Peter and immediately ascended with him into the ship! For then are we at once in the haven of rest.

'Thou Framer of the light and dark,
Steer through the tempest thine own ark;
Amid the howling wintry sea
We are in port if we have Thee!'—KEBLE.

CHAP. VII. 1-23.—DISCOURSE ON CEREMONIAL POLLUTION. (= Matt. xv. 1-20.) For the exposition, see on Matt. xv. 1-20.

24-37.—THE SYROPHENICIAN WOMAN AND HER

the word of God of none effect through your tradition, which ye have
delivered: and many such like things do ye.
14 And when he had called all the people *unto him*, he said unto them,
15 Hearken unto me every one *of you*, and understand: there is [g]nothing
from without a man, that entering into him can defile him: but the
16 things which come out of him, those are they that defile the man. If
[h]any man have ears to hear, let him hear.
17 And [i]when he was entered into the house from the people, his disciples
18 asked him concerning the parable. And he saith unto them, Are ye so
without understanding also? Do ye not perceive, that whatsoever thing
19 from without entereth into the man, *it* cannot defile him; because it
entereth not into his heart, but into the belly, and goeth out into the
20 draught, purging all meats? And he said, That which cometh out of
21 the man, that defileth the man. For [j]from within, out of the heart of
22 men, proceed evil thoughts, adulteries, fornications, murders, thefts,
[6]covetousness, wickedness, deceit, lasciviousness, an evil eye, blasphemy,
23 pride, foolishness: all these evil things come from within, and defile the
man.
24 And [k]from thence he arose, and went into the borders of Tyre and
Sidon, and entered into an house, and would have no man know *it:* but
25 he could not be hid. For a *certain* woman, whose young daughter had
26 an unclean spirit, heard of him, and came and fell at his feet: the woman
was a [7]Greek, a Syrophenician by nation; and she besought him that he
would cast forth the devil out of her daughter.
27 But Jesus said unto her, Let [l]the children first be filled: for it is not

A. D. 32.
g Acts 10. 14, 15. Rom 14.17. 1 Cor. 8. 8. 1 Tim. 4. 4. Titus 1. 15.
h Matt. 11.15.
i Matt. 15.15.
j Gen. 6. 5. Gen. 8. 21. Matt. 15.19. Acts 8. 22. Gal. 5. 19.
6 covetousnesses, wickednesses.
k Matt. 15.21.
7 Or, Gentile. Isa. 49. 12. Gal. 3 28. Col. 3. 11.
l Matt. 7. 6. Matt. 10. 5, 6. Matt. 15.23-28. Acts 13. 46. Acts 22. 21. Rom. 9. 4. Eph. 2. 12.

DAUGHTER—A DEAF AND DUMB MAN HEALED. (= Matt. xv. 21-31.)

The Syrophenician Woman and her Daughter (24-30). The first words of this narrative show that the incident followed, in point of time, immediately on what precedes it. **24. And from thence he arose, and went into,** or 'unto' **the borders of Tyre and Sidon**—the two great Phenician seaports, but here denoting the territory generally, to the frontiers of which Jesus now came. But did Jesus actually enter this heathen territory? The whole narrative, we think, proceeds upon the supposition that He did. His immediate object seems to have been to avoid the wrath of the Pharisees at the withering exposure He had just made of their traditional religion. **and entered into an house, and would have no man know it**—because He had not come there to minister to heathens. But though not "*sent* but to the lost sheep of the house of Israel" (Matt. xv. 24), He hindered not the lost sheep of the vast Gentile world from coming to Him, nor put them away when they did come—as this incident was designed to show. **but he could not be hid.** Christ's fame had early spread from Galilee to this very region (ch. iii. 8; Luke vi. 17). **25. For a certain woman, whose young daughter had an unclean spirit**—or, as in Matthew, 'was badly demonized' [κακῶς δαιμονίζεται], **heard of him**—one wonders how; but distress is quick of hearing; **and fell at his feet: 26. The woman was a Greek** [Ἑλληνὶς]—that is, 'a Gentile,' as in the margin; **a Syrophenician by nation**—so called as inhabiting the Phenician tract of Syria. *Juvenal* uses the same term, as was remarked by *Justin Martyr* and *Tertullian.* Matthew calls her "a woman of Canaan"—a more intelligible description to his Jewish readers (cf. Jud. i. 30, 32, 33). **and she besought him that he would cast forth the devil out of her daughter**—"She cried unto him, saying, Have mercy on me, O Lord, Son of David; my daughter is grievously vexed with a devil" (Matt. xv. 22). Thus, though no Israelite herself, she salutes Him as Israel's promised Messiah.

Here we must go to Matt. xv. 23-25, for some important links in the dialogue omitted by our Evangelist. 23. "But He answered her not a word." The design of this was first, perhaps, to show that He was not *sent* to such as she. He had said expressly to the Twelve, "Go not into the way of the Gentiles" (Matt. x. 5); and being now amongst them Himself, He would, for consistency's sake, let it be seen that He had not gone thither for *missionary* purposes. Therefore He not only kept silence, but had actually left the house and—as will presently appear—was proceeding on His way back, when this woman accosted Him. But another reason for keeping silence plainly was to try and to whet her faith, patience, and perseverance. And it had the desired effect: "She *cried after them,*" which shows that He was already on His way from the place. "And His disciples came and besought Him, saying, Send her away; for she crieth after us." They thought her troublesome with her importunate cries, just as they did the people who brought young children to be blessed of Him, and they ask their Lord to "send her away," that is, to grant her request and be rid of her; for we gather from His reply that they meant to solicit favour for her, though not for her sake so much as their own. 24. "But He answered and said, I am not sent but unto the lost sheep of the house of Israel"—a speech evidently intended for the disciples themselves, to satisfy them that, though the grace He was about to show to this Gentile believer was *beyond His strict* commission, He had not gone *spontaneously* to dispense it. Yet did even this speech open a gleam of hope, could she have discerned it. For thus might she have spoken: 'I am not SENT, did He say? Truth, Lord, Thou comest not hither in quest of *us*, but I come in quest of *Thee;* and must I go empty away? So did not the woman of Samaria, whom when Thou foundest her on Thy way

28 meet to take the children's bread, and to cast *it* unto the dogs. And
she answered and said unto him, Yes, Lord: yet the dogs under the
29 table eat of the children's crumbs. And he said unto her, For this
30 saying go thy way; the devil is gone out of thy daughter. And when
she was come to her house, she found [m]the devil gone out, and her
daughter laid upon the bed.
31 And [n]again, departing from the coasts of Tyre and Sidon, he came
unto the sea of Galilee, through the midst of the coasts of Decapolis.
32 And they bring unto him one that was deaf, and had an impediment
33 in his speech; and they beseech him to put his hand upon him. And [o]he
took him aside from the multitude, and put his fingers into his ears, and

A. D. 32.

[m] Jos. 21. 45. Matt. 9. 29. ch. 9. 23. 1 John 3. 8.
[n] Matt. 15. 29.
[o] 1 Ki. 17. 19-22. 2 Ki. 4. 4-6. 2 Ki. 11. 24. Matt. 4. 25. ch. 5. 20. ch. 5. 40. ch. 8. 23.

to Galilee, Thou sentest away to make many rich!' But this our poor Syrophenician could not attain to. What, then, can she answer to such a speech? Nothing. She has reached her lowest depth, her darkest moment; she will just utter her last cry: 25. "Then came she and worshipped Him, saying, Lord, help me!" This appeal, so artless, wrung from the depths of a believing heart, and reminding us of the Publican's "God be merciful to me a sinner," moved the Redeemer at last to break silence—but in what style?

Here we return to our own Evangelist. **27. But Jesus said unto her, Let the children first be filled.** 'Is there hope for me here?' 'Filled FIRST?' 'Then my turn, it seems, *is* coming!—but then, "The CHILDREN first?" Ah! when, on that rule, shall my turn ever come?' But ere she has time for these ponderings of His word, another word comes to supplement it. **for it is not meet to take the children's bread, and to cast it unto the dogs.** Is this the death of her hopes? Nay, but it is life from the dead. Out of the eater shall come forth meat (Jud. xiv. 14). At evening time it shall be light (Zec. xiv. 7). 'Ha! I have it now. Had He kept silence, what could I have done but go unblest? but He hath spoken, and the victory is mine.' **28. And she answered and said unto him, Yes, Lord**—or, as the same word [Ναί] is rendered in Matt. xv. 27, "Truth, Lord," **yet the dogs eat of the children's crumbs**—"which fall from their master's table" (Matt.) 'I thank Thee, O blessed One, for that word! That's my whole case. Not of the children? True. A dog? True also: *Yet* the dogs under the table are allowed to eat of the children's crumbs—the droppings from their master's full table: Give me that, and I am content: One crumb of power and grace from Thy table shall cast the devil out of my daughter.' O what lightning-quickness, what reach of instinctive ingenuity, do we behold in this heathen woman! **29. And he said unto her**—"O woman, great is thy faith" (Matt. xv. 28.) As *Bengel* beautifully remarks, Jesus "marvelled" only at two things—*faith* and *unbelief* (see on Luke vii. 9). **For this saying go thy way; the devil is gone out of thy daughter.** That moment the deed was done. **30. And when she was come to her house, she found the devil gone out, and her daughter laid upon the bed.** But Matthew is more specific: "And her daughter was made whole from that very hour." The wonderfulness of this case in all its features has been felt in every age of the Church, and the balm it has administered, and will yet administer, to millions will be known only in that day that shall reveal the secrets of all hearts.

Deaf and Dumb Man Healed (31-37). **31. And again, departing from the coasts of Tyre and Sidon, he came unto the sea of Galilee**—or, according to what has very strong claims to be regarded as the true text here, 'And again, departing from the coasts of Tyre, He came through Sidon [διὰ Σιδῶνος] to the sea of Galilee.' The MSS. in favour of this reading, though not the most numerous, are weighty, while the versions agreeing with it are among the most ancient; and all the best critical editors and commentators adopt it. In this case we must understand that our Lord, having once gone out of the Holy Land the length of Tyre, proceeded as far north as Sidon, though without ministering, so far as appears, in those parts, and then bent His steps in a south-easterly direction. There is certainly a difficulty in the supposition of so long a *detour* without any missionary object; and some may think this sufficient to cast the balance in favour of the received reading. Be this as it may, on returning from these coasts of Tyre, He passed **through the midst of the coasts**—or frontiers—**of Decapolis**—crossing the Jordan, therefore, and approaching the lake on its east side. Here Matthew, who omits the details of the cure of this deaf and dumb man, introduces some particulars, from which we learn that it was only one of a great number. "And Jesus," says that Evangelist (xv. 29-31), "departed from thence, and came nigh unto the sea of Galilee, and went up into a mountain"—the mountain-range bounding the lake on the north-east, in Decapolis: "And great multitudes came unto Him, having with them lame, blind, dumb, maimed" [κυλλούς]—not 'mutilated,' which is but a secondary sense of the word, but 'deformed'—"and many others, and cast them down at Jesus' feet; and he healed them: insomuch that the multitude"—'the multitudes' [τοὺς ὄχλους]—"wondered, when they saw the dumb to speak, the maimed to be whole, the lame to walk, and the blind to see: and they glorified the God of Israel"—who, after so long and dreary an absence of visible manifestation, had returned to bless His people as of old (compare Luke vii. 16). Beyond this it is not clear from the Evangelist's language that the people saw into the claims of Jesus. Well, of these cases Mark here singles out one, whose cure had something peculiar in it. **32. And they bring unto him one that was deaf, and had an impediment in his speech; and they beseech him to put his hand upon him.** In their eagerness they appear to have been somewhat too officious. Though usually doing as here suggested, He will deal with this case in His own way. **33. And he took him aside from the multitude**—as in another case He "took the blind man by the hand and led him out of the town" (ch. viii. 23), probably to fix his undistracted attention on Himself and, by means of certain actions He was about to do, to awaken and direct his attention to the proper source of relief. **and put his fingers into his ears.** As his indistinct articulation arose from his deafness, our Lord addresses Himself to this first. To the impotent man He said, "Wilt thou be made whole?" to the blind men, "What will ye that I shall do unto you?" and "Believe ye that I am able to do this?"

34 he [p]spit, and touched his tongue; and, [q]looking up to heaven, [r]he sighed,
35 and saith unto him, Ephphatha, that is, Be opened. And [s]straightway
his ears were opened, and the string of his tongue was loosed, and he
36 spake plain. And [t]he charged them that they should tell no man: but
the more he charged them, so much the more a great deal they published
37 *it;* and were beyond measure astonished, saying, He hath done all things
well: he maketh both the deaf to hear, and the dumb to speak.

A. D. 32.

p ch. 8. 23. John 9. 6.
q ch. 6. 41. John 11. 41.
r John 11. 33, 38.
s Ps. 33. 9.
t Isa. 42. 2.

(John v. 6; Matt. xx. 32; ix. 28). But as this patient could *hear* nothing, our Lord substitutes symbolical actions upon each of the organs affected. **and he spit and touched his tongue**—moistening the man's parched tongue with saliva from His own mouth, as if to lubricate the organ or facilitate its free motion; thus indicating the source of the healing virtue to be His own person. (For similar actions, see ch. viii. 23; John ix. 6.) **34. And looking up to heaven**—ever acknowledging His Father, even while the Healing was seen to flow from Himself (see on John v. 19), **he sighed**—'over the wreck,' says *Trench*, 'which sin had brought about, and the malice of the devil in deforming the fair features of God's original creation.' But, we take it, there was a yet more painful impression of that "evil thing and bitter" whence all our ills have sprung, and which, when Himself took our infirmities and bare our sicknesses" (Matt. viii. 17), became mysteriously His own.

> 'In thought of these His brows benign,
> Not even in healing, cloudless shine.'—KEBLE.

and saith unto him, Ephphatha, that is, Be opened. Our Evangelist, as remarked on ch. v. 41, loves to give such wonderful words just as they were spoken. **35. And straightway his ears were opened.** This is mentioned first, as the source of the other derangement. **and the string of his tongue was loosed, and he spake plain.** The cure was thus alike instantaneous and perfect. **36. And he charged them that they should tell no man.** Into this very region He had sent the man out of whom had been cast the legion of devils, to proclaim "what the Lord had done for him" (ch. v. 19). Now He will have them "tell no man." But in the former case there was no danger of obstructing His ministry by "blazing the matter" (ch. i. 45), as He Himself had left the region; whereas now He was sojourning in it. **but the more he charged them, so much the more a great deal they published it.** They could not be restrained; nay, the prohibition seemed only to whet their determination to publish His fame. **37. And were beyond measure astonished, saying, He hath done all things well**—reminding us, says *Trench*, of the words of the first creation (Gen. i. 31, LXX.), upon which we are thus not unsuitably thrown back, for Christ's work is in the truest sense "a new creation." **he maketh both the deaf to hear, and the dumb to speak**—"and they glorified the God of Israel" (Matt. xv. 31). See on *v.* 31 of this chapter.

Remarks.—1. The Syrophenician woman had never witnessed any of Christ's miracles, nor seen His face, but she had "heard of Him." Like the woman with the issue of blood (ch. v. 27), she had heard of His wondrous cures, particularly how He cast out devils; and she probably said within herself, O that He would but come hither, or I could come to Him—which her circumstances did not permit. But now He is within reach, and though desiring concealment, she finds Him out, and implores a cure for her grievously demonized daughter. Instead of immediately meeting her faith, He keeps a mysterious silence; nay, leaves her, and suffers her to cry after Him without uttering a word. Does she now give it up, muttering to herself as she leaves Him, 'It's a false report—He can't do it?' Nay, His silence only redoubles her entreaties, and His withdrawal does but draw her after Him. The disciples—ever studying their Master's ease, rather than penetrating into His deep designs—suggest whether, as she was "troubling Him," it might not be better to throw a cure to her, so to speak, and get rid of her, lest, like the importunate widow, "by her continual coming she weary" Him. His reply seemed to extinguish all hope. "I am not sent but to the lost sheep of the house of Israel." Is not this very like breaking the bruised reed, and quenching the smoking flax? But the bruised reed shall not break, the smoking flax shall not go out. There is a tenacity in her faith which refuses to give up. It seems to hear a voice saying to her—

> 'Know the darkest part of night
> Is before the dawn of light;
> Press along, you're going right,
> Try, try again.'

At His feet she casts herself, with a despairing cry, "Lord, help me!"—as strong in the confidence of His *power*, as now, at the very weakest, of His *willingness*, to give relief. But even as to that willingness, while she clings to hope against hope, what a word does He at length utter—"Let the children first be filled: for it is not meet to take the children's bread, and to cast it unto the dogs." Worse and worse. But her faith is too keen not to see her advantage. That faith of hers is ingenious. 'The children's bread! Ah, yes! that is too good for me. Thou art right, Lord. To take the children's bread, and cast it to a heathen dog like me, is what I dare not ask. It is the dogs' portion only that I ask—the crumbs that fall from the Master's table—from Thy fulness even a crumb is more than sufficient.' Who can wonder at the wonder even of Jesus at this, and His inability any longer to hold out against her? The woman with the issue of blood heard of Jesus, as did this Syrophenician woman, and from the mere report conceived a noble faith in His power to heal her. But that woman was a Jewess, nursed amid religious opportunities and fed on the oracles of God. This woman was born a heathen, and reared under all the disadvantages of a pagan creed. With that woman it was short work: with this one it was tough and trying. Like Jacob of old, she wept and made supplication unto Him; yea, she had power over the Angel, and prevailed. And this has been written for the generations following, that men may say, "I will not let Thee go except Thou bless me." 2. We have in this case an example of that *cross* procedure which Jesus was wont to observe when He only wished to train and draw forth and be gained over by persevering faith. And certainly, never was the invincible tenacity of living faith more touchingly and beautifully educed than here. But for His knowledge where it would all end, that tender, great Heart would

8 IN those days [a]the multitude being very great, and having nothing to
2 eat, Jesus called his disciples *unto him,* and saith unto them, I have
[b]compassion on the multitude, because they have now been with me
3 three days, and have nothing to eat: and if I send them away fasting to
their own houses, they will faint by the way: for divers of them came
4 from far. And his disciples answered him, From whence [c]can a man
5 satisfy these *men* with bread here in the wilderness? And [d]he asked
6 them, How many loaves have ye? And they said, Seven. And he commanded the people to sit down on the ground: and he took the seven
loaves, and [e]gave thanks, and brake, and gave to his disciples to set
7 before *them;* and they did set *them* before the people. And they had a
few small fishes: and he [f]blessed, and commanded to set them also before
8 *them.* So they did eat, and were filled: and they took up of the broken
9 *meat* that was left seven baskets. And they that had eaten were about
four thousand: and he sent them away.

A. D. 32.

CHAP. 8.
[a] Matt. 15. 32.
[b] Ps. 145. 9. Heb. 2. 17. Heb. 4. 15.
[c] Num. 11. 21, 22. 2 Ki. 4. 42, 43. 2 Ki. 7. 2. ch. 6. 52.
[d] Matt. 15. 34. ch. 6. 38.
[e] Deut. 8. 10. ch. 6. 41-44. 1 Tim. 4. 4, 5.
[f] Matt. 14. 19. ch. 6. 41.

never have stood such a melting importunity of true faith, nor have endured to speak to her as He did. And shall we not learn from such cases how to interpret His procedure, when our Joseph "speaks roughly" to His brethren, and seems to treat them so, and yet all the while it is if He would seek where to weep, and He only waits for the right moment for making Himself known unto them? 3. When we read that Jesus sighed over the case of this deaf and dumb man, and groaned and wept over the grave of Lazarus, we have faint glimpses of feelings the depth of which we shall never fathom, and the whole meaning of which it is hard to take in, but of which we know enough to assure us that all the ills that flesh is heir to, and the one root of them—sin—He made His own. And now that He has put away sin by the sacrifice of Himself, and so provided for the rolling away of the complicated ills that have come in its train, He sits in heaven to reap the fruits of Redemption, with all His rich experience of human ill. Shall we not, then, "come boldly to the throne of grace, that we may obtain mercy, and find grace to help in time of need? For we have not an High Priest which cannot be touched by the feeling of our infirmities, but was in all points tempted like as we are, yet without sin."

CHAP. VIII. 1-26.—FOUR THOUSAND MIRACULOUSLY FED—A SIGN FROM HEAVEN SOUGHT AND REFUSED—THE LEAVEN OF THE PHARISEES AND SADDUCEES—A BLIND MAN AT BETHSAIDA RESTORED TO SIGHT. (= Matt. xv. 32—xvi. 12.) This Section of miscellaneous matter evidently follows the preceding one in point of time, as will be seen by observing how it is introduced by Matthew.

Feeding of the Four Thousand (1-9). **1. In those days the multitude being very great, and having nothing to eat, Jesus called his disciples unto him, and saith unto them, 2. I have compassion on the multitude**—an expression of that deep emotion in the Redeemer's heart which always preceded some remarkable interposition for relief. (See Matt. xiv. 14; xx. 34; Mark i. 41; Luke vii. 13; also Matt. ix. 36, before the mission of the Twelve: compare Jud. ii. 18; x. 16.) **because they have now been with me,** in constant attendance, **three days, and have nothing to eat: 3. And if I send them away fasting to their own houses, they will faint by the way: for divers of them came from far.** In their eagerness they seem not to have thought of the need of provisions for such a length of time; but the Lord thought of it. In Matt. (xv. 32) it is, "I will not send them away fasting" [ἀπολῦσαι αὐτοὺς νήστεις οὐ θέλω]—or rather, 'To send them away fasting I am unwilling.' **4. And his disciples answered him, From whence can a man satisfy these men with bread here in the wilderness?** Though the question here is the same as when He fed the five thousand, they evidently *now* meant no more by it than that *they* had not the means of feeding the multitude; modestly leaving the Lord to decide what was to be done. And this will the more appear from His not now trying them, as before, by saying, "They need not depart, give ye them to eat;" but simply asking what they had, and then giving His directions. **5. And he asked them, How many loaves have ye? And they said, Seven.** It was important in this case, as in the former, that the precise number of the loaves should be brought out. Thus also does the distinctness of the two miracles appear. **6. And he commanded the people to sit down on the ground: and he took the seven loaves, and gave thanks, and brake, and gave to his disciples to set before them; and they did set them before the people** [τῷ ὄχλῳ]—'the multitude.' **7. And they had a few small fishes: and he blessed, and commanded to set them also before them. 8. So they did eat, and were filled: and they took up of the broken meat**—or 'fragments' [κλασμάτων], **that was left seven baskets. 9. And they that had eaten were about four thousand: and he sent them away.** Had not our Lord distinctly referred, in this very chapter and in two successive sentences to the feeding of the Five and of the Four Thousand, as two distinct miracles, many critics would have insisted that they were but two different representations of one and the same miracle, as they do of the two expulsions of the buyers and sellers from the temple, at the beginning and end of our Lord's ministry. But even in spite of what our Lord says, it is painful to find such men as *Neander* endeavouring to identify the two miracles. The localities, though both on the eastern side of the lake, were different: the time was different: the preceding and following circumstances were different: the period during which the people continued fasting was different—in the one case not one entire day, in the other three days: the number fed was different—five thousand in the one case, in the other four thousand: the number of the loaves was different—five in the one case, in the other seven: the number of the fishes in the one case is definitely stated by all the four Evangelists—two; in the other case both give them indefinitely—"a few small fishes" [ἰχθύδια ὀλίγα]: in the one case the multitude were commanded to sit down "upon the green grass;" in the other, "on the ground" [ἐπὶ τῆς γῆς]: in the one case the number of the

10 And [g]straightway he entered into a ship with his disciples, and came
11 into the parts of Dalmanutha. And [h]the Pharisees came forth, and began
to question with him, seeking of him a sign from heaven, tempting him.
12 And he sighed deeply in his spirit, and saith, Why doth this generation
seek after a sign? Verily I say unto you, There shall no sign be given
13 unto this generation. And he left them, and, entering into the ship
again, departed to the other side.
14 Now [i]*the disciples* had forgotten to take bread, neither had they in the
15 ship with them more than one loaf. And [j]he charged them, saying, Take
heed, beware of the leaven of the Pharisees, and *of* the leaven of Herod.
16 And they reasoned among themselves, saying, *It is* [k]because we have no

A. D. 32.

[g] Matt. 15 39.
[h] Matt 12.38. Matt. 16. 1. Matt. 19. 3. ch. 2. 16. Luke 11.53. John 6. 30.
[i] Matt. 16. 5.
[j] Num. 27.19. 1 Chr. 28. 9. Luke 12. 1. 1 Cor. 5. 7.
[k] Matt. 16. 7.

baskets taken up filled with the fragments was twelve; in the other seven: but more than all, perhaps, because apparently quite incidental, in the one case the name given to the kind of baskets used is the same in all the four narratives—the *cophinus* (see on ch. vi. 43); in the other case the name given to the kind of baskets used, while it is the same in both the narratives, is quite different—the *spuris* [σπυρίς], a basket large enough to hold a man's body, for Paul was let down in one of these from the wall of Damascus [ἐν σπυρίδι], (Acts ix. 25). It might be added, that in the one case the people, in a frenzy of enthusiasm, would have taken Him by force to make Him a king; in the other case no such excitement is recorded. In view of these things, who could have believed that these were one and the same miracle, even if the Lord Himself had not expressly distinguished them?

Sign from Heaven Sought (10-13). **10. And straightway he entered into a ship** [εἰς τὸ πλοῖον]—'into the ship,' or 'embarked,' **with his disciples, and came into the parts of Dalmanutha.** In Matthew (xv. 39) it is "the coasts of Magdala." [For this word *Tischendorf*, *Tregelles*, and others read 'Magadan'—Μαγαδάν—on weighty, but not, as we think, preponderating authority. It is indeed easier to see how "Magadan"—a place of which nobody seems ever to have known anything—should have been changed into the now pretty well identified "Magdala," than how the known place should have been changed into one totally unknown. But the authorities do not seem to authorize this change in the text.] Magdala and Dalmanutha were both on the western shore of the lake, and probably not far apart. From the former the surname "Magdalenē" was probably taken, to denote the residence of one of the Maries. Dalmanutha may have been a village, but it cannot now be identified with certainty. **11. And the Pharisees came forth, and began to question with him, seeking of him a sign from heaven, tempting him**—not in the least desiring evidence for their conviction, but hoping to entrap Him. The first part of the answer is given in Matthew alone (xvi. 2, 3): "He answered and said unto them, When it is evening, ye say, It will be fair weather: for the sky is red. And in the morning, It will be foul weather to-day: for the sky is red and lowring"—'sullen' or 'gloomy' [στυγνάζων]. "Hypocrites! ye can discern the face of the sky; but can ye not discern the signs of the times?" The same simplicity of purpose and careful observation of the symptoms of approaching events which they showed in common things would enable them to "discern the signs of the times"—or rather "seasons," to which the prophets pointed for the manifestation of the Messiah. The sceptre had departed from Judah; Daniel's seventy weeks were expiring, &c.; and many other significant indications of the close of the old economy, and preparations for a freer and more comprehensive one, might have been discerned. But all was lost upon them. **12. And he sighed deeply in his spirit** [ἀναστενάξας τῷ πνεύματι αὐτοῦ]. The language is very strong. These glimpses into the interior of the Redeemer's heart, in which our Evangelist abounds, are more precious than rubies. The state of the Pharisaic heart, which prompted this desire for a fresh sign, went to His very soul. **and saith, Why doth this generation**—"this wicked and adulterous generation" (Matt. xvi. 4), **seek after a sign?**—when they have had such abundant evidence already? **There shall no sign be given unto this generation** [εἰ δοθήσεται]—lit., 'If there shall be given to this generation a sign;' a Jewish way of expressing a solemn and peremptory determination to the contrary, (compare Heb. iv. 5; Ps. xcv. 11, marg.) 'A generation incapable of appreciating such demonstrations shall not be gratified with them.' In Matt. xvi. 4, He added, "but the sign of the prophet Jonas." See on Matt. xii. 39, 40. **13. And he left them**—no doubt with tokens of displeasure, **and entering into the ship again, departed to the other side.**

The Leaven of the Pharisees and Sadducees (14-21). **14. Now the disciples had forgotten to take bread, neither had they in the ship with them more than one loaf.** This is another example of that graphic circumstantiality which gives such a charm to this briefest of the four Gospels. The circumstance of the "one loaf" only remaining, as *Webster and Wilkinson* remark, was more suggestive of their Master's recent miracles than the entire absence of provisions. **15. And he charged them, saying, Take heed, beware of the leaven of the Pharisees**—"and of the Sadducees" (Matt. xvi. 6), **and of the leaven of Herod.** The teaching or "doctrine" (Matt. xvi. 12) of the Pharisees and of the Sadducees was quite different, but both were equally pernicious; and the Herodians, though rather a political party, were equally envenomed against our Lord's spiritual teaching. See on Matt. xii. 14. The *penetrating* and *diffusive* quality of leaven, for good or bad, is the ground of the comparison. **16. And they reasoned among themselves, saying, It is because we have no bread.** But a little ago He was tried with the obduracy of the Pharisees; now He is tried with the obtuseness of His own disciples. The *nine* questions following each other in rapid succession (*vv.* 17-21), show how deeply He was hurt at this want of spiritual apprehension, and worse still, their low thoughts of Him, as if He would utter so solemn a warning on so petty a subject. It will be seen, however—from the very form of their conjecture, "It is because *we* have no bread," and our Lord's astonishment that they should not by that time have known better what He took up His attention with—that He ever left *the whole care for His own temporal wants to the Twelve:* that He did this so

17 bread. And when Jesus knew *it*, he saith unto them, Why reason ye
because ye have no bread? [l]perceive ye not yet, neither understand?
18 have ye your heart yet hardened? Having eyes, see ye not? and having
19 ears, hear ye not? and do ye not remember? When [m]I brake the five
loaves among five thousand, how many baskets full of fragments took ye
20 up? They say unto him, Twelve. And [n]when the seven among four
thousand, how many baskets full of fragments took ye up? And they said,
21 Seven. And he said unto them, How is it [o]that ye do not understand?
22 And he cometh to Bethsaida; and they bring a blind man unto him,
23 and besought him to touch him. And he took the blind man by the
hand, and led him out of the town; and when [p]he had spit on his eyes,
24 and put his hands upon him, he asked him if he saw ought. And he
25 looked up, and said, I see men as trees, walking. After that he put *his*
hands again upon his eyes, and made him look up: and he was restored,
26 and saw every man clearly. And he sent him away to his house, saying,
Neither go into the town, [q]nor tell *it* to any in the town.

A. D. 32.

[l] Isa. 63. 17. Matt. 15. 17. Matt. 16. 8, 9. ch. 6. 52. ch. 16. 14. Luke 24. 25. Heb. 5. 11, 12.
[m] Matt. 24. 20. ch 6. 43. Luke 9. 17. John 6. 13.
[n] Matt. 15. 37.
[o] Ps. 94. 8. ch. 6. 52. John 14. 9.
[p] ch. 7. 33.
[q] Matt. 8. 4. ch. 5. 43.

entirely, that finding they were reduced to their last loaf they felt as if unworthy of such a trust, and could not think but that the same thought was in their Lord's mind which was pressing upon their own; but that in this they were so far wrong that it hurt His feelings—sharp just in proportion to His love—that such a thought of Him should have entered their minds! Who that, like angels, "desire to look into these things" will not prize such glimpses above gold? **17. And when Jesus knew it, he saith unto them, Why reason ye because ye have no bread? perceive ye not yet, neither understand? have ye your heart yet hardened?** How strong an expression to use of true-hearted disciples! See on ch. vi. 52. **18. Having eyes, see ye not? and having ears, hear ye not?** See on Matt. xiii. 13. **and do ye not remember? 19. When I brake the five loaves among**—'the'—**five thousand, how many baskets** [*κοφίνους*] **full of fragments took ye up? They say unto him, Twelve. 20. And when the seven among**—'the'—**four thousand, how many baskets** [*σπυρίδων*] **full of fragments took ye up? And they said, Seven. 21. And he said unto them, How is it that ye do not understand?**—'do not understand that the warning I gave you could not have been prompted by any such petty consideration as the want of loaves in your scrip?' Profuse as were our Lord's miracles, we see from this that they were not wrought at random, but that He carefully noted their minutest details, and desired that this should be done by those who witnessed, as doubtless by all who read the record of them. Even the different kind of baskets used at the two miraculous feedings, so carefully noted in the two narratives, are here also referred to; the one smaller, of which there were twelve, the other much larger, of which there were seven.

Blind Man at Bethsaida Restored to Sight (22-26). **22. And he cometh to Bethsaida**—Bethsaida-Julias, on the north-east side of the lake, whence after this He proceeded to Cesarea Philippi (*v.* 27)—**and they bring a blind man unto him, and besought him to touch him.** See on ch. vii. 32. **23. And he took the blind man by the hand, and led him out of the town.** Of the deaf and dumb man it is merely said that "He took him aside" (ch. vii. 33); but this blind man He *led by the hand* out of the town, doing it Himself rather than employing another—great humility, exclaims *Bengel!*—that He might gain his confidence and raise his expectation. **and when he had spit on his eyes**—the organ affected. See on ch. vii. 33. **and put his hands upon him, he asked him if he saw ought. 24. And he looked up, and said, I see men as trees, walking.** This is one of the cases in which one edition of what is called the received text differs from another. That which is decidedly the best supported, and has also internal evidence on its side is this: 'I see men; for I see [them] as trees walking' [*βλέπω τοὺς ἀνθρώπους, ὅτι ὡς δένδρα ὁρῶ περιπατοῦντας*]—that is, he could distinguish them from trees only by their motion; a minute mark of truth in the narrative, as *Alford* observes, describing how human objects had appeared to him during that gradual failing of sight which had ended in blindness. **25. After that he put his hands again upon his eyes, and made him look up: and he was restored, and saw every man clearly.** Perhaps the one operation perfectly restored the *eyes*, while the other imparted immediately the *faculty of using them.* It is the only recorded example of a *progressive* cure, and it certainly illustrates similar methods in the spiritual kingdom. Of the four recorded cases of sight restored, all the patients save one either *came* or *were brought* to the Physician. In the case of the man born blind, *the Physician came* to the patient. So some seek and find Christ; of others He is found who seek Him not. See on Matt. xiii. 44-46, Remark 1. **26. And he sent him away to his house, saying, Neither go into the town, nor tell it to any in the town.** Besides the usual reasons against going about "blazing the matter," retirement in this case would be salutary to himself.

Remarks.—1. When our Lord was about to open the ears and loose the tongue of the deaf man who had an impediment in his speech, our Evangelist says that He looked up to heaven and *sighed* (ch. vii. 34); but when He had to reply to the captious petulance which sought of Him, amidst a profusion of signs, a sign from heaven, he says He *sighed deeply in His spirit.* Nor can we wonder. For if the spectacle of what sin had done affected Him deeply, how much more deeply would sin itself affect Him, when exhibited in so trying a form! And occurring, as such things now did, almost daily, what a touching commentary do they furnish on the prophetic account of Him as "a Man of sorrows, and acquainted with grief"! 2. When men apply to religion none of the ordinary principles of judgment and action, it shows itself to be with them but an empty creed or an outward ritual, neither acceptable to God nor profitable to themselves. But when it becomes a nature and a life, we learn to bring all our natural judgment,

27 And [r]Jesus went out, and his disciples, into the towns of Cesarea
Philippi: and by the way he asked his disciples, saying unto them,
28 Whom do men say that I am? And they answered, [s]John the Baptist:
29 but some *say*, Elias; and others, One of the prophets. And he saith unto
them, But whom say ye that I am? And Peter answereth and saith
30 unto him, [t]Thou art the Christ. And [u]he charged them that they should
tell no man of him.
31 And [v]he began to teach them, that the Son of man must suffer many
things, and be rejected of the elders, and *of* the chief priests, and scribes,
32 and be killed, and after three days rise again. And he spake that saying
33 openly. And Peter took him, and began to rebuke him. But when he
had turned about, and looked on his disciples, he rebuked Peter, saying,
Get thee behind me, Satan: [w]for thou savourest not the things that be
of God, but the things that be of men.
34 And when he had called the people *unto him*, with his disciples also, he
said unto them, [x]Whosoever will come after me, let him deny himself,
35 and take up his cross, and follow me. For [y]whosoever will save his life
shall lose it; but whosoever shall lose his life for my sake and the
36 Gospel's, the same shall save it. For what shall it profit a man, if he
37 shall gain the whole world, and lose his own soul? Or what shall a man
38 give in exchange for his soul? Whosoever [z]therefore shall be ashamed of
me and of my words in this adulterous and sinful generation, of him also
shall the Son of man be ashamed, when he cometh in the glory of his
Father with the holy angels.

9 AND he said unto them, [a]Verily I say unto you, That there be some
of them that stand here, which shall not taste of death, till they have
seen [b]the kingdom of God come with power.
2 And [c]after six days Jesus taketh *with him* Peter, and James, and John,
and leadeth them up into an high mountain apart by themselves: and he
3 was transfigured before them. And his raiment became shining, exceeding
4 [d]white as snow; so as no fuller on earth can white them. And there
appeared unto them Elias with Moses: and they were talking with Jesus.
5 And Peter answered and said to Jesus, Master, it is good for us to be
here: and let us make three tabernacles; one for thee, and one for Moses,
6 and one for Elias. For he wist not what to say; for they were sore afraid.
7 And there was [e]a cloud that overshadowed them: and a voice came out
8 of the cloud, saying, This is my beloved Son: hear [f]him. And suddenly,
when they had looked round about, they saw no man any more, save
Jesus only with themselves.

A. D. 32.

[r] Matt. 16. 13. Luke 9. 18.
[s] Matt. 14. 2.
[t] Matt. 16. 6. John 1. 41, 49. John 6. 69. John 11. 27. Acts 8. 37. Acts 9. 20. 1 John 4. 15.
[u] Matt. 16. 20.
[v] Matt. 16. 21. Matt. 17. 22. Luke 9. 22.
[w] Rom. 8. 7. 1 Cor. 2. 14.
[x] Matt. 10. 38. Matt. 16. 24. Luke 9. 23. Luke 14. 27. Gal. 5. 24. Gal. 6. 14.
[y] John 12. 25. Rev. 12. 11.
[z] Matt. 10. 33. Luke 9. 26. Luke 12. 9. Rom. 1. 16. 2 Tim. 1. 8. 2 Tim. 2. 12. 1 John 2. 23.

CHAP. 9.
[a] Matt. 16. 28. Luke 9. 27.
[b] Matt. 24. 30. Matt. 25. 31. Luke 22. 18. Heb. 2. 8, 9.
[c] Matt. 17. 1. Luke 9. 28.
[d] Dan. 7. 9. Matt. 28. 3.
[e] Ex. 40. 34. Isa. 42. 1. 2 Pet. 1. 17.
[f] Heb. 1. 1, 2. Heb. 2. 3. Heb. 12. 25, 26.

worldly sagacity, ordinary shrewdness, and growing experience to bear upon religious matters; and thus our entire life acquires a unity—having to do now with things temporal, and now with things spiritual and eternal, but in both cases alike governed by the same principles and directed to the same ends. And yet, how often do even the children of God incur that rebuke of their Lord, that they can discern the signs of change in the material, mercantile, or political atmosphere, but are dull in their perceptions of what is passing, and in their ability to forecast what is coming, in the moral, religious, or spiritual world! 3. If the Redeemer was tried with enemies, He had not a little to bear from time to time even from His own chosen Twelve. How little did they comprehend much that He said to them; how unworthy of Him were many of the thoughts which they imagined to be passing through His mind; and how petty the motives by which they supposed Him to be actuated! How admirable is the long-suffering patience which bore with both! But is the need for this patience yet ended? Not to speak of the world's enmity to Him, His truth, His cause, His people, which time certainly has not changed, is there not much still in His own people, the endurance of which, when rightly apprehended, is matter of wonder? 4. As our Lord seems purposely to have varied His mode of healing the maladies that came before Him—having respect, doubtless, to the nature of each case—so is the history of every soul that is healed of its deadly malady by the Great Physician different, probably, from that of every other: some, in particular, being healed quickly, others slowly; some apparently by one word, others by successive steps. But as in all the result is one, so the hand of one mighty, gracious Healer is to be seen alike in all.

27-38.—Peter's noble Confession of Christ—Our Lord's First explicit Announcement of His Approaching Sufferings, Death, and Resurrection—His Rebuke of Peter, and Warning to all the Twelve. (=Matt. xvi. 13-27; Luke ix. 18-26.) For the exposition, see on Matt. xvi. 13-28.

CHAP. IX. 1-13.—Jesus is Transfigured—

9 And [g]as they came down from the mountain, he charged them that
they should tell no man what things they had seen, till the Son of man
10 were risen from the dead. And they kept that saying with themselves,
questioning one with another what the rising from the dead should
11 mean. And they asked him, saying, Why say the scribes [h]that Elias
12 must first come? And he answered and told them, Elias verily cometh
first, and restoreth all things; and [i]how it is written of the Son of man,
13 that he must suffer many things, and [j]be set at nought. But I say unto
you, That [k]Elias is indeed come, and they have done unto him whatsoever they listed, as it is written of him.
14 And [l]when he came to *his* disciples, he saw a great multitude about
15 them, and the scribes questioning with them. And straightway all the
people, when they beheld him, were greatly amazed, and running to *him*
16 saluted him. And he asked the scribes, What question ye [1]with them?
17 And [m]one of the multitude answered and said, Master, I have brought
18 unto thee my son, which hath a dumb spirit: and wheresoever he taketh
him, he [2]teareth him; and he foameth, and gnasheth with his teeth, and
pineth away: and I spake to thy disciples that they should cast him out;
19 and they could not. He answereth him, and saith, O faithless generation,
how long shall I be with you? how long shall I suffer you? Bring him

A. D. 32.

g Matt. 17. 9.
h Mal. 4. 5. Matt. 17. 10.
i Gen. 3. 15. Num. 21. 9. Ps. 22. 6. Isa. 50. 6. Isa. 53. 2. Dan. 9. 26. Zec. 13. 7. John 3. 14.
j Luke 23. 11. Phil. 2. 7.
k Matt. 11. 14. Matt. 17. 12. Luke 1. 17.
l Matt. 17. 14. Luke 9. 37.
1 Or, among yourselves?
m Matt. 17. 14. Luke 9. 38.
2 Or, dasheth him.

CONVERSATION ABOUT ELIAS. (= Matt. xvi. 28—xvii. 13; Luke ix, 27-36.) For the exposition, see on Luke ix. 27-36.

14-32.—HEALING OF A DEMONIAC BOY—SECOND EXPLICIT ANNOUNCEMENT OF HIS APPROACHING DEATH AND RESURRECTION. (= Matt. xvii. 14-23; Luke ix. 37-45.)

Healing of the Demoniac Boy (14-29). **14. And when he came to his disciples, he saw a great multitude about them, and the scribes questioning with them.** This was "on the next day, when they were come down from the hill" (Luke ix. 37). The Transfiguration appears to have taken place at night. In the morning, as He came down from the hill on which it took place—with Peter, and James, and John—on approaching the other nine, He found them surrounded by a great multitude, and the scribes disputing or discussing with them. No doubt these cavillers were twitting the apostles of Jesus with their inability to cure the demoniac boy of whom we are presently to hear, and insinuating doubts even of their Master's ability to do it; while they, zealous for their Master's honour, would no doubt refer to His past miracles in proof of the contrary. **15. And straightway all the people**—'the multitude' [ὁ ὄχλος], **when they beheld him, were greatly amazed** [ἐξεθαμβήθη]—or 'were astounded'—**and running to him saluted him.** The singularly strong expression of surprise, the sudden arrest of the discussion, and the rush of the multitude towards Him, can be accounted for by nothing less than something amazing in His appearance. There can hardly be any doubt that *His countenance still retained traces of His transfiguration-glory.* (See Exod. xxxiv. 29, 30.) So *Bengel, De Wette, Meyer, Trench, Alford.* No wonder, if this was the case, that they not only ran to Him, but saluted Him. Our Lord, however, takes no notice of what had attracted them, and probably it gradually faded away as He drew near; but addressing Himself to the scribes, He demands the subject of their discussion, ready to meet them where they had pressed hard upon His half-instructed, and as yet timid apostles. **16. And he asked the scribes, What question ye with them?** Ere they had time to reply, the father of the boy, whose case had occasioned the dispute, himself steps forward and answers the question; telling a piteous tale of deafness, and dumbness, and fits of epilepsy—ending with this, that the disciples, though entreated, could not perform the cure. **17. And one of the multitude answered and said, Master, I have brought unto thee my son**—"mine only child" (Luke ix. 38), **which hath a dumb spirit**—a spirit whose operation had the effect of rendering his victim speechless, and deaf also (*v.* 25). In Matthew's report of the speech (xvii. 15), the father says "he is lunatic;" this being another and most distressing effect of the possession. **18. And wheresoever he taketh him, he teareth him; and he foameth, and gnasheth with his teeth, and pineth away** [ξηραίνεται]—rather, 'becomes withered,' 'dried up,' or 'paralyzed;' as the same word is everywhere else rendered in the New Testament. Some additional particulars are given by Luke, and by our Evangelist below. "Lo," says he in Luke ix. 39, "a spirit taketh him, and he suddenly crieth out; and it teareth him that he foameth again, and bruising him hardly (or with difficulty) departeth from him." **and I spake to thy disciples that they should cast him out; and they could not.** Our Lord replies to the father by a severe rebuke to the disciples. As if wounded at the exposure before such a multitude, of the weakness of His disciples' faith, which doubtless He felt as a reflection on Himself, He puts them to the blush before all, but in language fitted only to raise expectation of what Himself would do. **19. He answereth him, and saith, O faithless generation**—"and perverse," or 'perverted' [διεστραμμένη] (Matt. xvii. 17; Luke ix. 41), **how long shall I be with you? how long shall I suffer you?**—language implying that it was a shame to them to want the faith necessary to perform this cure, and that it needed some patience to put up with them. It is to us surprising that some interpreters, as *Chrysostom* and *Calvin*, should represent this rebuke as addressed, not to the disciples at all, but to the scribes who disputed with them. Nor does it much, if at all, mend the matter to view it as addressed to both, as most expositors seem to do. With *Bengel, de Wette*, and *Meyer*, we regard it as addressed directly to the nine apostles who were unable to expel this evil spirit. And though, in ascribing this inability to their 'want of faith' and the 'perverted turn of mind' which they had drunk in with their early training, the rebuke

20 unto me. And they brought him unto him: and when [n]he saw him,
straightway the spirit tare him; and he fell on the ground, and wallowed
21 foaming. And he asked his father, How long is it ago since this came
22 unto him? And he said, Of a child. And ofttimes it hath cast him
into the fire, and into the waters, to destroy him: but if thou canst do
23 any thing, have compassion on us, and help us. Jesus said unto him,
24 [o]If thou canst believe, all things *are* possible to him that believeth. And
straightway the father of the child cried out, and said with tears, Lord, I
25 believe; [p]help thou mine unbelief. When Jesus saw that the people
came running together, he [q]rebuked the foul spirit, saying unto him,
Thou dumb and deaf spirit, I charge thee, come out of him, and enter no
26 more into him. And *the spirit* cried, and rent him sore, and came out

A. D. 32.

[n] ch. 1. 26. Luke 9. 42.
[o] 2 Chr. 20. 20. Matt. 17. 20. ch. 11. 23. Luke 17. 6. John 11. 40. Acts 14. 9.
[p] Phil. 1. 29. 2 Thes. 1. 3, 11. Heb. 12. 2.
[q] Acts 10. 38. 1 John 3. 8.

would undoubtedly apply, with vastly greater force, to those who twitted the poor disciples with their inability; it would be to change the whole nature of the rebuke to suppose it addressed to those who had *no faith at all*, and were *wholly perverted.* It was because faith sufficient for curing this youth was to have been expected of the disciples, and because they should by that time have got rid of the perversity in which they had been reared, that Jesus exposes them thus before the rest. And who does not see that this was fitted, more than anything else, to impress upon the bystanders the severe loftiness of the training He was giving to the Twelve, and the unsophisticated footing He was on with them? **Bring him unto me.** The order to bring the patient to Him was instantly obeyed; when, lo! as if conscious of the presence of his divine Tormentor, and expecting to be made to quit, the foul spirit rages and is furious, determined to die hard, doing all the mischief he can to this poor child while yet within his grasp. **20. And they brought him unto him: and when he saw him, straightway the spirit tare him.** Just as the man with the legion of demons, "when he *saw* Jesus, ran and worshipped Him" (ch. v. 6), so this demon, *when he saw Him*, immediately "tare him." The feeling of terror and rage was the same in both cases. **and he fell on the ground, and wallowed foaming.** Still Jesus does nothing, but keeps conversing with the father about the case—partly to have its desperate features told out by him who knew them best, in the hearing of the spectators; partly to let its virulence have time to show itself; and partly to deepen the exercise of the father's soul, to draw out his faith, and thus to prepare both him and the bystanders for what He was to do. **21. And he asked his father, How long is it ago since this came unto him? And he said, Of a child. 22. And ofttimes it hath cast him into the fire, and into the waters, to destroy him.** Having told briefly the affecting features of the case, the poor father, half dispirited by the failure of the disciples and the aggravated virulence of the malady itself in presence of their Master, yet encouraged too by what he had heard of Christ, by the severe rebuke He had given to His disciples for not having faith enough to cure the boy, and by the dignity with which He had ordered him to be brought to Him—in this mixed state of mind, he closes his description of the case with these touching words: **but if thou canst do any thing, have compassion on us, and help us**—"us," says the father; for it was a sore family affliction. Compare the language of the Syrophenician woman regarding her daughter, "Lord, help *me.*" Still, nothing is done; the man is but *struggling into faith;* it must come a step farther. But he had to do with Him who breaks not the bruised reed, and who knew how to inspire what He demanded. The man had said to Him, "*If Thou canst do;*" **23. Jesus**—retorting upon him, **said unto him, If thou canst believe:** The man had said, "If Thou canst do *any thing;*" Jesus replies, **all things are possible to him that believeth**—'My doing all depends on thy believing.' To impress this still more, He redoubles upon the believing: "If thou canst believe, all things are possible to him that believeth." Thus the Lord helps the birth of faith in that struggling soul; and now, though with pain and sore travail, it comes to the birth, as *Trench*, borrowing from *Olshausen*, expresses it. Seeing the case stood still, waiting not upon the Lord's power but his own faith, the man becomes immediately conscious of conflicting principles, and rises into one of the noblest utterances on record. **24. And straightway the father of the child cried out, and said with tears, Lord, I believe; help thou mine unbelief.**—*q. d.*, ''Tis useless concealing from Thee, O Thou mysterious, mighty Healer, the unbelief that still struggles in this heart of mine; but that heart bears me witness that I do believe in Thee; and if distrust still remains, I disown it, I wrestle with it, I seek help from Thee against it.' Two things are very remarkable here: First, *The felt and owned presence of unbelief*, which only the strength of the man's faith could have so revealed to his own consciousness. Second, *His appeal to Christ for help against his felt unbelief*—a feature in the case quite unparalleled, and showing, more than all protestations could have done, the insight he had attained into the existence of *a power in Christ more glorious than any he had besought for his poor child.* The work was done; and as the commotion and confusion in the crowd was now increasing, Jesus at once, as Lord of spirits, gives the word of command to the dumb and deaf spirit to be gone, never again to return to his victim. **25. When Jesus saw that the people came running together, he rebuked the foul spirit, saying unto him, Dumb and deaf spirit, I charge thee, come out of him, and enter no more into him. 26. And the spirit cried, and rent him sore, and came out of him: and he was as one dead; insomuch that many said, He is dead.** The malignant, cruel spirit, now conscious that his time was come, gathers up his whole strength, with intent by a last stroke to kill his victim, and had nearly succeeded. But the Lord of life was there; the Healer of all maladies, the Friend of sinners, the Seed of the woman, "the Stronger than the strong man armed," was there. The very faith which Christ declared to be enough for everything being now found, it was not possible that the serpent should prevail. Fearfully is he permitted to bruise the *heel*, as in this case; but his own *head* shall go for it—his works shall be destroyed (1 John iii. 8). **27. But Jesus took him by the hand, and lifted him up; and he arose.**

of him: and he was as one dead; insomuch that many said, He is dead.
27 But Jesus took him by the hand, and lifted him up; and he arose.
28 And [r]when he was come into the house, his disciples asked him
29 privately, Why could not we cast him out? And he said unto them,
This kind can come forth by nothing but by prayer and fasting.
30 And they departed thence, and passed through Galilee; and he would
31 not that any man should know *it*. For [s]he taught his disciples, and said
unto them, The Son of man is delivered into the hands of men, and they
shall kill him; and after that he is killed, he shall rise the third day.
32 But they understood not that saying, and were afraid to ask him.

A. D. 32.
r Matt.17.19.
s Matt.17.22. ch 8. 31. Luke 9. 44. Luke 22.24, 44, 46. John 2. 19. John 3. 14. John 10.18. Acts 2. 23, 24. 2 Tim. 2. 2.

28. And when he was come into the house, his disciples asked him privately, Why could not we cast him out? 29. And he said unto them, This kind can come forth by nothing but by prayer and fasting—that is, as nearly all good interpreters are agreed, 'this kind of evil spirits cannot be expelled,' or 'so desperate a case of demoniacal possession cannot be cured, but by prayer and fasting.' But since the Lord Himself says that His disciples could not fast while He was with them, perhaps this was designed, as *Alford* hints, for their after guidance—unless we take it as but a definite way of expressing the general truth, that great and difficult duties require special preparation and self-denial. But the answer to their question, as given by Matthew (xvii.), is more full: "And Jesus said unto them, Because of your unbelief" [ἀπιστίαν. *Tregelles*, on insufficient authority, as we think, substitutes what appears to be a mere interpretation—ὀλιγοπιστίαν, 'because of your little faith.' *Tischendorf* adheres to the received text.] "For verily I say unto you, If ye have faith as a grain of mustard seed, ye shall say unto this mountain, Remove hence to yonder place, and it shall remove; and nothing shall be impossible unto you" (*v.* 20). See on Mark xi. 23. "Howbeit this kind goeth not out but by prayer and fasting" (*v.* 21): that is, though nothing is impossible to faith, yet such a height of faith as is requisite for such triumphs is not to be reached either in a moment or without effort—either with God in prayer or with ourselves in self-denying exercises. Luke (ix. 43) adds, "And they were all amazed at the mighty power of God" [ἐπὶ τῇ μεγαλειότητι τοῦ θεοῦ]—'at the majesty' or 'mightiness of God,' in this last miracle, in the transfiguration, &c.; or, at the *divine grandeur* of Christ rising upon them daily.

Second Explicit Announcement of His Approaching Death and Resurrection (30-32). **30. And they departed thence, and passed** [παρεπορεύοντο]—'were passing along' **through Galilee; and he would not that any man should know it.** By comparing Matt. xvii. 22, 23, and Luke ix. 43, 44, with this, we gather, that as our Lord's reason for going through Galilee more privately than usual on this occasion, was to reiterate to them the announcement which had so shocked them at the first mention of it, and thus familiarize them with it by little and little, so this was His reason for enjoining silence upon them as to their present movements. **31. For he taught his disciples, and said unto them**—"Let these sayings sink down into your ears" (Luke ix. 44); not what had been passing between them as to His grandeur, but what He was now to utter, "for" **The Son of man is delivered** [παραδίδοται]. The use of the present tense expresses how near at hand He would have them to consider it. As *Bengel* says, steps were already in course of being taken to bring it about. **into the hands of men.** This remarkable antithesis—"the Son of *man* shall be delivered into the hands of *men*"—it is worthy of notice, is in all the three Evangelists. **and they shall kill him**:—*q. d.*, 'Be not carried off your feet by all that grandeur of Mine which ye have lately witnessed, but bear in mind what I have already told you and now distinctly repeat, that that Sun in whose beams ye now rejoice is soon to set in midnight gloom.' **and after he is killed, he shall rise the third day. 32. But they understood not that saying**—"and it was hid from them, [so] that they perceived it not" (Luke ix. 45), **and were afraid to ask him.** Their most cherished ideas were so completely dashed by such announcements, that they were afraid of laying themselves open to rebuke by asking Him any questions. But "they were exceeding sorry" (Matt. xvii. 23). While the other Evangelists, as *Webster and Wilkinson* remark, notice their ignorance and their fear, St. Matthew, who was one of them, retains a vivid recollection of their sorrow.

Remarks.—1. When the keen-edged rebuke which our Lord administers to his apostles (*v.* 19, and Matt. xvii. 17) is compared with the almost identical language of Jehovah Himself to His ancient people, on an occasion of the deepest provocation (Num. xiv. 11, 27), who can help coming to the conclusion, that He regarded Himself as occupying the same position towards His disciples which the Lord God of Israel did towards His people of old? Let this be weighed. And it tends greatly to confirm this, that never once do we find anything approaching to a rebuke of them, or a correction of mistake in them or any others, for attributing *too much* to Him or conceiving of Him *too loftily*. Here, as everywhere else, it is the reverse. He takes with every charge of His "making Himself equal with God," and what He says in reply is but designed to make that good. Here, He is hurt at His disciples because their confidence in His power to aid them, even when at a distance from them, was not such as to enable them to grapple successfully even with one of the most desperate manifestations of diabolical power. 2. Our Lord thinks such attachment to Him and confidence in Him as is found in all genuine disciples from the first, is not enough. As there are degrees in this—from the lowest to the highest, from the infancy to the manhood of faith—so He takes it ill when His people either make no progress, or inadequate progress; when, "for the time they ought to be teachers, they have need that one teach them" (Heb. v. 12); when they do not "grow in grace, and in the knowledge of our Lord and Saviour Jesus Christ" (2 Pet. iii. 18). 3. How often have we to remark that distress and extremity in honest hearts does more towards a right appreciation of the glory of Christ than all teaching without it! (See, for example, on Luke vii. 36-50; xxiii. 39-43.) Here is a man who, without any of the advantages of the Twelve, but out of the depths of his anguish,

33 And [t]he came to Capernaum: and, being in the house, he asked them,
34 What was it that ye disputed among yourselves by the way? But they
held their peace: [u]for by the way they had disputed among themselves,
35 who *should be* the greatest. And he sat down, and called the twelve, and
saith unto them, [v]If any man desire to be first, *the same* shall be last of
36 all, and servant of all. And [w]he took a child, and set him in the midst
of them: and when he had taken him in his arms, he said unto them,
37 Whosoever shall receive one of such children in my name, receiveth me:
[x]and whosoever shall receive me, receiveth not me, but him that sent me.
38 And [y]John answered him, saying, Master, we saw one casting out

A. D. 32.

t Matt. 18. 1. Luke 9. 46.
u Pro. 13. 10.
v Matt. 20.26, 27. ch. 10. 43.
w Matt. 18. 2. ch. 10. 16.
x Matt. 10.40. Luke 9. 48.
y Num. 11. 28. Luke 9. 49.

utters a speech more glorifying to Christ than all which they ever expressed during the days of His flesh—protesting his faith in the Lord Jesus, but in the same breath beseeching Him for help against his unbelief! To be conscious at once both of faith and of unbelief; to take the part of the one against the other; yet to feel the unbelief, though disowned and struggled against, to be strong and obstinate, while his faith was feeble and ready to be overpowered, and so to "cry out" even "with tears" for help against that cursed unbelief—this is such a wonderful speech, that, all things considered, the like of it is not to be found. The nearest to it is that prayer of the apostles to the Lord, "Increase our faith" (Luke xvii. 5). But besides that this was uttered by *apostles*, whose advantages were vastly greater than this man's, it was said *a good while after* the scene here recorded, and was evidently but an echo, or rather an adaptation of it. So that this man's cry may be said to have supplied the apostles themselves with a new idea, nay perhaps with a new view altogether of the power of Christ. And is it not true still, that "there are last which shall be first"? 4. Signal triumphs in the kingdom of grace are not to be won by an easy faith, or by stationary, slothful, self-indulgent believers: they are to be achieved only by much nearness to God and denial of ourselves. As to "fasting," if the question be, Whether and how far is it an evangelical duty? there is a preliminary question, What is its proper object? Evidently the mortification of the flesh; and generally, the counteracting of all earthly, sensual, grovelling tendencies, which eat out the heart of our spirituality. Hence it follows, that whatever abstinence from food is observed *without any reference to this object*, and for its own sake, is nothing but "bodily exercise" (1 Tim. iv. 8); and whatsoever abstinence is found by experience to have an exhausting, stupefying effect upon the spirit itself, is, so far as it is so, of the same nature. The true fasting is the opposite of "surfeiting" (Luke xxi. 34), which destroys all elasticity of spirit and all vigour of thought and feeling. And while Christians should habitually keep themselves far from this, by being sparing rather than otherwise in the satisfaction of their appetites, the lesson here taught us is that there are sometimes duties to be done and victories to be achieved, which demand even more than ordinary nearness to God in prayer, and more than ordinary denial of ourselves.

33-50.—STRIFE AMONG THE TWELVE WHO SHOULD BE GREATEST IN THE KINGDOM OF HEAVEN, WITH RELATIVE TEACHING—INCIDENTAL REBUKE OF JOHN FOR EXCLUSIVENESS. (=Matt. xviii. 1-9; Luke ix. 46-50.)

Strife among the Twelve, with Relative Teaching (33-37). **33. And he came to Capernaum: and, being in the house, he asked them, What was it that ye disputed among yourselves by the way?** From this we gather that after the painful communication He had made to them, the Redeemer had allowed them to travel so much of the way by themselves; partly, no doubt, that He might have privacy for Himself to dwell on what lay before Him, and partly that they might be induced to weigh together and prepare themselves for the terrible events which He had announced to them. But if so, how different was their occupation! **34. But they held their peace: for by the way they had disputed among themselves, who should be the greatest.** From Matt. xviii. 1 we should infer that the subject was introduced, not by our Lord, but by the disciples themselves, who came and asked Jesus who should be greatest. Perhaps one or two of them first referred the matter to Jesus, who put them off till they should all be assembled together at Capernaum. He had all the while "perceived the thought of their heart" (Luke ix. 47); but now that they were all together "in the house," He questions them about it, and they are put to the blush, conscious of the *temper* towards each other which it had kindled. This raised the whole question afresh, and at this point our Evangelist takes it up. The subject was suggested by the recent announcement of the Kingdom (Matt. xvi. 19-28), the transfiguration of their Master, and especially the preference given to three of them at that scene. **35. And he sat down, and called the twelve, and saith unto them, If any man desire to be first, the same shall be last of all, and servant of all**—that is, 'let him be' such; he must be prepared to take the last and lowest place. See on ch. x. 42-45. **36. And he took a child** [παιδίον]—'a little child' (Matt. xviii. 2); but the word is the same in both places, as also in Luke ix. 47. **and set him in the midst of them: and when he had taken him in his arms.** This beautiful trait is mentioned by our Evangelist alone. **he said unto them.** Here we must go to Matthew (xviii. 3, 4) for the first part of this answer:—"Verily I say unto you, except ye be converted, and become as little children, ye shall not enter into the kingdom of Heaven:"—*q. d.*, 'Conversion must be thorough; not only must the heart be turned to God in general, and from earthly to heavenly things, but in particular, except ye be converted from that carnal ambition which still rankles within you, into that freedom from all such feelings which ye see in this child, ye have neither part nor lot in the kingdom at all; and he who in this feature has most of the child, is highest there.' Whosoever, therefore, shall "humble himself as this little child, the same is greatest in the kingdom of heaven;" "for he that is (willing to be) least among you all, the same shall be great" (Luke ix. 48). And **Whosoever shall receive one of such children**—so manifesting the spirit unconsciously displayed by this child, **in my name**—from love to Me, **receiveth me; and whosoever shall receive me, receiveth not me, but him that sent me.** See on Matt. x. 40.

Incidental Rebuke of John for Exclusiveness (38-41). **38. And John answered him, saying, Master, we saw one casting out devils in thy**

devils in thy name, and he followeth not us: and we forbade him,
39 because he followeth not us. But Jesus said, Forbid him not: [z]for
there is no man which shall do a miracle in my name, that can lightly
40 speak evil of me. For [a]he that is not against us is on our part.
41 For [b]whosoever shall give you a cup of water to drink in my name,
because ye belong to Christ, verily I say unto you, he shall not lose his
reward.
42 And [c]whosoever shall offend one of *these* little ones that believe in me,
it is better for him that a millstone were hanged about his neck, and he
43 were cast into the sea. And if thy hand [3]offend thee, cut it off: it is
better for thee to enter into life maimed, than having two hands to go
44 into hell, into the fire that never shall be quenched; where [d]their worm
45 dieth not, and the fire is not quenched. And if thy foot offend thee, cut
it off: it is better for thee to enter halt into life, than having two feet to
46 be cast into hell, into the fire that never shall be quenched; where their
47 worm dieth not, and the fire is not quenched. And if thine eye [4]offend
thee, [e]pluck it out: it is better for thee to enter into the kingdom of God
48 with one eye, than having two eyes to be cast into hell-fire; where their

A. D. 32.

[z] 1 Cor. 12. 3.
[a] Matt. 12. 30. Luke 11. 23.
[b] Matt. 10. 42. Matt 25. 40.
[c] Matt. 18. 6. Luke 17. 1.
[3] Or, cause thee to offend. Deut. 13 6. Matt. 5. 29. Matt. 18. 8. Col. 3. 5. Heb. 12. 1.
[d] Isa. 66. 24. 2 Thes. 1. 9.
[4] Or, cause thee to offend.
[e] Rom. 8. 13. Gal. 5. 24.

name, and he followeth not us: and we forbade him, because he followeth not us. The link of connection here with the foregoing context lies, we apprehend, in the emphatic words which our Lord had just uttered, "in My name." 'O,' interposes John—young, warm, but not sufficiently apprehending Christ's teaching in these matters—'that reminds me of something that we have just done, and we should like to know if we did right. We saw one casting out devils "*in Thy name*," and we forbade him, because he followeth not us. Were we right, or were we wrong?' Answer—'Ye were wrong.' 'But we did it because he followeth not us?' 'No matter.' **39. But Jesus said, Forbid him not: for there is no man which shall do a miracle in my name, that can lightly** [ταχὺ]—or, 'soon,' that is, 'readily,' **speak evil of me. 40. For he that is not against us is on our part.** Two principles of immense importance are here laid down: 'First, No one will readily speak evil of Me who has the faith to do a miracle in My name; and Second, If such a person cannot be supposed to be *against* us, ye are to hold him *for* us.' Let it be carefully observed that our Lord does not say this man should *not* have "followed them," nor yet that it was indifferent whether he did or not; but simply teaches how such a person was to be regarded, *although he did not*—namely, as a reverer of His name and a promoter of His cause. **41. For whosoever shall give you a cup of water to drink in my name, because ye belong to Christ, verily I say unto you, he shall not lose his reward.** See on Matt. x. 42.

Continuation of Teaching suggested by the Disciples' Strife (42-50). What follows appears to have no connection with the incidental reproof of John, immediately preceding. As that had interrupted some important teaching, our Lord hastens back from it, as if no such interruption had occurred. **42. And whosoever shall offend** [σκανδαλίσῃ] **one of these little ones that believe in me**—or, shall cause them to stumble; referring probably to the effect which such unsavoury disputes as they had held would have upon the inquiring and hopeful who came in contact with them, leading to the belief that after all they were no better than others. **it is better for him that a millstone were hanged about his neck.** The word here is simply 'millstone' [λίθος μυλικὸς], without expressing of which kind. But in Matt. xviii. 6, it is the 'ass-turned' kind [μύλος ὀνικὸς], far heavier than the small hand-mill turned by female slaves, as in Luke xvii. 35. It is of course the same which is meant here. **and he were cast into the sea**—meaning, that if by such a death that stumbling were prevented, and so its eternal consequences averted, it would be a happy thing for them. Here follows a striking verse in Matt. xviii. 7, "Woe unto the world because of offences!"—'There will be stumblings and falls and loss of souls enough from the world's treatment of disciples, without any addition from you: dreadful will be its doom in consequence; see that ye share not in it.' "For it must needs be that offences come; but woe to that man by whom the offence cometh!" 'The struggle between light and darkness will inevitably cause stumblings, but not less guilty is he who wilfully makes any to stumble.' **43. And if thy hand offend thee, cut it off: it is better for thee to enter into life maimed, than having two hands to go into hell.** See on Matt. v. 29, 30, and Remark 8 on that Section. The only difference between the words there and here is, that there they refer to impure inclinations; here, to an ambitious disposition, an irascible or quarrelsome temper, and the like: and the injunction is, to strike at the root of such dispositions and cut off the occasions of them. **into the fire that never shall be quenched; 44. Where their worm dieth not, and the fire is not quenched. 45. And if thy foot offend thee, cut it off: it is better for thee to enter halt into life, than having two feet to be cast into hell.** See, as above, on Matt. v. 29, 30, and Remark 8 there. **into the fire that never shall be quenched; 46. Where their worm dieth not, and the fire is not quenched. 47. And if thine eye offend thee, pluck it out: it is better for thee to enter into the kingdom of God with one eye, than having two eyes to be cast into hell-fire; 48. Where their worm dieth not, and the fire is not quenched.** [We cannot but regret that the words of the 48th verse—which in the received text are thrice repeated, with a thrilling and deeply rhythmical effect—are in *Tischendorf's* text excluded in *vv.* 44 and 46, as being genuine only in *v.* 48; while *Tregelles* brackets them, as of doubtful genuineness. The MSS. by whose authority they are guided in this case are of formidable weight; but those in favour of the received text are far more numerous, and one (A) equal perhaps in value to the most ancient; while the authority of the most ancient and best versions is de-

49 worm dieth not, and the fire is not quenched. For every one shall be
salted with fire, and [f]every sacrifice shall be salted with salt.
50 Salt [g]*is* good; but if the salt have lost his saltness, wherewith will ye
season it? Have [h]salt in yourselves, and [i]have peace one with another.

A. D. 32.

f Lev. 2. 13.
g Luke 14. 34.
h Eph. 4. 29.
i Rom. 12. 18.

cidedly in favour of the received text. To us it seems not difficult to see how, though genuine, the repetition should have been excluded by copyists, to avoid an apparent tautology and to conform the text to that of Matthew, but very difficult to see how, if not genuine, it should have found its way into so many ancient MSS. *Lachmann* adheres to the received text, and even *Fritzsche* contends for it; while *Alford* says the triple repetition gives sublimity, and leaves no doubt of the discourse having been thus uttered *verbatim.*] See on Matt. v. 30; and on the words "hell" [γέεννα] and "hell-fire," or 'the hell of fire' [ἡ γέεννα τοῦ πυρὸς]: see on Matt. v. 22. The "unquenchableness" of this fire has already been brought before us (see on Matt. iii. 12); and the awfully vivid idea of an undying worm, everlastingly consuming an unconsumable body, is taken from the closing words of the Evangelical prophet (Isa. lxvi. 24), which seem to have furnished the later Jewish Church with its current phraseology on the subject of future punishment (see *Lightfoot*). **49. For every one shall be salted with fire, and every sacrifice shall be salted with salt.** [It is surprising that *Tregelles* should bracket the last clause, as doubtful—against very preponderating authority, and nearly all critics.] A difficult verse, on which much has been written —some of it to little purpose. "Every one" probably means, 'Every follower of mine;' and the "fire" with which he "must be salted" probably means 'a fiery trial' to season him, (Compare Mal. iii. 2, &c.) The reference to salting the sacrifice is of course to that maxim of the Levitical law, that every acceptable sacrifice must be sprinkled with salt, to express symbolically its soundness, sweetness, wholesomeness, acceptability. But as it had to be *roasted* first, we have here the further idea of a salting with fire. In this case, "every sacrifice," in the next clause, will mean, 'Every one who would be found an acceptable offering to God;' and thus the whole verse may perhaps be paraphrased as follows: 'Every disciple of Mine shall have a fiery trial to undergo, and every one who would be found an odour of a sweet smell, a sacrifice acceptable and well-pleasing to God, must have such a *salting*, like the Levitical sacrifices.' Another, but, as it seems to us, far-fetched as well as harsh, interpretation—suggested first, we believe, by *Michaelis*, and adopted by *Alexander*—takes the "every sacrifice which must be salted with fire" to mean those who are "cast into hell," and the *preservative* effect of this salting to refer to the preservation of the lost not only *in* but *by means of* the fire of hell. Their reason for this is that the other interpretation changes the meaning of the "fire," and the characters too, from the lost to the saved, in these verses. But as our Lord confessedly ends His discourse with the case of His own true disciples, the transition to them in the preceding verse is perfectly natural; whereas to apply the preservative salt of the sacrifice to the preserving quality of hell-fire, is equally contrary to the symbolical sense of salt and the Scripture representations of future torment. Our Lord has still in His eye the unseemly jarrings which had arisen among the Twelve, the peril to themselves of allowing any indulgence to such passions, and the severe self-sacrifice which salvation would cost them.

50. Salt is good; but if the salt have lost his saltness—its power to season what it is brought into contact with, **wherewith will ye season it?** How is this property to be restored? See on Matt. v. 13. **Have salt in yourselves**—'See to it that ye retain in yourselves those precious qualities that will make you a blessing to one another, and to all around you;' **and**—with respect to the miserable strife out of which all this discourse has sprung, in one concluding word—**have peace one with another.** This is repeated in 1 Thess. v. 13.

Remarks.—1. How little suffices to stir unholy jealousies and strifes, even in genuine disciples of the Lord Jesus and loving friends! In the present case they were occasioned, it would seem, by the recent extraordinary manifestations of their Master's glory, opening up to the half-instructed minds of the Twelve the prospect of earthly elevation, coupled with the preference shown to three of them on several occasions, and particularly to one; stirring the jealousy of the rest, and leading probably to insinuations that they were taking too much upon them—which, in the case of the two sons of Zebedee, was probably not quite groundless. The traitor, at least, though his real character had not yet come out, would probably be ready enough to resent any appearances of presumption among the rest. The flame, thus kindled, would soon spread; and this journey to Capernaum—probably their last in company with their blessed Master, who left them to travel part of the way by themselves—was embittered by dissensions which would leave a sting behind them for many a day! And did not the scene between Paul and Barnabas at Antioch, though of a very different nature, show how easily the holiest and dearest fellowships may be interrupted by miserable misunderstandings? See on Acts xv. 37-40; and on Matt. xviii. 10-35, Remark 1. 2. Of all the forms in which the great Evangelical Lesson is taught by our Lord—'that Humility is the entrance-gate into the kingdom of heaven, and that the humblest here is the highest there'—none is more captivating than this, under the lowly roof in Capernaum, when, surrounded by the Twelve and with a little child in His arms, He answered their question, Which of them should be greatest in the kingdom of heaven, by saying, 'He that is likest this unassuming child.' And what a Religion is that, at the foundation of which lies this divine principle! What a contrast to all that Paganism taught! Some bright manifestations were given of it under the ancient economy (Gen. xiii. 8, 9; Num. xii. 3; Ps. cxxxi. 1, 2, &c.), and some sublime expressions of it occur in the Old Testament, (Ps. xviii. 27; cxiii. 5, 6; cxlvii. 3-6; Isa. lvii. 15; Isa. lxvi. 1, 2, &c.) Nor could it well be otherwise, since the Religion of Israel was that of Christ in the bud, and the Old Testament Scriptures are the oracles of God (Rom. iii. 2). But as the Son of God Himself was the Incarnation of Humility, so it was reserved for Him to teach as well as exemplify it as before it had never been, nor ever again will be. See on ch. x. 42-45. 3. Alas, that with such lessons before them, the spirit of pride should have such free scope among the followers of Christ; that in particular the pride ecclesiastic should have become proverbial; and that so few who name the

10 AND [a]he arose from thence, and cometh into the coasts of Judea by
the farther side of Jordan: and the people resort unto him again: and,
as he was wont, he taught them again.
2 And [b]the Pharisees came to him, and asked him, Is it lawful for a man
3 to put away *his* wife? tempting him. And he answered and said unto
4 them, What did Moses command you? And they said, [c]Moses suffered
5 to write a bill of divorcement, and to put *her* away. And Jesus answered
and said unto them, For [d]the hardness of your heart he wrote you this
6 precept: but from the beginning of the creation God [e]made them male
7 and female. For [f]this cause shall a man leave his father and mother,
8 and cleave to his wife; and they twain shall be one flesh: so then they
9 are no more twain, but one flesh. What therefore God hath joined
together, let no man put asunder.
10 And in the house his disciples asked him again of the same *matter*.

A. D. 33.

CHAP. 10.
[a] Matt. 19. 1. John 10. 40. John 11. 7.
[b] Matt. 19. 3.
[c] Deut. 24. 1. Matt. 5. 31. Matt. 19. 7.
[d] Deut. 9. 6. Acts 13. 18.
[e] Gen. 1. 27. Gen. 2. 20-23. Gen. 5. 2.
[f] Gen. 2. 24. 1 Cor. 6. 16. Eph. 5. 31.

name of Christ should be distinguished for lowliness of mind! 4. The disposition which prompted John to forbid the man who cast out devils in Christ's name and yet followed not with Him and the Twelve, was extremely natural. Whether he was one of that small band of John's disciples who did not attach themselves to Christ's company but yet seem to have believed in Him, or whether, though a believer in Jesus, he had found some inconveniences in attending him statedly and so did not do it, we cannot tell. Though it is likely enough that he ought to have joined the company of Christ, the man had not seen his way to that himself. But the first question with John should have been, Have I any right to decide that point for him, or to judge him by my standard? 'You had not,' says our Lord. But further, 'Supposing the man does wrong in not following with us, is it right in me to forbid him, on that account, to cast out devils in my Master's name?' 'It was not,' says Christ. 'The deed itself was a good deed; it helped to destroy the works of the devil; and the Name in which this was done was that at which devils tremble. Thus far, then, the man was My servant, doing My work, and doing it not the less effectually and beneficially that he "followeth not us:" that is a question between him and Me; a question involving more points than you are aware of or able to deal with; a question with which you have nothing to do: Let such alone.' How instructive is this, and how condemning! Surely it condemns not only those horrible attempts *by force* to shut up all within one visible pale of discipleship, which have deluged Christendom with blood in Christ's name, but the same spirit in its milder form of proud ecclesiastic scowl upon all who "after the form which they call 'a sect' [αἵρεσιν] do so worship the God of their fathers" (see on Acts xxiv. 14). Visible unity in Christ's Church is indeed devoutly to be wished, and the want of it is cause enough of just sorrow and humiliation. But this is not the way to bring it about. It is not to be thought that the various ranks into which the Church of Christ is divided are all equally right in being what and where they are, if only they be sincere in their own convictions. But, right or wrong, they are as much entitled to exercise and act upon their conscientious judgment as we are, and to their own Master, in so doing, they stand or fall. It is the duty, and should be felt as the privilege, of all Christ's servants to rejoice in the promotion of His kingdom and cause by those they would wish, but cannot bring, within their own pale. Nor will anything contribute so much to bring Christians visibly together as just this joy at each other's success, although separate in the meantime; while on the other hand rancorous jealousies in behalf of our own sectional interests are the very thing to narrow these interests still further, and to shrivel ourselves. What a noble spirit did Moses display when the Spirit descended upon the seventy elders, and they prophesied and did not cease. Besides these the Spirit had come upon two men, who remained in the camp prophesying, *and did not join the seventy.* Whereupon there ran a zealous youth to Moses, saying, Eldad and Medad do prophesy in the camp; and even Joshua said, My lord Moses, forbid them. But what was the reply of the great leader of Israel? "Enviest thou for my sake? Would God that all the Lord's people were prophets, and that the Lord would pour out His Spirit upon them!" (Num. xi. 24-29). 5. The word "*hell*" thrice repeated here in the same breath is tremendous enough in itself; but how awful does it sound from the lips of *Love Incarnate!* And when to this He adds, thrice over in the same terms, "where their worm dieth not, and the fire is not quenched"—words enough to make both the ears of every one that heareth them to tingle—what shall be thought of the mawkish sentimentalism which condemns all such language in the mouths of His servants, as inconsistent with what they presume to call 'the religion of the meek and lowly Jesus?' Why, it is just the apostle who breathed most of His Master's love whose Epistles express what would be thought the harshest things against vital error and those who hold it. It is love to men, not hatred, that prompts such severity against what will inevitably ruin them. 6. Who that has any regard for the teaching of Christ can venture, in the face of these verses (42-48), to limit the duration of future torment? See on Matt. xxv. 31-46, Remark 4. 7. As Christians are to present themselves a living sacrifice to God, so when the sacrifice has had the fire applied to it, and stood the fire, it is an odour of a sweet smell, a sacrifice acceptable and well-pleasing to God. But let them not think that the only fiery trial they have to stand is persecution *from without.* The numberless things that tend to stir their corruptions, even in their intercourse with each other, constitute an almost daily trial, and sometimes fiery enough. Then it is that a living Christianity, subduing corruption and overcoming evil with good, shows its value. This is the true *salt of the sacrifice.* "Let your speech," says the apostle—and the same applies to every other feature of the Christian character—"be alway *with grace,*" or to speak sacrificially, "*seasoned with salt* that ye may know how ye ought to answer every man" (Col. iv. 6).

CHAP. X. 1-12.—FINAL DEPARTURE FROM

11 And he saith unto them, [g]Whosoever shall put away his wife, and marry
12 another, committeth adultery against her. And if a woman shall put
away her husband, and be married to another, she committeth adultery.
13 And [h]they brought young children to him, that he should touch them:
14 and *his* disciples rebuked those that brought *them*. But when Jesus saw
it, he was much displeased, and said unto them, Suffer the little children
to come unto me, and forbid them not: for [i]of such is the kingdom of God.
15 Verily I say unto you, [j]Whosoever shall not receive the kingdom of God
16 as a little child, he shall not enter therein. And he [k]took them up in
his arms, put *his* hands upon them, and blessed them.
17 And [l]when he was gone forth into the way, there came one running,
and kneeled to him, and asked him, Good Master, what shall I do that I
18 may inherit eternal life? And Jesus said unto him, Why callest thou
19 me good? *there is* none good but one, *that is*, God. Thou knowest the
commandments, [m]Do not commit adultery, Do not kill, Do not steal, Do
20 not bear false witness, Defraud not, Honour thy father and mother. And
he answered and said unto him, Master, all these have I observed from
21 my youth. Then Jesus, beholding him, loved him, and said unto him,
One thing thou lackest: go thy way, sell [n]whatsoever thou hast, and give
to the poor, and thou shalt have treasure [o]in heaven: and come, take up
22 the [p]cross, and follow me. And he was sad at that saying, and went
away grieved: for he had great possessions.
23 And [q]Jesus looked round about, and saith unto his disciples, How
24 hardly shall they that have riches enter into the kingdom of God! And
the disciples were astonished at his words. But Jesus answereth again,
and saith unto them, Children, how hard is it for them [r]that trust in
25 riches to enter into the kingdom of God! It is easier for a camel to go
through the eye of a needle, than for a rich man to enter into the
26 kingdom of God. And they were astonished out of measure, saying
27 among themselves, Who then can be saved? And Jesus, looking upon
them, saith, With men *it is* impossible, but not with God: for [s]with God
all things are possible.
28 Then [t]Peter began to say unto him, Lo, we have left all, and have
29 followed thee. And Jesus answered and said, Verily I say unto you,
There is no man that hath left house, or brethren, or sisters, or father, or
30 mother, or wife, or children, or lands, for my sake, and the Gospel's, but
[u]he shall receive an hundred-fold now in this time, houses, and brethren,
and sisters, and mothers, and children, and lands, [v]with persecutions;
31 and in the world to come eternal life. But [w]many *that are* first shall be
last; and the last first.
32 And [x]they were in the way going up to Jerusalem; and Jesus went
before them: and they were amazed; and as they followed, they were

A. D. 33.
[g] Matt. 5. 32. Matt. 19. 9. Luke 16.18. Rom. 7. 3.
[h] Matt. 19.13. Luke 18.15.
[i] 1 Cor. 14.20.
[j] Matt. 18. 3.
[k] Isa. 40. 11.
[l] Matt. 19.16. Luke 18.18.
[m] Ex. 20. Rom. 13. 9. Jas. 2. 11.
[n] Acts 2. 44. 1 Tim. 6.18.
[o] Matt. 6. 19, 20. Matt. 19.21. Luke 12.33. Luke 16. 9.
[p] Acts 14. 22. 2 Tim. 3.12.
[q] Matt. 19.23. Luke 18.24.
[r] Job 31. 24. Ps. 17. 14. Ps. 52. 7. Ps. 62. 10. 1 Tim. 6.17.
[s] Jer. 32. 17. Matt. 19.26. Luke 1. 37. Heb. 7. 25.
[t] Matt. 19.27. Luke 18.28.
[u] 2 Chr. 25. 9. Ps. 19. 11. Luke 18.30.
[v] Matt. 5. 11, 12. John 16.22, 23. Acts 14. 22. Rom. 5. 3. 1 Thes. 3.3. 2 Tim. 3.12. Heb. 12. 6. 1 Pet. 4. 12-16.
[w] Matt. 19.30. Matt. 20.16. Luke 13.30.
[x] Matt. 20.17. Luke 18.31.

GALILEE—DIVORCE. (= Matt. xix. 1-12; Luke ix. 51.) For the exposition, see on Matt. xix. 1-12.

13-16.—LITTLE CHILDREN BROUGHT TO CHRIST. (= Matt. xix. 13-15; Luke xviii. 15-17.) For the exposition, see on Luke xviii. 15-17.

17-31.—THE RICH YOUNG RULER. (= Matt. xix. 16-30; Luke xviii. 18-30.) For the exposition, see on Luke xviii. 18-30.

32-45.—THIRD EXPLICIT AND STILL FULLER ANNOUNCEMENT OF HIS APPROACHING SUFFERINGS, DEATH, AND RESURRECTION—THE AMBITIOUS REQUEST OF JAMES AND JOHN, AND THE REPLY. (= Matt. xx. 17-28; Luke xviii. 31-34.)

Third Announcement of His approaching Sufferings, Death, and Resurrection (32-34). **32. And they were in the way**—or on the road, **going up to Jerusalem**—in Perea, and probably somewhere between Ephraim and Jericho, on the farther side of the Jordan, and to the north-east of Jerusalem. **and Jesus went before them**—as *Grotius* says, in the style of an intrepid Leader. **and they were amazed** [ἐθαμβοῦντο]—or 'struck with astonishment' at His courage in advancing to certain death. **and as they followed, they were afraid**—for their own safety. These artless, life-like touches—not only from an eye-witness, but one whom the noble carriage of the Master struck with wonder and awe—are peculiar to Mark, and give the second Gospel a charm all its own; making us feel as if we ourselves were in the midst of the scenes it describes. Well might the poet exclaim,

'The Saviour, what a noble flame
Was kindled in His breast,
When, hasting to Jerusalem,
He march'd before the rest!'—COWPER.

And he took again the twelve—referring to His

afraid. [y]And he took again the twelve, and began to tell them what
33 things should happen unto him, *saying*, Behold, we go up to Jerusalem;
and the Son of man shall be delivered unto the chief priests, and unto
the scribes; and they shall condemn him to death, and shall deliver him
34 to the Gentiles: and they shall [z]mock him, and shall scourge him, and
shall spit upon him, and shall kill him: and the third day he shall rise
again.
35 And James and John, the sons of Zebedee, come unto him, saying,
Master, we would that thou shouldest do for us whatsoever we shall
36 desire. And he said unto them, What would ye that I should do for you?
37 They said unto him, Grant unto us that we may sit, one on thy right
38 hand, and the other on thy left hand, in thy glory. But Jesus said unto
them, Ye know not what ye ask: can ye drink of the cup that I drink
39 of? and be baptized with the baptism that I am baptized with? And
they said unto him, We can. And Jesus said unto them, [a]Ye shall
indeed drink of the cup that I drink of; and with the baptism that I am

A. D. 33.

[y] Matt. 11. 35. Matt. 13. 11. ch. 4. 34. ch. 8. 31. ch. 9. 31. Luke 9. 22. Luke 18. 31.

[z] Ps. 22. 6-8. Isa. 53. 3. Matt. 27. 27. Luke 22. 63. Luke 23. 11. John 19. 2.

[a] Matt 10. 25. ch. 14. 36. John 15. 20. John 17. 14. Acts 12. 2. Col. 1. 24. Rev. 1. 9.

previous announcements on this sad subject. **and began to tell them what things should happen unto him** [τὰ μέλλοντα αὐτῷ συμβαίνειν]—'were going to befall Him.' The word expresses something already begun but not brought to a head, rather than something wholly future. **33. Saying, Behold, we go up to Jerusalem**—for the last time, **and**—"all things that are written by the prophets concerning the Son of man shall be accomplished" (Luke xviii. 31). **the Son of man shall be delivered unto the chief priests, and unto the scribes; and they shall condemn him to death, and shall deliver him to the Gentiles.** This is the first express statement that the Gentiles would combine with the Jews in His death; the two grand divisions of the human race for whom He died thus taking part in crucifying the Lord of Glory, as *Webster and Wilkinson* observe. **34. And they shall mock him, and shall scourge him, and shall spit upon him, and shall kill him: and the third day he shall rise again.** Singularly explicit as this announcement was, Luke (xviii. 34) says "they understood none of these things: and this saying was hid from them, neither knew they the things which were spoken." The meaning of the words they could be at no loss to understand, but their import in relation to His Messianic kingdom they could not penetrate; the whole prediction being right in the teeth of their preconceived notions. That they should have clung so tenaciously to the popular notion of an *un*suffering Messiah, may surprise us; but it gives inexpressible weight to their after-testimony to a suffering and dying Saviour.

Ambitious Request of James and John—The Reply (35-45). **35. And James and John, the sons of Zebedee, come unto him, saying.** Matthew (xx. 20) says their "mother came to Him with her sons, worshipping Him and desiring," &c. (Compare Matt. xxvii. 56, with Mark xv. 40.) Salome was her name (ch. xvi. 1). We cannot be sure with which of the parties the movement originated; but as our Lord, even in Matthew's account, addresses Himself to James and John, making no account of the mother, it is likely the mother was merely set on by them. The thought was doubtless suggested to her sons by the recent promise to the Twelve of "thrones to sit on, when the Son of man should sit on the throne of His glory" (Matt. xix. 28); but after the reproof so lately given them (ch. ix. 33, &c.), they get their mother to speak for them. **Master, we would that thou shouldest do for us whatsoever we shall desire**—thus cautiously approaching the subject. **36. And he said unto them, What would ye that I should do for you?** Though well aware what was their mind and their mother's, our Lord will have the unseemly petition uttered before all. **37. They said unto him, Grant unto us that we may sit, one on thy right hand, and the other on thy left hand, in thy glory**—that is, Assign to us the two places of highest honour in the coming kingdom. The semblance of a plea for so presumptuous a request might possibly have been drawn from the fact that one of the two usually leaned on the breast of Jesus, or sat next Him at meals, while the other was one of the favoured three. **38. But Jesus said unto them, Ye know not what ye ask.** How gentle the reply to such a request, preferred at such a time, after the sad announcement just made! **can ye drink of the cup that I drink of?** To 'drink of a cup' is in Scripture a figure for getting one's fill either of good (Ps. xvi. 5; xxiii. 5; cxvi. 13; Jer. xvi. 7) or of ill (Ps. lxxv. 8; John xviii. 11; Rev. xiv. 10). Here it is the cup of suffering. **and be baptized with the baptism that I am baptized with?** (Compare, for the language, Ps. xlii. 7.) The object of this question seems to have been to try how far those two men were *capable* of the dignity to which they aspired; and this on the principle that he who is able to suffer most for His sake will be the nearest to Him in His kingdom. **39. And they said unto him, We can.** Here we see them owning their mother's petition for them as their own; and doubtless they were perfectly sincere in professing their willingness to follow their Master to any suffering He might have to endure. Well, and they shall have to do it. As for *James*, he was the first of the apostles who was honoured, and showed himself able, to be baptized with his Master's baptism of blood (Acts xii. 1, 2); while *John*, after going through all the persecutions to which the infant Church was exposed from the Jews, and sharing in the struggles and sufferings occasioned by the first triumphs of the Gospel among the Gentiles, lived to be the victim, after all the rest had got to glory, of a bitter persecution in the evening of his days, for the word of God and for the testimony of Jesus Christ. Yes, they were dear believers and blessed men, in spite of this unworthy ambition, and their Lord knew it; and perhaps the foresight of what they would have to pass through, and the courageous testimony He would yet receive from them, was the cause of that gentleness which we cannot but wonder at in His reproof. **And Jesus said**

40 baptized withal shall ye be baptized: but to sit on my right hand and on
my left hand is not mine to give; but *it shall be given* [b]to *them* for
whom it is prepared.
41 And [c]when the ten heard *it,* they began to be much displeased with
42 James and John. But Jesus called them *to him,* and saith unto them, [d]Ye
know that they which [1]are accounted to rule over the Gentiles exercise
lordship over them; and their great ones exercise authority upon them.
43 But [e]so shall it not be among you: but whosoever will be great among
44 you, shall be your minister; and whosoever of you will be the chiefest,
45 shall be servant of all. For even [f]the Son of man came not to be
ministered unto, but to minister, and to [g]give his life a ransom for many.

A. D. 33.

b Jas. 4. 3.
c Matt. 20. 24.
d Luke 22. 25.
1 Or, think good.
e ch. 9. 35. Luke 9. 48.
f John 13. 14. Phil. 2. 7. Heb. 5. 8.
g Isa. 53. 10. Dan. 9. 24, 26.

unto them, Ye shall indeed drink of the cup that I drink of; and with the baptism that I am baptized withal shall ye be baptized. No doubt this prediction, when their sufferings at length came upon them, cheered them with the assurance, not that they would sit on His right and left hand—for of that thought they would be heartily ashamed—but that "if they suffered with Him, they should be also glorified together." **40. But to sit on my right hand and on my left hand is not mine to give; but [it shall be given to them] for whom** [ἀλλ' οἷς] **it is prepared**—"of my Father" (Matt. xx. 23). The supplement which our translators have inserted is approved by some good interpreters, and the proper sense of the word rendered "but" [ἀλλά] is certainly in favour of it. But besides that it makes the statement too elliptical—leaving too many words to be supplied—it seems to make our Lord repudiate the right to assign to each of His people his place in the kingdom of glory; a thing which He nowhere else does, but rather the contrary. It is true that He says their place is "prepared for them by His Father." But that is true of their admission to heaven at all; and yet from His great white throne Jesus will Himself adjudicate the kingdom, and authoritatively invite into it those on His right hand, calling them the "blessed of His Father:" so little inconsistency is there between the eternal choice of them by His Father, and that public adjudication of them, not only to heaven in general, but each to his own position in it, which all Scripture assigns to Christ. The true rendering, then, of this clause, we take it, is this: 'But to sit on My right hand and on My left hand is not Mine to give, save to them for whom it is prepared.' [The use of ἀλλά in this sense, as equivalent to εἰ μή, occurs in ch. ix. 8, "They saw no man any more *save* Jesus only"—ἀλλὰ τὸν Ιησοῦν. And the very words of our Evangelist, ἀλλ' οἷς, occur in this sense in Matt. xix. 11]. When therefore He says, "It is not mine to give" the meaning is, 'I cannot give it as a *favour* to whomsoever I *please*, or on a principle of *favouritism:* it belongs exclusively to those for whom it is prepared,' &c. And if this be His meaning, it will be seen how far our Lord is from disclaiming the right to assign to each his proper place in His Kingdom; that on the contrary, He expressly asserts it, merely announcing that the principle of distribution is quite different from what these petitioners supposed. Our Lord, it will be observed, does not *deny* the petition of James and John, or say they shall *not* occupy the place in His kingdom which they now improperly sought:—for aught we know, *that may be their true place.* All we are sure of is, that their asking it was displeasing to Him "to whom all judgment is committed," and so was not fitted to gain their object, but just the reverse. (See what is taught in Luke xiv. 8-11.) One at least of these brethren, as *Alford* strikingly remarks, saw on the right and on the left hand of their Lord, as He hung upon the tree, the crucified thieves; and bitter indeed must have been the remembrance of this ambitious prayer at that moment.

41. And when the ten heard it, they began to be much displeased with James and John—or "were moved with indignation," as the same word [ἀγανακτεῖν] is rendered in Matt. xx. 24. The expression "*began* to be," which is of frequent occurrence in the Gospels, means that more passed than is expressed, and that we have but the result. And can we blame the ten for the indignation which they felt? Yet there was probably a spice of the old spirit of rivalry in it, which in spite of our Lord's recent lengthened, diversified, and most solemn warnings against it, had not ceased to stir in their breasts. **42. But Jesus called them to him, and saith unto them, Ye know that they which are accounted to rule**—are recognized or acknowledged as rulers, **over the Gentiles exercise lordship over them; and their great ones exercise authority upon them**—as superiors exercising an acknowledged authority over inferiors. **43. But so shall it not be among you: but whosoever will be great among you, shall be your minister** [διάκονος]—a subordinate servant. **44. And whosoever of you will be the chiefest**—or 'first' [πρῶτος], **shall be**—that is, 'let him be,' or 'shall be he who is prepared to be' **servant of all** [δοῦλος]—one in the lowest condition of service. **45. For even the Son of man came not to be ministered unto, but to minister, and to give his life a ransom for**—or, 'instead of'—**many** [λύτρον ἀντι πολλῶν]:—*q. d.*, 'In the kingdom about to be set up this principle shall have no place. All my servants shall there be equal; and the only "greatness" known to it shall be the greatness of humility and devotedness to the service of others. He that goes down the deepest in these services of self-denying humility shall rise the highest and hold the "chiefest" place in that kingdom; even as the Son of man, whose abasement and self-sacrifice for others, transcending all, gives Him of right a place above all! As "the Word in the beginning with God," He *was* ministered unto; and as the risen Redeemer in our nature He now *is* ministered unto, "angels and authorities and powers being made subject unto Him" (1 Pet. iii. 22); but not for this came He hither. The Served of all came to be the Servant of all; and His last act was the grandest Service ever beheld by the universe of God—"HE GAVE HIS LIFE A RANSOM FOR MANY!" "Many" is here to be taken, not in contrast with *few* or with *all*, but in opposition to *one*—the one Son of man for the many sinners.

Remarks.—1. When we read of Jesus, on His last journey from Galilee to Jerusalem, going before the Twelve, with a courage which amazed and

46 And [h]they came to Jericho: and as he went out of Jericho with his
disciples and a great number of people, blind Bartimeus, the son of Timeus,
47 sat by the highway-side begging. And when he heard that it was Jesus
of Nazareth, he began to cry out, and say, Jesus, *thou* [i]son of David, have
48 mercy on me. And many charged him that he should hold his peace:
but he cried the more a great deal, *Thou* son of David, have mercy on
49 me. And Jesus stood still, and commanded him to be called. And they
call the blind man, saying unto him, Be of good comfort, rise; he calleth
50 thee. And he, casting away his garment, rose, and came to Jesus.
51 And Jesus answered and said unto him, What wilt thou that I should
do unto thee? The blind man said unto him, Lord, that I might receive
52 my sight. And Jesus said unto him, Go thy way; thy faith hath [2]made
thee whole. And immediately [j]he received his sight, and followed Jesus
in the way.

11 AND [a]when they came nigh to Jerusalem, unto Bethphage and
Bethany, at the mount of [b]Olives, he sendeth forth two of his disciples,
2 and saith unto them, Go your way into the village over against you: and
as soon as ye be entered into it, ye shall find a colt tied, whereon never
3 man sat; loose him, and bring *him.* And if any man say unto you, Why
do ye this? say ye that [c]the Lord hath need of him; and straightway he
4 will send him hither. And they went their way, and found the colt tied
by the door without in a place where two ways met; and they loose him.
5 And certain of them that stood there said unto them, What do ye, loosing
6 the colt? And they said unto them even as Jesus had commanded: and
7 they let them go. And they brought the colt to Jesus, and cast their
8 garments on him; [d]and he sat upon him. And [e]many spread their garments in the way; and others cut down branches off the trees, and
9 strawed *them* in the way. And they that went before, and they that
followed, cried, saying, [f]Hosanna! Blessed *is* he that cometh in the

A. D. 33.
[h] Matt. 20. 29. Luke 18. 35.
[i] Isa. 11. 1. Jer. 23. 5, 6. Rom. 1. 3. Rev. 22. 16.
[2] Or, saved thee. Matt. 9. 22.
[j] Isa. 29. 18. Isa. 32. 3. Isa. 35. 5. Isa. 42. 6, 7. Isa. 43. 8. Acts 26. 18.

CHAP. 11.
[a] Matt. 21. 1. Luke 19. 29. John 12. 14.
[b] Zec. 14. 4. Matt. 24. 3. John 8. 1. Acts 1. 12.
[c] Ps. 24. 1. Acts 10. 36. Heb. 1. 2. Heb. 2. 7-9.
[d] 1 Ki. 1. 33. Zec. 9. 9.
[e] Matt. 21. 8.
[f] Ps. 118. 26. Isa 62. 11. Matt. 21. 9. Matt. 23. 39. Luke 19, 37. 38. John 12. 13.

terrified them, it were well that we searched into the hidden springs of this, so far as we have scriptural light to guide us. Turning then to that glorious Messianic prediction, in the 50th of Isaiah, we find Him saying, "The Lord God hath given me the tongue of the learned, that I should know how to speak a word in season to Him that is weary: He wakeneth morning by morning; He wakeneth mine ear to hear as the learned (or 'as an instructed person'). The Lord God hath opened mine ear, and I was not rebellious, neither turned away back. I gave my back to the smiters, and my cheeks to them that plucked off the hair: I hid not my face from shame and spitting. For the Lord God will help me; therefore shall I not be confounded: therefore have I *set my face like a flint*, and I know that I shall not be ashamed," &c. (*vv.* 4-7). Here He speaks as if He went each successive morning to His Father, to receive His instructions for the work of each day; so that when He either spake a word in season to a weary soul, or showed unflinching courage in encountering opposition, or, as here, marched to the rude mockeries and cruel sufferings which awaited Him, with His "face set like a flint, knowing that He should not be ashamed," it was not mere impassive Godhead that did it, but the Son of man, keenly sensitive to shame and suffering, and only rising above them through the power of an all-subduing devotion to the great end of His mission into the world, and this, too, fed by daily communion with His Father in heaven. Thus is He to His people the perfect Model of self-devotion to the work given them to do. 2. How hard it is for even the plainest truths to penetrate through prejudice, we see once and again in these disciples of the Lord Jesus. The third Evangelist seems unable to say strongly enough how entirely hidden from them at that time was the *sense* of those exceeding plain statements in which our Lord now, for the third time, announced what lay before Him. And though this added prodigious, and, to the simple-hearted, irresistible weight to their subsequent testimony in behalf of a suffering, dying, and rising Messiah—now so incomprehensible to them—it teaches to us a lesson, of which we have as much need as they, to guard against allowing prepossessions and prejudices to thicken around us and shut out from our mind the clearest truth. 3. When the indignation of the ten was kindled against James and John for their offensive petition, how admirable was the wisdom of their Lord which then interposed, checking the hot quarrel which doubtless would have broken out at that moment, by calling them all equally around Him and opening to them calmly the relation in which they were to stand, and the spirit they were to cherish to each other in the future work of His kingdom, holding forth Himself as the sublime Model both for their feeling and for their acting! 4. The *sacrificial* and *vicarious* nature of Christ's death is here expressed by Himself (*v.* 45) as plainly as the *manner* of His death is foretold a few verses before. And to say that this was merely in accommodation to Jewish ideas, is to dishonour the teaching of our Lord, and degrade Judaism to a level with the rites of Paganism.

46-52.—BLIND BARTIMEUS HEALED. (= Matt. xx. 29-34; Luke xviii. 35-43.) For the exposition, see on Luke xviii. 35-43.

CHAP. XI. 1-11.—CHRIST'S TRIUMPHAL ENTRY

10 name of the Lord! Blessed *be* the kingdom of our father David, that
cometh in the name of the Lord! [g]Hosanna in the highest!
11 And [h]Jesus entered into Jerusalem, and into the temple: and when he
had looked round about upon all things, and now the even-tide was come,
he went out unto Bethany with the twelve.
12 And [i]on the morrow, when they were come from Bethany, he was
13 hungry: and [j]seeing a fig tree afar off having leaves, he came, if haply
he might find any thing thereon: and when he came to it, he found
14 nothing but leaves; for the time of figs was not *yet*. And Jesus
answered and said unto it, No man eat fruit of thee hereafter for ever.
And his disciples heard *it*.
15 And [k]they come to Jerusalem: and Jesus went into the temple, and
began to cast out them that sold and bought in the temple, and overthrew the tables of the money-changers, and the seats of them that sold
16 doves; and would not suffer that any man should carry *any* vessel
17 through the temple. And he taught, saying unto them, Is it not written,
[l]My house shall be called [1]of all nations the house of prayer? but [m]ye
18 have made it a den of thieves. And [n]the scribes and chief priests heard
it, and sought how they might destroy him: for they feared him, because
19 all [o]the people was astonished at his doctrine. And when even was come,
he went out of the city.
20 And [p]in the morning, as they passed by, they saw the fig tree dried

A. D. 33.

[g] Ps. 148. 1.
[h] Matt. 21. 12.
[i] Matt. 21. 18.
[j] Matt. 21. 19.
[k] Matt. 21. 12. Luke 19. 45. John 2. 14.
[l] Isa. 56. 7. Isa. 60. 7. Zec. 2. 11.
[1] Or, an house of prayer for all nations?
[m] Jer. 7. 11. Hos. 12. 7. John 2. 16.
[n] Matt. 21. 45, 46. Luke 19. 47.
[o] Matt. 7. 28. ch. 1. 22. Luke 4. 32.
[p] Matt. 21. 19. John 15. 6. Heb. 6. 8. Jude 12.

INTO JERUSALEM, ON THE FIRST DAY OF THE WEEK. (= Matt. xxi. 1-9; Luke xix. 29-40; John xii. 12. 19.) For the exposition of this majestic scene—recorded, as will be seen, by all the Evangelists—see on Luke xix. 29-40.

11-26.—THE BARREN FIG TREE CURSED, WITH LESSONS FROM IT—SECOND CLEANSING OF THE TEMPLE, ON THE SECOND AND THIRD DAYS OF THE WEEK. (= Matt. xxi. 12-22; Luke xix. 45-48.)

11. And Jesus entered into Jerusalem, and into the temple: and when he had looked round about upon—or 'surveyed' **all things, and now the even-tide was come, he went out unto Bethany with the twelve.** Thus briefly does our Evangelist dispose of this His first day in Jerusalem, after the triumphal entry. Nor do the Third and Fourth Gospels give us more light. But from Matthew (xxi. 10, 11, 14-16) we learn some additional and precious particulars, for which see on Luke xix. 45-48. It was not now safe for the Lord to sleep in the City, nor, from the day of His Triumphal Entry, did He pass one night in it, save the last fatal one.

The Barren Fig Tree Cursed (12-14). **12. And on the morrow.** The Triumphal Entry being on the First day of the week, this following day was Monday. **when they were come from Bethany**—"in the morning" (Matt. xxi. 18)—**he was hungry.** How was that? Had He stolen forth from that dear roof at Bethany to the "mountain to pray, and continued all night in prayer to God?" (Luke vi. 12); or, "in the morning," as on a former occasion, "risen up a great while before day, and departed into a solitary place, and there prayed" (Mark i. 35); not breaking His fast thereafter, but bending His steps straight for the city, that He might "work the works of Him that sent Him while it was day"? (John ix. 4). We know not, though one lingers upon and loves to trace out the every movement of that life of wonders. One thing, however, we are sure of—it was *real bodily hunger* which He now sought to allay by the fruit of this fig tree, "if haply He might find any thing thereon;" not a mere *scene* for the purpose of teaching a lesson, as some early heretics maintained, and some still seem virtually to hold. **13. And seeing a fig tree.** (In Matt. xxi. 19, it is 'one fig tree' [μίαν], but the sense is the same as here, 'a certain fig tree' [= τινα], as in Matt. viii. 19, &c.) Bethphage, which adjoined Bethany, derives its name from its being a *fig-region* [בֵּית־פַּגֵּי]—'House of figs.' **afar off having leaves**—and therefore promising fruit, which in the case of figs comes before the leaves. **he came, if haply he might find any thing thereon: and when he came to it, he found nothing but leaves; for the time of figs was not [yet].** What the precise import of this explanation is, interpreters are not agreed. Perhaps all that is meant is, that as the proper fig season had not arrived, no fruit would have been expected even of this tree but for the leaves which it had, which were in this case prematurely and unnaturally developed. **14. And Jesus answered and said unto it, No man eat fruit of thee hereafter for ever.** That word did not *make* the tree barren, but sealed it up in its own barrenness. See on Matt. xiii. 13-15. **And his disciples heard it**—and marked the saying. This is introduced as a connecting link, to explain what was afterwards to be said on the subject, as the narrative has to proceed to the other transactions of this day.

Second Cleansing of the Temple (15-18). For the exposition of this portion, see on Luke xix. 45-48.

Lessons from the Cursing of the Fig Tree (20-26). **20. And in the morning**—of Tuesday, the third day of the week: He had slept, as during all this week, at Bethany. **as they passed by**—going into Jerusalem again, **they saw the fig tree dried up from the roots**—no partial blight, leaving life in the root; but it was now dead, root and branch. In Matt. xxi. 19, it is said it withered away as soon as it was cursed. But the full blight had not appeared probably at once; and in the dusk perhaps, as they returned to Bethany, they had not observed it. The precision with which Mark distinguishes the days is not observed by Matthew, intent only on holding up the truths which the incident was designed to teach. In Matthew the whole is represented as taking place at once, just as the two stages of Jairus' daughter—dying and dead—are represented by him as one. The only

21 up from the roots. And Peter calling to remembrance saith unto him,
22 Master, behold, the fig tree which thou cursedst is withered away. And
23 Jesus answering saith unto them, [2]Have faith in God. For [q]verily I say
unto you, That whosoever shall say unto this mountain, Be thou removed,
and be thou cast into the sea; and shall not doubt in his heart, but shall
believe that those things which he saith shall come to pass; he shall have
24 whatsoever he saith. Therefore I say unto you, [r]What things soever ye
desire, when ye pray, believe that ye receive *them,* and ye shall have *them.*
25 And when ye stand praying, [s]forgive, if ye have ought against any; that
your Father also which is in heaven may forgive you your trespasses.
26 But [t]if ye do not forgive, neither will your Father which is in heaven
forgive your trespasses.
27 And they come again to Jerusalem: and [u]as he was walking in the
temple, there come to him the chief priests, and the scribes, and the

A. D. 33.

[2] Or, Have the faith of God.
[q] Matt. 17. 20. Matt. 21. 21. Luke 17. 6.
[r] Luke 11. 9. John 14. 13. John 15. 7. John 16 24. Jas. 1. 5, 6.
[s] Matt. 6. 14. Col. 3. 13. Eph. 4. 32.
[t] Matt. 18. 35.
[u] Matt 21. 23. Luke 20. 1.

difference is between a more summary and a more detailed narrative, each of which only confirms the other. **21. And Peter calling to remembrance saith unto him**—satisfied that a miracle so very peculiar, a miracle, not of *blessing,* as all his other miracles, but of *cursing,* could not have been wrought but with some higher reference, and fully expecting to hear something weighty on the subject: **Master, behold, the fig tree which thou cursedst is withered away**—so connecting the two things as to show that he traced the death of the tree entirely to the curse of his Lord. Matthew (xxi. 20) gives this simply as a general exclamation of surprise by the disciples "how soon" the blight had taken effect. **22. And Jesus answering saith unto them, Have faith in God. 23. For verily I say unto you, That whosoever shall say unto this mountain, Be thou removed, and be thou cast into the sea; and shall not doubt in his heart, but shall believe that those things which he saith shall come to pass; he shall have whatsoever he saith.** Here is the lesson now. From the nature of the case supposed—that they might wish a mountain removed and cast into the sea, a thing far removed from anything which they could be thought actually to desire—it is plain that not physical but moral obstacles to the progress of His kingdom were in the Redeemer's view, and that what He designed to teach was the great lesson, that *no obstacle should be able to stand before a confiding faith in God.* **24. Therefore I say unto you, What things soever ye desire, when ye pray, believe that ye receive them, and ye shall have them.** This verse only *generalizes* the assurance of the former verse; which seems to show that it was designed for the special encouragement of *evangelistic* and *missionary* efforts, while this is a directory for prevailing *prayer in general.* **25. And when ye stand praying, forgive, if ye have aught against any; that your Father also which is in heaven may forgive you your trespasses. 26. But if ye do not forgive, neither will your Father which is in heaven forgive your trespasses.** This is repeated from the Sermon on the Mount (see on Matt. vi. 14, 15); to remind them that if this was necessary to the acceptableness of *all* prayer, much more *when great things were to be asked and confidently expected.* [*Tischendorf* excludes *v.* 26 from his text, on what appears to us very insufficient evidence. He thinks it borrowed from Matt. vi. 15. *Tregelles* also excludes it; but *Lachmann* retains it. Of critical commentators, though *Fritzsche* brackets it and inclines against it, *Meyer* and *Alford* defend it, and *De Wette* is in favour of it.]

Remarks.—1. Needless difficulties have been raised, and indifferent solutions of them offered, on the subject of our Lord's expecting fruit from the fig tree when He must have known there was none. But the same difficulty may be raised about the structure of the parable of the Barren Fig Tree, in which it is said that the great Husbandman "came and sought fruit thereon, and found none" (Luke xiii. 6). The same difficulty may be raised about almost every human thought, feeling, and action of our Lord—that if He possessed Divine knowledge and infinite power, such thoughts, feelings, and actions could not have been real. Nay, such difficulties may be raised about the reality of human freedom and responsibility, if it be true that everything is under the supreme direction of the Lord of all. Let us have done with such vain speculations, which every well-regulated mind sees to involve no difficulty at all, though the principle which lies at the bottom of them is beyond the reach of the human mind at present—possibly beyond all finite comprehension. 2. Was there not another fig tree to which Christ came—not once only, but "lo, those three years—seeking fruit and finding none"? (See on Luke xiii. 6-9.) How really, how continuously, how keenly, He hungered for *that* fruit, is best understood by His lamentation over it—"How often would I have gathered thee, and ye would not!" (Matt. xxiii. 37). And is not this repeated from age to age? Well, just as the fig tree which Christ cursed was *dried* up from the roots long before it was *pulled* up by the roots, so was it with Israel, of whom Jesus said, whilst He was yet alive, "but *now* the things that belong to thy peace are hid from thine eyes;" and yet it was long after that before "the wrath came upon them to the uttermost." And so it is to be feared that many are blighted before they are cut down and cast into the fire, and that there may be a definite time when the curse is pronounced, when the transition takes place, and when the withering process begins, never to be arrested. (See Ezek. xvii. 24.) O that men were wise, that they understood these things, that they would consider their latter end! 3. What glorious encouragement to evangelistic and missionary effort is here held forth! And has not the promise of *v.* 23 been so abundantly fulfilled in past history as to put to flight all our fears about the future? Certainly when one thinks of the "mountains" that have already been "removed and cast into the sea" by the victorious faith of Christ's disciples—the towering paganisms of the old world which have fallen before the Church of Christ—we may well exclaim of the gigantic Indian superstitions, with the hoar of entire millenniums upon them, and of all other obstacles whatever to the triumphs of the Cross, "*Who art thou, O great mountain? Before Zerubbabel thou shalt become a plain*" (Zec. iv. 7).

27-33.—THE AUTHORITY OF JESUS QUESTIONED

28 elders, and say unto him, By what authority doest thou these things?
29 and who gave thee this authority to do these things? And Jesus
answered and said unto them, I will also ask of you one [3]question, and
30 answer me, and I will tell you by what authority I do these things. The
31 baptism of John, was *it* from heaven, or of men? answer me. And they
reasoned with themselves, saying, If we shall say, From heaven; he will
32 say, Why then did ye not believe him? But if we shall say, Of men;
they feared the people: for [v]all *men* counted John, that he was a prophet
33 indeed. And they answered and said unto Jesus, We cannot tell. And
Jesus answering saith unto them, [w]Neither do I tell you by what authority
I do these things.

12 AND [a]he began to speak unto them by parables. A *certain* man
planted a vineyard, and set an hedge about *it*, and digged *a place for*
the winefat, and built a tower, and let it out to husbandmen, and went
2 into a far country. And at the season he sent to the husbandmen a
servant, that he might receive from the husbandmen of the fruit of the
3 vineyard. And they caught *him*, and beat him, and sent *him* away
4 empty. And again he sent unto them another servant; and at him they
cast stones, and wounded *him* in the head, and sent *him* away shamefully
5 handled. And again he sent another; and him they killed, and many
6 others; beating some, and [b]killing some. Having yet therefore one son,
[c]his well-beloved, he sent him also last unto them, saying, They will
7 reverence my son. But those husbandmen said among themselves, This
is [d]the heir; come, let us kill him, and the inheritance shall be ours.
8 And they took him, and [e]killed *him*, and cast *him* out of the vineyard.
9 What shall therefore the lord of the vineyard do? He will come and
10 destroy the husbandmen, and [f]will give the vineyard unto others. And
have ye not read this scripture; The [g]stone which the builders rejected
11 is become the head of the corner: this was the Lord's doing, and [h]it is
marvellous in our eyes?
12 And [i]they sought to lay hold on him, but feared the people; for they
knew that he had spoken the parable against them: and they left him,
and went their way.
13 And [j]they send unto him certain of the Pharisees and of the Herodians,
to catch him in *his* words.
14 And when they were come, they say unto him, Master, we know
that thou art true, and carest for no man; for thou regardest not the
person of men, but teachest the way of God in truth: Is it lawful to give
15 tribute to Cesar, or not? Shall we give, or shall we not give? But he,
knowing their hypocrisy, said unto them, Why tempt ye me? bring me

A. D. 33.

[3] Or, thing.
[v] Matt. 3. 5. Matt. 14. 5. ch. 6. 20.
[w] Job 5. 13. Ps. 9. 15. Ps. 33. 10. Pro. 26. 4,5. Matt. 16. 4. 1 Cor. 3. 19.

CHAP. 12.
[a] Ps. 80. 8. Song 8. 11. Isa. 5. 1. Jer. 2. 21. Matt. 21.33. Luke 20. 9.
[b] 2 Chr. 24. 14. 2 Chr. 36. 16. Neh. 9. 26. Acts 7. 52. 1 Thes. 2. 15. Heb. 11. 36.
[c] Ps. 2. 7. Matt. 1. 23. Rom. 8. 3. Gal. 4. 4. 1 John 4. 9. 1 John 5. 11, 12.
[d] Ps 2. 8. Heb. 1. 2. Acts 4. 27.
[e] Acts 2. 23.
[f] Acts 28. 23-28.
[g] Ps. 118. 22. Matt. 21.42. Luke 20.17, 18. Rom. 9. 33. Eph. 2. 20. 1 Pet. 2. 7,8.
[h] 1 Tim. 3. 16.
[i] Matt. 21.45, 46. ch. 11. 18. John 7. 25, 30, 44.
[j] Matt. 22.15. Luke 20.20.

—HIS REPLY. (=Matt. xxi. 23-27; Luke xx. 1-8.) For the exposition, see on Matt. xxi. 23-27.

CHAP. XII. 1-12.—PARABLE OF THE WICKED HUSBANDMEN. (Matt. xxi. 33-46; Luke xx. 9-18.) For the exposition, see on Matt. xxi. 33-46.

13-40.—ENTANGLING QUESTIONS ABOUT TRIBUTE, THE RESURRECTION, AND THE GREAT COMMANDMENT, WITH THE REPLIES—CHRIST BAFFLES THE PHARISEES BY A QUESTION ABOUT DAVID, AND DENOUNCES THE SCRIBES. (=Matt. xxii. 15-46; Luke xx. 20-47.) The time of this Section appears to be still the third day of Christ's last week—Tuesday. Matthew introduces the subject by saying (xxii. 15), "Then went the Pharisees and took counsel how they might entangle Him in His talk."

13. And they send unto him certain of the Pharisees—"their disciples," says Matthew; probably young and zealous scholars in that hardening school. **and of the Herodians.** See on Matt. xxii. 16. In Luke xx. 20 these willing tools are called "spies, which should feign themselves just (or 'righteous') men, that they might take hold of His words, that so they might deliver Him unto the power and authority of the governor." Their plan, then, was to entrap Him into some expression which might be construed into disaffection to the Roman government; the Pharisees themselves being notoriously discontented with the Roman yoke.

Tribute to Cesar (14-17). **14. And when they were come, they say unto him, Master**—or 'teacher' [Διδάσκαλε]—**we know that thou art true, and carest for no man; for thou regardest not the person of men, but teachest the way of God in truth.** By such flattery—though they said only the truth—they hoped to throw Him off His guard. **Is it lawful to give tribute** [κῆνσον] **to Cesar, or not?** It was the civil poll-tax paid by all enrolled in the 'Census.' See on Matt. xvii. 25. **15. Shall we give, or shall we not give? But he, knowing their hypocrisy** [ὑπό-

16 a [1]penny that I may see *it*. And they brought *it*. And he saith unto
them, Whose *is* this image and superscription? And they said unto him,
17 Cesar's. And Jesus answering said unto them, Render to Cesar the
things that are Cesar's, and to God the things that are God's. And they
marvelled at him.
18 Then [k]come unto him the Sadducees, which [l]say there is no resurrec-
19 tion; and they asked him, saying, Master, [m]Moses wrote unto us, If a
man's brother die, and leave *his* wife *behind him*, and leave no children,
that his brother should take his wife, and raise up seed unto his brother.
20 Now there were seven brethren: and the first took a wife, and dying left
21 no seed. And the second took her, and died, neither left he any seed:
22 and the third likewise. And the seven had her, and left no seed: last of
23 all the woman died also. In the resurrection therefore, when they shall
24 rise, whose wife shall she be of them? for the seven had her to wife. And
Jesus answering said unto them, Do ye not therefore err, because ye know
25 not [n]the Scriptures, neither [o]the power of God? For when they shall
rise from the dead, they neither marry, nor are given in marriage; but
26 [p]are as the angels which are in heaven. And as touching the dead, that
they rise; have ye not read in the book of Moses, how in the bush God
spake unto him, saying, [q]I *am* the God of Abraham, and the God of
27 Isaac, and the God of Jacob? He is not the God of the dead, but the
God of the living: ye therefore do greatly err.

A. D. 33.

[1] In value sevenpence halfpenny.
[k] Matt. 22.23. Luke 20.27.
[l] Acts 23. 8. 1 Cor. 15.12.
[m] Gen. 38. 8. Deut. 25. 5. Ruth 4. 5.
[n] Dan. 12. 2. Hos. 6. 2. 1 Tim. 1, 7. 2 Pet. 1. 19.
[o] Luke 1. 37. Rom. 4. 17. Eph. 1. 19, 20. Heb. 11. 16.
[p] Matt. 22.30. Luke 20.35, 36. 1 Cor. 7. 29. 1 Cor. 15.42, 49, 52. Heb. 12. 22, 23.
[q] Ex. 3. 6.

κρισιν]—"their wickedness" [πονηρίαν] Matt. xxii. 18; "their craftiness" [πανουργίαν] Luke xx. 23. The malignity of their hearts took the form of craft, pretending what they did not feel—an anxious desire to be guided aright in a matter which to a scrupulous few might seem a question of some difficulty. Seeing perfectly through this, He **said unto them, Why tempt ye me?**—"hypocrites!" **bring me a penny** [δηνάριον], **that I may see it**—or "the tribute money" (Matt. xxii. 19). **16. And they brought it. And he saith unto them, Whose is this image** [εἰκὼν]—stamped upon the coin, **and superscription?** [ἐπιγραφή]—the words encircling it on the obverse side. **And they said unto him, Cesar's. 17. And Jesus answering said unto them, Render to Cesar the things that are Cesar's.** Putting it in this general form, it was impossible for sedition itself to dispute it, and yet it dissolved the snare. **and to God the things that are God's.** How much is there in this profound but to them startling addition to the maxim, and how incomparable is the whole for fulness, brevity, clearness, weight! **and they marvelled at him**—"at His answer, and held their peace" (Luke xx. 26), "and left Him, and went their way" (Matt. xxii. 22).

The Resurrection (18-27). **18. Then come unto him the Sadducees, which say there is no resurrection**—"neither angel nor spirit" (Acts xxiii. 7). They were the materialists of the day. See on Acts xxiii. 7. **and they asked him, saying, 19-22. Master, Moses wrote unto us** (Deut. xxv. 5), **If a man's brother die, and leave his wife behind him, &c. . . . And the seven had her, and left no seed: last of all the woman died also. 23. In the resurrection therefore [when they shall rise].** The clause in brackets is of doubtful authority, and *Tregelles* omits it; but *Lachmann* and *Tischendorf* retain it. **whose wife shall she be of them? for the seven had her to wife. 24. And Jesus answering said unto them, Do ye not therefore err, because ye know not the Scriptures**—regarding the future state, **neither the power of God?**—before which a thousand such difficulties vanish. **25. For when they shall rise from the dead, they neither marry, nor are given in marriage**—"neither can they die any more" (Luke xx. 36). Marriage is ordained to perpetuate the human family; but as there will be no breaches by death in the future state, this ordinance will cease. **but are as the angels which are in heaven.** In Luke it is "equal unto the angels" [ἰσάγγελοι]: but as the subject is death and resurrection, we are not warranted to extend the equality here taught beyond the one point—the *immortality* of their nature. A beautiful clause is added in Luke—"and are the children of God"—not in respect of *character*, which is not here spoken of, but of *nature*—"being the children of the resurrection," as rising to an undecaying existence (Rom. viii. 21, 23), and so being the children of their Father's immortality (1 Tim. vi. 16). **26. And as touching the dead, that they rise; have ye not read in the book of Moses**—"even Moses" (Luke xx. 37), whom they had just quoted for the purpose of entangling Him, **how in the bush God spake unto him** [ἐπὶ τοῦ βάτου]—either 'at the bush,' as the same expression is rendered in Luke xx. 37, that is, when he was there; or 'in the (section of his history regarding the) bush.' The structure of our verse suggests the latter sense, which is not unusual. **saying** (Exod. iii. 6), **I am the God of Abraham, and the God of Isaac, and the God of Jacob? 27. He is not the God of the dead, but [the God] of the living** [ὁ Θεὸς νεκρῶν ἀλλὰ Θεὸς ζώντων]—not 'the God of dead but [the God] of living persons.' The word in brackets is almost certainly an addition to the genuine text, and critical editors exclude it. "For all live unto Him" [αὐτῷ] Luke xx. 38—'in His view,' or 'in His estimation.' This last statement—found only in Luke—though adding nothing to the argument, is an important additional illustration. It is true, indeed, that to God no human being is dead or ever will be, but all mankind sustain an abiding conscious relation to Him; but the "all" here mean "those who shall be accounted worthy to obtain that world." These sustain a gracious covenant-relation to God which cannot be dissolved. (Compare Rom. vi. 10, 11.) In this sense our Lord affirms that for Moses to call the Lord the "God" of His patriarchal servants, if at that

28 And [r]one of the scribes came, and having heard them reasoning
together, and perceiving that he had answered them well, asked him,
29 Which is the first commandment of all? And Jesus answered him, The
first of all the commandments *is*, [s]Hear, O Israel; The Lord our God is
30 one Lord: and thou shalt love the Lord thy God with all thy heart, and
with all thy soul, and with all thy mind, and with all thy strength. This
31 *is* the first commandment. And the second *is* like, *namely* this, Thou
[t]shalt love thy neighbour as thyself. There is none other commandment

A. D. 33.

[r] Matt. 22.35.
[s] Deut. 6. 4. Pro. 23. 26. Luke 10.27.
[t] Lev. 19. 18. Rom. 13. 9. 1 Cor. 13. 1. Gal. 5. 14. Jas. 2. 8.

moment they had no existence, would be unworthy of Him. He "would be *ashamed* to be called their God, if He had not prepared for them a city" (Heb. xi. 16). It was concluded by some of the early Fathers, from our Lord's resting His proof of the Resurrection on such a passage as this, instead of quoting some much clearer testimonies of the Old Testament, that the Sadducees, to whom this was addressed, acknowledged the authority of no part of the Old Testament but the Pentateuch; and this opinion has held its ground even till now. But as there is no ground for it in the New Testament, so *Josephus* is silent upon it; merely saying that they rejected the Pharisaic traditions. It was because the Pentateuch was regarded by all classes as the fundamental source of the Hebrew Religion, and all the succeeding books of the Old Testament but as developments of it, that our Lord would show that even there the doctrine of the Resurrection was taught. And all the rather does He select this passage, as being not a bare annunciation of the doctrine in question, but as expressive of that glorious truth *out of which the Resurrection springs.* "And when the multitude heard this (says Matt. xxii. 33), they were astonished at His doctrine." "Then (adds Luke xx. 39, 40) certain of the scribes answering said, Master"—'Teacher' [Διδάσκαλε], "thou hast well said"—enjoying His victory over the Sadducees. "And after that they durst not ask Him any [question at all]"—neither party could; both being for the time utterly foiled.

The Great Commandment (28-34). "But when the Pharisees had heard that He had put the Sadducees to silence, they were gathered together" (Matt. xxii. 34). **28. And one of the scribes** [γραμματέων]—"a lawyer" [νομικὸς], says Matthew (xxii. 35); that is, a teacher of the law, **came, and having heard them reasoning together, and perceiving that he had answered them well, asked him**—manifestly in no bad spirit. When Matthew therefore says he came "tempting," or "trying him," as one of the Pharisaic party who seemed to enjoy the defeat He had given to the Sadducees, we may suppose that though somewhat priding himself upon his insight into the law, and not indisposed to measure his knowledge with One in whom he had not yet learned to believe, he was nevertheless an honest-hearted, fair disputant. **Which is the first commandment of all?**—first in importance; the primary, leading commandment, the most fundamental one. This was a question which, with some others, divided the Jewish teachers into rival schools. Our Lord's answer is in a strain of respect very different from what He showed to cavillers—ever observing His own direction, "Give not that which is holy to the dogs, neither cast ye your pearls before swine; lest they trample them under their feet, and turn again and rend you" (Matt. vii. 6). **29. And Jesus answered him, The first of all the commandments is.** The readings here vary considerably. *Tischendorf* and *Tregelles* read simply [Πρώτη ἐστὶν] 'the first is;' and they are followed by *Meyer* and *Alford*. But though the authority for the precise form of the received text is slender, a form almost identical with it seems to have most weight of authority. Our Lord here gives His explicit sanction to the distinction between commandments of a more *fundamental* and *primary* character, and commandments of a more *dependent* and *subordinate* nature; a distinction of which it is confidently asserted by a certain class of critics that the Jews knew nothing, that our Lord and his apostles nowhere lay down, and which has been invented by Christian divines. (Compare Matt. xxiii. 23.) **Hear, O Israel; the Lord our God is one Lord.** This every devout Jew recited twice every day, and the Jews do it to this day; thus keeping up the great ancient national protest against the polytheisms and pantheisms of the heathen-world: it is the great utterance of the national faith in One Living and Personal God—"ONE JEHOVAH!" **30. And thou shalt love the Lord thy God with all thy heart, and with all thy soul, and with all thy mind, and with all thy strength. This is the first commandment. 31. And the second is like, namely this, Thou shalt love thy neighbour as thyself. There is none other commandment greater than these.** As every word here is of the deepest and most precious import, we must take it in all its details. **30. And thou shalt.** We have here the language of *law*, expressive of God's *claims*. What then are we here bound down to do? One word is made to express it. And what a word! Had the essence of the divine law consisted in *deeds*, it could not possibly have been expressed in a single word; for no one deed is comprehensive of all others embraced in the law. But as it consists in *an affection of the soul*, one word suffices to express it—but only one. *Fear*, though due to God and enjoined by Him, is *limited* in its sphere and *distant* in character. *Trust*, *Hope*, and the like, though essential features of a right state of heart towards God, are called into action only by *personal necessity*, and so are—in a good sense, it is true, but still are properly—*selfish* affections; that is to say, they have respect to *our own well-being*. But LOVE is an *all-inclusive* affection, embracing not only every other affection proper to its Object, but all that is proper to be *done* to its Object; for as love spontaneously seeks to please its Object, so, in the case of men to God, it is the native well-spring of a voluntary obedience. It is, besides, the most *personal* of all affections. One may fear an *event*, one may hope for an *event*, one may rejoice in an *event*; but one can love only a *Person*. It is the *tenderest*, the most *unselfish*, the most *divine* of all affections. Such, then, is the affection in which the essence of the divine law is declared to consist—**Thou shalt love.** We now come to the glorious Object of that demanded affection. Thou shalt love **the Lord, thy God**—that is, Jehovah, the Self-Existent One, who has revealed Himself as the "I AM," and there is "*none else;*" who, though by his name JEHOVAH apparently at an unapproachable distance from His finite creatures, yet bears to *Thee* a real and definite relationship, out of which arises *His claim* and *Thy duty*—of LOVE. But with what are we to love Him? Four things

32 greater than these. And the scribe said unto him, Well, Master, thou
hast said the truth: for there is one God; [u]and there is none other but
33 he: And to love him with all the heart, and with all the understanding,
and with all the soul, and with all the strength, and to love *his* neighbour
34 as himself, [v]is more than all whole burnt offerings and sacrifices. And
when Jesus saw that he answered discreetly, he said unto him, Thou art
not far from the kingdom of God. [w]And no man after that durst ask
him *any question.*
35 And [x]Jesus answered and said, while he taught in the temple, How say

A. D. 33.

[u] Deut. 4. 39. Isa. 45. 6,14. Isa. 46. 9. 1 Cor. 8. 4,6.
[v] 1 Sam. 15. 22. Hos. 6. 6. Mic. 6. 6.
[w] Matt. 22. 46.
[x] Luke 20. 41.

are here specified. First, "Thou shalt love the Lord thy God" **with thy heart.** This sometimes means 'the whole inner man' (as Prov. iv. 23): but that cannot be meant here; for then the other three particulars would be superfluous. Very often it means 'our emotional nature'—the seat of *feeling* as distinguished from our intellectual nature or the seat of *thought*, commonly called the "mind" (as in Phil. iv. 7). But neither can this be the sense of it here; for here the heart is distinguished both from the "mind" and the "soul." The "heart," then, must here mean the *sincerity* of both the thoughts and the feelings; in other words, '*uprightness*' or '*true-heartedness*,' as opposed to a *hypocritical* or *divided* affection. [So the word—לֵב and καρδία—is used in Gen. xx. 6; Heb. x. 22; and see particularly Jer. iii. 10.] But next, "Thou shalt love the Lord thy God" **with thy soul.** This is designed to command our emotional nature: 'Thou shalt put *feeling* or *warmth* into thine affection.' Further, "Thou shalt love the Lord thy God" **with thy mind.** This commands our intellectual nature: 'Thou shalt put *intelligence* into thine affection'—in opposition to a blind devotion, or mere devoteeism. Lastly, "Thou shalt love the Lord thy God" **with thy strength.** This commands our energies: 'Thou shalt put *intensity* into thine affection'—"Do it with thy might" (Eccl. ix. 10). Taking these four things together, the command of the Law is, 'Thou shalt love the Lord thy God *with all thy powers*—with a *sincere*, a *fervid*, an *intelligent*, an *energetic* love.' But this is not all that the Law demands. God will have all these qualities in their most perfect exercise. "Thou shalt love the Lord thy God," says the Law, "with *all* thy heart," or, with perfect sincerity; "Thou shalt love the Lord thy God with *all* thy soul," or, with the utmost fervour; "Thou shalt love the Lord thy God with *all* thy mind," or, in the fullest exercise of an enlightened reason; and "Thou shalt love the Lord thy God with *all* thy strength," or, with the whole energy of our being! So much for the First Commandment. **31. And the second is like**—"unto it" (Matt. xxii. 39); as demanding the same affection, and only the extension of it, in its proper measure, to the creatures of Him whom we thus love—our *brethren* in the participation of the same nature, and *neighbours*, as connected with us by ties that render each dependent upon and necessary to the other. **Thou shalt love thy neighbour as thyself.** Now, as we are not to love ourselves supremely, this is virtually a command, in the first place, *not* to love our neighbour with all our heart and soul and mind and strength. And thus it is a condemnation of the idolatry of the creature. Our supreme and uttermost affection is to be reserved for God. But as *sincerely* as ourselves we are to love all mankind, and with *the same readiness to do and suffer for them* as we should reasonably desire them to show to us. The golden rule (Matt. vii. 12) is here our best interpreter of the nature and extent of these claims. **There is none other commandment greater than these**—or, as in Matt. xxii. 40, "On these two commandments hang all the Law and the Prophets" (see on Matt. v. 17). It is as if He had said, 'This is all Scripture in a nutshell; the whole law of human duty in a portable, pocket form.' Indeed, it is so *simple* that a child may understand it, so *brief* that all may remember it, so *comprehensive* as to embrace all possible cases. And from its very nature it is *unchangeable.* It is inconceivable that God should require from his rational creatures anything *less*, or in substance anything *else*, under any *dispensation*, in any *world*, at any *period* throughout eternal duration. He cannot but claim this—all this—alike in *heaven*, in *earth*, and in *hell!* And this incomparable summary of the Divine Law belonged to *the Jewish Religion!* As it shines in its own self-evidencing splendour, so it reveals its own true source. The Religion from which the world has received it could be none other than a *God-given Religion.* **32. And the scribe said unto him, Well, Master**—'Teacher' [Διδάσκαλε], **thou hast said the truth: for there is one [God]; and there is none other but he.** The genuine text here seems clearly to have been, "There is one," without the word [Θεὸς] "God;" and so nearly all critical editors and expositors read. **33. And to love him with all the heart, and with all the understanding, and with all the soul, and with all the strength, and to love his neighbour as himself, is more than all whole burnt offerings and sacrifices**—more, that is, than all positive institutions; thereby showing insight into the essential difference between what is *moral* and in its own nature *unchangeable*, and what is obligatory only *because enjoined* and only *so long as enjoined.* **34. And when Jesus saw that he answered discreetly** [νουνεχῶς]—rather, 'intelligently,' or 'sensibly;' not only in a good spirit, but with a promising measure of insight into spiritual things, **he said unto him, Thou art not far from the kingdom of God**—for he had but *to follow out a little further* what he seemed sincerely to own, to find his way into the kingdom. He needed only the experience of another eminent scribe who at a later period said, "We know that *the law is spiritual*, but *I am carnal*, sold under sin;" who exclaimed, "O wretched man that I am! Who shall deliver me?" but who added, "I thank God through Jesus Christ!" (Rom. vii. 14, 24, 25). Perhaps among the "great company of the priests" and other Jewish ecclesiastics who "were obedient to the faith," almost immediately after the day of Pentecost (Acts vi. 7) this upright lawyer was one. But for all his nearness to the Kingdom of God, it may be he never entered it. **And no man after that durst ask any question**—all feeling that they were no match for Him, and that it was vain to enter the lists with Him.

Christ Baffles the Pharisees regarding David (35-37). **35. And Jesus answered and said, while he taught in the temple**—and "while the Pharisees were gathered together" (Matt. xxii. 41).

36 the scribes that Christ is the son of David? For David himself said [y]by
the Holy Ghost, [z]The LORD said to my Lord, Sit thou on my right hand,
37 till I make thine enemies thy footstool. David therefore himself calleth
him Lord; and [a]whence is he *then* his son? And the common people
heard him gladly.
38 And [b]he said unto them in his doctrine, [c]Beware of the scribes, which
love to go in long clothing, and [d]*love* salutations in the market-places,
39 and the chief seats in the synagogues, and the uppermost rooms at feasts;
40 which [e]devour widows' houses, and for a pretence make long prayers:
these shall receive greater damnation.

A. D. 33.

y 2 Sam. 23.2. 2 Tim. 3.16.
z Ps. 110. 1. 1 Cor.15.25. Heb. 1. 13.
a Rom. 1. 3. Rom. 9. 5.
b ch. 4. 2.
c Matt. 23. 1. Luke 20.46.
d Luke 11.43.
e Matt.23.14.

How say the scribes that Christ is the son of David?—How come they to give it out, that Messiah is to be the son of David? In Matthew, Jesus asks them, "What think ye of Christ?" or of the promised and expected Messiah? "Whose son is He (to be)? They say unto Him, The son of David." The sense is the same. "He saith unto them, How then doth David in spirit call Him Lord?" (Matt. xxii. 42, 43). **36. For David himself said by the Holy Ghost** (Ps. cx. 1), **The Lord said to my Lord, Sit thou on my right hand, till I make thine enemies thy footstool. 37. David therefore himself calleth him Lord; and whence is he then his son?** There is but one solution of this difficulty. Messiah is at once inferior to David as his son according to the flesh, and superior to him as the Lord of a kingdom of which David is himself a subject, not the sovereign. The Human and Divine natures of Christ, and the spirituality of His kingdom—of which the highest earthly sovereigns are honoured if they be counted worthy to be its subjects—furnish the only key to this puzzle. **And the common people** [ὁ πολὺς ὄχλος]—or, 'the immense crowd,' **heard him gladly.** "And no man was able to answer Him a word; neither durst any man from that day forth ask Him any more questions" (Matt. xxii. 46).

The Scribes Denounced (38-40). **38. And he said unto them in his doctrine** [ἐν τῇ διδαχῇ αὐτοῦ]—rather, 'in His teaching;' implying that this was but a specimen of an extended Discourse, which Matthew gives in full (ch. xxiii.) Luke says (xx. 45) this was "in the audience of all the people said unto his disciples." [The reading, 'unto them'—πρὸς αὐτοὺς—which *Tischendorf* adopts there is ill supported: *Lachmann* and *Tregelles* take the received text.] **Beware of the scribes, which love**—or 'like' [θελόντων] **to go in long clothing** (see on Matt. xxiii. 5), **and** [love] **salutations in the market-places, 39. And the chief seats in the synagogues, and the uppermost rooms**, or positions, **at feasts.** See on this love of distinction, Luke xiv. 7; and on Matt. vi. 5. **40. Which devour widows' houses, and for a pretence make long prayers: these shall receive greater damnation.** They took advantage of their helpless condition and confiding character, to obtain possession of their property, while by their "long prayers" they made them believe they were raised far above "filthy lucre." So much the "greater damnation" awaited them. (Compare Matt. xxiii. 33). A life-like description this of the Romish clergy, the true successors of "the scribes."

Remarks.—1. What an exalted illustration does our Lord's example here afford of His own direction to the Twelve and His servants in every age, "Behold, I send you forth as sheep among wolves: be ye therefore wise as serpents and harmless as doves"! And shall not we, the deeper we drink into His spirit, approach the nearer to that matchless wisdom with which, in the midst of "wolves" hungry for their prey, He not only avoided their snares but put them to silence and shame; with wise speech, even as by well-doing, putting to silence the ignorance of foolish men? 2. The things of Cesar and the things of God—or things civil and things sacred—are essentially distinct, though quite harmonious. Neither may overlap or intrude itself into the sphere of the other. In the things of God we may not take law from men (Acts iv. 19; v. 29); while in honouring and obeying Cesar in his own sphere, we are rendering obedience to God Himself (Rom. xiii. 1, 2, 5). 3. In matters which lie entirely beyond the present sphere—as the Resurrection of the dead—the authority of "the Scriptures" must decide everything; and all difficulties arising out of their teaching on this and kindred subjects must be referred, as here, to "the power of God." A seasonable directory this in our day, when physical difficulties in the way of any corporeal resurrection of the dead have well-nigh annihilated the faith of it in the minds of many scientific Christians. While "the Scriptures" must be the sole rule of faith with Christians on this subject, let us learn to refer every difficulty in the way of believing its testimony to "the power of God" to accomplish whatever He promises. So much for the doctrine of the Resurrection generally. As to the difficulty with which the Sadducees plied our Lord—the difficulty of adjusting, in the resurrection-state, the relationships of the present life—His reply not only dissolves it, but opens to us some beautiful glimpses into the heavenly state. The Sadducean difficulty proceeded on the supposition that the marriage-relations of the present life would require to reappear in the resurrection-state, if there was to be any. This was but one of those gross conceptions of the future life to which some minds seem prone. As marriage is designed to supply the waste of human life here which death creates, it can have no place in a state where there is no death. The future life of the children of God, as it will be sinless, so it will be deathless. This supposes new and higher laws stamped upon their physical system, to which the purer and higher element in which they are to move will be adapted. In respect of this undecaying life they will be on a level with the angels, and a faint reflection of their Father's own immortality. Yet there is an extreme on the other side to be guarded against, of so attenuating our ideas of the resurrection-state as to amount to scarcely more than the immortality of the *soul.* Were this all, the resurrection of the dead would have no meaning at all. It is the *body* only which does or can rise from the dead; and however "spiritual" the resurrection-body is to be (1 Cor. xv, 44), it must be a body still, and therefore possessed of all the essential characteristics of a body. Never let us lose hold of this truth, one of the brightest and most distinguishing of the Christian verities. 3. What a light is here thrown upon the historical

41 And [f] Jesus sat over against the treasury, and beheld how the people
cast money into the [g] treasury: and many that were rich cast in much.

A. D. 33.

f Luke 21. 1.
g 2 Ki. 12. 9.

truth and inspiration of the Pentateuch! On any lower supposition, it is incredible that our Lord should have rested the divine authority of the doctrine of the Resurrection upon such words as He has quoted from it; and when, in His subsequent question about David, He quotes the 110th Psalm as what David said "in spirit" or "by the Holy Ghost," and throughout all His teaching refers to every portion of the Old Testament Scriptures as of equal divine authority, we must set our seal also to that great truth, if we would not charge our Lord either with inability to rise above the errors of His age or with unworthy accommodation to them, knowing them to be errors. 4. Our Lord's selection of an implied evidence of the resurrection in the Pentateuch, in preference to a direct proof which He might have found in the prophets, is worthy of note, not as showing His wish to confine Himself to the Pentateuch, but as encouraging us to penetrate beneath the surface of Scripture, and, in particular, to take God's own words in their most comprehensive sense. When the Lord said to Moses, "I am the God of Abraham, and the God of Isaac, and the God of Jacob," He might seem to mean no more than that He had neither forgotten nor grown indifferent to the promises which He made, some centuries before, to those patriarchs, whose God He *was* when they were alive. But as our Lord read, and would have us to read, those words, they were an assurance to Moses that He and the patriarchs, dead though they were, sustained the same relation still, and that as "all (of them) lived to Him," He held Himself under pledge to them; and in now sending Moses to redeem their children from Egypt and bring them to the promised land, He was but fulfilling His engagements to the patriarchs themselves, as living and not dead men. To superficial readers this may seem, if not far-fetched, yet not the most cogent reasoning. But the views which it opens up of the indissoluble relation that God sustains to His redeemed—which death cannot for a moment interrupt, much less destroy or impair (John xi. 25, 26)—as they necessarily imply a resurrection of the dead, will be deemed by all deeper thinkers to be as cogent in point of argument as they are precious in themselves. In fact, the strongest arguments for a Future State in the Old Testament are derived, not so much from explicit statements—which however are not wanting—as from the essentially indestructible character of those relations and intercourses which the saints sustained to God, and the consciousness of this which the saints themselves seemed to feel; as if they took it for granted rather than reasoned it out, or even reflected upon it. 5. The intelligent reader of the New Testament will not fail to perceive that "life" in the future world is never once ascribed to the wicked as their portion, even though a life of misery. That they *exist* for ever is but too clear. That they will "rise" as well as the righteous, is explicitly declared; but never "from the dead" [ἐκ νεκρῶν]—as if they would rise to *live:* They "rise to the resurrection of *damnation*" (John v. 29), even as in the Old Testament they are said to "awake to shame and everlasting contempt" (Dan. xii. 2). But the word "life," as expressive of the future state, is invariably reserved for the condition of the saints. Hence, when our Lord here says, "For all live unto Him," we might conclude, even although the connection did not make it clear, that He meant 'all His saints'—all the dead that die in the Lord—and they only. 6. How unscriptural as well as gloomy is the doctrine of *the sleep of the soul* between death and the resurrection! The argument of our Lord here for the resurrection of the patriarchs, and consequently of the saints in general, is founded on their being *even now alive.* Yes; and not only are their souls in conscious life, but as God is the God of themselves—the embodied Abraham and Isaac and Jacob—"though worms have destroyed their bodies, yet in their flesh must they see God," in order to be their full selves again, and get in full the promised inheritance. Sweet consolation this "concerning them which are asleep, that we sorrow not, even as others which have no hope." They are not dead. They have but fallen asleep. Their souls are still awake; "for all live unto Him." And as to their sleeping dust, "If we believe that Jesus died and rose again, even so them also which sleep in Jesus will God bring with Him" (1 Thess. iv. 13, 14). 7. In the light of the Great Commandment, what shall we think of those who talk of the Pentateuch as but fragments of the early Jewish literature, and this as embodying none but narrow and rude ideas of Religion, suited to a gross age of the world, but not worthy to give law to the religious thinking of all time? Whether we compare the religious and ethical views opened up in that Commandment with the best religious thinking to be found outside the pale of Judaism during any period whatever before Christ; or compare it with the light which the teaching of Christ has shed upon Religion, and with the most advanced ideas of the present time—the peerless perfection of this monument of the Mosaic Religion stands equally forth before the unsophisticated, reflecting mind, as evidence of its *supernatural* origin and *revealed* character. And just as the deeper view of those words of the Pentateuch, "I am the God of Abraham, and the God of Isaac, and the God of Jacob," suggest the continued life and ultimate resurrection of those patriarchs, so does the deeper study of the Great Commandment, like a "schoolmaster, bring us unto Christ, that we may be justified by faith." For who, in the view of its requirements, must not exclaim, "By the deeds of the law there shall no flesh be justified in His sight; for by the law is the knowledge of sin;" but "Christ hath redeemed us from the curse of the law, being made a curse for us;" and this redemption, or rather "the love of Christ" which prompted it, "constraineth us to live no longer to ourselves, but to Him who died for us and rose again." And thus is the Law reinstated in its rightful place in our hearts; and, despairing of life through the Great Commandment, the life which we fetch out of Christ's death is a life of real, loving, acceptable obedience to that Great Commandment. O the depth of the riches both of the wisdom and knowledge of God, in that wonderful invention! 8. The doctrine of the two natures—the Divine and the Human—in the one Person of Christ, is the only key to the satisfactory solution of many enigmas in Scripture, of which that which our Lord propounded to the scribes regarding David was but one. Accordingly, none who repudiate this doctrine have been able to retain their hold of almost any of the cardinal doctrines of Scripture, nor have held firmly even by the Scriptures themselves, of which this may be called the chief corner stone—elect, precious.

41-44.—The Widow's Two Mites. (= Luke xxi. 1-4.) For the exposition, see on Luke xxi. 1-4.

42 And there came a certain poor widow, and she threw in two [3]mites,
43 which make a farthing. And he called *unto him* his disciples, and saith
unto them, Verily I say unto you, That [h]this poor widow hath cast more
44 in than all they which have cast into the treasury: for all *they* did cast
in of their abundance; but she of her want did cast in all that she had,
[i]*even* all her living.

13 AND [a]as he went out of the temple, one of his disciples saith unto
him, Master, see what manner of stones and what buildings *are here!*
2 And Jesus answering said unto him, Seest thou these great buildings?
[b]there shall not be left one stone upon another, that shall not be thrown
down.
3 And as he sat upon the mount of Olives, over against the temple, Peter
4 and James and John and Andrew asked him privately, Tell [c]us, when
shall these things be? and what *shall be* the sign when all these things
shall be fulfilled?
5 And Jesus answering them began to say, [d]Take heed lest any *man*
6 deceive you: for many shall come in my name, saying, I am *Christ;*
7 and shall deceive many. And when ye shall hear of wars and rumours
of wars, be ye not troubled: for *such things* must needs be; but

A. D. 33.

[3] It is the seventh part of one piece of that brass money.
[h] 2 Cor. 8. 12.
[i] 1 John 3.17.

CHAP. 13.
[a] Matt. 24. 1. Luke 25. 1.
[b] 1 Ki. 9. 7. 2 Chr 7. 20. Jer. 26. 18. Mic. 3. 12. Luke 19.44.
[c] Dan. 12. 6. Matt. 24. 3. Luke 21. 7. John 21.22.
[d] Jer. 29. 8. Matt. 24. 5. Luke 21. 8. Eph. 5. 6.

CHAP. XIII. 1-37.—CHRIST'S PROPHECY OF THE DESTRUCTION OF JERUSALEM, AND WARNINGS SUGGESTED BY IT TO PREPARE FOR HIS SECOND COMING. (= Matt. xxiv. 1-51; Luke xxi. 5-36.)

Jesus had uttered all His mind against the Jewish ecclesiastics, exposing their character with withering plainness, and denouncing, in language of awful severity, the judgments of God against them for that unfaithfulness to their trust which was bringing ruin upon the nation. He had closed this His last public Discourse (Matt. xxiii.) by a passionate Lamentation over Jerusalem, and a solemn Farewell to the Temple. "And (says Matthew, xxiv. 1) Jesus went out, and departed from the temple"—never more to re-enter its precincts, or open His mouth in public teaching. *With this act ended His public ministry.* As He withdrew, says *Olshausen*, the gracious presence of God left the sanctuary; and the Temple, with all its service, and the whole theocratic constitution, was given over to destruction. What immediately followed is, as usual, most minutely and graphically described by our Evangelist.

1. And as he went out of the temple, one of his disciples saith unto him. The other Evangelists are less definite. "As some spake," says Luke: "His disciples came to Him," says Matthew. Doubtless it was the speech of one, the mouth-piece, likely, of others. **Master**—'Teacher' [Διδάσκαλε], **see what manner of stones and what buildings are here!**—wondering, probably, how so massive a pile could be overthrown, as seemed implied in our Lord's last words regarding it. *Josephus*, who gives a minute account of the wonderful structure, speaks of stones forty cubits long (Jewish War, v. 5. 1.), and says the pillars supporting the porches were twenty-five cubits high, all of one stone, and that the whitest marble (Ib., v. 5. 2). Six days' battering at the walls, during the siege, made no impression upon them (Ib., vi. 4. 1.) Some of the under-building, yet remaining, and other works, are probably as old as the first temple. **2. And Jesus answering said unto him, Seest thou these great buildings?** 'Ye call my attention to these things? I have seen them. Ye point to their massive and durable appearance: now listen to their fate.' **there shall not be left**—"left here" (Matt. xxiv. 2). [*Tregelles* adds ὧδε—"here"—in Mark also, on authority of some weight; but we think *Tischendorf* right in adhering to the received text here]. **one stone upon another, that shall not be thrown down.** Titus ordered the whole city and temple to be demolished (*Joseph.* J. W., vii. 1. 1.); Eleazar wished they had all died before seeing that holy city destroyed by enemies' hands, and before the temple was so profanely *dug up.* (Ib. vii. 8. 7.)

3. And as he sat upon the mount of Olives, over against the temple. On their way from Jerusalem to Bethany they would cross mount Olivet; on its summit He seats Himself, over against the temple, having the city all spread out under His eye. How graphically is this set before us by our Evangelist. **Peter and James and John and Andrew asked him privately.** The other Evangelists tell us merely that "the disciples" did so. But Mark not only says it was four of them, but names them; and they were the first *quaternion* of the Twelve. See on Matt. x. 1-5, Remarks 6 and 7. **4. Tell us, when shall these things be? and what shall be the sign when all these things shall be fulfilled?**—"and what shall be the sign of thy coming, and of the end of the world?" [συντελείας τοῦ αἰῶνος]. They no doubt looked upon the date of all these things as one and the same, and their notions of the things themselves were as confused as of the times of them. Our Lord takes His own way of meeting their questions.

Prophecies of the Destruction of Jerusalem (5-31). **5. And Jesus answering them.** [The words ἀποκριθεὶς αὐτοῖς are, without reason, we think, excluded from the text by *Tischendorf* and *Tregelles. Lachmann* inserts them.] **began to say, Take heed lest any man deceive you: 6. For many shall come in my name, saying, I am [Christ]** (see Matt. xxiv. 5)—"and the time draweth nigh" (Luke xxi. 8); that is, the time of the kingdom in its full splendour. **and shall deceive many.** "Go ye not therefore after them" (Luke xxi. 8). The reference here seems not to be to pretended Messiahs, deceiving those who rejected the claims of Jesus, of whom indeed there were plenty—for our Lord is addressing His own genuine disciples—but to persons pretending to be Jesus Himself, returned in glory to take possession of His kingdom. This gives peculiar force to the words, "Go ye not therefore after them." **7. And when ye shall hear of**

8 [e]the end *shall* not *be* yet. For nation shall rise against nation, and
kingdom against kingdom; and there shall be earthquakes in divers
places, and there shall be famines and troubles. These *are* the beginnings
of [1]sorrows.
9 But [f]take heed to yourselves: for they shall deliver you up to councils;
and in the synagogues ye shall be beaten: and ye shall be brought before
10 rulers and kings for my sake, for a testimony against them. And [g]the
11 gospel must first be published among all nations. But [h]when they shall
lead *you*, and deliver you up, take no thought beforehand what ye shall
speak, neither do ye premeditate; but whatsoever shall be given you in
that hour, that speak ye: for it is not ye that speak, [i]but the Holy
12 Ghost. Now [j]the brother shall betray the brother to death, and the
father the son; and children shall rise up against *their* parents, and shall
13 cause them to be put to death. And ye shall be hated of all *men* for my
name's sake: but [k]he that shall endure unto the end, the same shall be
saved.
14 But [l]when ye shall see the abomination of desolation, [m]spoken of by
Daniel the prophet, standing where it ought not, (let him that readeth
15 understand,) then let [n]them that be in Judea flee to the mountains: and

A. D. 33.

[e] Jer. 4. 27. Jer. 5. 10.
[1] The word in the original importeth the pains of a woman in travail.
[f] Matt. 10. 17. Rev. 2. 10.
[g] Matt. 24. 14. Rom. 10. 18.
[h] Ex. 24. 12. Luke 12. 11.
[i] Acts 2. 4. Acts 4. 8, 31.
[j] Mic. 7. 6. Luke 21. 16.
[k] Dan. 12. 12. 2 Tim 4. 7, 8.
[l] Matt. 24. 15.
[m] Dan. 9. 27.
[n] Luke 21. 21.

wars and rumours of wars, be ye not troubled—see on *v.* 13, and compare Isa. viii. 11-14, **for such things must needs be; but the end shall not be yet.** In Luke (xxi. 9), "the end is not by and by" [εὐθέως] or 'immediately.' Worse must come before all is over. **8. For nation shall rise against nation, and kingdom against kingdom; and there shall be earthquakes in divers places, and there shall be famines and troubles. These are the beginnings of sorrows** [ὠδίνων]—'of travail-pangs,' to which heavy calamities are compared. (See Jer. iv. 31, &c.) The annals of *Tacitus* tell us how the Roman world was convulsed, before the destruction of Jerusalem, by rival claimants of the imperial purple.

9. But take heed to yourselves: for—"before all these things" (Luke xxi. 12); that is, before these public calamities come, **they shall deliver you up to councils; and in the synagogues ye shall be beaten.** These refer to *ecclesiastical* proceedings against them. **and ye shall be brought before rulers and kings**—before *civil* tribunals next, **for my sake, for a testimony against them**—rather 'unto them' [εἰς μαρτύριον αὐτοῖς]—to give you an opportunity of bearing testimony to Me before them. In the Acts of the Apostles we have the best commentary on this announcement. (Compare Matt. x. 17, 18.) **10. And the gospel must first be published among all nations**—"for a witness, and then shall the end come" (Matt. xxiv. 14). God never sends judgment without previous warning; and there can be no doubt that the Jews, already dispersed over most known countries, had nearly all heard the Gospel "as a witness," before the end of the Jewish state. The same principle was repeated and will repeat itself to "*the* end." **11. But when they shall lead you, and deliver you up, take no thought beforehand** [μὴ προμεριμνᾶτε]—'be not anxious beforehand,' **what ye shall speak, neither do ye premeditate:** 'Be not filled with apprehension, in the prospect of such public appearances for Me, lest ye should bring discredit upon My name, nor think it necessary to prepare beforehand what ye are to say.' **but whatsoever shall be given you in that hour, that speak ye: for it is not ye that speak, but the Holy Ghost.** See on Matt. x. 19, 20. **12. Now the brother shall betray the brother to death, and the father the son; and children shall rise up against their parents, and shall cause them to be put to death. 13. And ye shall be hated of all men for my name's sake.** Matthew (xxiv. 12) adds this important intimation: "And because iniquity shall abound, the love of many" [τῶν πολλῶν]—'of the many,' or 'of the most;' that is, of the generality of professed disciples—"shall wax cold." Sad illustrations of the effect of abounding iniquity in cooling the love even of faithful disciples we have in the *Epistle of James*, written about the period here referred to, and too frequently ever since. **but he that shall endure unto the end, the same shall be saved.** See on Matt. x. 21, 22; and compare Heb. x. 38, 39, which is a manifest allusion to these words of Christ; also Rev. ii. 10. Luke adds these re-assuring words: "But there shall not an hair of your heads perish" (xxi. 18). Our Lord had just said (Luke xxi. 16) that they should be *put to death;* showing that this precious promise is far above immunity from mere bodily harm, and furnishing a key to the right interpretation of Ps. xci., and such like.

14. But when ye shall see—"Jerusalem compassed by armies" [στρατοπέδων]—'by encamped armies;' in other words, when ye shall see it *besieged*, and **the abomination of desolation** [τὸ βδέλυγμα τῆς ἐρημώσεως], **spoken of by Daniel the prophet, standing where it ought not**—that is, as explained in Matthew (xxiv. 15), "standing in the holy place." (**let him that readeth**—readeth that prophecy, **understand.**) That "the abomination of desolation" here alluded to was intended to point to the Roman ensigns, as the symbols of an idolatrous, and so unclean Pagan power, may be gathered by comparing what Luke says in the corresponding verse (xxi. 20); and commentators are agreed on it. It is worthy of notice, as confirming this interpretation, that in 1 Macc. i. 54—which, though Apocryphal *Scripture*, is authentic *history*—the expression of Daniel is applied to the idolatrous profanation of the Jewish altar by Antiochus Epiphanes. **then let them that be in Judea flee to the mountains.** The ecclesiastical historian, *Eusebius*, early in the fourth century, tells us that the Christians fled to *Pella*, at the northern extremity of Perea, being "prophetically directed"—perhaps by some prophetic intimation more explicit than this, which would be their chart—and that thus they escaped the predicted calamities by which the nation was overwhelmed. **15. And let him that is on the house-top not go down into the house, neither**

let him that is on the house-top not go down into the house, neither
16 enter *therein,* to take any thing out of his house: and let him that
is in the field not turn back again for to take up his garment.
17 But [o]woe to them that are with child, and to them that give suck,
18 in those days! And pray ye that your flight be not in the winter.
19 For [p]*in* those days shall be affliction, such as was not from the beginning
20 of the creation which God created unto this time, neither shall be. And
except that the Lord had shortened those days, no flesh should be saved:
but for the elect's sake, whom he hath chosen, he hath shortened the
21 days. And [q]then, if any man shall say to you, Lo, here *is* Christ; or, lo,
22 *he is* there; believe *him* not: for false Christs and false prophets shall
rise, and shall show signs and wonders, to seduce, [r]if *it were* possible,
23 even the elect. But [s]take ye heed: behold, I have foretold you all
things.

A. D. 33.

[o] Luke 23.29.
[p] Deut.28.15. Dan. 9. 26. Dan. 12. 1. Joel 2. 2. Matt.24.21.
[q] Luke 17.23. Luke 21. 8.
[r] Rom. 8. 28-39. 1 Pet. 1. 5. 1 John 2.19, 26, 27.
[s] Matt. 7. 15. Luke 21. 8, 34. 2 Pet. 3. 17.

enter therein, to take any thing out of his house:—that is, let him take the outside flight of steps from the roof to the ground; a graphic way of denoting the extreme urgency of the case, and the danger of being tempted, by the desire to save his property, to delay till escape should become impossible. **16. And let him that is in the field not turn back again for to take up his garment. 17. But woe to them**—or, 'alas for them,' **that are with child, and to them that give suck in those days**—in consequence of the aggravated suffering which those conditions would involve. **18. And pray ye that your flight be not in the winter**—making escape perilous, or tempting you to delay your flight. Matthew (xxiv. 20) adds, "neither on the sabbath day," when, from fear of a breach of its sacred rest, they might be induced to remain. **19. For in those days shall be affliction, such as was not from the beginning of the creation which God created unto this time, neither shall be.** Such language is not unusual in the Old Testament with reference to tremendous calamities. But it is matter of literal fact, that there was crowded into the period of the Jewish War an amount and complication of suffering perhaps unparalleled; as the narrative of *Josephus*, examined closely and arranged under different heads, would show. **20. And except that the Lord had shortened those days, no flesh**—that is, no human life—**should be saved: but for the elect's sake, whom he hath chosen, he hath shortened the days.** But for this merciful "shortening," brought about by a remarkable concurrence of causes, the whole nation would have perished, in which there yet remained a remnant to be afterwards gathered out. This portion of the prophecy closes, in Luke, with the following vivid and important glance at the subsequent fortunes of the chosen people: "And they shall fall by the sword, and shall be led away captive into all nations: and Jerusalem shall be trodden down of the Gentiles, until the times of the Gentiles be fulfilled" (Luke xxi. 24). The language as well as the idea of this remarkable statement is taken from Dan. viii. 10, 13. What, then, is its import here? It implies, first, that a time is coming when Jerusalem shall cease to be "trodden down of the Gentiles;" which it was then by Pagan, and since and till now is by Mohammedan unbelievers: and next, it implies that the period when this treading down of Jerusalem by the Gentiles is to cease will be when "the times of the Gentiles are fulfilled" or 'completed.' But what does this mean? We may gather the meaning of it from Rom. xi., in which the divine purposes and procedure towards the chosen people from first to last are treated in detail. In *v.* 25 of that chapter, these words of our Lord are thus reproduced: "For I would not, brethren, that ye should be ignorant of this mystery, lest ye should be wise in your own conceits; that blindness in part is happened to Israel, until the fulness of the Gentiles be come in." See the exposition of that verse, from which it will appear that—"till the fulness of the Gentiles be come in"—or, in our Lord's phraseology, "till the times of the Gentiles be fulfilled"—does not mean 'till the general conversion of the world to Christ,' but 'till the Gentiles have had their *full time* of that place in the Church which the Jews had before them.' After that period of *Gentilism*, as before of *Judaism*, "Jerusalem" and Israel, no longer "trodden down by the Gentiles" but "grafted into their own olive tree," shall constitute, with the believing Gentiles, one Church of God, and fill the whole earth. What a bright vista does this open up! **21. And then, if any man shall say to you, Lo, here is Christ; or, lo, [he is] there; believe him not.** So Luke xvii. 23. **22. For false Christs and false prophets shall rise, and shall show signs and wonders.** No one can read *Josephus*' account of what took place before the destruction of Jerusalem without seeing how strikingly this was fulfilled. **to seduce, if it were possible, even the elect**—implying that this, though all *but* done, will prove impossible. What a precious assurance! (Compare 2 Thess. ii. 9-12.) **23. But take ye heed: behold, I have foretold you all things.** He had just told them that the seduction of the elect would prove impossible; but since this would be all but accomplished, He bids them be on their guard, as the proper means of averting that catastrophe. In Matthew (xxiv. 26-28) we have some additional particulars: "Wherefore, if they shall say unto you, Behold, He is in the desert; go not forth: behold, He is in the secret chambers; believe it not. For as the lightning cometh out of the east, and shineth even unto the west; so shall also the coming of the Son of man be." See on Luke xvii. 23, 24. "For wheresoever the carcase is, there will the eagles be gathered together." See on Luke xvii. 37.

The preceding portion of this prophecy is by all interpreters applied to the destruction of Jerusalem by the Romans. But on the portion that follows some of the most eminent expositors are divided; one class of them considering that our Lord here makes an abrupt transition to the period and the events of His Second Personal Coming and the great Day of Judgment; while another class think there is no evidence of such transition, and that the subject is still the judicial vengeance on Jerusalem, ending not only in the destruction of the city and temple, but in the breaking up of the entire polity, civil and ecclesiastical, of which Jerusalem

24 But [t] in those days, after that tribulation, the sun shall be darkened, and
25 the moon shall not give her light, and the stars of heaven shall fall, and
26 the powers that are in heaven shall be shaken. And [u] then shall they see

A. D. 33.

[t] Dan. 7. 10.
[u] Dan. 7. 13.

was the centre. From the remarkable analogy, however, which subsists between those two events, they admit that the language gradually swells into what is much more descriptive of the events of Christ's Personal Coming and the final Judgment than of the destruction of Jerusalem; and in the concluding warnings most of this latter class see an exclusive reference to the Personal Coming of the Lord to judgment. For the following reasons we judge that this latter is the correct view of the Prophecy. FIRST, the connection between the two parts of the prophecy is that of *immediate sequence of time.* In Matt. xxiv. 29 it is said, "Immediately after [Εὐθέως δὲ μετὰ] the tribulation of those days"—shall all the following things happen. What can be plainer than that the one set of events was to happen in close succession after the other? Whereas, on the other supposition, they were to be so far from happening "immediately" after the others, that after eighteen centuries the time for them has not even yet come. The inconvenience of this is felt to be so great, that "the tribulation of those days" is taken to mean, not the calamities which issued in the destruction of Jerusalem at all, but the tribulation which is to usher in the Personal Coming of Christ and the Judgment of the great day. But though this *might* do, as an exposition of the words of Matthew, the words of Mark (xiii. 24) seem in flat contradiction to it: "But in those days, after *that* tribulation" emphatically [μετὰ τὴν θλίψιν ἐκείνην]. How can this possibly mean any tribulation but the one just described? And were we to try the other sense of it, how very unnatural is it—after reading a minute account of the tribulations which were to bring on the destruction of Jerusalem, and then that "immediately after the tribulation of those days" certain other events are to happen — to understand this to mean, 'Immediately after the tribulation of another and far distant day, a tribulation not here to be described at all, shall occur the following events!' What object could there be for alluding so abruptly to "the tribulation of those days," if that tribulation was not to be described at all, but only something which was to happen *after* it? But, SECONDLY, at the conclusion of the second part of this prophecy, our Lord says (*v.* 30), "Verily I say unto you, that this generation shall not pass away till all these things be done," or "fulfilled" (as in Matt. xxiv. 34; Luke xxi. 32). This, on the face of it, is so decisive that those who think the second half of the Prophecy refers to the Second Coming of Christ and the Final Judgment are obliged to translate the words [ἡ γενεὰ αὕτη]. 'This (Jewish) *nation*,' or 'This (human) *race* shall not pass away,' &c. But besides that this is quite contrary to the usage of the word—just think how inept a sense is brought out by translating 'this race;' for who could require to be told that the human family would not have passed away before certain events occurred which were to befall the human race? and how pointless is the other sense, that the Jewish *nation* would not be extinct before those events! Whereas, if we understand the words in their natural sense—that the generation then running should see all those predictions fulfilled—all is intelligible, deeply important, and according to literal fact. But the exposition will throw further light upon this question.

24. But in those days, after that tribulation— "Immediately after the tribulation of those days" (Matt. xxiv. 29); see introductory remarks on this latter portion of the prophecy, **the sun shall be darkened, and the moon shall not give her light. 25. And the stars of heaven shall fall**— "and upon the earth distress of nations, with perplexity; the sea and the waves roaring; men's hearts failing them for fear, and for looking after those things which are coming on the earth" (Luke xxi. 25, 26). **and the powers that are in heaven shall be shaken.** Though the grandeur of this language carries the mind over the head of all periods but that of Christ's Second Coming, nearly every expression will be found used of the Lord's coming in terrible national judgments: as of Babylon (Isa. xiii. 9-13); of Idumea (Isa. xxxiv. 1, 2, 4, 8-10); of Egypt (Ezek. xxxii. 7, 8): compare also Ps. xviii. 7-15; Isa. xxiv. 1, 17-19; Joel ii. 10, 11, &c. We cannot therefore consider the mere strength of this language a proof that it refers exclusively or primarily to the precursors of the final day, though of course in "*that day*" it will have its most awful fulfilment. **26. And then shall they see the Son of man coming in the clouds with great power and glory.** In Matt. xxiv. 30, this is given most fully: "And then shall appear the sign of the Son of man in heaven; and then shall all the tribes of the earth mourn, and they shall see the Son of man," &c. That this language finds its highest interpretation in the Second Personal Coming of Christ, is most certain. But the question is, whether that be the primary sense of it as it stands here? Now, if the reader will turn to Dan. vii. 13, 14, and connect with it the preceding verses, he will find, we think, the true key to our Lord's meaning here. There the powers that oppressed the Church–symbolized by rapacious wild beasts—are summoned to the bar of the great God, who as the Ancient of days seats Himself, with His assessors, on a burning Throne; thousand thousands ministering to Him, and ten thousand times ten thousand standing before Him. "The judgment is set, and the books are opened." Who that is guided by the *mere words* would doubt that this is a description of the Final Judgment? And yet nothing is clearer than that it is *not*, but a description of a vast *temporal* judgment, upon organized bodies of men, for their incurable hostility to the kingdom of God upon earth. Well, after the doom of these has been pronounced and executed, and room thus prepared for the unobstructed development of the kingdom of God over the earth, what follows? "I saw in the night visions, and, behold, one like THE SON OF MAN came with the clouds of heaven, and came to the Ancient of days, and they (the angelic attendants) brought Him near before Him." For what purpose? To receive investiture in the kingdom, which, as Messiah, of right belonged to Him. Accordingly, it is added, "And there was given Him dominion, and glory, and a kingdom, that all peoples, nations, and languages should serve Him: His dominion is an everlasting dominion, which shall not pass away, and His kingdom that which shall not be destroyed." Comparing this with our Lord's words, He seems to us, by "the Son of man (on which phrase, see on John i. 51) coming in the clouds with great power and glory," to mean, that when judicial vengeance shall once have been executed upon Jerusalem, and the ground thus cleared for the unobstructed establishment of His own kingdom, His true regal claims and rights would be visibly

27 the Son of man coming in the clouds with great power and glory. And
then shall he send his angels, and shall gather together his elect from the
four winds, from the uttermost part of the earth to the uttermost part of
heaven.
28 Now learn a parable of the fig tree; When her branch is yet tender,
29 and putteth forth leaves, ye know that summer is near: so ye, in like
manner, when ye shall see these things come to pass, know that it is nigh,
30 *even* at the doors. Verily I say unto you, that this generation shall not
31 pass, till all these things be done. Heaven and earth shall pass away;
but my [v] words shall not pass away.
32 But of that day and *that* hour knoweth no man, no, not the angels
which are in heaven, neither the Son, but the Father.

A. D. 33.

[v] Num. 23. 19. Jos. 23. 14, 15. Ps. 19. 7. Ps. 102. 26. Ps. 119. 89. Isa. 40. 8. Isa. 46. 10. Isa. 51. 6. Zec. 1. 6. Luke 21. 33. 2 Tim. 2. 13. Titus 1. 2.

and gloriously asserted and manifested. See on Luke ix. 28 (with its parallels in Matthew and Mark), in which nearly the same language is employed, and where it can hardly be understood of anything else than *the full and free establishment of the kingdom of Christ on the destruction of Jerusalem.* But what is that "sign of the Son of man in heaven"? Interpreters are not agreed. But as before Christ came to destroy Jerusalem some appalling portents were seen in the air, so before His Personal appearing it is likely that something *analogous* will be witnessed, though of what nature it would be vain to conjecture. **27. And then shall he send his angels**—"with a great sound of a trumpet" (Matt. xxiv. 31), **and shall gather together his elect from the four winds, from the uttermost part of the earth to the uttermost part of heaven.** As the tribes of Israel were anciently gathered together by sound of trumpet (Exod. xix. 13, 16, 19; Lev. xxiii. 24; Ps. lxxxi. 3-5), so any mighty gathering of God's people, by divine command, is represented as collected by sound of trumpet (Isa. xxvii. 13; compare Rev. xi. 15); and the ministry of angels, employed in all the great operations of Providence, is here held forth as the agency by which the present assembling of the elect is to be accomplished. *Lightfoot* thus explains it: 'When Jerusalem shall be reduced to ashes, and that wicked nation cut off and rejected, then shall the Son of man send His ministers with the trumpet of the Gospel, and they shall gather His elect of the several nations, from the four corners of heaven: so that God shall not want a Church, although that ancient people of His be rejected and cast off; but that ancient Jewish Church being destroyed, a new Church shall be called out of the Gentiles.' But though something like this appears to be the primary sense of the verse, in relation to the destruction of Jerusalem, no one can fail to see that the language swells beyond any gathering of the human family into a Church upon earth, and forces the thoughts onward to that gathering of the Church "at the last trump," to meet the Lord in the air, which is to wind up the present scene. Still, this is not, in our judgment, the *direct* subject of the prediction; for the next verse limits the whole prediction to the generation then existing.

28. Now learn a parable of the fig tree ['Ἀπὸ δὲ τῆς συκῆς μάθετε τὴν παραβολήν]—'Now from the fig tree learn the parable,' or the high lesson which this teaches: **When her branch is yet tender, and putteth forth leaves** [τὰ φύλλα]—'its leaves,' **ye know that summer is near: 29. So ye, in like manner, when ye shall see these things come to pass** [γινόμενα]—rather, 'coming to pass,' **know that it**—"the kingdom of God" (Luke xxi. 31), **is nigh, even at the doors**—that is, the full manifestation of it; for till then it admitted of no full development. In Luke (xxi. 28) the following words precede these: "And when these things begin to come to pass, then look up, and lift up your heads; for your redemption draweth nigh"—their redemption, in the first instance certainly, from Jewish oppression (1 Thess. ii. 14-16; Luke xi. 52): but in the highest sense of these words, redemption from all the oppressions and miseries of the present state at the Second Appearing of the Lord Jesus. **30. Verily I say unto you, that this generation shall not pass till all these things be done**—or "fulfilled" (Matt. xxiv. 34; Luke xxi. 32). See introductory remarks on this second half of the prophecy. Whether we take this to mean that the whole would be fulfilled within the limits of the generation then current, or, according to a usual way of speaking, that the generation then existing would not pass away without seeing a *begun* fulfilment of this prediction, the facts entirely correspond. For either the whole was fulfilled in the destruction accomplished by Titus, as many think; or if we stretch it out, according to others, till the thorough dispersion of the Jews a little later, under Adrian, every requirement of our Lord's words seems to be met. **31. Heaven and earth shall pass away; but my words shall not pass away**—the strongest possible expression of the divine authority by which He spake; not as Moses or Paul might have said of their own inspiration, for such language would be unsuitable in any merely human mouth.

Warnings to Prepare for the Coming of Christ Suggested by the foregoing Prophecy (32-37). It will be observed that, in the foregoing prophecy, as our Lord approaches the crisis of the day of vengeance on Jerusalem, and redemption for the Church—at which stage the analogy between that and the day of final vengeance and redemption waxes more striking—His language rises and swells beyond all temporal and partial vengeance, beyond all earthly deliverances and enlargements, and ushers us resistlessly into the scenes of the final day. Accordingly, in these six concluding verses it is manifest that preparation for "THAT DAY" is what our Lord designs to inculcate.

32. But of that day and that hour—that is, the precise time, **knoweth no man** [οὐδεὶς]—lit., 'no one,' **no, not the angels which are in heaven, neither the Son, but the Father.** This very remarkable statement regarding "the Son" is peculiar to Mark. Whether it means that the Son was *not at that time in possession of the knowledge* referred to, or simply that it was not *among the things which He had received to communicate*—has been matter of much controversy even amongst the firmest believers in the proper Divinity of Christ. In the latter sense it was taken by some of the most eminent of the ancient Fathers, and by *Luther*, *Melancthon*, and most of the elder Lutherans; and it is so taken by *Bengel, Lange, Webster and Wilkin-*

33 Take [w]ye heed, watch and pray: for ye know not when the time is.
34 *For [x]the Son of man is* as a man taking a far journey, who left his house,
and gave authority to his servants, and to every man his work, and com-
35 manded the porter to watch. Watch [y]ye therefore; for ye know not
when the master of the house cometh, at even, or at midnight, or at the
36 cock-crowing, or in the morning; lest, coming suddenly, he find you
37 sleeping. And what I say unto you I say unto all, Watch.

A. D. 33.

w Matt. 24.42. Luke 12.40. Rom. 13.11.
x Matt. 24.45. Matt. 25.14.
y Matt. 24.42, 44. Rev. 3.3.

---

son. *Chrysostom* and others understood it to mean that *as Man* our Lord was ignorant of this. It is taken literally by *Calvin, Grotius, de Wette, Meyer, Fritzsche, Stier, Alford,* and *Alexander.* Beyond all doubt, as the word "knoweth" [οἶδεν] in this verse is the well-known word for the knowledge of any fact, this latter sense is the one we should naturally put upon the statement; namely, that our Lord did not at that time know the day and hour of His own Second Coming. But *the nature of the case*—meaning by this the speaker, His subject, and the probable design of the statement in question—is always allowed to have its weight in determining the sense of any doubtful utterance. What, then, is the nature of this case? First, The Speaker was One who, from the time when He entered on His public ministry, spoke ever, acted ever, as One *from whom nothing was hid;* and *to Whom was committed the whole administration of the Kingdom of God* from first to last; nor when Peter ascribed *omniscience* to Him (John xxi. 17), can He be supposed to have pointed to any enlargement of the sphere of his Lord's knowledge since His resurrection, or to aught save what he had witnessed of Him "in the days of His flesh." Second, There seems nothing so peculiar in the knowledge of *the precise time of His Second Coming,* much less of *the destruction of Jerusalem,* more than of other things which we are certain that our Lord knew at that time, that *it* should be kept from Him, while those other things were all full before His view. We are ill judges indeed of such matters, but we are obliged to give this consideration some weight. So far as we may presume to judge, there was no benefit to the disciples to be gained by the concealment from *Him*—as certainly there could be no danger to Himself from the knowledge—of the precise time of His coming. But, Third, When we have familiarized ourselves with our Lord's way of speaking of His communications to men, we shall perhaps obtain a key to this remarkable saying of His. Thus: "And what He hath seen and heard, that He testifieth;" "I speak to the world those things that I have heard of Him;" "The Father which sent me, He gave me a commandment what I should say and what I should speak" (John iii. 32; viii. 26; xii. 49). And in a remarkable prophecy (Isa. l. 4) to which we have already adverted (see on ch. x. 32-45, Remark 1)—in which beyond doubt He is the Speaker—He represents Himself as receiving His instructions daily, being each morning instructed what to communicate for that day. In this view, as the precise time of His coming was certainly not in His instructions; as He had not "*seen* and *heard*" it, and so could not "testify" it; as He had no communication from His Father on that subject—might He not, in this sense, after saying that neither men nor angels knew it, add that *Himself knew it not,* without the danger of lowering, even in the minds of any of His half-instructed disciples, the impression of His Omniscience, which every fresh communication to them only tended to deepen? What recommends this opinion is not any inconsistency in the opposite view with the supreme Divinity of Christ. That view might quite well be maintained, if only there appeared sufficient ground for it. But while the one argument in its favour is the natural sense of the words—a very strong argument, however, we are constrained to admit—everything else which one is accustomed to take into account, in weighing the sense of a doubtful saying, is in favour of a *modified* sense of the words in question.

Here follow, in Matt. xxiv. 37-41, some additional particulars: 37. "But as the days of Noe were, so shall also the coming of the Son of man be. 38. For as in the days that were before the flood they were eating and drinking, marrying and giving in marriage, until the day that Noe entered into the ark, 39. And knew not until the flood came, and took them all away; so shall also the coming of the Son of Man be" (see on Luke xvii. 26, 27). 40. "Then shall two (men) be in the field"—at their ordinary work—"the one shall be taken, and the other left. 41. Two women shall be grinding at the mill (see on Mark ix. 42); the one shall be taken, and the other left"—the children of this world and the children of light mingled to the last. See on Luke xvii. 34-36.

33. Take ye heed, watch and pray: for ye know not when the time is. 34. [For the Son of man is] as a man taking a far journey, who left his house, and gave authority to his servants, and to every man his work. The idea thus far is similar to that in the opening part of the parable of the talents (Matt. xxv. 14,15). **and commanded the porter** [τῷ θυρωρῷ]—or 'the gate-keeper,' **to watch**—pointing to the official duty of the ministers of religion to give warning of approaching danger to the people. **35. Watch ye therefore; for ye know not when the master of the house cometh, at even, or at midnight, or at the cock-crowing, or in the morning**—an allusion to the four Roman watches of the night. **36. Lest, coming suddenly, he find you sleeping.** See on Luke xii. 35-40, 42-46. **37. And what I say unto you**—this Discourse, it will be remembered, was delivered in private, **I say unto all, Watch**—anticipating and requiring the diffusion of His teaching by them amongst all His disciples, and its perpetuation through all time.

The closing words of the Discourse, as given by Luke, xxi. 34-36, are remarkable. "And take heed to yourselves, lest at any time your hearts be overcharged" [βαρυνθῶσιν], or 'weighted down,' "with surfeiting" [κραιπάλῃ]—'debauchery,' or its effects; "and drunkenness"—meaning all animal excesses, which quench spirituality; "and cares of this life"—engrossing the interest, absorbing the attention, and so choking spirituality: "and so that day come upon you unawares. For as a snare"—a trap catching them when least expecting it—"shall it come on all them that dwell on the face of the whole earth. Watch ye therefore, and pray always"—the two great duties which, in prospect of trial, are always enjoined—"that ye may be accounted worthy to escape all these things that shall come to pass, and to stand before the Son of man." These warnings, though suggested by the need of preparedness for the tremen-

14 AFTER [a] two days was *the feast of* the passover, and of unleavened
bread: and the chief priests and the scribes sought how they might take

A. D. 33.

CHAP. 14
[a] Matt. 26. 2.

dous calamities approaching, and the total wreck of the existing state of things, have reference to a Coming of another kind, for judicial Vengeance of another nature and on a grander and more awful scale—not ecclesiastical or political but *personal*, not temporal but *eternal*—when all safety and blessedness will be found to lie in being able to "STAND BEFORE THE SON OF MAN" in the glory of His Personal appearing.

The nine concluding verses of Matthew's account (ch. xxiv. 43-51) are peculiar to that Gospel, but are in the same strain of warning to prepare for His Second Coming and the Final Judgment. "But know this, that if the goodman of the house had known in what watch the thief would come, he would have watched, and would not have suffered his house to be broken up. Therefore be ye also ready: for in such an hour as ye think not the Son of man cometh. Who then is a faithful and wise servant, whom his lord hath made ruler over his household, to give them meat in due season? Blessed is that servant whom his lord when he cometh shall find so doing. Verily I say unto you, That he shall make him ruler over all his goods. But and if that evil servant shall say in his heart, My lord delayeth his coming; and shall begin to smite his fellow-servants, and to eat and drink with the drunken; the lord of that servant shall come in a day when he looketh not for him, and in an hour that he is not aware of. And shall cut him asunder, and appoint him his portion with the hypocrites: there shall be weeping and gnashing of teeth." On this whole passage, see on Luke xii. 35-40, 42-46, which is almost identical with it; and on the last words, see on Matt. xiii. 42.

In Luke's account (xxi. 37, 38) the following brief summary is given of our Lord's proceedings until the fifth day (or the Thursday) of His last week: "And in the daytime" [τὰς ἡμέρας]—'during the days'—"He was teaching in the temple; and at night" [τὰς νύκτας]—'during the nights'—"He went out and abode in the mount that is called the mount of Olives"—that is, at Bethany.

Remarks.—1. In the destruction of Jerusalem, and the utter extinction of all that the Jews prided themselves in, on the one hand; and in the preservation, on the other, of the little flock of Christ's disciples, and their secure establishment and gradual diffusion, as now the only visible kingdom of God upon earth—we see an appalling illustration of those great principles of the Divine Government: "Yet a little while, and the wicked shall not be: yea, thou shall diligently consider his place, and it shall not be. But the meek shall inherit the earth; and shall delight themselves in the abundance of peace." "Behold, the day cometh that shall burn as an oven; and all the proud, yea, and all that do wickedly, shall be stubble: and the day that cometh shall burn them up, saith the Lord of Hosts, that it shall leave them neither root nor branch. But unto you that fear my name shall the Sun of Righteousness arise, with healing in His wings; and ye shall go forth, and grow up as calves of the stall." "Every plant which my heavenly Father hath not planted shall be rooted up." (Ps. xxxvii. 10, 11; Mal. iv. 1, 2; Matt. xv. 13.) Every spiritual edifice that is not built of living stones has the rot in it, and will sooner or later crumble down. Like the house built upon the sand, the storm of divine indignation will sweep it away. *He* only *that doeth the will of God abideth for ever* (1 John ii. 17). "Well; because of unbelief they were broken off, and thou standest by faith. Be not high-minded, but fear: for if God spared not the natural branches, take heed lest He also spare not thee" (Rom. xi. 20, 21). 2. We here see the falsity of that shallow view of prophecy which used to be so generally accepted, and even yet is advocated by too many who speak contemptuously of all study of unfulfilled prophecy—that it was designed exclusively for the benefit of those who live *after* its fulfilment, to confirm their faith in the inspiration by which it was uttered, and generally, in the Religion of which it forms a part. Certainly this was not the primary object of our Lord's prophecy of the destruction of Jerusalem; for throughout He gives it forth expressly as a directory *in prospect of it*, for the guidance of those who heard it. "Take heed lest any man deceive you: for many shall come in my name, &c. And when ye shall hear of wars and rumours of wars, be not troubled. When ye shall see the abomination, spoken of by Daniel the prophet, standing where it ought not, (LET HIM THAT READETH UNDERSTAND,) then let them which be in Judea flee, &c. False Christs and false prophets shall rise, and shall show signs and wonders, to seduce, if it were possible, even the elect. But take heed: *behold, I have foretold you all things.* Now learn a parable of the fig tree: . . So ye, in like manner, *when ye shall see these things come to pass, know that it is nigh, even at the doors.*" And if this prophecy was intended directly for those who lived *before* its fulfilment, why not others? Even the darkest prophecy—the Apocalypse—bears on its face throughout a reference to those who should live, not after, but before its accomplishment—to forewarn them of coming dangers, to indicate at least the general nature of them, to prepare and animate them to encounter these, and to assure them of the ultimate safety and triumph of Christ's cause and the glorious reward awaiting the steadfast followers of the Lamb. It is the rashness and dogmatism of the students of prophecy, and the fantastic principles which have often been applied to the interpretation of it, that have scared away sensible Christians and grave theologians from this study, despairing of success. But let us take heed of being thus spoiled of so precious a portion of our Scripture inheritance; missing the blessing pronounced on those who read and keep what is written in prophecy (Rev. i. 3), and disobeying our Lord's own solemn injunction: "*Whoso readeth let him understand*" (*v.* 14). 3. As temperance in animal indulgences is indispensable to that wakefulness and elevation of spirit which fits us for welcoming Christ when He comes, so that spirit of excess which goes to the utmost lawful indulgence wars against the soul, leaving it a prey to surprises even the most fatal (Luke xxi. 34-36; 1 Cor. ix. 27; 1 Pet. ii. 11). 4. In whatever providential events Christ may come to us (Rev. iii. 3; xvi. 15)—even in the summons to "depart and be with Him, which is far better"—it is to His Personal Appearing the second time, without sin unto salvation," that the hearts of believers must ever supremely rise; nor is it a healthy state of soul to stop short of this—as most certainly it is not scriptural. Let us, then, "love His appearing."

CHAP. XIV. 1-11.—THE CONSPIRACY OF THE JEWISH AUTHORITIES TO PUT JESUS TO DEATH—THE SUPPER AND THE ANOINTING AT BETHANY—

2 him by craft, and put *him* to death. But they said, Not on the feast
day, lest there be an uproar of the people.

A. D. 33.

[a] Luke 22. 1.

JUDAS AGREES WITH THE CHIEF PRIESTS TO BETRAY HIS LORD. (= Matt. xxvi. 1-16; Luke xxii. 1-6; John xii. 1-11.) The events of this Section appear to have occurred on the fourth day of the Redeemer's Last Week—the *Wednesday.*

Conspiracy of the Jewish Authorities to Put Jesus to Death (1, 2). **1. After two days was the feast of the passover, and of unleavened bread.** The meaning is, that two days after what is about to be mentioned the Passover would arrive; in other words, what follows occurred two days *before* the feast. **and the chief priests and the scribes sought how they might take him by craft, and put him to death.** From Matthew's fuller account (ch xxvi.) we learn that our Lord announced this to the Twelve as follows, being the first announcement to them of the precise time: "And it came to pass, when Jesus had finished all these sayings"—referring to the contents of ch. xxiv., xxv., which He delivered to His disciples; His public ministry being now closed: from His *prophetical* He is now passing into His *Priestly* office, although all along Himself took our infirmities and bare our sicknesses—"He said unto His disciples, Ye know that after two days is [the feast of] the Passover, and the Son of man is betrayed to be crucified." The *first* and the *last* steps of his final sufferings are brought together in this brief announcement of all that was to take place. The *Passover* [τὸ πάσχα = פֶּסַח] was the first and the chief of the three great annual festivals, commemorative of the redemption of God's people from Egypt, through the sprinkling of the blood of a lamb divinely appointed to be slain for that end; the destroying angel, "when he saw the blood, *passing over*" the Israelitish houses, on which that blood was seen, when he came to destroy all the first-born in the land of Egypt (Exod. xii.)—bright typical foreshadowing of the great Sacrifice, and the Redemption effected thereby. Accordingly, "by the determinate counsel and foreknowledge of God, who is wonderful in counsel and excellent in working," it was so ordered that precisely at the Passover-season, "Christ our Passover should be sacrificed for us." On the day following the Passover commenced "the feast of unleavened bread" [τὰ ἄζυμα], so called because for seven days only unleavened bread was to be eaten (Exod. xii. 18-20). See on 1 Cor. v. 6-8. We are further told by Matthew (xxvi. 3) that the consultation was held in the palace of Caiaphas the high priest, between the chief priests, [the scribes], and the elders of the people, how "they might take Jesus by subtlety and kill Him." [The words καὶ οἱ γραμματεῖς are probably not genuine here. *Tischendorf* and *Tregelles* exclude them. It is likely they were introduced from Matthew and Luke.] **2. But they said, Not on the feast** [day]—rather, 'not during the feast' [ἐν τῇ ἑορτῇ]; not until the seven days of unleavened bread should be over. **lest there be an uproar of the people.** In consequence of the vast influx of strangers, embracing all the male population of the land who had reached a certain age, there were within the walls of Jerusalem at this festival some two millions of people; and in their excited state, the danger of tumult and bloodshed among "the people," who for the most part took Jesus for a prophet, was extreme. (See *Joseph.* Antt. xx. 5. 3.) What plan, if any, these ecclesiastics fixed upon for seizing our Lord, does not appear. But the proposal of Judas being at once and eagerly gone into, it is probable they were till then at some loss for a plan sufficiently quiet and yet effectual. So, just at the feast time shall it be done; the unexpected offer of Judas relieving them of their fears. Thus, as *Bengel* remarks, did the divine counsel take effect.

The Supper and the Anointing at Bethany Six Days before the Passover (3-9). The time of this part of the narrative, as we shall presently see, is *four days before* what has just been related. Had it been part of the regular train of events which our Evangelist designed to record, he would probably have inserted it in its proper place, before the conspiracy of the Jewish authorities. But having come to the treason of Judas, he seems to have gone back upon this scene as what probably gave immediate occasion to the awful deed. The best introduction to it we have in the Fourth Gospel.

John xii. 1, 2.—"Then Jesus, six days before the Passover, came to Bethany" (see on Luke xix. 29)—that is, on the sixth day before it; probably after sunset on *Friday* evening, or the commencement of the Jewish *Sabbath* that preceded the Passover: "where Lazarus was which had been dead, whom He raised from the dead. There they made Him a supper"—in what house is not here stated; but the first two Evangelists expressly tell us it was "in the house of Simon the leper" (Matt. xxvi. 6; Mark xiv. 3). But for this statement, we should have taken it for granted that the scene occurred in the house of Lazarus. At the same time, as Martha served (John xii. 2), he was probably some near relative of her family. Who this "Simon the leper" was, is quite unknown. A leper at that time, while entertaining guests at his own table, he could not have been, as this would have been contrary to the Jewish law. But he *had been* one, perhaps long one, and so came to be best known by his old name, "Simon the leper." And just as Matthew, long after he was transformed into "an apostle of Jesus Christ," continued to call himself what none of the other Evangelists do, "Matthew the publican;" so, perhaps, this healed leper, after the Saviour had cleansed him, and won his heart—healing soul and body together—felt it pleasant to be known ever after as "Simon the leper:" and just as Matthew, again, "made Him a great feast in his own house," this Simon, out of the fulness of a grateful heart, made Him this supper. And what if he was that very leper whose case is the first recorded in the Gospel History, who, immediately after the Sermon on the Mount," as Jesus descended from the hill on which it was delivered, came running and kneeling to Him, saying, "Lord, if thou wilt, thou canst make me clean," and whose leprosy immediately departed from him, when the Lord said, "I will; be thou clean"! (See on Matt. viii. 1-4.) The time when this supper was made to Jesus was affecting. As it was His last visit to His quiet and loved retreat at Bethany, so He honoured it by making it His longest. He made it His nightly home during His final week; going thence daily into the city, but never sleeping there. And, says the beloved disciple, "Martha served." Active, busy, but true-hearted, Martha is here at her proper vocation—serving her Lord. A blessed employment. She got a gentle check once when so engaged, though not for so doing. But there is no rebuke here; nay, it seems recorded here as her privilege that she served. Service to Christ there must be; somebody must do it; and Martha on this occasion was the honoured servant; "but

3 And [b]being in Bethany, in the house of Simon the leper, as he sat at
meat, there came a woman having an alabaster box of ointment of
[1]spikenard very precious; and she brake the box, and poured *it* on his
4 head. And there were some that had indignation within themselves, and
5 said, Why was this waste of the ointment made? for it might have been
sold for more than three hundred [c]pence, and have been given to the
6 poor. And they murmured against her. And Jesus said, Let her alone;
7 why trouble ye her? she hath wrought a good work on me. For [d]ye
have the poor with you always, and whensoever ye will ye may do them
8 good: but me ye have not always. She hath done what she could: she
9 is come aforehand to anoint my body to the burying. Verily I say unto
you, Wheresoever this gospel shall be preached throughout the whole
world, *this* also that she hath done shall be spoken of for a memorial of
her.
10 And [e]Judas Iscariot, one of the twelve, went unto the chief priests, to

A. D. 33.

[b] Matt. 26. 6. Luke 7. 37. John 12. 1, 3.

[1] Or, pure nard, or, liquid nard.

[c] Matt. 18. 28. John 6. 7.

[d] Deut. 15. 11. Pro. 22. 2. Matt. 26. 11. Matt. 25. 35. John 12. 8. 2 Cor. 9. 13.

[e] Matt. 26. 14. John 13. 2, 30.

Lazarus," says John, "was one of them that sat at the table with him"—a trophy of his Master's resurrection-power and glory. So much for John's introduction to the scene. Let us now return to our own narrative:

3. And being in Bethany, in the house of Simon the leper, as he sat at meat, there came a woman. It was "Mary," as we learn from John xii. 3. **having an alabaster box of ointment of spikenard** [νάρδου]—pure *nard*, a celebrated aromatic. (See Cant. i. 12.) **very precious** —"very costly" (John xii. 3), **and she brake the box, and poured it on his head**—"and anointed," adds John, "the feet of Jesus, and wiped His feet with her hair: and the house was filled with the odour of the ointment." The only use of this was to refresh and exhilarate—a grateful compliment in the East, amidst the closeness of a heated atmosphere, with many guests at a feast. Such was the form in which Mary's love to Christ, at so much cost to herself, poured itself out. **4. And there were some that had indignation within themselves, and said.** Matthew says (xxvi. 8), "But when His disciples saw it, they had indignation, saying." The spokesman, however, was none of the true-hearted Eleven—as we learn from John (xii. 4): "Then saith one of His disciples, Judas Iscariot, Simon's son, which should betray Him." Doubtless the thought stirred first in his breast, and issued from his base lips; and some of the rest, ignorant of his true character and feelings, and carried away by his plausible speech, might for the moment feel some chagrin at the apparent waste. **Why was this waste of the ointment made? 5. For it might have been sold for more than three hundred pence**—between nine and ten pounds sterling, **and have been given to the poor. And they murmured against her.** "This he said," remarks John, and the remark is of exceeding importance, "not that he cared for the poor; but because he was a thief, and had the bag" [τὸ γλωσσόκομον]—the scrip or treasure-chest; "and bare what was put therein" [ἐβάσταζεν]—not 'bare it off' by theft, as some understand it. It is true that he did this; but the expression means simply that he had charge of it and its contents, or was treasurer to Jesus and the Twelve. What a remarkable arrangement was this, by which an avaricious and dishonest person was not only taken into the number of the Twelve, but entrusted with the custody of their little property! The purposes which this served are obvious enough; but it is farther noticeable, that the remotest hint was never given to the Eleven of his true character, nor did the disciples most favoured with the intimacy of Jesus ever suspect him, till a few minutes before he voluntarily separated himself from their company —for ever! **6. And Jesus said, Let her alone; why trouble ye her? she hath wrought a good work on me.** It was good in itself, and so was acceptable to Christ; it was eminently seasonable, and so more acceptable still; and it was "what she could," and so most acceptable of all. **7. For ye have the poor with you always**—referring to Deut. xv. 11, **and whensoever ye will ye may do them good: but me ye have not always**—a gentle hint of His approaching departure, by One who knew the worth of His own presence. **8. She hath done what she could**—a noble testimony, embodying a principle of immense importance. **she is come aforehand to anoint my body to the burying**—or, as in John (xii. 7), "Against the day of my burying hath she kept this." Not that she, dear heart, thought of His burial, much less reserved any of her nard to anoint her dead Lord. But as the time was so near at hand when that office would have to be performed, *and she was not to have that privilege even after the spices were brought for the purpose* (ch. xvi. 1), He lovingly *regards it as done now.* **9. Verily I say unto you, Wheresoever this gospel shall be preached throughout the whole world, this also that she hath done shall be spoken of for a memorial of her.** 'In the act of love done to Him,' says *Olshausen* beautifully, 'she has erected to herself an eternal monument, as lasting as the Gospel, the eternal Word of God. From generation to generation this remarkable prophecy of the Lord has been fulfilled; and even we, in explaining this saying of the Redeemer, of necessity contribute to its accomplishment.' 'Who but Himself,' asks *Stier*, 'had the power to ensure to any work of man, even if resounding in His own time through the whole earth, an imperishable remembrance in the stream of history? Behold once more here the majesty of His royal judicial supremacy in the government of the world, in this "Verily I say unto you."'

10. And Judas Iscariot, one of the twelve, went unto the chief priests, to betray him unto them—that is, to make his proposals, and to bargain with them, as appears from Matthew's fuller statement (ch. xxvi.), which says, he "went unto the chief priests, and said, What will ye give me, and I will deliver Him unto you? And they covenanted with him for thirty pieces of silver" (*v.* 15). The thirty pieces of silver were thirty shekels, the fine paid for man or maid-servant accidentally killed (Exod. xxi. 32), and equal to between four and five pounds sterling

11 betray him unto them. And when they heard *it*, they were glad, and
promised to give him [f] money. And he sought how he might conveniently
betray him.

A. D. 33.

[f] Zec. 11. 12. 1 Tim. 6. 10.

—"a *goodly* price that I was prized at of them"! (Zec. xi. 13). **11. And when they heard it, they were glad, and promised to give him money.** Matthew alone records the precise sum, because a remarkable and complicated prophecy, which he was afterwards to refer to, was fulfilled by it. **And he sought how he might conveniently betray him**—or, as more fully given in Luke (xxii. 6), "And he promised, and sought opportunity to betray Him unto them in the absence of the multitude." That he should avoid an "uproar" or 'riot' among the people, which probably was made an essential condition by the Jewish authorities, was thus assented to by the traitor; into whom, says Luke (xxii. 3), "Satan entered," to put him upon this hellish deed.

Remarks.—1. Among the 'undesigned coincidences' in the narratives of the Four Evangelists which so strongly confirm their truth, not the least striking are the representations given of the respective characters of Martha and Mary by the Third and Fourth Evangelists. While in Luke we have a scene omitted by John, in which the active services of Martha and the placid affection, the passive docility, of Mary come strikingly out (see on Luke x. 38-42), we have in John (xii. 1, &c.) a very different scene, omitted by Luke, in which, nevertheless, the same characteristics appear. Martha serves, while Mary diffuses over her Lord the odour of her love, in the costly ointment which she spent upon Him. What are these but different rays from one bright historic Reality? 2. In this feast, beheld in its inner character, may we not see on a small scale something like what is from age to age realized in the kingdom of grace? Here is the Redeemer surrounded by the varied trophies of His grace. First, we have Simon the leper—the healed man; next, Lazarus—the risen man; and here is the man that leaned on Jesus' breast, nearest to his Lord—type of seraphic affection; and that other "son of thunder," James, the brother of John, who was honoured to drink of his Lord's cup, and be baptized with the baptism which He was baptized withal—the man of impulsive but robust devotion to Christ; and here was blessed Simon Bar-jona—the man of commanding energy—first among the Twelve; and all the diversified types of Christian character, as exemplified in the rest: But, lo! in the midst of these, and one of their number, was "a devil"—type of that traitorous spirit from which probably the Christian Church has hardly ever been quite free. But woman also is here represented—redeemed womanhood; and in its two great types—active and passive, or doing and feeling. And yet there was doing in both, and feeling in both; although the hands were the characteristic in the one case, the heart in the other. And what would the Church and the world be without both? Active service laid the foundations of the infant Church, and has ever since diffused and preserved it; active service has rolled back the tide of corruption when it had settled over the Church, and restored its evangelical character; and the active services of woman have been in every age of quickened Christianity as precious as they have been beautiful. But it is the service of love which Christ values. Love to Christ transfigures the humblest services. All, indeed, who have themselves a heart value its least outgoings above the most costly mechanical performances; but how does it endear the Saviour to us to find Himself endorsing that principle, as His own standard in judging of character and deeds!

'What though in poor and humble guise
Thou here didst sojourn cottage-born?
Yet from thy glory in the skies
Our earthly gold thou dost not scorn.
For Love delights to bring her best,
And where Love is, that offering evermore is blest.

'Love on the Saviour's dying head
Her spikenard drops unblam'd may pour,
May mount His cross and wrap Him dead
In spices from the golden shore,' &c.—KEBLE.

3. Works of *utility* are never to be set in opposition to the promptings of self-sacrificing *love*, and the sincerity of those who do so is to be suspected. What a number of starving families might those "three hundred pence" have cheered (would Judas exclaim, if time had been allowed him to enlarge upon this waste)! In like manner, under the mask of concern for the poor at home, how many excuse themselves from all care of the perishing heathen abroad! The bad source of such complaints and the insincerity of such excuses may reasonably be suspected. 4. Amidst conflicting duties, that which our hand presently findeth to do is to be preferred to that which can be done at any time. "Ye have the poor always with you; but Me ye have not always." 5. The Lord Jesus has an exalted consciousness of the worth of His own presence with His people, and will have them alive to it too. There is, indeed, a sense in which He is with them always, even to the world's end (Matt. xxviii. 20). But there are special opportunities of which it may be said, "Me ye have not always;" and it is the part of wisdom to avail ourselves of these while we have them, even though it should interfere with duties, which, however important, are of such a nature that opportunities for doing them never cease. 6. To those who are oppressed with the little they can do for Christ, what unspeakable consolation is there in that testimony borne to Mary, "She hath done what she could"! Not the poorest and humblest of Christ's loving followers but may, on this principle, rise as high in the esteem of Christ as the wealthiest and those who move in the widest spheres of Christian usefulness. "If there be first a willing mind, it is accepted according to what a man hath, and not according to what he hath not" (2 Cor. viii. 12). On this delightful subject, see also on Luke xxi. 1-4, with Remarks at the close of that Section. 7. As Jesus beheld in spirit the universal diffusion of His Gospel, while His lowest depth of humiliation was only approaching, so He regarded the facts of His earthly History as constituting the substance of "this Gospel," and the proclamation of them as just the "preaching of this Gospel." Not that preachers are to confine themselves to a bare narration of these facts, but that they are to make their whole preaching revolve around them as its grand centre, and derive from them its proper vitality; all that goes before this in the Bible being but the *preparation* for them, and all that follows but the *sequel*. 8. The crime of Judas is too apt to be viewed as something exceptional in character and atrocity. But the study of its different stages is fitted to dissipate that delusion. First, *Covetousness* being his master-passion, the Lord suffered it to reveal itself and gather strength, by entrusting him with "the bag" (John xii. 6), as treasurer to Himself and the Twelve. Next, in the dis-

12 And [g]the first day of unleavened bread, when they [2]killed the passover,
his disciples said unto him, Where wilt thou that we go and prepare that
13 thou mayest eat the passover? And he sendeth forth two of his disciples,
and saith unto them, Go ye into the city, and there shall meet you a man
14 bearing a pitcher of water: follow him. And wheresoever he shall go in,
say ye to the goodman of the house, The Master saith, Where is the
15 guest-chamber, where I shall eat [h]the passover with my disciples? And
he will show you a large upper room furnished *and* prepared: there make
16 ready for us. And his disciples went forth, and came into the city, and
found as he had said unto them: and they made ready the passover.
17 And [i]in the evening he cometh with the twelve. And as they sat and
18 did eat, Jesus said, Verily I say unto you, One of you which eateth with
19 me shall betray me. And they began to be sorrowful, and to say unto
20 him one by one, *Is* it I? and another *said, Is* it I? And he answered
and said unto them, *It is* one of the twelve, that dippeth with me in the
21 dish. The [j]Son of man indeed goeth, as it is written of him: but woe to
that man by whom the Son of man is betrayed! good were it for that
man if he had never been born.
22 And [k]as they did eat, Jesus took bread, and blessed, and brake *it,* and
23 gave to them, and said, Take, eat: this [3]is my body. And he took the
cup, and when he had given thanks, he gave *it* to them: and they all
24 drank of it. And he said unto them, This is [l]my blood of the new
25 testament, which is shed for many. Verily I say unto you, I will drink
no more of the fruit of the vine, until that day that I drink it new in the
kingdom of God.
26 And [m]when they had sung an [4]hymn, they went out into the mount of
27 Olives. And [n]Jesus saith unto them, All ye shall be offended because of
me this night: for it is written, [o]I will smite the Shepherd, and the sheep

A. D. 33.
[g] Luke 22. 7.
[2] Or, sacrificed.
[h] Ex. 12. 6. Lev. 23. 5.
[i] Matt. 26. 20. Luke 22. 14. John 13. 21.
[j] Gen. 23. 15. Isa. 53. 1-12. Dan. 9. 26. Zec. 13. 7. Matt. 26. 24. Luke 22. 22.
[k] Matt. 26. 26. Luke 22. 19. 1 Cor. 11. 23.
[3] Or, represents. 1 Cor. 10. 4, 16.
[l] Ex. 24. 8. Zec. 9. 11. 1 Cor. 11. 25. Heb. 9. 14.
[m] Matt. 26. 30.
[4] Or, psalm.
[n] Matt. 26. 31. Luke 22. 31, 32. John 16. 31, 32. 1 Tim. 4. 16.
[o] Isa. 53. 2-10. Dan. 9. 26. Zec. 13. 7.

charge of that most sacred trust, he began to pilfer, and became "a thief," appropriating the store from time to time to his own use. Then Satan, walking about seeking whom he might devour, and seeing this door standing wide open, determined to enter by it; but cautiously (2 Cor. ii. 11)—at first merely "putting it into his heart to betray him" (John xiii. 2), or whispering to him the thought that by this means he might enrich himself, and that possibly, when the danger became extreme, He who had wrought so many miracles, might miraculously extricate Himself. The next stage was the conversion of that thought into the settled purpose to do it; to which we may well suppose he would be loath to come till something occurred to fix it. That something, we apprehend, was what took place at the house of Simon the leper; from which he probably withdrew with a chagrin which was perhaps all that was now wanted to decide him. Still starting back, however, or mercifully held back for some time, the determination to carry it into immediate effect was not consummated, it would appear, till, sitting at the Paschal supper, "*Satan entered into him,*" John xiii. 27; and conscience, now effectually stifled, only rose, after the deed, to drive him to despair. O, what warnings do these facts sound forth to every one! Could the traitor but be permitted to send a messenger from "his own place" (Acts i. 25) to warn the living—as the rich man in the parable wished that Lazarus might be to his five brethren—with what a piercing cry would he utter these words, "They that will be rich fall into temptation and a snare, and into many foolish and hurtful lusts, which drown men in destruction and perdition. For the love of money is the root of all evil; which while some coveted after, they have erred from the faith, and pierced themselves through with many sorrows." "Your adversary the devil, as a roaring lion, walketh about, seeking whom he may devour: whom resist steadfast in the faith." "Resist the devil, and he will flee from you." (1 Tim. vi. 9, 10; 1 Pet. v. 8, 9; Jas. iv. 7.) 9. How sublime is the self-possession with which Jesus, four days after this scene at Bethany, announced to the Twelve that in two days more He should be betrayed to be crucified! At that very moment, perhaps, the Jewish authorities were assembled in the palace of the high priest, consulting together how they might do it; and Judas, who had stolen away from the rest of the Twelve, and got admission to the Council, was just concluding his bargain, perhaps, when He to whose mind every step of the process lay open, disclosed to His true-hearted ones the near-approaching consummation. What a study have we here: on the one hand, of incomparable placidity in One of acutest sensibility; and on the other, of the harmonious working of man's perfectly free will, and the determinate counsel and foreknowledge of God that what men freely resolve on and do shall come to pass for His own high ends! "For *of* Him, and *through* Him, and *to* Him, are all things: to Whom be glory for ever. Amen." (See on Rom. xi. 36.)

12-26.—Preparation for, and Last Celebration of, the Passover—Announcement of the Traitor—Institution of the Supper. (= Matt. xxvi. 17-30; Luke xxii. 7-23, 39; John xiii. 21-30.) For the exposition, see on Luke xxii. 7-23, 39; and on John xiii. 10, 11, 18, 19, 21-30.

27-31.—The Desertion of Jesus by His Disciples, and the Fall of Peter, Foretold. (= Matt. xxvi. 31-35; Luke xxii. 31-38; John xiii. 36-38.) For the exposition, see on Luke xxii. 31-46.

28 shall be scattered. But [p] after that I am risen, I will go before you into
29 Galilee. But [q] Peter said unto him, Although all shall be offended, yet
30 *will* not I. And Jesus saith unto him, Verily I say unto thee, That this
day, *even* in this night, before the cock crow twice, thou shalt deny me
31 thrice. But he spake the more vehemently, If I should die with thee, I
will not deny thee in any wise. Likewise also said they all.
32 And [r] they came to a place which was named Gethsemane: and he
33 saith to his disciples, Sit ye here, while [s] I shall pray. And he taketh
with him Peter and James and John, and began to be sore amazed, and
34 to be very heavy; and saith unto them, [t] My soul is exceeding sorrowful
35 unto death: tarry ye here, and watch. And he went forward a little,
and fell on the ground, and prayed that, if it were possible, the hour
36 might pass from him. And he said, [u] Abba, Father, [v] all things *are*
possible unto thee; take away this cup from me: [w] nevertheless not what
37 I will, but what thou wilt. And he cometh, and findeth them sleeping,
and saith unto Peter, Simon, sleepest thou? couldest not thou watch one
38 hour? Watch ye and pray, lest ye enter into temptation. [x] The spirit
39 truly *is* ready, but the flesh *is* weak. And again he went away, and
40 prayed, and spake the same words. And when he returned, he found
them asleep again, (for their eyes were heavy,) neither wist they what to
41 answer him. And he cometh the third time, and saith unto them, Sleep
on now, and take *your* rest: it is enough, [y] the hour is come; behold, the
42 Son of man is betrayed into the hands of sinners. Rise [z] up, let us go;
lo, he that betrayeth me is at hand.
43 And [a] immediately, while he yet spake, cometh Judas, one of the
twelve, and with him a great multitude with swords and staves, from the
44 chief priests and the scribes and the elders. And he that betrayed him
had given them a token, saying, Whomsoever I shall kiss, that same is he;
45 take him, and lead *him* away safely. And as soon as he was come, he
goeth straightway to him, and saith, [5] Master, master; and [b] kissed him.
46 And they laid their hands on him, and took him.
47 And one of them that stood by drew a sword, and smote a servant of
48 the high priest, and cut off his ear. And [c] Jesus answered and said unto
them, Are ye come out, as against a thief, with swords and *with* staves to
49 take me? I was daily with you in the temple teaching, and ye took me
50 not: but [d] the Scriptures must be fulfilled. And [e] they all forsook him,
51 and fled. And there followed him a certain young man, having a linen
cloth cast about *his* naked *body;* and the young men laid hold on him:
52 And he left the linen cloth, and fled from them naked.

A. D. 33.

[p] Matt. 16.21. Matt. 26.32. Matt. 28. 7, 10-16. ch. 16. 7. John 21. 1. 1 Cor. 15. 4-6.
[q] Matt. 26.33, 34. Luke 22.33, 34. John 13.37, 38.
[r] Matt. 26.36. Luke 22.39. John 18. 1.
[s] Heb 5. 7.
[t] John 12.27.
[u] Rom. 8. 15. Gal. 4. 6.
[v] Heb. 5. 7.
[w] John 5. 30. John 6. 38.
[x] Rom. 7. 23. Gal. 5. 17.
[y] John 13. 1.
[z] Matt. 26.46. John 18. 1, 2.
[a] Matt. 26.47. Luke 22.47. John 18. 3.
[5] Rabbi, Rabbi. Matt 23.10. John 20.16.
[b] 2 Sam. 20. 9.
[c] Matt. 26.55. Luke 22.52.
[d] Ps. 22. 6. Isa. 53. 7. Dan. 9. 26. Luke 22.37. Luke 24.44.
[e] Job 19. 13, 14. Ps. 38. 11. Ps. 88. 8. John 16.32.

32-42.—THE AGONY IN THE GARDEN. (=Matt. xxvi. 36-46; Luke xxii. 39-46.) For the exposition, see on Luke xxii. 39-46.

43-52.—BETRAYAL AND APPREHENSION OF JESUS —FLIGHT OF HIS DISCIPLES. (= Matt. xxvi. 47-56; Luke xxii. 47-53; John xviii. 1-12.) For the exposition, see on John xviii. 1-12.

53-72.—JESUS ARRAIGNED BEFORE THE SANHEDRIM, CONDEMNED TO DIE, AND SHAMEFULLY ENTREATED—THE FALL OF PETER. (=Matt. xxvi. 57-75; Luke xxii. 54-71; John xviii. 13-18, 24-27.)

Had we only the first three Gospels, we should have concluded that our Lord was led immediately to Caiaphas, and had before the Council. But as the Sanhedrim could hardly have been brought together at the dead hour of night—by which time our Lord was in the hands of the officers sent to take Him—and as it was only "as soon as it was day" that the Council met (Luke xxii. 66), we should have had some difficulty in knowing what was done with Him during those intervening hours. In the fourth Gospel, however, all this is cleared up, and a very important addition to our information is made (John xviii. 13, 14, 19-24). Let us endeavour to trace the events in the true order of succession, and in the detail supplied by a comparison of all the four streams of text.

Jesus is brought privately before Annas, the Father-in-law of Caiaphas (John xviii. 13, 14). 13. "And they led Him away to Annas first; for he was father-in-law to Caiaphas, which was the high priest that same year." This successful Annas, as *Ellicott* remarks, was appointed high priest by Quirinus A.D. 12, and after holding the office for several years, was deposed by Valerius Gratus, Pilate's predecessor in the procuratorship of Judea, (*Joseph.* Antt. xviii. 2. 1, &c.) He appears, however, to have possessed vast influence, having obtained the high priesthood, not only for his son Eleazar, and his son-in-law Caiaphas, but subsequently for four other sons, under the last of whom James, the brother of our Lord, was put to death (Ib. xx. 9. 1). It is thus highly probable that, besides having the title of "high priest" merely as one who had filled the office, he to a great degree

53 And [f]they led Jesus away to the high priest: and with him were
54 assembled all the chief priests and the elders and the scribes. And Peter
followed him afar off, even into the palace of the high priest: and he sat
with the servants, and warmed himself at the fire.

A. D. 33.

[f] Matt. 26. 67. Luke 22. 54. John 18. 13.

retained the powers he had formerly exercised, and came to be regarded practically as a kind of rightful high priest. 14. "Now Caiaphas was he which gave counsel to the Jews, that it was expedient that one man should die for the people." See on John xi. 50. What passed between Annas and our Lord during this interval the beloved disciple reserves till he has related the beginning of Peter's fall. To this, then, as recorded by our own Evangelist, let us meanwhile listen.

Peter obtains Access within the Quadrangle of the High Priest's Residence, and Warms Himself at the Fire (53, 54). **53. And they led Jesus away to the high priest: and with him were assembled** [συνέρχονται αὐτῷ]—or rather, 'there gathered together unto him,' **all the chief priests and the elders and the scribes.** It was then a full and formal meeting of the Sanhedrim. Now, as the first three Evangelists place all Peter's denials of his Lord after this, we should naturally conclude that they took place *while our Lord stood before the Sanhedrim.* But besides that the natural impression is that the scene around the fire took place *over-night*, the *second crowing of the cock*, if we are to credit ancient writers, would occur about the beginning of the fourth watch, or between three and four in the morning. By that time, however, the Council had probably convened, being warned, perhaps, that they were to prepare for being called at any hour of the morning, should the Prisoner be successfully secured. If this be correct, it is pretty certain that only the *last* of Peter's three denials would take place while our Lord was under trial before the Sanhedrim. One thing more may require explanation. If our Lord had to be transferred from the residence of Annas to that of Caiaphas, one is apt to wonder that there is no mention of His being marched from the one to the other. But the building, in all likelihood, was one and the same; in which case He would merely have to be taken, perhaps across the court, from one chamber to another. **54. And Peter followed him afar off, even into** [ἀπο μακρόθεν ἕως ἔσω]—or 'from afar, even to the interior of,' **the palace of the high priest** [εἰς τὴν αὐλήν]. 'An Oriental house,' says *Robinson*, 'is usually built around a quadrangular interior court; into which there is a passage (sometimes arched) through the front part of the house, closed next the street by a heavy folding gate, with a smaller wicket for single persons, kept by a porter. The interior court, often paved or flagged, and open to the sky, is the *hall* [αὐλή], which our translators have rendered "palace," where the attendants made a fire; and the passage beneath the front of the house, from the street to this court, is the *porch* [προαύλιον, Mark xiv. 68, or πυλών, Matt. xxvi. 71]. The place where Jesus stood before the high priest may have been an open room, or place of audience on the ground-floor, in the rear or on one side of the court; such rooms, open in front, being customary. It was close upon the court, for Jesus heard all that was going on around the fire, and turned and looked upon Peter (Luke xxii. 61).'

In the fourth Gospel we have an extremely graphic description of the way in which Peter obtained access within the court or hall of the high priest (John xviii. 15, 16): "And Simon Peter followed Jesus." Natural though this was, and safe enough had he only "watched and prayed that he might not enter into temptation" as his Master bade him (Matt. xxvi. 41)—it was in his case a fatal step. "And so did another (rather 'the other') disciple." This was the beloved disciple himself, no doubt. "That disciple was known unto the high priest (see on John xviii. 15), and went in with Jesus into the palace of the high priest. But Peter stood at the door without"—by a preconcerted arrangement with his friend, till he should procure access for him. "Then went out that other disciple, which was known unto the high priest, and spake unto her that kept the door, and brought in Peter." The *naturalness* of these small details is not unworthy of notice. This other disciple having first made good his own entrance, on the score of acquaintance with the High Priest, goes forth again, now as a privileged person, to make interest for Peter's admission. But thus our poor disciple is in the coils of the serpent.

54. And he sat with the servants, and warmed himself at the fire. The graphic details, here omitted, are supplied in the other Gospels. John xviii. 18, "And the servants and officers stood there (that is, in the hall, within the quadrangle, open to the sky), who had made a fire of coals" [ἀνθρακιὰν], or 'charcoal' (in a brazier probably), "for it was cold." John alone of all the Evangelists mentions the *material*, and the *coldness* of the night, as *Webster and Wilkinson* remark. The elevated situation of Jerusalem, observes *Tholuck*, renders it so cold about Easter, as to make a watch-fire at night indispensable. "And Peter stood with them and warmed himself." "He went in (says Matt. xxvi. 58), and sat with the servants *to see the end.*" These two minute statements throw an interesting light on each other. His wishing to "see the end," or issue of these proceedings, was what led him into the palace, for he evidently feared the worst. But once in, the serpent-coil is drawn closer; it is a cold night, and why should not he take advantage of the fire as well as others? Besides, in the talk of the crowd about the all-engrossing topic, he may pick up something which he would like to hear. Poor Peter! But now, let us leave him warming himself at the fire, and listening to the hum of talk about this strange case by which the subordinate officials, passing to and fro and crowding around the fire in this open court, would while away the time; and, following what appears the order of the Evangelical Narrative, let us turn to Peter's Lord.

Jesus is Interrogated by Annas—His Dignified Reply—Is Treated with Indignity by one of the Officials—His Meek Rebuke (John xviii. 19-23). We have seen that it is only the Fourth Evangelist who tells us that our Lord was sent to Annas first, over-night, until the Sanhedrim could be got together at earliest dawn. We have now, in the same Gospel, the deeply instructive scene that passed during this non-official interview. 19. "The high priest [Annas] then asked Jesus of His disciples and of His doctrine"—probably to entrap Him into some statements which might be used against Him at the trial. From our Lord's answer it would seem that "His disciples" were understood to be some secret party. 20. "Jesus answered him, I spake openly to the world"—compare ch. vii. 4. He speaks of His public teaching as now a past thing—as now all over [ἐλάλησα]. "I ever

55 And [g] the chief priests and all the council sought for witness against
56 Jesus to put him to death; and [h] found none: for many bare [i] false witness
57 against him, but their witness agreed not together. And there arose cer-

A. D. 33.

[g] Matt 26. 59.
[h] Dan. 6. 4.
[i] Ps. 35. 11.

taught in the synagogue and in the temple, whither the Jews always resort," courting publicity, though with sublime noiselessness, "and in secret have I said nothing" [ἐλάλησα οὐδὲν]—rather, 'spake I nothing;' that is, nothing different from what He taught in public; all His private communications with the Twelve being but explanations and developments of His public teaching. (Compare Isa. xlv. 19; xlviii. 16). 21. "Why askest thou Me? ask them which heard Me what I have said to them" [ἐλάλησα]—rather, 'what I said unto them:' "behold, they know what I said." From this mode of replying, it is evident that our Lord saw the attempt to draw Him into self-crimination, and resented it by falling back upon the right of every accused party to have some charge laid against Him by competent witnesses. 22. "And when He had thus spoken, one of the officers which stood by struck Jesus with the palm of his hand, saying, Answerest thou the high priest so?" (see Isa. l. 6). It would seem, from Acts xxiii. 2, that this summary and undignified way of punishing what was deemed insolence in the accused had the sanction even of the high priests themselves. 23. "Jesus answered him, If I have spoken evil" [ἐλάλησα]—rather, 'If I spoke evil,' in reply to the high priest, "bear witness of the evil; but if well, why smitest thou Me?" He does not say, 'if *not* evil,' as if His reply had been merely unobjectionable; but "if *well*," which seems to challenge something altogether fitting in the remonstrance He had addressed to the high priest. From our Lord's procedure here, by the way, it is evident enough that His own precept in the Sermon on the Mount—that when smitten on the one cheek we are to turn to the smiter the other also (Matt. v. 39)—is not to be taken to the letter.

Annas Sends Jesus to Caiaphas (24). 24. "[Now] Annas had sent Him bound unto Caiaphas the high priest." [The particle "Now"—οὖν—though in the *Elzevir*, is not in the *Stephanic* form of the received text, and is rejected by most critics as wanting authority, and even by those who understand the verse as our translators did: the evidence for it is considerable; but it is rather stronger against it. *Lachmann* prints it in his text; *Tregelles* brackets it; but *Tischendorf* excludes it, and *Alford* follows him—concluding, as we think, rightly from the variations between οὖν and δὲ in the MSS. that it crept in as a connecting particle.] On the meaning of this verse there is much diversity of opinion; and according as we understand it will be the conclusion we come to, whether there was but *one hearing* of our Lord before Annas and Caiaphas together, or whether, according to the view we have given above, there were *two hearings*—a preliminary and informal one before Annas, and a formal and official one before Caiaphas and the Sanhedrim. If our translators have given the right sense of the verse, there was but one hearing before Caiaphas; and then this 24th verse is to be read as a *parenthesis*, merely supplementing what was said in *v.* 13. This is the view of *Calvin*, *Beza*, *Grotius*, *Bengel*, *de Wette*, *Meyer*, *Lücke*, *Tholuck*. But there are decided objections to this view. First, We cannot but think that the *natural* sense of the whole passage, embracing *vv.* 13, 14 and 19-24, is that of a preliminary non-official hearing before "Annas first," the particulars of which are accordingly recorded; and then of a transference of our Lord from Annas to Caiaphas. Second, On the other view, it is not easy to see why the Evangelist should not have inserted *v.* 24 immediately after *v.* 13; or rather, how he could well have done otherwise. As it stands, it is not only quite out of its proper place, but comes in most perplexingly. Whereas, if we take it as a simple statement of fact, that after Annas had finished his interview with Jesus, as recorded in *vv.* 19-23, he transferred Him to Caiaphas to be formally tried, all is clear and natural. Third, The pluperfect sense "*had* sent" is in the translation only; the sense of the original word [ἀπέστειλεν] being simply 'sent.' And though there are cases where the aorist here used has the sense of an English pluperfect, this sense is not to be put upon it unless it be obvious and indisputable. Here that is so far from being the case, that the pluperfect 'had sent' is rather an unwarrantable *interpretation* than a simple *translation* of the word; informing the reader that, *according to the view of our translators*, our Lord "had been" sent to Caiaphas *before* the interview just recorded by the Evangelist; whereas, if we translate the verse literally—"Annas *sent* Him bound unto Caiaphas the high priest"—we get just the information we expect, that Annas, having merely '*precognosced*' the prisoner, hoping to draw something out of Him, "sent Him to Caiaphas" to be formally tried before the proper tribunal. This is the view of *Chrysostom* and *Augustin* among the Fathers; and of the moderns, of *Olshausen*, *Schleiermacher*, *Neander*, *Ebrard*, *Wieseler*, *Lange*, *Luthardt*. This brings us back to the text of our second Gospel, and in it to—

The Judicial Trial and Condemnation of the Lord Jesus by the Sanhedrim (55-64). But let the reader observe, that though this is introduced by the Evangelist before any of the denials of Peter are recorded, we have given reasons for concluding that probably *the first two denials* took place while our Lord was with Annas, and the last only during the trial before the Sanhedrim.

55. And the chief priests and all the council sought for witness against Jesus to put him to death: Matthew (xxvi. 59) says they "sought *false* witness." They knew they could find nothing valid; but having their Prisoner to bring before Pilate, they behoved to *make a case.* **and found none**—none that would suit their purpose, or make a decent ground of charge before Pilate. **56. For many bare false witness against him.** From their debasing themselves to "*seek*" them, we are led to infer that they were *bribed* to bear false witness; though there are never wanting sycophants enough, ready to sell themselves for nought, if they may but get a smile from those above them: see a similar scene in Acts vi. 11-14. How is one reminded here of that complaint, "False witnesses did rise up: they laid to my charge things that I knew not!" (Ps. xxxv. 11). **but their witness agreed not together.** If even *two* of them had been agreed, it would have been greedily enough laid hold of, as all that the law insisted upon even in capital cases (Deut. xvii. 6). But even in this they failed. One cannot but admire the providence which secured this result; since, on the one hand, it seems astonishing that those unscrupulous prosecutors and their ready tools should so bungle a business in which they felt their whole interests bound up, and, on the other hand, if they *had* succeeded in making even a plausible case, the effect on the progress of the Gospel might for a time have been injurious. But

58 tain, and bare false witness against him, saying, We heard him say, [j]I will
destroy this temple that is made with hands, and within three days I will
59 build another made without hands. But neither so did their witness agree
60 together. And [k]the high priest stood up in the midst, and asked Jesus,
saying, Answerest thou nothing? what *is it which* these witness against
61 thee? But [l]he held his peace, and answered nothing. [m]Again the high
priest asked him, and said unto him, Art thou the Christ, the Son of
62 the Blessed? And Jesus said, I am: [n]and ye shall see the Son of man
sitting on the right hand of power, and coming in the clouds of heaven.

A. D. 33.

j ch. 15. 29. John 2. 19.
k Matt. 26. 62.
l Isa. 53. 7. 1 Pet. 2. 23.
m Matt. 26. 63.
n Matt. 24. 30. Matt. 26. 64. Luke 22. 69. Acts 1. 11.

at the very time when His enemies were saying, "God hath forsaken Him; persecute and take Him; for there is none to deliver Him" (Ps. lxxi. 11), He whose Witness He was and whose work He was doing was keeping Him as the apple of His eye, and while He was making the wrath of man to praise Him, was restraining the remainder of that wrath (Ps. lxxvi. 10). **57. And there arose certain, and bare false witness against him.** Matthew (xxvi. 60) is more precise here: "*At the last* came two false witnesses." As no two had before agreed in anything, they felt it necessary to secure a duplicate testimony to something, but they were long of succeeding. And what was it, when at length it was brought forward? **saying, 58. We heard him say, I will destroy this temple that is made with hands, and within three days I will build another made without hands.** On this charge, observe, first, that eager as His enemies were to find criminal matter against our Lord, they had to go back to the outset of His ministry, His first visit to Jerusalem, more than three years before this. In all that He said and did after that, though ever increasing in boldness, they could find nothing: Next, that even then, they fix only on one speech, of two or three words, which they dared to adduce against Him: Further, they most manifestly pervert the speech of our Lord. We say not this because in Mark's form of it, it differs from the report of the words given by the Fourth Evangelist (John ii. 18-22)—the only one of the Evangelists who reports it at all, or mentions even any visit paid by our Lord to Jerusalem before his last—but because the one report bears truth, and the other falsehood, on its face. When our Lord said on that occasion, "Destroy this temple, and in three days I will raise it up," they *might*, for a moment, have understood Him to refer to the temple out of whose courts He had swept the buyers and sellers. But *after* they had expressed their astonishment at His words, in that sense of them, and reasoned upon the time it had taken to rear the temple as it then stood, since *no answer* to this appears to have been given by our Lord, it is hardly conceivable that they should continue in the persuasion that this was really His meaning. But finally, even if the more ignorant among them had done so, it is next to certain that *the ecclesiastics*, who were *the prosecutors* in this case, *did not believe that this was His meaning.* For, in less than three days after this, they went to Pilate, saying, "Sir, we remember that that deceiver said, while he was yet alive, *after three days I will rise again*" (Matt. xxvii. 63). Now what utterance of Christ, known to his enemies, *could* this refer to, if not to this very saying about destroying and rearing up the temple? And if so, it puts it beyond a doubt that by this time, at least, they were perfectly aware that our Lord's words referred to *His death by their hands and His resurrection by His own.* But this is confirmed by the next verse. **59. But neither so did their witness agree together**—that is, not even as to so brief a speech, consisting of but a few words, was there such a concurrence in their mode of reporting it as to make out a decent case. In such a charge *everything depended on the very terms alleged to have been used.* For every one must see that a very slight turn, either way, given to such words, would make them either something like *indictable matter*, or else *a ridiculous ground for a criminal charge*—would either give them a colourable pretext for the charge of impiety which they were bent on making out, or else make the whole saying appear, on the worst view that could be taken of it, as merely some mystical or empty boast. **60. And the high priest stood up in the midst, and asked Jesus, saying, Answerest thou nothing? what is it which these witness against thee?** Clearly, they felt that *their case had failed*, and by this artful question the high priest hoped to get *from his own mouth* what they had in vain tried to obtain from their false and contradictory witnesses. But in this, too, they failed. **61. But he held his peace, and answered nothing.** This must have nonplussed them. But they were not to be easily baulked of their object. **Again the high priest**—arose (Matt. xxvi. 62), matters having now come to a crisis, and **asked him, and said unto him, Art thou the Christ, the Son of the Blessed?** Why our Lord should have answered this question, when He was silent as to the former, we might not have quite seen, but for Matthew, who says (xxvi. 63) that the high priest *put Him upon solemn oath*, saying, "I adjure thee by the living God, that thou tell us whether thou be the Christ, the Son of God." Such an adjuration was understood to render an answer legally necessary (Lev. v. 1). **62. And Jesus said, I am**—or, as in Matt. xxvi. 64, "Thou hast said [it]." In Luke, however (xxii. 70), the answer, "Ye say that I am" [Ὑμεῖς λέγετε, ὅτι ἐγώ εἰμι], should be rendered—as *de Wette*, *Meyer*, *Ellicott*, and the best critics agree that the preposition requires —'Ye say [it], for I am [so].' Some words, however, were spoken by our Lord before giving His answer to this solemn question. These are recorded by Luke alone (xxii. 67, 68): "Art thou the Christ (they asked)? tell us. And He said unto them, If I tell you, ye will not believe: and if I also ask"—or 'interrogate' [ἐρωτήσω] "you, ye will not answer me, nor let me go." This seems to have been uttered before giving His direct answer, as a calm remonstrance and dignified protest against the prejudgment of His case and the unfairness of their mode of procedure. But now let us hear the rest of the answer, in which the conscious majesty of Jesus breaks forth from behind the dark cloud which overhung Him as He stood before the Council: **and** (in that character) **ye shall see the Son of man sitting on the right hand of power, and coming in the clouds of heaven.** In Matthew (xxvi. 64) a slightly different but interesting turn is given to it by one word: "Thou hast said [it]: nevertheless"—We prefer this sense of the word [πλήν] to 'besides,' which some recent critics decide for—"I say

63 Then the high priest rent his clothes, and saith, What need we any
64 further witnesses? ye have heard [o]the blasphemy: what think ye? And
they all condemned him to be guilty of death.
65 And some began to [p]spit on him, and to cover his face, and to buffet
him, and to say unto him, Prophesy: and the servants did strike him
with the palms of their hands.

A. D. 33.

[o] Lev. 24. 16. 1 Ki. 21. 9, 13. Acts 6. 13.

[p] Isa. 50. 6. Isa. 53. 3.

unto you, Hereafter shall ye see the Son of man sit on the right hand of power, and coming in the clouds of heaven:" 'I know the scorn with which ye are ready to meet such an avowal: To your eyes, which are but eyes of flesh, there stands at this bar only a mortal like yourselves, and he at the mercy of the ecclesiastical and civil authorities: *Nevertheless*, a day is coming when ye shall see another sight: those eyes, which now gaze on me with proud disdain, shall see this very prisoner at the right hand of the Majesty on high, and coming in the clouds of heaven. Then shall the Judged One be revealed as the Judge, and His judges in this chamber appear at His august tribunal: then shall the *unrighteous* judges be *impartially* judged; and while they are wishing that they had never been born, He for whom they now watch as their Victim shall be greeted with the hallelujahs of heaven and the welcome of Him that sitteth upon the Throne!' The word rendered "hereafter" [ἀπ'ἄρτι] means, not 'at some future time' (as now "hereafter" commonly does), but what the English word originally signified, 'after here,' 'after now,' or 'from this time.' Accordingly, in Luke xxii. 69, the words used [ἀπὸ τοῦ νῦν] mean 'from now.' So that though the reference we have given it to the day of His glorious Second Appearing is too obvious to admit of doubt, He would, by using the expression, 'From this time,' convey the important thought which He had before expressed, immediately after the traitor left the Supper-table to do his dark work, "*Now* is the Son of Man glorified" (John xiii. 31). At this moment, and by this speech, did He "witness *the* good confession" [τὴν καλὴν ὁμολογίαν], emphatically and properly, as the apostle says, 1 Tim. vi. 13. Our translators render the words there, "Who *before* Pontius Pilate witnessed;" referring it to the admission of His being a *King*, in the presence of Cesar's own chief representative. But it should be rendered, as *Luther* renders it, and as the best interpreters now understand it, 'Who *under* Pontius Pilate witnessed, &c. [Compare the sense of ἐπὶ τινος in such passages as Matt. i. 11; Mark ii. 26; Luke iii. 2; Acts xi. 28; as also in the Apostles' Creed—"suffered *under* Pontius Pilate."] In this view of it, the apostle is referring not to what our Lord confessed *before* Pilate—which, though noble, was not of such primary importance—but to that sublime confession which, under Pilate's administration, He witnessed before the only competent tribunal on such occasions, the Supreme Ecclesiastical Council of God's chosen nation, that He was THE MESSIAH, and THE SON OF THE BLESSED ONE; in the former word owning His Supreme *Official*, in the latter His Supreme *Personal* Dignity. **63. Then the high priest rent his clothes.** On this expression of *horror at blasphemy*, see 2 Ki. xviii. 37. **and saith, What need we any further witnesses? 64. Ye have heard the blasphemy.** (See John x. 33.) In Luke (xxii. 71), "For we ourselves have heard of his own mouth"—an affectation of religious horror. **what think ye?** 'Say what the verdict is to be.' **And they all condemned him to be guilty of death**—or of a capital crime, which *blasphemy* against God was according to the Jewish law (Lev. xxiv. 16). Yet *not absolutely all;* for *Joseph* of Arimathea, "a good man and a just," was one of that Council, and '*he was not a consenting party* to the counsel and deed of them,' for that is the strict sense of the words of Luke xxiii. 50, 51 [οὐκ ἦν συγκατατεθειμένος τῇ βουλῇ καὶ τῇ πράξει αὐτῶν]. Probably he absented himself, and *Nicodemus* also, from this meeting of the Council, the temper of which they would know too well to expect their voice to be listened to; and in that case, the words of our Evangelist are to be taken strictly, that, without one dissentient voice, "all [present] condemned Him to be guilty of death."

The Blessed One is now Shamefully Entreated (65). Every word here must be carefully observed, and the several accounts put together, that we may lose none of the awful indignities about to be described. **65. And some began to spit on him**—or, as in Matt. xxvi. 67, "to spit in [or 'into'—εἰς] His face." Luke (xxii. 63) says in addition, "And the men that held Jesus mocked him"—or cast their jeers at Him. **and to cover his face** [περικαλύπτειν]—or 'to blindfold him' (as in Luke xxii. 64), **and to buffet him** [κολαφίζειν]. Luke's word, which is rendered "smote Him" (xxii. 63), is a stronger one [δέροντες], conveying an idea for which we have an exact equivalent in English, but one too colloquial to be inserted here. **and [began] to say unto him, Prophesy.** In Matt. xxvi. 68 this is given more fully: "Prophesy unto us, thou Christ, Who is he that smote thee?" The sarcastic fling at Him as "*the Christ*," and the demand of Him in this character to name the unseen perpetrator of the blows inflicted on Him, was in them as infamous as to Him it must have been, and was intended to be, stinging. **and the servants did strike him with the palms of their hands**—or "struck Him on the face" (Luke xxii. 64). Ah! Well did He say prophetically, in that Messianic prediction which we have often referred to, "I gave my back to the smiters, and my cheeks to them that plucked off the hair: I hid not my face from shame and spitting"! (Isa. l. 6). "And many other things blasphemously spake they against Him" (Luke xxii. 65). This general statement is important, as showing that virulent and varied as were the *recorded* affronts put upon Him, they are but a *small specimen* of what He endured on that dark occasion.

But this brings us back to our poor disciple, now fairly within the coils of the serpent. It is extremely difficult so to piece together the several charges thrown against Peter, and his replies, as perfectly to harmonize and exhaust the four streams of text. But the following, in which the best critics concur, comes as near to it, perhaps, as we shall succeed in getting. Nothing could better show how independently of each other the Evangelists must have written, than the almost hopeless difficulty of putting all the accounts of Peter's denials into their exact order, so as to make one harmonious record out of them. But the circumstantial differences are just of that nature which is so well understood in sifting a mass of complicated evidence on a public trial, which, instead of throwing doubt over them, only confirms the more strongly the truth of the facts reported.

66 And [q]as Peter was beneath in the palace, there cometh one of the maids
67 of the high priest: and when she saw Peter warming himself, she looked
68 upon him, and said, And thou also wast with Jesus of Nazareth. But he
denied, saying, I know not, neither understand I what thou sayest. And
69 he went out into the porch; and the cock crew. And [r]a maid saw him

A. D. 33.
[q] Matt. 26. 58, 69. Luke 22. 55.
[r] Matt. 26. 71. Luke 22. 58.

Peter's First Denial *of his Lord* (66-68). **66. And as Peter was beneath in the palace.** This little word "*beneath*" [κάτω]—one of our Evangelist's graphic touches—is most important for the right understanding of what we may call the topography of the scene. We must take it in connection with Matthew's word (xxvi. 69). "Now Peter sat *without* [ἔξω] in the palace"—or quadrangular court, in the centre of which the fire would be burning; and crowding around and buzzing about it would be the menials and others who had been admitted within the court. At the upper end of this court, probably, would be the memorable chamber in which the trial was held—*open to the court*, likely, and *not far from the fire* (as we gather from Luke xxii. 61), but *on a higher level;* for (as our verse says) the court, with Peter in it, was "beneath" it. The ascent to the Council-chamber was perhaps by a short flight of steps. If the reader will bear this explanation in mind, he will find the intensely interesting details which follow more intelligible. **there cometh one of the maids of the high priest**—"the damsel that kept the door" (John xviii. 17). The Jews seem to have employed women as porters of their doors (Acts xii. 13). **67. And when she saw Peter warming himself, she looked upon him.** Luke (xxii. 56) is here more graphic; "But a certain maid beheld him as he sat by the fire" [πρὸς τὸ φῶς]—literally, 'by the *light*,' which, shining full upon him, revealed him to the girl—"and earnestly looked upon him" [καὶ ἀτενίσασα αὐτῷ]—or, 'fixed her gaze upon him.' His demeanour and timidity, which must have attracted notice, as so generally happens, 'leading,' says *Olshausen*, 'to the recognition of him.' **and said, And thou also wast with Jesus of Nazareth**—'with Jesus the Nazarene,' or, "with Jesus of Galilee" (Matt. xxvi. 69). The *sense* of this is given in John's report of it (xviii. 17), "Art not thou also one of this man's disciples?" that is, thou as well as "that other disciple," whom she knew to be one, but did not challenge, perceiving that he was a privileged person. In Luke (xxii. 56) it is given as a remark made by the maid to one of the bystanders—"this man was also with Him." If so expressed in Peter's hearing—drawing upon him the eyes of every one that heard it (as we know it did, Matt. xxvi. 70), and compelling him to answer to it—that would explain the different forms of the report naturally enough. But in such a case this is of no real importance. **68. But he denied**—"before all" (Matt. xxvi. 70). **saying, I know not, neither understand I what thou sayest**—in Luke, "I know Him not." **And he went out into the porch** [τὸ προαύλιον]—the vestibule leading to the street—no doubt finding the fire-place too *hot* for him; possibly also with the hope of escaping—but that was not to be, and perhaps he dreaded that too. Doubtless, by this time his mind would be getting into a sea of commotion, and would fluctuate every moment in its resolves. **AND THE COCK CREW.** See on Luke xxii. 34. This, then, was the First Denial.

Peter's Second Denial *of his Lord* (69, 70). There is here a verbal difference among the Evangelists, which, without some information which has been withheld, cannot be quite extricated. **69. And a maid saw him again**—or, 'a girl' [ἡ παιδίσκη]. It might be rendered 'the girl;' but this would not necessarily mean the same one as before, but might, and probably does, mean just the female who had charge of the door or gate near which Peter now was. Accordingly, in Matt. xxvi. 71, she is expressly called "another [maid]" [ἄλλη]. But in Luke it is a *male* servant: "And after a little while (from the time of the first denial) another"—that is, as the word signifies, 'another male' servant [ἕτερος]. But there is no real difficulty, as the challenge, probably, after being made by one was reiterated by another. Accordingly, in John, it is "*They* said therefore unto him," &c., as if more than one challenged him at once. **and began to say to them that stood by, This is one of them**—or, as in Matt. xxvi. 71—"This [fellow] was also with Jesus the Nazarene" [τοῦ Ναζωραίου]. **70. And he denied it again.** In Luke, "Man, I am not." But worst of all in Matthew—"And again he denied with an oath, I do not know the man." (xxvi. 72). This was the Second Denial, more vehement, alas! than the first.

Peter's Third Denial *of His Lord* (70-72). **70. And a little after**—"about the space of one hour after" (Luke xxii. 59), **they that stood by said again to Peter, Surely thou art one of them: for thou art a Galilean, and thy speech agreeth thereto**—"bewrayeth (or 'discovereth') thee" (Matt. xxvi. 73). In Luke it is "Another confidently affirmed, saying, Of a truth this [fellow] also was with him; for he is a Galilean." The Galilean dialect had a more *Syrian* cast than that of Judea. *If Peter had held his peace*, this peculiarity had not been observed; but hoping, probably, to put them off the scent by joining in the *fireside-talk*, he only thus discovered himself. The Fourth Gospel is particularly interesting here: "One of the servants of the high priest, being his kinsman (or kinsman to him) whose ear Peter cut off, saith, Did not I see thee in the garden with Him?" (John xviii. 26). No doubt his relationship to Malchus drew his attention to the man who had smitten him, and this enabled him to identify Peter. 'Sad reprisals!' exclaims *Bengel.* Thus everything tended to identify him as a disciple of the Prisoner—his being introduced into the interior by one who was known to be a disciple, as the maid who kept the gate could testify; the recognition of him by the girl at the fire, as one whom she had seen in His company; his broad guttural Galilean dialect; and there being one present who recognized him as the man who, at the moment of the prisoner's apprehension, struck a blow with his sword at a relative of his own. Poor Peter! Thou art caught in thine own toils; but like a wild bull in a net, thou wilt toss and rage, filling up the measure of thy terrible declension by one more denial of thy Lord, and that the foulest of all. **71. But he began to curse** [ἀναθεματίζειν]—'to anathematize,' or wish himself accursed if what he was now to say was not true, **and to swear**—or to take a solemn oath, **saying, I know not this man of whom ye speak. 72. And THE SECOND TIME THE COCK CREW.** The other three Evangelists, who mention but one crowing of the cock—and that not the first, but the second and last one of Mark—all say the cock crew "immediately," but Luke says, "Im-

70 again, and began to say to them that stood by, This is *one* of them. And
he denied it again. [s]And a little after, they that stood by said again
to Peter, Surely thou art *one* of them: [t]for thou art a Galilean, and thy

A. D. 33.

[s] Matt 26.73.
[t] Acts 2. 7.

mediately, while he yet spake, the cock crew" (xxii. 60). Alas!—But now comes the wonderful sequel.

The Redeemer's Look upon Peter, and Peter's Bitter Tears (72; Luke xxii. 61, 62). It has been observed that while the beloved disciple is the only one of the four Evangelists who does not record the repentance of Peter, he is the only one of the four who records the affecting and most beautiful scene of his complete restoration. (John xxi. 15-17.)

Luke xxii. 61: "And the Lord turned and looked upon Peter." How? it will be asked. We answer, From the chamber in which the trial was going on, in the direction of the court where Peter then stood—in the way already explained. See on ch. xiv. 66. Our Second Evangelist makes no mention of this look, but dwells on the warning of his Lord about the double crowing of the cock, which would announce his triple fall, as what rushed stingingly to his recollection and made him dissolve in tears. **And Peter called to mind the word that Jesus said unto him, Before the cock crow twice, thou shalt deny me thrice. And when he thought thereon, he wept.** To the same effect is the statement of the First Evangelist (Matt. xxvi. 75), save that like "the beloved physician," he notices the "bitterness" of the weeping. The most precious link, however, in the whole chain of circumstances in this scene is beyond doubt that "look" of deepest, tenderest import reported by Luke alone. Who can tell what lightning flashes of wounded love and piercing reproach shot from that "look" through the eye of Peter into his heart! "And Peter remembered the word of the Lord, how He had said unto him, Before the cock crow, thou shalt deny Me thrice. And Peter went out and wept bitterly." How different from the sequel of Judas's act! Doubtless the hearts of the two men towards the Saviour were perfectly different from the first; and the treason of Judas was but the consummation of the wretched man's resistance of the blaze of light in the midst of which he had lived for three years, while Peter's denial was but a momentary obscuration of the heavenly light and love to his Master which ruled his life. But the immediate cause of the blessed revulsion which made Peter "weep bitterly" was, beyond all doubt, this heart-piercing "look" which his Lord gave him. And remembering the Saviour's own words at the table, "Simon, Simon, Satan hath desired to have you, that he may sift you as wheat; *but I prayed for thee, that thy faith fail not,*" may we not say that *this prayer fetched down all that there was in that "look"* to pierce and break the heart of Peter, to keep it from despair, to work in it "repentance unto salvation not to be repented of," and at length, under other healing touches, to "restore his soul"? (See on Mark xvi. 7.)

Remarks.—1. The demeanour of the Blessed One before Annas first, and then before Caiaphas and the Sanhedrim, is best left to speak its own mingled meekness and dignity. *We*, at least, are not able to say aught—beyond what has come out in the exposition—that would not run the risk of weakening the impression which the Evangelical Narrative itself leaves on every devout and thoughtful mind. But the reader may be asked to observe the *wisdom* which to Annas speaks, but before the Sanhedrim keeps silence while the witnesses against Him are uttering their lies and contradictions. In the former case, silence might have been liable to misconstruction; and the opportunity which the questions of Annas about "His disciples and His doctrine" afforded, of appealing to the *openness* of all His movements from first to last, was too important not to be embraced: whereas, in the latter case, the silence which He preserved—while the false witnesses were stultifying themselves and the case was breaking down of itself the further they proceeded—was the most dignified, and to His envenomed judges most stinging reply to them. It was only when, in despair of evidence save from His own mouth, the high priest demanded of Him on solemn oath to say whether He were the Christ, the Son of the Blessed, and the moment had thus arrived when it was right and fitting in itself, and according to the law, that He should "witness" *the* "*good confession,*" that He broke silence accordingly—and in how exalted terms! 2. Perhaps the best commentary on the Sixth Petition of the Lord's Prayer —"Lead us not into temptation"—is to be found in the conduct of Peter, and the circumstances in which he found himself, after our Lord warned him to "pray that he might not enter into temptation." See on Matt. vi. 13, and Remark 9 at the close of that Section. The explicit announcement that all the Eleven should be stumbled in Him and scattered that very night, might have staggered him; but it did not. The still more explicit announcement addressed immediately to Peter, that Satan had sought and obtained them all—to the extent of being permitted to sift them as wheat—but as to Peter in particular, that He had prayed for *him*, that his faith might not fail, was fitted, surely, to drive home upon his conscience a sense of more than ordinary danger, and more than ordinary need to watch and pray; but it did not. Above all, the appalling announcement, that—instead of the certainty of his standing, even if all the rest should fall, and of his readiness to go to prison and to death for his blessed Master—the cock should not crow twice before he had thrice denied that he knew Him, was fitted, one should think, to dash the confidence of the most self-confident believer; but it made no impression upon Peter. Once more, in the Garden his Lord found him sleeping, along with the other two, in the midst of His agony and bloody sweat; and He chided him for his inability to watch with Him one hour on that occasion. He gave him and the rest a last warning, almost immediately before Judas and the officers approached to take Him, to "watch and pray, that they entered not into temptation." But how did he take it? Why, he insisted on admission within that fatal quadrangle, which from that time he would never forget. We wonder not at his eagerness to learn all that was going on within that court; but one who had been so warned of what he would do that very night should have kept far away from a spot which must have seemed, even to himself, the most likely to prove the fatal one. The coil of the serpent, however, was insensibly but surely drawing him in, and he was getting, by his own act and deed, sucked into the vortex—"led into temptation." Through the influence of "that disciple who was known to the high priest," the door which was shut to the eager crowd was opened to him. No doubt he now thought all was right, and congratulated himself on his good fortune. He lounges about, pre-

71 speech agreeth *thereto.* But [u]he began to curse and to swear, *saying,* I
72 know not this man of whom ye speak. And the second time the cock
crew. And Peter called to mind the word that Jesus said unto him,

A. D. 33.

[u] Pro. 29. 25. 1 Cor. 10. 12.

tending indifference or the mere general curiosity of others. But it is bitterly cold, and an inviting fire is blazing in the court. He will join the knot that is clustering around it—perhaps he will pick up some of the current talk about the Prisoner, the trial, and its probable issue. He has got close to the fire, and a seat too—so near, that his countenance is lighted up by the blazing fuel. He has now gained his end, and in so cold a night how comfortable he feels—"*till a dart strikes through his liver*"*!* (Pro. vii. 22, 23.) O, if this true-hearted and noble disciple had but retained the spirit which prompted him to say, along with others, of the unnamed traitor that sat at the Supper-Table, "Lord, Is it I?" (see on John xiii. 21-25)—if he had watched and gone to his knees, when his Master was on His, agonizing in the Garden, his danger had not been so great, even within the court of the high priest. *There,* indeed, *he had no business to be,* considering the sad prediction which hung over him—this, in fact, was what sold him into the enemy's hands. But, if we could have supposed him sitting at that fire in a "watching and praying" spirit, the challenge of him by the maid, as one who had been "with Jesus the Nazarene," had drawn forth a "good confession." And what though he had had to "go to prison and to death for His sake"? it had been but what he was undoubtedly prepared for as he sat at the Supper-Table, and what he afterwards did cheerfully in point of fact. But he was caught without his armour. The fear of man now brought a snare (Pro. xxix. 25). His locks were shorn. The secret of his great strength was gone, and he had become weak as other men. O, let these mournful facts pierce the ears of the children of God, and let them listen to One who knows them better than they do themselves, when He warns them to "watch and pray, that they enter not into temptation." 3. See how the tendency of all sin is to aggravate as well as multiply itself. Peter's first fall naturally led to his second, and his second to his third; each denial of his Lord being now felt as but one and the same act—as only the keeping up of the character which he would regret that he had been driven to assume, but, once assumed, needed to keep up for consistency's sake. 'The deed was done, and could not be undone—he must now go through with it.' But merely to reiterate, even in a different form, his first denial, would not do for the second, nor the second for the third, if he was to be believed. He must exaggerate his denials; he must repudiate his Master in such a style that people would be forced to say, We *must* be mistaken—that man *cannot* be a disciple, so unlike all we have ever heard of His character and teaching. So Peter at length comes to "anathematize" himself if he should be uttering a lie in ignoring the Nazarene, and solemnly "swears" that he knows nothing of Him. Nor, although there was about an hour's interval between the first and the second denials, is there any reason to suppose that he had begun to give way, or seriously meditated confessing his Lord within that court. His mind, from the first moment that he fell before the maid, would be in a burning fever—his one object being to avoid detection; and this would keep the warning about the cock-crowing from ever coming up to his recollection; for it is expressly said that it was only after his last denial and the immediate crowing of the cock, that "Peter remembered" his Lord's warning. Well, these details will not have been recorded in vain, if they convince believers that, besides the danger of the strongest giving way, there is no length in defection to which they may not quickly go, when once that has been done. Times of persecution, especially when unto death, have furnished sad enough evidence that Peter's case was no abnormal one; that he acted only according to the stable laws of the human mind and heart in such circumstances, and only illustrated the laws of the Kingdom of God as to the sources of weakness and of strength; and that in similar circumstances the children of God in every age, when like him they flatter themselves, in spite of warnings, that they will never be moved, will act a similar part. 4. Secret things indeed belong unto the Lord our God, but those which are revealed unto us and to our children for ever (Deut. xxix. 29). We intrude not into those things which we have not seen, vainly puffed up by our fleshly mind (Col. ii. 18); but the few glimpses with which Scripture favours us of what is passing on the subject of men's eternal interests in the unseen world are of too vital a nature to be overlooked. In the book of Job we have revelations to which there is a manifest allusion in our Lord's warning to Peter, and without which it could not perhaps be fully understood. The all-seeing Judge is seen surrounded by His angelic assessors on human affairs, and Satan presents himself among them. "Whence comest thou?" the Lord says. "From going to and fro in the earth, and walking up and down in it," is the reply—watching men's actions, studying their character, seeking whom he might devour. 'In these roamings, hast thou seen My servant Job (asks the Lord), a saint above all saints on the earth?' 'O yes (is the reply), I have seen him, and weighed his religion too: 'Tis easy for him to be religious, with a divine hedge about him, and laden with prosperity. But only let me have him, that I may sift him as wheat, and we shall soon see what becomes of his religion. Why, touch but his substance, and he will curse Thee to Thy face.' 'Behold, he is in thine hand (is the divine response), to sift him to the uttermost; only upon his person lay not a hand.' So Satan goes forth, strips him of substance and family at once, leaving him only a wife worse than none, who did but aid the tempter's purposes. Observe now the result. "So Job arose and rent his mantle, and shaved his head, and fell upon the ground, and worshipped, and said, Naked came I out of my mother's womb, and naked shall I return thither: The Lord gave, and the Lord hath taken away; blessed be the name of the Lord. In all this Job sinned not, nor charged God foolishly." But the enemy of men's souls is not to be easily foiled. He has missed his mark once, to be sure; but the next time he will succeed. He mistook the patriarch's weak point. Now, however, he is sure of it. Again he enters the councils of heaven, is questioned as before, and rebuked, in language unspeakably comforting to the tempted, for moving the Lord to destroy His dear saint without cause. 'Not without cause (replies the tempter): Skin for skin; yea, all that a man hath will he give for his life: suffer me once more to sift him as wheat, and it will be seen what chaff his religion is.' 'Then, behold, he is in thine hand, to smite his person even as thou wilt; only save his life.' So Satan

Before the cock crow twice, thou shalt deny me thrice. And [v]when he thought thereon, he wept.

A. D. 33.

[v] 2 Cor. 7. 10.

went forth, and did his worst; the body of this saint is now a mass of running sores; he sits among the ashes, scraping himself with a potsherd; while his heartless wife advises him to have done with this at once, by sending up to God such a curse upon Him for His cruelty as would bring down a bolt of vengeance, and end his sufferings with his life. Now hear the noble reply: "Thou speakest as one of the foolish women speaketh. What? Shall we receive good at the hand of God, and shall we not receive evil? In all this did not Job sin with his lips." He is seen to be wheat and no chaff, and the enemy disappears from the stage. This now is what our Lord alludes to in His warning at the Supper-Table. Satan, still at his old work, had demanded to have these poor disciples, to sift them too; and he had gotten them—in that sense and to that extent. [The reader is requested to refer to the remarks on the sense of the word ἐξῃτήσατο, Luke xxii. 31.] But while that transaction was going on in the unseen world, a counteraction, in the case of Peter, was proceeding at the same time. He whom the Father heareth alway "prayed for Peter that his faith might not fail." And (as implied in the tenses of the verbs employed—see the remarks on the above passage) when the one action was *completed*, so was the other—the bane and the antidote going together. Poor Peter! Little thinkest thou what is passing between heaven and hell about thee, and thy one source of safety. That thou gottest that "look" of wounded love from thy suffering Lord; that thy heart, pierced by it, was not driven to despair; that the warning of the triple denial and the double cock-crowing did not send thee after the traitor, by the nearest road to "his own place:" what was all this due to but to that "*prayer* for thee, that thy faith fail not"? Now, for the first time, thou knowest the meaning of that word "fail." Perhaps it deluded thee into the persuasion that thou wouldst not give way at all, and thou wert thyself confident enough of that. Now thou knowest by sad experience what "shipwreck of faith and of a good conscience" thou hadst made, but that the means of preventing it were fetched down by the great Intercessor's "prayer." 5. If Christ's praying for Peter, even in the days of His flesh here below, availed so much, what a glorious efficacy must attach to His pleadings for them that are dear to Him within the veil? For here, His proper work was to give His life a Ransom for them: there, to sue out the fruit of His travail in their behalf. But along with these intercessions, are there no such "looks" now cast upon His poor fallen ones, such as He darted upon Peter, just when he had gone down to his lowest depth in shameful repudiation of Him? Let the fallen and recovered children of God answer that question. 6. What light does this last thought, in connection with Christ's special prayer in behalf of Peter, cast upon the eternal safety of believers? "While I was with them in the world I kept them in Thy name: those that Thou hast given Me I kept [δέδωκας—ἐφύλαξα], and none of them is lost but the son of perdition, that the Scripture might be fulfilled. But now I am no more in the world, but these are in the world, and I come to Thee: Holy Father, keep through thine own name those whom Thou hast given Me, that they may be one as We are" (John xvii. 11, 12). 7. If prayer on the part of Christ for His people is so essential to their safety, shall their own prayer for it be less so? He who said, "*I prayed* for thee," said also, "Watch and pray *ye*, that ye enter not into temptation." And who that verily believes that Jesus within the veil is praying for *him* that his faith fail not, can choose but cry, "Hold Thou me up, and I shall be safe"? 8. Was it while those false witnesses were rising up against Thee, blessed Saviour, and laying to Thy charge things that Thou knewest not, that Thou didst cast towards Peter that soul-piercing "look"? Or was it in the midst of those heart-rending indignities, at the reading of which one almost covers his face, and the calm endurance of which must have filled even heaven with wonder—was it during one of those dreadful moments when they were proceeding to blindfold that blessed Face, that Thou lookedst full on Thy poor disciple with that never-to-be-forgotten look? I know not. But I can well believe that no indignities from enemies wounded Thee at that hour like that which was done unto Thee by thine own familiar friend and dear disciple, and that this quite absorbed the sense of that. And if in heaven He *feels* the slight put upon Him by those who will not suffer Him to "gather" them, shall He not feel even more acutely (if the word may be allowed) "the wounds wherewith He is wounded in the house of His friends"? 9. In reviewing the contents of this Section, who can be insensible to the self-evidencing reality which is stamped upon the facts of it, both in their general bearing and in their minute details! What mere inventor of a Story would have so used the powerful influence of Annas as to hand over the Prisoner to him first, relating what passed between them in the dead of night, ere the Council could be got together for the formal trial? And who would have thought of making Him answer with *silence* the lies and contradictions of the witnesses against Him; when these failed to make any decent charge, bringing forward at the last two more, only to neutralize each other by the inconsistency of their statements; and, when all failed, and the high priest in despair had to put it to Him on oath to say if He were the Christ, the Son of the Blessed, *then* drawing from Him a sublime affirmative? The condemnation and the indignities which followed would be natural enough; but the particulars now enumerated lie quite beyond the range of conceivable fiction. But far more so are the details of Peter's denials. That the most eminent of the Eleven should be made to inflict on his Master the deepest wound, and this in the hour of greatest apparent weakness, when a Prisoner in the hands of His enemies—is unlike enough the work of fiction. But those minute details — the "following Him from afar" [ἀπὸ μακρόθεν]; the introduction into the quadrangle through the influence of "that disciple who was known to the high priest;" the cold night, and the blazing fire, and the clustering of the menials and others around it, with Peter among them, and the detection of him by a maid, through the reflection of the fire-light on his countenance, the first denial in that moment of surprise, and the crowing of the cock; his uneasy removal "out into the porch," the second denial, more emphatic than the first, and then the last and foulest, and the second cock-crowing; but beyond every other thought that would never occur to an inventor, that "look upon Peter" by his wounded Lord, and that rush of recollection which brought the sad warning at the Supper-Table fresh to view, and

15 AND [a]straightway in the morning the chief priests held a consultation
with the elders and scribes and the whole council, and bound Jesus, and
2 carried *him* away, and delivered *him* to Pilate. And [b]Pilate asked
him, Art thou the King of the Jews? And he answering said unto
3 him, [c]Thou sayest *it*. And the chief priests accused him of many
4 things: but [d]he answered nothing. And [e]Pilate asked him again, saying,
Answerest thou nothing? behold how many things they witness against
5 thee. But [f]Jesus yet answered nothing; so that Pilate marvelled.
6 Now [g]at *that* feast he released unto them one prisoner, whomsoever
7 they desired. And there was *one* named Barabbas, *which lay* bound with
them that had made insurrection with him, who had committed murder
8 in the insurrection. And the multitude, crying aloud, began to desire
9 *him to do* as he had ever done unto them. But Pilate answered them,
10 saying, Will ye that I release unto you the King of the Jews? For he
11 knew that the chief priests had delivered him for [h]envy. But [i]the
chief priests moved the people, that he should rather release Barabbas
12 unto them. And Pilate answered and said again unto them, What
will ye then that I shall do *unto him* whom ye call [j]the King of
13 the Jews? And they cried out again, Crucify him. Then Pilate said
14 unto them, Why, what evil hath he done? And they cried out the more
15 exceedingly, Crucify him. And *so* Pilate, [k]willing to content the people,
released Barabbas unto them, and delivered Jesus, when he had scourged
him, to be crucified.
16 And the soldiers led him away into the hall called Pretorium; and
17 they call together the whole band. And they clothed him with purple,
18 and platted a crown of thorns, and put it about his *head*, and began to
19 salute him, Hail, King of the Jews! And they smote him on the head
with a reed, and did spit upon him, and bowing *their* knees worshipped
20 him. And when they had mocked him, they took off the purple from
him, and put his own clothes on him, and led him out to crucify him.
21 And [l]they compel one Simon a Cyrenian, who passed by, coming out
of the country, the father of Alexander [m]and Rufus, to bear his cross.
22 And [n]they bring him unto the place Golgotha, which is, being inter-
23 preted, The place of a skull. And they gave him [o]to drink wine
24 mingled with myrrh: but he received *it* not. And when they had
crucified him, they [p]parted his garments, casting lots upon them, what
25 every man should take. And [q]it was the third hour, and they crucified
26 him. And [r]the superscription of his accusation was written over, THE
27 KING OF THE JEWS. And with him they crucify two thieves; the
28 one on his right hand, and the other on his left. And the scripture
was fulfilled, which saith, [s]And he was numbered with the transgressors.
29 And [t]they that passed by railed on him, wagging their heads, and saying,
30 Ah! thou [u]that destroyest the temple, and buildest *it* in three days, save

A. D. 33.

CHAP. 15.
[a] Ps. 2. 2. Matt. 21. 38. Matt. 27. 1. Luke 22. 66. Luke 23. 1. John 18. 28. Acts 3. 13. Acts 4. 26.
[b] Matt. 27. 11.
[c] 1 Tim. 6. 13.
[d] 1 Pet. 2. 23.
[e] Matt. 27. 13.
[f] Isa. 53. 7. John 19. 9.
[g] Matt. 27. 15. Luke 23. 17. John 18. 39.
[h] Acts 7. 9, 51. 1 John 3. 12.
[i] Matt. 27. 20. Acts 3. 14.
[j] Jer. 23. 5, 6. Mic. 5. 2.
[k] Pro. 29. 25.
[l] Matt. 27. 32. Luke 23. 26.
[m] Rom. 16. 13.
[n] John 19. 17. Acts 7. 58. Heb. 13. 12.
[o] Ps. 69. 21.
[p] Ps. 22. 18. Matt. 27. 35, 36. Luke 23. 34. John 19. 23, 24.
[q] Matt. 27. 45. Luke 23. 44. John 19. 14.
[r] Deut. 23. 5. Ps. 76. 10. Pro. 21. 1. Isa. 10. 7. Isa. 46. 10. Matt. 27. 37.
[s] Isa. 53. 12. Luke 22. 37.
[t] Ps. 22. 7. Ps. 35. 15, 16. Matt. 9. 24. Luke 16. 14.
[u] ch. 14. 58. John 2. 19.

his "going out and weeping bitterly,"—who that reads all this with unsophisticated intelligence, can doubt its reality, or fail to feel as if himself had been in the midst of it all? But what puts the crown upon the self-evidencing truth of all this is, that we have four Records of it, so harmonious as to be manifestly but different reports of the same transactions, yet differing to such an extent in minute details, that hostile criticism has tried to make out a case of irreconcilable contradiction, which has staggered some—while the most friendly and loving criticism has not been able to remove all difficulties. This at least shows that none of them wrote to prop up the statements of the others, and that the facts of the Gospel History are bound together by a fourfold cord that cannot be broken. Thanks, then, be unto God for this inestimable treasure, but above all for the Unspeakable Gift of Whom it tells its wondrous Tale—a Tale as new while we now write as when the Evangelists themselves were holding the pen—a Tale, like the new song, that will never grow old!

CHAP. XV. 1-20.—Jesus is Brought Before Pilate—At a Second Hearing, Pilate, after Seeking to Release Him, Delivers Him Up—After being Cruelly Entreated, He is Led Away to be Crucified. (= Matt. xxvi. 1, 2, 11-31; Luke xxiii. 1-6, 13-25; John xviii. 28—xix. 16.) For the exposition, see on John xviii. 28—xix. 16.

21-37.—Crucifixion and Death of the Lord Jesus. (= Matt. xxvii. 32-50; Luke xxiii. 26-46; John xix. 17-30.) For the exposition, see on John xix. 17-30.

31 thyself, and come down from the cross. Likewise also the chief priests
mocking said among themselves with the scribes, He saved others; him-
32 self he cannot save. Let Christ the King of Israel descend now from the
cross, that we may see and believe. And [v]they that were crucified with
him reviled him.
33 And [w]when the sixth hour was come, there was darkness over the
34 whole land until the ninth hour. And at the ninth hour Jesus cried
with a loud voice, saying, [x]Eloi! Eloi! lama sabachthani? which is,
35 being interpreted, My God! my God! why hast thou forsaken me? And
some of them that stood by, when they heard *it*, said, Behold, he calleth
36 Elias. And [y]one ran and filled a sponge full of vinegar, and put *it* on a
reed, and [z]gave him to drink, saying, Let alone; let us see whether Elias
will come to take him down.
37, And [a]Jesus cried with a loud voice, and gave up the ghost. And
38 [b]the veil of the temple was rent in twain from the top to the bottom.
39 And [c]when the centurion, which stood over against him, saw that he so
cried out, and gave up the ghost, he said, Truly this man was the Son of
40 God. There [d]were also women looking on afar [e]off: among whom was
Mary Magdalene, and Mary the mother of James the less and of Joses,
41 and Salome; (who also, when he was in Galilee, followed [f]him, and
ministered unto him;) and many other women which came up with him
unto Jerusalem.
42 And [g]now when the even was come, because it was the preparation,
43 that is, the day before the sabbath, Joseph of Arimathea, an honourable
counsellor, which also [h]waited for the kingdom of God, came, and went
44 in boldly unto Pilate, and craved the body of Jesus. And Pilate marvelled if he were already dead: and, calling *unto him* the centurion, he
45 asked him whether he had been any while dead. And when he knew *it*
46 of the centurion, he gave the body to Joseph. And [i]he bought fine
linen, and took him down, and wrapped him in the linen, and laid him
in a sepulchre which was hewn out of a rock, and rolled a stone unto the
47 door of the sepulchre. And Mary Magdalene and Mary *the mother* of
Joses beheld where he was laid.

16 AND [a]when the sabbath was past, Mary Magdalene, and Mary the
mother of James, and Salome, [b]had bought sweet spices, that they might
2 come and anoint him. And [c]very early in the morning, the first *day*
3 of the week, they came unto the sepulchre at the rising of the sun. And
they said among themselves, Who shall roll us away the stone from the
4 door of the sepulchre? And when they looked, they saw that the stone

A. D. 33.

[v] Matt. 27. 44. Luke 23. 39. Heb. 12. 3. 1 Pet. 2. 23.
[w] Luke 23. 44.
[x] Ps. 22. 1. Matt. 27. 46. Heb. 5. 7.
[y] Matt. 27. 48. John 19. 29.
[z] Ps. 69. 21.
[a] Matt. 27. 50. Luke 23. 46. John 19. 30.
[b] Ex. 26. 31. Ex. 40. 20, 21. 2 Chr. 3. 14. Matt. 27. 51-53. Luke 23. 45. Heb. 4. 14-16. Heb. 6. 19. Heb. 9. 3-12. Heb. 10. 19.
[c] Deut. 32. 31. Matt. 27. 54.
[d] Ps. 38. 11. Matt. 27. 55, 56. Luke 23. 49. John 19. 26, 27.
[e] Ps. 38. 11.
[f] Luke 8. 2.
[g] John 19. 38.
[h] Ps. 25. 2. Ps. 27. 14. Isa. 8. 16. Lam. 3. 25, 26. Luke 2. 25.
[i] Isa. 53. 9.

CHAP. 16.
[a] Matt. 28. 1.
[b] Luke 23. 56.
[c] Matt. 28. 1. Luke 24. 1. John 20. 1.

38-47.—Signs and Circumstances following the Death of The Lord Jesus—He is Taken Down from the Cross and Buried—The Sepulchre is Guarded. (= Matt. xxvii. 51-66; Luke xxiii. 45, 47-56; John xix. 31-42.) For the exposition, see on Matt. xxvii. 51-56; and on John xix. 31-42.

CHAP. XVI. 1-20.—Angelic Announcement to the Women on The First Day of the Week, that Christ is Risen—His Appearances after His Resurrection—His Ascension—Triumphant Proclamation of His Gospel. (= Matt. xxviii. 1-10, 16-20; Luke xxiv. 1-51; John xx. 1, 2, 11-29.)

The Resurrection Announced to the Women (1-8).

1. And when the sabbath was past—that is, at sunset of our Saturday, **Mary Magdalene**—see on Luke viii. 2, **and Mary the Mother of James**—James the Less (see on ch. xv. 40), **and Salome**—the mother of Zebedee's sons (compare ch. xv. 40 with Matt. xxvii. 56), **had bought sweet spices, that they might come and anoint him.** The word is simply 'bought' [ἠγόρασαν]. But our translators are perhaps right in rendering it here 'had bought,' since it would appear, from Luke xxiii. 56, that they had purchased them immediately after the Crucifixion, on the *Friday* evening, during the short interval that remained to them before sunset, when the Sabbath rest began; and that they had only deferred using them to anoint the body till the Sabbath rest should be over. On this "anointing," see on John xix. 40. **2. And very early in the morning**—see on Matt. xxviii. 1, **the first day of the week, they came unto the sepulchre at the rising of the sun**—not quite literally, but 'at earliest dawn;' according to a way of speaking not uncommon, and occurring sometimes in the Old Testament. Thus our Lord rose on the third day; having lain in the grave part of Friday, the whole of Saturday, and part of the following First day. **3. And they said among themselves**—as they were approaching the sacred spot, **Who shall roll us away the stone from the door of the sepulchre? 4. And when they looked, they saw that the stone was rolled away: for it was very great.**

5 was rolled away: for it was very great. And [d]entering into the
sepulchre, they saw a young man sitting on the right side, clothed in a
6 long white garment; and they were affrighted. And [e]he saith unto
them, Be not affrighted: Ye seek Jesus of Nazareth, which was crucified:
7 he is [f]risen; he is not here: behold the place where they laid him. But
go your way, tell his disciples and Peter that he goeth before you into
8 Galilee: there shall ye see him, [g]as he said unto you. And they went
out quickly, and fled from the sepulchre; for they trembled and were
amazed: [h]neither said they any thing to any *man;* for they were
afraid.
9 Now when *Jesus* was risen early the first *day* of the week, [i]he appeared

A. D. 33.

[d] Luke 24. 3. John 20. 8.
[e] Matt. 28. 5.
[f] ch. 10. 34. John 2. 19. 1 Cor. 15. 3-7.
[g] Matt. 26.32. Matt 28.10, 16, 17. ch. 14. 28.
[h] Matt. 28. 8.
[i] John 20. 14.

This last clause is added, both to account for their wonder how with such a stone on it the grave was to be laid open for them, and to call attention to the power which had rolled it away. Though it was too great for themselves to remove, and without that their spices had been useless, they come notwithstanding; discussing their difficulty, yet undeterred by it. On reaching it they find their difficulty gone—the stone already rolled away by an unseen hand. *And are there no others who, when advancing to duty in the face of appalling difficulties, find their stone also rolled away?* **5. And entering into the sepulchre, they saw a young man.** In Matt. xxviii. 2, he is called "the angel of the Lord;" but here he is described as he appeared to the eye, in the bloom of a life that knows no decay. In Matthew he is represented as sitting on the stone *outside* the sepulchre; but since even there he says, "*Come*, see the place where the Lord lay" (xxviii. 6), he seems, as *Alford* says, to have gone in with them from without; only awaiting their arrival to accompany them into the hallowed spot, and instruct them about it. **sitting on the right side**—having respect to the position in which His Lord had lain there. This trait is peculiar to Mark; but compare Luke i. 11. **clothed in a long white garment.** On its *length*, see Isa. vi. 1; and on its *whiteness*, see on Matt. xxviii. 3. **and they were affrighted** [ἐξεθαμβήθησαν]. **6. And he saith unto them, Be not affrighted** [Μὴ ἐκθαμβεῖσθε]—a stronger word than "Fear not" [μὴ φοβεῖσθε] in Matthew. **Ye seek Jesus of Nazareth, which was crucified** [τὸν Ναζαρηνὸν, τὸν ἐσταυρωμένον]—'the Nazarene, the Crucified.' **he is risen; he is not here.** See on Luke xxiv. 5, 6. **behold the place where they laid him.** See on Matt. xxviii. 6. **7. But go your way, tell his disciples and Peter.** This Second Gospel, being drawn up—as all the earliest tradition states—*under the eye of Peter*, or from materials chiefly furnished by him, there is something deeply affecting in the preservation of this little clause by Mark alone, and in the clause itself, which it is impossible not to connect with the cloud under which Peter lay in the eyes of the Eleven, not to say in his own also. Doubtless the "look" of Jesus and the "bitter weeping" which followed upon it (Luke xxii. 61, 62) contained all the materials of a settlement and a reconciliation. But such wounds are not easily healed; and this was but the first of a series of medicinal touches, the rest of which will follow anon. **that he goeth before you into Galilee: there shall ye see him, as he said unto you.** See on Matt. xxviii. 7. **8. And they went out quickly, and fled from the sepulchre; for they trembled and were amazed** [εἶχε δὲ αὐτὰς τρόμος καὶ ἔκστασις]—'for tremor and amazement seized them.' **neither said they any thing to any man; for they were afraid.** How intensely natural and simple is this!

Appearances of Jesus After His Resurrection (9-18). [All the verses of this chapter, from the 9th to the end, are regarded by *Griesbach*, *Tischendorf*, and *Tregelles* as no part of the original text of this Gospel, but as added by a later hand: Because, first, they are wanting in B and ℵ—the well-known *Vatican* and the recently discovered *Sinaitic*, being the oldest MSS. yet known; in one copy of the *Old Latin* Version; in some copies of the Armenian Version; and in an Arabic Lectionary or Church Lesson; while a few of the Cursive or later MSS. of this Gospel have the verses with marks indicative of doubt as to their genuineness: Again, because *Eusebius* and *Jerome*—most competent witnesses and judges, of the fourth century—pronounce against them, affirming that the genuine text of this Gospel ended with verse 8: And further, because the style of this portion so differs from the rest of this Gospel as to suggest a different author; while the variations in the text itself are just ground of suspicion. For these reasons, *Meyer*, *Fritzsche*, *Alford*, and other critical commentators, decide against the passage. But these reasons seem to us totally insufficient to counterbalance the evidence in favour of the verses in question. First, they are found in *all* the Uncial or earlier Greek MSS., except the two above-mentioned—including A, or the Alexandrian MS., which is admitted to be not more than fifty years later than the two oldest, and of scarcely less, if indeed of any less, authority; in one or two MSS. in which they are not found, a space is left to show that something is wanting—not large enough, indeed, to contain the verses, but this probably only to save space; nor do the variations in the text exceed those in some passages whose genuineness is admitted: They are found in *all* the Cursive or later Greek MSS.: They are found in all the most ancient Versions: They are quoted by *Irenæus*, and so must have been known in the *second* century; by one father at least in the *third* century, and by two or three in the *fourth*, as part of this Gospel. The argument from difference of style is exceedingly slender—confined to a few words and phrases, which vary, as every one knows, in different writings of the same author and even different portions of the same writing, with the varying aspects of the subject and the writer's emotions. That so carefully constructed a Narrative as that of this Gospel terminated with the words, "for they were afraid"—ἐφοβοῦντο γάρ—is what one wonders that any can bring themselves to believe. Accordingly, *Lachmann* inserts it as part of his text; and *de Wette*, *Hug*, and *Lange* in Germany, with *Ellicott* and *Scrivener* among ourselves, defend it. The conjecture of some recent critics, that it may have been added by the Evangelist himself, after the copies first issued had been for some time in circulation, is too far-fetched to be entitled to consideration.]

9. Now when Jesus was risen early the first day of the week, he appeared first to Mary Magdalene,

10 first to Mary Magdalene, [j]out of whom he had cast seven devils. *And*
she went and told them that had been with him, as they mourned and
11 wept. And [k]they, when they had heard that he was alive, and had been
seen of her, believed not.
12 After that he appeared in another form unto two of them, as they
13 walked, and went into the country. And they went and told *it* unto
the residue: neither believed they them.
14 Afterward [l]he appeared unto the eleven as they sat [1]at meat, and
upbraided them with their unbelief and hardness of heart, because they
believed not them which had seen him after he was risen.
15 And [m]he said unto them, Go ye into all the world, [n]and preach the
16 Gospel to every creature. He [o]that believeth and is baptized shall be
17 saved; [p]but he that believeth not shall be damned. And these signs
shall follow them that believe: [q]In my name shall they cast out devils;
18 [r]they shall speak with new tongues: they [s]shall take up serpents; and
if they drink any deadly thing, it shall not hurt them; [t]they shall lay
hands on the sick, and they shall recover.
19 So then, [u]after the Lord had spoken unto them, he was [v]received up
20 into heaven, and [w]sat on the right hand of God. And they went forth,
and preached every where, the Lord working with *them*, and [x]confirming
the word with signs following. Amen.

A. D. 33.

[j] Luke 8. 2.
[k] Luke 24. 11.
[l] Luke 24. 36. 1 Cor. 15. 5.
[1] Or, together.
[m] John 15. 16.
[n] Col. 1. 23.
[o] John 3. 18, 36.
[p] John 12. 48.
[q] Luke 10. 17.
[r] Acts 2. 4. 1 Cor. 12. 10, 28.
[s] Acts 28. 5.
[t] Acts 9. 17. Jas. 5. 14.
[u] Acts 1. 2, 3.
[v] Luke 24. 51.
[w] Ps. 110. 1. Acts 7. 55. Heb. 1. 3. Rev. 3. 21.
[x] Acts 14. 3. 1 Cor. 2. 4, 5.

out of whom he had cast seven devils. There is some difficulty here, and different ways of removing it have been adopted. She had gone with the other women to the sepulchre (*v.* 1), parting from them, perhaps, before their interview with the angel, and on finding Peter and John she had come with them back to the spot; and it was at this second visit, it would seem, that Jesus appeared to this Mary, as detailed in John xx. 11-18. *To a woman was this honour given to be the first that saw the risen Redeemer; and that woman was* NOT *his virgin-mother.* **10. And she went and told them that had been with him, as they mourned and wept. 11. And they, when they had heard that he was alive, and had been seen of her, believed not.** This, which is once and again repeated of them all, is most important in its bearing on their subsequent testimony to His resurrection, at the risk of life itself.

12. After that he appeared in another form (compare Luke xxiv. 16) **unto two of them, as they walked, and went into the country.** The reference here, of course, is to His manifestation to the two disciples going to Emmaus, so exquisitely told by the third Evangelist (see on Luke xxiv. 13, &c.). **12. And they went and told it unto the residue: neither believed they them.**

14. Afterward he appeared unto the eleven as they sat at meat, and upbraided them with their unbelief and hardness of heart, because they believed not them which had seen him after he was risen. 15. And he said unto them, Go ye into all the world, and preach the Gospel to every creature. See on John xx. 19-23; and on Luke xxiv. 36-49. **16. He that believeth and is baptized.** Baptism is here put for the external signature of the inner faith of the heart, just as "confessing with the mouth" is in Rom. x. 10; and there also as here this *outward* manifestation, once mentioned as the proper fruit of faith, is not repeated in what follows (Rom. x. 11). **shall be saved; but he that believeth not shall be damned.** These awful issues of the reception or rejection of the Gospel, though often recorded in other connections, are given in this connection only by Mark. **17. And these signs shall follow them that believe: In my name shall they cast out devils; they shall speak with new tongues; 18. They shall take up serpents; and if they drink any deadly thing, it shall not hurt them; they shall lay hands on the sick, and they shall recover.** These two verses also are peculiar to Mark.

The Ascension and Triumphant Proclamation of the Gospel thereafter (19-20). **19. So then, after the Lord**—an epithet applied to Jesus by this Evangelist only in the two concluding verses, when He comes to His glorious Ascension and its subsequent fruits. It is most frequent in Luke. **had spoken unto them, he was received up into heaven.** See on Luke xxiv. 50, 51. **and sat on the right hand of God.** This great truth is here only related as a fact in the Gospel History. In that exalted attitude He appeared to Stephen (Acts vii. 55, 56); and it is thereafter perpetually referred to as His proper condition in glory. **20. And they went forth, and preached every where, the Lord working with them, and confirming the word with signs following. Amen.** We have in this closing verse a most important link of connection with the Acts of the Apostles, where He who directed all the movements of the infant Church is perpetually styled "THE LORD;" thus illustrating His own promise for the founding and building up of the Church, "Lo, I AM WITH YOU alway!"

For Remarks on this Section, see those on the corresponding Section of the First Gospel—Matt. xxviii. 1-15.

THE GOSPEL ACCORDING TO

ST. LUKE.

---

1 FORASMUCH as many have taken in hand to set forth in order a
declaration of [a]those things which are most surely believed among
2 us, even [b]as they delivered them unto us, which [c]from the beginning
3 were eye-witnesses, and ministers of the word; it [d]seemed good to me
also, having had perfect understanding of all things from the very first,
4 to write unto thee [e]in order, most [f]excellent Theophilus, that [g]thou
mightest know the certainty of those things, wherein thou hast been
instructed.
5 THERE was, [h]in the days of Herod the king of Judea, a certain priest
named Zacharias, [i]of the course of Abia: and his wife *was* of the
6 daughters of Aaron, and her name *was* Elisabeth. And they were
both [j]righteous before God, walking in all the commandments and
7 ordinances of the Lord blameless. And they had no child, because
that Elisabeth was barren; and they both were *now* well stricken in
years.
8 And it came to pass, that, while he executed the priest's office before

A. M. 4000.

CHAP. 1.
[a] John 20. 31. Acts 1. 1-3. 1 Tim. 3.16.
[b] Heb. 2. 3. 1 Pet. 5. 1. 2 Pet. 1. 16. 1 John 1. 1.
[c] John 15.27.
[d] 1 Cor. 7. 40.
[e] Acts 11. 4.
[f] Acts 1. 1.
[g] John 20. 31.
[h] Matt. 2. 1.
[i] 1 Chr. 24.10. Neh. 12. 4.
[j] 1 Ki. 9. 4. 2 Ki. 20. 3. Ps. 119. 6. 2 Cor. 1. 12.

CHAP. I. 1-17.—INTRODUCTION—ANNOUNCEMENT OF THE FORERUNNER.

Introduction (1-4). **1. Forasmuch as many have taken in hand to set forth in order a declaration** [ἐπεχείρησαν ἀνατάξασθαι διήγησιν]—'have undertaken to draw up a narrative,' **of those things which are most surely believed** [τῶν πεπληροφορημένων] **among us**—not 'believed confidently,' but 'believed on sure grounds.' So the word "surely" is used by our translators in Prov. x. 9, "He that walketh uprightly walketh *surely*." **2. Even as they delivered them unto us, which from the beginning** [ἀπ' ἀρχῆς]—that is, of Christ's ministry, **were eye-witnesses, and ministers of the word** [αὐτόπται καὶ ὑπηρέται τοῦ λόγου]. Though it would not be strictly proper to understand "the word" here of Christ Himself—since only John applies to Him this exalted title, and He seems never to have been actually so denominated—yet since the term rendered "ministers" [ὑπηρέται] denotes the servants of a *person*, it must refer to those apostles of the Lord Jesus, who, in proclaiming everywhere that word which they had heard from His own lips, acted as *His* servants. **3. It seemed good to me also, having had perfect understanding of** [παρηκολουθηκότι]—rather, 'having closely followed,' or 'traced along' **all things from the very first** [ἄνωθεν πᾶσιν ἀκριβῶς]—'all things with precision from the earliest;' referring particularly to the precious contents of his first two chapters, for which we are indebted to this Evangelist alone, **to write unto thee in order** [καθεξῆς = ἐφεξῆς]—*i. e., consecutively;* probably in contrast with the disjointed productions he had just referred to. But we need not take this as a claim to rigid chronological accuracy in the arrangement of his materials (as some able Harmonists insist that we should do); a claim which, on a comparison of this with the other Gospels, it would be difficult in every case to make good. **most excellent** [κράτιστε] **Theophilus.** As the term here applied to Theophilus was given to Felix and Festus, the Roman governors (Acts xxiii. 26; xxiv. 3; xxvi. 25), he probably occupied some similar official position. **4. That thou mightest know**—'know thoroughly' [ἐπιγνῷς]—**the certainty of those things wherein thou hast been instructed** [κατηχήθης]—'orally instructed;' *i. e.*, as a catechumen, or candidate for Christian baptism.

5. There was, in the days of Herod the king of Judea (see on Matt. ii. 1), **a certain priest named Zacharias, of the course of Abia**—or Abijah, the eighth of the twenty-four courses or orders into which David divided the priests (1 Chr. xxiv. 1, 4, 10). Of these courses only four returned after the captivity (Ezra ii. 36-39), which were again divided into twenty-four courses, retaining the ancient name and the original order; and each of these took the whole Temple-service for a week. **and his wife was of the daughters of Aaron.** Though the priests, says *Lightfoot*, might marry into any tribe, it was most commendable of all to marry one of the priests' line. **and her name was Elisabeth. 6. And they were both righteous**—not merely virtuous before men, but righteous **before God** who searcheth the heart. What that comprehended is next explained. **walking**—a familiar biblical term denoting the habitual tenor of one's life, (Ps. i. 1, &c.) **in all the commandments and ordinances of the Lord**—the one denoting the *moral*, the other the *ceremonial* precepts of the law—a distinction which it is falsely alleged that the ancient Jews were strangers to (see on Mark xii. 33; and see Ezek. xi. 20; Heb. ix. 1). **blameless**—irreproachable. **7. And they had no child, because that Elisabeth was barren; and they both were now well stricken in years.** This quiet couple have one trial. Almost every one has some crook in his lot; but here it was a link in the great chain of the divine purposes. As with Abraham and Sarah before Isaac was given; with Elkanah and Hannah before Samuel was granted them; and with Manoah and his wife before Samson was born; so here with Zacharias and Elisabeth before the Forerunner was bestowed—in each case, doubtless, to make the gift more prized, and raise high expectations from it.

8. And it came to pass, that, while he executed

9 God [k]in the order of his course, according to the custom of the priest's
office, his lot was [l]to burn incense when he went into the temple of the
10 Lord. And [m]the whole multitude of the people were praying without
11 at the time of incense. And there appeared unto him an angel of the
12 Lord standing on the right side of the altar of incense. And when
13 Zacharias saw *him,* [n]he was troubled, and fear fell upon him. But the
angel said unto him, Fear not, Zacharias: for [o]thy prayer is heard; and
thy wife Elisabeth shall bear thee a son, and thou shalt call his name
14 John. And thou shalt have joy and gladness; and many shall rejoice
15 at his birth. For he shall be [p]great in the sight of the Lord, and [q]shall
drink neither wine nor strong drink; and he shall be filled with the

A. M. 4000.

k 2 Chr. 8. 14.
l Ex. 30. 7. 8.
m Lev. 16. 17.
n Dan. 10. 8. Acts 10. 4. Rev. 1. 17.
o Gen. 25. 21. 1 Sam. 1. 19.
p Matt. 11. 11. John 5. 35.
q Num. 6. 3. Jud. 13. 4. ch. 7. 33.

the priest's office before God in the order of his course, 9. According to the custom of the priest's office, his lot was to burn incense when he went into the temple. The part assigned to each priest during his week of service was decided by lot. Three were employed at the offering of incense: to remove the ashes of the former service; to bring in and place on the golden altar the pan filled with hot burning coals taken from the altar of burnt offering; and to sprinkle the incense on the hot coals, and, while the smoke of it ascended, to make intercession for the people. This was the most distinguished part of the service (Rev. viii. 3), and this was what fell to the lot of Zacharias at this time [*Lightfoot*]. **10. And the whole multitude of the people were praying without**—outside the court fronting the temple, where stood the altar of burnt offering; the men and women worshipping in separate courts, but the altar visible to all. **at the time of incense**—which was offered twice every day, along with the morning and evening sacrifice, at the third and ninth hours (or 9 A.M. and 3 P.M.)—a beautiful symbol, first of *the acceptableness of the sacrifice* which was then burning on the altar of burnt offering, with coals from which the incense laid on the golden altar was burnt (Lev. xvi. 12, 13); but next, of the *acceptableness of themselves and all their services,* as "living sacrifices" presented daily to God. Hence the language of Ps. cxli. 2, "Let my prayer come up before thee as incense, and the lifting up of my hands as the evening sacrifice;" and see Gen. viii. 3, 4. That the acceptableness of this *incense-offering* depended on the *expiatory* virtue pre-supposed in the *burnt offering,* and pointed to the Lamb of God that taketh away the sin of the world, is clear from Isa. vi. 6, 7, where the symbolic action of touching the prophet's lips with a live coal from off the altar is interpreted to mean the "taking away of his iniquity, and the purging of his sin," in order that his lips might be clean to speak for God. **11. And there appeared unto him an angel of the Lord**—not while at home, but in the act of discharging his sacerdotal duties; yet not when engaged *outside,* at the altar of burnt offering, but during his week of inside-service, and so while *alone* with God. It is impossible not to observe here a minuteness of providential arrangement, proclaiming in every detail the hand of Him who is "wonderful in counsel and excellent in working." **standing**—the attitude of service, **on the right side of the altar of incense**—*i. e.,* the south side, between the golden altar and the candlestick or lamp-stand; Zacharias being on the north side, and fronting the altar as he offered the incense. Why did the angel appear on the right side? Because, say some, the right was regarded as the favourable side [*Schöttgen,* and *Wetstein* in *Meyer*]. See Matt. xxv. 33; and cf. Mark xvi. 5. But perhaps it was only to make the object more visible. **12. And when Zacharias saw him, he was troubled**—'discomposed,' **and fear fell upon him.** And what wonder? The unseen world is so veiled from us, and so different from ours in its nature and laws, that when in any of its features it breaks in unexpectedly upon mortals, it cannot but startle and appal them, as it did Daniel (Dan. x. 7, 8, 17), and the beloved disciple in Patmos (Rev. i. 17). 'He that had wont to live and serve in presence of the Master was now astonished at the presence of the servant. So much difference is there betwixt our faith and our senses, that the apprehension of the presence of the God of spirits by faith goes down sweetly with us, whereas the sensible apprehension of an angel dismays us. Holy Zachary, that had wont to live by faith, thought he should die when his sense began to be set on work. It was the weakness of him that served at the altar without horror, to be daunted with the face of his fellow-servant' (*Bp. Hall.*) **13. But the angel said unto him, Fear not.** Thus by two familiar, endeared, exhilarating words, was the silence of four centuries broken, and thus unexpectedly, yet all noiselessly, was the curtain of a stupendous and enduring Economy in this world's history at once drawn up! And was it not worth all the terror which Zacharias experienced to be greeted with so gladsome a salutation! It is God's prerogative, indeed, to dispel our fears—"Thou drewest near (sings Jeremiah) in the day that I called upon Thee; Thou saidst, Fear not" (Lam. iii. 57)—but angels, we see, are privileged to convey the message from heaven; nay, all who have themselves been divinely cheered are bidden "Say to them that are of a fearful heart, Be strong, fear not" (Isa. xxxv. 4). **Zacharias!** How sweet is it to hear the name of this lowly mortal man sounded forth by an exalted messenger from the very presence-chamber of the Most High! Does it not bring vividly before us the nearness of heaven to earth, God's intimate knowledge of those who serve Him here below, and the tender interest which He takes in them? **for thy prayer is heard**—doubtless for *offspring,* which, by some presentiment, perhaps, he had even till now been kept from quite despairing of. **and thy wife Elisabeth shall bear thee a son, and thou shalt call his name John** [=יוֹחָנָן, יְהוֹחָנָן]—the "Johanan" so frequent in the Old Testament, meaning Jehovah's gracious gift. **14. And thou shalt have joy and gladness**—'exultation,' **and many shall rejoice**—*i. e.,* shall have cause to rejoice **at his birth**—through whose ministry they were "turned to the Lord their God." **15. For he shall be great in the sight of the Lord**—*i. e.,* great *officially* beyond all the prophets that went before him (as is evident from Matt. xi. 11). In personal character John was indeed among the greatest of men; but it is the supereminent dignity of his office, as Messiah's Forerunner, that is here meant. **and shall drink neither wine nor strong drink**

16 Holy Ghost, [r]even from his mother's womb. And [s]many of the children
17 of Israel shall he turn to the Lord their God. And [t]he shall go before
him in the spirit and power of Elias, to turn the hearts of the fathers to
the children, and the disobedient [1]to the wisdom of the just; to make
ready a people prepared for [u]the Lord.

A. M. 4000.
[r] Jer. 1. 5.
[s] Mal 4. 5,6.
[t] Matt.11.14.
[1] Or, by.
[u] Isa. 40. 3.

—that is, he shall be a *Nazarite*, or 'separated one.' See Num. vi. 1, &c. As the leper was the living symbol of *sin*, so was the Nazarite of *holiness:* nothing inflaming was to cross his lips; no razor was to come on his head; no ceremonial defilement was to be contracted. Thus was he to be ceremonially "holy to the Lord all the days of his separation." In ordinary cases this separation was voluntary and temporary: we read of three only who were Nazarites from the womb—*Samson* (Jud. xiii. 7), *Samuel* (1 Sam. i. 11), and here *John Baptist.* It was fitting that the utmost severity of legal consecration should be in the Forerunner. In Christ Himself we see the REALITY and PERFECTION of the Nazarite without the symbol, which perished in that living realization of it. "Such an high priest became us, who is holy, harmless, undefiled, SEPARATE FROM SINNERS" (Heb. vii. 26). **and he shall be filled with the Holy Ghost** (see Matt. i. 18), **even from his mother's womb**—a holy vessel for future service. This is never said of the supernatural endowments of ungodly men; and indeed of John it is expressly said that he "did no miracle" (John x. 41). Nor can the reference be to inspiration, for this does not appear to have come on John till his public ministry commenced, when "the word of God came to John the son of Zacharias in the wilderness" (Luke iii. 2). It is *sanctification from the womb*—a truth of high import in personal Christianity, of weighty bearing on the standing of the infants of believers in the Church of God, and ministering precious encouragement to religious parents. **16. And many of the children of Israel shall he turn to the Lord their God. 17. And he shall go before him**—*i. e.*, before "the Lord their God" just spoken of; showing that Messiah, before whom John was to go, as a *herald* to announce his approach and as a *pioneer* to prepare his way, was to be "the Lord God of Israel" manifested in the flesh (Isa. xl. 3; Mal. iii. 1). So *Calvin, Olshausen*, &c. **in the spirit and power of Elias**—*i. e.*, after the model of that distinguished reformer, and with like success, in "turning hearts." Strikingly indeed did John resemble Elias: both fell on evil times; both witnessed fearlessly for God; neither was much seen save in the direct exercise of their ministry; both were at the head of schools of disciples; the result of the ministry of both might be expressed in the same terms—"*many* (not all, nor even the majority, but still many) of the children of Israel did they turn to the Lord their God." **to turn the hearts of the fathers to the children.** This, if taken literally, with *Meyer* and others, denotes the restoration of parental fidelity, the decay of which is certainly the beginning of religious and social corruption. In this case it is just one prominent feature of the coming revival put for the whole. But the next clause, **and the disobedient to the wisdom of the just**—which seems designed to give the sense of the preceding one, rather suggests a *figurative* meaning: 'He shall bring back the ancient spirit of the nation to their degenerate children.' So *Calvin, Bengel*, &c. Thus prayed Elijah, "Lord God of Abraham, Isaac, and Israel, hear me, that this people may know that thou art the Lord God, and that thou hast *turned their heart back again*" (1 Ki. xviii. 36, 37). **to make ready a people prepared for the Lord** [ἑτοιμάσαι Κυρίῳ λαὸν κατεσκευασμένον]—rather, 'to make ready for the Lord a prepared people;' prepared, that is, to welcome Him. Such preparation for welcoming the Lord is required, not only in every age, but in every soul.

Remarks.—1. Works such as Jesus wrought and Teaching such as poured from His lips, as He walked up and down Judea and Galilee, in the days of His flesh, could not but be carried on the wings of the wind, especially after He rose from the dead, ascended up into heaven, and at the Pentecostal festival made His handful of adherents proclaim, in the tongues of all the nationalities then assembled at Jerusalem, the wonderful works of God. These Jewish strangers and proselytes would carry them to their homes, and the first preachers—and every Christian would be more or less a preacher—would tell the tale to all who had ears to hear them. Of such astonishing tidings eager listeners would take notes; and digests, more or less full, would be put into circulation. For lack of better, such summaries would be read aloud at prayer-meetings and other small assemblies of Christians; and of these a few would be pretty full, and, on the whole, pretty correct narratives of the Life, Acts, and Sayings of Christ. To such it is that our Evangelist here refers, and in terms of studied respect, as narratives of what was 'on sure grounds believed among Christians, and drawn up from the testimony of eye-witnesses and ministers of the word.' But when he adds that it seemed good to him also, having traced down all things with exactness from its first rise, to write a consecutive History, he virtually claims, by this Gospel of his own, to supersede all these narratives. Accordingly, while not one of them has survived the wreck of time, this and the other canonical Gospels live, and shall live, the only worthy vehicles of those life-bringing facts which have made all things new. Apocryphal or spurious gospels—such as sprang up in swarms at a later period to feed a prurient curiosity and minister to the taste of those who could not rise to the tone of the canonical Gospels—have *not* altogether perished: but those well-meant and substantially correct narratives here referred to, used only while better were not to be had, were by tacit consent allowed to merge in the four peerless documents which, as one Gospel, have from age to age, even from the very time of their publication, and with astonishing unanimity, been accepted as the written Charter of all Christianity. 2. The diversity which obtains among these Four Gospels is as beautiful a feature of them as their inner harmony. Each has an invaluable character of its own which the others want. And although a comparison of the four different streams of narration with each other, with the view of tracing out the unity of incident and discourse, and so shaping out as perfectly as possible *The Life of Jesus*, has been the laudable, and delightful, and fruitful occupation of biblical students in every age; one cannot but feel, the longer he studies these matchless productions, that every detail of them is so much fresher just *where it lies* than in any combination of them into one, that every such attempt as Tatian's DIATESSARON (about A.D. 170), and that of Professor White of Oxford (1803)—that is, one continuous History woven out of the text of the

18 And Zacharias said unto the angel, Whereby [v]shall I know this? for
19 I am an old man, and my wife well stricken in years. And the angel
answering said unto him, I am [w]Gabriel, that stand in the presence of
God; and am sent to speak unto thee, and to show thee these glad
20 tidings. And, behold, [x]thou shalt be dumb, and not able to speak,
until the day that these things shall be performed, because thou believest
21 not my words, which shall be fulfilled in their season. And the people
[y]waited for Zacharias, and marvelled that he tarried so long in the
22 temple. And when he came out, he could not speak unto them: and
they perceived that he had seen a vision in the temple; for he beckoned
unto them, and remained speechless.
23 And it came to pass, that, as soon as the [z]days of his ministration
24 were accomplished, he departed to his own house. And after those days
25 his wife Elisabeth conceived, and hid herself five months, saying, Thus
hath the Lord dealt with me in the days wherein he looked on *me*, to
[a]take away my reproach among men.
26 And in the sixth month the angel Gabriel was sent from God unto a

[v] Gen. 15. 8. Gen. 17. 17. Gen. 18. 12. Jud. 6. 36. Isa. 38. 22.
[w] Dan. 8. 16. Dan. 9. 21. Matt. 18. 10. Heb. 1. 14.
[x] Ex. 4. 11. Ezek. 3. 26 Ezek. 24. 27 ch. 1. 62.
[y] Num. 6. 23. Lev. 9. 22.
[z] 2 Ki. 11. 5. 1 Chr. 9. 25
[a] Gen. 30. 23. 1 Sam. 1. 6. Isa. 4. 1. Isa. 54. 1.

Four Gospels—is a mistake. Let that river, the streams whereof make glad the city of God, flow, like the river that watered the garden of Eden, in its four crystal streams and in their own native beds, until that which is perfect is come, when that which is in part shall be done away. 3. How beautiful is the spectacle of husband and wife, in advancing years, when "joint-heirs [συγκληρονόμοι] of the grace of life," and "their prayers [together] are not hindered" (1 Pet. iii. 7) by misunderstandings or inconsistencies! (*vv.* 7, 13). 4. When God has any special blessing in store for His people, He usually creates in them a longing for it, and yet withholds it from them till all hope of it is dying within them. By this He makes the blessing, when at length it comes, the more surprising and the more welcome, an object of deeper interest and dearer delight (*v.* 7). 5. The most cheering visitations of Heaven are wont to come to us in the discharge of duty. It was when Elijah "*still went on and talked*" with Elisha, who was to succeed him in office, that the chariots and horses of fire appeared to take him up to heaven (2 Ki. ii. 11): more gloriously still—when Jesus had led His disciples out "as far as to Bethany, and lifted up His hands and blessed them—it came to pass, *while He blessed them*, He was parted from them, and carried up into heaven" (Luke xxiv. 50, 51). So here, it was "while Zacharias was executing the priest's office in the order of his course, burning incense in the temple of the Lord, and the whole multitude of the people were praying without," that the angel of the Lord appeared to him with the glad announcement of a son who should usher in and prepare the way of Christ Himself (*vv.* 8-11). 6. If the heart is ready to sink when the thin partitions between heaven and earth are, even in a small degree, rent asunder, how re-assuring is it to find such exceptional visitations only confirming the teaching of Moses and the prophets, and strengthening the expectations built upon them! (*vv.* 13-17).

18-38.—Unbelief and Punishment of Zacharias—Annunciation of Christ, and Faith of His Virgin-Mother.

Unbelief and Punishment of Zacharias (18-25). **18. And Zacharias said unto the angel, Whereby** [κατὰ τί] **shall I know this? for I am an old man, and my wife well stricken in years.** Had such a promise never been made and fulfilled before, the unbelief of Zacharias would have been more easily accounted for, and less sinful. But when the like promise was made to Abraham, at a more advanced age, "he staggered not at the promise of God through unbelief, but was strong in faith, giving glory to God" (Rom. iv. 20). "Through faith Sara herself also received strength to conceive seed, and was delivered of a child when she was past age, because she judged Him faithful who had promised" (Heb. xi. 11). As God is glorified by implicit confidence in His promises—and just in proportion to the natural obstacles in the way of their fulfilment—so unbelief like that of Zacharias here is regarded as a dishonour put upon His word, and resented accordingly. **19. And the angel answering said unto him, I am Gabriel** —'man of God' [גַּבְרִיאֵל]. He appeared to Daniel, and at the same time of incense (Dan. ix. 21); to Mary also he was sent (*v.* 26). **that stand in the presence of God**—as His attendant (cf. 1 Ki. xvii. 1) **and am sent to speak unto thee, and to show thee these glad tidings. 20. And, behold, thou shalt be dumb** —'speechless' [σιωπῶν]—**until the day that these things shall be performed, because thou believest not my words, which shall be fulfilled in their season.** He asked for a sign, and now he got one. **21. And the people waited for Zacharias**—to receive from him the usual benediction (Num. vi. 23-27). **and marvelled that he tarried so long in the temple.** It was not usual to tarry long, lest it should be thought vengeance had stricken the people's representative for something wrong. (*Lightfoot*). **22. And when he came out, he could not speak unto them: and they perceived that he had seen a vision in the temple; for he beckoned unto them**—by some motion of his hands and eyes, signifying what had happened, **and remained speechless**—'dumb' [κωφός], and deaf also, as appears from *v.* 62.

23. And it came to pass, that, as soon as the days of his ministration were accomplished, he departed to his own house. 24. And Elisabeth conceived, and hid herself five months—that is, till the event was put beyond doubt. **saying, 25. Thus hath the Lord dealt with me in the days wherein he looked on me, to take away my reproach among men.** There was here more than true womanly simplicity and gratitude to the Lord for the gift of offspring. She has respect to the *manner* in which that reproach was to be taken away, in connection with the great Hope of Israel.

Annunciation of Christ, and Faith of His Virgin-Mother (26-38). The curtain of the first scene of this wonderful story has dropt, but only to rise again and disclose a scene of surpassing sacredness

27 city of Galilee, named Nazareth, to a [b]virgin espoused to a man whose
name was Joseph, of the house of David; and the virgin's name *was*
Mary.
28 And the angel came in unto her, and said, Hail! *thou that art* [2]highly
29 favoured, the Lord *is* with thee: blessed *art* thou among women! And
when she saw *him*, she was troubled at his saying, and cast in her mind
30 what manner of salutation this should be. And the angel said unto
31 her, Fear not, Mary; for thou hast found favour with God. And,
[c]behold, thou shalt conceive in thy womb, and bring forth a son, and
32 shalt call his name JESUS. He shall be [d]great, and shall be called the
Son of the Highest: and [e]the Lord God shall give unto him the throne
33 of his father David: and [f]he shall reign over the house of Jacob for ever;
34 and of his kingdom there shall be no end. Then said Mary unto the
35 angel, How shall this be, seeing I know not a man? And the angel
answered and said unto her, The Holy Ghost shall come upon thee, and
the power of the Highest shall overshadow thee: therefore also that holy

A. M. 4000.

[b] Isa. 7. 14. Matt. 1. 18.
[2] Or, graciously accepted, or, much graced.
[c] Gal. 4. 4.
[d] 1 Tim. 6. 15. Phil. 2. 10.
[e] 2 Sam. 7. 11. Ps. 132. 11. Isa. 9. 6, 7. Isa. 16. 5. Jer. 23. 5.
[f] Dan. 2. 44. Dan. 7. 14. Oba. 21. Mic. 4. 7. John 12. 34.

and delicacy, simplicity and grandeur. **26. And in the sixth month** of Elisabeth's conception **the angel Gabriel was sent from God.** I could envy thee, O Gabriel, these most exalted of all errands. But I remember that true greatness lies, not in the dignity of our calling, but in the right discharge of its duties—not in the loftiness of our talents, but in the use we make of them. **unto a city named Nazareth.** "Can any good thing come out of Nazareth?" asked the guileless Nathanael, having respect to its proverbially bad name. But the Lord selects His own places as well as persons. **27. To a virgin espoused**—rather 'betrothed' [μεμνηστευμένην] **to a man whose name was Joseph, of the house of David.** See on Matt. i. 16. **and the virgin's name was Mary** [=מִרְיָם]—equivalent to *Miriam* in the Old Testament.

28. And the angel came in unto her, and said, Hail! highly favoured—a word [κεχαριτωμένη] only once used elsewhere (Eph. i. 6, "made accepted"). That our translators have given the right sense of it here seems plain not only from the import of verbs of that termination, but from the next clause, **the Lord is with thee,** and *v.* 30, "Thou hast found favour with God." The Vulgate's mistaken rendering—"full of grace" [*gratiâ plena*]—has been taken abundant advantage of by the Romish Church. As the mother of our Lord, she was indeed "the most blessed among women;" but His own reply to the woman who once said this to Himself (see on ch. xi. 27, 28) is enough to teach us that this blessedness of His virgin-mother is not to be mixed up or confounded with her personal character—high as no doubt that was. **blessed art thou among women!** This clause is excluded from the text here by *Tischendorf*, and *Tregelles* brackets it as of doubtful authority, though admitted to be without question in *v.* 42. *Alford* excludes it from his text, and *Meyer* pronounces against it. But the authority in favour of the clause here also is immensely preponderating. *Lachmann* inserts it. The expression, "Blessed among women," is Old Testament language for "Most blessed of women." **29. And when she saw him, she was troubled, &c. 30. And the angel said unto her, Fear not, &c. 31. And, behold, thou shalt conceive in thy womb, and bring forth a son, and shalt call his name JESUS.** See on Matt. i. 21-23. **32, 33. He shall be great, &c.** The whole of this magnificent announcement is purposely couched in almost the terms of Isaiah's sublime prediction (Isa. ix. 6). **He shall be great.** Of His Forerunner too it had been said by the same Gabriel, "He shall be great;" but it was immediately added, "in the sight of the Lord"—an explanation highly suitable in the case of a *mere servant*, but omitted, with evident purpose, in the present case. Indeed, the words that follow, **and shall be called the Son of the Highest**—or, "of the Most High" [υἱὸς ὑψίστου = בֶּן־עֶלְיוֹן], would have forbidden such an explanation, as altogether unsuitable here. And is there one reader of unsophisticated and teachable spirit who can take these last words as designed to express a merely figurative relation of a creature to God? But see on John v. 18; and on Rom. viii. 32. **33. And he shall reign over the house of Jacob**—God's visible people, who then stood in Jacob's descendants, but soon to take in all the families of the earth who should come under the Redeemer's ample wing; **and of his kingdom there shall be no end.** The perpetuity of Messiah's kingdom, stretching even into eternity, was one of its brightest prophetic features. See 2 Sam. vii. 13; Ps. lxxii. 5, 7, 17; lxxxix. 36, &c.; Dan. ii. 44; vii. 13, 14. **34. Then said Mary, How shall this be, seeing I know not a man?** There was here none of the unbelief of Zacharias. On the contrary, taking the fact for granted, the simple import of the question seems to be—*On what principle is* this to be, so contrary to the hitherto unbroken law of human generation? Accordingly, instead of reproof, she receives an explanation on that very point, and in mysterious detail. **35. And the angel answered and said unto her, The Holy Ghost shall come upon thee** (see on Matt. i. 18), **and the power of the Highest**—the immediate energy of the Godhead, conveyed by the Holy Ghost, **shall overshadow thee.** What exquisite delicacy is there in the use of this word, suggesting how gentle, while yet efficacious, would be this power, and its mysterious secrecy too, as if withdrawn by a cloud from human scrutiny—as *Calvin* hints. **therefore also that holy thing which shall be born [of thee]** [τὸ γεννώμενον ἅγιον]—an expression denoting the singularity and consequent sanctity of this birth. The words "of thee" [ἐκ σου] are wanting in the best MSS., and even in the received text as printed by *Stephens* and the *Elzevirs*. **shall be called the Son of God.** That Christ is the Son of God in His Divine and eternal nature is clear from all the New Testament; yet here we see that Sonship efflorescing into human and palpable manifestation by His being born, through "the power of the Highest," an Infant of days. We must neither think of a double Sonship—a divine and a human—as some

36 thing which shall be born of thee shall be called the [g]Son of God. And,
behold, thy cousin Elisabeth, she hath also conceived a son in her old
37 age: and this is the sixth month with her, who was called barren. For
38 [h]with God nothing shall be impossible. And Mary said, Behold the
handmaid of the Lord; be it unto me according to thy word. And the
angel departed from her.
39 And Mary arose in those days, and went into the hill country with
40 haste, [i]into a city of Juda; and entered into the house of Zacharias, and
41 saluted Elisabeth. And it came to pass, that, when Elisabeth heard the
salutation of Mary, the babe leaped in her womb; and Elisabeth was
42 filled [j]with the Holy Ghost; and she spake out with a loud voice, and
said, [k]Blessed *art* thou among women, and blessed *is* the fruit of thy
43 womb. And whence *is* this to me, that the mother of my Lord should

A. M. 4000.

[g] Matt. 14. 33. Matt. 26. 63. Mark 1. 1. John 1. 34. John 20. 31. Acts 8. 37. Rom. 1. 4.
[h] Gen. 18. 14. Jer. 32. 17. Zec. 8. 6. Rom. 4. 21.
[i] Jos. 21. 9.
[j] Acts 6. 3. Eph. 5. 18. Rev. 1. 10.
[k] Jud. 5. 24.

do, harshly and groundlessly, nor yet deny what is here plainly expressed, the connection between His human birth and His proper personal Sonship. **36. And, behold, thy cousin**—rather, 'relative' [συγγενής]; for how nearly they were related the word does not decide. Though Elisabeth was of the tribe of Levi and Mary of Judah, as will afterwards appear, they might still be related, as intermarriage among the tribes was permitted. **she hath also conceived a son in her old age: and this is the sixth month with her, who was called barren.** This was to Mary an *unsought* sign, in reward of a faith so simple; and what a contrast to the demanded sign which unbelieving Zacharias got! **37. For with God nothing shall be impossible**—reminding her, for her encouragement, of what had been said to Abraham in like case (Gen. xviii. 14). The future tense here employed [ἀδυνατήσει], "shall be impossible," is designed to express an enduring principle—*q. d.*, 'With God nothing ever has been nor ever shall be impossible.' **38. And Mary said, Behold the handmaid of the Lord; be it unto me according to thy word.** Marvellous faith, in the teeth of natural law, and in a matter which to one betrothed and already in law the wife of one of the royal line, fitted to inspire feelings in the last degree painful and embarrassing! Meet vessel for such a treasure!

Remarks.—The reflections most naturally suggested by this Section are best conveyed by the blessed Virgin herself, in the exalted Hymn which she uttered under the roof of Elisabeth. But such as she could not express may here be indicated. 1. The language in which the angel conveyed to the Virgin the mode in which her Offspring was to come into the world is nearly as remarkable as the event itself. It is too far removed from ordinary phraseology, and, considering the low state of tone and feeling then prevalent—which is well reflected in the apocryphal gospels of a somewhat later date—too lofty in its delicate simplicity to admit of any doubt that it is the very phraseology employed by the angel. And when it is remembered how every word and turn of expression in this most remarkable verse—containing all the information we possess on this subject—has been scrutinized by friends and foes in every age, and compared with all we otherwise know of the Person and Character of Jesus of Nazareth; and that not a word or shade of thought in it has been found unsuitable to the occasion, but everything in keeping with circumstances of surpassing sacredness and delicacy, what a character of *divine authority* does it stamp upon this Third Gospel! 2. The information given us in this verse furnishes the only adequate key to the sinless life of the Virgin's Son. As the facts of His recorded History show Him to have been throughout the "Undefiled and Separate from sinners," so we have here the root of it all, in that operation of the Holy Ghost which after His birth had merely to be continued as an indwelling energy, in order to develop all that was seminally there from the first.

39-56.—Visit of Mary to Elisabeth. This is the third scene in the great Story of Redemption, beautifully knitting up the two former.

39. And Mary arose in those days, and went into the hill country—a mountain-range, running north to south from the one extremity of Palestine to the other, in a parallel course to the Jordan, and nearly dividing the country in two. It is the most striking of all the physical features of the country. In Judea this "hill country" stands well out from the flat parts around it, and it was thither that Mary hied her. **with haste**—the haste, not of trepidation, but of transport, not only at the wonderful announcement she had to make to her relative, but at the scarcely less astonishing news she expected to receive from her of her own condition. **into a city of Juda.** Writing in the first instance to Gentiles, it was not necessary to be more particular; but without doubt the city was Hebron: see Jos. xx. 7; xxi. 11. **40. And entered into the house of Zacharias, and saluted Elisabeth**—now returned from her seclusion (*v.* 24). **41. And it came to pass, that, when Elisabeth heard the salutation, the babe leaped in her womb.** That this was like nothing of the same kind which she had felt before, and with which mothers are familiar, is plain from *v.* 44: nor does Elisabeth ascribe to it merely an extraordinary character; she describes it, and this when "filled with the Holy Ghost," as a sympathetic emotion of the unconscious babe at the presence of her and his Lord. **and Elisabeth was filled with the Holy Ghost; 42. And she spake out.** This word [ἀνεφώνησε] is often used classically of persons who burst into poetic exclamations: **with a loud voice, and said, Blessed art thou among women**—that is, most blessed of all women, **and blessed is the fruit of thy womb.** In the case of Mary, there was, as yet, no visible evidence that she had even conceived, nor does she appear to have had time to communicate to Elisabeth the tidings she came to bring her. But the rapt spirit of this honoured woman sees all as already accomplished. **43. And whence is this to me, that the mother of my Lord should come to me?** What beautiful superiority to *envy* have we here? High as was the distinction conferred upon herself, Elisabeth loses sight of it altogether, in presence of one more honoured still; upon whom, and on her unborn Babe, in an ecstasy of inspiration, she pronounces a benediction, feeling it to be a wonder unaccountable that "the mother of her Lord should come to *her*." 'Turn this as we will,' says *Olshausen*, 'we shall never

44 come to me? For, lo, as soon as the voice of thy salutation sounded in
45 mine ears, the babe leaped in my womb for joy. And blessed *is* she
[3] that believed: for there shall be a performance of those things which
46 were told her from the Lord. And Mary said,
[l] My soul doth magnify the Lord,
47 And my spirit hath rejoiced in God my Saviour.
48 For [m] he hath regarded the low estate of his handmaiden:
For, behold, from henceforth [n] all generations shall call me blessed.
49 For he that is mighty hath done to me great things;
And holy *is* his name.
50 And [o] his mercy *is* on them that fear him
From generation to generation.
51 He [p] hath showed strength with his arm:
[q] He hath scattered the proud in the imagination of their hearts.
52 He [r] hath put down the mighty from *their* seats,
And exalted them of low degree.
53 He [s] hath filled the hungry with good things;
And the rich he hath sent empty away.
54 He hath holpen his servant Israel, [t] in remembrance of *his* mercy,
55 As [u] he spake to our fathers, to Abraham, and to his seed for ever.
56 And Mary abode with her about three months, and returned to her
own house.

A. M. 4000.

[3] Or, which believed that there.
[l] 1 Sam. 2. 1.
[m] 1 Sam. 1. 11. Ps. 138. 6.
[n] Mal. 3. 12. ch. 11. 27.
[o] Gen. 17. 7. Ex. 20. 6. Ps. 85. 9. Ps. 118. 4. Ps. 145. 19. Ps. 147. 11. Mal. 3. 16-18. Rev. 19. 5.
[p] Ps. 98. 1. Ps. 118. 15.
[q] Ps. 33. 10. 1 Pet. 5. 5.
[r] 1 Sam. 2. 6. Ps. 113. 6.
[s] Ps. 34. 10.
[t] Ps. 98. 3. Jer. 31. 3, 20.
[u] Gen. 17. 19. Gal. 3. 16.

---

be able to see the propriety of calling an unborn child "Lord," but by supposing Elisabeth, like the prophets of old, enlightened to perceive the Messiah's *Divine nature.*' Cf. ch. xx. 42; John xx. 28. **44. For, lo, as soon, &c. 45. And blessed is she that believed: for** [ὅτι] **there shall be a performance of those things which were told her from the Lord**—or, rather, perhaps (as in *marg.*) "Blessed is she that believed that there shall be a performance," &c. But the word will bear either sense. This is an additional benediction on the Virgin for her implicit faith, in tacit and delicate contrast with her own husband. **46. And Mary said**—Magnificent canticle! in which the strain of Hannah's ancient song, in like circumstances, is caught up, and just slightly modified and sublimed. Is it unnatural to suppose that the spirit of the blessed Virgin had been drawn beforehand into mysterious sympathy with the ideas and the tone of this hymn, so that when the life and fire of inspiration penetrated her whole soul it spontaneously swept the chords of this song, enriching the Hymnal of the Church with that spirit-stirring canticle which has resounded ever since from its temple walls? In both songs those holy women—filled with wonder to behold "the proud, the mighty, the rich," passed by, and, in their persons, the lowliest chosen to usher in the greatest events—sing of this as being no exceptional movement but a great law of the kingdom of God, by which He delights to "put down the mighty from their seats, and exalt them of low degree." In both songs the strain dies away on CHRIST; in Hannah's, under the name of "Jehovah's King," to whom, through all His line from David onwards to Himself, He will "give strength," and as His "Anointed," whose horn He will exalt (1 Sam. ii. 10); in the Virgin's song, it is as the "Help" promised to Israel by all the prophets.

My soul doth magnify the Lord, 47. And my spirit—or, "all that is within me" (Ps. ciii. 1), **hath rejoiced in God my Saviour.** Mary never dreamt, we see, of her 'own immaculate conception'—to use the offensive language of the Romanists—any more than of her own immaculate life. **48. For he hath regarded the low estate of his handmaiden**—for the family of David was now very low in Israel (as predicted, Isa. xi. 1). **for, behold, from henceforth all generations shall call me blessed.** In spirit, her eye stretching into all succeeding time, and beholding the blessed fruits of Messiah's benign and universal sceptre, her heart is overpowered with the honour in which herself shall be held in every succeeding age, as having been selected to give Him birth. **49-53. For he that is mighty hath done to me great things . . . 50. And his mercy is on them that fear him from generation to generation. 51. He hath showed strength with his arm . . . 52. He hath put down the mighty . . . 53. He hath filled the hungry, &c.** [The *aorists* here—ἐποίησεν, down to ἐξαπέστειλεν—express a general principle, as seen in a succession of single examples; according to a known, though peculiar application of that tense.] Mary here recognizes, in God's procedure towards herself—in His passing by all those families and individuals whom He might have been expected to select for such an honour, and pitching upon one so insignificant as herself—one of the greatest laws of His kingdom in overpowering operation, (cf. ch. xiv. 11; xviii. 14, &c.) **54. He hath holpen his servant Israel, in remembrance of his mercy.** Cf. Ps. lxxxix. 19, "I have laid *help* on One that is mighty." **55. (As he spake to our fathers)**—*These words should be read as a parenthesis,* **to Abraham**—that is, in remembrance of His mercy to Abraham, **and to his seed for ever.** See on *v.* 33, and cf. Mic. vii. 20; Ps. xcviii. 3.

56. And Mary abode with her about three months—that is, till there should be visible evidence of the fulfilment of the promise regarding her, **and returned to her own house**—at Nazareth. She had not yet been taken home by Joseph; but that was the next, or fourth, scene in this divine History. See on Matt. i. 18-25, where alone it is recorded.

Remarks.—1. 'Only the meeting of saints in heaven,' as *Bishop Hall* well remarks, 'can parallel the meeting of these two cousins: the two wonders of the world are met under one

57 Now Elisabeth's full time came that she should be delivered; and
58 she brought forth a son. And her neighbours and her cousins heard
how the Lord had showed great mercy upon her; and they rejoiced
with her.
59 And it came to pass, that [v]on the eighth day they came to circumcise
the child; and they called him Zacharias, after the name of his father.
60 And his mother answered and said, Not *so;* but he shall be called John.
61 And they said unto her, There is none of thy kindred that is called by
62 this name. And they made signs to his father, how he would have him
63 called. And he asked for a writing table, and wrote, saying, His name
64 is John. And they marvelled all. And his mouth was opened im-
65 mediately, and his tongue *loosed,* and he spake, and praised God. And
fear came on all that dwelt round about them: and all these [4]sayings
66 were noised abroad throughout all the hill country of Judea. And
all they that heard *them* [w]laid *them* up in their hearts, saying, What
manner of child shall this be! And [x]the hand of the Lord was with
him.
67 And his father Zacharias [y]was filled with the Holy Ghost, and prophesied, saying,

A. M. 4000.
[v] Gen. 17. 12. Gen. 21. 4. Lev. 12. 3. ch. 2. 21. Acts 7. 8. Phil. 3. 5.
[4] Or, things.
[w] Gen. 37. 11. Dan. 7. 28. ch. 2. 19. ch. 9. 44.
[x] Gen. 39. 2. Jud. 13. 24. 1 Sam. 2. 18. 1 Sam. 16. 18. 1 Ki. 18. 46. Ps. 80. 17. Ps. 89. 21. Acts 11. 21.
[y] Num. 11. 25. 2 Sam. 23. 2. 2 Chr. 20. 14. Joel 2. 28. 2 Pet. 1. 21.

roof, and congratulate their mutual happiness.' 2. What an honoured roof was that which for the period of three months overarched those holy women, whose progeny—though the one was but the herald of the other—have made the world new! And yet not a trace of it is now to be seen, nor can it even be known, save by inference, what "city of Juda" is meant to which the Virgin hied her to visit her relative. This remark, applicable to most of the so-called 'holy places,' not only rebukes the childish superstition of the Greek and Latin Churches, which have built convents at nearly all these places, and filled them with lazy monks, whose monotonous and dreary services are designed to commemorate the events of which they were the scenes, but may also suggest matter for useful reflection to a class of Protestants whose religion is not free from the same tincture. 3. How beautiful does womanhood appear in the light of the foregoing scenes—the grace of God making the "spices" of modesty, simplicity, and religious susceptibility, which are the characteristics of the sex, so charmingly to "flow out!" And yet these are but premonitions of what we shall meet with throughout all this History of Him to whom woman owes not only the common salvation but the recovery of her proper relation to the other sex. 4. 'How should our hearts leap within us,' to use again the words of *Bishop Hall,* 'when the Son of God vouchsafes to come into the secret of our souls, not to visit us, but to dwell with us, to dwell in us!'

57-80.—Birth, Circumcision, and Naming of the Forerunner—Song of Zacharias, and Progress of the Child.

Birth, Circumcision, and Naming of the Forerunner (57-66). **57. Now Elisabeth's full time came . . . and she brought forth a son. 58. And her neighbours . . . rejoiced with her. 59. And it came to pass, that on the eighth day they came to circumcise the child.** The law which required circumcision to be performed on the eighth day (Gen. xvii. 12) was so strictly observed, that it was done even on the Sabbath if it fell on that day; although it was of the nature of servile work, which on the Sabbath day was prohibited. See John vii. 22, 23; and Phil. iii. 5. **and they called him** [ἐκάλουν]—rather, 'were calling,' that is, 'were going to call him' **Zacharias.** The naming of children at baptism has its origin in this Jewish custom at circumcision (Gen. xxi. 3, 4; ch. ii. 21), and the names of Abram and Sarai were changed at its first performance (Gen. xvii. 5, 15). **after the name of his father. 60-63. And his mother answered and said, Not so; but he shall be called John . . . And they made signs to his father, how he would have him called**—showing that he was deaf as well as dumb. **And he asked for a writing table, and wrote, saying, His name is John. And they marvelled all**—at his concurring with his wife in giving to the child a name so new in the family; not knowing of any communication between them on the subject. **64. And his mouth was opened immediately, and his tongue loosed**—on his thus showing how entirely the unbelief for which he had been struck dumb had passed away. Probably it ceased immediately on his receiving the *sign,* so different from what he expected; and as the truth of the promise became palpable in Elisabeth, and was so gloriously confirmed during the visit of Mary, it would ripen doubtless into full assurance. But the words of the angel behoved to be fulfilled to the letter, "Thou shalt be dumb *until the day that these things shall be performed;*" and since one of these things was "*Thou shalt call his name John,*" it was fitting that not before, but "immediately" upon his doing this, his mouth should be opened. **and he spake, and praised God.** The song in which he did this being long, the Evangelist postpones it till he has recorded the effect which these strange doings produced upon the neighbourhood. **65. And fear**—or a religious awe, **came on all that dwelt round about them**—under the conviction that God's hand was specially in these events (cf. ch. v. 26; vii. 16): **and all these sayings were noised abroad throughout all the hill country of Judea. 66. And all they that heard them laid them up in their hearts, saying, What manner of child shall this be!** Yet there is every reason to believe that long ere John appeared in public all these things were forgotten, nor were recalled even after that by his wonderful success. **And the hand of the Lord was with him**—by special tokens marking him out as destined to some great work (cf. 1 Ki. xviii. 46; 2 Ki. iii. 15; Acts xi. 21).

67. And Zacharias was filled with the Holy Ghost, and prophesied—or, spake by inspiration, according to the Scripture sense of that term. It

68 Blessed *be* the Lord God of Israel;
For he hath visited and redeemed his people,
69 And hath raised up an horn of salvation for us
In the house of his servant David;
70 As [z]he spake by the mouth of his holy prophets,
Which have been since the world began;
71 That we should be saved from our enemies,
And from the hand of all that hate us;
72 To [a]perform the mercy *promised* to our fathers,
And to remember his holy covenant,
73 The [b]oath which he sware to our father Abraham,
74 That he would grant unto us,
That we, being delivered out of the hand of our enemies,
Might [c]serve him without fear,
75 In [d]holiness and righteousness before him, all the days of our life.
76 And thou, child, shalt be called the Prophet of the Highest:
For [e]thou shalt go before the face of the Lord to prepare his ways:
77 To give knowledge of salvation unto his people,
[5]By the remission of their sins,

A. M. 4000.
[z] Jer. 23. 5. Jer. 30. 10. Dan. 9. 24. Acts 3. 21. Rom. 1. 2.
[a] Gen. 12. 3. Lev. 26. 42. Ps 98. 3. Acts 3. 25.
[b] Gen. 12. 3. Heb. 6. 13.
[c] Rom. 6. 18. Heb. 9. 14.
[d] Jer. 32. 39. Eph. 4. 24. 2 Thes. 2. 13. 2 Tim. 1. 9. Titus 2. 12. 1 Pet. 1. 15. 2 Pet. 1. 4.
[e] Isa. 40. 3. Mal 3. 1. Matt 11. 10.
[5] Or, for.

did not necessarily include the prediction of future events, though here it certainly did. **saying,**

68. Blessed. There is not a word in this noble burst of divine song about his own relationship to this child, nor about the child at all, till it has expended itself upon Christ. Like rapt Elisabeth, Zacharias loses sight entirely of self in the glory of a Greater than both. **be the Lord God of Israel**—the ancient covenant-God of the peculiar people; **for he hath visited and redeemed**—that is, visited in order to redeem **his people**—returning to His own after long absence, and now for the first time breaking the silence of centuries. In the Old Testament God is said to "visit" chiefly for *judgment*, in the New Testament for *mercy*. Zacharias—looking from the Israelitish point of view—would as yet have but imperfect apprehensions of the design of this "visit" and the nature of this "redemption." But though, when he sang of "salvation from our enemies, and from the hand of all that hated us," the *lower* and more *outward* sense would naturally occur first to Zacharias as a devout Jew, his words are equally adapted, when viewed in the light of a loftier and more comprehensive kingdom of God, to convey the most spiritual conceptions of the redemption that is in Christ Jesus. (But see on *v.* 77.) **69. And hath raised up an horn of salvation for us**—that is, a 'strength of salvation,' or 'a mighty salvation;' meaning the Saviour Himself, whom Simeon in his song calls "Thy Salvation" (ch. ii. 30). The metaphor is taken from those animals whose strength lies in their horns, and was familiar in the Psalmody of the agricultural Jews, (Ps. cxxxii. 17; lxxv. 10; xviii. 2, &c.) **in the house of his servant David.** *This shows that Mary must have been of the royal line*, independent of Joseph—of whom Zacharias could not know that after this he would recognize his legal connection with Mary. The Davidic genealogy of the Messiah, as it was one of the most prominent of His predicted characteristics, and one by which the Jews were warranted and prepared to test the pretensions of any claimant of that office who should arise, so it is here emphatically sung of as fulfilled in the unborn Offspring of the blessed Virgin. **70. As he spake by the mouth of his holy prophets, which have been since the world began**—or, from the earliest period. **71. That we should be saved from our enemies, and from the hand of all that hate us; 72. To perform the mercy promised to our fathers, and to remember his holy covenant, 73. The oath which he sware to our father Abraham.** The whole work of Messiah, and the kingdom He was to establish on the earth, are represented here as a mercy promised, and pledged on oath, to Abraham and his seed, to be at an appointed period—"the fulness of time"—gloriously made good. Hence, not only "*grace*," or the thing promised, but "*truth*," or fidelity to the promise, are said to "come by Jesus Christ" (see on John i. 14, 16, 17). **74. That he would grant unto us, that we, being delivered out of the hand of our enemies, might serve him without fear, 75. In holiness and righteousness before him, all the days of our life.** How rich and comprehensive is the view here given of Messiah's work! First, the grand *purpose* of redemption—"that we should serve Him," that is, "the Lord God of Israel" (*v.* 68): the word [λατρεύειν] signifies *religious* service, and points to the priesthood of believers under the New Testament (Heb. xiii. 10, 15). Second, the *nature* of this service—"in holiness and righteousness before Him"—or, in His presence (cf. Ps. lvi. 13). Third, its *freedom*—"being delivered out of the hand of our enemies." Fourth, its *fearlessness*—"might serve Him without fear." Fifth, its *duration*—"all our days." [The words τῆς ζωῆς are quite wanting in authority.]

76-79. Here are the dying echoes of this song: and very beautiful are these closing notes—like the setting sun, shorn indeed of its noon-tide radiance, but skirting the horizon with a wavy and quivering light, as of molten gold—on which the eye delights to gaze, till it disappears from the view. The song passes not here from Christ to John, but only from Christ direct, to Christ as heralded by his Forerunner. **76. And thou, child**—not, 'thou, my son,' for this child's relation to himself was lost in his relation to a Greater than either; **shalt be called the Prophet of the Highest: for thou shalt go before the face of the Lord**—that is, "before the face of the Most High." As this epithet is in Scripture applied to the supreme God, it is inconceivable that Inspiration should here so plainly apply it to Christ, if He were not "over all, God blessed for ever" (Rom. ix. 5). **77. To give knowledge of salvation.** To sound the note of a needed and provided salvation—now at the

78 Through the [6] tender mercy of our God,
Whereby the [7] dayspring from on high hath visited us,
79 To [f] give light to them that sit in darkness and *in* the shadow of death,
To guide our feet into the way of peace.
80 And the child grew, and waxed strong in spirit, and was in the deserts
till the day of his showing unto Israel.

2 AND it came to pass in those days, that there went out a decree from
2 Cesar Augustus, that all the world should be [1] taxed. (*And* this taxing
3 was first made when Cyrenius was governor of Syria.) And all went to

A. M. 4000.

[6] Or, bowels of the mercy.
[7] Or, sunrising.
[f] Isa 9. 2.

CHAP. 2.
[1] Or, enrolled in order to be taxed.

door—was the noble, the distinguishing office of the Forerunner. **by**—rather, 'in' **the remission of their sins** [ἐν ἀφέσει ἁμαρτιῶν αὐτῶν]—this remission being, not the way, but rather the primary element of salvation (cf. 1 John ii. 12). This view of salvation throws great light upon the *Jewish* language of verses 71 and 74, about "deliverance from enemies," stamping an undeniably *spiritual* character upon it. **78. Through the tender mercy of our God**—which is, and must be, the sole spring of all salvation for sinners; **whereby the dayspring from on high hath visited us.** This may mean either Christ Himself, as "the Sun of Righteousness" arising on a dark world (so *Calvin*, *Beza*, *Grotius*, *de Wette*, *Olshausen*, &c., understand it), or the glorious light which He sheds: the sense is the same. **79. To give light to them that sit in darkness and in the shadow**—rather, 'in the darkness and shadow' **of death**—meaning, 'in the most utter darkness.' So this expression should always be understood in the Old Testament, from which it is taken. Even in Ps. xxiii. 4, its application to the *dying hour* is but one, though certainly the most resistless and delightful, application of a great comprehensive truth—that believers have no reason to fear the most unrelieved darkness through which, in the mysterious providence of "the Lord their Shepherd," they may be called to pass. **to guide our feet into the way of peace.** Christianity is distinguished from all other religions, not only in bringing to men *what* the troubled spirit most needs—"peace," even "the peace of God, which passeth all understanding"—but in opening up the one only "*way* of peace."

80. And the child grew, and waxed strong [ηὔξανεν καὶ ἐκραταιοῦτο] **in spirit.** The grammatical tenses here employed denote the continuance of the action—'kept growing (that is, bodily) and waxing strong in spirit,' or in mental development. **and was in the deserts**—probably "the wilderness of Judea," whence we find him issuing on his entrance into public life (Matt. iii. 1). **till the day of his showing unto Israel**—or of his presenting himself before the nation as Messiah's Forerunner. Retiring into this wilderness in early life, in the true Nazarite spirit, and there free from rabbinical influences and alone with God, his spirit would be educated, like Moses in the desert of Sinai, for his future high vocation.

Remarks.—1. While to the believing Gentiles—"aliens from the commonwealth of Israel, and strangers from the covenants of promise"—the Gospel came with all the freshness of an overpowering novelty; it came to the devout Israelite with all the charm of ancient and oft-repeated promises at length fulfilled, of hopes, divinely kindled but long deferred, in the end unexpectedly realized. It is this latter view of the Gospel which reigns in Zacharias' noble song, in which God is seen 'mindful of His grace and truth' to the house of Israel, accomplishing the high objects of the ancient economy, and introducing His people into the blessedness of a realized salvation, and the dignity of a free and fearless service of their covenant-God. 2. The "Fearlessness" of the Christian life is no less emphatically celebrated here (*v.* 74) than its priestly sanctity and enduring character (*v.* 75): but is this a leading and manifest feature in our current Christianity? 3. If "the remission of our sins" be the primary element of our salvation (*v.* 77), why is it that there are so many of God's dear children who "through fear of death are all their lifetime subject to bondage"? For if "the sting of death be [unpardoned] sin," what else than the sense of forgiveness can dissolve that fear? And surely it cannot be God's will that His children should have to meet the last enemy without that weapon which effectually disarms him. 4. Seasons of comparative retirement have usually preceded and proved a precious preparative for great public usefulness: for example, Moses' sojourn in Midian; the Baptist's stay in the Judean desert (*v.* 80); our Lord's own privacy at Nazareth; Paul's three years in Arabia; Luther's ten month's seclusion at Wartburg; and Zwingli's two years and a half at Einsiedeln.

CHAP. II. 1-7.—THE BIRTH OF CHRIST.

1. And it came to pass in those days—a general reference to the foregoing transactions, particularly the birth of John, which preceded that of our Lord by about six months (ch. i. 26). **that there went out a decree from Cesar Augustus**—the first of the Roman emperors—**that all the world**—that is, the Roman empire; so called as being now virtually world-wide. **should be taxed**—or 'enrolled,' or 'register themselves.' **2. (And this taxing was first made when Cyrenius was governor of Syria)**—a very perplexing verse, inasmuch as Cyrenius, or Quirinus, appears not to have been governor of Syria for about ten years after the birth of Christ, and the taxing under his administration was what led to the insurrection alluded to in Acts v. 37 (cf. *Joseph.* Antt. xviii. 1. 1). That Augustus took steps towards introducing uniform taxation throughout the empire, has been proved beyond dispute (by *Savigny*, the highest authority on the Roman law); and candid critics, even of sceptical tendency, are forced to allow that no such glaring anachronism as the words, on the first blush of them, seem to imply, was likely to be fallen into by a writer so minutely accurate on Roman affairs as our Evangelist shows himself, in the Acts, to be. Some superior scholars would render the words thus: 'This registration was *previous to* Cyrenius being governor of Syria.' In this case, of course, the difficulty vanishes. But, as this is a very precarious sense of the word [πρώτη], it is better, with others, to understand the Evangelist to mean; that though the registration was now ordered with a view to the taxation, the taxing itself—an obnoxious measure in Palestine—was not carried out till the time of Quirinus. **3. And all went to be taxed, every one into his own city**—*i.e.*, the city of his *extraction*, according to the Jewish custom; not of his *abode*, which was the usual Roman method. **4. And Joseph also went up from Galilee, out of the**

4 be taxed, every one into his own city. And Joseph also went up from
Galilee, out of the city of Nazareth, into Judea, unto [a]the city of David,
which is called Bethlehem, ([b]because he was of the house and lineage of
5 David,) to be taxed with Mary his espoused wife, being great with child.
6 And so it was, that, while they were there, the days were accomplished
7 that she should be delivered. And [c]she brought forth her first-born
son, and wrapped him in swaddling clothes, and laid him in [d]a manger;
because there was no room for them in the inn.

A. M. 4000.

[a] 1 Sam. 16. 1. Mic. 5. 2. John 7. 42.
[b] Matt. 1. 16. ch. 1. 27.
[c] Matt. 1. 25. Gal. 4. 4.
[d] Isa. 53. 2. 2 Cor. 4. 4.

city of Nazareth, into Judea, unto the city of David, which is called Bethlehem, (because he was of the house and lineage of David.) The transfer from the one province to the other, and from the one city to the other, is carefully noted. **5. To be taxed with Mary his espoused**—'betrothed' **wife.** She had sometime before this been taken home by Joseph (see on Matt. i. 18-24); but she is so called here, perhaps, for the reason mentioned in Matt. i. 25. **being great with child.** Not only does Joseph, as being of the royal line, go to Bethlehem (1 Sam. xvi. 1), but Mary too; not from choice, surely, in her tender condition. It is possible that in this they simply followed the Roman method, of the wife accompanying the husband; but the more likely reason would seem to be that she herself was of the family of David.

6. And so it was, that, while they were there, the days were accomplished that she should be delivered. Mary had up to this time been living at the wrong place for Messiah's birth. A little longer stay at Nazareth, and the prophecy of His birth at Bethlehem would have failed. But, lo! with no intention on her part—much less on the part of Cesar Augustus—to fulfil the prophecy, she is brought from Nazareth to Bethlehem, and at that very nick of time her period for delivery arrives. **7. And she brought forth her first-born son** (see on Matt. i. 25), **and wrapped him in swaddling clothes, and laid him**—that is, the mother herself did so. Had she then none to assist her in such circumstances? All we can say is, it would seem so. **in a manger**—or crib, in which was placed the horses' food, **because there was no room for them in the inn**—a square erection, open inside, where travellers put up, and whose back parts were used as stables. The ancient tradition, that our Lord was born in a grotto or cave, is quite consistent with this, the country being rocky. In Mary's condition the journey would be a slow one, and ere they arrived the inn would be preoccupied—affecting anticipation of the reception He was throughout to meet with (John i. 11).

> 'Wrapt in His swaddling bands,
> And in His manger laid,
> The hope and glory of all lands
> Is come to the world's aid.
> No peaceful home upon His cradle smiled,
> Guests rudely went and came where slept the royal Child.'
> KEBLE.

But some '**guests went and came**,' *not* 'rudely,' but reverently. God sent visitors of His own to pay court to the new-born King.

Remarks.—1. Cesar Augustus had his own ends to serve in causing steps to be taken for a general census of his kingdom. But God had ends in it too, and infinitely higher. Augustus must bring Joseph and Mary to Bethlehem, and bring them just before the time for the Virgin's delivery, that the mark of His Son's birth-place, which He had set up seven centuries before, might not be missed. Even so must Pharaoh dream, that Joseph might be summoned from prison to read it; and dream such a dream as required Joseph's elevation to be governor of all Egypt, in order to the fulfilment of divine predictions (Gen. xl., &c.); and king Ahasuerus must pass a sleepless night, and beguile the weary hours with the chronicles of the kingdom, and read there of his obligations to Mordecai for the preservation of his life, in order that at the moment when he was to be sacrificed he might be lifted into a position to save his whole people (Esth. vi.); and Belshazzar must dream, and his dream must pass from him, and the wise men of Babylon must be required both to tell and to interpret it on pain of death, and all of them fail, in order that Daniel, by doing both, might be promoted along with his companions, for the present good and ultimate deliverance of his people, (Dan. ii., &c.) 2. In the Roman edict, which brought the Jews of Palestine to their several tribal towns, we see one of the badges of their lost independence. The splendour of the theocracy was now going fast down: but this was doubtless divinely ordered, that the new glory of Messiah's kingdom, which it dimly shadowed forth, might the more strikingly appear. 3. Our Evangelist simply records the fact, that the new-born Babe of Bethlehem was laid in a manger, because there was no room for them in the inn; leaving his readers from age to age to their own reflections on so stupendous a dispensation. 'Thou camest,' exclaims *Bp. Hall*, 'to Thine own, and Thine own received thee not: how can it trouble us to be rejected of the world, which is not ours?'

8-20.—ANGELIC ANNUNCIATION TO THE SHEPHERDS OF THE SAVIOUR'S BIRTH—THEIR VISIT TO THE NEW-BORN BABE.

Annunciation to the Shepherds (8-14). **8. And there were in the same country shepherds abiding in the field**—staying there, probably in huts or tents, **keeping watch** [φυλάσσοντες φυλακὰς τῆς νυκτὸς]—rather, 'keeping the night watches,' or taking their turn of watching **by night.** From this most critics, since *Lightfoot*, conclude that the time which, since the fourth century, has been ecclesiastically fixed upon for the celebration of Christ's birth—the 25th of December, or the midst of the rain season—cannot be the true time, as the shepherds drove their flocks about the spring or passover time out to the fields, and remained out with them all summer, under cover of huts or tents, returning with them late in the autumn. But recent travellers tell us that in the end of December, after the rains, the flowers come again into bloom, and the flocks again issue forth. The nature of the seasons in Palestine could hardly have been unknown to those who fixed upon the present Christmas-period: the difficulty, therefore, is perhaps more imaginary than real. But leaving this question undecided, another of some interest may be asked—Were these shepherds chosen to have the first sight of the blessed Babe without any respect to their own state of mind? That, at least, is not God's way. No doubt, as *Olshausen* remarks, they were, like Simeon (*v.* 25), among the waiters for the Consolation of Israel; and if the simplicity of their rustic minds, their quiet occupation, the stillness of the midnight hours, and the amplitude of the deep

8 And there were in the same country shepherds abiding in the field,
9 keeping [2]watch over their flock by night. And, lo, the angel of the
Lord came upon them, and the glory of the Lord shone round about
10 them; and they were sore afraid. And the angel said unto them, Fear
not; for, behold, I bring you good tidings of great joy, [e]which shall be
11 to all people. For [f]unto you is born this day, in the city of David, a
12 Saviour, [g]which is Christ the Lord. And this *shall be* a sign unto you;
Ye shall find the babe wrapped in swaddling clothes, lying in a manger.
13 And [h]suddenly there was with the angel a multitude of the heavenly
14 host praising God, and saying, Glory to God in the highest, and on
earth peace, good will toward men.

A. M. 4000.

2 Or, the night watches.
e Gen. 12. 3. Col. 1. 23.
f Isa. 9. 6. Matt. 1. 21 Gal. 4. 4. 2 Tim. 1. 9. 1 John 4. 14.
g Phil. 2. 11.
h Gen. 28. 12. Ps. 103. 20.

blue vault above them for the heavenly music which was to fill their ear, pointed them out as fit recipients for the first tidings of an Infant Saviour, the congenial meditations and conversations by which, we may suppose, they would beguile the tedious hours would perfect their preparation for the unexpected visit. Thus was Nathanael engaged, all alone but not unseen, under the fig tree, in unconscious preparation for his first interview with Jesus. (See on John i. 48.) So was the rapt seer on his lonely rock "in the spirit on the Lord's day," little thinking that this was his preparation for hearing behind him the trumpet-voice of the Son of Man, (Rev. i. 10, &c.) But if the shepherds in his immediate neighbourhood had the *first*, the sages from afar had the *next* sight of the new-born King. Even so still, simplicity first, science next, finds its way to Christ. Whom,

'In quiet ever and in shade
Shepherd and Sage may find;
They who have bowed untaught to Nature's sway,
And they who follow Truth along her star-pav'd way.'

KEBLE.

9. And, lo, the angel of the Lord came upon them, and the glory of the Lord—'the brightness or glory which is represented as encompassing all heavenly visions,' to use the words of *Olshausen*, **and they were sore afraid.** See on ch. i. 12. **10. And the angel said unto them, Fear not** (see on ch. i. 13); **for, behold, I bring you good tidings of great joy, which shall be to all people** [παντὶ τῷ λαῷ]—or rather, 'to the whole people;' meaning the chosen people of Israel, but only to be by them afterwards extended to the whole world, as a message of "good will to *men*" (*v.* 14). **11. For unto you is born this day, in the city of David, a Saviour, which is Christ the Lord.** Every word here contains transporting intelligence from heaven. For whom provided? "To *you*"—shepherds, Israel, mankind. Who is provided? "A SAVIOUR." What is He? "CHRIST THE LORD." How introduced into the world? He "is *born*"—as said the prophet, "Unto us a child is born" (Isa. ix. 6); "the Word was made flesh" (John i. 14). When? "*This Day.*" Where? "*In the city of David.*" In the predicted line, and at the predicted spot, where prophecy bade us look for Him and faith accordingly expected Him. How dear to us should be these historical moorings of our faith, with the loss of which all historical Christianity vanishes! By means of them how many have been kept from making shipwreck, and have attained to a certain admiration of Christ, ere yet they have fully "beheld His glory"! Nor does the angel say that One is born who *shall be* a Saviour, but He "is *born* a Saviour;" adding, "which is CHRIST THE LORD." 'Magnificent appellation!' exclaims devout *Bengel*. *Alford* notices that these words come together nowhere else, and sees no way of understanding this "Lord" but as corresponding to the Hebrew word JEHOVAH. **12. And this shall be a sign** [τὸ σημεῖον]—'the sign,' **unto you; Ye shall find the babe** [βρέφος]—'a Babe.' Pity that our translators so often insert the definite article where it is emphatically wanting in the original, and omit it where in the original it is emphatically inserted. **wrapped in swaddling clothes, lying in a manger.** Here the article, though existing in the received text, ought not to be there, having but weak authority: our translators, therefore, are right here. The sign, it seems, was to consist solely in the overpowering *contrast* between the lofty things just said of Him and the lowly condition in which they would find Him. 'Him whose goings forth have been from of old, from everlasting, ye shall find a Babe: Whom the heaven of heavens cannot contain ye shall find "wrapped in swaddling bands and lying in a manger!"' Thus early were those amazing contrasts, which are His chosen style, held forth. (See 2 Cor. viii. 9.) **13. And suddenly**—as if eager to break in as soon as the last words of the wonderful tidings had dropped from their fellow's lips, **there was with the angel**—not in place of him; for he retires not, and is only joined by others, come to seal and to celebrate the tidings which he was honoured first to announce, **a multitude of the heavenly host**—or 'army;' 'An army,' as *Bengel* quaintly remarks, 'celebrating peace!' come down to let it be known here how this great event is regarded in heaven: **praising God, and saying, 14. Glory to God in the highest, and on earth peace, good will toward men**—brief but transporting hymn, not only in articulate human speech for our behoof, but in tunable measure, in the form of a Hebrew parallelism of two complete members, and a third one, as we take it, only explaining and amplifying the second, and so without the connecting "and." The "glory to God" which the new-born Saviour was to bring is the first note of this exalted hymn, and was sounded forth probably by one detachment of the choir. To this answers the "peace on earth," of which He was to be the Prince (Isa. ix. 6), probably sung responsively by a second detachment of the celestial choir; while quick follows the glad echo of this note—"good will to men"—by a third detachment, we may suppose, of these angelic choristers. Thus:—

First division of the celestial choir—

"GLORY TO GOD IN THE HIGHEST."

Second——

"AND ON EARTH PEACE."

Third——

"GOOD WILL TO MEN."

Peace with God is the grand necessity of a fallen world. To bring in this, in whose train comes all other peace worthy of the name, was the prime errand of the Saviour to this earth. This effected, Heaven's whole "good will to men" or the Divine complacency [εὐδοκία, cf. Eph. i. 5, 9; Phil. ii. 13, &c.] descends now on a new footing to rest upon men, even as upon the Son Himself, "in

15 And it came to pass, as the angels were gone away from them into
heaven, [3]the shepherds said one to another, [i]Let us now go even unto
Bethlehem, and see this thing which is come to pass, which the Lord
16 hath made known unto us. And they came with haste, and found Mary
17 and Joseph, and the babe lying in a manger. And when they had seen
it, they made known abroad the saying which was told them concerning
18 this child. And all they that heard *it* wondered at those things which
19 were told them by the shepherds. But [j]Mary kept all these things, and
20 pondered *them* in her heart. And the shepherds returned, glorifying
and praising God for all the things that they had heard and seen, as it
was told unto them.

A. M. 4000.

[3] The men the shepherds.

[i] Ex. 3. 3. Ps. 111. 2. Matt. 2. 1. Matt. 12. 42. John 20. 1-10.

[j] Gen. 37. 11. 1 Sam. 21. 12. Pro. 4. 4. Hos. 14. 9.

whom God is well pleased" [εὐδόκησα, Matt. iii. 17]. *Bengel* notices that they say not 'glory to God in heaven,'—but using a rare expression—"in the highest" heavens [ἐν ὑψίστοις], whither angels aspire not (Heb. i. 3, 4). [The reading, 'to men of good will'—ἐν ἀνθρώποις εὐδοκίας—is introduced into the text by *Tischendorf* and *Tregelles*, after *Lachmann*—on the authority of the Alexandrian and Beza MSS. (A and D); but chiefly on the strength of the Latin versions, and from the difficulty of accounting for so uncommon a reading occurring at all if not genuine. In this case the sense will still be agreeable to Scripture doctrine—'to men of (His, that is, God's) good will,' or the objects of the Divine complacency; not as the Romish Church, after the Vulgate, take it to mean, 'to men of good disposition.' But the great preponderance of MSS. and versions is in favour of the received reading; nor will the objections to it, as spoiling the rhythm, appear of the least force in the view we have given of it above, but just the reverse. *De Wette*, *Meyer*, *Alford*, and *van Osterzee*, are decidedly in favour of the received reading.]

Visit of the Shepherds to the New-born Babe (15-20). **15. And it came to pass, as the angels were gone away from them into heaven, the shepherds** [οἱ ἄνθρωποι οἱ ποιμένες]—'the men, the shepherds,' in contrast with the angelic party, **said one to another, Let us now go even unto Bethlehem, and see this thing which is come to pass, which the Lord hath made known unto us.** Lovely simplicity of devoutness and faith this! They say not, Let us go and see if this be true—for they have no misgivings—but, "Let us go and see this thing *which is come to pass*, which the Lord hath *made known unto us*." Does not this confirm the view we have given (on *v.* 8) of the previous character of these humble shepherds? Nor are they taken up with the angels, the glory that invested them, and the lofty strains with which they filled the air. It is the Wonder itself, the Babe of Bethlehem, that absorbs these devout shepherds. **16. And they came with haste** (see on ch. i. 39; Matt. xxviii. 8), **and found Mary**—'mysteriously guided,' says *Olshausen*, 'to the right place through the obscurity of the night,' **and Joseph, and the babe lying in a manger**—[ἐν τῃ φάτνῃ] 'the manger', of which the angel had told them. **17. And when they had seen it, they made known abroad the saying which was told them concerning this child**—that is, as is evident from *v.* 20, before they left the neighbourhood. And so they were, as *Bengel* remarks, the first evangelists; having, indeed, no commission, but feeling with Peter and John, "We cannot but speak the things which we have seen and heard." **18. And all they that heard it wondered at those things which were told them by the shepherds. 19. But Mary kept all these things, and pondered**—or 'revolved' **them in her heart**—seeking to gather from them, in combination, what light she could as to the future of this wondrous Babe of hers. **20. And the shepherds returned, glorifying and praising God for all the things that they had heard and seen, as it was told unto them.** The word for "praising" [αἰνοῦντες]—used of the song of the angels (*v.* 13), and in ch. xix. 37, and xxiv. 53—would lead us to suppose that theirs was a song too, and perhaps some canticle from the Psalter; meet vehicle for the swelling emotions of their simple hearts at what "they had seen and heard."

Remarks.—1. Not in the busy hum of day, but in the profound stillness of night, came these heavenly visitants to the shepherds of Bethlehem. So came the Lord to Abraham (Gen. xv.); and once and again to Jacob, (Gen. xxviii.; xxxii.; xlvi. 2, &c.) It was in the night season that Jesus Himself was transfigured on the mount. And who can tell what visits of Heaven were paid Him when He spent whole nights alone in prayer? See Ps. iv. 4; lxiii. 6; cxix. 55, 62, 147, 148; Isa. xxvi. 9; Job xxxv. 10.

'Sun of my soul, Thou Saviour dear,
It is not night if Thou be near:
O may no earth-born cloud arise
To hide Thee from thy servant's eyes.

'Abide with me from morn till eve,
For without Thee I cannot live:
Abide with me when night is nigh,
For without Thee I cannot die.'—KEBLE.

2. What a view of heaven is here disclosed to us! As it teems with angels (cf. Deut. xxxiii. 2; 1 Ki. xxii. 19; Ps. lxviii. 17; ciii. 20, 21; cxlviii. 2; Dan. vii. 10; Matt. xxvi. 53; xxv. 31; Rev. v. 11), all orderly, harmonious, and vocal, so their uniting principle, the soul of all their harmony, the Object of their chiefest wonder and transport, is the Word made flesh, the Saviour born in the city of David, Christ the Lord. Accordingly, as Moses and Elias, when they appeared in glory on the mount of transfiguration and talked with Him, "spake of His decease which He should accomplish at Jerusalem" (Luke ix. 31); so we are told that "these things the angels desire to look into" (1 Pet. i. 12); and among the wonders of the Incarnation, this is said to be one, that He "was seen of angels" (1 Tim. iii. 16). Is this our element upon earth? Would our sudden transportation to heaven bring us to "our own company" (Acts iv. 23), and "our own place"—as Judas went to his? (Acts i. 25). By this may all men know whether they be travelling thither. 3. If we would thoroughly sympathize with heaven in its views of Salvation, and be prepared at once to unite in its music, we must take the elements of which salvation consists as heaven here presents them to us. As the "peace on earth" of which they sing—expounded by that "good will to men" which is its abiding result—means God's own peace, or His "reconciling the

21 And [k]when eight days were accomplished for the circumcising of the
child, his name was called [l]JESUS, which was so named of the angel
before he was conceived in the womb.
22 And when [m]the days of her purification according to the law of Moses
were accomplished, they brought him to Jerusalem, to present *him* to

A. M. 4000.

k Gen. 17. 12. Lev. 12. 3. Phil. 2. 8.
l Matt. 1. 21.
m Lev. 12. 2.

world unto Himself by Jesus Christ," we must regard this as the proper spring of all peace between man and man that is thoroughly solid and lasting. And even in experiencing, exemplifying, and diffusing this, let that "glory to God in the highest" which is due on account of the birth into our world of the Prince of peace, and for all that He has done to unite earth to heaven and man to man, be uppermost and first in all our thoughts, affections, and praises. 4. What wondrous contrasts are those shepherds of Bethlehem invited to contemplate—the Lord of glory, a Babe; Christ the Lord, born; the Son of the Highest, wrapped in swaddling bands and lying in a manger! Yet what was this but a foretaste of like overpowering contrasts of Infinite and finite, Divine and human, Fulness and want, Life and death, throughout all His after-history upon earth? "Ye know the grace of our Lord Jesus Christ, that though He was rich, yet for your sakes He became poor, that ye through His poverty might be rich" (2 Cor. viii. 9). Nor is the Church which He hath purchased with His own blood and erected upon earth a stranger to analogous contrasts. 5. When the Evangelist says, "It came to pass, as the angels *were gone away* from them into heaven," we are reminded that this was but a momentary visit—sweet but short. Like their Master, they "ascended up where they were before," even as the shepherds returned to their flocks. But the time is coming when they and we shall dwell together. And so shall we all and ever be with the Lord. 6. Our Evangelist tells us that the shepherds "found Mary and Joseph, and the Babe lying in a manger." But he does *not* tell us what passed between the visitors and the visited in that rude birth-place of the Son of God. Apocryphal gospels would probably manufacture information enough on such topics, and gaping readers would greedily enough drink it in. But the silences of Scripture are as grand and reverend as its disclosures. In this light, when we merely read in the next verse, "And when they had seen [it], they made known abroad the saying that was told them concerning this Child," we feel that there is a Wisdom presiding over these incomparable Narratives, alike in the dropping as in the drawing of the veil, which fills the soul with ever-growing satisfaction. 7. The shepherds, not lifted off their feet, "returned"—"glorifying and praising God," indeed, but still returned—to their proper business. So Jesus Himself, at twelve years of age, after sitting in the temple among the doctors, and filling all with astonishment at His understanding and His answers, "went down with His parents, and came to Nazareth, and was subject unto them" (*v.* 51). Thus should it ever be; and O what a heaven upon earth would this hallowing of earthly occupations and interests and joys and sorrows by heavenly intercourses make!

21-24.—CIRCUMCISION OF THE INFANT SAVIOUR—PURIFICATION OF THE VIRGIN-MOTHER—PRESENTATION OF THE BABE IN THE TEMPLE.

Circumcision of the Infant Saviour (21). **21. And when eight days were accomplished** (see on ch. i. 59) **for the circumcising of the child**—'for circumcising Him' is the better supported reading, **his name was called JESUS, which was so named of the angel before he was conceived,** &c. Circumcision was a symbolical and bloody removal of the body of sin (Col. ii. 11, 13; cf. Deut. x. 16; Jer. iv. 4; Rom. ii. 29). But as if to proclaim, in the very act of performing this rite, that there was no body of sin to be removed in His case, but rather that He was the destined Remover of it from others, the name JESUS, in obedience to express command from heaven, was given Him at His circumcision, and given Him "*because*," as said the angel, "He shall save His people from their sins" (Matt. i. 21). So significant was this, that His circumciser, had he been fully aware of what he was doing, might have said to Him, as John afterwards did, "I have need to be circumcised of Thee, and comest Thou to me?" and the answer, in this case as in that, would doubtless have been, "Suffer it to be so now: for thus it becometh us to fulfil all righteousness" (Matt. iii. 14, 15). Still, the circumcision of Christ had a profound bearing on His own work. For since he that is "circumcised is a debtor to do the whole law" (Gal. v. 3), the circumcised Saviour thus bore about with Him, in His very flesh, the seal of a voluntary *obligation* to do the whole law—by Him only possible in the flesh, since the fall. But further, as it was only to "redeem (from its curse) them that were under the law," that He submitted at all to be "made under the law" (Gal. iv. 4, 5; iii. 13), the obedience to which Jesus was bound over was purely a *redeeming* obedience, or the obedience of a "Saviour." Once more, as it was only by being made a curse for us that Christ could redeem us from the curse of the law (Gal. iii. 13), the circumcision of Christ is to be regarded as a virtual *pledge to die;* a pledge not only to yield obedience in general, but to be "obedient unto death, even the death of the cross" (Phil. ii. 8).

'Like sacrificial wine
Pour'd on a victim's head
Are those few precious drops of thine
Now first to offering led.'—KEBLE.

Purification of the Virgin-Mother and Presentation of the Babe in the Temple (22-24). **22. And when the days of her purification.** This reading [αὐτῆς] has hardly any support at all. All the best and most ancient MSS. and versions read 'their purification' [αὐτῶν]—which some late transcribers had been afraid to write. But whether this is to be understood of mother and Babe together, or of Joseph and Mary, as the parents, the great fact that "we are shapen in iniquity, and in sin by our mothers conceived," which the Levitical rite was designed to proclaim, had no real place, and so could only be symbolically taught, in the present case; since "that which was conceived in the Virgin was of the Holy Ghost," and Joseph was only the Babe's legal father. **according to the law of Moses were accomplished.** The days of purification, in the case of a male child, were forty in all (Lev. xii. 2, 4): **they brought him to Jerusalem, to present him to the Lord.** All the first-born males had been claimed as "holy to the Lord," or set apart to sacred uses, in memory of the deliverance of the first-born of Israel from destruction in Egypt, through the sprinkling of blood (Exod. xiii. 2). In lieu of these, however, one whole tribe, that of Levi, was accepted, and set apart to occu-

23 the Lord; (as it is written in the law of the Lord, Every ^{n}male that
24 openeth the womb shall be called holy to the Lord;) and to offer a
sacrifice according to that which is said in the law of the Lord, A pair
of turtle doves, or two young pigeons.
25 And, behold, there was a man in Jerusalem, whose name *was* Simeon;
and the same man *was* just and devout, ^{o}waiting for the consolation of
26 Israel: and the Holy Ghost was upon him. And it was revealed unto
him by the Holy Ghost, that he should not ^{p}see death, before he had
27 seen the Lord's Christ. And he came by ^{q}the Spirit into the temple:
and when the parents brought in the child Jesus, to do for him after

A. M. 4000.
[n] Ex. 13. 2. Ex. 22. 29. Num. 3. 13.
[o] Isa. 40. 1. Mark 15 43.
[p] Ps. 89. 48. Heb. 11. 5.
[q] Acts 8. 29. Acts 10. 19. Acts 16. 7. Rev. 1. 10. Rev. 17. 3.

pations exclusively sacred (Num. iii. 11-38); and whereas there were fewer Levites than first-born of all Israel on the first reckoning, each of these supernumerary first-born was to be redeemed by the payment of five shekels, but not without being "*presented* [publicly] *unto the Lord*," in token of His rightful claim to them and their service. (Num. iii. 44-47; xviii. 15-16). It was in obedience to this "law of Moses," that the Virgin presented her Babe unto the Lord, 'in the east gate of the court called Nicanor's Gate, where herself would be sprinkled by the priest with the blood of her sacrifice' [*Lightfoot*]. By that Babe, in due time, we were to be redeemed, "not with corruptible things as silver and gold, but with the precious blood of Christ" (1 Pet. i. 18, 19); and the consuming of the mother's burnt offering, and the sprinkling of her with the blood of her sin offering, were to find their abiding realization in the "living sacrifice" of the Christian mother herself, in the fulness of a "heart sprinkled from an evil conscience" by "the blood which cleanseth from all sin." **23. (As it is written in the law of the Lord, Every male that openeth the womb shall be called holy to the Lord;) 24. And to offer a sacrifice according to that which is said in the law of the Lord, A pair of turtle doves, or two young pigeons.** The proper sacrifice was a lamb for a burnt offering, and a turtle-dove or young pigeon for a sin offering. But if a lamb could not be afforded, the mother was to bring two turtle-doves or two young pigeons; and if even this was beyond the family means, then a portion of fine flour, but without the usual fragrant accompaniments of oil and frankincense, because it represented a sin offering (Lev. xii. 6-8; v. 7-11). From this we gather that our Lord's parents were in poor circumstances (2 Cor. viii. 9), and yet not in abject poverty; as they neither brought the lamb, nor availed themselves of the provision for the poorest, but presented the intermediate offering of "a pair of turtle-doves, or two young pigeons."

Remarks.—1. We have here the first example of that double aspect of Christ's conformity to the law which characterized it throughout. Viewed simply in the light of obedience—an obedience in the highest sense voluntary, and faultlessly perfect—it is for men the model-obedience: He hath left us an example that we should follow His steps (1 Pet. ii. 21). But as He was made under the law only to redeem them that were under the law, His obedience was more than voluntary—it was strictly *self-imposed* obedience; and since it is by the obedience of this One that the many are made righteous (Rom. v. 19), it had throughout, and in every part of it, a *substitutionary* character, which made it altogether unique. As it was *human* obedience, it is our glorious exemplar: but as it is *mediatorial* obedience—strictly self-imposed and vicarious—a stranger doth not intermeddle with it. Thus, Christ is at once imitable and inimitable; and—paradoxical though it may sound—it is just the inimitable character of Christ's obedience that puts us in a condition to look at it in its imitable character, with the humble but confident assurance that we shall be able to follow His steps. 2. That He who was rich should for our sakes have become, in the very circumstances of His birth, so poor that His parents should not have been able to afford a lamb for a burnt offering on His presentation in the temple—is singularly affecting; but that this poverty was not so abject as to awaken the emotion of *pity*—is one of those marks of Wisdom in the arrangement even of the comparatively trivial circumstances of His history, which bespeak the Divine presence in it all, stamp the Evangelical Record with the seal of truth, and call forth devout admiration.

25-39.—SIMEON AND ANNA RECOGNIZE THE INFANT SAVIOUR IN THE TEMPLE—THE RETURN TO NAZARETH, AND ADVANCEMENT OF THE CHILD JESUS.

Simeon's Recognition of the Infant Saviour (25-35). **25. And, behold, there was a man in Jerusalem, whose name was Simeon.** The attempts that have been made to identify this Simeon with a famous man of the same name, but who died long before, and with the father of Gamaliel, who bore that name, are quite precarious. The name was a common one. **and the same man was just**—upright in his moral character, **and devout**—of a religious frame of spirit, **waiting for the consolation of Israel**—or, for the Messiah; a beautiful and pregnant title of the promised Saviour: **and the Holy Ghost was upon him**—supernaturally. Thus was the Spirit, after a dreary absence of nearly four hundred years, returning to the Church, to quicken expectation and prepare for coming events. **26. And it was revealed unto him by the Holy Ghost, that he should not see death before he had seen the Lord's Christ.** *Bengel* notices the 'sweet antithesis' here between the two sights—his "seeing the Lord's Christ" ere he should "see death." How would the one sight gild the gloom of the other! He was probably by this time advanced in years. **27. And he came by the Spirit into the temple**—the Spirit guiding him, all unconsciously, to the temple at the very moment when the Virgin was about to present the Infant to the Lord. Let it here be observed, once for all, that whenever the priests are said to go, or come, into "the temple," as in ch. i. 9, the word always used [ὁ ναὸς] is that which denotes the *temple proper*, into which none might enter save the priests; and never is this word used when our Lord, or any *not* of the priestly family, is said to go into the temple: in such case the word used [τὸ ἱερὸν] is one of wider signification, denoting any place *within the sacred precincts*. So here of Simeon. **and when the parents brought in the child Jesus, to do for him after the custom of the law, 28. Then took he him up in his arms**—the same Spirit that drew

28 the custom of the law, then took he him up in his arms, and blessed God,
and said,
29 Lord, [r]now lettest thou thy servant depart
In peace, according to thy word:
30 For mine eyes [s]have seen thy salvation,
31 Which thou hast prepared before the face of all people;
32 A [t]light to lighten the Gentiles,
And the glory of thy people Israel.
33 And Joseph and his mother marvelled at those things which were
34 spoken of him. And Simeon blessed them, and said unto Mary his
mother, Behold, this *child* is set for the [u]fall and rising again of many
35 in Israel: and for [v]a sign which shall be spoken against; (yea, [w]a sword
shall pierce through thy own soul also,) that [x]the thoughts of many
hearts may be revealed.
36 And there was one Anna, [y]a prophetess, the daughter of Phanuel, of
the tribe of Aser: she was of a great age, and had lived with an husband
37 seven years from her virginity; and she *was* a widow of about fourscore
and four years, which departed not from the temple, but served *God* with

A. M. 4000.

[r] Gen. 46. 30. 1 Cor. 15. 54. Phil. 1. 23. Rev. 14. 13.
[s] Isa. 52. 10. Acts 4. 12.
[t] Isa. 9. 2. Acts 13. 47.
[u] Isa. 8. 14. Hos. 14. 9. Rom. 9. 32. 1 Cor. 1. 23. 2 Cor. 2. 16. 1 Pet. 2. 7, 8.
[v] Matt. 11. 19. Acts 28. 22. 1 Pet. 2. 12. 1 Pet. 4. 14.
[w] Ps. 42. 10. John 19. 25.
[x] 1 Cor 11. 19.
[y] Ex. 15. 20.

him thither revealing to him at once the glory of that blessed Babe. Now, since all that he uttered might as well have been simply *pronounced over* the Child, there is to be seen in this act of taking Him into his arms a most affecting, personal, and, so to speak, palpable appropriation of this new-born, unconscious, helpless Babe, as "all his salvation and all his desire," which it were a pity we should miss. **and blessed God, and said, 29. Lord.** The word is 'Master' [Δέσποτα], a word but rarely used in the New Testament, and never but to mark emphatically the sovereign rights of Him who is so styled, as Proprietor of the persons or things meant. Here it is selected with peculiar propriety, when the aged saint, feeling that his last object in wishing to live had now been attained, only awaited his Master's word of command to "depart." **now lettest thou thy servant depart in peace, according to thy word.** Most readers probably take this to be a prayer for permission to depart, not observing that "lettest Thou" is just 'Thou art letting,' or 'permitting thy servant to depart.' It had been clearer as well as more literal thus—"Lord, now art Thou releasing Thy servant"—a placid, reverential intimation that having now "seen the Lord's Christ," his time, divinely indicated, for "seeing death" had arrived, and he was ready to go. **30. For mine eyes have seen thy salvation.** How many saw this Child, nay the full-grown "Man, Christ Jesus," who never saw in Him "God's Salvation!" This estimate of Simeon's was an act of pure faith. While gazing upon that Infant, borne in his own arms, he "beheld His glory." In another view it was prior *faith* rewarded by present *sight.* **31. Which thou hast prepared before the face of all people** [πάντων τῶν λαῶν]—'of all the peoples,' or mankind at large. **32. A light to lighten the Gentiles**—then in thick darkness, **and the glory of thy people Israel**—already Thine, and now, in the believing portion of it, to be more gloriously so than ever. It will be observed that this 'swan-like song, bidding an eternal farewell to this terrestrial life,' to use the words of *Olshausen,* takes a more comprehensive view of the kingdom of Christ than that of Zacharias (cf. ch. i. 68-79), though the kingdom they sing of is one.

33. And Joseph and his mother—or, according to what is probably the true reading here, 'And his father and mother,' **marvelled at those things which were spoken of him**—each successive recognition of the glory of this Babe filling them with fresh wonder. **34. And Simeon blessed them**—the parents, **and said unto Mary his mother, Behold, this child is set** [κεῖται]—'lieth,' or, 'is appointed:' compare Isa. xxviii. 16, "Behold, I *lay* in Zion," &c. Perhaps, this Infant's lying in his own arms at that moment suggested this sublime allusion. **for the fall and rising again of many in Israel: and for a sign which shall be spoken against.** If the latter of these two expressions refer to the determined rejecters of Christ, perhaps the former refers, not to two classes—one "falling" from a higher to a lower, the other "rising" from a lower to a higher state—but to one and the same class of persons, who after "falling," through inability to discern the glory of Christ in the days of His flesh, "rose again" when, after the effusion of the Spirit at Pentecost, a new light dawned upon their minds. The like treatment do the claims of Christ experience from age to age. **35. Yea, a sword shall pierce through thy own soul also.** 'Blessed though thou art among women, thou shalt have thine own deep share of the struggles and sufferings which this Babe is to occasion'—pointing not only to the obloquy to which He would be exposed through life, to those agonies of His on the cross which she was to witness, and to her own desolate condition thereafter, but perhaps also to dreadful alternations of faith and unbelief, of hope and fear regarding Him which she should have to pass through: **that the thoughts of many hearts may be revealed**—for men's views and decisions regarding Christ are a mirror in which the very thoughts of their hearts are seen.

Anna's Recognition of the Infant Saviour (36-38). **36. And there was one Anna**—or Hannah, **a prophetess**—another sign that "the last times" in which God was to "pour out His Spirit upon all flesh" were at the door, **the daughter of Phanuel, of the tribe of Aser**—one of the ten tribes, of whom many were not carried captive, and not a few, particularly of this very tribe, re-united themselves to Judah after the return from Babylon (2 Chr. xxx. 11). The distinction of tribes, though practically destroyed by the captivity, was well enough known up to their final dispersion (Rom. xi. 1; Heb. vii. 14); nor even now is it entirely lost. **she was of a great age, and had lived with an husband seven years from her virginity. 37. And she was a widow of about fourscore and four years.** If this mean that she had been 84 years in a state of widow-

38 fastings and prayers [z]night and day. And she coming in that instant
gave thanks likewise unto the Lord, and spake of him to all them that
[a]looked for redemption in [4]Jerusalem.
39 And when they had performed all things according to the law of the
40 Lord, they returned into Galilee, to their own city Nazareth. And the
child grew, and waxed strong in spirit, filled with wisdom; and the grace
of God was upon him.

A. M. 4000.

[z] Acts 26. 7. 1 Tim. 5. 5.
[a] Lam. 3. 25, 26. Mark 15. 43. ch. 24. 21.
[4] Or, Israel.

hood, then, since her married life extended to seven years, she could not now have been less than 103 years old, even though she had married at the age of twelve, the earliest marriageable age of Jewish females. But probably the meaning is that her whole present age was 84, of which there had been but seven years of a married life. **which departed not from the temple**—that is, at any of the stated hours of day-service, and was found there even during the night-services of the temple-watchmen (see Ps. cxxxiv. 1, 2); **but served God**—the word here used denotes religious services, **with fastings and prayers night and day.** It is this statement about Anna that appears to have suggested to the apostle his description of the "widow indeed and desolate," that she "trusteth in God, and continueth in supplications and prayers night and day" (1 Tim. v. 5). **38. And she coming in that instant** [ἐπιστᾶσα]—rather, 'standing by' or 'presenting herself;' for she had been there already. When Simeon's testimony to the blessed Babe was dying away, she was ready to take it up. **gave thanks likewise unto the Lord** [ἀνθωμολογεῖτο]—rather, 'gave thanks in turn,' or responsively to Simeon, **and spake of him to all them that looked for redemption in Jerusalem.** [The reading, adopted by recent critics, 'the redemption of Jerusalem,' has not, as we think, sufficient authority. The meaning appears to be, 'She spake of Him to all them in Jerusalem that were looking for redemption,' meaning, the expectants of Messiah who were then in the city. Saying in effect—In that Babe are wrapt up all your expectations. If this took place at the hour of prayer, it would account, as *Alford* remarks, for her having such an audience as the words imply.

Return to Nazareth and Advancement of the Child Jesus (39, 40). **39. And when they had performed all things according to the law of the Lord, they returned into Galilee, to their own city Nazareth.** Are we to conclude from this that the parents of Jesus went straight back to Nazareth from these temple scenes, and that the visit of the Magi, the flight into Egypt, and the return thence, recorded by Matthew (ch. ii.), all took place *before* the presentation of the Babe in the temple? So some think, but in our judgment very unnaturally. To us it seems far more natural to suppose that the presentation in the temple took place during the residence of the parents at Bethlehem, where they appear at first to have thought it their duty henceforth to reside (see on Matt. ii. 22). In this case all that is recorded by Luke in the preceding verses was over before the Magi arrived in Jerusalem. Nor is there any difficulty in Luke's saying here, that "when they had performed all they returned to Galilee." If, indeed, we had no account of any intermediate transactions, we should of course conclude that they went *straight* from Jerusalem to Nazareth. But if we have reason to believe that the whole transactions of Matt. ii. occurred in the interval, we have only to conclude that our Evangelist, having no information to communicate to his readers between those events, just passes them by. A precisely similar, and at least equally important, omission by Matthew himself occurs at ch. iv. 12 (on which see note). **40. And the child grew, and waxed strong in spirit**—His mental development keeping pace with His bodily: **filled with wisdom**—yet a fulness ever enlarging with His capacity to receive it; **and the grace of God**—the divine favour, **was upon him**—resting upon Him, manifestly and increasingly. Compare *v.* 52. [*Tischendorf* and *Tregelles* omit πνεύματι—"in spirit," but, as we think, on insufficient authority.]

Remarks.—1. Now began to be fulfilled that beautiful prediction—uttered as an encouragement to rebuild the temple after the captivity—"I will fill this house with glory, saith the Lord of Hosts: the glory of this latter house shall be greater than of the former, saith the Lord of Hosts; and in this place will I give peace, saith the Lord of Hosts" (Hag. ii. 7, 9). The peculiar glory of the first temple was wholly wanting in the second. "The ark of the covenant, overlaid round about with gold, wherein was the golden pot that had manna, and Aaron's rod that budded, and the tables of the covenant, and over it the cherubim of glory shadowing the mercy seat"—all these had been lost, and the impossibility of recovering them was keenly felt. By what other "glory" was the second temple to eclipse the first? Not certainly by its architectural and ornamental beauty; and if not, what greater glory had it than the first, save this only, that the Lord of the temple in human flesh came into it, bringing peace? 2. By what glorious premonitions of future greatness was the Infancy of Christ distinguished—fitted to arrest the attention, to quicken the expectation, and to direct the views of all who were waiting for the Consolation of Israel! 3. To be prepared to welcome death as the peaceful release of a servant by his divine Master, in the conscious enjoyment of His salvation, is the frame of all others most befitting the aged saint. 4. The reception or rejection of Christ is in every age the great test of real character. 5. How richly rewarded was Anna for the assiduousness with which she attended all the temple-services! Not only was she privileged in consequence to behold the Infant Saviour, and to give public thanks to the Lord for so precious a gift, but she got an audience of devout worshippers to hear her, to whom, as expectants of the coming Redemption, she spake of Him, proclaiming Him the Hope and Consolation of Israel. 6. How beautiful is age when mellowed, as in Simeon and Anna, by a devout and heavenly spirit, and gladdened with the joy of God's salvation! 7. Those whose hearts are full of Christ will hardly be able to refrain, whether they be male or female, from speaking of Him to others, as did Anna here.

41-52.—First Conscious Visit of Jesus to Jerusalem—Return to Nazareth, Subjection to His Parents, and gradual Advancement. After following with rapt interest the minute details of the Redeemer's Birth and Infancy, one is loath to see the curtain suddenly drop, to be but once raised, and disclose but one brief scene, before His thirtieth year. How curiosity yearns for more, may be seen by the puerile and degrading information regarding the boyhood of Jesus, with which some of the

41 Now his parents went to Jerusalem every [b]year at the feast of the
42 passover. And when he was twelve years old, they went up to Jerusalem
after the custom of the feast.
43 And when they had fulfilled the days, as they returned, the child Jesus
tarried behind in Jerusalem; and Joseph and his mother knew not *of it.*
44 But they, supposing him to have been in the company, went a day's jour-
45 ney; and they sought him among *their* kinsfolk and acquaintance. And
when they found him not, they turned back again to Jerusalem, seeking him.
46 And it came to pass, that after three days they found him in the
temple, sitting in the midst of the doctors, [c]both hearing them, and

A. M. 4000.

b Ex. 12. 14. Ex. 23. 14-17. Ex. 34. 23. Lev. 23. 5. Deut. 12. 5, 7, 11. Deut. 16. 1. 1 Sam. 1. 3, 21.

c Isa. 49. 1, 2. Isa. 50. 4.

apocryphal Gospels pandered to the vicious taste of that class of Christians for which they were written. What a contrast to these are our Four Gospels, whose *historical chastity*, as *Olshausen* well says, chiefly discovers their divine character. As all great and heroic characters, whether of ancient or of modern times, have furnished glimpses in early life of their commanding future, so it was meet, perhaps, that something of this nature should distinguish the Youth of Jesus. One incident is given: one, to show what budding glory, the glory of the Only Begotten of the Father, lay concealed for nearly thirty years under a lowly Nazarene roof; and but one, that the life of secret *preparation* and patient *waiting* for public work might not draw off that attention which should be engrossed with the work itself, and that edification might be imparted rather than curiosity fed. In this view of it, let us reverently approach that most wonderful scene, of our Lord's first visit to Jerusalem, since the time that He was carried thither a Babe hanging upon His mother's breast.

First Conscious Visit to Jerusalem (41-50). **41. Now his parents went** [ἐπορεύοντο]—'were wont' or, 'used to go' **to Jerusalem every year at the feast of the passover.** Though the males only were required to go up to Jerusalem at the three annual festivals (Exod. xxiii. 14-17), devout women, when family duties permitted, went also. So did Hannah (1 Sam. i. 7), and, as here appears, the mother of Jesus. **42. And when he was twelve years old, they went up to Jerusalem after the custom of the feast.** At the age of twelve every Jewish boy was styled 'a son of the law;' being then put under a course of instruction, and trained to fasting and attendance on public worship, besides being set to learn a trade. About this age the young of both sexes have been in use to appear before the bishop for confirmation, where this rite is practised; and at this age, in Scotland, they were regarded as *examinable* by the minister for the first time—so uniform has been the view of the Church, both Jewish and Christian, that about the age of twelve the mind is capable of a higher discipline than before. At this age, then, our Lord is taken up for the first time to Jerusalem, at the Passover-season, the chief of the three annual festivals. But, O, with what thoughts and feelings must this Youth have gone up! Long ere He beheld it, He had doubtless "loved the habitation of God's house, and the place where His honour dwelt" (Ps. xxvi. 8); a love nourished, we may be sure, by that "word hid in His heart," with which in after life He showed so perfect a familiarity. As the time for His first visit approached, could one's ear have caught the breathings of His young soul, he might have heard Him whispering, "As the hart panteth after the water brooks, so panteth my soul after Thee, O God. The Lord loveth the gates of Zion more than all the dwellings of Jacob. I was glad when they said unto me, Let us go into the house of the Lord. Our feet shall stand within thy gates, O Jerusalem"! (Ps. xlii. 1; lxxxvii. 2; cxxii. 1, 2). On catching the first view of "the city of their solemnities," and high above all in it, "the place of God's rest," we hear Him saying to Himself, "Beautiful for situation, the joy of the whole earth, is Mount Zion, on the sides of the north, the city of the great King. Out of Zion, the perfection of beauty, God hath shined" (Ps. xlviii. 2; l. 2). Of His feelings or actions during all the seven days of the feast, not a word is said. As a devout Child, in company with His parents, He would go through the services, keeping His thoughts to Himself; but methinks I hear Him, after the sublime services of that feast, saying to Himself, "He brought me to the banqueting house, and His banner over me was love. I sat down under His shadow with great delight, and His fruit was sweet to my taste" (Song ii. 3, 4).

43. And when they had fulfilled the days—the seven days of the festival; **as they returned.** Yes, they had to return. For if the duties of life must give place to worship, worship in its turn must give place to them. *Jerusalem* is good; but *Nazareth* is good too. Let him then who neglects the one, on pretext of attending to the other, ponder this scene. Work and Worship serve to relieve each other, and beautifully alternate. **the child Jesus tarried behind in Jerusalem; and Joseph and his mother knew not of it.** Accustomed to the discretion and obedience of the lad, as *Olshausen* says, they might be thrown off their guard. **44. But they, supposing him to have been in the company** [ἐν τῇ συνοδίᾳ]—'the travelling-company,' **went a day's journey; and they sought him among their kinsfolk and acquaintance.** On these sacred journeys whole villages and districts travelled in groups together, partly for protection, partly for company; and as the well-disposed would beguile the tediousness of the way by good discourse, to which the Child Jesus would be no silent listener, they expect to find Him in such a group. **45. And when they found him not, they turned back again to Jerusalem, seeking him. 46. And it came to pass, that after three days they found him.** Do you inquire how he subsisted all this time? I do not. This is one of those impertinences which we should avoid indulging. The spurious gospels, we daresay, would tell their readers all that: how everybody vied with his neighbour who should have Him to keep, and how angels came and fed Him with nectar, or how He needed neither food nor sleep, and so on. But where God has dropt the veil, let us not seek to raise it. Well, they found Him. Where? Not gazing on the architecture of the sacred metropolis, or studying its forms of busy life, but **in the temple**—not of course in the "sanctuary" [τῷ ναῷ], as in ch. i. 9, to which only the priests had access (see on *v.* 27), but in some one of the en-

47 asking them questions. And [d]all that heard him were astonished at his
48 understanding and answers. And when they saw him, they were amazed:
and his mother said unto him, Son, why hast thou thus dealt with us?
49 behold, thy father and I have sought thee sorrowing. And he said unto
them, How is it that ye sought me? wist ye not that I must be about
50 [e]my Father's business? And [f]they understood not the saying which he
spake unto them.
51 And he went down with them, and came to Nazareth, and was subject
unto them: but his mother [g]kept all these sayings in her heart.
52 And Jesus [h]increased in wisdom and [5]stature, and in favour with God
and man.

A. M. 4000.

d Matt. 7. 28. Mark 1. 22. John 7. 15.
e Matt. 21. 12. John 2. 16. John 4. 34. John 8. 29.
f ch. 9. 45. ch. 18. 34.
g Gen. 37. 11. Dan. 7. 28.
h 1 Sam. 2. 26.
5 Or, age.

closures around it, where the rabbins, or "doctors," taught their scholars. **sitting in the midst of the doctors, both hearing them, and asking them questions.** The method of question and answer was the customary form of rabbinical teaching; teacher and learner becoming by turns questioner and answerer, as may be seen from their extant works. This would give full scope for all that "astonished them in His understanding and answers." Not that He assumed the office of *teaching*—"His hour" for that "was not yet come," and His furniture for that was not complete; for He had yet to "increase in wisdom" as well as "stature" (*v.* 52). In fact, the beauty of Christ's example lies very much in His never at one stage of His life anticipating the duties of another. All would be in the style and manner of a learner, "opening His mouth and panting—His soul breaking for the longing that it had unto God's judgments at all times," and now more than ever before, when finding Himself for the first time in His Father's house. Still there would be in His *questions* far more than in their *answers;* and, if we may take the frivolous interrogatories with which they afterwards plied Him—about the woman that had seven husbands and such like—as a specimen of their present drivelling questions, perhaps we shall not greatly err, if we suppose that the "questions," which He now "asked them" in return, were just the germs of those pregnant questions with which He astonished and silenced them in after years:—"*What think ye of Christ?—Whose Son is He? If David call him Lord, how is he then his son?*"—"*Which is the first and great commandment?*"—"*Who is my neighbour?*" **47. And all that heard him were astonished at his understanding and answers.** This confirms what we have said above, that while His "*answers*" to their questions made His attitude appear throughout to be that of a *learner*, "His understanding" peered forth to the amazement of all. **48. And when they saw him, they were amazed: and his mother said unto him, Son, why hast thou thus dealt with us? behold, thy father and I have sought thee sorrowing.** Probably this was said, not before the group, but in private. **49. And he said unto them, How is it that ye sought me? wist (knew) ye not that I must be about my Father's business** [ἐν τοῖς τοῦ Πατρός μου]. These, as THE FIRST RECORDED WORDS OF CHRIST, have a peculiar interest, over and above their intrinsic preciousness. They are somewhat elliptical. The meaning may be, as our translators have taken it, 'about my Father's affairs' or 'business' [*sc.* πράγμασιν]. So *Calvin, Beza, Maldonat, de Wette, Alford, Stier, van Osterzee,* &c. Or the sense may be, 'in my Father's house' [*sc.* οἰκήμασιν, or δώμασιν]. This latter shade of meaning, besides being the primary one, includes the former. So most of the fathers and of the moderns, *Erasmus, Grotius, Bengel, Olshausen, Meyer, Trench, Webster and Wilkinson.* In His Father's house Jesus felt Himself at home, breathing His own proper air, and His words convey a gentle rebuke of their obtuseness in requiring Him to *explain this.* 'Once here, thought ye I should so readily hasten away? Let ordinary worshippers be content to keep the feast and be gone; but is this all ye have learnt of Me?' Methinks we are here let into the holy privacies of Nazareth; for sure what He says they *should* have known He must have given them *ground* to know. She tells Him of the sorrow with which *His father* and she had sought Him. He speaks of *no father but one,* saying, in effect, 'My Father has *not* been seeking Me; I have been with Him all this time; the King hath brought me into His chambers: His left hand is under my head, and His right hand doth embrace Me (Song i. 4; ii. 6). How is it that ye do not understand (Mark viii. 21)?' **50. And they understood not the saying which he spake unto them.** Probably He had never *said* so much to them, and so they were confounded; though it was but the true interpretation of many things which they had seen and heard from Him at home. We have an example of this way of speaking in John xiv. 4, 5, where the disciples are presumed to know more than had been told them in so many words.

Return to Nazareth, Subjection to His Parents, and gradual Advancement (51-52). **51. And he went down with them, and came to Nazareth, and was subject unto them, &c.** This is added lest it should be thought that He now threw off the filial yoke, and became henceforth His own master, and theirs too. The marvel of such condescension as this verse records lies in its coming after such a scene, and such an assertion of His higher Sonship; and the words are evidently meant to convey this. **but his mother kept all these sayings in her heart.** *N.B.* After this it will be observed that *Joseph entirely disappears* from the Sacred Narrative. Henceforth, it is always "His mother and His brethren." From this it is inferred, that before the next appearance of our Lord in the History Joseph had *died.* Having now served the double end of being the protector of our Lord's Virgin-mother, and affording Himself the opportunity of presenting a matchless pattern of subjection to both parents, he is silently withdrawn from the stage.

52. And Jesus increased in wisdom and stature. So our translators have rendered the word [ἡλικίᾳ], with *Beza, Grotius, Bengel, Meyer.* But it may be rendered 'age'; and so the *Vulgate, Erasmus, Calvin, de Wette, Olshausen, Alford, Webster and Wilkinson, van Osterzee,* and the best interpreters. Probably this latter idea is the one intended; as filling up, by a general expression, the long interval until the age at which He emerged from this mysterious privacy. **and in favour with God and man.** (See on *v.* 40.) This is all the record we

3 NOW in the fifteenth year of the reign of Tiberius Cesar, Pontius
Pilate being governor of Judea, and Herod being tetrarch of Galilee, and
his brother Philip tetrarch of Iturea and of the region of Trachonitis,
2 and Lysanias the tetrarch of Abilene, Annas [a] and Caiaphas being the
high priests, the word of God came unto John the son of Zacharias in
the wilderness.
3 And [b] he came into all the country about Jordan, preaching the baptism
4 of repentance [c] for the remission of sins; as it is written in the book of
the words of Esaias the prophet, saying, [d] The voice of one crying in the
wilderness, Prepare ye the way of the Lord, make his paths straight.
5 Every valley shall be filled, and every mountain and hill shall be
brought low; and the crooked shall be made straight, and the rough
6 ways *shall be* made smooth; and [e] all flesh shall see the salvation of
7 God. Then said he to the multitude that came forth to be baptized of
him, [f] O generation of vipers, who hath warned you to flee from the
8 wrath to come? Bring [g] forth therefore fruits [1] worthy of repentance,
and begin not to say within yourselves, We have Abraham to *our*
father: for I say unto you, That God is able of these stones to raise
9 up children unto Abraham. And now also the ax is laid unto the root

A. D. 26.

CHAP. 3.
[a] John 11.49. John 18.13. Acts 4. 6.
[b] Mal. 4. 6. Matt. 3. 1. Mark 1. 4. Acts 13. 24. Acts 19. 4.
[c] ch. 1. 77.
[d] Isa. 40. 3. Matt. 3. 3. Mark 1. 3. John 1. 23.
[e] Ps. 98. 2. Isa. 52. 10.
[f] Matt. 3. 7.
[g] Isa. 1. 16. Ezek 18.27. Acts 26. 20. 2 Cor. 7. 10. Heb. 6. 7.
[1] Or, meet for.

have of the next eighteen years of that wondrous life.

Remarks.—1. Those who love the habitation of God's house and the place where His honour dwelleth, will not be ready to take advantage of permitted absence from it, but, like the mother of Jesus, be found there at all stated seasons when necessary duties allow. 2. The children of Christian parents are the children of the Church; they should be early taught to feel this, and—like the Child Jesus—trained to early attendance on its public ordinances and more private arrangements for instruction and edification. 3. One of the most decisive marks of early piety is a delight in the gates of Zion. And if we cannot attain to all that was in the mind of Jesus, when in language so remarkable He gently rebuked His earthly parents for their anxiety on His account (*v.* 49), let us imbibe and manifest the spirit of His words. 4. Let us realize the glorious identity with ourselves of the Infant Saviour, the Child, the Youth, the Man, Christ Jesus. 5. What an overpowering Example of filial obedience have we here! That the Child Jesus, so long as He *was* a Child, should be subject to His parents, though He was Lord of all, is not so wonderful; but that after His glory broke forth so amazingly in his Father's house, He still "went down with them to Nazareth, and was subject unto them;" continuing so, as we cannot doubt, until, at the appointed time, He emerged into public life—this is that marvel of filial obedience which even angels cannot but desire to look into. 6. Is it asked how "that holy thing," which was born of the Virgin, the sinless Seed of the woman, could increase "in wisdom, and in favour with God and man"? This is but to ask how He could become an Infant of days at all, and go through the successive stages of human life, up to full-grown manhood. But a simple illustration may perhaps aid our conceptions. Suppose a number of golden vessels, from the smallest conceivable size up to the largest, all filled to the brim with pure water, clear as crystal, so full that the least drop added to any one of them would make it to run over. Of all these vessels alike it may be said that they are quite full; and yet there is, in point of fact, less in the smallest than the largest, and each of them has less in it than in the next larger one. Such was Jesus. The golden vessels of all different sizes are His human nature at each successive period of His life up to the age of thirty, when He came to full maturity; and the crystal-clear water in them is the holy excellences and graces with which He was filled. He was never otherwise than full of these to the whole measure of His capacity. His understanding was ever as full as it could hold of intelligence and wisdom; His heart ever as full as it could hold of grace. But as it could hold more and more the further He advanced, so He might be said to become more and more lovely, more and more attractive, as He advanced, and so to "increase in favour with God and man." True, the favour of men was afterwards turned into frown and rage, when His fidelity irritated their corruption and dashed their expectations. But at this early period, there being nothing in Him to prejudice them against Him, His ever-unfolding loveliness could not fail to be increasingly attractive to all who observed it. 6. See the patience of Jesus, who, though doubtless conscious of His high destination, yet waited thirty years, not only for the entire development and maturity of all His powers and graces, but for the appointed time of His public appearance. Not so Moses, who, burning with the consciousness of his divine destination to deliver Israel, waited not his full time and the manifest call to act, but took this into his own hand, and was punished for it by having forty years longer to wait, far from the scene of his future work. Yet such patient waiting has unspeakable reliefs and consolations. The conviction that the best things ever take the longest to come to maturity would doubtless minister quiet satisfaction. But besides this, what seasons of tranquil meditation over the lively oracles, and holy fellowship with His Father; what inlettings, on the one hand, of light, and love, and power from on high, and on the other, what outgoings of filial supplication, freedom, love, joy, and what glad consecration to the work before Him, would these last eighteen years of His private life embrace! And would they not "seem but a few days" when thus spent, however ardently He might long to be more directly "about His Father's business."

CHAP. III. 1-20.—PREACHING, BAPTISM, AND IMPRISONMENT OF JOHN. (=Matt. iii. 1-12; Mark i. 1-8.) For the exposition, see on Matt. iii. 1-12.

21, 22.—BAPTISM OF CHRIST, AND DESCENT OF THE SPIRIT UPON HIM IMMEDIATELY THEREAFTER. (=Matt. iii. 13-17; Mark i. 9-11; John

of the trees: [h]every tree therefore which bringeth not forth good fruit
is hewn down, and cast into the fire.
10, And the people asked him, saying, What [i]shall we do then? He
11 answereth and saith unto them, He [j]that hath two coats, let him impart
to him that hath none; and he that hath meat, let him do likewise.
12 Then [k]came also publicans to be baptized, and said unto him, Master,
13 what shall we do? And he said unto them, [l]Exact no more than that
14 which is appointed you. And the soldiers likewise demanded of him,
saying, And what shall we do? And he said unto them, [2]Do violence
to no man, [m]neither accuse *any* falsely; and be content with your
[3]wages.
15 And as the people were [4]in expectation, and all men [5]mused in their
16 hearts of John, whether he were the Christ, or not; John answered,
saying unto *them* all, I [n]indeed baptize you with water; but one mightier
than I cometh, the latchet of whose shoes I am not worthy to unloose:
17 he shall baptize you with [o]the Holy Ghost and with fire: whose fan *is*
in his hand, and he will throughly purge his floor, and [p]will gather the
wheat into his garner; but the chaff he will burn with fire unquenchable.
18 And many other things in his exhortation preached he unto the people.
19 But [q]Herod the tetrarch, being reproved by him for Herodias his
20 brother Philip's wife, and for all the evils which Herod had done, added
yet this above all, that he shut up John in prison.
21 Now when all the people were baptized, [r]it came to pass, that Jesus
22 also being baptized, and praying, the heaven was opened, and the Holy
Ghost descended in a bodily shape like a dove upon him, and a voice
came [s]from heaven, which said, Thou art my beloved Son; in thee I
am well pleased.
23 And Jesus himself began to be [t]about thirty years of age, being (as
24 was supposed) the [u]son of Joseph, which was *the* [6]*son* of Heli, which was
the son of Matthat, which was *the son* of Levi, which was *the son* of
25 Melchi, which was *the son* of Janna, which was *the son* of Joseph, which
was *the son* of Mattathias, which was *the son* of Amos, which was *the son*
26 of Naum, which was *the son* of Esli, which was *the son* of Nagge, which
was *the son* of Maath, which was *the son* of Mattathias, which was *the son*
27 of Semei, which was *the son* of Joseph, which was *the son* of Juda, which
was *the son* of Joanna, which was *the son* of Rhesa, which was *the son* of
[7]Zorobabel, which was *the son* of Salathiel, which was *the son* of Neri,
28 which was *the son* of Melchi, which was *the son* of Addi, which was *the
son* of Cosam, which was *the son* of Elmodam, which was *the son* of Er,

A. D. 26.

h Matt. 7. 19. John 15. 2, 6.
i Acts 2. 37.
j 2 Cor. 8. 14. 1 Tim. 6. 18. Jas. 2. 15. 1 John 3. 17.
k Matt. 21. 32.
l Mic. 6. 8. ch. 19. 8.
2 Or, put no man in fear.
m Ex. 23. 1. Lev. 19. 11.
3 Or, allowance.
4 Or, in suspense.
5 Or, reasoned, or, debated.
n Matt. 3. 11.
o 1 Cor. 12. 13.
p Mic. 4. 12.
q Pro. 28. 15, 16. Matt. 11. 2. Matt. 14. 3. Mark 6. 17.
r Matt. 3. 13. John 1. 32.
s 2 Pet. 1. 17.
t Num. 4. 3, 35, 39, 47.
u Matt. 13. 55. John 6. 42.
6 Son-in-law.
7 It is uncertain whether Zorobabel and Salathiel are the same as those mentioned in Matt. 1. 12, 13, and 1 Chr. 3. 17, 19.

i. 31-34.) For the exposition, see on Matt. iii. 13-17.

23-38.—Genealogy of Christ. (= Matt. i. 1-18.)

23. And Jesus himself began to be about thirty years of age [ὡσεὶ ἐτῶν τριάκοντα ἀρχόμενος]—or, 'was about entering on His thirtieth year.' So our translators have taken the word, and so *Calvin*, *Beza*, *Bloomfield*, *Webster and Wilkinson;* but 'was about thirty years of age when He began [His ministry]' makes better Greek, and is probably the true sense. So *Bengel*, *Olshausen*, *de Wette*, *Meyer*, *Alford*, &c. At this age the priests entered on their office (Num. iv. 3), and the commencement of the ministry both of our Lord and His Forerunner appears to have been fixed on this principle. **being (as was supposed) the son of Joseph.** By this expression the Evangelist reminds his readers of His miraculous conception by the Virgin, and His being thus only the *legal* son of Joseph. **which was the son of Heli, &c.** Have we in this genealogical table the line of *Joseph* again, as in Matthew; or is this the line of *Mary?*—a point on which there has been great difference of opinion and much acute discussion. Those who take the *former* opinion contend that it is the natural sense of this verse, and that no other would have been thought of but for its supposed improbability and the uncertainty which it seems to throw over our Lord's real descent. But it is liable to another difficulty, viz., that in this case Matthew makes "*Jacob,*" while Luke makes "*Heli,*" to be Joseph's father; and though the same person had often more than one name, we ought not to resort to that supposition, in such a case as this, without necessity. And then, though the descent of Mary from David would be liable to no real doubt, even though we had no table of her line preserved to us (see, for example, ch. i. 32, and on ch. ii. 4), still it does seem unlikely—we say not incredible—that two genealogies of our Lord should be preserved to us, neither of which gives his *real* descent. Those who take the *latter* opinion, that we have here the line of *Mary*, as in Matthew that of *Joseph*—here his *real*, there his *reputed* line—explain the statement about Joseph, that he was "*the son* of

29 which was *the son* of Jose, which was *the son* of Eliezer, which was *the son*
30 of Jorim, which was *the son* of Matthat, which was *the son* of Levi, which
was *the son* of Simeon, which was *the son* of Juda, which was *the son* of
31 Joseph, which was *the son* of Jonan, which was *the son* of Eliakim, which
was *the son* of Melea, which was *the son* of Menan, which was *the son* of
Mattatha, which was *the son* of [v]Nathan, which [w]was *the son* of David,
32 which [x]was *the son* of Jesse, which was *the son* of Obed, which was *the son*
of Booz, which was *the son* of Salmon, which was *the son* of Naasson,
33 which was *the son* of Aminadab, which was *the son* of Aram, which was
the son of Esrom, which was *the son* of Phares, which was *the son* of Juda,
34 which was *the son* of Jacob, which was *the son* of Isaac, which was *the son*
of Abraham, [y]which was *the son* of Thara, which was *the son* of Nachor,
35 which was *the son* of Saruch, which was *the son* of Ragau, which was *the*
son of Phalec, which was *the son* of Heber, which was *the son* of Sala,
36 which [z]was *the son* of Cainan, which was *the son* of Arphaxad, [a]which
was *the son* of Sem, which was *the son* of Noe, which was *the son* of
37 Lamech, which was *the son* of Mathusala, which was *the son* of Enoch,
which was *the son* of Jared, which was *the son* of Maleleel, which was *the*
38 *son* of Cainan, which was *the son* of Enos, which was *the son* of Seth,
which was *the son* of Adam, [b]which was *the son* of God.

4 AND [a]Jesus, being full of the Holy Ghost, returned from Jordan, and
2 [b]was led by the Spirit into the wilderness, being forty days [c]tempted
of the devil. And [d]in those days he did eat nothing: and when they
3 were ended, he afterward hungered. And the devil said unto him, If
thou be the Son of God, command this stone that it be made bread.
4 And Jesus answered him, saying, [e]It is written, That man shall not live
5 by bread alone, but by every word of God. And the devil, taking him
up into an high mountain, showed unto him all the kingdoms of the
6 world in a moment of time. And the devil said unto him, All this
power will I give thee, and the glory of them: for [f]that is delivered unto
7 me; and to whomsoever I will I give it. If thou therefore wilt [1]worship
8 me, all shall be thine. And Jesus answered and said unto him, Get thee
behind me, Satan: [g]for it is written, Thou shalt worship the Lord thy
9 God, and him only shalt thou serve. And [h]he brought him to Jerusalem,
and set him on a pinnacle of the temple, and said unto him, If thou be
10 the Son of God, cast [i]thyself down from hence: for [j]it is written, He
11 shall give his angels charge over thee, to keep thee; and in *their* hands
they shall bear thee up, lest at any time thou dash thy foot against a

A. D. 30.
[v] Zec. 12. 12.
[w] 2 Sam. 5. 14. 1 Chr. 3. 5.
[x] Ruth 4. 18. 1 Sam. 17. 58. 1 Chr. 2. 10. Ps. 72. 20. Isa. 11. 1, 2. Matt. 1. 3-6. Acts 13. 22, 23.
[y] Gen. 11. 24, 26.
[z] Gen. 11. 12.
[a] Gen. 5. 6. Gen. 11. 10.
[b] Gen. 1. 26, 27. Gen. 2. 7. Gen. 5. 1, 2. Isa. 64. 8.

CHAP. 4.
[a] Isa. 11. 2. Isa 61. 1. Matt. 4. 1. Mark 1. 12. John 1. 33. John 3. 34.
[b] ch. 2. 27.
[c] Gen. 3. 15. Heb. 2. 18. Heb. 4 15.
[d] Ex. 34. 28. 1 Ki. 19. 8.
[e] Deut. 8. 3. Eph. 6. 17.
[f] John 12 31. John 14 30. Rev. 13. 2, 7.
[1] Or, fall down before me.
[g] Deut. 6. 13. Deut. 10 20.
[h] Matt. 4. 5.
[i] Matt. 8. 29. Rom. 1. 4. 1 Pet. 5. 8.
[j] Ps. 91. 11.

Heli," to mean that he was his *son-in-law*, as being the husband of his daughter Mary (so in Ruth i. 11, 12), and believe that Joseph's name is only introduced instead of Mary's, in conformity with the Jewish custom in such tables. Perhaps this view is attended with fewest difficulties, as it certainly is the best supported. However we decide, it is a satisfaction to know that not a doubt was thrown out by the bitterest of the early enemies of Christianity as to *our Lord's real descent from David.* On comparing the two genealogies, it will be observed that Matthew, writing more immediately for *Jews*, deemed it enough to show that the Saviour was sprung from Abraham and David; whereas Luke, writing more immediately for *Gentiles*, traces the descent back to Adam, the parent stock of the whole human family, thus showing Him to be the promised "Seed of the woman." Without going into the various questions raised by this and the corresponding genealogical line in the First Gospel, we merely quote the following striking remarks of *Olshausen*:—'The possibility of constructing such a table, comprising a period of thousands of years, in an uninterrupted line from father to son, of a family that dwelt for a long time in the utmost retirement, would be inexplicable, had not the members of this line been endowed with *a thread* by which they could extricate themselves from the many families into which every tribe and branch was again subdivided, and thus hold fast and know *the* member that was destined to continue the lineage. This thread was the hope that Messiah would be born of the race of Abraham and David. The ardent desire to behold Him and be partakers of His mercy and glory suffered not the attention to be exhausted through a period embracing thousands of years. Thus the member destined to continue the lineage, whenever doubtful, became easily distinguishable, awakening the hope of a final fulfilment, and keeping it alive until it was consummated.'

For general Remarks on this Section, see on Matt. i. 1-17, Remarks 1 and 2.

CHAP. IV. 1-15.—TEMPTATION OF CHRIST—BEGINNING OF HIS GALILEAN MINISTRY. (=Matt. iv. 1-25; Mark i. 12-20, 35-39.) For the exposition, see on Matt. iv. 1-25, and Mark i. 35-39.

12 stone. And Jesus answering said unto him, It [k]is said, Thou shalt not
13 tempt the Lord thy God. And when the devil had ended all the
temptation, he [l]departed from him [m]for a season.
14 And [n]Jesus returned in the power of the Spirit into [o]Galilee: and
15 there went out a fame of him through all the region round about. And
he taught in their synagogues, being [p]glorified of all.
16 And he came to [q]Nazareth, where he had been brought up: and, as
his custom was, [r]he went into the synagogue on the sabbath day, and

A. D. 30.

k Deut. 6. 16.
l Jas. 4. 7.
m John 14. 30.
n Matt. 4. 12.
o Acts 10. 37.
p Isa. 52. 13.
q Matt. 2. 23. Mark 6. 1.
r Acts 13. 14.

16-30. — Christ's Rejection at Nazareth. (= Matt. xiii. 54-58; Mark vi. 1-6.) As observed on Matt. iv. 13, the prevalent opinion has always been that our Lord paid two visits to Nazareth: the first being that recorded here; the second that recorded in Matt. xiii. 54-58, and Mark vi. 1-6. This is maintained on the following grounds:—First, The most natural sense of the words in Matt. iv. 13, "And leaving Nazareth, He came down and dwelt in Capernaum," is that He then paid a visit to it, though the particulars of it are not given. In this case the visit recorded in ch. xiii. 54-58 must be a second visit. Next the visit recorded in Luke bears on its face to have been made at the outset of our Lord's ministry, if not the very first opening of it; whereas that recorded in Matt. xiii. and in Mark vi. is evidently one paid at a somewhat advanced period of His ministry. Further, at the visit recorded by Luke, our Lord appears to have wrought no miracles; whereas it is expressly said that at the visit recorded in Mark He did work some miracles. Once more it is alleged of the wonder expressed by the Nazarenes at our Lord's teaching, that the language is noticeably different in Luke and in Mark. In reply to this, we observe: First, That as none of the Evangelists record more than one public visit to Nazareth, so we have shown in our exposition of Matt. iv. 13, that it is not necessary to infer from that verse that our Lord actually visited Nazareth at that time. Thus are we left free to decide the question—of one or two visits—on internal evidence alone. Secondly, The unparalleled violence with which the Nazarenes treated our Lord, at the visit recorded by Luke, suits far better with a somewhat advanced period of His ministry than with the very opening scene of it, or any very near its commencement. Thirdly, The visit, accordingly, recorded by Luke, though it reads at first like the opening scene of our Lord's ministry, gives evidence, on closer inspection, of its having occurred at a somewhat advanced period. The challenge which they would be ready to throw out to Him, and which He here meets, was *that He ought to work among His Nazarene townsmen as wonderful miracles as had made His stay at Capernaum so illustrious.* Does not this prove not only that His ministry did not begin at Nazareth, but that He had stayed so long away from it after His public ministry began, that the Nazarenes were irritated at the slight thus put upon them, and would be ready to insinuate that He was afraid to face them? Fourthly, Supposing our Lord to have framed His own procedure according to the instructions which He gave to His disciples —"Give not that which is holy unto the dogs, neither cast ye your pearls before swine;" and "When they persecute you in one city, flee ye into another" (Matt. vii. 6; x. 23)—it is in the last degree improbable that He would again expose Himself to those who had, at a former visit, rushed upon Him and thrust Him out of their city, and attempted to hurl Him down a precipice to kill Him; and though, if recorded, it is of course to be believed, the evidence of the fact would require to be much clearer than we think it is to warrant the conclusion that He actually did so. Fifthly, If our Lord did pay a second public visit to Nazareth, we might expect, in the record of it, some allusion to the first; or, if that be not necessary, it is surely reasonable to suppose that the impression made upon the Nazarenes, and the observations that fell from them would differ somewhat at least from those produced by the first visit. But, instead of this, not only do we find the impression produced upon them by the visit recorded by Matthew (xiii.) and by Mark (vi.), to be just what might have been expected from such a people on hearing Him *for the first time;* but we find their remarks to be identical with those recorded by Luke as made at *his* visit. Who can readily believe this of two distinct visits? Can anything be more unnatural than to suppose that after these Nazarenes had attempted the life of our Lord, and been disappointed of their object at one visit, they should at a subsequent one express their surprise at His teaching precisely in the terms they had before employed, and just as if they had never heard him before? As for the attempts to show that the questions are not put so strongly in Matthew and Mark, as they are in Luke (see *Birks'* "Horæ Evangelicæ"), it is astonishing to us that this should be urged—so devoid of all plausibility does it appear. The one argument of real force in favour of two visits is, that at the visit recorded by Mark (which is the same as that of Matthew) our Lord is expressly said to have wrought miracles, while it would seem that at that of Luke He wrought none. But the very way in which Mark records those miracles suggests its own explanation: "He could there do no mighty work" [δύναμιν], or, "*He could there do no miracle,* save that He laid His hands upon a few sick folk, and healed them" (Mark vi. 5)—suggesting that the unbelief of the Nazarenes tied up His hands, so to speak, from any display of His miraculous power. But as that unbelief evidently refers to what was displayed *in public,* so the inability is clearly an inability, in the face of that unbelief, to give any manifestation *in the synagogue,* or *in public,* of His miraculous power, as He did in the synagogue of Capernaum and elsewhere. Hence His "laying His hands on a few sick folk," being expressly recorded as *exceptional,* had been done in private, and in all likelihood before His public appearance in the synagogue had kindled the popular rage, and made it impossible. If this be correct, the demand of the Nazarenes for miracles and our Lord's refusal of them, as recorded by Luke, is quite consistent with the statement of what He wrought as given in Mark. A striking confirmation of the conclusion we have formed on this question will be found in the exposition of John iv. 43, 44, and Remark 1 at the close of that Section.

16. And he came to Nazareth, where he had been brought up, and, as his custom was [κατὰ τὸ εἰωθὸς αὐτῷ]—compare Acts xvii. 2, **he went into the synagogue on the sabbath day, and stood up**

17 stood up for to read. And there was delivered unto him the book of the
prophet Esaias. And when he had opened the book, he found the place
18 where it was written, The [s]Spirit of the Lord *is* upon me, because he
hath anointed me to preach the Gospel to the poor; he hath sent me
to heal the broken-hearted, to preach deliverance to the captives, and
19 recovering of sight to the blind, to set at liberty them that are bruised, to
20 preach the [t]acceptable year of the Lord. And he closed the book, and
he gave *it* again to the minister, and sat down. And the eyes of all
21 them that were in the synagogue were fastened on him. And he began
22 to say unto them, This day is this scripture fulfilled in your ears. And
all bare him witness, and [u]wondered at the gracious words which proceeded out of his mouth. And they said, Is [v]not this Joseph's son?
23 And he said unto them, Ye will surely say unto me this proverb,
Physician, heal thyself: whatsoever we have heard done in [w]Capernaum,
24 do also here in [x]thy country. And he said, Verily I say unto you, No

A. D. 30.

[s] Ps. 45. 7. Isa. 11. 2-5. Isa. 42. 1. Isa. 50. 4. Isa. 59. 21. Dan. 9. 24.
[t] Lev. 25. 8. 2 Cor. 6. 2.
[u] Ps. 45. 2. Pro. 10. 32. Matt. 13. 54. Mark 6. 2. ch. 2. 47.
[v] John 6. 42.
[w] Matt. 4. 13. Matt. 11. 23.
[x] Matt. 13. 54. Mark 6. 1.

for to read. Does this read like the opening of our Lord's public ministry? Does it not expressly tell us, on the contrary, that His ministry had already continued long enough to acquire a certain uniformity of procedure on the Sabbath days? As others besides Rabbins were allowed to address the congregation (see Acts xiii. 15), our Lord took advantage of that liberty. **17. And there was delivered unto him the book of the prophet Esaias. And when he had opened the book, he found the place where it was written** (Isa. lxi. 1, 2). There is no sufficient ground for supposing that our Lord fixed upon the *portion for the day.* The language used rather implies the contrary—that it was a portion selected by Himself for the occasion. **18. The Spirit of the Lord is upon me, because**—or 'inasmuch as' [οὗ ἕνεκεν]—**he hath anointed me to preach the Gospel to the poor; he hath sent me to heal the broken-hearted, to preach deliverance to the captives, and recovering of sight to the blind, to set at liberty them that are bruised, 19. To preach the acceptable**—or 'accepted' [τὸ δεκτὸν]—**year of the Lord.** To have fixed on any portion relating to His *sufferings* (as Isa. liii.) would have been unsuitable at that early stage of His ministry. But He selects a passage announcing the sublime object of His whole mission, its Divine character, and His special endowments for it; expressed in the first person, and so singularly adapted to the first opening of the mouth in His prophetic capacity, that it seems as if made expressly for the occasion when He first opened His mouth where He had been brought up. It is from the well-known section of Isaiah's prophecies whose burden is that mysterious "SERVANT OF THE LORD" [עֶבֶד יְהוָה], despised of man, abhorred of the nation, but before whom kings on seeing Him are to arise, and princes to worship; in visage more marred than any man, and his form than the sons of men, yet sprinkling many nations; labouring seemingly in vain, and spending His strength for nought and in vain, yet Jehovah's Servant to raise up the tribes of Jacob, and be His Salvation to the ends of the earth, (Isa. xlix., &c.) The quotation is chiefly from the Septuagint version, used, it would seem, in the synagogues. **acceptable year**—an allusion to the Jubilee year (Lev. xxv. 10), a year of universal *release* for person and property. See also Isa. xlix. 8; 2 Cor. vi. 2. As the maladies under which humanity groans are here set forth under the names of *poverty, broken-heartedness, bondage, blindness, bruisedness,* (or *crushedness*), so Christ announces Himself, in the act of reading it, as the glorious HEALER of all these maladies; stopping the quotation just before it comes to "the day of vengeance," which was only to come on the rejecters of His message (John iii. 17). The first words, "THE SPIRIT of THE LORD is upon ME," have been noticed since the days of the Church Fathers, as an illustrious example of *Father, Son, and Holy Ghost* being exhibited as in distinct yet harmonious action in the scheme of salvation. **20. And he closed the book, and he gave it again to the minister**—the *Chazan* or synagogue-officer. **And the eyes of all them that were in the synagogue were fastened on him**—astounded at His putting in such Messianic claims; for that, they saw, was what He meant. **21. And he began to say unto them**—language implying that only the substance, or even the general drift, of His address is here given. **This day is this scripture fulfilled in your ears.** The Evangelist means to say in a word, that His whole address was just a detailed application to Himself of this, and perhaps other like prophecies. **22. And all bare him witness, and wondered at the gracious words which proceeded out of his mouth** [ἐπὶ τοῖς λόγοις τῆς χάριτος]—'the words of grace,' referring to the richness of His matter and the sweetness of his manner (Ps. xlv. 2). **And they said, Is not this Joseph's son?** See on Matt. xiii. 54-56. They knew He had received no rabbinical education, and could not imagine how one who had gone in and out amongst them, as one of themselves, during all his boyhood and youth, up to within a short time before, could be the predicted Servant of the Lord who was to speak comfort to all mourners, to bring healing for all human maladies, and be, in fact, the Consolation of Israel. **23. And he said unto them, Ye will surely** [πάντως]—'Ye will no doubt' **say unto me this proverb, Physician, heal thyself**—not unlike our proverb, 'Charity begins at home.' **whatsoever we have heard done in Capernaum, do also here in thy country.** 'Strange rumours have reached our ears of thy doings at Capernaum; but if such power resides in thee to cure the ills of humanity, why has none of it yet come nearer home, and why is all this alleged power reserved for strangers?' His choice of Capernaum as a place of residence since entering on public life was, it seems, already well known at Nazareth; and when He did come thither, that he should give no displays of his power when distant places were ringing with His fame wounded their pride. He had indeed "laid His hands on a few sick folk, and healed them" (Mark vi. 5); but this, as we have said, seems to have been done quite privately—the general unbelief precluding anything more open. **24. And he said, Verily I say unto you. No prophet is accepted in his own country,**

25 prophet [y]is accepted in his own country. But I tell you of a truth,
[z]many widows were in Israel in the days of Elias, when the heaven was
shut up three years and six months, when great famine was throughout
26 all the land; but unto none of them was Elias sent, save unto Sarepta,
27 *a city* of Sidon, unto a woman *that was* a widow. And [a]many lepers
were in Israel in the time of Eliseus the prophet; and none of them was
cleansed, saving Naaman the Syrian.
28 And all they in the synagogue, when they heard these things, were
29 filled with wrath, and rose up, and thrust him out of the city, and led
him unto the [2]brow of the hill whereon their city was built, that they
30 might cast him down headlong. But he [b]passing through the midst of
them went his way,

A. D. 30.

[y] Matt. 13. 57. Mark 6. 4. John 4. 44. Acts 22. 3, 18-22.
[z] 1 Ki. 17. 9. 1 Ki. 18. 1. Jas. 5. 17.
[a] 2 Ki. 5. 14.
[2] Or, edge.
[b] John 8. 59. John 10. 39. John 18. 6, 7. Acts 12. 18.

In Mark vi. 4, "A prophet is not without honour, but in his own country, and among his own kin, and in his own house." He replies to one proverb by another equally familiar, which we express in rougher forms, such as, 'Too much familiarity breeds contempt.' Our Lord's long residence in Nazareth merely as a townsman had made Him *too common*, incapacitating them for appreciating Him as others did who were *less familiar with His every-day demeanour in private life.* A most important principle, to which the wise will pay due regard. **25. But I tell you of a truth, many widows were in Israel in the days of Elias, when the heaven was shut up three years and six months.** So Jas. v. 17, including perhaps the six months *after the last fall of rain*, when there would be little or none at any rate; whereas in 1 Ki. xviii. 1, which says the rain returned "in the third year," that period is probably not reckoned. **when great famine was throughout all the land; 26. But unto none of them was Elias sent, save** [εἰ μὴ]—rather, 'but only,' as the same phrase means in Mark xiii. 32, **unto Sarepta**—or "Zarephath" (1 Ki. xvii. 9), far beyond the northern border of Palestine, and near to Sidon (see Mark vii. 24): **unto a woman that was a widow.** Passing by all the famishing widows in Israel, the prophet was sent to one who was not an Israelite at all. **27. And many lepers were in Israel in the time of Eliseus**—or Elisha, **the prophet; and none of them was cleansed, saving** [εἰ μὴ again]—rather, 'but only' **Naaman the Syrian.** Thus, in defending the course which He had taken in passing by the place and the people that might be supposed to have the greatest claim on Him, our Lord falls back upon the well-known examples of Elijah and Elisha, whose miraculous power—passing by those who were *near*—expended itself on those *at a distance*, yea on *heathens;* 'these being,' to use the words of *Stier*, 'the two great prophetic prophets who stand at the commencement of prophetic antiquity, and whose miracles strikingly prefigured those of our Lord. As He intended like them to feed the poor and cleanse the lepers, He points to these *miracles of mercy*, and not to the *fire* from heaven and the *bears* that tore the mockers.' **28. And all they in the synagogue, when they heard these things, were filled with wrath**—maddened at the severity with which it reflected upon them, and at those allusions to the *heathen* which brought such a storm of violence afterwards on His apostle at Jerusalem (Acts xxii. 21, 22): **29. And rose up**—breaking up the service irreverently and rushing forth, **and thrust him out of the city**—with violence, as a prisoner in their hands. **and led him unto the brow of the hill whereon their city was built.** Nazareth, though not built on the ridge of a hill, is in part surrounded by one to the west, having several such precipices. It was a mode of capital punishment not unusual in ancient times among the Jews (see 2 Chr. xxv. 12; 2 Ki. ix. 33), the Romans, and others; and to this day examples of it occur in the East. This was the first open insult which the Son of God received, and it came from "them of His own household"! (Matt. x. 36). **30. But he passing through the midst of them went his way**—evidently in a miraculous manner, though perhaps quite noiselessly, leading them to wonder afterwards what spell could have come over them that they allowed Him to escape. Escapes, however, remarkably similar and beyond dispute, in times of persecution, stand on record.

Remarks.—1. Was there ever a more appalling illustration of human depravity than the treatment which the Lord Jesus received from His Nazarene townsmen? Real provocation there was none. Demonstrations of His miraculous power they had no right to demand; and if without these they declined to believe in Him, they had their liberty to do so unchallenged. He knew them too well to indulge them with bootless displays of His divine power; and by an allusion to the Lord's sovereign procedure in ancient times, in dispensing His compassion to whom He would, and quite differently from what might have been expected, He indicated to them intelligibly enough why He declined to do at Nazareth what He had done exuberantly at Capernaum. But, as if to compensate for this, and gain them otherwise, if that were possible, He seems to have spoken in their synagogue with even more than His usual suavity and grace; insomuch that "all bore Him witness, and wondered at the gracious words which proceeded out of His mouth." Yet all was in vain. Nor were they contented with venting their rage in malignant speeches; but, unable to restrain themselves, they broke through the sanctities of public worship and the decencies of ordinary life, and like lions roaring for their prey they rushed upon Him to destroy Him. After this, we may indeed wonder the less at the question, "Can any good thing come out of Nazareth?" But instead of contenting ourselves with ascribing such procedure to the exceptional perversity of the Nazarene character, we shall do well to inquire whether there be not in it a revelation of human malignity, which hateth the light, neither cometh to the light, lest its deeds should be reproved, and which, if it would speak out its mind on the Redeemer's gracious approach to it, would say, "What have we to do with Thee, Jesus, thou Son of God most High? We know Thee who thou art; the Holy One of God"! 2. Did the Lord Jesus become so common amongst His Nazarene townsmen, with whom He had mingled in the ordinary intercourse of society during His early life, that they were unable to take in His divine claims when at length presented to them with matchless benignity and grace? Then must there be a deep principle in the proverb by which

A. D. 30.

31 And [c] came down to Capernaum, a city of Galilee, and taught them on
32 the sabbath days. And they were astonished at his doctrine: [d] for his
33 word was with power. And [e] in the synagogue there was a man
which had a spirit of an unclean devil, and cried out with a loud voice,
34 saying, [3] Let *us* alone; what have we to do with thee, *thou* Jesus of
Nazareth? art thou come to destroy us? I know thee who thou art; [f] the
35 Holy One of God. And Jesus rebuked him, saying, Hold thy peace, and
come out of him. And when the devil had thrown him in the midst, he
36 came out of him, and hurt him not. And they were all amazed, and
spake among themselves, saying, What a word *is* this! for with authority
37 and power he commandeth the unclean spirits, and they come out. And
[g] the fame of him went out into every place of the country round about.
38 And [h] he arose out of the synagogue, and entered into Simon's house.
And Simon's wife's mother was taken with a great fever; and they
39 besought him for her. And he stood over her, and [i] rebuked the fever;
and it left her. And immediately she arose and ministered unto them.
40 Now [j] when the sun was setting, all they that had any sick with divers
diseases brought them unto him; and he laid his hands on every one of
41 them, and healed them. And [k] devils also came out of many, crying

[c] Matt. 4. 13. Mark 1. 21.
[d] Matt. 7. 28, 29. Tit. 2. 15.
[e] Mark 1. 23.
[3] Or, away.
[f] Ps. 16. 10. Isa. 49. 7. Dan. 9. 24. ch. 1. 35. Acts 2. 31. Ac's 4. 37.
[g] Ps. 72. 8. Mic. 5. 4.
[h] Matt. 8. 14. Mark 1. 29. 1 Cor. 9. 5.
[i] Ps. 103. 3. ch. 8. 24.
[j] Matt. 8. 16. Mark 1. 32.
[k] Mark 1. 34. Mark 3. 11.

He explains it, "A prophet is not without honour, but in his own country, and among his own kin, and in his own house." As if He had said, 'The nearer the vision, the less the attraction.' We must not descend so low as to recall our own analogous maxims; but in fact, almost every language has such sayings, showing that there is a principle in it, everywhere arresting attention. In the case of mere showy virtues, there is no difficulty in explaining it. It is merely this, that nearer inspection discovers the tinsel which distance concealed. The difficulty is to account for the ordinary intercourses of life destroying, or at least blunting, the charm of real excellence, and in this case taking down, in the eyes of His Nazarene townsmen, even the matchless excellences of the Lord Jesus. In all other cases there is an element which cannot be taken into account here. There are foibles of character invisible at a distance, which the familiarities of ordinary life never fail to reveal. But if it be asked on what principle, common to the Holy One of God with all other men, the fact in question is to be accounted for, perhaps two things may explain it. As novelty charms, so that to which we are accustomed has one charm less, however intrinsically worthy of admiration. But in addition to this, there is such a tendency to dissociate loftiness of spirit from the ordinary functions and intercourses of life, that if the one be seen without the other it is likely to be appreciated at its full value; whereas, when associated with languor and want, waste and dust, and the consequent necessity of eating and drinking, sleeping and waking, and such like, then that loftiness of spirit is apt to be less lofty in our esteem, and we say in our hearts, 'After all, they are much like other people'—as if in such things they could or ought to be otherwise. This, however, would be a small matter, if it did not intrude itself into the spiritual domain. But there also its operation is painfully felt, occasioning a false and unholy separation between natural and spiritual, human and divine, earthly and heavenly things. 'Is not this the carpenter's son? Is not his mother called Mary? And his brothers—James and Joses and Simon and Judas—don't we all know them? Haven't we done business with them? Haven't they been in our houses? and this Jesus himself, have we not seen Him in boyhood and youth moving about amongst us? Can this be He of whom Moses and all the prophets wrote? Can this be He who is sent to heal the broken-hearted, and comfort all that mourn? Incredible!' Nor can it be doubted that a nearer view of Him than even ordinary Nazarenes could have was the very thing that stumbled His own "brethren," who for a while, we are told, "did not believe in Him," and that made even the whole family think He was "beside Himself" (Mark iii. 21). Well, if these things be so, let Christians learn wisdom from it. Recognizing the principle which lies at the bottom of the proverb quoted by our Lord, it will be their wisdom, with Him, to bring their character and principles to bear rather upon *strangers* than upon those to whom they have become too familiar in the ordinary walks of life; for the rare exceptions to this only prove the rule. On the other hand, let Christians beware of being too slow to recognize eminent graces and gifts in those whom they have known very intimately *before* these discovered themselves. 3. As we read that Jesus, when about to be hurled down a precipice, glided through the midst of them and went His way, we perhaps think only of His own peculiar resources for self-preservation. But when we remember how He only refused to avail Himself wantonly of the promise rehearsed to Him by the Tempter, "He shall give His angels charge over Thee, to keep Thee in all Thy ways; and in their hands they shall bear Thee up, lest at any time Thou dash Thy foot against a stone," may we not suppose that the unseen ministry of angels, now if ever legitimately available, had something to do with the marvellous preservation of Jesus on this occasion? Nor can it well be doubted that their interposition in similar ways since in behalf of "the heirs of salvation" (Heb. i. 14) is the secret of the many and marvellous escapes of such which are on record.

31-44.—HEALING OF A DEMONIAC IN THE SYNAGOGUE OF CAPERNAUM, AND THEREAFTER OF SIMON'S MOTHER-IN-LAW AND MANY OTHERS—NEXT DAY, JESUS IS FOUND IN A SOLITARY PLACE, AND IS ENTREATED TO RETURN, BUT DECLINES, AND GOES FORTH ON HIS FIRST MISSIONARY CIRCUIT. (= Matt. viii. 14-17; iv. 23-25; Mark i. 29-39.) For the exposition of this Section—embracing, as appears, the first recorded transactions of our Lord on the Sabbath day in Galilee,

out, and saying, Thou art Christ, the Son of God. And [l]he, rebuking
them, suffered them not [4]to speak: for they knew that he was Christ.
42 And [m]when it was day, he departed and went into a desert place; and
the people sought him, and came unto him, and stayed him, that he
43 should not depart from them. And he said unto them, [n]I must preach
44 the kingdom of God to other cities also: for therefore am I sent. And
[o]he preached in the synagogues of Galilee.
5 AND [a]it came to pass, that, as the people pressed upon him to hear
2 the word of God, he stood by the lake of Gennesaret, and saw two ships
standing by the lake: but the fishermen were gone out of them, and were
3 washing *their* nets. And he entered into one of the ships, which was
Simon's, and prayed him that he would thrust out a little from the land.
And he sat down, and taught the people out of the ship.
4 Now when he had left speaking, he said unto Simon, [b]Launch out into
5 the deep, and let down your nets for a draught. And Simon answering
said unto him, Master, we have toiled all the night, and have taken
6 nothing: nevertheless at thy word I will let down the net. And when
they had this done, they inclosed a great multitude of fishes: and their
7 net brake. And they beckoned unto *their* partners, which were in the
other ship, that they should come and help them. And they came, and
8 filled both the ships, so that they began to sink. When Simon Peter
saw *it,* he fell down at Jesus' knees, saying, [c]Depart from me; for I am a
9 sinful man, O Lord. For he was astonished, and all that were with him,
10 at the draught of the fishes which they had taken: and so *was* also
James and John, the sons of Zebedee, which were partners with Simon.
And Jesus said unto Simon, Fear not; [d]from henceforth thou shalt catch
11 men. And when they had brought their ships to land, [e]they forsook all,
and followed him.

A. D. 31.
[l] Mark 1. 25, 34.
[4] Or, to say that they knew him to be Christ
[m] Mark 1. 35.
[n] Mark 1. 14, 15. Acts 10. 38. Rom. 15. 8.
[o] Mark 1. 39.

CHAP. 5.
[a] Matt. 4. 18. Mark 1. 16. ch. 12. 1.
[b] John 21. 6.
[c] Ex. 20. 19. Jud. 13. 22. 1 Sam. 6. 20. 2 Sam. 6. 9. 1 Ki. 17. 18. 1 Chr. 13. 12. Job 42. 5, 6. Dan. 8. 17.
[d] Ezek. 47. 9, 10. Matt. 4. 19. Mark 1. 17.
[e] Matt. 4. 20. Matt. 19. 27. Mark 1. 18. ch. 18. 28. Phil. 3. 7, 8.

and those of the following morning—see on Mark i. 29-39; and on Matt. iv. 23-25.

CHAP. V. 1-11.—MIRACULOUS DRAUGHT OF FISHES, AND CALL OF PETER, JAMES, AND JOHN. In our exposition of Matt. iv. 18-22, we have shown, as it appears to us, that this was quite a different occasion from that, and consequently that the calling of the disciples there and here recorded were different callings. This one, as we take it, was neither their first call, recorded in John i. 35-42; nor their second, recorded in Matt. iv. 18-22; but their *third* and last before their appointment to the apostleship. These calls are to be viewed as progressive stages in their preparation for the great work before them, and something similar is observable in the providential preparation of other eminent servants of Christ for the work to which they are destined.

1. And it came to pass, that, as the people pressed upon him [ἐπικεῖσθαι]—lit., 'lay upon Him' **to hear the word of God, he stood by the lake of Gennesaret, 2, 3. And saw two ships, &c. And he entered into one of the ships, which was Simon's . . . And he sat down, and taught the people out of the ship**—as in Matt. xiii. 2.

4. Now when he had left speaking, he said unto Simon, Launch out into the deep, and let down your nets for a draught—munificent recompense for the use of his boat! **5. And Simon answering said unto him, Master** ['Επιστάτα]—betokening not surely a first acquaintance, but a relationship already formed. **we have toiled all night**—the usual time of fishing then (John xxi. 3), and even now. **and have taken nothing: nevertheless at thy word I will let down the net.** Peter, as a fisherman, knew how hopeless it was to "let down his net" again at that time, save as a mere act of faith, "at His word" of command, which carried in it, as it ever does, assurance of success. This is a further proof that he must have been already and for some time a follower of Christ. **6. And when they had this done, they inclosed a great multitude of fishes: and their net brake** [διεῤῥήγνυτο]. This should have been rendered, 'was breaking,' or 'was beginning to break;' for evidently it did not break. **7. And they beckoned unto their partners which were in the other ship, that they should come and help them. And they came, and filled both the ships, so that they began to sink** [βυθίζεσθαι]—'were sinking,' or 'were beginning to sink.' **8. When Simon Peter saw it, he fell down at Jesus' knees, saying, Depart from me; for I am a sinful man, O Lord.** Did Peter then wish Christ to leave him? Verily no. His all was wrapt up in Him. (See John vi. 68.) 'Twas rather, 'Woe is me, Lord! How shall I abide this blaze of glory? A sinner such as I am is not fit company for Thee.' Compare Isa. vi. 5. **9, 10. For he was astonished, and all that were with him . . . And Jesus said unto Simon, Fear not.** This shows that the Lord read Peter's speech very differently from many learned and well-meaning commentators on it. **from henceforth**—marking a new stage in their connection with Christ. **thou shalt catch men.** 'What wilt thou think, Simon, overwhelmed by this draught of fishes, when I shall bring to thy net what will dim all this glory?' **11. And when they had brought their ships to land, they forsook all and followed him.** They did this before (Matt. iv. 20); now they do it again: and yet after the Crucifixion they are at their boats once more (John xxi. 3). In such a business this is easily conceivable. After Pentecost, however, they appear to have finally abandoned their secular calling.

12 And [f]it came to pass, when he was in a certain city, behold a man full
of leprosy; who, seeing Jesus, fell on *his* face, and besought him, saying,
13 Lord, if thou wilt, thou canst [g]make me clean. And he put forth *his*
hand, and touched him, saying, I will: be thou clean. And immediately
14 the leprosy departed from him. And [h]he charged him to tell no man:
but go, and show thyself to the priest, and offer for thy cleansing,
15 [i]according as Moses commanded, for a testimony unto them. But so
much the more went there a fame abroad of him: and [j]great multitudes
came together to hear, and to be healed by him of their infirmities.
16 And [k]he withdrew himself into the wilderness, and prayed.
17 And it came to pass on a certain day, as he was teaching, that there
were Pharisees and doctors of the law sitting by, which were come out of
every town of Galilee, and Judea, and Jerusalem: and the power of the
18 Lord was *present* to heal them. And, [l]behold, men brought in a bed
a man which was taken with a palsy: and they sought *means* to bring
19 him in, and to lay *him* before him. And when they could not find by
what *way* they might bring him in because of the multitude, they went
upon the housetop, and let him down through the tiling with *his* couch
20 into the midst before Jesus. And when he saw their [m]faith, he said
21 unto him, Man, [n]thy sins are forgiven thee. And [o]the scribes and the
Pharisees began to reason, saying, Who is this which speaketh blasphemies?

A. D. 31.

[f] Matt. 8. 2. Mark 1. 40.
[g] Gen. 18. 14. Jer. 32. 17, 27. Matt. 8.8,9. Matt. 9. 28. Mark 9. 22-24. Heb. 7. 25.
[h] Matt. 8. 4.
[i] Lev. 13. 1. Lev. 14. 4,10, 21, 22.
[j] Matt. 4. 25. Mark 3. 7. ch. 12. 1. ch. 14. 25. John 6. 2.
[k] Mark 14.23. Mark 6. 46.
[l] Matt. 9. 2. Mark 2. 3.
[m] Rev. 2. 23.
[n] Acts 5. 31.
[o] Matt. 9. 3. Mark 2 6,7.

Remarks.—1. Did Jesus give His disciples this miraculous draught of fishes after they had toiled all the previous night and caught nothing? Did He do the same thing after His resurrection in precisely similar circumstances? Did He heal the impotent man at the pool of Bethesda, who had endured his infirmity thirty and eight years, but not till he had long vainly endeavoured to obtain a cure by stepping into the pool? In a word, Did He let the woman endure her issue of blood twelve years, and spend all that she had upon physicians, only to find herself worse instead of better, before she found instant healing under His wings? Let us not doubt that "all these things happened unto them for ensamples, and are written for our admonition on whom the ends of the world are come," to the intent we should not doubt that at evening time it shall be light, that God *will* hear His own elect that cry unto Him day and night, though He hold out long, as if deaf to them. 2. If the exclamation of Peter, "Depart from me, for I am a sinful man, O Lord," be compared with that of Isaiah, when the thrice-Holy One was revealed to him in his temple-vision, "Woe is me! for I am undone; because I am a man of unclean lips . . . for mine eyes have seen the King the Lord of hosts" (Isa. vi. 5), can any right-thinking mind fail to see that such a speech, if from one creature to another, ought to have been met as Paul met the attempts of the Lycaonians to do sacrifice to him and Barnabas, when he ran in among them, exclaiming with horror—"Sirs, why do ye these things? We also are men of like passions with you, and preach unto you that ye should turn from these vanities unto the living God" (Acts xiv. 14, 15); and that when Jesus, instead of rebuking it, only comforted His trembling disciple with the assurance that wonders far surpassing what he had just witnessed would follow his own labours, He set His seal to views of His Person and character, which only the Word made flesh was entitled to accept? In fact, the more highly they deemed of Him, ever the more grateful it seemed to be to the Redeemer's spirit. Never did they pain Him by manifesting too lofty conceptions of Him. 3. 'Simon,' says *Bishop Hall* most admirably, 'doth not greedily fall upon so unexpected and profitable a booty, but he turns his eyes from the draught to Himself, from the act to the Author, acknowledging vileness in the one, in the other majesty: "Go from me, Lord, for I am a sinful man." It had been a pity the honest fisher should have been taken at his word. O Simon, thy Saviour is come into thine own ship to call thee, to call others by thee, unto blessedness; and dost thou say, "Lord, go from me?" as if the patient should say to the physician, Depart from me, for I am sick. [But] it was the voice of astonishment, not of dislike; the voice of humility, not of discontentment: yea, because thou art a sinful man, therefore hath thy Saviour need to come to thee, to stay with thee; and because thou art humble in the acknowledgment of thy sinfulness, therefore Christ delights to abide with thee, and will call thee to abide with Him. No man ever fared the worse for abasing himself to his God. Christ hath left many a soul for froward and unkind usage; never any for the disparagement of itself, and entreaties of humility. Simon could not devise how to hold Christ faster than by thus suing Him to be gone, than by thus pleading his unworthiness.' 4. Did Jesus teach Simon to regard the ingathering of souls to Himself by the Gospel as transcending all physical miracles? O that the ministers of the everlasting Gospel would rise to such a view of their calling, and travail in birth until Christ be formed in men's souls! But it is not they only whom Christ's words to Peter are fitted to stimulate. "He that winneth souls is wise" (Prov. xi. 30)—be he who he may. "They that be wise shall shine as the brightness of the firmament; and they"—whoever they be—"that turn many to righteousness as the stars for ever and ever" (Dan. xii. 3). "Brethren, if any of you do err from the truth, and *one* convert him"—no matter who—"let him know that he which converteth the sinner from the error of his way shall save a soul from death, and shall hide a multitude of sins" (Jas. v. 19, 20).

12-16.—HEALING OF A LEPER. (= Matt. viii. 1-4; Mark i. 40-45.) For the exposition, see on Matt. viii. 1-4.

17-26.—HEALING OF A PARALYTIC. (= Matt. ix.

22 [p]Who can forgive sins but God alone? But when Jesus perceived their
thoughts, he answering said unto them, What reason ye in your hearts?
23 Whether is easier to say, Thy sins be forgiven thee; or to say, Rise up
24 and walk? But that ye may know that [q]the Son of man hath power
upon earth to forgive sins, (he said unto the sick of the palsy,) I say
unto thee, Arise, and take up thy couch, and go unto thine house.
25 And immediately he rose up before them, and took up that whereon he
26 lay, and departed to his own house, [r]glorifying God. And they were all
amazed, and they glorified God, and were filled with fear, saying, We
have seen strange things to-day.
27 And [s]after these things he went forth, and saw a publican, named
Levi, sitting at the receipt of custom: and he said unto him, Follow me.
28 And he left all, rose up, and followed him. And [t]Levi made him a great
29 feast in his own house: and [u]there was a great company of publicans and
30 of others that sat down with them. But their scribes and Pharisees
murmured against his disciples, saying, Why do ye eat and drink with
31 publicans and sinners? And Jesus answering said unto them, They that
32 are whole need not a physician; but they that are sick. I [v]came not to
call the righteous, but sinners to repentance.
33 And they said unto him, [w]Why do the disciples of John fast often,
and make prayers, and likewise *the disciples* of the Pharisees; but thine
34 eat and drink? And he said unto them, Can ye make the children of the
35 bride-chamber fast while the [x]bridegroom is with them? But the days
will come, when the bridegroom shall [y]be taken away from them, and
36 then shall they [z]fast in those days. And [a]he spake also a parable unto
them; No man putteth a piece of a new garment upon an old: if otherwise, then both the new maketh a rent, and the piece that was *taken* out
37 of the new agreeth not with the old. And no man putteth new wine into
old bottles; else the new wine will burst the bottles, and be spilled, and
38 the bottles shall perish. But new wine must be put into new bottles;
39 and both are preserved. No man also having drunk old *wine* straightway
desireth new; for he saith, The old is better.

A. D. 31.
[p] Ex. 34. 7. Is. 32. 5. Ps. 103. 3. Isa. 1. 18. Isa. 43. 25. Dan. 9. 9.
[q] Isa. 53. 11. Matt. 9. 6. Matt. 28. 18. John 5. 22, 23. Acts 5. 31. Col. 3. 13.
[r] Ps. 103. 1.
[s] Matt. 9. 9. Mark 2. 13, 14.
[t] Matt. 9. 10. Mark 2. 15.
[u] ch. 15. 1.
[v] Matt. 9. 13. 1 Tim. 1. 15.
[w] Matt. 9. 14. Mark 2. 18.
[x] Matt. 22. 2. ch. 14. 16-23. 2 Cor. 11. 2. Rev. 19. 7. Rev. 21. 2.
[y] Dan. 9. 26. Zec. 13. 7. John 7. 33.
[z] Matt. 6. 16, 17. Acts 13. 2, 3. 1 Cor. 7. 5. 2 Cor. 6. 4, 5. 2 Cor. 11. 27.
[a] Matt. 9. 16, 17. Mark 2. 21, 22.

1-8; Mark ii. 1-12.) For the exposition, see on Mark ii. 1-12.

27-32.—LEVI'S (OR MATTHEW'S) CALL AND FEAST. (= Matt. ix. 9-13; Mark ii. 14-17.) For the exposition, see on Matt. ix. 9-13.

33-39.—DISCOURSE ON FASTING. (= Matt. ix. 14-17; Mark ii. 18-22.) As this discourse is recorded by all the three first Evangelists immediately after their account of the Feast which Matthew made to his Lord, there can be no doubt that it was delivered on that occasion.

Mark introduces the subject thus (ii. 18): "And the disciples of John and of the Pharisees used to fast." These disciples of John, who seem not to have statedly followed Jesus, occupied a position intermediate between the Pharisaic life and that to which Jesus trained His own disciples; further advanced than the one, not so far advanced as the other. "And they come and say unto him"—or, according to our Evangelist, to whose narrative we now come, they brought their difficulty to Him through our Lord's own disciples. **33. And they said unto him, Why do the disciples of John fast often, and make prayers, and likewise the disciples of the Pharisees?** These seem to have fasted twice in the week (Luke xviii. 12), besides the prescribed seasons, **but thine eat and drink**—or, as in Matt. and Mark, "thy disciples fast not?" **34. And he said unto them, Can ye make the children of the bride-chamber**—the bridal attendants, **fast while the bridegroom is with them?** Glorious title for Jesus to take to Himself! The Old Testament is full of this conjugal tie between Jehovah and His people, to be realized in Messiah. See on Matt. xxii. 2, and Remark 1 on that Section; and compare John iii. 29. **35. But the days will come** [Ἐλεύσονται δὲ ἡμέραι]—rather, 'But days will come,' **when the bridegroom shall be taken away from them**—a delicate and affecting allusion to coming events, and the grief with which these would fill the disciples, **and then shall they fast in those days**—*q.d.*, 'In My presence such exercises were unseemly: when bereft of Me, they will have time enough and cause enough.' **36. And he spake also a parable unto them; No man putteth a piece of a new garment upon an old.** In Matthew and Mark the word employed [ἀγνάφου] signifies 'uncarded,' 'unfulled,' or 'undressed' cloth, which, as it is apt to shrink when wetted, would rend the old cloth to which it was sewed: **if otherwise**—if he *will* do so unwise a thing, **then both the new maketh a rent, and the piece that was taken out of the new agreeth not with the old. 37. And no man putteth new wine into old bottles** [ἀσκοὺς]—'wine-skins.' They were made usually of goat-skins, and of course would be liable to burst in the case supposed: **else** [εἰ δέ μήγε, again]—if he do such a thing, **the new wine will burst the bottles, and be spilled, and the bottles shall perish. 38. But new wine must be put into new bottles; and both are preserved. 39. No man also having drunk old wine straightway desireth new; for he saith, The old is better.** These are just examples of *incon-*

6 AND [a]it came to pass, on the second sabbath after the first, that he
went through the corn fields; and his disciples plucked the ears of corn,
2 and did eat, rubbing *them* in *their* hands. And certain of the Pharisees
said unto them, [b]Why do ye that which is not lawful to do on the
3 sabbath days? And Jesus answering them said, Have ye not read so
much as this, [c]what David did, when himself was an hungered, and they
4 which were with him; how he went into the house of God, and did take
and eat the showbread, and gave also to them that were with him;
5 [d]which it is not lawful to eat but for the priests alone? And he said
unto them, That the Son of man is Lord also of the sabbath.
6 And [e]it came to pass also on another sabbath, that he entered into the
synagogue and taught: and there was a man whose right hand was
7 withered. And the scribes and Pharisees watched him, whether he would
heal on the sabbath day; that they might find an accusation against
8 him. But he [f]knew their thoughts, and said to the man which had the
withered hand, Rise up, and stand forth in the midst. And he arose and
9 stood forth. Then said Jesus unto them, I will ask you one thing; [g]Is
it lawful on the sabbath days to do good, or to do evil? to save life, or to
10 destroy *it?* And looking round about upon them all, he said unto the
man, Stretch forth thy hand. And he did so: and his hand was restored
11 whole as the other. And they were filled with madness; and communed
one with another what they might do to Jesus.

A. D. 31.

CHAP. 6.

a Matt. 12. 1. Mark 2. 23.

b Ex. 20. 10. Matt. 12. 2. Matt. 15. 2. Mark 7. 2.

c 1 Sam. 21. 6.

d Ex. 29. 23, 33. Lev. 24. 9.

e Matt. 12. 9. Mark 3. 1. ch. 13. 14. ch. 14. 3. John 9. 16.

f 1 Sam. 16. 7. ch. 5. 22. John 2. 24, 25. John 6. 64. John 21. 17. Acts 1. 24. Rev. 2. 23.

g Matt. 12. 12, 13. Mark 3. 4. ch. 14. 3. John 7. 23.

gruities in common things. As men's good sense leads them to avoid these in ordinary life, so are there analogous incongruities in spiritual things which the wise will shun. But what has this to do with the question about fasting? Much every way. The genius of the old economy—of whose *sadness* and *bondage* "fasting" might be taken as the symbol—was quite different from that of the new, whose characteristic is *freedom* and *joy:* the one of these, then, was not to be mixed up with the other. As, in the one case adduced for illustration, "the rent is made worse," and in the other "the new wine is spilled," so 'by a mongrel mixture of the ascetic ritualism of the old with the spiritual freedom of the new economy both are disfigured and destroyed.' The parable about preferring the old wine to the new, which is peculiar to our Gospel, has been variously interpreted. But the "new wine" seems plainly to be the evangelical freedom which Christ was introducing; and "the old," the opposite spirit of Judaism: men long accustomed to the latter could not be expected "straightway," or all at once, to take a liking for the former:—*q. d.*, 'These inquiries about the difference between My disciples, and the Pharisees, and even John's ways of living, are not surprising; they are the effect of *a natural revulsion against sudden change*, which time will cure; *the new wine will itself in time become old, and so acquire all the added charms of antiquity.*'

Remarks.—1. There may seem to be some inconsistency between the freedom and joy which our Lord here indirectly teaches to be characteristic of the new economy, and that sadness at His departure in Person from the Church which He intimates would be the proper feeling of all that love Him during the present state. But the two are quite consistent. We may sorrow for one thing and rejoice for another, even at the same time. The one, indeed, will necessarily chasten the other; and so it is here. The liberty wherewith Christ hath made us free is a well-spring of resistless and commanded joy; nor is this a jot abated, but only chastened and refined, by the widowed feeling of Christ's absence. But neither is this sense of Christ's absence the less real and sad that we are taught to "rejoice in the Lord alway," "Whom having not seen we love, in whom believing we rejoice with joy unspeakable and full of glory," in the assurance that "when He who is our Life shall appear, we also shall appear with Him in glory." 2. In all transition-states of the Church, or of any section of it, from the worse to the better, two classes appear among the true-hearted, representing two extremes. In the one, the *conservative* element prevails; in the other, the *progressive.* The one, sympathizing with the movement, are yet afraid of its going too fast and too far: the other are impatient of half-measures. The sympathy of the one class with what is good in the movement is almost neutralized and lost by their apprehension of the evil that is likely to attend the change: the sympathy of the other class with it is so commanding, that they are blind to danger, and have no patience with that caution which seems to them only timidity and trimming. There are dangers on both sides. Of many who shrink in the day of trial, when one bold step would land them safely on the right side, it may be said, "The children are brought to the birth, and there is not strength to bring forth." To many reckless reformers, who mar their own work, it may be said, "Be not righteous overmuch, neither make thyself overwise: why shouldest thou destroy thyself?" Our Lord's teaching here, while it has a voice to those who unreasonably cling to what is antiquated, speaks still more clearly to those hasty reformers who have no patience with the timidity of their weaker brethren. What a gift to the Church, in times of life from the dead, are even a few men endued with the wisdom to steer the ship between those two rocks!

CHAP. VI. 1-5.—PLUCKING CORN-EARS ON THE SABBATH DAY. (= Matt. xii. 1-8; Mark ii. 23-28.) For the exposition, see on Matt. xii. 1-8.

6-11.—THE HEALING OF A WITHERED HAND. (= Matt. xii. 9-14; Mark iii. 1-6.) For the exposition, see on Matt. xii. 9-14.

12-49.—THE TWELVE APOSTLES CHOSEN—GATHERING MULTITUDES AND GLORIOUS HEALINGS—THE SERMON IN THE PLAIN (OR LEVEL PLACE). (= Matt. x. 2-4; v.—vii.; Mark iii. 13-19.)

12 And [h]it came to pass in those days, that he went out into a mountain
13 to pray, and continued all night in prayer to God. And when it was
day, he called *unto him* his disciples: [i]and of them he chose twelve,
14 whom also he named Apostles; Simon, ([j]whom he also named Peter,)
and Andrew his brother, James and John, Philip and Bartholomew,
15 Matthew and Thomas, James the *son* of Alpheus, and Simon called
16 Zelotes, and Judas [k]*the brother* of James, and Judas Iscariot, which also
was the traitor.
17 And he came down with them, and stood in the plain, and the
company of his disciples, [l]and a great multitude of people out of
all Judea and Jerusalem, and from the sea coast of Tyre and Sidon,
18 which came to hear him, and to be healed of their diseases; and they
19 that were vexed with unclean spirits: and they were healed. And the
whole multitude [m]sought to touch him: for [n]there went virtue out of
him, and healed *them* all.
20 And he lifted up his eyes on his disciples, and said, [o]Blessed *be ye*
21 poor: for yours is the kingdom of God. Blessed [p]*are ye* that hunger
now: for ye shall be filled. [q]Blessed *are ye* that weep now: for ye shall
22 laugh. Blessed [r]are ye when men shall hate you, and when they [s]shall
separate you *from their company*, and shall reproach *you*, and cast out your

A. D. 31.

[h] Matt. 14. 23.
[i] Matt. 10. 1.
[j] John 1. 42.
[k] John 14. 22. Acts 1. 13. Jude 1.
[l] Matt. 4. 25. Mark 3. 7.
[m] Matt. 14. 36.
[n] Mark 5. 30. ch. 8. 46.
[o] Matt. 5. 3. Matt. 11. 5. Acts 14. 22. Jas. 2. 5.
[p] Isa. 55. 1. 1 Cor. 4. 11.
[q] Isa. 61. 3. Rev. 7. 14-17.
[r] Matt. 5. 11. 1 Pet. 2. 19. 1 Pet. 3. 14. 1 Pet. 4. 14.
[s] John 16. 2.

Our Lord has now reached the most important period in His public ministry, when His Twelve Apostles have to be chosen; and it is done with a solemnity corresponding to the weighty issues involved in it.

The Twelve Chosen (12-16). **12. And it came to pass in those days, that he went out**—probably from Capernaum, **and continued all night in prayer to God. 13. And when it was day, he called unto him his disciples: and of them he chose twelve, whom also he named apostles** [ἀποστόλους]—'sent,' or 'commissioned;' as if to put upon the very name by which they were in all future time to be known the seal of their Master's appointment. The work with which the day began shows what had been the burden of this whole night's devotions. As He directed His disciples to pray for "labourers" just before sending themselves forth (see on Matt. ix. 35—x. 5, Remarks 1 and 2), so here we find the Lord Himself in prolonged communion with His Father in preparation for the solemn appointment of those men who were to give birth to His Church, and from whom the world in all time was to take a new mould. How instructive is this! They appear all to have been first selected from amongst those who had been disciples of John the Baptist (see Acts i. 21, 22), as probably the most advanced or the most teachable; with a view also, no doubt, to diversity of gifts. And after watching the steadiness with which they had followed Him, the progress they had made in the knowledge of the truth, and their preparedness to enter the higher school to which they were now to be advanced, He solemnly "ordained" [ἐποίησεν], or 'constituted' these Twelve men, "that they should be with Him" (Mark iii. 14) as a Family, and enjoy His most private fellowship, as none of His other followers were permitted to do. By this they would not only hear much more from Him, and have it impressed upon them as it could not else have been, but catch His spirit, and take on a stamp which, when He was removed from them, and they had to prosecute His work, would bring their Master Himself to the recollection, of His enemies. (See on Acts iv. 13.) **14-16. Simon, &c.** See on Matt. x. 1-4.

Gathering Multitudes and Glorious Healings (17-19). **17. And he came down with them, and stood in the plain** [ἐπὶ τόπου πεδινοῦ]—or, 'on a level place;' that is, probably on some level plat below the mountain, while the listening multitudes lay beneath Him on what was more strictly "the plain." **and the company of his disciples**—the outer circle of His stated followers, **and a great multitude . . . which came to hear him, and to be healed of their diseases; 18. And they that were vexed with unclean spirits: and they were healed. 19. And the whole multitude sought to touch him: for there went virtue** [δύναμις]—or healing 'efficacy'—compare Mark v. 30, **out of him, and healed them all** [ἰᾶτο]—or 'kept healing,' denoting successive acts of mercy, till it went over "*all*" that needed it. There is something unusually grand in this touch of description, giving to the reader the impression of a more than usual exuberance of His majesty and grace in this succession of healings, which made itself felt among all the vast multitude.

Sermon in the Plain or Level Place (20-49). **20. And he lifted up his eyes on his disciples, and said.** Referring to our ample comments on the Sermon on the Mount (Matt. v.-vii.), we here only note a few things suggested by the present form of the Discourse, which could not be so properly taken up under the other form of it. **Blessed be ye poor: for yours is the kingdom of God. 21. Blessed are ye that hunger now: for ye shall be filled.** In the Sermon on the Mount the benediction is pronounced upon the "poor *in spirit*" and those who "hunger and thirst *after righteousness*." Here it is simply on the "poor" and the "hungry now." In this form of the Discourse, then, our Lord seems to have had in view "*the poor of this world*, rich in faith, and heirs of the kingdom which God hath promised to them that love Him," as these very beatitudes are paraphrased by James (ii. 5). **Blessed are ye that weep now: for ye shall laugh** [γελάσατε]. How charming is the liveliness of this word, to express what in Matthew is calmly set forth by the word "comfort!" **22. Blessed are ye when men shall hate you, and when they shall separate you [from their company]** [ἀφορίσωσιν]—whether from Church-fellowship, by excommunition, or from their social circles—both hard to flesh and blood. **and shall reproach you, and cast out your name as evil, for the Son of**

23 name as evil, for the Son of man's sake. Rejoice [t]ye in that day, and
leap for joy: for, behold, your reward *is* great in heaven: for [u]in the like
24 manner did their fathers unto the prophets. But [v]woe unto you that
25 are rich! for ye [w]have received your consolation. Woe [x]unto you that
are full! for ye shall hunger. [y]Woe unto you that laugh now! for ye
26 shall mourn and weep. Woe [z]unto you when all men shall speak well of
you! for so did their fathers to the false prophets.
27 But [a]I say unto you which hear, Love your enemies, do good to them
28 which hate you, bless them that curse you, and [b]pray for them which
29 despitefully use you. And [c]unto him that smiteth thee on the *one* cheek
offer also the other; [d]and him that taketh away thy cloak forbid not *to*
30 *take thy* coat also. Give [e]to every man that asketh of thee; and of him
31 that taketh away thy goods ask *them* not again. And [f]as ye would that
32 men should do to you, do ye also to them likewise. For [g]if ye love them
which love you, what thank have ye? for sinners also love those that
33 love them. And if ye do good to them which do good to you, what
34 thank have ye? for sinners also do even the same. And [h]if ye lend *to*
them of whom ye hope to receive, what thank have ye? for sinners also
35 lend to sinners, to receive as much again. But love ye your enemies,
and do good, and [i]lend, hoping for nothing again; and your reward shall
be great, and [j]ye shall be the children of the Highest: for [k]he is kind
36 unto the unthankful and *to* the evil. Be [l]ye therefore merciful, as your
37 Father also is merciful. Judge [m]not, and ye shall not be judged: condemn not, and ye shall not be condemned: forgive, and ye shall be
38 forgiven: give, [n]and it shall be given unto you; good measure, pressed
down, and shaken together, and running over, shall men give into your
[o]bosom. For [p]with the same measure that ye mete withal it shall be
measured to you again.
39 And he spake a parable unto them: Can [q]the blind lead the blind?
40 shall they not both fall into the ditch? The [r]disciple is not above his
master: but every one [1]that is perfect shall be as his master.
41 And [s]why beholdest thou the mote that is in thy brother's eye, but
42 perceivest not the beam that is in thine own eye? Either how canst thou
say to thy brother, Brother, let me pull out the mote that is in thine eye,
when thou thyself beholdest not the beam that is in thine own eye?
Thou hypocrite, [t]cast out first the beam out of thine own eye, and then
shalt thou see clearly to pull out the mote that is in thy brother's eye.

A. D. 31.

[t] Acts 5. 41. Col. 1. 24. Jas. 1. 2.
[u] Acts 7. 51.
[v] Amos 6. 1. ch. 12. 21. Jas. 5. 1.
[w] Matt. 6. 2. ch. 16. 25.
[x] Isa. 65. 13.
[y] Pro. 14. 13.
[z] John 15. 19. 1 John 4. 5.
[a] Ex. 23. 4. Pro. 25. 2. Matt. 5. 44. Rom. 12. 20.
[b] ch. 23. 34. Acts 7. 60.
[c] Matt. 5. 39
[d] 1 Cor. 6. 7.
[e] Deut. 15. 7. Pro. 3. 27. Pro. 21. 26. Matt. 5. 42.
[f] Matt. 7. 12. Phil. 4. 8.
[g] Matt. 5. 46.
[h] Matt. 5. 42.
[i] Lev. 25. 35. Ps. 37. 26.
[j] Matt. 5. 45. 1 John 3. 1.
[k] Acts 14. 17.
[l] Matt. 5. 48. Eph. 5. 1, 2.
[m] Matt. 7. 1.
[n] Pro. 19. 17.
[o] Ps. 79. 12.
[p] Matt. 7. 2.
[q] Matt. 15. 14.
[r] Matt. 10. 24.
[1] Or, shall be perfected as his master.
[s] Matt. 7. 3.
[t] Pro. 18. 17

man's sake. Compare the following: "Being reviled, we bless; being persecuted, we suffer it; being defamed, we entreat; we are made as the filth of the world, and are the offscouring of all things unto this day" (1 Cor. iv. 12, 13). Observe the language of our Lord in regard to the cause of all this ill treatment "For the Son of man's sake," says He in *v.* 22: "For My sake," says He in Matt. v. 11: "For righteousness' sake," says He in the immediately preceding *v.* 10. *Thus does Christ bind up the cause of Righteousness in the world with the reception of Himself.* **23. Rejoice ye in that day, and leap [for joy]** [σκιρτήσατε]—a livelier word than even "be exceeding glad," or 'exult' in Matt. v. 12; **for, behold, your reward is great in heaven: for in the like manner did their fathers unto the prophets.** As five of the benedictions in the Sermon on the Mount are omitted in this Discourse, so now follow four *woes* not to be found there. And yet, being but the opposites of the benedictions pronounced, they need hardly any illustration. **24. But woe unto you that are rich! for ye have received your consolation. 25. Woe unto you that are full! for ye shall hunger**—your inward craving strong as ever, but the materials of satisfaction for ever gone. **Woe unto you that laugh now! for ye shall mourn and weep**—who have all your good things and joyous feelings *here* and *now*, in perishable objects. See on ch. xvi. 25. **26. Woe unto you when all men shall speak well of you! for so did their fathers to the false prophets**—paying court to them because they flattered them with peace when there was no peace. See Mic. ii. 11. For the principle of this woe and its proper limits, see John xv. 19.

37, 38. Judge not, and ye shall not be judged: condemn not . . . forgive . . . give, and it shall be given unto you; good measure, pressed down, &c. It will be observed, on comparing this with Matt. vii. 1, 2, that here it is much fuller and more graphic. **39. And he spake a parable unto them: Can the blind lead the blind? shall they not both fall into the ditch?** This is not in the Sermon on the Mount; but it is recorded by Matthew in another and very striking connection (ch. xv. 14). **40. The disciple is not above his master: but every one that is perfect shall be as his master**—*q. d.*, 'The disciple's aim is to come up to his master, and he

43 For [u]a good tree bringeth not forth corrupt fruit: neither doth a corrupt
44 tree bring forth good fruit. For [v]every tree is known by his own fruit.
For of thorns men do not gather figs, nor of a bramble bush gather they
45 [2]grapes. A [w]good man out of the good treasure of his heart bringeth
forth that which is good; and an evil man out of the evil treasure of his
heart bringeth forth that which is evil: for of the abundance of the heart
his mouth speaketh.
46 And [x]why call ye me, Lord, Lord, and do not the things which I say?
47 Whosoever [y]cometh to me, and heareth my sayings, and doeth them, I
48 will show you to whom he is like: he is like a man which built an house,
and digged deep, and laid the foundation on a rock: and when [z]the
flood arose, the stream beat vehemently upon that house, and could not
49 shake it; for it was founded upon [a]a rock. But he that heareth, and
doeth not, is like a man that without a foundation built an house upon
the earth; against which the stream did beat vehemently, and immediately it fell; and [b]the ruin of that house was great.
7 NOW when he had ended all his sayings in the audience of the people,
2 [a]he entered into Capernaum. And a certain centurion's servant, who
3 was dear unto him, was sick, and ready to die. And when he heard of
Jesus, he sent unto him the elders of the Jews, beseeching him that he
4 would come and heal his servant. And when they came to Jesus, they
besought him instantly, saying, That he was worthy for whom he should
5 do this: for he loveth our nation, and he hath built us a synagogue.
6 Then Jesus went with them.
And when he was now not far from the house, the centurion sent

A. D. 31

[u] Matt. 7. 16. Gal. 5. 19, 23. 2 Tim. 3. 1-9.
[v] Matt. 12. 33.
[2] A grape.
[w] Rom. 8. 5-8.
[x] Mal. 1. 6. Matt. 25. 11. ch. 13. 25. Rom. 2. 13. Jas. 1. 22.
[y] Matt. 7 24.
[z] Acts 14. 22. 2 Tim. 3. 12.
[a] Ps. 125. 1. 2 Tim. 2. 19. 1 Pet 1. 5. Jude 1.
[b] Job 8. 13. Heb. 10. 28-31. 2 Pet. 2. 20, 21.

CHAP. 7.
[a] Matt. 8. 5. Matt. 27 54. ch. 23. 47. Acts 10. 1, 2. Acts 22. 26. Acts 23. 17.

thinks himself complete when he does so: if ye then be but blind leaders of the blind, the perfection of your training will be but the certain and complete ruin of both.'

For Remarks on this Section, see those on the Sermon on the Mount generally, and particularly on the portions of it with which this Discourse corresponds.

CHAP. VII. 1-10.—HEALING OF THE CENTURION'S SERVANT. (= Matt. viii. 5-13.) The time of this scene seems to have been just after the preceding Discourse; the healing of the Leper (Matt. viii. 1-4, and Mark i. 40-45) only intervening—on the way, probably, from the Mount to Capernaum.

1. Now when he had ended all his sayings in the audience of the people, he entered into Capernaum. 2. And a certain centurion's servant, who was dear unto him, was sick, and ready to die. These centurions were Roman officers, so called from being captains over a hundred soldiers. Though a heathen by birth and early training, he had become acquainted with the Jewish Religion probably either while quartered at Capernaum or in some other Galilean town; although there were so many proselytes to the Jewish Religion in all the principal Greek and Roman cities that he might have embraced the true Faith even before his arrival in the Holy Land. The same may be said of Cornelius (Acts x. 1). His character appears here in the most beautiful light. The value which he set upon this dying servant and his anxiety for his recovery—as if he had been his own son—is the first feature in it; for, as *Bp. Hall* observes, he is unworthy to be well served who will not sometimes wait upon his followers. This servant was "sick of the palsy, grievously tormented" (Matt. viii. 6). **3. And when he heard of Jesus**—like the woman with the issue of blood (Mark v. 27), and the Syrophenician woman (Mark vii. 25). **he sent unto him the elders** [πρεσβυτέρους]—rather 'elders' **of the Jews.** His reason for this is best given in his own words of profound humility: "wherefore neither thought I myself worthy to come unto Thee" (*v.* 7). Matthew represents him as coming himself (viii. 5, 6): but this is only as James and John are said to have petitioned their Lord (Mark x. 35), when they got their mother to do it for them (Matt. xx. 20); and as Jesus made and baptized more disciples than John, though Jesus Himself baptized not, but His disciples (John iv. 1, 2); and as Pilate scourged Jesus (John xix. 1), when he ordered it to be done. **beseeching him that he would come and heal his servant. 4. And when they came to Jesus, they besought him instantly** [σπουδαίως]—or 'in haste,' **saying, That he was worthy for whom he should do this: 5. For he loveth our nation, and he hath built us a synagogue.** These elders content not themselves with delivering the humble petition of the centurion himself, but urge their own arguments in support of it. And how precious is the testimony they bear to this devout soldier; all the more so as coming from persons who were themselves probably strangers to the principle from which he acted. "He loveth our nation," they say; for he had found, in his happy experience, as our Lord said to the woman of Samaria, that "Salvation is of the Jews" (John iv. 22); "and (they add) he hath built us a synagogue" [καὶ τὴν συναγωγὴν αὐτὸς ᾠκοδόμησεν ἡμῖν]—'and himself built us the synagogue;' rebuilding the synagogue of the place at his own sole expense. His love to the Jews took this appropriate and somewhat costly form. He would leave a monument in Capernaum of the debt he owed to the God of Israel by providing for His worship and the comfort of His worshippers. If "a good name is better than precious ointment" (Eccl. vii. 1), this military proselyte certainly had it. **6. Then Jesus went with them.**

And when he was now not far from the house, the centurion sent friends to him. This

friends to him, saying unto him, Lord, trouble not thyself; for I am not
7 worthy that thou shouldest enter under my roof: wherefore neither thought
I myself worthy to come unto thee: [b]but say in a word, and my servant
8 shall be healed. For I also am a man set under authority, having under
me soldiers; and I say unto [1]one, Go, and he goeth; and to another,
Come, and he cometh; and to my servant, Do this, and he doeth *it*.
9 When Jesus heard these things, he marvelled at him, and turned him
about, and said unto the people that followed him, I say unto you, I
10 have not found so great faith, no, not in [c]Israel. And they that were
sent, returning to the house, found the servant whole that had been
sick.

A. D. 31.

[1] This man.

[b] Ex. 15. 16. Deut. 32. 39. 1 Sam. 2. 6. Ps. 33. 9. Ps. 107. 20. Mark 1. 27. ch. 4. 36. ch. 5. 13.

[c] Ps. 147. 19. Matt. 9. 33. Rom. 3. 1, 2. Rom. 9. 4.

was a second message; and here again, what Matthew represents as said to our Lord by the centurion himself is by Luke, who is more specific and full, put into the mouth of the centurion's friends. **saying unto him, Lord, trouble not thyself; for I am not worthy that thou shouldest enter under my roof.** What deep humility! **7. Wherefore neither thought I myself worthy to come unto thee: but say in a word.** In Matthew it is "but speak the word only" [ἀλλὰ μόνον εἰπὲ λόγον]—or more expressively, 'but speak only a word.' **and my servant shall be healed.** No such faith as this had been before displayed. **8. For I also am a man set under authority, having under me soldiers; and I say unto one, Go, and he goeth; and to another, Come, and he cometh; and to my servant, Do this, and he doeth it**—*q. d.*, 'I know both to obey and command: though but a subaltern, my orders are implicitly obeyed: Shall not diseases, then, obey their Lord, and at His word be gone?' **9. When Jesus heard these things, he marvelled at him.** As *Bengel* hints, Jesus marvelled but at two things—*faith* (as here) and *unbelief* (Mark vi. 6): at the one, considering the general blindness in spiritual things; at the other, considering the light that shone around all who were privileged to hear Him and behold His works. But the unprecedented faith of this heathen convert could not fail to fill His soul with peculiar admiration. **and turned him about, and said unto the people that followed him**—Jews, no doubt, **I have not found so great faith, no, not in Israel**—among the chosen people; this Gentile outstripping all the children of the covenant. A most important addition to this statement is given by Matthew (viii. 11, 12), who wrote specially for the Jews: "And I say unto you, that many shall come from the east and west"—from all parts of the heathen world—"and shall sit down" [ἀνακλιθήσονται]—'shall recline,' as at a feast, "with Abraham, and Isaac, and Jacob"—the fathers of the ancient covenant: Luke, reporting a solemn repetition of these words on a later occasion (ch. xiii. 28-30), adds, "and all the prophets;" "in the kingdom of heaven:" "but the children of the kingdom"—born to its privileges, but void of faith, "shall be cast out into outer darkness," the darkness outside the banqueting-house; "there (or in this outside-region) shall be weeping and gnashing of teeth"—the one expressive of *anguish*, the other of *despair*. **10. And they that were sent, returning to the house, found the servant whole that had been sick.** In Matthew we read, "And Jesus said unto the centurion, Go thy way: and as thou hast believed, so be it done unto thee. And his servant was healed the self-same hour" (Matt. viii. 13), teaching, that as in these *bodily* diseases, so in the salvation of the *soul*, all hinges on *faith*. No doubt this was conveyed to him in the form of a message through the "friends" that brought the second message. Whether Jesus now visited this centurion we are not informed.

Remarks.—1. How devoutly would this centurion, as he thought of the Providence that brought him into contact with the chosen people, and thus turned his heathen darkness into light, exclaim with the sweet Psalmist of Israel, "The lines are fallen unto me in pleasant places; yea, I have a goodly heritage"! (Ps. xvi. 6). And Cornelius also (Acts x. 1, &c.); and Lydia (Acts xvi. 14). And by what wonderful providences have hundreds and thousands since then been brought, as by accident and through circumstances the most trivial, into contact with the truth which has set them free! But, perhaps, if we knew all, it would be found that in every case it is in a way perfectly casual and all unexpected that the ear first hears effectually the loving Voice which says, "Look unto me, and be saved." And if so, what materials will this afford for wonder in heaven, when the whole story of each one's life will stand up before his view distinct and vivid; and what a fund of blissful intercourse will be thus provided, when the redeemed will, as we may reasonably believe, exchange with each other their past experience, as each says to the other, "Come, all ye that fear God, and I will declare what He hath done for my soul!"

'When this passing world is done,
When has sunk yon glaring sun,
When we stand with Christ in glory,
Looking o'er life's finished story,
Then, Lord, shall I fully know—
Not till then, how much I owe.'—M'Cheyne.

2. Bright as was the radiance which shone from the Old Testament upon this mind that had been reared in Pagan darkness, it rested not there, but was only guided by it to Him of whom Moses, in the law, and the Prophets did write. Nor was his a hesitating or superficial faith. Capernaum being the place of Christ's stated residence while in Galilee, this devout officer seems to have not only heard His public addresses, but made himself sufficiently acquainted with the wonders of His gracious hand to have every doubt as to His claims removed, and a profound conviction implanted in his mind of His Divine dignity. When, therefore, he has need of His interposition, he applies for it with undoubting confidence, "beseeching Him to come and heal His servant." But he shrinks from a personal application as "unworthy to come to Him;" and though he had petitioned Jesus to come and heal his servant, he sends again to say that it was too much honour to him that He should come under his roof, but that since one word of command from Him would suffice, he would be content with that. What wonderful faith is this for a convert from heathenism to reach! The arguments by which he illustrates the power of Jesus to order diseases to be gone—as servants in entire subjection to their Master and Lord—are singularly expressive of a

11 And it came to pass the day after, that he went into a city called
12 Nain; and many of his disciples went with him, and much people. Now
when he came nigh to the gate of the city, behold, there was a dead man
carried out, the only son of his mother, and she was a widow: and much
13 people of the city was with her. And when the Lord saw her, he [d]had
14 compassion on her, and said unto her, Weep not. And he came and
touched the [2]bier: and they that bare *him* stood still. And he said,
15 Young man, I say unto thee, [e]Arise. And he that was dead sat up, and
16 began to speak. And he delivered him to his mother. And there came
a fear on all: and they glorified God, saying, [f]That a great prophet is
17 risen up among us; and, [g]That God hath visited his people. And this
rumour of him went forth throughout all Judea, and throughout all the
region round about.

A. D. 31.

[d] Lam. 3. 32. John 11. 33, 35. Heb. 2. 17. Heb. 4. 15.
[2] Or, coffin.
[e] ch. 8. 54. John 11. 43. Acts 9. 40. Rom. 4. 17.
[f] ch. 24 19. John 4. 19. John 6. 14. John 9. 17.
[g] ch. 1. 68. ch. 19. 44.

faith in the sovereignty of Christ over the elements of nature and the forces of life to which nothing was impossible. And when we "see how faith wrought with his works (in loving God's nation and building them a synagogue), and by works his faith was made perfect;" and when we observe how all this anxiety of his was not like that of Jairus for the life of an only *daughter* (ch. viii. 42), nor like that of the nobleman for his *son* (John iv. 47), but for a *servant* that was dear to him, can we wonder that Jesus should say, "I have not found so great faith, no, not in Israel"? 3. If the Lord Jesus had been a mere creature, could He have suffered such views of Him to pass uncorrected? But instead of this—as on every other occasion—*the more exalted were men's views of Him, ever the more grateful it was to His spirit.* See on ch. v. 1-11, Remark 2. 4. There is too good reason to fear that those very elders of the Jews who besought Jesus to come and heal the Centurion's servant, and enforced their petition so well, had themselves none of the centurion's faith in the Lord Jesus. Our Lord's words seem to imply as much. And when He says that this centurion was, after all, but one of a class which, from the most distant and unpromising spots, would occupy the highest places and be in the most favoured company in the kingdom of heaven—while those that had been nursed in the arms and dandled upon the knees and had sucked the breasts of God's lawgivers and prophets, and basked in the sunshine of supernatural truth and divine ordinances, without any inward transformation, would be thrust out, and found weltering in anguish and despair—what a warning does it utter to the religiously favoured, and what encouragement does it hold out to work hopefully amongst the heathen abroad and the outcasts at home, that "there are first which shall be last, and there are last which shall be first!"

11-17.—The Widow of Nain's Son Raised to Life. This incident is peculiar to our Evangelist, and its occurrence in Luke's Gospel alone illustrates that charming characteristic of it—its liking for those scenes, circumstances, and sayings of Jesus which manifest His *human tenderness, compassion, and grace.* The time is expressly stated in the opening words.

11. And it came to pass the day after—that is, the day after He had healed the centurion's servant, **that he went into a city called Nain**—a small village not elsewhere mentioned in Scripture, and only this once probably visited by our Lord: it lay a little to the south of mount Tabor, about twelve miles from Capernaum. **and many of his disciples went with him, and much people** [ὄχλος πολύς]—'a great multitude.' **12. Now when he came nigh to the gate of the city, behold, there was a dead man carried out** [ἐξεκομίζετο]—in the act of being so. Dead bodies, being ceremonially unclean, were not allowed to be buried within the cities—though the kings of David's house were buried in the city of David—and the funeral was usually on the same day as the death. **the only son of his mother, and she was a widow**—affecting particulars, and told with delightful simplicity. **13. And when the Lord saw her.** This sublime appellation of Jesus—"the Lord"—is more usual, as *Bengel* notes, with Luke and John than Matthew, while Mark holds the mean. **he had compassion on her, and said unto her, Weep not.** What consolation to thousands of the bereaved has this single verse carried from age to age! **14. And he came and touched the bier**—no doubt with a look and manner which said, Stand still. **and they that bare him stood still. And he said, Young man, I say unto thee, Arise. 15. And he that was dead sat up**—the bier [σορὸς] was an open one, **and began to speak**—evidencing that he was both alive and well. **And he delivered him to his mother.** What mingled majesty and grace shines here! Behold, the Resurrection and the Life in human flesh, with a word of command, bringing back life to the dead body, and Incarnate Compassion putting forth its absolute power to dry a widow's tears. **16. And there came a fear on all**—a religious awe, **and they glorified God, saying, That a great prophet is risen up among us; and, That God hath visited his people**—after long absence, more than bringing back the days of Elijah and Elisha. For they, though they raised the dead, did so *laboriously;* Jesus immediately, and with a word: they confessedly as servants and creatures, by a power *not their own;* Jesus by that inherent "virtue," which "went out of Him," in every cure which He wrought. Compare 1 Ki. xvii. 17-24; 2 Ki. iv. 32-37; and see on Mark v. 30. **17. And this rumour of him went forth throughout all Judea, and throughout all the region round about.**

For Remark on this Section, see on Mark v. 21-43, Remark 5.

18-35.—The Imprisoned Baptist's Message to His Master—The Reply, and Discourse regarding John and His Mission, on the Departure of the Messengers (=Matt. xi. 2-19.) For the circumstances of the Baptist's imprisonment, see on Mark vi. 17-20.

He had now lain in prison probably a full year, far away from the scene of his Master's labours. But his faithful disciples appear from time to time to have kept him informed of them. At length the tidings they brought him, including no doubt those of the resurrection of the widow of Nain's son from the dead, appear to have determined the lonely prisoner to take a step

18, And [h]the disciples of John showed him of all these things. And John
19 calling *unto him* two of his disciples, sent *them* to Jesus, saying, Art thou
20 [i]he that should come? or look we for another? When the men were
come unto him, they said, John Baptist hath sent us unto thee, saying,
21 Art thou he that should come? or look we for another? And in the
same hour he cured many of *their* infirmities and plagues, and of evil
22 spirits; and unto many *that were* blind he gave sight. Then [j]Jesus
answering said unto them, Go your way, and tell John what things ye
have seen and heard; [k]how that the blind see, the lame walk, the lepers
are cleansed, the deaf hear, the dead are raised, [l]to the poor the Gospel
23 is preached. And blessed is *he,* whosoever shall not be offended in me.
24 And [m]when the messengers of John were departed, he began to speak
unto the people concerning John, What went ye out into the wilderness
25 for to see? A reed shaken with the wind? But what went ye out for to
see? A man clothed in soft raiment? Behold, they which are gorgeously
26 apparelled, and live delicately, are in kings' courts. But what went ye

A. D. 31.

h Matt. 11. 2.
i Ezek. 21.27.
Ezek 34.23, 29.
Dan. 9. 24-26.
Mic. 5. 2.
Hag. 2. 7.
Zec. 9. 9.
Mal. 3. 1-3.
j Matt. 11. 5.
k Isa. 29. 18.
Isa. 35. 5.
Isa. 42. 6.
Acts 26. 18.
l Isa. 61. 1.
Zeph. 3. 12.
ch. 4. 18.
Jas. 2. 5.
m Matt. 11. 7.

which probably he had often thought of, but till now shrunk from. **18. And the disciples of John showed him of all these things. 19. And John calling unto him two of his disciples** [δύο τινὰς]—'two certain disciples;' that is, two picked, trusty ones. [In Matt. xi., instead of δύο, *Lachmann, Tischendorf, and Tregelles,* on certainly powerful evidence, print διὰ—'sent by his disciples.' *Fritzsche* and *Alford* follow them in their text; and *Meyer* and *de Wette* approve of the change. But as the external evidence is not overpowering, so there is, in our judgment, the strongest internal evidence against it, and in favour of the received reading, which differs only by a letter and a half from the other reading.] **sent them to Jesus, saying, Art thou he that should come? or look we for another? 20. When the men were come unto him, they said, John Baptist hath sent us unto thee, saying, Art thou he that should come? or look we for another?** Was this a question of doubt as to the Messiahship of his Lord, as Rationalists are fain to represent it? Impossible, from all we know of him. Was it then purely for the satisfaction of his disciples, as some expositors, more concerned for the Baptist's reputation than for simple and natural interpretation, take it? Obviously not. The whole strain of our Lord's reply shows that it was designed for John himself. Clearly it was a message of *impatience,* and almost of *desperation.* It seemed, no doubt, hard to him that his Master should let him lie so long in prison for his fidelity—useless to his Master's cause and a comparative stranger to His proceedings—after having been honoured to announce and introduce Him to His work and to the people. And since the wonders of His hand seemed only to increase in glory as He advanced, and it could not but be easy for Him who preached deliverance to the captives, and the opening of the prison to them that were bound, to put it into the heart of Herod to set him at liberty, or to effect his liberation in spite of him, he at length determines to see if, through a message from the prison by his disciples, he cannot get Him to speak out His mind, and at least set his own at rest. This, we take it, was the real object of his message. The message itself, indeed, was far from a proper one. It was peevish; it was presumptuous; it was all but desperate. He had got depressed; he was losing heart; his spirit was clouded; Heaven's sweet light had, to some extent, departed from him; and this message was the consequence. As it was announced that he should come in the spirit and power of Elijah, so we find him treading in that prophet's steps rather more than was desirable (see 1 Ki. xix. 1-4). **21. And in the same hour**—no doubt expressly with a view to its being reported to John, **he cured many of their infirmities and plagues, and of evil spirits; and unto many that were blind he gave sight** [ἐχαρίσατο τὸ βλέπειν]—'granted [the gift of] sight.' **22. Then Jesus answering said unto them, Go your way, and tell John what things ye have seen and heard.** No doubt along with the miracles which they "saw," they would "hear" those magic words with which He rolled away the maladies that came before Him. Nor would He fail to drop some other words of grace, fitted to impress the minds of the messengers, and, when reported, to cheer the spirit of their lonely master. **how that the blind see, the lame walk, the lepers are cleansed, the deaf hear, the dead are raised.** As the article is wanting in each of these clauses, the sense would be better perceived by the English reader thus, though scarcely tunable enough: 'Blind persons are seeing, lame people are walking, leprous persons are getting cleansed, deaf people are hearing, dead persons are being raised.' **to the poor the Gospel is preached** [εὐαγγελίζονται]—or 'is [in course of] being preached;' alluding to the great Messianic prediction, as it was uttered and appropriated by Himself at Nazareth, "The Spirit of the Lord is upon me, because He hath anointed me to preach the Gospel to the *poor.*" **23. And blessed is he, whosoever shall not be offended in me.** 'Let these things convince him that My hand is not shortened that it cannot save; but blessed is he who can take Me with just as much light as to his future lot as is vouchsafed to him.' This was all the reply that the messengers received. Not a ray of light is cast on his prospects, nor a word of commendation uttered while his disciples are present; he must die in simple faith, and as a martyr to his fidelity. But no sooner are they gone, than Jesus breaks forth into a glorious commendation of him.

24. And when the messengers of John were departed, he began to speak unto the people concerning John, What went ye out into the wilderness for to see? A reed shaken with the wind? —'a man driven about by every gust of popular opinion, and uttering an uncertain sound? Such is not John.' **25. But what went ye out for to see? A man clothed in soft raiment?**—'a self-indulgent, courtly preacher? Such was not John.' **Behold, they which are gorgeously apparelled, and live delicately, are in kings' courts.** 'If that be the

out for to see? A prophet? Yea, I say unto you, and much more than
27 a prophet. This is *he* of whom it is written, [n]Behold, I send my mes-
28 senger before thy face, which shall prepare thy way before thee. For I
say unto you, Among those that are born of women there is not a greater
prophet than John the Baptist: but he that is least in the kingdom of
God is greater than he.
29 And all the people that heard *him*, and the publicans, justified God,
30 [o]being baptized with the baptism of John. But the Pharisees and lawyers
[3]rejected [p]the counsel of God [4]against themselves, being not baptized of
him.
31 And the Lord said, [q]Whereunto then shall I liken the men of this
32 generation? and to what are they like? They are like unto children
sitting in the market-place, and calling one to another, and saying, We
have piped unto you, and ye have not danced; we have mourned to you,
33 and ye have not wept. For [r]John the Baptist came neither eating bread

A. D. 31.

[n] Isa. 40. 3. Mal 3. 1. Mal. 4. 5. ch 1. 16, 17, 76.
[o] Matt. 3. 5. ch. 3. 12.
[3] Or, frustrated.
[p] Acts 20. 27.
[4] Or, within themselves.
[q] Lam. 2. 13. Matt. 11.16. Mark 4. 30.
[r] Matt. 3. 4. Mark 1. 6. ch. 1. 15.

man ye wanted, ye must go in quest of him to royal palaces.' **26. But what went ye out for to see? A prophet?**—a faithful straightforward utterer of the testimony given him to bear? **Yea, I say unto you, and much more than a prophet.** 'If that was what ye flocked to the wilderness to see in John, then ye have not been disappointed; for he is that, and much more than that.' **27. This is he of whom it is written** (Mal. iii. 1), **Behold, I send my messenger before thy face, which shall prepare thy way before thee.** See on Mark i. 3; and on Luke i. 17. 'There were many prophets, but only one Forerunner of the Lord's Christ; and this is he.' **28. For I say unto you, Among those that are born of women there is not**—"there hath not risen" (Matt. xi. 11) **a greater prophet than John the Baptist: but he that is least in the kingdom of God is greater than he.** The point of comparison is manifestly not personal character; for as it could hardly be said that in this respect he excelled every human being that preceded him, so it would be absurd to say that he was outstripped by the least advanced of the disciples of Christ. It is of his official *standing* or *position* in the economy of grace that our Lord is speaking. In that respect he was above all that ever went before him, inasmuch as he was the last and most honoured of the Old Testament prophets, and stood on the very edge of the new economy, though belonging to the old: but for this very reason, the humblest member of the new economy was *in advance of him.* In Matt. xi. 12-15, we have the following important additions:—"And from the days of John the Baptist until now the kingdom of heaven suffereth violence, and the violent take it by force" [βιάζεται, καὶ βιασταὶ ἁρπάζουσιν αὐτήν]; 'is being forced, and violent persons are seizing it.' The sense of these remarkable words is best seen in the form in which they were afterwards repeated, as preserved by our Evangelist alone (Luke xvi. 16): "The law and the prophets were until John"—who stood midway between the old economy of the law and the prophets and the new; above the one, but below the other—"since that time the kingdom of God is preached, and every man presseth into it" [εἰς αὐτὴν βιάζεται], or 'is forcing his way into it.' The idea is that of a *rush* for something unexpectedly and transportingly brought within their reach. In the one passage the *struggle* to obtain entrance is the prominent idea; in the other and later one it is the *multitude* that were thus pressing or forcing their way in. And what our Lord says of John in both places is that his ministry constituted the honourable point of transition from the one state of things to the other. "For," to continue Matthew's additions to this Discourse, "all the prophets and the law prophesied until John. And if ye will receive it, this is Elias, which was for to come. He that hath ears to hear, let him hear." They expected the literal Elijah the Tishbite to reappear before the coming of Messiah; misinterpreting the closing words of the prophet Malachi (iv. 5), and misled by the LXX., which rendered it, "Behold, I send you Elijah *the Tishbite.*" But our Lord here tells them plainly that this promised messenger was no other than John the Baptist of whom he had been speaking; although, knowing that this would be a startling and not very welcome announcement to those who confidently looked for the reappearance of the ancient prophet himself from heaven, He first says it was intended *for those who could take it in,* and then calls the attention of all who had ears to hear it to what he had said. Coming back now to our own Evangelist,

29. And all the people that heard [him] [ἀκούσας]—rather, 'on hearing [this],' **and the publicans, justified God, being baptized** [βαπτισθέντες]—rather, 'having been baptized' **with the baptism of John. 30. But the Pharisees and lawyers rejected the counsel of God against themselves, being not**—or rather, 'not having been' **baptized of him**—a striking remark of the Evangelist himself on the different effects produced by our Lord's testimony to John. The spirit of it is, that all those of the audience who had surrendered themselves to the great preparatory ministry of John, and submitted themselves to his Baptism—including the publicans, amongst whom there had been a considerable awakening—were grateful for this encomium on one to whom they owed so much, and gave glory to God for such a gift, through whom they had been led to Him who now spake to them (ch. i. 16, 17); whereas the Pharisees and lawyers, true to themselves in having refused the Baptism of John, now set at nought the merciful design of God in the Saviour Himself, to their own undoing.

31. [And the Lord said], Whereunto then shall I liken the men of this generation? and to what are they like? [The introductory words of this verse—Εἶπεν δὲ ὁ Κύριος—have scarcely any authority at all, and were evidently no part of the original text. They were added probably at first to some Church Lesson, to introduce what follows, and thence found their way into the text.] **32-35. They are like unto children . . . saying, We have piped . . . and ye have not danced . . . mourned . . . and ye have not wept. For John . . . came neither eating . . . nor drinking . . . and ye say, He hath a devil. The Son of man**

34 nor drinking wine; and ye say, He hath a devil. The Son of man is
come eating and drinking; and ye say, Behold a gluttonous man, and a
35 wine-bibber, a friend of publicans and sinners! But [s]Wisdom is justified
of all her children.

A. D. 31.

[s] Hos. 14. 9. Matt. 11. 19. 1 Cor. 1. 23, 24.

is come eating and drinking; and ye say, Behold a gluttonous man . . . a friend of publicans and sinners! But Wisdom is justified of all her children. As cross, capricious children, invited by their playmates to join them in their amusements, will play with them neither at weddings nor at funerals (juvenile imitations of the joyous and mournful scenes of life), so that generation rejected both John and his Master: the one because he was too unsocial—as if under some dark demoniacal influence; the other, because he was too much the reverse, lax in his habits, and consorting with the lowest classes of society. But the children of Wisdom recognize and honour her whether in the austere garb of the Baptist or in the more attractive style of his Master, whether in the Law or in the Gospel, whether in rags or in royalty; as it is written, "The full soul loatheth an honeycomb: but to the hungry soul every bitter thing is sweet" (Prov. xxvii. 7).

Remarks.—1. Among the internal evidences of the truth of the Gospel History, none is more striking, and to an unsophisticated mind more resistless, than the view which it gives of John the Baptist. Who, in the first place, would not have expected that the ministry of the Forerunner should cease as soon as that of his Master commenced; and yet it did not, but both continued for some time the same work of preaching and baptizing. Next, who would not have expected that the disciples of John would all attach themselves to his Master, especially after what he said when questioned on that subject? (John iii. 25-36). And yet, to the very last, there was a company known by the name of "John's disciples," who not only remained with him, but followed a more austere rule of life than the disciples of Jesus Himself, a mode of life suited to the man who seems never to have mixed in general society, but kept himself, in a great measure, secluded; and only when John was beheaded, and by his affectionate and faithful disciples decently interred, do this class seem to have joined themselves to Jesus in a body. Then, Christ's not only letting John be imprisoned, but lie in prison so long without even a message of sympathy being sent him; and, after the patience of the lonely prisoner was well-nigh worn out, and all the more tried by the tidings that reached him of Christ's triumphant career, when he sent a message to his Master, couched in terms almost of desperation, that he should receive no other answer than that the tidings that had reached him of his Master's glory were true to the full, and that blessed was he who did not allow himself to be staggered and stumbled at Him—all this is the very reverse of anything one would expect. But further still, that while uttering not one word in commendation of John in the hearing of his disciples, the reporting of which might have lifted up his depressed spirit, our Lord should, as soon as they were gone, break forth into a lofty encomium on his character and office—who would have expected Him to act so? Finally, that He should allow him to be beheaded, to gratify a base woman, and when tidings of this were brought to Jesus by his sorrowing disciples, that not a word should be uttered by Him on the subject:—these things, which surprise and almost perplex us as *facts*, it is impossible to conceive of as pure *inventions;* being the very opposite of all that the history of such inventions would lead us to expect. But, 2. When we come to deal with them *as* facts, we see in them but vivid illustrations of certain features of the Divine procedure for which we ought to be prepared. When the three Hebrew youths were threatened with the burning fiery furnace if they would not worship Nebuchadnezzar's golden idol, they expressed their full conviction that the God they served both could and would deliver them; but even should they be mistaken in this expectation, they were still resolved rather to suffer than to sin. And they suffered not. But John did. He had indeed counted the cost, but he had it to pay. 'Wilt thou be faithful even unto death?' was the question, and his spirit answered, Yes. 'Canst thou lie in prison unrescued, and even uncheered, save by the light thou already hast, and at length in a moment be despatched by those whom thy fidelity hath stung to the quick?' To this also his true heart doubtless bowed, though the trying question was never explicitly submitted to him. And such is what thousands of the martyrs of Jesus have undergone for His name. Nor can we doubt that this very record of the Lord's procedure towards the Baptist has soothed many a one when called to pass through a like dreary period of comfortless suffering, ending in death, for Jesus' sake. And may we not please ourselves with the thought that, like as the words wrung from the Saviour Himself in Gethsemane—"O my Father, if it be possible, let this cup pass from me"—were followed by the placid words, "Father, into thy hands I commend my spirit;" so the deep depression which prompted the question, "Art Thou He that should come, or look we for another?" was followed by a serene contentment and placid hope which might thus sing its pensive song, and only be interrupted by the murderer with his bloody axe?—

> 'God moves in a mysterious way
> His wonders to perform:
> He plants His footsteps in the sea,
> And rides upon the storm.
>
> 'Deep in unfathomable mines
> Of never-failing skill,
> He treasures up His bright designs,
> And works His sovereign will.
>
> 'His purposes will ripen fast,
> Unfolding every hour;
> The bud may have a bitter taste,
> But sweet will be the flower.'—COWPER.

3. As when John the Baptist ushered in an era of new light and liberty in the kingdom of God, "every man pressed into it;" so there have been periods in the history of the Church ever since, in which a light and a freedom altogether unwonted have been infused into the Christian ministry, or men have been raised up outside the regular ministry, but gifted specially for special work, and particularly for rousing the impenitent to flee from the coming wrath and lay hold on eternal life, whose labours God designs to bless to the shaking of the dry bones and the turning of many to righteousness. Publicans and sinners—the most unlikely classes—are then to be seen flocking to Christ; while scribes and Pharisees—the respectably religious and the formal amongst the ministers of the Gospel—stand aloof,

36 And [t]one of the Pharisees desired him that he would eat with him.
And he went into the Pharisee's house, and sat down to meat.
37 And, behold, a [u]woman in the city, which was a sinner, when she knew
that *Jesus* sat at meat in the Pharisee's house, brought an alabaster box
38 of ointment, and stood at his feet behind [v]*him* weeping, and began to
wash his feet with tears, and did wipe *them* with the hairs of her head,
39 and kissed his feet, and anointed *them* with the ointment. Now when
the Pharisee which had bidden him saw *it*, he spake within himself,

A. D. 31.

[t] Matt. 26. 6. Mark 14. 3. John 11. 2.
[u] ch. 8. 2. John 9. 24.
[v] Zec. 12. 10. Rom. 5. 20. 1 Tim. 1.15, 16.

and cannot easily conceal their dislike at what they deem irregularities, and fanaticism, and dangers. At such a time it will be the part of the simple-hearted and the wise to hail, on the one hand, the ingathering of souls to Christ, however it be effected, and, on the other hand, by prudent and kindly guidance of it, to keep so glorious a work from being marred by human folly. 4. Is it not extraordinary that, after our Lord's most explicit declaration here, that John the Baptist was *the* Elias that prophecy taught the Church to look for before the coming of Messiah, there are Christian students of prophecy who affirm that the Jews were quite right in expecting the literal Elijah from heaven; and who, while admitting that John was *an* Elias, sent to announce the *first* coming of Christ, maintain that the prophecy will only be properly fulfilled in the coming of the Tishbite himself to prepare men for His *second* coming? The thing to be condemned here is not so much the extravagance of the expectation itself, which, the more one thinks of it, will appear the more extravagant, but the manifest distortion which it puts upon our Lord's words, and the violence which it does to the prophecy. But all this comes of an out-and-out literalism in the interpretation of prophecy, which in some cases brings out conclusions, not only very harsh, but scarcely consistent with the principle itself. 5. When men want an excuse for rejecting or disregarding the grace of the Gospel, they easily find it. And there are none more ready and common than those arising out of something objectionable in the mode of presenting the truth. One preacher is too austere; another too free: one is too long; another too short: one is too sentimental; another too hard. Nothing pleases; nobody quite suits them. But O, when the soul is hungry, how welcome is God's solid truth, Christ's precious Gospel, however it comes! And so "Wisdom is justified of her children," who know her, hail her, clasp her to their bosom, however humbly clad; while those who do otherwise only show themselves to be "full souls," to whom even an honey-comb is distasteful—"the whole, who need not the Physician" and prize Him not.

36-50. THE WOMAN THAT WAS A SINNER, AND SIMON THE PHARISEE. This exquisite scene is peculiar to Luke. The time is quite uncertain. Perhaps it is introduced here as being suggested by "the publicans" and others of similar character, whom the preceding Section brought before us as welcoming Christ, while "the Pharisees and lawyers rejected the counsel of God against themselves" (*vv.* 29, 30).

36. And one of the Pharisees desired—or 'requested' **him that he would eat with him. And he went into the Pharisee's house, and sat down to meat.** This Pharisee seems to have been in a state of mind regarding Jesus intermediate between that of the few who, like Nicodemus, were led to believe on Him, and of the overwhelming majority who regarded Him with suspicion from the first, which soon grew into deadly dislike. We shall see that, though not free from cold suspicion, He was desirous of a closer acquaintance with our Lord, under the impression that He might perhaps at least be a prophet. And our Lord, knowing the opportunity it would afford Him of receiving the love of a remarkable convert from the worst class of society, and expounding the great principles of saving truth, accepts His invitation.

37. And, behold, a woman in the city—what city is not known: it may have been Capernaum, **which was a sinner**—who had led a profligate life. But *there is no ground whatever for the prevalent notion that this woman was Mary Magdalene* (see on ch. viii. 2); nor do we know what her name was. It may have been concealed from motives of delicacy; but indeed the names of very few women are given in the Gospels. **when she knew that Jesus sat at meat in the Pharisee's house, brought an alabaster box of ointment**—a perfume-vessel, in some cases very costly, as we know from John xii. 5. If the ointment, as *Alford* suggests, had been an accessory to her unhallowed work of sin, the offering of it as here described has a tender interest; but there is no certainty of that. **38. And stood at his feet behind him weeping**—the posture at meals being a reclining one, with the feet out behind, **and began**—or proceeded **to wash his feet with tears.** The word here translated "wash" [βρέχειν] signifies to 'bathe' or 'bedew.' **and did wipe them with the hairs of her head**—the long tresses of that hair on which before she had bestowed too much attention. Had she come for such a purpose, she had not been at a loss for a towel. But tears do not come at will, especially in such plenty. No, they were quite involuntary, pouring down in a flood upon His naked feet, as she bent down to kiss them; and deeming them rather fouled than washed by this, she hastened to wipe them off with the only towel she had, the long tresses of her own hair, with which, as *Stier* observes, slaves were wont to wash their masters' feet. **and kissed his feet** [κατεφίλει]. The word signifies to 'caress,' or 'kiss tenderly and repeatedly'—which *v.* 45 shows to be the meaning here. What prompted all this? He who knew her heart tells us it was *much love, springing from a sense of much forgiveness.* Where she had met with Christ before, or what words of His had brought life to her dead heart and a sense of Divine pardon to her guilty soul, we know not. But probably she was of the crowd of "publicans and *sinners*" whom incarnate Compassion drew so often around Him, and heard from His lips some of those words such as never man spake, "Come unto me, all ye that labour," &c. No personal interview had up to this time taken place between them; but she could keep her feelings no longer to herself, and having found her way to Him (and entered along with him, *v.* 45), they burst forth in this surpassing, yet most art less style, as if her whole soul would go out to Him. **39. Now when the Pharisee which had bidden him saw it.** Up to this time He seems to have formed no definite opinion of our Lord, and invited him apparently to obtain materials for a judgment. **he spake within himself, saying, This man, if he were a prophet**—one

saying, [w]This man, if he were a prophet, would have known who and
what manner of woman *this is* that toucheth him; for she is a sinner.
40 And Jesus answering said unto him, Simon, I have somewhat to say
41 unto thee. And he saith, Master, say on. There was a certain creditor
which had two debtors: the one owed five hundred [x]pence, and the other
42 fifty. And when they had nothing to pay, he frankly [y]forgave them
43 both. Tell me therefore, which of them will love him most? Simon
answered and said, I suppose that *he* to whom he forgave most. And he
44 said unto him, Thou hast rightly judged. And he turned to the woman,
and said unto Simon, Seest thou this woman? I entered into thine house,
thou gavest me no [z]water for my feet: but she hath washed my feet with
45 tears, and wiped *them* with the hairs of her head. Thou gavest me no
[a]kiss: but this woman since the time I came in hath not ceased to kiss
46 my feet. My [b]head with oil thou didst not anoint: but this woman hath
47 anointed my feet with ointment. Wherefore [c]I say unto thee, Her sins,
which are many, are forgiven; for she loved much: but to whom little is
48 forgiven, *the same* loveth little. And he said unto her, [d]Thy sins are
49 forgiven. And they that sat at meat with him began to say within

A. D. 31.

[w] ch. 15. 2.
[x] Matt. 18. 28.
[y] Isa. 1. 18. Isa. 43. 25. Isa. 44. 22.
[z] Gen. 18. 4. 1 Tim. 5. 10.
[a] 1 Cor. 16. 20. 2 Cor. 13. 12.
[b] Ps. 23. 5. Eccl. 9. 8. 1 John 2. 20, 27.
[c] 1 Tim. 1. 14.
[d] Matt. 9. 2. Mark 2. 5. ch. 5. 20. Acts 13. 38, 39. Rom. 4. 6-8. Col. 1. 12-14.

possessed of supernatural knowledge. The form of expression here employed is to this effect—'If he were a prophet—but that he cannot be,' [εἰ ἦν προφήτης] **would have known who and what manner of woman this is that toucheth him; for she is a sinner.** 'I have now discovered this man: If he were what he gives himself forth to be, he would not have suffered a wretch like this to come near him; but plainly he knows nothing about her, and therefore he can be no prophet.' Not so fast, Simon; thou hast not seen through thy Guest yet, but He hath seen through thee. Too courteous to expose him nakedly at his own table, He couches His home-thrusts, like Nathan with David, in the first instance under the veil of a parable, and makes him pronounce both the woman's vindication and his own condemnation; and then he lifts the veil.

40, 41. And Jesus answering said unto him, Simon . . . There was a certain creditor which had two debtors: the one owed five hundred pence, the other fifty. 42. And when they had nothing to pay, he frankly forgave them both. Tell me therefore, which of them will love him most? 43. Simon answered and said, I suppose he to whom he forgave most. And he said unto him, Thou hast rightly judged. Now for the unexpected and pungent application. The two debtors are the woman and Simon; the criminality of the one was *ten times* that of the other—or in the proportion of *five hundred* to *fifty;* but both being equally insolvent, both are with equal frankness forgiven; and Simon is made to own that the greatest debtor to forgiving mercy will cling to her Divine Benefactor with the deepest gratitude. Does our Lord then admit that Simon and the woman were both truly forgiven persons? Let us see. **44. And he turned to the woman, and said unto Simon, Seest thou this woman? I entered into thine house, thou gavest me no water for my feet**—'a compliment from a host to his guest which love surely would have prompted; but I got it not: Was there much love in that? *Was there any?*' **but she hath washed my feet with tears, and wiped them with the hairs of her head.** Dear penitent! Thy tears fell faster and fuller than thou thoughtest endurable on those blessed feet, and thou didst hasten to wipe them off, as if they had been a stain: but to Him who forgave thee all that debt, the water from those weeping eyes of thine is more precious than would crystal streams from fountains in the Pharisee's house have been; for they welled forth from a bursting heart. That, indeed, was 'much love.' Again, **45. Thou gavest me no kiss**—of salutation. 'How much love was there here? *Any at all?*' **but this woman since the time I came in hath not ceased to kiss my feet.** She would, in so doing, both hide her head, and get her womanly feelings in a womanly way all expressed. That indeed was 'much love.' But once more, **46. My head with oil thou didst not anoint: but this woman hath anointed my feet with ointment.** The double contrast is here to be observed—between *his* not anointing the *head* and *her* anointing the *feet;* and between his withholding even common *olive oil* for the higher purpose, and her expending that precious *aromatic balsam* for the humbler. *What evidence did the one afford of any feeling which forgiveness prompts? But what beautiful evidence of this did the other furnish!* Our Lord speaks this with delicate politeness, as if *hurt* at these inattentions of His host, which though not *invariably* shown to guests, were the customary marks of studied respect and regard. The inference is plain—*Only one of the debtors was really forgiven,* though in the first instance, to give room for the play of withheld feeling, the forgiveness of both is supposed in the parable. Our Lord now confines Himself to the woman's case. **47. Wherefore I say unto thee, Her sins, which are many, are forgiven** [ἀφέωνται αἱ ἁμαρτίαι αὐτῆς αἱ πολλαί]—'those many sins of hers are forgiven.' As He had acknowledged before how deep was her debt, so now He reiterates it: her sins were indeed many; her guilt was of a deep dye; but in terms the most solemn He proclaims it all cancelled. **for she loved much.** The "for" here [ὅτι] is plainly *evidential,* and means, 'inasmuch as' or 'seeing that.' Her love was not the *cause,* but the *proof* of her forgiveness; as is evident from the whole structure of the parable. **but to whom little is forgiven, the same loveth little**—a delicately ironical intimation of there being *no love* in the present case, and so *no forgiveness.* **48. And he said unto her, Thy sins are forgiven**—an unsought assurance of what she had felt, indeed, in the simple appropriation to herself of the first words of grace which she had heard—we know not where—but how precious, now that those blessed Lips addressed it to herself! **49. And they that sat at meat with him began to say within themselves** [ἐν ἑαυτοῖς]—or, 'among themselves,' **Who is this**

50 themselves, [e]Who is this that forgiveth sins also? And he said to the
woman, [f]Thy faith hath saved thee; go in peace.

A. D. 31.

[e] Isa. 53. 3.
[f] Matt. 9. 22.

that forgiveth sins also? 50. And he said to the woman, Thy faith hath saved thee; go in peace. No wonder they were startled to hear One who was reclining at the same couch, and partaking of the same hospitalities with themselves, assume the awful prerogative of 'even forgiving sins.' But so far from receding from this claim, or softening it down, our Lord only repeats it, with two precious additions: one, announcing what was the secret of the "forgiveness" she had experienced, and which carried "salvation" in its bosom—her "faith;" the other, a glorious dismissal of her in that "peace" which she had already felt, but is now assured she has His full warrant to enjoy! The expression, "in peace," is literally "into peace" [εἰς εἰρήνην]—'into the assured and abiding enjoyment of the peace of a pardoned state.'

Remarks.—1. What a glorious exhibition of the grace of the Gospel have we in this Section? A woman of the class of profligates casually hears the Lord Jesus pour forth some of those wonderful words of majesty and grace, which dropped as an honey-comb. They pierce her heart; but, as they wound, they heal. Abandoned of men, she is not forsaken of God. Hers, she had thought, was a lost case; but the prodigal, she finds, has a Father still. She will arise and go to Him; and as she goes He meets her, and falls on her neck and kisses her. Light breaks into her soul, as she revolves what she heard from those Lips that spake as never man spake, and draws from them the joyful assurance of Divine reconciliation for the chief of sinners, and the peace of a pardoned state. She cannot rest; she must see that wonderful One again, and testify to Him what He hath done for her soul. She inquires after His movements, as if she would say with the Spouse, "Tell me, O Thou whom my soul loveth, where Thou feedest, for why should I be as one that turneth aside by the flocks of Thy companions?" She learns where He is, and follows in His train till she finds herself at His feet behind Him at the Pharisee's table. At the sight of Him, her head is waters and her eyes a fountain of tears, which drop copiously on those beautiful feet. What a spectacle, which even angels might desire—and doubtless did—to look into! But, how differently is it regarded by one at least at that table! Simon the Pharisee thinks it conclusive evidence against the claims of his Guest, that He should permit such a thing to be done to Him by such a person. So the matter shall be expounded, the woman vindicated, and the Pharisee's suspicions courteously yet pointedly rebuked. And what a rich statement of Gospel truth is here conveyed in a few words. Though there be degrees of guilt, yet insolvency—or inability to wipe out the dishonour done to God by sin—is common to all sinners alike. The debtors are sinners, and sin is a debt incurred to Heaven. The debtor of "five hundred" represents the one extreme of them; the debtor of "fifty" the other—those at the bottom and those at the top of the scale of sinners, the greatest and the least sinners, the profligate and the respectable, the publicans and the Pharisees. A great difference there is between these. But it is a difference only of degree; for of both debtors alike it is said that they had nothing to pay. They were both alike insolvent. The debtor of "fifty" could no more pay his fifty than the debtor of five hundred her's. The least sinner is insolvent; the greatest is no more. "There is no difference, for all have sinned, and come short of the glory of God." But when they had nothing to pay, the Creditor frankly forgave them both. The least sinner, to have peace with God and get to heaven, needs a frank forgiveness, and the greatest needs only that. Reputable Simon must be saved on the same terms with this once profligate and still despised woman; and she, now that she has tasted that the Lord is gracious, is on a level with every other pardoned believer. "Such *were* some of you: but ye are washed, but ye are sanctified, but ye are justified, in the name of the Lord Jesus, and by the Spirit of our God" (1 Cor. vi. 11). But the working of this doctrine of Grace comes out here as beautifully as the doctrine itself. Love to its Divine Benefactor, reigning in the heart of the pardoned believer, is seen seeking Him, finding Him, broken down at the sight of Him, embracing His very feet, and pouring out its intensest emotions in the most expressive form. Even so, "the love of Christ constraineth us . . . to live not unto ourselves, but unto Him that died for us and rose again." It casts its crown at His feet. It lives for Him; and, if required, it lays down its life for Him. Thus, what law could not do love does, writing the law in the heart. But, now, turning from the sinner to the Saviour, 2. In what light does this Section exhibit Christ? He plainly represents Himself here as the great Creditor to Whom is owing that debt, and Whose it is to cancel it. For, observe His argument. 'The more forgiveness, the greater the debtor's love to his generous Creditor.' Such is the general principle laid down by Simon and approved by Christ. Well, then, says our Lord, let the conduct of these two be tried by this test. So He proceeds, by the woman's treatment of Himself, to show how much she loved Him, and consequently how much forgiveness she felt that she had received from Him; and by the Pharisee's treatment of Him, to show what an absence of the feeling of love to Him there was, and consequently of the sense of forgiveness. The more that the structure and application of the parable of this Section is studied, the more will the intelligent reader be struck with the high claim which our Lord here puts forth—a claim which would never have entered into the mind of a mere creature, with reference to the Person to whom sin lays us under obligation, and whose prerogative accordingly it is with royal "frankness" to remit the debt. Should any hesitate about the force of this indirect—but just on that account the more striking—argument for the proper Divinity of Christ, let him look on to the close of this Section, where he will find the Lord Jesus putting forth His royal prerogative of publicly *pronouncing* that forgiveness which had been already *experienced;* and when it was manifest to His fellow-guests that He was assuming a Divine prerogative, and it seemed nothing short of blasphemy that one who reclined at the same table and partook of the same hospitalities with themselves, should speak and act *as God,* He not only did not correct them by retreating out of the supposed claim, but reiterated the august language, and with even increased majesty and grace: "Thy faith hath saved thee, Go in peace!" Let the Person of Christ be studied in the light of these facts. 3. How cheering is it to be assured that love gives beauty and value, in the eye of Christ, to every the least act of His genuine people! But on this subject,

8 AND it came to pass afterward, that he went throughout every city
and village, preaching and showing the glad tidings of the kingdom of
2 God: and the twelve *were* with him, and [a]certain women, which had
been healed of evil spirits and infirmities, Mary called Magdalene, [b]out of
3 whom went seven devils, and Joanna the wife of Chuza Herod's steward,
and Susanna, and many others, which ministered unto him of their
substance.
4 And [c]when much people were gathered together, and were come to
5 him out of every city, he spake by a parable: A sower went out to sow
his seed: and as he sowed, some fell by the way-side; and it was trodden

A. D. 31.

CHAP. 8.
[a] Matt. 27.55, 56.
Mark 15.40, 41.
Mark 16. 1.
ch. 23. 27.
John 19.25.
Acts 1. 14.
[b] Mark 16. 9.
[c] Matt. 13. 2.
Mark 4. 1.

---

see on Mark xiv. 1-11, Remark 2. 4. As this woman came not for the purpose of shedding tears, so neither did she come to get an assurance from Jesus of her pardon and reconciliation. But as the evidences of the change that had passed upon her flowed forth, the balm of a pronounced acceptance was poured in. And thus do the most delightful assurances of our forgiveness usually spring up unsought, in the midst of active duty and warm affections; while they fly from those who hunt for them in the interior of an anxious heart, and not finding them there go mourning and weak for want of them.

CHAP. VIII. 1-3.—Jesus makes a Second Galilean Circuit with the Twelve and Certain Ministering Women. This exquisite Section is peculiar to Luke. It seems to follow, in point of time, the events of the preceding chapter.

1. And it came to pass afterward, that he went [καὶ αὐτὸς διώδευε]—'that He travelled about,' or 'made a progress.' The "He" is emphatic here. **throughout every city and village** [κατὰ πόλιν καὶ κώμην]—'through town and village,' **preaching and showing the glad tidings of the kingdom of God**—the Prince of itinerant preachers scattering far and wide the seed of the Kingdom: **and the twelve were with him, 2. And certain women, which had been healed of evil spirits and infirmities**—on whom He had the double claim of having brought healing to their bodies and new life to their souls. Drawn to Him by an attraction more than magnetic, they accompany Him on this tour as His *almoners*—ministering unto Him of their substance. **Mary called Magdalene** [Μαγδαληνή]—probably 'of Magdala,' as to which see on Mark viii. 10, **out of whom went** [ἐξεληλύθει]—rather, 'had gone,' **seven devils.** The same thing being said in Mark xvi. 9, it seems plain that this was what distinguished her amongst the Maries. It is a great wrong to this female to identify her with the once profligate, though afterwards marvellously changed, woman who is the subject of the preceding Section (ch. vii. 37, &c.), and to call all such penitents *Magdalenes.* The mistake has arisen from confounding unhappy demoniacal possession with the conscious entertainment of diabolic impurity, or supposing the one to have been inflicted as a punishment for the other—for which there is not the least scriptural ground. See on ch. xiii. 1-9, Remark 2, at the close of that Section. **3. And Joanna the wife of Chuza Herod's steward.** If the steward of such a godless, cruel, and licentious sovereign as Herod Antipas (see on Mark vi. 14, &c.) differed greatly from himself, his post would be no easy or enviable one. That he was a disciple of Christ is very improbable, though he might be favourably disposed towards Him. But what we know not of him, and may fear he wanted, we are sure his wife possessed. Healed either of "evil spirits" or of some one of the "infirmities" here referred to—the ordinary diseases of humanity—she joins in the Saviour's train of grateful, clinging followers. **and Susanna.** Of her we know nothing but the name, and that in this one place only; but her services on this memorable occasion have immortalized her name—"Wheresoever this Gospel shall be preached throughout the whole world, this also that she hath done," in ministering to the Lord of her substance on this Galilean tour, "shall be spoken of as a memorial of her" (Mark xiv. 9). **and many others** [καὶ ἕτεραι πολλαί]—that is, 'many other healed women,' **which ministered unto him**—rather, according to the better supported reading, 'unto them;' that is, to the Lord and the Twelve.

Remarks.—1. What a train have we here! all ministering to the Lord of their substance, and He allowing them to do it, and subsisting upon it. Blessed Saviour! It melts us to see Thee living upon the love of Thy ransomed people. That they bring Thee their poor offerings we wonder not. Thou hast sown unto them spiritual things, and they think it, as well they might, a small thing that Thou shouldst reap their carnal things (1 Cor. ix. 11). But dost Thou take it at their hand, and subsist upon it? "O the depth of the riches"—of this poverty of His! Very noble are the words of *Olshausen* upon this scene: 'He who was the support of the spiritual life of His people disdained not to be supported by them in the body. He was not ashamed to penetrate so far into the depths of poverty as to live upon the alms of love. He only fed others miraculously: for Himself, He lived upon the love of His people. He gave all things to men His brethren, and received all things from them, enjoying thereby the pure blessing of love; which is then only perfect when it is at the same time both giving and receiving. Who could invent such things as these? *It was necessary to live in this manner that it might be so recorded.*' See more on this exalted subject, on ch. xix. 28-44, Remark 2, at the close of that Section. But 2. May not His loving people, and particularly those of the tender clinging sex, still accompany Him as He goes from land to land preaching, by His servants, and showing the glad tidings of the kingdom of God? and may they not minister to Him of their substance by sustaining and cheering these agents of His? Verily they may; and they do. "Inasmuch as ye have done it unto the least of these My brethren, ye have done it unto Me." Yes, as He is with them "alway, even unto the end of the world," in preaching and showing the glad tidings of the kingdom of God, even so, as many as are with the faithful workers of this work, and helpful to them in it, are accompanying Him and ministering to Him of their substance. But see on Matt. xxv. 31-46, concluding Remarks.

4-18.—Parable of the Sower. (=Matt. xiii. 1-23; Mark iv. 1-23.) For the exposition, see on Mark iv. 1-23.

19-21.—His Mother and Brethren Seek to

6 down, and the fowls of the air devoured it. And some fell upon a rock;
and as soon as it was sprung up, it withered away, because it lacked
7 moisture. And some fell among thorns; and the thorns sprang up with
8 it, and choked it. And other fell on good ground, and sprang up, and
bare fruit an hundred-fold. And when he had said these things, he
cried, He that hath ears to hear, let him hear.
9 And [d]his disciples asked him, saying, What might this parable be?
10 And he said, Unto you it is given to know the mysteries of the kingdom
of God: but to others in parables; [e]that seeing they might not see, and
11 hearing they might not understand. Now [f]the parable is this: The
12 [g]seed is the word of God. Those by [h]the way-side are they that hear;
then cometh [i]the devil, and taketh away the word out of their hearts,
13 lest they should believe and be saved. They on the rock *are they*, which,
when they hear, receive the word with joy; and these have no root,
14 which for a while believe, and in time of temptation fall away. And
that which fell among thorns are they, which, when they have heard, go
forth, and are choked with cares [j]and riches and pleasures of *this* life,
15 and bring no fruit to perfection. But that on the good ground are they,
which in an honest and good heart, having heard the word, keep *it*, and
[k]bring forth fruit with patience.
16 No [l]man, when he hath lighted a candle, covereth it with a vessel, or
putteth *it* under a bed; but setteth *it* on a candlestick, that they which
17 enter in may see the light. For [m]nothing is secret that shall not be
made manifest; neither *any thing* hid that shall not be known and
18 come abroad. Take heed therefore how ye hear: [n]for whosoever hath,
to him shall be given; and whosoever hath not, from him shall be taken
even that which he [1]seemeth to have.
19 Then [o]came to him *his* mother and his brethren, and could not come
20 at him for the press. And it was told him *by certain*, which said, Thy
21 mother and thy brethren stand without, desiring to see thee. And he
answered and said unto them, My mother and my brethren are these
which hear the word of God, and do it.
22 Now [p]it came to pass on a certain day, that he went into a ship with
his disciples: and he said unto them, Let us go over unto the other side
23 of the lake. And they launched forth. But as they sailed he fell asleep:
and there came down a storm of wind on the lake; and they were filled
24 *with water*, and were in jeopardy. And they came to him, and awoke
him, saying, Master, master, we perish! Then he [q]arose, and rebuked
the wind and the raging of the water: and they ceased, and there was a
25 calm. And he said unto them, Where is your faith? And they being
[r]afraid wondered, saying one to another, What manner of man is this!
for he commandeth even the winds and water, and they obey him.
26 And [s]they arrived at the country of the Gadarenes, which is over
27 against Galilee. And when he went forth to land, there met him out of
the city a certain man, which had devils long time, and ware no clothes,
28 neither abode in *any* house, but in the tombs. When he saw Jesus, he
[t]cried out, and fell down before him, and with a loud voice said, What
have I to do with thee, Jesus, *thou* Son of God most high? I beseech
29 thee, torment me not. (For he had commanded the unclean spirit to
come out of the man. For oftentimes it had caught him: and he was
kept bound with chains and in fetters; and he brake the bands, and was
30 driven of the devil into the wilderness.) And Jesus asked him, saying,
What is thy name? And he said, Legion: because many devils were

A. D. 31.

[d] Matt. 13. 10. Mark 4. 10.
[e] Isa. 6. 9. Mark 4. 12.
[f] Matt 13. 18. Mark 4. 14.
[g] Mark 4. 14. Acts 20. 27, 32. 1 Cor. 3. 6, 7, 9-12. Jas. 1. 21. 1 Pet. 1. 23.
[h] Jas. 1. 23, 24.
[i] 2 Cor. 2. 11. 2 Cor. 4. 3. 2 Thes. 2. 10. 1 Pet. 5. 8.
[j] Matt. 19 23. 1 Tim. 6. 9, 10. 2 Tim. 4. 10.
[k] Eph. 2. 4. 2 Pet. 1. 5-10.
[l] Matt. 5. 15. Mark 4. 21. ch. 11. 33. Phil. 2. 15, 16.
[m] Matt. 10. 26. ch. 12. 2.
[n] Matt. 13. 12. Matt. 25. 29. Mark 4. 25. ch. 19. 26. John 15. 2. Rev. 22. 11.
[1] Or, thinketh that he hath.
[o] Matt. 12. 46. Matt. 13. 55. Mark 3. 31. John 7. 5. Acts 1. 14. 1 Cor. 9. 5. Gal. 1. 19.
[p] Matt. 8. 23. Mark 4. 35.
[q] Job 28. 11. Job 38. 11. Ps. 29. 10. Ps. 46. 1. Ps. 65. 7. Ps. 89. 9. Ps. 93. 4. Ps. 107. 29. Ps. 135. 6. Nah. 1. 4.
[r] Ps. 33. 8, 9. Mark 4. 41. Mark 6. 51.
[s] Matt. 8. 28. Mark 5. 1.
[t] Acts 16. 16, 17. Phil. 2. 10, 11.

Speak with Him, and the Reply. (=Matt. xii. 46-50; Mark iii. 31-35.) For the exposition, see on Matt. xii. 46-50.

22-39.—Jesus, Crossing the Sea of Galilee, Miraculously Stills a Tempest—He Cures the Demoniac of Gadara. (=Matt. viii. 23-34; Mark iv. 35—v. 20.) For the exposition, see on Mark iv. 35—v. 20.

31 entered into him. And they besought him that he would not command
them to go out [u]into the deep.
32 And there was there an herd [v]of many swine feeding on the mountain:
and they besought him that he would suffer them to enter into them.
33 And [w]he suffered them. Then went the devils out of the man, and
entered into the swine: and the herd ran violently down a steep place
34 into the lake, and were choked. When they that fed *them* saw what was
done, they fled, and went and told *it* in the city, and in the country.
35 Then they went out to see what was done: and came to Jesus, and
found the man out of whom the devils were departed, sitting at the feet
36 of Jesus, clothed, [x]and in his right mind: and they were afraid. They
also which saw *it* told them by what means he that was possessed of the
devils was healed.
37 Then [y]the whole multitude of the country of the Gadarenes round about
besought [z]him to depart from them; for they were taken with great fear.
38 And he went up into the ship, and returned back again. Now [a]the man
out of whom the devils were departed besought him that he might be
39 with him: but Jesus sent him away, saying, Return to thine own house,
and show how great things God hath done unto thee. And he went his
way, and published throughout the whole city how great things Jesus
had done unto him.
40 And it came to pass, that, when Jesus was returned, the people *gladly*
41 received him: for they were all waiting for him. And, [b]behold, there
came a man named Jairus, and he was a ruler of the synagogue: and he
fell down at Jesus' feet, and besought him that he would come into his
42 house: for he had one only daughter, about twelve years of age, and she
lay a-dying. But as he went the people thronged him.
43 And [c]a woman, having an issue of blood twelve years, which had spent
44 all her living upon physicians, neither could be healed of any, came
behind *him*, and [d]touched the border of his garment: and immediately
45 her issue of blood stanched. And Jesus said, Who touched me? When
all denied, Peter and they that were with him said, Master, the multitude
46 throng thee and press *thee*, and sayest thou, Who touched me? And
Jesus said, Somebody hath touched me: for I perceive that [e]virtue is
47 gone out of me. And when the woman saw that she was not hid, she
came trembling, and falling down before him, she declared unto him
before all the people for what cause she had touched him, and how she
48 was healed immediately. And he said unto her, Daughter, be of good
comfort: thy faith hath made thee whole; go in peace.
49 While [f]he yet spake, there cometh one from the ruler of the synagogue's
house, saying to him, Thy daughter is dead; trouble not the Master.
50 But when Jesus heard *it*, he answered him, saying, Fear not: [g]believe
51 only, and she shall be made whole. And when he came into the house,
he suffered no man to go in, save Peter and James and John, and the
52 father and the mother of the maiden. And all wept, and bewailed her:
53 but he said, Weep not; she is not dead, [h]but sleepeth. And they
54 laughed him to scorn, knowing that she was dead. And he put them
55 all out, and took her by the hand, and called, saying, Maid, [i]arise. And
her spirit came again, and she arose straightway: and he commanded to
56 give her meat. And her parents were astonished: but he [j]charged them
that they should tell no man what was done.
9 THEN [a]he called his twelve disciples together, and [b]gave them power
2 and authority over all devils, and to cure diseases. And [c]he sent them

A. D. 31.
[u] Rev. 20. 3.
[v] Lev. 11. 7. Deut. 14. 8.
[w] Job 1. 12. Job 12. 16. Rev. 20. 7.
[x] 1 John 3. 8. Rom. 16. 20.
[y] Matt. 8. 34.
[z] Deut. 5. 25. 1 Sam. 6. 20. 1 Sam. 16. 4. 2 Sam. 6. 8, 9. Job 21. 14. Matt. 8. 34. Mark 1. 24. Mark 5. 17. ch. 4. 34. ch. 5. 8. Acts 16. 39. 1 Cor. 2. 14.
[a] Ps. 103. 1. Ps. 116. 12. Mark 5. 18. ch. 18. 43.
[b] Matt. 9. 18. Mark 5. 22.
[c] Lev. 15. 25. Matt. 9. 20. Mark 5. 25.
[d] Deut. 22. 12. Mark 5. 27, 28. Mark 6. 56. Acts 5. 15. Acts 19. 12.
[e] Mark 5. 30. ch. 5. 17. ch. 6. 19.
[f] Mark 5. 35.
[g] 2 Chr. 20. 20. Isa. 1. 10. Mark 9. 23. Mark 11. 22-24. John 11. 25, 40.
[h] John 11. 11, 13.
[i] ch. 7. 14. John 11. 43. Acts 9. 40.
[j] Matt. 8. 4. Matt. 9. 30. Mark 5. 43.

CHAP. 9.
[a] Matt. 10. 1. Mark 3. 13. Mark 6. 7.
[b] John 14. 12. Acts 3. 6.
[c] Matt. 10. 7, 8. Mark 6. 12. ch. 10. 1, 9. Tit. 1. 9. Tit. 2. 12, 14.

40-56.—Re-crossing the Lake, the Daughter of Jairus is Raised to Life, and the Woman with the Issue of Blood is Healed. (= Matt. ix. 18-26; Mark v. 21-43.) For the exposition, see on Mark v. 21-43.

CHAP. IX. 1-6.—Mission of the Twelve

3 to preach the kingdom of God, and to heal the sick. And [d]he said unto
them, Take nothing for *your* journey, neither staves, nor scrip, neither
4 bread, neither money; neither have two coats apiece. And [e]whatsoever
5 house ye enter into, there abide, and thence depart. And [f]whosoever
will not receive you, when ye go out of that city, [g]shake off the very dust
6 from your feet for a testimony against them. And [h]they departed, and
went through the towns, preaching the Gospel, and healing every where.
7 Now [i]Herod the tetrarch heard of all that was done by him: and he
was perplexed, because that it was said of some, that John was risen from
8 the dead, and of some, that Elias had appeared; and of others, that
9 one of the old prophets was risen again. And Herod said, John have I
beheaded: but who is this of whom I hear such things? And [j]he desired
to see him.
10 And [k]the apostles, when they were returned, told him all that they had
done. And [l]he took them, and went aside privately into a desert place
11 belonging to the city called Bethsaida. And the people, when they knew
it, followed him: and he received them, and spake unto them of the
kingdom of God, and healed them that had need of healing.
12 And [m]when the day began to wear away, then came the twelve, and
said unto him, Send the multitude away, that they may go into the
towns and country round about, and lodge, and get victuals: for we are
13 here in a desert place. But he said unto them, [n]Give ye them to eat.
And they said, [o]We have no more but five loaves and two fishes; except
14 we should go and buy meat for all this people. (For they were about five
thousand men.) And he said to his disciples, Make them sit down by
15 fifties in a company. And they did so, and made them all sit down.
16 Then he took the five loaves and the two fishes, and looking up to heaven,
he blessed them, and brake, and gave to the disciples to set before the
17 multitude. And they [p]did eat, and were all filled: and there was taken
up of fragments that remained to them twelve baskets.
18 And [q]it came to pass, as he was alone praying, his disciples were with
him: and he asked them, saying, Whom say the people that I am?
19 They answering said, [r]John the Baptist; but some *say*, Elias; and others
20 *say*, that one of the old prophets is risen again. He said unto them, But
21 whom say ye that I am? [s]Peter answering said, The Christ of God. And
[t]he straitly charged them, and commanded *them* to tell no man that
22 thing; saying, [u]The Son of man must suffer many things, and be rejected
of the elders and chief priests and scribes, and be slain, and be raised the
third day.
23 And [v]he said to *them* all, If any *man* will come after me, let him deny
24 himself, and take up his cross daily, and follow me. For whosoever will
save his life shall lose it: but whosoever will lose his life for my sake, the
25 same shall save it. For [w]what is a man advantaged, if he gain the whole
26 world, and lose himself, or be cast away? For [x]whosoever shall be
ashamed of me and of my words, of him shall the Son of man be ashamed,
when he shall come in his own glory, and *in his* Father's, and of the holy
27 angels. But [y]I tell you of a truth, there be some standing here, which
shall not taste of death, till they see the kingdom of God.

A. D. 31.

[d] Ps. 37. 3. Matt. 10. 9. Mark 6. 8. ch. 10. 4. ch. 22. 35. 2 Tim. 2. 4.
[e] Matt. 10. 11. Mark 6. 10.
[f] Matt. 10. 14.
[g] Acts 13. 51.
[h] Mark 6. 12.
[i] Matt. 14. 1. Mark 6. 14.
[j] ch. 23. 8.
[k] Mark 6. 30.
[l] Matt. 14. 13.
[m] Matt. 14. 15. Mark 6. 35. John 6. 1, 5.
[n] 2 Ki. 4. 42, 43.
[o] Num. 11. 22. Ps. 78. 19, 20.
[p] Ps. 145. 15, 16.
[q] Matt. 16. 13. Mark 8. 27.
[r] Matt. 14. 2.
[s] Matt. 16. 16. Mark 8. 29. Mark 14. 61. John 1. 41, 49. John 4. 29, 42. John 6. 69. John 7. 41. John 11. 27. John 20. 31. Acts 8. 37. Acts 9. 22. Rom. 10. 9. 1 John 4. 14, 15. 1 John 5. 5.
[t] Matt. 16. 20.
[u] Matt. 16. 21. Matt. 17. 22. Matt. 20. 17. Mark 9. 31. ch. 18. 31. ch. 24. 6, 7.
[v] Matt. 10. 38. Matt. 16. 24. Mark 8. 34. ch. 14. 27.
[w] Matt. 16. 26. Mark 8. 36.
[x] Matt. 10. 33. Mark 8. 38. 2 Tim. 2. 12.
[y] Matt. 16. 28. Mark 9. 1.

APOSTLES. (=Matt. x. 1, 5-15; Mark vi. 7-13.) For the exposition, see on Matt. x. 1, 5-15.

7-9.—HEROD THINKS JESUS A RESURRECTION OF THE MURDERED BAPTIST. (=Matt. xiv. 1, 2; Mark vi. 14-16.) For the exposition, see on Mark vi. 14-16.

10-17.—THE TWELVE, ON THEIR RETURN, HAVING REPORTED THE SUCCESS OF THEIR MISSION, JESUS CROSSES THE SEA OF GALILEE WITH THEM, TEACHES THE PEOPLE, AND MIRACULOUSLY FEEDS FIVE THOUSAND. (=Matt. xiv. 13-21; Mark vi. 30-44.) For the exposition, see on Mark vi. 30-44.

18-27.—PETER'S NOBLE CONFESSION OF CHRIST—FIRST EXPLICIT ANNOUNCEMENT OF HIS APPROACHING SUFFERINGS, DEATH, AND RESURRECTION, WITH WARNINGS TO THE TWELVE. (=Matt. xvi. 13-28; Mark viii. 27—ix. 1.) For the exposition, see on Matt. xvi. 13-28.

28-36.—JESUS IS TRANSFIGURED—CONVERSATION ABOUT ELIAS. (= Matt. xvii. 1-13; Mark ix.

28 And [z]it came to pass, about an eight days after these [1]sayings, he took
29 Peter and John and James, and went up into a mountain to pray. And
as he prayed, the [a]fashion of his countenance was altered, and his raiment
30 *was* white *and* glistering. And, behold, there talked with him two men,
31 which were Moses and [b]Elias; who appeared in [c]glory, and spake of his
32 decease which he should accomplish at Jerusalem. But Peter and they
that were with him were [d]heavy with sleep: and when they were awake,

A. D. 31.

[z] Matt. 17. 1.
[1] Or, things.
[a] Ex. 34. 29, 35.
[b] 2 Ki. 2. 11.
[c] Phil. 3. 21.
[d] Dan. 8. 18. Dan. 10. 9.

2-13.) The time and occasion of this Section, which are of the utmost importance to the right comprehension of it, are most definitely fixed in the opening words of it.

28. And it came to pass, about an eight days after these sayings—meaning, after the first startling announcement of His approaching Sufferings and Death. Matthew and Mark say it was "after six days;" but they *exclude* the day on which "these sayings" were uttered and the Transfiguration-day, while our Evangelist *includes* them. Now, since all the three Evangelists so definitely connect the Transfiguration with this announcement of His Death—so unexpected by the Twelve and so depressing—there can be no doubt that the primary intention of it was to manifest the glory of that Death in the view of Heaven, to irradiate the Redeemer's sufferings, to transfigure the Cross. It will appear, by and by, that the scene took place *at night.* **he took Peter and John and James**—partners before in secular business, now selected, as a kind of sacred triumvirate, to be sole witnesses, first, of the resurrection of Jairus' daughter (Mark v. 37), next, of the Transfiguration, and finally, of the Agony in the garden (Mark xiv. 33), **and went up into a mountain**—probably not mount *Tabor*, according to long tradition, with which the facts scarcely comport, but rather some mountain in the vicinity of the sea of Galilee, **to pray**—for the period He had now reached was a critical and anxious one. But who can adequately express those "strong cryings and tears"? Methinks, as I steal by His side, I hear from Him these plaintive cries, 'Lord, Who hath believed our report? I am come unto mine own, and mine own receive Me not; I am become a stranger unto my brethren, an alien to my mother's children: Consider mine enemies, for they are many, and they hate me with cruel hatred. Arise, O Lord, let not man prevail. Thou that dwellest between the cherubim, shine forth: Show me a token for good: Father, glorify thy name.' These strong cryings and tears pierced the skies: they entered into the ears of the Lord of Sabaoth. **29. And as he prayed, the fashion of his countenance was altered.** Before He cried He was answered, and whilst he was yet speaking He was heard. Blessed interruption to prayer this! **and his raiment was white and glistering.** [ἐξαστράπτων]. Matthew says "His face did shine as the sun, and his raiment was white as the light" (xvii. 2). Mark's description is, as usual, intense and vivid: "His raiment became shining" [στίλβοντα] or 'glittering,' "exceeding white as snow [λευκὰ λίαν ὡς χιών], so as no fuller on earth can white them" (ix. 3). These particulars were doubtless communicated to Mark by Peter, on whom they made such deep impression, that in his second Epistle he refers to them in language of peculiar strength and grandeur (2 Pet. i. 16-18). Putting all the accounts together, it would appear that the light shone, not *upon* Him *from without*, but *out of Him from within:* He was all irradiated: It was one blaze of dazzling, celestial glory; it was Himself glorified. What a contrast now to that "visage more marred than any man, and His form than the sons of men"! (Isa. lii. 14). **30. And, behold, there talked with him two men, which were Moses and Elias.** Who, exclaims *Bengel*, would not have believed these were *angels* (compare Acts i. 10; Mark xvi. 5), had not their *human* names been subjoined? Moses represented "the law," Elijah "the prophets," and both together the whole testimony of the Old Testament Scriptures and the Old Testament saints, to Christ; now not borne in a *book*, but by *living men*, not to a *coming*, but a *come* Messiah, *visibly*, for they "appeared," and *audibly*, for they "spake." **31. Who appeared in glory, and spake** [ἔλεγον]—rather, 'and were speaking' **of his decease** [τὴν ἔξοδον αὐτοῦ]—'of His exodus;' 'His exit,' or 'His departure.' Beautiful euphemism (or softened expression) for *death*, which Peter, who witnessed the scene, uses in his second Epistle to express his own death, and the use of which single term seems to have recalled the whole scene by a sudden rush of recollection, which he accordingly describes in language of uncommon grandeur (2 Pet. i. 15-18). **which he should accomplish** [ἣν ἔμελλεν πληροῦν]—'which He was going to fulfil' **at Jerusalem.** Mark the *historical* and *local* character which Christ's death possessed in the eye of these glorified men, as vital as it is charming; and see on ch. ii. 11. What now may be gathered from this statement? First, That a dying Messiah is the great article of the true Jewish Theology. For a long time the Church had fallen clean away from the faith of this article, and even from a preparedness to receive it. But here we have that jewel brought forth from the heap of Jewish traditions, and by the true representatives of the Church of old made the one subject of talk with Christ Himself. Next, The adoring gratitude of glorified men for His undertaking to accomplish such a decease; their felt dependence upon it for the glory in which they appeared; their profound interest in the progress of it; their humble solaces and encouragements to go through with it; and their sense of its peerless and overwhelming glory. 'Go, matchless, adored One, a Lamb to the slaughter! rejected of men, but chosen of God and precious; dishonoured, abhorred, and soon to be slain by men, but worshipped by cherubim, ready to be greeted by all heaven! In virtue of that decease we are here; our all is suspended on it and wrapt up in it. Thine every step is watched by us with ineffable interest; and though it were too high an honour to us to be permitted to drop a word of cheer into that precious but now clouded spirit, yet, as ourselves the first-fruits of harvest, the very joy set before Him, we cannot choose but tell Him that what is the depth of shame to Him is covered with glory in the eyes of heaven, that the Cross to Him is the Crown to us, that that "decease" is all our salvation and all our desire.' And who can doubt that such a scene *did* minister deep cheer to that spirit? 'Tis said they "talked" not to Him, but "*with* Him;" and if they told Him how glorious His decease was, might He not fitly reply, 'I know it all, but your voice, as messengers from heaven come down to tell it me, is music in mine ears.' **32. But Peter and they that were with him were heavy with sleep: and when they were awake** [διαγρηγορήσαντες δὲ]. So certainly most interpreters understand the expres-

33 they saw his glory, and the two men that stood with him. And it came
to pass, as they departed from him, Peter said unto Jesus, Master, it is
good for us to be here: and let us make three tabernacles; one for thee,
34 and one for Moses, and one for Elias: not knowing what he said. While
he thus spake, there came a cloud and overshadowed them: and they
35 feared as they entered into the cloud. And there came a voice out of
36 the cloud, saying, [e]This is my beloved son: hear [f]him. And when the
voice was past, Jesus was found alone. [g]And they kept *it* close, and
told no man in those days any of those things which they had seen.

A. D. 32.

[e] Matt. 3. 17. 2 Pet. 1. 16, 17.

[f] Ex. 23. 21. Deut. 18. 15-18. Acts 3. 22. Heb. 2. 3. Heb. 12. 25.

[g] Matt. 17. 9.

sion. But as the word signifies, not 'to awake,' but 'to keep awake,' which agrees much better with the manifest intention of the Evangelist, we should either, with *Meyer* and *Alford*, render the words, 'but having kept awake,' or, better still perhaps, with *Olshausen*, 'having roused themselves up,' or shaken off their drowsiness. From *v.* 37 it would appear that this Transfiguration-scene took place during night, and that the Lord must have passed the whole night on the mountain; for it was "the next day" before He and the three "came down from the hill." This will account for the drowsiness of the disciples. **they saw his glory, and the two men that stood with him.** The emphasis here lies on the word "saw;" so that they were "*eye-witnesses* of His majesty," as one of them long afterwards testifies that they were (2 Pet. i. 16). In like manner, Elijah made it the one condition of Elisha's getting a double portion of his spirit after he went away, that he should see him ascend: "If thou *see me* taken from thee, it shall be so unto thee; but if not, it shall not be so." Accordingly, immediately after the record of Elijah's translation, it is added, "And Elisha *saw it*" (2 Ki. ii. 10, 12). **33. And it came to pass, as they departed from him, Peter said unto Jesus, Master, it is good for us to be here: and let us make three tabernacles; one for thee, and one for Moses, and one for Elias: not knowing what he said.** Peter's speech was so far not amiss. It was indeed good, very good to be there; but for the rest of it, the best that can be said is what our Evangelist says, that he knew not what he said. The poor man's words in such circumstances must not be scrutinized too closely. The next step put an end to the hallucination. The cloud and the voice effectually silenced him. **34. While he thus spake, there came a cloud**—not one of our watery clouds, but the Shechinah-cloud, the pavilion of the manifested presence of God with His people on earth, what Peter calls "the excellent" or "magnificent glory" [τῆς μεγαλοπρεποῦς δόξης], 2 Pet. i. 17. **and overshadowed them: and they feared as they entered into the cloud. 35. And there came a voice out of the cloud**—"*such a voice*," says Peter emphatically [φωνῆς τοιᾶσδε]. "And this voice," he adds, "we heard when we were with him in the holy mount" (2 Pet. i. 17, 18). There must have been something very unearthly and awe-striking in the sound, especially as the articulate vehicle of such a testimony to Christ, to be thus recalled. **saying, This is my beloved Son**—"in whom I am well pleased" (Matt. xvii. 5): **hear him**: Hear Him *reverentially*, hear Him *implicitly* hear Him *alone*. **36. And when the voice was past, Jesus was found alone.** Moses and Elias are gone. Their work is done, and they have disappeared from the scene, feeling no doubt with their fellow-servant the Baptist, "He must increase, but I must decrease." The cloud too is gone, and the naked majestic Christ, braced in spirit, and enshrined in the reverent affection of His disciples, is left—to suffer! Matthew (xvii. 6-8) is more full here: "And when the disciples heard [the voice], they fell on their face, and were sore afraid (*v.* 6). And Jesus came and touched them, and said, Arise, and be not afraid (*v.* 7.) And when they had lifted up their eyes, they saw no man save Jesus only" (*v.* 8). **And they kept it close, and told no man in those days any of those things which they had seen**—feeling, for once, at least, that such things were unmeet as yet for general disclosure.

Remarks.—1. We know how the first announcement which our Lord made to the Twelve of His approaching Sufferings and Death startled and shocked them. We know, too, with what sternness Peter's entreaty that his Lord would spare Himself was met and put down, (Matt. xvi. 21, &c.) But it is only by studying the recorded connection between these disclosures and the Transfiguration that we gather how protracted had been the depression produced upon the Twelve, and how this probably reacted upon the mind even of our Lord Himself. After the lapse of a week, and during a night of prayer spent on a mountain, that Death, the announcement of which had been so trying to His most select disciples, is suddenly presented in a new and astonishing light, as engaging the wonder and interest of heaven. No doubt, such a view of it was needed. As the Twelve were beyond all doubt reassured by it, so it is not to be doubted that the Redeemer's own spirit was cheered and invigorated by it. 2. We have tried to conceive what might be the strain of those "prayers and supplications, with strong crying and tears" which Jesus poured out on that mountain, ere the glory broke forth from Him. But much must be left unimagined. 'He filled the silent night with His crying,' says *Traill* beautifully, 'and watered the cold earth with His tears, more precious than the dew of Hermon, or any moisture, next unto His own blood, that ever fell on God's earth since the creation.' 3. "As He prayed the fashion of His countenance was altered." Thanks to God, transfiguring manifestations are not quite strangers here. Ofttimes in the deepest depths, out of groanings which cannot be uttered, God's dear children are suddenly transported to a kind of heaven upon earth, and their soul is made as the chariots of Ammi-nadib. Their prayers fetch down such light, strength, holy gladness, as makes their face to shine, putting a kind of celestial radiance upon it. (Compare 2 Cor. iii. 18, with Exod. xxxiv. 29-35.) 4. What a testimony have we here to the *evangelical* scope of the whole ancient economy. Not only is *Christ* the great End of it all, but a *dying* Christ. Nor are we to dissever the *economy* from the *saints* that were reared under it. In heaven, at least, they regard that "Decease" as all their salvation and all their desire, as we see beautifully here. For here, fresh from heaven, and shining with the glory of it, when permitted to talk with Him, they speak not of His miracles, nor of His teaching, nor of the honour which he put upon their Scriptures, nor upon the unreasonable opposition to Him and His patient endurance of it: They speak not of the

37 And [h]it came to pass, that on the next day, when they were come down
38 from the hill, much people met him. And, behold, a man of the company cried out, saying, Master, I beseech thee, look upon my son; for he
39 is mine only child: and, lo, a spirit taketh him, and he suddenly crieth out; and it teareth him that he foameth again, and, bruising him, hardly
40 departeth from him. And I besought thy disciples to cast him out; and
41 they could not. And Jesus answering said, O faithless and [i]perverse generation! how long shall I be with you, and suffer you? Bring thy son
42 hither. And as he was yet a-coming, the devil threw him down, and tare *him*. And Jesus rebuked the unclean spirit, and healed the child, and

A. D. 32.

h Matt. 17.14, 21. Mark 9. 14, 17.

i Deut. 32. 5. Ps. 78. 8. Matt. 3. 7. Matt.12.39, 45. Matt. 16. 4. Matt.23.36. Acts 2. 40.

glory they were themselves enshrined in, and the glory which He was so soon to reach. Their one subject of talk is "His *decease* which he was going to accomplish at Jerusalem." One fancies he might hear them saying, "Worthy is the Lamb that *is to be* slain!" Those, then, who see no suffering, dying Messiah in the Old Testament read it amiss, if this Transfiguration-scene mean anything at all. 5. In the light of this interview between the two great representatives of the ancient economy and Christ, what are we to think of that theory which some modern advocates of the Personal Reign of Christ on earth during the Millennium contend for—that the saints of the Old Testament are never to be glorified with the Church of the New, but to occupy the lower sphere of a resurrection to some earthly or Adamic condition? The speculation in itself is repulsive enough, and void enough of anything like Scripture support. But in the light of such a scene as this, may we not call it intolerable? 6. What think ye of Christ? Are ye in sympathy with heaven about Him? Doubtless the hymn of the New-Testament Church which best accords with this celestial talk on the mount of Transfiguration is that of the rapt seer in Patmos: "Unto Him that loved us, and washed us from our sins in His own blood, and hath made us kings and priests unto God and His Father, to Him be glory and dominion for ever and ever. Amen" (Rev. i. 5, 6). 7. How cheering is the view here given of the intermediate state between death and the resurrection! No doubt Elijah was translated that He should not see death. But Moses died and was buried. We speak not of those shining bodies, which we know that even angels put on when they came down to talk to the women at the sepulchre of their Lord. But the disembodied saints cannot be conceived to have come down from heaven and talked with Christ as living conscious beings, if the state of the soul between death and the resurrection be one of *unconscious sleep;* no, nor if it be in a state *perfectly passive*, as some good but too speculative divines endeavour to make out. For here is active thought and feeling, aye, and deepest interest in what is passing on earth, particularly what relates to the work, and so, the kingdom of Christ. We presume not to "intrude into those things which we have not seen, vainly puffed up by a fleshly mind." But to the extent we have just expressed, we seem to be on sure Scripture ground. 8. "This is my beloved Son." Is He our Beloved? 9. "Hear Him." Are we doing that? Is His word law to us? Do we like it when it speaks sharp as well as smooth things; when it tells of the worm that dieth not, and the fire that is not quenched, as well as of the many mansions in His Father's house? Does Christ's word carry it over everything that comes into collision with it? And would it not help us just to think, that whatever Christ speaks, the Father is standing over us, as it enters our ears, and saying, 'Hear that.' Thus, "Except a man be born again, he cannot enter into the kingdom of God"—'*Hear* Him.' "Come unto Me, all ye that labour and are heavy laden, and I will give you rest"—'Hear that.' When dark and crushing events are ready to overwhelm us, "What I do thou knowest not now, but thou shalt know hereafter"—'*Hear* Him.' When walking through the valley of the shadow of death, "I am the Resurrection and the Life: he that believeth in Me, though he were dead, yet shall he live; and he that liveth and believeth in Me shall never die"—'Hear Him!' 10. "It came to pass, as they departed from Him." Ah! Bright manifestations in this vale of tears are always "departing" manifestations. But the time is coming when our sun shall no more go down, and the glory shall never be withdrawn. 11. "Jesus was left alone." And alone He abidingly is and ever will be in the eyes of all heaven, earth, and hell—unique, sole: the Alpha and Omega of all God's purposes, the Church's hopes, and hell's fears! 12. When the three disciples heard the voice from heaven, "they fell on their face, and were sore afraid." But Jesus was not. He was not in the least discomposed. He "came and touched them, and said, Arise, and be not afraid" (Matt. xvii. 6, 7). How was this? Why, it was His proper element. A mere man would, as we say, have had his head turned by such a demonstration in His behalf. At least he would have taken time to recover himself, and get down to his proper level. But Jesus—amidst all this blaze of glory, and celestial talk, and the voice from within the cloud, the voice of God Himself, proclaiming Him His beloved Son, whom all are to hear—is perfectly at home. But indeed it was only a faint anticipation of what He will be when He shall come in His own glory and in the glory of the Father and of the holy angels. 13. Well might Peter, looking back, near the close of his life, to this scene, say, "We have not followed cunningly devised fables, when we made known unto you the power and coming of our Lord Jesus Christ, but were eye-witnesses of His majesty. For He received from God the Father honour and glory, when there came such a voice to Him from the excellent glory [*μεγαλοπρεπους δόξης*], This is my beloved Son, in whom I am well pleased. And this voice which came from heaven, we heard, when we were with Him in the holy mount" (2 Pet. i. 16-18). But, as that chastened disciple delightfully adds, there is something better than even this: "We have also what is firmer, the prophetic word [*Καὶ ἔχομεν βεβαιότερον τὸν προφητικὸν λόγον*]; whereunto ye do well that ye take heed, as unto a light that shineth in a dark place, until the day dawn, and the day star arise in your hearts" (see on 2 Pet. i. 19). "Until the day break, and the shadows flee away, turn, my Beloved, and be thou like a roe, or a young hart, upon the mountains of Bether" (Song ii. 17).

37-45.—Healing of a Demoniac Boy—Secon

43 delivered him again to his father. And they were all amazed at the
mighty power of God.
But, while they wondered every one at all things which Jesus did, he
44 said unto his disciples, Let these sayings sink down into your ears: for
45 the Son of man shall be delivered into the hands of men. But [j]they
understood not this saying, and it was hid from them, that they perceived
it not: and they feared to ask him of that saying.
46 Then [k]there arose a reasoning among them, which of them should be
47 greatest. And Jesus, perceiving the thought of their heart, took a child,
48 and set him by him, and said unto them, [l]Whosoever shall receive this
child in my name receiveth me; and whosoever shall receive me receiveth
him that sent me: [m]for he that is least among you all, the same shall be
great.
49 And [n]John answered and said, Master, we saw one casting out devils
in thy name; and we forbade him, because he followeth not with us.
50 And Jesus said unto him, Forbid *him* not: for [o]he that is not against us
is for us.
51 And it came to pass, when the time was come that [p]he should be
52 received up, he stedfastly set his face to go to Jerusalem, and sent messengers before his face: and they went, and entered into a village of the
53 Samaritans, to make ready for him. And [q]they did not receive him,
54 because his face was as though he would go to Jerusalem. And when his
disciples James and John saw *this*, they said, Lord, wilt thou that we
command fire to come down from heaven, and consume them, even as

A. D. 32.

j Matt. 16. 22. Mark 8. 16. Mark 9. 32. ch. 2. 50. ch. 18. 34. John 12. 16. John 14. 5. 2 Cor. 3. 14.
k Matt. 18. 1. Mark 9. 34.
l Matt. 10. 40. Matt. 18. 5. Mark 9. 37. John 12. 44. John 13. 20. 1 Thes. 4. 8.
m Matt. 23. 11, 12.
n Mark 9. 38. Num. 11. 28.
o Matt. 12. 30. Mark 9 39-41. ch. 11. 23. 1 Cor. 12. 3.
p 2 Ki. 2. 1. Mark 16. 19. John 6. 62. Acts 1. 2. Heb. 6. 20.
q John 4. 4, 9.

EXPLICIT ANNOUNCEMENT OF HIS APPROACHING SUFFERINGS. (=Matt. xvii. 14-23; Mark ix. 14-32.) For the exposition, see on Mark ix. 14-32.

46-50.—STRIFE AMONG THE TWELVE WHO SHOULD BE GREATEST, WITH RELATIVE TEACHING—INCIDENTAL REBUKE OF JOHN FOR EXCLUSIVENESS. (= Matt. xviii. 1-5; Mark ix. 33-37.) For the exposition, see on Mark ix. 33-37.

51-56.—THE PERIOD OF HIS ASSUMPTION APPROACHING, CHRIST TAKES HIS LAST LEAVE OF GALILEE—THE SAMARITANS REFUSE TO RECEIVE HIM. (= Matt. xix. 1; Mark x. 1.) It is a remarkable characteristic of this Gospel that the contents of nearly nine chapters of it—beginning with this Section (ch. ix. 51), and going down to ch. xviii. 14—are, with the exception of two or three short passages, peculiar to itself. As there are scarcely any marks of time and place in all this peculiar portion, it is difficult to fix these with any certainty. But there is reason to believe that the earlier portion of it belongs to the period of our Lord's final journey from Galilee—which was probably a circuitous journey, with the view, perhaps, of ministering in localities not before visited; and that the latter portion of it belongs to the intervals between the Feast of Tabernacles and that of the Dedication, in our Lord's last year (see on John x. 22), and between the Feast of the Dedication and that of His Last Passover—during which intervals our Lord appears to have sojourned chiefly in Peræa, within the jurisdiction of Herod Antipas.

Farewell to Galilee, and Refusal of the Samaritans to Receive Him (51-56). **51. And it came to pass, when the time was come that he should be received up** [ἐν τῷ συμπληροῦσθαι τὰς ἡμέρας τῆς ἀναλήμψεως αὐτοῦ]—rather, 'when the days of His assumption were fulfilling,' or 'in course of fulfilment:' meaning not His *death*, as *Calvin* and some others take it, but His *exaltation* to the Father, as *Grotius*, *Bengel*, *de Wette*, *Meyer*, *Olshausen*, *Alford*, *van Osterzee* understand it. It is a sublime expression, taking the sweep of His whole career, as if at one bound He was about to vault into glory. It divides the work of Christ in the flesh into *two great stages;* all that preceded this belonging to the one, and all that follows it to the other. During the one, He formally "came to His own," and "would have gathered them;" during the other, the awful consequences of "His own receiving Him not," rapidly revealed themselves. **he stedfastly set his face to go to Jerusalem** [καὶ αὐτὸς τὸ πρόσωπον αὐτοῦ ἐστήριξε]. The "He" is emphatic here; and the spirit in which He "set (or fixed) his face steadfastly" [= שׂוּם פָּנִים, Jer. xxi. 10; Ezek. vi. 2, which in the LXX. is the same as here] "to go to Jerusalem," is best expressed in His own prophetic language, "I have set my face like a flint" (Isa. l. 7). See on Mark x. 32, and Remark 1 at the close of that Section. Jerusalem was His goal; but the reference here to His final visit must be understood as including two preparatory visits to it, at the feasts of Tabernacles and of Dedication (John vii. 2, 10; and x. 22, 23), with all the intermediate movements and events. **52. And sent messengers before his face: and they went, and entered into a village of the Samaritans, to make ready for him.** He had given no such orders before; but now, instead of avoiding, He seems to court publicity—all now hastening to maturity. **53. And they did not receive him, because his face was as though he would go to Jerusalem.** The Galileans, in going to the festivals at Jerusalem, usually took the Samaritan route (*Joseph.* Antt. xx. 6. 1), and yet seem to have met with no such inhospitality. But if they were asked to prepare quarters *for the Messiah*, in the person of one whose face was as though He would *go to Jerusalem*, their national prejudices would be raised at so marked a slight upon their claims. (See on John iv. 20). **54. And when his disciples James and John saw this, they said, Lord, wilt thou that we command fire to come down from**

55 [r]Elias did? But he turned, and rebuked them, and said, Ye know not
56 [s]what manner of spirit ye are of. For [t]the Son of man is not come to
destroy men's lives, but to save *them.* And they went to another village.
57 And [u]it came to pass, that, as they went in the way, a certain *man*
58 said unto him, Lord, I will follow thee whithersoever thou goest. And
Jesus said unto him, Foxes have holes, and birds of the air *have* nests;
59 but the Son of man hath not where to lay *his* head. And [v]he said unto
another, Follow me. But he said, Lord, suffer me first to go and bury
60 my father. Jesus said unto him, Let the dead bury their dead: but go
61 thou and preach the kingdom of God. And another also said, Lord, [w]I
will follow thee; but let me first go bid them farewell which are at home
62 at my house. And Jesus said unto him, [x]No man, having put his hand
to the plough, and looking back, is fit for the kingdom of God.

10 AFTER these things the Lord appointed other seventy also, and [a]sent
them two and two before his face into every city and place, whither
2 he himself would come. Therefore said he unto them,

A. D. 32.

r 2 Ki. 1. 10, 12. Acts 4. 29. 30. Rev. 13. 13.
s Num. 20. 10-12. Job 2. 10. Job 26. 4. Rom. 10. 2.
t John 3. 17. John 12. 47.
u Matt. 8. 19.
v Matt. 8. 21.
w 1 Ki. 19. 20.
x Heb. 6. 4.

CHAP. 10.
a Matt. 10. 1. Mark 6. 7.

heaven, and consume them. It was not *Peter* who spoke this, as we should have expected, but those "*sons of thunder*" (Mark iii. 17), who afterwards would have all the highest honours of the Kingdom to themselves, and the younger of whom had been rebuked already for his exclusiveness (*vv.* 49, 50). Yet this was "the disciple whom Jesus loved," while the other willingly drank of His Lord's bitter cup. (See on Mark x. 38-40, and on Acts xii. 2.) And that same fiery zeal, in a mellowed and hallowed form, in the beloved disciple, we find kindling up—in view of deadly error and ecclesiastical presumption—in 2 John 10, and 3 John 10. **even as Elias did?**—a plausible precedent, and the more so, perhaps, as it also occurred in *Samaria* (2 Ki. i. 10-12). **55. But he turned, and rebuked them, and said, Ye know not what manner of spirit ye are of.** 'The thing ye demand, though in keeping with the *legal*, is unsuited to the genius of the *evangelical* dispensation.' The sparks of *un*holy indignation would seize readily enough on this example of Elias; but our Lord's rebuke, as is plain from *v.* 56, is directed to the *principle* involved rather than the animal heat which doubtless prompted the reference. **56. For the Son of man is not come to destroy men's lives, but to save them**—a saying truly divine, of which all His miracles—for salvation, never destruction—were one continued illustration. **And they went to another village**—illustrating His own precept (Matt. x. 23), "When they persecute you in one city, flee ye to another." *Tischendorf* and *Tregelles* greatly curtail the text in this passage, leaving out all that we here inclose in brackets: 54. [Even as Elias.] 55. But he turned and rebuked them, [and said, Ye know not what manner of spirit ye are of. 56. For the Son of man is not come to destroy men's lives, but to save them.] *Lachmann* admits, "Even as Elias," but excludes all the rest. The authority on which this is done, though ancient and weighty, is decidedly inferior, in our judgment, to that in favour of the received text—so far as *vv.* 54, 55, are concerned. For the exclusion of *v.* 56 the authorities are more formidable; and some critics, who abide by the received text up to that verse, think themselves bound to reject it, as probably inserted from Matt. xviii. 11, and Luke xix. 10. But we agree with *Alford* in retaining the whole, on internal as well as external evidence. The saying in Matt. xviii. 11 cannot fairly be identified with this one.

Remarks.—1. How easily may the heat of human anger mingle with zeal for the Lord, and be confounded with it, as in the case of James and John here; and how slow are we to learn that "the wrath of man worketh not the righteousness of God" (Jas. i. 20). Confounding the Legal and the Evangelical dispensations, has been the fruitful source, as of woeful corruption of the worship of God, so of hateful persecution in the name of religion. While attempts to graft the spirit of the ancient ritual upon the worship of the Christian Church has led to a monstrous caricature of the temple-service and the Aaronic priesthood in the Church of Rome, the merciless vengeance which was required to be taken, and which sometimes miraculously descended, upon the despisers of Moses' law has been regarded as the model and law of the Christian Church; and Christian magistrates have been hounded on—not by the Church of Rome only, but, alas! by others also—to execute what was called the just judgment of God upon the unbelieving and the heretical. But that great saying of Christ, "The Son of man is not come to destroy men's lives, but to save them," should for ever banish and brand such a mode of treating errorists as contrary to the entire genius of the Gospel. It is a golden saying of *Tillotson,* as *Webster and Wilkinson* remark, that we should never do anything for religion which is against religion.

57-62.—Incidents illustrative of Discipleship. (= Matt. viii. 18-22.) For the exposition, see on Matt. viii. 18-22.

CHAP. X. 1-4.—Mission of the Seventy Disciples—their Return, and Discourse occasioned by their Report. As our Lord's end approaches, the preparations for the establishment of the coming Kingdom are quickened and extended.

Mission of the Seventy Disciples (1-16).—**1. After these things**—but how long after does not appear. See introductory remarks on the large portion of this Gospel commencing with ch. ix. 51. **the Lord.** This august appellation is here in the highest degree suitable, the appointment about to be mentioned being, as *Bengel* remarks, truly *lordly.* **appointed other seventy also** [καὶ ἑτέρους, ἑβδομήκοντα]—an unhappy rendering. It should be, as we have pointed the Greek, 'appointed others also, seventy [in number]'—that is, others in addition to the Twelve, to the number of seventy. In all likelihood, as the number Twelve had reference to the number of the tribes of Israel, so the number Seventy had reference to the number of elders on whom the Spirit rested in the wilderness (Num. xi. 24, 25).

[b]The harvest truly *is* great, but the labourers *are* few: [c]pray ye therefore the [d]Lord of the harvest, that he would send forth labourers into his
3 harvest. Go your ways: [e]behold, I send you forth as lambs among wolves.
4 Carry [f]neither purse, nor scrip, nor shoes: and [g]salute no man by the
5 way. And [h]into whatsoever house ye enter, first say, Peace *be* to this
6 house. And if the son of peace be there, your peace shall rest upon it:
7 if not, it shall turn to you again. And [i]in the same house remain, [j]eat-
ing and drinking such things as they give: for the [k]labourer is worthy of
8 his hire. Go not [l]from house to house. And into whatsoever city ye
9 enter, and they receive you, eat such things as are set before you: and
[m]heal the sick that are therein; and say unto them, [n]The kingdom of
10 God is come nigh unto you. But into whatsoever city ye enter, and they
receive you not, go your ways out into the streets of the same, and say,
11 Even [o]the very dust of your city, which cleaveth on us, we do wipe off
against you: notwithstanding, be ye sure of this, that the kingdom of
12 God is come nigh unto you. But I say unto you, That [p]it shall be more
13 tolerable in that day for Sodom, than for that city. Woe [q]unto thee,
Chorazin! woe unto thee, Bethsaida! [r]for if the mighty works had been
done in Tyre and Sidon which have been done in you, they had a great
14 while ago [s]repented, sitting in sackcloth and ashes. But it shall be more
15 tolerable for Tyre and Sidon at the judgment, than for you. And [t]thou
Capernaum, which art exalted [u]to heaven, [v]shalt be thurst down to hell.
16 He [w]that heareth you heareth me; and he [x]that despiseth you despiseth
me; [y]and he that despiseth me despiseth him that sent me.
17 And the seventy returned again with joy, saying, Lord, even the devils
18 are subject unto us through thy name. And he said unto them, [z]I
19 beheld Satan as lightning fall from heaven. Behold, [a]I give unto you
power to tread on serpents and scorpions, and over all the power of the

A. D. 32.

[b] Matt. 9. 37, 38. John 4. 35.
[c] 2 Thes. 3. 1.
[d] Jer. 3. 15. 1 Cor. 12. 28.
[e] Matt. 10. 16.
[f] Matt. 10. 9, 10. Mark 6. 8. ch. 9. 3.
[g] 2 Ki. 4. 29.
[h] Matt 10. 12.
[i] Matt. 10. 11.
[j] 1 Cor. 10. 27.
[k] Matt 10. 10. 1 Cor. 9. 4.
[l] Eph. 5. 15.
[m] ch. 9. 2.
[n] Isa. 2. 2.
[o] Matt 10. 14.
[p] Matt. 10. 15.
[q] Matt. 11. 21.
[r] Ezek. 3. 6.
[s] Jon. 3. 5.
[t] Matt. 11. 23.
[u] Gen. 11. 4. Deut. 1. 28.
[v] Ezek. 26. 20. Ezek. 32. 18.
[w] Mark 9. 37. John 13. 20.
[x] 1 Thes. 4. 8.
[y] John 5. 23.
[z] John 12. 31.
[a] Mark 16. 18.

This appointment, unlike that of the Twelve, was evidently quite *temporary*. All the instructions are in keeping with a brief and hasty *pioneering* mission, intended to supply what of general preparation for coming events the Lord's own visit afterwards to the same "cities and places" (*v.* 1), would not, from want of time, now suffice to accomplish; whereas, the instructions to the Twelve, besides embracing all those given to the Seventy, contemplate *world-wide* and *permanent* effects. Accordingly, after their return from this single missionary tour, we never again read of the Seventy. **and sent them two and two before his face into every city and place, whither he himself would come** [ἔμελλεν αὐτὸς ἔρχεσθαι]—or 'was going to come.' **2. Therefore said he**—or, 'So He said' **unto them, The harvest, &c.** See on Matt. ix. 37, 38, and Remarks 1 and 2 at the close of that Section. **3-12. Go your ways, &c.** See on Matt. x. 7-16. **13-15. Woe unto thee, Chorazin, &c.** See on Matt. xi. 21-24. **16. He that heareth you, &c.** See on Matt. x. 40.

Return of the Seventy, and Discourse occasioned by their Report (17-24). **17. And the seventy returned again**—evidently they had not been long away, **with joy, saying, Lord, even the devils are subject unto us through**—or, 'in' [ἐν] **thy name.** 'Lord, thou hast exceeded thy promise: We had not expected this.' The power to cast out devils, not being expressly in their commission, as it was in that to the Twelve (ch. ix. 1), seems to have filled them with more astonishment and joy than the higher object of their mission. Yet they say, "in Thy name"—taking no credit to themselves, but feeling lifted into a region of unimagined superiority to the powers of evil, simply through their connection with Christ. **18. And he said, I beheld** ['Εθεώρουν] **Satan as lightning fall from heaven.** As much of the force of this glorious statement depends on the nice shade of sense indicated by the *imperfect tense* in the original, it might have been well to bring it out in the translation:—'I was beholding Satan as lightning falling from heaven:'—*q. d.*, 'I followed you on your mission, and watched its triumphs; while ye were wondering at the subjection to you of devils in My name, a grander spectacle was opening to My view; sudden as the darting of lightning from heaven to earth Satan was beheld by Mine eye falling from heaven!' By that law of association which connects a part with the whole, those feeble triumphs of the Seventy seem to have not only brought vividly before the Redeemer the whole ultimate result of His mission, but compressed it into a moment and quickened it into the rapidity of lightning! We have repeatedly observed that the word rendered "devils" [δαιμόνια] is always used for those spiritual agents employed in *demoniacal possessions*—never for the ordinary agency of Satan in rational men. When, therefore, the Seventy say, "the *demons* are subject to us," and Jesus replies, 'Mine eye was beholding *Satan* falling,' it is plain that He meant to raise their minds not only from the *particular* to the *general*, but from a very *temporary* form of satanic operation to *the entire kingdom of evil*. See John xii. 31, and compare Isa. xiv. 17. **19. Behold, I give unto you**—not with a view to the renewal of their mission, though probably many of them afterwards became ministers of Christ, but simply as disciples. **power to tread on serpents and scorpions**—the latter more venomous than the former. This was to be literally fulfilled at the first starting of the Gospel ministry (Mark xvi. 17, 18; Acts xxviii. 5). But the following words, **and over all the power**

20 enemy: and nothing shall by any means hurt you. Notwithstanding in
this rejoice not, that the spirits are subject unto you; but rather rejoice,
because [b]your names are written in heaven.
21 In [c]that hour Jesus rejoiced in spirit, and said, I thank thee, O Father,
Lord of heaven and earth, that thou hast hid these things from [d]the
wise and prudent, and hast revealed them unto babes: even so, Father;
22 for so it seemed good in thy sight. [1]All things [e]are delivered to me
of my Father: and [f]no man knoweth who the Son is, but the Father;
and who the Father is, but the Son, and *he* to whom the Son will reveal
him.
23 And he turned him unto *his* disciples, and said privately, [g]Blessed *are*
24 the eyes which see the things that ye see: for I tell you, [h]that many
prophets and kings have desired to see those things which ye see, and
have not seen *them;* and to hear those things which ye hear, and have
not heard *them.*
25 And, behold, a certain lawyer stood up, and tempted him, saying,
26 [i]Master, what shall I do to inherit eternal life? He said unto him,
27 What is written in the law? how readest thou? And he answering said,
[j]Thou shalt love the Lord thy God with all thy heart, and with all thy
soul, and with all thy strength, and with all thy mind; and [k]thy
28 neighbour as thyself. And he said unto him, Thou hast answered
29 right: this do, and [l]thou shalt live. But he, willing to [m]justify himself,
said unto Jesus, And who is my neighbour?

A. D. 32.

[b] Ex. 32. 32. Ps. 69. 28.
[c] Matt. 11. 25.
[d] 1 Cor. 1. 19. 2 Cor. 2. 6.
1 Many ancient copies add these words, And turning to his disciples, he said.
[e] Matt. 28. 18. John 3. 35.
[f] John 1. 18. John 6. 44.
[g] Matt. 13. 16.
[h] 1 Pet. 1. 10.
[i] Matt. 22 35.
[j] Deut. 6. 5.
[k] Lev. 19. 18.
[l] Lev. 18. 5. Neh. 9. 29. Ezek. 20. 11. Rom. 10. 5.
[m] ch. 16. 15.

of the enemy: and nothing shall by any means hurt you—show that what is meant is the glorious power of faith to "overcome the world" and "quench all the fiery darts of the wicked one," by the communication and maintenance of which to His people He makes them *innocuous* (1 John v. 4; Eph. vi. 16). **20. Notwithstanding in this rejoice not**—that is, not so much **that the spirits are subject unto you; but rather rejoice, because your names are written in heaven.** So far from forbidding this joy at the expulsion of demons by their instrumentality, He told them the exultation with which He followed it Himself; but since power over demons might unduly elate them, He gives them a higher joy to *balance* it, the joy of having their own names in Heaven's register. (Phil. iv. 3).

21. In that hour Jesus rejoiced [ἠγαλλιάσατο]—or 'exulted,' **in spirit**—giving visible expression to His unusual emotions, while the words "in spirit" express the depth of them, **and said, I thank thee** [Ἐξομολογοῦμαί σοι]—rather, 'I assent to thee;' but with the idea of full or cordial concurrence, expressed by the preposition. (See on Matt. xi. 25.) **that thou hast hid these things from the wise and prudent, and hast revealed them unto babes: even so, Father; for so it seemed good in thy sight. 22. [And turning to his disciples, he said,]** The words in brackets are in the received text of *Stephens*, though not of the *Elzevirs*, nor in *Beza's* text; and our version, which in some places follows *Beza's* text in preference to the other, omits them here. But the authority for the insertion of them is preponderating. *Tischendorf* inserts them, though *Tregelles* does not. **All things are delivered to me of my Father: and no man knoweth who the Son is, but the Father; and who the Father is, but the Son, and he to whom the Son will reveal him.** This sublime utterance has been regarded by some acute harmonists as but a repetition by Luke of what is recorded in Matt. xi. 25-27, and so, as spoken only once. But besides that the occasions were not the same, the words in the First Gospel merely are, "Jesus answered and said," whereas here they are, "Jesus exulted in spirit, and said." If this should be thought of less moment, let it be observed that there it is merely said, "At that time," or 'season' [καιρῷ], He spoke thus—with a general reference to the rejection of His Gospel by the self-sufficient; whereas here it is, "*In that hour* Jesus said," with express reference probably to the humble class from which He had had to draw the Seventy, and the similar class that had chiefly welcomed their message. **23, 24. And he turned him unto his disciples, and said privately, Blessed are the eyes that see the things that ye see, &c.** See on Matt. xiii. 16, 17.

For Remarks on the Mission of the Seventy, see those on the analogous Mission of the Twelve, Matt. x.; and for Remarks on the lofty utterance with which this Section closes, see those on the same in Matt. xi. 25-27.

25-37.—QUESTION OF A LAWYER ABOUT THE WAY TO INHERIT ETERNAL LIFE, AND THE PARABLE OF THE GOOD SAMARITAN.

How to Inherit Eternal Life (25-29). **25. And, behold, a certain lawyer stood up, and tempted him**—'tried,' or 'tested Him' [ἐκπειράζων]; in no hostile spirit, yet with no tender anxiety for light on that question of questions, but just to see what insight this great Galilean teacher had. **saying, Master**—'Teacher' [Διδάσκαλε]; **what shall I do to inherit eternal life? 26. He said unto him, What is written in the law? how readest thou?**—'an apposite question,' says *Bengel*, 'to a doctor of the law, and putting himself in turn to the test.' **27. And he answering said, Thou shalt love the Lord thy God, &c.**—precisely as Christ Himself had answered another lawyer. See on Mark xii. 29-33. **28. And he said unto him, Thou hast answered right: this do, and thou shalt live.** 'Right: THIS do, and life is thine'—laying such emphasis on "this" as to indicate, without expressing it, *where the real difficulty to a sinner lay*, and thus nonplussing the questioner himself. **29. But he, willing**—or 'wishing' [θέλων], **to justify himself**—to get himself out of the difficulty by throwing upon Jesus the definition of

30 And Jesus answering said, A certain *man* went down from Jerusalem
to Jericho, and fell among thieves, which stripped him of his raiment,
31 and wounded *him*, and departed, leaving *him* half dead. And by chance
there came down a certain priest that way: and when he saw him, [n]he
32 passed by on the other side. And likewise a Levite, when he was at the
33 place, came and looked *on him*, and passed by on the other side. But a
certain [o]Samaritan, as he journeyed, came where he was: and when he
34 saw him, he had compassion *on him*, and went to *him*, and bound up his
wounds, pouring in oil and wine, and set him on his own beast, and
35 brought him to an inn, and took care of him. And on the morrow, when
he departed, he took out two [p]pence, and gave *them* to the host, and said
unto him, Take care of him: and whatsoever thou spendest more, when
36 I come again, I will repay thee. Which now of these three, thinkest
37 thou, was neighbour unto him that fell among the thieves? And he
said, He that showed mercy on him. Then said Jesus unto him, [q]Go,
and do thou likewise.

A. D. 32.

[n] Job 6.14,21. Ps 38. 11. Ps. 69. 20. Pro. 21. 13. Jas. 2. 13. 1 John 3.16.
[o] Pro. 27. 10. Jer. 38. 7. Jer. 39. 16. John 4. 9. John 8. 48.
[p] Matt. 20. 2.
[q] ch. 6. 32. John 13.15. Rom. 12.20. 1 Pet. 2. 21. 1 John 3.16, 18. 1 John 4.10, 11.

"neighbour," 'which,' as *Alford* remarks, 'the Jews interpreted very narrowly and technically, as excluding Samaritans and Gentiles; **said unto Jesus, And who is my neighbour?**

Parable of the Good Samaritan (30-37). **30. And Jesus answering said, A certain man**—a Jew, as the story shows, **went down from Jerusalem to Jericho**—a distance of eighteen miles northeast, a deep and very fertile hollow, and, as *Trench* says, the *Tempe* of Judea; **and fell among thieves** [λῃσταῖς]—rather 'robbers.' The road, being rocky and desolate, was a notorious haunt of robbers, then and for ages after, and is even to this day. **which stripped him of his raiment, and wounded him, and departed, leaving him half dead. 31. And by chance there came down a certain priest that way.** Jericho, the second city of Judea, was a city of the priests and Levites, and thousands of them lived there. **and when he saw him**—so it was not *inadvertently* that he acted, **he passed by on the other side**—although the law expressly required the opposite treatment even of the *beast* not only of their *brethren* but of their *enemy* (Deut. xxii. 4; Exod. xxiii. 4, 5; and compare Isa. lviii. 7). **32. And likewise a Levite, when he was at the place, came and looked on him**—a further aggravation, **and passed by on the other side.** If we suppose this priest and Levite to have been returning from their temple duties at Jerusalem, as *Trench* says, it would show that whatever else they had learnt there, they had not learnt what that meaneth, "I will have mercy, and not sacrifice." **33. But a certain Samaritan**—one of a race excommunicated by the Jews; a byword among them, and synonymous with heretic and devil (John viii. 48; and see on ch. xvii. 18); **as he journeyed, came where he was: and when he saw him, he had compassion on him.** Compare what is said of the Lord Himself: "And when the Lord saw her (the widow of Nain), He had compassion on her" (ch. vii. 13). No doubt the priest and Levite had their excuses for passing by their wounded brother.—''Tisn't safe to be lingering here; besides, he's past recovery; and then, mayn't suspicion rest upon ourselves?' So might the Samaritan have reasoned—*but did not.* Nor did he say, 'He would have had no dealings with me (John iv. 9), and why should I with him?' **34. And went to him, and bound up his wounds, pouring in oil and wine**—the remedies used in such cases all over the East (Isa. i. 6), and elsewhere; the *wine* to cleanse the wounds, the *oil* to assuage their smartings. **and set him on his own beast**—himself going on foot, **and brought him to an inn, and took care of him. 35. And on the morrow, when he departed, he took out two pence**—equal to two days' wages of a labourer, and enough for several days' support, **and gave them to the host, and said unto him, Take care of him: and whatsoever thou spendest more, when I come again, I will repay thee. 36. Which now of these three, thinkest thou, was neighbour unto him that fell among the thieves?**—a most dexterous way of putting the question: first, turning it from the lawyer's form of it, 'Whom am I to love as my neighbour?' to the more pointed question, 'Who is the man that shows that love?' and next, compelling the lawyer to give a reply very different from what he would like—not only condemning his own nation, but those of them who should be the most exemplary; and finally, making him commend one of a deeply-hated race. And he does so, but it is almost extorted. **37. And he said, He that showed mercy on him.** He does not answer, 'The Samaritan'—that would have sounded heterodox, heretical—but "He that showed mercy on him." It comes to the same thing, no doubt, but the circumlocution is significant. **Then said Jesus unto him, Go, and do thou likewise.**

Remark.—O exquisite, matchless teaching! What new fountains of charity has not this opened up in the human spirit—rivers in the wilderness, streams in the desert! what noble Christian Institutions have not such words founded, all undreamed of till that Divine One came to bless this heartless world of ours with His incomparable love—first in words, and then in deeds which have translated His words into flesh and blood, and poured the life of them through that humanity which He made His own! But was this parable designed merely to magnify the law of love, and show who fulfils it and who not? Is not the mind irresistibly directed to Him who, as our Brother Man, "our Neighbour," did this as never man did it? The priests and Levites, says *Trench*, had not strengthened the diseased, nor bound up the broken (Ezek. xxxiv. 4), while He bound up the broken-hearted (Is. lxi. 1), and poured into all wounded spirits the balm of sweetest consolation. All the Church-fathers saw, through the thin veil of this noblest of stories, *the* Story of love, and never wearied of tracing the analogy, though sometimes fancifully enough. 'He hungered'—exclaims *Gregory* of Nazianzum, in the fourth century, in a passage of singular eloquence, in one of his Sermons—'but He fed thousands; He was weary, but He is the Rest of the weary; He is saluted "Samaritan" and "Demoniac," but He *saves him*

38 Now it came to pass, as they went, that he entered into a certain
village: and a certain woman named [r]Martha received him into her
39 house. And she had a sister called Mary, which also [s]sat at Jesus' feet,
40 and heard his word. But Martha was [t]cumbered about much serving,
and came to him, and said, Lord, dost thou not care that my sister
41 hath left me to serve alone? bid her therefore that she help me. And
Jesus answered and said unto her, Martha, Martha, thou art care-
42 ful and troubled about many things: but one thing is needful: and
Mary hath chosen that good part, which shall not be taken away from
her.

11 AND it came to pass, that, as he was praying in a certain place,
when he ceased, one of his disciples said unto him, Lord, [a]teach us to
pray, as John also taught his disciples.

A. D. 32.

[r] John 11. 1.
[s] Deut. 33. 3. Acts 22. 3.
[t] 1 Cor. 7. 32.

CHAP. 11.
[a] Ps. 10. 17. Ps. 19. 14. Rom. 8. 26, 27. 2 Cor. 3. 5. Jas. 4. 2, 3. Jude 20.

---

that went down from Jerusalem and fell among thieves,' &c. More of this noble passage will be found on chap. xix. 28-44, Remark 2, at the close of that Section.

38-42.—JESUS IN THE HOUSE OF MARTHA AND MARY. **38. Now it came to pass, as they went, that he entered into a certain village.** The village was Bethany—as to which, see on ch. xix. 29. It will be seen how void of all definite note of time and place are the incidents recorded in this large portion of our Gospel, as noticed on ch. ix. 51. **and a certain woman named Martha received him into her house.** From this way of speaking we gather that the house belonged to her, and from all the notices of her it would seem that she was the elder sister. **39. And she had a sister called Mary, which also**—or 'who for her part,' as *Webster and Wilkinson* put it, as opposed to Martha, **sat**—or 'seated herself' [παρακαθίσασα] **at Jesus' feet.** From the custom of sitting *beneath* an instructor, the phrase 'sitting at one's feet' came to mean being his disciple (Acts xxii. 3). **and heard** [ἤκουε]—or 'kept listening' to **his word. 40. But Martha was cumbered**—or 'distracted' [περιεσπᾶτο] **about much serving, and came to him** [ἐπιστᾶσα]—presenting herself, as from another apartment, in which her sister had "*left* her to serve, or make preparation, *alone*," **and said, Lord, dost thou not care that my sister hath left me to serve alone?**—'Lord, here am I with everything to do, and this sister will not lay a hand to anything; thus I miss something from Thy lips, and Thou from our hands.' **bid her therefore that she help me.** She presumes not to stop Christ's teaching by calling her sister away, and thus leaving Him without His rapt auditor, nor did she hope perhaps to succeed if she had tried. **41. And Jesus answered and said unto her, Martha, Martha**—emphatically redoubling upon the name, **thou art careful and troubled** [μεριμνᾷς καὶ τυρβάζῃ]. The one word expresses the inward *fretting anxiety* that her preparations should be worthy of her Lord; the other, the outward *bustle* of those preparations. **about many things**—"much serving" (*v.* 40); too elaborate preparation, which so engrossed her attention that she missed her Lord's teaching. **42. But one thing is needful.** The idea of 'Short work and little of it sufficeth for Me' is not so much the lower *sense* of these weighty words, as *implied* in them as the basis of something far loftier than any precept on economy. Underneath that idea is couched another, as to the littleness both of elaborate preparation for the present life and *of that life itself* compared with another. **and Mary hath chosen that**—or 'the' **good part**—not in the general sense of Moses' choice (Heb. xi. 25), and Joshua's (Josh. xxiv. 15), and David's (Ps. cxix. 30); that is, of good in opposition to *bad;* but, of two good ways of serving and pleasing the Lord, choosing *the better.* Wherein, then, was Mary's better than Martha's? What follows supplies the answer: **which shall not be taken away from her.** Martha's choice would be taken from her, for *her services would die with her;* Mary's *never*, being spiritual and eternal. Both were true-hearted disciples, but the one was absorbed in the higher, the other in the lower of two ways of honouring their common Lord. Yet neither would deliberately despise, or willingly neglect, the other's occupation. The one represents the *contemplative,* the other the *active* style of the Christian character.

Remark.—This rebuke of Martha was but for the excess of a valuable quality, which on another occasion appears without that excess. See on Mark xiv. 3, and Remark 1 at the close of that Section. The quality which was commended in Mary has its excesses too. It is true that a predominance of the impulsive activity of the one sister is unfavourable to depth of thought and elevation of feeling; but a predominance of the passive docility of the other sister is apt to generate an unhealthy tone, and lead rather to dreamy speculation or sentiment than to sound knowledge and wisdom. A Church full of Maries would perhaps be as great an evil as a Church full of Marthas. Both are needed, each to be the complement of the other.

CHAP. XI. 1-13.—JESUS TEACHES HIS DISCIPLES TO PRAY, AND GIVES ENCOURAGEMENTS TO IMPORTUNITY AND FAITH IN THE EXERCISE OF IT.

1. And it came to pass, that, as he was praying in a certain place—where, it is impossible to say; see introductory remarks on ch. ix. 51, **when he ceased, one of his disciples**—struck, no doubt, with both the matter and the manner of our Lord's own prayers, **said unto him, Lord, teach us to pray, as John also taught his disciples.** From this reference to John, it is probable this disciple had not heard the Sermon on the Mount, containing very specific instructions on the subject of Prayer. It is worthy of notice that we have no record of John's teaching on this subject, and that but for this allusion to it we should never have known that he had touched on it. It shows that the Baptist's inner or more private teaching was of a much more detailed nature than we should have supposed; the specimens of it which we have in the Gospels being chiefly what he taught to the general multitude. One would like to have known more of his teaching on the subject of Prayer. But whatever it was, we may be sure he never taught his disciples, when they prayed, to say, "Our Father." That was reserved for a Greater than he.

The Model Prayer (2-4). **2. And he said unto them, When ye pray, say, Our Father,** [*Tischen-*

2 And he said unto them, When ye pray, say, [b]Our Father which art
in heaven, Hallowed be thy name. [c]Thy kingdom come. Thy will be
3 done, as in heaven, so in earth. Give us [1]day by day our daily bread.
4 And forgive us our sins: for [d]we also forgive every one that is indebted
to us. And [e]lead us not into temptation; but deliver us from evil.
5 And he said unto them, Which of you shall have a friend, and shall
go unto him at midnight, and say unto him, Friend, lend me three
6 loaves; for a friend of mine [2]in his journey is come to me, and I have
7 nothing to set before him? And he from within shall answer and say,
Trouble me not: the door is now shut, and my children are with me in
8 bed; I cannot rise and give thee. I say unto you, [f]Though he will not
rise and give him, because he is his friend, yet because of his importunity
9 he will rise and give him as many as he needeth. And [g]I say unto you,
Ask, and it shall be given you; seek, and ye shall find; knock, and it
10 shall be opened unto you. For every one that asketh receiveth; and he
that seeketh findeth; and to him that knocketh it shall be opened.
11 If [h]a son shall ask bread of any of you that is a father, will he give
12 him a stone? or if *he ask* a fish, will he for a fish give him a serpent? or
13 if he shall ask an egg, will he [3]offer him a scorpion? If ye then,
being evil, know how to give good gifts unto your children: how much
more shall *your* heavenly Father give the Holy [i]Spirit to them that ask
him?

A. D. 32.
[b] 2 Chr. 20. 6. Ps. 11. 4. Isa. 63. 16. Matt. 5. 16. Matt. 10. 32.
[c] Isa. 11. 9. Dan. 7. 14.
[1] Or, for the day.
[d] Matt. 6. 14, 15. Eph. 4. 32. Jas. 2. 13.
[e] Matt. 6. 13. ch. 8. 13. ch. 22. 46. 1 Cor. 10. 13. Jas. 1. 13. Rev. 3. 10.
[2] Or, out of his way.
[f] ch. 18. 1.
[g] 1 John 5. 14.
[h] Matt. 7. 9.
[3] Give.
[i] Isa. 44. 3 Matt. 7. 11. John 4. 10.

dorf and *Tregelles*—whom *Alford* follows, and *Meyer* approves—here omit both the word ἡμῶν, "our," and the following words, ὁ ἐν τοῖς οὐρανοῖς, "which art in heaven." But the authority for inserting those words is most decisive, as we judge. *Lachmann* inserts them.] **which art in heaven, Hallowed be thy name. Thy kingdom come. Thy will be done, as in heaven, so in earth.** [Here again the same critical editors, on the same authority, omit the entire petition—Γενηθήτω τὸ θέλημά σου, ὡς ἐν οὐρανῷ καὶ ἐπὶ τῆς γῆς, "Thy will," &c. But here, also, as we judge, the evidence is clear in favour of the disputed words.] **3. Give us day by day our daily bread.** This is an extension of the petition in Matthew for "*this* day's" supply, to *every* day's necessities. **4. And forgive us our sins, for we also forgive every one that is indebted to us. And lead us not into temptation; but deliver us from evil.** [This last clause is, by the above editors, on the same authority, excluded from the text, but on insufficient warrant, as we judge.] See on Matt. vi. 9-13, with the corresponding Remarks at the close of that Section. There is no closing doxology here. On the question, whether it formed part of the Lord's Prayer in the Sermon on the Mount, see on Matt. vi. 13. Perhaps our Lord purposely left that part *open;* and as the grand Jewish doxologies were ever resounding, and passed, immediately and naturally, in all their hallowed familiarity into the Christian Church, probably this Prayer was never used in the Christian assemblies but in its present form, as we find it in Matthew, while in Luke it has been allowed to stand as originally uttered.

Encouragements to Importunity and Faith in Prayer (5-13). **5. And he said unto them, Which of you shall have a friend, and shall go unto him at midnight, and say unto him, Friend, lend me three loaves; 6. For a friend of mine in his journey** [ἐξ ὁδοῦ]—the marginal rendering, 'out of his way,' is to be rejected, **is come to me, and I have nothing to set before him.** The heat in warm countries makes evening preferable to day for travelling; but "midnight" is everywhere a most *unseasonable* hour of call, and for that very reason it is here selected. **7. And he from within shall answer and say, Trouble me not**—the *trouble* making him insensible both to the urgency of the case and the claims of friendship: **the door is now shut, and my children are with me in bed; I cannot rise and give thee**—without such exertion as he was unwilling to make. **8. I say unto you, Though he will not rise and give him, because he is his friend**—or for friendship's sake, **yet because of his importunity** [ἀναίδειαν]. The word is a strong one, signifying 'shamelessness;' expressing his persistency, in the face of all that seemed reasonable, and refusing to take a denial. **he will rise and give him as many as he needeth.** His reluctance once overcome, all the claims of friendship and necessity are felt to the full. The sense is obvious: If the churlish and self-indulgent—deaf both to friendship and necessity—can, after a positive refusal, be won over by sheer persistency to do all that is needed, *how much more* may the same determined perseverance in prayer be expected to prevail with Him whose very nature it is to be "*rich* unto all that call upon Him" (Rom. x. 12). **9-12. And I say unto you, Ask, and it shall be given you . . . If a son shall ask bread of any of you that is a father, &c.** See on Matt. vii. 7-10. **Or if he shall ask an egg, will he offer him a scorpion?**—looking quite like an egg at some distance, but of a deadly nature. **13. If ye then, being evil**—evil though ye be, **know how to give good gifts unto your children: how much more shall your heavenly Father give the Holy Spirit to them that ask him?** In Matt. vii. 11, it is "give *good gifts* to them that ask Him:" here, at a riper stage of His teaching, and to His disciples apart from the multitude, He says "*the Holy Spirit;*" to teach us that this, the Gift of gifts, descending on the Church through Christ, comprehends all "good gifts."

For Remarks on the subjects embraced in this Section, see those on Matt. vi. 2-15, at the close of that Section; and on Matt. vii. 7-11, at the close of that Section.

14-36.—A BLIND AND DUMB DEMONIAC HEALED, AND REPLY TO THE MALIGNANT EXPLANATION PUT UPON THIS—THE REMARK OF A WOMAN IN THE

14 And [j]he was casting out a devil, and it was dumb. And it came to
pass, when the devil was gone out, the dumb spake; and the people
15 wondered. But some of them said, [k]He casteth out devils through
16 [4]Beelzebub the chief of the devils. And others, tempting *him*, [l]sought
17 of him a sign from heaven. But [m]he, knowing their thoughts, said unto
them, Every kingdom divided against itself is brought to desolation; and
18 a house *divided* against a house falleth. If Satan also be divided against
himself, how shall his kingdom stand? because ye say that I cast out
19 devils through Beelzebub. And if I by Beelzebub cast out devils, by
whom do [n]your sons cast *them* out? therefore shall they be your judges.
20 But if I [o]with the finger of God cast out devils, no doubt the kingdom of
God is come upon you.
21 When [p]a strong man armed keepeth his palace, his goods are in peace:
22 But [q]when a stronger than he shall come upon him, and overcome him,
he taketh from him all his armour wherein he trusted, and divideth his
23 spoils. He [r]that is not with me is against me; and he that gathereth
not with me scattereth.
24 When [s]the unclean spirit is gone out of a man, he walketh through
dry places, seeking rest; and finding none, he saith, I will return unto
25 my house whence I came out. And when he cometh, he findeth *it* swept
26 and garnished. Then goeth he, and taketh *to him* seven other spirits
more wicked than himself; and they enter in, and dwell there: and [t]the
last *state* of that man is worse than the first.

A. D. 33.

j Matt. 9. 32. Matt. 12. 22.
k Matt. 9. 34. Matt. 12. 24.
4 Beelzebul.
l Matt. 12. 38. Matt. 16. 1.
m Matt. 12. 25. Mark 3. 24. John 2. 25. Rev. 2. 23.
n Mark 9. 38. ch. 9. 49.
o Ex. 8. 19.
p Matt. 12. 29. Mark 3. 27. Eph. 6. 12. Eph. 2. 2. 1 Pet. 5. 8.
q Isa. 9. 6. Isa. 53. 12. Col. 2. 15. Heb. 7. 25.
r Matt. 12. 30.
s Matt. 12. 43.
t John 5. 14. Heb. 6. 4. Heb. 10. 26. 2 Pet. 2. 20.

CROWD, AND THE ANSWER—WARNING ON SEEKING A SIGN. (=Matt. xii. 22-45; Mark iii. 22-30.) See on Matt. xii. 22-28.

Healing of a Demoniac, and Reply to the Malignant Explanation put upon it (14-20). For the exposition of this portion, see on Matt. xii. 22-28.

Parables of the Strong Man and the Unclean Spirit (21-26).

Parable of The Strong Man (21, 22). **21. When a**—or 'the,' **strong man armed keepeth**—or 'guardeth' [φυλάσσῃ] **his palace** [αὐλήν]. 'This stands for "palace" (says *Olshausen*), a great pile surrounded with fore-courts and halls.' *Meyer* repudiates this sense, contending for the primary meaning of the word, an open 'court.' But though this does not materially affect the statement itself, the secondary meaning is most suitable here, as interpreters generally agree. The palace here meant by our Lord is *man*, whether viewed more largely or in individual souls—men as nations, churches, or individuals: the "strong man" is Satan. His being "armed" points to all the subtle and varied methods by which he wields his dark power over men. **his goods are in peace**—undisturbed, securely in his possession. **22. But when a stronger**—or 'the Stronger' **than he.** Glorious title of the Lord Jesus in relation to Satan! (1 John iii. 8). **shall come upon him, and overcome him**—sublimely expressing the Redeemer's approach, as the Seed of the woman, to bruise the Serpent's head. **he taketh from him all his armour** [τὴν πανοπλίαν αὐτοῦ]—'his panoply,' 'his complete armour.' Vain would be the victory, were not the *means of regaining* his lost power wrested from him. It is this that completes the triumph and ensures the utter overthrow of his kingdom. **23. He that is not with me is against me; and he that gathereth not with me scattereth.** The nature and force of this statement, in relation to the foregoing parable will be best perceived when we have taken up the one that follows.

Parable of The Unclean Spirit (24-26). **24. When the unclean spirit is gone out of a man, he walketh through dry places** [ἀνύδρων]—literally, 'un-watered,' and so desert, uninhabited places; where are no men to possess and destroy; **seeking rest; and finding none**—because out of his element, which is human misery and destruction: **he saith, I will return unto my house whence I came out**: 'It may be I shall find it tired of its new religious ways, and not unwilling to entertain overtures of reconciliation with its old friend.' **25. And when he cometh, he findeth it**—"empty" (Matt. xii. 44); *occupied by no rival:* but further, **swept and garnished**—not only empty, but all ready to receive him; nay, decked out as if to invite his return. **26. Then goeth he, and taketh to him seven other spirits more wicked than himself.** Seven being the number of completeness, a sevenfold diabolic force, the wickedness of each of which exceeds that of the first, is the strongest conceivable expression of a power sufficient to secure them against all disturbance for the future. **and they enter in.** No resistance now. As we say, they walk the course. **and dwell there.** No temporary sojourn or precarious stay do they make now. They *dwell* there as in their own proper and permanent abode. **and the last state of that man is worse than the first.** Matthew adds this important application to the second parable (xii. 45), "Even so shall it be also unto this wicked generation:" implying that the illustration of this parable which that wicked generation was to furnish was but one example of the working of a great general principle. But an awful illustration of it it was which that generation was to furnish. By the ministry of the Baptist their 'heart was turned to the Lord,' to a large extent: then was their opportunity to receive Christ and live; but they did not: so they became worse than at the first, and soon put their very Deliverer to death. These exceedingly vivid parables bear a strong resemblance to each other; but they differ far more widely than they agree. The subject of both is the same —the soul of man changing from the worse to the better. In both the soul is pictured to us as the residence of the Evil One; in the one parable as his "palace," in the other as his "house." In

27 And it came to pass, as he spake these things, a certain woman of the
company lifted up her voice, and said unto him, [u]Blessed *is* the womb
28 that bare thee, and the paps which thou hast sucked. But he said, Yea
[v]rather, blessed *are* they that hear the word of God, and keep it.
29 And [w]when the people were gathered thick together, he began to say,
This is an evil generation: they seek a sign; and there shall no sign be
30 given it, but the sign of Jonas the prophet. For as [x]Jonas was a sign unto
31 the Ninevites, so shall also the Son of man be to this generation. The
[y]queen of the south shall rise up in the judgment with the men of this
generation, and condemn them: for she came from the utmost parts of
the earth to hear the wisdom of Solomon; and, behold, a [z]greater than
32 Solomon *is* here. The men of Nineve shall rise up in the judgment
with this generation, and shall condemn it: for [a]they repented at the
preaching of Jonas; and, behold, a greater than Jonas *is* here.
33 No [b]man, when he hath lighted a candle, putteth *it* in a secret place,
neither under a [c]bushel, but on a candlestick, that they which come in
34 may see the light. The [d]light of the body is the eye: therefore when
thine eye is single, thy whole body also is full of light; but when *thine*
35 *eye* is evil, thy body also *is* full of darkness. Take heed therefore that
36 the light which is in thee be not darkness. If thy whole body therefore
be full of light, having no part dark, the whole shall be full of light, as
when [5]the bright shining of a candle doth give thee light.

A. D. 33.

[u] ch. 1. 28, 48.
[v] Matt. 7. 21. Matt. 12. 49. ch. 8. 21. Jas. 1. 25.
[w] Matt. 12. 38, 39.
[x] Jon. 1. 17. Jon. 2. 10.
[y] 1 Ki. 10. 1.
[z] Isa. 9. 6. Rom. 9. 5. Tit. 2. 13. Phil. 2. 10.
[a] Jon. 3. 5.
[b] Matt. 5. 15. Mark 4. 21.
[c] Matt. 5. 15.
[d] Ps. 119. 18. Matt. 6. 22. Mark 8. 18. Acts 26. 18. Eph. 1. 17, 18.
[5] A candle by its bright shining.

the one parable the *strength* of this mysterious enemy is the prominent idea; in the other his *uncleanness.* In both parables the soul is delivered from this mighty and filthy enemy. But here the resemblance terminates, and the vast difference between the two parables comes out. The unclean spirit goes out only to come in again; but the strong man is grappled with and mastered, and the palace is permanently occupied by the Victor. The one is a temporary, if not a voluntary departure; the other is a total defeat, and an absolute, resistless expulsion. In the one case the last state of the soul is worse than the first; in the other the last is its best and noblest state. Both are cases of *conversion;* but in the one case the conversion is partial and abortive; in the other it is thorough and enduring. And the cause of this difference is most strikingly depicted. Why was it that the unclean spirit, after going out of the man, entered in again without a struggle, never more to be dislodged? Because on his return he found no rival to dispute the ground with him: *the devil was out, but Christ was not in.* Precisely the reverse of this was the reason why, in the other parable, his return was hopeless. As it was the Stronger than he that put him out, so *His presence,* as the rightful Occupant of the palace henceforth, *secures it* against all successful assault for the future. And now we are prepared to listen to the great saying that comes in between the two parables (*v.* 23), and to apprehend both its import and its weight: "He that is not with Me is against Me; and he that gathereth not with Me scattereth." This last clause seems to be an allusion to gleaners, whose labour is lost if they follow not in the wake, or work not in the company, of their leader. Thus are proclaimed these great maxims: '*Whatever in religion is disconnected from Christ comes to nothing;*' '*Neutrality in religion there is none;*' '*The absence of positive attachment to Christ involves hostility to Him.*'

Remark of a Woman in the Crowd, and the Reply (27-28). **27. And it came to pass, as he spake these things, a certain woman of the company** [ἐκ τοῦ ὄχλου]—or 'from the crowd,' **lifted up her voice, and said, Blessed is the womb that bare thee, and the paps which thou hast sucked. 28. But he said, Yea rather, blessed are they that hear the word of God, and keep it.** A charming little incident, and profoundly instructive. With true womanly feeling, she envies the mother of such a wonderful Teacher. Well, and higher and better than she had said as much before her, ch. i. 28, 42; and our Lord is far from condemning it. He only holds up, as "blessed rather," the hearers and keepers of God's word; in other words, *the humblest real saint of God.* See on Matt. xii. 49, 50. How utterly alien is this sentiment from the teaching of the Church of Rome, which would excommunicate any one of its members that dared to talk in the spirit of this glorious saying!

Seeking a Sign (29-36). **29-32. And when the people**—rather, 'the multitudes' [τῶν ὄχλων] **were gathered thick together, he began to say, This is an evil generation: they seek a sign.** Matthew tells us (xii. 38) that certain of the scribes and Pharisees said, "Master, we would see a sign from thee;" and it was to this that our Lord here replied. **and there shall no sign be given it, but the sign of Jonas the prophet, &c.** On this and the three following verses, see on Matt. xii. 38-42. **33-36. No man, when he hath lighted a candle, putteth it in a secret place, &c.** On this and the three following verses, see on Matt. v. 14-16; and on Matt. vi. 22, 23. But *v.* 36, here, is peculiarly vivid, expressing what pure, beautiful, broad perceptions the *clarity of the inward eye* imparts.

For Remarks on *vv.* 14-20, and 29-32, see those on the corresponding verses of Matt. xii.: and for Remarks on *vv.* 33-36, see those on the corresponding verses of Matt. v. and vi. above noted: it only remains, then, on this Section, that we add two on the parables here illustrated (*vv.* 21-26), to bring out more in detail the distinctive features of the two cases.

Remarks.—1. In the second parable we have three successive stages in the history of a soul. The first is a change for the better: *The unclean spirit goes out of the man.* When is this? Seldom is it seen in a period of general religious indifference. Then the strong man hardly needs to guard his palace; his goods are in undisturbed peace.

37 And as he spake, a certain Pharisee besought him to dine with him:
38 and he went in, and sat down to meat. And [e] when the Pharisee saw *it*,
39 he marvelled that he had not first washed before dinner. And [f] the Lord
said unto him, Now do ye Pharisees make clean the outside of the cup

A. D. 33.

[e] Mark 7. 3. John 3. 25.
[f] Matt. 23. 25. Gal. 1. 14.

But where a ministry like the Baptist's is attended with great success, and men are stirred to their depths, and many are fleeing from the wrath to come, then may be seen, amongst real conversions, not a few that are but partial, temporary, abortive. For a while, under the terrors of the coming wrath or the joys of the Gospel, all seems changed, and a thorough conversion appears to have taken place—the unclean spirit has gone out of the man. The house has become uncongenial to him. As an unwelcome guest, and out of his element, he takes his leave—"going" rather than "cast out." But there is no real exchange of masters, of services, of felicities; of Christ for Belial, of spiritual principles for carnal, of heavenly for earthly affections. If the old man seems put off, the new man has not been put on; if old things seem to have passed away, all things have not become new. A heap of negatives make up the change: the man has not been born again. Accordingly, when the unclean spirit returns, he finds the house as "empty" as when he left it. But worse—it is now "swept and garnished." This seems to point to such a relapse in the interval as has transformed it out of the unsympathetic state which drove him forth, into a prepared and inviting habitation for him. The soul's lively interest in religion and relish for divine things has cooled down; the standard has been by little and little lowered; carnal interests and affections have returned; the world has re-assumed its faded charms, and sin its enticing forms; devotion, when not intermitted, has dwindled into wretched and hurried generalities. At length sin is tampered with, and the unclean spirit sees his advantage. But he is in no haste to seize his prey. On the contrary, "he goeth and taketh with him seven other spirits more wicked than himself; and they enter in, and dwell there"—never more to go or be put out. And so, "the last state of that man is worse than the first." Not, it may be, in the way of abandoning itself to greater abominations. But it is more utterly hopeless. There are several laws of the moral system which explain this. There is such a thing as God giving men over to a reprobate mind. Nor is the rage of the wicked one to be overlooked in these mysterious escapes from him for a time and subsequent welcomings back. And over and above these, there is the well-known and terrific law, in virtue of which habits and practices, abandoned with difficulty and afterwards taking fresh possession, become more inveterate than ever before—the power of a resisting will being destroyed. Thus is there no medium between the unclean spirit going out of the man, only to come in again, and the effectual expulsion of the strong man by the Stronger than he. There is no safety for the heart of man but in cordial subjection to Christ. 2. In the first parable, see the palace of the soul in secure, but not unguarded, possession of the strong man. This dark master of the soul—"the prince, the god of this world"—is "armed" and "guards" his palace. Some are easily guarded against serious thought and alarm about their eternal state—drowned in fleshly lusts, or engrossing secularities, or scientific pursuits; the cravings of the spirit after peace and fellowship with God, holiness and heaven, either systematically quenched, or never consciously—at least painfully—felt. But when religious convictions and alarms refuse to be lulled, false principles are made to play about the soul, if possible to seduce it out of its cravings for that relief which only the Gospel of Christ supplies. But when "the Stronger than the strong man" takes the case in hand, this ruler of the darkness of this world must quit his hold. Glorious name of Jesus this—"The Stronger than the Strong One"—to as many as are sighing for emancipation from felt bondage, and not less, but rather more so, to those whom the Son hath made free indeed. Majestic and varied are the manifestations of His superiority to the strong one in this matchless Gospel History. But the secret of His strength to expel this enemy from the soul of man lies in the victory which He achieved over him in His Cross. "*Now*," says He Himself, "*shall the prince of this world be cast out*, and I, *if I be lifted up from the earth*, will draw all men unto me." As it was sin that sold us into the enemy's hands, so when He put away sin by the sacrifice of Himself, He opened the prison-doors and set us free. And now hath He gone up to receive, as His fitting reward, the Gift of the Holy Ghost, by whose agency in the souls of men He grapples with the enemy, and casts Him out, that He may get Him a temple for God, a palace for Himself to dwell in—"When the Stronger than he shall *come upon him*." Sublime expression this of Christ's approach to the stronghold for a deadly encounter with the strong man. But it may be quick or slow, simple or elaborate in preparation. Now is the "armour" of the strong man put to busy use:—'God is merciful; there have been many worse than thou, with whom, if thou perish, it will go harder still; thou art sorry for sin; thou sighest after holiness; thou hast made some progress; all will yet come right; and there is no such urgent haste.' These whispers of the father of lies lull for a time, but do not last. The urgency of the case is borne in with resistless power by the sinner's mighty Friend, and now the last thrust is given—'Thine is a gone case; it is now all too late.' But this last piece of his infernal "armour" is at length "taken from him;" the soul falls sweetly into the arms of its mighty Friend; the strong man is made to quit his palace, and the Stronger than he, now its real as before its rightful owner, divides the spoil. Fain would the bruised serpent, in his retreat, hiss for rage after the woman's Seed—'What hast Thou gained by the pardon and restoration of this rebel? he hath no taste for Thy company; he is of his father the devil, and the lusts of his father he will continue to do.' But the Stronger than he cries after him, 'I have put my fear in his heart, that he may *not* turn away from Me—Get thee behind Me!'

What, now, is the conclusion of this whole matter? *Freedom from both masters*, or entire moral independence, *is impossible*. The palace is freed from the usurped dominion of the strong man, only to become the willing recipient of the Stronger than he. But subjection to Christ is no bondage; it is the very law of liberty. "If the Son," then, O my readers, "shall make you free, ye shall be free indeed!"

37-54.—AT THE HOUSE OF A PHARISEE JESUS VEHEMENTLY DENOUNCES THE PHARISEES, WHO ARE EXASPERATED, AND TRY TO ENSNARE HIM.

37. And as he spake, a certain Pharisee besought him to dine with him: and he went in, and sat down to meat. 38. And when the Pharisee saw

and the platter; but [g]your inward part is full of ravening and wickedness.
40 *Ye* fools, did not he that made that which is without make that which is
41 within also? But [h]rather give alms [6]of such things as ye have; and,
42 behold, all things are clean unto you. But [i]woe unto you, Pharisees!
[j]for ye tithe mint and rue, and all manner of herbs, and pass over judgment and the love of God: these ought ye to have done, and not to leave
43 the other undone. Woe [k]unto you, Pharisees! for ye love the uppermost
44 seats in the synagogues, and greetings in the markets. Woe [l]unto you,
scribes and Pharisees, hypocrites! [m]for ye are as graves which appear not,
and the men that walk over *them* are not aware *of them.*
45 Then answered one of the lawyers, and said unto him, Master, thus
46 saying thou reproachest us also. And he said, Woe unto you also, *ye*
lawyers! [n]for ye lade men with burdens grievous to be borne, and ye
47 yourselves touch not the burdens with one of your fingers. Woe [o]unto
you! for ye build the sepulchres of the prophets, and your fathers killed
48 them. Truly ye bear witness that ye allow the deeds of your fathers:
49 for [p]they indeed killed them, and ye build their sepulchres. Therefore
also said the [q]wisdom of God, [r]I will send them prophets and apostles,
50 and *some* of them they shall slay and persecute: that the blood of all the
prophets, which was shed from the foundation of the world, may be
51 required of this generation; from [s]the blood of Abel, unto the blood of
Zacharias, which perished between the altar and the temple: verily I say
52 unto you, It shall be required of this generation. Woe [t]unto you,
lawyers! for ye have taken away the key of knowledge: ye enter not in
yourselves, and them that were entering in ye [7]hindered.
53 And as he said these things unto them, the scribes and the Pharisees
began to urge *him* vehemently, and to provoke him to speak of many
54 things; laying wait for him, and [u]seeking to catch something out of his
55 mouth, that they might accuse him.
12 IN [a]the mean time, when there were gathered together an innumerable
multitude of people, insomuch that they trode one upon another, he
began to say unto his disciples first of all, [b]Beware ye of the leaven of
2 the Pharisees, which is hypocrisy. For [c]there is nothing covered, that
3 shall not be revealed; neither hid, that shall not be known. Therefore
whatsoever ye have spoken in darkness shall be heard in the light; and

A. D. 33.

g 2 Tim. 3. 5. Tit. 1. 15.
h Isa. 58. 7. Dan. 4. 27. ch. 12. 33.
6 Or, as you are able.
i Matt. 23. 23.
j 1 Sam. 15. 22. Hos. 6. 6.
k Matt. 23. 6. Mark 12. 38, 39.
l Matt. 23. 27.
m Ps. 5. 9. Acts 23. 3.
n Matt. 23. 4.
o Matt. 23. 29.
p Acts 7. 51, 52. 1 Thes. 2. 15. Heb. 11. 36-38. Jas. 5. 10.
q Pro. 1. 20. 1 Cor. 1. 24.
r Matt. 23. 34.
s Gen. 4. 8.
t Matt. 23. 13
7 Or, forbade.
u Mark 12. 13.

CHAP. 12.
a Matt. 16. 6. Mark 8. 15.
b Matt. 16. 12. 1 Cor. 5. 7, 8.
c Eccl. 12. 14. Matt. 10. 26. Mark 4. 22. ch. 8. 17. 1 Cor. 4. 5. Rev. 20. 11, 12.

it, he marvelled that he had not first washed before dinner. See on Mark vii. 2-4. **39-52. And the Lord said unto him, Now do ye Pharisees make clean the outside, &c.** For the exposition of all these verses, see on Matt. xxiii. 1-36. **53. And as he said these things unto them, the scribes and the Pharisees began to urge him vehemently, and to provoke him to speak of many things; 54. Laying wait for him, and seeking to catch something out of his mouth, that they might accuse him.** How exceedingly vivid and affecting! They were stung to the quick—and can we wonder?—yet had not materials for the charge they were preparing against Him. For Remarks on this Section, see those on Matt. xxiii. 1-39, at the close of that Section.

CHAP. XII. 1-59.—WARNINGS AGAINST HYPOCRISY, AND AGAINST COVETOUSNESS—WATCHFULNESS INCULCATED, AND SUPERIORITY TO EARTHLY ENTANGLEMENTS AT THE CALL OF HIGHER DUTY —DISCERNING THE SIGNS OF THE TIME.

Hypocrisy (1-12). **1. In the mean time**—in close connection, probably, with the foregoing scene. Our Lord had been *speaking out* more plainly than ever before, as matters were coming to a head between Him and His enemies, and this seems to have suggested to His own mind the warning here. He had just Himself illustriously exemplified His own precepts. **when there were gathered together an innumerable multitude of people, insomuch that they trod one upon another, he began to say unto his disciples first of all**—and afterwards to the multitudes (*v.* 54), **Beware ye of the leaven of the Pharisees, which is hypocrisy.** As leaven is *concealed* within the mass on which it operates, yet works diffusively and masterfully, so is it with hypocrisy. Hypocrisy is of two kinds. *Pretending to be what we are not*, and *concealing what we are.* Though these are so closely allied that the one runs into the other, it is the latter form of it against which our Lord here warns His disciples. When His name could not be confessed but at the risk of reputation, liberty, property, and life itself, the temptation to unworthy concealment of what they were would of course be exceedingly strong; and it is the consequences of such cowardly and traitorous concealment that our Lord is now to point out. Elsewhere He would have us count the cost of *Discipleship* ere we undertake it: Here He would have us count the *cost of hypocrisy*—in the sense of shrinking from the confession of His name before men—ere we resolve on or give way to that fatal step. **2, 3. For there is nothing covered**—from view, **that shall not be revealed; neither hid**—from knowledge, **that shall not be**

that which ye have spoken in the ear in closets shall be proclaimed upon
the house-tops.
4 And [d]I say unto you, my friends, Be not afraid of them that kill the
5 body, and after that have no more that they can do. But I will forewarn
you whom ye shall fear: Fear him, which after he hath killed hath
6 [e]power to cast into hell; yea, I say unto you, Fear him. Are not five
sparrows sold for two [f]farthings? and [g]not one of them is forgotten
7 before God: but even the very hairs of your head are all numbered.
Fear not therefore: ye are of more value than many sparrows.
8 Also [h]I say unto you, Whosoever shall confess me before men, him
9 shall the Son of man also confess before the angels of God: but he that
10 denieth me before men shall be denied before the angels of God. And
[i]whosoever shall speak a word against the Son of man, it shall be forgiven
him: but unto him that blasphemeth against the Holy Ghost it shall not
11 be forgiven. And [j]when they bring you unto the synagogues, and *unto*
magistrates, and powers, take ye no thought how or what thing ye shall
12 answer, or what ye shall say: for [k]the Holy Ghost shall teach you in the
same hour what ye ought to say.
13 And one of the company said unto him, Master, speak to my brother,
14 that he divide the inheritance with me. And he said unto him, [l]Man,
15 who made me a judge or a divider over you? And he said unto them,
[m]Take heed, and beware of covetousness: for a man's life consisteth not
in the abundance of the things which he possesseth.
16 And he spake a parable unto them, saying, The ground of a certain
17 rich man brought forth plentifully: and he thought within himself,
saying, What shall I do, because I have no room where to bestow my
18 fruits? And he said, This will I do: I will pull down my barns, and
19 build greater; and there will I bestow all my fruits and my goods. And

A. D. 33.

[d] Isa. 8.12,13. Isa. 51. 7, 8, 12, 13. Jer. 1. 8. Matt. 10.28. Acts 20. 24. Phil. 1. 28. 1 Pet. 3. 14.
[e] Ps. 9. 17. Matt. 10.28. Matt. 25.41, 46. 2 Pet. 2. 4. Rev. 1. 18.
[f] Matt. 10 29.
[g] Acts 15. 18.
[h] Matt. 10.32. Mark 8. 38. Rom. 10. 9, 10. 2 Tim. 2.12. 1 John 2.23. Rev. 2. 13.
[i] Matt. 12.31, 32. Mark 3. 28. 1 John 5.16.
[j] Matt. 10.19. Mark 13.11. ch. 21. 14.
[k] Ex. 4. 12. 1 Pet. 5. 7.
[l] John 18.36.
[m] Pro. 28. 16. 1 Tim. 6. 7. Heb. 13. 5.

known. Therefore whatsoever ye have spoken in darkness, &c. See on Matt x. 26, 27.

4. And I say unto you, my friends. He calls them "friends" here, not in any loose sense, but, as we think, from the feeling He then had that in this "killing of the body" *He and they* were going to be affectingly one with each other. **Be not afraid of them that kill the body, and after that have no more that they can do**—they *may* go that length, but there their power ends. **5. But I will forewarn you whom ye shall fear: Fear him which after he hath killed**—that is, taken away the life of the body, as at length He does even by natural death, **hath power to cast into hell; yea, I say unto you, Fear him.** How striking the repetition of this word "Fear!" Only the fear of the Greater will effectually expel the fear of the less. **6. Are not five sparrows sold for two farthings?** In Matt. x. 29, it is, "two for one farthing:" so, if one took two farthings' worth, he got one in addition—of such insignificant value were they. **and** (yet) **not one of them is forgotten before God: 7. But even the very hairs of your head are all numbered. Fear not therefore: ye are of more value than many sparrows.** What incomparable teaching—its simplicity imparting to it a wonderful charm!

8, 9. Also I say unto you, Whosoever shall confess me before men, &c. See on Matt. x. 32, 33. **10. And whosoever shall speak a word against the Son of man . . . but unto him that blasphemeth against the Holy Ghost, &c.** See on Matt. xii. 31, 32. **11, 12. And when they bring you unto the synagogues, &c.** See on Matt. x. 19, 20.

Covetousness (13-34). **13. And one of the company said unto him, Master**—'Teacher' [Διδάσκαλε], **speak to my brother, that he divide the inheritance with me:**—*q. d.*, 'Great Preacher of righteousness, help; there is need of Thee in this rapacious world; here am I the victim of injustice, and that from my own brother, who withholds from me my rightful share of the inheritance that has fallen to us.' In this most inopportune intrusion upon the solemnities of our Lord's teaching, there is a mixture of the absurd and the irreverent, the one however occasioning the other. The man had not the least idea that his case was not of as urgent a nature, and as worthy the attention of our Lord, as anything else He could deal with. **14. And he said unto him, Man.** What a contrast is there between this style of address and "*My friends*," when encouraging His own faithful disciples resolutely to confess Him in the face of all dangers (*v.* 4)! **Who made me a judge or a divider over you?** A remarkable question, coming from such lips, explicitly repudiating an office which Moses assumed (Exod. ii. 14), and afterwards was divinely called to exercise. Not for such a purpose was the Son of God manifested. **15. And he said unto them**—the immense multitude before Him, (*v.* 1), **Take heed, and beware of covetousness**—'of all covetousness,' or, 'of every kind of covetousness,' is beyond doubt the true reading here. As this was one of the more plausible forms of it, the Lord would strike at once at the root of the evil. **for a man's life consisteth not in the abundance of the things which he possesseth.** A singularly weighty maxim, and not the less so, because its meaning and its truth are equally evident. **16-19. And he spake a parable . . . The ground of a certain rich man brought forth plentifully: And he thought within himself, saying, What shall I do . . . I will pull down my barns, and build greater; and there will I bestow all**

I will say to my soul, [n]Soul, thou hast much goods laid up for many
20 years; take thine ease, eat, drink, *and* be merry. But God said unto
him, *Thou* fool, this night [1]thy soul shall be required of thee: then
21 [o]whose shall those things be which thou hast provided? So *is* he that
layeth up treasure for himself, [p]and is not rich toward God.
22 And he said unto his disciples, Therefore I say unto you, [q]Take no
thought for your life, what ye shall eat; neither for the body, what ye
23 shall put on. The life is more than meat, and the body *is more* than
24 raiment. Consider the ravens: for they neither sow nor reap; which
neither have storehouse nor barn; and [r]God feedeth them: how much more
25 are ye better than the fowls? And which of you with taking thought can
26 add to his stature one cubit? If ye then be not able to do that thing
27 which is least, why take ye thought for the rest? Consider the lilies how
they grow: they toil not, they spin not; and yet I say unto you, that
28 Solomon in all his glory was not arrayed like one of these. If then God
so clothe the grass, which is to-day in the field, and to-morrow is cast
into the oven; how much more *will he clothe* you, O ye of little faith?
29 And seek not ye what ye shall eat, or what ye shall drink, [2]neither be
30 ye of doubtful mind. For all these things do the nations of the world
seek after: and your Father knoweth [s]that ye have need of these things.
31 But [t]rather seek ye the kingdom of God; and [u]all these things shall be
32 added unto you. Fear not, little flock; for [v]it is your Father's good
33 pleasure to give you the kingdom. Sell [w]that ye have, and give alms;
provide [x]yourselves bags which wax not old, a treasure in the heavens
that faileth not, where no thief approacheth, neither moth corrupteth.
34 For where your treasure is, there will your heart be also.
35, Let [y]your loins be girded about, [z]and *your* lights burning; and ye
36 yourselves like unto men that wait for their lord, when he will return

A. D. 33.
[n] Pro. 27. 1. Eccl. 11. 9. 1 Cor.15.32. Jas 5. 5
[1] Or, do they require thy soul. Job 20. 22. Job 21. 13. Job 27. 8. Ps. 52. 7. Dan. 4. 31. 1 Thes. 5. 3. Jas. 4. 14.
[o] Ps. 39. 6. Jer. 17. 11.
[p] Matt. 6. 20. 1 Tim. 6.18, 19. Jas. 2. 5.
[q] Matt. 6. 25. Phil. 4. 6.
[r] Job 38. 41. Ps. 147. 9.
[2] Or, live not in careful suspense.
[s] 2 Chr. 16.9.
[t] Matt. 6. 33.
[u] Rom. 8. 31.
[v] Matt. 11.25.
[w] Matt.19.21.
[x] Matt. 6. 20.
[y] Eph. 6. 14. 1 Pet. 1. 13.
[z] Matt. 25. 1.

my fruits and my goods. And I will say to my soul, Soul, thou hast much goods laid up for many years; take thine ease, eat, drink, and be merry. Why is this man called a "fool"? First, Because he deemed a life of secure and abundant earthly enjoyment the summit of human felicity; and next, because, having acquired the means of realizing this, through prosperity in his calling, he flattered himself that he had a long lease of such enjoyment, and nothing to do but to give himself up to it. *Nothing else is laid to his charge.* **20. But God said unto him, Fool, this night thy soul shall be required of thee.** This sudden cutting short of his career is designed to express not only the folly of building securely upon the future, but of throwing one's whole soul into what may at any moment be gone. "His *soul* being required of him" is put in opposition to his own treatment of it—"I will say to my soul, Soul," &c. **then whose shall those things be which thou hast provided?** Compare Ps. xxxix. 6, "He heapeth up riches, and knoweth not who shall gather them." **21. So is he that layeth up treasure for himself, and is not rich toward God.** Here is a picture of present folly, and of its awful issue. Such is the man "who is not rich toward God:" he lives to amass and enjoy such riches only as terminate on *self,* and end with *time;* but as to God's favour which is life (Ps. xxx. 5), and precious faith (2 Pet. i. 1; James ii. 5), and riches in good works (1 Tim. vi. 18), and the wisdom which is better than rubies (Prov. iii. 15), and, in a word, all that the Lord esteems true riches (Rev. ii. 9; iii. 18), he lives and dies *a beggar!*

22-34. And he said unto his disciples, Therefore I say unto you, Take no thought, &c. This and the twelve following verses are but a repetition, with slight verbal difference, of part of the Sermon on the Mount. See on Matt. vi. 25-34. But a word or two of explanation on one or two of the verses may be added here. **25. And which of you with taking thought can add to his stature one cubit? 26. If ye then be not able to do that thing which is least, why take ye thought for the rest?** 'Corroding solicitude will not bring you the least of the things ye fret about, though it may double the evil of wanting them. And if not the least, why vex yourselves about things of more consequence?' **29. And seek not ye what ye shall eat, or what ye shall drink, neither be ye of doubtful mind** [μὴ μετεωρίζεσθε]—'be not of unsettled mind,' or put off your balance. **32. Fear not, little flock** [τὸ μικρὸν ποίμνιον]—a double diminutive, which in German can be expressed, but in English only in colloquial language. The tenderness it is designed to convey is plain enough. **for it is your Father's good pleasure** [ὅτι εὐδόκησεν ὁ Πατὴρ ὑμῶν]. On this expression, see on Matt. iii. 17. **to give you the kingdom.** Every word of this little verse is more to be desired than fine gold. How sublime and touching is the contrast between the tender and pitying appellation, "little flock," and the "Good Pleasure" of the Father to give them the Kingdom: the one recalling the insignificance and helplessness of the at that time truly little flock, that literal handful of disciples; the other holding up to their view the eternal love that encircled them, the everlasting arms that were underneath them, and the high inheritance awaiting them! "To give you *the Kingdom:*" Grand word, exclaims *Bengel;* then why not bread? Well might He say, "Fear not"! **33. Sell that ye have, and give alms, &c.** This is but a more vivid expression of Matt. vi. 19, 20.

Watchfulness (35-48). **35. Let your loins be**

from the wedding; that, when he cometh and knocketh, they may open
37 unto him immediately. Blessed [a]*are* those servants, whom the lord when
he cometh shall find watching: verily I say unto you, that he shall gird
himself, and make them to sit down to meat, and will come forth and serve
38 them. And if he shall come in the second watch, or come in the third
39 watch, and find *them* so, blessed are those servants. And [b]this know,
that if the goodman of the house had known what hour the thief would
come, he would have watched, and not have suffered his house to be
40 broken through. Be [c]ye therefore ready also: for the Son of man cometh
at an hour when ye think not.
41 Then Peter said unto him, Lord, speakest thou this parable unto us,
42 or even to all? And the Lord said, [d]Who then is that faithful and wise
steward, whom *his* lord shall make ruler over his household, to give *them*
43 *their* portion of meat in due season? Blessed *is* that servant, whom his
44 lord when he cometh shall find so doing. Of a truth I say unto you,
45 [e]that he will make him ruler over all that he hath. But and if that
servant say in his heart, My lord delayeth his coming; and shall begin
to beat the men-servants and maidens, and to eat and drink, and to be
46 drunken; the lord of that servant will come in a day when he looketh

A. D. 33.

[a] Matt. 24.46. Matt. 25.21-23. 2 Tim. 4. 7, 8. 1 Pet. 5. 1-4. 2 Pet. 1. 11. 2 Pet. 3. 14. Rev. 14. 13.
[b] 1 Thes. 5. 2. Rev. 16. 15.
[c] Matt 25.13. Mark 13.33. Rom. 13.11-14. 2 Pet. 3. 12 14.
[d] Matt. 24.45, 46. Matt. 25.21. ch. 19.15-19.
[e] 1 Pet. 5. 4. Rev. 3. 21.

girded about—to fasten up the long outer garment, which was always done before travel and before work (See 2 Ki. iv. 29; Acts xii. 8; and compare, for the sense, Eph. vi. 14; 1 Pet. i. 13.) The meaning is, *Be prepared.* **and your lights burning; 36. And ye yourselves like unto men that wait for their lord, &c.** In the corresponding parable of the Virgins (Matt. xxv. 1, &c.) the preparedness is *for* the wedding; here it is for *return from* the wedding. But in both, the thing intended is *Preparedness for Christ's Coming.* **37. Blessed are those servants, whom the lord when he cometh shall find watching: verily I say unto you, that he shall gird himself, and make them to sit down to meat, and will come forth and serve them.** A promise the most august of all. Thus will the Bridegroom entertain His friends on the solemn Nuptial Day, says *Bengel* sweetly. **38. And if he shall come in the second watch, or come in the third watch, and find them so, blessed are those servants.** To find them ready to receive Him at any hour of day or night, when one might least of all expect Him, is peculiarly blessed. A servant may be truly faithful, even though taken so far unawares that he has not everything in *such* order and readiness for his master's return as he thinks is due to him, and as he both could and would have had if he had had notice of the time of his coming. In this case he would not be willing to open to him "*immediately*," but would fly to preparation, and let his master knock again ere he admit him, and even then *not with full joy.* A too common case this with Christians. But if the servant have himself and all under his charge in such a state that at any hour when his master knocks he can open to him "immediately," and hail his return—what an enviable, "blessed" servant is that! **39. And this know, that if the goodman of the house had known what hour the thief would come, he would have watched, and not have suffered his house to be broken through**—of course; but no credit, no thank to him. **40. Be ye therefore ready also: for the Son of man cometh at an hour when ye think not.** So Matt. xxiv. 42, 44; xxv. 13, &c. How frequently does this recur in the teaching of our Lord; nor less so in that of His apostles! 1 Thess. v. 2; 2 Pet. iii. 10, &c. *Is it as frequently heard now?*

41. Then Peter said unto him, Lord, speakest thou this parable unto us, or even to all? He had addressed Himself on this occasion alternately to the Twelve and to the vast assemblage; and Peter, feeling the solemn import of what had just been said coming home to himself, would fain know for which of the two classes it was specially intended. **42. And the Lord said, Who then is.** Our Lord answers the question indirectly by another question, from which they were left to gather what it would be:—'To you certainly, in the first instance, representing the "stewards" of the "household" I am about to collect, but generally to all "servants" in My house.' **that faithful and wise steward** [οἰκονόμος]—'house-steward,' whose it was to distribute to the servants their allotted portion of food. *Fidelity* is the first requisite in a servant; but *wisdom*—discretion and judgment in the exercise of his functions—is the next. **whom his lord shall make**—or will deem fit to be made **ruler over his household, to give them their portion of meat in due season?**—that is, whom his lord will advance to the highest post: The reference is of course to the world to come. (See Matt. xxv. 21, 23.) **43-45. Blessed is that servant, whom his lord when he cometh shall find so doing. Of a truth . . . he will make him ruler over all that he hath. But and if that servant say in his heart, My lord delayeth his coming; and shall begin to beat the men-servants and maidens, and to eat and drink, and to be drunken.** The picture here presented is that of a servant who, in the confidence that his lord's return will not be speedy, throws off the servant and plays the master, maltreating those faithful servants who refuse to join him, seizing on and revelling in the fulness of his master's board; intending, when he has got his fill, to resume the mask of fidelity ere his master appear. **46. The lord of that servant will come in a day when he looketh not for him, and at an hour when he is not aware, and will cut him in sunder** [διχοτομήσει αὐτόν]. *Dichotomy*, or cleaving a person in two, was a punishment not unknown in the East. Compare Heb. xi. 37, "Sawn asunder;" and 1 Sam. xv. 33; Dan. ii. 5. **and will appoint him his portion with the unbelievers** [μετὰ τῶν ἀπίστων]—rather, 'with the unfaithful,' meaning those servants who are found unworthy of trust. In Matt. xxiv. 51 it is, "with

not for *him*, and at an hour when he is not aware, and will [3]cut him in
47 sunder, and will appoint him his portion with the unbelievers. And
[f]that servant, which knew his lord's will, and prepared not *himself*,
48 neither did according to his will, shall be beaten with many *stripes*. But
[g]he that knew not, and did commit things worthy of stripes, shall be
beaten with few *stripes*. For unto whomsoever much is given, of him
shall be much required; and to whom men have committed much, of him
they will ask the more.
49 I am come to send fire on the earth; and what will I, if it be already
50 kindled? But [h]I have a baptism to be baptized with; and how am I
51 [4]straitened till it be accomplished! Suppose [i]ye that I am come to give
52 peace on earth? I tell you, Nay; [j]but rather division: for [k]from henceforth there shall be five in one house divided, three against two, and two
53 against three. The father shall be divided against the son, and the son
against the father; the mother against the daughter, and the daughter
against the mother; the mother-in-law against her daughter-in-law, and
the daughter-in-law against her mother-in-law.
54 And he said also to the people, When [l]ye see a cloud rise out of the
55 west, straightway ye say, There cometh a shower; and so it is. And
when *ye see* [m]the south wind blow, ye say, There will be heat; and it
56 cometh to pass. *Ye* [n]hypocrites, ye can discern the face of the sky and
57 of the earth; but how is it that ye do not discern [o]this time? Yea, and
why even of yourselves judge ye not what is right?

A. D. 33.

[3] Or, cut him off. Matt. 24. 51.
[f] Num. 15. 30. Deut. 25. 2. John 9. 41. John 15. 22. Acts 17. 30. Jas. 4. 17.
[g] Lev. 5. 17. 1 Tim. 1. 13.
[h] Matt. 20. 22. Mark 10. 38.
[4] Or, pained.
[i] Matt. 10. 34.
[j] Mic. 7. 6. John 7. 43. John 9. 16. John 10. 19.
[k] Matt. 10. 35.
[l] Matt. 16. 2.
[m] Job 37. 17.
[n] 1 Cor. 1. 19-27.
[o] Matt. 16. 3. ch. 19. 42-44. Gal. 4. 4.

the hypocrites;" that is, those falsely calling themselves servants. **47. And that servant, which knew his lord's will, and prepared not himself, neither did according to his will, shall be beaten with many stripes**—his guilt being aggravated by the extent of his knowledge. **48. But he that knew not**—that is, knew it but *partially;* for some knowledge is presupposed both in the name "servant" of Christ, and in his being liable to punishment at all. **and did commit things worthy of stripes, shall be beaten with few stripes.** So that there will be degrees of future punishment, proportioned to the light enjoyed—the knowledge sinned against. Even heathens are not without knowledge enough for future judgment (see on Rom. ii. 12-16); but the reference here is not to such. It is a solemn truth, and though *general*, like all other revelations of the future world, discloses a tangible and momentous principle in its awards. **For unto whomsoever much is given, of him shall be much required; and to whom men have committed much, of him they will ask the more.** So that when we are told that men are to be judged according to the *deeds* done in the body (Matt. xvi. 27; Rom. ii. 6), we are to understand not the actions only, but the *principles on* which and the whole *circumstances in* which they were done. Thus equitable will the Judgment be.

Superiority to Earthly Entanglements (49-53). **49. I am come to send** [βαλεῖν]—rather, 'to cast' **fire on the earth.** By "fire" here we are to understand, as *Olshausen* expresses it, the higher spiritual element of life which Jesus came to introduce into this earth (compare Matt. iii. 11), with reference to its mighty effects in quickening all that is akin to it and destroying all that is opposed. To cause this element of life to take up its abode on earth, and wholly to pervade human hearts with its warmth, was the lofty destiny of the Redeemer. So *Calvin*, *Stier*, *Alford*, &c. **and what will I, if it be already kindled?** [καὶ τί θέλω εἰ ἤδη ἀνήφθη]—an obscure expression, uttered under deep and half-smothered emotion. In its general import all are agreed, but interpreters differ as to the precise shade of meaning intended. The nearest to the precise meaning seems to be, 'And what should I have to desire if it were but once kindled?' **50. But I have a baptism to be baptized with**—clearly His own bloody baptism, which had first to take place. **and how am I straitened**—not, 'how do I long for its accomplishment,' as many understand it, thus making it but a repetition of the former verse; but 'what a pressure of spirit is upon me' **till it be accomplished**—completed, over! Before a promiscuous audience, such obscure language was perhaps fitting on a theme like this; but O what surges of mysterious emotion in the view of what was now so near at hand does it reveal! **51. Suppose ye that I am come to give peace on earth? I tell you, Nay**—'in the first instance, the reverse.' **but rather division.** See on Matt. x. 34-36. **52, 53. For from henceforth there shall be five in one house divided, three against two, and two against three. The father . . . against the son, and the son against the father; the mother . . . the daughter . . . the mother-in-law, &c.** The connection of all this with the foregoing warnings about Hypocrisy, Covetousness, and Watchfulness, is deeply solemn: 'My conflict hastens apace; Mine over, yours begins; and then, let the servants tread in their Master's steps, uttering their testimony entire and fearless, neither loving nor dreading the world, anticipating awful wrenches of the dearest ties in life, but looking forward, as I do, to the completion of their testimony, when, after the tempest, reaching the haven, they shall enter into the joy of their Lord.'

Discerning the Signs of the Time (54-59). **54-56. And he said also to the people**—rather, 'to the multitudes' [τοῖς ὄχλοις]: it is a word of special warning to the thoughtless crowd, before dismissing them. **When ye see a cloud rise out of the west, straightway ye say, There cometh a shower; and so it is. And when ye see the south wind blow, ye say, There will be heat. . . . Hypocrites, ye can discern the face of the sky and of the earth; but how is it that ye do not discern this time?** See on Mark viii. 11. They were wise in their fore-

58 When [p] thou goest with thine adversary to the magistrate, [q] *as thou*
art in the way, give diligence that thou mayest be delivered from him;
lest he hale thee to the judge, and the judge deliver thee to the officer,
59 and the officer cast thee into prison. I tell thee, thou shalt not depart
thence, till thou hast paid the very last [r] mite.

A. D. 33

p Pro. 25. 8. Matt. 5. 25.
q Ps. 32. 6. Isa. 55. 6.
r Mark 12.42.

castings as to the things of time, but applied not the same sagacity to things spiritual, and were unable to perceive what a critical, decisive period for the chosen people they had fallen upon. **57. Yea, and why even of yourselves judge ye not what is right?** They might say, To do this requires more knowledge of Scripture and Providence than we possess; but He sends them to their own conscience, as enough to show them who He was, and win them to immediate discipleship.

58. When thou goest with thine adversary to the magistrate, as thou art in the way, give diligence that thou mayest be delivered from him; lest he hale thee to the judge, and the judge deliver thee to the officer, and the officer cast thee into prison. See on Matt. v. 25, 26. It was the urgency of the case with them, and the necessity of immediate decision for their own safety, that drew forth this repetition of those striking words of the Sermon of the Mount.

Remarks.—1. It will be observed that in dealing with hypocrisy—as indeed with everything else—our Lord passes by all *inferior considerations*, holding forth only its *eternal issues.* It is not that these inferior arguments against hypocrisy and other forms of inconsistency in Christians are of no weight. But since apart from the higher considerations they are powerless against the evil tendencies of the heart, and it is from the higher that the lower derive all their real influence, our Lord will not descend to them in His teaching, but concentrates attention upon the final issues of such conduct. This imparted to His teaching a loftiness and a weight perfectly new to those accustomed only to the drivel of the rabbins. In modern times both kinds of teaching have been exemplified in the Christian Church. In times of spiritual death, or prevailing insensibility to eternal things, preachers of ability have wasted their strength in the pulpit, in analyzing the human faculties and expatiating on the natural operation of the principles and passions of our nature. On such a subject as hypocrisy they would show how unmanly it was to conceal one's sentiments, what a crooked, sneaking, pusillanimous, vacillating disposition it tended to generate, and what general distrust it was apt to beget when it assumed formidable proportions. Such discourses are little else than lectures on practical ethics—very proper in a chair of philosophy, but below the dignity and sanctity of the pulpit. And what has been the effect? Attentive hearers have been *entertained* perhaps; and the preachers have been *complimented* upon their ability. But never have the souls of the people been stirred, and never have the evils so exposed been a whit diminished in consequence. But whenever there is any general awakening from spiritual torpor, and the reality of eternal things comes in any good degree to be felt, the pulpit rises to a higher tone, and our Lord's way of treating spiritual things is adopted; the attention of the people is riveted, their souls are stirred, and the fruits of righteousness more or less appear. On this subject it deserves notice, too, that our Lord knows nothing of that false and mawkish refinement which would represent the *fear of hell* as a selfish and gross motive to present, especially to Christians, to deter them from basely denying or being ashamed of Him. As the meekness and gentleness of Christ were not compromised by such harsh notes as these, so those servants of Christ who soften down all such language, to please 'ears polite,' have little of their Master's spirit. See on Mark ix. 43-48, and Remark 5 at the close of that Section. 2. The refusal of our Lord to intermeddle with the affairs of this life as a Judge carries with it a great lesson to all religious teachers. Immense indeed is the influence of religious teachers in the external relations of life, but only when it is *indirectly* exercised: whenever they interfere *directly* with secular and political matters, the spell of that influence is broken. If they take a side, as in that case they must do, those on the opposite side cannot help regarding them as adversaries; and this necessarily diminishes, if it does not destroy—with such at least—their professional influence, or the weight they would otherwise carry in their own proper sphere. Whereas, when the ministers of Christ keep themselves aloof from secular disputes and political parties, abiding within their proper sphere, all parties look up to them, and they are often the means of mollifying the bitterest feelings and reconciling the most conflicting interests. Will the servants of Christ weigh this? 3. Though there is a *general* preparedness for Christ's coming which belongs to the character of all who truly love Him, even believers may be more or less taken *by surprise* when He comes. A faithful servant, whose master's return has been delayed long beyond expectation, may cease expecting him at any particular time, and so slacken his preparations for receiving him. When at length he comes and demands admittance, that servant, though not wholly unprepared, may, on hastily glancing over what is under his hand, see many things which *might* have been in better order, and *would*, if he had got but a very little warning. But he must open to his master without delay. He does so, conscious of his general fidelity, and trusting this will appear to his master's kindly eye, yet unable to welcome him with that *full cordiality* which he should have wished to feel. And his master *is* satisfied of his honest fidelity, but fails not to observe, both in the state of his house and the symptoms of confusion which his servant betrays, that He has been taken somewhat by surprise. How different the feeling of that servant who is "always ready," determined that his Master shall *not* take him by surprise! O the gladness of that welcome which Christ's servants are enabled to give Him when always watching and habitually ready! Is not this what is meant by "having an entrance ministered to us abundantly [πλουσίως] into the everlasting kingdom of our Lord and Saviour Jesus Christ?" (2 Pet. i. 11). 4. If Christ's religion be as fire cast into the earth, burning up whatever is opposed to it, admitting of no compromise, and working towards its own unimpeded power over men, it is easy to see why its operation is so slow and small at many periods, and in many places and persons. The fire is too often quenched by the systematic attempt to serve two masters. Jesus will have uncompromising decision, even though it set friends or families at variance—whether rending distant or dearest ties. But if this be trying, it has a natural termination. The more resolute the

13 THERE were present at that season some that told him of [a]the Gali-
2 leans, whose blood Pilate had mingled with their sacrifices. And Jesus
answering said unto them, Suppose [b]ye that these Galileans were sinners
3 above all the Galileans, because they suffered such things. I tell you,
4 Nay: but, except ye repent, ye shall all likewise perish. Or those
eighteen, upon whom the tower in Siloam fell, and slew them, think ye
5 that they were [1]sinners above all men that dwelt in Jerusalem? I tell
you, Nay: but, except [c]ye repent, ye shall all likewise perish.
6 He spake also this parable; [d]A certain *man* had a fig tree planted in
his vineyard; and he came and sought fruit thereon, and found none.
7 Then said he unto the dresser of his vineyard, Behold, these [e]three years
I come seeking fruit on this fig tree, and find none: cut it down; why
8 cumbereth it the ground? And he answering said unto him, Lord, let
9 [f]it alone this year also, till I shall dig about it, and dung *it:* and if it
bear fruit, *well;* and if not, *then* after that thou shalt cut it down.

A. D. 33.

CHAP. 13.
[a] Acts 5. 37.
[b] Job 22. 5-16.
John 9. 2.
Acts 28. 4.
[1] Or, debtors.
Matt. 18. 24.
ch. 11. 4.
[c] Ezek. 18. 30.
[d] Isa. 5. 2.
Matt. 21. 19.
[e] Lev. 25. 21.
Rom. 2. 4, 5.
2 Pet. 3. 9.
[f] Ex. 32. 11.
Joel 2. 17.
Heb. 7. 25.

servants of Christ are, the sooner usually does the opposition to them cease. Besides, active opposition, when seen to be hopeless, is often desisted from, while consistency and strength of character command respect, and are often blessed to the gaining even of the most determined enemies.

CHAP. XIII. 1-9.—THE LESSON 'REPENT OR PERISH,' SUGGESTED BY TWO RECENT INCIDENTS, AND ILLUSTRATED BY THE PARABLE OF THE BARREN FIG TREE.

The Slaughter of certain Galileans (1-3). **1. There were present at that season**—showing that what is here recorded comes, in order of time, immediately after ch. xii. But what the precise season was, cannot certainly be determined. See opening remarks on ch. ix. 51. **some that told him of the Galileans, whose blood Pilate had mingled with their sacrifices.** Possibly these were the followers of Judas of Galilee, who, some twenty years before this, taught that Jews should not pay tribute to the Romans, and of whom we learn, from Acts v. 37, that he drew after him a multitude of followers, who, on his being slain, were all dispersed. About this time that party would be at its height, and if Pilate caused this detachment of them to be waylaid and put to death, as they were offering their sacrifices at one of the festivals, that would be "mingling their blood with their sacrifices." So *Grotius*, *Webster and Wilkinson*, but doubted by *de Wette*, *Meyer*, *Alford*, &c. News of this—whatever the precise matter referred to may be—having been brought to our Lord, to draw out His views of it, and particularly, whether it was not a judgment of Heaven, He simply points them to the practical view of the matter. **2. And Jesus answering said unto them, Suppose ye that these Galileans were sinners above all the Galileans, because they suffered such things? 3. I tell you, Nay: but, except ye repent, ye shall all likewise perish.** 'These men are not signal examples of divine vengeance, as ye suppose; but every impenitent sinner—*ye yourselves*, except ye repent—shall be like monuments of the judgment of Heaven, and in a more awful sense.' The reference here to the impending destruction of Jerusalem is far from exhausting our Lord's weighty words; they manifestly point to a "perdition" of a more awful kind—*future, personal, remediless.*

The Eighteen on whom the Tower in Siloam Fell (4, 5). **4. Or those eighteen, upon whom the tower in Siloam fell**—probably one of the towers of the city-wall, near the pool of Siloam. Of its fall nothing is known. **and slew them, think ye that they were sinners above all men that dwelt in Jerusalem? 5. I tell you, Nay: but, except ye repent, ye shall all likewise perish.**

The Barren Fig Tree (6-9). **6. He spake also this parable; A certain man had a fig tree**—meaning Israel as the visible witness for God in the world; but generally, all within the pale of the visible Church of God: a familiar figure—compare Isa. v. 1-7; John xv. 1-8, &c. **planted in his vineyard**—a spot selected for its fertility, separated from the surrounding fields, and cultivated with special care, with a view solely to fruit. **and he came and sought fruit thereon**—a heart turned to God, the fruits of righteousness. Compare Matt. xxi. 33, 34, and Isa. v. 2. "He *looked* that it should bring forth fruit:" He has a *right* to it, and will *require* it. **and found none. 7. Then said he unto the dresser of his vineyard**—to him whom he employed to take charge of his vineyard, which in this case we know to be Christ. **Behold, these three years**—a long enough trial for a fig tree, and so denoting probably just a *sufficient* period of culture for spiritual fruit. The supposed allusion to the duration of our Lord's ministry is precarious. **I come seeking fruit on this fig tree, and find none: cut it down.** There is a certain indignation in this language. **why cumbereth it the ground?**—not only doing no good, but wasting ground. **8. And he answering said unto him.** This represents Christ as Intercessor, loath to see it cut down so long as there was any hope. (See *v.* 34). **Lord, let it alone this year also, till I shall dig about it, and dung it**—loosen the earth about it and enrich it with manure: pointing to changes of method in the Divine treatment of the impenitent, in order to fresh spiritual culture. **9. And if it bear fruit, [well]**—all then will yet be right; **and if not, then after that thou shalt cut it down**—I will then no longer interpose: all is over.

Remarks.—1. The small incidents recorded at the beginning of this chapter bear irresistible marks of historical truth in the Evangelical Records. Who that had been drawing up an unreal Story would ever have thought of inserting in it such incidents as these? Much less would they ever have occurred to such untutored writers as these Records show their authors to have been. 2. How slow have even Christians been, notwithstanding the explicit teaching of Christ here, to be convinced that extraordinary outward calamities are not necessarily the vengeance of Heaven against unusual criminality! From the days of Job's friends until now the tendency to explain the one of these by the other has been too prevalent. Is it not to this that the prevalent view of Mary Magdalene's character is to be

10, And he was teaching in one of the synagogues on the sabbath. And,
11 behold, there was a woman which had a spirit of infirmity eighteen years,
12 and was bowed together, and could in no wise lift up *herself*. And when
Jesus saw her, he called *her to him*, and said unto her, [g]Woman, thou art

A. D. 33.

[g] Ps. 107. 20. Isa. 65. 1. Matt. 8. 16.

traced? (See on ch. viii. 2.) 3. To be within the pale of Revealed Religion and the Church of the living God is a high privilege, and involves a solemn responsibility. The owner of the vineyard, having planted a fig tree in it, "came and sought fruit thereon;" for in the natural course of things fruit, in such a case, was to be expected. But when does God *come*, seeking fruit from men thus privileged? Not at the day of judgment; for though He *will* come and demand it then, the parable represents the tree as still in the ground after the lord of the vineyard has come seeking fruit, and as allowed to remain with a view to further trial. It is *now*, therefore, or during our present state, that God is coming seeking fruit from us. Are we favoured with a Christian education and example? He comes, saying, 'Any fruit?' Have we been placed under a faithful, rousing ministry of the Gospel? He comes, asking, 'What fruit?' Have we been visited with crushing trials, fitted to bring down pride, and soften the heart, and give the lessons of Religion an entrance they never had before? He comes, demanding the fruit. Alas, of multitudes the report must still be—"and found none"! 4. The Lord, we see, notes the length of time that men continue fruitless under the means of spiritual culture. "Behold, *these three years* I come seeking fruit on this fig tree, and find none." Thoughtless men heed this not, but One does. "*How long*, ye simple ones, will ye love simplicity?" is His question. "O Jerusalem, wash thine heart from wickedness, that thou mayest be saved: *how long* shall thy vain thoughts lodge within thee?" "Wilt thou not be made clean? when shall it once be?" "*It is time* to seek the Lord, till He come and rain righteousness upon you," (Prov. i. 22; Jer. iv. 14; xiii. 27; Hos. x. 12). 5. To be cut down is the rich desert of all the fruitless: "Cut it down; why cumbereth it the ground?" As if they were a burden to the earth that bears them, to the place they fill, deforming the beauty and hindering the fruitfulness of God's vineyard. They are borne with, but with a certain impatience and indignation. And even when the fruitless are borne with, it is because of the good offices of an Intercessor, and solely with a view to fresh culture. Were there no one in the kingdom of God answering to this dresser of the vineyard, who pleads; and as is here supposed successfully, for a respite to the tree, we might take this feature of the parable as but a part of its drapery, not to be pressed into the exposition of it. But, with the great facts of mediation before us, it is impossible not to see here something more than drapery. And what is that fresh culture for which He pleads? Why, anything by which truths and lessons hitherto neglected may come with a force upon the heart before unknown, may justly be so regarded. A change of the means of grace; a change of sphere—sometimes in the way of banishing one from all the privileges in which he basked, leading him in a far distant land, when sighing over removal from dear objects and scenes, to reflect upon religious privileges never before valued—the remarkable conversion of some companion; or a religious awakening within the immediate sphere of one's observation: these and a thousand other such things are fitted to give truths and lessons, never heeded before, a new power to impress the heart. And it is with a view to this that many are in mercy spared after their long-continued impenitence under high religious culture seemed to be but preparing them to be cut down. 7. It is worthy of notice that the respite sought in the parable was not another three years, but just "one year." As in the natural culture, this would be sufficient to determine whether any fruit was to be got out of the tree at all, so in the spiritual husbandry, the thing intended is just *one sufficient trial more*. And surely it is a loud call to immediate repentance when one has any good reason to think that *he* is on his last trial! 8. Genuine repentance, however late, avails to save: "If it bear fruit (well);" and only *if not*, was it to be cut down. The case of the thief on the cross decides this for all time and for every soul. There is not a sinner out of hell—though the most hardened, the furthest gone, the nearest to the flames—but if he only begin to bear fruit, if he do but turn to God with all his heart in the Gospel of His Son, it will deliver him from going down to the pit, it will stay the hand of justice, it will secure his eternal salvation. "Let the wicked forsake his way, and the unrighteous man his thought, and let him return unto the Lord, and He will have mercy upon him, and to our God, and He will abundantly pardon." "As I live, saith the Lord, I have no pleasure in the death of the wicked, but rather that he should turn from his way and live. Turn ye, turn ye, why will ye die, O house of Israel?" 9. The final perdition of such as, after the utmost limits of divine forbearance, are found fruitless, will be pre-eminently and confessedly just: "If not, after that thou shalt cut it down." It is the Intercessor Himself that says this. Mercy herself, who before pleaded for a respite, now acquiesces in, if not demands, the execution. "He that, being often reproved, hardeneth his neck, shall *suddenly* be destroyed, and that *without remedy*" (Prov. xxix. 1). Be wise now, therefore, O ye fruitless; be instructed, ye foolish and unwise: Kiss the Son, lest He be angry, and ye perish from the way, when His wrath is kindled but a little. Blessed are all they that put their trust in Him! Beware lest that come upon you which is spoken of by the prophet, "Because I have purged thee, and thou wast not purged, thou shalt not be purged from thy filthiness any more, till I have caused my fury to rest upon thee" (Ezek. xxiv. 13).

10-17.—A WOMAN OF EIGHTEEN YEARS' INFIRMITY HEALED ON THE SABBATH DAY.

10. And he was teaching in one of the synagogues on the sabbath—time and place left indefinite. (See opening remarks on ch. ix. 51.) **11. And, behold, there was a woman which had a spirit of infirmity eighteen years.** From the expression used in *v.* 16, "whom *Satan* hath bound," it has been conjectured that her protracted infirmity was the effect of some milder form of *possession;* but this is a precarious inference. At all events she was "a daughter of Abraham," in the same gracious sense, no doubt, as Zaccheus after his conversion was "a son of Abraham" (ch. xix. 9). **and was bowed together, and could in no wise lift up herself. 12. And when Jesus saw her, he called her to him, and said unto her, Woman, thou art loosed from thine infirmity. 13. And he laid his hands on her.** The word and the act were simultaneous; and the effect was instant. **and immediately she was made straight, and gloried God.**

13 loosed from thine infirmity. And [h]he laid *his* hands on her: and immediately she was made straight, and glorified God.
14 And the ruler of the synagogue answered [i]with indignation, because
that Jesus had healed on the sabbath day, and said unto the people,
There are six days in which men ought to work: in them therefore come
15 and be healed, and [j]not on the sabbath day. The Lord then answered
him, and said, *Thou* hypocrite, [k]doth not each one of you on the sabbath
loose his ox or *his* ass from the stall, and lead *him* away to watering?
16 And ought not this woman, [l]being a daughter of Abraham, whom Satan
hath bound, lo, these eighteen years, be loosed from this bond on the
17 sabbath day? And when he had said these things, all his adversaries
were ashamed: and all the people rejoiced for all the glorious things that
were done by him.
18 Then [m]said he, Unto what is the kingdom of God like? and whereunto
19 shall I resemble it? It is like a grain of mustard seed, which a man
took, and cast into his garden; and it grew, and waxed a great tree; and
20 the fowls of the air lodged in the branches of it. And again he said,
21 Whereunto shall I liken the kingdom of God? It is like leaven,
which a woman took and hid in three [n]measures of meal, till the
whole was leavened.
22 And [o]he went through the cities and villages, teaching and journeying
toward Jerusalem.
23 Then said one unto him, Lord, are there few that be saved? And he
24 said unto them, [2]Strive to enter in at the strait gate: for [p]many, I say

A. D. 33.

h Mark 16. 18. ch 17. 14-17. Acts 9. 17.
i John 5. 15, 16. Rom. 10. 2.
j Matt. 12. 10. Mark 3. 2. ch. 6. 7. ch. 14. 3.
k ch 14. 5. John 7. 21-24.
l ch. 19. 9. Rom. 4. 12-16.
m Matt. 13. 31. Mark 4. 30.
n Matt. 13. 33.
o Matt. 9. 35. Mark 6. 6. Acts 10. 38.
2 Strive as in agony. Matt. 7. 13.
p John 7. 34. John 8. 21. John 13. 33. Rom. 9. 31. Rom. 10. 2, 3.

14. And the ruler of the synagogue answered with indignation, because that Jesus had healed on the sabbath day, and said unto the people—or 'the multitude' [ὄχλῳ]. 'Not daring,' as *Trench* remarks, 'directly to find fault with the Lord, he seeks circuitously to reach Him through the people, who were more under his influence, and whom he feared less.' **There are six days in which men ought to work: in them therefore come and be healed, and not on the sabbath day.** From the "hypocrisy" with which the Lord charges him (*v.* 15), we may conclude that zeal for the honour of the Sabbath was only the pretence, and that the glory which this miracle shed upon the Lord Jesus was the real cause of this ruler's "indignation," as the same writer observes. See Matt. xxi. 15. **15. The Lord** (see on ch. x. 1) **then answered him, and said, Hypocrite!** How "the faithful and true Witness" tears off the masks which men wear! **doth not each one of you on the sabbath loose his ox or his ass from the stall, and lead him away to watering?** See on Matt. xii. 10-13. **16. And ought not this woman, being a daughter of Abraham**—that is, not *after the flesh*, or a Jewess, which would be a poor view of His meaning; but *in spirit* (compare ch. xix. 9, and 1 Pet. iii. 6). **whom Satan hath bound.** Probably there is nothing more intended by this expression than a strong contrast between the exalted character of the woman, and the suffering of which the dark author of all evil had so long made her the victim. **lo, these eighteen years.** The "behold" here calling attention to the long duration of her malady is not to be overlooked; attesting, as it does, the lively sensibility to human suffering of our great High Priest. **be loosed from this bond on the sabbath day?** How gloriously the Lord vindicates the superior claims of this woman, in consideration of the sadness and long duration of her suffering, and of her dignity notwithstanding, as an heir of the promise! **17. And when he had said these things, all his adversaries were ashamed: and all the people**—or 'multitude' [ὁ ὄχλος], **rejoiced for all the glorious things that were done by him.** This remark of the Evangelist attests its own artless truth: the resistless force and pungency of the rebuke not only stung His adversaries, but made them feel themselves thoroughly exposed; while the instantaneous cure of this chronic malady, and more than all, the outburst of divine benevolence which vindicated the act, from its own intrinsic superiority to all acts of mercy towards the lower creation, carried the acclaim of the unsophisticated people.

For remarks on this Section, see on Matt. xii. 9-21, Remarks 1, 2, 4, at the close of that Section.

18-30.—PARABLES OF THE MUSTARD SEED AND THE LEAVEN—REPLY TO THE QUESTION, ARE FEW SAVED?

Parables of the Mustard Seed and the Leaven (18-21). For the exposition of this portion, see on Matt. xiii. 31-33, with Remarks.

Are Few Saved? (22-30). **22. And he went through the cities and villages, teaching and journeying toward Jerusalem**—on His final but circuitous journey from Galilee. See introductory remarks on the portion commencing with ch. ix. 51. **23. Then said one unto him, Lord, are there few that be saved?** This is one of those curious questions which a time of religious inquiry and excitement usually suggests, by taking up their attention with which some flatter themselves that they are religious, but thus only lulling the inward craving after something more substantial. **And he said unto them**—that is, the multitude; taking no notice of the man or his question, save as furnishing the occasion of a solemn warning not to trifle with so momentous a matter as "salvation." **24. Strive to enter in** [Ἀγωνίζεσθε]. The word signifies to 'contend' as for the mastery, to 'struggle,' expressive of the *difficulty* of being saved, as if one would have to *force his way in* **at the strait gate**—another figure of the same. See on Matt. vii. 13, 14. **for many will seek to enter in, and shall not be able. 25.**

25 unto you, will seek to enter in, and shall not be able. When [q] once the
Master of the house is risen up, and [r] hath shut to the door, and ye begin
to stand without, and to knock at the door, saying, [s] Lord, Lord, open
unto us; and he shall answer and say unto you, [t] I know you not whence
26 ye are: then shall ye begin to say, [u] We have eaten and drunk in thy
27 presence, and thou hast taught in our streets. But [v] he shall say, I tell
you, I know you not whence ye are: [w] depart from me, all *ye* workers of
28 iniquity. There [x] shall be weeping and gnashing of teeth, [y] when ye shall
see Abraham, and Isaac, and Jacob, and all the prophets, in the kingdom
29 of God, and you *yourselves* thrust out. And [z] they shall come from the
east, and *from* the west, and from the north, and *from* the south, and
30 shall sit down in the kingdom of God. And, [a] behold, there are last
which shall be first, and there are first which shall be last.
31 The same day there came certain of the Pharisees, saying unto him,
32 Get thee out, and depart hence: for Herod will kill thee. And he said
unto them, Go ye, and tell that fox, Behold, I cast out devils, and I do
cures to-day and to-morrow, and the third *day* [b] I shall be perfected.

A. D. 33.
[q] Ps. 32. 6. Isa. 55. 6.
[r] Matt. 25. 10.
[s] ch. 6. 46.
[t] Matt. 7. 23.
[u] Tit. 1. 16.
[v] Matt. 7. 23. Matt. 25. 41.
[w] Ps. 6. 8. Matt. 25. 41.
[x] Matt. 8. 12. Matt. 13. 42. Matt. 24. 51.
[y] Matt. 8. 11.
[z] Gen. 28. 14. Isa. 60. 3.
[a] Matt. 19. 30. Matt. 20. 16. Mark 10. 31.
[b] Heb. 2. 10. Heb. 5. 8.

When once the Master of the house is risen up, and hath shut to the door. Awfully sublime and vivid picture! At present He is represented as in a *sitting* posture, as if calmly looking on to see who will "strive," while entrance is practicable. But this is to have an end, by the great Master of the house Himself rising and shutting the door, after which there will be no admittance. **and ye begin to stand without, and to knock at the door, saying, Lord, Lord**—emphatic reduplication, expressive of the earnestness *now* felt, but too late. See on Matt. vii. 21, 22. **open unto us; and he shall answer and say unto you, I know you not whence ye are: 26. Then shall ye begin to say, We have eaten and drunk in thy presence, and thou hast taught in our streets. 27. But he shall say, I tell you, I know you not whence ye are: depart from me, all ye workers of iniquity.** 'What! not know *us*, Lord? Astonishing! Why, we have eaten and drunk in Thy presence. Were we not at that great feast which Matthew the publican made to Thee in his own house? Did we not sit opposite to Thee at his table? Heard we not from Thy lips on that occasion the precious saying, "I came not to call the righteous, but sinners to repentance," a saying which, *in the midst of our sins*, has proved so great a comfort to us?'—"Never knew you, workers of iniquity!" 'But, Lord, in addition to all this, Thou hast taught in our streets. At Capernaum, did we not live next door to Thee, and what glorious teachings of Thine have we not heard there? When the woman with the issue of blood was healed by touching the hem of Thy garment, we were in the crowd that followed Thee through the streets; and when Thou spakest from Peter's boat to the thronging multitudes that lined the shore of the beautiful lake, we stood right opposite to Thee, and could repeat every word of those seven charming parables which were then delivered. Nay, we followed Thee from place to place, from city to city, enchained by Thy matchless teaching: we could repeat most of the Sermon on the Mount, and we heard Thee utter that great word, "Come unto Me, all ye that labour and are heavy laden, and I will give you rest;" and *what a comfort was that to us!* And that glorious word uttered in the streets of Jerusalem on the last, that great day of the feast, we heard, "If any man thirst, let him come unto me and drink." O what scores of such beautiful sayings of Thine did our ears drink in. Never knew *us*, Lord? Impossible!'—"NEVER KNEW YOU, workers of iniquity!" 'But, Lord—' 'Enough: begone!' 28, 29. **There**—in the place of separation from Me, **shall be weeping**—for anguish, **and gnashing of teeth**—for despair, **when ye shall see Abraham, &c. And they shall come from the east, and from the west, &c.** See on ch. vii. 9.

For Remarks on this Section, see on Matt. vii. 13-29, Remarks 3, 4, 5, at the close of that Section. But we may call attention to the two following points here standing out with peculiar vividness:—1. No nearness of external communion with Christ will avail at the Great Day, in place of that "holiness without which no man shall see the Lord." 2. The *style* which Christ announces that He will then assume—that of absolute Disposer of men's eternal destinies—and contrast this with His "despised and rejected" condition when He uttered these words!

31-35.—MESSAGE TO HEROD, AND LAMENTATION OVER JERUSALEM, SUGGESTED BY IT.

Message to Herod (31-33). **31. The same day there came certain of the Pharisees, saying unto him, Get thee out, and depart hence**—'Push on without delay, if thou regardest thine own safety.' **for Herod** (Antipas) **will kill thee** [θέλει σε ἀποκτεῖναι]—'is minded to kill thee.' He was now on His way out of Perea, on the east side of the Jordan, and so out of Herod's dominions, "journeying towards Jerusalem" (*v.* 22). Haunted, probably, by guilty fears, Herod wanted to get rid of Him (see on Mark vi. 14), and seems, from our Lord's answer, to have sent these Pharisees, under pretence of a friendly hint, to persuade Him that the sooner He got beyond Herod's jurisdiction the better it would be for His own safety. Our Lord saw through both of them, and sends the cunning ruler a message couched in dignified and befitting irony. **32. And he said unto them, Go ye, and tell that fox**—that crafty, cruel enemy of God's innocent servants, **Behold, I cast out devils, and I do cures to-day and to-morrow, and the third day I shall be perfected**—or, finish My course, attain completion. 'Plot on and ply thy wiles; I also have My plans; My works of mercy are nearing completion, but some yet remain; I have work for to-day and to-morrow too, and the third day; by that time I shall be where his jurisdiction reaches not; the guilt of My blood shall not lie at his door; that dark deed is reserved for others.' He does not say, as *Bengel* remarks, I preach the Gospel—that would have made little impression upon Herod. In the light of the *merciful* character of Christ's *actions* the *malice* of Herod's *snares* is laid bare. **33. Nevertheless I must walk to-day, and**

33 Nevertheless I must walk to-day, and to-morrow, and the *day* following:
for it cannot be that a prophet perish out of Jerusalem.
34 O [c]Jerusalem, Jerusalem, which killest the prophets, and stonest them
that are sent unto thee; how often would I have gathered thy children
together, as a hen *doth gather* her brood under *her* wings, and ye would
35 not! Behold, [d]your house is left unto you desolate: and verily I say
unto you, Ye shall [e]not see me, until *the time* come when ye shall say,
[f]Blessed *is* he that cometh in the name of the Lord.

14 AND it came to pass, as he went into the house of one of the chief
2 Pharisees to eat bread on the sabbath day, that they watched him. And,
3 behold, there was a certain man before him which had the dropsy. And
Jesus answering spake unto the lawyers and Pharisees, saying, [a]Is it
4 lawful to heal on the sabbath day? And they held their peace. And he
5 took *him,* and healed him, and let him go: and answered them, saying,
[b]Which of you shall have an ass or an ox fallen into a pit, and will not
6 straightway pull him out on the sabbath day? And they could not
answer him again to these things.
7 And he put forth a parable to those which were bidden, when he
8 marked how they chose out the chief rooms; saying unto them, When
thou art bidden of any *man* to a wedding, sit not down in the highest
9 room; lest a more honourable man than thou be bidden of him; and he
that bade thee and him come and say to thee, Give this man place; and
10 thou begin with shame to take the lowest room. But [c]when thou art

A. D. 33.

[c] 2 Chr. 24. 21, 22. Neh. 9. 26. Matt. 21. 35, 36. Matt. 23. 37.
[d] Lev. 26. 31, 32. Ps. 69. 25. Isa. 1. 7. Dan. 9. 27. Mic. 3. 12. Luke 21. 24.
[e] Pro. 1. 24-30. John 8. 21, 24.
[f] Ps. 118. 26. Matt. 21. 9. Mark 11. 10. ch. 19. 38. John 12. 13.

CHAP. 14.
[a] Matt. 12. 10.
[b] Ex. 23. 5. Deut. 22. 4. ch. 13. 15.
[c] Pro. 15. 33. Pro. 18. 12. Pro. 25. 6, 7.

to-morrow, and the day following. Remarkable language, expressive of *successive steps* of His work yet remaining, of the calm *deliberateness* with which He meant to go through with them, one after another, to the last, unmoved by Herod's threat, but of the *rapid march* with which they were now hastening to completion! (Compare Luke xxii. 37.) **for it cannot be that a prophet perish out of Jerusalem.** Awful severity of satire this upon 'the bloody city'! 'He seeks to "kill me" does He? Ah! I must be out of Herod's jurisdiction for that: Go tell him I neither fly from him nor fear him, but Jerusalem has ever been, and is once more to become, the prophet's slaughter-house.'

Lamentation over Jerusalem (34-35). **34. O Jerusalem, Jerusalem, which killest the prophets, and stonest them that are sent unto thee; how often would I have gathered thy children together, as a hen doth gather her brood under her wings, and ye would not! 35. Behold, your house is left unto you desolate: and verily I say unto you, Ye shall not see me, until the time come when ye shall say, Blessed is he that cometh in the name of the Lord.** How naturally this melting Lamentation would be wrung from Christ's heart after the words just uttered, let the devout and intelligent reader judge. And yet there are critics of some weight who regard it as but a repetition by the Third Evangelist of the Lamentation uttered considerably later, on His final departure from the Temple, and recorded in its proper place by Matthew (xxiii. 37-39). For the exposition, see on Matt. xxiii. 37-39, with Remarks at the close of that Section.

CHAP. XIV. 1-24.—HEALING OF A DROPSICAL MAN, AND MANIFOLD TEACHINGS AT A SABBATH-FEAST.

Healing of a Dropsical Man on the Sabbath day (1-6). **1. And it came to pass, as he went into the house of one of the chief Pharisees** [τινος τῶν ἀρχόντων τῶν Φαρισαίων]—rather, 'of one of the rulers of the Pharisees,' that is, one of the rulers who belonged to the sect of the Pharisees. The place and time, as usual in this portion of the present Gospel, are not indicated. See remarks prefixed to ch. ix. 51. **to eat bread on the sabbath day, that they watched him. 2. And, behold, there was a certain man before him which had the dropsy**—not one of the invited guests probably, but one who presented himself in hope of a cure, though not expressly soliciting it; and it may be that this was all the more readily allowed, to see what He would do. This is confirmed by our Lord "letting Him go" immediately after curing him (*v.* 4). The company, it will be observed, had not yet sat down. **3-6. And Jesus answering spake unto the lawyers and Pharisees, saying, Is it lawful to heal on the sabbath day? &c.** For the exposition of these verses, see on Matt. xii. 10-13, and Remarks 1, 2, at the close of that Section.

Lessons on Humility (7-11). **7. And he put forth a parable to those which were bidden, when he marked how they chose out the chief rooms** [τὰς πρωτοκλισίας]—that is, the couches or seats at the table reserved for the most honoured guests, or the middle parts of the couches which were esteemed the most honourable. His mode of conveying the instruction intended is called a "parable," as teaching something deeper than the outward form of it expressed—because His design was not so much to inculcate mere politeness, or good manners, but, underneath this, universal humility, as appears by *v.* 11. **8. When thou art bidden of any man to a wedding**—'and,' as is implied, 'art taking thy place at the wedding-feast.' Our Lord, as *Bengel* remarks, avoids the appearance of personality by this delicate allusion to a different kind of entertainment from this of His present host. **sit not down in the highest room; lest a more honourable man than thou be bidden of him; 9. And he that bade thee and him come and say to thee, Give this man place; and thou begin with shame to take the lowest room.** To be lowest, says *Bengel,* is only ignominious to him who affects to be highest. **10. But when thou art bidden, go and sit down in the lowest room; that when he that bade thee cometh, he may say unto thee, Friend**—said to the modest guest

bidden, go and sit down in the lowest room; that when he that bade
thee cometh, he may say unto thee, Friend, go up higher: then shalt
thou have worship in the presence of them that sit at meat with thee.
11 For [d]whosoever exalteth himself shall be abased; and he that humbleth
himself shall be exalted.
12 Then said he also to him that bade him, When thou makest a dinner
or a supper, call not thy friends, nor thy brethren, neither thy kinsmen,
nor *thy* rich neighbours; lest they also bid thee again, and a recompence
13 be made thee. But when thou makest a feast, [e]call the poor, the maimed,
14 the lame, the blind: and thou shalt be blessed; for they cannot recompense
thee: for thou shalt be recompensed at [f]the resurrection of the
just.
15 And when one of them that sat at meat with him heard these things,
he said unto him, [g]Blessed *is* he that shall eat bread in the kingdom of
16 God. Then [h]said he unto him, A certain man made a great supper, and
17 bade many: and [i]sent his servant at supper time to say to them that
18 were bidden, Come; for all things are now ready. And they all with one
consent began to make excuse. The first said unto him, [j]I have bought
a piece of ground, and I must needs go and see it: I pray thee have me
19 excused. And another said, I have bought five yoke of oxen, and I go
20 to prove them: I pray thee have me excused. And another said, I have

A. D. 33.

d Job 22. 29. Ps. 18. 27. Pro. 29. 23. Matt. 23. 12. ch. 18. 14. Jas. 4. 6. 1 Pet. 5. 5.

e Neh. 8. 10, 12. Job 31. 14-20. Pro. 3. 9, 28.

f Dan. 12. 2. Matt. 25. 36. John 5. 29. Acts 24. 15.

g Rev. 19. 9.

h Matt. 22. 2.

i Pro. 9. 2, 5.

j Matt. 6. 24. Matt. 13. 22. Luke 8. 14. John 5. 40. 1 Tim. 6. 9, 10. 2 Tim. 4. 10.

only, says the same critic, not the proud one (*v.* 9). **then shalt thou have worship** [δόξα]—or 'honour.' The whole of this is but a reproduction of Prov. xxv. 6, 7. But it was reserved for the matchless Teacher to utter articulately, and apply to the regulation of the minutest features of social life, such great laws of the Kingdom of God as the following: **11. For whosoever exalteth himself shall be abased; and he that humbleth himself shall be exalted.** The chaste simplicity and proverbial terseness of this great maxim impart to it a charm only inferior to that of the maxim itself. But see further on ch. xviii. 14.

Entertaining the Poor (12-14.) **12. Then said he also to him that bade him, When thou makest a dinner or a supper, call not thy friends, nor thy brethren, neither thy kinsmen, nor thy rich neighbours; lest they also bid thee again, and a recompense be made thee**—a fear the world is not afflicted with. Jesus certainly did not mean us to dispense with the duties of ordinary fellowship. But since there was no exercise of *principle* involved in it, save of reciprocity, and selfishness itself would suffice to prompt it, His object was to inculcate, over and above everything of this kind, such attentions to the helpless and provision for them as, from their inability to make any return, would manifest their own disinterestedness, and, like every other exercise of high religious principle, meet with a corresponding gracious recompense. **13. But when thou makest a feast, call the poor, the maimed, the lame, the blind.** Compare this with the classes God himself invites to the great Gospel Feast, *v.* 21. **14. And thou shalt be blessed; for they cannot recompense thee: for thou shalt be recompensed at the resurrection of the just**—as acting from disinterested, God-like compassion for the wretched.

The Great Supper (15-24). **15. And when one of them that sat at meat with him heard these things, he said unto him, Blessed is he that shall eat bread in the kingdom of God.** As our Lord's words seemed to hold forth the future "recompense" under the idea of a great Feast, the thought passes through this man's mind, how blessed they would be who should be honoured to sit down to it. A pious exclamation it seemed to be; but, from our Lord's reply, it would appear to have sounded in His ears more like Balaam's wish, "Let me die the death of the righteous, and let my last end be like his" (Numb. xxiii. 10)—a wish only to be safe and happy *at last*, while rejecting all *present* invitations to turn to God and live. 'The Great Feast of which you sigh to partake,' says our Lord, 'is prepared already: the invitations are issued, but declined: the Feast, notwithstanding, shall have guests enough, and the table shall be filled: but when its present contemners come to sue for admission to it—as they will yet do—not one of them shall taste of it.' **16. Then said he unto him, A certain man made a great supper.** The blessings of Salvation are in Scripture familiarly set forth as a *Feast*, to signify not merely the rich abundance and variety of them, but their suitableness to our spiritual wants, and the high satisfaction and enjoyment which they yield. Thus, Isa. xxv. 6, "And in this mountain (mount Zion, Heb. xii. 22) shall the Lord of hosts make unto all peoples [לְכָל־הָעַמִּים] a feast of fat things," or rich delicacies, "a feast of wines on the lees," freed from all mixture, "of fat things full of marrow, of wines on the lees well refined." **and bade many.** *Historically*, the Jews are here meant, whom, by taking them into visible covenant, God first invited to partake of salvation; but generally it denotes all within the pale of professed discipleship. **17. And sent his servant at supper time to say to them that were bidden, Come; for all things are now ready**—pointing undoubtedly to the lengthened, but now ripening preparations for the great Gospel call. See on Matt. xxii. 4. **18. And they all with one consent began to make excuse. The first said unto him, I have bought a piece of ground, and I must needs go and see it: I pray thee have me excused. 19. And another said, I have bought five yoke of oxen, and I go to prove them: I pray thee have me excused. 20. And another said, I have married a wife, and therefore I cannot come.** None give a naked refusal. Each has some reason of his own why he ought to be held excused. Three excuses are given as specimens of all the rest; and it will be observed that they answer to the three things which are said to "choke the word" in the parable of the Sower (ch. viii. 14),—

21 married a wife, and therefore I cannot come. So that servant came, and
showed his lord these things. Then the master of the house, being angry,
said to his servant, Go [k]out quickly into the streets and lanes of the city,
and bring in hither the poor, and the maimed, and the halt, and the
22 blind. And the servant said, Lord, it is done as thou hast commanded,
23 and yet there is room. And the lord said unto the servant, Go out into
the highways and hedges, [l]and compel *them* to come in, that my house
24 may be filled. For I say unto you, [m]That none of those men which were
bidden shall taste of my supper.

A. D. 33.

k Matt. 28. 18, 19. Acts 13. 46.
l Pro. 1. 20. 2 Cor. 5. 20.
m Matt. 8. 11, 12. Matt. 21. 43. Matt. 22. 8. Acts 13. 46. Heb. 3 19.

"the care of this world," *v.* 18; "the deceitfulness of riches," *v.* 19; and "the pleasures of this life," *v.* 20. Each differs from the other, and each has its own plausibility; but all arrive at the same result—'We have other things to attend to, more pressing just now.' So far from saying, I decline to come, each represents himself as *only* hindered by something in the way just now: when these are removed, they will be ready. But, notwithstanding these plausibilities, they are held as *refusers;* and when at length they *call*, the Master in turn will *refuse* them. **21. So that servant came, and showed his lord these things.** It is the part of ministers, says *Bengel*, to report to the Lord in their prayers the compliance or refusal of their hearers; and certainly, of those first bidden, it could only be said, "Lord, who hath believed our report, and to whom is the arm of the Lord revealed?" (Isa. liii. 1.) **Then the master of the house, being angry**—at the slight put upon him. At the same time there is *grace* in this anger, showing how sincere he was in issuing his invitation (Ezek. xxxiii. 11). **said to his servant, Go out quickly**—all now being ready, and waiting, **into the streets and lanes of the city.** *Historically*, this must mean those within the limits of the city of God (Ps. lxxxvii. 3), but the despised and outcast classes of it—the "publicans and sinners," as *Trench* rightly conceives it; but generally it comprehends all similar classes, usually overlooked in the first provision for supplying the means of grace to a community—half heathen in the midst of revealed light, and in every sense miserable. **and bring in hither the poor, and the maimed, and the halt, and the blind. 22. And the servant said, Lord, it is done as thou hast commanded, and yet there is room**—implying, first, that these classes *had* embraced the invitation (see Matt. xxi. 32; Mark xii. 37, last clause; John vii. 48, 49); but further, beautifully expressing the longing that should fill the hearts of ministers to see their Master's table filled. **23. And the lord said unto the servant, Go out into the highways and hedges**—outside the city altogether. *Historically*, this denotes the heathen, sunk in the lowest depths of spiritual wretchedness, as being beyond the pale of all that is revealed and saving—"without Christ, strangers from the covenant of promise, having no hope, and without God in the world" (Eph. ii. 12): generally, it comprehends all similar classes. Thus, this parable *prophetically* contemplates the extension of the kingdom of God to the whole world; and *spiritually*, directs the Gospel invitations to be carried to the lowest strata, and be brought in contact with the outermost circles, of human society. **and compel them to come in.** This is not meant to intimate *unwillingness*, as in the first class, but that it would be hard to get them over two difficulties. First, 'We, homeless wretches, that are fain to creep under a "hedge" for shelter, what company are we for such a feast?' Next, 'We who are on the dusty, weary "highway," have no proper dress for such a feast, and are ill in order for such a presence.' How fitly does this represent the difficulties and fears of the *sincere!* Well, and how is this met? 'Take no excuse; beat them out of all their difficulties; dispel all their fears: Tell them you have orders to bring them *just as they are;* make them come without preparation, and without delay.' **that my house may be filled**—for, as *Bengel* quaintly says, grace as well as nature abhors a vacuum. **24. For I say unto you, That none of those men which were bidden shall taste of my supper.** Our Lord here appears to throw off the veil of the parable, and proclaim the Supper *His Own*, intimating that when transferred and transformed into its final glorious form, and the refusers themselves would give all for another opportunity, *He* will not allow one of them to taste of it.

Remarks.—1. Some of the richest of our Lord's teachings were quite *incidental*—drawn forth by casual circumstances occurring in His daily course. Thus, having accepted the invitation of this Pharisee to dine on the Sabbath day, the presence of a dropsical person, whom He resolves to cure, gives occasion to some important teaching on the right observance of that holy day. Then, observing the eagerness of the guests to occupy the places of honour at the table, He instructs them on the subject of Humility. Further, from the quality of the guests—apparently "brethren, kinsmen, rich neighbours"—He takes occasion to inculcate hospitality of a diviner sort, compassionate provision for the wants of those who could make no return, looking to the time when a return of another kind would be made them—when "the merciful should obtain mercy." 'Blessed lot that will be'—exclaims one of the guests, fired for the moment at the thought of a Feast in the kingdom above—'Happy they who shall have the honour of sitting down to it!' Happy indeed, replies the Great Teacher and loving Redeemer; but the present despisers of it shall not be the future partakers of it. Thus did His heavenly wisdom stream forth at every opening, however incidental. "Grace was poured into His lips," and was ready to pour out again whenever it would not be as pearls cast before swine. And should not His disciples strive to copy Him in this? "The lips of the righteous feed many" (Prov. x. 21). There is a certain advantage in *set* discourses, to which the hearers set themselves to listen, expecting something lengthened, formal, solid. But the wisdom that comes out unexpectedly and casually has a freshness and charm peculiar to itself. And it impresses the hearer, far more than all set discoursing, with the conviction that it is the *genuine* and *spontaneous* expression of the speaker's present judgment and feeling. And when it comes as "line upon line, line upon line; precept upon precept, precept upon precept; here a little, and there a little" (Isa. xxviii. 10), its weight is all the greater. (Compare Deut. vi. 7.) 2. The punishment attached to pride, and the reward promised to humility, make themselves good even in the ordinary workings of human society. When a man insists on thrusting himself, as *Lord Bacon*

25 And there went great multitudes with him: and he turned, and said
26 unto them, If [n]any *man* come to me, [o]and hate not his father, and
mother, and wife, and children, and brethren, and sisters, [p]yea, and his
27 own life also, he cannot be my disciple. And [q]whosoever doth not bear
28 his cross, and come after me, cannot be my disciple. For [r]which of you,
intending to build a tower, sitteth not down first, and counteth the cost,
29 whether he have *sufficient* to finish *it?* Lest haply, after he hath laid
the foundation, and is not able to finish *it*, all that behold *it* begin to
30 mock him, saying, This man began to build, and was not able to finish.

A. D. 33.

n Deut. 13. 6. Deut. 33. 9. Matt. 10. 37.
o Rom. 9. 13.
p Rev. 12. 11.
q Matt. 16. 24. Mark 8. 34. ch. 9. 23.
r Pro. 24. 27. 1 Pet. 2. 5.

somewhere expresses it, into the centre of things, there is a kind of social instinct that leads others to resist and take him down; but when one gives place to others, he not only disarms every disposition to take advantage of it, but is usually made to go before his neighbours. Thus, in the ordinary working of the social system, the great principles of the divine administration are revealed; on a small scale, indeed, and often without the smallest reference, on the part of men, to the divine will, but just on that account all the more strikingly manifesting and illustrating a moral government. 3. It is a mistake in religion, alike common and fatal, to regard heaven as a state of simple happiness—mere bliss; higher and more refined than anything conceivable now, but not essentially dependent upon *present character*. If one thing is clearer than another in the Scripture view of the future state, it is that, in point of moral and religious character, it will be but the perfection and development of the present state, both in the righteous and the wicked; and all the conclusions, even of Natural Theology, confirm that view of it. In vain, therefore, do worldlings, living without God and minding only earthly things, exclaim, Blessed is he that shall eat bread in the kingdom of God! Let me die the death of the righteous, and let my last end be like his! The best of heaven's bliss is but getting face to face with Him whom not having seen we love, in whom, though now we see him not, yet believing, we rejoice with joy unspeakable and full of glory. But if we have never felt any of this love to Him and joy in Him, are we capable of heaven? To be "for ever with the Lord," is transport, even in prospect, to such as have tasted that He is gracious, experienced the blessedness of reconciliation, learned to cry, Abba, Father, walk daily in the light of His countenance, and live to please Him. In such as these, it is but a change of sphere, and the new life perfected; it is but the bursting of the flower, the ripening of the fruit. Amidst all its novelties, the children of God will find themselves *at home* in heaven—its company congenial, its services familiar, its bliss not strange. But if so, how is it possible that those who disrelished its language, its exercises, its fellowship here, should have any capacity for it, and, wanting this, be admitted to it? No, "none of those men who were bidden"—but only insulted Him who prepared the feast by slighting His invitation—"shall taste of His Supper." "Be not deceived: God is not mocked; for whatsoever a man soweth, that shall he also reap." 4. How often is it found that while the Gospel is slighted by the classes who enjoy the greatest advantages, who might be expected the most to appreciate it, and whom one would most gladly see brought under its power, it is embraced by those to whom it has last of all been presented, and—judging as we are apt to do—the least likely to value it. Thus it ever is, that there are last which come to be first, and first last. 5. The call addressed to those in the highways and hedges is a glorious directory to the preachers of the Gospel. If such are invited and expected to come straight to the feast, all *preparation* is out of the question; and all misgivings on their own part, or obstructions on the part of others, on the ground of want of preparation, must be met with one answer—'The invitation found us in that condition, and required immediate compliance.' If this great Gospel truth is not clearly apprehended, and by the preacher himself felt as the sole ground of his own standing in Christ, he cannot urge it upon others, and still less so deal with them as to "compel them to come in." But having got over all his own scruples on that one principle, that the invitations of the Gospel are to sinners *as such*—to sinners *just as they are*—he can and will then effectually meet all difficulties and scruples of earnest, anxious souls; and as he cries to them—

'Come, ye sinners, poor and needy,
Weak and wounded, sick and sore,
Jesus ready stands to save you,
Full of pity, love, and power:
He is able,
He is willing, ask no more'—

he shall hear of one and another falling down before the cross, and saying—

'Just as I am—without one plea,
But that Thy blood was shed for me,
And that Thou bidd'st me come to Thee—
O Lamb of God! I come.

'Just as I am—and *waiting not*
To rid my soul of one dark blot,
To Thee, whose blood can cleanse each spot—
O Lamb of God! I come.'

25-35.—ADDRESS ON COUNTING THE COST OF FOLLOWING HIM, DELIVERED BY JESUS TO GREAT MULTITUDES WHO WENT AFTER HIM. **25. And there went great multitudes with him**—on His final journey to Jerusalem. If they were going up to the Passover, moving along, as they were wont to do, in clusters (see on ch. ii. 44), and forming themselves into one mass about the Lord Jesus, this must have occurred after the Feast of Tabernacles and the winter Feast of Dedication, at both of which our Lord was present, after His final departure from Galilee. But the precise time cannot be determined. See remarks prefixed to the portion of this Gospel beginning with ch. ix. 51. **and he turned, and said unto them, 26, 27. If any man come to me, and hate not his father, &c., he cannot be my disciple. And whosoever doth not bear his cross, and come after me, cannot be my disciple.** See on Matt. x. 37, 38. **28. For which of you, intending to build a tower, sitteth not down first, and counteth the cost, whether he have sufficient to finish it? 29. Lest haply, after he hath laid the foundation, and is not able to finish it, all that behold it begin to mock him, 30. Saying, This man began to build, and was not able to finish.** Common sense teaches men not to *begin* any costly work without first seeing that they have wherewithal to *finish* it. And he who does otherwise exposes himself to

31 Or what king, going to make war against another king, sitteth not down
first, and consulteth whether he be able with ten thousand to meet him
32 that cometh against him with twenty thousand? Or else, while the
other is yet a great way off, he sendeth [s]an ambassage, and desireth
33 conditions of peace. So likewise, whosoever [t]he be of you that forsaketh
not all that he hath, he cannot be my disciple.
34 Salt [u]*is* good: but if the salt have lost his savour, wherewith shall it be
35 seasoned? It is neither fit for the land, nor yet for the dunghill; *but*
men cast it out. He that hath ears to hear, let him hear.
15 THEN [a]drew near unto him all the publicans and [b]sinners for to hear
2 him. And the Pharisees and scribes murmured, saying, This man re-

A. D. 33.

[s] Job 22. 21. Matt. 5. 25. ch. 12. 58. 2 Cor. 6. 2.
[t] Matt. 19.27, 28. ch. 18. 22.
[u] Matt. 5. 13. Mark 9. 50.

CHAP. 15.
[a] Matt. 9. 10.
[b] Ezek. 18. 23. 1 Tim. 1.15.

general ridicule. **31. Or what king, going to make war against another king, sitteth not down first, and consulteth whether he be able with ten thousand to meet him that cometh against him with twenty thousand?** No wise potentate will enter on a war with any hostile power without first seeing to it that, despite formidable odds—of "twenty" to "ten thousand," or two to one—he be able to stand his ground. **32. Or else, while the other is yet a great way off, he sendeth an ambassage, and desireth conditions of peace.** If he see that he has no hope of bearing up against such odds, he will feel that nothing remains for him but to make the best terms he can. **33. So likewise, whosoever he be of you that forsaketh not all that he hath, he cannot be my disciple.** 'In the warfare you will each have to wage as My disciples, despise not your enemy's strength, for the odds are all against you; and you had better see to it that, despite every disadvantage, you still have wherewithal to hold out and win the day, or else not begin at all, but make the best you can in such awful circumstances.' In place of this simple and natural sense of the latter parable, *Stier*, *Alford*, &c., go wide of the mark, making the enemy here meant to be *God*, because of the "conditions of peace" which the parable speaks of. It is the *spirit* of such a case, rather than the mere phraseology, that is to be seized.

34, 35. Salt is good: but if the salt have lost his savour, &c. He that hath ears to hear, let him hear. See on Matt. v. 13; and on Mark iv. 9.

Remarks.—1. Better not begin the Christian course, than begin and not finish it. Inconsistency is offensive even to men, and, in the matter of religion, is apt to draw down ridicule and contempt; as is so admirably portrayed in "Pliable" by *Bunyan* in the "Pilgrim's Progress." But to Him whose eyes are as a flame of fire, it is abhorrent. "I would thou wert cold or hot. So then, because thou art lukewarm, and neither cold nor hot, I will spue thee out of my mouth" (Rev. iii. 15, 16). 2. Though the contest for salvation be on our part an awfully unequal one, *the human will*, in the exercise of that "faith which overcometh the world" (1 John v. 4), and nerved by power from above, which "out of weakness makes it strong" (Heb. xi. 34; 1 Pet. i. 5), becomes heroical, and will come off "more than conqueror." But without *absolute surrender of self*, the contest is hopeless.

CHAP. XV. 1-32.—Publicans and Sinners Welcomed by Christ—Three Parables opening the Divine Principle of this.

1. Then—but when, is not stated and cannot be determined. See remarks prefixed to ch. ix. 51. **drew near** [Ἦσαν δὲ ἐγγίζοντες]. The phrase implies something *habitual*. See on the same imperfect tense in ch. i. 22, &c. **unto him all the publicans and sinners for to hear him.** Strange auditory for such a Preacher! In fact, among the marvels of this most marvellous History, none is more marvellous than the fact that the most sunken classes of society—we might almost say, its refuse and scum—seem, as by some spell, to have been attracted to the Holy, Harmless, Undefiled One, the Separate from sinners! What could the secret of this be? What but the discovery in *Him* of a compassion for their case against which they had found every other breast steeled. 'Abandoned of men, we had thought ourselves much more so of God: Heaven and earth seemed alike shut against us, and we were ready to conclude that, as outcasts from both, we must live on the wretched life we are living, and then lie down and die without hope. But compassion for the chief of sinners beams in that Eye, and streams forth from those Lips; God is in that Heart, Heaven in that Voice; Never man spake like this Man: As He speaks, God Himself seems to draw near even to us, and say to us in accents of melting love, Return unto Me, and I will return unto you: Who and what He is, we are too ignorant to tell; but we *feel* what He is to us; when *He* is with us, we seem to be in the precincts of heaven.' How far these were the thoughts and feelings of that class, would of course depend on the extent to which they were sick of their evil ways, and prepared to welcome divine encouragement to turn from them and live. But that what drew to Him "all the publicans and sinners for to hear Him" must have something *of this nature*—that of Him and Him alone, if we except His like-minded Forerunner, they saw clearly it could not be said, "No man careth for my soul"—will be evident from the sequel. **2. And the Pharisees and scribes murmured, saying, This man receiveth sinners, and eateth with them.** They were scandalized at His procedure, and insinuated—on the principle that a man is known by the company he keeps—that He must have some secret sympathy with their *character*. But what a truth of unspeakable preciousness do their lips, as on other occasions, unconsciously utter! And Jesus will show them how divine the deed is. Here, accordingly, follow three parables, illustrating the principle on which He drew them to Himself and hailed any symptoms in them of return to God. The three parables, though the same in their general import, present the sinner each of them under a different aspect. The first, as *Bengel* acutely and laconically remarks, represents him, in his *stupidity*, as a silly sheep going astray; the second, like lost property, as '*unconscious of his lost condition;*' the third, as '*knowingly and wilfully estranged from God.*' The first two, as *Trench* well observes, set forth the *seeking* love of God; the last His *receiving* love.

The Parable of The Lost Sheep, *with the Moral of it* (3-7). This parable occurs again, and is recorded in Matt. xviii. 12-14; but there it is to show

3 ceiveth sinners, and [c]eateth with them. And he spake this parable unto
them, saying,
4 What [d]man of you, having an hundred sheep, if he [e]lose one of
them, doth not leave the ninety and nine in the wilderness, and go
5 after that which is lost, until he find it? And when he hath found *it*,
6 he layeth *it* on his shoulders, rejoicing. And when he cometh home, he
calleth together *his* friends and neighbours, saying unto them, Rejoice
7 with me; for I have found my sheep [f]which was lost. I say unto you,
That likewise joy shall be in heaven over one sinner that repenteth, [g]more
than over ninety and nine just persons, which need no repentance.
8 Either what woman, having ten [1]pieces of silver, if she lose one piece,
doth not light a candle, and sweep the house, and seek diligently till she
9 find *it?* And when she hath found *it*, she calleth *her* friends and *her*
neighbours together, saying, Rejoice with me; for I have found the piece
10 which I had lost. Likewise, I say unto you, There is joy in the presence
of the angels of God over one sinner that repenteth.
11, And he said, A certain man had two sons: and the younger of them
12 said to *his* father, Father, give me the portion of goods that falleth *to me.*

A. D. 33.

[c] Acts 11. 3.
[d] Matt. 18.12.
[e] 1 Pet. 2. 25.
[f] 1 Pet. 2. 10, 25.
[g] Pro. 30. 12.
1 Drachma, here translated a piece of silver, is the eighth part of an ounce, which cometh to seven-pence halfpenny, and is equal to the Roman penny.

how precious one of his sheep is to the good Shepherd; here, to show that the shepherd, though it stray never so widely, will seek it out, and when he hath found, will rejoice over it. **3. And he spake this parable unto them, saying, 4. What man of you, having an hundred sheep, if he lose one of them, doth not leave the ninety and nine in the wilderness.** Instead of saying, ''Tis but one; let it go; enough remain,' will he not bend all his attention and care, as it were, to the one object of recovering the lost sheep? **and go after that which is lost, until he find it?**—pointing to all the diversified means which God sets in operation for recovering sinners, and the patience and perseverance with which He continues to ply them. **6. And when he cometh home, he calleth together his friends and neighbours, saying unto them, Rejoice with me; for I have found my sheep which was lost.** It is a beautiful principle of our nature, that deep feeling, either of sorrow or of joy, is almost too much for one to bear alone, and that there is a feeling of positive relief in having others to share it. This principle our Lord here proclaims to be in operation even in the divine procedure. **7. I say unto you, That likewise joy shall be in heaven over one sinner that repenteth, more than over ninety and nine just persons, which need no repentance.** It is not *angels* who are meant here as needing no repentance. The angels' place in these parables is very different from this. The class here meant, as needing no repentance, are those represented by *the prodigal's well-behaved brother*, who have "served their Father many years," and not at any time transgressed His commandment—in the outrageous sense of the prodigal. (But see on *v.* 29, 31.) In other words, *such as have grown up from childhood* in the fear of God and as the sheep of His pasture. Our Lord does not say "the Pharisees and scribes" were such; but as there *was* undoubtedly such a class, while "the publicans and sinners" were confessedly the strayed sheep and the prodigal children, He leaves them to fill up the place of the other class, *if they could.*

The Parable of THE LOST COIN, *with the Moral of it* (8-10). **8. Either what woman, having ten pieces of silver, if she lose one piece, doth not light a candle, and sweep the house, and seek diligently till she find it? 9. And when she hath found it, she calleth her friends and her neighbours together, saying, Rejoice with me; for I have found the piece which I had lost. 10. Likewise**—that is, on the same principle, **there is joy in the presence of the angels of God over one sinner that repenteth.** Note carefully the language here employed: it is not, 'joy among' or 'on the part of,' but "joy before" [ἐνώπιον] or "*in the presence* of the angels of God." True to the idea of the parables, it is the Great Shepherd, the Great Owner Himself, *Whose* properly *the joy is over His own recovered property;* but so vast and exuberant is it (Zeph. iii. 17), that as if He could not keep it to Himself, He "calleth His friends and neighbours together"—His whole celestial family—"saying, Rejoice WITH ME, for I have found MY sheep, I have found MY property, which was lost. In this sublime sense it is "joy," *before* "*or in the presence of* the angels:" they only 'catch the flying joy,' sharing it *with Him!* The application of this to the reception of those publicans and sinners that stood around our Lord is grand in the extreme: 'Ye turn from these lost ones with disdain, and because I do not, ye murmur at it; but a very different feeling is cherished in heaven: There, the recovery of even one such outcast is watched with interest and hailed with joy; nor are they left to come home of themselves or perish; for, lo! even now the great Shepherd is going after His lost sheep, and the Owner is making diligent search for His lost property; and He is finding it too, and bringing it back with joy, and all heaven is full of it.' Let the reader mark what sublime claims for Himself our Lord covertly puts in here—as if in Him these outcasts beheld, though all unknown to themselves, nothing less than Heaven disclosing itself in the habiliments of earth, the Great Shepherd above, clothed in a garment of flesh, come "to seek and to save that which was lost"!

The Parable of THE PRODIGAL SON, *and the Case of his Elder Brother* (11-32). **11. And he said, A certain man had two sons: 12. And the younger of them**—as the more thoughtless, **said to his father, Father, give me the portion of goods that falleth to me**—weary of restraint, panting for independence, unable longer to abide the check of a father's eye. *This is man*, impatient of divine control, desiring to be independent of God, seeking to be his own master—that sin of sins, as *Trench* well says, in which all subsequent sins are included as in their germ, for they are but the unfolding of this one. **And he divided unto them his living.** Thus God, to use the words of

13 And he divided unto them [h]*his* living. And not many days after, the
younger son gathered all together, and took his journey into [i]a far
14 country, and there wasted his substance with riotous living. And when
he had spent all, there arose a mighty famine in that land; and he began
15 to be in want. And he went and joined himself to a citizen of that
16 country; and he sent him into his fields to feed swine. And he would
fain have filled his belly with the husks that the swine did eat: and no
17 man gave unto him. And when he came to himself, he said, How many
hired servants of my father's have bread enough, and to spare, and I
18 perish with hunger! I will [j]arise and go to my father, and will say unto

A. D. 33.

h Mark 12.44.
i Gen. 6. 5. Ps. 81. 12. Jer. 2. 5. Rom. 1. 21. Tit. 3. 3.
j 1 Ki. 20. 30. 2 Chr. 33.12, 13. Lam. 3. 40. Hos. 14. 3-7. Jon. 2. 4.

the same penetrating and accurate expositor of the parables, when His service no longer appears a perfect freedom, and man promises himself something far better elsewhere, allows him to make the trial; and he shall discover, if need be by saddest proof, that to depart from Him is not to throw off the yoke, but only to exchange a light yoke for a heavy one, and one gracious Master for a thousand imperious tyrants and lords. **13. And not many days after**—intoxicated with his new-found resources, and eager for the luxury of using them at will, **he took his journey into a far country**—away from the paternal eye, beyond all danger of rebuke or interference from home, **and there wasted his substance with riotous living** [ἀσώτως]—or 'to the destroying of himself.' His brother's charge against him, that he had "devoured his father's living with harlots," shows what is meant. But ah! this reaches deeper than sensuality. As the whole story is designed to set forth the degradation of our sonship, and the prostitution of our powers to purposes unworthy of our dignity and true destiny, we must understand the language as intended to express all that life of estrangement from God, self-seeking and low desire which are common, in different forms and degrees, to all who live "without God," who "have their portion in this life," who mind "earthly things." So long as his substance lasted, the inward monitor would be silenced, and the prodigal would take his ease, eat, drink, and be merry. At times, he would hear the whisper of expostulation, "Wherefore do ye spend money for that which is not bread, and your labour for that which satisfieth not?" (Isa. lv. 2). But though his means were fast fading, he would say to himself, "The bricks are fallen down, but we will build with hewn stones; the sycamores are cut down, but we will change them into cedars" (Isa. ix. 10). So long as anything remained, he would hold out. "Thou art wearied in the greatness of thy way: yet saidst thou not, There is no hope: thou hast found the life of thine hand: therefore thou wast not grieved" (Isa. lvii. 10). **14. And when he had spent all, there arose a mighty famine in that land**—a mysterious providence holding back the famine till he was in circumstances to feel it in all its rigour. Thus, like Jonah, whom the storm did not overtake till on the mighty deep at the mercy of the waves, does the sinner feel as if "the stars in their courses were fighting against" him (Jud. v. 20). **and he began to be in want**—the first stage of his bitter experience, and preparation for a change. **15. And he went and joined himself to a citizen of that country; and he sent him into his fields to feed swine.** His pride, it seems, was not yet humbled; he could not brook the shame of a return. Glad to keep life in any how, behold the son sunk into a swineherd; among the Jews, to whom swine's flesh was prohibited, emphatically vile! He, says *Trench*, who begins by using the world as a servant, to minister to his pleasure, ends by reversing the relationship. **16. And he would fain have filled his belly with the husks** [τῶν κερατίων] **that the swine did eat** [καὶ ἐπεθύμει γεμίσαι]—rather, 'was fain to fill,' or ate greedily of the only food he could get. These husks, or pulse-pods, were in the East the food of cattle and swine, and in times of distress were the nourishment of the very poorest people, as *Stier* remarks. **and no man gave unto him**—that is, no one minded him, to give him anything better than this. "All thy lovers have forgotten thee; they seek thee not: for I have wounded thee with the wound of an enemy, with the chastisement of a cruel one, for the multitude of thine iniquity; because thy sins were increased" (Jer. xxx. 14). This was his lowest depth: he was perishing unpitied; he was alone in the world; he was ready to disappear from it unmissed. But this is just the blessed turning-point—the midnight before dawn of day. "Thine own wickedness shall correct thee, and thy backslidings shall reprove thee: know therefore and see that it is an evil thing and bitter, that thou hast forsaken the Lord thy God" (Jer. ii. 19). "The Lord brought upon Manasseh's people the captains of the host of the king of Assyria, which took Manasseh among the thorns, and bound him with fetters, and carried him to Babylon. And when he was in affliction, he besought the Lord his God, and humbled himself greatly before the God of his fathers, and prayed unto Him; and He was entreated of him, and heard his supplication, and brought him again to Jerusalem into his kingdom. Then Manasseh knew that the Lord he was God" (2 Chron. xxxiii. 11-13; and see 2 Chr. xii. 7, 8). **17. And when he came to himself**—as if before he had been "beside himself." How truly does the wise man say, "*Madness* is in the heart of the sons of men while they live, and after that they go to the dead" (Eccl. ix. 3). But in what sense men far from God are beside themselves will presently appear more clearly. **he said, How many hired servants of my father's have bread enough, and to spare, and I perish with hunger!** What a testimony to the *nature* of the home he had left! But did he not know all this ere he departed, and every day of his voluntary exile? He did, and he did not. His heart being wholly estranged from home and steeped in selfish gratifications, his father's house never came within the range of his vision, or but as another name for bondage and gloom. Now empty, desolate, withered, perishing—*home*, with all its peace, plenty, freedom, dignity, starts into view, fills all his vision as a warm and living reality, and breaks his heart. **18. I WILL ARISE AND GO TO MY FATHER.** The change has come at last, and what a change!—couched in terms of such exquisite simplicity and power as if expressly framed for all heart-broken penitents. **and will say unto him, Father, I have sinned against Heaven, and before thee, 19. And am**

19 him, Father, [k]I have sinned against Heaven, and before thee, and am no
more worthy to be called thy son: make me as one of thy hired servants.
20 And he arose, and came to his father. But [l]when he was yet a great way
off, his father saw him, and had compassion, and ran, and fell on his neck,
21 and kissed him. And the son said unto him, Father, I have sinned
against Heaven, [m]and in thy sight, and am no more worthy to be called
22 thy son. But the father said to his servants, Bring forth [n]the best robe,
and put *it* on him; and put a ring on his hand, and shoes on *his* feet:
23 and bring hither the fatted calf, and kill *it;* and let us eat, and be
24 merry: for [o]this my son was dead, and is alive again; he was lost, and
is found. And they [p]began to be merry.
25 Now his elder son was in the field: and as he came and drew nigh to the
26 house, he heard music and dancing. And he called one of the servants, and
27 asked what these things meant. And he said unto him, Thy brother is
come; and thy father hath killed the fatted calf, because he hath received

A. D. 33.

k Lev. 26. 40, 41. 1 Ki. 8. 47, 48. Job 33. 27, 28.
l Isa. 49. 15. Acts 2. 39. Eph. 2. 13, 17.
m Ps. 51. 4.
n Matt. 22. 11. Gal. 3. 27. Rev. 19. 8.
o Eph. 2. 1. Eph. 5. 14. Col. 1. 13.
p Isa. 35. 10.

no more worthy to be called thy son: make me as one of thy hired servants. Mark the term, "Father." Though "no more *worthy* to be called his son," the prodigal sinner is taught to claim the *degraded* and *defiled*, but *still existing* relationship, asking, not to be *made* a servant, but *remaining a son* to be made "*as* a servant," willing to take the lowest place and do the meanest work. Ah! and is it come to this? Once it was, 'Any place rather than home.' Now, 'O that home! could I but dare to hope that the door of it would not be closed against me, how gladly should I take any place and do any work, happy only to be there at all!' Well, *that is conversion*—nothing absolutely new, yet all new; old familiar things seen in a new light, and for the first time as realities of overwhelming magnitude and power. By what secret supernatural power upon the heart this change upon the sinner's views and feelings is effected, the parable says not, and could not say, without an incongruous and confusing mixture of the figure and the thing figured—the human story and the spiritual reality couched under it. We have that, however, abundantly elsewhere, (Phil. ii. 13; 1 Cor. xv. 10, &c.) The one object of the parable is to paint the glad WELCOME HOME of the greatest sinners, when—no matter for the present *how*—they "arise and go to their father." **20. And he arose, and came to his father.** Many a one says, "I will arise," yet sits still. But this is the story of a real conversion, in which purpose is presently turned into practice. **But when he was yet a great way off, his father saw him, and ran.** O yes! when the face is turned homeward, though as yet far, far away, our Father recognizes his own child in us, and bounds to meet us—not saying, 'Let him come to me and sue for pardon first,' but Himself taking the first step. **and fell on his neck, and kissed him.** What! In all his filth? Yes. In all his rags? Yes. In all his haggard, shattered wretchedness? Yes. "Our Father who art in heaven," is this Thy portraiture? It is even so. And because it is so, I wonder not that such incomparable teaching hath made the world new. "Is Ephraim my dear son? Is he a pleasant child? For since I spake against him, I do earnestly remember him still: therefore my bowels are troubled for him; I will surely have mercy upon him, saith the Lord" (Jer. xxxi. 20). **21. And the son said unto him, Father, I have sinned against Heaven, and in thy sight, and am no more worthy to be called thy son.** This humiliating confession he might have spared, if his object had been mere re-admission to the *advantages* of the parental roof. But the case depicted is one in which such heartless selfishness has no place, and in which such a thought would be abhorred. No, this confession was uttered, as *Trench* well remarks, *after the kiss of reconciliation.* **22. But the father said.** The son has not said all he purposed, but the explanation of this given by *Trench*, &c., appears to us to miss the mark—that the father's demonstrations had rekindled the filial, and swallowed up all servile feeling. It is, in our judgment, rather because the father's heart is made to appear too full to listen at such a moment to more in this strain. **to his servants.** We know who these represent, in all the three parables spoken on this occasion: they are "the angels of God" (*vv.* 7-10). **Bring forth the best robe, and put it on him.** Compare Zec. iii. 4, 5, "And He answered and spake unto those that stood by, saying, Take away the filthy garments from him. And unto him he said, Behold, I have caused thine iniquity to pass from thee, and I will clothe thee with change of raiment. . . And they clothed him with garments. And the angel of the Lord stood by." See also Isa. lxi. 10; Rev. iii. 18. **and put a ring on his hand.** Compare Gen. xli. 42. **and shoes on his feet.** Slaves went barefoot. Thus have we here a threefold symbol both of *freedom* and of *honour* as the fruit of *perfect reconciliation.* **23. And bring hither the fatted calf**—kept for festive occasions, **and kill it; and let us eat, and be merry**—denoting the exultation of the whole household: "Likewise, I say unto you, there is joy in the presence of the angels of God over one sinner that repenteth" (*v.* 10). But though the joy ran through the whole household, it was properly the *father's* matter. Accordingly it is added, **24. For this my son was dead, and is alive again; he was lost, and is found.** Now, twice his son. "He was lost"—both to his Father and to himself, lost to his Father's service and satisfaction, lost to his own dignity, peace, profit. But he "is alive again"—to all these.

But what of the elder brother all this time? That we are now to see.

25. Now his elder son was in the field—engaged in his father's business. Compare *v.* 29, "Lo, these many years do I *serve* thee." **and as he came and drew nigh to the house, he heard music and dancing. 26. And he called one of the servants.** [The *Stephanic* form of the received text has "his servants;" but our Version properly follows the *Elzevir* form, "the servants," which has decisive weight of external evidence, while the internal evidence is even more decisive.] **and asked what these things meant. 27. And he said unto him, Thy brother is come; and thy father hath killed the fatted calf, because he hath received him safe and sound. 28. And he was**

28 him safe and sound. And [q] he was angry, and would not go in: therefore
29 came his father out, and entreated him. And he answering said to *his* father,
Lo, these many years do I serve thee, neither transgressed I at any time thy
commandment; and [r] yet thou never gavest me a kid, that I might make
30 merry with my friends: but as soon as this thy son was come, which hath
devoured thy living with harlots, thou hast killed for him the fatted calf.
31 And he said unto him, Son, thou art ever with me, and all that I have
32 is thine. It [s] was meet that we should make merry and be glad: for this
thy brother was dead, and is alive again; and was lost, and is found.

A. D. 33.

[q] 1Sam. 17. 28. Isa. 65. 5. Jon. 4. 1-3. Acts 11. 2.
[r] Matt. 20. 11, 12.
[s] Ps. 51. 8. Isa. 35. 10. Jon. 4. 10. Rom. 15. 9-12.

angry, and would not go in: therefore came his father out, and entreated him. As it is the elder brother who now errs, so it is *the same paternal compassion* which had fallen on the neck of the younger that comes forth and pleads with the elder. "Like as a father pitieth his children, so the Lord pitieth them that fear him" (Ps. ciii. 13). **29. And he answering said to his father, Lo, these many years do I serve thee, neither transgressed I at any time thy commandment.** These last words are not to be pressed beyond their manifest intention—to express the constancy of his own love and service as a son towards his father, in contrast with the conduct of his brother. So Job, when resenting the charge of *hypocrisy*, brought against him by his friends, speaks as if nothing whatever could be laid to his charge: "When he hath tried me, I shall come forth as gold," &c. (Job xxiii. 10-12). And David too (Ps. xviii. 20-24); and the Church, in a time of persecution for righteousness' sake (Ps. xliv. 17-22). And the father in the sequel of this parable (*v.* 31) attests the truth of his son's protestation. **and yet thou never gavest me a kid**—'I say not a *calf*, but not even a *kid*,' **that I might make merry with my friends.** Here lay his misapprehension. It was no entertainment for the gratification of the prodigal: it was a *father's* expression of the joy *he* felt at his recovery. **30. But as soon as this thy son was come, which hath devoured thy living with harlots, thou hast killed for him the fatted calf.** Mark the unworthy reflection on the common father of both, implied in these expressions—"*thy* son," "*thy* living;" the one brother not only disowning the other, but flinging him back upon his father, as if he should say, 'If such be the emotions which his return awakens, take him, and have joy of him!' **31. And he said unto him, Son, thou art ever with me, and all that I have is thine.** The father resents not the insult—how could he, after the largeness of heart which had kissed the returning prodigal? He calmly expostulates with him, 'Son, listen to reason. What need for special, exuberant joy over thee? Saidst thou not, "Lo, these many years do I serve thee"? Wherefore then set the whole household a rejoicing over thee? For thee is reserved *what is higher still*—the tranquil lifelong satisfaction of thy father in thee, as a true-hearted faithful son in thy father's house; nor of the inheritance reserved for thee is aught alienated by this festive and fitting joy over the once foolish but now wise and newly recovered son.' **32. It was meet that we should make merry and be glad: for this thy brother was dead, and is alive again; and was lost, and is found.** Should he simply take his long-vacant place in the family, without one special sign of wonder and delight at the change? Would that have been *nature?* But *this* being the meaning of the festivity, it would for that very reason be *temporary.* In time, the dutifulness of even the younger son would become the *law* and not the *exception:* he too at length might venture to say, "Lo, these many years do I serve thee;" and of him the father would say, "Son, thou art ever with me." And then it would *not* be "meet that they should make merry and be glad"—as at his first return.

Remarks.—1. The estrangement of the human spirit from God is the deepest and most universal malady of our nature. It may take the form either of impatience of divine authority or of want of sympathy with the things wherein He delighteth. But important as is the distinction between these two forms of estrangement from God, they naturally run into each other, and are inseparable. In placid and amiable natures, what shows itself chiefly is *disrelish of spiritual things.* This may not take any active form, and in that case it is only perceptible in the heart's entire satisfaction *without God.* No fellowship with Him, or even thought of Him, is necessary to such. They get on perfectly well, and even better, when every such thought is away. This is truly a godless life, but it is the life of many of the most attractive and accomplished members of society. In young men it is apt to take the form of dislike of the restraints which divine authority imposes, and a desire to get free from them. But in all, it is the same malady at bottom, with which our fallen nature is smitten. 2. The extent to which men *go from God* varies as much as men themselves; but the freedom they assert in this condition is but bondage under another name. 3. It is not every discovery of the folly and bitterness of departure from God that will move the heart to retrace its steps; often matters go from bad to worse before any decisive change is resolved on; and in most cases it is only when the soul is brought to extremities that it says in earnest, "I will arise and go to my Father." And when, upon so doing, we are welcomed back, and feel the bond that binds us to our Father even firmer and dearer than if we had never departed, we find ours to be just such a case as the sweet Psalmist of Israel sings of: "Such as sit in darkness, and in the shadow of death, being bound in affliction and iron; because they rebelled against the words of God, and contemned the counsel of the Most High: therefore he brought down their heart with labour: they fell down, and there was none to help. Then they cried unto the Lord in their trouble, and he saved them out of their distresses. He brought them out of darkness and the shadow of death, and brake their bands in sunder:—O that men would praise the Lord for his goodness, and for his wonderful works to the children of men!" (Ps. cvii. 10-15.) 4. The pardon of sin is absolutely gratuitous, and reaches down to the lowest depths of estrangement from God and rebellion against his precepts. The one thing required is to "arise and go to our Father." "Go and proclaim these words toward the north, and say, *Return,* thou backsliding Israel, saith the Lord; and I will not cause mine anger to fall upon you: Only acknowledge thine iniquity, and I

16 AND he said also unto his disciples, There was a certain [a]rich man
which had a steward; and the same was accused unto him that he had
2 wasted his goods. And he called him, and said unto him, How is it that
I hear this of thee? give an account [b]of thy stewardship; for thou mayest
3 be no longer steward. Then the steward said within himself, What shall
I do? for my lord taketh away from me the stewardship: I cannot dig;
4 to beg I am ashamed. I am resolved what to do, that, when I am put
out of the stewardship, they may receive me into their houses.
5 So he called every one of his lord's debtors *unto him*, and said unto the
6 first, How much owest thou unto my lord? And he said, An hundred
[1]measures of oil. And he said unto him, Take thy bill, and sit down

A. D. 33.

CHAP. 16.
[a] Ps. 24. 1.
[b] Matt. 12. 36. Rom. 14. 12.
[1] The word Batus, in the original, containeth nine gallons three quarts. Ezek. 45. 10, 11, 14.

will not cause mine anger to fall upon thee." 5. The sense of reconciliation to God, instead of checking, only deepens the grief of the pardoned believer for the sin that has been forgiven: "That thou mayest remember, and be confounded, and never open thy mouth any more because of thy shame, *when I am pacified toward thee for all that thou hast done*, saith the Lord God." (Ezek. xvi. 63). 'True repentance,' says Dr. Owen, 'waters a free pardon with tears, detests forgiven sin, and aims at the ruin of that which we are assured shall never ruin us.' 6. The deeper sunk and the longer estranged from God any sinner is, the more exuberant is the joy which his recovery occasions. All heaven is represented as ringing with it, while he himself breaks forth into such songs as these—"He brought me up out of a horrible pit, out of the miry clay, and set my feet upon a rock, and established my goings. And He hath put a new song into my mouth, even praise unto our God: Many shall see it, and fear, and trust in the Lord" (Ps. xl. 2, 3). But, 7. This joy over returning prodigals is *not* the portion of those whose whole lives have been spent in the service of their Father in heaven. Yet, instead of grudging the want of this, they should deem it the highest testimony to their life-long fidelity, that something better is reserved for them—the deep, abiding complacency of their Father in heaven. 8. In giving such an interpretation of the parable of the Prodigal Son as, in our judgment, bears consistency with all Scripture truth on its face, we have not adverted to interpretations which seem to us to miss the mark. The notion of not a few, that the younger son represents the *Gentiles*, who early strayed from God, and the elder the *Jews*, who abode true to Him, is rejected by the best expositors; and no wonder, since the publicans and sinners, whose welcome back to God is illustrated by the reception of the prodigal, were Jews and not Gentiles. Clearly this parable has to do, not with nationalities, but with classes or characters. But most interpreters—even such as *Trench*—misapprehend, we think, almost entirely the truth intended to be taught by the conduct of the elder son—who, he thinks, 'represents a form of legal righteousness, not altogether false, but low; who has been kept by the law from gross offences,' &c. Let the reader judge whether this interpretation, or that which we have given is the more consistent and eligible. 9. Was ever teaching like this heard on earth? Did even the Mouth that spake as never man spake utter such words of grace to the vilest—for fulness and melting tenderness of love—on any other recorded occasion? This is the *Gospel within the Gospel*, as it has been well called; and it will stand, while the world lasts, an evidence which no unsophisticated mind can resist, that He who uttered it must have come forth from the very bosom of the Father to declare it, and that him that cometh to Him He will in no wise cast out.

CHAP. XVI. 1-31.—THE PARABLE OF THE UNJUST STEWARD, AND FURTHER TEACHING SUGGESTED BY IT—THE PARABLE OF THE RICH MAN AND LAZARUS. No indication is given of the time and occasion of these two parables—as usual in this portion of our Gospel. (See opening remarks on ch. ix. 51.) But they appear to be in their natural order after the preceding, and a certain distant connection with them has been traced.

The Parable of the Unjust Steward (1-9). This parable has occasioned more discussion and diversity of opinion than all the rest. But judicious interpreters are now pretty much agreed as to its general import. **1. And he said also unto his disciples**—not the Twelve exclusively, but His followers in the wider sense: **There was a certain rich man**—denoting the Great Lord of all, "the most high God, Possessor of heaven and earth," **which had a steward** [οἰκονόμον]—the manager of his estate; representing all who have gifts divinely committed to their *trust*, and so answering pretty nearly to the "servants" in the parable of the *Talents*, to whom were committed their lord's "goods." **and the same was accused** [διεβλήθη] **unto him that he had wasted his goods** [διασκορπίζων]—rather, 'was wasting his goods.' The word signifies to 'scatter,' and so to 'waste.' Information to this effect was lodged with his master. **2. And he called him, and said unto him, How is it that I hear this of thee?** And thus does God from time to time—now by startling providences, and now in the secret whispers of conscience—charge home its abuse of gifts, and manifold guilt, very sharply upon the soul. **give an account of thy stewardship**—render up whatever has been entrusted to thee, that I may transfer it to other hands, **for thou mayest be no longer steward. 3. Then the steward said within himself, What shall I do? for my lord taketh away from me the stewardship.** His guilt is tacitly admitted, and his one question now is, what is to become of him? **I cannot dig**—brought up as I have been to higher work; **to beg I am ashamed**—his pride could not stand that. What, then, was to be done to prevent starvation? **4. I am resolved what to do, that, when I am put out of the stewardship, they may receive me into their houses**—'in grateful return for the services I am going to do them.' Thus his one object was, *when cast out of one home to secure another.* This will be found to be the great lesson of the parable.

5. So he called every one of his lord's debtors unto him, and said unto the first, How much owest thou unto my lord? 6. And he said, An hundred measures of oil [βάτους]. The word indicates a prodigious debt. **And he said unto him, Take thy bill, and sit down quickly**—the business being urgent, **and write fifty**—'write a receipt for only half that quantity: the master, to be sure, will be defrauded, but he will never discover it, and thus half your debt is at once wiped out.' **7. Then**

7 quickly, and write fifty. Then said he to another, And how much owest
thou? And he said, An hundred [2]measures of wheat. And he said unto
8 him, Take thy bill, and write fourscore. And the lord commended the
unjust steward, because he had done wisely: for the children of this
world are in their generation wiser than [c]the children of light.
9 And I say unto you, [d]Make to yourselves friends of the [3]mammon of
unrighteousness; that, when ye fail, they may receive you into everlasting

A. D. 33.

[2] About fourteen bushels and a pottle.
[c] John 12.36.
[d] ch. 11. 41.
[3] Or, riches.

said he to another, And how much owest thou? And he said, An hundred measures [κόρους] **of wheat**—also a heavy debt. **And he said unto him, Take thy bill, and write fourscore**—or a fifth less than the actual debt. There is nothing of spiritual significance in these amounts. They represent merely the shrewdness with which the steward dealt with each debtor, with sole reference probably to the greater or less ability of each to render a grateful return to himself when cast upon the world. **8. And the lord**—that is, the steward's lord, as he is expressly called in *vv.* 3, 5, **commended the unjust steward**—not the injustice of the steward; for what master would praise his servant for defrauding him? but he commended the man, **because he had done wisely** [φρονίμως]—'shrewdly,' 'sagaciously,' 'prudently;' with commendable promptitude, foresight, and skilful adaptation of means to end: for "men will praise thee when thou doest well to thyself" (Ps. xlix. 18): **for**—this, now, is the reflection of the glorious Speaker of the parable, **the children of this world are in their generation** [εἰς τὴν γενεὰν τὴν ἑαυτῶν]—rather, 'for their own generation;' that is, for the purposes of their own kind, or sort, or class; their own sphere of interest and action, **wiser** [φρονιμώτεροι]—'shrewder' **than the children of** [the] **light** [τοῦ φωτός]. Let us examine this most weighty saying. It divides all men, according to the all-pervading doctrine of Scripture, into two great classes. The one is called "THE CHILDREN OF THIS WORLD" [τοῦ αἰῶνος τούτου]—(see on Eph. ii. 2), meaning what we call *worldlings.* The Psalmist, after calling this class "men of this world," gives the following striking definition of what he means—"who *have their portion in this life*" (Ps. xvii. 14); and of the same class the apostle says, they "mind" [φρονοῦντες] or 'are taken up with,' "earthly things" (Phil. iii. 19). Their whole ambition, whether their inclinations be grovelling or refined, is bounded by the present sphere, and they have no taste for anything beyond it. The other class are beautifully called "THE CHILDREN OF LIGHT," as being the offspring of supernatural heavenly teaching, for "God, who commanded the light to shine out of darkness, hath shined in our hearts, to give the light of the knowledge of the glory of God in the face of Jesus Christ" (2 Cor. iv. 6). "While ye have the Light [τὸ φῶς], believe in the light, that ye may be the children of light" (John xii. 36). "Ye are all the children of the light and of the day" (1 Thess. v. 5). See also Eph. v. 8. And yet, though the latter class are to the former as superior as light is to darkness, the children of this world have in one point the advantage of the children of light—they excel them in the shrewdness with which they prosecute their proper business. It is not that they are more truly wise; but that in their own sphere they display a sagacity which the children of light may well emulate, and should strive to outdo. Their sphere is indeed a wretched enough one. But let the children of light observe what a definite and firm grasp they take of the objects at which they aim; how shrewdly they adapt their means to their ends, and with what untiring energy, determination, and perseverance they prosecute their purposes. All these are wasted, to be sure, on perishable objects and in fleeting enjoyments. Spiritual and eternal realities are a region they never penetrate—the new life is an air they never breathe, an undiscovered world, an unborn existence: they know nothing, sympathize with nothing, live for nothing but "their own generation." But why should such excel the children of light *in anything?* This is exactly what our Lord here says they *should not;* and in giving forth this parable He would stir up our jealousy to roll away that reproach—just as on another occasion He sends us for lessons of this same "wisdom" to venomous "serpents" (Matt. x. 16).

Further Teaching suggested by this Parable (9-18). Having laid down the great general principle, that 'it is not enough to have a high and holy *sphere* of action, but there must be such a discreet and determined prosecution of its objects as the children of this world so much excel in'—our Lord now comes to particulars; and, first, to that point of wisdom which the parable most directly illustrates. **9. And I say unto you, Make to yourselves friends of** [ἐκ]—rather, 'out of' **the mammon of unrighteousness**—that is, by the help of it. The word "mammon" [μαμωνᾶς]—on which see on Matt. vi. 24—stands here just for those *riches* which the children of this world idolize, or live supremely for; and it is called "the mammon of unrighteousness," or "the unrighteous mammon" (*v.* 11), apparently because of the unrighteous abuse of it which so prevails. The injunction, then, is to this effect: 'Turn to your own highest advantage those riches which the unrighteous so shamefully abuse, in the spirit of that forecasting sagacity which this unjust steward displayed.' **that when ye fail** [ὅταν ἐκλίπητε]—that is, in respect of life: a remarkable expression, but suggested here, as we think, from a certain analogy which our departure from this world has to the *breaking up* of the steward's comfortable condition, and his being forced to *quit.* [*Lachmann* and *Tregelles,* retaining the same aoristic tense, adopt the singular ἐκλίπῃ—'when it has failed;' while *Tischendorf* prefers the present tense, ἐκλείπῃ, also in the singular—'when it fails.' *Meyer* and *Alford,* too, decide in favour of the singular, for which the authority is perhaps greater than for the plural of the received text. But even if we should have to adopt this reading, the sense must be held the same; we must still understand our Lord to speak, on that supposition, of the failure of mammon solely by our removal from the present scene.] **they may receive you**—that is, the "friends" ye make by the mammon of unrighteousness. **into everlasting habitations**—into "mansions" more durable than this steward was welcomed into when turned out of doors. But how are these friends to receive us into everlasting habitations? By rising up as witnesses of what we did in their behalf for Jesus' sake. Thus, the only difference between this view of the saints' admission to heaven and that in our Lord's grand description of the Last Judgment (Matt. xxv. 34-40) is, that there Christ Himself as Judge speaks for them, in the character of omniscient

10 habitations. He [e]that is faithful in that which is least is faithful also in
11 much; and he that is unjust in the least is unjust also in much. If
therefore ye have not been faithful in the unrighteous [4]mammon, who will
12 commit to your trust the [f]true *riches?* And if ye have not been faithful
in that which is another man's, who shall give you that which is your own?
13 No [g]servant can serve two masters: for either he will hate the one, and
love the other; or else he will hold to the one, and despise the other.
Ye cannot serve God and mammon.
14 And the Pharisees also, [h]who were covetous, heard all these things:
15 and they derided him. And he said unto them, Ye are they which
[i]justify yourselves before men; but God [j]knoweth your hearts: for [k]that
which is highly esteemed among men is abomination in the sight of
16 God. The [l]Law and the Prophets *were* until John: since that time the
17 kingdom of God is preached, and every man presseth into it. And [m]it
is easier for heaven and earth to pass, than one tittle of the Law to fail.
18 Whosoever [n]putteth away his wife, and marrieth another, committeth
adultery: and whosoever marrieth her that is put away from *her* husband
committeth adultery.

A. D. 33.
[e] Matt. 25. 21. ch. 19. 17.
[4] Or, riches.
[f] Eph. 3. 8. Rev. 3 18.
[g] Matt. 6. 24.
[h] Matt. 23. 14.
[i] ch. 10. 29. ch. 11. 39, 40. Jas. 2. 21-25.
[j] Ps. 7. 9. Jer. 17. 10. Rev. 2. 23.
[k] 1 Sam. 16. 7. Jas. 4. 4.
[l] Matt. 11. 12.
[m] Ps. 102. 26, 27. Isa. 40. 8. Isa. 51. 6. 1 Pet. 1. 25.
[n] 1 Cor. 7. 10.

Spectator of their acts of beneficence to "His brethren;" while here, these brethren of Jesus are supposed to be the speakers in their behalf. There, Christ says, "I was an hungered, and ye gave Me meat;" for "inasmuch as ye did it unto the least of these my brethren, ye did it unto me." Here, these least of Christ's brethren themselves come forward, one after another, saying, 'I was hungry, and that dear saint gave me bread;' 'and I was naked, and that other saint clothed me;' 'and I was sick, and that saint there paid me such heavenly visits;' 'and I was in prison for Thy name's sake, but that fearless one came unto me, and was not ashamed of my chain.' 'And they did it unto Thee, Lord!' "Come, then," will the King say unto them, "ye blessed of My Father, inherit the kingdom prepared for you from the foundation of the world." 'Thus, like this steward (so teaches Jesus here), when turned out of one home shall ye secure another; but better than he, a heavenly for an earthly, an everlasting for a temporary habitation.' Money is not here made the key to heaven, more than "the deeds done in the body" in general, according to which, as a test of character—not by the merit of which—men are to be judged (2 Cor. v. 10). See on Matt. xxv. 31-40, with the corresponding Remarks at the close of that Section. **10. He that is faithful in that which is least is faithful also in much; and he that is unjust in the least is unjust also in much.** A maxim of great pregnancy and value; advancing now from the *prudence* which the steward had, to the *fidelity* which he had not; to that "*harmlessness* of the dove" to which "the serpent," with all his "*wisdom*" or subtilty is a total stranger. But what bearing has this maxim on the subject of our parable? A very close connection. 'As for me (some would say) I have too little of "the unrighteous mammon" to be much interested in this parable.' 'You are wrong,' is the reply: 'That is the speech of the slothful servant, who, because he was entrusted with but one talent by his master, went and hid it in the earth instead of using it. Fidelity depends not on the *amount entrusted*, but on the *sense of responsibility*. He that feels this in little will feel it in much, and conversely.' **11. If therefore ye have not been faithful in the unrighteous mammon**—or, "the mammon of unrighteousness" (*v.* 9), **who will commit to your trust the true riches?**—that which makes one truly rich, the riches of the kingdom above. **12. And if ye have not been faithful in that which is another man's**—the pecuniary and other earthly means which are but *lent* us, and must be held at best as only *entrusted* to us, **who shall give you that which is your own?** This verse gives an important turn to the subject. Here all we have is *on trust* as stewards, who have an account to render. Hereafter, what the faithful have will be *their own property*, being no longer on probation, but in secure, undisturbed, rightful, everlasting possession and enjoyment of all that is graciously bestowed on us. Thus money is neither to be *idolized* nor *despised:* we must sit loose to it, but use it for God's glory. **No servant can serve**—or, *be entirely at the command of* **two masters.** This is true even where there is no hostility between them: how much more where they are in deadly opposition! **for either he will hate the one, and love the other; or else he will hold to the one, and despise the other. Ye cannot serve God and mammon.** This shows that the two masters here intended are such as are in uncompromising hostility to each other. (See on the same saying in the Sermon on the Mount, Matt. vi. 24.)

14. And the Pharisees also, who were covetous, heard all these things: and they derided him. [ἐξημυκτήριζον]—sneered at Him; their master, sin, being too plainly struck at. But it was easier to *ridicule* than to *refute* such teaching. **15. And he said unto them, Ye are they which justify yourselves**—make a show of righteousness **before men; but God knoweth your hearts: for that which is highly esteemed among men**—who are easily carried away by plausible appearances (see 1 Sam. xvi. 7; and ch. xiv. 11), **is abomination in the sight of God**—who, Himself true, loathes all hypocrisy. **16. The Law and the Prophets were until John: since that time the kingdom of God is preached, and every man presseth into it.** 'While publicans and sinners are eagerly pressing into the kingdom of God, ye, interested adherents of the mere forms of an economy which is passing away, "discerning not the signs of this time," are allowing the tide to go past you, and will be found a stranded monument of blindness and obstinacy.' **17. And it is easier for heaven and earth to pass, than one tittle of the Law to fail.** See on Matt. v. 17, 18. **18. Whosoever putteth away his wife, and marrieth another, committeth adultery: and whosoever marrieth her that is put away from her husband committeth adultery.** See on Matt. xix. 3-9. Far from intend-

19 There was a certain rich man, which was clothed in purple and fine
20 linen, and fared sumptuously every day: and there was a certain beggar
21 named Lazarus, which was laid at his gate, [o]full of sores, and desiring to
be fed with the crumbs which fell from the rich man's table: moreover
22 the dogs came and licked his sores. And it came to pass, that the
beggar died, and [p]was carried by the angels into Abraham's [q]bosom: the
23 rich man also died, and was buried; and in hell he lifted up his eyes,
being in torments, and seeth Abraham afar off, and Lazarus in his bosom.
24 And he cried and said, Father Abraham, have mercy on me, and send
Lazarus, that he may dip the tip of his finger in water, and [r]cool my
25 tongue; for I [s]am tormented in this flame. But Abraham said, Son,
[t]remember that thou in thy lifetime receivedst thy good things, and
likewise Lazarus evil things: but now he is comforted, and thou art

A. D. 33.

o Heb. 11. 37.
p Ps. 34. 7. Ps. 91. 10, 12. Ps. 103. 20. Heb 1. 14. Jas. 2. 5.
q Matt. 8. 11.
r Zec. 14. 12.
s Isa. 66. 24. Mark 9. 44. Heb. 10. 31.
t Job 21. 13. Ps. 17. 14. ch. 6. 24. Rom. 8. 7.

ing to weaken the force of the law, by these allusions to a new economy, our Lord only sends home, in this unexpected way, its high requirements with a pungency which the Pharisees would not fail to feel.

The Parable of the Rich Man and Lazarus (19-31). This parable, being precisely the converse of the former, was evidently spoken immediately after it, and designed to complete the lesson of *The Right Use of Riches.* As the steward made himself *friends* out of the mammon of unrighteousness, so this rich man made himself, out of the same mammon, an *enemy*—in the person of Lazarus—of a kind to make the ears of every one that heareth it to tingle. As, by acting for eternity, in the spirit of this steward for time, the friends we thus make will on our removal from this scene "receive us into everlasting habitations," so by acting, even while professing to be Christians, in the spirit of this rich man, the enemies we thus make will rise up to shut us out for ever from the mansions of the blest. Such is the striking connection between these two parables. This last one, however, is altogether of a higher order and deeper significance than the former. The thin veil—of exclusion from one earthly home only to be followed by admission into others equally earthly—is thrown off; and the awful bearing of the use we now make of the mammon of unrighteousness upon our eternal state is presented before the eye in the light of the eternal flames, insomuch that the lurid glare of the scene abides with even the most cursory reader.

19. There was a certain rich man [Ἄνθρωπος δὲ τις]. The connecting particle should not have been omitted here—'But there was a certain rich man;' in contrast with the man of the former parable: **which was clothed in purple and fine linen** (See Esth. viii. 15; Rev. xviii. 12), **and fared sumptuously every day**—wanting for nothing which appetite craved, and taste fancied, and money could procure. **20. And there was a certain beggar named Lazarus**—equivalent to the Old Testament *Eleazer.* The naming of this precious saint adds much to the liveliness of the picture; but to conclude from this that the story was founded on fact, is going rather far. Cases of this heartless nature are, alas, but too common everywhere. **which was laid at his gate.** So he had to be carried and laid down at it. **full of sores**—open, running sores, which, as appears from the next verse, had not been closed, nor bound up, nor mollified with ointment (Isa. i. 6). **21. And desiring to be fed** [ἐπιθυμῶν χορτασθῆναι] **with the crumbs which fell from the rich man's table.** The meaning may either be (as in ch. xv. 16), that 'he was fain to feed' or 'gladly fed,' as *Alford, Webster and Wilkinson*, &c., take it; or he 'desired to be fed,' but was not: so *Grotius, Bengel, Meyer, Trench*, &c., understand it. The context seems rather to favour this latter view. **moreover the dogs came and licked his sores**—a touching act of brute pity in the absence of human relief. Thus have we here a case of heartless indifference, amidst luxuries of every kind, to one of God's poorest and most afflicted ones, presented daily before the view. **22. And it came to pass, that the beggar died, and was carried by the angels into Abraham's bosom**—as if he had been seen reclining next to him at the heavenly feast (see on ch. vii. 9). **the rich man also died, and was buried.** The burial of the beggar was too unimportant to mention; but it is said, "the rich man died, and was *buried*"—his carcase borne in pomp to its earthly resting-place. **23. And in hell he lifted up his eyes** [ἐν τῷ ᾅδῃ]—not the final region of the lost, for which another word is used [γέεννα] (Mark ix. 43, 45, 47, &c.), but what we call 'the unseen world.' Yet since the object here is certainly to depict *the whole torment* of the one and *the perfect bliss* of the other, it comes in this case to much the same thing. **being in torments, and seeth Abraham afar off**—quite beyond his reach, yet not beyond his view. **and Lazarus in his bosom. 24. And he cried and said, Father Abraham**—a well-founded but unavailing claim of natural descent (see ch. iii. 8; John viii. 37), **have mercy on me**—'Have mercy on me who never showed any mercy to my fellow-men.' Not daring to cry to God, he applies in his desperation to one who has no power to help him. **and send Lazarus**—the pining victim of his merciless neglect, **that he may**—do what? take him out of that place of torment? No, that he presumes not to ask; but merely, **that he may dip the tip of his finger in water, and cool my tongue; for I am tormented in this flame.** What does this wretched man ask? He asks the *least* conceivable and the *most momentary* abatement of his torment—that is all. But even that is denied him, for two awfully weighty reasons. First, IT IS UNREASONABLE. **25. But Abraham said, Son**—a stinging acknowledgment this of the *natural* relationship to him which he had claimed: **remember that thou in thy lifetime receivedst thy good things, and likewise Lazarus evil things: but now he is comforted, and thou art tormented.** As it is a great law of God's kingdom that 'the nature of our present desires shall rule that of our future bliss,' so by that law, he whose "good things," craved and enjoyed, were all bounded by time, could look for none after his connection with time had come to an end (see ch. vi. 24). But by the same law, he whose "evil things," all crowded into the present life, drove him to seek, and find, consolation in a

26 tormented. And besides all this, between us and you there is [u]a great
gulf fixed: so that they which would pass from hence to you cannot;
27 neither can they pass to us, that *would come* from thence. Then he said,
I pray thee therefore, father, that thou wouldest send him to my father's
28 house: for I have five brethren; that he may testify unto them, lest
29 they also come into this place of torment. Abraham saith unto him,
30 [v]They have Moses and the Prophets; let them hear them. And he said,
Nay, father Abraham: but if one went unto them from the dead, they

A. D. 33.

[u] 2 Thes. 1. 9.

[v] Isa. 8. 20. Isa. 34. 16. John 5. 39, 45. Acts 15. 21. Acts 17. 11. 2 Tim. 3. 15.

life beyond the grave, is by death released from all evil and ushered into unmixed and uninterrupted good. See ch. vi. 21. But secondly, IT IS IMPOSSIBLE. **26. And besides all this**—independently of this consideration, **between us and you there is a great gulf fixed: so that they which would pass from hence to you cannot; neither can they pass to us, that would come from thence.** 'By an irrevocable decree there has been established [ἐστήρικται] a vast impassable abyss between the two states and the occupants of each.' **27. Then he said**—now abandoning all hope, not only of release but relief for himself, and directing his thoughts to others, **I pray thee therefore, father, that thou wouldest send him to my father's house: 28. For I have five brethren; that he may testify unto them, lest they also come into this place of torment.** There is here no waking up of good in the heart of the lost, but, as *Trench* acutely remarks, bitter reproach against God and the old economy, as not having warned him sufficiently. Abraham's answer rolls back the reproach with calm dignity, as unmerited: 'They *are* sufficiently warned.' **29. Abraham saith unto him, They have Moses and the Prophets; let them hear them.** Still this does not satisfy. **30. And he said, Nay, father Abraham**—giving him the lie, **but if one went unto them from the dead, they will repent.** What a reply now is given to this, shutting up the dialogue where it ought to close—when nothing more remains to be said on the one hand, and nothing can be replied on the other. **31. And he said unto him, If they hear not Moses and the Prophets, neither will they be persuaded though one rose from the dead.** A principle of awful magnitude and importance. The greatest miracle will have no effect on those who are determined not to believe. A *real* Lazarus soon "rose from the dead;" but the sight of him by crowds of people, who were thereby drawn so far towards Christ, only crowned the unbelief and hastened the murderous plots of the Pharisees against the Lord of glory; nor has *His own resurrection*, far more overpowering, yet won over that "crooked and perverse nation."

Remarks.—1. The parable of the Unjust Steward has this in common with the Parable of the *Talents* (Matt. xxv. 14-30), that both represent all we possess as a sacred *Trust* committed to us; for the right use of which we are responsible; and the actual use made of which shall go to determine our eternal state. But in the Parable of the Talents the trust intended comprehends *all endowments* whatsoever that may be turned to the service of Christ; here it is *money* alone, the love of which is the root of all evil (1 Tim. vi. 10), and whose slaves and worshippers were among the audience to which it was addressed (*v.* 13, 14). There, the talents are to be used for the *Master's* interest; here, the immediate object is to enforce such a use of money as may promote *our own* interest in the highest sense of it. Thus, the same general subject has different aspects, which, though consistent, are not to be confounded. 2. Let us ponder the Lord's weighty saying, that the children of this world are in their generation wiser than the children of light. 'These religious people (methinks I hear some supercilious observer of Christians say—so very impartial as to be "neither cold nor hot") may be all very good, but they have small common sense; their principles are fine—most unexceptionable—but they are wonderfully airy: they somehow want the substance of things earthly; they cannot be grasped; and even those who make so much of them go about them in so unbusiness-like a fashion, and with so little of the shrewdness and energy we are used to in common matters, that one may be excused for not surrendering himself to such notions, and resting contented with those general views which commend themselves to every one, and about which there is no dispute.' This witness is true: spiritual things are all too airy for such persons; they have substance only to faith here, and of that they have none: Theirs is a world of sense; the things which are *seen* are their sphere; and right easily are they grasped, and all congenial to the natural man: in hunting after them they go with the stream—to which the remonstrances of conscience and of Scripture oppose but a feeble barrier. No wonder, then, that shrewdness is stamped upon all that is done in this sphere, and no thanks for it to them and theirs. But ours is a world of faith and hope; and hope that is *seen* is not hope; for what a man seeth, why doth he yet hope for? but if we hope for that we *see not*, then do we with patience wait for it. We know Whom we have believed; we have made our choice, and mean to abide by it, nor will it ever be taken from us. Nevertheless, we stand rebuked. 'Thou hast said too much truth of us, thou cold, supercilious critic of our poor Christianity, but our gracious Master said it before thee. We thank thee not, but we thank Him, and mean, with His help, to wipe away this reproach.' And now, will not my Christian readers try to do it? We know very well it is because the things of this present world are "seen" that they are more vividly apprehended, and so —all "temporal," though they be—more powerfully grasped, than the things which are "not seen," even though they be "eternal." We know full well how keenly we feel the one, and how languidly the other; what sacrifices of time and strength, yea, what risks of life itself men will readily incur, to promote their temporal interests, and how little of all this even the children of God will go through with for those which are eternal. But as our Lord holds this up as a reproach, and here sends us to the worldling for wisdom—even as the sluggard is sent to the ant for activity—let us not rest in *explanations* of the fact, but rather strive to reverse it. What we want from the men of the world is not so much their shrewd management of affairs, as that *vivid apprehension of our own sphere* which shall convert our world of *faith* into substance and *sense* to us; then shall we have grasp enough and energy enough; for "this is the victory that overcometh the world, even our faith." Yet along with this—as in

31 will repent. And he said unto him, If they hear not Moses and the
Prophets, [w]neither will they be persuaded though one rose from the
dead.

A. D. 33.

[w] John 12.10. 2 Cor. 4. 3.

temporal things—*habits* of steady vigilance and activity have much to do with success in spiritual things; and this parable will not have produced its proper fruit till the children of light, ashamed of being excelled in anything for eternity by the worldly wisdom of the children of this world, shall bend their efforts to rise above them in all such things, commanding its respect and compelling its admiration for this superiority. "If any of you lack wisdom, let him ask of God, who giveth to all liberally, and upbraideth not; and it shall be given him" (Jas. i. 5). 3. This and similar portions of Scripture have been so sadly abused to support the fatal doctrine of the merit of good works, and especially of charity to the poor and needy, that not a few Christians have been scared away from such scriptures, and are little aware what a test of character at the great day will be the use they make of the pecuniary means with which they are entrusted. Should any say, That can hardly apply to those who have so little of this world's goods as I have, let them consider whether they are not acting the unprofitable servant in the parable of the Talents, who, because his lord had given him but one talent, went and hid it in the earth; and let them remember the pregnant and comprehensive maxim, "He that is faithful in the least is faithful also in much, and he that is unfaithful in the least is unfaithful also in much." 4. How entirely is the divinest teaching thrown away upon those who, like the Pharisaic portion of our Lord's audience, are resolved not to part with the sinful courses which it exposes and condemns! But the "derision" of those "covetous" Pharisees at such teaching as that of this Section was the best evidence of its power. 5. In the parable of the rich man and Lazarus, were the poverty and disease of this dear saint of God so extreme as is here represented, and, to add to all, when laid down at the rich man's gate, in hope of at length moving his compassion, is he represented as dying just as he was? Then, let no one so interpret the promises of divine compassion and provision for the godly poor as to think that they may not be left to live and die as poor and as neglected of men as this Lazarus. But neither let God's providence be maligned on this account, until we know how He deals with the *spirits* of such. Did we know what unseen ministrations of angels He sends them, and with what seasons of nearness to Himself He favours them, in the absence of human consolation, with what light He irradiates their darkness, how out of weakness He makes them strong, and how in patience and hope He makes them to possess their souls—giving them "songs in the night," unknown to the prosperous even of His own children (Rev. xiv. 3)—we should perhaps change our mind, and be almost tempted to envy "Lazarus" with all his miseries. As he looked at the sycophantish visitors who went in and out of the rich man's gate, regardless of him, methinks I hear him saying with the sweet singer of Israel, "There be many that say, Who will show us any good? Lord, lift thou up the light of Thy countenance upon us: Thou hast put gladness in my heart more than in the time when their corn and their wine increased. Deliver my soul from the wicked, from men of the world, which have their portion in this life, and whose belly Thou fillest with Thy hid treasure: As for me, I shall behold Thy face in righteousness; I shall be satisfied, when I wake, with Thy likeness" (Ps. iv. 6, 7; xvii. 13-15). And see him at last: Those angels are not ashamed of his poverty, nor repelled away by his sores. His wasted skeleton—to men a sightless carcase—is to them beautiful as the shrine of a redeemed spirit; and that spirit is more beautiful still, in its resemblance to God, its likeness to themselves, its meetness for glory. They hover over the beggarly habitation, and surround the mean pallet, and watch the last effort of the spirit to break away from its falling tenement, that at the appointed hour they may convey it in triumph to its celestial home. O that men—that even Christians—would judge less by the outward appearance, and try, like the Lord, to look upon the heart! 6. And how beautiful is the view here given us of the ministrations of angels, especially at the death-bed of the saints. Often do they tell us, they *see* them waiting for them and smiling on them. They are ready to stretch out their arms to them, to signify their readiness at that moment to be taken up by them; and they ask us, sometimes, if *we* do not see them too. Of course we don't, for we live in a world of sense. But they are then leaving it; it has all but closed upon them, and they are getting within the precincts of heaven. Who, then, shall say that they see not what is hid from us; and since what they affirm they see is only what is here represented as a reality, who, with this parable before him, shall say that such sights are but the fruit of a distempered imagination, a picture of the fevered or languid brain? 7. How frequently do the terrors of hell recur, and how terrific are the representations given of it, in the teaching of our Lord! Here, its unutterable and inconceivable horrors are depicted with a vividness altogether astonishing. And the unreasonableness and impossibility of the *slightest* and *briefest* abatement of them, which is here proclaimed as from the other world itself, only completes the representation. And mark how this unreasonableness is grounded wholly on the life and conduct of the lost in the present world—rendering any change in their condition in eternity as hopeless as their being able to undo their past life by living over again and acting otherwise. Need it be asked whether the *perpetuity of hell-torments*, and the *character* of them too—as but the natural development and fitting termination of a life of ungodliness—could be more emphatically taught? 8. Though we are not to press the *language* of the parables unduly, does it not seem a legitimate inference from the whole strain of this Parable, that the lost will, as an aggravation of their torment, in some way or other, either *see* the bliss of the saved in heaven, or have such a vivid knowledge of what it is as will amount to a kind of sight? And are not those other words of Christ confirmatory of this? "Ye shall *see* Abraham, and Isaac, and Jacob, and all the prophets, in the kingdom of God, and you yourselves thrust out"? (ch. xiii. 28). 9. Nowhere is the sufficiency of revealed truth in general, and of the *Old Testament* Scriptures in particular, for all the purposes of *salvation*, so emphatically stated as by our Lord in the closing verses of this chapter, who puts it into the mouth of Abraham from the unseen world. Men are fain to believe that if they had this or that evidence which they have not, they would repent and be converted. And because they are not startled into faith—because their impenitence is not overpowered by resistless occurrences—they think

17 THEN said he unto the disciples, [a]It is impossible but that offences
2 will come: but [b]woe *unto him* through whom they come! It were better
for him that a millstone were hanged about his neck, and he cast into the
3 sea, than that he should offend one of these little ones. Take heed to
yourselves: [c]If thy brother trespass against thee, [d]rebuke him; and if he
4 repent, [e]forgive him. And if he trespass against thee seven times in a
day, and seven times in a day turn again to thee, saying, I repent; thou
shalt forgive him.
5, And the apostles said unto the Lord, Increase our faith. And [f]the
6 Lord said, If ye had faith as a grain of mustard seed, ye might say unto
this sycamine tree, Be thou plucked up by the root, and be thou planted
in the sea; and it should obey you.
7 But which of you, having a servant plowing or feeding cattle, will say
unto him by and by, when he is come from the field, Go and sit down to
8 meat? And will not rather say unto him, Make ready wherewith I may
sup, and gird thyself, [g]and serve me, till I have eaten and drunken; and
9 afterward thou shalt eat and drink? Doth he thank that servant because
10 he did the things that were commanded him? I trow not. So likewise
ye, when ye shall have done all those things which are commanded you,
say, We are [h]unprofitable servants: we have done that which was our
duty to do.
11 And it came to pass, [i]as he went to Jerusalem, that he passed through

A. D. 33.

CHAP. 17.
[a] Matt. 18. 6, 7.
Mark 9. 42.
1 Cor 11.19.
[b] 2 Thes. 1.6.
[c] Matt. 18.15.
[d] Lev. 19. 17.
Pro. 17. 10.
Jas. 5. 19.
[e] 1 Cor. 13. 4.
Col. 3. 12.
[f] Matt 17.20.
Matt. 21. 21.
Mark 9. 23.
Mark 11.23.
[g] ch. 12. 37.
[h] Job 22. 3.
Job 35. 7.
Ps. 16. 2.
Matt 25.37-40.
Rom. 3. 12.
Rom. 11.35.
1 Cor 9. 16.
Phile. 11.
[i] Luke 9. 51.
John 4. 4.

there will be some excuse for them if at last they are found unchanged. But the Lord here shuts us absolutely up to THE REVEALED WORD, as *God's ordained means of all saving effect upon the heart and life.* (See 2 Pet. i. 19; John v. 39, 46, 47; xvii. 17.) And if this be true, need we add, that the *right* and the *duty* of all to "search the Scriptures," and the apostasy from a Scripture foundation of any Church that would prohibit the general searching of them—as the Church of Rome does—follow by necessary consequence?

CHAP. XVII. 1-19.—FURTHER DISCOURSE ON OFFENCES, FAITH, AND HUMILITY.—TEN LEPERS CLEANSED.—Whether this was delivered in continuation of what is recorded in the preceding chapter, it is impossible to say; but probably it came close upon it.

Offences (1-4). **1, 2. Then said he unto the disciples, It is impossible but that offences, &c. It were better for him that a millstone, &c.** See on Mark ix. 42. **3. Take heed to yourselves**—Guard your spirit: **If thy brother trespass against thee, rebuke him; and if he repent, forgive him. 4. And if he trespass against thee seven times in a day, and seven times in a day turn again to thee, saying, I repent; thou shalt forgive him**—that is, 'however often;' seven being the number of completeness. So that this is not a *lower* measure of forgiving love than the "seventy-times seven times" was, enjoined upon Peter; for that was merely because Peter had asked if he was to *stop* at seven times—to which the reply was, 'No, not though it should come to seventy times that number.' See on Matt. xviii. 21, 22.

Faith (5, 6). **5. And the apostles said unto the Lord** (see on Luke xi. 1), **Increase our faith.** What prompted so peculiar a petition? No doubt the felt difficulty of carrying into effect such holy directions—the difficulty first of avoiding offences, and next of forgiving them so divinely. This is the only instance in which *a spiritual operation upon their souls* was solicited of Christ by the Twelve; but a kindred and even higher prayer had been offered to Him before, by one with far fewer opportunities, which in all likelihood first suggested to them this prayer. See on Mark ix. 24, and Remark 3 at the close of that Section. **6. And the Lord said, If ye had faith as a grain of mustard seed, ye might say unto this sycamine**—or mulberry **tree, Be thou plucked up by the root, and be thou planted in the sea; and it should obey you.** See on Mark xi. 22-24, and Remark 3 at the close of that Section.

Humility (7-10). **7. But which of you, having a servant plowing or feeding cattle, will say unto him by and by**—or 'directly' [εὐθέως]—**when he is come from the field, Go and sit down to meat?** By this way of arranging and pointing the words, the sense is obscured. It would be clearer thus: 'Which of you, having a servant ploughing or feeding cattle, will say unto him, when he is come from the field, Go directly, and sit down to meat.' **8. And will not rather say unto him, Make ready wherewith I may sup, and gird thyself, and serve me, till I have eaten and drunken; and afterward thou shalt eat and drink? 9. Doth he thank that servant because he did the things that were commanded him? I trow not** [οὐ δοκῶ]—or as we say, when much more is meant, 'I presume not,' or 'I should think not.' **10. So likewise ye, when ye shall have done all those things which are commanded you, say, We are unprofitable servants.** The word 'unprofitable' [ἀχρεῖοι], though in modern English denoting the *opposite* of profit, is here used in its proper *negative* sense, 'We have not profited' or 'benefited God at all by our services.' The connection of this with the subject discoursed of may be thus expressed—'But when your faith has been so increased as both to avoid and forgive offences, and do things impossible to all but faith—even then, be not puffed up as though you had laid the Lord under any obligations to you.' (Compare Job xxii. 2, 3; Rom. xi. 35.)

Ten Lepers Cleansed (11-19). **11. And it came to pass, as he went to Jerusalem, that he**—The 'He' is emphatic [καὶ αὐτὸς]—**passed through the midst of Samaria and Galilee** [διὰ μέσου Σαμαρείας]. This may mean, '*between* Samaria and Galilee,' that is, on the frontiers of both, but

12 the midst of Samaria and Galilee. And as he entered into a certain
village, there met him ten men that were lepers, which [j]stood afar off:
13 and they lifted up *their* voices, and said, Jesus, Master, have mercy on
14 us. And when he saw *them*, he said unto them, [k]Go show yourselves unto
the priests. And it came to pass, that, as they went, they were cleansed.
15 And one of them, when he saw that he was healed, turned back, and with
16 a loud voice [l]glorified God, and fell down on *his* face at his feet, giving
17 him thanks: and he was [m]a Samaritan. And Jesus answering said,
18 Were there not ten cleansed? but where *are* the nine? There are not
19 found that returned to give glory to God, save this stranger. And [n]he
said unto him, Arise, go thy way: thy faith hath made thee whole.
20 And when he was demanded of the Pharisees, when the kingdom of
God should come, he answered them and said, The kingdom of God
21 cometh not [1]with observation: neither shall they say, Lo here! or, lo
there! for, behold, [o]the kingdom of God is [2]within you.

A. D. 33.

[j] Lev. 13. 46.
[k] Lev. 13. 2. Lev. 14. 2. Matt. 8. 4.
[l] Ps. 103. 1.
[m] 2 Ki. 17. 24. John 8. 48.
[n] Matt. 9. 22. Mark 5. 34.
[1] Or, with outward show. John 18. 36.
[o] Rom. 14. 17. Col. 1. 27.
[2] Or, among you. John 1. 26. Gal. 6 15.

without passing through them—as *Meyer*, *Alford*, *Webster and Wilkinson*, &c., take it: or, it may mean, "through the midst of Samaria and Galilee," in the sense of passing through those regions —as *de Wette* and *Olshausen* understand it. But in this sense the phrase is scarcely a natural one; nor does it seem to us likely that our Evangelist means his readers to understand that this was a fresh journey through those great divisions of the country. We prefer, therefore, the former sense. But the whole chronology of this large portion of our Gospel is difficult. See remarks prefixed to ch. ix. 51. **12. And as he entered into a certain village, there met him ten men that were lepers, which stood afar off.** See the affecting directions laid down for such in Lev. xiii. 45, 46. That there should be so many as ten in one locality shows how numerous they, as well as possessed persons, must have been in Palestine in our Lord's time—no doubt with a view to the manifestation of His glory in healing them. **13. And they lifted up their voices**—their common misery, as *Trench* remarks, drawing these poor outcasts together (see 2 Ki. vii. 3), nay, causing them to forget the fierce national antipathy which reigned between Jew and Samaritan. **and said, Jesus, Master** [ἐπιστάτα], **have mercy on us.** How quick a teacher is felt misery, even though in some cases (as in all but one here) the teaching may be soon forgotten! **14. And when he saw them, he said unto them, Go show yourselves unto the priests**—that is, as cleansed persons. See on Matt. viii. 4. One of these was a Samaritan; but he too was required to go with the rest, thus teaching him that "Salvation was of the Jews" (John iv. 22). And yet when ordered to do this, *they had not been cleansed.* A great trial of faith this was. But they obeyed. **And it came to pass, that, as they went, they were cleansed.** In how many different ways were our Lord's cures wrought, and this different from all the rest! Yet it closely resembled the cure of the nobleman's son (John iv. 50-53). **15. And one of them, when he saw that he was healed, turned back, and with a loud voice glorified God.** Forgetting all about the priests, or unable to proceed further, on discovering the change upon him, he returns to His wondrous Benefactor, his emotions finding vent in a loud burst of praise. **16. And fell down on his face at his feet, giving him thanks: and he was a Samaritan.** While he rendered his tribute to Him from whom cometh down every good and perfect gift, he gave thanks at the same time to the mysterious, beneficent Hand by which the cure was wrought. And as these men must have had their faith kindled by the reported wonders of His hand on others like themselves, no doubt they saw in Jesus what the Samaritans of Sychar did—"the Christ, the Saviour of the world" (John iv. 42), however imperfect their conceptions. **17. And Jesus answering said, Were there not ten cleansed?** [οὐχὶ οἱ δέκα ἐκαθαρίσθησαν]—rather, 'Were not the ten cleansed?'—that is, the whole ten. A striking example this of Christ's omniscience, as *Bengel* notices. **but where are the nine?** [οἱ δὲ ἐννέα ποῦ] —'but the nine, where [are they]?' **18. There are not found that returned to give glory to God, save this stranger** [ὁ ἀλλογενὴς οὗτος]—'this alien,' 'this of another race.' The language is that of wonder and admiration, as is expressly said of another exhibition of Gentile faith (Matt. viii. 10). **19. And he said unto him, Arise**—for he was on his face at Jesus' feet, and there, it seems, lay prostrate. **go thy way: thy faith hath made thee whole**—not as the others, merely in body, but in that higher spiritual sense with which His constant language has so familiarized us.

For Remarks on this Section, see those on the Sections referred to in the exposition.

20-37.—The Coming of the Kingdom of God and of the Son of Man. As usual in this portion of our Gospel, we have no notice of time or place. (See opening remarks on ch. ix. 51.) To meet the erroneous views not only of the Pharisees, but of the disciples themselves, our Lord addresses both, announcing the coming of the Kingdom under different aspects.

20. And when he was demanded of the Pharisees, when the kingdom of God should come, he answered them and said, The kingdom of God cometh not with observation [μετὰ παρατηρήσεως]. The word signifies 'watching' or 'lying in wait for' a person or thing. In this sense, they "watched" our Lord once and again (ch. xiv. 1; xx. 20; Mark iii. 2); and so they "watched" the gates to kill Paul (Acts ix. 24). Here, the precise meaning would seem to be, The kingdom of God cometh not with 'watching' or 'lying in wait for it,' 'straining after it,' as for something outwardly imposing, and at once revealing itself. What follows confirms this. **21. Neither shall they say, Lo here! or, lo there!**—shut up within *this* or *that* sharply defined or visible limit, geographical or ecclesiastical. **for the kingdom of God is within you**—[ἐντὸς ὑμῶν]. This may either mean, 'inside of you;' meaning, that it is of an internal and spiritual character, as opposed to their *outside* views of it: so the best expositors among the Fathers understood it; and so, of the moderns, *Luther*, *Erasmus*, *Calvin*,

22 And he said unto the disciples, [p]The days will come, when ye shall
desire to see one of the days of the Son of man, and ye shall not see
23 *it.* And [q]they shall say to you, See here! or, see there! go [r]not after
24 *them,* nor follow *them.* For as the lightning, that lighteneth out of
the one *part* under heaven, shineth unto the other *part* under heaven;
25 so shall also [s]the Son of man be in his day. But [t]first must he
26 suffer many things, and be rejected of this generation. And [u]as it
was in the days of Noe, so shall it be also in the days of the Son of
27 man. They did eat, they drank, they married wives, they were given
in marriage, until the day that Noe entered into the ark, and the flood
28 came, and destroyed them all. Likewise [v]also as it was in the days
of Lot; they did eat, they drank, they bought, they sold, they planted,
29 they builded; but the same day that Lot went out of Sodom it rained
30 fire and brimstone from heaven, and destroyed *them* all. Even thus shall
31 it be in the day when the Son of man [w]is revealed. In that day, he
[x]which shall be upon the house-top, and his stuff in the house, let him
not come down to take it away: and he that is in the field, let him like-

A. D. 33.

p Matt. 9. 15. John 17.12.
q Matt. 24.23. Mark 13.21. ch. 21. 8.
r 1 John 4. 1.
s 1 Tim 6.15.
t ch. 9. 22.
u Gen. 7. 1. Matt. 24.37.
v Gen. 19. 1.
w Matt. 24. 3, 27-30. Mark 13.26. ch. 21. 22, 27. 2 Thes. 1. 7.
x Job 2. 4. Jer. 45. 5. Mark 6. 25. Mark 13.15.

Campbell, Olshausen. Or, it may mean, 'in the midst of you,' or 'amongst you'—as already set up in its beginnings, if they had but eyes to discern it: so *Beza, Grotius, Bengel, Meyer, de Wette, Alford, Webster and Wilkinson.* It seems a weak argument against the former sense, though urged by nearly all who adopt the latter, that the kingdom of God could not be said to be within or in the hearts of the Pharisees, to whom our Lord was addressing himself. For, all that the phrase, in that sense, implies is, that it is 'within men,' as its general character. The question must be decided by the whole scope of the statement; and though others judge this to be in favour of the second sense, we incline, on this ground, to the first. Compare Deut. xxx. 11-14; Rom. xiv. 17.

22. And he said unto the disciples—for they needed light on this subject, as well as the Pharisees, **The days will come** ['Ελεύσονται ἡμέραι]—rather, 'There shall come days,' **when ye shall desire to see one of the days of the Son of man, and ye shall not see it**—that is, one day of His own presence amongst them, such as they now had. See Matt. ix. 15. 'So far will the kingdom I speak of be from bringing with it My personal presence, that amidst the approaching calamities and confusion, and the anxiety ye will be in for the infant cause—which will then be felt to lie all upon your own feeble shoulders—ye will be fain to say, O that we had the Master amongst us again but for one day! But ye shall not have Him.' He was to make other and more suitable provision, in the mission of the Comforter, for their fluttering hearts; but of that it was not now the time and place to speak. **23. And they shall say to you, See here! or, see there! go not after them, nor follow them.** A warning, says *Alford,* to all so-called expositors of prophecy and their followers, who cry, Lo there and see here, every time that war breaks out, or revolutions occur. **24. For as the lightning, that lighteneth out of the one part under heaven, shineth unto the other part under heaven; so shall also the Son of man be in his day.** That is, it will be as *manifest* as the lightning. So that the kingdom here spoken of has its *external* and *visible* side too. 'The Lord,' says *Stier* correctly, 'speaks here of His coming and manifestation in a prophetically indefinite manner, and in these preparatory words *blends into one the distinctive epochs.*' When the whole polity of the Jews, civil and ecclesiastical alike, was broken up at once, and its continuance rendered impossible, by the destruction of Jerusalem, it became as manifest to all as the lightning of heaven that the Kingdom of God had ceased to exist in its old, and had entered on a new and perfectly different, form. So it may be again, ere its final and greatest change at the personal coming of Christ, of which the words in their highest sense are alone true. **25. But first must he suffer many things, and be rejected of this generation.** This shows that the more immediate reference of the previous verse is to an event *soon* to follow the death of Christ. It was designed to withdraw the attention of "His disciples" from the *glare* in which His foregoing words had invested the approaching establishment of His kingdom. **26. And as it was in the days of Noe, so shall it be also in the days of the Son of man. 27. They did eat, . . . drank . . . married . . . were given in marriage, until the day that Noe entered into the ark, and the flood came, and destroyed them all. 28. Likewise also as it was in the days of Lot; they did eat . . . drank, . . . bought . . . sold . . . planted . . . builded; 29. But the same day that Lot went out of Sodom it rained fire and brimstone from heaven, and destroyed them all. 30. Even thus shall it be in the day when the Son of man is revealed.** It will be observed here that what the *flood* and the *flames* found the antediluvians and the Sodomites engaged in were just all the ordinary and innocent occupations and enjoyments of life—eating and drinking, marrying and giving in marriage, in the one case; eating and drinking, buying and selling, planting and building, in the other. Though the antediluvian world and the cities of the plain were awfully wicked, it is not their *wickedness,* but their *worldliness,* their unbelief and indifference to the future, their *unpreparedness,* that is here held up as a warning. Let the reader mark how these great events of Old Testament History—denied, or explained away, now-a-days by not a few who profess to reverence our Lord's authority—are here referred to by Him as facts. The wretched theory of *accommodation* to the popular belief—as if our Lord could lend Himself to this in such cases—is now nearly exploded. **31. In that day, he which shall be upon the house-top, and his stuff in the house, let him not come down to take it away: and he that is in the field, let him likewise not return back.** A warning against that *lingering reluctance to part with present treasures* which induces some to remain in a burning house, in hopes of saving this and that precious article, till consumed and buried in its ruins. The cases here supposed, though

32 wise not return back. Remember [y]Lot's wife. Whosoever [z]shall seek to
33 save his life shall lose it; and whosoever shall lose his life shall preserve
34 it. I [a]tell you, in that night there shall be two *men* in one bed; the one
35 shall be taken, and the other shall be left. Two *women* shall be grinding
36 together; the one shall be taken, and the other left. [3]Two *men* shall be
37 in the field; the one shall be taken, and the other left. And they
answered and said unto him, [b]Where, Lord? And he said unto them,
Wheresoever the body *is*, thither will the eagles be gathered together.

18 AND he spake a parable unto them *to this end*, that men ought
2 [a]always *to* pray, and not to faint; saying, There was [1]in a city a judge,
3 which feared not God, neither regarded man: and there was a widow
in that city; and she came unto him, saying, Avenge me of mine
4 adversary. And he would not for a while: but afterward he said within
5 himself, Though I fear not God, nor regard man; yet [b]because this
widow troubleth me, I will avenge her, lest by her continual coming she
6 weary me. And the Lord said, Hear what the unjust judge saith.
7 And [c]shall not God avenge his own elect, which cry day and night unto

A. D. 33.

y Gen. 19. 26.
z Matt. 16. 25. John 12. 25.
a 1 Thes. 4. 17.
3 This verse is wanting in many Greek copies.
b Job 39. 30.

CHAP. 18.
a ch. 11. 5. ch. 21. 36. Rom. 12. 12. Eph. 6. 18. Col. 4. 2. 1 Thes. 5. 17.
1 In a certain city.
b ch. 11. 8.
c 2 Thes. 1. 6.

different, of course, are similar. **32. Remember Lot's wife**—her "*look back*" and her *doom*. Her heart was in Sodom still, and that "look" just said, 'Ah, Sodom! and shall I never enter, never see thee again? must I bid thee a final adieu?' **33. Whosoever shall seek to save his life shall lose it; and whosoever shall lose his life shall preserve it.** See on Matt. x. 39. **34. I tell you, in that night there shall be two men in one bed; the one shall be taken, and the other shall be left. 35. Two women shall be grinding together** (see on Mark ix. 42); **the one shall be taken, and the other left. 36.** [**Two men shall be in the field; the one shall be taken, and the other left.**] The evidence against the genuineness of this verse is too strong to admit of its being printed without brackets, as at least doubtful, and probably taken from Matt. xxiv. 40. All the critical editors exclude it from their text, and nearly all critical expositors concur with them. *De Wette*, however, inclines to receive it. The prepared and the unprepared will, says our Lord, be found mingled in closest intercourse together in the ordinary walks and fellowships of life when the moment of severance arrives. Awful truth! realized before the destruction of Jerusalem, when the Christians found themselves forced by their Lord's directions (ch. xxi. 21) at once and for ever away from their old associates; but most of all, when the second coming of Christ shall burst upon a heedless world. **37. And they answered and said unto him, Where, Lord?** Where shall this occur? **And he said unto them, Wheresoever the body is, thither will the eagles be gathered together.** Though what is here said of the eagles is true rather of the vultures, yet as both are birds of prey, the former are named here (and in Matt. xxiv. 28), with an evident allusion to the *Roman eagles*—the standard of the Roman army—to signify the vengeance more immediately referred to. 'As birds of prey scent out the carrion, so wherever is found a mass of incurable moral and spiritual corruption, there will be seen alighting the ministers of Divine judgment;' a proverbial saying terrifically verified at the destruction of Jerusalem, and many times since, though its most tremendous illustration will be at the world's final day. For Remarks on this Section, see those at the close of Mark xiii.

CHAP. XVIII. 1-8.—THE PARABLE OF THE IMPORTUNATE WIDOW. This delightful parable was evidently designed to follow up the subject of the last Section, on the Coming of the Son of man (*v.* 8). In so far as the closing verses directed the thoughts to the Second Personal Appearing of the Lord Jesus, it was as an event which would occur *when least expected*. But lest this should lead—as it has led—to the inference that it would be very speedy, or was *quite near at hand*, the more immediate design of this parable was to guard against that impression, by intimating that it might, on the contrary, be so long delayed as nearly to extinguish the expectation of His coming at all. Accordingly, while the duty of persevering prayer in general is here enforced, the more direct subject of the parable is unceasing prayer by the widowed and oppressed Church for redress of all its wrongs, for deliverance out of all its troubles, for transition from its widowhood to its wedded state, by the glorious appearing of its heavenly Bridegroom.

1. And he spake a parable unto them to this end, that men ought always to pray. Compare *v.* 7, "His own elect which cry unto Him day and night." **and not to faint** [ἐκκακεῖν, or, as the better supported reading, perhaps, is, ἐγκακεῖν]—'and not to lose heart,' or 'slacken.' **2. Saying, There was in a** [certain] **city** [ἔν τινι πόλει] **a judge, which feared not God, neither regarded man**—regardless alike of Divine and human judgment; void of all principle. **3. And there was a widow in that city**—weak, desolate, defenceless. Compare 1 Tim. v. 5, a verse evidently alluding to what is here said, "Now she that is a widow indeed, and desolate, trusteth in God, and continueth in supplications and prayers night and day." **and she came** [ἤρχετο]—rather, 'kept coming,' as the imperfect tense implies. Indeed it was to get rid of this "*continual coming*" that the judge at length gave her redress. **saying, Avenge me** ['Εκδίκησόν με ἀπὸ] **of mine adversary**—that is, by a judicial interposition. **4. And he would not for a while: but afterward he said within himself, Though I fear not God, nor regard man; 5. Yet**—I have some regard to my own comfort: so **because this widow troubleth me, I will avenge her, lest by her continual coming** [εἰς τέλος ἐρχομένη]—'her incessant coming.' In 1 Thess. ii. 16 the same expression is rendered 'to the uttermost.' **she weary**—or 'annoy' **me** [ὑπωπιάζῃ με]. **6. And the Lord**—a name expressive of the authoritative style in which He now interpreted His own parable, **said, Hear what the unjust judge saith. 7. And shall not God**—not like that unprincipled man, but the infinitely righteous "Judge of all the earth," **avenge**—redeem from oppression, **his own elect**—who are not like this poor widow in the eye of that selfish wretch, the objects of indifference and

8 him, though he bear long with them? I tell you [d]that he will avenge
them speedily. Nevertheless when the Son of man cometh, shall he find
faith on the earth?
9 And he spake this parable unto certain [e]which trusted in themselves
10 [2]that they were righteous, and despised others: Two men went up into
11 the temple to pray; the one a Pharisee, and the other a publican. The
Pharisee [f]stood and prayed thus with himself, [g]God, I thank thee, that I
am not as other men *are*, extortioners, unjust, adulterers, or even as this
12 publican. I fast twice in the week, I give tithes of all that I possess.

A. D. 33.

d Heb. 10. 37. 2 Pet. 3. 8, 9.
e ch. 10. 29. ch. 16. 15.
2 Or, as being righteous.
f Ps. 135. 2.
g Isa. 1. 15. Isa. 58. 2. Rev. 3. 17.

contempt, but dear to Him as the apple of the eye (Zec. ii. 8). **which cry day and night unto him**—whose every cry enters into the ears of the Lord of Sabaoth (Jas. v. 4); and how much more their incessant and persevering cries, **though he bear long with them?** [καὶ μακροθυμῶν, or, according to the preferable reading, μακροθυμεῖ ἐπ' αὐτοῖς]. This rendering is apt to perplex the English reader, to whose ear it fails to convey the obvious sense. The same expression is used in Jas. v. 7—"The husbandman waiteth for the precious fruit of the earth, and *hath long patience for it*" [μακροθυμῶν ἐπ' αὐτῷ]. So we should render it here, 'though he bear long *for them*,' or 'on their account;' that is, with their oppressors. It is not with His own elect that God has to bear in the case here supposed, but with those that oppress them. And the meaning is, that although He *tolerates* those oppressions for a long time, He will at length interpose in behalf of His own elect. **8. I tell you, he will avenge them speedily** [ἐν τάχει]. As when "His soul was grieved for the misery of Israel" (Judg. x. 16), so "His bowels are troubled" for His own elect, crying to Him day and night from the depths of their oppressions: He is pained, as it were, at the long delay which His wisdom sees necessary, and at the sore trial to which it puts their faith, and is impatient, so to speak, till "the time, the set time," arrive to interpose. **Nevertheless when the Son of man cometh, shall he find faith**—that is, any belief that He will come at all, **on the earth?** 'Yet, ere the Son of man comes to redress the wrongs of His Church, so low will the hope of relief sink, through the length of the delay, that one will be fain to ask, Is there any faith of a coming Avenger, any expectation that the Church's Lord will ever return to her, left on the earth?'

Remarks.—1. Thus the *primary*, the *historical* reference of this parable is to the Church in her widowed, desolate, oppressed, defenceless condition, during the present absence of her Lord in the heavens. And the lessons it teaches, in this view of it, which are two-fold, are most precious. One lesson is, that though we are to be "always ready, not knowing when our Lord may come," we are at the same time not to be surprised though "the Bridegroom should tarry," and tarry so long as to wear out the patience of the most, and almost extinguish the hope of His coming. And the more so, as His coming will be needed, not only because the Bride can never be contented with anything short of the presence of her Beloved, but because in her widowed state she is exposed to all manner of indignities and wrongs, from which her Lord's coming alone will set her completely free. But another lesson is, that in these circumstances prayer is her proper resource, that though He seems to turn a deaf ear to her, she is to "pray always, and not faint," assured that she is dear to her Lord even when He seems to deny her; nay, that her incessant crying to Him is that which will bring Him to her at length; but yet, that the faith of His coming, through the length of the delay, will have reached its lowest ebb, and nearly died out, ere the day dawn and the shadows flee away! It may be added that it would seem a law of the divine administration, that both *judgment* and *mercy*, when long delayed, come at last with a rapidity proportioned to the length of that delay. Of *judgment* it is said, "He that, being often reproved, hardeneth his neck, shall *suddenly* be destroyed, and that without remedy" (Prov. xxix. 1); and so it is said, "Their foot shall *slide* in due time" (Deut. xxxii. 35). Of *mercy* it is here said, When at length it comes, it will come "speedily." But, 2. The application of this delightful parable to *prayer in general* is so obvious as to have nearly hidden from most readers its *more direct* reference; and this general application is so resistless and invaluable that it cannot be allowed to disappear in any public and historical interpretation.

9-14.—The Parable of the Pharisee and the Publican. As the subject of this Section has no connection with the two preceding ones, so the precise time and place of it are, as usual in this portion of our Gospel, left quite indefinite. But the purpose for which it was spoken—the lesson it was intended to convey—is more precisely expressed than in most other cases; for it is expressed both as a preface to it and as the concluding moral of it.

9. And he spake this parable unto certain which trusted in themselves that they were righteous, and despised others: 10. Two men went up into the temple to pray; the one a Pharisee, and the other a publican. On these classes, see on Matt. iii. 1-12, Remark 2, at the close of that Section. **11. The Pharisee stood**—as the Jews did in prayer (Mark xi. 25), **and prayed thus with himself, God, I thank thee, that I am not as other men are, extortioners, unjust, adulterers, or even as this publican.** To have been kept from gross iniquities was undoubtedly a just cause of thankfulness to God; but instead of the devoutly humble, admiring frame which this should inspire, he arrogantly severs himself from the rest of mankind, as quite above them, and with a contemptuous look at the poor publican, thanks God that he has not to stand afar off like him, to hang down his head like a bulrush, and beat his breast like him. But these are only his *moral* excellences. His *religious* merits complete his grounds for self-congratulation. **12. I fast twice in the week, I give tithes**—or the tenth **of all that I possess** [κτῶμαι]—or 'acquire;' 'of all my gains' or 'increase.' Not confining himself to the one divinely prescribed annual fast (Lev. xvi. 29), he was not behind the most rigid, who, as *Lightfoot* says, fasted on the second and fifth days of every week, and gave the tenth not only of what the law laid under tithing, but of "all his gains." Thus, besides doing *all his duty*, he did *works of supererogation;* while sins to confess and spiritual wants to be supplied he seems to have felt none. What a picture of the Pharisaic character and religion! **13. And the publican, standing afar off**

13 And the publican, [h]standing afar off, would not lift up so much as *his*
eyes unto heaven, but smote upon his breast, saying, God be merciful to
14 me a sinner. I tell you, this man went down to his house justified *rather*
than the other: [i]for every one that exalteth himself shall be abased; and
he that humbleth himself shall be exalted.
15 And [j]they brought unto him also infants, that he would touch them:
16 but when *his* disciples saw *it*, they rebuked them. But Jesus called
them *unto him*, and said, [k]Suffer little children to come unto me, and

A. D. 33.

h Ps. 40. 12.
i Job 22. 29. Job 40. 9-13. Isa. 2. 11-17. Jas. 4. 6. 1 Pet. 5. 5, 6.
j Matt. 19. 13. Mark 10. 13.
k Pro. 8. 7.

—as unworthy to draw near; but that was the way to *get* near (Ps. xxxiv. 18; Isa. lvii. 15), **would not lift up so much as his eyes unto heaven**—"blushing and ashamed" to do so (Ezra ix. 6), **but smote** [ἔτυπτε]—rather, 'kept smiting' **upon his breast**—for anguish (ch. xxiii. 48) and self-reproach (Jer. xxxi. 19), **saying, God be merciful** [ἱλάσθητι]—'be propitiated' or 'propitious:' a very unusual word to occur here, and in only one other place used in the New Testament, in the sense of "making reconciliation" by sacrifice (Heb. ii. 17). There *may* therefore be some allusion to this here, though it can hardly be pressed. **to me a sinner** [μοι τῷ ἁμαρτωλῷ]—literally 'to me the sinner;' as if he should say, 'If ever there was a sinner, I am he.' **14. I tell you**—authoritatively, **this man went down to his house justified rather than the other.** The meaning is, 'and not the other.' **for every one that exalteth himself shall be abased; and he that humbleth himself shall be exalted.** This great law of the Kingdom of God is, in the teaching of Christ, inscribed over its entrance-gate as in letters of gold; but how vividly is it here depicted?

Remarks.—1. The grand peculiarity of the Religion of the Bible is *Salvation by Grace;* a Salvation, however, unto holiness—not *by*, but *unto*, good works. It pervades the Old Testament (Ex. xxxiv. 6, 7; Ps. xxv. 7; xxxiv. 18; cxxxviii. 6; cxlvii. 6; Isa. lvii. 15, &c.); though its full disclosure, in connection with the Lamb of God which taketh away the sin of the world, was naturally reserved for the New Testament. And yet, so natural is self-righteousness to the pride of the human heart, that it has found its way even into the doctrinal system of the Church; and by that Apostasy which panders to all the corrupt inclinations of our nature, while preserving the form of evangelical truth, it has been erected into a most subtle scheme which, while apparently ascribing all to *Grace*, is in reality a doctrine of Salvation by *works.* (See the Canons and Decrees of the Council of Trent, Sess. VI. *Decretum de Justificatione;* particularly c. vii. ix. with *Can.* ix. xi. xii. xiii.) Even into Protestant Churches the very same doctrine has found entrance, under different forms of language, and in times of religious indifference and general degeneracy has spread its deadly virus over whole regions once blooming with health; nor is it effectually dislodged in any heart save by Divine teaching. 2. To be self-emptied, or "poor in spirit," is the fundamental and indispensable preparation for welcoming the "grace which bringeth salvation." Wherever this exists, that "mourning" which precedes comfort, that "hungering and thirsting after righteousness" which is rewarded with the "fulness" of it, is invariably found—as in this publican. Such, therefore, and such only, are the truly justified ones. "He hath filled the hungry with good things; and the rich he hath sent empty away". (ch. i. 53).

15-17.—Little Children Brought to Christ. (= Matt. xix. 13-15; Mark x. 13-16.) *Here at length our Evangelist—after travelling over three hundred and fifty-one verses almost alone—gets again upon the line, travelling, as will be seen, in company with the two preceding Evangelists, though each,* if one might so speak, *on separate rails.*

15. And they brought unto him also infants [τὰ βρέφη]. This shows that some, at least, of those called "little" or "young children" in Matt. xix. 13, and Mark x. 13, were literally "babes." **that he would touch them**—or, as more fully given in Matthew, "that He should put his hands on them and *pray*," that is, invoke a blessing on them (Mark x. 16); according to venerable custom (Gen. xlviii. 14, 15). **but when his disciples saw it, they rebuked them.** Repeatedly the disciples thus interposed, to save annoyance and interruption to their Master, but, as the result showed, *always against the mind of Christ.* (Matt. xv. 23, &c.; ch. xviii. 39, 40.) Here, it is plain from our Lord's reply, that they thought the intrusion a useless one, since *infants* were not capable of receiving anything from Him—His ministrations were for *grown people.* **16. But Jesus called them unto him, and said.** In Mark, however, we have a precious addition, "But when Jesus saw it, He was *much displeased*" [ἠγανάκτησε], and said unto them," **SUFFER [THE] LITTLE CHILDREN** [τὰ παιδία] **TO COME UNTO ME, AND FORBID THEM NOT.** What words are these from the lips of Christ! The price of them is above rubies. But the *reason* assigned, in the words that follow, crowns the statement—**FOR OF SUCH IS THE KINGDOM OF GOD**—or, as in Matt., "of heaven." **17. Verily I say unto you, Whosoever shall not receive the kingdom of God as a little child shall in no wise enter therein.** See on Mark ix. 36. But the action that followed—omitted by our Evangelist, and only partially given by Matthew, but fully supplied by Mark—is the best of all: "And He took them up in His arms, put His hands upon them, and blessed them" (Mark x. 16). Now, is it to be conceived that all our Lord meant by this was to teach a lesson, not about children at all, but about *grown people;* namely, that they must become childlike if they would be capable of the kingdom of God, and for this reason they should not hinder *infants* from coming to Him, and therefore He took up and blessed *the infants themselves?* Did not the grave mistake of the disciples, which so "much displeased" the Lord Jesus, consist just in this, that they thought infants should not be brought to Christ, *because only grown people could profit by Him?* And though He took the irresistible opportunity of lowering their pride of reason, by informing them that, in order to enter the Kingdom, *instead of the children first becoming like them, they must themselves become like the children*—as a German writer has well expressed it—yet this was but by the way; and returning to the *children themselves*, He took them up in His gracious arms, put His hands upon them, and blessed them, for no conceivable reason but to show that *they were thereby made capable*, as infants, *of the Kingdom of God.*

17 forbid them not: for [l]of such is the kingdom of God. Verily I say unto you, Whosoever shall not receive the kingdom of God as a little child shall in no wise enter therein.

A. D. 33.

[l] 1 Cor. 14. 20.

Remarks.—1. How different the feelings of Jesus from those of His disciples, in this as in so many other cases! They "marvelled that He talked with the woman" of Samaria, while that "talk" was "meat to Him that they knew not of" (John iv. 27, 32): The cries of the Syrophenician woman after Jesus were harsh in their ears, but they were music in His (Matt. xv. 23, 28): And here, they think He has grown people enough to attend to, without being annoyed with untaught children and unconscious babes, who could get no possible good from Him; and so they administer to the expectant parents their damping, miserable "rebuke." But this was not more false in doctrine than the feeling that expressed it was at variance with His. It 'grievously vexed' Him, as the word signifies. His heart yearned after these babes, just as "babes" and "little children;" nor are we capable of knowing the whole heart of Christ towards us if we leave out of it this most touching and beautiful element—the feeling that grievously vexed Him when infants were held back from Him. O what a spectacle was that which presented itself to the eye that was capable (if, indeed, there was one) of seeing into the interior of it—The Only begotten of the Father with an unconscious Babe in His arms; His gentle, yet mighty hands upon it; and His eyes upraised to heaven as the blessing descended upon it! Was not this one of those things which "angels desired to look into?" For He was "seen of angels."

> 'He raised them in His holy arms,
> He blessed them from the world and all its harms:
> Heirs though they were of sin and shame,
> He blessed them in his own and in His Father's name.
>
> 'Then, as each fond, unconscious child
> *On th' everlasting Parent sweetly smil'd,*
> *Like infants sporting on the shore,*
> *That tremble not at ocean's boundless roar,'* &c.—KEBLE.

3. If Christ was "much displeased" with His disciples for interfering with those who were bringing their infants to Him, surely it is not enough that *we* do not positively *hinder* them. Whatsoever on our part is *fitted* to keep back children from Christ is in effect the same thing, and may be expected to cause the same displeasure. But that is not all. For, as it is an acknowledged rule, that whenever any sin is forbidden, the contrary duty is commanded, so the displeasure of Christ at the attempt to keep back these children from Him carries with it the duty of bringing, or having them brought to Him, and the assurance of His benignant satisfaction with parents that bring them, and every one who does anything to cause them to be brought to Him. Be stirred up, then, and emboldened, believing parents, to bring your babes, even from their first breath, to Jesus; and let the ministers of Christ, and all who would have His gracious complacency resting upon them, as the first and the last step in "feeding His lambs," bring them to Jesus! 4. As the parable of the Good Samaritan has filled Christendom with Institutions for the relief of the wretched, over and above all that individuals have done in private, so this little incident—recorded by three of the Evangelists, yet occupying, even in the most detailed narrative of it, only four brief verses—has, over and above all that it has given birth to in private, filled Christendom with classes for the Christian training of the young; in the earlier ages, in a less systematic and comprehensive form, and chiefly by pastoral superintendence of parental instruction, but in these latter days on a vast scale, and to admirable effect. Nor can we doubt that the eye of Him who, in the days of His flesh, took up little children in His arms, put his hands on them, and blessed them, looks down from the skies in sweet complacency upon such efforts, blesses richly those that in obedience and love to Him engage in them, gathers many a lamb from amongst such flocks, to fold them in His own bosom above, and sends the rest as they grow up into the great world as "a seed to serve Him," a leaven to leaven the lump, that He may not come and smite it with a curse (Mal. iv. 6). 5. Let the intelligent reader note carefully the *standing* which this incident gives to children—even unconscious "infants"—in the Kingdom of God. "Suffer the little children to come unto me, for *of such* is the Kingdom of God." We have given reasons why this cannot mean merely, 'Let little *children* come to me, because *grown people* must be like them if they would enter the Kingdom.' What can be balder than such an interpretation of our Lord's words? But how natural and self-commending is the following sense of them: 'Ye are wrong in thinking that not till these children have grown to manhood can they get any good from Me. They also, even these unconscious babes, have their place, and not the least place, in the Kingdom of Heaven.' But if there could be any doubt whether our Lord was here speaking of the *children themselves*, or only of child-like *men*, surely His putting His hands upon them, and blessing them, ought to set that question at rest. What *could* such actions mean, if not to convey some spiritual blessing, some saving benefit, to the babes themselves? Does any one doubt that children, dying in infancy, are capable of going to heaven? Or, does any Christian think that without the new birth, and the blood that cleanseth from all sin, they will be fit company for heaven's inhabitants, or find themselves in an atmosphere congenial to their nature, or without this will ever see it? But, if infants are capable *of all that saves the soul*, before they are capable of consciously believing in Christ, and even though they die before ever doing so, what follows? "*Can any man forbid water*"—said Peter of the Gentile Cornelius and his company—"*that these should not be baptized, which have received the Holy Ghost as well as we?*" (Acts x. 47). Of course, such application of the baptismal water *to infants* can have no warrant from our incident, save where the infants have been *previously brought to Christ Himself* for his benediction, and only as *the sign and seal* of His promised benediction. But you may say, 'Is not *faith* explicitly and peremptorily required *in order to baptism?*' Yes, and *in order to salvation* too. Nay, "he that believeth not shall be damned." Are those who die in infancy, then, damned—because incapable of believing? 'O no,' it will be said; 'they were not *contemplated* in the demand for faith, in order to salvation.' Just so; and for that reason, since they are capable of the new birth, and forgiveness, and complete salvation—all in infancy and without any faith at all, just as truly as grown people—they are surely capable of the mere outward symbol of it, which brings them within the sacred enclosure, and separates them to a holy service and society, and inheritance amongst the people of God (1 Cor. vii. 14). Within this sacred enclosure, the apostle regards them as "in the Lord," and addresses them as such (Eph. vi. 1), in-

18 And [m] a certain ruler asked him, saying, Good Master, what shall I do
19 to inherit eternal life? And Jesus said unto him, Why callest thou me

A. D. 33.

[m] Matt. 19. 16.

culcating on them obedience to their parents, as "*well pleasing unto the Lord*" (Col. iii. 20). The Christian household is thus to be *a Christian nursery.* Sweet view this of the standing of children that have been from their very birth brought to Christ, and blessed of Him, as believers may not doubt that their children are, and loved as dearly as if He took them up in His very arms, and made the blessing to descend upon them, even life for evermore! For more on this subject, see on ch. xix. 28-44, Remark 5 at the close of that Section.

18-30.—THE RICH YOUNG RULER, AND DISCOURSE SUGGESTED BY HIS CASE. (= Matt. xix. 16-30; Mark x. 17-31.)

The Rich Young Ruler (18-23). **18. And a certain ruler asked him, saying.** Mark says, "And when He was gone forth into the way"—the high road, by this time crowded with travellers on their way to Jerusalem, to keep the Passover—"there came one running, and kneeled to Him, and asked Him," **Good Master, what shall I do**—in Matthew, "What good thing shall I do," **to inherit eternal life? 19. And Jesus said unto him, Why callest thou me good? none is good, save one, that is, God** [Τί με λέγεις ἀγαθόν; οὐδεὶς ἀγαθὸς, εἰ μὴ εἷς ὁ Θεός. So Mark x. 18; and so in the received text of Matt. xix. 17, with trifling variation. But all recent critical editors—*Griesbach, Lachmann, Tischendorf,* and *Tregelles*—give the text of Matt. xix. 17 thus—Τί με ἐρωτᾷς περὶ τοῦ ἀγαθοῦ; εἷς ἐστιν ὁ ἀγαθός: '*Why askest thou me concerning what is Good? One is the Good One:*' *Alford* adopts this into his text; *de Wette* and *Meyer* approve of it; and *Olshausen* thinks it admits of no doubt that this is the genuine reading. In spite of this, we venture to think that nothing but such overwhelming evidence in its behalf as it certainly does not possess would entitle it even to favourable consideration. And this for two reasons: First, It makes our Lord's reply to this sincere and anxious enquirer incredibly inept. The man's question was, "Good Master, what good thing shall I do to inherit eternal life?" Our Lord answers by asking him why he questioned Him regarding what was good—according to this reading. Is it likely our Lord would so answer him? especially as He presently tells him the thing he really wanted to know. But the conclusion of our Lord's reply, according to this reading, crowns its absurdity in our judgment: 'One is the Good One.' If this has any connection at all with what goes before, it must mean that the man had no need to enquire what was the good which men were to do, because One was the Good Being! But if there be no connection here, there is as little in what follows. And looking at this reading of our Lord's reply to a sincere and anxious enquirer after eternal life, nothing could persuade us that our Lord did utter it—in the absence, at least, of overpowering evidence from ancient MSS. and versions. But secondly, Since no one pretends that this is the reading of Mark and Luke, and since *their* account of our Lord's reply, while it gives a clear and pregnant answer to the man's question, differs totally from the sense of this peculiar reading of Matthew, is it not a strong argument against this reading that it yields no proper sense at all, while the received reading gives the clear sense of the other two Gospels? We are well aware of the tendency of early transcribers to assimilate the readings of one Gospel to those of another, especially of two others which agree together; and we could give that consideration some weight here if the evidence otherwise were in favour of the peculiar reading. Nor do we forget that, *other things being equal,* the more peculiar a reading is the more probably is it the right one. But other things are *not* equal here, but far from it. It only remains, then, that we advert to the external evidence on the subject. Only one MS. of the oldest date—the celebrated *Vatican* (B)—was thought to have this reading; but the recently discovered *Sinaitic* MS. (א), we now know, has it too. Two others (D and L) have it, together with three of the cursive or more recent MSS. Two of the *Syriac* versions, nearly all copies of the *Old Latin* and of the *Vulgate,* and the *Memphitic* or Lower-Egyptian, have it. *Origen,* in the third century, has the first part of it at least; and *Eusebius, Jerome,* and *Augustin* in the fourth. Such is the evidence for this unnatural reading. Now, how stands the evidence on the other side? The only other MS. of oldest date and greatest authority (A) is defective here; but the MSS. with which it usually agrees have the received text. The next weightiest MS. has it—the *Codex Ephraemi rescriptus* (C)—and with it *all other known MSS. of the Gospels,* except those above referred to. An overwhelming number; and in weight, surely counterbalancing those above-mentioned. It is found in the oldest and most venerable of all the *Syriac* versions, the 'Peshito,' and in the text of the most critical one, the 'Philoxenian' or 'Harclean;' though the other reading is inserted in the margin. And it is found in the *Thebaic* or Upper-Egyptian version, which is thought to have claims to great antiquity. Of the Fathers, it is found in *Irenæus,* and substantially in *Justin Martyr,* both of the second century, besides most of the later Fathers. On a review of the whole case, we hesitate not to say, that while the weight of *external* evidence appears to us to be clearly in favour of the received text, the *internal* evidence, arising from the inept character which the other reading gives to our Lord's reply, is decisive against it. We have been the more full in our statement upon this passage, because, while we hold that the true text of the New Testament must in every case be determined by the *whole evidence* which we possess, this passage affords a good example of the tendency of critics to be carried away, in opposition to their own principles, in favour of startling readings, and of the necessity, in such cases—even though one should stand almost alone—of expressing the result of the entire evidence in terms as strong as that evidence warrants. *Scrivener* ("Criticism of the New Testament") vindicates the received text, though with no reference to the inept character which the other one stamps upon our Lord's reply, and admitting too much in favour of the other reading from its *harshness,* and the tendency to *assimilation.* The only able critic who speaks out upon the 'absurdity' of this various reading is *Fritzsche.*]

Our Lord's response consists, first, of a hint by the way, founded on the appellation, "Good Master;" and next, of a direct reply to the enquiry itself. "Why callest thou me good? There is none good but One, [that is], God." Did our Lord mean by this to teach that God only ought to be called "good?" Impossible: for that had been to contradict all Scripture teaching *and His own too.* "A *good* man showeth favour and lendeth" (Ps. cxii. 5); "A *good* man out of the good treasure of his heart, bringeth forth good things" (Matt. xii. 35); "Well done, *good* and faithful servant"

Z

20 good? none *is* good, save one, *that is,* God. Thou knowest the commandments, [n]Do not commit adultery, Do not kill, Do not steal, Do not
21 bear false witness, [o]Honour thy father and thy mother. And he said,
22 All these have I kept from my youth up. Now when Jesus heard these
things, he said unto him, Yet lackest thou one thing: sell [p]all that thou
hast, and distribute unto the poor, and thou shalt have treasure in
23 heaven: and come, follow me. And when he heard this, he was very
sorrowful: for he was very rich.
24 And when Jesus saw that he was very sorrowful, he said, [q]How hardly
25 shall they that have riches enter into the kingdom of God! For it is
easier for a camel to go through a needle's eye, than for a rich man to

A. D. 33.

[n] Ex. 20. 12. Deut. 5. 16. Rom. 13. 9.
[o] Eph. 6. 2. Col. 3. 20.
[p] Matt. 6. 19. Matt. 19. 21. 1 Tim. 6. 19.
[q] Pro. 11. 28. Pro. 18. 11. Jer. 5. 5. 1 Tim. 6. 9. Jas. 2. 5.

(Matt. xxv. 21); "Barnabas was a *good* man, and full of the Holy Ghost" (Acts xi. 24). Unless, therefore, we are to ascribe captiousness to our Lord, He could have had but one object—to teach this youth, on the one hand, that *He declined to be classed along with other "good" people and "good masters;"* and on the other hand, by reminding him that the only *other* sort of goodness, namely, *supreme goodness*, belonged to God alone, to leave him to draw the startling inference—that *that* was the goodness which belonged to Him. Unless this object is seen in the *background* of our Lord's words, nothing worthy of Him can be made out of this first part of His reply. But this hint once given, our Lord at once passes from it to the proper subject of the youth's inquiry. **20. Thou knowest the commandments.** In Matthew (xix. 17, 18) this is more fully given: "But," passing from that point, "if thou wilt enter into life, keep the commandments. He saith unto Him, Which?"—as if He had said, 'Point me out one of them which I have not kept.' "Jesus saith unto him," **Do not commit adultery, Do not kill, Do not steal, Do not bear false witness, Honour thy father and thy mother.** Our Lord purposely confines Himself to the commandments of what is called the *second* table of the law, which he would consider easy to keep, enumerating them all—for in Mark x. 19, "Defraud not" stands for the *tenth* commandment; otherwise the eighth is twice repeated. In Matthew the *sum* of this second table of the law is added, "Thou shalt love thy neighbour as thyself," as if to see if he would venture to say he had kept *that.* **21. And he said, All these have I kept from my youth up:**—"What lack I yet?" (Matt. xix. 20) is an important addition in Matthew, though implied in the shorter answer of the other Evangelists. Ah! this gives us a glimpse of his heart. Doubtless he was perfectly sincere; but something within whispered to him that *his* keeping of the commandments was *too easy* a way of getting to heaven. He felt something beyond this to be necessary; but since after keeping all the commandments he was at a loss to know what that could be, he came to Jesus just upon that point. "Then," says Mark (x. 21), "Jesus, beholding him, loved him," or 'looked lovingly upon him.' His sincerity, frankness, and nearness to the kingdom of God, in themselves most winning qualities, won our Lord's regard even though he turned his back upon Him—a lesson to those who can see nothing loveable save in the regenerate. **22. Now when Jesus heard these things, he said unto him, Yet lackest thou one thing**—but that, alas! was a fundamental, a fatal lack. **sell all that thou hast, and distribute unto the poor, and thou shalt have treasure in heaven: and come, follow me.** As riches were his idol, our Lord, who knew this from the first, lays His great authoritative grasp at once upon it, saying, 'Now give Me up that, and all is right.' No general direction about the disposal of riches, then, is here given, save that we are to sit loose to them and lay them at the feet of Him who gave them. He who does this with all he has, whether rich or poor, is a true heir of the kingdom of heaven. **23. And when he heard this, he was very sorrowful: for he was very rich.** Matthew, more fully, "he *went away* sorrowful:" Mark, still more fully, "he was sad at that saying, and went away grieved, for he had great possessions." Sorry he was, very sorry, to part with Christ; but to part with his riches would have cost him a pang more. When Riches or Heaven on Christ's terms were the alternatives, the result showed to which side the balance inclined. Thus was he shown to lack the one all-comprehensive requirement of the law—the *absolute subjection of the heart to God,* and this want vitiated all his other obediences. Let us now gather up the favourable points in this man's case, as here presented. First, He was of irreproachable moral character; and this amidst all the temptations of *youth,* for he was a "young man" (Matt. xix. 22), and of *wealth,* for he was "very rich." Secondly, He was restless notwithstanding: his heart craved eternal life. Thirdly, Unlike the "rulers," to whose class he belonged (*v.* 18), he so far believed in Jesus as to be persuaded He could authoritatively direct him on this vital point. And, Fourthly, So earnest was he that he came "running," and even "kneeling" before Him; and that not in any quiet corner, but "when He was gone forth into the *way*"—the open road—undeterred by the virulent opposition of the class to which he belonged, and by the shame he might be expected to feel at broaching such a question in the hearing of so many. How much that is interesting, attractive, loveable, promising, is there here! And yet all was in vain. Eternal life could not be his, for he was not prepared to *give up all* for it. He had not *found* the treasure hid in the field; he had not found the one pearl of great price; for he was not prepared to sell all that he had to possess himself of them (Matt. xiii. 44-46).

Discourse suggested by this case (24-30). **24. And when Jesus saw that he was very sorrowful**—as he "went away," **he said.** Mark says "He looked round about," as if first He would follow the departing youth with His eye, "and saith unto His disciples," **How hardly shall they that have riches enter into the kingdom of God!** In Mark (x. 24) an explanation of the difficulty is added, "How hard is it for them that *trust* in riches to enter," &c., that is, 'With what difficulty is this idolatrous trust conquered, without which they cannot enter;' and this is introduced by the word, "Children" [Τέκνα]—that sweet diminutive of affection and pity. (See John xxi. 5.) **25. For it is easier for a camel to go through a needle's eye, than for a rich man to enter into the kingdom of God**—a proverbial expression, denoting literally a thing impossible, but figuratively a thing very

26 enter into the kingdom of God. And they that heard *it* said, Who then
27 can be saved? And he said, [r]The things which are impossible with men
are possible with God.
28, Then [s]Peter said, Lo, we have left all, and followed thee. And he said
29 unto them, Verily I say unto you, [t]There is no man that hath left house,
or parents, or brethren, or wife, or children, for the kingdom of God's
30 sake, who [u]shall not receive manifold more in this present time, and [v]in
the world to come life everlasting.

A. D. 33.

r Jer. 32. 17. Zec. 8. 6. Eph. 1. 19, 20.
s Matt. 19. 27.
t Deut. 33. 9.
u Job 42. 10.
v Rev. 2. 17. Rev. 3. 21.

difficult. **26. And they that heard it said, Who then can be saved?** 'At that rate, how is any one to be saved?' **27. And he said, The things which are impossible with men are possible with God**—'Well, it does pass *human*, but not *divine* power.'

28. Then Peter said—in the simplicity of his heart, as is evident from our Lord's reply, **Lo, we have left all, and followed thee.** He was conscious that the required surrender, which that young ruler had not been able to make, had been made, not only by himself but by his brethren along with him, whom he generously takes in—"*we* have left all." Little, indeed, was Peter's "all." But, as *Bengel* says, the workman's little is as much to him as the prince's much. In Matthew's narrative Peter adds, "What shall we have therefore?" How shall it fare with us? **29, 30. And he said unto them, Verily I say unto you, There is no man that hath left house, or parents, or brethren, or wife, or children, for the kingdom of God's sake, Who shall not receive manifold more in this present time, and in the world to come life everlasting.** In Mark (x. 29, 30) the specification is so full as to take in *every* form of self-sacrifice: "There is no man that hath left house, or brethren, or sisters, or father, or mother, or wife, or children, or lands, for My sake, and the Gospel's, but he shall receive an hundred-fold now in this present time, houses, and brethren, and sisters, and mothers, and children, and lands, with persecutions; and in the world to come eternal life." This glorious promise is worthy of minute study. First, Observe how graciously the Lord Jesus acknowledges at once the completeness and the acceptableness of the surrender, as a thing already made by the attached followers whom He had around Him. 'Yes, Peter, thou and thy fellows have indeed given up all for Me, and it makes you beautiful in Mine eyes; but ye shall lose nothing by this, but gain much.' Next, Observe how our Lord identifies the interests of the kingdom of God with the Gospel's and with His own—saying alternatively, "For the kingdom of God's sake," and "for My sake and the Gospel's." See on Matt. v. 11; and on Luke vi. 22. Further, Observe the very remarkable promise—not of comfort and support, in a mere general sense, under persecution, and ultimate deliverance out of all this into eternal life—but of "an hundred-fold *now in this time;*" and this in the form of a *re-construction of all human relationships and affections, on a Christian basis and amongst Christians, after they have been sacrificed in their natural form, on the altar of love to Christ.* This He calls "manifold more," yea, "an hundred-fold more," than what they sacrificed for His sake. Our Lord was Himself the first to exemplify this in a *new adjustment of His own relationships.* (See on Matt. xii. 49, 50, and Remark 3 at the close of that Section; see also on 2 Cor. vi. 14, 18.) But this, it is added, "with persecutions;" for how could such a transfer take place without the most cruel wrenches to flesh and blood? Nay, the persecution would haply follow them into their new and higher circle, breaking that up too. Well, but "in the world to come life everlasting." And

> 'When the shore is won at last,
> Who will count the billows past?'—KEBLE.

The foregoing promises are for *every one* that forsakes his all for Christ—"There is no man," &c. But in Matthew xix. 28, these promises are prefaced by a special promise *to the Twelve:* "And Jesus said unto them, That ye which have followed me, in the regeneration, when the Son of man shall sit in the throne of His glory, ye also shall sit upon twelve thrones, judging the twelve tribes of Israel." The words "in the regeneration" [ἐν τῇ παλιγγενεσίᾳ] may be joined either to what goes *before* or to what follows *after;* and this, of course, materially affects the sense. In the former case it is, "Ye which have followed Me in the regeneration;" the meaning of which is, 'Ye who have followed Me in the new kingdom or economy which I am now erecting—the new life now begun.' Among the few who take this view of it are *Hilary* among the Fathers; *Erasmus* and *Calvin*, among the moderns. But by far the most and best interpreters, with whom we agree, connect the words with what follows: "Ye which have followed Me shall, in the regeneration," &c. But opinions are divided as to what is meant in this case by "the regeneration," and consequently, as to what is meant by the promise that the Twelve should "sit on twelve thrones, judging the twelve tribes of Israel." One class of interpreters, understanding by "the regeneration" the new Gospel kingdom which Christ was erecting, would paraphrase the words thus: 'Ye who have forsaken all and followed Me as no others have done shall, in the new kingdom which I am setting up, and which shall soon become more visible and stable than it now is, give law to and rule the great Christian world'—which is here set forth in Jewish dress, as the Twelve tribes of Israel, to be presided over by the Twelve apostles on Twelve judicial thrones. In this sense certainly the promise has been illustriously fulfilled; and so *Grotius, Lightfoot,* &c., take it. But the majority of interpreters refer it to the yet future glory; and ch. xxii. 28-30 seems to confirm that interpretation. In this case it points to the time of the restitution of all things, when the great apostolic founders of the Christian Church shall be exalted to a distinction corresponding with the services they have rendered. Perhaps there is no need to draw a very sharp line of separation between these two views of the promise here made to the Twelve; and we do better, probably (with *Calvin*), to see in the present *fact*, that the "holy temple" of the Christian Church is "built upon the foundation of the apostles," and those "prophets" that supplemented their labours, "Jesus Christ Himself being the Chief Corner-Stone," the *assurance* that in the future glory their place would correspond with their services in that high office. The reply of our Lord to Peter closes, in Matthew and Mark, with the oft-repeated words, "But many

31 Then [w]he took *unto him* the twelve, and said unto them, Behold, we
go up to Jerusalem, and all things [x]that are written by the prophets
32 concerning the Son of man shall be accomplished. For [y]he shall be
delivered unto the Gentiles, and shall be mocked, and spitefully entreated,
33 and spitted on: and they shall scourge *him*, and put him to death: and
34 the third day he shall rise again. And [z]they understood none of these
things: and this saying was hid from them, neither knew they the things
which were spoken.
35 And [a]it came to pass, that, as he was come nigh unto Jericho, a certain

A. D. 33.
[w] Matt. 16. 21. Matt. 17. 22.
[x] Ps. 22. Isa. 53.
[y] Matt. 27. 2. ch. 23. 1.
[z] Mark 9. 32. ch. 2. 50.
[a] Matt. 20. 29. Mark 10. 46.

that are first shall be last, and the last first." See on Matt. xx. 16, and Remark 4 at the close of that Section.

Remarks.—1. Is it not affecting to think how near this rich young ruler came to the kingdom of God without entering it? His irreproachable morals and his religious earnestness, amidst so much that was hostile to both; the ingenuousness with which he looked up to the Lord Jesus as qualified to solve his difficulties and relieve his anxieties on the subject of salvation, though belonging to a class that regarded Him with bitter hostility; and the courage with which he ran to Him, and knelt before Him in the presence of so many, with the eager enquiry, "What shall I do to inherit eternal life?"—when one thinks of all this, and then reads that, after all, "he went away" from Christ, how sad does it make the heart! But we must get to the bottom of this case if we would fully profit by it. What, then, was the defect? One thing only he lacked; but that, as we have said, was fundamental and fatal. "If any man love the world," says the apostle, "the love of the Father is not in him" (1 John ii. 15). Now this was just what this youth did. Others might not have detected it; but He whose eyes were as a flame of fire stood before him. Had anything else been asked of him, he might have stood the test. But the one thing that was demanded of him was the one thing he could not part with—his possessions. He might have kept these and gone to heaven if the Lord had not expressly demanded them. But for this, had he only sat loose to them, and been *prepared* to part with them at the call of duty, that had been quite enough. For while many a one covets the world he does not possess, some sit loose to the world they do possess. The former are idolaters, and "no idolater hath any inheritance in the kingdom of Christ and of God." The latter have, in the eye of Christ, "left all and followed Him, and they shall have treasure in heaven." Thus this youth, instead of keeping, as he thought, all the commandments from his youth up, never kept the first and great commandment, which is to love the Lord our God with all our heart. Had he done so he would not have gone away from Christ. And thus, too, just as in the human body, one may want an eye, or a hand, or a foot, or all of these, and other members too, and yet be a living man, because none of these are *vital;* whereas the heart, being essential to life, cannot be wanted: so the soul may be spiritually alive, and on its way to glory, notwithstanding many imperfections; but there are defects, even one of which is incompatible with life: "Without *faith* it is impossible to please God;" and "If any man have not *the Spirit of Christ*, he is none of His;" and "*Covetousness* is idolatry." 2. While every condition in life has its own snares, the danger of wealth lies in the tendency to idolize it; and it is not unlikely that the apostle had this incident and the reflections that follow it in view when he thus directed Timothy: "Charge them that are rich in this world, that they be not high-minded, nor *trust* in uncertain riches, but in the living God, who giveth us richly all things to enjoy; that they do good, that they be rich in good works, ready to distribute, willing to communicate; laying up in store for themselves a good foundation against the time to come, that they may lay hold on eternal life" (1 Tim. vi. 17-19). At the same time, this and numberless exhortations to the rich show the folly of taking our Lord's directions to the rich young ruler as a general direction to part with all worldly possessions to the poor in order to get to heaven. In that case such passages as those just quoted would have no meaning at all. Christianity was not designed to obliterate the distinction of ranks and conditions in life, but to teach and beget in the different classes of society the proper feelings towards each other, and towards the common Lord of all. 3. Christians should learn from Christ Himself to appreciate the excellences even of the unconverted, while not blinded by these to what they fundamentally and fatally lack. 4. The Human excellences of the Lord Jesus are not to be regarded as on a level with those of mere men. Though human in their *nature*, they are the excellences of the Only begotten of the Father, which take them quite out of the category of *ordinary* excellences, even though these were faultless. If something of this kind was not underneath our Lord's hint to the young man about there being none good but One, it will be difficult to make any dignified sense out of it at all; but if it was, all is intelligible and worthy of Jesus. And thus *Socinianism*, instead of finding the support here which it is so fain to catch at, is only baffled by it.

31-34.—Third Explicit Announcement of His approaching Sufferings, Death, and Resurrection. (= Matt. xx. 17-19; Mark x. 32-34.) For the exposition, see on Mark x. 32-34.

35-43.—A Blind Man Healed. (= Matt. xx. 29-34, "Two Blind Men;" Mark x. 46-52, "Blind Bartimeus.")

35. And it came to pass, that, as he was come nigh unto Jericho—on his way through Peræa to his last Passover, **a certain blind man sat by the way-side begging.** In Mark the name is given—"blind Bartimæus, the son of Timæus." But there and in Matthew it was "as they departed from," or "went out of Jericho;" and in Matthew it is not one, but "two blind men," beggars, that on this occasion received their sight. Several critics —as *Greswell, Ebrard, Ellicott, Neander, Wieseler*, with some of the Fathers—suppose one to have been healed on *entering*, the other on *leaving* Jericho. Others to whom this seems far-fetched, would leave the facts as recorded to speak independently for themselves. One thing seems clear, that these three narratives must have been written quite apart from each other; and another, that these divergences in the circumstantial details strongly corroborate the historical truth of the facts. Perhaps, *if we knew all the particulars*, we should see no difficulty; but that we have been left so far in the dark, shows that the thing is of

36 blind man sat by the way-side begging: and hearing the multitude pass
37 by, he asked what it meant. And they told him, that Jesus of Nazareth
38 passeth by. And he cried, saying, Jesus, *thou* son of David, have mercy
39 on me! And they which went before rebuked him, that he should hold
his peace: but he cried so much the more, *Thou* son of David, have mercy
40 on me! And Jesus [b]stood, and commanded him to be brought unto
41 him: and when he was come near, he asked him, saying, What wilt thou
that I shall do unto thee? And he said, Lord, that I may receive my
42 sight. And Jesus said unto him, Receive thy sight: [c]thy faith hath
43 saved thee. And immediately [d]he received his sight, and followed him,
[e]glorifying God: and all the people, when they saw *it*, gave praise unto
God.

A. D. 33.

[b] Heb. 2. 17. Heb. 5. 2.
[c] ch. 17. 19.
[d] Ps. 33. 9. Isa. 35. 5.
[e] Ps. 103. 1. Isa. 43. 7, 8, 21. ch. 4. 39. ch. 5. 26. ch. 17. 15-18. Acts 4. 21. Acts 11. 18. 1 Pet. 2. 9.

no moment any way. Had there been any collusion among the authors of these Gospels, they would certainly have taken care to remove these 'spots on the sun'—as *Chrysostom*, of the Fathers, with *Olshausen*, *van Osterzee*, and *Alford*, fail not to observe. **36. And hearing the multitude pass by, he asked what it meant**—a most graphic and natural touch; the *sound* being all he had to tell him what was going on. **37. And they told him, that Jesus of Nazareth passeth by. 38. And he cried, saying, Jesus, son of David,** in other words, 'Thou promised Messiah.' That this was the understood sense of the phrase is evident from the acclamation with which the multitude greeted Him on his triumphal entry into Jerusalem (Matt. xxi. 9; see also Matt. xii. 23). **have mercy on me! 39. And they which went before**—"the multitude" (Matt. xx. 31), **rebuked him, that he should hold his peace**—and not annoy, or impede the progress of Jesus; very much in the spirit of the Twelve themselves but a little before, when infants were brought to Him (see on verse 15, and Remark 1 at the close of that Section), and when the Syrophenician woman "cried after Him" (see on Mark vii. 26). But O, how differently from them did Jesus feel! **but he cried so much the more, Son of David, have mercy on me!** This is that *importunity*, so highly commended and richly rewarded in the Syrophenician woman, and so often enjoined, (ch. xi. 5, &c.; xviii. 1, &c.) **40. And Jesus stood**—or "stood still," as rendered in Matthew and Mark, **and commanded him to be brought unto him.** Mark (x. 49-50) has this interesting addition: "And they call the blind man, saying unto him, Be of good comfort: rise, He calleth thee." It is just as one earnestly desiring an interview with some exalted person, but told by one official after another that it is vain to wait, for he will not succeed—they know it—yet persists in waiting for some answer to his suit, and at length the door opens, and a servant appears, saying, 'You are to be admitted—He has called you.' No doubt those who thus encouraged the poor man, knew well the cure that would follow. "And he, casting away his garment, rose, and came to Jesus." How lively is this touch about the casting away of his garment! It is evidently the remark of an eye-witness, expressive of the exhilarating hope with which he was immediately filled. **And when he was come near, he asked him, 41. Saying, What wilt thou that I shall do unto thee?** It was plain enough to all present what the poor blind man wanted: but Jesus, by this question, would try him; would deepen his present consciousness of need; and would draw out his faith in Him. See on John v. 6. **and he said, Lord** [Κύριε]. In Mark the term rendered "Lord" is "*Rabboni*"—an emphatic and confiding exclamation (see on John xx. 16). **that I may receive my sight. 42. And Jesus**—"had compassion on them, and touched their eyes," says Matthew, "and" **said unto him, Receive thy sight, thy faith hath saved thee. 43. And immediately he received his sight, and**—now as a grateful disciple, **followed him, glorifying God: and all the people, when they saw it, gave praise unto God.**

Remark.—This gracious cure, it will be observed, was quite casual. Blind Bartimeus sat that day, as usual, by the way-side begging; not dreaming that ere its shadows fell he should see the light of heaven. But, like other blind people, his ears had doubtless been all the quicker to hear whatever was flying about. And there can be no doubt that the tidings sent to the imprisoned Baptist—"The blind receive their sight"—had flown to him, with, very possibly, the details of some of the cures. And just, as in the case of the Syrophenician woman, and in that of the woman with the issue of blood, these tidings had wrought in his heart the conviction that He was the promised Messiah, and such a confidence in His power and grace, that he would say within himself, 'O if He would but pass this way, how should I cry to Him, as "He that cometh in the name of the Lord;" and, poor beggar though I be, the Son of David would not shut His ear against me—*for they tell me He never yet did that to any suppliant.* And who knows but He will come? They say he is even now in this region, and if He goes up to Jerusalem to keep the approaching Passover, He likely *will* come this way. But He may not come when I am here; and yet there is hope:—but what is that stir I hear? What is it? "Jesus of Nazareth passeth by!" O transport! He comes, He comes! Now is my time.' So, ere He comes up, the loud cry is heard, "Jesus, Son of David, have mercy on me!" In a moving crowd, accompanying some great person on a progress, there are always some who keep ahead of the main body. These, catching the sound first, officiously try to silence him, that there may be no commotion, no interruption:—'Stop that dense crowd in order that the case of a beggar may be attended to? why, at that rate He would never get on at all.' But the earnest suppliant is not to be moved by that. His opportunity has come, for which he had longed but scarce dared to hope; and he shall not be silenced. Nay, "so much the more" did he cry, "Son of David, have mercy on me!" At length the glorious Healer comes up to the spot, and the whole crowd must halt, while He cures this believing beggar. And first, He commands him to be called. They hasten through the crowd to the road-side, and bid the poor man be of good cheer, for the Lord has sent for him. This gives his faith time to ripen. 'I thought it would come to that: Long looked for—come at last: my hopes refused to be damped: they could not silence me; my soul went forth to Him in yet louder cries, and not in

19, AND *Jesus* entered and passed through [a]Jericho. And, behold, *there*
2 *was* a man named Zaccheus, which was the chief among the publicans,
3 and he was rich. And he sought to see Jesus who he was; and could
4 not for the press, because he was little of stature. And he ran before,
and climbed up into a sycamore tree to see him: for he was to pass that
5 *way*. And when Jesus came to the place, he looked up, and saw him,
and said unto him, Zaccheus, make haste, and come down; [b]for to-day I
6 must abide at thy house. And he made haste, and came down, and
7 received him joyfully. And when they saw *it*, they all murmured,

A. D. 33.

CHAP. 19.
[a] Jos. 6. 26.
1 Ki. 16. 34.
2 Ki. 2. 18-22
Jos. 2. 1.
[b] Gen. 18. 3, 5.
Gen. 19. 1, 3.
Ps. 101. 2, 3.
John 14. 23.

vain: I'm to succeed; I shall, I shall!' Thus he comes into the presence of Jesus. "What wilt thou that I shall do unto thee?" As he could not *see* Him, the Lord takes this way of awakening, through his *ears*, the expectation of relief, and gives him an opportunity of presenting in explicit terms the desire of his heart. "Lord," is his ready answer, "that I may receive my sight." It is enough. The Redeemer's heart yearns with compassion; He touches his eyes, and immediately He sees as other men. Like the man out of whom went the legion of devils, he clings to his wondrous Benefactor, pouring out his grateful feelings, in which the wondering people also join. Thus did this man catch his favourable moment, seize his opportunity, and obtain a rich reward. At other times he had cried in vain. And are there no opportunities—no favourable moments still—*analogous* to this, for getting the higher sight, for being healed in the higher sense? Are there not some seasons, rather than others, of which it may be said that "Jesus of Nazareth *passeth by*"? Seasons of affliction are such; but pre-eminently, seasons of religious awakening, of revival, and the effusion of the Spirit. And just as when, after a long, dull calm at sea, the wind gets up, all hands are astir to hoist the sails and catch the breeze, so then, if ever, as Jesus of Nazareth passeth by, should all that feel their need of healing stir up their expectations, and lift up their cries; and though there may be here also officious people who rebuke them, that they should hold their peace, their wisdom will be only to "cry so much the more." Nor can they more readily draw down His compassion and ensure relief, than by refusing to be silenced by such pretended friends.

CHAP. XIX. 1-10.—CONVERSION OF ZACCHEUS THE PUBLICAN. The opening verse shows that this remarkable incident occurred at the same time with the foregoing.

1. **And Jesus entered.** As the word "Jesus" is not in the original, it should not have been inserted here. The rendering should be, 'And He entered,' showing that the occasion is the same as before. **and passed through** [διήρχετο]—rather, 'was passing through' **Jericho**—as to which, see on chap. x. 30, 31. 2. **And, behold, there was a man named Zaccheus**—the same as *Zacchai*, Ezra ii. 9; Neh. vii. 14. From *v.* 9 it is evident that he was a Jew, and what he says in *v.* 8 would have proved it too. **which was** [καὶ αὐτὸς]—'and the same was' **the chief among the publicans**—a high revenue official, **and he was rich.** Ill-gotten riches some of it certainly was, as we shall see on *v.* 8. For the office and character of the publicans, see on Matt. v. 46, and on ch. xv. 1. 3. **And he sought to see Jesus**—not to listen to His teaching, or obtain anything from Him, but merely to see **who he was**—what sort of person this was, about whom there was so much speculation, and after whom such crowds were following. *Curiosity*, then, was his only motive, though his determination not to be baulked was overruled for more than he sought. **and could not for the press, because he was little of stature.** 4. **And he ran before, and climbed up into a sycamore tree**—the Egyptian fig, with leaves like the mulberry—**to see him: for he was to pass that way.** Thus eager to put himself in the way of Jesus, low as his motive was, he was rewarded by what he little dreamt of. 5. **And when Jesus came to the place, he looked up**—in the full knowledge of who was in that tree, and preparatory to addressing him, **and saw him, and said unto him, Zaccheus**—whom He had never before seen in the flesh, nor probably heard of by report; but "He calleth His own sheep *by name*, and leadeth them out" (John x. 3). **make haste, and come down; for to-day I must abide at thy house.** Our Lord *invites Himself*, and that in right *royal* style, which waits not for invitations, but—since the honour is done to the subject, not the sovereign—announces the purpose of royalty to partake of the subject's hospitalities. Manifestly our Lord speaks as knowing how the privilege would be appreciated. Accordingly, with an alacrity which in such a person surprises us, he does exactly as bidden. "Make haste;" 6. **And he made haste**—"and come down," **and came down**—"for to-day I must abide at thy house," **and received him joyfully.** Whence this so sudden "joy" in the cold bosom of an avaricious publican? The internal revolution was as perfect as it was instantaneous. He who spake to Matthew the publican but those witching words, "Follow me," and "he arose, left all, and followed Him"—He who said to the man with the withered hand, "Stretch forth thine hand," and "he stretched it out, and it was restored whole as the other"—the same said to the *heart* of Zaccheus at one and the same moment as to his ear, "Make haste and come down; for to-day I must abide at thy house." He with whom Zaccheus had to do had but to "speak, and it was done;" though few penetrated to the secret of this as the centurion did, at whose faith Jesus "marvelled" (ch. vii. 7-9). At the same time one can trace the steps of this revolution in the mind of Zaccheus. In the *look* which Christ gave him—"When Jesus came to the place, He looked up," singling him out from all others—he must have seen something of a *purpose* towards himself, which would at once arrest his attention. Then, His addressing him by *name*, as perfectly familiar with him, though He had never seen or heard of him before—this would fill him with amazement, and make the thought instantly flash across his mind, 'This *must* be the Christ He claims to be!' But when the *call* followed, in such wonderful terms—"Make haste, and come down, for to-day I must abide at thy house"—the conscious majesty of it, and the power with which it was spoken, as if sure of instant and glad obedience, doubtless completed the conquest of his mind and heart. But these, though the *avenues* through which Christ found His way into Zaccheus's heart, must not be regarded as the whole explanation of the change upon him. (See on Acts xvi. 14.) 7. **And when they saw it, they all murmured.** We have got so

8 saying, [c]That he was gone to be guest with a man that is a sinner. And
Zaccheus stood, and said unto the Lord; Behold, Lord, the half of my
goods I give to the poor; and if I have taken any thing from any man
9 by false accusation, I [d]restore *him* four-fold. And Jesus said unto him,
This day is salvation come to this house, forsomuch as [e]he also is a son
10 of Abraham. For [f]the Son of man is come to seek and to save that
which was lost.

A. D. 33.

[c] Matt. 9. 11, 21, 28, 31. ch. 5. 30.
[d] Ex. 22. 1. 1 Sam. 12. 3.
[e] ch. 13. 16.
[f] Matt. 10. 6. Matt. 15. 24.

accustomed to this in the Gospel History, that we know the classes that must be here referred to—"the Pharisees and scribes" (ch. xv. 2), or their echoes among the multitude. **saying, That he was gone to be guest** [καταλῦσαι]—or, 'take up His lodging,' as the same word is rendered in ch. ix. 12. The word signifies to 'unloose' or 'unyoke,' as travellers do where they are to rest for the night. (See Gen. xxiv. 23, in LXX.) **with a man that is a sinner.** No, captious Pharisees; he *was* a sinner up till a minute ago, but now he is a new creature, as his own lips shall presently make manifest. **8. And Zaccheus stood**—stood forth, openly before all; **and said unto the Lord, Behold, Lord.** Mark how frequently our Evangelist uses this title, especially where lordly *authority*, *dignity*, *grace*, or *power* is intended. **the half of my goods I give to the poor; and if I have taken any thing from any man by false accusation**—'defrauded,' 'overcharged,' any man, assessing him on a false representation of his means, or of the value of the articles for which he was rated, which was but too common with this class (see ch. iii. 12, 13), **I restore him four-fold.** The "if" here is not meant to express any doubt of the *fact*, but only the difficulty, where there had been so much of this, to fix upon the cases and the extent of the unrighteous exactions. The meaning, then, is, 'in so far as I have done this.' The Roman law required this four-fold restitution; the Jewish law, but the principal, and a fifth more (Num. v. 7). There was no *demand* made for either; but, as if to revenge himself on his hitherto reigning sin (see on John xx. 28), and to testify the change he had experienced, besides surrendering the half of his *fair* gains to the poor, he voluntarily determines to give up all that was ill gotten, quadrupled. And what is worthy of notice, in the presence of all he gratefully addressed this to "the Lord," to whom he owed the wonderful change. **9. And Jesus said unto him**—and this also before all, and for the information of all, **This day is salvation come to this house.** Memorable saying! Salvation has already come, but it is not a day nor an hour old. The word "to this *house*" was probably designed to meet the taunt, 'He is gone to lodge at a sinner's house.' The house, says Jesus, is no longer a sinner's house, polluted and polluting: ''Tis now a saved house, all meet for the reception of Him who came to save.' What a precious idea is *salvation to a house*, expressing the new air that would henceforth breathe in it, and the new impulses from its head which would reach its members. **forsomuch as he also** [καθότι καὶ αὐτὸς]—'inasmuch as even he,' publican though he be, and acting till now in the unprincipled way which even himself has confessed—even he **is a son of Abraham.** He was that by birth, but here it means a partaker of Abraham's *faith*, being mentioned as the sufficient explanation of *salvation* having come to him. (Gal. iii. 26, 29; and for Abraham's faith as evidenced by *works*, as here, see Jas. ii. 22.) **10. For the Son of man is come to seek and to save that which was lost.** A remarkable expression—not '*them*,' but 'that' which was lost [τὸ ἀπολωλός]; that is, the *mass* of lost sinners. Zaccheus was simply one such; and in saving him, Jesus says He was not going out of His way, but just doing His proper work. He even explains why He waited not for Zaccheus to apply to Him; for, says He, 'My business is to *seek* as well as save such.'

Remarks.—1. Whatever brings souls in contact with Christ is hopeful. When Zaccheus "sought to see Jesus, who He was," nothing probably was further from his mind than becoming His disciple, and a new creature. But that mere *curiosity* of his, and the step he took to gratify it, were the "cords of a man" by which he was drawn into the position for Christ's eye and voice of love and power to reach him. On his part, all was the operation of natural, ordinary, every-day principles of action: on Christ's part, all was supernatural, divine. But *so it is in every conversion.* Hence the importance of bringing those we love, and for whose conversion we long and pray, within the atmosphere of those means, and in contact with those truths, on the wings of which Christ's power and grace are wont to reach the heart. What thousands have thus, all unexpectedly to themselves, been transformed into new creatures! 2. What a testimony to *instantaneous conversion* have we here! Against this there are groundless prejudices even among Christians; which, it is to be feared, arise from want of sufficient familiarity with the laws and activities of the spiritual life. Though the fruit of a sovereign operation of Grace upon their own hearts, Christians are nevertheless in danger of sinking into such a secular spirit, that the *supernatural* character of their Christian life is scarcely felt, and lively spirituality hardly known. No wonder, then, that such should view with suspicion changes like this, which by their instantaneousness reveal a *kind* of divine operation to which they are themselves too great strangers. But what else than *instantaneous* can any conversion be? The *preparation* for it may be very gradual; it may take a hundred or a thousand steps to bring the very means which are to be effectual right up to the heart, and the heart itself into a frame for yielding to them. But once let it come to that, and the transition from death to life *must* be instantaneous—the last surrender of the heart must be so. The result of such words from heaven as "Live"! (Ezek. xvi. 6): "Be thou clean"! (Matt. viii. 3): "Thy sins be forgiven thee"! (Mark xi. 5): "Make haste, and come down; for to-day I must abide at thy house"!—cannot but be instantaneous, as when they issued from the lips of Jesus in the days of His flesh. The "taking away of the stone" *before* Lazarus's resurrection, and "loosing and letting him go" *after* it, as they were human operations, so they took a little time, though not a great deal. But when "the Resurrection and the Life" said, "Lazarus, come forth!" his resuscitation was instantaneous, and could not but be. See on John xi. 39, 44. 3. The best evidence of conversion lies in the undoing or reversal of those things by which our former sinfulness was chiefly marked—the conquest of what

11 And as they heard these things, he added and spake a parable, because
he was nigh to Jerusalem, and because [g] they thought that the kingdom
12 of God should immediately appear. He [h] said therefore,
A certain nobleman went into a far country to receive for himself a
13 kingdom, and to return. And he called his ten servants, and delivered
14 them ten [1] pounds, and said unto them, Occupy till I come. But [i] his
citizens hated him, and sent a message after him, saying, We will not
15 have this *man* to reign over us. And it came to pass, that, when he was
returned, having received the kingdom, then he commanded these servants
to be called unto him, to whom he had given the [2] money, that he might
16 know how much every man had gained by trading. Then came the first,
17 saying, Lord, thy pound hath gained ten pounds. And he said unto
him, Well, thou good servant: because thou hast been [j] faithful in a very

A. D. 33.

g Acts 1. 6.
h Matt. 25.14. Mark 13.34.
1 A Pound is twelve ounces and a half; which, at five shillings the ounce, is 3*l.* 2*s.* 6*d.*
i John 1. 11.
2 Silver.
j Matt. 25.21. ch. 16. 10.

are called 'besetting sins.' Had Zaccheus lived before chiefly to *hoard up?* Now, "Behold, Lord, the half of my goods I give to the poor." A large proportion of his means this, to part with at once to those who were in want. But further, did Zaccheus become "rich" by appropriating to himself the excess of his exactions "by false accusation"? "If I have taken any thing from any man by false accusation, I restore him four-fold." The frozen heart had melted down, the clenched fist had opened, and—unlike the rich young ruler (ch. xviii. 23)—the idol had been dethroned. This was a change indeed. See on the wise injunctions of the Baptist to the different classes that asked him how they were to manifest their repentance—on ch. iii. 12. 4. When religion comes into the *heart*, it will find its way into the *house*, as into that of Zaccheus. For it is in one's house that one is most *himself*. There, he is on no stiff ceremony; there, if anywhere, he opens out; there he acts as he *is*. Where religion is not, the home is the place to reveal it; where it is, it is the air of home that draws it out, like perfumes which the zephyr wafts to all around. Hence the bold language of the apostle to the jailer of Philippi, "Believe in the Lord Jesus Christ, and thou shalt be saved, and *thy house*" (Acts xvi. 31; and see also *vv.* 14, 15). "The voice of rejoicing and salvation is" not only in the hearts but in the houses, not only in the temples but "in the tabernacles of the righteous" (Ps. cxviii. 15). 5. Till men are converted and become new creatures, they are "*lost*," in the account of Christ—in what sense may be seen in the case of the Prodigal son, who was "*lost*" when a run-away from his father, and "*found*" when he returned and was welcomed back as a penitent. (See on ch. xv. 24.) Accordingly, as being the common condition of all whom Christ came to save, they are represented as "*that* which is lost." But if the worst features of men's fallen state are held forth without disguise in the teaching of Christ, it is only to commend the remedy, and encourage those who have felt it most deeply not to despair. For "the Son of Man is come to seek and to save that which is lost." It was His errand; it is His business; and this glorious case of Zaccheus—He Himself assures us—is but a specimen-case. Multitudes of them there have since been, but there are more to come; and when any are ready to sink under insupportable discoveries of their lost state, we are warranted to tell them that theirs is just a *case* for the Lord Jesus—"for the Son of Man is come to seek and to save that which was lost!"

11-27.—The Parable of the Pounds. That this parable is quite a different one from that of The Talents (in Matt. xxv. 14-30)—although *Calvin, Olshausen, Meyer*, &c., but not *de Wette* and *Neander*, identify them—will appear from the following considerations:—First, This parable was spoken "when He was *nigh* to Jerusalem" (*v.* 11); that one, some days after entering it, and from the Mount of Olives. Second, This parable was spoken to the promiscuous crowd; that, to the Twelve alone. Accordingly, Third, Besides the "*servants*" in this parable, who profess subjection to Him, there is a class of "*citizens*" who refuse to own Him, and who are treated differently; whereas in the Talents, spoken to the *former* class alone, this latter class is omitted. Fourth, In the Talents, each *servant* receives a different number of them—five, two, one; in the Pounds, all receive the same one pound (which is but about the sixtieth part of a talent); also, in the Talents, each of the faithful servants shows the *same* fidelity by doubling what he received—the five are made ten, the two four; in the Pounds, each, receiving the same, renders a *different* return—one making his pound ten, another five. Plainly, therefore, the intended lesson is different; the one illustrating *equal fidelity with different degrees of advantage;* the other, *different degrees of improvement of the same opportunities.* And yet, with all this difference, the parables are remarkably similar.

11. And as they heard—or were listening to, **these things, he added and spake** [προσθεὶς εἶπεν]—or 'went on to speak;' which shows that this followed close upon the preceding incident: **a parable, because he was nigh to Jerusalem, and because they thought that the kingdom of God should immediately appear** [ἀναφαίνεσθαι]—or be visibly set up as soon as He reached the capital. So that this was designed more immediately for His own disciples, as is also evident from the nature of the parable itself. **12. He said therefore, A certain nobleman went into a far country**—said to put down the notion that He was just on His way to set up His kingdom, and to inaugurate it by His personal presence. **to receive for himself a kingdom**—to be invested with royalty; as when Herod went to Rome and was there made king: a striking expression of what our Lord went away for and received, "sitting down at the right hand of the majesty on high." **and to return**—at His Second coming. **13. And he called his ten servants, and delivered them ten pounds, and said unto them, Occupy** [Πραγματεύσασθε]—'Negociate,' 'do business,' with the resources entrusted to you. **till I come. 14. But his citizens hated him, and sent a message after him, saying, We will not have this man to reign over us.** It is a great misconception of this parable to confound these "citizens" with the "servants." The one repudiate all subjection to Him; the other, not excepting the unfaithful one, acknowledge Him as Master. By the "**citizens**"

18 little, have thou authority over ten cities. And the second came, saying,
19 Lord, thy pound hath gained five pounds. And he said likewise to him,
20 Be thou also over five cities. And another came, saying, Lord, behold,
21 *here is* thy pound, which I have kept laid up in a napkin: for [k]I feared
thee, because thou art an austere man: thou takest up that thou layedst
22 not down, and reapest that thou didst not sow. And he saith unto him,
[l]Out of thine own mouth will I judge thee, *thou* wicked servant. [m]Thou
knewest that I was an austere man, taking up that I laid not down, and
23 reaping that I did not sow: wherefore then gavest not thou my money
into the bank, that at my coming I might have required mine own with
24 usury? And he said unto them that stood by, Take from him the pound,
25 and give *it* to him that hath ten pounds. (And they said unto him,
26 Lord, he hath ten pounds.) For I say unto you, [n]That unto every one
which hath shall be given; and from him that hath not, even that he
27 hath shall be taken away from him. But those mine enemies, which
would not that I should reign over them, bring hither, and slay *them*
before me.

28 And when he had thus spoken, [o]he went before, ascending up to
Jerusalem.

29 And [p]it came to pass, when he was come nigh to Bethphage and
Bethany, at the mount called *the mount* of Olives, he sent two of his

A. D. 33.

k Ex. 20. 19, 20. 1Sam. 12. 20. Matt. 25. 24. 2 Tim. 1. 7. Rom. 8. 15. Jas. 2. 19. 1 John 4. 18. Rev. 21. 8.
l 2 Sam. 1. 16. Job 15. 6. Matt. 12. 37. Tit. 3. 11.
m Matt. 25. 26.
n Matt. 13. 12. Matt. 25. 29. Mark 4. 25. ch. 8. 18.
o Mark 10. 32. ch. 9. 51. ch. 12. 50. John 18. 11. 1 Pet. 4. 1.
p Matt. 21. 1. Mark 11. 1. John 12. 12, 16.

---

historically are here meant the Jews as a nation, who were Christ's "own," as "King of the Jews," but who expressly repudiated Him in this character, saying, "We have no king but Cesar" (John xix. 15.) But *generally*, and in Christendom, this class comprehends all infidel, open rejecters of Christ and Christianity, as distinguished from professed Christians. 15-26. The *reckoning* here is so very similar to that in Matt. xxv. 19-29, that the same exposition will answer for both; if only it be observed that here we have different degrees of future gracious reward, proportioned to the measure of present fidelity. **27. But those mine enemies, which would not that I should reign over them, bring hither, and slay them before me.** Compare 1 Sam. xv. 32, 33. The reference is to the awful destruction of Jerusalem; but it points to the final perdition of all who shall be found in open rebellion against Christ.

For Remarks on this Section, see those on Matt. xxv. 14-30, at the close of that Section.

28-44.—CHRIST'S TRIUMPHAL ENTRY INTO JERUSALEM ON THE FIRST DAY OF THE WEEK—HIS TEARS OVER IT, AND ITS DOOM PRONOUNCED. (=Matt. xxi. 1-11; Mark xi. 1-11; John xii. 12-19.) It will be seen, from the parallels, that we are now coming to those scenes of which we have the concurrent records of all the Four Evangelists. And no wonder, considering how pregnant with the life of the world are those scenes of majesty and meekness, of grace and glory, of patience and power, of death, with elements of unutterable anguish, and life, with issues in its bosom inconceivably glorious. The river, the streams whereof make glad the City of God—but O, with what an awful gladness!—now parts, as befits the river of our Paradise, into its "four heads."

28. And when he had thus spoken, he went before. See on Mark x. 32, and Remark 1 at the close of that Section; **ascending up to Jerusalem.** Here occurs an important gap, supplied in the Fourth Gospel.

John xii. 1: "Then Jesus, six days before the Passover"—probably after sunset on the *Friday* Evening, or at the commencement of the Jewish *Sabbath*, which preceded the Passover—"**came to Bethany,** where **Lazarus was,** which had been dead, whom He [had] raised from the dead." There, if we are right as to the time of His arrival, He would spend His last Sabbath amongst friends peculiarly dear to Him, and possibly it was on the evening of that Sabbath that "there they made Him a supper, at the house of Simon the leper." See on Mark xiv. 3, &c. At all events, it was on the day following, which was *the First Day of the Week*, that He made this His triumphal Entry into Jerusalem. This corresponded to the *tenth* day of the month *Nisan*, in the Jewish year, the day on which the paschal lamb was separated from the rest of the flock, and *set apart for sacrifice*: it was "*kept up until the fourteenth day*," on which "the whole assembly of the congregation of Israel were to kill it in the evening" [בֵּין הָעַרְבָּיִם] literally, 'between the two evenings' (as in the *margin*); that is, between *three* o'clock—the hour of the evening sacrifice—and six o'clock, or the close of the Jewish day (Exod. xii. 3, 6). Who can believe that this was a mere coincidence? Who that observes how every act in the final scenes was alluded to, arranged and carried out with a calm dignity, as seeing the end from the beginning, can doubt that "Christ *our Passover*" who was to be "*sacrificed for us*," designed, by His solemn entry into the bloody city, yet the appointed place of sacrifice, to hold Himself forth as from this time *set apart for sacrifice?* Accordingly, He never after this properly left Jerusalem—merely sleeping at Bethany, but spending the whole of every day in the city.

The Triumphal Entry into Jerusalem (29-40). **29. And it came to pass, when he was come nigh to Bethphage and Bethany, at the mount called [the mount] of Olives.** Our Evangelist alludes thus generally to Bethany, as if our Lord had merely passed by it, on His way to Jerusalem, because He was not to relate anything about His *stay* there, but only that He took it on His route to the capital. The word "Bethphage" [=בֵּית פַּגָּא] means '*Fig-house*,' no doubt from the profusion of that fruit which this spot produced. That it lay, as Bethany did, on the eastern side of the mount of Olives, or the side farthest from the capital, is certain: but no

30 disciples, saying, Go ye into the village over against *you;* in the which
at your entering ye shall find a colt tied, whereon yet never man sat:
31 loose him, and bring *him hither.* And if any man ask you, Why do ye
loose *him?* thus shall ye say unto him, Because [q] the Lord hath need of
him.
32 And they that were sent went their way, and found even as he had
33 said unto them. And as they were loosing the colt, the owners thereof
34 said unto them, Why loose ye the colt? And they said, The Lord hath
35 need of him. And they brought him to Jesus: [r] and they cast their garments upon the colt, and they set Jesus thereon.

A. D. 33.

[q] Ps. 24. 1. Ps. 50. 10-12. Matt. 21. 2, 3. Mark 11. 2-6. Acts 10. 36.

[r] 2 Ki. 9. 13. Matt. 21. 7. Mark 11. 7. John 12. 14. Gal. 4. 15.

traces of it are now to be found, and whether it was east or west, north or south, of Bethany, is not agreed. The small village of Bethany [בֵּית עֲנִיָּה], meaning '*Date-house*,' yet remains, 'pleasantly situated,' says *Thomson*, 'near the south-eastern base of the mount, and having many fine trees about and above it.' **he sent two of his disciples, 30. Saying, Go ye into the village over against you**—that is, Bethphage; **in the which at your entering ye shall find a colt tied, whereon yet never man sat.** This last remarkable particular is mentioned both by Matthew and Mark. On its significance, see on John xix. 41. **loose him, and bring him hither. 31. And if any man ask you, Why do ye loose him? thus shall ye say unto him, Because the Lord hath need of him**—"and straightway he will send him hither" (Mark xi. 3). Remarkable words! But the glorious Speaker knew all, and had the key of the human heart. (See on verse 5.) It is possible the owner was a disciple; but whether or no, the Lord knew full well what the result would be. A remarkable parallel to it will be found in the case of Samuel (see 1 Sam. x. 2-7); but with this noteworthy difference, that it is impossible to read the narrative of Samuel's directions without observing that he knew himself all the while to be but a *servant* of the Lord, whereas *the Lord Himself* is in every utterance and act of Jesus on this occasion.

32. And they that were sent went their way, and found even as he had said unto them. Mark is so singularly precise here, that it is impossible to doubt that the description is fresh from one of the two disciples sent on this errand; and in that case, who can it be but *Peter*, of whose hand in this Gospel all antiquity testifies and internal evidence is so strong? Probably *John* was the other (compare Mark xiv. 13, with Luke xxii. 8). "And they went their way (says Mark), and found the colt *tied by the door without in a place where two ways met;* and they loose him." Had not the minutest particulars of this grand entry into Jerusalem burned themselves into the memory of those dear disciples that were honoured to take part in the preparations for it, such unimportant details had never been recorded. **33. And as they were loosing the colt, the owners thereof said unto them, Why loose ye the colt? 34. And they said, The Lord hath need of him**—"and (says Mark) they let them go." **35. And they brought him to Jesus.** Matthew here gives an important particular, omitted by the other Evangelists. He says "they brought *the ass and the colt.*" Of course, the unbroken colt would be all the more tractable by having its dam to go along with it. The bearing of this minute particular on the prophecy about to be quoted is very striking. **and they cast their garments upon the colt, and they set Jesus thereon**—He allowing them to act this part of attendants on royalty, as befitting the *state* He was now, for the first and only time, assuming.

Matthew here notes the well-known prophecy which was fulfilled in all this, on which we must pause for a little: "All this was done, that it might be fulfilled which was spoken by the prophet (Zec. ix. 9), saying, Tell ye (or, 'Say ye to') the daughter of Zion"—quoting here another bright Messianic prophecy (Isa. lxii. 11) in place of Zechariah's opening words, "Rejoice greatly, O daughter of Zion; shout, O daughter of Jerusalem: Behold, thy King cometh unto thee." Here the prophet adds, "He is just, and having salvation" or 'helped'—[נוֹשָׁע]; but the Evangelist omits these, passing on to what relates to the *lowly* character of His royalty: "meek, and sitting upon an ass, and a colt, the foal of an ass." It was upon the *foal* that our Lord sat, as Mark and Luke expressly state. While the *horse* was an animal of war, the *ass* was used for purposes of peace. In the times of the Judges, and for a considerable time afterwards, horses were not used at all by the Israelites, and so even distinguished persons rode on asses (Jud. v. 10; x. 4; xii. 14)—but not from any nobleness in that animal, or its being an emblem of royalty, as some say. 'Nor,' to use the words of *Hengstenberg*, 'in all our accounts of the asses of the East, of which we have a great abundance, is there a single example of an ass being ridden by a king, or even a distinguished officer, on any state occasion; whereas here it is expressly *in His royal capacity* that the prophet says Jerusalem's King is to ride upon an ass.' And there are not wanting proofs, adduced by this able critic, that in the East the ass was and is regarded with a measure of *contempt.* And does not the fulfilment of the prophecy which we behold here itself show that *lowliness* was stamped upon the act, royal though it was? 'Into the same city,' adds the critic just quoted, 'which David and Solomon had so frequently entered on mules or horses richly caparisoned, and with a company of proud horsemen as their attendants, the Lord rode on a borrowed ass, which had never been broken in; the wretched clothing of His disciples supplying the place of a saddle-cloth, and His attendants consisting of people whom the world would regard as a mob and rabble.' This critic also, by an examination of the phrase used by the prophet, "the foal of asses," infers that it means an ass still mostly dependent upon its mother, and regards the use of this as a mark of yet greater humiliation in a King. In short, it was the *meekness of majesty* which was thus manifested, entering the city with royal *authority*, yet waiving, during His humbled state, all the external *grandeur* that shall yet accompany that authority. On this remarkable prophecy, so remarkably fulfilled, we notice two other points. First, the familiar and delightful name given to the chosen people, "The daughter of Zion," or, as we might conceive of it, '*the offspring of Zion's ordinances*,' born and nursed amid its sanctities—deriving all their spiritual life from the Religion which had its centre and seat in Zion;

36, And [s]as he went, they spread their clothes in the way. And when he
37 was come nigh, even now at the descent of the mount of Olives, the whole
multitude of the disciples began to rejoice and praise God with a loud
38 voice for all the mighty works that they had seen, saying, [t]Blessed *be* the
King that cometh in the name of the Lord: [u]peace in heaven, and glory
in the highest.
39 And some of the Pharisees from among the multitude said unto him,
40 Master, rebuke thy disciples. And he answered and said unto them, I

A. D. 33.

[s] Matt. 21. 8.
[t] Ps. 72. 17, 19. Ps. 118. 26. Zec. 9. 9. Matt. 21. 9. ch. 13. 35. 1 Tim. 1. 17.
[u] ch. 2. 14. Eph. 2. 14.

next, the prophetic call to the chosen people to "*Rejoice greatly*" at this coming of their King to His own proper city. And the joy with which Jesus was welcomed on this occasion into Jerusalem was all the more striking a fulfilment of this prophecy, that it was far from being that intelligent, deep, and exultant welcome which the prophetic Spirit would have had Zion's daughter to give to her King. For if it was so superficial and fickle a thing as we know that it was, all the more does one wonder that it was so immense in its reach and volume; nor is it possible to account for it save by a wave of feeling—a mysterious impulse—sweeping over the mighty mass from above, in conformity with high arrangements, to give the King of Israel for once a visible, audible, glad welcome to His Own regal City.

36. **And as he went**—or proceeded onwards towards the city, **they spread their clothes in the way**—that is, the gathering crowds did so; attracted, probably, in the first instance, by the novelty of the spectacle, but a higher view of it by and by flashing across them. Matthew says, "And a very great multitude"—or 'the immense multitude' [Ὁ δὲ πλεῖστος ὄχλος] "spread their garments in the way; others cut down branches from the trees, and strawed them in the way." This casting of their garments beneath His feet was an ancient Oriental way of expressing the homage of a people towards their sovereign, or one whom they wished to welcome as such—as we see in the case of Jehu (2 Ki. ix. 13). And spreading a gorgeous cloth over the pathway that is to be trodden by a monarch on any great occasion, is our modern way of doing the same thing. **37. And when he was come nigh, even now at the descent of the mount of Olives**—just as He approached the city, **the whole multitude of the disciples**—in the wider sense of that term—"that went before and that followed" (Matt. xxi. 9.)—both the van and the rear of this immense mass, **began**—or proceeded, **to rejoice and praise God with a loud voice.** The language here is unusually grand, intended to express a burst of admiration far wider and deeper than ever had been witnessed before. **for all the mighty works**—or 'miracles' [δυνάμεων] **that they had seen**—the last and grandest, the resurrection of Lazarus, only crowning a series of unparalleled wonders. **38. Saying,**—"Hosanna" (Matthew, Mark, and John); that is, "*Save now*" [הוֹשִׁיעָה נָּא] Ps. cxviii. 25. **Blessed [be]**—or 'is,' as rendered in Matthew and John. Either way, it is their glad welcome to **the King that cometh in the name of the Lord**—in John (xii. 13), "the King of Israel;" in Matthew (xxi. 9), "the Son of David;" in Mark (xi. 9, 10), after "Blessed is He that cometh in the name of the Lord," another exclamation is added, "Blessed be the Kingdom of our father David, that cometh in the name of the Lord." In all likelihood, the exclamation was variously uttered by the multitude, and the same voices may have varied their acclaim, as they repeated it over and over again, **peace in heaven, and glory in the highest.** The multitude of the *heavenly* host, remarks *Bengel*, said at His birth, "Peace on *earth*" (ch. ii. 14), this *earthly* multitude say, "Peace in *heaven.*" A great truth, indeed, but uttered in ignorance. Christ's entry into Jerusalem now meant peace in both senses; but, alas, they "knew not the things that belonged to their peace." In Matthew and Mark another "Hosanna in the highest" is substituted for this; and, doubtless, it was repeated often enough. In thus uttering the grand Messianic words of Ps. cxviii. 25—which lie embosomed in those rich Evangelical anticipations that formed part of the *Great Hallel*, as it was called, or Passover-Psalms, to be sung by all the people in a few days, and which were understood to refer to the Messiah—they acted, all unconsciously, as the representatives of the true Church welcoming Her King, aye, and of the literal Israel, who will one day hail Him with a transport of joy, but mingled with weeping. (Compare Matt. xxiii. 39, with Zec. xii. 10).

A very important addition is here made in the Fourth Gospel:

John xii. 16-19. "These things understood not His disciples at the first; but when Jesus was glorified, then remembered they (see John xiv. 26) that these things were written of Him"—referring more immediately to the prophecies just quoted from Ps. cxviii. and Zec. ix., but generally to those Messianic portions of the Old Testament which had till then been overlooked—"and that they had done these things unto him." The Spirit, descending on them from the glorified Saviour at Pentecost, opened their eyes suddenly to the true sense of the Old Testament, brought vividly to their recollection this and other Messianic predictions, and to their unspeakable astonishment showed them that they, and all the actors in these scenes, had been unconsciously fulfilling those predictions. "The people therefore that was with Him when He called Lazarus out of His grave, and raised Him from the dead, bare record"—probably telling others in the crowd what they had so recently witnessed, as additional evidence that this *must* be "He that cometh in the name of the Lord." "For this cause the people"—or 'the multitude' [ὁ ὄχλος] "also met Him, for that they heard that He had done this miracle." The crowd was thus largely swelled in consequence of the stir which the resurrection of Lazarus made in and about the city. "The Pharisees therefore said among themselves, Perceive ye"—or 'Ye perceive' [Θεωρεῖτε], "how ye prevail nothing? behold, the world is gone after Him"—a popular way of speaking: 'He is drawing all men after Him;' a saying, as *Bengel* remarks, in which there lay something prophetic, like that of Caiaphas (John xi. 50-52), and that of Pilate (John xix. 19). This was spoken evidently with deep indignation; and was as much as to say, 'We cannot allow this to go any further, steps must be immediately taken to get rid of Him, else all will be lost.'

39. And some of the Pharisees from among the multitude said unto him, Master—'Teacher'—[Διδάσκαλε], **rebuke thy disciples**—a bold throw

tell you that, if these should hold their peace, [v]the stones would immediately cry out.
41 And when he was come near, he beheld the city, and [w]wept over it,
42 saying, If thou hadst known, even thou, at least in this thy day, the

A. D. 33.

[v] Hab. 2. 11.
[w] Hos. 11. 8. John 11.35.

this, evidently to try Him, for they could hardly think that it would be done. **40. And he answered and said unto them**—using this Pharisaic interruption as but an opportunity for giving vent to His pent up feelings in the hearing of all around Him, **I tell you that, if these should hold their peace, the stones would immediately cry out** [κεκράξονται, *paulo-post fut.* This rare tense is better supported here, we think, than the simple future, κράξουσιν, 'will cry out,' adopted by *Tischendorf, Tregelles*, and *Alford*, but not *Lachmann*]. In Hab. ii. 11 we have nearly the same saying. But it was proverbial even among the Greeks and Romans, and *Webster and Wilkinson* quote a Greek couplet and a passage from Cicero precisely the same. Hitherto the Lord had discouraged all demonstrations in his favour; latterly He had *begun* an opposite course; on this one occasion He seems to yield His whole soul to the wide and deep acclaim with a mysterious satisfaction, regarding it as *so necessary* a part of the regal dignity in which as Messiah He for this last time entered the city, that if not offered by the vast multitude, it would have *been wrung out of the stones* rather than be withheld!

The Redeemer's Tears over Jerusalem (41, 42). **41. And when he was come near, he beheld the city, and wept over it.** "Mine eye" said the weeping prophet, "affecteth mine heart" (Lam. iii. 51); and the heart in turn fills the eye. Under this sympathetic law of the relation of mind and body, Jesus, in His beautiful, tender humanity, was constituted even as we. What a contrast to the immediately preceding profound joy! But He yielded Himself alike freely to both. **42. Saying, If thou hadst known**—'But, alas! thou hast not.' This "If" is the most emphatic utterance of a *wish* for that which cannot be, or is not likely to be realized. (Compare Jos. vii. 7, in Hebrew, and Job. xvi. 4.) **even thou.** This may be joined to the preceding —'If even thou hadst known' [εἰ ἔγνως καὶ σύ]. There is deep and affecting emphasis on this "*Thou:*"—'Far as thou art gone, low as thou hast sunk, all but hopeless as thou art, yet if even *thou* hadst known!' **at least in this thy day**—even at this most moving moment. See on ch. xiii. 9. **the things [which belong] unto thy peace!** [τὰ πρὸς εἰρήνην σου]—or, as *Luther* and *Beza* render it, 'which make for thy peace' (*was zu deinem Frieden dienet—quæ ad pacem tuam faciunt*). It has been thought, by *Wetstein* and others since, that there is some allusion here to the original name of the city—"Salem," meaning 'Peace' [שָׁלוֹם]. **but now they are hid from thine eyes.** This was among His *last* open efforts to "gather" them, but their eyes were judicially closed. (See on Matt. xiii. 13, 14.)

Jerusalem's Doom Pronounced (43, 44). **43. For the days shall come** ["Οτι ἥξουσιν ἡμέραι]—'For there shall come days' **upon thee, that thine enemies shall cast a trench about thee** [χάρακα] —rather a palisaded 'rampart.' The word signifies any 'pointed stake;' but here it denotes the Roman military *vallum*, a mound or rampart with palisades. In the present case, as we learn from *Josephus*, it was made first of wood; and when this was burnt, a wall of four miles' circuit was built in three days—so determined were the besiegers. This 'cut off all hope of escape,' and consigned the city to unparalleled horrors. (*Joseph.* Jewish War, v. 6. 2; and xii. 3. 4.) **and compass thee round, and keep thee in on every side, 44. And shall lay thee even with the ground, and thy children within thee; and they shall not leave in thee one stone upon another.** All here predicted was with dreadful literality fulfilled, and the providence which has preserved such a remarkable commentary on it as the record of *Josephus*—an eye-witness from first to last, a Jew of distinguished eminence, an officer of high military capacity in the Jewish army, and when taken prisoner living in the Roman camp, and acting once and again as a negotiator between the contending parties—cannot be too devoutly acknowledged.

Our Evangelist gives no record of the first day's proceedings in Jerusalem, after the triumphal Entry; for what follows (*vv.* 45-48) belongs to the second and subsequent days. Mark disposes of this in a single verse (ch. xi. 11), while in the Fourth Gospel there is nothing on the subject. But in Matt. xxi. 10, 11, 14-16, we have the following precious particulars:

Stir about Him in the City (Matt. xxi. 10, 11). 10. "And when he was come into Jerusalem, all the city was moved"—as the cavalcade advanced—"Saying, Who is this? 11. And the multitude" —rather 'the multitudes' [οἱ ὄχλοι] from the procession itself—"said, This is Jesus, the prophet of," or 'from'—[ὁ ἀπὸ] "Nazareth of Galilee." By this they evidently meant something more than a mere prophet; and from John vi. 14, 15, and this whole scene, it seems plain that they meant by this exclamation that it was the expected Messiah.

Miracles wrought in the Temple (Matt. xxi. 14). 14. "And the blind and the lame came to him in the temple" [ἐν τῷ ἱερῷ]—in the large sense of that word (see on ch. ii. 27), "and He healed them." If these miracles were wrought *after* the cleansing of the temple—as one would gather from Matthew —since they were wrought in the very temple-court from which the money changers had been cleared out—they would set a divine seal on that act of mysterious authority. But as the second Gospel is peculiarly precise as to the order of these events, we incline to follow it, in placing the cleansing of the Temple on the second day. Yet these miracles wrought in the temple on the lame and the blind are most touching, as the *last* recorded miraculous displays of His glory—with the single exception of the majestic Cleansing of the Temple—which He gave in public.

Glorious Vindication of the Children's Testimony (Matt. xxi. 15, 16). 15. "And when the chief priests and scribes saw the wonderful things which he did, and the children crying in the temple, and saying, Hosanna to the Son of David"—which was just the prolonged echo of the popular acclamations on His triumphal entry, but drawn forth anew from these children, on witnessing what doubtless filled their unsophisticated minds with wonder and admiration—"they were sore displeased. 16. And said unto him, Hearest thou what these say?"—stung most of all by this novel testimony to Jesus, as showing to what depths His popularity was reaching down, and from the mysterious effect of *such* voices upon the human spirit. "And Jesus saith unto them, Have ye never read (in Ps. viii. 2) Out of the mouth of babes and sucklings thou hast

things *which belong* unto thy peace! but now they are hid from thine
43 eyes. For the days shall come upon thee, that thine enemies shall [x]cast
a trench about thee, and compass thee round, and keep thee in on every

A. D. 33.

[x] Isa. 29. 3, 4. Jer. 6. 3, 6.

perfected praise?" This beautiful psalm is repeatedly referred to as prophetic of Christ, and this is the view of it which a sound interpretation of it will be found to yield. The testimony which it predicts that Messiah would receive from "babes"—a very remarkable feature of this prophetic psalm—was indeed here literally fulfilled, as was that of His being "numbered with the transgressors" (Isa. liii. 12), and "pierced" (Zec. xii. 10); but like those and similar predictions, it reaches deeper than literal babes, even the "babes" to whom are revealed the mysteries of the Gospel. See on Matt. xi. 25.

Thus, it would seem, ended the first memorable day of the Redeemer's last week in Jerusalem. Of the close of it the following is the brief account of the First and Second Gospels, which we combine into one: "And He left them; and when now the eventide was come, He went out of the city into Bethany, with the Twelve, and he lodged there" (Matt. xxi. 17; Mark xi. 11).

Before proceeding to the *Remarks* which this grand scene suggests, let us first retrace it. And here we copy entire the most graphic and beautiful description of it which we have read, by one of the most recent travellers, whose minute and patient accuracy is only equalled by his rare faculty of word-painting. 'From Bethany,' says *Dr. Stanley*, 'we must begin. A wild mountain-hamlet screened by an intervening ridge from the view of the top of Olivet, perched on its broken plateau of rock, the last collection of human habitations before the desert hills which reach to Jericho—this is the modern village of El-Lazarieh, which derives its name from its clustering round the traditional site of the one house and grave which give it an undying interest. High in the distance are the Peræan mountains; the foreground is the deep descent to the Jordan valley. On the further side of that dark abyss Martha and Mary knew that Christ was abiding when they sent their messenger; up that long ascent they had often watched His approach—up that long ascent He came, when, outside the village, Martha and Mary met Him, and the Jews stood round weeping. Up that same ascent He came also at the beginning of the week of His Passion. One night He halted in the village, as of old; the village and the Desert were then all alive,—as they still are once every year at the Greek Easter,—with the crowd of Paschal pilgrims moving to and fro between Bethany and Jerusalem. In the morning He set forth on His journey. Three pathways lead, and probably always led, from Bethany to Jerusalem; one, a steep footpath from the summit of mount Olivet; another, by a long circuit over its northern shoulder, down the valley which parts it from Scopus; the third, the natural continuation of the road by which mounted travellers always approach the city from Jericho, over the southern shoulder, between the summit which contains the Tombs of the Prophets and that called the 'Mount of Offence.' There can be no doubt that this last is the road of the Entry of Christ, not only because, as just stated, it is and must always have been the usual approach for horsemen and for large caravans, such as then were concerned, but also because this is the only one of the three approaches which meets the requirements of the narrative which follows. Two vast streams of people met on that day. The one poured out from the city (John xii. 12); and as they came through the gardens [Dr. S. here would read, ἐκ τῶν ἀγρῶν, with *Tischendorf* and *Tregelles*—but not *Lachmann*—instead of δένδρων, of the received text], whose clusters of palm rose on the south-eastern corner of Olivet, they cut down the long branches, as was their wont at the Feast of Tabernacles, and moved upwards towards Bethany, with loud shouts of welcome. From Bethany streamed forth the crowds who had assembled there on the previous night, and who came testifying (John xii. 17) to the great event at the sepulchre of Lazarus. The road soon loses sight of Bethany. It is now a rough, but still broad and well-defined mountain track, winding over rock and loose stones; a steep declivity below on the left; the sloping shoulder of Olivet above it on the right; fig-trees below and above, here and there growing out of the rocky soil. Along the road the multitudes threw down the branches which they cut as they went along, or spread out a rude matting formed of the palm-branches they had already cut as they came out. The larger portion—those, perhaps, who escorted Him from Bethany—unwrapped their loose cloaks from their shoulders, and stretched them along the rough path, to form a momentary carpet as He approached. (Matt. xxi. 8; Mark xi. 8.) The two streams met midway. Half of the vast mass, turning round, preceded; the other half followed (Mark xi. 9). Gradually the long procession swept up and over the ridge, where first begins "the descent of the Mount of Olives" towards Jerusalem. At this point the first view is caught of the south-eastern corner of the city. The Temple and the more northern portions are hid by the slope of Olivet on the right; what is seen is only Mount Zion, now for the most part a rough field, crowned with the Mosque of David and the angle of the western walls, but then covered with houses to its base, surmounted by the Castle of Herod, on the supposed site of the palace of David, from which that portion of Jerusalem emphatically the "city of David" derived its name. It was at this precise point, "As He drew near, at the descent of the mount of Olives"—that is, at the point where the road over the mount begins to descend (may it not have been from the sight thus opening upon them?)—that the shout of triumph burst forth from the multitude, "Hosanna to the Son of David! Blessed is He that cometh in the name of the Lord. Blessed is the kingdom that cometh of our father *David*. Hosanna . . . peace . . . glory in the highest." There was a pause as the shout rang through the long defile; and, as the Pharisees who stood by in the crowd (Luke xix. 39) complained, He pointed to the stones which, strewn beneath their feet, would immediately cry out, if "these were to hold their peace." Again the procession advanced. The road descends a slight declivity, and the glimpse of the city is again withdrawn behind the intervening ridge of Olivet. A few moments, and the path mounts again, it climbs a rugged ascent, it reaches a ledge of smooth rock, and in an instant the whole city bursts into view. As now the dome of the Mosque El-Aksa rises like a ghost from the earth before the traveller stands on the ledge, so then must have risen the Temple tower; as now the vast enclosure of the Mussulman sanctuary, so then must have spread the Temple courts; as now the gray town on its broken hills, so then the magnificent city, with its background—long since vanished away—of gardens and suburbs on the

44 side, and [y]shall lay thee even with the ground, and thy children within
thee; and they [z]shall not leave in thee one stone upon another; [a]because
thou knewest not the time of thy visitation.

A. D. 33.

[y] 1 Ki. 9. 7, 8.
[z] Matt. 24. 2.
[a] Dan. 9. 24.

western plateau behind. Immediately below was the Valley of the Kedron, here seen in its greatest depth as it joins the Valley of Hinnom, and thus giving full effect to the great peculiarity of Jerusalem, seen only on its eastern side—its situation as of a city rising out of a deep abyss. It is hardly possible to doubt that this rise and turn of the road—this rocky ledge—was the exact point where the multitude paused again, and "He, when He beheld the city, wept over it."' ("Sinai and Palestine," chap. iii.)

Remarks.—1. Often as we have had occasion to observe how unlike the Gospel History is, in almost everything, to an invented Story, it is impossible not to be struck with it in the present Section. That our Lord should at some time or other be made to enter Jerusalem in triumph, would be no surprising invention, considering the claim to be King of the Jews which the whole Narrative makes for Him. But that He should enter it on an ass, and that an unbroken foal attended by its dam; that it should be found by the two who were sent for it precisely "by the door without, in a place where two ways met," and that they should be allowed to carry it away on simply telling the owners that "the Lord had need of it;" that notwithstanding this feeblest of all assumptions of royal state, the small following should grow to the proportions of a vast state-procession, covering His path with their garments as He drew near to the city; and that, aided by the flying reports of Lazarus's resurrection, the multitude should get into such enthusiasm as to hail Him, in terms the most august and sacred which the Jewish Scriptures could furnish, as the long-promised and expected Messiah; that instead of being elated with this, He should at the sight of the city and in the midst of the popular acclamations, dissolve into tears, and that not so much at the prospect of His own approaching sufferings, as at the blindness of the nation to its own true interests; and yet, on the other hand, should feel those acclamations so grateful and befitting, as to tell those irritated ecclesiastics who found fault with them that they *behoved* to be uttered, and if withheld by human lips, the predicted welcome of Jerusalem to its King would be wrung out of the very stones; that the whole of this should be a mystery to the Twelve, at the time of its occurrence, and that not till the resurrection and glorification of Jesus, when the Spirit shed down at Pentecost lighted up all these events, did they comprehend their significance and behold the Grand Unity of this matchless life; that after He had reached Jerusalem, and was amongst the temple-buildings, the echoes of the popular acclaim to Him should be caught up by the children in so marked and emphatic a style as to deepen the ecclesiastic hate, and call forth a demand to Him to stop it, which only rebounded upon themselves by the glorious Scriptural vindication of it which He gave them:—these are circumstances so very different from anything which could be supposed to be an invention, especially when *taken together*, that no unsophisticated mind can believe it possible. And as the first three narratives can be shown to be independent productions, and yet each—while agreeing in the main with all the rest—varies in minute and important details from the others, and only out of all Four can the full account of the whole transaction be obtained, have we not in this the most convincing evidence of the *historic reality* of what we read? No wonder that myriads of readers and hearers of these wondrous Narratives over all Christendom—of the educated classes as well as the common people—drink them in as indubitable and living History, without the need of any laboured arguments to prove them true! 2. The blended meekness and majesty of this last entry into Jerusalem is but one of a series of contrasts, studding this matchless History, and attracting the wonder of every devout and intelligent reader. What, indeed, is this whole History but a continued meeting of Lord and Servant, of riches and poverty, of strength and weakness, of glory and shame, of life and death? The early Fathers of the Church delighted to trace these stupendous contrasts in the life of Christ, arising out of the two natures in His mysterious Person—in the one of which He was to humble Himself to the uttermost, while the glory of the other could never be kept from breaking through it. Infested as those early Fathers of the Church were with all manner of heresies on this subject, these facts of the Gospel History formed at once the rich nourishment of their own souls, and the ready armoury whence they drew the weapons of their warfare in defence and illustration of the truth. Hear, for example, how the eloquent Greek, Gregory of Nazianzum (born A.D. 300—died, A.D. 390), regales himself and his audience in one of his discourses, kindling at the assaults to which the Person of his Lord was subjected:—'He was wrapt, indeed, in swaddling clothes; but rising, He burst the wrappings of the tomb. He lay, it is true, in a manger; but He was glorified by angels, and pointed out by a star, and worshipped by Magi. Why do you stumble at the visible [in Him], not regarding the invisible? He had no form nor comeliness to the Jews; but to David He was fairer than the children of men, yea, He glisters on the Mount, with a light above the brightness of the sun, foreshadowing the glory to come. He was baptized, indeed, as man, but He washed away sins as God; not that He needed purification, but that He might sanctify the waters. He was tempted as man, but He overcame as God; nay, He bids us be of good cheer, because He hath overcome the world. He hungered, but He fed thousands; yea, He is Himself the living and Heavenly Bread. He thirsted, but He cried, If any man thirst, let him come unto Me and drink; nay, He promised that those who believe in Him should themselves gush like a well. He was weary, but He is Himself the Rest of the weary and heavy-laden. He was overpowered with sleep; but He is upborne upon the sea, but He rebukes the winds, but He upbears sinking Peter. He pays tribute, but out of a fish; but He is the Prince of dependents. He is saluted "Samaritan," and "Demoniac," but He saves him that went down from Jerusalem and fell among thieves; nay, devils own Him, devils flee before Him, legions of spirits He whelms in the deep, and sees the prince of the devils falling as lightning. He is stoned, but not laid hold of; He prays, but He hears prayer. He weeps, but He puts an end to weeping. He inquires where Lazarus is laid, for He was man, but He raises Lazarus, for He was God. He is sold, and at a contemptible rate, even thirty pieces of silver; but He ransoms the world, and at a great price, even His own blood." After carrying these contrasts down to the Judgment, the eloquent preacher apologizes for the

45 And [b]he went into the temple, and began to cast out them that sold
46 therein, and them that bought; saying unto them, [c]It is written, My
house is the house of prayer: but [d]ye have made it a den of thieves.

A. D. 33.

[b] Matt. 21. 12.
[c] Ps. 93. 5.
[d] Jer. 7. 11.

artificial style in which he had indulged, to meet the arts of the adversaries. (Orat. xxxv.) 3. Often as we have had occasion to notice the mysterious *light and shade* which marked the emotions of the Redeemer's soul (as in Matt. xi. 16-30), nowhere are these more vividly revealed than in the present Section. The acclamations of the multitude as He approached Jerusalem were indeed shallow enough, and He was not deceived by them. He had taken their measure, and knew their exact value. But they were the *truth*, and the truth uttered for the first time by a multitude of voices. "Hosanna to the Son of David! Blessed is the King of Israel that cometh in the name of the Lord? Peace in heaven, and glory in the highest!" His soul, from its inmost depths, echoed to the sound. It was to Him as the sound of many waters. When the Pharisees, therefore, bade Him rebuke it—for it was as wormwood to them—He rose to a sublime pitch at the very thought, and, in words which revealed the intense complacency with which He drank in the vast acclaim, "He answered and said unto them, I tell you that if these should hold their peace, the stones would immediately cry out!" Yet, scarcely has this utterance died away from His lips, when, on the City coming into view, He is in tears! What emotions they were which drew the water from those eyes, we shall do better to try to conceive than attempt to express. We do desire to look into them; yet, on such a subject, at least, we say with the poet,—

> 'But peace—still voice and closed eye
> Suit best with hearts beyond the sky.'

Our object in here again alluding to it, is merely to note the impressive fact, that this deep *shade* came over the Redeemer's spirit almost immediately after the *light* with which the acclamations of the multitude seemed to irradiate His soul. 4. If Christ thus felt on *earth* the wilful blindness of men to the things that belong to their peace, shall He feel it less in heaven? The *tears* doubtless are not there; but can that which wrung them from His eyes be absent? The mental *pain* which the spectacle occasioned Him on earth is certainly a stranger to His bosom now; but I, for one, shall never believe that there is nothing at all there which a benevolent heart would feel on earth to see men rushing wilfully on their own destruction. Is it said of the Father, that He "spared not His own Son, but delivered Him up for us all"? (see on Rom. viii. 32). And what is immediately to our point, Does God Himself protest to us, "As I live, saith the Lord God, I have no pleasure in the death of the wicked, *but that the wicked turn* from his way *and live*"? (Ezek. xxxiii. 11). In a word, Is there "joy in the presence," indeed, but not exclusively on the part, "of the angels of God over one sinner that repenteth"—the joy properly of the Shepherd Himself over His recovered sheep, of the Owner Himself over His found property, of the Father Himself over His prodigal son for ever restored to Him? (see on Luke xv.)—and can it be doubted that in the bosom of Him who descended to ransom and went up to gather lost souls, as He watches from His seat in the heavens the treatment which His Gospel receives on earth, while the cordial acceptance of it awakens His deepest joy, the wilful rejection of it, the whole consequences of which He only knows, must go to His heart with equal acuteness—though beyond that we may not describe it? And who that reads this can fail to see in it an argument of unspeakable force for immediate flight to Jesus on the part of all who till now have held out? You take such matters easy, perhaps; but Christ did not—nor will you one day. 5. What a beautiful light does Christ's complacency in the Hosannas of the children throw upon His delight in drawing the young to Him! And what Christian parent will not deem himself, or herself, honoured with a rare honour whose children's voices, trained by them to sing Hosannas to the Son of David, send up into the soul of the now glorified Redeemer a wave of delight? See on ch. xviii. 15-17, with the Remarks at the close of that Section.

45-48.—Second Cleansing of the Temple, and Summary of Subsequent Proceedings. (= Matt. xxi. 12, 13; Mark xi. 15-19.) That there was but one cleansing of the temple—either that recorded in the Fourth Gospel, at His first visit to Jerusalem and His first Passover, or that recorded in the other three Gospels, at His last visit to it at the time of the Passover—some critics have endeavoured to make out; but all they have to allege for this is the supposed improbability of two such similar and unusual occurrences, and the fact that while each of the Evangelists records one cleansing, none of them records two. The Evangelists do indeed differ from each other considerably as to the order in which they place certain events; but if a cleansing of the temple occurred at the *outset* of our Lord's ministry—as recorded by John, who ought certainly to know the fact—and if it was never afterwards repeated, it cannot be believed that all the other Evangelists, whose Gospels may be shown to have been written independently of each other, should agree in transferring it to the very *close* of His ministry. Accordingly, most, if not all the Fathers recognized two cleansings of the temple—the one at the outset, the other at the close of our Lord's public life: and with them agree nearly all the best modern critics, *Calvin*, *Grotius*, *Lampe*, *Tholuck*, *Olshausen*, *Ebrard*, *Meyer*, *Stier*, *Alford;* compared with whom, those who regard both as one, though acute and learned critics, are, on a question of this nature, of inferior weight, *Wetstein*, *Pearce*, *Priestley*, *Neander*, *de Wette*, *Lücke*. *Lange* once took the latter view, but now contends decidedly for the double cleansing. That our Lord should put forth His *authority* in this remarkable way at His first visit to the city and temple, and so command attention to His claims from the highest authorities at the very outset, was altogether natural and appropriate. And that He should reassert it when He came to the city and temple for the last time, when the echoes of the popular acclaim to Him as the Son of David had scarce died away, but were about to be followed by cries of a very different nature, and His life was to pay the penalty of those claims—that in these circumstances He should vindicate them once more was surely in the highest degree natural. Nor are there wanting in the narratives of the two cleansings, evidences of a *progress* in the state of things from the time of the first to that of the last, which corroborates the fact of the deed being repeated. (See on John ii. 13-22, Remark 1, at the close of that Section.)

Second Cleansing of the Temple (45, 46). **45. And he went into the temple, and began**—or proceeded **to cast out**—but no mention is here made of the "whip of small cords" with which this was done

47 And he taught daily in the temple. But the [e]chief priests and the
48 scribes and the chief of the people sought to destroy him, and could
not find what they might do: for all the people [3]were very attentive to
hear him.

20 AND [a]it came to pass, *that* on one of those days, as he taught the
people in the temple, and preached the Gospel, the chief priests and the
2 scribes came upon *him* with the elders, and spake unto him, saying, Tell
us, by what [b]authority doest thou these things? or who is he that gave
3 thee this authority? And he answered and said unto them, I will also ask
4 you one thing; and answer me: The baptism of John, was it from heaven,
5 or of men? And they reasoned with themselves, saying, If we shall say,
6 From heaven; he will say, Why then believed ye him not? But and if
we say, Of men; all the people will stone us: [c]for they be persuaded that
7 John was a prophet. And they answered, That [d]they could not tell
8 whence *it was.* And Jesus said unto them, [e]Neither tell I you by what
authority I do these things.
9 Then began he to speak to the people this parable: [f]A certain man
planted a vineyard, and let it forth to husbandmen, and went into a far
10 country for a long time. And at the season [g]he sent a servant to the
husbandmen, that they should give him of the fruit of the vineyard: but
11 the husbandmen beat him, and sent *him* away empty. And again he
sent another servant: and they beat him also, and entreated *him* shame-
12 fully, and sent *him* away empty. And [h]again he sent a third: and they

A. D. 33.
[e] Mark 11.18. John 7. 19. John 8. 37.
[3] Or, hanged on him. Acts 16. 14.

CHAP. 20.
[a] Matt. 21.23.
[b] Acts 4. 7. Acts 7. 27.
[c] Matt. 14. 5. Matt. 21.26. ch. 7. 29.
[d] Job 24. 13. Rom. 1. 18, 21. 2 Cor. 4. 3. 2 Thes. 2. 9, 10.
[e] Job 5.12,13.
[f] Matt. 21.33. Mark 12. 1.
[g] 2 Ki. 17. 13, 14. 2 Chr. 36.15, 16. Acts 7. 52.
[h] Neh. 9. 29, 30.

the first time (John ii. 15). It is simply said now, He cast out **them that sold therein, and them that bought**—"and overthrew the tables of the money-changers, and the seats of them that sold doves, and would not suffer that any man should carry any vessel through the temple"—that is, the temple-court. 'There was always,' says *Lightfoot,* 'a constant market in the temple, in that place which was called "The Shops," where every day was sold wine, salt, oil, and other requisites to sacrifices; as also oxen and sheep, in the spacious court of the Gentiles.' The "money-changers" were those who, for the convenience of the people, converted the current Greek and Roman money into Jewish coins, in which all temple dues had to be paid. The "doves" being required for sacrifice, as well as young pigeons on several prescribed occasions, could not conveniently be brought from great distances at the annual festivals, and so were naturally provided for them by dealers, as a matter of merchandise (see Deut. xiv. 24-26). Thus the whole of these transactions were, *in themselves*, not only harmless, but nearly indispensable. The one thing about them which kindled the indignation of the Lord of the Temple, now traversing its sacred precincts in the flesh, was the *place* where they were carried on—the *profanation* involved in such things being done within an inclosure sacred to the worship and service of God—and the effect of this in destroying in the minds of the worshippers the sanctity that should attach to everything on which that worship cast its shadow. On His "not suffering any man to carry a vessel through the temple," *Lightfoot* has a striking extract from one of the rabbinical writings, in answer to the question, What is the reverence due to the temple? The reply is, That none go through the court of it with his staff and shoes and purse, and dust upon his feet, and that none make it a common thoroughfare, or let any of his spittle fall upon it. **46. Saying unto them, It is written** (Isa. lvi. 7), **My house is the house of prayer: but ye have made it a den of thieves** [σπήλαιον λῃστῶν]—rather, 'of robbers;' of men banded together for plunder, reckless of principle. So in Matthew and Mark. This also is a quotation, but from Jeremiah (vii. 11)—"Is this house, which is called by my name, become a den of robbers in your eyes? Behold, even I have seen it, saith the Lord." Our Lord uses the very words of the LXX [σπήλαιον λῃστῶν]. The milder charge, made on the former occasion—"Ye have made it a house of merchandise"—was now unsuitable. Nor was the authority of the prophet expressly referred to on that occasion, so far at least as recorded, though it was certainly implied in the language of the rebuke. The second Gospel is more exact and full in the quotation from the prophet: "And He taught, saying unto them, Is it not written, My house shall be called of all nations the house of prayer?" (Mark xi. 17). The translation should be, as in the margin, '*for* all nations' [πᾶσι τοῖς ἔθνεσιν], and as in the prophet "for all people," or rather, 'all the nations' [לְכָל־הָעַמִּים]. The glimpse here given of the extension of the Church to "every people and tongue and nation," and consequently beyond the ancient economy—which is the burden of the original passage—was not the immediate point for which our Lord referred to it, but the *character* of the house as God's—"*My* house"—and "a house of prayer." And it was the desecration of it *in this light* that our Lord so sternly rebuked.

Summary of Subsequent Proceedings (47, 48). **47. And he taught daily in the temple. But the chief priests and the scribes and the chief of the people sought** [ἐζήτουν]—or 'kept seeking;' that is, from day to day, **to destroy him, 48. And could not find what they might do: for all the people were very attentive to hear him** [ἐξεκρέματο αὐτοῦ ἀκούων]—or 'hung upon His lips.'

For Remarks on this Section, see those on John ii. 13-25, at the close of that Section.

CHAP. XX. 1-19.—THE AUTHORITY OF JESUS QUESTIONED, AND THE REPLY—THE PARABLES OF THE TWO SONS AND OF THE WICKED HUSBANDMEN. (=Matt. xxi. 23-46; Mark xi. 27—xii. 12.) For the exposition, see on Matt. xxi. 23-46.

13 wounded him also, and cast *him* out. Then said the lord of the vineyard,
What shall I do? I will send [i]my beloved son: it may be they will
14 reverence *him* when they see him. But when the husbandmen saw him,
they reasoned among themselves, saying, This is [j]the heir: come, let us
15 kill him, that the inheritance may be ours. So they cast him out of the
vineyard, and [k]killed *him*. What therefore shall the lord of the vineyard
16 do unto them? He shall come and destroy these husbandmen, and shall
give the vineyard to others. And when they heard *it*, they said, God
forbid.
17 And he beheld them, and said, What is this then that is written, [l]The
stone which the builders rejected, the same is become the head of the
18 corner? Whosoever shall fall upon that stone shall be broken; but [m]on
19 whomsoever it shall fall, it will grind him to powder. And the chief
priests and the scribes the same hour sought to lay hands on him; and
they feared the people: for they perceived that he had spoken this
parable against them.
20 And [n]they watched *him*, and sent forth spies, which should feign
themselves just men, that they might take hold of his words, that so
they might deliver him unto the power and authority of the governor.
21 And they asked him, saying, [o]Master, we know that thou sayest and
teachest rightly, neither acceptest thou the person *of any*, but teachest
22 the way of God [1]truly: Is it lawful for us to give tribute unto Cesar, or
23 no? But he perceived their craftiness, and said unto them, Why tempt
24 ye me? Show me a [p]penny. Whose image and superscription hath it?
25 They answered and said, Cesar's. And he said unto them, Render therefore unto Cesar the things which be Cesar's, and unto God the things
26 which be God's. And they could not take hold of his words before the
people: and they marvelled at his answer, and held their peace.
27 Then [q]came to *him* certain of the Sadducees, [r]which deny that there is
28 any resurrection; and they asked him, saying, Master, [s]Moses wrote unto
us, If any man's brother die, having a wife, and he die without children,
that his brother should take his wife, and raise up seed unto his brother.
29 There were therefore seven brethren: and the first took a wife, and died
30 without children. And the second took her to wife, and he died child-
31 less. And the third took her; and in like manner the seven also: and
32 they left no children, and died. Last of all the woman died also.
33 Therefore in the resurrection whose wife of them is she? for seven had
her to wife.
34 And Jesus answering said unto them, The children of this world marry,
35 and are given in marriage: but they which shall be [t]accounted worthy
to obtain that world, and the resurrection from the dead, neither marry,
36 nor are given in marriage: neither can they die any more: for they [u]are
equal unto the angels; and are the children of God, [v]being the children
37 of the resurrection. Now, that the dead are raised, [w]even Moses showed
at the bush, when he calleth the Lord the God of Abraham, and the God
38 of Isaac, and the God of Jacob. For [x]he is not a God of the dead, but
39 of the living: for [y]all live unto him. Then certain of the scribes
40 answering said, Master, thou hast well said. And after that they durst
not ask him any *question at all*.
41 And he said unto them, [z]How say they that Christ is David's son?
42 And David himself saith in the book of Psalms, [a]The LORD said unto my
43 Lord, Sit thou on my right hand, till I make thine enemies thy footstool.
44 David therefore calleth him Lord, how is he then his son?
45 Then, [b]in the audience of all the people, he said unto his disciples,

A. D. 33.
[i] Isa. 7. 14. John 3. 16. Rom. 8. 3. Gal. 4. 4.
[j] Ps. 2. 6. Isa. 9. 6. Col. 1. 15, 16. Phil. 2. 9-11. Heb. 1. 2.
[k] John 19. Acts 3. 15. 1 Cor. 2. 8.
[l] Ps. 118. 22. Matt. 21. 42. 1 Pet. 2. 7.
[m] Isa. 8. 15. Dan. 2. 34, 35. Matt. 21. 44.
[n] Matt. 22. 15.
[o] Matt. 22. 16. Mark 12. 14.
1 Of a truth.
[p] Matt. 18. 28.
[q] Matt. 16. 1, 6, 12. Matt. 22. 23. Mark 12. 18. Acts 4. 1, 2. Acts 5. 17.
[r] Acts 23. 6.
[s] Gen. 38. 8. Deut. 25. 5.
[t] 2 Thes. 1. 5. Rev. 3. 4.
[u] Zec. 3. 7. Matt. 22 30. Mark 12. 25. 1 Cor. 15. 42, 49, 52. 1 John 3. 2. Rev. 5. 6-14. Rev. 7. 9-12. Rev. 22. 9.
[v] Rom. 8. 23.
[w] Ex. 3. 6. Acts 7. 32. Heb. 11. 9, 35.
[x] Ps. 16. 5-11. Ps. 73. 23-26. Ps. 145. 1, 2. John 11. 25. Rom. 4. 17. Col. 3. 3, 4. Heb. 11. 16.
[y] Rom. 6. 10, 11. Rom. 14. 7-9. 2 Cor. 6. 16. 2 Cor. 13. 4. Col. 3. 3, 4.
[z] Matt. 22. 42. Mark 12. 35.
[a] Ps. 110. 1. Acts 2. 34. 1 Cor. 15. 25.
[b] Matt. 23. 1. Mark 12. 38.

20-40.—ENTANGLING QUESTIONS ABOUT TRIBUTE AND THE RESURRECTION, WITH THE REPLIES. (=Matt. xxii. 15-33; Mark xii. 13-27.) For the exposition, see on Mark xii. 13-27.

46 Beware [c]of the scribes, which desire to walk in long robes, and [d]love
greetings in the markets, and the highest seats in the synagogues, and
47 the chief rooms at feasts; which [e]devour widows' houses, and for a show
make long prayers: [f]the same shall receive greater damnation.
21 AND he looked up, [a]and saw the rich men casting their gifts into the
2 treasury. And he saw also a certain poor widow casting in thither two
3 mites. And he said, Of a truth I say unto you, that [b]this poor widow
4 hath cast in more than they all: for all these have of their abundance
cast in unto the offerings of God: but she of her penury hath cast in all
the living that she had.

A. D. 33.

c Matt. 23. 5.
d ch. 11. 43.
e Matt. 23 14.
f Matt. 11. 22, 24.
ch. 10. 10-16.
ch. 12. 47, 48.

CHAP. 21.
a Mark 12. 41.
b Pro. 3. 9.
2 Cor. 8. 12.

41-47.—CHRIST BAFFLES THE PHARISEES BY A QUESTION ABOUT DAVID AND MESSIAH, AND DENOUNCES THE SCRIBES. (=Matt. xxii. 41-46, and xxiii. 14; Mark xii. 35-40.) For the exposition, see on Mark xii. 35-40.

CHAP. XXI. 1-4.—THE WIDOW'S TWO MITES. (=Mark xii. 41-44.) Most touching is the connection between the denunciations against those grasping ecclesiastics who "devoured *widows' houses*"—which, according both to Mark and Luke, our Lord had just uttered—and the case of this poor widow, of highest account in the eye of Jesus. The incident occurred, as appears, on that day of profuse teaching—the third day (or the *Tuesday*) of His last week. In Mark's account of it we read that "Jesus sat," or 'sat down' [καθίσας] "over against the treasury" (Mark xii. 41)—probably to rest; for he had continued long teaching on foot in the temple-court (Mark xi. 27). This explains the opening words of our Evangelist.

1. And he looked up—from his sitting posture, **and saw**—doubtless as in Zaccheus's case, not quite casually, **the rich men casting their gifts into the treasury** [γαζοφυλάκιον]—a court of the temple where thirteen chests were placed to receive the offerings of the people towards its maintenance (2 Ki. xii. 9; John viii. 20.) These chests were called trumpets, from the trumpet-like shape of the tubes into which the money was dropped, wide at the one end and narrow at the other. Mark (xii. 41) says, "He beheld how the multitude [ὁ ὄχλος] cast money [χαλκὸν] into the treasury"—literally 'brass,' but meaning copper-coin, the offering of the common people—"and many that were rich cast in much" [πολλά], literally, 'many [coins]' or 'large [sums].' **2. And he saw a certain poor**—or 'indigent' [πενιχρὰν] **widow casting in two mites** [λεπτὰ]—"which make a farthing" (Mark xii. 42); that is, the smallest Jewish coin. The term here rendered "farthing" [κοδράντης=*quadrans*] is the eighth part of the Roman *as;* and thus her whole offering would amount to no more than about the fifth part of our penny. But it was *her all.* "And He called His disciples" (Mark xii. 43) for the purpose of teaching from this case a great general lesson. **3. And he said, Of a truth I say unto you, that this poor widow hath cast in more than they all**—in proportion to her means, which is God's standard of judgment (2 Cor. viii. 12). **4. For all these have of their abundance** [ἐκ τοῦ περισσεύοντος αὐτοῖς]—'of their superfluity;' of what they had *to spare*, beyond what they needed. **cast in unto the offerings**—or 'gifts' [δῶρα] **of God**—the gifts dedicated to the service of God, **but she of her penury** [ὑστερήματος]—'her deficiency;' out of what was *less* than her own wants required, **hath cast in all the living that she had.** In Mark it is "her whole subsistence" [ὅλον τὸν βίον αὐτῆς].

Remarks.—1. Even under the ancient elaborate and expensive economy, God made systematic provision for drawing out the voluntary liberality of His people for many of the purposes of His worship and service. And here we have a quantity of treasure-chests laid out expressly to receive the free-will offerings of the people; and on this the incident before us turns. Much more is the Christian Church dependent upon the voluntary liberalities of its members for the maintenance, efficiency, and extension of its ordinances, at home and abroad. 2. As Jesus "looked up" in the days of His flesh, so He looks down now from the height of His glory, upon "the treasury;" observing who cast in much, and who little, who "of their superfluity," and who "of their penury." 3. Christ's standard of commendable liberality to His cause is not what we give of our abundance, but what we give of our deficiency—not *what will never be missed*, however much that may be, but *what costs us some real sacrifice*, what we give at a pinch; and just in proportion to the relative amount of that sacrifice is the measure of our Christian liberality in His eye. Do the majority of real Christians act upon this principle? Are not those who do so the exceptions rather than the rule? Can it be doubted that if this principle were faithfully carried out by those who love the Lord Jesus Christ, the wants of all our Churches, our schemes of missionary enterprise, and all that pertains to the maintenance and propagation of the Kingdom of Christ, would be abundantly supplied; or if not quite that, supplied to an extent, at least, as yet unknown? The apostle testifies to the Corinthians of "the grace of God bestowed on the churches of Macedonia; how that in a great trial of affliction the abundance of their joy and their deep poverty abounded unto the riches of their liberality. For to their power (he says), yea, and *beyond their power*, they were willing of themselves; (not needing to be asked, but) praying us with much entreaty that we would receive the gift (towards the maintenance of the poor saints at Jerusalem), and their share [τὴν κοινωνίαν] of the ministering to the saints. And this they did, not as we hoped, but (far beyond our expectation) first gave their own selves unto the Lord, and (then) to us by the will of God" (2 Cor. viii. 1-5). Are there many in our day like these Macedonian churches? But it would seem that even then they were the exception; for this same apostle says, even of the bulk of Christians with whom he mixed, that "all sought their own, not the things which were Jesus Christ's" (Phil. ii. 21). In a comparative sense, no doubt, this was meant. But in any sense it was humiliating enough. O will not the touching incident of this Section rouse those who love the Lord Jesus to *raise their standard* of what He claims at their hands? "How much owest thou unto thy Lord?" is a question which, if but heard by each believer within the recesses of his conscience, in the light of what himself hath experienced of the grace of Christ,

5 And [c]as some spake of the temple, how it was adorned with goodly
6 stones and gifts, he said, *As for* these things which ye behold, the days
will come, in the which [d]there shall not be left one stone upon another,
7 that shall not be thrown down. And they asked him, saying, Master, but
when shall these things be? and what sign *will there be* when these things
8 shall come to pass? And he said, [e]Take heed that ye be not deceived:
for many shall come in my name, saying, I am *Christ;* [1]and the time
9 draweth near: go ye not therefore after them. But when ye shall hear
of wars and commotions, be not terrified: for these things must first come
10 to pass; but the end *is* not by and by. Then [f]said he unto them, Nation
11 shall rise against nation, and kingdom against kingdom: and great earthquakes shall be in divers places, and famines, and pestilences; and fearful
sights and great signs shall there be from heaven.
12 But [g]before all these, they shall lay their hands on you, and persecute
you, delivering *you* up to the synagogues, and into [h]prisons, [i]being
13 brought before kings and rulers [j]for my name's sake. And [k]it shall
14 turn to you for a testimony. Settle [l]*it* therefore in your hearts, not to
15 meditate before what ye shall answer: for I will give you a mouth and
wisdom, [m]which all your adversaries shall not be able to gainsay nor resist.
16 And [n]ye shall be betrayed both by parents, and brethren, and kinsfolks,
17 and friends; and [o]*some* of you shall they cause to be put to death. And
18 [p]ye shall be hated of all *men* for my name's sake. But there shall not
19 an hair of your head perish. In your patience possess ye your souls.
20 And [q]when ye shall see Jerusalem compassed with armies, then know
21 that the desolation thereof is nigh. Then let them which are in Judea
flee to the mountains; and let them which are in the midst of it depart
22 out; and let not them that are in the countries enter thereinto. For
these be the days of vengeance, that [r]all things which are written may be
23 fulfilled. But woe unto them that are with child, and to them that give
suck, in those days! for there shall be great distress in the land, and
24 wrath upon this people. And they shall fall by the edge of the sword,
and shall be led away captive into all nations: and Jerusalem shall be
trodden down of the Gentiles, [s]until the times of the Gentiles be fulfilled.
25 And [t]there shall be signs in the sun, and in the moon, and in the
stars; and upon the earth distress of nations, with perplexity; the sea
26 and the waves roaring; men's hearts failing them for fear, and for looking
after those things which are coming on the earth: [u]for the powers of
27 heaven shall be shaken. And then shall they see the Son of man coming
28 [v]in a cloud, with power and great glory. And when these things begin
to come to pass, then look up, and lift up your heads; for your redemption draweth nigh.
29 And [w]he spake to them a parable; Behold the fig tree, and all the
30 trees; when they now shoot forth, ye see and know of your own selves
31 that summer is now nigh at hand. So likewise ye, when ye see these
things come to pass, know ye that the kingdom of God is nigh at hand.

A. D. 33.

[c] Matt. 24. 1. Mark 13. 1.
[d] 1 Ki. 9. 7-9. Isa. 64. 10, 11. Jer. 5. 10. Jer. 7. 11, 14. Lam. 2. 6-8. Ezek. 7. 20-22. Mic. 3. 12. Matt. 24. 2. Mark 13. 2. ch. 19. 44.
[e] Matt. 24. 4. Mark 13. 5. 2 Cor. 11. 13-15. Eph. 5. 6. 2 Thes. 2. 3. 2 Tim. 3. 13. 1 John 4. 1. Rev. 12. 9.
[1] Or, and, The time. Matt. 3. 2. Matt. 4. 17.
[f] Matt. 24. 7.
[g] John 15. 20. Rev. 2. 10.
[h] Acts 4. 3. Acts 5. 18. Acts 12. 4. Acts 16. 24.
[i] Acts 25. 23.
[j] 1 Pet. 2. 13.
[k] Phil. 1. 28. 2 Thes. 1. 5.
[l] Matt. 10. 19.
[m] Acts 6. 10.
[n] Mic. 7. 6.
[o] Acts 7. 59. Acts 12. 2.
[p] Matt. 10. 22. 2 Tim. 3. 12.
[q] Matt. 24. 15.
[r] Dan. 9. 26, 27. Zec. 11. 1.
[s] Dan. 9. 27. Rom. 11. 25.
[t] 2 Pet. 3. 10, 12.
[u] Matt. 24. 29.
[v] Acts 1. 11. Rev. 1. 7. Rev. 14. 14.
[w] Mark 13. 28.

might put all his past givings and doings to shame. What an encouraging word is this of Christ, concerning the poor widow and her two mites, to the poor of His flock in every age! Let them not hide their talent in the earth, because it is but one, but put it out to usury, by "lending it to the Lord." But, indeed, this class go beyond the rich in their givings to Christ. Only we would that each vied with the other in this matter. See, on this delightful subject, on Mark xiv. 1-11, Remark 6 at the close of that Section. And, perhaps, much of the fault of the stinted givings of Christians lies with the ministers of Christ for not pressing upon them such duties, and such considerations in support of them, frequently enough, urgently enough, lovingly enough. That is a maxim which deserves to be written in letters of gold (2 Cor. viii. 12): "*If there be first a willing mind, it is accepted according to what a man hath, and not according to what he hath not.*" "Ye know the grace of our Lord Jesus Christ, that though He was rich, yet for your sakes He became poor, that ye through His poverty might be rich" (2 Cor. viii. 9).

5-38.—Christ's Prophecy of the Destruction of Jerusalem, and Warnings suggested by it to Prepare for His Second Coming—Summary of Proceedings during His Last Week. (= Matt. xxiv. 1-51; Mark xiii. 1-37.) For the exposition, see on Mark xiii. 1-37.

32 Verily I say unto you, This generation shall not pass away till all be
33 fulfilled. Heaven and earth shall pass away; but my words shall not
pass away.
34 And [x]take heed to yourselves, lest at any time your hearts be overcharged with surfeiting, and drunkenness, and cares of this life, and *so*
35 that day come upon you unawares. For [y]as a snare shall it come on all
36 them that dwell on the face of the whole earth. Watch [z]ye therefore,
and [a]pray always, that ye may be accounted worthy to escape all these
things that shall come to pass, and [b]to stand before the Son of man.
37 And [c]in the day-time he was teaching in the temple; and [d]at night he
went out, and abode in the mount that is called *the mount* of Olives.
38 And all the people came early in the morning to him [e]in the temple, for
to hear him.

22 NOW [a]the feast of unleavened bread drew nigh, which is called the
2 Passover. And [b]the chief priests and scribes sought how they might
3 kill him; for they feared the people. Then [c]entered Satan into Judas
surnamed Iscariot, being of the number of the twelve.
4 And he went his way, and communed with the chief priests and
5 captains, how he might betray him unto them. And they were glad,
6 and [d]covenanted to give him money. And he promised, and sought
opportunity to betray him unto them [1]in the absence of the multitude.
7 Then [e]came the day of unleavened bread, when the passover must be

A. D. 33.

[x] Rom. 13. 13. 1 Pet. 4. 7.
[y] 1 Thes. 5. 2. 2 Pet. 3. 10. Rev. 3. 3.
[z] Matt. 25. 13. Mark 13. 33.
[a] ch. 18. 1.
[b] Ps. 1. 5. Eph. 6. 13. 1 John 2. 28.
[c] John 8. 1, 2.
[d] ch. 22. 39.
[e] Hag. 2. 7. Mal. 3. 1.

CHAP. 22.
[a] Matt. 26. 2. Mark 14. 1.
[b] Ps. 2. 2. John 11. 47.
[c] Matt. 26. 14.
[d] Zec. 11. 12. 1 Tim. 6. 10.
[1] Or, without tumult.
[e] Matt. 26. 17. Mark 14. 12.

CHAP. XXII. 1-6.—THE CONSPIRACY OF THE JEWISH AUTHORITIES TO PUT JESUS TO DEATH—JUDAS AGREES WITH THE CHIEF PRIESTS TO BETRAY HIS LORD. (= Matt. xxvi. 1-5, 14-16; Mark xiv. 1, 2, 10, 11.) For the exposition, see on Mark xiv. 1, 2, 10, 11, with the corresponding Remarks at the close of that Section.

7-30.—PREPARATION FOR AND LAST CELEBRATION OF THE PASSOVER—INSTITUTION OF THE SUPPER—ANNOUNCEMENT OF THE TRAITOR—FRESH STRIFE WHO SHOULD BE GREATEST. (= Matt. xxvi. 17-30; Mark xiv. 12-26; John xiii. 10, 11, 18, 19, 21-30.)

Preparation for the Passover (7-13). We have now arrived, in the progress of the Redeemer's earthly history, at the fifth day of His last week—the *Thursday*—on which the preparations now to be described were made. Here arises a question of extreme difficulty, a question very early discussed in the Church, a question which has divided, and to this day divides, the ablest critics: 'Did our Lord eat the passover with His disciples at all? and if He did, was it on the same day on which it was eaten by the rest of the Jews, or was it a day earlier?' Had we only the testimony of the first three Evangelists, there could be no doubt both that He ate the Passover, and that He ate it on the usual statutory evening—on the fourteenth day of the month Nisan; for their testimony to this effect is concurrent and decisive (Mark xiv. 12; Luke xxii. 7; with which the whole of Matt. xxvi. 17, &c., though less explicit, accords). But, on the other hand, if we had only the testimony of the Fourth Evangelist, we should not be perfectly sure that our Lord ate the paschal supper at all; or if it should seem clear enough, though not explicitly stated, that the "supper" of John xiii. was no other than the Passover, one would certainly have been apt to conclude, from some expressions in that Gospel, that up to the morning of the *Friday*—when our Lord was before the ecclesiastical and civil tribunals for judgment—the Jews had *not* eaten their Passover, and consequently, that Jesus and His disciples, if they ate it at all, must have eaten it a day before the proper time. One general remark on this question may here be made:—That from the nature of the case, a mistake on such a point by all the three first Evangelists, whose accounts coincide and yet evince themselves to be independent narratives, was hardly possible; and as to the Fourth Evangelist—who was himself so largely concerned in the whole transaction, and whose Gospel, written after the other three had been long in circulation, bears evidence of having been drawn up to supplement the others—it is not conceivable that there should have been any error on his part. And as there is not a trace in his Gospel of any design to correct an error on this subject in the other three, one is forced to conclude—apart altogether from the divine authority of the Gospels—that the first three Evangelists and the fourth must be at one on this important point. Now since the testimony of the first three is explicit and cannot be set aside, while that of the fourth is but general and presumptive, the conclusion to which we feel ourselves shut up is, that the Passover was eaten by our Lord and His apostles on the usual evening. The expressions in the Fourth Gospel, which seem to imply the reverse, but which may all, as we think, be interpreted consistently with the view we have stated, will be taken up at the places where they occur.

7. Then came the day of unleavened bread, when the passover must be killed. The day here alluded to—"the first day of unleavened bread" (Matt. xxvi. 17)—was the 14th Nisan, when, about mid-day, labour was intermitted, and all leaven removed from the houses (Exod. xii. 15-17). Then, "between the two evenings" (Exod. xii. 6, *margin*)—or between three and six o'clock—the paschal lamb was killed, and in the evening, when the 15th Nisan began, was eaten. And though "the days of unleavened bread" properly began with the 15th, the preparations for the festival being made on the 14th, it was popularly called, as here, the "first" day of unleavened bread—as we learn from *Josephus*, whose way of speaking agrees with that here employed. The two disciples being sent from Bethany to make the necessary preparations on the Thursday, our Lord and the other disciples followed them to the city later in the day, and probably as evening drew near. **8. And he sent**

8 killed. And he sent Peter and John, saying, Go and prepare us the pass-
9 over, that we may eat. And they said unto him, Where wilt thou that
10 we prepare? And he said unto them, Behold, when ye are entered into
the city, there shall a man meet you, bearing a pitcher of water; follow
11 him into the house where he entereth in. And ye shall say unto the
goodman of the house, The Master saith unto thee, Where is the guest-
12 chamber, where I shall eat the passover with my disciples? And he shall
13 show you a large upper room furnished: there make ready. And they
went, and found as he had said unto them: and they made ready the
passover.
14 And when the hour was come, he sat down, and the twelve apostles
15 with him. And he said unto them, [2]With desire I have desired to eat
16 this passover with you before I suffer: for I say unto you, I will not any
17 more eat thereof, [f]until it be fulfilled in the kingdom of God. And he
took the cup, and gave thanks, and said, Take this, and divide *it* among
18 yourselves: for [g]I say unto you, I will not drink of the fruit of the vine,
until the kingdom of God shall come.
19 And he took bread, and gave thanks, and brake *it*, and gave unto
them, saying, This is my body, which is given for you: this [h]do in

A. D. 33.

[2] Or, I have heartily desired.

[f] ch. 12. 37. ch. 14. 15. Acts 10. 41. John 6. 27, 50. 1 Cor. 5. 7, 8. Heb. 10. 1-10. Rev. 19. 9.

[g] Jud. 9. 13. Ps. 104. 15. Pro. 31. 6, 7. Isa. 24. 9, 11. Isa. 25. 6. Isa. 55. 1. Zec. 9. 15. Matt. 26. 29. Mark 14. 25.

[h] Ps. 78. 4, 6. Ps. 111. 4. 1 Cor. 11. 24.

Peter and John, saying, Go and prepare us the passover, that we may eat. 9. And they said unto him, Where? . . . 10. And he said unto them, Behold, when ye are entered into the city, there shall a man meet you, bearing a pitcher of water; follow him into the house where he entereth in. 11. And ye shall say unto the goodman of the house, The Master saith unto thee, Where is the guest-chamber, where I shall eat the passover with my disciples? 12. And he shall show you a large upper room furnished [*ἐστρωμένον*]—or 'spread;' with tables, and couches, and covering, all ready for supper. Such large apartments were set apart by the inhabitants of the city, for the accommodation of parties from the country. **13. And they went, and found as he had said unto them: and they made ready the passover.** See the similarly minute directions to the two who were sent to procure the ass on which He rode into Jerusalem, ch. xix. 30-32.

Last Celebration of the Passover (14-18). **14. And when the hour was come**—about six o'clock, **he sat down, and the twelve apostles with him**—the whole twelve, Judas included. **15. And he said unto them, With desire I have desired** [*'Επιθυμίᾳ ἐπεθύμησα*]—the strongest expression of intense desire. In Gen. xxxi. 30 the same expression [נִכְסֹף נִכְסַפְתָּה, *ἐπιθυμίᾳ ἐπεθύμησας*] is rendered "thou sore longedst." **to eat this passover with you before I suffer.** The last meal one is to partake of with his family or friends before his departure even for a far distant land, in all probability never to see them again, is a solemn and fond one to any thoughtful and loving person. The last meal of a martyr of Jesus with his friends in the truth, before being led forth to execution, is still more touching. But faint are these illustrations of the emotions with which Jesus now sat down to supper with the Twelve. All the sweetness and all the sadness of His social intercourse with them, from the day that He first chose them to be with Him, were now to be concentrated and heightened to their utmost intensity during the brief hour or two of this their last meal together. But this was no common meal, nor even common passover. It was to be *the point of transition between two divine economies and their respective festivals;* the one to close for ever, the other to run its majestic career through all time, until from a terrestrial form it should dissolve into a form celestial. No wonder, then, that He said, "With desire I have desired to eat *this* passover with you before I suffer." This, as *Alford* remarks, is the only instance in the Gospels in which the word "suffer" [*πάσχω*] is used in its absolute sense—as in the Creed, 'He *suffered* under Pontius Pilate.' **16. For I say unto you, I will not any more eat thereof, until it be fulfilled in the kingdom of God**—or, as in Matt. xxvi. 29, "I will not drink henceforth of this fruit of the vine, until that day when I drink it new with you in my Father's kingdom," or "in the kingdom of God" (Mark xiv. 25). The primary application of this, no doubt, is to the *new* Gospel kingdom to be fully erected when the old economy, with its Passover and temple-rites, should disappear. But the best interpreters agree that its only full and proper application is to that celestial kingdom of which He speaks so beautifully in *v.* 30—"that ye may eat and drink at My table in My kingdom," &c.

17. And he took the cup. Several cups of wine were partaken of, or tasted, during the somewhat elaborate rites observed in the celebration of the Passover. This was probably the first one: but it is not to be confounded with the Eucharistic cup mentioned in *v.* 20, and then partaken of for the first time; this *Paschal* cup was now partaken of for the *last* time. **and gave thanks, and said, Take this, and divide it among yourselves.** A false inference has been drawn from this by some expositors—that Christ did not Himself drink of it. The contrary is obvious from His earnest desire to "eat this Passover with them," and of course to drink the Paschal cup; and in what follows He expressly says that He did drink of it. **18. For I say unto you, I will not drink of the fruit of the vine, until the kingdom of God shall come.** See on *v.* 16, of which this is but a repetition, in a form adapted to the cup, as there it was uttered in a form adapted to the paschal lamb and the bread eaten with it.

Institution of the Supper (19, 20). **19. And he took bread, and gave thanks** (see on Mark vi. 41). In Matthew and Mark it is "and blessed it." The one act includes the other. He "gave thanks," not so much here for the literal bread, as for that higher food which was couched under it; and He "blessed" it as the ordained channel of spiritual nourishment. **and brake it, and gave unto them, saying, This is my body, which is**

20 remembrance of me. Likewise also the cup after supper, saying, [i]This
cup *is* the new testament in my blood, which is shed for you.
21 But, [j]behold, the hand of him that betrayeth me *is* with me on the
22 table. And truly the Son of man goeth, as [k]it was determined: but
23 woe unto that man by whom he is betrayed! And they began to enquire
among themselves, which of them it was that should do this thing.
24 And [l]there was also a strife among them, which of them should be
25 accounted the greatest. And [m]he said unto them, The kings of the
Gentiles exercise lordship over them; and they that exercise authority
26 upon them are called benefactors. But [n]ye *shall* not *be* so: [o]but he that
is greatest among you, let him be as the younger; and he that is chief, as

A. D. 33.

i 1 Cor.10.16.
j Ps. 41. 9. Mark 14.18. John 13.21, 26.
k Acts 2. 23. Acts 4. 28.
l Mark 9. 34. ch. 9. 46.
m Matt. 20. 25.
n Jas. 4. 6. 1 Pet. 5. 3.
o ch. 9. 48.

given for you: this do in remembrance of me. 'The expression, "This is my body,"' says *Alexander* most truly, 'which is common to all the accounts, appears so unambiguous and simple an expression, that it is hard to recognize in it the occasion and the subject of the most protracted and exciting controversy that has rent the Church within the last thousand years. That controversy is so purely theological that it has scarcely any basis in the exposition of the text; the only word upon which it could fasten (the verb *is*) being one which in Aramaic (or Syro-Chaldaic), would not be expressed, and therefore belongs merely to the Greek translation of our Saviour's language. [But this supposes our Lord now spoke in Aramaic—the contrary of which we believe.] Until the strong unguarded figures of the early Fathers had been petrified into a dogma, at first by popular misapprehension, and at last by theological perversion, these words suggested no idea but the one which they still convey to every plain unbiased reader, that our Saviour calls the bread His body in the same sense that He calls Himself a door (John x. 9), a vine (John xv. 1), a root (Rev. xxii. 16), a star, and is described by many other metaphors in Scripture. The bread was an emblem of His flesh, as wounded for the sins of men, and as administered for their spiritual nourishment and growth in grace.' **20. Likewise also the cup after supper**—not after the *Lord's* Supper, as if the taking of the bread and of the cup in it were separated so far as that; but after the *paschal* supper, and consequently immediately after the distribution of the bread. The accounts of Matthew and of Mark would seem to imply that He gave thanks on taking the cup, as well as with the bread; but here, at any rate, and in the most authoritative account, perhaps, which we have, in 1 Cor. xi. 23, &c., that is not said. **saying, This cup is the new testament in my blood, which is shed for you.** In Matthew (xxvi. 28), "This is my blood of the new testament, which is shed for many for the remission of sins." In 1 Cor. (xi. 25) "This cup is the new testament in my blood: this do ye, as oft as ye drink it, in remembrance of me." Most critics now maintain that the word here rendered "testament" [διαθήκη] should be rendered *covenant*, not only here but wherever else it occurs in the New Testament; being used in the Old Testament constantly by the LXX. translators for the well-known Hebrew word signifying 'covenant' [בְּרִית], which never signifies 'testament.' Here, in particular, there is a manifest allusion to Exod. xxiv. 8, "Behold, *the blood of the covenant* [דַם־הַבְּרִית] which the Lord hath made with you concerning all these words." Now it is beyond doubt that 'covenant' is the fundamental idea, and that in the Old Testament the word is correctly rendered "covenant." But let it be observed, first, that 'testament' or 'will' is the proper classical sense of the Greek word, and 'disposition' or 'covenant' but a secondary sense; and next, that in Heb. ix. 15, &c., the sense of 'testament' appears to be so obviously what the apostle reasons on, that to exclude it there, and restrict the meaning to 'covenant,' can only be made to yield the harshest sense. But the true harmony of both senses of the word, and how, in the case of Christ's death, the one runs into the other, will be seen, not by any criticism on the *word*, but by reflecting on the *thing*. If it be true that by 'covenant,' or eternal divine arrangement, all the blessings of salvation become the rightful possession of believers solely *in virtue of Christ's death*, does not this almost irresistibly suggest to every reflecting mind the idea of a *testator's* death as a most true and exalted conception of the virtue of it? What can be a more natural view of the *principle* on which the fruits of Christ's death become ours than that of a testamentary disposition? Then, observe how near to this idea of His death our Lord Himself came in what He said, when the Greeks sought to "see Jesus" on the eve of His last Passover, "The hour is come when the Son of man should be glorified: Except a corn of wheat fall into the ground and die, it abideth *alone; but if it die, it bringeth forth much fruit*" (John xii. 23, 24). Observe, too, His mode of expression twice over at the Supper-table, "I *appoint* [διατίθεμαι] unto you, as My Father appointed [διέθετο] unto Me, a kingdom" (Luke xxii. 29); "Peace I *leave* with you; My peace I *give* unto you" (see on John xiv. 27): and it will be seen, we think, how each idea suggests the other. While that of '*covenant*' is confessedly the fundamental one, that of '*testament*' is accessory or illustrative only. Yet the one is as real as the other, and presents a phase of the truth exceeding precious. In this view *Bengel* substantially concurs, and *Stier* entirely.

Announcement of the Traitor (21-23). **21-23. But, behold, the hand of him that betrayeth me is with me on the table, &c.** See on John xiii. 21-26.

Fresh Strife Who should be Greatest (24-30). **24. And there was**—rather, here, 'there had been' **a strife among them, which of them should be accounted the greatest.** Some symptoms of the former contention on this subject seem to have reappeared once more; probably just before sitting down to the paschal supper, and perhaps in consequence of seeing the whole paschal arrangements committed to two of the Twelve. (See on Mark ix. 33, &c.) But of all occasions for giving way to such petty ambition and jealousy, this was the worst, and to our Lord must have been the most painful. And if so, who can but wonder at the gentleness with which He here rebukes it? **25. And he said unto them, The kings of the Gentiles exercise lordship over them; and they that exercise authority upon them are called benefactors** [εὐεργέται]—a title which the vanity of princes eagerly coveted.

27 he that doth serve. For whether *is* greater, he that sitteth at meat, or
he that serveth? *is* not he that sitteth at meat? but [p]I am among you as
28 he that serveth. Ye are they which have continued with me in [q]my
29 temptations. And [r]I appoint unto you a kingdom, as my Father hath
30 appointed unto me; that [s]ye may eat and drink at my table in my
kingdom, [t]and sit on thrones judging the twelve tribes of Israel.

A. D. 33.
p John 13. 13. Phil. 2. 7.
q Heb. 4. 15.
r ch. 12. 32.
s ch. 14. 15.
t Ps. 49. 14.

26. But ye shall not be so: but he that is greatest among you, let him be as the younger; and he that is chief, as he that doth serve. Of how little avail has this condemnation of "lordship" and other vain titles been against the vanity of Christian ecclesiastics! **27. For whether is greater, he that sitteth at meat, or he that serveth? is not he that sitteth at meat? but I am among you as he that serveth.** See on Mark x. 42-45, with Remarks 3 and 4 at the close of that Section; also, on John xiii. 6-8, with Remark 2 at the close of that Section. **28. Ye are they which have continued with me in my temptations.** Affecting evidence this, of Christ's tender susceptibility to human sympathy and support! See on *v.* 40; and on John vi. 66, 67; xvi. 32. **29. And I appoint unto you a kingdom, as my Father hath appointed unto me**—or, according to the order of the original text, 'And I appoint unto you, as My Father hath appointed unto Me, a kingdom.' Who is this that dispenses kingdoms, nay, the Kingdom of kingdoms, within an hour or two of His apprehension, and less than a day of His shameful death? These sublime contrasts, however, perpetually meet and entrance us in this matchless History. The 'giving of a given' Kingdom is in our Lord's usual style of speaking, in which He ever holds forth His oneness in counsel with the Father. 'So far from the high claims I advance being an unwarrantable usurpation of divine prerogatives, dishonouring to the Father, it is from Him I have My commission to be here, to do all I do, and dispense all I bestow.' See on Matt. xxviii. 18; and on John v. 19, &c. **30. That ye may eat and drink at my table in my kingdom, and sit on thrones judging the twelve tribes of Israel.** See on ch. xviii. 29.

Remarks.—1. The *feelings of Jesus Himself* have been too much lost sight of in attention to His *work*, in such portions of the History—a somewhat selfish way of reading it, which punishes itself by the dry and not very satisfactory views thence resulting. Blessed Jesus! Do I hear thee, on seating Thyself at the Paschal table, laying open the burden of Thy heart to the Twelve, saying, "With desire I have desired to eat this Passover with you before I suffer," telling them it was the last Passover Thou wouldst eat with them on earth, and the last time Thou wouldst drink with them here below of the fruit of the vine? In this I read, so as I am not able to express it, Thy oneness with us even in our social sympathies. All that makes a last meeting and a last meal with one's family, whole and unbroken, or with friends with whom one has gone in and out for years in joy and sorrow, alike in the commonest and the loftiest intercourse, an occasion of peculiar solemnity and tender interest—all this, it seems, was felt by Thee; and if felt at all, felt surely on this occasion with an intensity unknown to us. For it was more than Thy last meal—it was the last Paschal meal ever to be partaken of even by Thy disciples. Ere another such season came round, the typical Passover was to be exchanged for the commemorative Supper; and even at that very table, the one was sweetly to be transfigured into the other. One can understand, then, the emotion that filled Thy heart, when, surrounded by the Twelve in that upper room, Thou foundest Thyself arrived at this stage. And yet, how can we enough bless Thee for giving utterance to this; for who else would have ventured to presume it? But there is something else here, which is at least as noteworthy as this. The treason-hatching, the traitor, the plan, the end—and all so near, so very imminent—were full before Thee, blessed Saviour; yea, the traitor himself was sitting at that table: and yet, with what holy calmness Thou reclinest at this meal! One word thou utterest of direct allusion to it—"Before I *suffer*"—just to reveal the spring of surpassing interest Thou didst feel in *that* Passover; but only one. When after this the new Feast was instituted for all that should believe on Thee through their word to the world's end, it was only to explain the deep intent of that Feast that the bloody scene was again alluded to—and so serenely! not at all in the light of the dishonour done to *Thee*, but of the benefit thereby accruing to *them*—not in the light of Thy suffering, but of the expiatory virtue of that blood of Thine to the salvation of a lost world! But here I see another thing, which at once ravishes and melts me. This Feast Thou wouldst have kept up "IN REMEMBRANCE OF THEE"—not Thy death merely, and the benefits thence resulting, but *Thyself*. No one who has a heart at all would like to be forgotten of those he loves; every one would like to be remembered when he is gone. And is it even so with Thee, O Thou whom my soul loveth? Thy love, it seems—like all other love—seeks a response; it will have itself appreciated and reciprocated, and in that Thou hast all Thy desire; thus to see of the travail of Thy soul is Thy satisfaction, Thy reward (Isa. liii. 11). But had sufficient provision not been made for that without this Supper—in that Thy love is shed abroad in Thy people's hearts by the Holy Ghost given unto them—a love *constraining* them to live not unto themselves, but unto Him that died for them and rose again? True, but Thou art not yet contented. Thou wilt be enshrined in the Church's visible services—and that not in the glory of Thy Person, Thy character, Thy teaching, Thy miracles, or all of these together, but of that Decease which was accomplished at Jerusalem, of that dearest act of Self-sacrifice by which Thy people's ransom was paid; Thou wilt be held visibly up as the bruised Messiah, the bleeding Lamb that taketh away the sin of the world. And who shall say what shallow faith has not been deepened, what languishing affections have not been afresh enkindled by this most blessed ordinance, and how much of its spiritual *nourishment* in all time to come the Church of Christ will not owe to this ordinance? O yes, as we sit at that eucharistic table with robes washed and made white in the blood of the Lamb, and as our faith gazes, through its instituted elements of bread and wine, on that bleeding Lamb, now in the midst of the Throne, does not the hymn of redeeming love go up to Him fresher and warmer than ever before, "Unto Him that loved us, and washed us from our sins in His own blood, and hath made us kings and priests unto God and His Father; to Him be glory and dominion for ever and ever, Amen"? 2. In

31 And the Lord said, Simon, Simon, behold, [u]Satan hath desired *to*
32 *have* you, that he may [v]sift *you* as wheat: but [w]I have prayed for thee,
that thy faith fail not: [x]and when thou art converted, strengthen thy

[u] 1 Pet. 5. 8.
[v] Amos 9. 9.
[w] John 17. 9.
[x] Ps. 51. 13.

the light of these views, what are we to think of the monstrous abuses of this ordinance, on the one hand by *Unitarians*—who can celebrate it and yet see in it no Atonement, and nothing beyond a memorial banquet in honour of a most heroic Sufferer for virtue—and, on the other hand, by *Romanists*, who bury its precious truths and destroy its quickening efficacy under the detestable abuses of transubstantiation and the mass! On the 'Real Presence' and other eucharistic controversies, see on 1 Cor. xi. 23, &c.

31-39.—The Fall of Peter Foretold—The Disciples Warned of Coming Trials. (=Matt. xxvi. 31-35; Mark xiv. 27-31; John xiii. 36-38.)

Here must be taken in an important particular, omitted by our Evangelist, but supplied in the first two Gospels.

Desertion of Jesus by the Apostles Foretold (Matt. xxvi. 31, 32; Mark xiv. 27, 28). Had we only the first two Gospels, we should have concluded that this was spoken after our Lord had left the upper room, and either reached or was on His way to the Mount of Olives. But from the Third and Fourth Gospels, it would appear to have been spoken while they were yet at the Supper-table. Some suppose that part of it was spoken before they left the supper-room, and the rest during that last and most mournful of all His walks with them, from the city to the Mount of Olives. But we prefer to conceive of that walk as taken *in silence*. Matt. xxvi. 31, "Then saith Jesus unto them, All ye shall be offended because of Me this night" [σκανδαλισθήσεσθε ἐν ἐμοὶ]—'shall be stumbled in me;' temporarily staggered on seeing their Master apprehended. In the expression, "*All ye*," there may be a reference to the *one* who had just "gone out." Great as was the relief, now for the first time experienced by the Saviour Himself, on the traitor's voluntary separation from a fellowship to which He never in heart belonged (see on John xiii. 31), even in those who remained there was something which burdened the spirit and wounded the heart of the Man of Sorrows. It saddened Him to think that, within one brief hour or two of the time when their hearts had warmed towards Him more than ever at the Paschal and Communion table, they should every one of them be 'stumbled' because of Him: "for it is written (Zec. xiii. 7), I will smite the Shepherd, and the sheep of the flock shall be scattered abroad." 32. "But after I am risen again, I will go before you into Galilee." He falls back upon this striking prophecy, partly to confirm their faith in what they would otherwise hardly think credible; and partly to console Himself with the reflection that it was but one of "the things concerning him" which "would have an end"—that they would be but links in the chain, "doing what God's hand and purpose determined before to be done." The whole of this marvellous prediction, as it stands in the prophet, runs thus: "Awake, O sword, against My Shepherd, and against the Man that is My Fellow [עַל-גֶּבֶר עֲמִיתִי], saith the Lord of hosts: smite the Shepherd, and the sheep shall be scattered; and I will turn mine hand upon the little ones." Here observe, first, that in the prophet, Jehovah calls upon the sword to awake against His Shepherd and smite Him; here, Jesus receives the thrust direct from the Father's own hand: compare John xviii. 11, "The cup which my Father hath given me, shall I not drink it?" Each view of it presents an aspect of sublime and affecting truth. Next, in the passage, as it stands in Zechariah, two classes are spoken of—"the *sheep*," who are "scattered" on the striking down of their Shepherd (as might be expected, whether literally or figuratively); and "the *little ones*," on whom Jehovah's hand is to be lovingly "turned," to gather or collect them. The former class are the unbelieving nation, who, being staggered and stumbled at a suffering Messiah, turned away from Jesus, and were thereafter nationally scattered or dispersed. The latter are, of course, the little flock of Christ's disciples, who, on the dispersion of the nation, were gathered not only into safety, but to honour and blessedness unspeakable as a redeemed Church. Now mark what turn our Lord here gives to the prophecy. Making no mention, at that solemn moment, of the dispersion of the unbelieving nation, He represents the disciples themselves as both the *dispersed* and the *gathered*. When He their Shepherd, who up to that moment had been their one Bond of dear union, should be smitten—even that night, when the first blow was to be struck at Him by His apprehension—their faith in Him would be momentarily shaken, and "for a small moment" their unbelief would have the same effect as on the nation at large, making them start back and run away, like a flock of sheep when their shepherd is struck down. "But"—now viewing them as "the little ones" on whom Jehovah was to turn His hand—"after I am risen, I will go before you into Galilee;" like a true Shepherd, who, "when He putteth forth His own sheep, *goeth before them*, and *the sheep follow Him*" (John x. 4). The scattered in Gethsemane were to be the gathered in Galilee! How very explicit He is in His announcements now, when on the eve of parting with them till after His resurrection. This manifest allusion to the remainder of the prophecy—"I will turn mine hand upon the little ones"—how beautiful is it! This He only began to do when He went before them into Galilee; for though after His resurrection He had several interviews with them at Jerusalem before this, it was in Galilee that He appears to have collected and rallied them, as the Shepherd of His lately scattered flock, and to have given them some at least of those parting instructions and commissions which may be termed *the initial organization of the Church*. But to return to our Evangelist, whose narrative now is the fullest.

The Fall of Peter Foretold (31-34). **31. And the Lord said, Simon, Simon.** On this reduplication of the name, see on ch. x. 41, and on Matt. xxiii. 37. **Satan hath desired to have you** [ἐξῃτήσατο ὑμᾶς]. The meaning is, 'obtained (by asking) you'—not *thee*, Peter, but *you*, all. **that he may sift you as wheat**—is sifted. "The accuser of the brethren, who accuseth them before God day and night" (Rev. xii. 10), is here represented as accusing these disciples of Christ of hollowness in their attachment to Him; and alleging that if, as in the case of Job (i. 6-12; ii. 1-6), he were only permitted to "sift them," it would soon be seen that there was chaff enough among the wheat, if indeed there would be found, after that sifting, any wheat at all. So he first '*asks* them,' and then he '*obtains* them' (for both ideas are required to complete the sense of the word used) for this sifting purpose. And observe, it is not '*hath* obtained,' but '*obtained;*' that is, it is a transaction *past*, and you are already *given*

33 brethren. And he said unto him, Lord, I am ready to go with thee,
34 both into prison, and to death. And [y]he said, I tell thee, Peter, the
cock shall not crow this day, before that thou shalt thrice deny that
thou knowest me.
35 And [z]he said unto them, When I sent you without purse, and scrip,
36 and shoes, lacked ye any thing? And they said, Nothing. Then said

A. D. 33.

y Matt 26. 34. John 13 38.
z Matt. 10. 9. Mark 6. 8, 9. ch. 9. 3. ch. 10. 4.

over to him—to the extent of his petition—to be allowed to sift you. **32. But I have prayed for thee, that thy faith fail not** ['Εγὼ δὲ ἐδεήθην περὶ σοῦ ἵνα μὴ ἐκλείπῃ ἡ πίστις σου]. Here again, it is not, "I *have* prayed for thee," but 'I *prayed* regarding thee.' The "*I*" too is emphatic: *q. d.*, 'While Satan was soliciting and obtaining you all to sift you as wheat, I was engaged in praying regarding thee—as in greater danger than all the rest—that thy faith fail not; and when the transaction between God and SATAN was completed by your being, every one of you, given over for sifting purposes into the enemy's hand, the transaction between God and ME about thee, Peter, was a completed one too—for Me the Father heareth always.' Such is the *import* of these pregnant words of Jesus. But all this was not fully *expressed.* So far from that, it is not improbable that a misapprehension of what our Lord meant by Peter's faith not "*failing*" helped to bolster him up in his false security. What, then, did our Lord mean by this? Not, certainly, that Peter's faith might not give way at all, or to any extent; for in that sense it did fail, and that foully enough. Clearly His prayer was that Peter's faith might not utterly fail—altogether give way—or *perish.* How near it came to that, and how it only stopped short of that, the sequel affectingly showed. See on *v.* 62. **and when thou art converted**—brought back afresh as a penitent disciple, **strengthen thy brethren**—'fortify them against like falls by holding up to them thine own bitter experience.' **33. And he said unto him, Lord, I am ready to go with thee, both into prison, and to death.** In Matthew and Mark it was when our Lord told them they should all be stumbled in Him that night, that Peter said, "Though all men"—or rather, "all," meaning all that sat with him at the table—"shall be offended in Thee, yet will I never be offended" (Matt. xxvi. 33; Mark xiv. 29). But as the answer there given by our Lord is the same as that recorded by our Evangelist, he probably uttered both protestations in his vehemence at one time; his feeling being roused by our Lord singling him out from all the rest. Poor Peter, thou shalt yet pay dear for that unlovely elevation of thyself above the rest of thy brethren, when thy risen Lord shall wring thy heart by asking thee, in presence of these very brethren, "Simon, son of Jonas, lovest thou Me *more than these?*" (see on John xxi. 15-17). Yet no vain-glorious vaunt was this of Peter. It was just the outcoming of conscious attachment: insomuch that all the rest, feeling a cord touched in their own hearts by this protestation, immediately repeated it for themselves. For, add our two first Evangelists, "*Likewise also said all the disciples.*" Dear disciples! Ye spoke out but the feelings of your heart then; your Lord knew that, and doubtless was comforted by it, as a spontaneous utterance of your hearts' affection. But little thought ye how soon it was to be seen—in all of you, but in Peter pre-eminently—that "he that trusteth in his own heart is a fool" (Prov. xxviii. 26). **34. And he said, I tell thee, Peter, the cock shall not crow this day, before that thou shalt thrice deny that thou knowest me.** Most interesting and touching is the fact, that whereas in the first, third, and fourth Gospels only *one* crowing of the cock is mentioned as sounding the note of Peter's fall, in the second Gospel—which all ancient tradition proclaims, and internal evidence suggests, to have been drawn up under the immediate eye of Peter—it is said that *two* crowings of the cock would sound his fall. And as it is Mark alone who records the fact that the cock did crow twice—the first time after one denial of his Lord, and the second immediately after the last—we have thus an affecting announcement, almost from his own pen, that warning after warning passed unheeded, till the second knell rung in his ears and bitterly revealed how much wiser his Lord was than he.

The fourth Gospel gives all this in a somewhat different and beautiful connection—John xiii. 36-38. Our Lord had been saying (*v.* 33), "Whither I go, ye cannot come. Simon Peter," not prepared for that, "said unto Him, Lord, whither goest Thou? Jesus answered him, Whither I go, thou canst not follow Me now, but thou shalt follow Me afterwards"—meaning to glory through the gate of martyrdom (John xxi. 18, 19). "Peter"—getting a glimpse of His meaning, but only rising to a higher feeling of readiness for anything, "said unto Him, Lord, why cannot I follow Thee now? I will lay down my life for Thy sake. Jesus answered him, Wilt thou lay down thy life for my sake?" What deep though tender irony is in this repetition of his words, which Peter, as he retraced the painful particulars, would feel for many a day after his recovery! "Verily, verily, I say unto thee, the cock shall not crow, till thou hast denied Me thrice."

The Disciples Warned of Coming Trials (35-38). **35. And he said unto them, When I sent you without purse, and scrip, and shoes, lacked ye any thing? And they said, Nothing.** 'Ye see, then, your sufficiency in Me.' **36. Then said he unto them, But now, he that hath a purse, let him take it, and likewise his scrip: and he that hath no sword, let him sell his garment, and buy one.** 'But now that ye are going forth, not as before on a temporary mission, provided for without purse or scrip, but into scenes of continued and severe trial, your *methods* must be different; for purse and scrip will now be needed for support, and the usual means of defence.' **37. For I say unto you, that this that is written** (Isa. liii. 12) **must yet be accomplished in me** [ἔτι]—or, yet remains to be fulfilled, **And he was reckoned among the transgressors.** This is among the very last and most pregnant of that most remarkable series of details which have made the 53rd chapter of Isaiah to read to the Church in every age more like a history, than a prophecy, of the sufferings of Christ and the glories that were to follow them (see on John xix. 18). **for the things concerning me have an end** [τέλος ἔχει]—'are having an end,' or drawing rapidly to a close. **38. And they said, Lord, behold, here are two swords.** Honest souls! They thought He referred to present defence, for which they declare themselves ready, no matter what might be the issue; though they significantly hint that two swords would make sorry enough work. But His answer shows that He meant something else. **And he said unto them, It is enough**—not 'Two will suffice,' but 'Enough of this for the present.'

he unto them, But now, he that hath a purse, let him take *it*, and likewise *his* scrip: and he that hath no sword, let him sell his garment, and
37 buy one. For I say unto you, that this that is written must yet be
accomplished in me, And [a]he was reckoned among the trangressors: for
38 the things concerning me have an end. And they said, Lord, behold,
here *are* two swords. And he said unto them, It is enough.

A. D. 33.

[a] Isa. 53. 12. Mark 15.28, 29. ch. 23. 32. 2 Cor. 5. 21. Gal. 3. 13.

The warning had been given, and preparation for coming dangers hinted at; but as His meaning had not been apprehended in the comprehensive sense in which it was meant, He wished to leave the subject.

The Evening in the upper room had now passed into night; for Jesus seemed to linger over that hallowed scene, breathing forth heavenly discourse after the Paschal and Eucharistic services were over, not caring to break up His last and sweetest fellowship with them a moment sooner than the dark work before Him required. But the closing act of that heavenly fellowship is omitted by our Evangelist, though happily supplied in the first two Gospels.

The Closing Hymn (Matt. xxvi. 30; Mark xiv. 26). "And when they had sung an hymn, they went out unto the mount of Olives [ὑμνήσαντες]—literally, 'having hymned;' that is, having chanted, according to the Jewish practice at the close of the Passover, the second part of what the Jews call *The Great Hallel.* It consisted of Ps. cxv., cxvi., cxvii., cxviii.; the first part of it, embracing Ps. cxiii., cxiv., having been sung *during* the Paschal supper. Or, if our Lord and His apostles sang the second part of this immediately after the Passover, and before instituting the Supper, what they closed their hallowed meeting with may have been portions of Ps. cxx.—cxxxvi., which were sometimes sung on that occasion. At any rate, the strain was from a portion of the Psalter eminently Messianic; a portion in which the mystery of redemption is richly conveyed to the spiritual mind. *Bengel* has a remark here, more quaint than correct. 'That Jesus *prayed*,' he says, 'we often read; that He *sang*, never.' But to "sing forth the honour of God's name, and make His praise glorious," is a duty so frequently and peremptorily inculcated on men, that it is inconceivable that "the Man Christ Jesus" should have passed His life without ever so using His voice; and if the saints feel this independently of the command, to be the most exalted and delightful exercise of heart and flesh, and a bright earnest of heaven itself, who shall say that Jesus, amidst the "sorrows" with which He was so familiar, and the "grief" with which He was "acquainted," did not get such "songs in the night," as turned His darkness into light? What a spectacle would that have been—the eleven disciples trying, as best they could, to cheer their sorrowing hearts with those songs of Zion which the Paschal season invariably brought round, and their Lord standing dumb beside them. To me this is inconceivable. But the Hymn is over. The scenes of the upper room have closed, and for the last time the disciples go forth with their blessed Master to the Mount of Olives, in whose garden was now to be transacted the most mysterious of all passages in the Redeemer's History.

Remarks.—1. The heart-breaking reproach which Jesus had already experienced, but which was soon to come down upon Him in its cruelest and most cutting form would seem enough to bear without being aggravated by the desertion of His own disciples. But both these were in the cup which was given him to drink, and both seem to be comprehended in that affecting prophetic complaint, "Reproach hath broken My heart, and I am full of heaviness, and I looked for some to take pity, but there was none; and for comforters, but I found none" (Ps. lxix. 20). See on John xvi. 32. 2. Who can fathom the mingled bitterness and sweetness of the cup which was given to Christ to drink? That there were high ends of righteousness and grace which *demanded* that penal death, who can doubt with those words of Jehovah ringing in his ears, "Awake, O sword, against My Shepherd, and against the Man that is My Fellow, saith the Lord of hosts; smite the Shepherd!" Jesus heard those words, and knew that, summoned by *that call*, the Jewish officers, with Judas at their head, were coming to apprehend Him, and even then making their arrangements. Little did any one then think that Jewish malignity and the awful treachery of covetous Judas were but "doing what God's hand and counsel determined before to be done." But Jesus knew it, and knew that those unconscious instruments of His approaching apprehension, condemnation, and death, were only held back till the Voice should say, Awake now, and smite the Shepherd! Mysterious words, considering Whence they came, and against Whom they were directed! Who, in the view of this, shall say that the death of Christ had not *penal* ingredients, of bitterest taste? But O the sweetness of those words, "MY Shepherd—the Man that is MY FELLOW!" What inconceivable solace would they carry in their bosom to Him who now referred to them! Accordingly, as if this predicted smiting was hardly present to His mind at all, it is the desertion of Him by those whom most He loved—their being "stumbled in Him" that very night—that seemed so painfully to occupy His thoughts. And yet, with what affecting gentleness and love does He announce it—adding, as if unwilling to leave the wound sticking in them, "But after I am risen, I will go before you into Galilee!" a bright glimpse of the coming fruits of His sufferings which to Himself, who understood it better than they, would be like sunshine from out the cloud. 3. After Peter, let none trust to the conscious strength of his attachment and the warmth of his love to Christ, as any security against the foulest denial of Him in the hour of trial. Of all the Eleven, Peter was foremost in these. Whatever others might afterwards prove themselves to be, none up to that time had stood so high as he. Yet this is the disciple whom His loving yet penetrating and faithful Master singles out and warns as of all the Eleven in the greatest peril; and we know what an affecting commentary on this the result gave. Yet the last to discern such danger as Peter was in are just those who are most exposed to it and least prepared successfully to meet it. 'Me, Lord, me? Why single out me? Once at least have I been singled out from all the rest for clear perception of Thy glory and firm attachment to Thy Person; and am I to be the one man to give way on the approach of danger? Others may, but I never.' This was just the stone at which Peter stumbled. Had he distrusted himself, and betaken himself to his knees, he had there got strength to stand. "The name of the Lord is a strong tower: the righteous runneth into it, and is safe" (Prov. xviii. 10). But what needed Peter this? He was safe enough—

39 And he came out, and went, as he was wont, to the mount of Olives;
40 and his disciples also followed him. And [b]when he was at the place, he
41 said unto them, Pray that ye enter not into temptation. And he was

A. D. 33.

[b] Matt 6. 13. Mark 14. 38.

he knew it. His Master knew better, and bid him "watch and pray, that he enter not into temptation;" but we do not read that he did it. O if believers would but know that the secret of all their strength lies in that consciousness of their own weakness which sends them to the "Strong Tower" to find it, how many such falls would be averted!

39-46.—The Agony in the Garden. (=Matt. xxvi. 36-46; Mark xiv. 32-42; John xviii. 1.)

This is one of those scenes in the Evangelical History which, to have been *written*, must have been *real*. If we could conceive the life of Christ to be but a pious Romance or a mythical Legend, such a scene would have been the last to be thought of, or imagined only to be rejected as a discordant note, a literary blemish. But the existence of such a scene in the Gospel History does more than prove the historic reality of the scene itself: it is a bright testimony to the severe fidelity of the Narrative that contains it. Had the three Evangelists who record this scene, and the fourth who has one remarkably like it (John xii. 27, &c.), been guided in their selection of the materials before them by the desire to glorify their Master in the eyes of their readers, we may be pretty sure they would have omitted what could not fail to repel many well-inclined readers, to stagger for a time even attached disciples, and occasion perplexity and discordance among the most established in the faith. Certain it is that in the age immediately succeeding that of the apostles, some vindication of it was felt to be necessary even for those who were well affected to Christianity (see a remarkable allusion to this scene in the Apocryphal "Gospel of Nicodemus," or "Acts of Pilate," ch. xx.); while its enemies—as *Celsus* at the beginning of the second century, and *Julian* in the fourth—held it up to contempt for the pusillanimity which it displayed, in contrast with the magnanimity of dying Pagans. Some of the vindications of this scene in later times have laid themselves open to the hostile criticism of *Strauss* ("Leben Jesu," iii. 3, § 125, 4th edit.); although his own *mythical* theory cuts a pitiful figure when it has to deal with such unique materials as those of Gethsemane.

The three narratives of this scene, when studied together, will be found to have just that diversity which throws additional light on the whole transaction. That the fourth Evangelist, though himself an eye-witness, has not recorded it, is only in accordance with the plan of his Gospel, which omits the other two scenes of which he was one of three chosen witnesses—the resurrection of Jairus' daughter, and the transfiguration. But just as in place of the one of these—the resurrection of Jairus' daughter—it is the beloved disciple alone who records the grander resurrection of Lazarus; and in place of the other of these—the transfiguration—that beloved disciple records a series of passages in the life, and discourses from the lips, of his Master, which are like a continued transfiguration: so it is he alone who records that mysterious *prelude* to Gethsemane, which the visit of the Greeks to Him, after His last entry into Jerusalem, seems to have occasioned, (John xii. 27, &c.) In the three priceless narratives of this scene, the fulness of the picture is such as to leave nothing to be desired, except what probably could not have been supplied in any narrative; the lines are so vivid and minute and life-like, that we seem ourselves to be eye and ear-witnesses of the whole transaction; and no one who has had it brought fully before him can ever again have it effaced from his mind.

In this instance, we must deviate somewhat from our usual plan of comment first, and Remarks following. We shall try to sketch the scene, interweaving the triple text, with such slight expository remarks as it requires; and in place of closing Remarks, we shall expatiate at some length upon the successive phases of the scene as they open upon us.

Jesus had passed through every stage of His suffering history except the last, but that last was to be the great and dreadful stage. Nothing now remained but that He should be apprehended, arraigned, condemned, and led forth to Calvary. And how far off was this seizure? Not more probably than *one brief hour*. Like the "silence in heaven for the space of half an hour," between the breaking of the apocalyptic *seals* and the peal of the *trumpets of war*, so was this brief, breathless silence, before the final stage of Christ's career. How, then, was it spent? It was night. Men slept. A profound, Sodom-like security overspread the city that "killed the prophets and stoned them that were sent unto it." But our Shepherd of Israel slept not. "He went forth"—from the upper room and from the city—"over the brook Cedron, where was a garden, into the which he entered, with his (eleven) disciples. And Judas which betrayed him knew the place; for Jesus ofttimes resorted thither with his disciples" (John xviii. 1, 2). With what calm sobriety does the basest of all treacheries begin here to be related! No straining after effect. The traitor knows His favourite resort, and takes it for granted he shall find Him there. Perhaps the family of Bethany were told the night before, in the hearing of the Twelve, that that night the Lord would not be with them. Be this as it may, if Jesus had wished to elude His enemies, nothing would have been easier. But he would not. Already He had said, "No man taketh My life from me; but I lay it down of myself." So He "went as a lamb to the slaughter." The spot selected was well suited to His present purpose. The upper room would not have done; nor would he cloud the hallowed associations of the last Passover, and the first Supper, the heaven-breathing discourse at the supper table and the high-priestly prayer which wound up the whole, by discharging the anguish of His soul *there*. Nor was Bethany so suitable, But the garden was ample enough, while the stillness, and the shady olives, and the endeared recollections of former visits, rendered it congenial to His soul. Here He had space enough to withdraw from His disciples, and yet be within view of them; and the solitude that reigned here would only be broken, at the close of the scene, by the tread of the traitor and his accomplices.

The walk to Gethsemane, we incline to think, was taken in silence. But no sooner was He on the spot, than having said to the whole of them, "Pray that ye enter not into temptation" (Luke xxii. 40), the internal commotion—which may have begun as soon as the "hymn" that closed the proceedings of the upper room died away in silence—would no longer conceal. As soon as He was "at the place," having said to eight out of the eleven, "Sit ye here while I go and pray yonder," He took Peter and James and John aside by themselves, or a little in advance of the rest, and

withdrawn from them about a stone's cast, and kneeled down, and prayed,
42 saying, Father, if thou be [3]willing, remove this cup from me: nevertheless
43 [c]not my will, but thine, be done. And there appeared [d]an angel unto

[3] Willing to remove.
[c] John 6 38.
[d] Matt. 4. 11.

"saith unto them, My soul is exceeding sorrowful, even unto death: tarry ye here and watch with Me" (Matt. xxvi. 38; Mark xiv. 34). Not, Come and *see* Me, to be My witnesses; but, Come and *watch with Me*, to bear Me company. It did Him good, it seems, to have them by Him. For He had a true humanity, only all the more tender and susceptible than ours, that it was not blunted and dulled by sin. You may say, indeed, if company was what He wanted, He got little of it. True enough. They fell asleep. "I looked for some to take pity, but there was none; and for comforters, but I found none" (Ps. lxix. 20). It *would* have soothed His burdened spirit to have had their sympathy, contracted at its best though it behoved to be. But He did not get it. They were broken reeds. And so He had to tread the wine-press alone. Yet was their presence, even while asleep, not quite in vain. Perhaps the spectacle would only touch His sensibilities the more, and rouse into quickened action His great-hearted compassions. In fact, He did not want even them *too near* Him. For it is said, "He went forward a little;" or, as Luke (xxii. 41), more precisely expresses it, "was withdrawn from them about a stone's cast." Yes, company is good, but there are times when even the best company can hardly be borne.

But now let us reverently draw near and see this great sight, the Son of God in a tempest of mysterious internal commotion—"the bush burning, and the bush not consumed." Every word of the three-fold record is weighty, every line of the picture awfully bright. "Let us put off the shoes from off our feet, for the place whereon we stand is holy ground." "He began," says Matthew, "to be sorrowful and very heavy," or, "to be sorrowful and oppressed" [λυπεῖσθαι καὶ ἀδημονεῖν], Matt. xxvi. 37. Mark uses the last of these words, but places before it one more remarkable: "He began to be sore amazed, and to be very heavy;" or better, perhaps, "to be appalled and to be oppressed" [ἐκθαμβεῖσθαι καὶ ἀδημονεῖν], Mark xiv. 33; and see the former word again in ch. xvi. 5, 6. Although through life He had been "a man of sorrows, and acquainted with grief," there is no ground to think that even the selectest circle of His followers was made privy to them, save on one occasion before this, after His final entry into Jerusalem, when, upon the Greeks "desiring to see Jesus"—which seems to have brought the hour of His "uplifting" overwhelmingly before Him—He exclaimed, "Now is my soul troubled, and what shall I say? Father, save me from this hour? But for this cause came I unto this hour. Father, glorify thy name" (John xii. 27, 28). This was just *Gethsemane anticipated.* But now the tempest rose as never before. "He *began* to be sorrowful," as if till this moment unacquainted with grief. So new to Him, indeed, was the feeling, that Mark, using a singularly bold word, says, He was "appalled" at it; and under the joint action of this "sorrow" and "amazement," He was "very heavy," oppressed, weighed down—so much so, that He was fain to tell it to the three He had taken aside, and most affectingly gave this as His reason for wishing their company: "My soul is exceeding sorrowful, even unto death; tarry ye here and watch with me." 'I feel as if nature were sinking under this load—as if life were ebbing out—as if death were coming before its time—as if I could not survive this.' It is usual to compare here such passages as that of Jonah, "I do well to be angry *even unto death*" (ch. iv. 9), and even some classical passages of similar import; but these are all too low. In dealing with such scenes as this, one feels as if even the most ordinary phraseology must be interpreted with reference to the unique circumstances of the case.

What next? He "kneeled down," says Luke; He "fell on his face," says Matthew; or "fell on the ground," as Mark expresses it (Luke xxii. 41; Matt. xxvi. 39; Mark xiv. 35). Perhaps the kneeling posture was tried for a moment, but quickly became intolerable: and unable to bear up under a pressure of spirit which felt like the ebbing out of life itself, He was fain to seek the dust! And now went up a cry such as never before ascended from this earth; no, not from those lips which dropt as an honeycomb: "O my Father, if it be possible, let this cup pass from me; nevertheless not as I will, but as thou wilt (Matt. xxvi. 39). The variations in Mark (xiv. 36) and Luke (xxii. 42) are worthy of note. Mark's double form of the invocation, "Abba, Father," we may pretty confidently conjecture was the very one our Lord used—the hallowed, endeared form of the mother-tongue "Abba," followed emphatically by the term "Father," that of educated life (Rom. viii. 15). Then Mark breaks up the one expression of Matthew, "If it be possible, let this cup pass," into these two, identical in meaning, "All things are possible unto thee; take away this cup;" while Luke's expression, "If thou be *willing* to remove this cup" (as in the Greek), shows that the "possibility" of the other two Evangelists was understood to be one purely of Divine *will* or arrangement, insomuch that the one word came naturally to be interchanged with the other. (To suppose that our Lord used the identical words of all the three accounts is absurd.) That *tears* accompanied this piercing cry, is not reported by any of the Evangelists—who appear to give rigidly what was *seen* by the three favoured disciples in the clear moonlight, and *heard* by them in the unbroken stillness of the night-air of Gethsemane, ere sleep overpowered their exhausted frames. But those remarkable words in the Epistle to the Hebrews—which, though they seem to express what often took place, have, beyond all doubt, a special reference to this night of nights—leave no doubt of it, as a fact well known in the Christian churches, that on this occasion the tears of the Son of God fell fast upon the earth, while His cries rent the heavens: "Who in the days of His flesh, when He had offered up prayers and supplications, *with strong crying and tears,*" &c. (Heb. v. 7). Exquisite here are the words of old Traill, which, though before quoted, are peculiarly appropriate here: "He filled the silent night with His crying, and watered the cold earth with His tears, more precious than the dew of Hermon, or any moisture, next unto His own blood, that ever fell on God's earth since the creation."

But now let us listen to the cry itself. "The cup" to which the Son of God was so averse—"the cup," the very prospect of drinking which so appalled and oppressed Him—"the cup," for the removal of which, if it were possible, He prayed so affectingly—that cup was assuredly no other than the *death* He was about to die. Come, then, thoughtful reader, and let us reason together about this matter. Ye that see nothing in Christ's death but the injustice of it at the hands of men, the excruciating mode of it, and the uncomplaining sub-

44 him from heaven, strengthening him. And [e]being in an agony he prayed
more earnestly: and his sweat was as it were great drops of blood falling
45 down to the ground. And when he rose up from prayer, and was come

A. D. 33.

[e] John 12. 27. Heb. 5. 7.

mission to it of the innocent victim—put me through this scene of agonies and cries at the near approach of it. I will not ask you whether you go the length of those pagan enemies of the Gospel, *Celsus* and *Julian*, who could see nothing but cowardice in this Gethsemane-scene, as compared with the last hours of Socrates and other magnanimous pagans; or whether you are prepared to applaud that wretch who, in the days of Henry IV. of France, went to execution jeering at our Lord for the bloody sweat which the prospect of death drew from Him, while he himself was about to die unmoved. But I do ask you, in view of hundreds, if not thousands of the martyrs of Jesus who have gone to the rack or to the flames for His sake, rejoicing that they were counted worthy to suffer for His name, Are you prepared to exalt the servants above their Master, or, if not, can you give any rational account of the amazing difference between them, to the *advantage* of the Master? You cannot, nor on your principles is the thing possible. Yet which of these dear servants of Jesus would not have shuddered at the thought of comparing themselves with their Lord? Is not your system, then, radically at fault? I am not now addressing myself to professed Unitarians, who, with the Atonement, have expunged the Divinity of Christ from their biblical beliefs. If any such would but give me a hearing, I think I have something to say which is not unworthy of their attention. But I address myself more immediately to an increasing class within the pale of orthodox Christianity—a class embracing many cultivated minds—a class who, while clinging sincerely, though vaguely, to the Divinity of Christ, have allowed themselves to let go, as something antiquated and scholastic, the *vicarious* element in the sufferings and death of Christ, and now view them purely in the light of a sublime model of *self-sacrifice*. According to this view, Christ suffered nothing whatever *in the stead* of the guilty, or in order that *they* might *not* suffer, but rather that men might learn from Him how to suffer: Christ simply inaugurated in His own Person a new Humanity, to be "made perfect through sufferings," and hath thus "left us an Example that we should follow His steps." Now, I have no quarrel with this *exemplary* theory of Christ's sufferings. It is too clearly expressed by our Lord Himself, and by His apostles too frequently echoed, for any Christian to have a doubt of it. But my question is, *Will it solve the mystery of Gethsemane?* Will any one venture to say that for a Christian man, who would know how to suffer and die, the best model he can follow is *Christ in Gethsemane*—Christ, in the prospect of His own death, "sore amazed and very heavy, exceeding sorrowful even unto death"—Christ piercing the heavens with that affecting cry, thrice repeated, with His face upon the ground, "O my Father, *if it be possible*, let this cup pass from me" —Christ agonizing till the sweat fell in bloody drops from His face upon the ground: and all this at the mere prospect of the death He was going to die? But He added, you say, "Nevertheless, not my will, but thine be done." I know it well. It is my sheet-anchor. But for this, my faith in the Son of God as the Redeemer of the world would reel to and fro and stagger like a drunken man. But with all this, will you affirm that these feelings of Christ in Gethsemane are those which best befit any other dying man? You cannot. And if not, does not the hollowness of this view of Christ's sufferings, as an *exhaustive* account of them, or even as the chief feature of them, stand frightfully revealed!

How, then, do *you* explain them? may the reader ask. It is a pertinent question, and I refuse not to meet it. Tell me, then, what means that statement of the apostle Paul, "*He hath made Him to be sin for us, Who knew no sin;* that we might be made the righteousness of God in Him" (2 Cor. v. 21); and that other, "Christ hath redeemed us from the curse of the law, *being made a curse for us*" (Gal. iii. 13). The ablest and most recent rationalizing critics of Germany—*de Wette*, for example—candidly admit that such statements can mean nothing but this, that the absolutely Sinless One was regarded and treated as the Guilty one, in order that the really guilty might in Him be regarded and treated as righteous. If it be asked in what sense and to what extent Christ was regarded and treated as the Guilty One, the second passage replies, "He was "made a curse for us"—language so appallingly strong, that *Bengel* with reason exclaims, as he does also on the other passage, 'Who would have dared to use such language if the apostle had not gone before him?' Says *Meyer*—a critic not over fastidious in his orthodoxy but honest as an interpreter—'The curse of the law would have had to be realized; all who render not complete satisfaction to the law (which no one can do) must experience the infliction of the Divine "wrath;" but that Christ, to rescue them from this outlawry by the curse, is introduced dying *as the Accursed One*, and as *by a purchase-price*, dissolving that curse-relation of the law to them. Compare 1 Cor. vi. 20; vii. 23.'

Now, is this to be regarded as a true representation of the *character* in which Christ suffered and died? With those who sit quite loose to apostolic authority, and regard all such statements as expressing merely Paul's *opinions*, we have here nothing to do. Strange to say, we have now-a-days men high in our schools of learning and in ecclesiastical place, who scruple not to affirm this and many other strange things. But we write for those who regard the statements of the apostle as authoritative, and to them we submit this question: If Christ felt the *penal* character of the sufferings and death which He had to undergo—if, though feeling this more or less throughout all His public life, it was now borne in upon His spirit in unrelieved, unmitigated, total force, during the dread, still hour between the transactions of the upper room and the approach of the traitor—does not this furnish an adequate key to the horror and sinking of spirit which he then experienced? Just try it with this key. In itself, the death He had to die—being in that case not the mere surrender of life in circumstances of pain and shame, but the surrender of it *under the doom of sin*, the surrender of it *to the vengeance of the law*, which regarded Him as the Representative of the guilty (to use again the language even of *de Wette*), could not but be purely revolting. Nor is it possible for us otherwise to realize the horror of His position, as the absolutely Sinless One, now emphatically made sin for us. In this view of it we can understand how He could only brace Himself up to drink the cup because it was the Father's will that He should do it, but that in *that* view of it He was quite

46 to his disciples, he found them sleeping for sorrow, and said unto them,
[f] Why sleep ye? rise and pray, lest ye enter into temptation.

A. D. 33.

f Jon. 1. 6.

prepared to do it. And thus have we here no struggle between a *reluctant* and a *compliant* will, nor between a *human* and a *divine* will; but simply between two views of one event: between penal sufferings and death considered in themselves—in other words, being "bruised, put to grief, made an offering for sin"—and all this considered as the Father's will. In the one view, this was, and could not but have been, appalling, oppressing, ineffably *repulsive:* in the other view, it was sublimely *welcome.* When He says, "If it be possible, let this cup pass from Me," He tells me He didn't like it, and couldn't like it; its ingredients were too bitter, too revolting; but when He says, "Nevertheless, not my will, but thine be done," He proclaims in mine ear His absolute obediential subjection to the Father. This view of the cup quite changed its character, and by the expulsive power of a new affection—I will not say, turned its bitterness into sweetness, for I see no signs of sweetness even in that sense, but—absorbed and dissolved His natural repugnance to drink it up. If you still feel the theology of the matter encompassed with difficulty, let it alone. It will take care of itself. You will never get to the bottom of it here. But take it as it stands, in all its wonderful naturalness and awful freshness, and rest assured that just as, if this scene had not actually occurred, it never would nor could have been written down, so on any other view of the Redeemer's extraordinary repugnance to drink the cup than the *penal* ingredient which He found in it, His magnanimity and fortitude, as compared with those of myriads of His adoring followers, must be *given up.*

But to return to the conflict, whose crisis is yet to come. Getting a momentary relief—for the agitation of His spirit seems to have come upon Him by surges—He returns to the three disciples, and finding them sleeping, He chides them, particularly Peter, in terms deeply affecting: "He saith unto Peter, What! could ye not watch with me one hour?" In Mark (which may almost be called Peter's own Gospel) this is particularly affecting, "He saith unto Peter, Simon, sleepest thou? Couldest not thou watch one hour? Watch ye and pray, lest ye enter into temptation. The spirit truly is ready, but the flesh is weak." How considerate and compassionate this allusion to the weakness of the flesh was at that moment, appears by the explanation which Luke gives of the cause of it—an explanation beautifully in accordance with his profession as "the beloved physician" (Col. iv. 14)—"that He found them sleeping *for sorrow*" (Luke xxii. 45). What now? "Again He went away, and prayed, and spake the same words" (Mark xiv. 39). He had nothing more, it seems, and nothing else to say. But now the surges rise higher, beat more tempestuously, and threaten to overwhelm Him. To fortify Him against this, "there appeared an angel unto Him from heaven, strengthening Him:" not to minister to Him *spiritually*, by supplies of heavenly light or comfort—of that He was to have none during this awful scene; nor if it had been otherwise, would it seem competent for an angel to convey it—but simply to sustain and brace up sinking nature for a yet hotter and fiercer struggle. (On this interesting subject, see on John v. 1-47, Remark 1 at the close of that Section.) And now that He *can* stand it, "He is in an agony, and prays more earnestly" [ἐκτενέστερον], 'more intensely or vehemently.' What! Christ pray at one time more earnestly than at another? will some exclaim. O if people would but think less of a systematic or theological Christ, and believe more in the biblical, historical Christ, their faith would be a warmer, aye, and a mightier thing, because it would then be not human but divine. Take it as it stands in the record. Christ's prayer, it teaches you, did at this moment not only admit of more vehemence, but demand it. For "His sweat was as it were great drops," literally, 'clots' [θρόμβοι] "of blood falling down to the ground." [We cannot stay to defend the text here.] What was this? It was just the internal struggle, apparently hushed somewhat before, but now swelling up again, convulsing His whole inner man, and this so affecting His animal nature, that the sweat oozed out from every pore in thick drops of blood, falling to the ground. It was just *shuddering nature* and *indomitable will* struggling together. Now, if death was to Christ only the separation of soul and body in circumstances of shame and torture, I cannot understand this in one whom I am asked to take as my Example, that I should follow His steps. On this view of His death, I cannot but feel that I am asked to copy a model far beneath that of many of His followers. But if death in Christ's case had those elements of *penal vengeance*, which the apostle explicitly affirms that it had—if the Sinless One felt Himself divinely regarded and treated as the Sinful and Accursed One, then I can understand all this scene; and even its most terrific features have to me something sublimely congenial with *such* circumstances, although only its having *really* occurred could explain its being so *written.*

But again there is a lull; and returning to the three, "He found them asleep again (for their eyes were heavy), neither wist they what to answer Him" (Mark xiv. 40), when He chid them, perhaps in nearly the same terms. And now, once more, returning to His solitary spot, He "prayed the third time," saying the same words; but this time slightly varied. It is not now, "O my Father, if it be possible, let this cup pass from me;" but, "O my Father, *if this cup may not pass from me*, except I drink it, thy will be done." Had only one of these two forms of the petition occurred in the same Gospel, we might have thought that they were but verbal differences in the different reports of one and the same petition. But as they both occur in the same Gospel of Matthew, we are warranted in regarding the second as an intentional, and in that case momentous, modification of the first. The worst is over. The bitterness of death is past. He has *anticipated and rehearsed* His final conflict. The victory has now been won on the theatre of an *invincible will*—to "give His life a ransom for many." He shall win it next on the arena of *the Cross*, where it is to become an accomplished fact. "I *will* suffer," is the result of Gethsemane: "It is finished," bursts from the Cross. Without the *deed*, the *will* had been all in vain. But His work was then consummated when into the palpable deed He carried the now manifested will—"*by the which* WILL *we are sanctified* THROUGH THE OFFERING OF THE BODY OF JESUS CHRIST ONCE FOR ALL" (Heb. x. 10).

At the close of the whole scene, returning once more to His three disciples, and finding them still sleeping, worn out with continued sorrow and racking anxiety, He says to them, with an irony of tender but deep emotion, "Sleep on now, and

47 And while he yet spake, behold a multitude, and he that was called
Judas, one of the twelve, went before them, and drew near unto Jesus to
48 kiss him. But Jesus said unto him, Judas, betrayest thou the Son of
49 man with a kiss? When they which were about him saw what would
50 follow, they said unto him, Lord, shall we smite with the sword? And
[g]one of them smote a servant of the high priest, and cut off his right ear.
51 And Jesus answered and said, Suffer ye thus far. And he touched his
52 ear, and healed him. Then Jesus said unto the chief priests, and
captains of the temple, and the elders, which were come to him, Be ye
53 come out, as against a thief, with swords and staves? When I was daily
with you in the temple, ye stretched forth no hands against me: [h]but
54 this is your hour, and the power of darkness. Then [i]took they him,
and led *him*, and brought him into the high priest's house. [j]And Peter
followed afar off.
55 And [k]when they had kindled a fire in the midst of the hall, and
56 were set down together, Peter sat down among them. But a certain
maid beheld him as he sat by the fire, and earnestly looked upon him,
57 and said, This man was also with him. And he denied him, saying,
58 Woman, I know him not. And, [l]after a little while, another saw him,
59 and said, Thou art also of them. And Peter said, Man, I am not. And
about the space of one hour after, another confidently affirmed, saying,
60 Of a truth this *fellow* also was with him; for he is a Galilean. And
Peter said, Man, I know not what thou sayest. And immediately, while
61 he yet spake, the cock crew. And the Lord turned, and looked upon
Peter. [m]And Peter remembered the word of the Lord, how he had said
62 unto him, Before [n]the cock crow, thou shalt deny me thrice. And Peter
went out, and [o]wept bitterly.
63 And [p]the men that held Jesus mocked him, and smote *him*. And
64 when they had blindfolded him, they struck him on the face, and asked
65 him, saying, Prophesy, who is it that smote thee? And many other
things blasphemously spake they against him.
66 And [q]as soon as it was day, [r]the elders of the people, and the chief
priests, and the scribes, came together, and led him into their council,
67 saying, Art [s]thou the Christ? tell us. And he said unto them, If I tell
68 you, ye will not believe: and if I also ask *you*, ye will not answer me, nor
69 let *me* go. Hereafter [t]shall the Son of man sit on the right hand of the
70 power of God. Then said they all, Art thou then the Son of God? And
71 he said unto them, [u]Ye say that I am. And [v]they said, What need we
any further witness? for we ourselves have heard of his own mouth.

A. D. 33.

[g] Matt. 26. 51. Mark 14. 47. John 18. 10. Rom 12. 19. 2 Cor. 10. 4.
[h] Gen. 3. 15. John 12. 27. Acts 2. 23. Acts 4. 27.
[i] Matt. 26. 57. Acts 8. 32.
[j] John 18. 15.
[k] Matt. 26 69. Mark 14 66. John 18. 17, 18.
[l] Matt. 26. 71. Mark 14. 69. John 18 25.
[m] Matt. 26. 75. Mark 14. 72.
[n] John 13. 38.
[o] Isa. 66. 2. Ezek. 7. 16. 2 Cor. 7. 10.
[p] Ps. 69. 1-21. Isa. 50. 6. Isa. 52. 14. Matt. 26. 67, 68. Mark 14 65.
[q] Matt. 27. 1.
[r] Ps. 2. 1. Ps. 22. 12, 16. Acts 4. 26. Acts 22. 5.
[s] Matt. 26. 63. Mark 14. 61.
[t] Ps. 110. 1. Dan. 7. 13, 14. Acts 1. 11. Acts 3. 21. 1 Thes. 4. 16. Heb. 1. 3. Heb 8. 1.
[u] Matt. 26. 64. Mark 14. 62.
[v] Matt 26. 65. Mark 14. 63.

take your rest: behold, the hour is at hand, and the Son of man is betrayed into the hands of sinners. Rise, let us be going: behold, he is at hand that doth betray me" (Matt. xxvi. 45, 46). While He yet spake, Judas appeared with his armed band, and so they proved miserable comforters, broken reeds. But thus in His whole work He was *alone*, and "of the people there was none with Him."

Much is said about the *necessity* of an atonement, some stoutly affirming it, while others accuse the thought of presumption. Of antecedent necessity, on such subjects, I know nothing at all; and it is possible that some who dispute the position mean nothing more than this. But one thing I know, that God under the law did so *educate the conscience* that there was seen written, as in letters of fire, over the whole Levitical economy—

WITHOUT THE SHEDDING OF BLOOD NO REMISSION;
while the great proclamation of the Gospel is—

PEACE THROUGH THE BLOOD OF THE CROSS.

And ever as I deal with God on this principle, I find my whole ethical nature so exalted and purified—my views and feelings as to sin and holiness and the sinner's relation to Him with Whom he has to do, so deepened, enlarged, and sublimed—while on no other do I find any footing at all—that I feel I have been *taught* what I am sure I could never have antecedently *discovered*, the necessity, in its highest sense—the necessity, that is, in order to any right relation between God and me—of the expiatory death of the Lord Jesus; and when, thus *educated*, I anew approach Gethsemane, that I may witness the conflict of the Son of God there, and listen to His "strong crying and tears to Him that was able to save Him from death," I seem to myself to have found that key to it all, without which it is a blot in His life that will not wipe out, but in the use of which I can open its most difficult wards, and let in light upon its darkest chambers.

47-54.—BETRAYAL AND APPREHENSION OF JESUS. (=Matt. xxvi. 47-56; Mark xiv. 43-52; John xviii. 1-12.) For the exposition, see on John xviii. 1-12.

55-71.—JESUS ARRAIGNED BEFORE CAIAPHAS, CONDEMNED TO DIE, AND SHAMEFULLY EN-

23 AND [a]the whole multitude of them arose, and led him unto Pilate.
2 And they began to accuse him, saying, We found this *fellow* [b]perverting
the nation, and [c]forbidding to give tribute to Cesar, saying [d]that he
3 himself is Christ a king. And [e]Pilate asked him, saying, Art thou the
King of the Jews? And he answered him and said, Thou sayest *it*.
4 Then said Pilate to the chief priests and *to* the people, [f]I find no fault
5 in this man. And they were the more fierce, saying, He stirreth up the
people, teaching throughout all Jewry, beginning from Galilee to this
6 place. When Pilate heard of Galilee, he asked whether the man were a
7 Galilean. And as soon as he knew that he belonged unto [g]Herod's
jurisdiction, he sent him to Herod, who himself also was at Jerusalem
at that time.
8 And when Herod saw Jesus, he was exceeding glad: for [h]he was
desirous to see him of a long *season*, because [i]he had heard many
things of him; and he hoped to have seen some miracle done by him.
9 Then he questioned with him in many words; but he answered him
10 nothing. And the chief priests and scribes stood and vehemently accused
11 him. And [j]Herod with his men of war set him at nought, and mocked
him, and arrayed him in a gorgeous robe, and sent him again to Pilate.
12 And the same day [k]Pilate and Herod were made friends together: for
before they were at enmity between themselves.
13 And [l]Pilate, when he had called together the chief priests and the
14 rulers and the people, said unto them, Ye have brought this man unto
me, as one that perverteth the people: and, behold, I, having examined
him before you, have [m]found no fault in this man touching those things
15 whereof ye accuse him: no, nor yet Herod: for I sent you to him; and,
16 lo, nothing worthy of death is done unto him. I [n]will therefore chastise
17 him, and release *him*. (For [o]of necessity he must release one unto them
18 at the feast.) And [p]they cried out all at once, saying, Away with this
19 *man*, and release unto us Barabbas: (who for a certain sedition made in
20 the city, and for murder, was cast into prison.) Pilate therefore, willing
21 to release Jesus, spake again to them. But they cried, saying, Crucify
22 *him*, crucify him. And he said unto them the third time, Why, what
evil hath he done? I have found no cause of death in him: I will there-
23 fore chastise him, and let *him* go. And they were instant with loud
voices, requiring that he might be crucified: and the voices of them and
24 of the chief priests prevailed. And Pilate [1]gave sentence that it should
25 be as they required. And [q]he released unto them him that for sedition and murder was cast into prison, whom they had desired; but he
delivered Jesus to their will.
26 And [r]as they led him away, they laid hold upon one Simon, a Cyrenian, coming out of the country, and on him they laid the cross, that he
27 might bear *it* after Jesus. And there followed him a great company of
28 people, and of women, which also bewailed and lamented him. But
Jesus, turning unto them, said, Daughters of Jerusalem, weep not for me,
29 but weep for yourselves, and for your children. For, [s]behold, the days
are coming, in the which they shall say, Blessed *are* the barren, and the
30 wombs that never bare, and the paps which never gave suck. Then [t]shall
they begin to say to the mountains, Fall on us; and to the hills, Cover
31 us. For [u]if they do these things in a green tree, what shall be done in
the dry?

A. D. 33.

CHAP. 23.
[a] Matt. 27. 2. Mark 15. 1. John 18.28.
[b] 1 Ki. 21. 10-13. Ps. 35. 11. Ps. 62. 4. Ps. 64. 3-6. Jer. 20. 10. Jer. 37. 13-15. Dan. 3. 12. Acts 17. 7. Acts 24. 5. 1 Pet. 3. 16-18.
[c] Matt. 17.27. Matt. 22. 21. Mark 12.17.
[d] John 19.12.
[e] Matt. 27.11. 1 Tim. 6.13.
[f] Matt. 27.19, 24. Mark 15.14. John 18.38. 2 Cor. 5. 21. 1 Pet. 2. 22.
[g] ch. 3. 1.
[h] ch. 9. 9.
[i] Matt. 14. 1. Mark 6. 14.
[j] Isa. 53. 3.
[k] Acts 4. 27. Jas. 4. 4.
[l] Matt. 27. 23. Mark 15 14. John 18.38.
[m] Dan. 6. 4.
[n] Matt. 27.26. Mark 15.15. John 19. 1. Acts 5. 40, 41.
[o] Matt. 27.15. Mark 15. 6. John 18.39.
[p] Acts 3. 14.
[1] Or, assented. Ex. 23. 2. John 19. 16.
[q] Pro. 17. 15.
[r] John 19.17.
[s] ch. 21. 23.
[t] Isa. 2. 19. Hos. 10. 8. Rev. 6. 16. Rev. 9. 6.
[u] Pro. 11. 31. Jer. 25. 29. Ezek. 20. 47. Ezek. 21. 3, 4. 1 Pet. 4. 17.

TREATED—THE FALL OF PETER. (=Matt. xxvi. 57-75; Mark xiv. 53-72; John xviii. 13-27.) For the exposition, see on Mark xiv. 53-72.

CHAP. XXIII. 1-12.—JESUS IS BROUGHT BEFORE PILATE, WHO PRONOUNCES HIM INNOCENT, AND SENDS HIM TO HEROD—FAILING TO DRAW ANYTHING OUT OF HIM, HEROD, WITH HIS MEN OF WAR, SETS HIM AT NOUGHT, AND SENDS HIM BACK TO PILATE. (=Matt. xxvii. 1, 2; Mark xv. 1-5; John xviii. 28-38.) For the exposition, see on John xviii. 28-38.

13-38.—JESUS IS AGAIN BEFORE PILATE, WHO, AFTER AGAIN PROCLAIMING HIS INNOCENCE AND SEEKING TO RELEASE HIM, DELIVERS HIM UP—

32 And [v] there were also two others, malefactors, led with him to be put
33 to death. And [w] when they were come to the place which is called
[2] Calvary, there they crucified him, and the malefactors, one on the right
34 hand, and the other on the left. Then said Jesus, Father, [x] forgive them;
for [y] they know not what they do. And [z] they parted his raiment, and
35 cast lots. And [a] the people stood beholding. And the rulers also with
them derided *him*, saying, He saved others; let him save himself, if he
36 be Christ, the chosen of God. And the soldiers also mocked him, coming
37 to him, and offering him vinegar, and saying, If thou be the King of the
38 Jews, save thyself. And [b] a superscription also was written over him in
letters of Greek, and Latin, and Hebrew, THIS IS THE KING OF
THE JEWS.
39 And [c] one of the malefactors which were hanged railed on him, saying,
40 If thou be Christ, save thyself and us. But the other answering [d] rebuked
him, saying, Dost not thou fear God, seeing thou art in the same con-
41 demnation? And we indeed justly; for we receive the due reward of

A. D. 33.

v Isa. 53. 12. Matt. 27. 38.
w Mark 15. 22. John 19. 17.
2 Or, the place of a skull. Heb. 13. 12.
x Matt. 5. 44. Acts 7. 60. 1 Cor. 4. 12.
y Acts 3. 17.
z Mark 15. 24. John 19. 24.
a Ps. 22. 17. Zec. 12. 10.
b John 19. 19.
c Matt. 27. 44. Mark 15. 32.
d Eph. 5. 11.

TOUCHING INCIDENTS ON THE WAY TO CALVARY AND AT THE PLACE OF EXECUTION—THE CRUCIFIXION. (=Matt. xxvii. 31-50; Mark xv. 6-37; John xviii. 38—xix. 30.) For the exposition, see on John xviii. 38—xix. 30.

39-43.—THE TWO THIEVES BETWEEN WHOM JESUS WAS CRUCIFIED. This episode—peculiar to Luke—is one of the grandest in the Gospel History. If only hellish ingenuity could have suggested the expedient of crucifying our Lord between two malefactors, in order to hold Him forth as the worst of the three, only that wisdom which "taketh the wise in their own craftiness" could have made this very expedient irradiate the Redeemer, in His hour of deepest gloom, with a glory as bright to the spiritual eye as it was unexpected.

39. And one of the malefactors (see on John xix. 18) **which were hanged railed on him.** The first two Evangelists say that the *thieves* did so (Matt. xxvii. 44; Mark xv. 32). Now, if we had no more than this general statement, we should naturally conclude that both of them were meant. But after reading what is here recorded—of *one* that did so, and the other that rebuked him for doing it—it is to us astonishing that some sensible commentators should think it necessary to take the statement of the first two Evangelists so strictly as to imply that both of them reviled our Lord; and then to *infer*, without a shadow of ground for it in the text, that some sudden change came over the *penitent* one, which turned him from an unfeeling railer into a trembling petitioner. Is it conceivable that this penitent thief, after first himself reviling the Saviour, should then, on his views of Christ suddenly changing, have turned upon his fellow-sufferer and fellow-reviler, and rebuked him, not only with dignified sharpness, but in the language of *astonishment* that he should be capable of such conduct? Besides, there is a deep calmness in all that he utters, extremely unlike what we should expect from one who had been the subject of a mental revolution so sudden and so total. No, when it is said that "the *thieves* which were crucified with Him cast the same in His teeth," it is merely what grammarians call an 'indeterminate' plural, denoting no more than the unexpected *quarter* or *class* whence, in addition to all others, the taunts proceeded. The Evangelists had been telling us that scoffs at the Redeemer proceeded from the *passers by*, from the *ecclesiastics*, and from the *soldiery;* but, as if that had not been enough, they tell us that they proceeded even from *the thieves*—a mode of speaking which no one would think *necessarily* meant both of them. Thus Matthew says, "*They say* unto Him, We have here but five loaves," &c.; whereas we learn from the Fourth Gospel that it was *one* only—Andrew, Simon Peter's brother—that said this (Matt. xiv. 17; John vi. 8). And when Mary poured her precious ointment on her Lord's head, Matthew says that "*His disciples* had indignation at it," and exclaimed against such waste; whereas from the Fourth Gospel we learn that it was *the traitor* that said this. It was but one of the malefactors, then, that, catching up the general derision, "cast the same in His teeth." But *his* taunt had a turn of its own, a sting which the others had not. **saying, If thou be** ('the') **Christ** [ὁ Χριστὸς], **save thyself and us.** Jesus, "reviled, reviles not again;" but another voice from the cross shall nobly wipe out this dishonour, and turn it to the unspeakable glory of the divine Redeemer. **40. But the other answering rebuked him, saying, Dost not thou fear God** [Οὐδὲ φοβῇ σὺ τὸν Θεόν]—rather, 'Dost thou too not fear God?' or, 'Dost not even thou fear God?' There is a tacit reference to the godless, reckless spirit which reigned among the bystanders and shot such envenomed shafts at the meek Sufferer that hung between them. In *them* such treatment might be bad enough; but was it indeed coming from one of themselves? 'Let others jeer; but dost *thou?*' "Dost not thou *fear God?*" he asks. 'Hast thou no fear of meeting Him so soon as thy righteous Judge? Thou art within an hour or two of eternity, and dost thou spend it in reckless disregard of coming judgment?' **seeing thou art in the same condemnation?** 'He has been condemned to die, indeed, but is it better with thee? Doth even a common lot kindle no sympathy in thy breast?' But he goes on with his expostulations, and rises higher. **41. And we indeed justly; for we receive the due reward of our deeds.** Owning his crimes, and the justice with which he was paying their awful penalty, he would fain shame his fellow-sufferer into the same feeling, which would have quickly closed his mouth. **but this man hath done nothing amiss** [οὗτος δὲ οὐδὲν ἄτοπον ἔπραξεν]—'this person did nothing amiss;' literally, 'out of place,' and well rendered here "amiss." A very remarkable declaration. He does not acquit Him of all *ordinary crimes*, such as bring men to a judicial death; for with these he knew that our Lord was not charged. The charge of treason had not even a show of truth, as Pilate told His enemies. The one charge against Him was His claim to office and

42 our deeds: but this man hath done nothing amiss. And he said unto
43 Jesus, Lord, remember me when thou comest into [e] thy kingdom. And
Jesus said unto him, Verily I say unto thee, To-day shalt thou be with
me in [f] paradise.

A. D. 33.

e Heb. 1. 3. Heb. 8. 1.
f Rev. 2. 7.

honours, which in the eyes of His judges amounted to blasphemy. Hear, then, this remarkable testimony in that light: 'He made Himself the promised Messiah, the Son of God—but in this He "*did nothing amiss:*" He ate with publicans and sinners, and bid all the weary and heavy laden come and rest under His wing—but in this He "*did nothing amiss:*" He claimed to be Lord of the Kingdom of God, to shut it at will, but also to open it at pleasure even to such as we are—but in this He "*did nothing amiss!*"' Does his next speech imply *less* than this? Turning now to the Lord Himself, how wonderful is his address! **42. And he said unto Jesus, Lord, remember me when thou comest into thy kingdom** [ἐν τῃ βασιλεία σου]—rather, 'in thy kingdom;' that is, in the glory of it (Matt. xxv. 31; Luke ix. 26). Let us analyze and study this marvellous petition. First, the "Kingdom" he meant could be no *earthly* one, but one *beyond the grave;* for it is inconceivable that he should have expected Him to come down from the cross to erect any *temporal* kingdom. Next, he calls this Christ's own Kingdom—"thy Kingdom." Then, he sees in Christ the absolute right to dispose of that Kingdom to whom He pleased. But further, he does not presume to *ask* a place in that kingdom—though no doubt that is what he means—but with a humility quite affecting, just says, "Lord, *remember me* when," &c. Yet was there mighty faith in that word. If Christ will but "think upon him" (Neh. v. 19), at that august moment when He "cometh in His kingdom," it will do. 'Only assure me that then Thou wilt not forget such a wretch as I, that once hung by Thy side, and I am content.' Now contrast with this bright act of faith the darkness even of the apostles' minds, who could hardly be got to believe that their Master would die at all, who now were almost despairing of Him, and who when dead had almost buried their hopes in His grave. Consider, too, the man's previous *disadvantages* and *bad life.* And then mark how his faith comes out—not in protestations, 'Lord, I cannot doubt—I am firmly persuaded that Thou art Lord of a kingdom—that death cannot disannul Thy title nor impede the assumption of it in due time,' and so on—but as having no shadow of doubt, and rising above it as a question altogether, he just says, "Lord, remember me *when* thou comest," &c.—Was ever faith like this exhibited upon earth? It looks as if the brightest crown had been reserved for the Saviour's head at His darkest moment! **43. And Jesus said unto him.** To the taunt of the other criminal He answered nothing; but a response to this was resistless. The dying Redeemer had not seen so great faith, no not in His nearest and dearest apostles. It was to Him a "song in the night." It ministered cheer to His spirit in the thick midnight gloom that now enwrapt it. **Verily I say unto thee.** 'Since thou speakest as to the King, with kingly authority speak I to thee.' **To-day shalt thou be with me in paradise.** 'Thou art prepared for a long delay ere I come in My Kingdom, but not a day's delay shall there be for thee; thou shalt not be parted from Me even for a moment, but together we shall go, and with Me, ere this day expire, shalt thou be in paradise.' On the meaning of this word "paradise"—employed by the LXX. for the Garden of Eden (Gen. ii. 8, &c.)—it is only necessary to observe that it was employed by the Jews to express the state of future bliss, both in its lower and higher stages; that, in keeping with this general idea, it is used by the apostle to express "the third heaven" (2 Cor. xii. 2, 4); and that our Lord Himself, in His apocalyptic epistle to the church of Ephesus, manifestly uses it to express the final glory and bliss of the redeemed, under the figure of Paradise Restored: "To him that overcometh will I give to eat of the tree of life, which is in the midst of the paradise of God" (Rev. ii. 7). In our passage, of course, the *immediate* reference is to such bliss as the disembodied spirit is capable of, and experiences, immediately after death; for it was to be on *that very day* that the penitent thief was to be with his dying Lord in paradise. But this is viewed as a thing understood, and so the promise amounts to this, that they were never more to be parted; that he would go with Him into heavenly bliss immediately on his departure; and though the One was to reassume His body in a few days, while the dust of the other would sleep till the resurrection, that their fellowship would never be interrupted!

Remarks.—1. Of all the possible conceptions of a writer of imaginary history, this incident is about the last that would enter the mind even of the most ingenious. While its presence in the Gospel History is to every unsophisticated reader its own evidence of actual occurrence, the glory with which it invests the Cross of Christ is beyond the power of language to express. Verily "He disappointeth the devices of the crafty, so that their hands cannot perform their enterprise: He taketh the wise in their own craftiness, and the counsel of the froward is carried headlong: with Him is strength and wisdom; the deceived and the deceiver are His. He leadeth counsellors away spoiled, and maketh the judges fools" (Job v. 12, 13; xii. 16, 17). 2. How true is that saying of Christ, "One shall be taken and another left!" (ch. xvii. 34-36). It is possible, indeed, that the religious opportunities of the penitent criminal may have been superior to his fellow's. But we have too much evidence, even in this Gospel History, that far better opportunities than he could possibly have enjoyed left the heart all unsoftened. Nor is it the reach of this man's *knowledge* which contrasts so remarkably with the demeanour of the impenitent criminal. It is his ingenuous self-condemnation; his mingled astonishment and horror at the very different temper of his fellow's mind; his anxiety to bring him to a better state of mind, while yet there was hope; and the pain with which he listened to the scoffs of his companion in crime at suffering innocence. Such deep and tender feeling, in contrast with the other's heartlessness on the brink of eternity, is but superficially apprehended until we trace it up to that distinguishing grace which, while it "*left*" one hardened criminal to go to his own place, "*took*" the other as a brand from the fire, lighted up into a blaze of light the few scattered rays of information about Jesus which beamed into his mind, and made him a bright jewel in that crown of glory that encircled the dying Redeemer! 3. How easily can divine grace elevate the rudest and the worst above the best instructed and most devoted servants of Christ! We are such slaves of *average experience* in morals and religion, that we are apt to treat whatever greatly tran-

44 And [g]it was about the sixth hour, and there was a darkness over all
45 the [3]earth until the ninth hour. And the sun was darkened, and [h]the
46 veil of the temple was rent in the midst. And when Jesus had cried
with a loud voice, he said, [i]Father, into thy hands I commend my spirit:
[j]and having said thus, he gave up the ghost.
47 Now [k]when the centurion saw what was done, he glorified God, saying,

A. D. 33.

[g] Mark 15 33.
[3] Or, land.
[h] Matt 27.51.
[i] Ps. 31. 5.
[j] John 19.30.
[k] Matt. 27.54.

scends it, however well attested, with a measure of scepticism. But however exceptional such cases may seem, the laws of the divine administration in spiritual things—of which our knowledge is but very partial—will be found comprehensive enough to embrace them all. Think how limited must have been the means of knowledge which the Centurion possessed; and yet, in regard to the power and glory of Christ, what a reach of perception and deep humility did he display, with a faith at which Jesus Himself marvelled! (Luke vii. 6-9). And did not the faith of the Syrophenician woman—heathen though her upbringing had been—draw forth the Redeemer's admiration? (Matt. xv. 28). And what an unwonted spectacle was the woman that washed the Saviour's feet with her tears! (Luke vii. 36, &c.) And who, even of the Twelve, got such a grasp of the Redeemer's power over the subtlest exercises of the human spirit as the man that, without any such opportunities as they enjoyed, exclaimed, "Lord, I believe; help Thou mine unbelief"? And what but a very unusual display of converting grace was that in the case of Zaccheus? (Luke xix). And yet, in some of these cases at least, it is not difficult to see what principles were at work, and how they wrought. As trials are fitted to open the heart, to direct it to the true source of relief, and to make it accessible to divine compassion and grace, so a deep sense of sin and a consciousness of hell-deserving draw the spiritual eye with a quick instinct to Him who came to seek and to save the lost, and rivet it upon Him with reviving and transforming efficacy. While others fasten on features of divine truth of lesser moment, and miss, through prejudice, the right view even of these, such deep-taught souls, with a kind of unerring scent, discover the direction in which relief for them is alone to be found. What to the penitent woman whose tears watered His blessed feet, and what to this poor dying criminal, who felt himself ready to drop into hell, were all the Messianic honours and dignities about which the Twelve kept dreaming and disputing till within an hour or two of their Lord's apprehension? To them one gracious look from that eye of His was more than all such things:

> 'Poor fragments all of this low earth;
> Such as in sleep would hardly soothe
> A soul that once had tasted of immortal truth.'—KEBLE.

And thus it was that, divinely taught in *the school of conscious unworthiness and soul-distress*, they shot far ahead of the best instructed but less schooled disciples. And so it still is. Schools of theological and critical training in the knowledge of Scripture are excellent things. But he who trusts in them as his sole key to divine truth and guide to heaven will find them blind guides, while many a one, ignorant of all but his own tongue, and little versed in the literature even of that, has made religious attainments that might put divines and scholars to shame. 4. *Presumption* and *despair*, it has been long ago and well remarked, are equally discountenanced here; the one in the impenitent thief, the other in his penitent fellow. He who flatters himself in his sins, hoping that, as one man was saved in the agonies of death, another may—and why not he?—should turn to the man who, in the same circumstances and at the same moment, died *unsaved*. But, on the other hand, he who, conscious that he has worse than wasted his life, is sceptical as to both the reality and the value of what are called death-bed repentances, and so is ready to sink into despair, should study the case of this penitent thief. If *real*, the *value* of such death-bed changes is beyond dispute; since Jesus took this man, dying for his crimes, straight with Him to paradise. What, in fact, is wanting to any one's entering into the kingdom of God? Only that he be born again. How instantaneous that change may be, and in fact in every case essentially is, we have already had occasion to observe. See on ch. xix. 1-10, Remark 2 at the close of that Section. And what though there be no time left in one's life to *develop* the change and make it manifest to the world? If it be *real*—and the Searcher of hearts, the Judge of quick and dead, at least knows that—it is enough. And just as we nothing doubt that infants dying ere they attain to the sense of responsibility are capable of heaven, so the undeveloped infancy of the new life in dying penitents has in it a germ which will surely expand in the paradise of God. On the one hand, then, "Be not high-minded, but fear," O sinner, sleeping on a pillow of baseless hope that, after a reckless life, one dying glance at the Saviour will set thee all right. But, on the other hand, fear not, poor despairing sinner, to behold even at the last the Lamb of God that taketh away the sin of the world. For His word is not, "Him that cometh unto me" early, or up to a certain period of life and measure of guilt; but, "*Him that cometh*"—if only he *do come*, and come "UNTO ME, I will in no wise cast out." No limitation at all, either of *time* or *measure of guilt*. It is the 'coming unto Jesus' that secures the sinner against being cast out. 5. How false as well as cheerless, in the light of our Lord's words to this penitent, is the notion of the soul's *sleep*, or total unconsciousness, during the intermediate state between death and the resurrection! "To-day shalt thou be with Me in paradise." Who can take that to mean the mere transference of the soul to some place or state of *safety*, without the consciousness of it, or to the mere certainty of bliss *at the resurrection?* Nor is it that notion only which is rebuked here, but along with it the speculations of not a few who would so cripple the *capacities* of the disembodied spirit as to admit little beyond that 'sleep of the soul' before its re-union with the body. The more our Lord's words here are considered—in the light of such passages as 2 Cor. v. 6-8—the more will it be seen, that the spirits of the just, on their being disengaged from this earthly tabernacle, are immediately ushered into paradise in the bud, and find themselves tasting the bliss of heaven in substance; and thus it is that the language which describes the one merges naturally in that which properly describes only the other So let us labour that whether present or absent, we may be accepted of Him!

44-56.—THE CRUCIFIXION COMPLETED—SIGNS AND CIRCUMSTANCES FOLLOWING THE DEATH OF THE LORD JESUS—HE IS TAKEN DOWN FROM THE

48 Certainly this was a righteous man. And all the people that came
together to that sight, beholding the things which were done, smote their
49 breasts, and returned. And [l]all his acquaintance, and the women that
followed him from Galilee, stood afar off, beholding these things.
50 And, [m]behold, *there was* a man named Joseph, a counsellor; *and he*
51 *was* a good man, and a just: (the same [n]had not consented to the
counsel and deed of them:) *he was* of Arimathea, a city of the Jews:
52 [o]who also himself waited for the kingdom of God. This *man* went unto
53 Pilate, and begged the body of Jesus. And [p]he took it down, and
wrapped it in linen, and laid it in [q]a sepulchre that was hewn in stone,
54 wherein never man before was laid. And that day was the preparation,
and the sabbath drew on.
55 And the women also, [r]which came with him from Galilee, followed
56 after, and beheld [s]the sepulchre, and how his body was laid. And they
returned, and [t]prepared spices and ointments; and rested the sabbath
day, [u]according to the commandment.

24 NOW [a]upon the first *day* of the week, very early in the morning, they
came unto the sepulchre, [b]bringing the spices which they had prepared,
2 and certain *others* with them. And they found the stone rolled away
3 from the sepulchre. And [c]they entered in, and found not the body of
4 the Lord Jesus. And it came to pass, as they were much perplexed
5 thereabout, [d]behold, two men stood by them in shining garments: and as
they were afraid, and bowed down *their* faces to the earth, they said unto
6 them, Why seek ye [1]the living among the dead? He is not here, but is
7 risen: [e]remember how he spake unto you when he was yet in Galilee, saying, The Son of man must be delivered into the hands of sinful men, and
8 be crucified, and the third day rise again. And [f]they remembered his words,
9 And [g]returned from the sepulchre, and told all these things
10 unto the eleven, and to all the rest. It was Mary Magdalene, and
[h]Joanna, and Mary *the mother* of James, and other *women that were*
11 with them, which told these things unto the apostles. And their words
seemed to them as idle tales, and they believed them not. Then

A. D. 33.

l Ps. 38. 11. John 19.25.
m Matt.27.57. Mark 15.42. John 19.38.
n Gen 37. 21, 22. Gen. 42. 21, 22. Ex. 23. 2. 1 Tim 5. 22.
o ch. 2. 25,38.
p Matt.27. 59.
q Isa. 53. 9.
r ch. 8. 2.
s Mark 15.47.
t Mark 16. 1.
u Ex. 20. 10. Isa. 56. 2, 6. Isa. 58. 13. Jer. 17. 24.

CHAP. 24.

a Matt. 28. 1. Mark 16. 1. John 20. 1.
b ch. 23. 56.
c Mark 16. 5.
d John 20. 12. Acts 1. 10.
1 Or, Him that liveth? 1 Tim. 1.17. Rev. 1. 18.
e Matt.16.21. Mark 8. 31. ch. 9. 22.
f John 2. 22.
g Matt. 28. 8. Mark 16.10.
h ch. 8. 3.

CROSS AND BURIED—THE WOMEN OBSERVE THE SPOT. (= Matt. xxvii. 51-66; Mark xv. 38-47; John xix. 31-42.) For the exposition, see on Matt. xxvii. 51-66; and on John xix. 31-42.

CHAP. XXIV. 1-12.—ANGELIC ANNOUNCEMENT TO THE WOMEN, ON THE FIRST DAY OF THE WEEK, THAT CHRIST IS RISEN—THEY CARRY THE TRANSPORTING NEWS TO THE ELEVEN, WHO RECEIVE IT INCREDULOUSLY — PETER'S VISIT TO THE EMPTY SEPULCHRE. (=Matt. xxviii. 1-8; Mark xvi. 1-8; John xx. 1-10.)

The Resurrection Announced to the Women (1-8). **1. Now upon the first day of the week, very early in the morning, they came unto the sepulchre, bringing the spices which they had prepared, and certain others with them. 2. And they found the stone rolled away from the sepulchre. 3. And they entered in, and found not the body of the Lord Jesus.** See on Matt. xxviii. 1-4; and on Mark xvi. 1-4. **4. And it came to pass, as they were much perplexed thereabout.** Mark reports their perplexity, before they reached the sepulchre, as to who should roll them away the stone that covered the body of their dear Lord; while our Evangelist here, who simply tells us that they found the stone rolled away, records their next and still greater perplexity at finding the sepulchre empty. But as the one vanished as soon as they arrived at the spot, so the other was soon dissipated by the shining ones that appeared to them. **behold, two men stood by them in shining garments** [ἀστραπτούσαις]—garments of dazzling brightness. See on Mark xvi. 5. **5. And as they were afraid, and bowed down their faces to the earth** (see on ch. i. 12), **they said unto them, Why seek ye the living** [τὸν ζῶντα]—'the Living One,' **among the dead?** Astonishing question! It is not, Why seek ye the *risen* One? but "Why seek ye the Living One among the dead?" See on Rev. i. 18. The surprise expressed in the question implies a certain incongruity in His being there at all; as if, though He might *submit* to it, "it was impossible that He should be *holden* of it" (Acts ii. 24). **6. He is not here, but is risen: remember how he spake unto you when he was yet in Galilee**—to which these women themselves belonged (ch. xxiii. 55.) **7. Saying**—in those explicit announcements, which He made once and again, of His approaching sufferings, death, and resurrection, **The Son of man must be delivered into the hands of sinful men, and be crucified, and the third day rise again.** How remarkable it is to hear angels quoting a whole sentence of Christ's to the disciples, mentioning where it was uttered, and wondering it was not fresh on their memory, as doubtless it was in theirs! See 1 Tim. iii. 16, "Seen of angels;" and 1 Pet. i. 12. **8. And they remembered his words.**

The Incredulity of the Eleven—Peter's Visit to Christ's Sepulchre (9-12). **9. And returned from the sepulchre, and told all these things unto the eleven, and to all the rest. 10. It was Mary Magdalene, and Joanna** (see on ch. viii. 1-3), **and Mary the mother of James, and other** [καὶ αἱ

12 [i]arose Peter, and ran unto the sepulchre; and stooping down, he beheld
the linen clothes laid by themselves, and departed, wondering in himself
at that which was come to pass.
13 And, behold, two of them went that same day to a village called
14 Emmaus, which was from Jerusalem *about* threescore furlongs. And
15 they [j]talked together of all these things which had happened. And it
came to pass, that, while they communed *together* and reasoned, [k]Jesus
16 himself drew near, and went with them. But [l]their eyes were holden
17 that they should not know him. And he said unto them, What manner
of communications *are* these that ye have one to another, as ye walk,
18 and are sad? And the one of them, [m]whose name was Cleopas, answering
said unto him, Art thou only a stranger in Jerusalem, and hast not
19 known the things which are come to pass there in these days? And he
said unto them, What things? And they said unto him, Concerning
Jesus of Nazareth, [n]which was a prophet [o]mighty in deed and word
20 before God and all the people: and [p]how the chief priests and our rulers
21 delivered him to be condemned to death, and have crucified him. But
we trusted [q]that it had been he which should have redeemed Israel: and
besides all this, to-day is the third day since these things were done.
22 Yea, and certain women also of our company made us astonished, which
23 were early at the sepulchre; and when they found not his body, they
came, saying, that they had also seen a vision of angels, which said that
24 he was alive. And certain of them which were with us went to the
sepulchre, and found *it* even so as the women had said: but him they

A. D. 33.

i John 20. 3, 10.
j Deut. 6. 7. Mal. 3. 16. ch. 6. 45.
k Matt. 18. 20. John 14. 18, 19.
l 2 Ki. 6. 18, 20. Mark 16. 12. John 20. 14. John 21. 4.
m John 19. 25.
n John 3. 2. John 6. 14. Acts 2. 22.
o Acts 7. 22.
p Matt. 27. 1, 2, 20. Mark 15. 1. ch. 22. 66, 71. ch. 23. 1, 5. Acts 3. 13, 15. Acts 4. 8, 10, 27. Acts 5. 30, 31. Acts 13. 27.
q Acts 1. 6.

λοιπαὶ]—rather, 'and the others,' **that were with them, which told these things unto the apostles.** See on Mark xvi. 1. **11. And their words seemed to them as idle tales, and they believed them not.** See on *v.* 41, and on Mark xvi. 11. **12. Then arose Peter, &c.** For the details of this, see on John xx. 1, &c.

For Remarks on this Section, see those on the corresponding Section of the First Gospel, Matt. xxviii. 1-15.

13-53.—Jesus Appears to the Two Going to Emmaus—Then to the Assembled Disciples—His Glorious Ascension, and Return of the Eleven to Jerusalem. (=Mark xvi. 12-19; John xx. 19-23.)

Jesus Appears to The Two Going to Emmaus, &c. (13-35). This most exquisite scene is peculiar to our Evangelist. **13. And, behold, two of them.** For the name of the one, see on *v.* 18. Who the other was is mere conjecture. **went**—or 'were proceeding' [ἦσαν πορευόμενοι] **that same day to a village called Emmaus, which was from Jerusalem about threescore furlongs**—or, about seven and a half miles; but the spot has not been satisfactorily determined. Perhaps they were returning home after the Passover. **14. And they talked together of all these things which had happened. 15. And it came to pass, that, while they communed together and reasoned**—as they exchanged views and feelings, weighing afresh all the facts detailed in *vv.* 18-24, **Jesus himself drew near, and went with them**—coming up behind them, as from Jerusalem (*v.* 18). **16. But their eyes were holden that they should not know him** [τοῦ μὴ ἐπιγνῶναι]—or 'did not recognize Him.' Certainly, as they did not believe that He was alive, His company, as a Fellow-traveller, was the last thing they would expect. But the words, "their eyes were holden," and the express intimation, in another Gospel, that "He appeared to them in another form" (Mark xvi. 12), make it evident that there was a divine operation hindering the recognition of Him until the fitting time. **17. And he said unto them, What manner of communications are these that ye have one to another** [ἀντιβάλλετε]. The word "have" is too weak. Literally it is, 'that ye cast about' from one to the other, and denotes the earnest discussion that seemed to be going on between them. **as ye walk, and are sad? 18. And the one of them, whose name was Cleopas** (see on Matt. x. 3), **answering said unto him, Art thou only a stranger in Jerusalem, and hast not known the things which are come to pass there in these days?** If he knew not the events of the last few days in Jerusalem, he must be a mere sojourner; if he did, how could he suppose they would be talking of anything else? How artless is all this! **19. And he said unto them, What things? And they said unto him, Concerning Jesus of Nazareth, which was a prophet mighty in deed and word before God and all the people: 20. And how the chief priests and our rulers delivered him to be condemned to death**—that is, handed Him over to Pilate, that he might order Him to be put to death. **and have crucified him.** As if feeling it a relief to have some one to unburden his thoughts and feelings to, this disciple goes over the main facts, in his own desponding style, and this was just what our Lord wished. **21. But we trusted that it had been he which should have redeemed Israel** [Ἡμεῖς δὲ ἠλπίζομεν ὅτι αὐτός ἐστιν ὁ μέλλων λυτροῦσθαι]—rather, 'But we were hoping that it was He that was to redeem,' &c. The "we" is emphatic:—*q. d.*, 'Others, we know, thought differently; but for our part we,' &c., implying expectations kept up till the recent events so dashed them. They expected, indeed, the promised Deliverance at His hand; but certainly not by His death. **and besides all this, to-day is the third day since these things were done. 22. Yea, and certain women also of our company made us astonished, which were early at the sepulchre; 23. And when they found not his body, they came, saying, that they had also seen a vision of angels, which said that he was alive. 24. And certain of them which were with us went to the sepulchre,**

25 saw not. Then he said unto them, O fools, and slow of heart to believe
26 all that the prophets have spoken! ought [r]not Christ to have suffered
27 these things, and to enter into his glory? And beginning at [s]Moses and
[t]all the Prophets, he expounded unto them in all the Scriptures the
28 things concerning himself. And they drew nigh unto the village whither
29 they went: and [u]he made as though he would have gone farther. But
they constrained him, saying, Abide with us; for it is toward evening,
30 and the day is far spent. And he went in to tarry with them. And it
came to pass, as he sat at meat with them, he took bread, and blessed *it*,
31 and brake, and gave to them. And their eyes were opened, and they
32 knew him; and he [2]vanished out of their sight. And they said one to
another, Did not our heart burn within us, while he talked with us by
the way, and while he opened to us the Scriptures?
33 And they rose up the same hour, and returned to Jerusalem, and found
34 the eleven gathered together, and them that were with them, saying, The
35 Lord is risen indeed, and hath [v]appeared to Simon. And they told what

A. D. 33.

r Acts 17. 3. Phil 2. 6-11. 1 Pet. 1. 11.
s Gen. 3. 15. Gen. 22. 18. Gen. 26. 4. Num. 21. 9.
t Ps. 16. 9. Ps. 22. Jer. 23. 5. Jer. 33. 14. Ezek. 34. 23. Ezek. 37. 25. Dan. 9. 24. Mic. 7. 20.
u Gen. 32. 26.
2 Or, ceased to be seen of them.
v 1 Cor. 15. 5.

and found it even so as the women had said; but him they saw not. Not only did His death seem to give the fatal blow to their hopes, but He had been two days dead already, and this was the third. 'It is true,' they add, 'some of our women gave us a surprise, telling us of a vision of angels they had at the empty grave this morning that said He was alive, and some of ourselves who went thither confirmed their statement; but then, Himself they saw not.' A doleful tale truly, and told out of the deepest despondency. **25. Then he said unto them, O fools** [῏Ω ἀνόητοι]—This is too strong a word. Our Lord never calls His true disciples "fools" [μωροί]. It should be, 'O senseless;' that is, void of discernment. **and slow of heart to believe all that the prophets have spoken!**—or 'spake' [ἐλάλησαν]. **26. Ought not Christ** [ἔδει παθεῖν τὸν Χριστὸν] **to have suffered these things, and to enter into his glory?**—'Behoved it not the Messiah to suffer these things, and to enter into His glory;' that is, Was it not necessary to the fulfilment of the Scriptures that the predicted Messiah should, through the gate of these very sufferings, enter into His glory? It is doubtless to these words that the apostle Peter alludes, when he speaks of the Spirit of Christ who testified in the prophets 'the sufferings that were to light upon Messiah and the following glories' [προμαρτυρόμενον τὰ εἰς Χριστὸν παθήματα καὶ τὰς μετὰ ταῦτα δόξας], 1 Pet. i. 11. 'Ye have had your eye fixed so exclusively on the "glories" (says our Lord), that ye have overlooked the "sufferings" which the prophets told you were to go before and pave the way for them.' **27. And beginning at Moses and all the Prophets, he expounded unto them in all the Scriptures the things concerning himself**—the great Burden of all the Old Testament Scriptures. **28. And they drew nigh unto the village whither they went**—or 'were going' [ἐπορεύοντο]. **and he made as though he would have gone farther**—but only "as though;" for He had no intention of going farther. So when He walked towards them on the sea of Galilee, "He would have passed by them"—but never meant to do it. So Gen. xxxii. 26. (Compare Gen. xviii. 3, 5; xlii. 7.) **29. But they constrained him, saying, Abide with us; for it is toward evening, and the day is far spent. And he went in to tarry with them.** But for this, the whole design of the interview had been lost; but *it was not to be lost*, for He who only wished to be constrained had kindled a longing in the hearts of His travelling companions which was not to be so easily put off. **30. And it came to pass, as he sat at meat with them, he took bread, and blessed it, and brake, and gave to them. 31. And their eyes were opened, and they knew**—or 'recognized' [ἐπέγνωσαν] **him; and he vanished out of their sight** [καὶ αὐτὸς ἄφαντος ἐγένετο ἀπ' αὐτῶν]—or 'ceased to be seen of them;' supernaturally disappearing. The stranger first startles them by taking the place of Master at their own table, but on proceeding to that act which reproduced the whole scene of the last Supper, a rush of associations and recollections disclosed their Guest, and He stood confessed before their astonished gaze—THEIR RISEN LORD! They were going to gaze on Him, perhaps embrace Him, but that moment He is gone! It was enough; the end of the whole interview had been gained. **32. And they said one to another, Did not our heart burn within us, while he talked with us by the way, and while he opened to us the Scriptures?** The force of the imperfect tenses here [καιομένη ἦν—ἐλάλει—διήνοιγεν], denoting what they felt *during the whole time* of His walk and talk with them, should if possible be preserved; as thus: 'Was not our heart burning within us whilst He was talking with us on the way, and whilst He was opening to us the Scriptures?' 'Ah! this accounts for it: We could not understand the glow of self-evidencing light, love, glory, that ravished our hearts; but now we do.' They cannot rest—how could they?—they must go straight back and tell the news. They cannot think of sleeping over it.

33. And they rose up the same hour, and returned to Jerusalem, and found the eleven gathered together. This does not show that the two disciples themselves were not of "the Eleven;" for the expression is used here to denote the *company* or *class*, not the fact of the whole number of them being present on this occasion. **and them that were with them. 34. Saying, The Lord is risen indeed, and hath appeared to Simon.** They think they will bring strange tidings—thrilling intelligence—to their downcast brethren. But ere they have time to tell their tale, their own ears are saluted with tidings not less thrilling: "The Lord is risen indeed [ὄντως], and hath appeared to SIMON." Most touching and precious intelligence this. The only one of the Eleven to whom He appeared *alone* was he, it seems, who had so shamefully denied Him. *What passed at that interview we shall never know here. Probably it was too sacred for disclosure.* See on Mark xvi. 7. **35. And they told what things were done in the way, and how he was known of them in breaking of**

things *were done* in the way, and how he was known of them in breaking
of bread.
36 And as they thus spake, Jesus himself stood in the midst of them,
37 and saith unto them, Peace *be* unto you. But they were terrified and
38 affrighted, and supposed that they had seen a spirit. And he said unto
them, Why are ye troubled? and why do thoughts arise in your hearts?
39 Behold my hands and my feet, that it is I myself: handle me, and see;
40 for a spirit hath not flesh and bones, as ye see me have. And when he
41 had thus spoken, he showed them *his* hands and *his* feet. And while
they yet believed not for joy, and wondered, he said unto them, Have ye
42 here any meat? And they gave him a piece of a broiled fish, and of an
43 honey-comb. And [w]he took *it*, and did eat before them.
44 And he said unto them, [x]These *are* the words which I spake unto you,
while I was yet with you, that all things must be fulfilled which were
written in the law of Moses, and *in* the Prophets, and *in* the Psalms,
45 concerning me. Then [y]opened he their understanding, that they might
46 understand the Scriptures, and said unto them, Thus it is written, and
thus it behoved Christ to suffer, and to rise from the dead the third day:
47 and that repentance and [z]remission of sins should be preached in his
48 name among all [a]nations, beginning at Jerusalem. And [b]ye are witnesses
49 of these things. And, [c]behold, I send the promise of my Father upon
you: but tarry ye in the city of Jerusalem, until ye be endued with
power from on high.

A. D. 33.

[w] Acts 10. 41.
[x] Matt. 16. 21. Mark 8. 31, 32. Mark 9. 31. ch. 9. 22. ch. 18. 31, 32.
[y] Acts 16. 14. 2 Cor. 4. 6.
[z] Dan. 9. 24. Acts 13. 38. 1 John 2. 12.
[a] Gen. 12. 3. Ps. 22. 27. Isa. 49. 6. Jer. 31. 34. Hos. 2. 23. Mic. 4. 2. Mal. 1. 11. Gal. 3. 28.
[b] John 15. 27. Acts 1. 22.
[c] Isa. 44. 3. Joel 2. 28. John 14. 16, 17. John 15. 26. Acts 2. 1.

bread. The two from Emmaus have now their turn, and relate the marvellous manifestation made to them. While thus comparing notes of their Lord's appearances, lo! Himself stands in the midst of them.

Jesus Appears to the Assembled Disciples—Convinces them wondrously of the Reality of His Resurrection—Opens to them the Scriptures on the Subject, and Directs them to Wait for the promised Spirit (36-49). **36. And as they thus spake, Jesus himself stood in the midst of them, and saith unto them, Peace be unto you.** See on John xx. 19-21. **37. But they were terrified and affrighted, and supposed that they had seen a spirit**—the ghost of their dead Lord rather than Himself in the body. (See on Acts xii. 15; and Matt. xiv. 26.) **38. And he said unto them, Why are ye troubled? and why do thoughts arise in your hearts?** [*διαλογισμοὶ*]—rather 'reasonings;' that is, whether He were risen or no, and whether this was His very Self. **39. Behold my hands and my feet, that it is I myself: handle me, and see**—lovingly offering them both *ocular* and *tangible* demonstration of the reality of His resurrection. **for a spirit hath not flesh and bones, as ye see me have**—an important statement regarding 'spirits.' He says not "flesh and *blood;*" for the blood is the life of the animal and corruptible body (Gen. ix. 4) which "cannot inherit the kingdom of God" (1 Cor. xv. 50); but "flesh and bones"—implying the *identity*, but *with diversity of laws*, of the resurrection-body. **40. And when he had thus spoken, he shewed them his hands and his feet.** See on John xx. 24-28. **41. And while they yet believed not for joy, and wondered.** They did believe, else, as *Bengel* beautifully remarks, they had not "joyed." But it seemed *too good* to be true. Like the captives from Babylon, "they were as men that dreamed" (Ps. cxxvi. 1, 2). **he said unto them, Have ye here any meat? 42. And they gave him a piece of a broiled fish, and of an honey-comb**—common, frugal fare, anciently. **43. And he took it, and did eat before them**—that is, so as to let them see Him eating; not for His own necessity, but their conviction.

44. And he said unto them, These are the words which I spake unto you, while I was yet with you. Mark this last expression—"while I was yet with you"—that is, in the days of His flesh. Now, He was as good as removed from them; His life being a new one, the atmosphere He breathed no longer that of this lower world, and His proper home, even for their interests, His Father's house. But 'now ye will understand what I said to you, once and again, to your so great surprise and distress, about the Son of man requiring to be put to death and to rise again. **that all things must be fulfilled which were written in the law of Moses, and in the Prophets, and in the Psalms**—the three current Jewish divisions of the Old Testament Scriptures, **concerning me. 45. Then opened he their understanding, that they might understand the Scriptures.** A statement of unspeakable value: expressing, on the one hand, Christ's *immediate access to the human spirit* and *absolute power over it*, to the adjustment of its vision, and its permanent rectification for spiritual discernment; and, on the other hand, showing that the *apostolic manner of interpreting the Old Testament*, in the Acts and Epistles, *has the direct sanction of Christ Himself.* **46. And said unto them, Thus it is written, and thus it behoved Christ**—or 'the Messiah' [*τὸν Χριστὸν*], **to suffer, and to rise from the dead the third day**—see on *v.* 26. **47. And that repentance and remission of sins should be preached in his name among all nations, beginning at Jerusalem;** first, because Jerusalem was the metropolitan centre of the then existing kingdom of God (see Rom. i. 16—"to the Jew first;" Acts xiii. 46; Isa. ii. 3; and see on Matt. x. 6); and next, because it was the great laboratory and reservoir of all the sin and all the crime of the nation (ch. xiii. 33), and by beginning *there*, it would be proclaimed for all time that there was mercy in Christ for the chief of sinners (see on Matt. xxiii. 37). **48. And ye are witnesses of these things** (see on Acts i. 8, 22). **49. And, behold, I send** [*ἀποστέλλω*]—or, 'I am sending,' in the present tense, to intimate its nearness. **the promise of my Father**—that is, what my Father hath promised; or the Holy Ghost, of which Christ is the

50 And he led them out as far as to Bethany; and he lifted up his hands,
51 and blessed them. And [d]it came to pass, while he blessed them, he was
52 parted from them, and carried up into heaven. And they worshipped

A. D. 33.

[d] 2 Ki. 2. 11. Eph. 1. 20.

authoritative Dispenser (John xiv. 7; Rev. iii. 1; v. 6); **but tarry ye in the city of Jerusalem, until ye be endued** [ἐνδύσασθε]—or 'clothed' **with power from on high**—implying (as the parallels show—Rom. xiii. 14; 1 Cor. xv. 53; Gal. iii. 27; Col. iii. 9, 10) their being so penetrated and acted upon by conscious supernatural "power" as to stamp with divine authority the whole exercise of their apostolic office, including, certainly, their *pen* as well as their *mouth.*

Glorious Ascension of the Risen Redeemer (50, 51). **50. And he led them out as far as to Bethany**—not to the village itself, which would be no congenial spot; but "as far as to Bethany"—meaning, probably, to that side of the mount of Olives where the road strikes down to Bethany; for there is every reason to concur in the early tradition that from Mount Olivet our Lord took His flight on high. But how came Jesus and the Eleven to be now together at Bethany, having been last together in Galilee? The feast of Pentecost, now within ten days, would bring the disciples to Jerusalem, and no doubt their Lord appointed to meet them in the neighbourhood of it, probably somewhere on the way to Bethany. **and he lifted up his hands, and blessed them. 51. And it came to pass, while he blessed them, he was parted from them, and carried up into heaven.** Sweet intimation! The Incarnate, Crucified, Risen One, now on the wing for heaven—waiting only for those odorous gales which were to waft Him to the skies—goes away in benedictions, only to continue them, in yet higher style, as the Glorified and Enthroned One, until He come again. And O, if angels were so transported at His birth into this scene of tears and death, what must have been their ecstasy as they welcomed and attended Him up "far above all heavens" into the presence-chamber, and conducted Him to the right hand, of the Majesty on High! Thou hast an everlasting right, O my Saviour, to that august place. The Brightness of the Father's glory, enshrined in our nature, hath won it well, for He poured out His soul unto death. Therefore hath He ascended on high, and led captivity captive, receiving gifts for men, yea for the rebellious, that the Lord God might dwell among them. 'Thou art the King of glory, O Christ.' Lift up your heads, O ye gates, be lifted up, ye everlasting doors, that the King of glory may come in! Even so wilt thou change these vile bodies of ours, that they may be like unto Thine own glorious body; and then, with gladness and rejoicing shall they be brought, they shall enter into the King's palace! For fuller particulars of the Ascension, by the same Evangelist, see on Acts i. 9-11.

Return of the Eleven to Jerusalem (52, 53). **And they worshipped him**—beyond all doubt, in the sense of supreme worship. In the whole Gospel of St. Luke, remarks *Stier*, we have this word to 'worship' [προσκυνεῖν] but in one other place—ch. iv. 7, 8—where it is used of the honour due to God alone; and in the Acts only in the following passages, all in the same sense: ch. [vii. 43]; viii. 27; xxiv. 11; x. 25, 26. In this last passage, though Cornelius meant only subordinate worship, Peter rejected it—as only a *man.* And what was the worship of His bright escort on His way upwards, and of His reception above? (Ps. lxviii. 18, 19). **and returned to Jerusalem**—as instructed to do; but not till, after gazing as if entranced up into the blue vault in which He had disappeared, they were gently checked by two shining ones, who assured them He would come again to them in the like manner as He had gone into heaven. (See on Acts i. 10, 11.) This made them return, not with disappointment at His removal, but **with great joy: 53. And were continually in the temple**—that is, every day at the regular hours of prayer until the day of Pentecost, **praising and blessing God**—in higher than Jewish strains now, though in the accustomed forms. **Amen.** This "Amen" is excluded from the text by *Tischendorf* and *Tregelles*, in which they are followed by *Alford.* But the authorities in its favour are, in our judgment, decisive. *Lachmann* inserts it. Probably some might less see the import of it *here* than in the other Gospels. But who that has followed our Evangelist, till he leaves his readers with the Eleven, "praising and blessing God" after their Lord's ascension to the Father, could refrain from adding his own "Amen," even though the Evangelist had not written it? It is as though he had said, 'For such wonders, the record of which is here closed, let every reader join with those Eleven continually in praising and blessing God.'

For Remarks on the Resurrection-scene, see those on the corresponding Section of the First Gospel—Matt. xxviii. 1-15. But on the remaining portion of this chapter we add the following—

Remarks.—1. Were we asked to select from the Four Gospels the six verses which bear the most indubitable marks of exact historic reality, we might be at some loss, from the profusion of such that stud the pages of the Evangelical Narrative. But certainly the doleful tale of the two disciples going to Emmaus—of expectations regarding Jesus of Nazareth, raised only to be crushed to the lowest, with the half-trembling, half-hoping allusion to the reports of His resurrection by "certain women of their company," and all this poured into the ear of the risen Saviour Himself, who had overtaken and made up to them as an unknown fellow-traveller (*vv.* 19-24)—this must be held by every competent and candid judge to pass all the powers of human invention. Some, perhaps, will think that the subsequent manifestation in the breaking of bread is stamped with a self-evidencing glory at least equally great. Perhaps it is. Or that scene in the apartment at Jerusalem, where the disciples were met the same evening, when the two who had hastened back from Emmaus entered it to tell their tale of transport, but were anticipated by one equally thrilling, and while they were all unburdening themselves, breathless with joy, the Redeemer made His own appearance in the midst of them! But the difficulty of deciding which is most life-like arises from the multitude of such scenes, whose reality those *photographic* Records have printed indelibly on the minds of all unsophisticated readers in every age and all lands. And what those Records do *not* relate bears higher testimony to them, perhaps, than even their positive statements. Apocryphal Gospels would have been ready enough to tell us what passed between the risen Redeemer and the disciple who thrice denied Him, at their first meeting on the resurrection-morn. But while only one of the Four Evangelists notices the fact at all, even from him all the information we have is contained in the thrilling announcement by the company assembled in the evening to the two from Emmaus, "The Lord is risen indeed, and hath appeared to *Simon!*" Not for the perplexed only do we recur to this subject

53 him, and returned to Jerusalem with great joy: and were continually [e]in
the temple, praising and blessing God. Amen.

A. D. 33.

[e] Acts 2. 46.

again and again. To look into these things is an exercise as healthy as delightful to those who love the Lord Jesus. For thus do we find ourselves in the midst of them; and the views which such scenes disclose to us of the person of the Lord Jesus, His Work in the flesh, His dying love, His resurrection-power and glory, have such a *historical* form as imparts to them undying life, immortal youth and beauty. 2. How often in hours of darkest despondency are the disciples of the Lord Jesus favoured with His presence, though their eyes for a time are holden that they shall not know Him? For all He does, perhaps, at such seasons is to keep them from sinking, and cheer them with hopes of relief, through the talk, it may be, of some friend who speaks to their case and reminds them of forgotten truths and promises. But this is itself relief enough to be sweet in the meantime; and dimly though Himself may be discerned in all this, the feeling which it begets finds vent in such strains as these,—

'Abide with me from morn to eve,
For without Thee I cannot live:
Abide with me when night is nigh,
For without Thee I cannot die.'—Keble.

But there are times when the presence of Jesus makes itself almost as manifest as when the eyes of the two at Emmaus were opened and they knew Him. And never, perhaps, more than "in the breaking of bread." It was indeed a common meal which those two prepared for their unknown Guest. But His taking the place of Master at their own table, and His "taking the bread, and blessing, and breaking, and giving to them"—bringing up the whole scene of the Last Supper, and disclosing to them in this Guest their own risen Lord—converted it into a communion in the most exalted sense. And thus sometimes, when we sit down to that table which He hath ordered to be spread, with no higher feeling at the moment than of simple obedience to a commanded duty, He "makes Himself known to us in the breaking of bread" as evidently as if Himself said to us with His own lips, "This is my body which is broken for thee. This cup is the New Testament in my blood shed for many, for the remission of sins; drink thou and all of it." But such vivid disclosures of Jesus to the spirit, like cordials to a sinking frame, are not what we live upon; and just as, when the end was answered, He vanished out of the sight of the two wondering disciples, and, when on the mount of transfiguration the voice was past, Jesus was left alone, the glory gone, and Jesus only, as before, with the three astonished disciples—so are we left to go up through this wilderness leaning on our Beloved through the medium of the *word*, of which Jesus Himself says, "Sanctify them through thy truth: Thy word is truth." 3. What a testimony to the *divine authority* and *evangelical sense* of the Old Testament Scriptures have we in the expositions of them by the Lord Jesus, first to the two going to Emmaus, and afterwards to the company of disciples assembled at Jerusalem on the same evening of the resurrection-day? He who denies, or would explain away, either of these—and both certainly stand or fall together—must settle it with Christ Himself; but with those who, in our day, dispute even His authority, and yet call themselves Christians, this is not the place to dispute—nor, perhaps, would it be of much avail. But, 4. Who that reads with simple faith what is here written of Christ's direct access to the human spirit, and power to open its faculties to the reception of truth (*v.* 45), can doubt His proper Divinity? It is, indeed, no more than He is said to have done to Lydia (see on Acts xvi. 14); nor is it more than the father of the lunatic boy ascribed to Him with tears (see on Mark ix. 24); and we must get rid of the whole Gospel History ere we can free ourselves of the necessity of believing that Jesus *has* this glorious power over the human heart. But to free ourselves from this obligation we want not. It is our joy that it is written in the Evangelical Narrative as with a sunbeam, and reflected in all the subsequent writings of the New Testament. But for this, who would commit the keeping of his eternal all to Him? But "we know in Whom we have believed, and are persuaded that He is able to keep that which we have committed unto Him against that day" (see on 2 Tim. i. 12). 5. The *identity* of the Risen with the Crucified body of the Lord Jesus is beyond all doubt what our Lord intended to convince His disciples of, by eating before them, and by showing them His hands and His feet, with "the print of the nails." This is a truth of unspeakable importance, and delightful beyond the power of language to express. The varying forms in which He appeared to the disciples, in consequence of which He was not always immediately recognized by them, suggests the high probability that the resurrection bodies of the saints too will possess the same or analogous properties; and the conjecture that a process of progressive glorification during the forty days of His sojourn on earth, and consummated as He "went up where He was before"—though it derives but slender support from the words of John xx. 17, "I am *not yet* ascended"—may possibly have something in it. But one little fact speaks volumes on the perfect identity of the Risen Jesus Himself with Him who in the days of His flesh endeared Himself to the disciples in the familiar intercourses of life—that when His appearance in the garden quite deceived Mary Magdalene, that one word "*Mary!*" fixed His identity to *her* beyond what all other proofs perhaps could have done (see on John xx. 16). And is it beyond the bounds of legitimate inference from this, that *personal recognition*, implying of course the vivid recollection of those scenes of the present life which constitute the ties of dearest fellowship, will be found so to connect the future with the present state—the perfection and glory of the one with the weakness, and wants, and tears, and vanities of the other—as to make it for ever delightfully manifest that with all its glory it is but the efflorescence of the present life of the redeemed? 6. And Thou art gone up to the Father, O Thou whom my soul loveth! It is Thy proper home. Thou hast but ascended up where Thou wast before. And it was expedient for us that Thou shouldst go away. For otherwise the Comforter would not have come. But He *is* come. Thou hast sent Him to us; and He hath glorified Thee as Thou never wast nor, without Him, would have been in the Church. Now, repentance and remission of sins is in course of being preached in Thy name among all nations. Beginning at Jerusalem, bloody Jerusalem, it shall reach in its triumphs the most desperate cases of human guilt. But Thou shalt come again, and receive us to Thyself, that where Thou art we may be also. Even so, come, Lord Jesus! The grace of our Lord Jesus Christ be with all that read these lines. Amen.

THE GOSPEL ACCORDING TO

ST. JOHN.

---

1 IN the beginning [a]was the Word, and the Word was [b]with God, [c]and
2 the Word was God. The same was in the beginning with God.
3 All things were made by him; and without him was not any thing made
4 that was made. In him was life; and the life was the light of men.

CHAP. 1.
a Rev. 19. 13.
b Zec. 13. 7.
c Isa. 9. 6.
ch. 10. 30.
Phil. 2. 6.

CHAP I. 1-18.—THE WORD MADE FLESH. As the Fourth Gospel was not written until the other three had become the household words and daily bread of the Church of Christ—thus preparing it, as babes are by milk, for the strong meat of this final Gospel—so, even in this Gospel, the great key-note of it, that "*The Word was made Flesh,*" is not sounded until, by thirteen introductory verses, the reader has been raised to the altitude and attempered to the air of so stupendous a truth. **1. In the beginning was the Word, and the Word was with God, and the Word was God.**

Three great things are here said of The Word: First, He was "in the beginning" [ἐν ἀρχῇ = בְּרֵאשִׁית, Gen. i. 1]. Thus does our Evangelist commence his Gospel with the opening words of the book of Genesis. Only, as *Meyer* remarks, he raises the historical conception of the phrase, which in Genesis denotes the first moment of *time*, to the absolute idea of *pre-temporality*. That the words "In the beginning" are here meant to signify, 'Before all time' and all created existence, is evident from *v.* 3, where all creation is ascribed to this Word, who Himself, therefore, is regarded as uncreated and eternal. See ch. xvii. 5, 24; Col. i. 17.

Second, The Word "was with God" [πρὸς τὸν Θεόν]. This conveys two ideas—that He 'had a conscious personal existence distinct from God,' as one is distinct from the person he is "with;" and that He 'was associated with Him in mutual fellowship.' See on *v.* 18, and observe Zec. xiii. 7, "My Fellow, saith the Lord of hosts" [עֲמִיתִי, '*My Associate*']. Observe, that He who is called "God" here, is in 1 John i. 1, 2, called "THE FATHER:"—"The Word of Life (says this same exalted penman) was with the Father, and was manifested unto us." And such is the familiar language of Scripture, with respect to Him who *absolutely* is "God," but *personally*, and relatively to the Son, is "the Father."

Third, The Word "was God" [Θεὸς ἦν ὁ λόγος]. No other translation of this great clause is grammatically possible. Even should the order of the original words be retained (as in *Luther's* German version)—"and God was the Word," the sense will still be the same: 'and God the Word was.' But this is against the genius of the English language.

Each of these three pregnant statements is the complement of the other; each successive one correcting any misapprehension to which the others might give rise. Thus: The Word, says the Evangelist, was eternal. Yet this was not the eternity of the Father, nor the eternity of a mere attribute of the Father, but of One who is consciously and personally distinct from, and associated with, the Father. But neither is this the distinctness and fellowship of two different Beings—as if there were a plurality of Gods, but of two subsistences in the one absolute Godhead: in such sort that the absolute Unity of the Godhead—the great principle of all Religion—instead of being thereby compromised, is only transferred from the region of shadowy abstraction to that of warm personal life and love.

But why all these sharp definitions? it may be asked. Not to tell us of certain mysterious internal distinctions in the Godhead, which but for the Incarnation could never, perhaps, have been apprehended at all; but for the purpose of throwing light upon that stupendous assumption of our nature about to be announced, even as that assumption throws light back again upon the eternal distinctions and fellowships of the Godhead.

2. The same was in the beginning with God. Here the first and second statements are combined into one; emphatically reiterating the eternal distinctness of the Word from God ("the Father"), and His association with Him in the Unity of the Godhead. But now what does this peculiar title "The Word" import? The simplest explanation of it, we think, is this: that what a man's *word* is to *himself*—the index, manifestation, or expression of himself to others—such, in some faint sense, is "The Word" in relation to God; "He hath *declared* Him" (*v.* 18). For the origin and growth of this conception, see Remark 3 at the close of this Section. So much for the *Person* of The Word. Now for His *actings*. **3. All things were made by him**—that is, "all things" in the most absolute sense; as the next clause is intended to make evident; **and without him was not any thing made that was made** [οὐδὲ ἓν ὃ γέγονεν]. The statement is most emphatic—'without Him was not one thing made that hath been made.' To blunt the force of this, it is alleged that the word "by" [διὰ] in "by him" here means no more than 'through,' or 'by means of'—in the sense of subordinate instrumentality, not efficient agency. But this same preposition is once and again used in the New Testament of God's own efficient agency in the production of all things. Thus, Rom. xi. 36, "Of Him" [ἐξ]—as their eternal Source—"and *through* Him" [δι' αὐτοῦ]—by His efficient Agency—"and to Him" [εἰς]—as their last End—"are all things." And in Col. i. 16 the creation of all things—in the most absolute sense and in the way of efficient agency—is ascribed to Christ: "For by Him [ἐν αὐτῷ] were created all things" [τὰ πάντα]—that is, the entire universality of created things, as the all-comprehensive details that follow are intended to show—"whether they be thrones, or dominions, or principalities, or powers: all things were created *by* Him and for Him" [τὰ πάντα δι' αὐτοῦ καὶ εἰς αὐτὸν ἔκτισται]. See also Heb. i. 10-12, where creation, in the most absolute sense, is ascribed to Christ. **4. In him was life.** From simple *creation*, or calling into existence, the Evangelist now advances to a higher idea—the communication of *life*. But he begins by announcing its essential and original existence in Himself, in virtue of which He became the great *Fontal Principle* of life in all living, but specially in the high-

5 And [d]the light shineth in darkness; and the darkness comprehended
it not.
6, There [e]was a man sent from God, whose name *was* John. The same
7 came for a witness, to bear witness of the Light, that all *men* through
8 him might believe. He [f]was not that Light, but *was sent* to bear witness
of that Light.
9 *That* [g]was the true Light, which lighteth every man that cometh into
10 the world. He was in the world, and [h]the world was made by him, and
11 the world knew him not. He [i]came unto his own, and his own received
12 him not. But [j]as many as received him, to them gave he [1]power to

d ch. 3. 19.
e Mal. 3. 1.
f Acts 13. 25.
g Isa. 49. 6.
h Ps. 33. 6. 1 Cor. 8. 6.
i Luke 19. 14.
j Isa. 56. 5. Rom. 8. 15. Gal. 3. 26.
1 Or, the right, or, privilege.

est sense of life. Accordingly, He is styled "The Word of life" (1 John i. 1, 2). **and the life was the light of men.** It is remarkable, as *Bengel* notes, how frequently in Scripture *light* and *life*, on the one hand, and on the other, *darkness* and *death*, are associated: "I am the Light of the world," said Christ: "he that followeth Me shall not walk in darkness, but shall have the *light of life*" (John viii. 12). Contrariwise, "Yea, though I walk," sings the sweet Psalmist, "in the valley of the *shadow of death*, I will fear no evil" (Ps. xxiii. 4). Compare Job x. 21, 22. Even of God, it is said, "Who only hath *immortality*, dwelling in the *light* which no man can approach unto" (1 Tim. vi. 16). Here "the light of men" seems to denote all that distinctive light in men which flows from the life given them—intellectual, moral, spiritual: "For with Thee," says the Psalmist, "is the fountain of *life: in* Thy *light* shall we see light" (Ps. xxxvi. 9). **5. And the light shineth in darkness**—that is, in this dark fallen world; for though the Life was the light of men," they were "sitting in darkness and the shadow of death" when He came of whom our Evangelist is about to speak, with no ability to find the way either of truth or of holiness. In this thick darkness, then—in this obliquity, intellectual and moral, the light of the Living Word "shineth;" that is, by all the rays of natural or revealed teaching with which men were favoured *before* the Incarnation. **and the darkness comprehended it not** [οὐ κατέλαβεν]—'did not take it in.' Compare Rom. i. 28, "They did not like to retain God in their knowledge." Thus does our Evangelist, by hinting at the inefficacy of all the strivings of the *unincarnate* Word, gradually pave the way for the announcement of that final remedy—the Incarnation. Compare 1 Cor. i. 21.

6. There was a man sent from God, whose name was John. In approaching his grand thesis—the historical manifestation of the Word—our Evangelist begins with him who was at once a *herald* to announce Him and a *foil* to set off His surpassing glory. This—by the way—is sufficient to show that the five foregoing verses are not to be understood of the Incarnate Word, or of Christ's life and actions while He was upon the earth; as is alleged, not by Socinians only, but by some sound critics too—over-jealous of anything that seems to savour of the mystical, metaphysical, or transcendental in Scripture. **7. The same came for a witness**—[εἰς μαρτυρίαν]—rather, 'for witness,' **to bear witness of the Light, that all men through him** (John) **might believe. 8. He was not that Light**—rather, 'The Light' [τὸ Φῶς], **but [was sent] to bear witness of that**—or 'The' **Light.** Noble testimony this to John, that it should be necessary, or even pertinent, to explain that *he* was *not* The Light! But John found it necessary himself to make this disavowal (*v.* 19-21); and certainly none could be more deeply penetrated and affected by the contrast between himself and his blessed Master than he. (See on Luke iii. 15, 16; and on John iii. 27-34.) From the very first he saw and rejoiced to think that his own night-taper was to wax dim before the Day-spring from on high (ch. iii. 30).

9. That was the true Light, which lighteth every man that cometh into the world. So certainly this verse may be rendered (with most of the Fathers and the Vulgate; and of the moderns, with *Luther*, *Erasmus*, *Calvin*, *Beza*, *Bengel*, *Meyer*, *van Osterzee*). But "coming into the world," besides being rather a superfluous, is in Scripture quite an unusual, description of "every man." [It has been observed too—and the remark has great force—that the article τὸν should in that case have been inserted before ἐρχόμενον.] On the other hand, of all our Evangelist's descriptions of Christ, none is more familiar than His "coming into the world." See ch. iii. 19; vi. 14; xii. 46; xviii. 37; and compare 1 John iv. 9; 1 Tim. i. 15, &c. In this view of the words the sense will be, 'That was the true Light which, coming into the world, lighteth every man,' or became "The Light of the World." [So substantially *Lampe*, *Lücke*, *de Wette*, *Tholuck*, *Olshausen*, *Luthardt*, *Ewald*, *Alford*, *Webster and Wilkinson.*] If this be the Evangelist's meaning, it beautifully carries on his train of thought in *vv.* 4 and 5: *q. d.*, 'The Life was the Light of men; and though men resisted it when it shone but faintly before the Incarnation, yet when it came into the world (by the Personal assumption of flesh, about to be mentioned), it proved itself the one all-illuminating Light.' **10. He was in the world**—as already hinted, and presently to be more explicitly announced, **and the world was made by him**—for, as has been said, "all things were made by Him," **and the world**—that is, the intelligent world, **knew him not.** The language here is hardly less wonderful than the thought. Observe its compact simplicity and grand sonorousness—"the world" resounding in each successive member of the sentence, and the enigmatic form in which it is couched startling the reader, and setting his ingenuity a-working to solve the vast enigma of 'The world's Maker treading on and yet ignored by the world He made! **11. He came unto his own** [τὰ ἴδια], **and his own** [οἱ ἴδιοι]. It is impossible to give in English the full force of this verse. In the first clause it is 'His own [things]'—meaning 'His own Messianic rights and possessions:' in the second clause, it is 'His own [people];' meaning the peculiar people who were the more immediate subjects of His Messianic kingdom (see on Matt. xxii. 1). **received him not**—that is, as a *people;* for there were some noble exceptions, to whose case the Evangelist comes in the next clause. As for the nation, they said of Him, "This is THE HEIR, come let us kill Him" (Luke xx. 14). **12. But as many as received him**—as many *individuals*, out of the mass of that "disobedient and gainsaying people," as owned and embraced Him in His true character, **to them**

13 become the sons of God, *even* to them that believe on his name: which
[k]were born, not of blood, nor of the will of the flesh, nor of the will of
14 man, but of God. And [l]the Word [m]was made [n]flesh, and dwelt among
us, (and [o]we beheld his glory, the glory as of the only begotten of the
Father,) [p]full of grace and truth.

[k] Deut. 30. 6.
[l] Matt. 1. 20.
[m] Rom. 1. 3.
[n] Heb. 2. 14.
[o] Isa. 40. 5.
[p] Col. 2. 3, 9.

gave he power [ἐξουσίαν]. The word signifies either *authority* ('potestas') or *ability* ('potentia') or both. Here certainly both are included; nor is it easy to say which is the prevailing shade of thought. **to become the sons of God** [τέκνα Θεοῦ]—or rather, 'to become children of God;' not in *name* and *dignity* only, but in *nature* also, as the next verse makes evident. **even to them that believe on his name** [εἰς τὸ ὄνομα αὐτοῦ]. This is a phrase *never used of any creature* in Scripture. To 'believe one' [πιστεύειν τινί] means to 'give credit to a person's testimony.' This is used not only of prophets and apostles, but of Christ Himself, to signify the credit due to His testimony (as ch. iv. 21; v. 46, 47). But to 'believe *upon* one,' or '*on the name* of one,' signifies that *trust* which is proper to be placed on God only; and when applied, as it is here and in so many other places, to the Lord Jesus, it signifies that the persons spoken of placed *supreme faith* in Him. But what kind of sonship is this to which Christ introduces such believers in Him? The next verse tells us. **13. Which were born** [ἐγεννήθησαν]. Observe this word "born," or 'begotten.' It was not a name only, a dignity only, which Christ conferred on them: it was a new *birth*, it was a change of *nature*—the soul being made conscious, in virtue of it, of the vital capacities, perceptions, and emotions of a 'child of God,' to which before it was a total stranger. But now for the Source and Author of that new birth—both negatively and positively. **not of blood**—not of 'superior human descent,' as we judge the meaning to be, **nor of the will of the flesh**—not of 'human generation' at all, **nor of the will of man**—not of man in any of the ways in which his will brings anything about. By this elaborate, three-fold denial of the human and earthly source of this sonship, how emphatic does the following declaration of its real source become! **but of God.** A sonship strictly divine, then, in its source this was which Christ conferred on as many as received Him. Right royal gift, which Whoso confers must be absolutely Divine. For who would not worship Him who can bring him into the family, and evoke within him the life, of the children of God? Now comes the great climax, to introduce and raise us to the altitude of which the foregoing thirteen verses were penned.

14. And the Word was made flesh—or 'made *man*,' or took Human Nature in its present state of frailty and infirmity—in contrast both with what it was before the fall, and with what it will be in the state of Glory—without reference to its sinfulness. So we read, "All flesh is Grass" (1 Pet. i. 24); "I will pour out my Spirit upon all flesh" (Acts ii. 17); "Thou hast given Him power over all flesh" (ch. xvii. 2); "All flesh shall see the salvation of God" (Luke iii. 6). In this sense the word "flesh" is applied to Christ's human nature before His resurrection in Heb. v. 7, "Who in *the days of His flesh*," &c. And this is plainly the meaning of "flesh" here—'The Word was made,' or became Man, in the *present* condition of manhood, apart from its sinfulness in us. The other sense of "flesh" as applied to man in Scripture—'human nature under the law of sin and death,' as in Gen. vi. 3; John iii. 6; Rom. vii. viii.—is wholly inapplicable to Him who was born "the Holy Thing;" who in life was "holy, harmless, undefiled, separate from sinners;" and who in death "offered Himself without spot to God." Thus, by His Incarnation, married to our nature, He is henceforth and for ever personally conscious of all that is strictly human, as truly as of all that is properly divine; and our nature in His Person is redeemed and quickened, ennobled and transfigured. This glorious statement of our Evangelist was probably directed specially against those who alleged that Christ took flesh not really, but only apparently (afterwards called '*Docetæ*', or advocates of 'the *apparent* theory'). Against these this gentle spirit is vehement in his Epistles—1 John iv. 3; 2 John 7, 10, 11. Nor could he be too much so; for with the verity of the Incarnation all that is substantial in Christianity vanishes. **and dwelt among us** [ἐσκήνωσεν ἐν ἡμῖν]. The word strictly signifies 'tabernacled' or 'pitched His tent;' a word peculiar to John, who uses it four times in the Revelation—and in every case in the sense, not of a temporary sojourn, as might be supposed, but of a *permanent stay:* Rev. vii. 15, "Therefore are they before the Throne of God, and serve Him day and night in His temple, and He that sitteth upon the Throne shall *dwell* [σκηνώσει] among them;" and ch. xxi. 3, "And I heard a great voice out of heaven, saying, Behold, the tabernacle of God is with men, and He will *dwell* [σκηνώσει] with them." (So Rev. xii. 12; xiii. 6.) Thus, then, is He wedded for ever to our flesh; He has entered this tabernacle to go no more out. But the specific allusion in this word is doubtless to that tabernacle where dwelt the *Shechinah*, as the Jews called the manifested "glory of the Lord" (see on Matt. xxiii. 38, 39): and this again shadowed forth God's glorious residence, in the person of Christ, in the midst of His redeemed people: Ps. lxviii. 18, "Thou hast ascended on high, Thou hast led captivity captive: Thou hast received gifts for men; yea, for the rebellious also, that the Lord God might dwell [among them]" [לִשְׁכּוֹן, τοῦ κατασκηνῶσαι]. See also Lev. xxvi. 11, 12, "And I will set my tabernacle among you, and my soul shall not abhor you. And I will walk among you, and be your God, and ye shall be my people;" and Ps. cxxxii. 13, 14; Ezek. xxxvii. 27. That all this was before the Evangelist's mind, is put almost beyond doubt by what immediately follows. So *Lücke*, *Olshausen*, *Meyer*, *de Wette*—which last critic, rising higher than usual, says that thus were perfected all former partial manifestations of God in *an essentially personal and historically human manifestation.* (**and we beheld his glory.** The word [ἐθεασάμεθα] is more emphatic than the simple "saw" [εἴδομεν]: 'This glory,' the Evangelist would say, 'was revealed to our gaze; yet not to *sense*, which saw in Him only "the carpenter"—no, it was spiritually discerned' (1 Cor. ii. 14). Hence it was that Peter's noble testimony is ascribed, by Him who knew its Source, to Divine teaching (Matt. xvi. 16, 17). **the glory as** [ὡς] **of the only begotten of the Father**)—not a glory 'resembling' or 'like to;' but, according to a well-known sense of the word, a glory 'such as became' or 'was befitting' the Only begotten of the Father. (So *Chrysostom*, *Calvin*, *Lücke*, *Tho-*

15 John bare witness of him, and cried, saying, This was he of whom I
spake, He that cometh after me is preferred before me: [q]for he was
16 before me. And of his [r]fulness have all we received, and grace for grace.
17 For the [s]Law was given by Moses, [t]*but* grace and [u]truth came by Jesus
Christ.

A. D. 30.

[q] Col. 1. 17.
[r] Eph. 1. 6.
[s] Ex. 20. 1.
[t] Rom. 5. 21.
[u] ch. 14. 6.

luck, *Olshausen*, &c.) On the meaning of the word "Only begotten" [*μονογενὴς*], see on *v.* 18. But the whole phrase is expressed somewhat peculiarly here: it is 'the Only begotten'—not of [*ἐκ*], but '[forth] from the Father' [*παρὰ Πατρός*]; on the sense of which, see on *v.* 18. **full of grace and truth.** Our translators have here followed the grammatical construction of the verse, connecting this last clause with "the Word" [*ὁ Λόγος—πλήρης*], and thus throwing the intermediate words into a long parenthesis. But if we take it otherwise, and view this last as an independent clause, not unusual in the New Testament, and not requiring to be *grammatically* connected with any of the preceding words—which we prefer—the sense will still be the same. These words "Grace and Truth"—or in Old Testament phraseology, "Mercy and Truth"—are the great key-notes of the Bible. By "GRACE" is meant 'the whole riches of God's redeeming love to sinners of mankind in Christ.' Up to the period of the Incarnation, this was, strictly speaking, only in *promise;* but in the fulness of time it was turned into *performance* or "TRUTH"—that is, fulfilment. The Old Testament word, "Mercy," denotes the rich Messianic promises made to David; while "Truth" stands for God's faithfulness to these promises. Thus, Psalm lxxxix. sings, almost from beginning to end, of these two things, and pleads upon them, as the two great features of one and the same thing: "I will sing of the *mercies* of the Lord for ever: with my mouth will I make known thy *faithfulness* to all generations. For I have said, *Mercy* shall be built up for ever: thy *faithfulness* shalt thou establish in the very heavens. I have found David my servant . . . my *faithfulness* and my *mercy* shall be with Him. My *loving-kindness* will I not utterly take from Him, nor suffer my *faithfulness* to fail. O Lord, where are thy former *loving-kindnesses* which thou swearest unto David in thy *truth?*" And, not to quote more passages, in one great word of the evangelical prophet, and in one of his richest evangelical predictions, we have both ideas combined in that one now familiar expression, "The *Sure Mercies* of David." (Isa. lv. 3; see also Acts xiii. 34; 2 Sam. xxiii. 5.) In Christ's Person all that Grace and Truth which had for long ages been floating in shadowy forms, and darting into the souls of the poor and needy its broken beams, took everlasting possession of human flesh, and filled it full. By this Incarnation of Grace and Truth, the teaching of thousands of years was at once transcended and beggared, and the family of God sprang into manhood.

15. John bare witness of him, and cried—in testimony of the certainty and grandeur of the truth he was proclaiming, and the deep interest of all in it. The strict sense of the words [*μαρτυρεῖ καὶ κέκραγεν*] is, 'beareth witness and hath cried;' as if the testimony were still continued and the cry still resounding. But such delicate shades of meaning cannot easily be conveyed in any tolerable translation. **saying, This was he of whom I spake, He that cometh after me is preferred before me** ['Ο *ὀπίσω μου ἐρχόμενος ἔμπροσθέν μου γέγονεν*] or better, perhaps, 'has got before (that is, 'above') me.' **for he was before me** [*πρῶτός μου*]. Our translators have here used one English word, "before," to convey the sense of two different Greek words—the one [*ἔμπροσθεν*] primarily signifying 'before' in respect of *place*, and here of *official rank;* the other [*πρῶτος*] 'before' in point of *time.* Nor would it be easy to improve the translation without either marring the intentional terseness of the saying by too many words, or departing from the chaste simplicity required in any version of the Scriptures, and so characteristic of ours. Were we to render it, 'My Successor has become my Superior, for He was my Predecessor,' we should, indeed, convey to the mere English reader some idea of the *enigmatic* character and quaint structure of the saying, but we should fail to convey the true sense of the statement; for Christ, though posterior to John, was in no sense his Successor, and though prior to Him was in no proper sense his Predecessor. Doubtless, this enigmatic play upon the different senses of the words "before" and "after" was purposely devised by the Baptist to startle his readers, to set their ingenuity a-working to resolve his riddle, and when found, to rivet the truth conveyed by it upon their mind and memory. It may here be observed, that though it was no part of our Evangelist's plan to relate in detail the calling and ministry of John the Baptist—that having been sufficiently done in the preceding Gospels—he studiously introduces all his weightiest testimonies to his blessed Master; and the one now given seems to have been suggested by what had just been said of the glory of the Only begotten, and designed to confirm it. **16. And of his fulness**—that is, of grace and truth; resuming the thread of *v.* 14, which had only been interrupted for the purpose of inserting that testimony of John. **have all we received, and grace for grace** [*χάριν ἀντὶ χάριτος*]—that is, as we say, 'grace upon grace;' in successive communications and larger measures, as each was able to take it in. So the best critics understand the clause: other and older interpretations are less natural, and not more accordant with the Greek. The word "truth," it will be observed, is dropt here; and "GRACE" stands alone, as the chosen New Testament word for "all spiritual blessings" with which believers are enriched out of the fulness of Christ. **17. For the Law was given by Moses, but grace and truth came by Jesus Christ.** The law is here placed in opposition both to "grace" and to "truth"—but in different respects, of course. The law is opposed to *grace* only in that sense in which the law contains *no grace.* "The law," says the apostle, "worketh wrath" (Rom. iv. 15), that is, against all who break it; pronouncing a curse upon "every one that continueth not in all things which are written in the book of the law to do them" (Gal. iii. 10). If, then, under Moses, there was any grace for the guilty, it could not issue out of the bosom of the law, as a proclamation of moral duty; for "by the deeds of the law there shall no flesh be justified in His sight, for by the law is the knowledge of sin" (Rom. iii. 20). But the law was not given only to condemn. It "had a shadow of good things to come, though not the very image of the things" (Heb. x. 1); and it was this *shadow* of Gospel blessings which was given by Moses, while the "truth" or substance of them came by Jesus Christ. The law was but "a figure for the time then present, that could not make the worshippers perfect as

18 No [v] man hath seen God at any time; the [w] only begotten Son, which
is in the bosom of the Father, he hath declared *him*.

A. D. 30.
[v] Ex. 33. 20.
[w] 1 John 4. 9.

pertaining to the conscience; for it was not possible that the blood of bulls and of goats should take away sins" (Heb. ix. 9; x. 4). All the salvation, therefore, that was gotten under Moses was *on the credit* of that one offering for sins which perfects for ever them that are sanctified; and so they without us could not be made perfect (Heb. xi. 40).

18. No man—'No one' [οὐδεὶς] **hath seen God at any time**—that is, by immediate gaze; by direct, naked perception. In the light of this emphatic negation of all creature vision of God, how striking is what follows! **the only begotten Son, which is in the bosom of the Father, he hath declared him.** Had such a statement not come from the pen of apostolic authority and inspiration, who could have ventured to write or to utter it? Let us study it a little. [The extraordinary and extremely harsh reading which *Tregelles* here adopts, in deference to three of the oldest MSS., and some other authorities—'the only begotten God'—reading ΘC for YC—is met by such a weight of counter-authority in favour of the received reading, so thoroughly Joannean, that *Tischendorf* abides by it, and all but every critic approves it.] What now is the import of this phrase, "*The Only begotten Son,*" as applied to Christ here by the beloved disciple, and in three other places (ch. iii. 16, 18; 1 John iv. 9), and of "*the Only begotten from the Father,*" in *v.* 14? To say, with the Socinians and some others, that it means no more than "well beloved," is quite unsatisfactory. For when our Lord Himself spoke to the Jews of "*His Father,*" they understood Him to mean that God was His 'proper Father' [πατέρα ἴδιον], and so to claim equality with God; nor did He deny the charge (see on ch. v. 18). And that precious assurance of the Father's love which the apostle derives from His "not sparing His own Son" depends for its whole force on His being His *essential* Son, or partaker of His very nature [τοῦ ἰδίου Υἱοῦ οὐκ ἐφείσατο]; see on Rom. viii. 32. We are shut up, then, to understand the phrase, "Only begotten," as applied to Christ, of the Son's *essential* relation to the Father. The word "begotten," however—like every imaginable term on such a subject—is liable to be misunderstood, and care must be taken not to press it beyond the limits of what is clearly sustained by Scripture. That the Son is essentially and eternally related to the Father, in some real sense, as Father and Son; but that while *distinct* in Person (for "The Word was with God"), He is neither *posterior* to Him in time (for "In the beginning was The Word"), nor *inferior* to Him in nature (for "The Word was God"), nor *separate* from Him in being (for "The same was in the beginning with God"), but *One Godhead* with the Father:—this would seem to come as near to the full testimony of Scripture on this mysterious subject as can be reached by our finite understanding, without darkening counsel by words without knowledge. The peculiar expression in the 14th verse—"The Only begotten Son [forth] from the Father" [παρὰ Πατρὸς], and that equally remarkable one in *v.* 18, "The Only begotten Son which is in (or 'into,' or 'upon') the bosom of the Father" [εἰς τὸν κόλπον τοῦ Πατρὸς] seem to be the complement of each other: the one expressing, as we might say, His relation to the Father's essence—as 'forth from' it; the other, if we might so speak, His non-separation from Him, but this in the form of inconceivable Personal and loving nearness to Him. Thus does our Evangelist positively affirm of Christ, not only what he had just before denied of all creatures—that He "hath seen God" (see ch. vi. 46)—but that being 'in,' 'into,' or 'on' the bosom of the Father, He had access to His very heart, or, without a figure, that He, and He only, *has absolute knowledge of God*. Well, **he hath declared him** [ἐκεῖνος ἐξηγήσατο]—'He declared him' who only could, as The Word, the Reflection, the Expression of His very Self; He, who, living ever on His bosom, gazes on Him ever, knows Him ever, with an intimate perception, an absolute knowledge peculiar to Himself—He it is whom the Father hath sent to "declare Him." And thus does our Evangelist close this great Introductory Section of his Gospel as he began it, with The Word.

Remarks.—1. Since God so ordered it that the first converts and the infant churches should be thoroughly familiarized with the History of His Son's work in the flesh on the lower platform of the First Three Gospels, ere they were lifted up by this Fourth Gospel to the highest view of it, we may infer, that just as we also have thriven upon the milk of the other Gospels will be our ability to digest and to grow upon the strong meat of this last and crowning Gospel. And might it not be well, in the public exposition of the Gospel History, to advance from the *corporeal* Gospels, as the Fathers of the Church were wont to call them, [τὰ σωματικὰ], to what by way of eminence they called the *spiritual* Gospel [τὸ πνευματικόν]? Nevertheless, even in this Gospel there is an exquisite net-work of concrete outward History, which captivates even the rudest and youngest readers; and it breathes such an atmosphere of love and heaven, that the deep truths which are enshrined in it possess attractions they would not otherwise have had. Thus, each is perfect in its own kind, and all are one pearl of great price. 2. Did our Evangelist, before uttering the key-note of his whole Gospel, pave the way for it by so many introductory verses? What need, then, to put off the shoe from off our feet when we come to tread such holy ground! 3. With respect to the origin and growth of this term, "The Word," in the sense in which it is here used—for it certainly was not used by our Evangelist for the first time—we find the teaching of the Old Testament from the first tending gradually towards that conception of it which is here presented: "The word of the Lord" is said to have given birth to creation, and to carry into effect all the divine purposes; "wisdom" is spoken of as eternally with God, and rejoicing in the habitable parts of His earth; "The Angel of Jehovah" is identified with Jehovah Himself; men are warned to "kiss the Son, lest He be angry, and they perish from the way;" and the form of that fourth mysterious Person who was seen walking in Nebuchadnezzar's burning fiery furnace, with the three Hebrew youths, was "like the Son of God." These conceptions, combined, would familiarize the thoughtful with something very like what is here said of The Word. Accordingly, the more profound Jewish theologians constantly represented "The Word of the Lord" [מֵימְרָא דַי״] as the Personal Agent by whom all divine operations were performed. In a word, about the time of our Lord the Alexandrian Jews, with *Philo* at their head, engrafting the Platonic philosophy upon their own reading of the Old Testament, had fallen into the familiar use of language closely resembling that employed here; and this phraseology was doubtless current throughout all the region in which our Evangelist

19 And this is the record of John, when the Jews sent priests and Levites
20 from Jerusalem to ask him, Who art thou? And [x]he confessed, and
21 denied not; but confessed, I am not the Christ. And they asked him,
What then? Art thou [y]Elias? And he saith, [z]I am not. Art thou

A. D. 30.

x ch. 3. 28. Acts 13. 25.
y Mal. 4. 5.
z Luke 1. 17.

probably wrote his Gospel, and must have been familiar to him. And yet, in two important points, this language of the Jewish Platonists, even where it seems to come the nearest to that of our Evangelist, is vastly removed from it. First, it was so *hazy*, that scholars who have studied their writings the most deeply are not agreed whether by The Word [ὁ Λόγος] they meant a *Person* at all; and next, even if that were certain, this "Word" was never identified by them with the promised *Messiah.* The truth seems to be, that this beloved disciple, having often reflected on such matters in the stillness of his own meditative and lofty spirit, and now, after so long a silence, addressed himself to the task of drawing up one more and final Gospel, did, under the guidance of the Spirit, *advisedly* take up the current phraseology, and not only thread his way through the corrupt elements which had mixed themselves up with the true doctrine of "The Word," but stamp upon that phraseology new conceptions, and enshrine for ever in these eighteen introductory verses of his Gospel the most sublime of all truths regarding the Incarnate Redeemer. 4. Within the limits of this Section all the heresies that have ever been broached regarding the Person of Christ—and they are legion—find the materials of their refutation. Thus, to the *Ebionites* and the *Artemonites* of the second century, to *Noetus* and *Paul of Samosata* of the third, and to *Socinus* and his followers at and since the Reformation—who all affirmed that Christ was a mere man, more or less filled with the Divinity, but having no existence till He was born into our world—our Evangelist here cries, "IN THE BEGINNING was the Word." To *Arius*, in the fourth century, and to a host of modern followers—who affirmed that Christ, though he existed before all other created beings, was himself but a creature; the first and highest indeed, but still a creature —our Evangelist here cries, "The Word WAS GOD:" All things were made by Him, and without Him was not one thing made that was made: In Him was life, and the life was the light of men: as many as received Him to them gave He power to become children of God. The Only begotten Son, who is in the bosom of the Father, He declared Him." To *Sabellius*, in the third century, and not a few speculative moderns—who held that there is but one Person in the Godhead; the Father, Son, and Holy Ghost being but three *modes* in which the one Person has been pleased to manifest Himself for man's salvation—our Evangelist cries, "The Word was in the beginning WITH GOD: He is the Only begotten from the Father, and He it is that declared Him." To those afterwards called *Docetæ*—who, as early as the first century, held that Christ took only an apparent, not a real, humanity; and *Apollinaris*, in the fourth century, and some modern followers—who affirmed that Christ, though He took a human body, took no rational human spirit, the Word supplying its place as the only intelligence by which He acted; and the *Nestorians* of the fifth century—who held, or were charged with holding, that that Holy Thing which was born of the virgin was not "the Son of God," but only the son of Mary, to whom the Son of God joined Himself, making two separate persons, though closely united; and finally to the *Eutychians*—who, in the same century, affirmed that the divine and human natures were so blended as to constitute together but one nature, having the properties of both: to one and all of these errorists (in language at least, though there is reason to think not always in actual belief) our Evangelist here cries, in words of majestic simplicity and transparent clearness, "THE WORD WAS MADE FLESH;" using that term "Flesh" in its well-known sense when applied to human nature, and leaving no room for doubt in the unsophisticated reader that He *became Man* in the only sense which those words naturally convey. The Fathers of the Church, who were driven to the accurate study of this subject by all sorts of loose language and floating heresies regarding the person of Christ, did not fail to observe how warily our Evangelist changes his language from "WAS" to "BECAME" [ἦν-ἐγένετο] when he passes from the *pre-existent* to the *incarnate* condition of the Word, saying, "In the beginning *was* the Word—and the Word *was made* flesh." To express this they were wont to say, 'Remaining what He was, He became what He was not.' 5. Did the truth of Christ's Person cost the Church so much study and controversy from age to age against persevering and ever-varying attempts to corrupt it? How dear, then, should it be to us, and how jealously should we guard it, at the risk of being charged with stickling for human refinements, and prolonging fruitless and forgotten controversies! At the same time, 7. The glory of the Only begotten of the Father is best seen and felt, not in the light of mere abstract phraseology—sanctioned though it be by the whole orthodox Church, unexceptionable in form, and in its own place most valuable—but by tracing in this matchless History His footsteps upon earth, as He walked amid all the elements of nature, the diseases of men, and death itself, amidst the secrets of the human heart, and the rulers of the darkness of this world—in all their number, subtlety, and malignity—not only with absolute ease as their conscious Lord, but as if themselves had been conscious of their Master's presence and felt His will to be their resistless law.

19-51.—TESTIMONIES OF THE BAPTIST TO JESUS ADDRESSED TO A JEWISH DEPUTATION AND TO HIS OWN DISCIPLES—JESUS BEGINS TO GATHER DISCIPLES.

Testimony Addressed to a Jewish Deputation (19-28). **19. And this is the record**—or 'testimony,' **of John, when the Jews sent priests and Levites from Jerusalem to ask him, Who art thou?** By "*the Jews*" here, and almost always in this Gospel, is meant—not the Jewish nation, as contrasted with the Gentiles, but—'*the rulers*' of the nation. **20. And he confessed, and denied not; but confessed, I am not the Christ.** In thus disclaiming the Messiahship for himself, he resisted a strong temptation; for many were ready to hail the Baptist as himself the Christ. But as he gave not the least ground for such impressions of him, so neither did he give them a moment's entertainment. **21. And they asked him, What then? Art thou Elias? And he saith, I am not**—that is, not Elijah in his own proper person, whom the Jews expected, and still expect, before the coming of their Messiah. **Art thou that prophet?** [ὁ προφήτης]—rather, 'the prophet;' announced in Deut. xviii. 15, &c., about whom they seem not to have been agreed whether he were the same with the promised Messiah or no. **And he answered, No. 22. Then said they unto him, Who art thou? that we may give an**

22 [2]that prophet? And he answered, No. Then said they unto him, Who
art thou? that we may give an answer to them that sent us. What sayest
23 thou of thyself? He said, I *am* the voice of one crying in the wilderness,
24 Make straight the way of the Lord, as [a]said the prophet Esaias. And
25 they which were sent were of the Pharisees. And they asked him, and
said unto him, Why baptizest thou then, if thou be not that Christ, nor
26 Elias, neither that prophet? John answered them, saying, I baptize with
27 water: [b]but there standeth one among you, whom ye know not; he it
is, who coming after me, is preferred before me, whose shoe's latchet I
28 am not worthy to unloose. These things were done in Bethabara beyond
Jordan, where John was baptizing.
29 The next day John seeth Jesus coming unto him, and saith, Behold
30 [c]the Lamb of God, [d]which [3]taketh away the sin of the world! This is
he of whom I said, After me cometh a man which is preferred before me:
31 for he was before me. And I knew him not: but that he should be
made manifest to Israel, therefore am I come baptizing with water.
32 And John bare record, saying, I saw the Spirit descending from heaven

A. D. 30.

[2] Or, a prophet.
[a] Isa. 40. 3.
[b] Mal. 3. 1.
[c] Gen. 22. 7,8. Ex. 12. 3. Num. 28. 3-10. Isa. 53. 7. 1 Pet. 1. 19. Rev. 5. 6.
[d] 1 Cor. 15. 3. Gal. 1. 4. Heb. 1. 3. Heb. 2. 17. Heb. 9. 28. 1 Pet. 2. 24. 1 John 2. 2. Rev. 1. 5.
[3] Or, beareth.

answer to them that sent us. What sayest thou of thyself? 23. He said, I am the voice of one crying in the wilderness. His Master was "The Word;" the herald was but a *voice* crying through the Judean desert, Make ready for the coming Lord! See on Matt. iii. 1-3. **24. And they which were sent were of the Pharisees.** As the Sadducees could hardly be expected to take much interest in such matters, this explanation is probably intended to do more than tell the reader that this deputation was of the other sect. It probably refers to their peculiar jealousy about any innovations on the traditional way of thinking and acting, and to prepare the reader for their question in the next verse. **25. And they asked him, and said unto him, Why baptizest thou then, if thou be not that**—'the' **Christ, nor Elias, neither that**—'the' **prophet?** Thinking that he disclaimed any special connection with the Messiah's kingdom, they very naturally demand his right to gather disciples by baptism. (See on ch. iii. 28.) **26. John answered them, saying, I baptize with water**—with water only; the higher, internal, baptism with the Holy Ghost being the exclusive prerogative of his Master. (See on Matt. iii. 11.) **but there standeth one among you, whom ye know not.** This must have been spoken after Christ's Baptism, and probably almost immediately after it. **27. He it is, who coming after me, is preferred before me**—see on *v.* 15. **whose shoe's latchet I am not worthy to unloose**—see on Matt. iii. 11. **28. These things were done in Bethabara** [בֵּית עֲבָרָה]—'ferry-house' or 'crossing-place.' But the true reading, as nearly all the best and most ancient MSS. attest, is 'Bethany:' not, of course, the well-known Bethany, at the foot of mount Olivet, but some village lying on the east side of the Jordan, which in the time of *Origen* had disappeared. **beyond Jordan, where John was baptizing.**

Testimony of the Baptist, addressed to his own disciples (29-36). **29. The next day**—the crowd, as we take it, having dispersed, and only his own disciples being present, **John seeth Jesus coming unto him.** This was probably immediately after the Temptation, when Jesus, emerging from the wilderness of Judea on His way to Galilee (*v.* 43), came up to the Baptist. But it was not to hold intercourse with him, however congenial that would have been; for *of this there appears to have been none at all from the time of His baptism even till the Baptist's imprisonment and death.* The sole object of this approach to the Baptist would appear to have been to receive from him that wonderful testimony which follows: **and saith**—immediately catching a sublime inspiration at the sight of Him approaching: **Behold the Lamb of God, which taketh away the sin of the world!** Every word here is emphatic, and precious beyond all expression. "THE LAMB" here, beyond all doubt, points to the *death* of Christ, and the *sacrificial* character of that death. The offering of a lamb every morning and evening, and of two on the morning and evening of every Sabbath day, throughout all the ages of the Jewish economy, had furnished such a language on this subject as to those who heard these words of the Baptist could need no explanation, however the truth thus expressed might startle them. But in calling Jesus "*the* Lamb," and "the Lamb *of God*," he held Him up as the one 'God-ordained, God-gifted, God-accepted' sacrificial offering. If, however, there could remain a doubt whether this was what the words were designed to convey, the explanation which follows would set it at rest—"Which taketh away the sin of the world." The word [αἴρων] here used, and the corresponding Hebrew word [נָשָׂא] signify both 'taking up' and 'taking away.' Applied to sin, they mean to 'be chargeable with the guilt of it' (Exod. xxviii. 38; Lev. v. 1; Ezek. xviii. 20), and to 'bear it away' (as in many places). In the Levitical victims both ideas met, as they do in Christ; the people's guilt being viewed as transferred to them, avenged in their death, and thus borne away by them (Lev. iv. 15; xvi. 15, 21, 22; and compare Isa. liii. 6-12; 2 Cor. v. 21). "The *sin*," says the Baptist, using the singular number to denote the collective burden laid upon the Lamb, and the all-embracing efficacy of the great Sacrifice; and "the sin of *the world*"—in contrast with the typical victims which were offered for Israel exclusively: 'Wherever there shall live a sinner throughout the wide world, sinking under that burden too heavy for him to bear, he shall find in this "Lamb of God" a shoulder equal to the weight.' Thus was the right note struck at the very outset. And what balm must it have been to Christ's own spirit to hear it! Never, indeed, was a more glorious utterance heard on earth; no, nor ever shall be. But it was uttered, as we think, in the hearing only of those who were in some measure prepared for it. **30. This is he of whom I said, After me cometh, &c.**—recalling the testimony he had borne before, and recorded in *v.* 15. **31. And I knew him not: but that he should be made manifest to Israel,**

33 like a dove, and it abode upon him. And I knew him not: but he that
sent me to baptize with water, the same said unto me, Upon whom thou
shalt see the Spirit descending, and remaining on him, the [e]same is he
34 which baptizeth with the Holy Ghost. And I saw, and bare record that
this is the Son of God.
35, Again, the next day after, John stood, and two of his disciples; and
36 looking upon Jesus as he walked, he saith, Behold the Lamb of God!
37 And the two disciples heard him speak, and they followed Jesus.
38 Then Jesus turned, and saw them following, and saith unto them,
What seek ye? They said unto him, Rabbi, (which is to say, being
39 interpreted, Master,) where [4]dwellest thou? He saith unto them, Come
and see. They came and saw where he dwelt, and abode with him that
40 day: for it was [5]about the tenth hour. One of the two which heard
John *speak*, and followed him, was Andrew, Simon Peter's brother.

A. D. 30.

[e] ch. 14. 26. ch. 20. 22. Acts 1. 5. Acts 2. 4. Acts 4. 8, 31. Acts 6. 3, 5, 8. Acts 7. 55. Acts 9. 17. Titus 3. 5, 6.

[4] Or, abidest.

[5] That was two hours before night.

therefore am I come baptizing with water. 32. And John bare record, saying, I saw [τεθέαμαι]—or 'I have seen' **the Spirit descending from heaven like a dove, and it abode upon him. 33. And I knew him not: but he that sent me to baptize with water, the same said unto me, Upon whom thou shalt see the Spirit descending, and remaining on him, the same is he which baptizeth with the Holy Ghost. 34. And I saw**—or 'have seen'—[ἑώρακα] **that this is the Son of God.** There is some appearance of inconsistency between the First and the Fourth Gospels, as to the Baptist's knowledge of his Master before the descent of the Holy Ghost upon Him. Matthew seems to write as if the Baptist had immediately recognized Him, and accordingly recoiled, as a servant, from baptizing his Master: whereas John makes the Baptist himself to say that he "knew Him not," and *seem* to say that until the Spirit descended upon Him he perceived no difference between Him and the other applicants for baptism that day. But by viewing the transaction in the following light the two statements may be harmonized. Living mostly apart—the One at Nazareth, the other in the Judean desert, to prevent all appearance of collusion—John only knew that at a definite time after his own call his Master would show Himself. As He drew near for baptism one day, the last of all the crowd, the spirit of the Baptist, perhaps, heaving under a divine presentiment that the moment had at length arrived, and an air of unwonted serenity and dignity—not without traits, probably, of the family features—appearing in this Stranger, the Spirit, we may imagine, said to him as to Samuel of his youthful type, "Arise, anoint Him, for this is He!" (1 Sam. xvi. 12). But just then would the incongruity be felt of the servant baptizing the Master, nay, a sinner the Saviour Himself; and then would take place the dialogue, recorded by Matthew, between John and Jesus. Then followed the Baptism, and thereupon the descent of the Spirit. And this visible descent of the Spirit upon Him, as He emerged out of the baptismal water, being the very sign which he was told to expect, he now knew the whole transaction to be divine; and catching up the voice from heaven, "he saw, and bare record that this is the Son of God." So, substantially, the best interpreters.

35. Again, the next day after, John stood [εἱστήκει—or 'was standing;' probably at his accustomed place. The reader will do well to observe that here, and in *v.* 29, we have the beginning of that chronological precision which is so marked a characteristic of this Gospel. **and two of his disciples; 36. And looking** [ἐμβλέψας]—fixing his eyes with significant gaze **upon Jesus as he walked.** Observe, it is not said this time that Jesus was coming to John. To have done that once (*v.* 29) was humility enough, as *Bengel* notes. But John saw Him simply "walking" [περιπατοῦντι], as if in solitary meditation; yet evidently designing to bring about that interview with two of John's disciples which was to be properly His first public act. **he saith, Behold the Lamb of God!** The repetition, in brief, of that wonderful proclamation, in identical terms and without an additional word, was meant both as a gentle hint to go after Him, and to fix the light in which they were to regard Him. And it had the desired effect—as we are now to hear.

The Calling of John and Andrew (37-40). **37. And the two disciples heard him speak, and they followed Jesus. 38. Then Jesus turned, and saw them following** [καὶ θεασάμενος αὐτοὺς ἀκολουθοῦντας]—'and looked upon them as they followed' (see on *v.* 36), **and saith unto them, What seek ye?** Gentle, winning question; remarkable as the Redeemer's *first public utterance.* **They said unto him, Rabbi (which is to say, being interpreted, Master,)**—an explanation which shows that this Gospel was designed for those who had little or no knowledge of Jewish phraseology or usages. **where dwellest thou?** As if to say, 'Lord, that is a question not to be answered in a moment; but had we Thy company for a calm hour in private, gladly should we open our burden.' **39. He saith unto them, Come and see**—His *second utterance;* more winning still. **They came and saw where he dwelt** [μένει]—'where He stayed' or 'abode,' **and abode**—rather 'remained' [ἔμειναν] **with him that day: [for].** This word "for" [δὲ] is no part of the original text, as the evidence decisively shows. **it was about the tenth hour.** According to the Roman reckoning—from midnight to midnight—this would be with us ten o'clock in the morning: according to the Jewish reckoning—from six in the morning to six in the evening—the tenth hour here would be with us four in the afternoon, or within two hours of the close of the day. *Olshausen, Tholuck, Ebrard, Ewald* understand the Evangelist in the former sense; in which case they must have spent with our Lord a far greater length of time than, we think, is at all probable. To us there appears to be no reasonable doubt that the latter reckoning is here meant, which would make their stay about two hours, if they left precisely at the close of the Jewish day, though there is no reason to suppose this. Indeed, the Greeks of Asia Minor and the Romans themselves had latterly begun to reckon time popularly by the *working* day—from six to six. In this sense, *Calvin, Beza, Bengel, Meyer, de Wette, van Osterzee, Alford, Webster*

41 He first findeth his own brother Simon, and saith unto him, We have
42 found the Messias, which is, being interpreted, [6] the Christ. And he
brought him to Jesus. And when Jesus beheld him, he said, Thou art
Simon the son of Jona: thou shalt be called Cephas, which is, by interpretation, [7] A stone.
43 The day following Jesus would go forth into Galilee, and findeth Philip,
44 and saith unto him, Follow me. Now Philip was of Bethsaida, the city
of Andrew and Peter.
45 Philip findeth Nathanael, and saith unto him, We have found him
of whom Moses [f] in the Law, and the [g] Prophets, did write, Jesus
46 of Nazareth the son of Joseph. And Nathanael said unto him,
Can there any good thing come out of Nazareth? Philip saith unto
47 him, Come and see. Jesus saw Nathanael coming to him, and saith

A. D. 30.

[6] Or, the Anointed. Ps. 2. 2. Dan. 9. 25.
[7] Or, Peter. Matt. 16. 18.
[f] Gen. 3. 15. Gen. 22. 18. Num. 21. 9. Deut. 18. 18.
[g] Isa. 9. 6. Isa. 53. Mic. 5. 2. Zec. 6. 12. Zec. 9. 9. Mal. 3. 1.

and Wilkinson, understand the Evangelist. **40. One of the two which heard John speak, and followed him, was Andrew, Simon Peter's brother.** It would appear that Andrew was Peter's elder brother. The other was certainly our Evangelist himself—because otherwise there seems no reason why he should not have named him; because, if not, he has not even alluded to his own calling; but chiefly, because it is according to his usual manner to allude to himself while avoiding the express mention of his name, and the narrative here is so graphic and detailed as to leave an irresistible impression on the reader's mind that the writer was himself a party to what he describes. His great sensitiveness, as *Olshausen* says, is touchingly shown in his representation of this first contact with the Lord; the circumstances are present to him in the minutest details; he still remembers the very hour: but he reports no particulars of those discourses of the Lord, by which he was bound to Him for the whole of his life; he allows everything personal to retire.

The Calling of Simon (41, 42). **41. He first findeth his own brother Simon.** Possibly, this may mean 'own brother' in contrast with step-brothers in the family. But the expression may here be used merely for emphasis. According to the received text [πρῶτος], the meaning is, 'He was the first to find;' but, according to what we think with *Lachmann* and *Tregelles*—but not *Tischendorf*—the better supported reading [πρῶτον], our English version gives the true sense. The meaning probably is, as we familiarly express it, 'the first thing;' that is, immediately on returning home. But the word "findeth" seems to imply that he had to seek for him, and could not rest until he was able to open to him his swelling heart. **and saith unto him, We have found the Messias, which is, being interpreted, the Christ.** See on Matt. i. 16, 21. The previous preparation of their simple hearts, under the Baptist's ministry, made quick work of this blessed conviction, while others kept hesitating till doubt settled into obduracy. And so it is still. **42. And he brought him to Jesus.** Happy brothers, thus knit together by a new tie! If Peter soon outstripped not only Andrew but all the rest, he would still remember that his brother "was in Christ before him," and was the blessed instrument of bringing him to Jesus. **And when Jesus beheld him** (see on 36), **he said, Thou art Simon the son of Jona**, or rather, "*Jonas*," as rendered in ch. xxi. 17—the full name serving, as *Tholuck* says, to give solemnity to the language (Matt. xvi. 17; John xxi. 17): **thou shalt be called Cephas** [כֵּיפָא, 'rock'], **which is, by interpretation, A stone** [Πέτρος]—'Rock.' See on Matt. xvi. 18.

The Calling of Philip (43, 44). **43. The day following Jesus would go forth** [ἠθέλησεν]—or, 'was minded to go forth' **into Galilee.** From the time when He "came from Nazareth" to be baptized of John, He had lived in Judea until now, when He was on His way back to Galilee. This makes it quite evident that the calling of Simon and Andrew at the sea of Galilee, recorded in Matt. iv. 18, must have been a subsequent transaction. But see on Matt. iv. 18; and on Luke v. 1. **and findeth Philip, and saith unto him, Follow me.** The other three might be said to find Jesus, but Philip was found of Jesus. Yet in every case, "we love Him because He first loved us," and in every case the response on our part must be as cordial as the call on His. **44. Now Philip was of**—rather, 'from' [ἀπὸ] **Bethsaida, the city** [ἐκ τῆς πόλεως]—it should be 'of the city' **of Andrew and Peter**—the city of their *birth* probably; for their place of residence was Capernaum (Mark i. 29). The fact mentioned in this verse throws light on a very small incident in ch. vi. 5 (on which see). That Philip did follow Jesus is not here recorded; but the next two verses more than express this.

The Calling of Nathanael (45-51). **45. Philip findeth Nathanael.** For the evidence that this disciple was no other than "Bartholomew," in the catalogues of the Twelve, see on Matt. x. 3. **and saith unto him, We have found him of whom Moses in the Law**—"for he wrote of Me," says our Lord Himself, ch. v. 46, **and the Prophets**—"who testified beforehand the sufferings of Christ, and the glory that should follow" [τὰς μετὰ ταῦτα δόξας], 1 Pet. i. 11, **did write, Jesus of Nazareth the son of Joseph.** This was the current way of speaking, and *legally* true. See on Matt. i. **46. And Nathanael said unto him, Can there any good thing come out of Nazareth?** Bethlehem, he perhaps remembered, was Messiah's predicted birth-place: Nazareth as a town had no place in prophecy, nor in the Old Testament at all. But its proverbial ill-repute may have been what directly suggested the doubt whether that could possibly be the place, of all places, whence Messiah was to issue. **Philip saith unto him, Come and see.** Noble remedy against pre-conceived opinions! exclaims *Bengel*. Philip, though probably unable to solve the difficulty, could show him where to get rid of it; and Nathanael takes his advice. See on ch. vi. 68. **47. Jesus saw Nathanael coming to him, and saith of him, Behold an Israelite indeed, in whom is no guile!**—not only no hypocrite, but, with a guileless simplicity not always found even in God's own people, ready to follow wherever truth might lead him, saying, Samuel-like, "Speak, Lord, for thy servant heareth." **48. Nathanael saith unto him, Whence knowest thou me?** Conscious that his very heart had been read, and that at this critical moment that which he most deeply felt—a single desire to

48 of him, Behold an Israelite indeed, in whom is no guile! Nathanael
saith unto him, Whence knowest thou me? Jesus answered and said
unto him, Before that Philip called thee, when thou wast under the fig
49 tree, I saw thee. Nathanael answered and saith unto him, Rabbi, thou
50 art the Son of God; thou art [h]the King of Israel. Jesus answered and
said unto him, Because I said unto thee, I saw thee under the fig tree,

A. D. 30.

h Ps. 2. 6. Ps. 110. 1. Isa. 9. 7. Ezek. 37. 21. Dan. 9. 25. Hos. 3. 5.

know and embrace the truth—had been expressed. **Jesus answered and said unto him, Before that Philip called thee**—showing He knew all that had passed at a distance between Philip and him, **when thou wast under the fig tree, I saw thee.** Of His being there at all the Evangelist says nothing, but tells us that Jesus, to the amazement of Nathanael, saw him there, and what he was there engaged in. What could He be doing? Fortunately we can answer that question with all but certainty. *Lightfoot* and *Wetstein* quote passages from the Jewish rabbins, showing that little knots of earnest students were wont to meet with a teacher early in the morning, and sit and study under a shady fig tree. Thither, probably—hearing that his master's Master had at length appeared, and heaving with mingled eagerness to behold Him and dread of deception—he had retired to pour out his guileless heart for light and guidance. "Good and upright is the Lord," we think we hear him saying; "therefore will He teach sinners in the way: The meek will He guide in judgment, and the meek will He teach His way: The secret of the Lord is with them that fear Him, and He will show them His covenant. My heart is inditing a good matter, I will speak of the things which I have made touching the King, my tongue shall be the pen of a ready writer: Thou art fairer than the children of men, Grace is poured into Thy lips, therefore God hath blessed Thee for ever. O that the salvation of Israel were come out of Zion! Why is His chariot so long in coming? Why tarry the wheels of His chariot? O that Thou wouldest rend the heavens, that Thou wouldest come down, that the mountains might flow down at Thy presence. For from the beginning of the world men have not heard, nor perceived by the ear, neither hath the eye seen, O God, beside Thee, what He hath prepared for him that waiteth for Him. My soul, wait thou only upon God, for my expectation is from Him. Let integrity and uprightness preserve me, for I wait on Thee. Till the day dawn, and the shadows flee away, I will get me to the mountain of myrrh, to the hill of frankincense. Show me a token for good!" (See on Luke ii. 8.) At that moment, of calm yet outstretched expectancy, returning from his fig tree, "Philip"—missing him probably at his house, whither he had gone to seek him, and coming out in search of him—"findeth Nathanael, and saith unto him, We have found Him of whom Moses and the prophets wrote, Jesus of Nazareth, the son of Joseph." 'Of Nazareth? How can that be?' 'I cannot tell, but Come and see, and that will suffice.' He comes; and as he draws near, the first words of Jesus, who breaks the silence, fill him with wonder. 'Would ye see a guileless, true-hearted Israelite, whose one object is to be right with God, to be taught of Him, and be led by Him? this is he!' 'Rabbi, whence knowest thou me?' 'Guileless soul! that fig tree, with all its heaving anxieties, earnest pleadings, and tremulous hopes—without an eye or an ear, as thou thoughtest, upon thee—Mine eye saw it, Mine ear heard it all!' The first words of Jesus had astonished, but this quite overpowered and more than won him. Accordingly, **49. Nathanael answered and saith unto him, Rabbi, thou art the Son of God; thou art the King of Israel**—the one denoting His Personal, the other His Official dignity. How much loftier this than anything Philip had said to him! But just as the earth's vital powers, the longer they are frost-bound, take the greater spring when at length set free, so souls, like Nathanael and Thomas (see on ch. xx. 28), the outgoings of whose faith are hindered for a time, take the start of their more easy-going brethren when once loosed and let go. It may, indeed, be asked how Nathanael came so far ahead of the current views of his day as these words of his express. For though "The King of Israel" was a phrase familiar enough to the Jews, in their own sense of it, the phrase "Son of God" was so far from being familiar to them as a title of their promised Messiah, that they never took up stones to stone our Lord till He called Himself, and claimed the prerogatives of, God's own Son. We think there can be no doubt that Nathanael got this from the Baptist's teaching—not his *popular* teaching, recorded in detail, but his *inner* teaching to the circle of his own select disciples, whom he taught to recognize in the Messiah not only "the Lamb of God," but "the Son of God" (see on ch. iii. 27-36). **50. Jesus answered and said unto him, Because I said unto thee, I saw thee under the fig tree, believest thou?** 'So quickly convinced, Nathanael, and on this evidence only?'—an expression of admiration. Jesus saw in the quickness and the rapture of this guileless Israelite's faith a noble susceptibility, which He tells him should soon have food enough. And, no doubt, He felt the fragrance to His own spirit of such a testimony. **thou shalt see greater things than these. 51. And he saith unto him, Verily, verily, I say unto you, Hereafter.** [This phrase "hereafter"—ἀπ' ἄρτι—is excluded from the text by *Lachmann*, *Tregelles*, and *Tischendorf*, in his earlier editions, whom *Alford* follows. But the evidence in its favour is, in our judgment, decisive, and *Tischendorf* has restored it to the text in his last edition. *De Wette*, *Meyer*, and *Olshausen* concur in regarding it as part of the original text.] **ye shall see heaven open, and the angels of God ascending and descending upon the Son of man.** The key to this great saying is Jacob's vision on his way to Padanaram, (Gen. xxviii. 12, &c.) To show the patriarch that though alone and friendless on earth his interests were busying all heaven, he was made to see "heaven opened, and the angels of God ascending and descending upon a" mystic "*ladder* reaching from heaven to earth." 'By and by,' says Jesus here, 'ye shall see this communication between heaven and earth thrown wide open, and the Son of Man to be the real *Ladder* of this intercourse.' On the meaning of the word "hereafter"—or, as it should rather be, 'henceforth'—see on Mark xiv. 62. Here, for the first time, and at the very opening of His public ministry, our Lord gives Himself that peculiar title—"THE SON OF MAN"—by which He designates Himself almost invariably throughout, even till just before He was adjudged to die, when to the Jewish Sanhedrim He said, "Nevertheless I say unto you, Henceforth [ἀπ' ἄρτι] shall ye see *The Son of Man* sitting at the right hand of

51 believest thou? thou shalt see greater things than these. And he saith
unto him, Verily, verily, I say unto you, [i]Hereafter ye shall see heaven
open, and the angels of God ascending and descending upon the Son
of man.

A. D. 30.

[i] Gen. 28. 12. Matt. 3. 16. Luke 3. 21. Acts 7. 56.

power, and coming in the clouds of heaven" (Matt. xxvi. 64). But whilst our Lord hardly ever called Himself by any other name, it is a striking fact that by that name He was never once addressed, and never once spoken of, while He was on earth, and that, with two exceptions, He is never so styled in the succeeding parts of the New Testament. And even these two passages are no proper exceptions. For in the one (see on Acts vii. 56) the martyr Stephen is only recalling our Lord's own words to the Jewish council, as already fulfilled before His own vision in the presence of that same council: in the other passage (see on Rev. i. 13) the beloved disciple—having a vision of Jesus in the symbols of majesty and glory, power and grace, in the midst of the churches, as their living Lord—only recalls the language of Daniel's night vision of "*The Son of Man*," and tells us how he was able to identify this glorious One with Him on whose bosom himself had leaned at every meal when He was on earth, saying that He was "like unto the Son of Man." These peculiar passages, then, instead of contradicting, only confirm the remark, that by this name He was never spoken to, never spoken of, and in the churches never styled, and that it stands alone as His own chosen designation of Himself. Of the seventy-nine times in which it occurs in the Gospels, it is found seldomest in John—only eleven times—being there overshadowed by a still more august name, "The Son of God." Mark uses it but one time more; Luke twenty-six times; but in Matthew it occurs thirty times. This suggests a *Hebraic* origin of the phrase; and indeed there can be no doubt that it is fetched directly from Dan. vii. 13, 14 (on the occasion and scope of which, see on Mark xiii. 26): "I saw in the night visions, and behold [one] like THE SON OF MAN [כְּבַר אֱנָשׁ, *ὡς υἱὸς 'Ανθρώπου*] came with the clouds of heaven," &c. But what is the import of this peculiar title? It has a two-fold significance, we apprehend. Putting the emphasis on the last word, "The Son of *Man*," or of Humanity, it expresses the great fact that He took flesh of our flesh, that He "was made in the likeness of men," that "as the children were partakers of flesh and blood, He also Himself likewise took part of the same." Accordingly, in several passages it will be found that our Lord designed by this phrase to express emphatically the humiliation to which He had submitted in "being formed in fashion as a man." But when we put the emphasis upon the definite article, "*The* Son of Man," it will be seen that He thereby severs Himself from all other men, or takes Himself out of the category of ordinary humanity. And we believe that He thus holds Himself forth as "The Second Man," in contrast with "the first man, Adam," or, as He is otherwise called, "The Second Adam;" that is, the second Representative Man, in whose Person Humanity stood and was recovered, in opposition to the first Representative man, in whom Humanity fell and was ruined. So much for this peculiar phrase. But what is meant by "the angels of God ascending and descending upon the Son of Man?" Almost all expositors of any depth, from *Origen* to *Calvin*, and from *Calvin* to *Lücke*, and *Olshausen*, and *Tholuck*, and *Stier*, and *Alford*, set aside all reference to miraculous events, and see in it the opening up of a gracious intercourse between heaven and earth through the mediation of the Lord Jesus. If it be asked why, both in Jacob's vision and in our Lord's reference to it here, the angels are not said to "descend and ascend"—as we should expect, from and to their proper abode—but to "ascend and descend," we may give *Lücke's* beautiful suggestion, that they are *left* in their descending office, as if they went up only to come down to us again on yet other errands, and exercise an *abiding* ministry.

Remarks.—1. How sublimely noiseless were the first footsteps of that Ministry whose effects were to be world-wide and for all time—reaching even into eternity! How quietly were those five disciples first called—under one of whom the Christian Church rose first into visible existence, and achieved its earliest triumphs; while another—the youngest of them all, and Peter's companion and coadjutor in all his early sufferings and labours—after surviving them all, contributed to the Canon of Scripture writings which transcend, may we not say, all the rest in the impress which they bear of Christ Himself! See on Matt. xii. 16-21, with Remark 6 at the close of that Section. 2. Every disciple of the Lord Jesus is called in his own way. John and Andrew are drawn to Jesus, after the training they had received from the Baptist, by the sublime strain in which their master directed their attention to Him, and the Saviour's winning encouragement of their own advances. Simon is brought to Jesus by his brother Andrew. Jesus "findeth" Philip, and at once gives him that call to follow Him which needed not to be repeated. But Philip "findeth" Nathanael and fetches him to Jesus. Difficulties exist in that guileless man; but they vanish in a transport of wonder and exultation, on the Saviour revealing him all to himself. Even so it is still. But as He to Whom all come is One, so the grace that worketh in all to bring them is one; and a goodly fellowship it is, whose diversity only enhances the charm of their unity. Even as in the Kingdom of Nature,

'Wisely Thou givest—all around
Thine equal rays are resting found,
Yet varying so on various ground
They pierce and strike
That not two roseate cups are crown'd
With dew alike,'

so in the kingdom of grace. 3. What a glorious note was that to strike at the very outset of the Gospel—ere yet the Lord Jesus had opened His own 'mouth most sweet'—"Behold the Lamb of God, which taketh away the sin of the world!" and as it was so soon again repeated to the same audience, is it not clear that this was designed to be the great primary proclamation of Christ's servants in every land and in all ages? They are not to think it enough to show to sinners of mankind that there has been given a Lamb of God for the taking away of the sin of the world, and that this is the one all-availing sacrifice for sin; but when they have done this, they are to hold Him forth and bid burdened sinners *behold* Him, and know their burden removed in Him. Never, we may safely say, was any ministry divinely owned and honoured of which this has not been the alpha and the omega; nor has any *such* ministry been without the seals of Heaven's approval. 4. Difficulties in religion are best dealt with by taking a firm

2 AND the third day there was a marriage in Cana of Galilee; and
2 the mother of Jesus was there: and both Jesus was called, and his disci-
3 ples, to the marriage. And when they wanted wine, the mother of Jesus
4 saith unto him, They have no wine. Jesus saith unto her, [a]Woman,

A. D. 30.

[a] Matt. 15. 28. ch. 19. 26. ch. 20. 13, 15.

grasp of fundamental and undeniable truths. Nathanael's difficulties, though they were those of a sincere enquirer, were certainly not removed before he consented to come to Jesus; nor did Christ Himself remove them as a preliminary to Nathanael's believing on Him. But being furnished with transparent evidence of His claims, that honest heart waited not for more, but uttered forth its convictions at once. Difficulties may be removed, but even if they never be on this side of time, let us not spend our days in doubt and darkness; let us plant our foot upon the rock of manifest truth, and for the rest wait till the day dawn and the shadows flee away. 5. As guile in every form vitiates the religious character and shuts out divine teaching, so to be "without guile" is the beginning of all that is acceptable to God (Ps. xxxii. 2), and carries with it the assurance of Divine guidance in the path of truth and duty. It is one of the great characteristics of the predicted Christ that no deceit should be found in His mouth (Isa. liii. 9); and of a class of Christians distinguished for their fidelity to Him in times of general defection, that in their mouth was found no guile (Rev. xiv. 5); and of the restored remnant of Israel that they shall not speak lies; neither shall a deceitful tongue be found in their mouth (Zeph. iii. 13). All this would seem to imply that entire simplicity and freedom from guile is a character remarkable rather for its rarity even among God's own people. 6. As the joy of discovered truth is in proportion to the difficulties experienced in finding it, so when firmness of conviction bursts forth from the heart that has found Christ in a tide of emotion, it is to Him peculiarly grateful, as was that noble exclamation of Nathanael's. 7. If Christ be *Immanuel*, "God with us," we can understand His being the Ladder of mediatorial communication between heaven and earth—uniting in his glorious Person the nature of both, but on no other view of Christ is this explainable; and, in fact, none who dispute the one really believe the other. But 8. What thoughts does this idea of the "Ladder" suggest! Never a groaning that cannot be uttered enters into the ears of the Lord of sabaoth, but it first passes *up* this Ladder—for no man cometh unto the Father but by Him: Never a ray of light, never a breath of love divine, irradiates and cheers the dark and drooping spirit, but it first passes *down* this Ladder; for the Father loveth the Son and hath given all things into his hand, and, if we are "blessed with all spiritual blessings," it is "in Christ." Thus is He not only our "way" to the Father, but the Father's "way" to us. Needest thou, then, poor burdened heart, aught from thy Father, to keep thee from sinking, to bear thee through the trials of life, and to bring thee home at length to thy Father's house in peace? Lie like Jacob at the foot of this glorious Ladder, planted close by thee on this ground but whose top reacheth to heaven, and send up thy petition on this Ladder—make known thy request through Him: then look and listen, and thou shalt see, as Jacob did, "the Lord standing above it, and hear Him speaking down this Ladder into thine own ear the rich assurances of His love and power, His grace and truth, pledged "not to leave thee until He hath done that which He hath spoken to thee of." And with Jacob thou shalt say, "How dreadful is this place! This is none other than the house of God, and this is the gate of heaven." Well may the angels of God be the winged messengers of such an intercourse; and what a crowded Ladder, and what busy activities, are suggested to us by their thus "ascending and descending" on errands of love to us, the "*descending*" flight of them being the thought with which the curtain of this beautiful scene drops upon us!

CHAP. II. 1-12.—CHRIST'S FIRST MIRACLE, OR THE TURNING OF WATER INTO WINE, AT THE MARRIAGE IN CANA—BRIEF VISIT TO CAPERNAUM. The time of this Section is clearly expressed in the opening verse; and here, again, let the reader note the chronological precision of this Gospel.

Water Turned into Wine (1-11). **1. And the third day there was a marriage in Cana of Galilee.** It would take two days to travel from the Judean valley of the Jordan, where He parted with John—never to meet again, so far as we are informed—to Cana; and this marriage-day was the day following, or the third. It is not called Cana in Galilee to distinguish it, as *Eusebius* and *Jerome* thought, from Kaneh in the tribe of Asher (Jos. xix. 28), for that also would be reckoned to Galilee, according to the New Testament division of the country—but merely to note its geographical locality, and to let the reader know that Jesus had now returned to His own region, which He left in order to be baptized of John in Jordan. No remains of the village of Cana now exist; but the most probable site of it was a spot about three hours northward of Nazareth. Nathanael belonged to this village (ch. xxi. 2). **and the mother of Jesus was there**—whether as a relative or as an intimate acquaintance we have no means of knowing. Our Evangelist, it will be observed, never names the Virgin, but styles her "the mother of Jesus," from that reverence, probably, with which he had learnt to look up to her, especially since he "took her to his own home." **2. And both Jesus was called, and his disciples, to the marriage**—by special invitation, probably, at the instance of Jesus' mother. **3. And when they wanted wine** [ὑστερήσαντος οἴνου]—'the wine having failed;' perhaps, as *Bengel* suggests, from more being present than had been arranged for, **the mother of Jesus saith unto him, They have no wine**—evidently expecting some display of His glory, and hinting that now was His time. Not that she had witnessed any displays of His miraculous power before this at home, as *Calvin* thinks. The Evangelist, indeed, by calling this the "beginning of His miracles" (*v.* 11), seems to say the reverse; nor can we suppose He would make such needless displays before the time. But she had gathered probably enough from Him regarding the miraculous credentials which He was to furnish of His divine commission, to infer that He would on this occasion make a beginning; and with a natural impatience for the revelation to others of what she knew Him to be, and a certain womanly eagerness—mixed possibly with feelings of a less commendable kind—she brings the state of matters before Him. **4. Jesus saith unto her, Woman** [γύναι]—no term of disrespect in the language of that day. (See ch. xix. 26; xx. 13.) **what have I to do with thee?** [Τί ἐμοὶ καὶ σοὶ;= מַה לִּי וָלָךְ]. If such passages as Jos. xxii. 24; Jud. xi. 12; 2 Sam.

5 [b]what have I to do with thee? [c]mine hour is not yet come. His mother
6 saith unto the servants, Whatsoever he saith unto you, do *it*. And there
were set there six water-pots of stone, [d]after the manner of the puri-
7 fying of the Jews, containing two or three firkins apiece. Jesus saith
unto them, Fill the water-pots with water. And they filled them up to
8 the brim. And he saith unto them, Draw out now, and bear unto the
9 governor of the feast. And they bear *it*. When the ruler of the feast
had tasted the [e]water that was made wine, and knew not whence it was,
(but the servants which drew the water knew,) the governor of the feast
10 called the bridegroom, and saith unto him, Every man at the beginning
doth set forth good wine; and when men have well drunk, then that
11 which is worse: *but* thou hast kept the good wine until now. This
beginning of miracles did Jesus in [f]Cana of Galilee, [g]and manifested
forth his glory; and his disciples believed on him.
12 After this he went down to Capernaum, he, and his mother, and [h]his
brethren, and his disciples: and they continued there not many days.

A. D. 30.

[b] 2Sam.16.10. 2Sam.19.22. Luke 2. 49. 2 Cor. 5. 16.
[c] Eccl. 3. 1. ch. 7. 6.
[d] Mark 7. 3. Eph. 5. 26. Heb. 6. 2. Heb. 9. 10-19. Heb. 10. 22.
[e] ch. 4. 46.
[f] Jos. 19. 28.
[g] Deut. 5. 24. Ps. 72. 19. ch. 1. 14. ch. 5. 23. ch. 12. 41.
[h] Matt. 12. 46.

xvi. 10, be compared with Matt. viii. 29; Mark i. 24; Luke viii. 28, it will be seen that this, in the current language of the Old and New Testament, is the strongest expression of *no-connection* between the party speaking and the party spoken of. Here, it is an intimation on the part of Jesus to His mother that in thus officiously interfering with Him she was entering a region from which all creatures were excluded. A gentle, yet decided rebuke. (See Acts iv. 19, 20.) **mine hour is not yet come**—a hint that He *would*, nevertheless, do something, but at His own time; and so she understood it, as the next verse shows. **5. His mother saith unto the servants, Whatsoever he saith unto you, do it. 6. And**—or, 'Now' [δὲ] **there were set there six water-pots of stone, after the manner of the purifying of the Jews, containing two or three firkins apiece.** The "firkin" here mentioned [μετρητής], when it stands for the Jewish "bath," is a measure containing about seven and a half gallons; in Attic measure it held nine and a half gallons. Each of these huge water-jars, then, must have held some twenty gallons; designed for "the purifying" of the Jews (see Mark vii. 4). **7. Jesus saith unto them, Fill the water-pots with water. And they filled them up to the brim. 8. And he saith unto them, Draw out now, and bear unto the governor of the feast. And they bare it.** It will be observed that our Lord here *directs* everything, but Himself touches nothing: thus excluding all appearance or suspicion of collusion. Compare Elijah's methods on Carmel, 1 Ki. xviii. 33-35. **9. When the ruler of the feast had tasted the water that was made wine**—the total quantity being about a hundred gallons! **and knew not whence it was (but the servants which drew the water knew,) the governor**—or, 'the ruler;' it is the same word as before [ἀρχιτρίκλινος], **of the feast called**—or 'calleth' [φωνεῖ] **the bridegroom, 10. And saith unto him, Every man at the beginning doth set forth**—or 'place,' that is, on his table, ['the'] **good wine; and when men have well drunk** [μεθυσθῶσιν = יִשְׁכְּרוּ], or 'drunk freely,' as Song v. i. The man is speaking of the general practice. **then that which is worse**—or inferior: **but thou hast kept the good wine until now**—thus testifying, while ignorant of the source of supply, not only that it was real wine, but better than any at the feast. **11. This beginning of miracles did Jesus in Cana of Galilee, and manifested forth his glory.** Nothing in the least like this is said of the miracles of either prophets or apostles, nor could be said without manifest blasphemy of any mere creature. Being said here, then, by our Evangelist of the very first miracle of Christ, it is as if he had said, 'This was but the first of a series of such manifestations of the glory of Christ.' **and his disciples believed on him**—that is, were confirmed in the faith which they had reposed in Him before they had any miraculous attestation of what He was.

Brief Visit to Capernaum (12). **12. After this he went down to Capernaum**—said to be "down" because it lay on the shore of the Sea of Galilee. See on Matt. iv. 13. **he, and his mother, and his brethren.** See on Matt. xiii. 55, 56. **and his disciples**—the five so recently gathered, **and they continued there not many days**—for the reason mentioned in the next verse, because the Passover was at hand.

Remarks.—1. All sorts of attempts have been made to reduce this miracle to the level of something natural; some of them too ridiculous to be worth a moment's notice, save to show how desperate are the shifts to which those are driven who are not able to dispute the genuineness of the text, and yet are determined not to bow to the miraculous. Nor is that half-and-half theory of a mere acceleration in the ordinary processes of nature in the vintage—first suggested, in the honesty of his heart, by *Augustin*, and since defended by *Olshausen*—nor *Neander's* theory, that He merely intensified the powers of water so as to produce the same effects as wine, more worthy of acceptance as a satisfactory explanation of the miracle; which stands, and while the world lasts will stand, a glorious monument of the power of the Lord Jesus, and in a form which, as we shall presently see, is pregnant with the richest lessons. 2. In this His first miracle Christ would show what He meant to be throughout His whole ministry—in entire contrast to the ascetic retirement which suited the *legal* position of John. "John came neither eating nor drinking" socially with others: "The Son of Man," says Christ Himself, "came eating and drinking" in that very sense. 3. At a marriage Christ made His first public appearance in any company, and at a marriage He wrought this His first miracle—the noblest sanction that could be given to that divinely appointed institution. 4. As all the miracles of Christ were designed to hold forth the characteristic features of His mission—not only to redeem humanity from the effects of the Fall, but to raise it to a higher platform of existence even than at first—so in the present miracle we see this gloriously set forth. For as the miracle did not make *bad good*, but *good better*, so Christianity only redeems, sanctifies, and

13 And [i]the Jews' passover was at hand; and Jesus went up to Jerusalem,
14 and [j]found in the temple those that sold oxen and sheep and doves, and
15 the changers of money sitting: and when he had made a scourge of small
cords, he drove them all out of the temple, and the sheep, and the oxen;
16 and poured out the changers' money, and overthrew the tables; and said
unto them that sold doves, Take these things hence; [k]make not my
17 Father's house an house of merchandise. And his disciples remembered
that it was written, [l]The zeal of thine house hath eaten me up.
18 Then answered the Jews and said unto him, What sign showest thou
19 unto us, seeing that thou doest these things? Jesus answered and said
unto them, Destroy [m]this temple, and in three days I will raise it up.
20 Then said the Jews, Forty and six years was this temple in building,
21 and wilt thou rear it up in three days? But he spake [n]of the temple of

A. D. 30.

[i] Ex. 12. 14. Num. 28. 16. ch. 5. 1.
[j] Matt. 21. 12. Mark 11. 15. Luke 19. 45.
[k] Ps. 93. 5. 1 Tim. 6. 9, 10.
[l] Ps. 69. 9.
[m] Matt. 26. 61. Matt. 27. 40. Mark 14. 58.
[n] 1 Cor. 3. 16. 1 Cor. 6. 19. Col. 2. 9.

ennobles the beneficent but abused institution of marriage; and Christ's whole work only turns the water of earth into the wine of heaven. Thus "this beginning of miracles" exhibited the character and "manifested forth the glory" of His entire Mission. 5. As Christ countenanced our seasons of *festivity*, so also that greater *fulness* which befits such; so far was He from encouraging that *asceticism* which has since been so often put for all religion. 6. In what a light does this scene place the Romish views of the blessed Virgin! The doctrine of the 'immaculate conception of the Virgin'—in our day for the first time, even in the Church of Rome, erected into a dogma of the faith—is so outrageous a contradiction of Scriptural truth that none who can take it in are likely to be staggered by the teaching of this or any other portion of Scripture. But even those Romanists who in past times have stopped short of this, as the sober and excellent *Maldonat*, while admitting that there was hardly one of the fathers who did not acknowledge some fault, or error at least, in the Virgin on this occasion, endeavour to explain it away, and refuse to admit that there ever was anything faulty in her, and much less here. But the passage may well be left to speak for itself with all candid readers. 7. Christ's presence is that which turns the water of this and all other social gatherings into wine.

13-22.—CHRIST'S FIRST PUBLIC VISIT TO JERUSALEM AT THE PASSOVER, AND FIRST PURIFYING OF THE TEMPLE.

13. And the Jews' passover—as to which see on Mark xiv. 1, **was at hand.** Here begins our Evangelist's distinct mention of the successive passovers which occurred during our Lord's public ministry, and which are our only sure materials for determining the duration of it. See more on this subject on ch. v. 1. **and Jesus went up to Jerusalem, 14. And found in the temple** [ἐν τῷ ἱερῷ]—in the large sense of that word, for which see on Luke ii. 27. Here it probably means the temple-court. **those that sold oxen and sheep and doves**—for the convenience of those who had to offer them in sacrifice. See Deut. xiv. 24-26. **and the changers of money**—of Roman into Jewish money, in which the temple dues, &c., had to be paid (see on Matt. xvii. 24). **sitting: 15. And when he had made a scourge** [φραγέλλιον=*flagellum*] **of small cords**—likely some of the rushes spread for bedding, and when twisted used to tie up the cattle there collected. 'Not by this slender whip,' says *Grotius* admirably, 'but by divine majesty was the ejection accomplished, the whip being but a sign of the scourge of divine anger.' **he drove them all out of the temple, and the sheep, and the oxen** [πάντας . . τά τε πρόβατα καὶ τοὺς βόας]—rather, 'drove out all, both the sheep and the oxen.' The men would naturally enough go with them. **and poured out the changers' money, and overthrew the tables**—expressing the mingled indignation and authority of the impulse. **16. And said unto them that sold doves, Take these things hence; make not my Father's house an house of merchandise.** How close is the resemblance of these remarkable words to those in Luke ii. 49, "Wist ye not that I must be about my Father's business!" or 'at my Father's' (see on that passage). Both express the same *consciousness of intrinsic relation to the Temple*, as the seat of His Father's most august worship, and so the symbol of all that is due to Him on earth. Only, when but a Youth *with no authority*, He was simply "a Son IN His own house;" now He was "a Son OVER His own house" (Heb. iii. 6), the proper Representative, and in flesh "the Heir," of His Father's rights. There was nothing wrong in the merchandise; but to bring it, for their own and others' convenience, into that most sacred place, was a high-handed profanation which the eye of Jesus could not endure. **17. And his disciples remembered that it was written** (Ps. lxix. 9), **The zeal of thine house hath eaten me up**—a glorious feature in the predicted character of the suffering Messiah, and rising high even in some not worthy to loose the latchet of His shoes. (See, for example, Exod. xxxii. 19, &c.)

18. Then answered the Jews and said unto him, What sign showest thou unto us, seeing that thou doest these things? Though the act itself, and the words that accompanied it, when taken together, were sign enough, they are not convinced. Yet were they *awed;* insomuch that though at His very next appearance at Jerusalem they "sought to kill him" for speaking of "His Father" just as He did now (ch. v. 18), they, at this early stage, only ask a sign. **19. Jesus answered and said unto them, Destroy this temple**—not now the mere *temple-court* [ἱερόν], but the *temple proper* [ναός], **and in three days I will raise it up.** See on Mark xiv. 58, 59. **20. Then said the Jews, Forty and six years was this temple in building.** From the eighteenth year of Herod, from which we are to date this building work of his, until this time, was just a period of forty-six years (*Joseph.* Antt. xv. 11. 1). The word [ᾠκοδομήθη] is rightly rendered 'was in building,' by a peculiar application of the tense—the same tense being similarly used by the LXX. in Ezra v. 16, where the sense is manifestly the same as here. **and wilt thou rear it up in three days? 21. But he spake of the temple of his body**—in which was enshrined the glory of the eternal Word. (See on ch. i. 14.) By its resurrection the true Temple of God upon earth was reared up, of which the stone temple was

22 his body. When therefore he was risen from the dead, [o]his disciples
remembered that he had said this unto them; and they believed the
Scripture, and the word which Jesus had said.

A. D. 30.

[o] Luke 24. 8, 25, 45. John 14. 26.

but a shadow; so that the allusion, though to Himself, may be said to take in that temple of which He is the Foundation, and all believers are the "lively stones" (1 Pet. ii. 4, 5). **22. When therefore he was risen from the dead, his disciples remembered that he had said this unto them; and they believed the Scripture**—that is, with an intelligent apprehension of what its testimony on this subject meant, which until then was hid from them. **and the word which Jesus had said.** They believed it before, as they did the Scripture; but their faith in both was another thing after they came to understand it by seeing it verified.

Remarks.—1. On the question, whether this purification of the temple is one and the same action with that recorded in the first three Gospels (Matt. xxi. 12, 13; Mark xi. 15-19; Luke xix. 45-48), see introductory remarks to Luke xix. 45-48. But the points of difference between the two scenes may here be stated: First, The one took place at the very outset of our Lord's public ministry, and at His first visit to Jerusalem; the other at the very close of it, and at His last visit to Jerusalem. Second, At the former cleansing He used a whip of small cords in clearing the temple-court; at the latter cleansing we read of nothing of this sort. If, then, they were one and the same action, how is it that three Evangelists have recorded it without any mention of this part of it; while the mention of so peculiar a procedure even by one Evangelist can only be explained by its having actually occurred? Third, At the first cleansing all that the Lord said was, "Take these things hence; make not my Father's house an house of merchandise." At the last cleansing His rebuke was withering—"It is written, My house shall be called the house of prayer; but ye have made it a den of robbers" [ληστῶν]. And it may be added, that on this second occasion He "would not suffer that any man should carry any vessel through the temple," which would hardly have been said, perhaps, of the first cleansing. Fourth, On the first occasion "the Jews," or members of the Sanhedrim (see on ch. i. 19), asked of our Lord a "sign" of His right to do such things; and it was then that He spake that saying about destroying the temple and rearing it up in three days which was adduced, though impotently, as evidence against Him on His trial before the Council; whereas nothing of this is recorded in any of the three accounts of the second cleansing. Indeed, the time for asking of Him signs of His authority was then over. Lastly, At the second cleansing "the chief priests and the scribes, and the chief of the people"—exasperated at His high-handed exposure of their temple-traffic, "sought how they might destroy Him," but could not find what they might do, "for all the people were astonished at His teaching"—all betokening that the crisis of our Lord's public life had arrived; whereas the first cleansing passed away with the simple demand for a sign, and our Lord's reply. However dissatisfied they may have been, the matter appears to have rested there, in the meantime—just as we might presume it would at so early a period in our Lord's ministry, when even many who were sincere enough might be unable to make up their minds, and the prejudices of others had not acquired depth and strength enough for any open opposition. 2. Had this remarkable clearing of the temple-court not actually occurred, what inventor of a life that never was lived would have thought of such a thing? Or, if the idea itself should not have been so entirely beyond the range of probable conception, who would ever have thought of introducing the idea of the whip of small cords? Of all things, this at least, one should think, must have been *real*, else it could never have been *written.* But if this was real, the whole scene must have been so—the sanctity claimed for the temple-service and the desecration which kindled the jealousy of this Holy One of God, the Son for the honour of His Father's house; the demand for a sign, tacitly owning the actual exercise of resistless authority, with the remarkable reply, too peculiar to have been penned save as having been uttered; and the darkness of the speech even to the disciples themselves until the resurrection of their Lord cleared it all up. No wonder that the bare reading of such a Narrative carries its own evidence in the minds of all the unprejudiced. 3. In Christ's jealousy for the sanctity and honour of His Father's house—both when He came first to it, in His official character, and when He came to it for the last time—what a glorious commentary have we on those words of the last of the prophets: "The Lord, whom ye seek, shall suddenly come to His temple, even the Messenger of the covenant, whom ye delight in: behold, He shall come, saith the Lord of hosts. But who may abide the day of His coming? and who shall stand when He appeareth? for He is like a refiner's fire, and like fuller's soap: And He shall sit as a refiner and purifier of silver: and He shall purify the sons of Levi, and purge them as gold and silver, that they may offer unto the Lord an offering in righteousness" (Mal. iii. 1-3). Thus was He revealed as "a Son over His own House," the Lord of the temple, the Refiner and Purifier of the Church, of all its assemblies, and of each of its worshippers. Compare this: "JEHOVAH is in His holy temple; His eyes behold, His eyelids try, the children of men" (Ps. xi. 4)—with this: "Unto the angel of the church in Thyatira write; These things saith THE SON OF GOD, who hath His eyes as a flame of fire, and His feet are like fine brass; I know thy works . . . and all the churches shall know that I am He which searcheth the reins and hearts: and I will give unto every one of you according to your works" (Rev. ii. 18, 19, 23). This whip of small cords was like the fan in His hand with which He purged His floor;" not "throughly" indeed, but sufficiently to foreshadow His last act towards that faithless people—*sweeping them out of God's house.* The sign which He gives of His authority to do this is a very remarkable one—the announcement, at this the very outset of His ministry, of that coming death by *their* hands and resurrection by *His own,* which were to pave the way for their judicial ejection. This, however, was uttered—as was fitting at so early a period—in language only to be fully understood, even by His disciples, after His resurrection. 4. When Christ says He will Himself rear up the temple of His body, in three days after they had destroyed it, He makes a claim and uses language which would be manifest presumption in any creature—claiming absolute power over His own life. But on this important subject, see more on ch. x. 18.

23—iii. 21.—RESULTS OF CHRIST'S FIRST PUBLIC

23 Now when he was in Jerusalem at the passover, in the feast *day*, many
24 believed in his name, when they saw the miracles which he did. But
25 Jesus did not commit himself unto them, because he knew all *men*, and
needed not that any should testify of man: for [p]he knew what was in
man.
3 THERE was a man of the Pharisees, named Nicodemus, a ruler of the
2 Jews: the same came to Jesus by night, and said unto him, Rabbi, we
know that thou art a teacher come from God: for [a]no man can do these
miracles that thou doest, except [b]God be with him.
3 Jesus answered and said unto him, Verily, verily, I say unto thee,
[c]Except a man be born [1]again, he cannot see the kingdom of God.

A. D. 30.

[p] 1 Sam. 16. 7. 1 Chr. 28. 9. Matt. 9. 4.

CHAP. 3.

[a] ch. 9. 16, 33. Acts 2. 22.
[b] Acts 10. 38.
[c] ch 1. 13. 2 Cor. 5. 17. Gal. 6. 15. Jas. 1. 18.
[1] Or, from above.

VISIT TO JERUSALEM, IN MANY SHALLOW CONVERSIONS AND ONE PRECIOUS ACCESSION. The three last verses of the second chapter, and the first twenty-one verses of the third, form manifestly one subject, in two divisions; the former one brief, because unsatisfactory, the latter of too deep importance in itself and too pregnant with instruction for all, not to be given in full detail.

Unsatisfactory Accessions to Christ at His First Visit to Jerusalem (23-25). **23. Now when he was in Jerusalem at the passover, in the feast** [day] [ἐν τῇ ἑορτῇ]—rather, 'during the feast,' which lasted seven days. What is now to be related is not the result of one day, but of the whole period of this festival. The Cleansing of the Temple, recorded in the preceding verses, occurred probably before the feast began. **many believed in his name** —see on ch. i. 12. These converts, persuaded that His claims were well founded, reposed trust in Him in that sense, and to that extent **when they saw the miracles which he did.** What these were is not here recorded; nor can we get any light from the other Evangelists, as they speak of no public visit to Jerusalem but the last. It is singular that none of these miracles are recorded, since in the very opening of the next chapter Nicodemus refers to the immense force of conviction which they carried (ch. iii. 2), and they are again referred to in ch. iv. 45. **24. But Jesus** [Αὐτὸς δὲ ὁ Ἰησοῦς]—'But Jesus Himself,' or 'Jesus, for His part,' **did not commit**—or 'trust' **himself unto them** [οὐκ ἐπίστευεν αὑτὸν αὐτοῖς]. Though they confided in Him, He did not confide in them, or let Himself down to them familiarly, as He did to His genuine disciples. **because he knew all men.** He saw through them, as He did through all men, and, perceiving the superficial character of the trust they reposed in Him, He reposed none in them. **25. And needed not**—'And because He needed not' [Καὶ ὅτι οὐ χρείαν εἶχεν] **that any should testify of man: for He knew** [αὐτὸς γὰρ]. The language is emphatic, as in the previous verse: 'For Himself knew' **what was in man**—in other words, that all-penetrating perception of what was in man *resided in Himself;* the strongest possible expression of absolute knowledge of *man*, as in ch. i. 18 of *God*.

CHAP. III.—*Night-Interview of Nicodemus with Jesus, issuing in His Accession as a genuine Disciple* (1-21). See introductory remark at the commencement of this Section.

1. There was a man of the Pharisees, named Nicodemus, a ruler of the Jews. The connecting particle [δὲ] with which the original introduces this scene should not have been omitted, as the Evangelist is now going to show, in continuation of his subject, that *all* the accessions to Christ during this His first public visit to Jerusalem were not like those of whom he had spoken at the close of the preceding chapter. It should have begun thus: 'But (or 'Now') there was a man,' &c. Nicodemus is a purely Greek name, of frequent occurrence among the later Greeks, whose names were often appropriated by the Jews, especially those of foreign extraction. This Nicodemus, besides being of the stricter sect of the Pharisees, was a "ruler" [ἄρχων], or one of the Sanhedrim. In *v.* 10 he is called a "master," or 'doctor' of the law. It is useless attempting, as *Lightfoot* has done, to identify him with a rabbi of this name who lived at the destruction of Jerusalem. **2. The same came to Jesus.** The true text here clearly is 'to Him' [πρὸς αὐτόν]; this being regarded as but a continuation of the same subject with which the preceding chapter closed. The word "Jesus" no doubt came in first in those Church Lessons which began with ch. iii., and so required it; just as many in the public reading of the Scriptures insert the name of the person instead of "he" or "him," for clearness' sake. So all recent critical editors agree. **by night**—"for fear of the Jews," as is evident from all we read of him: see on ch. vii. 50-52; and on ch. xix. 38, 39. **and said unto him, Rabbi** [= διδάσκαλος], **we know**—meaning, probably, that a general conviction to that effect had been diffusing itself through the thoughtful portion of the worshippers with whom Jerusalem was then crowded, though much yet remained for anxious enquiry regarding His claims, and that as the representative of this class he had now come to solicit an interview with Him. **that thou art a teacher come from God** [ἀπὸ Θεοῦ ἐλήλυθας]—not "sent from God," as is said of the Baptist, ch. i. 6. *Stier* and *Luthardt* call attention to this, as expressing more than a conviction that Jesus was divinely *commissioned*, as were all the prophets. Certain it is that the expression "come from God" is nowhere used of any merely *human messenger*, while this Gospel of ours teems with phraseology of this kind applied to Christ. It is possible, therefore, that Nicodemus *may* have designed to express something indefinite as to Christ's higher claims; though what follows hardly bears that out. **for no man can do these miracles that thou doest, except God be with him.** See on ch. ii. 23. From all these particulars about Nicodemus, we may gather that sincerity and timidity struggled together in his mind. The one impelled him, in spite of his personal and official position, to solicit an interview with Jesus; the other, to choose the "night" time for his visit, that none might know of it. The one led him frankly to tell the Lord Jesus what conviction he had been constrained to come to, and the ground of that conviction; the other, so to measure his language as not to commit himself to more than a bare acknowledgment of a miraculously attested commission from God to men.

3. Jesus answered and said unto him, Verily, verily, I say unto thee, Except a man be born again, he cannot see the kingdom of God. This blunt and curt reply was plainly meant to shake

4 Nicodemus saith unto him, How can a man be born when he is old?
can he enter the second time into his mother's womb, and be born?
5 Jesus answered, Verily, verily, I say unto thee, [d]Except a man be born
of water and *of* the Spirit, he cannot enter into the kingdom of God.
6 That which is born of the flesh is flesh; and that which is born of the
7 Spirit is spirit. Marvel not that I said unto thee, Ye must be born

A. D. 30.

[d] Isa. 44. 3, 4. Matt. 3. 11. Mark 16.16. Acts 2. 38. Titus 3. 5. 1 Pet. 3. 21.

the whole edifice of the man's religion, in order to lay a deeper and more enduring foundation. Nicodemus probably thought he had gone a long way, and expected, perhaps, to be complimented on his candour. Instead of this, he is virtually told that he has raised a question which he is not in a capacity to solve, and that before approaching it, *his spiritual vision required to be rectified by an entire revolution on his inner man.* Had the man been less sincere, this would certainly have repelled him; but with persons in his mixed state of mind—to which Jesus was no stranger (ch. ii. 25)—such methods speed better than more honeyed words and gradual approaches. Let us analyze this great brief saying. "Except a *man*" [τις]—'a person,' or 'one' "be born again," the most universal form of expression. The Jews were accustomed to say of a heathen proselyte, on his public admission into the Jewish faith by baptism, that he was a new-born child. But our Lord here extends the necessity of the new birth to Jew and Gentile alike—to every one. **be born again** [ἄνωθεν]—or, as the word admits of being rendered, 'from above.' Since both are undoubted truths, the question is, Which is the sense here intended? *Origen* and others of the fathers take the latter view, though *Chrysostom* leaves it undecided; and with them agree *Erasmus, Lightfoot, Bengel, Meyer, de Wette, Lücke, Lange,* and others. But as it is evident that Nicodemus understood our Lord in the sense of a *second* birth, so the scope of our Lord's way of dealing with him was to drive home the conviction of the *nature* rather than the *source* of the change. And accordingly, as the word employed is stronger than "again" [πάλιν] it should be rendered by some such word as 'anew,' 'of new,' 'afresh.' In this sense it is understood, with our translators, by the *Vulgate, Luther, Calvin, Beza, Maldonat, Lampe, Olshausen, Neander, Tholuck, Stier, Luthardt, Campbell, Alford, Webster and Wilkinson.* Considering this to be the undoubted sense of the term, we understand our Lord to say that unless one *begin life anew,* in relation to God—his manner of thinking, and feeling, and acting, in reference to spiritual things, undergoing a *fundamental and permanent revolution,* **he cannot see**—that is, 'can have no part in'—just as one is said to "see life," "see death," &c. **the kingdom of God**—whether in its beginnings here or its consummation hereafter. (See on Matt. v. 3; and compare Luke xvi. 16; Matt. xxv. 34; Eph. v. 5.)

4. Nicodemus saith unto him, How can a man be born when he is old? Nicodemus probably referred here to himself. **can he enter the second time into his mother's womb, and be born?** The figure of the new birth, as we have seen, would have been intelligible enough to Nicodemus if it had been meant only of Gentile proselytes to the Jewish Religion; but that *Jews themselves* should need a new birth was to him incomprehensible.

5. Jesus answered, Verily, verily, I say unto thee, Except a man be born of water and of the Spirit [ἐξ ὕδατος καὶ πνεύματος]—or, more simply, 'of water and the Spirit,' **he cannot enter into the kingdom of God.** We have here a two-fold explanation of the new birth, so startling to Nicodemus. To a Jewish ecclesiastic, so familiar with the symbolical application of water, in every variety of way and form of expression, this language was fitted to show that the thing intended was no other than 'a thorough spiritual purification by the operation of the Holy Ghost.' Indeed, this element of *water* and operation of *the Spirit* are brought together in a glorious evangelical prediction of Ezek. xxxvi. 25-27, which Nicodemus might have been reminded of had such spiritualities not been almost lost in the reigning formalism. Already had the symbol of water been embodied in an initiatory ordinance, in the baptism of the Jewish expectants of Messiah by the Baptist, not to speak of the baptism of Gentile proselytes before that; and in the Christian Church it was soon to become the great visible door of entrance into "the kingdom of God," the reality being the sole work of the Holy Ghost. In this way of viewing the two elements—"water" and "the Spirit"—we avoid the unsatisfactory interpretation of the "water," as if our Lord had meant no more than 'Except a man be regenerated by the ordinance of baptism and by the Holy Ghost.' We call this unsatisfactory, because, as the ordinance of baptism was not instituted until Jesus was on the wing for glory, we think it harsh to suppose any direct allusion here to that institution. But neither is it to be reduced, with *Lampe,* &c., to a mere figure for *the truth.* It is undoubtedly the cleansing or purifying property of water which is referred to, in conformity with the familiar ideas of the Jewish ritual and the current language of the Old Testament. But since this was already taking form in an initiatory ordinance, in the ways just mentioned, it would be unreasonable to exclude all reference to baptism; although it would be nearer the truth, perhaps, to say that Baptism itself only embodies in a public ordinance the great general truth here announced—that a cleansing or purifying operation of the Spirit in every one is indispensable to entrance into the kingdom of God. **6. That which is born of the flesh is flesh; and that which is born of the Spirit is spirit.** A most weighty general proposition. As *Olshausen* expresses it, 'That which is begotten partakes of the nature of that which begat it.' By "*flesh*" here is meant, not the mere material body, but all that comes into the world by birth—the entire man: yet since "flesh" is here opposed to "spirit," it plainly denotes in this place, not humanity merely, but humanity in its corrupted, depraved condition—humanity in entire subjection to the law of the fall, called in Rom. viii. "the law of sin and death." (See on Rom. viii. 1-9.) So that though a man *could* "enter a second time into his mother's womb, and be born," he would be no nearer this new birth than before. (See Job xiv. 4; Ps. li. 5.) Contrariwise, when it is said, "that which is born of the Spirit is spirit," the meaning is, that the fruit of that operation of the Holy Spirit upon the inner man, which had been pronounced indispensable, is the production of a spiritual nature, of the same moral qualities as His own. **7. Marvel not that I said unto thee, Ye must be born again.** If a spiritual nature only can see and enter the kingdom of God, if all we bring into the world with us be the reverse of spiritual, and if this spirituality be solely of the Holy Ghost—no wonder a new birth is indispens-

8 [2]again. The [e]wind bloweth where it listeth, and thou hearest the sound
thereof, but canst not tell whence it cometh, and whither it goeth: so is
every one that is born of the Spirit.
9 Nicodemus answered and said unto him, How [f]can these things be?
10 Jesus answered and said unto him, Art thou a master of Israel, and
11 knowest not these things? Verily, verily, I say unto thee, We speak that
we do know, and testify that we have seen: and ye receive not our
12 witness. If I have told you earthly things, and ye believe not, how shall
13 ye believe, if I tell you *of* heavenly things? And [g]no man hath ascended
up to heaven, but he that came down from heaven, *even* the Son of man
14 which is in heaven. And [h]as Moses lifted up the serpent in the wilder-

A. D. 30.

2 Or, from above.
e Eccl. 11. 5. 1 Cor. 2. 11.
f ch. 6. 52.
g Pro. 30. 4. ch. 6. 33. ch 16. 28. Acts 2. 34. 1 Cor. 15.47. Eph. 4. 9.
h Num. 21. 9. ch. 8. 28.

able. *Bengel*, with his usual acuteness, notices that our Lord here says, not 'we,' but '*ye* must be born again.' And surely after those universal propositions, about what "*a man*" must be, to "enter the kingdom of God," this is remarkable; showing clearly that our Lord meant to hold Himself forth as "*separate from sinners*." **8. The wind bloweth where it listeth, and thou hearest the sound thereof, but canst not tell whence it cometh, and whither it goeth: so is every one that is born of the Spirit.** The word for wind here is not that usually so rendered [ἄνεμος], which means a gale; but that which signifies the 'breath' of life [πνεῦμα = רוּחַ, *anima*], or the gentle *zephyr*. Hence it is that in the Old Testament, "breath" and "spirit" are constantly interchanged, as analogous (see Job xxvii. 3; xxxiii. 4; Ezek. xxxvii. 9-14). The laws which govern the motion of the *winds* have, indeed, been partially discovered; but the risings, fallings, and change in direction many times in a day, of those *gentle breezes* here referred to, will probably ever be a mystery to us: So of the operation of the Holy Ghost in the new birth.

9. Nicodemus answered and said unto him, How can these things be? Though the subject, says *Luthardt*, still confounds him, the necessity and possibility of the new birth is no longer the point with him, but the nature of it and how it is brought about. From this moment, to use the words of *Stier*, Nicodemus *says nothing more*, but has sunk into a disciple who has found his true teacher. *Therefore* the Saviour now graciously advances in His communications of truth, and once more solemnly brings to the mind of this teacher in Israel, now become a learner, his own not guiltless *ignorance*, that He may then proceed to utter, out of the fulness of His divine knowledge, such further testimonies, both of earthly and heavenly things, as his docile scholar may to his own profit receive. **10. Jesus answered and said unto him, Art thou a master** [Σὺ εἶ ὁ διδάσκαλος]—rather, 'Art thou the teacher.' Perhaps this means only, 'Dost thou occupy the important post of the teacher,' or doctor of the law; not, as some good critics understand it, 'Art thou the well-known,' or 'distinguished teacher,' **of Israel, and knowest not these things?** The question clearly implies that the doctrine of Regeneration was so far disclosed in the Old Testament as to render Nicodemus's ignorance of it culpable. Nor is it merely as something that should be experienced *under the Gospel* that the Old Testament holds it forth—as many distinguished critics allege, denying that there was any such thing as regeneration before Christ. For our Lord's proposition is universal, that no fallen man is or can be spiritual without a regenerating operation of the Holy Ghost; and surely the necessity of a *spiritual obedience*, under whatever name, in opposition to mere mechanical services, which is proclaimed throughout all the Old Testament, amounts to a proclamation of the necessity of regeneration. **11. Verily, verily, I say unto thee, We speak that we do know, and testify that we have seen**—that is, by *absolute* knowledge and *immediate* vision of God, which "the Only begotten Son in the bosom of the Father" claims as exclusively His own (ch. i. 18). **and ye receive not our witness**—referring to the *class* to which Nicodemus belonged, but from which he was now beginning to be separated. Though our Lord says, "*we* speak" and "*our* testimony," Himself only is intended—probably in emphatic contrast with the opening words of Nicodemus, "Rabbi, *we know*," &c. **12. If I have told you earthly things,** [τὰ ἐπίγεια], **and ye believe not, how shall ye believe, if I tell you of heavenly things?** [τὰ ἐπουράνια]—rather simply, 'tell you heavenly things.' By the "earthly things" which Christ had just told Nicodemus of is certainly meant *Regeneration*, the one subject of His teaching to him up to this point; and it is so called, it would seem—in contrast with the "heavenly things"—as being a truth even of that more *earthly* economy to which Nicodemus belonged, and as the gate of entrance to the kingdom of God upon *earth*. The "heavenly things" are the things of the new and more heavenly evangelical economy, especially that great truth of salvation by faith in the atoning death of the Son of God, which He was now about to "tell" Nicodemus; though He forewarns him of the probability of people stumbling much more at that than he had done at the former truth—since it had been but dimly unfolded under the *earthly* economy, and was only to be fully understood after the effusion of the Spirit from *heaven* through the exalted Saviour. **13. And no man hath ascended up to heaven, but he that came down from heaven, even the Son of man which is in heaven.** How paradoxical this sounds: 'No one has gone up but He that came down, even He who is at once both up and down.' Doubtless it was intended to startle and constrain his auditor to think that there must be mysterious elements in His Person. The old Socinians, to subvert the doctrine of the pre-existence of Christ, seized upon this passage as teaching that the man Jesus was secretly caught up to heaven to receive his instructions, and then "came down from heaven" to deliver them. But the sense manifestly is this: 'The perfect knowledge of God is not obtained by any man's going up from earth to heaven to receive it—no man hath so ascended; but He whose *proper habitation*, in His essential and eternal nature, is heaven, hath, by taking human flesh, descended as "the Son of Man" to disclose the Father, whom He knows by immediate gaze alike in the flesh as before He assumed it, being essentially and unchangeably "in the bosom of the Father," (ch. i. 18.) Now comes He to tell him the heavenly things. **14. And as**

15 ness, even so must the Son of man be lifted up; that whosoever believeth
16 in him should not perish, but have eternal life. For [i]God so loved the
world, that he gave his only begotten Son, that whosoever believeth in
17 him should not perish, but have everlasting life. For [j]God sent not his
Son into the world to condemn the world; but that the world through
18 him might be saved. He that believeth on him [k]is not condemned: but
he that believeth not is condemned already, because he hath not believed
19 in the name of the only begotten Son of God. And this is the condemna-

A. D. 30.

[i] Luke 2. 14. Rom. 5. 8. Titus 3. 4. 1 John 4. 9.
[j] Luke 9. 56. 1 John 4.14. Rom. 5 1.
[k] Rom. 8. 1. 1 John 5.12.

Moses lifted up the serpent in the wilderness (see Num. xxi. 4-9), **even so must the Son of man be lifted up; 15. That whosoever believeth in him should not perish, but have eternal life.** Since this most heavenly thing, for the reason just mentioned, might be apt to stumble, Jesus holds it forth under a somewhat veiled form, but with sublime precision—calling His death His 'up-lifting' (compare viii. 28; xii. 32, 33); and by comparing it to the up-lifting of the brazen serpent, He still further veiled it. And yet to *us*, who know what it all means, it is, by being cast in this form, unspeakably more lively and pregnant with instruction. But what instruction? Let us see. The venom of the fiery serpents, shooting through the veins of the rebellious Israelites, was spreading death through the camp—lively emblem of the perishing condition of men by reason of sin. In both cases the remedy was divinely provided. In both the way of cure strikingly resembled that of the disease. Stung by serpents, by a serpent they are healed. By "fiery serpents" bitten—serpents, probably, with skin spotted fiery-red—the instrument of cure is a serpent of brass or copper, having at a distance *the same appearance.* So in redemption, as by man came death, by Man also comes life—Man too, "*in the likeness of sinful flesh,*" differing in nothing *outward and apparent* from those who, pervaded by the poison of the serpent, were ready to perish. But as the uplifted serpent had none of the venom of which the serpent-bitten people were dying, so while the whole human family were perishing of the deadly wound inflicted on it by the old serpent, "the Second Man," who arose over humanity with healing in His wings, was without spot or wrinkle or any such thing. In both cases the remedy is *conspicuously displayed:* in the one case on a pole; in the other on the cross, to "draw all men unto Him" (ch. xii. 32). In both cases it is by *directing the eye to the uplifted Remedy* that the cure is effected: in the one case it was the bodily eye, in the other it is the gaze of the soul by "believing in Him," as in that glorious ancient proclamation—"*Look* unto me, and be ye saved, all the ends of the earth," &c. (Is. xlv. 22.) Both methods are stumbling to human reason. What, to any thinking Israelite, could seem more unlikely than that a deadly poison should be dried up in his body by simply looking on a reptile of brass? Such a stumbling-block to the Jews and to the Greeks foolishness was faith in the crucified Nazarene, as a way of deliverance from eternal perdition. Yet was the warrant in both cases to expect a cure equally rational and well-grounded. As the serpent was *God's ordinance* for the cure of every bitten Israelite, so is Christ for the salvation of every perishing sinner; the one however a purely *arbitrary* ordinance, the other divinely *adapted* to man's complicated maladies. In both cases the efficacy is the same. As one simple look at the serpent, however distant and however weak, brought an instantaneous cure; even so, real faith in the Lord Jesus, however tremulous, however distant—be it but *real* faith—brings certain and instant healing to the perishing soul. In a word, the consequences of disobedience are the same in both. Doubtless many bitten Israelites, galling as their case was, would *reason* rather than *obey*, would *speculate* on the absurdity of expecting the bite of a living serpent to be cured by looking at a piece of dead metal in the shape of one—speculate thus *till they died.* Alas! is not salvation by a crucified Redeemer subjected to like treatment? Has "the offence of the Cross" yet ceased? (compare 2 Ki. v. 12.) **16. For God so loved the world, that he gave his only begotten Son, that whosoever believeth in him should not perish, but have everlasting life.** Who shall speak or write worthily of such a verse? What proclamation of the Gospel has been so oft on the lips of missionaries and preachers in every age since it was first uttered—what has sent such thrilling sensations through millions of mankind—what has been honoured to bring such multitudes to the feet of Christ—what to kindle in the cold and selfish breasts of mortals the fires of self-sacrificing love to mankind, as these words of transparent simplicity yet overpowering majesty have done? The picture embraces several distinct compartments. First, we have the object of regard, "THE WORLD" [τὸν κόσμον]—in its widest sense, ready to "*perish:*" Next, "THE LOVE OF GOD" to that perishing world —measured by, and only measurable and conceivable by, the gift which it drew forth from Him —He *so* loved the world that He gave," &c.: Then, THE GIFT itself, He so loved the world, that He gave His Only begotten Son; or, in the language of the apostle, He "*spared not* His own Son" (Rom. viii. 32): Further, THE FRUIT of this stupendous gift—negatively, in deliverance from impending perdition, that they "might not perish;" and positively, in the bestowal of "everlasting life:" and finally, THE MODE in which all takes effect—simply by "believing on the Son of God." How would Nicodemus's narrow Judaism become invisible in the blaze of this Sun of righteousness seen rising on "the world" with healing in His wings! **17. For God sent not his Son into the world to condemn the world; but that the world through him might be saved.** A statement of vast importance. Though "condemnation" is to many the *issue* of Christ's mission (*v.* 19), it is not the *object* of His mission, which is purely a *saving* one. **18. He that believeth on him is not condemned** [οὐ κρίνεται]—lit., 'is not being judged,' or 'is not coming into judgment.' The meaning is, as the apostle expresses it, that "there is now no condemnation to them which are in Christ Jesus" (Rom. viii. 1). Compare ch. v. 24, "He that heareth my word, and believeth on Him that sent me hath everlasting life, and shall not come into condemnation, but is (or hath) passed from death unto life." **but he that believeth not is condemned already, because he hath not believed in the name of the only begotten Son of God.** Rejecting the one way of deliverance from that condemnation which God gave His Son to *remove*, they thus wilfully *remain* condemned. **19. And this is the condemnation**—emphatically so;

tion, [l]that light is come into the world, and men loved darkness rather
20 than light, because their deeds were evil. For every one that doeth evil
hateth the light, neither cometh to the light, lest his deeds should be

A. D. 30.

[l] Isa. 5. 20. ch. 1. 4.

revealing the condemnation already existing, and *sealing up* under it those who will not be delivered from it. **that light** [τὸ φῶς]—rather, 'the light' **is come into the world**—in the Person of Him to whom Nicodemus was listening. **and men loved** ['the'] **darkness** [τὸ σκότος] **rather than** ['the'] **light, because their deeds were evil.** [On the aorist —ἠγάπησαν—here, see on ch. x. 4.] The deliberate rejection of Himself was doubtless that to which Jesus here referred, as that which would fearfully reveal men's preference for the darkness. **20. For every one that doeth evil hateth the light, neither cometh to the light, lest his deeds should be reproved**—by being brought out to the light. **21. But he that doeth** ['the'] **truth** [τὴν ἀλήθειαν]—whose one object in life is to be, and to do what will bear the light, **cometh to the light, that his deeds may be made manifest, that they are wrought in God**—that all he is and does, being thus thoroughly tested, may be seen to have nothing in it but what is divinely wrought and divinely approved. This is the "Israelite indeed, in whom is no guile."

Remarks.—1. What an air of *naturalness* is there in the first part of this Section, regarding the "many" who believed in Jesus' name when they saw the miracles which He did at His first official visit to Jerusalem, and during the paschal feast. One might have expected that all with whom He came in contact would be divided simply into two classes—those who recognized and those who repudiated His claims; or, if another class should emerge, it would be of the undecided, or the waverers—either unable to make up their minds, or oscillating between the two opposing views of His claims. But here we have a fourth class, or the first class separated into two divisions—the cordial and thorough accessions to Him and the shallow and fickle believers; and of these latter it seems there were "many" who came over on this occasion. Another thing which strikes one—as betokening the absence of everything *artificial* in the drawing up of this narrative—is, that "the miracles" which He did during the feast are not recorded at all; although they were such that not only *they* were won over by them, but the class of which Nicodemus was the most hopeful specimen were convinced by them of our Lord's divine commission. No wonder that unprejudiced readers, even of the highest class, as they bend over these wonderful Records, *feel* them to be true without, perhaps, one conscious reflection on the question, whether they are so or not—guided by that experience and sound judgment which, with the force of an instinct, tells them that *such* a Tale cannot deceive. But 2. If this may be said of the first part of this Section, what shall be said of the sequel of it—the night interview of Nicodemus with Jesus—a historical picture which, for graphic vividness, interest, and power, surpasses almost everything even in the Gospel History? Two figures only appear on the canvas; but to us it seems that there must have been one other in the scene, whose young and meditative eye scanned, by the night-lamp, the Jewish ruler and Him he had come to talk with, and whose ear drank in every word that fell from both. Our Evangelist himself—was not he there? What pen but that of an eye-and-ear witness could have reported to us a scene whose minute details and life-like touches rivet, and have riveted from the beginning, the very children that read it, never again to forget it, while the depths and heights of its teaching keep the most mature ever bending over it, and its grandeur, undiminished by time, will stand out to arrest and astonish, to delight and feed the Church so long as a Bible shall be needed by it here below? If this Gospel was written when it probably was, some *sixty* or more years must have elapsed between the occurrence itself and this Record of it for the ages to come. And yet how fresh, how life-like, how new and warm it all is—as if our Evangelist had taken down every word of it that very night, immediately on the departure of Nicodemus. We think we see this anxious ruler—not unaware of his own importance, and the possible consequences of this step to one in his position, yet unable any longer to rest in doubt—stealing along, approaching the humble dwelling where lodged the Lord of glory, and, as he enters, surveying the countenance of this mysterious Person, who courteously receives him and asks him to seat himself. It is Nicodemus who first breaks that silence which was only to be resumed as the last words of the most wonderful announcements ever yet made to any human being fell from the lips of the Son of God, and he who came a trembling enquirer, departed a humble, though secret, disciple. If no other fruit had come of that first visit to Jerusalem but the accession of this disciple, would it not, even by angel-eyes, have been regarded as enough? For, as was said of the precious ointment which Mary purchased to anoint her Lord withal at the supper in Bethany, but in which the Lord Himself saw another and yet dearer purpose—"She is come aforehand to anoint My body to the burying"—so may we say of this Nicodemus, that he was gained, and kept in reserve all the time of Christ's public ministry even till His death, in order that, having purchased an hundred pound weight of myrrh and aloes wherewith to anoint the body, he and Joseph of Arimathea, another secret disciple, might be the honoured instruments of wrapping and laying it in the virgin-sepulchre. Nay, but even if this service had not been rendered by Nicodemus to his dead Lord, that such an interview should have taken place between them *in order to its being reproduced here for all time*, was itself alone sufficient fruit of this first visit to Jerusalem; and doubtless the Lord, as He sees of *this* travail of His soul, is satisfied. 3. Nothing is more remarkable in this scene than the varied lights in which the Lord Jesus is exhibited in it. Observe, first of all, how entirely this "Man, Christ Jesus," isolates Himself from all other men, as not within the category of that humanity whose regeneration He pronounces indispensable to entrance into the kingdom of God:—"Except one [τις] be born again." And after giving a reason for this, arising from that kind of human nature which is propagated from parent to child in every descendant of Adam, He adds, "Marvel not that I said unto thee, *Ye* must [Δεῖ ὑμᾶς] be born again." Nor can it be alleged that this is a strain upon the words, which need not be pressed so far as to exclude Himself. For in almost every succeeding verse He continues to speak of Himself as if, though truly man, His connection with humanity were something voluntarily assumed—something superinduced upon His own proper being—that by thus coming into our world He might discharge a great mission of love to the world from His Father in heaven: "We speak that we do *know*,

21 [3]reproved. But he that doeth truth cometh to the light, that his deeds
may be made manifest, that they are wrought in God.

A. D. 30.

[3] discovered.

and testify that we have *seen:* No man hath ascended up to heaven but He that *came down from heaven*, even the Son of Man which *is in heaven:* God *sent* His Only begotten Son." Putting all these statements together, how evident is it that our Lord does mean to isolate Himself as Man from that universal humanity which cannot without regeneration enter into the kingdom of God. And, in connection with this, it may be stated that He never once mixes Himself up with other individual men by the use of such pronouns as "we," and "us," and "our"—save where no false inference could possibly be drawn—but always says, "I" and "they," "I" and "you," "Me" and "them," "My" and "your:"—remarkable and most pregnant fact. But next, observe the lofty style into which He rises when speaking of Himself. He could suggest no measure by which to gauge the love of God to a perishing world save the gift of Himself for it: "God *so* loved the world that He *gave* His Only begotten Son." What creature, not lost to all sense of his proper place, would have dared to use such language as this? Then, notice how warily—if we may so express it—our Lord uses the two names by which Himself is designated, "The Son of Man" and "The Son of God." When He would speak of His *uplifting from beneath*, He uses the former—"Even so must the Son of Man be lifted up:" When He would speak of His *descending from above*, as the Father's gift to the world, He uses the latter—"God gave His Only begotten Son." And yet, as if to show that it is One glorious Person who is both these, He uses the one of these—and the lower one too—to express both His higher and His lower natures and His actings in both: "No one [οὐδεὶς] hath *ascended* up to heaven but He that *descended* from heaven, even the Son of man who *is in heaven.*" This was much observed and dwelt on by the Greek Fathers, who called it 'the communication' or 'interchange of properties' [κοινωνία ἰδιωμάτων], in virtue of the Oneness of the Person [διὰ τὴν τῆς ὑποστάσεως ταυτότητα]. But once more, with all this lofty bearing, when speaking of Himself, with what meekness, with what patience, with what spiritual skill, does He deal with this soul, in whom *candour* and *caution* seem to struggle for the mastery—a jealousy, on the one hand, for his own position, and an anxiety, on the other, to get to the bottom of Christ's claims! 4. What a directory for the preachers of the Gospel, and for all who would save souls, have we here! The two great truths, of *Regeneration by the Holy Ghost* and *Reconciliation by the death of Christ*, are here held forth as *the two-fold need* of every sinner who would be saved. Over the portals of the kingdom of God may be seen two inscriptions, as in great letters of fire,—

NO REGENERATION—NO ENTRANCE HERE:
WITHOUT THE SHEDDING OF BLOOD—
NO REMISSION.

Or, to turn it out of the negative into the positive form,—

THE PURE IN HEART SEE GOD:
BELIEVE IN THE LORD JESUS CHRIST AND
BE SAVED.

As the one of these gives us the *capacity* for the kingdom, so the other gives us the *right* to it. The one rectifies our *nature;* the other adjusts our *relation* to God. Without the one *we* cannot see *Him;* without the other *He* will not see *us.* As upon these two pivots saved souls must ever turn, so on these must turn all preaching and teaching that would be divinely owned. 5. Is it true that the quickening operations of the Holy Ghost are like the gentle breath of heaven—unseen but not unfelt—with laws of movement divinely ordained, yet to us inscrutable; or if to some small extent so to be traced that our expectations may be stimulated, yet as little to be laid down by us as the laws of heaven's breath? Then let the Church at large, let every section of it, and every Christian, beware of *tying down* the Spirit of God to their own notions of the *way* in which, the *measure* in which, the *time* in which, and the *agencies* by which He shall work. There has been far too much of this in all past time, and even until now; and how much the Spirit of the Lord has been thus hindered and restrained, grieved and quenched, who shall tell? He is a "FREE Spirit," but as Himself Divine, is saying, "I will work, and who shall let it?" The one test of His presence is its *effects.* "Every good gift and every perfect is from above." "Do men gather grapes of thorns or figs of thistles?" Since nothing can be done effectually without the Spirit, and Christ Himself without the Spirit is no Saviour at all to *us* (John xvi. 8-15; Rom. viii. 9), our business is to be lying in wait for His blessed breathings, *expecting* them from above (Luke xi. 13), and prepared both to welcome and use them, to hail them wheresoever and in whomsoever we find them, and to put ourselves alongside of those operations of His, giving them our countenance and lending them our agency for carrying them out to their proper ends—just as sailors in a calm watch for the moment when a breeze shall spring up, which they know well may be when they least expect it, and hoist and adjust their sails to it with a speed and a skill at which others wonder, so as to let none of it be lost. 6. Definite, sharp, authoritative, spiritual teaching of divine truth is what alone we may expect will be divinely blessed. It was our Lord's transparent perception of the difference between truth and error, and of what Nicodemus needed, as the *right beginning* of a religious character, that prompted His peculiar manner of dealing with him. But the weighty brevity, the sharpness of those lines of distinction between "perdition" and "salvation," the high authority with which He bore in these great truths upon this enquirer, mingled with such gentle and winning spirituality—it is this that is so remarkable and so pregnant with wisdom for all that would follow Him in dealing with souls. Nor is He in these inimitable. The authority with which *He* uttered these great truths is indeed His own; and of this God says from the excellent glory, "Hear Him." But when *we* utter them, we do it with *His* authority, and have a right to use it, as did the apostolic preachers. Nay, this is our strength. The apologetical tone, or the reasoning tone—if it be the main characteristic of our preaching—will leave no divine impress, no stamp of heaven, upon it. Weak in itself, its effects will be weak too. And do not the facts of the pulpit attest this? "My speech and my preaching was not with enticing words of man's wisdom, but in demonstration of the Spirit and of power; that your faith should not stand in the wisdom of men, but in the power of God."

22-36.—JESUS WITHDRAWS FROM THE CITY TO THE RURAL PARTS OF JUDEA, AND BAPTIZES—THE BAPTIST ALSO, STILL AT LARGE, CONTINUES HIS WORK, AND BEARS HIS LAST AND NOBLEST TESTIMONY TO HIS MASTER.

22. After these things came Jesus and his

22 After these things came Jesus and his disciples into the land of Judea;
23 and there he tarried with them, [m]and baptized. And John also was
baptizing in Ænon near to [n]Salim, because there was much water there:
24 and they came, and were baptized. For [o]John was not yet cast into
prison.
25 Then there arose a question between *some* of John's disciples and the
26 Jews about purifying. And they came unto John, and said unto him,
Rabbi, he that was with thee beyond Jordan, [p]to whom thou barest
witness, behold, the same baptizeth, and all *men* come to him.
27 John answered and said, [q]A man can [4]receive nothing, except it be
28 given him from heaven. Ye yourselves bear me witness, that I said, I
29 am not the Christ, but [r]that I am sent before him. He [s]that hath
the bride is the bridegroom: but [t]the friend of the bridegroom, which
standeth and heareth him, rejoiceth greatly because of the bridegroom's
30 voice. This my joy therefore is fulfilled. He [u]must increase, but [v]I
31 *must* decrease. He [w]that cometh from above [x]is above all: [y]he that is
of the earth is earthly, and speaketh of the earth: [z]he that cometh from

A. D. 30.

[m] ch. 4. 2.
[n] Gen. 14. 18. Gen. 33. 18. 1 Sam. 9. 4.
[o] Matt. 14. 3. Luke 3. 19, 20.
[p] ch. 1. 34.
[q] Heb. 5. 4.
[4] Or, take unto himself.
[r] Mal. 3. 1.
[s] Matt. 22. 2.
[t] Song 5. 1.
[u] Isa 9. 7.
[v] Phil 3. 8, 9.
[w] ch. 8. 23.
[x] Matt. 28. 18.
[y] 1 Cor. 15. 47.
[z] ch. 6. 33.

disciples into the land of Judea [εἰς τὴν Ἰουδαίαν γῆν]—not the *province* of Judea, as distinguished from Galilee and Samaria, for the foregoing conversation was held in its capital. But the meaning is, that leaving the city He withdrew to the rural districts, and, it would appear, to some part of the valley-district of the Jordan northward. **and there he tarried with them, and baptized** [ἐβάπτιζεν] or, as we should say, 'kept baptizing;' but only in the sense explained in ch. iv. 2. **23. And** [δὲ]—rather, 'Now,' or 'But' **John also was baptizing in Ænon** [=עֵינָן, עַיִן]—'an eye,' 'a fountain,' which accords with the Evangelist's explanation at the end of this verse. **near to Salim.** The site of these places cannot now be certainly ascertained. But the scenes of the Master's and the servant's labours could not have been very far apart. **because there was much water there: and they came, and were baptized** [παρεγίνοντο καὶ ἐβαπτίζοντο]—or 'kept coming and getting baptized.' **24. For John was not yet cast into prison.** From the first three Evangelists one would naturally conclude that our Lord's public ministry only began after the Baptist's imprisonment. But here, about six months, probably, after our Lord had entered on His public ministry, we find the Baptist still at his work. How much longer this continued cannot be determined with certainty; but probably not very long. For the great importance of this little verse for the right harmonizing of the Gospels, and determining the probable duration of our Lord's ministry, see on Matt. iv. 12.

25. Then there arose a question between [some of] John's disciples and the Jews [ἐκ τῶν μαθητῶν Ἰωάννου μετὰ Ἰουδαίων]—rather, 'on the part of John's disciples with the Jews.' But the true reading beyond doubt is, 'with a Jew' [Ἰουδαίου]. The received text has but inferior support. **about purifying**—that is, baptizing; the symbolical meaning of washing with water being put (as in ch. ii. 6) for the act itself. As John and Jesus were the only teachers who baptized *Jews*, discussions might easily arise between the Baptist's disciples and such Jews as declined to submit to that rite. **26. And they came unto John, and said unto him, Rabbi, he that was with thee beyond Jordan.** '*He* was with *thee*,' they say—not 'thou with him.' **to whom thou barest witness** [σὺ μεμαρτύρηκας]—rather, 'to whom thou hast borne witness;' that is, hast been doing it all this time; **behold, the same baptizeth, and all men come to him:**—*q. d.*, 'Master, this man tells us that he to whom thou barest such generous witness beyond Jordan is requiting thy generosity by drawing all the people away to himself. At this rate, thou shalt soon have no disciples at all.' The reply to this is one of the noblest and most affecting utterances that ever came from the lips of man.

27. John answered and said, A man can receive nothing [Οὐ δύναται ἄνθρωπος λαμβάνειν οὐδὲν]—rather, as in the *margin*, 'A man can take to himself,' or 'assume nothing;' that is, lawfully, and with any success, **except it be given**—or 'have been given' [ᾖ δεδομένον] **him from heaven:**—*q. d.*, 'Every divinely commissioned person has his own work and sphere assigned him from above.' Even Christ Himself came under this law. See on Heb. v. 4. **28. Ye yourselves bear me witness, that I said, I am not the Christ, but that I am sent before him. 29. He that hath the bride is the bridegroom: but the friend of the bridegroom, which standeth and heareth him, rejoiceth greatly**—or 'with joy' [χαρᾷ χαίρει] **because of the bridegroom's voice. This my joy therefore is fulfilled. 30. He must increase, but I must decrease:**—*q. d.*, 'I do my heaven-prescribed work, and that is enough for me. Would you have me mount into my Master's place? Said I not unto you, I am not the Christ? The Bride is not mine, why should the people stay with me? Mine it is to point the burdened to the Lamb of God that taketh away the sin of the world, to tell them there is balm in Gilead, and a Physician there. And shall I grudge to see them, in obedience to the call, flying as a cloud, and as doves to their windows? Whose is the Bride but the Bridegroom's? Enough for me to be the Bridegroom's *Friend*, sent by Him to negotiate the match, privileged to bring together the Saviour and those he is come to seek and to save, and rejoicing with joy unspeakable, if I may but "stand and hear the Bridegroom's voice," witnessing the blessed espousals. Say ye, then, they go from me to Him? Ye bring me glad tidings of great joy. He must increase, but I must decrease; this, my joy, therefore, is fulfilled.' **31. He that cometh from above is above all: he that is of the earth is earthly.** As the words in this last clause are precisely the same, they had better have been so rendered:—'He that is of the earth is of the earth;' although the sense is correctly given by our translators, namely, that those sprung of the earth, even though divinely commissioned, bear the stamp of earth in their very work: but, **he that cometh from heaven is above all.** Here, then, is the reason why He must increase, while all human

32 heaven is above all. And [a]what he hath seen and heard, that he testi-
33 fieth; and no man receiveth his testimony. He that hath received his
34 testimony hath [b]set to his seal that God is true. For [c]he whom God
hath sent speaketh the words of God: for God giveth not the Spirit [d]by
35 measure *unto him.* The [e]Father loveth the Son, and hath given all
36 things into his hand. He [f]that believeth on the Son hath everlasting
life: and he that believeth not the Son shall not see life; but [g]the wrath
of God abideth on him.

A. D. 30.

[a] ch. 15. 15.
[b] 2 Cor. 1. 22.
[c] ch. 7. 16.
[d] ch. 1. 16. Col. 1. 19.
[e] Dan. 7. 14.
[f] Hab. 2. 4.
[g] Gal. 3. 10. Heb. 10. 29.

teachers must decrease. The Master "cometh from above"—descending from *His proper element,* the region of those "heavenly things" which He came to reveal—and so, although mingling with men and things on the earth, He is not "of the earth," either in Person or Word: The servants, on the contrary, springing of earth, are of the earth, and their testimony, even though divine in authority, partakes necessarily of their own earthiness. So strongly did the Baptist feel this contrast that the last clause just repeats the first. It is impossible for a sharper line of distinction to be drawn between Christ and all human teachers, even when divinely commissioned and speaking by the power of the Holy Ghost. And who does not perceive it? The words of prophets and apostles are undeniable and most precious truth; but in the words of Christ we hear a voice as from the excellent Glory, the Eternal Word making Himself heard in our own flesh. **32. And what he hath seen and heard, that he testifieth.** See on *v.* 11, and on ch. i. 18. **and no man receiveth his testimony.** John's disciples had said, "*All* come to Him" (*v.* 26), Would it were so, says the Baptist, but, alas! they are next to none. Nay, they were far readier to receive himself, insomuch that he was obliged to say, I am not the Christ; and this seems to have pained him. **33. He that hath received his testimony hath set to his seal that God is true**—gives glory to God whose words Christ speaks, not as prophets and apostles, by a partial communication of the Spirit to them. **34. For he whom God hath sent speaketh the words of God: for God giveth not the Spirit by measure [unto him].** Here, again, the sharpest conceivable line of distinction is drawn between Christ and all human inspired teachers: 'They have the Spirit in a *limited* degree; but God giveth not [to him] the Spirit *by measure.*' It means, as *Olshausen* says, the entire fulness of divine life and divine power. The present tense "*giveth*" [δίδωσιν] very aptly points out the ever-renewed communication of the Spirit by the Father to the Son, so that a constant flow and re-flow of living power is to be understood (see ch. i. 51). **35. The Father loveth the Son** [ἀγαπᾷ, not φιλεῖ—*diligit,* not *amat*]. The word denotes the love of *character,* as distinguished from the mere love of *person.* But this shade of distinction cannot be expressed in the translation, nor in the present case ought they to be separated. **and hath given all things into his hand.** See on Matt. xi. 27, where we have the same *delivering over* of all things into the hand of the Son, while here, over and above that, we have the deep spring of that august act, in the Father's ineffable *love of the Son.* **36. He that believeth on the Son hath everlasting life**—already hath it. See on *v.* 18; and on ch. v. 24. **and**—or rather, 'but' [δὲ] **he that believeth not the Son shall not see life.** The contrast here is striking. The one has already a life that will endure for ever: the other not only has it not now, but shall never have it—never see it; **but the wrath of God abideth on him.** It was on Him before, and not being *removed* in the only possible way, by "believing on the Son," it necessarily *remaineth* on him.

Remarks.—1. Here again we have the marriage-relation of Jehovah to the Church—one of the leading Evangelical ideas of the Old Testament—which in Ps. xlv. is transferred to *Messiah,* and is here, as in the First Gospel, appropriated by Christ to Himself, who thereby serves Himself Heir to *all* that the Old Testament holds forth of Jehovah's gracious affections, purposes, and relations towards the Church. See on Matt. xxii. 2, and Remark 1 at the close of that Section. 2. What a beautiful and comprehensive idea of the office of the ministry is this, of "Friends of the Bridegroom"—instrumentally bringing the parties together; equally interested in both of them and in their blessed union; rejoicing as they listen to the Bridegroom's voice, with whom the whole originates, by whom all is effected, and from whom flows all the bliss of those united to Him! 3. No test of fidelity in the service of Christ can be more decisive than the spirit here displayed by the Baptist—absorption in his Master's interests, joy at the ingathering of souls to Him, and a willingness to decrease that He may increase, as stars before the rising sun. 4. The difference between Christ and all other, even inspired, teachers is carefully to be observed, and never lost sight of. By this the honour in which the early Church held the Gospels above every other portion of the inspired Scripture is fully justified; nor are the other portions of canonical Scripture thereby disparaged, but rather the contrary, being thus seen in their right place, as all either preparatory to or expository of THE GOSPEL, as the Four Evangelical Records were called—Christ Himself being the chief Corner-stone. 5. When Christ "speaketh the words of God," it is not simply as "The Word made flesh," but (according to the teaching of the Baptist in *v.* 34) as plenarily gifted with the Holy Ghost—that "oil of gladness with which God, even His God, anointed Him above His fellows." As this was prophetically announced in Isa. lxi. 1-3, so it was recognized by Christ Himself (Luke iv. 18). But to guard against the abuse of this truth, as if Christ differed from other teachers only in having the Spirit given Him in larger measure, we shall do well to observe how jealous the fathers of the Church found it necessary to be on this point, when, having to combat such abuses, they decreed in one of their councils, that if any one said that Christ 'spake or wrought miracles by the Spirit of God, as by *a power foreign to Himself,*' he was to be condemned. Thus then—as at His baptism and elsewhere, so here—we have the Father, the Son, and the Holy Ghost, all present, and each in His respective office in the work of redemption. 6. The Son of God is the great Administrator of the kingdom of grace. As this is part of the closing testimony of the Baptist to Him, so does the last book of the New Testament canon conclude with it—"Behold, I come quickly, and *My reward is with Me,* to give to every man according as his work is" (Rev. xxii. 12). But this is not held forth here merely as a great fact. It is to give meaning and weight to what follows (*v.* 36)—that the destinies of all that hear the Gospel, their

4 WHEN therefore the Lord knew how the Pharisees had heard that
2 Jesus made and baptized more disciples than John, (though Jesus himself
3 baptized not, but his disciples,) [a]he left Judea, and departed again into
Galilee.

A. D. 30.

CHAP. 4.
[a] ch. 10. 40.
Matt. 10. 23.
Mark 3. 7.

blissful or blighted eternity, hang upon their reception or rejection of the Son of God. 7. God's attitude towards the unbelieving is that of "wrath" [ὀργή], that is, righteous displeasure, whose judicial expression is called "vengeance" [ἐκδίκησις]. While it repays [ἀποδίδωσι] the unbelieving by excluding them from "seeing life," it does so still more awfully by leaving them under the weight of God's settled, abiding displeasure. And yet, with such teaching sounding in their ears, there are those who confidently teach that there never was, is not, nor can be anything *in God* against sinners, needing to be removed by Christ, but solely *in men* against God. Having formed to themselves certain notions of the *love* and *unchangeableness* of God, which they think incompatible with there being anything in Him against the sinner needing to be removed in order to his salvation, they make the Scripture to bend to these notions, instead of adjusting their own views to its indisputable teaching. This may be consistent enough in those who believe in no authoritative divine Revelation, and regard the Scripture, and Christianity itself, as only designed to quicken and develop the natural religiousness of the human heart. But none who profess to bow to the teaching of Scripture as authoritative and conclusive can, consistently with the concluding words of this chapter, deny that God's view and treatment of the sinner will be that of reconciliation, complacency, and admission to life everlasting, or of abiding wrath or judicial displeasure, and permanent exclusion from life, according as he believes or believes not on the Son; in other words, that we must be not only *internally* but *relatively* right with God, or that He must be gained to us as well as we to Him. That He is willing and waiting to be so is indeed most true, as His whole procedure in the matter of salvation shows; and that neither Christ's death nor our faith in it *make* Him so—as we be slanderously reported and as some affirm that we say—is equally true. But until the sinner meets Him at the Cross, and sets to his own seal to the reconciliation effected by it—until both the Offended and the offending parties embrace each other over the same Sacrifice that taketh away the sin of the world, that love of God which yearns towards the sinner cannot, and will not, reach him. See on Matt. v. 23-26, Remark 7 at the close of that Section. 8. The language of the last six verses of this chapter, regarding Christ, has been thought by not a few critics to go so far beyond the Baptist's point of view, that they cannot persuade themselves that he uttered it as it stands reported here; and they think that the Evangelist himself has, in the exercise of his apostolic illumination and authority, blended the Baptist's fainter and his own clearer views into one full-orbed testimony, as that of the Baptist himself—being his in sense if not in form. We have put this view of *Bengel, Wetstein, Lücke, Olshausen, de Wette, da Costa,* and *Tholuck,* as favourably as we could. But first, if this principle is to be admitted, we can have no confidence that even Christ's own discourses are correctly reported, save that they are too lofty to have been expressed as they are by any human pen; and though this may do very well to authenticate them in the general, there are some statements of our Lord of so peculiar a nature that we should not feel bound to abide by them *as they stand,* if we could persuade ourselves that they were, *in the form* of them at least, due to the Evangelist himself. Thus is a principle of uncertainty in the testimony of the Gospels introduced, of which no one can see the end, or rather, the end of which has been too sadly seen in the criticism of *Schleiermacher* (on the Gospel of Luke, for example), and after him of *Strauss.* But again, this whole testimony of the Baptist—from *v.* 27—is so homogeneous, as *Meyer* well remarks, so uniform, consistent, and continuous, that one cannot see why the former portion of it should be thought to be strictly his, and the rest betray the Evangelist's own pen. But once more, we have seen already how glorious are the rays of Gospel truth—regarding the Person and the Work of Christ alike—which darted from the lips of His honoured herald (see on ch. i. 29; and on i. 49): and as from Luke xi. 1 it is clear that John's teaching to his disciples took a wider range than anything expressly reported in the Gospels, we have no reason for doubting that this testimony—explicitly related as his, and so entirely in harmony with all his recorded testimonies—was really his, merely because it widens out into something singularly clear and lofty; more especially when we consider that it must have been among the very last testimonies, if not altogether the last, which he was permitted to bear to his blessed Master before his imprisonment.

CHAP. IV. 1-42.—THE RISING JEALOUSY OF THE PHARISEES AT THE SUCCESS OF OUR LORD'S MINISTRY INDUCES HIM TO WITHDRAW FROM JUDEA TO GALILEE—ON THE WAY, HE MEETS WITH AND GAINS THE WOMAN OF SAMARIA, AND THROUGH HER, MANY OF THE SAMARITANS, WITH WHOM HE ABIDES TWO DAYS. (=Matt. iv. 12; Mark i. 14; Luke iv. 14.)

Jesus Leaves Judea for Galilee (1-3). **1. When therefore**—referring back to ch. iii. 22, from which the narrative is now resumed, **the Lord knew how the Pharisees had heard that Jesus made and baptized** [ποιεῖ καὶ βαπτίζει]—or 'was making and baptizing' **more disciples than John.** Word to this effect may have been brought to Him; but, perhaps, by styling Him here "the Lord"—which he does only once again before His resurrection—our Evangelist means that He "knew" it as "knowing all men" (ch. ii. 24, 25). **2. (Though** [Καίτοιγε]—or, 'And yet' **Jesus himself baptized not, but his disciples.)** John, being but a servant, baptized with his own hand: Jesus, as the Master, whose exclusive prerogative it was to baptize with the Holy Ghost, seems to have deemed it fitting that He should administer the outward symbol only through His disciples. Besides, had it been otherwise, undue eminence might have been supposed to attach to the Christ-baptized. **3. He left Judea**—that opposition to Him might not be too soon organized, which at that early stage would have marred His work; **and departed again into Galilee**—by which time John had been cast into prison. Here, then, our Evangelist takes up the thread of the three first Gospels: Matt. iv. 12; Mark i. 14; Luke iv. 14. The period during which our Lord continued in Judea, from the time of His first Passover, appears to have been at least eight months—it being, as we shall see from *v.* 35, now "four months to harvest," which, as usually reckoned, would be late in the month of December; but as this makes the harvest, it would seem, too

DD

4 And he must needs go through Samaria. Then cometh he to a
5 city of Samaria, which is called Sychar, near to the parcel of ground
6 [b]that Jacob gave to his son Joseph. Now Jacob's well was there. Jesus
therefore, being wearied with *his* journey, sat thus on the well: *and* it
was about the sixth hour.
7 There cometh a woman of Samaria to draw water: Jesus saith unto
8 her, Give me to drink. (For his disciples were gone away unto the city
9 to buy meat.) Then saith the woman of Samaria unto him, How is it
that thou, being a Jew, askest drink of me, which am a woman of
Samaria? for [c]the Jews have no dealings with the Samaritans.
10 Jesus answered and said unto her, If thou knewest [d]the gift of God,
and who it is that saith to thee, Give me to drink; thou wouldest have

A. D. 30.
[b] Gen. 33. 19. Gen. 48. 22 Jos. 24. 32.
[c] 2 Ki. 17. 24. Ezra 4. 3. Neh. 4. 1,2. Luke 9. 52. Acts 1. 8. Acts 10. 28.
[d] Isa. 9. 6. Isa. 42. 6. Luke 11. 13. Rom. 8. 32. 1 Cor. 1. 30. 2 Cor. 9. 15.

early, perhaps our Lord did not leave till late in January.

Jesus at Jacob's Well Converses with and Gains the Woman of Samaria (4-26). **4. And** [δὲ]—or, 'Now' **he must needs go through Samaria**—for a geographical reason, no doubt; the nearest way from Judea to Galilee being through the intermediate province of Samaria: but certainly it was not without a higher design—He "needed" to meet with the woman at Jacob's well, and to reap the blessed fruit of that meeting. **5. Then cometh he to a city of Samaria, called Sychar**—the "Shechem" of the Old Testament, about thirty-four miles north of Jerusalem. From the Romans it got the name of "Neapolis," and is now called "Nablous." But see on *v.* 20. In "coming to" this town, however, He came only to its neighbourhood, remaining in the first instance, at Jacob's well. **near to the parcel of ground that Jacob gave to his son Joseph.** This fact, though not expressly stated in the Old Testament, was *inferred* by the Jews from Gen. xxxiii. 19; xlviii. 22 (according to the LXX. translation); Jos. xxiv. 32. **6. Now Jacob's well was there.** 'We enquired of the Samaritans,' says *Dr. Robinson*, 'respecting Jacob's well. They said they acknowledged the tradition, and regarded it as having belonged to the patriarch. It lies at the mouth of the valley (the narrow valley of Nablous) near the south-side. Late as it was, we took a guide and set off for Jacob's well. We were thirty-five minutes in coming to it from the city. The well bears evident marks of antiquity, but was now dry and deserted; it was said usually to contain living water, and not merely to be filled by the rains. A large stone was laid loosely over, or rather in its mouth, and as the hour was now late, we made no attempt to remove the stone and examine the vaulted entrance below. We had also no line with us at the moment, to measure the well; but by dropping in stones, we could perceive that it was *deep* (*v.* 11). *Maundrell*, who measured the well, found it dug in a firm rock, about three yards in diameter, and thirty-five in depth; five yards being full of water. In 1839, it was found to be only seventy-five feet deep below the vault by which it is covered, with only ten or twelve feet of water; while in 1843, the bottom was found scarcely covered with water.' Various difficulties in the way of this tradition and the identity of the well are satisfactorily disposed of by Dr. Robinson. **Jesus therefore, being wearied with his journey, sat thus** [οὕτως] **on the well** [ἐπὶ τῇ πηγῇ]—rather, 'by the well'—that is, just as one would do in such circumstances, loungingly or at ease; an instance of the graphic style of our Evangelist. In fact, this is perhaps the most *human* of all the scenes of our Lord's earthly history. We seem to be beside Him, overhearing all that is here recorded; nor could any painting of the scene on canvas, however perfect, do other than lower the conception which this exquisite narrative conveys to the devout and intelligent reader. But with all that is *human*, how much also of the *divine* have we here, both blended in one glorious manifestation of the majesty, grace, pity, patience with which "the Lord" imparts light and life to this unlikeliest of strangers, standing midway between Jews and heathens. **[and] it was about the sixth hour**—or *noon-day;* reckoning from six o'clock A.M. From Cant i. 7, we know, as from other sources, that the very flocks "rested at noon." But Jesus, whose maxim was, "I must work the works of Him that sent me while it is day" (ch. ix. 4), seems to have denied Himself that repose, at least on this occasion, probably that He might reach this well when He knew the woman would be there. Once there, however, He accepts the grateful ease of a seat on the patriarchal stone. But, while Himself is resting, what music is that which I hear from His lips, "Come unto Me all ye that labour and are heavy laden, and I will give you *rest?*" (Matt xi. 28).

7. There cometh a woman of Samaria to draw water: Jesus saith unto her, Give me to drink. For the heat of a noon-day sun had parched His lips. But, while Himself thirsting, "In the last, that great day of the feast, Jesus stood and cried, saying, If any man thirst, let him come unto me and *drink*" (ch. vii. 37). **8. (For his disciples were gone away unto the city to buy meat)** [τροφὰς]—'victuals,' or 'provisions.' This was wisely ordered, that Jesus might be alone with the woman; nor did the disciples return till the dialogue was concluded, and our Lord's object in it entirely gained. **9. Then saith the woman of Samaria unto him, How is it that thou, being a Jew, askest drink of me, which am a woman of Samaria?**—not altogether refusing, yet wondering at so unusual a request from a Jew, as His dress and dialect would at once discover Him to be, to a Samaritan. **for the Jews have no dealings with the Samaritans**—or better without the article, as in the original, 'Jews have no dealings with Samaritans.' Not absolutely none, for the disciples at this very time had gone to buy of the Sycharites, and brought their purchase with them. But the reference is to *friendly* dealings, such as exchange of hospitalities and acts of kindness. It is this national antipathy that gives point to the parable of The Good Samaritan (Luke x. 30, &c.), and to the thankfulness of the Samaritan leper, when he found himself cured by the Lord Jesus (Luke xvii. 16, 18). *Robinson* says the Samaritans 'still maintain their ancient hatred against the Jews, and neither eat, nor drink, nor marry, nor associate with the Jews; but only trade with them.'

10. Jesus answered and said unto her, If thou knewest the gift of God, and who it is that saith

11 asked of him, and he would have given thee [e]living water. The woman
saith unto him, Sir, thou hast nothing to draw with, and the well is
12 deep: from whence then hast thou that living water? Art thou greater
than our father Jacob, which gave us the well, and drank thereof himself,
and his children, and his cattle?
13 Jesus answered and said unto her, Whosoever drinketh of this water
14 shall thirst again: but whosoever drinketh of the water that I shall give
him shall never thirst; but the water that I shall give him [f]shall be in
15 him a well of water springing up into everlasting life. The [g]woman saith
unto him, Sir, give me this water, that I thirst not, neither come hither
to draw.
16 Jesus saith unto her, Go, call thy husband, and come hither. The
17 woman answered and said, I have no husband.
18 Jesus said unto her, Thou hast well said, I have no husband: for thou
hast had five husbands; and he whom thou now hast is not thy husband:
19 in that saidst thou truly. The woman saith unto him, Sir, [h]I perceive
20 that thou art a prophet. Our fathers worshipped in [i]this mountain; and
ye say, that in [j]Jerusalem is the place where men ought to worship.

A. D. 30.

[e] Ex. 17. 6. Isa. 12. 3. Isa. 44. 3. Jer. 2. 13. Zec. 13. 1. Zec. 14. 8. Rev. 7. 17.
[f] ch. 7. 38. ch. 10. 10. Rom. 5. 21. 2 Cor. 1. 22.
[g] Rom. 6. 23. 1 John 5. 20.
[h] Luke 7. 16. Luke 24. 19. ch. 6. 14. ch. 7. 40.
[i] Gen. 12. 6. Jud. 9. 7.
[j] Deut. 12. 5. 2 Chr. 7. 12. Ps. 78. 68.

to thee, Give me to drink; thou wouldest have asked of him, and he would have given thee living water:—*q. d.*, 'In Me thou seest only a petitioner to thee; but if thou knewest Who that Petitioner is, and the gift that God is giving to men, thou wouldst have changed places with Him, gladly suing of Him living water—nor shouldst thou have sued in vain,' gently reflecting on her for not immediately meeting His request. **11. The woman saith unto him, Sir, thou hast nothing to draw with, and the well is deep: from whence then hast thou that living water?** This is the language of one who, though startled by what was said to her, saw that it must have some meaning, and sought by this question to get at the bottom of it. **12. Art thou greater**—already perceiving in this Stranger a claim to some mysterious greatness, **than our father Jacob, which gave us the well, and drank thereof himself, and his children, and his cattle?** For, says *Josephus* (Antt. ix. 14. 3), when it went well with the Jews the Samaritans claimed kindred with them, as being descended from Joseph, but when misfortunes befell the Jews they disowned all connection with them. **13. Jesus answered and said unto her, Whosoever** [Πᾶς ὁ]—rather, 'Every one that' **drinketh of this water shall thirst again: 14. But whosoever drinketh of the water that I shall give him shall never thirst; but the water that I shall give him shall be in him** [γενήσεται ἐν αὐτῷ]—rather, 'shall become in him' **a well of water springing up into everlasting life.** The contrast here is fundamental and all-comprehensive. "This water" plainly means 'this natural water and all satisfactions of a like earthly and perishable nature.' Coming to us from without, and reaching only the superficial parts of our nature, they are soon spent, and need to be anew supplied as much as if we had never experienced them before, while the deeper wants of our being are not reached by them at all; whereas the "water" that Christ gives—*spiritual life*—is struck out of the very depths of our being, making the soul not a *cistern*, for holding water *poured into* it *from without*, but a *fountain*—the word [πηγὴ] had been better so rendered, to distinguish it from the word rendered "well" in *v.* 11 [φρέαρ]—springing, gushing, bubbling up and flowing forth from *within* us, ever fresh, ever living. *The indwelling of the Holy Ghost as the Spirit of Christ* is the secret of this life, with all its enduring energies and satisfactions, as is expressly said (ch. vii. 37-39). "Never thirsting," then, just means that such souls have the supplies *at home.* It is an internal well, "springing up into everlasting life"—by which words our Lord carries the thoughts up from the eternal freshness and vitality of these waters in *us* to the great ocean in which they have their confluence. 'Thither,' says devout *Bengel*, 'may I arrive!' **15. The woman saith unto him, Sir, give me this water, that I thirst not, neither come hither to draw.** This is not obtuseness, for that is giving way: it expresses a wondering desire after she scarce knew what from this mysterious Stranger.

16. Jesus saith unto her, Go call thy husband, and come hither—now proceeding to arouse her slumbering conscience by laying bare the guilty life she was leading, and, by the minute details which that life furnished, not only bringing her sin vividly up before her, but preparing her to receive in His true character that wonderful Stranger to whom her whole life, in its minutest particulars, evidently lay open. **17. The woman answered and said, I have no husband. Jesus said unto her, Thou hast well said, I have no husband: 18. For thou hast had five husbands; and he whom thou now hast is not thy husband: in that saidst thou truly. 19. The woman saith unto him, Sir, I perceive that thou art a prophet. 20. Our fathers worshipped in this mountain**—that is, mount *Gerizim* (Deut. xi. 29; xxvii. 12; Jos. viii. 33; Jud. ix. 7). In the Samaritan Pentateuch, instead of "*Ebal*" (Deut. xxvii. 4)—on which Moses commanded the altar to be erected, with the ten commandments written upon the stones of it (see Deut. xxvii. 1-8)—the word "*Gerizim*" stands; and the Samaritans are tenacious of this reading as their warrant for holding Gerizim to be the divinely-ordained place of public worship, on which they have acted from age to age, and do even to this day. 'There is,' says *Stanley*, 'probably no other locality in which the same worship has been sustained with so little change or interruption for so great a series of years as that of this mountain, from Abraham to the present day. In their humble synagogue, at the foot of the mountain, the Samaritans still worship—the oldest and the smallest sect in the world.' *Robinson* found their whole number scarcely to exceed a hundred and fifty souls. 'Mounts Gerizim and Ebal,' says this last distinguished traveller, 'rise in steep rocky precipices from the valley on each side, apparently some eight hundred feet in height. The sides of both these mountains,

21 Jesus saith unto her, Woman, believe me, the hour cometh, [k]when ye
shall neither in this mountain, nor yet at Jerusalem, worship the Father.
22 Ye worship [l]ye know not what: we know what we worship: for [m]salva-
23 tion is of the Jews. But the hour cometh, and now is, when the true
worshippers shall worship the Father in [n]spirit [o]and in truth: for the
24 Father seeketh such to worship him. God [p]*is* a Spirit: and they that
25 worship him must worship *him* in spirit and in truth. The woman saith
unto him, I know that [q]Messias cometh, which is called Christ: when he
26 is come, he will tell us all things. Jesus saith unto her, I that speak
unto thee am *he.*

A. D. 30.

[k] Mal. 1. 11. Matt. 18. 20. 1 Tim. 2. 8.
[l] 2 Ki. 17. 29.
[m] Isa. 2. 3. Luke 24. 47. Rom. 9. 4, 5.
[n] Phil. 3. 3.
[o] ch. 1. 17.
[p] 2 Cor. 3. 17.
[q] Deut. 18. 15. Dan. 9. 24.

as here seen, were to our eyes equally naked and sterile.' **and ye say, that in Jerusalem is the place where men ought to worship.** Was this question asked—as *Stier*, *Alford*, and others think—merely for information on an important religious question? In that case it seems a strange way of meeting our Lord's home-thrust. But if we view it as the question of one who had been stunned by so unexpected a revelation of her sinful life, made to her by one whom she had begun to regard in no common light—all seems clear enough. Though she saw herself all disclosed, she is not yet prepared to break down and ask what hopes there might be for one so guilty. Her convictions have come upon her too suddenly for that. She shifts the question, therefore, from a personal to a public one, though the sequel shows how this revelation of her past life had told upon her. So her reply is not, 'Alas, what a wicked life have I been leading!' but, 'Lo, what a wonderful prophet have I got into conversation with! He will be able to settle that interminable dispute between us and the Jews. Sir, our fathers hold to this mountain,' pointing to *Gerizim*, 'as the divinely consecrated place of worship, but ye Jews say that *Jerusalem* is the proper place: say, which of us is right, thou to whom all such things are doubtless known.' How slowly does the human heart submit to *thorough* humiliation! Compare the prodigal (see on Luke xv. 15). Doubtless our Lord saw through her, and perceived the more immediate object of her question. But how does He meet it? Does He say 'That is not the point just now; but how stands it with thy heart and life? Till that is disposed of theological controversies must be let alone?' The Prince of preachers takes another method: He humours the poor woman, letting her take her own way, allowing her to lead while He follows—but thus only the more effectually gaining His object. He answers her question, pours light into her mind on the *spirituality* of all true worship, even as of its glorious Object, and so brings her insensibly to the point at which He could disclose to her wondering mind Whom she was all the while speaking to.

21. Jesus saith unto her, Woman, believe me, the hour cometh [ἔρχεται ὥρα]—rather, 'there cometh an hour,' **when ye shall neither in this mountain, nor yet at Jerusalem, worship the Father**—that is, shall worship Him at neither place and at no place as an exclusively chosen, consecrated, central place of worship. (See Mal. i. 11; 1 Tim. ii. 8.) Observe how our Lord gently and indirectly raises the woman's views of the great Object of all acceptable worship. She had talked simply of "worship." He says, "The worship of THE FATHER" shall soon be everywhere. 'The point raised will very soon cease to be of any moment, for a total change of dispensation is about to come over the Church:—but now, as to the question itself.' **22. Ye worship ye know not what: we know what we worship** [ὃ οὐκ οἴδατε—ὃ οἴδαμεν]—rather, 'Ye worship what ye know not: we worship what we know'—*q. d.*, 'Ye worship without any revealed authority, and so, very much in the dark; but in this sense the Jews know what they are about.' **for salvation is of the Jews.** The Samaritans are wrong, not only as to the *place*, but the whole *grounds* and *nature* of their worship; while in all these respects the truth lies with us Jews. For Salvation is not a thing left to be reached by any one who may vaguely desire it of a God of mercy, but something that has been revealed, prepared, deposited with a particular people, and must be sought in connection with, and as issuing from them; and that people "the Jews." Here, and almost here only, our Lord uses the pronoun "we." But observe in what sense. It is not, He and other individual men: It is He and the Jewish nation, "of whom as concerning the flesh, Christ came" (Rom. ix. 5). It is, *We Jews.* In other words, Christ here identifies Himself with others only as touching the family to which as man He belonged; and even that but once or twice. Hence it seems no proper exception to Remark 3 at the close of the Section on Nicodemus (ch. iii. 1-21). **23. But the hour cometh**—or, 'But there cometh an hour,' **and now is**—evidently meaning her to understand that this new economy was in some sense in course of being set up while He was talking to her; a sense which would in a few minutes so far appear, when He told her plainly that He was *the Christ.* **when the true worshippers shall worship the Father in spirit and in truth**—or 'in spirit and truth' [ἐν πνεύματι καὶ ἀληθείᾳ]; **for the Father seeketh such to worship him**—or 'seeketh such to be His worshippers' [τοιούτους ζητεῖ τοὺς προσκυνοῦντας αὐτόν]. **24. God is a spirit: and they that worship him must worship [him] in spirit and [in] truth.** 'As God is a Spirit, so He both invites and demands a spiritual worship, and already all is in preparation for a spiritual economy, more in harmony with the true nature of acceptable service than the ceremonial worship by consecrated *persons*, *places*, and *times*, which God for a time has seen meet to keep up till the fulness of the time should come.' **25. The woman saith unto him, I know that Messias cometh, which is called Christ: when he is come, he will tell us all things.** If we take our Lord's immediate disclosure of Himself, in answer to these words, as the proper key to their meaning *to His ear*, we can hardly doubt that the woman was already all but prepared for even this startling announcement, which indeed she seems (from *v.* 29) to have already begun to suspect by His revealing her to herself. Thus quickly, under so matchless a Teacher, was she brought up from her sunken condition to a frame of mind and heart capable of receiving the noblest revelations. When she says of the expected Messiah, that He would "tell them all things," this belief was probably founded on Deut.

27 And upon this came his disciples, and marvelled that he talked with
the woman: yet no man said, What seekest thou? or, Why talkest thou
28 with her? The woman then left her water-pot, and went her way into
29 the city, and saith to the men, Come, see a man which told me all things
30 that ever I did: is not this the Christ? Then they went out of the city,
and came unto him.
31 In the meanwhile his disciples prayed him, saying, Master, eat.
32 But he said unto them, [r]I have meat to eat that ye know not of.
33 Therefore said the disciples one to another, Hath any man brought him
34 *ought* to eat? Jesus saith unto them, [s]My meat is to do the will of him

A. D. 30.

[r] Job 23. 12. Ps. 63. 5. Ps. 119. 103. Pro. 18. 20. Isa. 53. 11. Jer. 15. 16. Acts 20. 35.
[s] Job 23. 12. ch. 6. 38. ch. 17. 4. ch. 19. 30.

xviii. 15. **26. Jesus saith unto her, I that speak unto thee am he.** Never did our Lord utter Himself so nakedly to His own people the Jews. He had magnified them to the woman; but to themselves He was to the last far more reserved than to her—*proving* to them rather than plainly *telling* them that He was the Christ. But what would not have been *safe* among them was safe enough with her, whose *simplicity* and *docility* at this stage of the conversation appear from the sequel to have become perfect. What now will the woman say? We listen, but all is over. The curtain has dropped. The scene has changed. A new party has arrived.

The Disciples Return from Sychar, and the Woman Returns to it—What passed between Jesus and the Disciples on this case, and how the Woman Brought the Sycharites to Jesus (27-38). **27. And upon this came his disciples**—who had been to Sychar to buy provisions (*v.* 8). **and marvelled that he talked**—or 'was talking' [ἐλάλει] **with the woman.** Being a Samaritan, they would not expect such a thing. But though our Lord never went out of His way to *seek* either Samaritans or Gentiles—ever observing His own direction to the Twelve when they went forth to preach (see on Matt. x. 5, 6)—neither did He ever go out of His way to *avoid* them, when, as in the case of the Syrophenician Gentile, they came seeking Him (see on Mark vii. 24, 25), or, as in the case of this Samaritan woman, Providence threw them in His way. In this He acted on the great principle which He Himself laid down in regard to the Sabbath—that '*Not to do good, when it is in the power of our hand to do it, is to do evil.*' See on Matt. xii. 12. Had the disciples seen with the eyes and felt with the heart of their Master, they would less have marvelled that He "talked with the woman"—and many a time have marvelled that He talked with *themselves.* **yet no man**—'no one' **said, What seekest thou?**—'What object hadst Thou? **or, Why talkest thou with her?**—awed, no doubt, by the spectacle, and thinking there must be something under it, yet afraid to meddle with it. **28. The woman then left her water-pot, and went her way into the city, and saith to the men, 29. Come** [Δεῦτε], **see a man which told me all things that ever I did: is not this the Christ?** [μήτι οὗτός ἐστιν ὁ Χριστός;] The grammatical form of this question, which expects a *negative* answer, requires that it should be rendered, 'Is this'—or rather, 'Can this be the Christ?' The woman put it thus, as if they would naturally reply, 'Impossible.' But beneath that modest way of putting it was the conviction, that if they would but come and judge for themselves, she would have no need to obtrude upon them any opinions of hers—which she well knew would appear unworthy of attention. Thus, by asking if this could possibly be the Christ—and so, rather asking to be helped by them than pretending to be their teacher—she in reality drew their attention to the point, in the least offensive and yet most effectual way. Observe, too, how she confines herself to the marvel of His disclosing to her the particulars of her own life, without touching on what He had said of Himself. If the woman's past life was known to the Sycharites—as who can doubt it was, in so small a place?—this would at once disarm their prejudices and add weight to her statement. How exquisitely natural is all this! Up to our Lord's last words her attention had been enchained, and her awe deepened; and certainly the last disclosure was fitted to hold her faster to the spot than ever. But the arrival of strangers made her feel that it was time for her to withdraw; and He who knew what was in her heart, and what she was going to the city to do, having said all to her that she was then able to bear, let her go without exchanging a word with her in the hearing of others. Their interview was too sacred, and the effect on the woman too overpowering (not to speak of His own deep emotion), to allow of its being continued. But this one artless touch—that she "left her water-pot"—speaks volumes. The living water was already beginning to spring up within her; she found that man doth not live by bread nor by water only, and that there was a water of wondrous virtue that raised people above meat and drink, and the vessels that held them, and all human things. In short, she was transported, forgot everything but one, or felt that her water-pot now would be an encumbrance; and her heart running over with the tale she had to tell, she hastens home and pours it out. **30. Then they went out of the city, and came unto him.** How different, in this, from the Jews! and richly was this their openness to conviction rewarded. But first the Evangelist relates what passed between Jesus and the disciples after the woman's departure.

31. In the meanwhile—during her absence—**his disciples prayed him, saying, Master, eat.** *Fatigue* and *thirst* we saw He felt; here is revealed another of our common infirmities to which the Lord was subject—*hunger.* **32. But he said unto them, I have meat to eat that ye know not of.** What spirituality of mind does this answer breathe! The pronouns, "*I*" and "*ye*" are emphatically expressed ['Εγὼ—ὑμεῖς], sharply to mark the contrast between His thoughts and theirs at this time. 'As for Me, I have been eating all this time, and such food as ye dream not of.' What can that be? they ask each other; have any supplies been brought Him in our absence? He knows what they are saying, though He hears it not. **33. Therefore said the disciples one to another, Hath any man brought him [ought] to eat? 34. Jesus saith unto them, My meat** ['Εμὸν βρῶμα]. Here, again, the "My" is emphatic, in the same sense. **is to do**—or rather, 'to be doing' [ἵνα ποιῶ] **the will of Him that sent me, and to finish his work** [τελειώσω]—changing the tense to that of a *completed*

35 that sent me, and to finish his work. Say not ye, There are yet four
months, and *then* cometh harvest? behold, I say unto you, Lift up your
36 eyes, and look on the fields; [t]for they are white already to harvest. And
[u]he that reapeth receiveth wages, and gathereth fruit unto life eternal;
37 that both he that soweth and he that reapeth may rejoice together. And
38 herein is that saying true, One soweth, and another reapeth. I sent you
to reap that whereon ye bestowed no labour: [v]other men laboured, and
ye are entered into their labours.

A. D. 30.

t Matt. 9. 37. Luke 10. 2.
u Pro. 11. 18. Dan. 12. 3. 1 Cor. 3. 8. 2 John 8. Jas. 5. 20.
v Acts 10. 43. 1 Pet. 1. 12.

work. 'A Servant here to fulfil a prescribed work, to *do* and to *finish* that work is "meat" to Me; and of this, while ye were away, I have had my fill.' And of what does He speak thus? Of the condescension, pity, patience, wisdom, He had been laying out upon *one soul*—a very humble woman, and one in some respects repulsive too! But He had gained her, and through her was going to gain more, and lay perhaps the foundation of a great work in the country of Samaria; and this filled His whole soul, and raised Him above the sense of natural hunger. (See on Matt. iv. 4.) **35. Say not ye, There are yet four months, and then cometh harvest?** That this was intended to express the actual interval between the time when our Lord was speaking and the harvest-time that year, we cannot doubt. The arguments against it, by *Alford* and others, as if this were a proverbial speech without any definite reference to the actual time of its utterance—which to us is scarcely intelligible—seem feeble, and the best critics and harmonists regard it here as a note of the actual season of the year at which our Lord spoke—late in December, but more probably January, and, as *Stanley* affirms, from his own observation, even so late as February; though the year he refers to was perhaps an exceptional one, and the month of February seems too late. **behold, I say unto you, Lift up your eyes, and look on the fields; for they are white already to harvest.** 'It wants four months to harvest, ye would say at this season of the natural harvest: but lift up your eyes and look upon those fields in the light of *another* husbandry, for, lo! *in that sense*, it wants not four months nor four days, for they are even now white to harvest, ready for the sickle.' The simple beauty of this language is only surpassed by the glow of holy emotion in the Redeemer's own soul which it expresses. It refers to the *ripeness* of these Sycharites for accession to Him, and the joy of this great Lord of the reapers over the anticipated ingathering. O could we but *so* "lift up our eyes and look" upon many fields abroad and at home, which to dull sense appear unpromising, as *He* beheld those of Samaria, what movements, now scarce in embryo, and accessions to Christ, seemingly far distant, might we not discern as quite near at hand, and thus, amidst difficulties and discouragements too much for nature to sustain, be cheered—*as our Lord Himself was* in circumstances far more overwhelming—with "songs in the night"! [It is surprising that *Tischendorf* should adhere to the punctuation of some certainly ancient MSS. and versions here, in connecting the word "already"—ἤδη—with the following verse; no doubt, because the usual place of that adverb is before, not after, καί. But as this would utterly destroy the sense of our Lord's statements in the two verses, so in the matter of mere punctuation the MSS. and versions are of no authority; and we are as good judges as the ancient transcribers and translators where the punctuation in every case ought to be. Both *Lachmann* and *Tregelles* follow here the punctuation of the received text.] **36. And he that reapeth receiveth wages, and gathereth fruit unto life eternal; that both he that soweth and he that reapeth may rejoice together. 37. And herein is that saying true, One soweth, and another reapeth.** As our Lord could not mean that the reaper only, and not the sower, received "wages," in the sense of *personal reward* for his work, the "wages" here can be no other than the joy of having such a harvest to gather in—the joy of "gathering fruit unto life eternal." The blessed issue of the whole ingathering is the interest alike of the sower and of the reaper; it is no more the fruit of the last operation than of the first; and just as there can be no reaping without previous sowing, so have those servants of Christ, to whom is assigned the pleasant task of merely reaping the spiritual harvest, no work to do, and no joy to taste, that has not been prepared to their hand by the toilsome and often thankless work of their predecessors in the field. The joy, therefore, of the great harvest festivity will be the common joy of all who have taken any part in the work from the first operation to the last. (See Deut. xvi. 11, 14; Ps. cxxvi. 6; Isa. ix. 3). **38. I sent you** ['Εγὼ ἀπέστειλα]. The "I" here is emphatic: I, the Lord of the whole harvest. When He says, "I *sent* you," He refers back to their *past* appointment to the apostleship, though it points only to the *future* discharge of it, for they had nothing to do with the present ingathering of the Sycharites. **to reap that whereon ye bestowed no labour**—meaning that much of their future success would arise from the preparation already made for them. **other men laboured**—referring, as we think, to the Old Testament labourers, the Baptist, and *by implication* Himself, though He studiously keeps this in the background, that the line of distinction between Himself and all His servants might not be lost sight of.

The Sycharites, Believing the Woman's Testimony concerning Jesus, are Confirmed in their Faith by personal intercourse with Him—On their invitation Jesus spends two days in Sychar, by which the number of believers in Him is greatly increased (39-42). **39. And many of the Samaritans of that city believed on him for the saying of the woman, which testified, He told me all that ever I did.** What a commentary is this on *v.* 35, "Lift up your eyes, and look on the fields, for they are white already to harvest"! **40. So when the Samaritans were come unto him, they besought him that he would tarry with them: and he abode**—or 'tarried'—it is the same word [ἔμεινεν]—**there two days. 41. And many more believed because of his [own] word; 42. And said unto the woman, Now we believe, not because of thy saying** [οὐκ ἔτι διὰ τὴν σὴν λαλιὰν]—or, 'No longer do we believe because of thy saying;' **for we have heard him ourselves, and know that this is indeed the Christ, the Saviour of the world**—or, according to the order in the original, 'that this is indeed the Saviour of the world, the Christ.' What a marvellous simplicity and docility do these Samaritans display! They first credit the woman's simple testimony, and let her bring them to Jesus; then they are satisfied by one brief interview with Himself that

39 And [w]many of the Samaritans of that city believed on him for the
40 saying of the woman, which testified, He told me all that ever I did. So
[x]when the Samaritans were come unto him, they besought him that he
41 would tarry with them: and he abode there two days. And [y]many more

A. D. 30.

[w] Gen. 49. 10.
[x] Gen. 32. 26.
[y] Isa. 42. 1.
Rom. 15. 8.

He is the Christ, and invite Him to visit them; and when He condescends to do so, His two days' stay not only brings over many more to the same faith in Him, but raises that faith to a conviction—never reached by the Jews, and hardly as yet attained by His own disciples—that as the Christ He was "*the Saviour of the world.*" And yet, beyond the supernatural knowledge which He had displayed in His interview with the woman, He does not appear to have wrought any miracle before these Samaritans. Is there anything in the Gospel History more remarkable than this? those were two precious days, surely, to the Redeemer Himself! Unsought, He had come to His own, yet His own received Him not; now those who were not His own had come to Him, been won by Him, and invited Him to their town that others might share with them in the benefit of His wonderful ministry. Here, then, would He solace His already wounded spirit, and have in this outfield village-triumph of His grace a sublime foretaste of the inbringing of the whole Gentile world into the Church. *Olshausen* correctly notes this as 'a rare instance of the Lord's ministry *producing an awakening on a large scale.*'

Remarks.—1. Did He who, when the time to suffer arrived, "set His face like a flint," withdraw from Judea to Galilee when Pharisaic jealousy at Jerusalem would have come too soon to a head, and arrested the work given Him to do? Let His followers learn from Him this wisdom of the serpent while manifesting, with Him, the harmlessness of the dove. Needless exposure is as much to be avoided as a cowardly flight, in times when the truth cannot be confessed without personal danger. 2. In what a light do the condescension, the zeal, the skill, the patience, which Jesus bestowed upon the woman of Samaria place the value of a single soul! Apart from all that followed, what a rescue was effected in that one cause! See a similar care of one soul in the case of the Ethiopian eunuch, with a view to whose illumination Philip the Evangelist was taken out of full and glorious work in the city of Samaria, away to the desert road from Jerusalem to Gaza (Acts viii. 26, &c., on which see). "Brethren," says James, "if any [*one*] of you [τις ἐν ὑμῖν] do err from the truth, and one convert him, let him know that he which converteth a sinner from the error of his way shall save *a soul* from death, and shall hide a multitude of sins" (see on Jas. v. 19, 20). And observe how *casually* this woman of Samaria was gained. Jesus and she were each on their own business at this well; He on His way from Judea to Galilee, and she come from the neighbouring village to draw water. Doubtless such meetings of Jewish men and Samaritan women at that well were customary enough; and had Jesus preserved the usual silence, nothing had come of it. But the opportunity was to Him too precious to be lost. Though the thirst was as real as the weariness, and water as desirable as repose, He certainly disregarded the national antipathies, not so much to mark His superiority to them and disapprobation of them, nor yet merely to slake His thirst, but to draw this woman into a conversation which should not cease till He had gained her soul. O, if such casual opportunities of usefulness were embraced by the followers of Christ as by Christ Himself, how many might be won to Him without ever going out of their way! All that is wanted is that love of souls which burned in Him, that constant readiness to avail ourselves of openings for Christian usefulness, the present sense of the truth upon the heart, and a spirit of dependence upon Him for that power to open the mind and heart which He possessed and we must get from Him. If we could but say with Him—and just in proportion as we *can* say with Him—"My meat is to be doing the will of Him that sent me, and to finish His work;" if we do but remember that this was said of what He had been doing for one soul, and that of the fruit He was reaping in that one case, He said, "I have meat to eat that ye know not of"—we should need no stimulants to follow Him, and hardly any directions for doing it. But who can tell what may issue out of one conversion? Think of the little maid of Israel (2 Ki. v. 1-14.) See what this once disreputable woman of Samaria did for her fellow-villagers; and who shall say what wide-spread influences, preparing Samaria for the eventual reception of the Gospel, may not have flowed from the precious events of those two days which Jesus spent there? (See on Acts viii. 9-13.) No conversion ought to stand alone. Every disciple of the Lord Jesus should feel himself, like this woman, a missionary for Christ, and every conversion should be like a wave of the sea, begetting another. So that the pains taken on one soul—while of itself, if it issue in conversion, it will be "meat" to any who have the Spirit of Christ—ought to be taken with all the more eagerness and hope, as we have ground to believe that we are thus, in all likelihood, doing good on a large scale. 3. How vividly does the reality of our Lord's human nature—His warm, quivering humanity—His identity with ourselves, not only in all the essential properties but in all the sinless infirmities of our nature, come out here! He is weary with a journey, just as we are; His tongue, like ours, is parched with thirst; He feels, as we do, the cravings of hunger: So He rests Him by Jacob's well, as we should do in like case, and asks, as a thirsty man would do, for a draught of water from the woman of Samaria; and He is provided by His disciples with victuals from Sychar, just as other men. And the life-like, minute lines of detail are so drawn that we feel as if we saw and heard the whole, and the very children that read it feel the same. And yet this is the loftiest and deepest of all the Gospels. Nay, in the dialogue which the Evangelist reports between Jesus and the Woman, these details seem but like the finest net-work of gold in which are set jewels of heavenly lustre and incomparable price—the jewel of unfathomable Dignity, Authority, Grace, Penetration, Patience, in this Petitioner for water; besides all the jewels of spiritual truth never before uttered in such a style. No wonder that this should be regarded as emphatically the Gospel of the Person and Grace of the Lord Jesus, and that our Evangelist should get the surname of "the divine." 4. Mark how Jesus holds Himself forth here as the sovereign Giver, the authoritative Dispenser of the living water; which living water is nothing less than a well-spring of eternal satisfaction opened up in a man's soul, never to dry up. Such a claim on the part of a mere *creature* would not be more offensive than ridiculous. Search the whole Scripture, and see if anything approaching to it was ever taken into the lips of the most emi-

42 believed because of his own word; and said unto the woman, Now we
believe, not because of thy saying; for [z]we have heard *him* ourselves, and
know that this is indeed the Christ, [a]the Saviour of the world.

A. D. 30.

[z] ch. 17. 8. 1 John 4. 14.
[a] 1 John 2. 2.

nent and inspired servants of God. But how majestic, appropriate, and self-evidencing are such claims from the lips of this Speaker! As we read and re-read this dialogue, we feel ourselves in the presence of Grace Incarnate—enshrined, too, not in celestial humanity, but (O wonder of wonders!) in weary, thirsty, hungry flesh, just like our own; sitting down beside us, talking with us, breathing on us its tender love, and laying its warm, fleshly hand upon us, drawing us with cords of a man and bands of love. See on Matt. xi. 28, and Remark 5 at the close of that Section. 5. With what charming simplicity and transparent clearness does one line of this dialogue express the unsatisfactoriness of all earthly satisfactions—"Every one that drinketh of this water shall thirst again." Under the figure of cold waters to a thirsty soul, it covers the whole field of earth's satisfactions, but stamps them as external to us, and coming into us from without; while it represents the soul as the mere reservoir of them, drying up like other cisterns, and needing to be ever replenished. But what a contrast to this immediately follows. Still keeping to the figure of water, Jesus claims it as His prerogative to open in the soul a fountain of living waters that shall never cease to flow, a spring of enduring satisfaction and eternal freshness; thus expressing, with matchless brevity, force, and beauty, the *spirituality*, the *vitality*, the *joy*, the *perpetuity* of that religious change which He effects in all that believe on His name. But now, 6. When we advance to the woman's question about the place where men ought to worship, how wonderful is the breadth and richness of the answer given her. First, our Lord will not dash her by telling her that her countrymen were in the wrong, until He has first told her how soon the whole question will be at an end. But when He does do so, how definite and positive is the verdict pronounced upon the Samaritan worship. Men talk as if *sincerity* were the only thing of consequence in the worship of God. That the Samaritans were more wanting in this than the Jews there is no evidence; and the very different reception which our Lord met with from the one than the other would seem to show that they were the more unsophisticated of the two. And yet He says the Samaritans knew not the Object they worshipped, while the Jews did, because Salvation was of the Jews. What can this mean, if it be not that the Samaritans worshipped after ideas and modes of their own, and in doing so were wrong; while the Jews followed divinely communicated ideas and prescribed modes, and therefore theirs was, in that respect, *the only acceptable worship?* But again, when our Lord says that all was right with the Jewish worship, "because *Salvation* is of the Jews," He enunciates the great truth, that in the worship of *sinful* men, as all worshippers on earth are, SALVATION must ever be the key-note —Salvation needed, sought, obtained, extolled; that historically the whole economy of salvation in its preparatory form had been entrusted for conservation to the seed of Abraham; and that so long as they occupied the important position of the ordained depositaries of all Saving Truth, Jerusalem must be regarded as the city of divine solemnities, and its temple as the visible dwelling-place of the Most High. (See Isa. ii. 3.) What a recognition is this of the Old Testament and its Faith, and of the Jews and the Jewish Economy as the living embodiment of it up to that time! But further, mark how explicitly our Lord announces the speedy cessation of all religious distinction between Jew and Gentile, and between one place and another for the worship of God. "There cometh an hour, and now is," when a world-wide worship shall be set up. The rending of the veil of the temple in twain, from the top to the bottom, was the signal-note of that mighty event—the death of Christ—which dissolved for ever these distinctions. From that time forth the middle wall of partition was broken down, and in every place the true incense and a pure offering was free to rise to heaven (Mal. i. 11). How strange it seems (one cannot avoid adding) that notwithstanding these announcements, and the commentaries on them in Gal. iv. and the Epistle to the Hebrews throughout, there should be an influential section of the students of prophecy who contend that the temple-services and the ritual distinctions of Jew and Gentile have *not* been absolutely and finally abolished, and that they will all be re-established during the Millennium! Another thing worthy of especial notice in this comprehensive reply to the woman of Samaria, is the emphatic manner in which the *spirituality* of all acceptable worship is proclaimed, and—what is even of more importance—its being based upon the *Spirituality of God* Himself. This was as true under the Jewish Economy as it has been since its cessation. But since, under an elaborate external and exclusive worship, this neither was nor could be so manifest, nor yet so fully realized by the worshippers themselves, the Lord here speaks as if only now such a spiritual worship was going to be established, because now for the first time since Moses—and in one sense even since the fall itself—to be stripped of sacrificial rites and the observance of time and place. Once more, in this reply, our Lord raises the woman's views of the glorious Object of worship, saying, "*The Father* seeketh such to worship Him." This is the more remarkable, because to the unbelieving Jews He never so speaks of God, and seems studiously to avoid it (ch. viii. 38). In the Sermon on the Mount, addressing His own disciples, He calls Him "your Father," and He teaches them in prayer to say, "Our Father." In His own prayers He says ever, "Father," and once His Agony in the Garden drew from Him the emphatic form, "My Father." From these facts we infer that though this woman was not yet within the circle of those to whom He says, "Your Father," this was so soon to be, that He could with propriety invite her to regard Him as "The Father." So much for the dialogue between our Lord and the woman of Samaria. Turning next to that between Him and the disciples on the woman's departure, we may notice, 7. What rich encouragement it affords to those "fishers of men" who "have toiled all the night" of their official life, and, to human appearance, have "taken nothing." How little might any other than one Eye have seen that the fields of Samaria were white already to harvest; and yet the event proves it to a very remarkable degree, as far as Sychar was concerned. Even so may the desert all unexpectedly rejoice and blossom as the rose; yet never is a harvest reaped that has not first been sown. The sowers may live and die before the harvest-time arrive, and the fruit of their labours be gathered. Yet can the reapers not say to the sowers, We have no need of you. "They that

43 Now after two days he departed thence, and went into Galilee.
44 For [b]Jesus himself testified, that a prophet hath no honour in his
45 own country. Then, when he was come into Galilee, the Galileans
received him, [c]having seen all the things that he did at Jerusalem at
the feast: [d]for they also went unto the feast.
46 So Jesus came again into Cana of Galilee, [e]where he made the water
wine. And there was a certain [1]nobleman, whose son was sick at
Capernaum.
47 When he heard that Jesus was come out of Judea into Galilee, he went
unto him, and besought him that he would come down, and heal his son:
48 for he was at the point of death. Then said Jesus unto him, [f]Except ye

A. D. 30.

[b] Matt. 13. 57. Mark 6. 4. Luke 4. 24.
[c] ch. 2. 23. ch. 3. 2.
[d] Deut 16. 16.
[e] ch. 2. 1, 11.
[1] Or, courtier, or, ruler.
[f] Matt. 16. 1. Luke 16. 31. 1 Cor. 1. 22.

sow in tears shall reap in joy," though others may do the actual reaping work after they are in their graves. And if the work of the latter is the more joyous, it should bind them sweetly to the sowers to recollect that "*other* men laboured, and they have but *entered into their labours.*" But may not the spiritual eye be trained so as to see what Jesus here saw—the whitening fields, the yellow grain, all invisible to the eye of sense? We have, indeed, much to learn ere we come to this, and the Lord overrules our spiritual obtuseness to try our faith, and then overpower us with the spectacle of nations born in a day. But even then, all *might* probably be seen by the eye of faith. In Tahiti, after nearly twenty years' missionary labour, not one conversion was known to have occurred, and the abandonment of the Mission was all but agreed on. But on the return of the missionaries to the island, after a native war which had driven them from it, they found that two natives, who, unknown to them, had received serious impressions as servants in their families, and had met together for prayer in their absence, had been joined by a number more, and that little remained for the missionaries but to help forward what God Himself had so marvellously begun. Meanwhile, the Directors in London, urged by one or two of their number, who could not endure to see the Mission abandoned had, after a season of special prayer, despatched letters of encouragement to the missionaries. While these were on their way out, a ship was conveying the news to England of the entire overthrow of idolatry in the island.

43-54.—Jesus Reaches Galilee—He makes a brief stay at Cana, and there performs His second Galilean Miracle, Healing a Nobleman's Son lying dangerously ill at Capernaum.

43. Now after two days [τὰς δύο ἡμέρας]—it should be, 'after the two days;' that is, of His stay at Sychar (*v.* 40), **he departed thence, and went into Galilee. 44. For Jesus himself testified, that a prophet hath no honour in his own country** [ἐν τῇ ἰδίᾳ πατρίδι]. If "his own country" here meant Galilee, His having no honour in it would seem to be a reason why he should *not* go to it. Hence some of those who think so render the words, He "went into Galilee, *although* He Himself testified," &c. But this is against the sense of the word "for" [γὰρ], and is inadmissible. Others of those who understand "His own country" here to mean Galilee get over the difficulty by connecting the "for" with what follows in the next verse rather than with what goes before, thus: 'The Galileans received Him, not because they appreciated His character and claims—"for" He had grown too common among them for that, according to the proverb—but merely because they had seen His recent miracles at Jerusalem.' This is the view of *Tholuck*, supported by *Lücke* in his 3d Edition, *de Wette*, and *Alford*. But it is too far-fetched. Hence, some give up Galilee as "His own country," and think *Judea*, or *Bethlehem* as His birth-place, to be meant. So *Origen*, *Maldonat*, *Lücke*, 2d Edition, *Robinson*, *Wieseler*. But our Lord was never either at Bethlehem or in Judea at all from the time of His birth till the commencement of His ministry; and therefore "His own country" can only mean the place of His early life—the scene of such familiar intercourse with others as would tend to make Him grow common amongst them. And what can that be but *Nazareth?*—which is expressly called "His country" [τὴν πατρίδα αὐτοῦ] in Matt. xiii. 54, 57, in precisely the same connection; as also in Mark vi. 4; Luke iv. 24. In this sense all is clear and natural: 'Now after the two days, Jesus, having left the province of Samaria as He had done that of Judea, went into the province of Galilee; but not, as might have been expected, to that part of it where He had been brought up, for Jesus knew that there—in His own country—He would have no honour, according to the proverb: He went, therefore, as the reader shall learn presently, to Cana of Galilee.' So *Calvin*, *Beza*, *Grotius*, *Bengel*, *Olshausen*, &c. **45. Then, when he was come into Galilee, the Galileans received**—or welcomed **him, having seen all the things that he did at**—'in' [ἐν] **Jerusalem at the feast: for they also went unto the feast**—proud, perhaps, of their countryman's wonderful works at Jerusalem, and possibly won by this circumstance to regard His claims as at least worthy of respectful investigation. Even this our Lord did not despise, for saving conversion often begins in less than this (so Zaccheus, Luke xix. 3).

46. So Jesus came again into Cana of Galilee (see on ch. ii. 1), **where he made the water wine. And there was a certain nobleman** [βασιλικὸς]—'courtier,' or king's servant, one connected with a royal household; such as "Chuza" (Luke viii. 3) or Manaen (Acts xiii. 1). So *Josephus* often uses the word. **whose son was sick at Capernaum. 47. When he heard that Jesus was come out of Judea**—whence the report of His miracles at the paschal feast had doubtless reached him, begetting in Him the hope that He would extend His healing power to his dying son, **into Galilee, he went unto him, and besought him that he would come down**—Capernaum being "down" from Cana on the N.W. shore of the sea of Galilee, **and heal his son: for he was at the point of death. 48. Then said Jesus, Except ye see signs and wonders** [σημεῖα καὶ τέρατα]. The latter word expresses simply the *miraculous* character of an act; the former the *attestation* which it gave of a higher presence and a divine commission. (See on ch. vi. 26.) **ye will not believe.** The poor man *did* believe, as both his coming and his urgent entreaty show. But how imperfect that faith was, we shall see, and our Lord would

49 see signs and wonders, ye will not believe. The nobleman saith unto him,
50 Sir, come down ere my child die. Jesus saith unto him, [g]Go thy way;
thy son liveth. And the man believed the word that Jesus had spoken
51 unto him, and he went his way. And as he was now going down, his
52 servants met him, and told *him*, saying, Thy son liveth. Then enquired
he of them the hour when he began to amend. And they said unto him,
53 Yesterday at the seventh hour the fever left him. So the father knew
that *it was* at the same hour in the which Jesus said unto him, Thy
54 son liveth; and [h]himself believed, and his whole house. This *is* again
the second miracle *that* Jesus did, when he was come out of Judea into
Galilee.

5 AFTER [a]this there was a feast of the Jews; and Jesus went up to

A. D. 30.

g 1 Ki. 17. 13-15. Matt. 8. 13. Mark 7. 29. Luke 17.14. ch. 11. 40. Acts 14. 9.

h Luke 19. 9. Acts 2. 39. Acts 16 34.

CHAP. 5.

a Lev. 23. 2. Deut. 16. 1. ch. 2. 13.

deepen it by such a blunt, and seemingly rough, answer as He made to Nicodemus (ch. iii. 3). **49. The nobleman saith unto him, Sir, come down ere my child die.** 'Ah! while we talk, my child is dying, and if Thou come not instantly, all will be over.' This was faith, but partial, and our Lord would perfect it. The man cannot believe the cure could be wrought without the Physician coming to the patient—the thought of such a thing evidently never occurred to him. But Jesus will in a moment bring him up to this. **50. Jesus saith unto him, Go thy way; thy son liveth. And the man believed the word that Jesus had spoken unto him, and he went his way.** Both effects instantaneously followed: the man believed the word, and the cure shooting quicker than lightning from Cana to Capernaum, was felt by the dying youth. In token of faith, the father takes his leave of Christ—in the circumstances this evidenced full faith. The servants hasten to convey the joyful tidings to the anxious parent, whose faith now only wants one confirmation. **51. And as he was now going down, his servants met him, and told him, saying, Thy son liveth. 52. Then enquired he of them the hour when he began to amend. And they said unto him, Yesterday at the seventh hour the fever left him. 53. So the father knew that it was at the same hour in the which Jesus said unto him, Thy son liveth; and himself believed, and his whole house.** He *had* believed before this—first very imperfectly, then with assured confidence in Christ's word; but now with a faith crowned by "sight." And the wave rolled from the head to the members of his household. "To-day is salvation come to this *house*" (Luke xix. 9); and no mean house this. **54. This is again the second miracle that Jesus did, when he was come out of Judea into Galilee**—that is, not His second miracle after coming out of Judea into Galilee; but 'His second Galilean miracle, and it was wrought after his return from Judea'—as the former was before He went to it.

Remarks.—1. If we are right as to the sense of *vv.* 43, 44—if Jesus, on His return into Galilee, went to Cana, avoiding Nazareth as "His own country," in which He knew that He would have "no honour," according to the proverb which Himself uttered—we have here a strong confirmation of the judgment we have given on the much-disputed question, whether Jesus paid *two visits* to Nazareth after His public ministry commenced, or *only one*. See on Matt. iv. 12, and more fully on Luke iv. 16, &c. As in our view He avoided Nazareth on this occasion, because He had become too *common* among them during His early life, so when He did visit it (Luke iv. 16, &c.), it was only to be upbraided for *never* having yet exhibited to His own town's-people the miraculous powers with the fame of which other places were ringing; and His reception on that one occasion when He visited Nazareth was quite enough to show that a repetition of His visit would be but "giving that which was holy to the dogs." So He left it, as we believe, never to return. 2. On comparing the faith of the nobleman whose son Jesus healed, with that of the centurion whose servant was restored by the same healing power, we are not to conclude that the believing *disposition* of the one was at all behind that of the other. Did the nobleman "beseech Jesus that He would *come down* and heal his son"—as if the thing could not be done at a distance? The centurion also "sent elders of the Jews, beseeching Him that He would come and heal his servant." It is true that Jesus replied to the nobleman, "Except ye see signs and wonders ye will not believe"—referring to the general unpreparedness even of those who believed in Him to recognize His *unlimited* power—and it is true that the nobleman only proved this by replying, "Sir, come down ere my child die;" while the centurion sent a noble message to Jesus *not* to come to Him, as that would be too great an honour, and besides there was no need, as it could be done equally well by a word uttered at a distance. But we must remember that the nobleman's case occurred almost at the outset of our Lord's ministry, when faith had much less to work upon than when the centurion applied (Luke vii. 2, &c). But what shows that the two cases are as nearly as possible on a par is, that whereas even the centurion's noble message seems to have been an after thought—his faith rising, perhaps, after his first messengers were despatched—the nobleman, as his case became more urgent, reached to the very same faith by another method. For when Jesus answered his entreaty to "come down" by saying, "Go thy way; thy son liveth," "the man believed the word that Jesus had spoken unto him, and he went his way," persuaded the cure could and would be wrought without the great Healer's presence. Thus may two cases, differing in their circumstances and features, be essentially of one character, and thus may a weaker *manifestation* of faith be consistent with an equal *capacity* for faith—the opportunities and advantages of each being different. This might indeed baffle man's power to detect and determine. But it is our comfort to know that it is He with whom both had to do, and from Whom they both experienced such love and grace, who is "ordained to be the Judge of quick and dead."

CHAP. V. 1-47.—THE IMPOTENT MAN HEALED AT THE POOL OF BETHESDA ON THE SABBATH DAY—DISCOURSE OCCASIONED BY THE PERSECUTION ARISING THEREUPON.

The Impotent Man Healed (1-9). The first verse of this chapter raises the most difficult, perhaps, and most controverted, of all questions touching the Harmony of the Gospels and the Duration of

2 Jerusalem. Now there is at Jerusalem, [b]by the sheep [1]*market*, a pool,
3 which is called in the Hebrew tongue [2]Bethesda, having five porches. In
these lay a great multitude of impotent folk, of blind, halt, withered,

[b] Neh. 3. 1.
[1] Or, gate.
[2] House of mercy.

our Lord's ministry. **1. After this there was a feast of the Jews; and Jesus went up to Jerusalem.** Three Passovers are distinctly mentioned in this Gospel as occurring during our Lord's public ministry: the first in ch. ii. 13, when Jesus paid His first official visit to Jerusalem; another, quite incidentally mentioned in ch. vi. 4; and the last, when Jesus went up to become "our Passover, sacrificed for us" (ch. xii. 2, 12; xiii. 1, 2). If no other Passover occurred than these three, during Christ's public life, then it could not have lasted more than two years and a half: whereas, if the feast mentioned in the first verse of this chapter was a Passover—making four in all—then the Duration of our Lord's public ministry was towards three years and a half. That this feast *was* a Passover, was certainly the most ancient opinion, and it is the opinion of the great majority of critics, (being that of *Irenæus*, as early as the second century, *Eusebius* and *Theodoret*, among the fathers; and of *Luther*, *Beza*, *Maldonat*, *Grotius*, *Lightfoot*, *La Clerc*, *Lampe*, *Hengstenberg*, *Greswell*, *Robinson*, *Tholuck* in his 6th Edition, and apparently in his 7th and last, *Middleton*, *Trench*, *Webster and Wilkinson*, &c.) Those who object to this view all differ among themselves as to what other feast it was, and some of the most acute have given up the hope of determining which it was. (So *Lücke*, at length, *de Wette*, and *Alford*.) That it was a *Pentecost* (as *Cyril* of Alexandria, *Chrysostom* and *Theophylact*, among the fathers; and *Erasmus*, *Calvin*, and *Bengel* have since thought) is inadmissible, as this Feast—which occurred fifty days after the Passover, or towards the end of May—will appear too late, if we consider that our Lord returned to Galilee in the month of December or January (ch. iv. 35). The Feast of *Tabernacles* (as *Cocceius* and *Ebrard*) is, for the same reason, still more out of the question, as it did not occur till the end of September. All these theories are now given up, by those who object to the Passover, in favour of the Feast of *Purim*, which was observed rather less than a month before the Passover. (So *Keppler*—who first suggested it, but doubtfully—and now *Hug*, *Olshausen*, *Wieseler*, *Meyer*, *Neander*, *Tischendorf*, *Lange*, and *Ellicott*.) But there are very strong objections to this view. First, The Feast of Purim was celebrated over all the country equally with the capital; none went up to Jerusalem to keep it; and the observance of it consisted merely in the reading of the book of Esther in the different synagogues, and spending the two days of it in feasting (Esth. ix. 21, 22): whereas the "multitude" referred to in *v.* 13 seems to imply that it was one of those greater festivals that drew large numbers from the provinces to the capital. It is difficult, indeed, to see why our Lord should have gone up to Jerusalem expressly to keep a feast of this nature, as the words of the first verse clearly imply. For though He was there at the Feast of Dedication (ch. x. 22)—which also was not a principal one—He did not go on purpose to keep it, but was there, or thereabouts, at any rate. But once more the Impotent Man, healed at this feast, was healed on the *Sabbath*—and by comparing *vv.* 9 and 13, one would naturally conclude that this Sabbath was one of the days of the Feast; whereas there is good reason to believe that the Purim was so far from being celebrated on a *Sabbath*, that when it fell on that day, it was put off till after it was over. The only objections to its being a Passover worth noticing are two. First, that our Evangelist, when he means a Passover, expressly names it; whereas here he merely calls it "a feast of the Jews:" and next, that if this be a Passover, it leaves too little time between this one and that of ch. vi. 4, and further, that since Jesus confessedly did not go up to Jerusalem at the next Passover, mentioned in ch. vi. 4—"because the Jews sought to kill Him" (ch. vii. 1)—it would follow that our Lord was about a year and a half absent from Jerusalem—a thing hard to believe. These objections are certainly weighty; but they are not insuperable. We lay no stress upon the fact that the definite article [ἡ ἑορτή], '*the* feast of the Jews' is found in several MSS.—(eight *uncial*, and two of the best *cursive* ones)—supported by the two ancient Egyptian versions; for this reading has not support enough. At the same time it must be observed that all who held to this reading certainly understood the feast intended to be *the* feast, by way of distinction from all the rest, that is, the Passover. But even with the article omitted, it has been shown by *Middleton* (Greek Article I., iii. 1) and *Winer* (xix. 2. *b.*) that its presence is implied, and the sense definite, just in such cases as the present. As to the shortness of the interval between the Passover of ch. v. 1 (supposing it to be one) and that of ch. vi. 4, it does not follow that the interval of *time* was short, because the *events recorded* between them in this Gospel are so few; since it is manifest that our Evangelist, till he comes to the final scenes, confines himself almost wholly to what had been *omitted* by the other Evangelists. To them, therefore, we are to go for the Galilean events which occurred between those Passovers. Finally, as to the long interval of a year and a half between this His second Passover (if so it be), and the Feast of Tabernacles, after the third one, when He next went up to Jerusalem (ch. vii. 2, 10), the reason given for it, in ch. vii. 1, appears sufficient; and as He was to take His final leave of Galilee not very long after, He would have abundant occupation there to fill up the time, while His continuing either in the capital or its neighbourhood nearly all the time between the Feast of Tabernacles and His final Passover—a period of about seven months—would sufficiently compensate for His longer absence from it at an earlier period. On a review of the whole evidence, then, we are decidedly of opinion that the "Feast" here referred to by our Evangelist was THE PASSOVER—and consequently, the *second* of *four* occurring during our Lord's public ministry.

2. Now there is at Jerusalem, by the sheep [market]. The supplement here is an unhappy one, as no such market-place is known. But as the *sheep gate* is mentioned in Neh. iii. 1, 32, and is familiar in the Jewish references to the temple, no doubt the supplement ought to be, as in the *margin*, "by the sheep [gate]." **a pool, which is called in the Hebrew tongue Bethesda** [= בֵּית חִסְדָּא]—that is, 'Mercy-house;' doubtless from the cures wrought there, **having five porches**—for shelter to the patients. That Jerusalem was yet standing when this Gospel was written cannot be inferred, as *Bengel* thought, from the use of the present tense "is." The water here referred to did not necessarily disappear with the overthrow of the city. There are indeed two distinct sites yet to be seen which have been identified with this pool: one, and the more probable site, a ruined reservoir near St. Stephen's gate, which

4 waiting for the moving of the water. For an angel went down at a
certain season into the pool, and troubled the water: whosoever then
first after the troubling of the water stepped in was made whole of
5 whatsoever disease he had. And a certain man was there, which had
6 an infirmity thirty and eight years. When Jesus saw him lie, and [c]knew
that he had been now a long time *in that case,* he saith unto him, [d]Wilt
7 thou be made whole? The impotent man answered him, Sir, I have no
man, when the water is troubled, to put me into the pool: but while I
8 am coming, another steppeth down before me. Jesus saith unto him,
9 [e]Rise, take up thy bed, and walk. And immediately the man was made
whole, and took up his bed, and walked:

A. D. 30.

[c] Ps. 142. 3. ch. 21. 17. Heb. 4. 13.

[d] Ps. 72. 13. Ps. 113. 5, 6. Isa. 55. 1. Jer. 13. 27. Luke 18. 41.

[e] Matt. 9. 6. Mark 2. 11. Luke 5. 24. Acts 9. 34.

ancient tradition has fixed upon and late investigations strongly confirm; the other, what is known as the Fountain of the Virgin. But even though all remains of it had disappeared with the destruction of Jerusalem, the Evangelist might have no knowledge of the fact; nor did he require to know it, as its well-known existence at the time of this incident is all that the word necessarily implies. **3. In these lay a great multitude of impotent folk**—or infirm people, **of blind, halt, withered** [ξηρῶν]—or 'paralyzed' (as Mark iii. 1), **waiting for the moving of the water. 4. For an angel went down at a certain season into the pool, and troubled the water: whosoever then first after the troubling of the water stepped in was made whole of whatsoever disease he had.** The imperfect tense in which these verbs are expressed conveys the idea of use and wont [κατέβαινεν—ἐτάρασσε—ἐγίνετο]—'was wont to descend'—'to trouble the pool'—'to be made whole.' **5. And**—or rather, 'Now' [δὲ] **a certain man was there, which had an infirmity thirty and eight years**—a length of time which to the man himself might seem to render a cure hopeless, and on the principle of a mere *medicinal* virtue in this water, which some even sound critics are too ready to tamper with, undoubtedly would. This, then, was probably the most pitiable of all the patients assembled at the pool, and for that very reason, no doubt, was selected by the Lord for the display of His glory. **6. When Jesus saw him lie, and knew that he had been now a long time in that case.** As He doubtless visited the spot just to perform this cure, so He knew where to find His patient, and the whole previous history of His case (ch. ii. 25). **he saith unto him, Wilt thou be made whole?** Could any one doubt that a sick man would like to be made whole, or that the patients came thither, and this man had returned again and again, just in hope of a cure? But our Lord asked the question, first, to fasten attention upon Himself; next, by making him detail his case, to deepen in him the feeling of entire helplessness; and further, by so singular a question, to beget in his desponding heart the hope of a cure. (See on Mark x. 51.) **7. The impotent man answered him, Sir, I have no man, when the water is troubled, to put me into the pool: but while I am coming, another steppeth down before me.** Instead of *saying* he wished to be cured, he just tells with piteous simplicity how fruitless had been all his efforts to obtain it, and how *helpless* and all but *hopeless* he was. 'Yet not quite. For here he is at the pool, waiting on. It seemed of no use; nay, only tantalizing—"While I am coming, another steppeth down before me"—the fruit was snatched from His lips. Yet he will not go away. He may get nothing by staying; he may drop into his grave ere he get into the pool; but by going from the appointed, divine way of healing, he can get nothing. Wait therefore he will, wait he does, and when Christ comes to heal him, lo! he is waiting his turn. *What an attitude for a sinner* at Mercy's gate! The man's hopes seemed low enough ere Christ came to him. He might have said, just before "Jesus passed by that way," 'This is no use; I'll never get in; let me die at home.' Then all had been lost. But he *held on,* and his perseverance was rewarded with a glorious cure. Probably some rays of hope darted into his heart as he told his tale before those Eyes whose glance measured his whole case. But the word of command consummates his preparation to receive the cure, and instantaneously works it. **8. Jesus saith unto him, Rise, take up thy bed, and walk. 9. And immediately the man was made whole, and took up his bed, and walked.** "He *spake,* and it was *done.*" The slinging of his portable couch over his shoulders was designed to show the perfection of the cure.

Such is this glorious miracle. Now let us look at it, as it stands here in the received text; and next let us examine the *shortened* text presented by most modern Editors of the Greek Testament—which leaves out the last clause of *v.* 3, "waiting for the moving of the waters," and the whole of *v.* 4. The miracle, as it here stands, differs in two points from all other miracles recorded in Scripture: First, It was not one, but a succession of miracles periodically wrought: Next, As it was only wrought "when the waters were troubled," so only upon one patient at a time, and that the patient "who first stepped in after the troubling of the waters." But this only the more undeniably fixed its miraculous character. We have heard of many waters having a medicinal virtue; but what water was ever known to cure *instantaneously* a single disease? And who ever heard of any water curing all, even the most diverse diseases—"blind, halt, withered"—alike? Above all, who ever heard of such a thing being done only "at a certain season," and most singularly of all, doing it only to the first person who stepped in after the moving of the waters? Any of these peculiarities—much more all taken together—must have proclaimed the supernatural character of the cures wrought. If the text, then, be genuine, there can be no doubt of the miracle, as there were multitudes living when this Gospel was published who, from their own knowledge of Jerusalem, could have exposed the falsehood of the Evangelist, if no such cure had been known there. It only remains, then, that we enquire on what authority the omission of the last clause of *v.* 3, and the whole of *v.* 4, from the text (by *Tischendorf* and *Tregelles,* and approved by *Tholuck, Meyer, Olshausen, Alford,* &c.) is supported. The external evidence against it is certainly very strong. [It is wanting in the newly-discovered *Codex Sinaiticus,* and the *Codex Vaticanus*—א and B—the two earliest known MSS. of the New Testament; in C, not much later; in

10 And on [f]the same day was the sabbath. The Jews therefore said
unto him that was cured, It is the sabbath day: [g]it is not lawful
11 for thee to carry *thy* bed. He answered them, He that made me
12 whole, the same said unto me, Take up thy bed, and walk. Then
asked they him, What man is that which said unto thee, Take up thy
13 bed, and walk? And he that was healed wist not who it was; for
Jesus had conveyed himself away, [3]a multitude being in *that* place.
14 Afterward Jesus findeth him [h]in the temple, and said unto him, Behold,
thou art made whole: [i]sin no more, lest a worse thing come unto thee.
15 The man departed, and told the Jews that it was Jesus which had made
16 him whole. And therefore did the Jews persecute Jesus, and sought to
slay him, because he had done these things on the sabbath day.

A. D. 30.

[f] ch. 9. 14.
[g] Ex. 20. 10. Neh. 13. 19. Jer. 17. 21. Matt. 12. 2. Mark 2. 24. Mark 3. 4. Luke 6. 2.
[3] Or, from the multitude that was.
[h] Ps. 103. 2.
[i] Matt. 12. 45.

D—which, however, has the disputed clause of *v.* 3; and in three of the cursive or later MSS.; in the ancient version called the Curetonian *Syriac*, and in the two ancient *Egyptian* versions, according to some copies. Besides this, it is fair to add, that there is considerable variety in the words used by the MSS. that have the disputed passage, and that in some MSS. and versions the passage is so marked as to imply that it was not universally received.] But when all the evidence in favour of the disputed passage—external and internal—is combined and well weighed, we think it will appear quite decisive. The external evidence for it is much stronger in fact than in appearance. [It is found—though not in the first, but the second hand—in the *Alexandrian* MS. of date scarcely second to the two oldest, and, in the opinion of some of the best critics, of almost equal authority; in ten other uncial MSS.; in the oldest or Peshito, and indeed all but the Curetonian *Syriac*, and in both the *Old Latin* and *Vulgate* Latin versions—which very rarely agree with the Alexandrian MS. when it differs from the Vatican—showing how very early the disputed words were diffused and recognized: in confirmation of which we have an undoubted reference to the passage by *Tertullian*, in the end of the second and beginning of the third century. Moved by this consideration, no doubt, *Lachmann* inserts the passage.] But the internal evidence is, in our judgment, quite sufficient to outweigh even stronger external evidence against it than there is. First, While the very *strangeness* and, as some venture to say, the legendary air of the miracle may easily account for its *omission*, we cannot see how such a passage could have crept in if it did not belong to the original text. But secondly, The text seems to us to yield no sense, or but an inept sense, without the disputed words. Just try to explain without them this statement of *v.* 7: "Sir, I have no man, when the water is troubled, to put me into the pool: but while I am coming, another steppeth down before me." Who would ever understand how the mere inability of this impotent man to step *first* into the pool should deprive him of its virtue—from whence soever that proceeded—when the water was troubled? Clearly the explanation given in *v.* 4—along with the last clause of *v.* 3—is *necessary* to the understanding of *v.* 7. The two, therefore, must stand or fall together; and as the seventh verse is admitted to be genuine, so, in our judgment, must the rest.

Consequences of this Miracle being wrought on the Sabbath Day (9-16). **9. and on the same day was the sabbath.** Beyond all doubt this was intentional, as in so many other healings, in order that, when opposition arose on this account, men might be compelled to listen to the claims and teaching of the Lord Jesus. **10. The Jews**—that is, those in authority (see on ch. i. 19), **therefore said unto him that was cured, It is not lawful for thee to carry thy bed**—a glorious testimony to the cure, as *instantaneous* and *complete*, from the lips of the most prejudiced! In *ordinary* circumstances the rulers had the law on their side (Neh. xiii. 15; Jer. xvii. 21). But when the man referred them to "Him that had made him whole" as his authority, the argument was resistless. **11. He answered them, He that made me whole, the same said unto me, Take up thy bed, and walk. 12. Then asked they him, What man is that which said unto thee, Take up thy bed, and walk?** They ingeniously parry the man's thrust, asking him, not who had "made him whole"—that would have condemned themselves and defeated their purpose—but who had bidden him "take up his bed, and walk," in other words, who had dared to order a breach of the Sabbath? ''Tis time we were looking after him'—thus hoping to shake the man's faith in his Healer. **13. And** [δὲ]—or rather, 'But' **he that was healed wist not who it was.** That some one with unparalleled generosity, tenderness, and power had done it, the man knew well enough; but as he had never heard of Him before, so He had disappeared too quickly for any enquiries. **for Jesus had conveyed himself away** [ἐξένευσεν]—had 'slipped out' of the crowd that had gathered, **a multitude being in that place**—to avoid both too hasty popularity and too precipitate hatred (Matt. xii. 14-19; ch. iv. 1, 3). **14. Afterward Jesus findeth him in the temple**—saying, perhaps, "I will go into thy house with burnt offerings; I will pay my vows, which my lips have uttered, and my mouth hath spoken, when I was in trouble" (Ps. lxvi. 13, 14). Jesus, there Himself for His own ends, "findeth him there"—*not all accidentally*, be assured. **and said unto him, Behold, thou art made whole: sin no more, lest a worse thing come unto thee** [ἵνα μὴ χεῖρόν τί σοι γένηται]—or, 'lest some worse thing befal thee—a glimpse this of the reckless life he had probably led *before* his thirty-eight years' infirmity had come upon him, and which not improbably had brought on, in the just judgment of God, his chronic complaint. Fearful illustration this of "the severity of God," but glorious manifestation of our Lord's insight into "what was in man." **15. The man departed, and told the Jews that it was Jesus which had made him whole**—little thinking how unwelcome his grateful and eager testimony would be. "The darkness," as *Olshausen* says, "received not the light which was pouring its rays upon it" (ch. i. 5-11). **16. And therefore did the Jews persecute Jesus, and sought to slay him.** [This last clause—καὶ ἐζήτουν αὐτὸν ἀποκτεῖναι—is excluded from the text by *Tischendorf* and *Tregelles*, on weighty but, as we judge, insufficient authority. *Alford* does the same, and *Lücke*, *Meyer*, and *de Wette*, approve of the omission, which they regard as a gloss to

17 But Jesus answered them, [j]My Father worketh hitherto, and I work.
18 Therefore the Jews [k]sought the more to kill him, because he not only had
broken the sabbath, but said also that God was his Father, [l]making
himself equal with God.
19 Then answered Jesus and said unto them, Verily, verily, I say unto you,
[m]The Son can do nothing of himself, but what he seeth the Father do:
20 for what things soever he doeth, these also doeth the Son likewise. For
[n]the Father loveth the Son, and showeth him all things that himself
doeth: and he will show him greater works than these, that ye may
21 marvel. For as the Father raiseth up the dead, and quickeneth *them;*
22 [o]even so the Son quickeneth whom he will. For the Father judgeth no
23 man, but hath [p]committed all judgment unto the Son; that all *men*

A. D. 30.

j ch. 9. 4. ch. 14. 10.
k ch. 7. 19.
l Zec. 13. 7. ch. 10. 30.
m ch. 8. 28. ch. 9. 4.
n Matt. 3. 17. ch. 3. 35.
o Luke 7. 14. Luke 8. 54.
p Matt. 11. 27. ch. 3. 35. ch. 17. 2. Acts 17. 31.

explain *v.* 18. But the word μᾶλλον—"the more"—which none propose to exclude from the text, presupposes the clause in *v.* 16, and is the strongest argument in favour of it. *Lachmann* retains the clause.] **because he had done these things on the sabbath day.** What to these hypocritical religionists was the doing of the most glorious and beneficent miracles, compared with the atrocity of doing them on the Sabbath day! Having given them this handle, on purpose to raise the first public controversy with them, and thus open a fitting opportunity for laying His claims before them, He rises at once to the whole height of them, in a statement which for grandeur, weight, and terseness exceeds almost anything that ever afterwards fell from Him—at least to His enemies.

Discourse occasioned by the opposition of the rulers to Christ's Working His glorious Miracles on the Sabbath Day (17-47). **17. But Jesus answered them, My Father worketh hitherto, and I work.** The "I" here is emphatic [κἀγώ]—*q. d.*, 'The creative and conservative activity of My Father has known no Sabbath-cessation from the beginning until now, *and that is the law of My working.*' **18. Therefore**—or 'for this cause' [διὰ τοῦτο], **the Jews sought the more to kill him, because he not only had broken the sabbath, but said also that God was his Father** [πατέρα ἴδιον]. This is not strong enough. It should be, 'that God was His own Father;' in the sense of Rom. viii. 32 (see there). **making himself equal with God.** This last clause expresses the sense in which they understood His words. And they were right in gathering this to be His meaning, not from the mere words "My Father," but from His claim of right to act as His Father did, in the like high sphere and by the same law of ceaseless activity in that sphere. And since, instead of instantly disclaiming any such meaning—as He must have done if it was false—He positively sets His seal to it in the following verses, merely explaining how consistent such claim was with the prerogatives of His Father, it is beyond all doubt that we have here an assumption of *peculiar, personal Sonship*, or participation in the Father's essential nature.

19. Then answered Jesus and said unto them, The Son can do nothing of himself [ἀφ' ἑαυτοῦ]—or 'from Himself,' that is, as an originating and independent Actor, *apart from* and *in rivalry of* the Father; which was what they supposed; **but what he seeth the Father do** [ἐὰν μὴ τι βλέπῃ τὸν πατέρα ποιοῦντα]—'but only what He seeth the Father doing.' The meaning is, 'The Son has and can have no separate interest or action from the Father.' **for what things soever he doeth, these also doeth the Son likewise** [ὁμοίως]—or 'in the like manner:'—*q. d.*, 'On the contrary, whatever the Father doeth, that same doeth the Son, and just as He doeth it.' What claim to absolute equality with the Father could exceed this—not only to do *whatever* the Father does, but to do it *as* the Father does it? And yet, in perfect conformity with the natural relation of *Father* and *Son*, everything originates with the Former, and is carried out by the Latter. **20. For the Father loveth the Son.** The word here for "loveth" [φιλεῖ] is that which peculiarly denotes *personal* affection, as distinguished from that in the similar statement of the Baptist [ἀγαπᾷ], which peculiarly marks complacency in the *character* of the person loved (see on ch. iii. 35). **and showeth him all things that himself doeth.** As love has no concealments, so it results from the perfect fellowship and mutual endearment of the Father and the Son (see on ch. i. 1, 18,) Whose interests are one, even as Their nature, that the Father communicates to the Son all His counsels; and what has been thus shown to the Son is by Him executed in His mediatorial character. For, as *Alford* properly says, with the Father *doing* is *willing:* it is the Son only who *acts* in *Time.* **and he will show him greater works than these.** The order is more lively in the original—'and greater works than these will He show Him,' **that ye may marvel**—referring to what He goes on to mention (in *vv.* 21-31), and which may be comprised in two great words—"LIFE" and "JUDGMENT"—which *Stier* beautifully calls '*God's Regalia.*' Yet these Christ says the Father and He have, and put forth, in common. **21. For as the Father raiseth up the dead, and quickeneth them**—one act in two stages, the resurrection of the body and the restoration of life to it. This surely is the Father's absolute prerogative, if He have any. **even so the Son quickeneth whom he will**—not only doing the same divine act, but doing it *as the result of His own will*, even as the Father does it. This statement is of immense importance in relation to the miracles of Christ, distinguishing them from similar miracles of prophets and apostles, who as *human instruments* were employed to perform supernatural actions, while Christ did all—as the Father's *commissioned Servant* indeed, but—*in the exercise of His own absolute right of action.* **22. For the Father judgeth no man** [Οὐδὲ γὰρ ὁ πατὴρ κρίνει οὐδένα]—'For neither doth the Father judge any man:' implying that the same thing was meant in the former verse of the "quickening of the dead;" both acts being done, not by the Father *and* the Son, as though twice done, but by the Father *through* the Son as His voluntary Agent. Our Lord has now passed to the second of the "greater works" which He was to show them, to their astonishment (*v.* 20). **but hath committed all judgment unto the Son**—judgment in its most comprehensive sense, or as we should say, all *administration.* **23. That all [men] should honour the Son, even as they honour the Father.** As he who believes that Christ, in the

should [q]honour the Son, even as they honour the Father. He that
honoureth not the Son honoureth not the Father which hath sent him.
24 Verily, verily, I say unto you, He that heareth my word, and believeth
on him that sent me, hath everlasting life, and shall not come into
25 condemnation; [r]but is passed from death unto life. Verily, verily, I say
unto you, The hour is coming, and now is, when [s]the dead shall hear the
26 voice of the Son of God: and they that hear shall live. For as the
Father hath life in himself, so hath he given to the Son to have life
27 in himself; and [t]hath given him authority to execute judgment also,
28 [u]because he is the Son of man. Marvel not at this: for the hour is
29 coming, in the which all that are in the graves shall hear his voice, and
[v]shall come forth; [w]they that have done good, unto the resurrection of
life; and they that have done evil, unto the resurrection of damnation.
30 I can of mine own self do nothing: as I hear, I judge: and my judgment

A. D. 30.

[q] Matt. 28.19. 1 John 2.23. Rev. 5. 8.
[r] 1 John 3.14.
[s] Gal. 2. 20. Eph. 2. 1, 5. Eph. 5. 14. Col. 2. 13. Rev. 3. 1.
[t] Jer. 10. 10. Acts 10. 42. Acts 17. 31.
[u] Dan. 7. 13.
[v] 1 Thes. 4. 16. 1 Cor. 15. 52.
[w] Dan. 12. 2. Matt. 25. 32.

foregoing verses, has given a true account of His relation to the Father must of necessity hold Him entitled to the same *honour* as the Father, so He here adds that it was the Father's express intention, in making over all judgment to the Son, that men *should* thus honour Him. **He that honoureth not the Son honoureth not the Father which hath sent Him** [τὸν πέμψαντα αὐτὸν]—'which sent Him:' he does not do it in fact, whatever he may imagine, and will be held as not doing it by the Father Himself, who will accept no homage which is not accorded to His own Son. **24. Verily, verily, I say unto you, He that heareth my word, and believeth on him that sent me**—that is, 'believeth in Him *as having* sent Me,' **hath everlasting life**—hath it immediately on his believing: see on ch. iii. 18; and compare 1 John v. 12, 13; **and shall not come** [ἔρχεται]—rather, 'and cometh not' **into condemnation.** So absolved is he from guilt—so released from the sentence of condemnation, which as a sinner the divine law had fastened upon him—that the life which he enjoys is henceforth and for ever a life of uncondemned, unrebuked right to stand before a holy God on terms of peace and acceptance. **but is passed from** [μεταβέβηκεν ἐκ]—literally, 'hath passed over out of' **death unto life.** What a transition! But though 'freedom from condemnation' is that feature of this new life which our Lord *here* emphatically dwells on, it is quite evident—both from what goes before and what follows after—that it is *life from the dead* in the widest sense which our Lord means us to understand as communicated, of His own inherent will, to all who believe in Him. (Compare 1 John iii. 14.) It is as if He had said, 'I have spoken of the Son's right not only to heal the sick, but to raise from the dead, and quicken whom He will: And now I say unto you, That life-giving operation has already passed upon all who receive my words as the Sent of the Father on the great errand of mercy.' **25. Verily, verily, I say unto you, The hour is coming** [ἔρχεται ὥρα]—or, 'There cometh an hour;' that is, in its whole fulness it was only "coming," namely, at Pentecost, **and now is**—in its beginnings, **when the dead**—the *spiritually* dead, as is clear from *v.* 28, (see on Luke ix. 60,) **shall hear the voice of the Son of God.** Here our Lord rises from the calmer phrase "hearing *His word*" (*v.* 24) to the grander expression, "hearing *the voice of the Son of God*," to signify that as it finds men in a *dead* condition, so it carries with it a divine *resurrection-power*. **and they that hear shall live**—in the largest sense of the word, as at the close of *v.* 24. **26. For as the Father hath life in himself, so hath he given** [ἔδωκεν]—or 'gave He' **to the Son to have life in himself.** Does this refer to the essential life of the Son before all time? (in the sense of ch. i. 4)—as most of the fathers understood it, and *Olshausen*, *Stier*, *Alford*, &c., among the moderns understand it; or, does it refer to the purpose of God that this essential life should reside in the Person of the incarnate Son, and be manifested thus to the world?—as *Calvin*, *Lücke*, *Luthardt*, &c., view it. The question is as difficult as the subject is high. But as all that Christ says of His *essential* relation to the Father is intended to explain and exalt his *mediatorial* functions, so the one seems in our Lord's own mind and language mainly the starting-point of the other. **27. And hath given him**—or, as before, 'gave Him' **authority to execute judgment also**—as well as to quicken whom He will (*v.* 21), **because he is the Son of man.** This seems to confirm the last remark, that what Christ had properly in view was the indwelling of the Son's essential life in *humanity* as the great *theatre* and *medium* of divine display, in both the great departments of His work—*life-giving* and *judgment*. The appointment of *a Judge in our own nature* is one of the most august and beautiful arrangements of divine wisdom in Redemption. **28. Marvel not at this**—this committal of all judgment to the Son of Man, **for the hour is coming**—or, 'there cometh an hour.' But here our Lord adds not, "and now is," as in *v.* 25; because the hour there intended was to arrive almost immediately, and in one sense had already come, whereas the hour here meant was not to arrive till the close of the whole dispensation of mercy. **in the which all that are in the graves shall hear his voice, 29. And shall come forth; they that have done good, unto the resurrection of life**—that is, the resurrection *unto* life everlasting (Matt. xxv. 46), **and they that have done evil unto the resurrection of damnation** [κρίσεως]—or, 'of judgment,' but in the sense of *condemnation*. It would have been harsh, as *Bengel* remarks, to say, 'the resurrection of death,' though that is meant; for sinners rise only *from death to death*. The resurrection of both classes is an exercise of *sovereign authority;* but in the one case it is an act of *grace*, in the other of *justice*. Compare Dan. xii. 2, from which the language is taken. How awfully grand are these unfoldings of His dignity and authority from the mouth of Christ Himself! And they are all, it will be observed, uttered in the *third* person—as great principles and arrangements from everlasting, independent of the utterance of them on this occasion. Immediately after this, however, He resumes the *first* person. **30. I can of**—or 'from' [ἀφ'] **mine own self do nothing**—apart from, or in rivalry of, the Father, and in any separate interest of My own (see on *v.* 19): **as I hear, I judge: and my**

is just; because [x]I seek not mine own will, but the will of the Father
31 which hath sent me. If [y]I bear witness of myself, my witness is not
32 true. There is another that beareth witness of me; and I know that
the witness which he witnesseth of me is true.
33, Ye sent unto John, [z]and he bare witness unto the truth. But I receive
34 not testimony from man: but these things I say, that ye might be saved.
35 He was a burning and [a]a shining light: and [b]ye were willing for a season
36 to rejoice in his light. But [c]I have greater witness than *that* of John:
for [d]the works which the Father hath given me to finish, the same works
37 that I do, bear witness of me, that the Father hath sent me. And the
Father himself, which hath sent me, [e]hath borne witness of me. Ye have
38 neither heard his voice at any time, nor [f]seen his shape. And ye have
not his word abiding in you: for whom he hath sent, him ye believe not.
39 Search [g]the Scriptures; for in them ye think ye have eternal life: and
40 [h]they are they which testify of me. And ye will not come to me, that
41, ye might have life. I [i]receive not honour from men. But I know you,
42, that ye have not the love of God in you. I am come in my Father's

A. D. 30.
x Matt. 26. 39. ch. 4. 34. ch. 6. 38.
y ch. 8. 14. Rev. 3. 14.
z ch. 1. 15.
a 2 Pet. 1. 19.
b Matt 13. 20. Matt. 21. 26.
c 1 John 5. 9.
d ch. 15. 24.
e Matt. 3. 17. Matt. 17. 5.
f Deut. 4. 12. ch. 1. 18.
g Isa. 8. 20. Luke 16. 29.
h Deut. 18. 15. Luke 24. 27, 44.
i 1 Thes. 2. 6.

judgment is just; because I seek not mine own will, but the will of the Father which hath sent me:—*q. d.*, 'My judgments are all *anticipated* in the bosom of my Father, to which I have immediate access, and by Me they are only *responded to* and *reflected*. They cannot, therefore, err, since I live for one end only, to carry into effect the will of Him that sent Me.' **31. If I bear witness of myself** [περὶ]—'concerning Myself;' that is, in the sense already explained—standing alone, and setting up a separate interest of my own, **my witness is not true. 32. There is another that beareth witness of me**—meaning, The Father, as is plain from the connection. How brightly the distinction of the Persons shines out here! **and I know that the witness which he witnesseth of me is true.** How affecting is this allusion! Thus did Jesus cheer His own spirit under the cloud of human opposition which was already gathering over His head.

33. Ye sent unto John—referring to the deputation which these same rulers sent to the Baptist (ch. i. 19, &c.), of which, though not present, Jesus was fully cognizant, as of the answer which the Baptist returned. **and he bare witness unto the truth. 34. But I receive not testimony from man**—that is, I depend not on human testimony. That He should have permitted Himself to receive testimony from the Baptist, seemed to the Lord Jesus to need some explanation, lest it should be supposed that He stood in need of it, which therefore He here explicitly says He did not. **but these things I say, that ye might**—or 'may' **be saved.** 'If I refer to John's testimony at all, it is but to aid your faith, in order to your salvation.' **35. He was a burning and a shining light** [ὁ λύχνος ὁ καιόμενος καὶ φαίνων]—literally, 'the burning and shining lamp,' or 'torch:'—*q. d.*, 'the great light of his day.' Christ is never called by the humble word here applied to John—a *light-bearer*—studiously used to distinguish him from his Master, but ever *The Light* [τὸ φῶς] in the most absolute sense. See on ch. i. 6. **and ye were willing for a season**—that is, till they saw that it pointed whither they were not prepared to go, **to rejoice in his light.** There is a play of irony here, referring to the hollow delight with which his testimony excited them. **36. But I have greater witness** ['Εγὼ δὲ ἔχω τὴν μαρτυρίαν μείζω]—rather, 'The witness which I have is greater' **than that of John: for the works which the Father hath given me to finish, the same works that I do, bear witness of me, that the Father hath sent me**—not simply as *miracles*, nor even as miracles of *mercy*, but these miracles *as He did them*, with a *will* and a *power*, a *majesty* and a *grace* manifestly *His own*. **37. And the Father himself hath borne witness of me**—not referring, probably, to the voice at His baptism, but, as seems from what follows, to the testimony of the Old Testament Scriptures. (So *Calvin*, *Lücke*, *Meyer*, *Luthardt*.) **Ye have neither heard his voice at any time, nor seen his shape**—never recognized Him in this character. The words, as *Stier* remarks, are designedly mysterious, like many others which our Lord uttered. **38. And ye have not his word abiding in you**—passing now from the *Witness-bearer* to the *testimony* borne by the Father in "the lively oracles:" both were alike strangers to their breasts, as was evidenced by their rejecting Him to whom all that witness was borne. **39. Search the Scriptures** ['Ερευνᾶτε]—or 'Ye search.' As either sense may be adopted consistently with the word itself, we must be guided by what seems to be the strain of our Lord's statement. But on this interpreters are entirely divided, and most are satisfied that theirs is the only tenable sense. The *indicative* sense—'Ye search'—is adopted by *Cyril* among the fathers, and of moderns by *Erasmus*, *Beza*, *Lampe*, *Bengel*, *Campbell*, *Olshausen*, *Meyer*, *de Wette*, *Lücke*, *Tholuck*, *Webster and Wilkinson*. In the *imperative* sense—'Search'—our translators are supported by *Chrysostom* and *Augustin* among the fathers, and of moderns by *Luther*, *Calvin*, *Grotius*, *Maldonat*, *Wetstein*, *Stier*, *Alford*. Perhaps the former sense—'Ye search'—best accords with what follows. **for in them ye think** [δοκεῖτε]—'deem,' 'consider'; in a good sense, **ye have eternal life: and they are they which testify of me. 40. And ye will not come** [οὐ θέλετε ἐλθεῖν]—rather, 'ye are not willing to come' **to me, that ye might have life:**—*q. d.*, 'With disregarding the Scriptures I charge you not: Ye do indeed busy yourselves about them (He was addressing, it will be remembered, the *rulers*—see on *v.* 16); rightly deeming them your Charter of eternal life: But ye miss the great Burden of them: Of Me it is they testify; and yet to Me ye will not come for that eternal life which ye profess to find there, and of which they proclaim Me the ordained Dispenser.' (See Acts xvii. 11, 12.) Severe though this rebuke was, there is something most touching and gracious in it. **41. I receive not honour** [δόξαν]—'applause,' 'glory,' **from men**—contrasting His own end with theirs, which was to obtain human applause. **42. But I know you, that ye have not**

43 name, and ye receive me not: if another shall come in his own name,
44 him ye will receive. How can ye believe, which receive honour one of
45 another, and seek not [j]the honour that *cometh* from God only? Do not
think that I will accuse you to the Father: [k]there is *one* that accuseth
46 you, *even* Moses, in whom ye trust. For had ye believed Moses, ye
47 would have believed me: [l]for he wrote of me. But if [m]ye believe not
his writings, how shall ye believe my words?

A. D. 30.

j Rom. 2. 29.
k Rom. 2. 12.
l Gen. 3. 15. Gen. 12. 3. Gen. 18. 18. Acts 26. 22.
m Luke 16. 29, 31.

the love of God in you—which would have inspired you with a single desire to know His mind and will, and yield yourselves to it, in spite of prejudice, and regardless of consequences. **43. I am come in my Father's name, and ye receive me not: if another shall come in his own name, him ye will receive.** How strikingly has this been verified in the history of the Jews. From the time of the true Christ to our time, says *Bengel*, sixty-four false Christs have been reckoned, by whom the Jews have been deceived. **44. How can ye believe, which receive honour one of another, and seek not the honour that cometh from God only.** The "*can*" not here, and the "*will*" not of *v.* 40, are but different aspects of one and the same state of the human heart, under the conscious and entire dominion of corrupt principles and affections—as contrasted with that simplicity and godly sincerity which, as in Nathanael (ch. i. 47), seeks only to know and receive the truth. **45. Do not think that I will accuse you to the Father:**—*q. d.*, 'My errand hither is not to collect evidence to condemn you at God's bar.' **there is one that accuseth you, even Moses, in whom ye trust** [ἠλπίκατε]—or 'hope':—*q. d.*, 'Alas! that will be too well done by another, and him the object of all your religious boastings—Moses;' here put for "*the Law*," the basis of the Old Testament Scriptures. **46. For had ye believed Moses, ye would have believed me** [ἐπιστεύετε]—rather, 'If ye believed Moses, ye would believe Me,' **for he wrote of me**—an important testimony, as *Alford* remarks, to the subject of the whole Pentateuch, "of ME." **47. But if ye believe not his writings** (see on Luke xvi. 31), **how shall ye believe my words?**—a remarkable contrast, not absolutely putting Old Testament Scripture below His own words, but pointing to the office of those venerable documents to *prepare* Christ's way, to the necessity universally felt for *documentary* testimony in revealed religion, and perhaps, as *Stier* adds, to the relation which the comparative "*letter*" of the Old Testament holds to the more flowing "words" of "spirit and life" which characterize the New Testament.

Remarks.—1. The light in which the ministry of angels is presented to us in connection with the pool of Bethesda is most interesting and instructive. First, it would appear that one particular angel had charge over the miraculous virtue of this pool. And next, all that he did was to "trouble" the water. That the patient who first stepped in after this owed his cure to *angelical virtue* is not said. The contrary is rather implied, and is in accordance with all else that we read of their ministry. They ministered to the tempted Saviour, but only in the way of bringing Him, as one of them did to Elijah (1 Ki. xix. 5-8), the bodily sustenance for which He had so long confidingly waited (Matt. iv. 11). In the extremity of His agony, there appeared an angel unto Him from heaven, strengthening Him; but for *spiritual* strength there is no reason to suppose that Jesus was indebted to an angel, save in so far as the consciousness of supernatural vigour of body and spirit to sustain the Conflict, certainly imparted by this angel, would tend to reassure Him of His Father's love and presence with Him in that awful hour. When apprehended, He expressed His confidence that He could immediately have, for the asking, more than twelve legions of angels, to free Him—if He desired it—from the hands of men; but that only. In heaven, He tells us, the angels of His dear "little ones" always behold the face of His Father which is in heaven (Matt. xviii. 10)—to receive, we may suppose, His commands concerning them. And Lazarus, in the parable, when he died, was carried by angels into Abraham's bosom. But in no case do their ministrations extend beyond what is *outward.* That they have either command or ability to interfere *between the soul and God in things purely spiritual*, or to affect the spiritual life at all save in the way of external ministration, we are bound—with such Scripture statements before us—positively to deny. How different from this is the teaching of the Church of Rome, is known to all. 2. Those who can see in the Discourse which our Lord uttered on this occasion no claim to essential equality with God, and no assertion of the distinct conscious Personality of the Father and the Son, are not likely to see it anywhere else. It is not, in fact, more evidence that such want: it is the right appreciation of the evidence they possess. Nor can there be any doubt that unwillingness—whether conscious or not—to credit these truths *on any evidence* lies at the bottom of the rejection of them. But those who recognize in this Discourse the Personal distinctions in the Godhead should not overlook these further intimations clearly to be gathered from it—that *unity of action* among the Persons results from *unity of nature;* and that Their oneness of interest is no unconscious or involuntary thing, but a thing of glorious consciousness, will, and love, of which the Persons themselves are the proper Objects. 3. In the announcement that the *dead* shall *hear* the voice of the Son of God, and hearing shall *live*—first, spiritually at this present time, and then corporeally at the resurrection-day (*vv.* 25, 28, 29)—we have one of those apparent paradoxes which "the wise and prudent" ever stumble at, but to faith are full of glory. See on Matt. xii. 9-21, Remark 3 at the close of that Section. 4. Observe the honour accorded to the Scriptures generally, and the Old Testament Scriptures in particular, by the Lord Jesus. Whether we understand Him to bid them "Search the Scriptures," or in the way of commendation to say, "Ye do search the Scriptures," even though this was addressed more immediately to the rulers, the reason assigned for it—that in them they thought they had eternal life—is enough to show that in His view it was alike the *interest* and the *duty* of all to search them. How directly in the teeth of this is the teaching of the Church of Rome, none need to be told. See on Luke xvi. 1-31, Remark 9 at the close of that Section. But 5. In that miserable "searching of the Scriptures" to which the Jewish ecclesiastics certainly addicted themselves—and in which they have been even exceeded by the learned rabbins of later times—we see how possible it is to rest in the mere *Book* without the living *spirit* of it, and above all without the living *Christ* of it—to direct

6 AFTER [a]these things Jesus went over the sea of Galilee, which is *the*
2 *sea* of Tiberias. And a great multitude followed him, because they saw
3 his miracles which he did on them that were diseased. And Jesus went
4 up into a mountain, and there he sat with his disciples. And [b]the pass-
5 over, a feast of the Jews, was nigh. When [c]Jesus then lifted up *his* eyes,
and saw a great company come unto him, he saith unto Philip, Whence
6 shall we buy bread, that these may eat? (And this he said to prove him:
7 for he himself knew what he would do.) Philip answered him, [d]Two
hundred penny-worth of bread is not sufficient for them, that every one
8 of them may take a little. One of his disciples, Andrew, Simon Peter's
9 brother, saith unto him, There is a lad here, which hath five barley
10 loaves, and two small fishes: [e]but what are they among so many? And
Jesus said, Make the men sit down. Now there was much grass in the
11 place. So the men sat down, in number about five thousand. And Jesus
took the loaves; and when he had [f]given thanks, he distributed to the
disciples, and the disciples to them that were set down; and likewise of
12 the fishes as much as they would. When they were filled, he said unto
his disciples, Gather up the fragments that remain, that nothing be lost.
13 Therefore they gathered *them* together, and filled twelve baskets with the
fragments of the five barley loaves, which remained over and above unto
them that had eaten.
14 Then those men, when they had seen the miracle that Jesus did, said,
15 This is of a truth [g]that prophet that should come into the world. When
Jesus therefore perceived that they would come and take him by force, to
make him a king, he departed again into a mountain himself alone.
16 And [h]when even was *now* come, his disciples went down unto the sea,
17 and entered into a ship, and went over the sea toward Capernaum. And
18 it was now dark, and Jesus was not come to them. And the sea arose,
19 by reason of a great wind that blew. So when they had rowed about five
and twenty or thirty furlongs, they see Jesus walking on the sea, and
20 drawing nigh unto the ship: and they were afraid. But he saith unto
21 them, It is I; be not afraid. Then they willingly received him into the
ship: and immediately the ship was at the land whither they went.
22 The day following, when the people which stood on the other side of
the sea saw that there was none other boat there, save that one whereinto
his disciples were entered, and that Jesus went not with his disciples into
23 the boat, but *that* his disciples were gone away alone; (howbeit there
came other boats from Tiberias, nigh unto the place where they did eat

A. D. 32.

CHAP. 6.
[a] Matt 14. 15. Mark 6. 35. Luke 9. 10.
[b] Ex. 12. 6. Lev. 23. 5, 7. Num. 28. 16. Deut. 16. 1. ch. 2. 13. ch. 5. 1. ch. 11. 55. ch. 12. 1. ch 13. 1.
[c] Matt. 14. 14. Mark 6. 35. Luke 9. 12.
[d] Num. 11. 21, 22. 2 Ki. 7. 2. Matt. 15. 33. Mark 6. 37. Mark 8. 4.
[e] 2 Ki 4. 43. Ps. 78. 19, 20. Matt. 14. 16, 17. Luke 9. 13.
[f] Ex. 23. 25. 1 Sam. 9. 13. Matt. 14. 19. Matt. 15 36. Matt. 26. 26. Luke 24. 30. 1 Tim. 4. 5.
[g] Gen. 49. 10. Deut. 18. 15, 18. Isa. 7. 14. Isa. 9. 6. Isa. 35. 5. Matt. 11. 3. Matt. 21. 11. Luke 7. 16. ch. 1. 21. ch. 4. 19, 25. ch. 7. 40. Acts 7. 37.
[h] Matt. 14. 23. Mark 6. 47.

---

the soul to Whom is its main use and chiefest glory.

CHAP. VI. 1-21.—JESUS CROSSES TO THE EASTERN SIDE OF THE SEA OF GALILEE, FOLLOWED BY A GREAT MULTITUDE—HE FEEDS THEM MIRACULOUSLY TO THE NUMBER OF FIVE THOUSAND, AND SENDS HIS DISCIPLES BY SHIP AGAIN TO THE WESTERN SIDE, HIMSELF RETURNING AFTERWARDS WALKING ON THE SEA. (=Matt. xiv. 13-36; Mark vi. 30-56; Luke ix. 10-17.) For the exposition, see on Mark vi. 30-56. But the reader will do well to mark here again the important note of time introduced quite parenthetically at *v.* 4—**And the passover, the feast of the Jews, was nigh.** This, according to our reckoning, was the *third* passover since our Lord entered on His public ministry. See on Mark vi. 34.

22-71.—JESUS, FOLLOWED BY THE MULTITUDES TO CAPERNAUM, DISCOURSES TO THEM, CHIEFLY IN THE SYNAGOGUE, OF THE BREAD OF LIFE—EFFECT OF THIS ON TWO CLASSES OF DISCIPLES.

The Multitudes, finding Jesus gone, cross to the Western Side of the Lake, and find Him at Capernaum (22-25). These verses are a little involved, from the Evangelist's desire to mention every circumstance, however minute, that might call up the scene as vividly to the reader as it stood before his own view. **22. The day following**—that is, the day after the miracle of the loaves and the stormy night, or the day on which Jesus and His disciples landed at Capernaum, **when the people**—'the multitude' [ὁ ὄχλος], **which stood on the other side of the sea**—not the whole multitude that had been fed, but only such of them as remained over night about the shore, that is, on the *east* side of the lake; for we are supposed to have come, with Jesus and His disciples in the ship, to the *west* side, to Capernaum; **saw that there was none other boat there, save that one whereinto his disciples were entered . . . but that his disciples were gone away alone.** The meaning is, the people had observed that there had been only one boat on the East side where they were, namely, the one in which the disciples had crossed at night to the other, the West side, and they had also observed that Jesus had not gone on board that boat, but His disciples had put off without Him. **23. (Howbeit**—adds the Evangelist, in a lively parenthesis,

24 bread, after that the Lord had given thanks:) when the people therefore
saw that Jesus was not there, neither his disciples, they also took shipping,
and came to Capernaum, seeking for Jesus.
25 And when they had found him on the other side of the sea, they said
unto him, Rabbi, when camest thou hither?
26 Jesus answered them and said, Verily, verily, I say unto you, Ye seek
me, not because ye saw the miracles, but because ye did eat of the
27 loaves, and were filled. [1]Labour not for the meat which perisheth, but
[i]for that meat which endureth unto everlasting life, which the Son of
28 man shall give unto you: [j]for him hath God the Father sealed. Then
said they unto him, What shall we do, that we might work the works of
29 God? Jesus answered and said unto them, This [k]is the work of God,
30 that ye believe on him whom he hath sent. They said therefore unto
him, [l]What sign showest thou then, that we may see, and believe thee?

A. D. 32.

[1] Or, Work not.
[i] ch. 4. 14. Rom. 6. 23.
[j] Matt. 3 17. Matt. 17. 5. Mark 1. 11. Mark 9. 7. Luke 3. 22. Luke 9. 35. ch. 1. 33. ch. 5. 37. Acts 2. 22. 2 Pet. 1. 17.
[k] 1 John 3. 23.
[l] Mark 8. 11. 1 Cor. 1. 22.

there came other boats from Tiberias—which lay near the south-west coast of the lake, whose passengers were part of the multitude that had followed Jesus to the East side, and been miraculously fed: these boats were fastened somewhere, says the Evangelist, **nigh unto the place where they did eat bread, after that the Lord had given thanks)** —thus he refers to the glorious "miracle of the loaves:" and now these boats were put in requisition to convey the people back again to the West side. For, says our Evangélist, **24. When the people**—'the multitude,' **therefore saw that Jesus was not there, neither his disciples, they also took shipping**—in these boats, **and came to Capernaum, seeking for Jesus. 25. And when they had found him on the other side of the sea**—at Capernaum, probably, as may be gathered perhaps from *vv.* 17-59; although one would infer from the other Gospels that He and the disciples had landed rather somewhere else—it may be in the neighbourhood of it (Matt. xiv. 34, 35; Mark vi. 55).

Jesus, questioned by the Multitudes that had run after Him, about His having got the start of them, changes the Subject, and, from the Loaves they had been filled with, Discourses to them of the Bread of Life (25-59). **25. And when they had found him on the other side of the sea, they said unto him, Rabbi, when camest thou hither?**—astonished at His *being* there, and wondering *how* He could have accomplished it, whether by land or water, and *when* He came; for being quite unaware of His having walked upon the sea and landed with the disciples in the ship, they could not see how, unless He had travelled all night round the head of the lake alone, He could have reached Capernaum, and even then how He could have arrived before themselves. Jesus does not put them through their difficulty, says nothing of His treading on the waves of the sea, nor even notices their question, but takes advantage of the favourable moment for pointing out to them how forward, flippant, and superficial were their spirit and views, and how low their desires.

26. Jesus answered them, Verily, verily, I say unto you, Ye seek me, not because ye saw the miracles [σημεῖα]—literally 'signs;' that is, supernatural tokens of a higher presence and a divine commission, **but because ye did eat of the loaves, and were filled.** From this He proceeds at once to that *other Bread*, just as, with the woman of Samaria, to that *other Water*, (ch. iv.) We should have supposed all that follows to have been delivered by the way-side, or wherever they happened first to meet. But from *v.* 59 we gather that they had probably met about the door of the synagogue—'for that,' says *Lightfoot*, 'was the day in which they assembled in their synagogues'—and that on being asked, at the close of the service, if He had any word of exhortation to the people, He had taken the two breads, the *perishing* and the *living* bread, for the subject of His profound and extraordinary Discourse. **27. Labour** [Ἐργάζεσθε]—or 'work' **not for the meat which perisheth, but for that meat which endureth unto everlasting life, which the Son of man**—taking that title of Himself which denoted His incarnate life, **shall give unto you**—in the sense of *v.* 51: **for him hath God the Father sealed** [τοῦτον γὰρ ὁ πατὴρ ἐσφράγισεν ὁ Θεός]—rather, perhaps, 'for Him hath the Father sealed, even God;' that is, marked out and authenticated for that transcendent office, to impart to the world the bread of an everlasting life, and this in the character of "the Son of *Man*." **28. Then said they unto him, What shall we do, that we might work the works of God?**—such works, that is, as God will approve. To this question different answers may be given, according to the *spirit* which prompts the enquiry (see Mic. vi. 6-8; Luke iii. 12-14). Here our Lord, knowing whom He had to deal with, shapes His reply accordingly. **29. Jesus answered and said unto them, This is the work of God, that ye believe on him whom he hath sent** [ἀπέστειλεν]—'Him whom He sent.' This lies at the threshold of all acceptable obedience, being not only the pre-requisite to it but the proper spring of it—in that sense it is the work of works, emphatically "*the* work of God." **30. They said therefore unto him, What sign showest thou then, that we may see, and believe thee? what dost thou work?** But how could they ask "a sign," when many of them scarce a day before had witnessed such a "sign" as had never till then been vouchsafed to men; when after witnessing it they could hardly be restrained from making Him a king; when they followed Him from the one side of the lake to the other; and when, in the opening words of this very Discourse, He had chid them for seeking Him, "not because they *saw the signs*," but for the loaves? The truth seems to be, that they were confounded by the *novel claims* which our Lord had just advanced. In proposing to make Him a king, it was for far other purposes than dispensing to the world the bread of an everlasting life; and when He seemed to raise His claims even higher still, by representing it as the grand "work of God," that they should believe *on Himself* as His Sent One, they saw very clearly that He was making a demand upon them beyond anything they were prepared to accord to Him, and beyond all that man had ever before made. Hence their question, "What dost thou *work?*" **31. Our fathers did eat manna in the desert; as**

31 what dost thou work? Our [m]fathers did eat manna in the desert; as it
is written, [n]He gave them bread from heaven to eat.
32 Then Jesus said unto them, Verily, verily, I say unto you, Moses gave
you not that bread from heaven; but my Father giveth you the true
33 bread from heaven. For the bread of God is he which cometh down from
34 heaven, and giveth life unto the world. Then said they unto him, Lord,
35 evermore give us this bread. And Jesus said unto them, I am the bread
of life: [o]he that cometh to me shall never hunger; and he that believeth
36 on me shall never thirst. But I said unto you, That ye also have seen
37 me, and believe not. All that the Father giveth me shall come to me:
38 and [p]him that cometh to me I will in no wise cast out. For I came
down from heaven, [q]not to do mine own will, [r]but the will of him that
39 sent me. And this is the Father's will which hath sent me, [s]that of all
which he hath given me I should lose nothing, but should raise it up
40 again at the last day. And this is the will of him that sent me, that
[t]every one which seeth the Son, and believeth on him, may have everlasting life: and I will raise him up at the last day.

A. D. 32.

m Ex. 16. 15. Num. 11. 7. Neh. 9. 15. 1 Cor. 10. 3.
n Ps. 78. 24. Neh. 9. 15. 1 Cor. 10. 3. Rev. 2. 17.
o Matt. 11. 28. ch. 7. 37. Rev. 22. 17.
p 2 Tim. 2. 19. 1 John 2. 19.
q Matt. 26. 39. ch. 5. 30.
r ch. 4. 34.
s ch. 10. 28. ch. 18. 9. Col. 3. 3. Jude 1.
t ch. 4. 14.

it is written, He gave them bread from heaven to eat—insinuating the inferiority of Christ's miracle of the loaves to those of Moses:—*q. d.*, 'When Moses claimed the confidence of the fathers, "he gave them bread from heaven to eat"—not for a few thousands, but for millions, and not once only, but daily throughout their wilderness journey.'

32. Then—or 'therefore' [οὖν] **Jesus said unto them, Verily, verily, I say unto you, Moses gave you not that bread** [δέδωκεν τὸν]—'hath not given you the bread' **from heaven; but my Father giveth you the true bread from heaven.** Every word here is an emphatic contradiction to their statement. 'It was not Moses that gave you the manna, and even it was but from the lower heavens; "but *My Father* giveth you *the true bread*," and that "*from heaven.*"' **33. For the bread of God is he which cometh down from heaven, and giveth life unto the world.** This verse is perhaps best left in its own transparent grandeur—holding up, as it does, the Bread itself as divine, spiritual, and eternal; its ordained Fountain and essential Substance, Him who came down from heaven to give it, that Eternal Life which was with the Father, and was manifested unto us (1 John i. 2); and its designed objects, "the world." **34. Then**—or 'therefore' **said they unto him, Lord, evermore give us this bread**—speaking now with a certain reverence, as at *v.* 25; the perpetuity of the manna floating perhaps in their minds, and much like the Samaritan woman, when her eyes were but half opened, "Sir, give me this water," &c. (ch. iv. 15). **35. And**—or, 'But' **Jesus said unto them, I am the bread of life.** Henceforth the discourse is all *in the first person*—"I," "Me"—which occurs in one form or other, as *Stier* reckons, thirty-five times. **he that cometh to me**—to obtain what the soul craves, and as the only all-sufficient and ordained Source of supply, **shall never hunger; and he that believeth on me shall never thirst**—shall have conscious and abiding satisfaction. **36. But I said unto you, That ye also have seen me**—rather 'that ye have even seen Me,' **and believe not**—that is, seen Him not in His mere bodily presence, but in all the majesty of His life, His teaching, His works. **37. All that** [which] **the Father giveth me shall come to me: and him that cometh to me I will in no wise cast out. 38. For I came down**—or 'have come down' [καταβέβηκα] **from heaven, not to do mine own will, but the will of him that sent me. 39. And this is the Father's will which hath sent me.** The true reading beyond doubt here is, 'This is the will of Him that sent Me' [πατρὸς having no sufficient authority], **that of all** [that] **which he hath given me I should lose nothing, but should raise it up again at the last day. 40. And this is the will of him that sent me.** Here the reading of 'the Father which hath sent Me' has much better support than in *v.* 39, though scarcely sufficient, perhaps, to justify its insertion (with *Lachmann*, *Tischendorf*, and *Tregelles*). **that every one which seeth** [θεωρῶν]—rather, 'beholdeth' **the Son, and believeth on him, may**—or should **have everlasting life: and I will raise him up**—rather, 'and that I should raise him up' **at the last day.** This comprehensive and very grand passage is expressed with a peculiar artistic precision. The opening general statement (*v.* 37) consists of two members: First, "ALL THAT THE FATHER GIVETH ME SHALL COME TO ME:"—*q. d.*, 'Though ye, as I told you, have no faith in Me, My errand into the world shall in no wise be defeated; for all that the Father giveth Me shall infallibly come to Me.' Observe, what is *given* Him by the Father is expressed in the *singular* number and *neuter* gender—literally, 'all [that] which' [πᾶν ὃ]; while those who *come* to Him are put in the *masculine* gender and *singular* number—'him that cometh' [τὸν ἐρχόμενον]. The *whole mass*, so to speak, is gifted by the Father to the Son as a *unity*, which the Son evolves, one by one, in the execution of His trust; so (ch. xvii. 2) "that He should give eternal life to *all that which* thou hast given him" [πᾶν ὃ δέδωκας]. The "*shall* come" of *v.* 37 expresses the glorious *certainty* of it; the Father being pledged to see to it that the gift become a reality. Second, "AND HIM THAT COMETH TO ME I WILL IN NO WISE CAST OUT." As the former was the *divine*, this is just the *human* side of the same thing. True, the "coming" ones of the second clause are just the "given" ones of the first. But had our Lord merely said, '*When those* that have been given me of My Father shall come to Me, I will receive them,'—besides being very flat, the impression conveyed would have been quite different, sounding as if there were *no other laws in operation*, in the movement of sinners towards Christ, but such as are wholly *divine* and *inscrutable* to us; whereas, though He does speak of it as a sublime certainty which men's *refusals* cannot frustrate, He speaks of that certainty as taking effect only by men's *voluntary advances* to Him and acceptance of Him—"Him that cometh to me," "whosoever will"—thus throwing the door wide

41 The Jews then murmured at him, because he said, I am the bread
42 which came down from heaven. And they said, Is not this Jesus, the
Son of Joseph, whose father and mother we know? how is it then that he
43 saith, I came down from heaven? Jesus therefore answered and said
44 unto them, Murmur not among yourselves. No man can come to me,
except the Father which hath sent me draw him: and I will raise him up
45 at the last day. It [u]is written in the Prophets, And they shall be all
taught of God. Every man therefore that hath heard, and hath learned
46 of the Father, cometh unto me. Not [v]that any man hath seen the
47 Father, save [w]he which is of God, he hath seen the Father. Verily,
48 verily, I say unto you, [x]He that believeth on me hath everlasting life. I
49 am that bread of life. Your fathers did eat manna in the wilderness,
50 and are dead. This is the bread which cometh down from heaven, that

A. D. 32.

[u] Isa. 54. 13. Jer. 31. 34. Mic. 4. 2. Heb. 8. 10. Heb. 10. 16.
[v] ch. 1. 18. ch. 5. 37.
[w] Matt. 11. 27. Luke 10. 22. ch. 1. 18. ch 7. 29. ch 8. 19. 2 Cor. 4. 6.
[x] ch. 3. 16, 36. ch. 5. 24. 1 John 5. 12.

open. Only it is not the simply *willing*, but the actually *coming*, whom He will not cast out. "In no wise" [οὐ μὴ] is an emphatic negative, to meet the fears of the timid—as in Rev. xxi. 27, to meet the presumption of the hardened. These, then, being the emphatic members of the general opening statement, what follows is meant to resume and reiterate them both in another form. But first, we have a parenthetic and emphatic explanation that His mission from heaven to earth had but one object—to carry into effect the Father's purposes: "For I came down from heaven, not to do mine own will"—not to act an independent part—"but," in respect of both the foregoing things, both the *divine* and the *human* side of salvation, to do "the will of Him that sent Me" (*v.* 38). What this two-fold will of Him that sent Him is, we are next sublimely told, *vv.* 39, 40. Thus:

First, "ALL THAT WHICH THE FATHER GIVETH ME SHALL COME TO ME."
This is now emphatically reiterated:
"AND THIS IS THE WILL OF HIM THAT SENT ME, THAT OF ALL THAT WHICH HE HATH GIVEN ME I SHOULD LOSE NOTHING, BUT SHOULD RAISE IT UP AGAIN AT THE LAST DAY."
So much for the *divine* side of man's salvation, whose every stage and movement is inscrutable to us, but infallibly certain.

Secondly, "AND HIM THAT COMETH TO ME I WILL IN NO WISE CAST OUT."
This also is now emphatically reiterated:
"AND THIS IS THE WILL OF THE FATHER WHICH HATH SENT ME, THAT EVERY ONE WHICH SEETH THE SON, AND BELIEVETH ON HIM, MAY HAVE EVERLASTING LIFE: AND I WILL RAISE HIM UP AT THE LAST DAY."
This is just the *human* side of the same thing. (See on *v.* 54.)

Thus God has a two-fold will about the salvation of men. He wills that those whom He has given in trust to His Son shall be presented faultless before the presence of His glory—redeemed from all iniquity, and their sleeping dust raised incorruptible. But He further wills that if any poor sinner, all ignorant of this secret purpose, but attracted by the grace and glory of His Son, shall believe on Him, he shall have eternal life and be raised up at the last day.

41. The Jews then murmured at him—or 'muttered' [ἐγόγγυζον], not in our Lord's hearing, but He knew it (*v.* 43; ch. ii. 25), **because he said I am the bread which came down from heaven. 42. And they said, Is not this Jesus, the son of Joseph, whose father and mother we know? how is it then that he**—or 'this man' [οὗτος], **saith I came down from heaven?** Missing the sense and glory of this, and having no relish for such sublimities, they harp upon the "Bread from heaven." 'What *can* this mean? Do we not know all about him—where, when, and of whom he was born? And yet he says he came down from heaven?' **43. Jesus therefore answered and said unto them, Murmur not among yourselves. 44. No man can come to me** (in the sense of *v.* 35), **except the Father which hath sent me**—that is, except the Father as the Sender of Me, and to carry out the design of My mission **draw him**—by an internal and efficacious operation; though by all the means of rational conviction, and in a way altogether consonant to their moral nature. (Song i. 4; Jer. xxxi. 3; Hos. xi. 3, 4.) **and I will raise him up at the last day.** See on *v.* 54. Thus this weighty statement amounts to the following: 'Be not either startled or stumbled at these sayings; for it needs divine teaching to understand them, divine drawing to submit to them.' **45. It is written in the Prophets** (in Isa. liv. 13; Jer. xxxi. 33, 34.) Other similar passages may also have been in view. Our Lord thus falls back upon Scripture authority for this seemingly hard saying. **And they shall be all taught of God**—not by *external* revelation merely, but by *internal illumination*, corresponding to the "drawing" of *v.* 44. **Every man therefore that hath heard, and hath learned of the Father**—who hath been thus efficaciously taught of Him, **cometh unto me**—*with absolute certainty*, yet in every case voluntarily, as above explained:—*q. d.*, 'As none can come to Me save as divinely drawn, so none thus drawn shall fail to come.' **46. Not that any man hath seen the Father, save he which is of God** [παρὰ τοῦ Θεοῦ]—or 'from God;' but in the sense of ch. i. 14, "the Only begotten [forth] from the Father." Lest they should confound that "hearing and learning of the Father," to which believers are admitted by divine *teaching*, with His own immediate access to Him, He here throws in a parenthetical explanation; stating, as explicitly as words could do it, how totally different the two cases were, and that only He who is "from God" hath this naked, immediate access to the Father. **47. Verily, verily, I say unto you, He that believeth on me hath everlasting life.** See on ch. iii. 36; and on ch. v. 24. **48. I am that bread of life.** This is repeated from *v.* 35, 'As he that believeth in Me hath everlasting life, so I am Myself the everlasting *Sustenance* of that life.' **49. Your fathers**—of whom ye spake (*v.* 31). Observe, He does not say '*Our* fathers'—by which, as *Bengel* remarks, He would hint

51 a man may eat thereof, and not die. I am the living bread which came
down from heaven. If any man eat of this bread, he shall live for ever:
and [y]the bread that I will give is my flesh, which I will give for the life
of the world.
52 The Jews therefore [z]strove among themselves, saying, [a]How can this
53 man give us *his* flesh to eat? Then Jesus said unto them, Verily, verily,
I say unto you, Except [b]ye eat the flesh of the Son of man, and
54 drink his blood, ye have no life in you. Whoso eateth my flesh, and
drinketh my blood, hath eternal life; and I will raise him up at the
55 last day. For my flesh is meat indeed, and my blood is drink indeed.
56 He that eateth my flesh, and drinketh my blood, [c]dwelleth in me, and I
57 in him. As the living Father hath sent me, and I live by the Father; so

A. D. 32.

[y] Heb. 10. 5, 10.
[z] ch. 7. 43. ch. 9. 16. ch. 10. 19.
[a] ch. 3. 9.
[b] Matt. 26. 26.
[c] 1 Cor. 6. 17. 1 Cor. 12. 27. 2 Cor. 6. 16. Eph. 3. 17. Eph. 5. 30. 1 John 3. 24. 1 John 4. 15, 16.

that *He* had a higher descent of which they dreamt not. **did eat manna in the wilderness, and are dead**—recurring to their own point about the manna, as one of the noblest of the *ordained* preparatory illustrations of His own office: 'Your fathers, ye say, ate manna in the wilderness, and ye say well, for so they did; *but they are dead*—even they whose carcases fell in the wilderness did eat of that bread: the Bread whereof I speak cometh down from heaven, which the manna never did, that men, eating of it, may *live for ever*.' **50. This, &c. 51. I am the living bread which came down from heaven. If any man eat of this bread, he shall live for ever: and the bread** [καὶ ὁ ἄρτος δὲ]—'aye, and,' or 'yea, and the Bread' **that I will give is my flesh, which I will give for the life of the world.** 'Understand, it is of MYSELF I now speak as the Bread from heaven; of ME if a man eat he shall live for ever; and "THE BREAD WHICH I WILL GIVE IS MY FLESH WHICH I WILL GIVE FOR THE LIFE OF THE WORLD." Here, for the first time in this high discourse, our Lord explicitly introduces His sacrificial *death*—for what impartial student of Scripture can doubt this?—not only as that which constitutes Him the Bread of life to men, but as THAT very element IN HIM WHICH POSSESSES THE LIFE-GIVING VIRTUE. From this time forth, observes *Stier*—and the remark is an important one—we hear no more in this Discourse of "Bread:" that figure is dropped, and the Reality takes its place. The words "I will *give*" may be compared with the words of institution at the Supper, "This is My body which is *given* for you (Luke xxii. 19), and, as the apostle reports it, "*broken* for you" (1 Cor. xi. 24).

52. The Jews therefore strove among themselves—arguing the point keenly among themselves, **saying, How can this man give us his flesh to eat?**—'Give us his flesh to eat? Absurd.' **53. Then Jesus said unto them, Verily, verily, I say unto you, Except ye eat the flesh of the Son of man, and drink his blood, ye have no life in you.** This is the harshest word He had yet uttered in their ears. They asked how it was *possible* to eat His flesh. He answers with great solemnity, 'It is *indispensable*.' Yet even here a thoughtful hearer might find something to temper the harshness. He says they must not only "eat His *flesh*" but "drink His *blood*," which could not but suggest the idea of His *death*—implied in the separation of one's flesh from his blood. And as He had already hinted that it was to be something very different from a *natural* death, saying, "My flesh I will give for the life of the world" (*v.* 51), it must have been pretty plain to candid hearers that He meant something above the gross idea which the bare terms expressed. And farther, when He added that they "had no *life* in them unless they thus ate and drank," it was impossible they should think He meant that the *temporal* life they were then living was dependent on their eating and drinking, in this gross sense, His flesh and blood. Yet the whole statement was certainly confounding, and beyond doubt was meant to be so. Our Lord had told them that in spite of all they had "seen" in Him they "did not believe" (*v.* 36). For *their* conviction, therefore, He does not here lay Himself out; but having the ear not only of them but of the more *candid* and *thoughtful* in the crowded synagogue, and the miracle of the loaves having led up to the most exalted of all views of His Person and Office, He takes advantage of their very difficulties and objections to announce, for all time, those most profound truths which are here expressed, regardless of the disgust of the unteachable, and the prejudices even of the most sincere, which His language would seem only designed to deepen. The *truth* really conveyed here is no other than that expressed in *v.* 51, though in more emphatic terms—that Himself, in the virtue of His sacrificial death, is the spiritual and eternal life of men; and that unless men voluntarily appropriate to themselves this death, in its sacrificial virtue, so as to become the very life and nourishment of their inner man, they have no spiritual and eternal life at all. Not as if His death were the *only* thing of value, but it is what gives all else in Christ's Incarnate Person, Life, and Office, their whole value *to us sinners*. **54. Whoso**—or 'He that' **eateth my flesh, and drinketh my blood, hath eternal life.** This is just the positive expression of what in the former verse He had expressed negatively. There it was '*Unless* ye so partake of Me, ye have not life;' here it is, 'Whosoever does so *hath* life everlasting.' **and I will raise him up at the last day.** For the fourth time this is repeated (see *vv.* 39, 40, 44)—showing most clearly that the "eternal life" which such a man "*hath*" cannot be the same with the *future* resurrection-life, from which it is carefully distinguished each time, but a life communicated *here below* immediately on believing (ch. iii. 36; v. 24, 25); but at the same time giving to *the resurrection of the body*, as that which consummates the redemption *of the entire man*, a prominence which, in the current theology, it is to be feared, it has seldom had. (See on Rom. viii. 23; and on 1 Cor. xv. throughout.) **55. For my flesh is meat indeed, and my blood is drink indeed. 56. He that eateth my flesh, and drinketh my blood, dwelleth in me, and I in him.** As our food becomes incorporated with ourselves, so Christ and those who eat His flesh and drink His blood become spiritually *one life*, though *personally* distinct. **57. As the living Father hath sent me** [ἀπέστειλεν]—'sent Me,' to communicate His own life, **and I live by the Father** [διὰ τὸν πατέρα]—not 'through,' but 'by reason of the Father;' My life and His being one life, though Mine is that of *Son*, whose it is to be "*of* the Father" (see ch. i. 18; v. 26).

58 he that eateth me, even he shall live by me. This is that bread which
came down from heaven: not as your fathers did eat manna, and are
59 dead: he that eateth of this bread shall live for ever. These things said
he in the synagogue, as he taught in Capernaum.
60 Many [d] therefore of his disciples, when they had heard *this*, said, This
61 is an hard saying; who can hear it? When Jesus knew in himself that
his disciples murmured at it, he said unto them, Doth this offend you?
62 *What* [e] and if ye shall see the Son of man ascend up where he was before?
63 It [f] is the Spirit that quickeneth; the flesh profiteth nothing: the words
64 that I speak unto you, *they* [g] are spirit, and *they* are life. But there are
some of you that believe not. For [h] Jesus knew from the beginning who
65 they were that believed not, and who should betray him. And he said,
Therefore said I unto you, that no man can come unto me, except it were
66 given unto him of my Father. From that *time* many of his disciples
went [i] back, and walked no more with him.
67, Then said Jesus unto the twelve, Will ye also go away? Then

A. D. 32.

d Matt. 11. 6.
e ch. 3. 13. Mark 16.19. Acts 1. 9. Eph. 4. 8.
f 2 Cor. 3. 6.
g Ps. 119. 50. Eph. 1. 17. 1 Thes. 2.13. Heb. 4. 12.
h Matt. 9. 4. ch. 2. 24. ch. 13. 11. ch. 16. 30. Acts 15. 18. Rev. 2. 23.
i Luke 9. 62. Heb. 6. 4-6. Heb. 10. 38. 1 John 2 19.

so he that eateth me, even he shall live by me [δι' ἐμὲ]—not 'through,' but 'by reason of Me.' So that though *one spiritual life* with Him, "the Head of every man is Christ, as the head of Christ is God." (1 Cor. xi. 3; iii. 23.) **58. This is that bread which came down from heaven: not as your fathers did eat manna, and are dead: he that eateth of this bread shall live for ever.** This is a sort of summing up of the whole Discourse, on which let this one further remark suffice—that as our Lord, instead of softening down His figurative sublimities, or even putting them in naked phraseology, leaves the great truths of His Person and Office, and our participation of Him and it, enshrined for all time in those glorious forms of speech, so when we attempt to strip the truth of these figures, figures though they be, it *goes away* from us, like water when the vessel is broken; and hence our wisdom lies in raising our own spirit, and attuning our own ear, to our Lord's chosen modes of expression. It should be added that although this discourse has nothing to do with the Sacrament of the Supper, the Sacrament has everything to do with it, as *the visible embodiment* of these figures, and to the believing partaker giving a *real*, yea the most lively and affecting participation of His flesh and blood, and nourishment thereby of the spiritual and eternal life here below. **59. These things said he in the synagogue, as he taught**—or 'teaching' **in Capernaum.** This would seem to intimate the breaking up of the congregation; rendering it probable that what follows took place after, but probably just after, they had begun to disperse.

The Effect of this Discourse on Two Classes of Hearers: First, *On the prejudiced mass* (60-66). **60. Many therefore of his disciples**—His pretty constant followers, though an outer circle of them, **when they heard this, said, This is an hard saying**—not merely harsh, but insufferable, as the word often means in the Old Testament; **who can hear it?**—or submit to listen to it. **61. When Jesus knew in himself that his disciples murmured at it, he said unto them, Doth this offend you? 62. What and if ye shall see the Son of man ascend up where he was before?** 'If ye are stumbled at what I *have* said, how will ye bear what I *now* say?' Not that His ascension itself would stumble them more than His death, but that after recoiling from the *mention* of the one they would not be in a state of mind to take in the other. **63. It is the Spirit that quickeneth; the flesh profiteth nothing.** Much of His discourse had been about "flesh;" but flesh as such, mere flesh, and all religious notions which originate in the flesh, could profit nothing, much less impart that *life* which the Holy Spirit alone communicates to the soul. **the words that I speak unto you**—rather, 'have spoken' [for λελάληκα is the preferable reading], **they are spirit, and they are life**—the whole burden of this discourse was "*spirit*," not mere flesh, and "*life*" in its highest, not its lower sense; and the words I employed were to be interpreted solely in that sense. **64. But there are some of you that believe not. For Jesus knew from the beginning who they were that believed not, and who should betray him.** As if He had said, 'But it matters little to some of you in what sense I speak, for ye believe not.' This was said, adds the Evangelist, not merely of the outer, but of the inner circle of His disciples; for He knew the traitor, though it was not yet time to expose him. **65. And he said, Therefore said I unto you, that no man can come unto me, except it were given**—or, 'have been given' [ᾖ δεδομένον] **unto him of my Father:**—*q. d.*, 'That was why I spoke to you of the necessity of divine teaching, which some of you are strangers to.' This last expression—"except it have been given him of my Father"—plainly shows that by the Father's "drawing" (*v.* 44,) was meant an *internal* and *efficacious* operation; for in recalling the statement here, He says it must be "*given* to a man to come" to Christ. **66. From that time** [ἐκ τούτου]—or 'In consequence of this,' **many of his disciples went back.** Those last words of our Lord seem to have given them the finishing stroke—they could stand it no longer. **and walked no more with him.** Many a journey, it may be, they had taken with Him, but now they gave Him finally up!

Secondly, *On the Twelve* (67-71). **67. Then said Jesus unto the twelve.** This is the first time that they are so called by our Evangelist. **Will ye also go away?** [θέλετε ὑπάγειν]—'Are ye also minded to go away.' The "ye also" [καὶ ὑμεῖς] is specially emphatic, and the appeal is singularly affecting. Evidently Christ *felt* the desertion of Him even by those miserable men who could not abide His statements; and seeing a disturbance even of the *wheat* by the violence of the wind which blew away the *chaff* (not yet visibly showing itself, but open to His eyes of fire), He would nip it at once by this home question. Doubtless there were other hearers besides the Twelve in whose hearts there was some good thing towards the Lord Jesus in spite of their prejudices and difficulties. But matters were too critical with the Twelve at this moment to admit of attention

68 Simon Peter answered him, Lord, to whom shall we go? thou hast
69 the words of eternal life. And [k]we believe and are sure that thou art
70 that Christ, the Son of the living God. Jesus answered them, Have
71 not I chosen you twelve, and one of you is a devil? He spake of Judas
Iscariot *the son* of Simon: for he it was that should betray him, being
one of the twelve.

A. D. 32.

k Matt. 16.16. Mark 1. 1. Acts 8. 37. Rom. 1. 3. 1 John 5. 1.

being now given to any others. **68. Then Simon Peter**—whose forwardness in this case was noble, and to the wounded spirit of His Lord doubtless very grateful, **answered him, Lord, to whom shall we go? thou hast the words of eternal life.** 'We cannot deny that *we* have been staggered as well as they, and seeing so many go away who, as we thought, might have been retained by teaching a little less hard to take in, our own endurance has been severely tried, nor have we been able to stop short of the question, Shall *we* follow the rest, and give it up? But when it came to this, our light returned and our hearts were reassured. For as soon as we thought of going away, there rose upon us that awful question, "To WHOM shall we go?" To the lifeless formalism and wretched traditions of the elders? to the gods many and lords many of the heathen around us? or to blank unbelief? Nay, Lord, we are shut up. *They* have none of that "ETERNAL LIFE" to offer us whereof Thou hast been discoursing, in words rich and ravishing as well as in words staggering to human wisdom. That life we cannot want; that life we have learnt to crave as a necessity of the deeper nature which Thou hast awakened; "*the words* of that eternal life" (the *authority to reveal* it and the *power to confer* it) Thou hast: Therefore will we stay with Thee—we *must*.' **69. And we believe and are sure** [ἡμεῖς πεπιστεύκαμεν καὶ ἐγνώκαμεν]—'And we have believed and know.' The 'we' is emphatic:—'Whatever may be the case with others, *we*' &c. **that thou art that Christ** [ὁ Χριστὸς]—rather, 'the Christ,' **the Son of the living God.** (See on Matt. xvi. 16.) Peter seems to have added this not merely—probably not so much—as an assurance *to His Lord* of his heart's belief in Him, as for the purpose of fortifying *himself* and his faithful brethren against that recoil from those harsh statements of His which he was probably struggling against with difficulty at that moment. **70. Jesus answered them, Have not I chosen** [ἐξελεξάμην]—'Did I not choose' **you twelve, and one of you is a devil?** 'Well said, Simon Barjonas, but that "we" embraces not so wide a circle as in the simplicity of thine heart thou thinkest; for though I have chosen you but twelve, one even of you twelve is a "devil."' Remarkable expression, at a period comparatively so early, ere yet, probably, the slightest evidence of it had come out to any but His eyes that spake it. It is not "*hath*," but "*is*" a devil; not only the tool, but the temple of Satan [not δαίμων, but διάβολος]. **71. He spake of Judas Iscariot the son of Simon: for he it was that should betray him, being one of the twelve.** These explanatory remarks constitute one of the many striking characteristics of this Gospel—as observed in the Introduction to it.

Remarks.—1. We have seen how, in ch. v., our Lord teaches the essential Unity of the Father and the Son, and yet the Distinction of the Persons, and the Relations of Each to the Other—both in Their own Nature and in the economy of Redemption. Let us now see how the same things are here taught under new aspects. The essential Divinity of the Son is so obviously implied in the following statements, that without it they either are so many turgid nothings, or they are blasphemous assumptions: "I am the Bread of Life"—"The Bread which I will give is My flesh, which I will give for the life of the world." "If any man eat of this Bread, he shall live for ever"—"He that cometh to Me shall never hunger, and he that believeth on Me shall never thirst"—"Except ye eat the flesh and drink the blood of the Son of man, ye have no life in you"—"Whoso eateth My flesh and drinketh My blood hath eternal life, and I will raise him up at the last day." That His death should be the world's life, and men believing on Him—or drawing from Him thereby the virtue of His death—should never hunger and never thirst, but have in them even now an eternal life, and be by Him raised up at the last day, is what no other man ever ventured to affirm of himself, and no creature could affirm without absurdity. But Christ here affirms and reiterates it in every possible form. Nor, in doing so, does He go beyond what He taught to the woman of Samaria, what He taught afterwards in the streets of Jerusalem, regarding the living water (ch. iv. 10, 13, 14; vii. 37-39), and what He taught in His great proclamation of Rest for the weary (Matt. xi. 28-30). But while asserting these claims to what is essentially divine, how careful is our Lord, in those very statements, to intimate that His consecration, and mission from heaven to earth, to discharge these great functions for the world, was all of God, and that He is but the Father's voluntary Agent in every step of man's salvation: "The Son of man shall give unto you the meat that endureth to everlasting life, for Him hath God the Father sealed"—"My Father giveth you the true bread from heaven"—"This is the Father's will which hath sent Me, that of all which He hath given Me I should lose nothing, but should raise it up again at the last day"—"Every man that hath heard and learned of the Father cometh unto Me." But this introduces a new and still more striking expression both of the proper Divinity of the Son and of the ineffable harmony with which the Father and the Son co-operate in every step of man's salvation. After representing it as the very work of God that men should believe in Him whom He had sent, He says, "No man can come to Me except the Father which hath sent Me draw him." What *creature* could possibly say either of these things—that the work of works which God demands from every man is to believe on *him*, and yet, that this cannot be done by any man without a special divine operation upon his heart? But the glory of Christ's proper Divinity shines, if possible, yet brighter in such statements as these—that it is the express will of His Father, which He came down to do, that of all that which He had given Him He should lose nothing, and that every one that beholdeth the Son and believeth on Him should have everlasting life, and He should raise him up at the last day. Who could possibly credit this of a creature? And what creature, on the faith of it, would come to a creature to get eternal life? Even if he could hope thus to get it, how could he possibly be sure in coming to Him, that Christ would know that he *had* come, or would know *when* he came, so as not to cast him out? And what insufferable presumption would it be in

7 AFTER these things Jesus walked in Galilee: for he would not walk
in Jewry, [a]because the Jews sought to kill him.
2 Now [b]the Jews' feast of tabernacles was at hand. His [c]brethren there-
3 fore said unto him, Depart hence, and go into Judea, that thy disciples
4 also may see the works that thou doest. For *there is* no man *that* doeth
any thing in secret, and he himself seeketh to be known openly. If thou

A. D. 32.

CHAP. 7.
[a] ch. 5. 16.
[b] Lev. 23. 34.
[c] Matt. 12. 46. Mark 3. 31. Acts 1. 14.

any creature to say to any other creature, 'If you come to me for eternal life, I will not cast you out?' In short, He that can say without falsehood and without presumption to the whole world—'If any man come to Me, I will give unto him eternal life, and him that cometh I will in no wise cast out, since all that the Father hath given Me shall come to Me; I have got charge from Him accordingly to receive them, to lose nothing and none of them, but to give them even now eternal life, and to raise every one of them up at the last day'—He must be essentially and properly Divine, personally distinct from, yet in absolute harmony with the Father about the matter of man's salvation in general, and every individual's salvation in particular; nor will, nor can any soul, on the faith of such words, come to Jesus and surrender itself into His hands for salvation accordingly, unless in the perfect assurance that He knows the fact of his doing so—knows when he does it—knows "that He is able to keep that which He has committed unto Him against that day" (see on 2 Tim. i. 12). 2. See here the double view of *faith* ever presented in Scripture—as at once a *duty* comprehensive of all other duties, and a *grace*, of special divine communication. It is the duty of duties; for "This is the work of God, that ye believe in Him whom He hath sent:" and it is a grace comprehensive of every other; for though "him that cometh to Me I will in no wise cast out," yet "no man can come to Me except the Father which hath sent Me draw him"—"Every man that hath heard and hath learned of the Father cometh unto Me"—"Therefore said I unto you, that no man can come to Me except it were given unto Him of My Father." Pity that, in the attempts to reconcile these, so much vain and unsavoury controversy has been spent, and that one of them is so often sacrificed to the other; for then they are not what Jesus says they are, but rather a caricature of them. The link of connection between divine and human operation will probably never be reached on earth—if even in heaven. Let us, then, implicitly receive and reverentially hold both; remembering, however, that the *divine* in this case ever precedes, and is the cause of, the *human*—the "drawing" on God's part of the "coming" on ours; while yet our coming is as purely spontaneous, and the result of rational considerations presenting themselves to our minds, as if there were no supernatural operation in the matter at all. 3. What bright marks of truth does the concluding scene of this chapter exhibit! The last thing that would occur to any biographer of a *mythical Christ*—or even filling up from his own fancy a few meagre fragments of real history—would be the entrance of doubts into the innermost circle of those who believed in Him. Or, if even that be conceivable, who would ever have managed such a thought as it is here? The question, "Will *ye also* go away?" is not more the affecting language of wounded feeling—springing from conscious desert of other treatment—than is the reply of Peter the expression of a state of mind too profoundly natural and pregnant ever to have been conceived if it had not been actually uttered. And the answer to this again—to the effect that what Peter expressed would be all that could be desired if it were the mind and feeling of them all; but that, so far from this, out of only twelve men whom He had chosen one would be found a devil—this has such originality stamped upon it as secures its own reception, as true history, by every intelligent and guileless reader. 4. There are seasons when one's faith is tried to the utmost, particularly by speculative difficulties; the spiritual eye then swims, and all truth seems ready to depart from us. At such seasons, a clear perception, like that of Peter here, that to abandon the faith of Christ is to face blank desolation, ruin, and death; and, on recoiling from this, to be able to fall back, not merely on *first principles* and *immovable foundations*, but on *personal experience of a Living Lord*, in whom all truth is wrapt up and made flesh for us—this is a relief unspeakable. Under that blessed Wing taking shelter, until we are again fit to grapple with the questions that have staggered us, we at length either find our way through them, or attain to a calm satisfaction on the discovery that they lie beyond the limits of present apprehension. 5. The narrowness of the circle of those who rally around the truth, and the unpopularity of their profession, are no security that all of them are true-hearted; for one even of the Twelve was a devil. And the length of time during which Judas remained within the innermost circle of Christ's followers, without discovering to his brethren his real character, or probably being aware of it himself, and the fact that when it did come out, it was drawn forth, as appears, quite casually, and then was matured with such frightful rapidity—do not these things cry aloud to all who name the name of Christ, "Rejoice with trembling!" "Let him that thinketh he standeth, take heed lest he fall"! "Watch and pray, that ye enter not into temptation"!

CHAP. VII. 1-53.—CHRIST AT THE FEAST OF TABERNACLES.

Jesus Declines the Advice of His brethren, to Go Openly to Jerusalem, and Show Himself to the World; but at His own time Goes Quietly up, and about the midst of the feast Stands Forth in the temple Teaching (1-14). 1. **After these things**—that is, *all that is recorded after the Discourse of* ch. v. 19-47, **Jesus walked in Galilee**—continuing His labours there, for the reason about to be mentioned; **for he would not walk in Jewry**—or Judea, **because the Jews sought to kill him**—as related in ch. v. 18. This is an exceedingly important piece of information, as we thus learn that our Lord *did not attend the Passover mentioned in* ch. vi. 4—which, according to our reckoning, was the *third* since the opening of His public ministry.

2. **Now the Jews' feast of tabernacles was at hand.** This was the last of the three annual festivals, celebrated on the fifteenth of the seventh month—September (see Lev. xxiii. 33, &c.; Deut. xvi. 13, &c.; Neh. viii. 14-18). 3. **His brethren therefore** (see on Matt. xiii. 54-56) **said unto him, Depart hence, and go into Judea, that thy disciples also may see**—or 'may behold' [θεωρήσωσιν] **the works that thou doest. 4. For there is no man that doeth any thing in secret, and he himself seeketh to be known openly. If thou do these things, show thyself to the world. 5. For**

5 do these things, show thyself to the world. For [d]neither did his brethren
6 believe in him. Then Jesus said unto them, [e]My time is not yet come:
7 but your time is alway ready. The [f]world cannot hate you; but me it
8 hateth, [g]because I testify of it, that the works thereof are evil. Go ye
up unto this feast: I go not up yet unto this feast; [h]for my time is not
9 yet full come. When he had said these words unto them, he abode *still*
10 in Galilee. But when his brethren were gone up, then went he also up
unto the feast, not openly, but as it were in secret.
11 Then [i]the Jews sought him at the feast, and said, Where is he?
12 And [j]there was much murmuring among the people concerning him: for
some [k]said, He is a good man: others said, Nay; but he deceiveth the
13 people. Howbeit no man spake openly of him for fear of the Jews.
14 Now about the midst of the feast, Jesus went up into the temple,
and taught.
15 And [l]the Jews marvelled, saying, How knoweth this man [1]letters,

A. D. 32.

[d] Mark 3. 21.
[e] Ps. 102. 13. Eccl. 3. 1. ch. 2. 4. Acts 1. 7.
[f] ch 15. 19.
[g] ch. 3. 19.
[h] ch. 8. 20.
[i] ch. 11. 56.
[j] ch. 9. 16. ch. 10. 19.
[k] Matt. 21. 46. Luke 7. 16. Luke 18. 19. ch. 6. 14.
[l] Luke 4. 22. Acts 2. 7.
[1] Or, learning.

neither did his brethren believe in him. But as we find these "brethren" of the Lord in the "upper room" among the hundred and twenty disciples who waited for the descent of the Spirit after the Lord's ascension (Acts i. 14), they seem to have had their prejudices removed—perhaps after His resurrection. Indeed, here their language is more that of strong prejudice and suspicion—*such as near relatives, even the best, too frequently show in such cases*—than formed unbelief. There was also, probably, a tincture of *vanity* in it. 'Thou hast many disciples in Judea; here in Galilee they are fast dropping off; it is not like one who advances the claims thou dost to linger so long here, away from the city of our solemnities, where surely "the kingdom of our father David" is to be set up: "seeking," as thou dost, "to be known openly," those miracles of thine ought not to be confined to this distant corner, but submitted at headquarters to the inspection of the world.' On hearing such a speech, one might suppose Him going to His Father, and saying, "I am become a stranger unto my brethren, an alien unto my mother's children"! (Ps. lxix. 8). Does not this speech, by the way, tend to confirm the view we have taken of the number of Passovers which occurred during our Lord's public ministry, and which imply His absence from Jerusalem for a time which had appeared unaccountably long? For about a year and a half, according to our reckoning, He had not been there. This seems to many incredibly long. But it would seem as if it had been long enough at least to appear to His "brethren" inconsistent with His claims. **6. Then Jesus said unto them, My time**—for showing Myself to the world—**is not yet come: but your time is alway ready. 7. The world cannot hate you; but me it hateth, because I testify of it, that the works thereof are evil. 8. Go ye up unto this feast**—or, 'the feast,' as, perhaps, is the preferable reading here. **I go not up yet unto this feast; for my time is not yet full come:**—*q. d.*, 'It matters little when ye go up, for ye have no great plans in life, and nothing hangs upon your movements: With Me it is otherwise; on every movement of Mine there hangs what ye know not: The world has no quarrel with you, for ye bear no testimony against it, and so draw down upon yourselves none of its wrath; but I am here to lift up My voice against its hypocrisy, and denounce its abominations; therefore it cannot endure Me, and one false step might precipitate its fury on its Victim's head before the time: Away, therefore, to the feast as soon as it suits you; I follow at the fitting moment, but "My time is not yet full come."' **9. When**—'And when' **he had said these words unto them, he abode still in Galilee. 10. But when his brethren were gone up, then went he also up unto the feast, not openly, but as it were in secret** [ὡς ἐν κρυπτῷ]—'but in a manner secretly,' not in the caravan-company, as *Meyer* explains it,—see on Luke ii. 44: perhaps by some other route, and at any rate in such a way as not to attract notice.

11. Then the Jews sought him at the feast, and said, Where is he? "The Jews" here mean the *rulers;* see on ch. i. 19. They sought Him on this occasion certainly for no good end. **12. And there was much murmuring**—or 'muttering' [γογγυσμὸς] **among the people** [ἐν τοῖς ὄχλοις]—'among the multitudes;' the natural expression of a Jewish writer, indicating without design, as *Webster and Wilkinson* remark, the crowded state of Jerusalem at this festival. **concerning him: for some said, He is a good man: others said, Nay; but he deceiveth the people**—or 'the multitude' [τὸν ὄχλον]. These are just the two opposite views of Him and His claims, the one, that He was *honest;* the other, that He was an *impostor.* **13. Howbeit no man spake openly of him**—that is, in His favour—**for fear of the Jews.** As the people who feared the Jews were themselves Jews, this would suffice to show that by "the Jews" in this Gospel we are almost invariably to understand the *rulers* or *leaders* of the people.

14. Now about the midst of the feast [Ἤδη δὲ τῆς ἑορτῆς μεσούσης]—rather, 'Now when it was already the midst of the feast.' It might be the fourth or fifth of the eight days during which it lasted. **Jesus went up into the temple, and taught** [ἐδίδασκεν]. The imperfect tense used implies *continued*, and therefore *formal* teaching, as distinguished from mere casual sayings. In fact, this appears to have been *the first time* that He taught thus openly in Jerusalem. He had kept back till the feast was half through, to let the stir about Him subside; and entering the city unexpectedly, He had begun His "teaching" at the temple, and created a certain awe, before the wrath of the rulers had time to break in upon it.

Amidst many interruptions, Jesus boldly continues His temple-teaching (15-31). **15. And the Jews marvelled, saying, How knoweth this man letters**—or learning, **having never learned?**—that is, at any rabbinical school, like Paul under Gamaliel (see Acts xxii. 3; xxvi. 24.) These rulers knew well enough that He had never studied under any human teacher—an important admission, as *Meyer* remarks, against ancient and modern attempts to trace our Lord's wisdom to human sources. Probably His teaching on this occasion was *expository,* manifesting that unrivalled faculty and depth

16 having never learned? Jesus answered them, and said, [m]My doc-
17 trine is not mine, but his that sent me. If [n]any man will do his
will, he shall know of the doctrine, whether it be of God, or *whether* I
18 speak of myself. He [o]that speaketh of himself seeketh his own glory:
but he that seeketh his glory that sent him, the same is true, and no
19 unrighteousness is in him. Did [p]not Moses give you the law, and *yet*
20 none of you keepeth the law? [q]Why go ye about to kill me? The
people answered and said, [r]Thou hast a devil: who goeth about to kill
21 thee? Jesus answered and said unto them, I have done one work, and
22 ye all marvel. Moses [s]therefore gave unto you circumcision; (not because
it is of Moses, but [t]of the fathers;) and ye on the sabbath day circumcise
23 a man. If a man on the sabbath day receive circumcision, [2]that the law
of Moses should not be broken; are ye angry at me, because I [u]have
24 made a man every whit whole on the sabbath day? Judge [v]not according to the appearance, but judge righteous judgment.
25 Then said some of them of Jerusalem, Is not this he whom they seek
26 to kill? But, lo, he speaketh boldly, and they say nothing unto him.
27 Do the rulers know indeed that this is the very Christ? Howbeit we
know this man whence he is: but when Christ cometh, no man knoweth
whence he is.

A. D. 32.

[m] ch. 8. 28. ch. 12. 49. ch. 14. 10, 24.
[n] Hos. 6. 2, 3. ch. 8. 43.
[o] ch. 5. 41. ch. 8. 50.
[p] Acts 7. 38.
[q] Matt. 12. 14. Mark 3. 6. ch. 5. 16.
[r] ch. 8. 48.
[s] Lev. 12. 3.
[t] Gen. 17. 10.
[2] Or, without breaking the law of Moses.
[u] ch. 5. 8.
[v] Deut. 1. 16. Pro. 24. 23. ch. 8. 15. Jas. 2. 1.

which in the Sermon on the Mount had excited the astonishment of all—though now, no doubt, it would be in a different strain. **16. Jesus**—'Jesus therefore' (according to the true text) **answered them, and said, My doctrine is not mine**—that is, in the sense repeatedly explained on ch. v. and vi., 'not from Myself,' 'not unauthorized;' 'I am here by divine commission.' **but his that sent me. 17. If any man will do** [θέλῃ]—or better, 'is minded to do' **his will, he shall know of the doctrine, whether it be of God, or whether I speak of myself**—whether it be from above or from beneath, whether it be divine or an imposture of mine own. A principle of immense importance; showing, on the one hand, that singleness of desire to please God is the grand inlet to light on all questions vitally affecting one's eternal interest, and, on the other, that the want of this, whether perceived or not, is the chief cause of infidelity amidst the light of revealed religion. **18. He that speaketh of himself**—not concerning, 'but from himself' [ἀφ' ἑαυτοῦ] **seeketh his own glory: but he that seeketh his glory that sent him, the same is true, and no unrighteousness is in him.** See on ch. v. 41-44. **19. Did not Moses give you** [δέδωκεν]—'Hath not Moses given you' **the law, and yet none of you keepeth the law? Why go ye about**—or 'seek ye' [ζητεῖτε] **to kill me?** 'In opposing Me ye pretend zeal for Moses, but to the spirit and end of that law which he gave ye are total strangers, and in going about to kill Me, ye are its greatest enemies.' **20. The people** [ὁ ὄχλος]—'The multitude' **answered and said, Thou hast a devil: who goeth about to kill thee?** The *multitude* who said this had as yet no bad feeling to Jesus, and evidently were not in the secret of the plot now hatching, as our Lord knew, against Him. **21. Jesus answered and said unto them, I have done**—rather, 'I did' [ἐποίησα] **one work, and ye all marvel.** Taking no notice of the popular appeal, as there were those there who knew well enough what He meant, He recalls His cure of the impotent man, and the murderous rage it had kindled (ch. v. 9, 16, 18). It may seem strange that He should refer to an event a year and a half old, as if but newly done; and this is urged as a fatal objection to our Lord's having been so long absent from Jerusalem. But their present attempt "to kill Him" brought the past scene all fresh up, not only to Him, but without doubt to them too, if indeed they had ever forgotten it; and by this fearless reference to it, exposing their hypocrisy and dark designs, He gave His position great moral strength. **22. Moses therefore gave unto you**—or, 'For this cause hath Moses given you' [δέδωκεν] **circumcision; (not because it is**—'not that it is' **of Moses, but of the fathers;) and ye on the sabbath day circumcise a man. 23. If a man on the sabbath day receive circumcision, that the law of Moses should not be broken; are ye angry at me, because I have made**—or 'I made' [ἐποίησα] **a man every whit whole on the sabbath day?** Though servile work was forbidden on the sabbath, the circumcision of males on that day (which certainly was a servile work) was counted no infringement of the law: How much less ought fault to be found with One who had made a man "every whit whole"—or rather, 'a man's entire body whole' [ὅλον ἄνθρωπον ὑγιῆ]—on the sabbath day? What a testimony to the reality of the miracle, none daring to meet the bold appeal? **24. Judge not according to the appearance, but judge righteous judgment**—'Rise above the *letter* into the *spirit* of the law.'

25. Then said some of them of Jerusalem—'the Jerusalemites;' that is, the citizens—as distinguished from the multitudes from the provinces—and who, knowing the long formed purpose of the rulers to put Jesus to death, wondered they were now letting him teach openly, **Is not this he whom they seek to kill? 26. But, lo**—'And, lo' [Καὶ ἴδε], **he speaketh boldly, and they say nothing unto him. Do the rulers know indeed** [ἔγνωσαν]—'Have the rulers come to know indeed' **that this is the [very] Christ?** [The second ἀληθῶς in this verse is of very doubtful authority.] 'Have they got some new light in favour of His claims?' **27. Howbeit we know this man whence he is: but when ['the'] Christ cometh, no man knoweth whence he is.** This seems to refer to some current opinion that Messiah's origin would be mysterious—not *altogether* wrong—from which they concluded that Jesus could not be he, since they knew all about his family at Nazareth.

28. Then—or 'therefore' **cried Jesus**—in a louder tone, and more solemnly witnessing style than usual, **in the temple, as he taught, saying, Ye both**

28 Then cried Jesus in the temple, as he taught, saying, [w]Ye both know
me, and ye know whence I am: and [x]I am not come of myself, but he
29 that sent me [y]is true, whom [z]ye know not. But [a]I know him: for I am
30 from him, and he hath sent me. Then they sought to take him: but no
31 man laid hands on him, because his hour was not yet come. And many
of the people believed on him, and said, When Christ cometh, will he
do more miracles than these which this *man* hath done?
32 The Pharisees heard that the people murmured such things concerning
him; and the Pharisees and the chief priests sent officers to take him.
33 Then said Jesus unto them, [b]Yet a little while am I with you, and *then* I
34 go unto him that sent me. Ye [c]shall seek me, and shall not find *me:*
35 and where I am, *thither* ye cannot come. Then said the Jews among
themselves, Whither will he go, that we shall not find him? will he go
36 unto [d]the dispersed among the [3]Gentiles, and teach the Gentiles? What
manner of saying is this that he said, Ye shall seek me, and shall not
find *me:* and where I am, *thither* ye cannot come?
37 In the last day, that great *day* of the feast, Jesus stood and cried,
38 saying, [e]If any man thirst, let him come unto me, and drink. He [f]that

A. D. 32.

[w] ch. 8. 14.
[x] ch. 5. 43. ch. 8. 42.
[y] ch. 5. 32. ch. 8. 26. Rom. 3. 4.
[z] ch. 1. 18. ch. 8. 55.
[a] Matt. 11. 27. ch. 10. 15.
[b] ch. 13. 33.
[c] Hos. 5. 6. ch. 8. 21. ch. 13. 33.
[d] Isa. 11. 12. Jas. 1. 1. 1 Pet. 1. 1.
[3] Or, Greeks.
[e] Isa. 55. 1. Rev. 3. 20. Rev. 22. 17.
[f] Deut. 18. 15.

know me, and ye know whence I am: and I am not come of myself:—*q. d.*, 'True, ye both know myself and my earthly parentage; and *yet* I am not come of myself, &c. **but he that sent me is true** [ἀληθινὸς]—'real;' meaning probably, 'He that sent Me is the only *real* Sender of any one.' **whom ye know not. 29. But I know him: for I am from him, and he hath sent me**—'and He sent me' [ἀπέστειλεν]. **30. Then they sought to take him: but**—rather, 'and yet' [καὶ] **no man laid hands on him**—their *impotence* happily being equal to their *malignity*, **because his hour was not yet come. 31. And many of the people** [δὲ—ὄχλου]—'But many of the multitude' **believed on him, and said, When Christ cometh**—or, 'When the Christ is come' [ὁ Χ.—ἔλθῃ], **will he do more miracles than these which this man hath done?**—*q. d.*, 'If this be not the Christ, what can the Christ do, when he does come—which has not been anticipated and eclipsed by this man?' This was evidently the language of friendly persons, overborne by their spiteful superiors, but unable to keep quite silent.

Officers are sent by the Rulers to Apprehend Jesus; but they, Captivated by His Teaching, Return, confessing their inability to do it (32-46). **32. The Pharisees heard that the people murmured**—or 'heard the multitude muttering [τοῦ ὄχλου γογγύζοντος] **such things concerning him.** They heard whispers to this effect going about, and thought it high time to stop Him if He was not to be allowed to carry away the people. **and the Pharisees and the chief priests sent officers to take him**—subordinate officials of their own to seize Him. **33. Then said Jesus [unto them].** The words in brackets [αὐτοῖς] have scarcely any authority. **Yet a little while am I with you, and then I go unto him that sent me. 34. Ye shall seek me, and shall not find me: and where I am, thither ye cannot come:**—*q. d.*, 'Your desire to be rid of Me will be for you all too soon fulfilled: Yet a little while and we part company—for ever; for I go whither ye cannot come, nor, even though ye should at length seek to Him whom now ye despise, shall ye be able to find Him'—referring not to any penitential, but to purely selfish cries in their time of desperation. **35. Then said the Jews**—the *rulers* again, **among themselves, Whither will he**—or 'this man' [οὗτος], **go, that we shall not find him?** They cannot comprehend Him, but seem awed by the solemn grandeur of His warning. **Will he go unto the dispersed** [τὴν διασπορὰν] **among the Gentiles, and teach the Gentiles?** [Ἑλλήνων, Ἕλληνας]—'unto the dispersed among the Greeks, and teach the Greeks? Will He go to the Jews of the dispersion—scattered abroad everywhere—and from them extend His teaching even to the Gentiles? (So *Meyer*, *Lücke*, *Tholuck*, &c.) By the *Greeks* here are not meant Hellenistic or Greek-speaking Jews, but *Gentiles*. It is well observed by *Neander*, that a presentiment that His teaching was designed to be universal had probably a good deal to do with the irritation which it occasioned. **36. What manner of saying is this that he said, Ye shall seek me, and shall not find me: and where I am, thither ye cannot come?** Thinking this theory of His words too outrageous or contemptible, they are quite baffled as to its meaning, and yet cannot help feeling that something deep lay under it. Jesus, however, takes no notice of their questions; and so for the time the subject dies away. And yet, long after this, Jesus recurs to this warning of His, in discoursing to the Eleven at the Supper table (ch. xiii. 33).

And now we come to one of the grandest of all His utterances.

37. In the last day, that great day of the feast—or 'Now [δὲ] in the last, the great day of the feast;' that is, the eighth day of the feast of Tabernacles (Lev. xxiii. 39). It was a Sabbath, the last feast-day of the year, and distinguished by very remarkable ceremonies. 'The generally joyous character of this feast,' says *Olshausen*, 'broke out on this day into loud jubilation, particularly at the solemn moment when the priest, as was done on every day of this festival, brought forth, in golden vessels, water from the stream of Siloah, which flowed under the temple-mountain, and solemnly poured it upon the altar. Then the words of Isa. xii. 3 were sung, "*With joy shall ye draw water out of the wells of Salvation,*" and thus the symbolical reference of this act, intimated in *v.* 39, was expressed.' 'So ecstatic,' says *Lightfoot*, 'was the joy with which this ceremony was performed—accompanied with sound of trumpets—that it used to be said, Whoever had not witnessed it had never seen rejoicing at all.' On this high occasion, then, He who had already drawn all eyes upon Him by His supernatural power and unrivalled teaching—**Jesus stood**—probably in some elevated position, **and cried**—as if making proclamation in the audience of all the people, **saying, IF ANY MAN THIRST, LET HIM COME UNTO ME, AND DRINK.** What an offer! The deepest cravings of

believeth on me, as the Scripture hath said, [g]out of his belly shall flow
39 rivers of living water. (But [h]this spake he of the Spirit, which they that
believe on him should receive: for the Holy Ghost was not yet *given;*
40 because that Jesus was not yet [i]glorified.) Many of the people therefore,
41 when they heard this saying, said, Of a truth this is [j]the Prophet. Others
said, [k]This is the Christ. But some said, Shall Christ come [l]out of
42 Galilee? Hath [m]not the Scripture said, That Christ cometh of the seed
43 of David, and out of the town of Bethlehem, [n]where David was? So
44 there was a division among the people because of him. And some of
them would have taken him; but no man laid hands on him.
45 Then came the officers to the chief priests and Pharisees; and they

A. D. 32.
[g] Isa. 12. 3.
[h] Isa. 44. 3. Joel 2. 28. ch. 16. 7. Acts 2. 17.
[i] ch. 12. 16.
[j] Deut. 18. 15. ch. 1. 21. ch. 6. 14.
[k] ch. 4. 42.
[l] ch. 1. 46.
[m] Ps. 132. 11.
[n] 1 Sam. 16. 1.

the human spirit are here, as in the Old Testament, expressed by the figure of "*thirst*," and the external satisfaction of them by "*drinking*." To the woman of Samaria He had said almost the same thing, and in the same terms (John iv. 13, 14). But what to her was simply affirmed as a *fact* is here turned into a world-wide *proclamation;* and whereas there, the *gift* by Him of the living water is the most prominent idea—in contrast with her hesitation to give Him the perishable water of Jacob's well—here the prominence is given to *Himself* as the Well-spring of all satisfaction. He had in Galilee invited all the WEARY AND HEAVY-LADEN of the human family to come under His wing and they should find REST (Matt. xi. 28), which is just the same deep want, and the same profound relief of it, under another and equally grateful figure. He had in the synagogue of Capernaum (ch. vi.), announced Himself, in every variety of form, as "the BREAD of Life," and as both able and authorized to appease the "HUNGER," and quench the "THIRST," of all that apply to Him. There is, and there can be, nothing beyond that here. But what was on all those occasions uttered in private, or addressed to a provincial audience, is here sounded forth in the streets of the great religious metropolis, and in language of surpassing majesty, simplicity, and grace. It is just Jehovah's ancient proclamation now sounding forth through human flesh, "Ho, EVERY ONE THAT THIRSTETH, COME YE TO THE WATERS, AND HE THAT HATH NO MONEY!" (Isa. lv. 1). In this light, we have but two alternatives; either to say with Caiaphas of Him that uttered such words, "*He is guilty of death*," or, falling down before Him, to exclaim with Thomas, "MY LORD AND MY GOD!" **38. He that believeth on me, as the Scripture hath said, out of his belly shall flow rivers of living water.** The words, "as the Scripture hath said," refer, of course, to the promise in the latter part of the verse—yet not so much to any particular passage as to the general strain of Messianic prophecy, as Isa. lviii. 11; Joel iii. 18; Zec. xiv. 8; Ezek. xlvii. 1-12; in most of which passages the idea is that of waters issuing from beneath the Temple, to which our Lord compares Himself and those who believe in Him. The expression "out of his belly" means, out of his inner man, his soul, as in Prov. xx. 27. On the "rivers of living water," see on ch. iv. 13, 14. There, however, the figure is "a fountain;" here it is "rivers." It refers primarily to the *copiousness*, but indirectly also to the *diffusiveness*, of this living water to the good of others. **39. (But this spake he of the Spirit**—Who, by His direct Personal Agency, opens up these fountains, these rivers of living water, in the human spirit (ch. iii. 6), and by his indwelling in the renewed soul ensures their unfailing flow. **which they that believe on him should receive**—or 'were about to receive' [ἔμελλον λαμβάνειν]: **for the Holy Ghost was not yet [given].** Beyond all doubt the word "given," or some similar word, is the right supplement here, if we are to insert any supplement at all. In ch. xvi. 7 the Holy Ghost is represented not only as *the gift of Christ*, but a Gift the communication of which was *dependent upon His own departure to the Father*. Now, as Christ was not yet gone, so the Holy Ghost was not yet given, **because that Jesus was not yet glorified.)** This is one of those explanatory remarks of our Evangelist himself which constitute a marked feature of this Fourth Gospel. The word "*glorified*" is here used advisedly, to teach the reader not only that the *departure* of Christ to the Father was *indispensable* to the giving of the Spirit, but that this illustrious Gift, direct from the hands of the ascended Saviour, was God's intimation to the world that He whom it had cast out, crucified, and slain, was "His Elect, in whom His soul delighted," and that it was through the smiting of that Rock that the waters of the Spirit—for which the Church was waiting, and with pomp at the feast of Tabernacles proclaiming its expectation—had gushed forth upon a thirsty world. **40. Many of the people**—'the multitude' [ἐκ τοῦ ὄχλου], **when they heard this saying.** The true reading appears to be 'the' or 'His sayings' [τῶν λόγων]; referring not to the last one only, but the whole strain of His discourse, terminating with such a glorious proclamation. **said, Of a truth this is the Prophet.** The only wonder is they did not all say it. "But their minds were blinded." **41. Others said, This is the Christ.** See on ch. i. 21. **But some**—rather, 'others' [ἄλλοι] **said, Shall Christ come out of Galilee?** [Μὴ γὰρ—ὁ Χ. ἔρχεται]—'Doth the Christ then,' or 'What then! Is the Christ to come out of Galilee?' **42. Hath not the Scripture said, That** ['the'] **Christ cometh of the seed of David, and out of the town of Bethlehem, where David was?** We accept this spontaneous testimony to our David-descended, Bethlehem-born Saviour. Had those who gave it made the enquiry which the case demanded, they would have found that Jesus "came out of Galilee" and "out of Bethlehem," both alike in fulfilment of prophecy as in point of fact. (Matt. ii. 23; iv. 13-16.) **43. So there was a division among the people**—'the multitude' [ἐν τῷ ὄχλῳ], **because of him. 44. And some of them**—the more envenomed of those who had taken the adverse side of the question, **would have taken him**—or 'were minded to take Him' [ἤθελον πιάσαι], **but**—or 'yet' [ἀλλὰ], **no man laid hands on him.** See on *v.* 30.

45. Then came the officers to the chief priests and Pharisees—who had sent them to seize Him (*v.* 32), and who would appear from the sequel to have been sitting in Council when the officers returned. **and they said unto them, Why have ye not brought him?**—already thirsting for their Victim, and thinking it an easy matter to seize and bring Him. **46. The officers answered, Never**

46 said unto them, Why have ye not brought him? The officers answered,
Never man spake like this man.
47, Then answered them the Pharisees, Are ye also deceived? Have [o] any
48, of the rulers or of the Pharisees believed on him? But this people who
49, knoweth not the law are cursed. Nicodemus saith unto them, ([p] he
50, that came [4] to Jesus by night, being one of them,) Doth [q] our law judge
51, *any* man before it hear him and know what he doeth? They answered
52 and said unto him, Art thou also of Galilee? Search, and look: for
53 out [r] of Galilee ariseth no prophet. And every man went unto his own
house.

A. D. 32.

[o] ch. 12. 42. Acts 6. 7. 1 Cor. 1. 20.
[p] ch. 3. 2.
[4] to him.
[q] Deut. 1 17. Deut. 17. 8.
[r] 1 Ki. 17. 1. 2 Ki. 14. 25. Isa 9. 1, 2. Matt. 4. 15. ch. 1. 46.

man spake like this man—Noble testimony of unsophisticated men! Doubtless they were strangers to the profound intent of Christ's teaching, but there was that in it which, by its mysterious grandeur and transparent purity and grace, held them spell-bound. No doubt it was of God that they should so feel, that their arm might be paralyzed, as Christ's "hour was not come;" but even in human teaching there has sometimes been felt such a divine power, that men who came to kill the speaker have confessed to all that they were unmanned.

The Pharisees Break Forth upon the Officers with Rage, but are met with an Unexpected Protestation from Amongst Themselves against their Indecent Haste in Condemning the Untried (47-53). **47. Then answered them the Pharisees, Are ye also deceived?** In their own servants this seemed intolerable. **48. Have any of the rulers or of the Pharisees believed on him?** We are expressly told that "many of them" did, including Nicodemus and Joseph, but not one of these had openly "confessed Him" (ch. xii. 42); and this appeal must have stung such of them as heard it to the quick. **49. But this people** [ὁ ὄχλος οὗτος]—rather, 'this multitude,' this ignorant rabble. Pity these important distinctions between the different classes, so marked in the original of this Gospel, should not be also in our version. **who knoweth not the law**—meaning, by school-learning, which only perverted the law by human additions, **are cursed**—a kind of swearing at them, out of mingled rage and scorn. **50. Nicodemus**—reappearing to us after nearly three years' absence from the history, as a member of the council, then sitting, as would appear, **saith unto them, (he that came to Jesus by night, being one of them,) 51. Doth our law judge any man before it hear him**—rather, 'except it first hear from him' [ἐὰν μὴ ἀκούσῃ παρ' αὐτοῦ πρότερον], **and know what he doeth?**—a very proper but all too tame rejoinder, and evidently more from pressure of conscience than any design to pronounce *positively* in the case. The feebleness of his defence of Jesus, as *Webster and Wilkinson* well remark, presents a strong contrast to the fierceness of the rejoinders of the Pharisees. **52. They answered and said unto him, Art thou also of Galilee?**—in this taunt expressing their scorn of the party. Even a word of caution, or the gentlest proposal to enquire before condemning, was with them equivalent to an espousal of the hated One. **Search, and look: for** [καὶ ἴδε ὅτι]—or better, 'Search and see that' **out of Galilee ariseth no prophet.** Strange! For had not *Jonah*, of Gath-hepher, and even Elijah, so far as appears, arisen out of Galilee? and it may be more, of whom we have no record. But rage is blind, and deep prejudice distorts all facts. Yet it looks as if they were afraid of losing Nicodemus, when they take the trouble to reason the point at all. It was just *because* he had "searched," as they advised him, that he went the length even that he did. **53. And every man went unto his own house**—finding their plot could not at that time be carried into effect. Is your rage thus impotent, O ye chief priests? *N.B.*—On the genuineness of this verse, and of the first eleven verses of the following chapter, we reserve our observations till we come to that chapter.

Remarks.—1. The springs of judgment and of action revealed in the first part of this chapter are so minutely and delicately natural as to defy invention, and to verify the narrative not only as a whole but in all its features. Here are Jesus and "His brethren" according to the flesh: on the principles somewhat largely explained on Luke iv. 24, with Remark 2 at the close of that Section, they have great difficulty in recognizing His claims at all; but His present procedure—so different from all that they presume it ought to be and naturally would be in the great predicted *Messiah*—stumbles them most of all. 'Surely One making such claims should at once and in the most open manner lay them before the public authorities at the capital: but instead of this, Thou hast been absent from Jerusalem for a very unusual time; and now that the last of the yearly festivals is at hand, no symptoms appear of a purpose to attend it: how is this?' The answer to these insinuations is in singular keeping with our Lord's habitual estimate of His own position, and the mingled caution and courage with which He laid and carried out all His plans; while the *indifference* which He stamps upon their movements, and the ground on which He regards them as of no consequence at all—this bears the stamp of entire historical reality. But most of all, perhaps, His going up noiselessly by Himself, after the departure of "His brethren;" and not, as usual, before the commencement of the feast, nor till towards the midst of it; and then—after much speculation what had become of Him, and whether He would venture to appear at all—His proceeding to teach in the temple-court, and that so marvellously as to secure for Himself a footing not to be disturbed, insomuch that even the officers sent to seize Him found themselves unable, through the riveting effect of His teaching, to lay a hand upon Him; and then the rage of the ecclesiastics at this, and—while ascribing it all to a want of learned insight which, if they had been "rulers or Pharisees," they would not have shown—finding, to their mortification, a ruler and a Pharisee of their own number, one sitting beside them, taking the officers' part and rebuking their indecent desire to condemn without a trial: these are details which carry their own truth to the hearts of all readers not blinded by prejudice. 2. When Jesus proclaimed, in such ravishing terms, "If any man thirst, let him come unto Me, and drink," we may well ask, Is there any man who does *not* thirst? *Satisfaction*—if that be the word which covers all the cravings of our nature—is indeed as different as possible in the estimation of different men. With some the

8, JESUS went unto the mount of Olives. And early in the morning he
2 came again into the temple, and all the people came unto him; and he
sat down, and taught them.
3 And the scribes and Pharisees brought unto him a woman taken
4 in adultery; and when they had set her in the midst, they say unto
him, Master, this woman was taken in adultery, in the very act.
5 Now [a] Moses in the law commanded us, that such should be stoned:
6 but what sayest thou? This they said, tempting him, that they

A. D. 32.

CHAP. 8.
[a] Ex. 20. 14.
Lev. 18. 20.
Lev. 20. 10.
Deut. 5. 18.
Deut. 22. 22.
Job 31. 9.
Pro. 6. 29, 32.

gratification of the lusts of the flesh is all the satisfaction desired; others crave domestic and intellectual enjoyment; a third class find the approval of conscience indispensable to their comfort, but, unable to come up to their own standard of character and excellence, are inwardly restless; while a fourth and smaller class groan under felt sinfulness, and—conscious that peace with God and delight in His law after the inward man are the great necessity of their nature and condition, but that these are just what they want and cannot reach—are wretched accordingly. But to one and all of these—embracing every soul of man—Jesus here speaks; though to each His proclamation would be differently understood. The first class He would raise from a sensual to spiritual satisfaction—as from the hollow to the real, from wormwood to honey; the second class He would advance from what is good to what is better, from meat that perisheth—even in its most refined forms —to that which endureth to everlasting life; the third class He would draw upwards from toilsome and fruitless efforts to pacify an uneasy conscience by mere attempted obedience to the law, and when they have come to the fourth stage, of conscious inability to keep the law, and wretchedness for want of peace with God, He would then attract and invite them to *Himself*, as the Well-spring of complete and eternal Satisfaction. *How* He was so He does but partially explain here; but the proclamation of such an astonishing truth was itself enough in the meantime; and those whom its transcendant grace might win over to attach themselves cordially to Him would immediately find in their own experience how true it was, and very soon—on the pentecostal descent of the Spirit—discover the secret of their satisfaction more in detail. But 3. When the Evangelist says that by the "rivers of living water which were to flow out of the belly of them that believed in Him," Jesus meant "*the Spirit*, which believers were about to receive: for the Holy Ghost had not then been given; because Jesus was not yet glorified"—he expresses the great evangelical truth, that it is the Holy Ghost who opens up in the souls of them that believe in Jesus the fountain of a new life, and by His indwelling presence and ever-quickening virtue within them, causes rivers of living water to flow forth from this internal fountain—in other words, makes exuberant and heavenly satisfaction to spring up and flow forth from within their own nature. But whereas He says that this glorious gift of the Spirit was so dependent upon the "*glorification of Jesus*," that until the one occurred the other could not be looked for—this expresses these further and most precious truths, that *the formal and judicial acceptance of Christ's work* done on earth *by His Father in heaven* behoved to take place ere the Spirit could be permitted to carry it into effect; that the actual descent of the Spirit at Pentecost was the proclamation to the world that His Father had *taken His work off His hands*, so to speak, as a "*finished*" *work;* and that now the Spirit, in opening up the springs of this new and enduring life in the souls of them that believed in Jesus, was but carrying into effect *in* men what Christ did on earth *for* men, was but putting them in personal possession and actual experience of the virtue of Christ's work—even as Jesus Himself afterwards said in express terms to the Eleven at the Supper-table, "He shall glorify Me; for He shall receive of Mine, and shall show it"—or 'make it known' [ἀναγγελεῖ] "unto you" (see on ch. xvi. 14-16). Thus, as Jesus glorified the Father, so the Spirit glorifies the Son; and by one high, harmonious work of Father, Son, and Holy Ghost, are sinners saved.

CHAP. VIII. 1-11.—THE WOMAN TAKEN IN ADULTERY. The genuineness of this narrative—including the last verse of the foregoing chapter—will be best considered after the exposition.

1. Jesus—It should be, 'But Jesus' [Ἰησοῦς δὲ] **went unto the mount of Olives.** This verse should have formed the last verse of ch. vii. The information given will then be, that while "every man went unto his own house," Jesus, who had no home of His own to go to, "went unto the mount of Olives." As "the mount of Olives" nowhere else occurs in this Gospel, and Jesus' spending the night there seems to belong only to the time of His final visit to Jerusalem; this has been thought adverse to the genuineness of the whole Section. The following is *Stier's* explanation of this, with which, however, we are but indifferently satisfied. 'The return of the people to the inert quiet and security of their *dwellings* (ch. vii. 53), at the close of the feast, is designedly contrasted with our Lord's *homeless* way, so to speak, of spending the short night, who is early in the morning on the scene again. One cannot well see why what is recorded in Luke xxi. 37, 38, may not even thus early have taken place: it might have been the Lord's ordinary custom from the beginning to leave the brilliant misery of the city every night, that so He might compose His sorrowful and interceding heart, and collect His energies for new labours of love; preferring for His resting-place Bethany, and *the Mount of Olives*, the scene thus consecrated by many preparatory prayers for His final humiliation and exaltation.' But see the discussion of this question below. **2. And early in the morning he came again into the temple, and all the people came unto him; and he sat down, and taught them.**

The Scribes and Pharisees Bring to Jesus a Woman Taken in Adultery for His Decision, and how this Attempt to Entrap Him was foiled (3-11).

3. And the scribes and Pharisees—foiled in their yesterday's attempts, and hoping to entrap Him in this new way, **brought unto him a woman taken in adultery; and when they had set her in the midst, 4. They say unto him, Master, this woman was taken in adultery, in the very act. 5. Now Moses in the law commanded us, that such should be stoned.** The law said merely she should die (Deut. xxii. 22), but in aggravated cases, at least in later times, this was probably by stoning (Ezek. xvi. 40). **but what sayest thou?** [σὺ οὖν τί λέγεις;]—'what now sayest thou?' **6. This they said, tempting him, that they might**

might have to accuse him. But Jesus stooped down, and with *his*
7 finger wrote on the ground, *as though he heard them not.* So when
they continued asking him, he lifted up himself, and said unto them,
[b]He that is without sin among you, let him first cast a stone at her.
8 And again he stooped down, and wrote on the ground. And they
9 which heard it, [c]being convicted by *their own* conscience, went out one
by one, beginning at the eldest, *even* unto the last: and Jesus was left
10 alone, and the woman standing in the midst. When Jesus had lifted
up himself, and saw none but the woman, he said unto her, Woman,
11 where are those thine accusers? hath no man condemned thee? She
said, No man, Lord. And Jesus said unto her, [d]Neither do I condemn
thee: go, and sin no more.

A. D. 32.

[b] Deut. 17. 7. Job 5. 12. Ps. 50. 16-20. Matt. 7. 1-5. Rom. 2. 1.
[c] Gen. 41. 21, 22. Rom. 2. 22. 1 John 3. 20.
[d] Luke 9. 56. Luke 12. 14. ch. 3. 17. Rom. 13. 3, 4.

have to accuse him—hoping, whatever He might answer, to put Him in the wrong:—if He said, Stone her, that would seem a stepping out of His province; if He forbade it, that would hold Him up as a relaxer of the public morals. See now how these cunning hypocrites were overmatched. **But Jesus stooped down.** It will be observed He was "*sitting*" when they came to Him (*v.* 2). **and with his finger wrote on the ground.** The words of our translators in Italics—"as though he heard them not"—have hardly improved the sense, for it is scarcely probable He could wish that to be thought. Rather He wished to show them His aversion to enter on the subject. But this did not suit them. They pressed for an answer. **7. So when they continued asking him, he lifted up himself, and said unto them, He that is without sin**—not meaning 'sinless altogether;' nor yet 'guiltless of a literal breach of the Seventh Commandment;' but probably, 'He whose conscience acquits him of *any such* sin,' **let him first cast a stone** [τὸν λίθον]—rather, 'the stone,' referred to in the Mosaic statute, Deut. xvii. 11. **8. And again he stooped down, and wrote on the ground.** The design of this second stooping and writing on the ground was evidently to give her accusers an opportunity to slink away unobserved *by Him*, and so avoid an exposure to His eye which they could ill have stood. Accordingly it is added, **9. And they which heard it**—or, 'But they, when they heard it' [Οἱ δὲ, ἀκούσαντες], **being convicted by their [own] conscience, went out one by one, beginning at the eldest** [ἀπὸ τῶν πρεσβυτέρων]—rather, 'at the elders;' in the official sense, and not the seniors in age. **even unto the last: and Jesus was left alone**—that is, without one of her accusers remaining; for it is added, **and the woman standing in the midst**—in the midst, that is, of the remaining audience. While the trap failed to catch Him for whom it was laid, it caught those who laid it. Stunned by the unexpected home-thrust, they immediately made off—which makes the impudence of those impure hypocrites in dragging such a case before the public eye the more disgusting. **10. When**—'And when' **Jesus had lifted up himself, and saw none but the woman, he said unto her, Woman, where are those thine accusers? hath no man condemned thee? 11. She said, No man, Lord. And Jesus said unto her, Neither do I condemn thee: go, and sin no more.** What inimitable tenderness and grace! Conscious of her own guilt, and till now in the hands of men who had talked of stoning her, wondering at the *skill* with which her accusers had been dispersed and the *grace* of the few words addressed to herself, she would be disposed to listen, with a reverence and teachableness before unknown, to our Lord's admonition. "And Jesus said unto her, Neither do I condemn thee, go and sin no more." He pronounces no pardon upon the woman—like "Thy sins are forgiven thee;" "Go in peace"—much less does He say that she had done nothing condemnable; He simply leaves the matter where it was. He meddles not with the magistrate's office, nor acts the *Judge* in any sense (ch. xii. 47). But in saying "Go, and sin no more," which had been before said to one who undoubtedly believed (ch. v. 14), more is probably implied than expressed. If brought suddenly to conviction of sin, to admiration of her Deliverer, and to a willingness to be admonished and guided by Him, this call to begin a new life may have carried with it what would ensure and naturally bring about a permanent change.

[The genuineness of this whole Section, including the last verse of ch. vii.—twelve verses—is by far the most perplexing question of textual criticism pertaining to the Gospels. The external evidence against it is immensely strong. It is wanting in the four oldest MSS.—the newly discovered Codex *Sinaiticus* (א), the *Alexandrian* (A), the *Vatican* (B), and the *Ephraem* (C)—and in four other valuable Uncial MSS., although two of these have a blank space, as if something had been left out; it is wanting also in upwards of fifty Cursive MSS.: of ancient versions, it is wanting in the venerable Peshito *Syriac* and its *Philoxenian* revision, in one and probably both the Egyptian versions—the *Thebaic* and *Memphitic*—the *Gothic*, probably the *Armenian*, and two or three copies of the *Old Latin:* several of the fathers take no notice of it—as *Origen, Tertullian, Cyprian, Cyril, Chrysostom:* it is wanting in the most ancient tables of the Sectional contents of the Gospels, though afterwards inserted as an additional Section: the variations in the MSS. which insert it exceed in number and extent those in any other part of the New Testament: and of those MSS. which insert it, four Uncials and upwards of fifty Cursives have an asterisk or other critical mark attached to it, as subject to doubt or requiring investigation. The internal evidence urged against it is, that it unnaturally interrupts the flow of the narrative, whereas if ch. viii. 12 come immediately after ch. vii. 52, all is natural; that the language of this Section is strikingly dissimilar, especially in the particles, to that of John; and that the statement in ch. viii. 1, as to Jesus having gone to the mount of Olives, is one of the strongest grounds of suspicion, since nowhere else in this Gospel is "the mount of Olives" mentioned at all, nor does our Lord's passing the night there agree with this or any stage of His public life except the last. That we have here very strong evidence against the genuineness of this Section, no intelligent and impartial judge will deny. Moved by this evidence, *Lachmann* and *Tischendorf* exclude it from their text; *Tregelles* prints it in small type below the approved text, which *Alford* also does; and hardly any recent critics acknowledge it as

12 Then spake Jesus again unto them, saying, [e] I am the light of the world: he that followeth me shall not walk in darkness, but shall have the light

A. D. 32.

[e] Mal. 4. 2.

John's, except *Stier* and *Ebrard*, to whom may be added *Lange* and *Webster and Wilkinson* (though the latter do not, like the former, grapple with the difficulties). But let us look at the other side of the question. Of the four most ancient MSS. which want this Section, the leaves of two at this place have been lost—of A, from ch. vi. 50 to viii. 52; and of C, from ch. vii. 3 to viii. 33. We have, therefore, no certainty whether those MSS. contained it or not. As to the two (L and Δ) whose spaces are not long enough to make it *possible* that they contained this Section, the inference is precarious, since no more may have been intended by those spaces than simply to indicate that there a portion of text was wanting. But it is found in seven Uncial MSS., though the letters in that most remarkable one, the Codex *Bezæ* (D), are said to be very different from the others, while in one of the others but a small number of the verses is given, and in another one verse is wanting; it is found in above three hundred of the Cursive MSS. without any note of question, and above fifty more with an asterisk or other mark of doubt. Of versions, it is found in the *Old Latin*—which may be held to neutralize the fact of its absence in the Peshito Syriac, as the one appears to have been executed for the Western churches about as early as the other for the Eastern; and it is found in the *Vulgate;* while Jerome, to whom we owe that revision of the venerable Old Latin, states that in his time—the fourth century, and we have no MSS. of older date than that—this Section was found 'in many MSS. both Greek and Latin.' Turning now from external to *internal* evidence in favour of this Section, it appears to us to be almost overpowering. Requesting the reader to recall the exposition of it, we confidently ask if historical authenticity is not stamped upon the face of it, and—admitting that *some* such incident as this might not be beyond invention—whether the very peculiar and singularly delicate details of it *could* be other than real. And if the question be, Whether, supposing it genuine, there were stronger motives for its exclusion, or, if spurious, for its insertion? no one who knows anything of the peculiarities of the early Church can well hesitate. The notions of the early Church on such subjects were of the most ascetic description, and to them the whole narrative must have been most confounding. *Augustin* accordingly says, 'Some of slender faith, or rather enemies of the true faith, have removed it from their MSS., fearing, I believe, that an immunity to sin might be thought to be given by it.' Nor was he alone in ascribing the omission of it to this cause. Such a feeling in regard to this Section is sufficient to account for the remarkable fact that it was never publicly read along with the preceding and following context in the early churches, but reserved for some unimportant festivals, and in some of the service-books appears to have been left out altogether. In short, to account for its *omission*, if genuine, seems easy enough; but for its *insertion*, if spurious, next to impossible. Moved by these considerations, a middle course is taken by some. *Meyer* and *Ellicott*, while convinced that it is no part of the Gospel of John, are equally convinced of its historical truth and canonical authority; and observing how closely ch. viii. agrees with Luke xxi. 37, think that to be its proper place. Indeed, it is a singular fact that four of the Cursive MSS. actually place it at the end of Luke xxi. Something very like this is *Alford's* view. This, of course, would quite explain the mention (in ch. viii. 1) of "the mount of Olives," and our Lord's spending the night there being His last week. But this theory—of a fragment of authentic canonical Gospel History never known to have existed in its proper place (with the exception of four pretty good MSS.), and known only as part of a Gospel to which it did not belong, and with which it was out of keeping—can never, in our judgment, be admitted. *Scrivener*, while impressed with its internal excellence, thinks the evidence against it too strong to be resisted, except on the singular theory that the beloved disciple himself added it in a later edition of his Gospel, and that thus copies having it and copies wanting it ran parallel with each other from the very first—a theory, however, for which there is not the slightest external evidence, and attended, it seems to us, with greater difficulty than that which it is designed to remove. On the whole, though we admit the difficulties with which this question is encompassed, as the narrative itself bears that stamp of originality, truth, purity, and grandeur which accord so well with its place in the Gospel History, so the fact that wherever it is found it is as part of the Fourth Gospel, and among the transactions of the Feast of Tabernacles, is to us the best proof that this is, after all, its true place in the Gospel History; nor does it appear to us to interrupt the flow of the narrative, but entirely to harmonize with it—if we except ch. viii. 1, which must be allowed to remain among the difficulties that we, at least, find it not easy to solve.] But see P.S. p. 486.

Remark.—While a sanctimonious hypocrisy is not unfrequently found among unprincipled professors of religion, a compassionate purity which wins the fallen is one of the most beautiful characteristics of real religion. But till Christ appeared, this feature of religion was but dimly realized, and in the Old Testament but faintly held forth. It was reserved for the Lord Jesus to exhibit it in all its loveliness. In this incident, of the Woman Taken in Adultery, we have it in its perfection, while the spirit of the men that brought her to Jesus, appearing in such vivid contrast to it, acts but as a foil to set it off. See on Luke xv. 1, 2.

12-59.—JESUS CONTINUES HIS DISCOURSE IN THE TEMPLE AMIDST REPEATED INTERRUPTIONS, TILL, ON THEIR PROCEEDING TO STONE HIM, HE PASSES THROUGH THE MIDST OF THEM AND DEPARTS.

Jesus Addresses Himself chiefly to a Hostile Audience, in the way of solemn Testimony, at the climax of which many are won to Him, to whom He Addresses an Encouraging Word (12-32). **12. Then spake Jesus again unto them, saying, I am the light of the world.** As the former references to *water* (ch. iv. 10, 13, 14; and ch. vii. 37, &c.) and to *bread* (ch. vi. 27, &c.) were occasioned by outward occurrences, so possibly may this reference to *light* have been. For, in "the treasury," where it was spoken (see *v.* 20), stood two colossal golden lampstands, on which hung a multitude of lamps, lighted after the evening sacrifice (probably every evening) during the feast of Tabernacles, diffusing their brilliancy, it is said, over all the city. Around these the people danced with great rejoicing. Now, as amidst the festivities of the *water* from Siloam, Jesus cried, saying, "If any man thirst let him come unto me and drink," so now, amidst the blaze and joyousness of this illumination, He proclaims, "I AM THE LIGHT OF THE WORLD"—plainly in the most *absolute* sense. For

13 of life. The Pharisees therefore said unto him, Thou bearest record
14 of thyself; thy record is not true. Jesus answered and said unto them,
Though I bear record of myself, *yet* my record is true: for I know
whence I came, and whither I go; but [f]ye cannot tell whence I come,
15 and whither I go. Ye [g]judge after the flesh; [h]I judge no man.
16 And yet if I judge, my judgment is true; for [i]I am not alone, but I
17 and the Father that sent me. It [j]is also written in your law, that the
18 testimony of two men is true. I am one that bear witness of myself,
19 and [k]the Father that sent me beareth witness of me. Then said they
unto him, Where is thy Father? Jesus answered, [l]Ye neither know me,
nor my Father: [m]if ye had known me, ye should have known my Father
also.
20 These words spake Jesus in [n]the treasury, as he taught in the temple:
and [o]no man laid hands on him; for [p]his hour was not yet come.
21 Then said Jesus again unto them, I go my way, and [q]ye shall seek me,
22 and shall die in your sins: whither I go, ye cannot come. Then said the
Jews, Will he kill himself? because he saith, Whither I go, ye cannot
23 come. And he said unto them, [r]Ye are from beneath; I am from above:
24 [s]ye are of this world; I am not of this world. I said therefore unto you,
that ye shall die in your sins: [t]for if ye believe not that I am *he*, ye shall
25 die in your sins. Then said they unto him, Who art thou? And Jesus

A. D. 32.

f Ps. 58. 1. ch. 7. 28. ch. 9. 29.
g 1 Sam. 16. 7. ch. 7. 24.
h ch. 18. 36.
i ch. 16. 32.
j Deut. 17. 6. Deut. 19. 15. Matt. 18. 16. 2 Cor. 13. 1. Heb. 10. 28.
k ch. 5. 37. 2 Pet. 1. 17. 1 John 5. 6-12.
l ch. 16. 3.
m ch. 14. 7.
n Mark 12. 41.
o ch. 7. 30.
p ch. 7. 8.
q ch. 13. 33.
r ch. 3. 31.
s ch. 15. 19. ch. 17. 16. 1 John 4. 5.
t Mark 16. 16.

though He gives His disciples the same title (see on ch. v. 14), they are only "light *in the Lord*" (Eph. v. 8); and though He calls the Baptist "the burning and shining light" (or '*lamp*' of his day—see on ch. v. 35), yet "he was *not that Light*, but was sent to bear witness of that Light: That was THE TRUE LIGHT which, coming into the world, *lighteth every man*" (ch. i. 8, 9). Under this magnificent title Messiah was promised of old, Isa. xlii. 6; Mal. iv. 2, &c. **he that followeth me**—as one does a light going before him, and as the Israelites did the pillar of bright cloud in the wilderness, **shall not walk in darkness, but shall have the light of life**—the light as of a new world, the light of a newly awakened spiritual and eternal life. **13. The Pharisees therefore said unto him, Thou bearest record of thyself; thy record is not true.** How does He meet this specious cavil! Not by disputing the wholesome human maxim that 'self-praise is no praise,' but by affirming that He was *an exception to the rule*, or rather, that *it had no application to Him.* **14. Jesus answered and said unto them, Though I bear record of myself, yet my record is true: for I know whence I came, and whither I go; but ye cannot tell whence I come, and whither I go.** See on ch. vii. 28, 29. **15. Ye judge after the flesh**—with no spiritual apprehension; **I judge no man. 16. And yet if I judge** [Καὶ ἐὰν κρίνω δὲ Ἐγὼ]. The "*I*" here is emphatic:—*q. d.*, 'Yet in My case, even if I do judge,' **my judgment is true; for I am not alone, but I and the Father that sent me. 17. It is also written in your law, that the testimony of two men is true. 18. I am one that bear witness of myself, and the Father that sent me beareth witness of me:**—*q. d.*, 'Ye not only *form* your carnal and warped judgments of Me, but are bent on carrying them into effect; I, though I form and utter My judgment of you, am not here to carry this into execution—that is reserved to a future day; yet the judgment I now pronounce and the witness I now bear is not Mine only, as ye suppose, but His also that sent Me. (See on ch. v. 31, 32.) And these are the two witnesses which your law requires to any fact.' **19. Then said they unto him, Where is thy Father? Jesus answered, Ye neither know me, nor my Father: if ye had known me, ye should have known my Father also.** The same spiritual light and darkness would suffice to reveal to the mind, or to hide from it, at once the Father and the Son, the Sender and the Sent.

20. These words spake Jesus in the treasury—a division, so called, of the fore-court of the temple, part of the court of the women (*Joseph.* Antt. xix. 6. 2, &c.), which may confirm the genuineness of *vv.* 2, 11, as the place where the woman was brought. **as he taught in the temple: and no man laid hands on him; for his hour was not yet come.** See on ch. vii. 30. In the dialogue that follows, the conflict waxes sharper on both sides.

21. Then said Jesus again unto them, I go my way, and ye shall seek me, and shall die in your sins [ἐν τῇ ἁμαρτίᾳ ὑμῶν]—it should be 'in your sin:' **whither I go, ye cannot come. 22. Then said the Jews, Will he kill himself? because he saith, Whither I go, ye cannot come.** They evidently saw something more in His words than when He spake thus before (ch. vii. 33-36); but their question now is more malignant and scornful. **23. And he said unto them, Ye are from beneath; I am from above: ye are of this world; I am not of this world.** He contrasts Himself here, not as in ch. iii. 31, simply with *earth-born messengers of God*, but with *men sprung from and breathing an opposite element* from His, which rendered it impossible that He and they should have any present fellowship, or dwell eternally together. See again on ch. vii. 34, and on *v.* 44, below. **24. I said therefore unto you, that ye shall die in your sins: for if ye believe not that I am [he]** [ὅτι ἐγώ εἰμι], **ye shall die in your sins.** "That I am [He]." Compare Mark xiii. 6, *Greek*, and Matt. xxiv. 5. They knew well enough what He meant. But He would not, by speaking it out, give them the materials for a charge for which they were watching. At the same time, one is irresistibly reminded by such language, so far transcending what is becoming in *men*, of those ancient declarations of the God of Israel, "I AM HE," &c. (Deut. xxxii. 39; Isa. xliii. 10, 13; xlvi. 4; xlviii. 12.) See on Mark vi. 50. **25. Then said they unto him, Who art thou?**—hoping thus to extort an explicit answer; but they are disap-

saith unto them, Even *the same* that I said unto you from the beginning.
26 I have many things to say and to judge of you: but [u]he that sent me
is true; and I [v]speak to the world those things which I have heard of
27 him. They understood not that he spake to them of the Father.
28 Then said Jesus unto them, When ye have [w]lifted up the Son of man,
[x]then shall ye know that I am *he,* and [y]*that* I do nothing of myself;
29 but [z]as my Father hath taught me, I speak these things. And [a]he
that sent me is with me: the Father hath not left me alone; [b]for I do
always those things that please him.
30, As he spake these words many believed on him. Then said Jesus to
31 those Jews which believed on him, If ye continue in my word, *then*
32 are ye my disciples indeed; and ye shall know the truth, and [c]the
truth shall make you free.
33 They answered him, [d]We be Abraham's seed, and were never in
bondage to any man: how sayest thou, Ye shall be made free?
34 Jesus answered them, Verily, verily, I say unto you, [e]Whosoever com-

A. D. 32.

[u] ch. 7. 28.
[v] ch. 3. 32. ch. 15. 15.
[w] ch. 3. 14. ch. 12. 32.
[x] Rom. 1. 4.
[y] ch. 5. 19, 30.
[z] ch. 3. 11.
[a] ch. 14. 10. ch. 16. 32.
[b] ch. 4. 34. ch. 6. 38.
[c] Rom. 6. 14, 18, 22. Rom. 8. 2. Jas. 1. 25. Jas. 2. 12.
[d] Lev. 25. 42. Matt. 3. 9.
[e] 2 Pet. 2. 19.

pointed. **And Jesus saith**—'said' [εἶπεν] **unto them, Even the same that I said unto you from the beginning** [Tὴν αρχὴν ὅ τι καὶ λαλῶ ὑμῖν]. This clause is in the original somewhat obscure, and has been varibusly rendered and much discussed. But the sense given in our version seems the true one, and has on the whole the best support. **26. I have many things to say and to judge of you: but he that sent me is true; and I speak to the world those things which I have heard of him**:—*q. d.*, 'I could, and at the fitting time will say and judge many things of you (referring perhaps to the work of the Spirit, which is for *judgment* as well as *salvation*, ch. xvi. 8), but what I do say is just the message My Father hath given Me to deliver.' **27. They understood not that he spake to them of the Father.**

28. Then said Jesus unto them, When ye have lifted up the Son of man—the plainest intimation He had yet given *in public* of the *manner* and the *authors* of His death. **then shall ye know that I am [he], and that I do nothing of myself; but as my Father hath taught me**—or, 'as my Father taught Me' [ἐδίδαξεν] **I speak these things**—that is, they should find out, or have sufficient evidence, how true was all He said, though they would be far from owning it. **29. And he that sent me is with me: the Father hath not left me alone; for I do always those things that please him** [τὰ ἀρεστὰ αὐτῷ]—'the things that are pleasing to Him:'—*q. d.*, 'To you, who gnash upon Me with your teeth, and frown down all open appearance for Me, I seem to stand uncountenanced and alone; but I have a sympathy and support transcending all human applause; I came hither to do My Father's will, and in the doing of it have not ceased to please Him; therefore is He ever by Me with His approving smile, His cheering words, His supporting arm.'

30. As he spake these words many believed on him. Instead of wondering at this, the wonder would be if words of such unearthly, surpassing grandeur *could* be uttered without captivating *some* that heard them. And just as "all that sat in the council" to try Stephen "saw his face"—though expecting nothing but death—"as it had been the face of an angel" (Acts vi. 15), so may we suppose that, full of the sweet supporting sense of His Father's presence, amidst the rage and scorn of the rulers, a divine benignity beamed from His countenance, irradiated the words that fell from Him, and won over the candid "many" of His audience. **31. Then said Jesus to those Jews which believed on him, If ye continue in my word, then are ye my disciples indeed; 32. And ye shall know the truth, and the truth shall make you free.** The impression produced by the last words of our Lord may have become visible by some decisive movement, and here He takes advantage of it to press on them "*continuance*" in the faith, since then only were they "His real disciples" (compare ch. xv. 3-8), and then should they *experimentally* "know the truth," and "by the truth be made *spiritually* free."

The Hostile Part of His Audience here Breaking in upon the Words of Encouragement addressed to the Believing Portion, Jesus again addresses Himself to them, and in a yet higher strain of Solemn Testimony (33-53). **33. They answered him, We be Abraham's seed, and were never in bondage to any man: how sayest thou, Ye shall be made free?** Who said this? Not surely the very class just spoken of as won over by His divine words, and exhorted to continue in them. Most interpreters seem to think so; but it is hard to ascribe such a petulant speech to newly gained disciples, even in the lowest sense, much less persons *so* gained as they were. It came, probably, from persons mixed up with them in the same part of the crowd, but of a very different spirit. The *pride* of the Jewish nation, even now, after centuries of humiliation, is the most striking feature of their character. 'Talk of freedom to *us?* Pray, when or to whom were we ever in bondage?' This bluster sounds almost ludicrous from such a nation. Had they forgotten their long and bitter bondage in Egypt? their dreary captivity in Babylon? their present bondage to the Roman yoke, and their restless eagerness to throw it off? But probably they saw that our Lord pointed to something else—freedom, perhaps, from the leaders of sects or parties—and were not willing to allow their subjection even to these. Our Lord, therefore, though He knew what slaves they were even in this sense, drives the ploughshare somewhat deeper than this, to a bondage they little dreamt of.

34. Jesus answered them, Verily, verily, I say unto you, Whosoever—or 'Every one that' [πᾶς ὁ] **committeth sin**—that is to say, 'liveth in the commission of it' (compare 1 John iii. 8; Matt. vii. 23), **is the servant of sin**—the *bond-servant*, or *slave* of it; for the question is not about free-service, but Who are in *bondage?* (Compare 2 Pet. ii. 19; Rom. vi. 16). The great truth here expressed was not unknown to heathen moralists; but it was applied only to *vice*, for they were total strangers to what in Revealed Religion is called *sin*. But the thought of *slaves* and *freemen* in the house suggests

35 mitteth sin is the servant of sin. And [f]the servant abideth not in the
36 house for ever: *but* the Son abideth ever. If [g]the Son therefore shall
make you free, ye shall be free indeed.
37 I know that ye are Abraham's seed; but ye [h]seek to kill me, be-
38 cause my word hath no place in you. I speak that which I have
seen with my Father; and ye do that which ye have seen with your
39 father. They answered and said unto him, Abraham [i]is our father.
Jesus saith unto them, [j]If ye were Abraham's children, ye would do
40 the works of Abraham. But now ye seek to kill me, a man that hath
told you the truth, which I have heard of God: this did not Abraham.
41 Ye do the deeds of your father. Then said they to him, We be not
42 born of fornication; [k]we have one Father, *even* God. Jesus said
unto them, [l]If God were your Father, ye would love me: [m]for I proceeded forth and came from God; [n]neither came I of myself, but he
43 sent me. Why [o]do ye not understand my speech? *even* because ye
44 cannot hear my word. Ye [p]are of *your* father the devil, and the
lusts of your father ye will do. He was a murderer from the beginning,
and [q]abode not in the truth, because there is no truth in him. When he

A. D. 32.

[f] Gal. 4. 30.
[g] Isa 49. 24. Rom. 8. 2. 2 Cor. 3. 17. Gal. 5. 1. Rev. 1. 5. Rev. 2. 7, 10. Rev. 5. 9.
[h] ch. 7. 19.
[i] Matt. 3. 9.
[j] Rom. 2. 28. Rom. 9. 7. Gal. 3. 7, 29.
[k] Isa. 63. 16. Isa. 64. 8. Mal. 1. 6.
[l] 1 John 4. 19.
[m] ch. 1. 14. ch. 3. 16.
[n] ch. 5. 43.
[o] ch. 7. 17.
[p] Matt. 13. 38.
[q] Gen. 3. 1.

to our Lord a wider idea. **35. And the servant**—or, 'Now the [bond-]servant' **abideth not in the house for ever: [but] the Son abideth ever. 36. If the Son therefore shall make you free, ye shall be free indeed.** A very glorious statement, the sense of which may be thus expressed: 'And if your connection with the family of God be that of BOND-SERVANTS, ye have no *natural* tie to the house; your tie is essentially *uncertain* and *precarious.* But THE SON'S relationship to the FATHER is a *natural* and *essential* one; it is an indefeasible tie; His abode in it is *perpetual* and *of right:* That is My relationship, My tie: If, then, ye would have your connection with God's family made *real, rightful, permanent,* ye must by the Son be *manumitted* and *adopted* as sons and daughters of the Lord Almighty.' In this sublime statement there is no doubt a subordinate allusion to Gen. xxi. 10, "Cast out this bond-woman and her son, for the son of this bond-woman shall not be heir with my son, with Isaac." (Compare Gal. iv. 22-30).

37. I know that ye are Abraham's seed; but ye seek to kill me. He had said this to their face before; He now repeats it, and they do not deny it; yet are they held back, as by some marvellous spell—it was the awe which His combined dignity, courage, and benignity struck into them. **because my word hath no place in you** [οὐ χωρεῖ ἐν ὑμῖν]—'finds no entrance' or 'room in you.' When did ever *human prophet* so speak of his words? They tell us of "the word of the Lord" coming to them. But here is One who holds up "His word" as that which ought to find entrance and abiding room for itself in the souls of all who hear it. **38. I speak that which I have seen with my Father; and ye do that which ye have seen with your father.** See on *v.* 23. **39. They answered and said unto him, Abraham is our father. Jesus saith unto them, If ye were Abraham's children, ye would do the works of Abraham.** He had just said He "knew they were Abraham's children"—that is, according to the *flesh;* but the children of his *faith and holiness* they were not, but the reverse. **40. But now ye seek to kill me, a man that hath told you the truth, which I have heard**—or 'which I heard' [ἤκουσα] **of God: this did not Abraham.** In so doing ye act in direct opposition to him. **41. Ye do the deeds of your father. Then said they to him, We be not born of fornication; we have one father [even] God.** The meaning is, they were not an illegitimate race in point of *religion,* pretending only to be God's people, but were descended from His own chosen Abraham. **42. Jesus said unto them, If God were your Father, ye would love me: for I proceeded forth and came**—or 'am come' [ἥκω] **from God; neither came I of myself, but he sent me. 43. Why do ye not understand my speech? even because ye cannot hear my word:**—*q. d.*, 'If ye had anything of His moral image, as children have their father's likeness, ye would love Me, for I am immediately of Him and directly from Him. But "My speech" (meaning His peculiar style of expressing Himself on these subjects) 'is unintelligible to you' because ye cannot take in the truth which it conveys.'

44. Ye are of your father the devil. This, as *Alford* remarks, is one of the most decisive testimonies to the *objective personality* of the devil. It is quite impossible to suppose an accommodation to Jewish views, or a metaphorical form of speech, in so solemn an assertion as this. **and the lusts of your father**—his impure, malignant, ungodly propensities, inclinations, desires, **ye will do** [θέλετε ποιεῖν]—or 'are willing to do,' that is, 'willingly do;" not of any blind necessity of nature, but of pure natural inclination. **He was a murderer from the beginning.** The reference here is not to the murderous spirit which he kindled in Cain (as *Lücke, de Wette, Tholuck, Alford, Webster and Wilkinson*), which yields but a tame and very limited sense, but to that which he did to Man in the person of *Adam.* So the majority of ancient and modern interpreters, including *Grotius, Calvin, Meyer, Luthardt.* The death of the human race, in its widest sense, is ascribed to the murderous seducer of our race. **and abode not in the truth.** Since the word [ἕστηκεν] properly means '*abideth,*' it has been, by *Lücke* and others, denied that the *fall* of Satan from a former holy state is here expressed; and some superior interpreters, as *Olshausen,* think this only *implied.* But though the *form* of the thought is present—not past—this is to express the important idea, that his whole character and activity are just *a continual aberration from his own original truth or rectitude;* and thus his fall is not only the *implied basis* of the thought, but *part of the statement itself,* properly interpreted and brought out. **because there is no truth in him**—because he is void of all that holy, transparent rectitude which, as God's creature, he originally possessed. **When he speaketh a lie, he speaketh of his own** [ἐκ τῶν ἰδίων]. As the word here is plural, perhaps the

speaketh a lie, he speaketh of his own: for he is a liar, and the
45 father of it. And because I tell *you* the truth, ye believe me not.
46 Which of you convinceth me of sin? And if I say the truth, why do
47 ye not believe me? He [r] that is of God heareth God's words: ye therefore
48 hear *them* not, because ye are not of God. Then answered the Jews, and
said unto him, Say we not well that thou art a Samaritan, and hast a
devil?
49 Jesus answered, I have not a devil; but I honour my Father, and ye
50 do dishonour me. And [s] I seek not mine own glory: there is one that
51 seeketh and judgeth. Verily, verily, I say unto you, [t] If a man keep
52 my saying, he shall never see death. Then said the Jews unto him, Now
we know that thou hast a devil. [u] Abraham is dead, and the prophets;
and thou sayest, If a man keep my saying, he shall never taste of death.
53 Art thou greater than our father Abraham, which is dead? and the
prophets are dead: whom makest thou thyself?

A. D. 32.

[r] ch. 1. 12, 13. ch. 6. 45, 46, 65. ch. 10. 26, 27. ch. 17. 6, 8. 1 John 3. 10. 1 John 4. 6. 1 John 5. 1. 2 John 9. 3 John 11.
[s] ch. 3. 15, 16. ch. 5. 41. ch. 6. 50. ch. 7. 18. ch. 15. 20.
[t] ch. 5. 24. ch. 11. 26.
[u] Zec. 1. 5. Heb. 11. 13.

meaning is, as *Alford* expresses it, 'of his own resources,' his own treasures (Matt. xii. 35). It means that he has no temptation to it *from without;* it is purely *self-begotten*, springing from a nature which is nothing but obliquity. **for he is a liar, and the father of it**—that is, of lying itself: all the falsehood in the world owes its existence to him. What a verse is this! It holds up the devil, first, as the murderer of the human race; but as this is meant here in the more profound sense of *spiritual* death, it holds him up, next, as the parent of this fallen human family, communicating to his offspring his own evil passions and universal obliquity, and stimulating these into active exercise. But as there is "a Stronger than he," who comes upon him and overcomes him (Luke xi. 21-22), it is only such as "love the darkness" who are addressed as children of the devil (Matt. xiii. 38; 1 John iii. 8-10). **45. And**—or rather, 'But' **because I tell you the truth, ye believe me not**—not *although* He told it them, but *because* He did so, and for the reason given in the former verse. Had He been *less* true, they would have hailed Him the more readily.

46. Which of you convinceth [ἐλέγχει]—rather, 'convicteth' **me of sin?**—or can bring home against Me a charge of sin? **[And] if I say the truth**—the "and" appears not to belong to the genuine text, **why do ye not believe me?** Glorious dilemma! 'Convict me of sin, and reject me: But if ye cannot, why stand ye out against My claims?' Of course they could only be supposed to impeach His *life;* but in one who had already passed through unparalleled complications, and had continually to deal with friends and foes of every sort and degree, such a challenge, thrown wide amongst His bitterest enemies, can amount to nothing short of a claim to *absolute sinlessness.* **47. He that is of God heareth God's words: ye therefore** [διὰ τοῦτο]—or 'for this reason,' **hear them not, because ye are not of God.** How often and how sharply does our Lord in this Discourse draw the line of awful separation between those that *are* and those that *are not* "of God!" The hostile part of His audience were stung to the quick by it. **48. Then answered the Jews, and said unto him, Say we not well that thou art a Samaritan, and hast a devil?** What intense and virulent scorn! (See Heb. xii. 3.) The "say we not well" is a reference to their former charge, "Thou hast a devil," ch. vii. 20. "Samaritan" here means more than 'no Israelite at all:' it means one who *pretended, but had no manner of claim* to connection with Abraham—retorting, perhaps, His denial of their *true* descent from the father of the faithful. **49. Jesus answered, I have not a devil.** What calm dignity is here! Verily, "when reviled, He reviled not again" (1 Pet. ii. 23). Compare Paul before Festus, "I am not mad, most noble Festus" (Acts xxvi. 25). Our Lord adds not, 'Nor am I a Samaritan,' that He might not even seem to partake of their contempt for a race that had already welcomed Him as the Christ, and begun to be blessed by Him. **but I honour my Father, and ye do dishonour me.** This is the language of *wounded feeling.* But the *interior* of His soul at such moments is only to be seen in such prophetic utterances as these, "For thy sake I have borne reproach: shame hath covered my face: I am become a stranger unto my brethren, an alien unto my mother's children. For the zeal of thine house hath eaten me up, and the reproaches of them that reproached thee are fallen upon me" (Ps. lxix. 7-9). **50. And**—or, 'But' **I seek not mine own glory: there is one that seeketh and judgeth.** There should be a supplement here: 'There is one that seeketh [it]; that is, 'that seeketh My glory and judgeth'—Who requireth "all men to honour the Son even as they honour the Father;" Who will judicially treat him "who honoureth not the Son as honouring not the Father that hath sent Him" (ch. v. 23, and compare Matt. xvii. 5); but Who will yet give to Him (see ch. vi. 37) those who will one day cast their crowns before His throne, in whom He "shall see of the travail of His soul, and be satisfied" (Isa. liii. 11). **51. Verily, verily, I say unto you, If a man keep my saying, he shall never see death:**—thus vindicating His lofty claims, as Lord of the kingdom of life everlasting, and, at the same time, holding out even to His revilers the sceptre of grace. The word "keep" [τηρήσῃ] is in harmony with His former saying to those who believed in Him, "If ye *continue* in my word," expressing the permanency, as a living and paramount principle, of that faith to which He referred. This promise—"he shall never see death"—though expressed before (ch. v. 24; vi. 40, 47, 51), is the strongest and most naked statement yet given of a very glorious truth. In ch. xi. 26 it is repeated in nearly identical terms. **52. Then said the Jews unto him, Now we know that thou hast a devil. Abraham is dead**—or 'died' [ἀπέθανεν], **and the prophets; and thou sayest, If a man keep my saying, he shall never taste of death. 53. Art thou greater than our father Abraham, which is dead?**—or 'died,' **and the prophets are dead**—or 'died:' **whom makest thou thyself?** 'Thou art now self-convicted; only a demoniac could speak so; the most illustrious of our fathers

54 Jesus answered, If I honour myself, my honour is nothing: [v]it is my
55 Father that honoureth me; of whom ye say, that he is your God: yet
[w]ye have not known him; but I know him: and if I should say, I know
him not, I shall be a liar like unto you: but I know him, and keep his
56 saying. Your father Abraham [x]rejoiced to see my day; [y]and he saw *it*,
57 and was glad. Then said the Jews unto him, Thou art not yet fifty
years old, and hast thou seen Abraham?
58 Jesus said unto them, Verily, verily, I say unto you, Before Abraham
59 was, [z]I am. Then took they up stones to cast at him: but Jesus hid
himself, and went out of the temple, going through the midst of them,
and so passed by.

A. D. 32.
[v] ch. 16. 14. ch. 17. 1. Acts 3. 13.
[w] ch. 7. 28.
[x] Gen. 22. 18. Luke 10. 24. Gal. 3. 8, 16.
[y] Heb. 11. 13.
[z] Ex. 3. 14. Isa. 9. 6. Isa. 43. 13. Mic. 5. 2. Col. 1. 17.

are dead, and thou promisest exemption from death to any one who will keep *thy saying!* pray, who art thou?'

The Climax (54-59). **54. Jesus answered, If I honour myself, my honour is nothing: it is my Father that honoureth me; of whom ye say, that he is your God: 55. Yet ye have not known him; but I know him: and if I should say, I know him not, I shall be a liar like unto you: but I know him, and keep his saying** [λόγον]—or 'word.' Our Lord now rises to the summit of holy, naked severity, thereby to draw this long dialogue to a head. **56. Your father Abraham rejoiced to see my day** [ἠγαλλιάσατο ἵνα ἴδῃ]—'exulted,' or 'exceedingly rejoiced that he should see;' that is, exulted to see it *by anticipation;* **and he saw it, and was glad** —he *actually* beheld it to his joy. If this mean no more than that he had a prophetic foresight of the Gospel-day—the second clause just repeating the first—how could the Jews understand our Lord to mean that He "had seen Abraham?" And if it mean that Abraham was *then beholding*, in his disembodied spirit, the incarnate Messiah, as *Stier*, *Tholuck*, *Alford*, &c., understand it, the words seem very unsuitable to express it. Plainly it speaks of something *past*—he *saw* my day, and *was* glad—that is, surely, while he lived. We understand it therefore to refer to the familiar intercourse which Abraham had with that "Angel of the Lord" who in the History is repeatedly styled "The Lord" or *Jehovah*—the Angel of the covenant, with whom Christ here identifies Himself. On those occasions, says our Lord, Abraham "saw ME." Such is the view of *Olshausen;* but we need not suppose it, with him, to refer to some unrecorded scene. Taking the words in this sense, all that follows will, we think, be quite natural. **57. Then said the Jews unto him, Thou art not yet fifty years old.** No inference, as *Alford* properly says, can be drawn from this as to our Lord's age as man at that time. Fifty years was, with the Jews, the term of ripe manhood, and at that age the Levites ceased to officiate. **and hast thou seen Abraham?** He had not said He saw Abraham, but that Abraham saw *Him*, as being Abraham's peculiar privilege. They, however, give the opposite turn to it—"Hast thou seen Abraham?"—as an honour which it was insufferable for him to pretend to.

58. Jesus said unto them, Verily, verily, I say unto you, Before Abraham was [πρὶν Ἀβραὰμ γενέσθαι]—'Before Abraham came into existence' **I am** [ἐγώ εἰμί]. The difference between the two verbs applied to Abraham and Himself, in this great saying, is to be carefully observed. 'Before Abraham was *brought into being*, I *exist*. The statement, therefore, is not that *Christ came into existence before Abraham did*—as Arians affirm is the meaning: it is that he never *came into* being at all, but *existed* before Abraham had a being; which, of course, was as much as to say that He existed before all creation, or from eternity, as in ch. i. 1. In that sense, beyond all doubt, the Jews understood Him, as will appear from what follows. **59. Then took they up stones to cast at him**—precisely as they did on a former occasion when they saw that He was making Himself equal with God, ch. v. 18. **but Jesus hid himself, and went out of the temple, [going through the midst of them, and so passed by].** See on Luke iv. 30. [These bracketed words—διελθὼν διὰ μέσου αὐτῶν· καὶ παρῆγεν οὕτως—are excluded from the text, as spurious, by *Lachmann, Tischendorf, Tregelles, Alford;* while *Meyer, de Wette, Ebrard*, and nearly all recent critics, concur in that judgment. *Olshausen* says it is undoubtedly spurious; even *Stier* suspects it; only Lücke speaks doubtfully. Yet how stands the evidence? B wants it; but A has it: D wants it; but *all the other* Uncial MSS.—some of them of the greatest value—contain it, as well as the best Cursive MSS. The *Old Latin* and the *Vulgate* want it—early and weighty evidence, no doubt; but evidence about as early and weighty, that of both the principal *Syriac* versions, is in its favour. One of the ancient Egyptian versions, the *Thebaic*, wants it; but the other, the *Memphitic*, has it. With these facts before us, we must regard the unhesitating rejection of this clause as quite unwarrantable; and whereas it is said to be an unauthorized repetition of Luke iv. 30, the words are not quite the same, nor is there anything improbable in our Lord, when precisely the same in circumstances of danger as then, escaping their grasp in the very same way. We certainly think that the clause should be bracketed, as the evidence against it is undoubtedly strong; but more than this, in our judgment, it will not warrant.]

Remarks.—1. What a lurid brightness invests the scene of this long Discourse—the majesty of the one party and the malignity of the other combining to give it this aspect; while the welcome which the words of grace found in the breasts of "many," and the encouraging words addressed to them, threw for the moment a heavenly radiance over the scene, though only to be overcast again! Who could have written this, if it had not been matter of actual occurrence? And who but an eye-witness could have thrown in such details as these? And what eye-witness even could have penned it as it is here penned, save under the ever-present guidance of Him Whom Jesus promised that the Father should send in His name, Who should "teach them all things, and *bring all things to their remembrance* whatsoever He spake unto them?" (ch. xiv. 26). 2. Who can believe that One whose jealousy for His Father's honour even "consumed" Him, should have exposed Himself once and again to the imminent risk of being stoned to death for "making Himself equal with God," *if He was not so*, and *never meant to teach that He was so;* when—either by avoiding those

9 AND as *Jesus* passed by, he saw a man which was blind from *his*
2 birth. And his disciples asked him, saying, Master, who did [a]sin, this
3 man, or his parents, that he was born blind? Jesus answered, Neither
hath this man sinned, nor his parents: [b]but that the works of God should
4 be made manifest in him. I [c]must work the works of him that sent me,
5 while it is day: the night cometh, when no man can work. As long as
6 I am in the world, [d]I am the light of the world. When he had thus
spoken, [e]he spat on the ground, and made clay of the spittle, and he
7 [1]anointed the eyes of the blind man with the clay, and said unto him,
Go, wash [f]in the pool of Siloam, (which is, by interpretation, Sent.) He
went his way therefore, and washed, and came seeing.
8 The neighbours therefore, and they which before had seen him that he
9 was blind, said, Is not this he that sat and begged? Some said, This is

A. D. 32.

CHAP. 9.
[a] Matt. 16. 14. Acts 28. 4.
[b] ch. 11. 4.
[c] ch. 4. 34.
[d] ch. 1. 5, 9. ch. 3. 19.
[e] Mark 7. 33. Mark 8. 23.
[1] Or, spread the clay upon the eyes of the blind man.
[f] Neh. 3. 15. Isa. 8. 6.

speeches from which they drew that inference, or by a few words of explanation—He could so easily have avoided such a construction of His words, or explained it away? But as He did neither, but advisedly did the reverse, that Corner-Stone of the Christian religion—the essential Divinity of the Lord Jesus—must be seen to stand firmer than the everlasting hills.

CHAP. IX. 1-41.—JESUS ON THE SABBATH DAY OPENS THE EYES OF A BEGGAR BORN BLIND —WHAT FOLLOWED ON THIS.

Jesus Opens the Eyes of a Beggar Born Blind (1-7). The connection between the close of the preceding chapter and the opening of this one appears so close, that one is apt to conclude that all happened on one day, and that a Sabbath (*v.* 14). But the violence with which the former chapter closes, and the tranquillity with which this one opens, renders that somewhat doubtful. At all events, the transactions of both chapters could not have been far apart in time. **1. And as Jesus passed by, he saw a man which was blind from his birth**—and who "sat and begged" (*v.* 8). **2. And his disciples asked him, saying, Master, who did sin, this man, or his parents, that he was born blind?** [ἵνα τυφλὸς γεννηθῇ]—or 'should be born blind.' As the doctrine of the pre-existence of souls, and that of the 'metempsychosis' (the transmission of the soul of one person into the body of another), though held by certain of the more philosophical Jews, was never a current belief of the people, we are not to understand the disciples here to refer to sin committed in a former state of existence; and probably it is but a loose way of concluding that sin *somewhere* had surely been the cause of this calamity. **3. Jesus answered, Neither hath this man sinned, nor his parents: but that the works of God should be made manifest in him**:—*q. d.*, 'The cause was neither in himself nor his parents, but in order to the manifestation of "the works of God" in his cure.' **4. I must work the works of him that sent me, while it is day: the night cometh, when no man can work**—a most interesting statement this, from the mouth of Christ; intimating, first, that He had a precise work to do upon earth, with every particular of it arranged and laid out to Him; next, that all He did upon earth was just "the works of God"—particularly "going about *doing good*," though not exclusively by miracles; further, that each work had its precise *time* and *place* in His programme of instructions, so to speak; hence, again, that as His period for work had a definite termination, so by letting any one service pass by its allotted time, the whole would be disarranged, marred, and driven beyond its destined period for completion; finally, that as man He acted ever under the impulse of these considerations—"the night cometh when *no man* (or no one) can work." **5. As long as I am in the world, I am the light of the world.** Not as if he would cease, after that, to be so; but that He must make full proof of His fidelity, while His earthly career lasted, by displaying His glory. As before the resurrection of Lazarus, says *Alford*, He announces Himself as *the Resurrection and the Life* (ch. xi. 25), so now He holds Himself forth as the Source of that archetypal spiritual *light*, of which the natural, now about to be conferred, is only a derivation and symbol. **6. When he had thus spoken, he spat on the ground, and made clay of the spittle, and he anointed the eyes of the blind man with the clay, 7. And said unto him, Go, wash in the pool of Siloam, (which is, by interpretation, Sent.)** These operations were not so incongruous in their nature as might appear, though it were absurd to imagine that they contributed in the least degree to the effect which followed. (See on Mark vi. 13, and vii. 33, 34.) As the prescribed action was purely symbolical in its design, so in connection with it the Evangelist notices the symbolical name of the pool, as in this case bearing testimony to Him who was *sent* to do what it only *symbolized*. See Isa. viii. 6, where this same pool is used figuratively to denote "the streams that made glad the city of God," and which, humble though they be, betoken *a present God of Israel*. **He went his way therefore, and washed, and came seeing.** See 2 Kings v. 10, 14. But though he "came seeing," it does not appear that he came to Jesus. On the contrary, when he "came seeing," Jesus was not to be seen; nor did they meet at all, it would seem, until, after his expulsion from the synagogue, Jesus "found him" (*v.* 35).

The Beggar's Neighbours Question him as to the Cure, but, receiving only partial satisfaction, bring him to the Pharisees (8-14). **8. The neighbours therefore, and they which before had seen him that he was blind** [τυφλός]. The true reading here appears plainly to be, 'that he was a beggar' [ὅτι προσαίτης ἦν]—this being what would most immediately identify him, as the following words indeed show. So all recent critical editors, and nearly all critical expositors. **said, Is not this he that sat and begged? 9. Some said, This is he; others said, He is like him: but he said, I am he.** How graphically is the identity of the man thus ascertained; and his own testimony, coming in only to settle the point after it had been raised and occasioned some discussion, acquires thus additional importance. It is a good remark of *Webster and Wilkinson*, that the diversity of opinion is readily accounted for by the great difference in his appearance, which would be made by the removal of the most deforming of blemishes,

10 he; others *said,* He is like him: *but* he said, I am *he.* Therefore said
11 they unto him, [g]How were thine eyes opened? He answered and said, A
man that is [h]called Jesus made clay, and anointed mine eyes, and said
unto me, Go to the pool of Siloam, and wash: and I went and washed,
12 and I received sight. Then said they unto him, Where is he? He said,
I know not.
13, They brought to the Pharisees him that aforetime was blind. And it
14 was the sabbath day when Jesus made the clay, and opened his eyes.
15 Then again the Pharisees also asked him how he had received his sight.
He said unto them, He put clay upon mine eyes, and I washed, and do
16 see. Therefore said some of the Pharisees, This man is not of God,
because he keepeth not the sabbath day. Others said, How can a man
that is a sinner do such miracles? And [i]there was a division among
17 them. They say unto the blind man again, What sayest thou of him,
18 that he hath opened thine eyes? He said, [j]He is a prophet. But the
Jews did not believe concerning him, that he had been blind, and received
his sight, until they called the parents of him that had received his sight.
19 And they asked them, saying, Is this your son, who ye say was born
20 blind? how then doth he now see? His parents answered them, and
21 said, We know that this is our son, and that he was born blind: but by
what means he now seeth, we know not; or who hath opened his eyes,
22 we know not: he is of age; ask him: he shall speak for himself. These
words spake his parents, because they [k]feared the Jews: [l]for the Jews

A. D. 32.

[g] Eccl. 11. 5. Mark 4. 27. ch. 3. 9. 1 Cor. 15. 35.
[h] Jer. 36. 17, 18. Matt. 1. 21-25.
[i] Luke 12. 51-53. ch. 7. 12, 43. ch. 10. 19. Acts 14. 4.
[j] Deut. 18. 15. Luke 24. 19. ch. 4. 19. ch. 6. 14. Acts 2. 22. Acts 3. 22, 26. Acts 10. 38.
[k] ch. 7. 13. ch. 12. 42. ch. 19. 38. Acts 5. 13.
[l] Luke 6. 22. ch. 16. 2. Acts 4. 18. Acts 5. 40.

and the bestowal of the most distinguishing of features. But another remark, of more consequence, might have been made here—that the difficulty which his neighbours had in believing that this was the same man whom they had known as the Blind Beggar, and the need of his own testimony to put the fact beyond all question, is the best evidence of the perfection of the cure. Well, this settled, the next questions naturally are, *How* was it done? and *Who* did it? **10. Therefore said they unto him, How were thine eyes opened? 11. He answered and said, A man that is called Jesus made clay, and anointed mine eyes, and said unto me, Go to the pool of Siloam, and wash: and I went and washed, and I received sight.** This reply is so fresh and lively that, as *Meyer* says, our Evangelist probably received it from the man himself after he became a believer. **12. Then said they unto him, Where is he? He said**—'saith' [λέγει], **I know not.** No doubt, after the attempt to stone Him, Jesus would not deem it prudent at once to appear in public.

13. They brought to the Pharisees him that aforetime was blind. 14. And—or, 'Now' [δὲ] **it was the sabbath day when Jesus made the clay, and opened his eyes.** The connection between these two verses, and especially what is mentioned in *v.* 16, make it evident that it was our Lord's having wrought this cure on the Sabbath day which induced these people to bring the beggar under the notice of the Pharisees; and so far, therefore, it was done in a spirit of at least suspicion of the glorious Healer. On the systematic performance of such miracles on the Sabbath day, see on ch. v. 9.

The Pharisees Question and Cross-question the Healed Beggar, till, unable to prevail upon him to Repudiate His Blessed Benefactor, or refrain from Testifying to Him, they Excommunicate him (15-34). It is probable that the Pharisees were sitting in council when the following dialogue took place: **15. Then again the Pharisees also asked him how he had received his sight. He said unto them, He put clay upon mine eyes, and I washed, and do see. 16. Therefore said some of the Pharisees, This man is not of God, because he keepeth not the sabbath day. Others**—as Nicodemus and Joseph, **said, How can a man that is a sinner do such miracles? And there was a division among them. 17. They say unto the blind man again, What sayest thou of him, that he hath opened thine eyes? He said, He is a prophet**—rightly viewing the miracle as but a "sign" [σημεῖον] of His prophetic commission. **18. But**—'Then,' or 'therefore.' Seeing, if they admitted the truth of the cure, they would likely be shut up to the acknowledgment of His divine commission, *therefore* they took the course of discrediting the fact. **the Jews**—that is, these ruling ecclesiastics (see on ch. i. 19), **did not believe concerning him, that he had been blind, and received his sight, until they called the parents of him that had received his sight. 19. And they asked them, saying, Is this your son, who ye say was born blind? how then doth he now see?** Foiled by the testimony of the young man himself, they hope to throw doubt on the fact by close questioning his parents, who, perceiving the snare laid for them, ingeniously escape it by testifying simply to the identity of their son, and his birth-blindness, leaving it to himself, as a competent witness, to speak to the cure. **20. His parents answered them, and said, We know that this is our son, and that he was born blind: 21. But by what means he now seeth, we know not; or who hath opened his eyes, we know not: he is of age; ask him: he shall speak for himself.** Here, however, they prevaricate, in saying they "knew not who had opened his eyes;" for "they feared the Jews," who had come to an understanding—probably after what is recorded, ch. vii. 50, &c., and by this time pretty well known—that whoever owned Him as the Christ should be put out of the synagogue—*i. e.*, not simply *excluded*, but *excommunicated.* **22. These words spake his parents, because they feared the Jews: for the Jews had agreed already, that if any man did confess that he was Christ** [αὐτὸν ὁμολογήσῃ Χριστὸν]—or 'own Him as Christ,' **he should be put out of the synagogue** [ἀποσυνάγωγος γένηται]—not only expelled,

had agreed already, that if any man did confess that he was Christ, he
23 should be put out of the synagogue. Therefore said his parents, He is of
age; ask him.
24 Then again called they the man that was blind, and said unto him,
25 [m]Give God the praise: we know that this man is a sinner. He answered
and said, Whether he be a sinner *or no,* I know not: one thing I know,
26 that, whereas I was blind, now I see. Then said they to him again,
27 What did he to thee? how opened he thine eyes? He answered
them, I have told you already, and ye did not hear: wherefore would
28 ye hear *it* again? will ye also be his disciples? Then they reviled him,
29 and said, Thou art his disciple; but we are Moses' disciples. We know
that God spake unto Moses: *as for* this *fellow,* [n]we know not from
30 whence he is. The man answered and said unto them, Why [o]herein is
a marvellous thing, that ye know not from whence he is, and *yet* he hath
31 opened mine eyes. Now we know that [p]God heareth not sinners: but if
any man be a worshipper of God, and doeth his will, him he heareth.
32 Since the world began was it not heard that any man opened the eyes
33 of one that was born blind. If this man were not of God, he could do
34 nothing. They answered and said unto him, Thou wast altogether born
in sins, and dost thou teach us? And they [2]cast him out.

A. D. 32.

m Jos. 7. 19. 1 Sam. 6. 5. Isa. 66. 5. ch. 5. 23. ch. 8. 49. Rom. 10. 2.
n ch. 8. 14.
o ch. 3. 10.
p Job 27. 9. Job 35. 12. Ps. 18. 41. Ps. 34. 15. Ps. 66. 18. Pro. 1. 28. Pro. 15. 29. Pro. 28. 9. Isa. 1. 15. Jer. 11. 11. Jer. 14. 12. Ezek. 8. 18. Mic. 3. 4. Zec. 7. 13.
2 Or, excommunicated him.

but 'become' and be held 'unsynagogued,' or, as we say, 'unchurched.' See ch. xii. 42; xvi. 2. **23. Therefore**—or 'for this cause' [Διὰ τοῦτο], **said his parents, He is of age; ask him.**

24. Then again—'the second time' [ἐκ δευτέρου]—**called they the man that was blind.** Baffled and perplexed, they seem to have put him forth till they should agree among themselves how next to proceed with him, so as to break down the testimony to Jesus which this marvellous cure so plainly furnished, and then to have summoned him back. **and said unto him, Give God the praise**—or, 'Give glory to God' [Δὸς δόξαν τῷ Θεῷ]: **we know that this man is a sinner**—not wishing him to own, even to the praise of God, that a miracle had been wrought upon him, but to show more regard to the honour of God than ascribe any such act to one who was a sinner. **25. He answered and said, Whether he be a sinner or no, I know not: one thing I know, that, whereas I was blind, now I see.** Not that the man meant to insinuate any doubt in his own mind on the point of His being "a sinner;" but as his *opinion* on such a point would be of no consequence to others, he would speak only to what he *knew* as *fact* in his own case. **26. Then said they**—'They said' **to him again, What did he to thee? how opened he thine eyes?**—hoping by repeated questions to ensnare him; but the youth is more than a match for them. **27. He answered them, I have told you already, and ye did not hear: wherefore would ye hear it again? will ye also be his disciples?** In a vein of keen irony he treats their questions as those of anxious enquirers, almost ready for discipleship! Stung by this, they retort upon *him* as the disciple (and here they plainly were not wrong): for themselves, they fell back upon Moses—about *him* there could be no doubt—but who knew about this upstart? **28. [Then] they reviled him.** [The οὖν of the received text has hardly any authority.] **and said, Thou art his disciple; but we are Moses' disciples. 29. We know that God spake**—or 'hath spoken' [λελάληκεν] **unto Moses: as for this [fellow]**—or simply, 'this [man]:' it is the language of contempt, though probably more affected than real: **we know not from whence he is.** The youth had now no need to say another word; but waxing bolder in defence of his Benefactor, and his views brightening by the very courage which it demanded, he puts it to them how they could pretend inability to tell whether one who opened the eyes of a man born blind was "of God" or "a sinner"—from above or from beneath—and proceeds to argue the case with remarkable power. **30. The man answered and said unto them, Why herein is a marvellous thing, that ye know not from whence he is, and yet he hath opened mine eyes. 31. Now we know that God heareth not sinners: but if any man be a worshipper of God, and doeth his will, him he heareth. 32. Since the world began was it not heard that any man opened the eyes of one that was born blind. 33. If this man were not of God, he could do nothing.** So irresistible was this argument that their rage burst forth in a speech of the most intense Pharisaism. **34. They answered and said unto him, Thou wast altogether born in sins, and dost thou teach us?**—'Thou, a base-born, uneducated, impudent youth, teach *us*, the trained, constituted, recognized guides of the people in the things of God? Out upon thee!' **and they cast him out**—judicially, no doubt, as we have said (on *v.* 22), as well as in fact. (So *de Wette, Olshausen, Tholuck,* &c.) The allusion to his being "born in sins" seems a tacit admission of his being blind from birth—the very thing they had been so unwilling to own. But rage and enmity to truth are seldom consistent in their outbreaks. The friends of this excommunicated youth, crowding around him with their sympathy, would probably express surprise that one who could work such a cure should be unable to protect his patient from the persecution it had raised against him, or should possess the power without using it. Nor would it be wonderful if such thoughts should arise in the youth's own mind. But if they did, it is certain, from what follows, that they made no lodgment there, conscious as he was that "whereas he was blind, now he saw," and satisfied that if his Benefactor "were not of God, he could do nothing," (*v.* 33). There was a word for him too, which, if whispered in his ear from the oracles of God, would seem expressly designed to describe his case, and prepare him for the coming interview with his gracious Friend. "Hear the word of the Lord, ye that tremble at His word; *Your brethren that hated you, that cast you out for My name's sake,*

35 Jesus heard that they had cast him out; and when he had found him,
36 he said unto him, Dost thou believe on [q]the Son of God? He answered
37 and said, Who is he, Lord, that I might believe on him? And Jesus
said unto him, Thou hast both seen him, and [r]it is he that talketh
38 with thee. And he said, Lord, I believe. And he worshipped him.
39 And Jesus said, [s]For judgment I am come into this world, [t]that they
which see not might see, and that they which see might be made blind.
40 And *some* of the Pharisees which were with him heard these words,
41 [u]and said unto him, Are we blind also? Jesus said unto them, [v]If ye
were blind, ye should have no sin: but now ye say, We see; therefore
your sin remaineth.

A. D. 32.

[q] Matt. 14. 33. Matt. 16. 16. Mark 1. 1. ch. 10. 36.
[r] ch. 4. 26.
[s] ch. 5. 22. ch. 3. 17. ch. 12. 47.
[t] Matt. 13. 13. Luke 2. 34. 2 Cor. 2. 16.
[u] Rom. 2. 19.
[v] ch. 15. 22.

said, Let the Lord be glorified; BUT HE SHALL APPEAR TO YOUR JOY, *and they shall be ashamed*" (Isa. lxvi. 5). But how was *He* engaged to whom such noble testimony had been given, and for whom such persecution had been borne? Uttering, perhaps, in secret, "with strong crying and tears," the words of the prophetic psalm, "Let not them that wait on thee, O Lord God of hosts, be ashamed for My sake; let none that seek thee be confounded for My sake, O God of Israel; because for thy sake I have borne reproach . . . and the reproaches of them that reproached thee are fallen upon Me" (Ps. lxix. 6, 7, 9).

Touching Interview between the Healed Beggar and His Unknown Benefactor—On Recognizing, he Worships Him (35-38). **35. Jesus heard that they had cast him out**—by intelligence brought to Him, **and when he had found him**—shall we say by accident? Not very likely. Sympathy in that breast could not long keep aloof from its object. **he said unto him, Dost thou believe on the Son of God?** A question stretching purposely beyond his present attainments, in order the more quickly to lead him—in his present teachable frame—into the highest truth. **36. He answered and said, Who is he, Lord, that I might**—or rather, 'may' **believe on him?** This is evidently the language of one who *did* believe in Him who had wrought such a marvellous work on him, and who now only yearned to behold and personally to recognize Him. The next two verses show this to be the real state of His mind. **37. And Jesus said unto him, Thou hast both seen him, and it is he that talketh with thee.** The new sense of sight imparted to him had at that moment its highest exercise, in gazing upon "The Light of the world." **38. And he said, Lord, I believe. And he worshipped him**—a *faith* and a *worship*, beyond doubt, meant to express far more than he would think proper to any human "prophet" (*v.* 17); the unstudied, resistless expression, probably, of SUPREME faith and adoration, though without the full understanding of what that implied. **39. And Jesus said**—perhaps at the same time, but after a crowd, including some of the sceptical and scornful rulers, had, on seeing Jesus talking with the healed youth, hastened to the spot. **For judgment I am come**—or 'came I' [ἦλθον] **that they which see not might see**—rising to that *sight* of which the natural vision communicated to the youth was but the symbol (see on *v.* 5, and compare Luke iv. 18): **and that they which see might be made blind**—judicially incapable of apprehending and receiving the truth, to which they have wilfully shut their eyes. See on Matt. xiii. 12.

40. And some—rather, 'those' **of the Pharisees which were with him heard these words, and said unto him, Are we blind also?**—we, the constituted, recognized guides of the people in spiritual things? pride and rage prompting the question. **41. Jesus said unto them, If ye were blind**—If ye wanted light to discern My claims, and only waited to receive it, **ye should have no sin**—none of the guilt of shutting out the light: **but now ye say, We see; therefore your sin remaineth**—Your claim to possess light, while rejecting Me, is that which seals you up in the guilt of unbelief.

Remarks.—1. Although the resurrection of Lazarus was beyond all doubt the greatest of our Lord's miracles, there is one particular in which the miracle of this chapter is even more marvellous. In all our Lord's miracles of healing, and even in the resurrection of the dead, He did but restore what had been already in use by the objects of His power and grace—seeing, hearing, walking, living. But here is one to whom vision is not *restored*, but for the first time *imparted*. And though we are not to suppose that the organ of sight was then *created*—for such "works were finished from the creation of the world"—though the organ was doubtless there from his mother's womb, it had never been capable of action till now, that he was "of age;" and thus, by an act of marvellous power, this man for the first time beheld the light of heaven, and from that time forth saw as other men—insomuch that his neighbours would hardly believe that he was the same man whom they had known as the Blind Beggar, and, as already remarked, it needed his own testimony to put the fact beyond all question. And what is most worthy of notice, it is just in the record of these two greatest of all our Lord's miracles that *the details are the fullest*—so full, and embracing so many minute yet vivid particulars, that it is impossible to doubt that we have them from the very parties concerned; the beloved Evangelist himself being doubtless present wherever his Lord was in the action of this chapter, while for the rest—as already observed—he was indebted, we can hardly doubt, to the newly gained disciple himself, whose eyes the Lord had doubly opened. 2. That all our Lord's beneficent miracles on the bodies of men were designed to illustrate analogous and higher operations on the souls of men, which it was His errand and is His office to perform, has been once and again observed, see on Matt. iv. 12-25, Remark 5, at the close of that Section. But nowhere is this more grandly seen than at the beginning and end of this chapter. Before aught was done to this blind beggar—while the disciples were questioning our Lord as to the cause of the poor man's misfortune, and as soon as He had explained that the primary intention of it was to display in him the works of God which He had come to do, and must do whilst it was day—Jesus said, "As long as I am in the world, I am THE LIGHT OF THE WORLD;" and then it was that, to illustrate that office of His, He miraculously opened this man's eyes. And at the close of the chapter, recurring, in presence of enemies, to the opening of the man's

10 VERILY, verily, I say unto you, [a]He that entereth not by the door
into the sheep-fold, but climbeth up some other way, the same is a thief
2 and a robber. But he that entereth in by [b]the door is the shepherd of
3 the sheep. To him [c]the porter openeth; and the sheep hear his voice:
4 and he calleth his own sheep by name, and leadeth them out. And when
he putteth forth his own sheep, he goeth before them, and the sheep
5 follow him: for they know his voice. And [d]a stranger will they not
follow, but will flee from him: for they know not the voice of strangers.
6 This parable spake Jesus unto them: but they understood not what
things they were which he spake unto them.

A. D. 32.

CHAP. 10.
[a] Isa. 56. 10. Jer. 23. 21. Heb. 5. 4.
[b] Isa. 61. 1. Acts 20. 28. 1 Cor. 12. 28.
[c] 1 Pet. 1. 12. 1 Cor. 16. 9.
[d] Pro. 19. 27. Gal. 1. 8. Eph. 4. 44.

eyes, He testified, "For judgment came I into this world, that they which see not might see," on the one hand; or—as He afterwards expressed it from His glory in the heavens to Saul of Tarsus, when sending him as a preacher to the Gentiles—"to open their eyes, and turn them from darkness to light, and from the power of Satan unto God" (Acts xxvi. 18): "and," on the other hand, "that they which see might be made blind." Thus, then, let us learn to read in every record of Christ's miracles on the *body* assurances and illustrations of His power and grace in the higher sphere of the *soul.* 3. While in the parents of this youth we have a lively illustration of the terrors of ghostly authority —in inspiring which the priests of the Church of Rome have diabolically improved upon the Jewish ecclesiastics—we have in the youth himself a beautiful illustration of the *courage* which a conscious experience of divine power and grace inspires, of the *strength* which the exercise of that courage in trying circumstances imparts, and of the *wisdom*—above their own—which, in fulfilment of express promise, the Lord has so often from that time to this communicated to His disciples when standing before rulers for His name's sake. See on Matt. x. 19, 20. 4. The accession of this healed man to the ranks of genuine discipleship is one, and not the least instructive, of the many cases of Christ found *without seeking*, referred to on Matt. xiii. 44-46, Remark 1 at the close of that Section. Not like blind Bartimeus did this man cry after Jesus; but, "as Jesus *passed by* (compare Ezek. xvi. 6, 8), He *saw* "this beggar, who had been blind from his birth"—doubtless with that peculiar look with which He *saw* Zaccheus (Luke xix. 5), for His eye affected His heart, and He proceeded to heal him. Not like the other blind man did He first recognize in Jesus "the Son of David;" nor does it appear whether He had even heard of Him before. Certain it is that the first motion was not in the man, or any of his relatives or neighbours, towards Jesus, but in Jesus towards Him. And thus is there a large class, of whom it is said, "I am found of them that sought Me not; I am made manifest unto them that asked not after Me." 5. Was ever virulent determination not to believe on any evidence, and wilful resistance of ocular demonstration, more signally manifested than in those rulers of the Jews, who, after vainly endeavouring to brow-beat this poor unbefriended youth, scornfully expelled him from the synagogue, because he refused to lie before God, and repudiate and malign his unknown Benefactor? But this spirit has not ceased; nor is it to be doubted that, whenever occasions arise for the display of it, the hatred of the world to Christ, in His truth and people, will be found as virulent as it has ever been (ch. xv. 19; Gal. iv. 29).

CHAP. X. 1-42. —DISCOURSE ON THE GOOD SHEPHERD, AND SPECULATION OCCASIONED BY IT —DISCOURSE AT THE FEAST OF DEDICATION—JESUS TAKES REFUGE FROM THE FURY OF HIS ENEMIES BEYOND JORDAN, WHERE MANY BELIEVE ON HIM. The discourses and transactions of this chapter, though belonging to two different festivals, between which there was an interval of between two and three months, will be most conveniently embraced in one Section, as the subjects are so much the same that the Remarks which they suggest cannot well be separated.

Discourse on the Good Shepherd (1-18). This Discourse seems plainly a continuation of the closing verses of the preceding chapter. The figure of a shepherd and his sheep was familiar to the Jewish ear, (see Jer. xxiii.; Ezek. xxxiv.; Zec. xi., &c.) 'This simple creature, the sheep,' says *Luther*, as quoted by *Stier*, 'has this special note among all animals, that it quickly hears the voice of the shepherd, follows no one else, depends entirely on him, and seeks help from him alone, cannot help itself, but is shut up to another's aid.' **1. Verily, verily, I say unto you, He that entereth not by the door**—that is, by the legitimate way; without as yet saying what that was, **into the sheep-fold**—the sacred inclosure of God's true people, **but climbeth up some other way**—not referring to the assumption of ecclesiastical office without an external call—for those Jewish rulers who were specially aimed at had this (see on Matt. xxiii. 2)—but to the want of a true call, a spiritual commission, the seal of heaven going along with the outward authority: it is the assumption of the spiritual guidance of the people *without this* that is meant. **the same is a thief and a robber. 2. But he that entereth in by the door is the shepherd of the sheep**—is a true, divinely recognized shepherd. **3. To him the porter openeth**—'To him is given right of free access, by order of Him to whom the sheep belong'—for it is better not to give this allusion a more specific interpretation. So *Calvin, Meyer, Luthardt.* **and the sheep hear his voice: and he calleth his own sheep by name, and leadeth them out. 4. And when he putteth forth**—or 'turneth out.' [The *aorist*—ἐκβάλῃ—is here rightly rendered 'putteth forth,' as in Luke i. 51-53; the idea being that of 'a succession of definite acts constituting a habit of so acting.' So probably ἠγάπησαν is to be explained in ch. iii. 19, 'men *love* the darkness,' &c.] **his own sheep, he goeth before them, and the sheep follow him: for they know his voice. 5. And** [δὲ]—rather, 'But' **a stranger will they not follow, but will flee from him: for they know not the voice of strangers. 6. This parable spake Jesus unto them: but they understood not what things they were which he spake unto them.** What is said in these three verses, though admitting of important *application* to every faithful shepherd of God's flock, is in its direct and highest sense true only of "the great Shepherd of the sheep," who in the first five verses seems plainly, under the simple character of a true shepherd, to be drawing His own portrait. So *Lampe, Stier,* &c.

7. Then said Jesus unto them again, Verily,

7 Then said Jesus unto them again, Verily, verily, I say unto you, I am
8 [e]the door of the sheep. All [f]that ever came before me are thieves and
9 robbers: but the sheep did not hear them. I am the door: by me if any
man enter in, he shall be saved, and shall go in and out, and find pasture.
10 The [g]thief cometh not, but for to steal, and to kill, and to destroy: I
am come that they might have life, and that they might have *it* more
11 abundantly. I [h]am the good shepherd: the good shepherd giveth his
12 life for the sheep. But he that is an hireling, and not the shepherd,
whose own the sheep are not, seeth the wolf coming, and [i]leaveth the
sheep, and fleeth: and the wolf catcheth them, and scattereth the sheep.
13 The hireling fleeth, because he is an hireling, and careth not for the
14 sheep. I am the good shepherd, and [j]know my *sheep*, and [k]am known
15 of mine. As the Father knoweth me, even so know I the Father: and I

A. D. 32.
[e] Eph. 2. 18. Heb. 10. 19.
[f] Jer 23. 1. Jer. 50. 6. Acts 5. 36, 37.
[g] Acts 20. 29. 2 Pet. 2. 1.
[h] Isa. 40. 11. Ezek. 34 23. Ezek. 37. 24.
[i] Zec. 11. 16.
[j] 2 Tim. 2. 19.
[k] Eph. 1. 17. Phil. 3. 10. 1 John 5. 20.

verily, I say unto you, I am the door of the sheep—that is, *The Way in* to the fold, with all its blessed privileges, alike for the shepherds and the sheep. (Compare ch. xiv. 6; Eph. ii. 18.) **8. All that ever came before me**—the false prophets; not as claiming the prerogatives of Messiah, but as perverters of the people from the way of life leading to Him. So *Olshausen.* **are thieves and robbers: but the sheep did not hear them**—the instinct of their divinely taught hearts preserving them from seducers, and attaching them to the heaven-sent prophets of whom it is said that "the Spirit of Christ was in them" (1 Pet. i. 11). **9. I am the door: by me if any man enter in**—whether shepherd or sheep, **he shall be saved**—the great object of the pastoral office, as of all the divine arrangements towards mankind. **and shall go in and out and find pasture.** He "shall go *in,*" as to a place of safety and repose; and he "shall go *out,*" as to green pastures and still waters" (Ps. xxiii. 2), for nourishment and refreshing; and all this only transferred to another clime, and enjoyed in another manner, at the close of this earthly scene (Rev. vii. 17). **10. The thief cometh not, but for to steal, and to kill, and to destroy: I am come**—or, 'I came' [ἦλθον] **that they might have life, and that they might have it more abundantly** [περισσὸν]—or rather, simply, 'have it abundantly.' I came, not to *preserve* a life already possessed, but to *impart* a life before unknown, and to communicate it in rich and unfailing exuberance. What a claim! And yet it is but a repetition, under a new aspect, of what He had taught in the synagogue of Capernaum (ch. vi.); nay, but an echo of all His teaching; and He who uttered these and like words must be either a blasphemer, all worthy of the death He died, or "God with us:" there can be no middle course. **11. I am the good shepherd**—not '*a,*' but emphatically "The Good Shepherd," and, in the sense intended, exclusively so (see Isa. xl. 11; Ezek. xxxiv. 23; xxxvii. 24; Zec. xiii. 7). **the good shepherd giveth** [τίθησιν]—rather, 'layeth down;' as the word is properly rendered in *vv.* 15, 17, **his life for the sheep.** Though this may be said of literal shepherds who, even for their brute flock have, like David, encountered "the lion and the bear" at the risk of their own lives, and still more of faithful pastors, who, like the early bishops of Rome, have been the foremost to brave the fury of their enemies against the flock committed to their care; yet here, beyond doubt, it points to the struggle which was to issue in the willing surrender of the Redeemer's own life, to save His sheep from destruction. **12. But he that is an hireling, and not the shepherd, whose own the sheep are not**—who has no *property* in them. By this He points to His own peculiar relation to the sheep, the same as His Father's, the great Proprietor and Lord of the flock, who styles Him "My Shepherd, *the Man that is my Fellow*" (Zec. xiii. 7); and though faithful under-shepherds, who are in their Master's interest, feel a measure of His own concern for their charge, the language is strictly applicable only to "the Son over His own house" (Heb. iii. 6). **seeth**—or 'beholdeth' [θεωρεῖ] **the wolf coming.** By this is meant, not (as *Stier, Alford,* &c., take it) *the devil* distinctively, but generally, as we judge, whoever comes upon the flock with hostile intent, in whatever form; though the wicked one, no doubt, is *at the bottom* of such movements. So *Lücke, Luthardt.* **14. I am the good shepherd.** See on *v.* 11. **and know my [sheep], and am known of mine.** As the word "sheep" is a supplement, it is perhaps better to render the words, 'and know mine, and am known of mine' [γινώσκω τὰ ἐμὰ, καὶ γινώσκομαι ὑπὸ τῶν ἐμῶν]. *Lachmann* and *Tregelles* read, 'and mine know me' [γινώσκουσίν με τὰ ἐμὰ], but, as we judge, on insufficient evidence: *Tischendorf* abides by the received text. **15. As the Father knoweth me, even so know I the Father.** This ought not to have begun a new sentence; for it is properly part of the previous verse. The whole statement will then stand thus: "And I know mine, and am known of mine, even as the Father knoweth Me, and I know the Father." So the *Vulgate,* and *Luther's* version, *Bengel, de Wette, Lücke,* and nearly every modern critic; and so *Lachmann, Tischendorf,* and *Tregelles* print the text. When Christ says He "*knows* His sheep," He means it in the peculiar and endearing sense of 2 Tim. ii. 19; and when He says, "I am known of mine," He alludes to the soul's response to the voice that has inwardly and efficaciously called it; for in this mutual loving acquaintance, ours is the *effect* of His. The Redeemer's knowledge of us, as *Olshausen* finely says, is the *active* element, penetrating us with His power and life; that of believers is the *passive* principle, the reception of His life and light. In this reception, however, an assimilation of the soul to the sublime Object of its knowledge and love takes place; and thus an activity, though a derived one, is unfolded, which shows itself in obedience to His commands. But when our glorious Speaker rises from this mutual knowledge of Himself and His people to another and loftier reciprocity of knowledge—even that of Himself and His Father—and says that the former is *even as* [καθὼς] the latter, He expresses what none but Himself could have dared to utter; though it is only what He had in effect said before (Matt. xi. 27, taken in connection with the preceding and following verses; and Luke x. 21, 22), and what in another and almost higher form He expressed afterwards in His Intercessory

16 lay down my life for the sheep. And [l]other sheep I have, which are not
of this fold: them also I must bring, and they shall hear my voice; [m]and
17 there shall be one fold, *and* one shepherd. Therefore doth my Father
18 love me, [n]because I lay down my life, that I might take it again. No
man taketh it from me, but I lay it down of myself. I have power to
lay it down, and I have power to take it again. This [o]commandment
have I received of my Father.
19 There was a division therefore again among the Jews for these sayings.
20 And many of them said, He hath a devil, and is mad; why hear ye him?
21 Others said, These are not the words of him that hath a devil. [p]Can a
devil open the eyes of the blind?
22 And it was at Jerusalem the feast of the dedication, and it was winter.
23 And Jesus walked in the temple, [q]in Solomon's porch.

A. D. 32.

[l] Isa. 56. 8.
[m] Ezek. 37. 22. Eph. 2. 14.
[n] Isa. 53. 7. 2 Cor. 5. 15. Heb. 2. 9. 1 John 3. 16.
[o] Acts 2. 24.
[p] Ex. 4. 11. Ps. 94. 9. Ps. 146. 8. Pro. 20. 12. Isa. 35. 5, 6. Matt. 11. 5.
[q] Acts 3. 11. Acts 5. 12.

Prayer (ch. xvii. 21-23). **and I lay down my life for the sheep.** How sublime is this, following immediately on the lofty claim of the preceding clause! 'Tis just the riches and the poverty of "The Word made flesh;" one glorious Person reaching at once up to the Throne—in absolute knowledge of the Father—and down even to the dust of death, in the voluntary surrender of His life "for the sheep." A candid interpretation of this last clause—"for the sheep"—ought to go far to establish the special relation of the vicarious death of Christ to the Church. **16. And other sheep I have, which are not of this fold** [αὐλῆς]: **them also I must bring.** He means the perishing Gentiles, of whom He speaks as *already* His sheep—in the love of His heart and the purpose of His grace—to "*bring* them" in due time. **and they shall hear my voice.** This is not the language of mere foresight that they would believe, but the expression of a purpose to draw them to Himself by an inward and efficacious call, which would infallibly issue in their spontaneous accession to Him. **and there shall be one fold** [ποίμνη]—rather, 'one flock.' The word for 'fold' in the previous part of the verse, it will be seen, is different. **17. Therefore** [Διὰ τοῦτο]—'For this cause' **doth my Father love me, because I lay down my life.** As the highest act of the Son's love to the Father was the laying down of His life for the sheep at His "commandment," so the Father's love to Him as His *incarnate* Son reached its consummation, and finds its highest justification, in that sublimest and most affecting of all acts. **that I might take it again**—His resurrection-life being indispensable to the accomplishment of the fruit of His death. **18. No man taketh it from me, but I lay it down of myself. I have power to lay it down, and I have power to take it again.** It is impossible for language more plainly and emphatically to express the *absolute voluntariness* of Christ's death, such a voluntariness as it would be manifest presumption in any mere *creature* to affirm of his own death. It is beyond all doubt the language of One who was conscious that *His life was His own*, which no creature's is, and, therefore, His to surrender or retain *at will*. Here lay the glory of His sacrifice, that it was *purely* voluntary. The claim of "power to take it again" is no less important, as showing that His resurrection, though ascribed to the Father, in the sense we shall presently see, was nevertheless *His own assertion of His own right to life* as soon as the purposes of His voluntary death were accomplished. **This commandment**—that is, to "lay down His life, that He might take it again," **have I received** [ἔλαβον]—rather, 'received I' **of my Father.** So that Christ died at once by "*command*" of His Father, and by such a *voluntary obedience* to that command as has made Him, so to speak, infinitely dear to the Father. The *necessity* of Christ's death, in the light of these profound sayings, must be manifest to all but the superficial.

Speculation occasioned by this Discourse (19-21). **19. There was a division therefore again among the Jews for**—or 'because of' **these sayings. 20. And many of them said, He hath a devil, and is mad; why hear ye him? 21. Others said, These are not the words of him that hath a devil. Can a devil open the eyes of the blind?** Thus did the light and the darkness reveal themselves with increasing distinctness in the separation of the teachable from the obstinately prejudiced. The one saw in Him only "a devil and a madman;" the other revolted at the thought that *such words* could come from one possessed, and sight be given to the blind by a demoniac; showing clearly that a deeper impression had been made upon them than their words expressed.

Discourse at the Feast of Dedication (22-30). **22. And**—or rather, 'Now,' as beginning a new subject, **it was at Jerusalem the feast of the dedication.** Recent interpreters, with few exceptions, conclude, from the silence of the Evangelist, that our Lord must have remained during the whole interval between the Feast of Tabernacles and this of the Dedication—a period of about two months and a half—either in Jerusalem or its immediate neighbourhood. But the opening words of this section—"Now it was *at Jerusalem*," &c.—imply, we think, the reverse. If our Lord remained so very long at the capital at this time, it was contrary certainly to His invariable practice; and considering how the enmity and exasperation of His enemies were drawing to a head, it does not seem to us very likely. But to suppose, with some harmonists, that our Lord went back during this interval to Galilee, and that a not inconsiderable portion of the matter of the first three Gospels belongs to this period, seems to us against all probability. We therefore take a middle course; and think that our Lord spent the interval between the above festivals partly in Peræa, within the dominions of Herod Antipas (where certainly we find Him at Luke xiii. 31), and partly in Judea, approaching to the suburbs of the capital (where certainly we find Him at Luke x. 38).

This festival of the *Dedication* was celebrated between two and three months after the Feast of Tabernacles. It was instituted by Judas Maccabeus, to commemorate the purification of the temple from the profanations to which it had been subjected by Antiochus Epiphanes (B. C. 165), and kept for eight days, from the 25th Chisleu (about the 20th December)—the day on which Judas began the first joyous celebration of it (1 Macc. iv. 52, 56, 59, and *Joseph.* Antt. xii. 7. 7.) **and it was winter—**

24 Then came the Jews round about him, and said unto him, How long
dost thou [1]make us to doubt? If thou be the Christ, tell us plainly.
25 Jesus answered them, I told you, and ye believed not: the works that I
26 do in my Father's name, they bear witness of me. But [r]ye believe not,
27 because ye are not of my sheep, as I said unto you. My sheep hear my
28 voice, and I know them, and they follow me: and I give unto them
eternal life; and they shall never perish, neither shall any pluck them
29 out of my hand. My [s]Father, [t]which gave *them* me, is greater than all;
30 and none is able to pluck *them* out of my Father's hand. I [u]and *my*
Father are one.
31, Then the Jews took up stones again to stone him. Jesus an-
32 swered them, Many goods works have I showed you from my Father;
33 for which of those works do ye stone me? The Jews answered him,

A. D. 33.

1 Or, hold us in suspense.
r ch. 8. 47. 1 John 4. 6.
s ch. 14. 28.
t Ex. 18. 11. Ps. 145. 3. Dan. 4. 3. Mal. 1. 14. ch. 17. 2, 6.
u ch. 17. 11. 1 Cor. 8. 4,6. Eph. 3. 9. 1 Tim. 3. 16. 1 John 5. 7.

implying some *inclemency*. Accordingly it is added, **23. And Jesus walked in the temple, in Solomon's porch**—for shelter. This portico was on the east side of the temple, and *Josephus* says it was part of the original structure of Solomon. (Antt. xx. 9. 7.)

24. Then came the Jews—that is, as usual in this Gospel, the rulers, as observed on ch. i. 19. **round about him, and said unto him, How long dost thou make us to doubt?** [τὴν ψυχὴν ἡμῶν αἴρεις]—or better, as in the margin, 'hold us in suspense.' **If thou be the Christ, tell us plainly.** But when the plainest *evidence* of it was resisted, what weight could a mere *assertion* of it have? nor can it be doubted that they had an ensnaring purpose in the attempt to draw this out of Him. **25. Jesus answered them, I told you**—that is, in substance (see ch. vii. 37, 38; viii. 35, 36, 58), **and ye believed not: the works that I do in my Father's name, they bear witness of me. 26. But ye** ['Αλλ' ὑμεῖς]. The "ye" is here in emphatic contrast to the "sheep." **believe not, because ye are not of my sheep, as I said unto you.** Our Lord here manifestly refers back to His discourse about the Shepherd and the sheep at the Feast of Tabernacles (*vv.* 1-18). He did not there *expressly* say what is here mentioned; but the sharp line of demarcation there drawn between the sheep who hear only their own shepherd's voice, and those who are led away by deceivers, implied as much, and what follows shows that His object was, first, to resume that subject, and then to carry it out further and raise it higher than before. **27. My sheep hear my voice, and I know them, and they follow me.** See on *v.* 8. **28. And I give unto them eternal life**—not 'I will,' but 'I do give' it them: it is a present gift. See on ch. iii. 36; v. 24. **and they shall never perish, neither shall any pluck them out of my hand.** A very grand utterance, couched in the language of majestic, royal, supreme authority. **29. My Father, which gave**—rather, 'hath given' [δέδωκεν] **them me** (see on ch. vi. 37-39) **is greater than all**—with whom no adverse power can contend (Isa. xxvii. 4); **and none is able to pluck them out of my Father's hand.** The bearing of this statement on what is called by divines *the perseverance of the saints* has not escaped the notice of candid and reverential expositors, even of those churches which repudiate that doctrine. In this view the following remarks of *Olshausen* on these words of our Lord have peculiar value: —'The impossibility of true believers being lost, in the midst of all the temptations which they may encounter, does not consist in their fidelity and decision, but is founded upon the *power of God*. Here the doctrine of predestination is presented in its sublime and sacred aspect; there is a predestination of the holy, which is taught from one end of the Scriptures to the other; not, indeed, of such a nature that an "irresistible grace" *compels* the opposing will of man'—of course not—'but so that that will of man which receives and loves the commands of God is *produced* only by God's grace.' But the statement of *v.* 29 is designed only to introduce that of *v.* **30. I and my Father** ['Εγὼ καὶ ὁ Πατὴρ]. It should be 'I and the Father' **are one** [ἕν ἐσμεν]. Our language admits not of the precision of the original in this great saying, 'We (two *Persons*) are One (*Thing*).' Perhaps '*one interest*' expresses nearly, though not quite, the purport of the saying. There seemed to be some contradiction between His saying they had been given by His Father into *His own* hands, out of which they could not be plucked, and then saying that none could pluck them out of *His Father's* hands, as if they had not been given *out of* them. '*Neither they have*,' says He: 'Though He has given them to Me, they are as much in His own almighty hands as ever—they *cannot be*, and when given to Me they *are not*, given away from Himself; for HE AND I HAVE ALL IN COMMON.' Thus it will be seen, that, though *oneness of essence* is not the precise thing here affirmed, that truth is *the basis of what is affirmed*, without which it would not be true. And Augustin was right in saying the "*We are*" condemns the *Sabellians*, who denied the *distinction of Persons* in the Godhead, while the "*one*" condemns the *Arians*, who denied the unity of their essence. (*Bengel*, in his terse and pithy way, thus expresses it: Per *sumus* refutatur *Sabellius*; per *unum*, *Arius*.)

The Ruling Party, having Taken up Stones to Stone Him, our Lord Vindicates what He had said, but on their again Seeking to Seize Him, He Escapes beyond Jordan, where many believe on Him (31-42). **31. Then the Jews**—the *rulers* again, as in ch. i. 19, **took up stones again to stone him**—and for precisely the same thing as before, the claim of equality with God which they saw He was advancing (ch. v. 18; viii. 58, 59). **32. Jesus answered them, Many good works** [καλὰ ἔργα]—that is, works of pure benevolence; to which Peter thus alludes (Acts x. 38), "Who went about doing good" [εὐεργετῶν], or as a Benefactor: and see Mark vii. 37. **from my Father**—not so much by His power, but as directly *commissioned by Him to do them*. This He says, as *Luthardt* properly remarks, to meet the imputation of unwarrantable assumption of the divine prerogatives—**for which of those works do ye stone me?**—or 'are ye stoning Me;' that is, going to do it. **33. The Jews answered him, saying, For a good work we stone thee not; but for blasphemy**—whose legal punishment was stoning (Lev. xxiv. 11-16), **and because that thou, being a man**—that is, a man only,

saying, For a good work we stone thee not; but for blasphemy; and
34 because that thou, being a man, makest [v]thyself God. Jesus answered
35 them, [w]Is it not written in your law, I said, Ye are gods? If he called
them gods [x]unto whom the word of God came, and the Scripture cannot
36 be broken; say ye of him, [y]whom the Father hath sanctified, and [z]sent
into the world, Thou blasphemest; because I said, I am [a]the Son of
37, God? If [b]I do not the works of my Father, believe me not. But if I do,
38 though ye believe not me, believe the works; that ye may know and
believe [c]that the Father *is* in me, and I in him.
39 Therefore they sought again to take him: but he escaped out of their
40 hand, and went away again beyond Jordan, into the place [d]where John
41 at first baptized; and there he abode. And many resorted unto him,
and said, John did no miracle: [e]but all things that John spake of this
42 man were true. And [f]many believed on him there.

A. D. 33.

v ch. 5. 18.
w Ps. 82. 6.
x Rom. 13. 1.
y ch. 6. 27.
z ch. 3. 17. ch. 5. 36. ch. 8. 42.
a Luke 1. 35. ch. 9. 35.
b ch. 15. 24.
c ch. 14. 10. ch. 17. 21.
d ch. 1. 28.
e ch. 1. 29. ch. 3. 30.
f ch. 8. 30. ch. 11. 45.

makest thyself God. Twice before they understood him to advance the same claim, and both times, as we have seen, they prepared themselves to avenge what they took to be the insulted honour of God, as here, in the way directed by their law. **34. Jesus answered them, Is it not written in your law** (Ps. lxxxii. 6)—respecting judges or magistrates, **I said, Ye are gods?**—as being the *official representatives* and *commissioned agents* of God. **35. If he called them gods unto whom the word of God came, and the Scripture cannot be broken; 36. Say ye of him, whom the Father hath sanctified, and sent into the world.** The whole force of this reasoning, which has been but in part seized by the commentators, lies in what is said of the two parties compared. There is both a comparison and a contrast. The *comparison* of Himself with mere men, divinely commissioned, is intended to show, as *Neander* well expresses it, that the idea of a communication of the Divine Majesty to human nature was by no means foreign to the revelations of the Old Testament; but the *contrast* between Himself and all merely human representatives of God—the One, "*sanctified by the Father, and sent into the world*," the other, "*to whom the word of God*" merely "*came*"—is expressly designed to prevent His being massed up with them as only one of many human officials of God. *It is never said of Christ* that "the word of the Lord came to Him;" whereas this is the well-known formula by which the divine commission even to the highest of *mere men* is expressed, such as John the Baptist (Luke iii. 2): and the reason is that given by the Baptist himself (see on ch. iii. 31). The contrast is between those "to whom the word of God came"—men of the earth, earthy, who were merely privileged to get a divine *message* to utter, if prophets, or a divine *office* to discharge, if judges—and "Him whom (not being of the earth at all), *the Father sanctified* (or set apart), and *sent into the world*"—an expression *never used of any merely human messenger of God*, and *used only of Himself*. **Thou blasphemest, because I said, I am the Son of God?** Our Lord *had not said*, in so many words, that He was the Son of God, on this occasion. But He had said what beyond doubt amounted to it—namely, that He gave His sheep eternal life, and none could pluck them out of His hand; that He had gotten them from *His Father*, in whose hands, though given to Him, they still remained, and out of whose hand none could pluck them; and that they were *the indefeasible property of Both*, inasmuch as "He and His Father were One." Our Lord considers all this as just saying of Himself, "I am the Son of God"—*One nature* with Him, yet mysteriously *of Him*. The parenthesis, in *v.* 35—"And the Scripture cannot be broken"—'dissolved' or 'made void' [λυθῆναι]—referring as it does here to the terms used of magistrates in the 82d Psalm, has an important bearing on the *authority* of the living oracles. The Scripture, says *Olshausen*, as the expressed will of the unchangeable God, is itself unchangeable and indissoluble. (Matt. v. 18.) **37. If I do not the works of my Father, believe me not. 38. But if I do, though ye believe not me, believe the works.** There was in Christ's words, independently of any miracles, a self-evidencing truth, majesty, and grace, which those who had any spiritual susceptibility were unable to resist (ch. vii. 46; viii. 30). But, for those who wanted this, "the works" were a mighty help. When these failed, the case was desperate indeed. **that ye may know and believe that the Father is in me, and I in him**—thus reiterating His claim to essential *oneness with the Father*, which He had only *seemed* to soften down, that He might calm their rage and get their ear again for a moment.

39. Therefore they sought again to take him—true to their original understanding of His words, for they saw perfectly well that He *meant* to "make Himself God" throughout all this dialogue. **but he escaped** [ἐξῆλθεν]—'went' or 'passed' **out of their hand**—slipping, as it were, or gliding away out of their grasp, just when they thought themselves sure of having Him. (See on Luke iv. 30; and on ch. viii. 59.) **40. And went away again beyond Jordan, into the place where John at first baptized.** (See on ch. i. 28.) **41. And many resorted unto him**—on whom the Baptist's ministry appears to have left permanent impressions, **and said, John did no miracle: but all things that John spake of this man were true**—what they now heard and saw in Jesus only confirming in their minds the divinity of His forerunner's mission, a mission unaccompanied by any of His Master's miracles. And thus, **many believed on Him there.**

Remark.—As the malignity of His enemies increases, the benignity and grace with which Jesus addresses Himself to His own seem to grow also; as if the sharp drawing off of the one party made Him cling all the more to the other, drew out to them the more of His loving heart, and encouraged a fuller exhibition of the purposes and plans of saving mercy. In proportion, too, as His scornful adversaries seemed bent on depreciating Him, does He Himself seem to rise in the assertion of His own Divine dignity and authority. Thus, after the virulent enmity to Him manifested in the scenes of the former chapter, how lovely is the whole Discourse on the Shepherd and the sheep, extending

11 NOW a certain *man* was sick, *named* Lazarus, of Bethany, the town of
2 [a]Mary and her sister Martha. (It [b]was *that* Mary which anointed the
Lord with ointment, and wiped his feet with her hair, whose brother
3 Lazarus was sick.) Therefore his sisters sent unto him, saying, Lord,
behold, he whom thou lovest is sick.
4 When Jesus heard *that*, he said, This sickness is not unto death, [c]but
for the glory of God, that the Son of God might be glorified thereby.
5, Now Jesus loved Martha, and her sister, and Lazarus. When he had
6 heard therefore that he was sick, [d]he abode two days still in the same
7 place where he was. Then after that saith he to *his* disciples, Let us go

A. D. 33.

CHAP. 11.
[a] Luke 10.38.
[b] Matt. 26. 7.
Mark 14 3.
Luke 7. 37.
ch. 12. 3.
[c] ch. 9. 3.
Phil. 1. 11.
1 Pet. 4. 11, 14.
[d] Isa. 55. 8.
ch. 10 40.

over the first eighteen verses of this chapter! And where shall we find a livelier expression of the relation which Christ sustains both to men and to God, as the only way of access and entrance *for* the one and *to* the Other; of the absolute voluntariness and saving virtue of His death, as the secret of that self-exerting power in the exercise of which He resumed the life which He had of Himself laid down; of the sustenance which He provides for the continuance of the life He imparts, the pasture of His saved sheep; of the Father's love to Him for freely doing all this; and of the mutual knowledge of Himself and His sheep, as bearing no faint resemblance to that of Himself and the Father? But in the Discourse at the Feast of Dedication, we find Him rising if possible, yet higher; speaking of the security that the sheep have, for that eternal life which in the exercise of His royal authority He gives them, in the impossibility of plucking them out of His hand: and lest this should seem to His audience small security, considering how little different from other men He outwardly appeared, He adds that His Father, at least, who gave His sheep to Him, would be admitted even by themselves to be greater than all; and as none could pluck them out of *His* hand, that was all the same as inability to pluck them out of His own hand, for He and the Father were one. This seemed too much, and accordingly they took up stones to stone Him as a blasphemer. But though He addressed to them an argument fitted to soothe and mollify them, He took care, lest it should take down His dignity in their eyes, to close it by reiterating in substance the very statement for which they had attempted to stone Him; and only by divinely eluding their grasp, and retiring to the further side of the Jordan, did they fail to seize before His time the Holy One of God!

CHAP. XI. 1-57.—THE RESURRECTION OF LAZARUS, AND ITS EFFECTS—THE DEATH OF JESUS BEING RESOLVED ON BY THE JEWISH COUNCIL, HE RETIRES OUT OF PUBLIC VIEW—PREPARATIONS FOR THE APPROACHING PASSOVER, AND SPECULATION WHETHER JESUS WILL COME TO IT. It was stated at the close of the former chapter that our Lord, eluding the fury of His Pharisaic adversaries in Jerusalem, "went away again beyond Jordan into the place where John at first baptized, and there abode" (ch. x. 39, 40). The place was probably somewhere about the well-known fords of the Jordan, and not far from Jericho, which was about eighteen miles distant from Jerusalem. Here we now find Him when intelligence reached Him regarding Lazarus.

A Message arriving from Bethany that Lazarus is sick, Jesus, after waiting Two Days, and informing the Disciples that Lazarus had died, Departs thither for the purpose of Raising Him from the Dead (1-16). **1. Now a certain man was sick, named Lazarus, of**—or 'from' [ἀπὸ] **Bethany** (see on Luke xix. 29), 'of' [ἐκ] **the town of Mary and her sister Martha**—thus distinguishing this Bethany from the one "beyond Jordan" above referred to. **2. (It was that Mary which anointed the Lord with ointment, and wiped his feet with her hair, whose brother Lazarus was sick.)** The fact here referred to, though not recorded by our Evangelist till ch. xii. 3, &c., was so well known in the teaching of all the churches, according to our Lord's prediction (see on Mark xiv. 9), that it is here alluded to by anticipation, as the most natural way of identifying her; and Mary is first named, though the younger, as the more distinguished of the two. She "anointed THE LORD," says the Evangelist—led doubtless to the use of this term here, as He was about to exhibit Him illustriously as the *Lord of Life*. **3. Therefore his sisters sent unto him, saying, Lord, behold, he whom thou lovest is sick.** A most womanly appeal to the known affection of her Lord for the patient; yet how reverential! 'Those,' says *Trench*, 'whom Christ loves, are no more exempt than others from their share of earthly trouble and anguish; rather are they bound over to it more surely.'

4. When—'But when' [δὲ] **Jesus heard that, he said, This sickness is not unto death, but for the glory of God, that the Son of God might**—or 'may' **be glorified thereby** [δι' αὐτῆς]—that is, by this "glory of God." Remarkable language this, which from creature lips would have been intolerable. It means that the glory of GOD manifested in the resurrection of the dead Lazarus would be shown to be the glory, personally and immediately, of THE SON. **5. Now Jesus loved Martha, and her sister, and Lazarus.** What a picture! one that in every age has attracted the admiration of the whole Christian Church. No wonder that those sceptics who have so pitifully carped at the ethical system of the Gospel, as not embracing private friendships in the list of its virtues, have been referred to the Saviour's peculiar regard for this family, as a triumphant refutation—if such were needed. **6. When he had heard**—'When he heard' [ἤκουσεν] **therefore that he was sick, he abode two days still**—rather, 'then [τότε] he abode two days' **in the [same] place where he was.** Beyond all doubt this was just to let things come to their worst, in order to the display of His glory. But how trying, meantime, to the faith of his friends, and how unlike the way in which love to a dying friend usually shows itself, on which it is plain that Mary reckoned. But the ways of *divine* are not as the ways of *human* love. Often they are the reverse. When His people are sick, in body or spirit, when their case is waxing more and more desperate every day, when all hope of recovery is about to expire—just then and therefore it is that "*He abides two days still in the same place where He is.*" Can they still hope against hope? Often they do not; but "this is their infirmity." For it is His chosen style of acting. We have been well taught it, and should not *now* have the lesson to

8 into Judea again. *His* disciples say unto him, Master, [e]the Jews of late
9 sought to stone thee; and goest thou thither again? Jesus answered,
Are there not twelve hours in the day? [f]If any man walk in the day,
10 he stumbleth not, because he seeth the light of this world. But [g]if a man
11 walk in the night, he stumbleth, because there is no light in him. These
things said he: and after that he saith unto them, Our friend Lazarus
12 [h]sleepeth; but I go, that I may awake him out of sleep. Then said his
13 disciples, Lord, if he sleep, he shall do well. Howbeit Jesus spake of his
death: but they thought that he had spoken of taking of rest in sleep.
14, Then said Jesus unto them plainly, Lazarus is dead. And I am glad for
15 your sakes that I was not there, to the intent ye may believe; neverthe-
16 less let us go unto him. Then said Thomas, which is called Didymus,
unto his fellow-disciples, Let us also go, that we may die with him.
17 Then when Jesus came, he found that he had *lain* in the grave four

A. D. 33.

[e] ch. 10. 31.
[f] Ps. 97. 11. Ps. 119. 105, 130. Pro. 4. 18. Pro. 6. 23. Pro. 13. 9. ch. 9. 4.
[g] Job 12. 24. Ps. 27. 2. ch. 12. 35.
[h] Deut. 31. 16. Dan. 12. 2. Matt. 9. 24. Acts 7. 60. 1 Cor. 15. 18, 51.

learn. From the days of Moses was it given sublimely forth as the character of His grandest interpositions, that "the Lord will judge His people, and repent Himself for His servants—*when He seeth that their power is gone*" (Deut. xxxii. 36). **7. Then after that saith he to his disciples, Let us go into Judea again**—out of Peræa where He now was. **8. His disciples say unto him, Master, the Jews of late sought** [νῦν ἐζήτουν]—rather, 'were but now seeking' **to stone thee** (see ch. x. 31); **and goest thou thither again?**—to certain death, as *v.* 16 shows they thought. **9. Jesus answered, Are there not twelve hours in the day? If any man walk in the day, he stumbleth not, because he seeth the light of this world. 10. But if a man walk in the night, he stumbleth, because there is no light in him** [τὸ φῶς οὐκ ἔστιν ἐν αὐτῷ]—or 'because the light is not in him.' See on ch. ix. 4. Our Lord's day had now reached its eleventh hour, and having till now "walked in the day," He would not *mis-time* the remaining and more critical part of His work, which would be as fatal, He says, as omitting it altogether; for "if *a man*"—so He speaks, putting Himself under the same great law of duty as all other men—if a man "walk in the night, he stumbleth, because the light is not in him." **11. These things said he: and after that he saith, Our friend Lazarus**—illustrious title from such Lips! To Abraham only did the Lord under the Old Testament accord this, and not till hundreds of years after his death (2 Chr. xx. 7; Isa. xli. 8); to which, as something very unusual, our attention is called in the New Testament (Jas. ii. 23). When Jesus came in the flesh, His forerunner applied this name, in a certain official sense, to himself (ch. iii. 29); and into the same fellowship the Lord's chosen disciples are declared to have come (ch. xv. 13-15). *Lampe* well remarks that the phrase here employed—"our friend Lazarus"—means more than "he whom *Thou* lovest" (*v.* 3); for it implies that Christ's affection was *reciprocated* by Lazarus. **sleepeth** [κεκοίμηται]—or 'has fallen asleep;' **but I go, that I may awake him out of sleep.** Our Lord had been told only that Lazarus was "sick." But the change which his two days' delay had produced is here tenderly alluded to. Doubtless, His heart was all the while with His dying, and now dead "friend." The symbol of "sleep" for *death* is common to all languages, and familiar to us in the Old Testament. In the New Testament, however, a higher meaning is put into it, in relation to believers in Jesus (see on 1 Thes. iv. 14)—a sense hinted at, and pretty clearly too, in Ps. xvii. 15, as *Luthardt* remarks; and the "awaking out of sleep" acquires a corresponding sense far transcending bare resuscitation. **12. Then said his disciples, Lord, if he sleep, he shall do well** [σωθήσεται]—literally, 'be saved' or 'preserved'—that is, 'shall recover:' and if so, why run the risk of going to Judea? **13. Howbeit Jesus spake of his death: but they thought that he had spoken of taking of rest in sleep. 14. Then said Jesus unto them plainly, Lazarus is dead.** 'In the language of heaven,' says *Bengel* beautifully, 'sleep is the death of the saints; but this language the disciples here understood not. Incomparable is the generosity of the divine manner of discoursing; but such is the slowness of men's apprehension that Scripture often has to descend to the more miserable style of human discourse. (See Matt. xvi. 11, &c.)' **15. And I am glad for your sakes that I was not there.** This, as is finely remarked by *Luthardt*, certainly implies that if He had been present, Lazarus would not have died; not because He could not have resisted the importunities of the sisters, but because, in presence of the personal Life, death could not have reached His friend. And *Bengel* again makes this exquisite remark, that it is beautifully congruous to the divine decorum that in presence of the Prince of Life no one is ever said to have died. **to the intent ye may believe.** This is added to explain His "gladness" at not having been present. His friend's death, as such, could not have been to Him "joyous;" the sequel shows it was "grievous;" but "*for them* it was safe" (Phil. iii. 1). **16. Then said Thomas, called Didymus**—or 'the twin.' **Let us also go, that we may die with him.** Lovely spirit, though tinged with some sadness, such as re-appears at ch. xiv. 5, showing the tendency of this disciple to take the *dark* view of things. On a memorable occasion this tendency opened the door to downright, though but momentary, unbelief. (ch. xx. 25.) Here, however, though alleged by many interpreters, there is nothing of the sort. He perceives clearly how this journey to Judea will end, as respects His Master, and not only sees in it peril to themselves, as they all did, but feels as if he could not and cared not to survive His Master's sacrifice to the fury of His enemies. It was that kind of affection which, living only in the light of its Object, cannot contemplate, or has no heart for, life without it.

Martha, Hearing that Jesus was Coming, Goes to Meet Him—Precious Dialogue between These Two (17-27). **17. Then when Jesus came, he found that he had lain in the grave four days.** If he died on the day that the tidings came of his illness; if he was, according to the Jewish custom, buried the same day (see on Luke vii. 12; and Acts v. 5, 6, 10); and if Jesus, after two days' farther stay in Peræa, set out on the day following for Bethany

18 days already. Now Bethany was nigh unto Jerusalem, [1]about fifteen
19 furlongs off. And many of the Jews came to Martha and Mary, to
20 comfort them concerning their brother. Then Martha, as soon as she
heard that Jesus was coming, went and met him: but Mary sat *still* in
21 the house. Then said Martha unto Jesus, Lord, if thou hadst been here,
22 my brother had not died. But I know, that even now, [i]whatsoever thou
23 wilt ask of God, God will give *it* thee. Jesus saith unto her, Thy brother
24 shall rise [j]again. Martha saith unto him, [k]I know that he shall rise again
25 in the resurrection at the last day. Jesus said unto her, I am [l]the resurrection, and the [m]life: he [n]that believeth in me, though he were dead,
26 yet shall he live: and whosoever liveth and believeth in me shall never
27 die. Believest thou this? She saith unto him, Yea, Lord: [o]I believe
that thou art the Christ, the Son of God, which should come into the
world.

28 And when she had so said, she went her way, and called Mary her
29 sister secretly, saying, The Master is come, and calleth for thee. As
30 soon as she heard *that*, she arose quickly, and came unto him. Now
Jesus was not yet come into the town, but was in that place where
31 Martha met him. The Jews then which were with her in the house, and
comforted her, when they saw Mary, that she rose up hastily and went

A. D. 33.

[1] That is, about two miles.
[i] ch. 9. 31.
[j] Dan. 12. 2. 1 Thes. 4. 14. Phil. 3. 21.
[k] Luke 14. 14. ch. 5. 29.
[l] ch. 5. 21. ch. 6. 39, 40, 44. Rom. 8. 11.
[m] ch. 1. 4. ch. 6. 35. ch. 14. 6. Col. 3. 4. 1 John 1. 1, 2. 1 John 5. 11.
[n] ch. 6. 36. 1 John 5. 10.
[o] Matt. 16. 16. ch. 4. 42. ch. 6. 14, 69.

(some ten hours' journey)—that would make out the four days, the first and last being incomplete. (So *Meyer*.) **18. Now Bethany was nigh unto Jerusalem, about fifteen furlongs**—rather less than two miles: this is mentioned to explain the visits of sympathy, noticed in the following words, which the proximity of the two places facilitated. **19. And many of the Jews came** [ἐληλύθεισαν]—rather, 'had come' **to Martha and Mary, to comfort them concerning their brother.** Thus were provided, in a most natural way, so many witnesses of the glorious miracle that was to follow as to put the fact beyond possible question. **20. Then Martha, as soon as she heard that Jesus was coming, went and met him**—true to the *energy* and *activity* of her character, as seen in the beautiful scene recorded by Luke (x. 38-42—on which see exposition): **but Mary sat** [still] **in the house** [ἐκαθέζετο]—literally, 'was sitting in the house;' equally true to her *placid*, *still* character. These undesigned touches charmingly illustrate, not only the minute *historic fidelity* of both narratives, but their *inner harmony*. **21. Then said Martha unto Jesus, Lord, if thou hadst been here, my brother had not died.** As Mary afterwards said the same thing (*v.* 32), it is plain they had made this very natural remark to each other, perhaps many times during these four sad days, and not without having their confidence in His love at times overclouded. Such trials of faith, however, are not peculiar to them. **22. But I know, that even now** [Ἀλλὰ καὶ νῦν οἶδα]—'Nevertheless, even now, I know' **whatsoever thou wilt**—'shalt' **ask of God.** Energetic characters are usually sanguine, the rainbow of hope peering through the drenching cloud. **God will give it thee**—that is, 'even to the restoration of my dead brother to life,' for that plainly is her meaning, as the sequel shows. **23. Jesus saith unto her, Thy brother shall rise again**—purposely expressing Himself in general terms, to draw her out. **24. Martha saith unto him, I know that he shall rise again in the resurrection at the last day:**—*q. d.*, 'But are we never to see him in life till then?' **25. Jesus said unto her, I am the resurrection, and the life:**—*q. d.*, '*The whole power to impart, maintain, and restore* life, resides in Me.' (See on ch. i. 4; v. 21.) What higher claim to supreme Divinity than this grand saying can be conceived? **he that believeth in me, though he were dead** [κἂν ἀποθάνῃ]—'though he die,' **yet shall he live:**—*q. d.*, 'The believer's death shall be swallowed up in life, and his life shall never sink into death.' As death comes by sin, it is His to dissolve it; and as life flows through His righteousness, it is His to communicate and eternally maintain it. (See on Rom. v. 21.) **26. And whosoever liveth and believeth in me shall never die.** The temporary separation of soul and body is here regarded as not even interrupting, much less impairing, the new and everlasting life imparted by Jesus to His believing people. **Believest thou this?** Canst thou take this in? **27. She saith unto him, Yea, Lord: I believe** [Ἐγὼ πεπίστευκα]—'I have believed (and do believe).' The "I" is emphatic—'As for me.' **That thou art the Christ, the Son of God, which should come**—or 'that cometh' **into the world:**—*q. d.*, 'And having *such* faith in Thee, I can believe all which that comprehends.' While she had a glimmering perception that Resurrection, in every sense of the word, belonged to the Messianic office and Sonship of Jesus, she means, by this way of expressing herself, to cover much that she felt her ignorance of—as no doubt appertaining of right to Him.

Mary, being sent for, Comes to Jesus Weeping, followed by sympathizing Jews, who weep too. The spirit of Jesus is deeply moved, and He, weeping also, arrives at the Grave (28-38). **28. And when she had so said, she went her way, and called Mary her sister secretly, saying, The Master is come, and calleth for thee** [πάρεστι καὶ φωνεῖ σε]—'is here, and calleth thee.' The narrative does not give us this charming piece of information, but Martha's words do. **29. As soon as**—or, 'When' [ὡς] **she heard that, she arose quickly, and came unto him** [ἐγείρεται-ἔρχεται]—rather, 'ariseth,' and 'cometh.' Affection for her Lord, assurance of His sympathy, and hope of his interposition, put a spring into her depressed spirit. **30. Now Jesus, &c. 31. The Jews then which were with her in the house, and comforted**—or 'were comforting' her, **when they saw Mary, that she rose up hastily and went out, followed her.** Thus *casually* were provided witnesses of the glorious miracle that followed, witnesses not prejudiced, certainly, *in favour* of Him who wrought it. **saying, She goeth unto the grave to weep there**—according to Jewish practice for some days after burial. **32. Then when**

32 out, followed her, saying, She goeth unto the grave to weep there. Then
when Mary was come where Jesus was, and saw him, she fell down at his
feet, saying unto him, Lord, if thou hadst been here, my brother had not
33 died. When Jesus therefore saw her weeping, and the Jews also weeping
34 which came with her, he groaned in the spirit, and [2]was troubled, and
said, Where have ye laid him? They said unto him, Lord, come
35, and see. Jesus [p]wept. Then said the Jews, Behold how he loved
36, him! And some of them said, Could not this man, [q]which opened the
37 eyes of the blind, have caused that even this man should not have died?
38 Jesus therefore, again groaning in himself, cometh to the grave. It was
a cave, and a stone lay upon it.
39 Jesus said, Take ye away the stone. Martha, the sister of him that
was dead, saith unto him, Lord, by this time he stinketh: for he hath

A. D. 33.

[2] he troubled himself.

[p] Gen. 43. 30. Job 30. 25. Ps. 35. 13. Ps. 119. 136. Isa. 53. 3. Jer. 9. 1. Jer. 13. 17. Luke 19.41. Rom. 12. 15. Heb. 2. 17, 18. Heb. 4. 15.

[q] ch. 9. 6.

Mary was come where Jesus was, and saw him, she fell down at his feet—more impassioned than her sister, though her words were fewer. **saying unto him, Lord, if thou hadst been here, my brother had not died.** See on *v.* 21. **33. When Jesus therefore saw her weeping, and the Jews also weeping which came with her, he groaned in the spirit** [ἐνεβριμήσατο]. The word here is not that usually employed to express groaning. It denotes any 'strong manifestation of inward emotion;' but here it probably means, 'made a visible and powerful effort to check His emotion'—to restrain those tears which were ready to gush from His eyes. **and was troubled** [ἐτάραξεν ἑαυτὸν]—rather, as in the margin, 'troubled Himself;' that is, became mentally agitated. The tears of Mary and her friends acted sympathetically upon Him, and drew forth His emotions. What a vivid outcoming of *real* humanity! **34. And said, Where have ye laid him?** Perhaps it was in order to retain composure enough to ask this question, and on receiving the answer to proceed with them to the spot, that He checked Himself. **They said**—'say' [λέγουσιν] **unto him, Lord, come and see. 35. Jesus wept** [ἐδάκρυσεν]. This beautifully conveys the sublime brevity of the original word; else '*shed tears*' might have better conveyed the difference between the word here used and that twice employed in *v.* 33 [κλαίω], and there properly rendered "weeping"—denoting the loud wail for the dead, while that of Jesus consisted of *silent tears.* Is it for nothing that the Evangelist, some *sixty years* after it occurred, holds up to all ages with such touching brevity the sublime spectacle of *the Son of God in tears?* What a seal of His perfect oneness with us in the most redeeming feature of our stricken humanity! But was there nothing in those tears beyond sorrow for human suffering and death? Could these *effects* move Him without suggesting the *cause?* Who can doubt that in His ear every feature of the scene proclaimed that stern law of the Kingdom, "The wages of *sin* is *death,*" and that this element in His visible emotion underlay all the rest? See on Mark i. 29-31, Remark 2 at the close of that Section. **36. Then said the Jews, Behold how he loved him!** We thank you, O ye visitors from Jerusalem, for this spontaneous testimony to the *human softness* of the Son of God. **37. And** [δὲ]—rather, 'But' **some of them said, Could not this man, which opened the eyes of the blind** [τοῦ τυφλοῦ]—not 'of blind people' generally, but 'of the blind man;' referring to the specific case recorded in the ninth chapter. **have caused that even** [ἵνα καὶ οὗτος]—rather, 'have caused also that' **this man should not have died?** The former exclamation came from the better-feeling portion of the spectators; this betokens a measure of suspicion. It hardly goes the length of attesting the miracle on the blind man, but—'if, as everybody says, He did that, why could He not also have kept Lazarus alive?' As to the restoration of the dead man to life, they never so much as thought of it. But this disposition to dictate to Divine power, and almost to peril our confidence in it upon its doing our bidding, is not confined to men of no faith. **38. Jesus therefore, again groaning in himself**—in the sense explained on *v.* 33. But whereas there the rising emotion which He laboured to check was that of sorrow for suffering and its cause, here it is of sorrow, or something stronger, at the suspicious spirit which breathed through this speech. Yet here, too, the former emotion was the deeper of the two, now that His eye was about to rest on the spot where lay, in the still horrors of death, His *friend.* **cometh to the grave. It**—'Now it' **was a cave**—the cavity, natural or artificial, of a rock. This, with the number of condoling visitors from Jerusalem, and the costly ointment with which Mary afterwards anointed Jesus at Bethany, all go to show that the family were in good circumstances. **and a stone lay upon it**—or 'against it'; for as the Oriental sepulchres of the better classes were hewn out of the rock, the slab which shut them in might be laid either horizontally or perpendicularly.

The Act Preparatory to the Resurrection (39-41). **39. Jesus said**—'saith' [λέγει], **Take ye away the stone.** This, remarks *Grotius,* was spoken to the attendants of Martha and Mary, for it was a work of no little labour. According to the Talmudists, says *Lampe,* quoting from *Maimonides,* it was forbidden to open a grave after the stone was placed upon it. Besides other dangers, they were apprehensive of legal impurity by contact with the dead. Hence they avoided coming nearer a grave than four cubits. But He who touched the leper, and the bier of the widow of Nain's son, rises here also above these Judaic memorials of evils, every one of which He had come to roll away. *Observe here what our Lord did Himself, and what He made others do.* As Elijah himself repaired the altar on Carmel, arranged the wood, cut the victim, and placed the pieces on the fuel, but made the bystanders fill the surrounding trench with water, that no suspicion might arise of fire having been secretly applied to the pile (1 Ki. xviii. 30-35); so our Lord would let the most sceptical see that, without laying a hand on the stone that covered His friend, He could recall him to life. What could be done by human hands He orders to be done, reserving only to Himself what transcended the ability of all creatures. **Martha, the sister of him that was dead**—and as such the proper guardian of the precious remains; the relationship being *here* mentioned to account for her

40 been *dead* four days. Jesus saith unto her, Said I not unto thee, that, if
41 thou wouldest believe, thou shouldest see the glory of God? Then they
took away the stone *from the place* where the dead was laid.
And Jesus lifted up *his* eyes, and said, Father, I thank thee
42 that thou hast heard me. And I knew that thou hearest me always: but [r] because of the people which stand by I said *it*, that
43 they may believe that thou hast sent me. And when he thus had
44 spoken, he cried with a loud voice, Lazarus, [s] come forth. And he that
was dead came forth, bound hand and foot with grave-clothes; and [t] his
face was bound about with a napkin. Jesus saith unto them, Loose him,
and let him go.
45 Then many of the Jews which came to Mary, [u] and had seen the things
46 which Jesus did, believed on him. But some of them went their ways to
the Pharisees, and told them what things Jesus had done.
47 Then [v] gathered the chief priests and the Pharisees a council, and said,

A. D. 33.

[r] ch. 12. 30.
[s] Deut. 32. 39. 1 Sam. 2. 6. Ps. 33. 9. Luke 7. 14. Luke 8. 54. Acts 3. 15. Acts 9. 40. Rom. 4. 17.
[t] ch. 20. 7.
[u] ch. 2. 23. ch. 10. 42. ch. 12. 11, 18.
[v] Ps. 2. 2. Matt. 26. 3. Mark 14. 1. Luke 22. 2.

venturing gently to remonstrate against their exposure, in a state of decomposition, to eyes that had loved him so tenderly in life. **saith unto him, Lord, by this time he stinketh: for he hath been [dead] four days.** (See on *v.* 17.) It is wrong to suppose from this, as *Lampe* and others do, that, like the bystanders, she had not thought of his restoration to life. But certainly the glimmerings of hope which she cherished from the first (*v.* 22), and which had been brightened by what Jesus said to her (*vv.* 23-27), had suffered a momentary eclipse on the proposal to expose the now sightless corpse. *To such fluctuations all real faith is subject in dark hours*—as the example of *Job* makes sufficiently manifest. **40. Jesus saith unto her, Said I not unto thee, that, if thou wouldest believe, thou shouldest see the glory of God?** He had not said those very words; but that was the scope of all that He had uttered to her about His life-giving power (*vv.* 23, 25, 26)—a gentle yet emphatic and most instructive rebuke: 'Why doth the restoration of life, even to a decomposing corpse, seem hopeless in presence of the Resurrection and the Life? Hast thou yet to learn that "if thou canst believe, all things are possible to him that believeth"'? (Mark ix. 23). **41. Then they took away the stone from the place where the dead was laid.**

The Preparatory Prayer (41, 42). **41. And Jesus lifted up his eyes** [ἦρε—ἄνω]. The attitude is somewhat emphatically expressed—'lifted His eyes upward,' marking His calm solemnity (compare ch. xvii. 1). **and said, Father, I thank thee thou hast heard me** [ἤκουσας]—rather, 'heardest me;' referring, as we think, to a specific prayer offered by Him, probably on intelligence of the case reaching Him (*vv.* 3, 4); for His living and loving oneness with the Father was maintained and manifested in the flesh, not merely by the spontaneous and uninterrupted outgoing of Each to Each in spirit, but by specific actings of faith and exercises of prayer about each successive case as it emerged. He prayed, as *Luthardt* well says, 'not for what He wanted, but for the manifestation of what He had;' and having the bright consciousness of the answer in the felt liberty to ask it, and the assurance that it was at hand, He gives thanks for this with a grand simplicity before performing the act. **42. And**—or rather, 'Yet' **I knew that thou hearest me always: but because of the people** [διὰ τὸν ὄχλον]—or 'for the sake of the multitude' **which stand by**—or 'stand around' [περιεστῶτα], **I said it, that they may believe that thou hast sent me.** Instead of praying now, He simply gives thanks for answer to prayer offered ere He left Peræa, and adds that His doing even this, in the audience of the people, was not from any doubt of the prevalency of His prayers in any case, but to show the people that *He did nothing without His Father, but all by direct communication with Him.*

The Resurrection-Act (43, 44). **43. And when he thus had spoken, he cried with a loud voice, Lazarus, come forth.** On one other occasion only did He this—on the *Cross.* His last utterance was a "loud cry" (Matt. xxvii. 50). "He shall not *cry,*" said the prophet; nor, in His ministry, did He cry. What a sublime contrast is this "loud cry" to the magical "whisperings" and "mutterings" of which we read in Isa. viii. 19, 20. As *Grotius* well remarks, it is second only to the grandeur of that voice which shall raise all the dead (ch. v. 28, 29; 1 Thess. iv. 16). **44. And he that was dead came forth, bound hand and foot with grave-clothes; and his face was bound about with a napkin.**

The Act Disengaging the Risen Man (44). **44. Jesus saith unto them, Loose him, and let him go.** Jesus will no more do this Himself than roll away the stone. As the one was the necessary *preparation* for resurrection, so the other was the necessary *sequel* to it. THE LIFE-GIVING ACT ALONE HE RESERVES TO HIMSELF. Even so in the quickening of the dead to spiritual life, human instrumentality is employed first to *prepare the way,* and then to *turn it to account.*

The Effects of this Miracle on Two Classes (45, 46). **45. Then many**—or, 'Many therefore' **of the Jews which came**—or 'had come' **to Mary**—as sympathizing friends, **and had seen the things which Jesus did, believed on him.** These were of the *candid* class, on whom the effect of so stupendous a miracle, done before their own eyes, could not but be resistless. See on ch. xii. 9-11. **46. But some of them went their ways to the Pharisees, and told them what things Jesus had done.** These were of the *prejudiced* class, whom no evidence would convince. These two classes continually re-appear in the Gospel History; nor is there ever any great work of God which does not produce both.

The Chief Priests and Pharisees, Alarmed at the Convincing Effect of His Miracles, Resolve in Council to put Jesus to Death (47-53). **47. Then**—or, 'Therefore,' in consequence of the intelligence brought them of this last and grandest of the Lord's miracles, **gathered the chief priests and the Pharisees a council, and said, What do we? for this man doeth many miracles. 48. If we let him thus alone, all men will believe on him: and the Romans shall come and take away both our place and nation:**—*q. d.*, 'While we trifle, this

48 [w]What do we? for this man doeth many miracles. If we let him thus
alone, all *men* will believe on him: and [x]the Romans shall come and take
49 away both our place and nation. And one of them, *named* [y]Caiaphas,
being the high priest that same year, said unto them, Ye know nothing
50 at all, nor [z]consider that it is expedient for us, that one man should die
51 for the people, and that the whole nation perish not. And this spake he
not of himself: but being high priest that year, he prophesied that Jesus
52 should die for that nation; and [a]not for that nation only, [b]but that also
he should gather together in one the children of God that were scattered
abroad.
53 Then from that day forth they took counsel together for to put him to
54 death. Jesus [c]therefore walked no more openly among the Jews; but went
thence unto a country near to the wilderness, into a city called [d]Ephraim,
and there continued with his disciples.
55 And [e]the Jews' passover was nigh at hand: and many went out of
the country up to Jerusalem before the passover, to purify [f]themselves.
56 Then [g]sought they for Jesus, and spake among themselves, as they stood
57 in the temple, What think ye, that he will not come to the feast? Now
both the chief priests and the Pharisees had given a commandment,
that, if any man knew where he were, he should show *it*, that they might
take him.

A. D. 33.

w ch. 12. 19. Acts 4. 16.
x Dan 9. 26.
y Luke 3. 2. ch. 18. 14.
z ch. 18. 14. ch. 19. 12.
a Isa. 49. 6. 1 John 2. 2.
b ch. 10. 16. Acts 13. 47. Gal. 3. 28. Eph. 3. 6. 1 Pet. 5. 9.
c ch. 4. 1, 3.
d 2 Chr. 13. 19.
e ch. 2. 13. ch. 5. 1. ch. 6. 4.
f Gen. 35. 2. Ex. 19. 10. Num. 9. 6. 1 Sam. 16. 5. Job 1. 5. Ps. 26. 6. Acts 24. 18.
g ch. 7. 11.

man, by his many miracles, will carry all before him; the popular enthusiasm will bring on a revolution, which will precipitate the Romans upon us, and our all will go down in one common ruin.' What a testimony to the reality of our Lord's miracles, and their resistless effect, from His bitterest enemies! But how low the considerations are by which their whole decision is influenced—the fear of a national break-up, which would endanger their own position and interests! **49. And one of them, named Caiaphas, being the high priest that same year, said unto them, Ye know nothing at all, 50. Nor consider that it is expedient for us, that one man should die for the people, and that the whole nation perish not.** He meant nothing more than that there was no use in discussing the matter, since the right course was obvious: the way to prevent the apprehended ruin of the nation was to make a sacrifice of the Disturber of their peace. But in giving utterance to this suggestion of political expediency, he was so guided as to give forth a Divine prediction of deep significance; and God so ordered it that it should come from the lips of the high priest for that memorable year, the recognized head of God's visible people, whose ancient office, symbolized by the Urim and Thummim, was to decide, in the last resort, all vital questions as the oracle of the Divine will. **51. And**—or, 'Now' **this spake he not of himself: but being high priest that year, he prophesied that Jesus should die for that**—or rather, 'the' **nation** [τοῦ ἔθνους]; **52. And not for that**—'the' **nation only, but that also he should gather together in one the children of God that were**—or 'are' **scattered abroad.** This is one of those explanatory remarks of our Evangelist himself, which we have had once and again to notice as one of the characteristics of his Gospel. **53. Then**—or, 'Therefore' **from that day forth they took council together for to put him to death.**

Jesus, in consequence of this, Goes into comparative Retirement (54). **54. Jesus therefore walked no more openly among the Jews.** How could He, unless He had wished to die before His time? **but went thence unto a**—or rather, 'the' **country** [τὴν χώραν] **near to the wilderness**—of Judea, **into a city called Ephraim, and there continued**—or 'tarried' [διέτριβε] **with his disciples.** What this city of Ephraim was, and where precisely it was, is not agreed. But *Robinson* and *Stanley* identify it with a small village now called *Taijibeh*, about twenty miles north of Jerusalem.

Preparations for the approaching Passover, and Speculation whether Jesus will come to it (55-57). **55. And**—or, 'Now' **the Jews' passover was nigh at hand**—the *fourth*, according to our reckoning, during our Lord's public ministry; that at which He became "our Passover, sacrificed for us." **and many went out of the country up to Jerusalem before the passover, to purify themselves**—from any legal uncleanness which would have disqualified them from keeping the feast (see Num. ix. 10, &c.; 2 Chr. xxx. 17, &c.) This is mentioned to introduce the graphic statement which follows. **56. Then sought they for Jesus, and spake**—or 'said' [ἔλεγον] **among themselves, as they stood in the temple, What think ye, that he will not come to the feast?** giving forth their various conjectures and speculations about the probability of His coming or not coming to the feast. **57. Now [both] the chief priests and the Pharisees.** The word "both" [καί] should be excluded, as clearly not genuine. **had given a commandment, that, if any man knew where he were, he should show it, that they might take him.** This is mentioned to account for the conjectures whether He would come, in spite of this determination to seize Him.

Remarks.—1. We have already remarked, that as the Resurrection of Lazarus and the opening of the eyes of the Man Born Blind were the most wonderful of all our Lord's miracles, so it is precisely these two miracles which are recorded with the minutest detail, and which stand attested by evidence the most unassailable. One argument only has scepticism been able to urge against the credibility of these miracles—the entire silence of the First Three Evangelists regarding them. But even if we were unable to account for that silence, the positive evidence by which these miracles are attested can in no degree be affected by it. And then this silence of the First Three Evangelists embraces *the whole Judæan ministry* of our Lord, from the very beginning of it down to His Final Entry into Jeru-

12 THEN Jesus, six days before the passover, came to Bethany, [a]where
2 Lazarus was which had been dead, whom he raised from the dead. There
[b]they made him a supper; and Martha served: but Lazarus was one of
them that sat at the table with him.
3 Then took [c]Mary a pound of ointment of spikenard, very costly, and
anointed the feet of Jesus, and wiped his feet with her hair: and the
4 house was filled with the odour of the ointment. Then saith one of his
5 disciples, Judas Iscariot, Simon's *son*, which should betray him, Why was
not this ointment sold for three hundred pence, and given to the poor?
6 This he said, not that he cared for the poor; but because he was a thief,
7 and [d]had the bag, and bare what was put therein. Then said Jesus, Let
8 her alone: against the day of my burying hath she kept this. For [e]the
poor always ye have with you; but me ye have not always.
9 Much people of the Jews therefore knew that he was there: and they
came not for Jesus' sake only, but that they might see Lazarus also,
10 whom he had raised from the dead. But [f]the chief priests consulted that
11 they might put Lazarus also to death; because [g]that by reason of him
many of the Jews went away, and believed on Jesus.

A. D. 33.

CHAP. 12.
[a] ch. 11. 1, 43.
[b] Matt. 26. 6. Mark 14. 3.
[c] Song 1. 12. Song 4. 13. Luke 10. 38, 39. ch. 11. 2.
[d] Pro. 26. 25. Pro. 28. 20, 22. ch. 13. 29. Eph. 5. 5.
[e] Deut. 15. 11. Matt. 26. 11. Mark 14. 7.
[f] Pro. 1. 16. Pro. 4. 16. Luke 16. 31.
[g] Mark 15. 10. ch. 11. 45. Acts 13. 45.

salem. So that if this be any argument against the two miracles in question, it is an argument rather against the entire credibility of the Fourth Gospel—to which we have adverted in the Introduction. 2. If the resurrections from the dead were the most divine of all the miracles which our Lord performed, this resurrection of Lazarus was certainly the most divine of the three recorded in the Gospel History. On the great lesson which it teaches, even more gloriously than the other two, see on Mark v. 21-43, Remark 5 at the close of that Section. But 3. The true nature of all these resurrections must be carefully observed. They were none of them a resurrection from the dead to "die no more." They were a mere *reanimation of the mortal body*, until in the course of nature they should die again, to sleep till the Trumpet shall sound, and with all other sleeping believers awake finally to resurrection-life. 4. Did Jesus suffer the case of Lazarus to reach its lowest and most desperate stage before interposing, and his loving sisters to agonize and weep until their faith in His own power and love, which had done nothing all that time to arrest the hand of death and corruption, had been tried to the uttermost? What is this, but an illustration—the most signal, indeed, yet but one more illustration—of a feature observable in most of His miracles, where *only after all other help was vain* did He Himself step in? In so acting, is it necessary to say that He did but serve Himself Heir, so to speak, to God's own ancient style of procedure towards His people? (See Deut. xxxii. 36; Isa. lix. 16). And will not this help to assure us that "to the upright there ariseth light in the darkness"? (Ps. cxii. 4). 5. We have seen in Christ's tears over impenitent Jerusalem The Weeping *Saviour:* in Christ's tears over the grave of Lazarus we see The Weeping *Friend.* And just as in the other case, though the tears which bedewed those Cheeks at the sight of impenitence are now no more, He is not even in heaven, at the sight of similar impenitence, insensible to the feeling that drew them forth here below: so when some dear Lazarus has fallen asleep, and his Christian relatives and friends are weeping over his bier and at his grave, we are not to be chilled by the apprehension that Jesus in the heavens merely looks on and drops comfort into the wounded heart—Himself all void of sympathetic emotion—but are warranted to assure ourselves that His heart there is quite as tender and warm, and quite as quick in its sensibilities, as ever it showed itself to be here; or, in language that will come better home to us, that "we have not an High Priest that cannot," even now, "be touched with the feeling of our infirmities, but was in all points tried like as we are, yet without sin," and this on very purpose to acquire experimentally the capacity to identify Himself to perfection, in feeling as well as in understanding, with the whole circle of our trials. What rivers of divine consolation, O ye suffering disciples of the Lord Jesus, are there here opened up for you! Drink, then, yea, drink abundantly, O beloved! 6. What a commentary is the determined and virulent resistance even of such evidence, by the ruling Jewish party, on those words of the Parable of the Rich Man and Lazarus—"If they hear not Moses and the prophets, neither will they be persuaded though one rose from the dead!"

CHAP. XII. 1-11.—THE SUPPER AND THE ANOINTING AT BETHANY, SIX DAYS BEFORE THE PASSOVER—THE DEATH OF LAZARUS PLOTTED, TO ARREST THE ACCESSIONS TO CHRIST IN CONSEQUENCE OF HIS RESURRECTION. (= Matt. xxvi. 6-13; Mark xiv. 3-9.)

The Supper and the Anointing at Bethany (1-8). For the exposition of this portion, see on Mark xiv. 3-9, and Remarks 1 to 8 at the close of that Section.

The Death of Lazarus is Plotted, to arrest the Triumphs of Jesus in consequence of his Resurrection (9-11). **9. Much people of the Jews therefore knew that he was there: and they came not for Jesus' sake only, but that they might see Lazarus also, whom he had raised from the dead. 10. But the chief priests consulted that they might put Lazarus also to death; 11. Because that by reason of him many of the Jews went away, and believed on Jesus.** Crowds of the Jews of Jerusalem hastened, it seems, to Bethany (scarce two miles distant), not so much to see Jesus, whom they knew to be there, as to see the dead Lazarus who had been raised to life. This, as was to be expected, issued in immense accessions to Christ (*v.* 19); and, as the necessary means of arresting these triumphs of the hated One, a plot is laid against the life of Lazarus also:—to such a pitch had these ecclesiastics come of diabolical determination not only to shut out the light from their own minds, but to extinguish it from the earth!

For Remarks on these three verses, see those on ch. xi.

12 On [h]the next day much people that were come to the feast, when they
13 heard that Jesus was coming to Jerusalem, took branches of palm trees,
and went forth to meet him, and cried, [i]Hosanna: Blessed *is* the King of
14 Israel that cometh in the name of the Lord. And Jesus, when he had
15 found a young ass, sat thereon; as it is written, Fear [j]not, daughter of
16 Sion: behold thy King cometh, sitting on an ass's colt. These things
[k]understood not his disciples at the first: [l]but when Jesus was glorified,
[m]then remembered they that these things were written of him, and *that*
they had done these things unto him.
17 The people therefore that was with him when he called Lazarus out of
18 his grave, and raised him from the dead, bare record. For this cause the
people also met him, for that they heard that he had done this miracle.
19 The Pharisees therefore said among themselves, Perceive ye how ye prevail
nothing? behold, the world is gone after him.
20 And there [n]were certain Greeks among them [o]that came up to worship
21 at the feast: the same came therefore to Philip, which was of Bethsaida
22 of Galilee, and desired him, saying, Sir, we would see Jesus. Philip
cometh and telleth Andrew: and again Andrew and Philip tell Jesus.
23 And Jesus answered them, saying, The [p]hour is come, that the Son of
24 man should be glorified. Verily, verily, I say unto you, [q]Except a corn
of wheat fall into the ground and die, it abideth alone: but if it die, it
25 bringeth forth much fruit. He [r]that loveth his life shall lose it; and he
26 that hateth his life in this world shall keep it unto life eternal. If any

A. D. 33.
h Luke 19.35.
i Ps. 72. 17-19. Ps. 118. 25. Matt. 21. 9, 11. Matt. 23. 39. Mark 11. 8, 10. 1 Tim. 1. 17.
j Isa. 62. 11. Mic. 4. 8. Zeph. 3. 16. Zec. 9. 9.
k Luke 18. 34. Luke 24. 25.
l ch. 7. 39. Heb. 1. 3.
m ch. 14. 26.
n Acts 17. 4.
o 1 Ki. 8. 41. Acts 8. 27.
p ch. 13. 32. ch. 17. 1.
q 1 Cor. 15. 36. Heb. 2. 10. 1 John 4. 14. Rev. 5. 9.
r Luke 9. 24. Luke 17. 33.

12-19.—CHRIST'S TRIUMPHAL ENTRY INTO JERUSALEM, ON THE FIRST DAY OF THE WEEK. (= Matt. xxi. 1-9; Mark xi. 1-11; Luke xix. 29-40.) For the exposition, see on Luke xix. 29-40.

20-50.—JESUS IS INFORMED THAT CERTAIN GREEKS DESIRE TO SEE HIM—THE EXALTED DISCOURSE AND THE MYSTERIOUS SCENE WHICH FOLLOWED THEREUPON—GENERAL RESULTS OF CHRIST'S MINISTRY, AND CONCLUDING SUMMARY OF HIS PUBLIC TEACHING.

Jesus, being informed that certain Greeks Desire to See Him, Discourses in an exalted strain on the great truths which that circumstance suggested (20-26). **20. And**—or, 'Now' [δὲ] **there were certain Greeks** ["Ελληνες]—not Grecian Jews ['Ελληνισται] but Greek or Gentile proselytes to the Jewish faith, who were wont to attend the annual festivals, and particularly this primary one—the Passover. **21. The same came therefore to Philip, which was of**—or 'from' [ἀπὸ] **Bethsaida.** Possibly they came from the same quarter. **and desired**—'requested' or 'prayed' **him, saying, Sir, we would see Jesus**—certainly with far higher objects than Zaccheus (Luke xix. 3). Perhaps our Lord was then in that part of the temple-court to which Gentile proselytes had no access. These men from the *west*, as *Stier* says, represent, at the end of Christ's life what the wise from the *east* represented at the beginning: only these come to the Cross of the King, while those came to His Manger. **22. Philip cometh and telleth Andrew.** As fellow-townsmen of Bethsaida, these two seem to have drawn to each other. **and again Andrew and Philip tell Jesus**—or, according to the reading adopted by *Lachmann*, *Tischendorf*, and *Tregelles*, 'Andrew and Philip come and tell Jesus,' [ἔρχεται 'Α. καὶ Φ. καὶ λέγουσιν 'Ι.] The minuteness of these details, while they add to the graphic force of the narrative, serve to prepare us for something important to come out of this introduction. **23. And**—or, 'But' [δὲ] **Jesus answered them, saying, The hour is come, that the Son of man should be glorified:**—*q. d.*, 'They would see Jesus, would they? Yet a little moment, and they shall see Him so as now they dream not of. The middle wall of partition that keeps them out from the commonwealth of Israel is on the eve of breaking down, "and I, if I be lifted up from the earth, shall draw all men unto Me:" I see them "flying as a cloud, and as doves to their cots," and a glorious event for the Son of Man will that be, by which this is to be brought about.' It is His *death* He thus sublimely and delicately alludes to. Lost in the scenes of triumph which this desire of the Greeks to see Him called up before His view, He gives no direct answer to their petition for an interview, but sees that cross which was to bring them in gilded with glory. **24. Verily, verily, I say unto you, Except a corn**—or 'grain' [κόκκος] **of wheat fall into the ground and die, it abideth alone** [αὐτὸς μόνος μένει]—'by itself alone,' **but if it die, it bringeth forth much fruit.** The *necessity* of His death is here brightly expressed, and its proper operation and fruit—*life springing forth out of death*—imaged forth by a beautiful and deeply significant law of the vegetable kingdom. For a double reason, no doubt, this was uttered—to explain what He had said of His death, as the hour of His own glorification, and to sustain His own spirit under the agitation which was mysteriously coming over it in the view of that death. **25. He that loveth his life shall lose it; and he that hateth his life in this world shall keep it unto life eternal.** (See on Matt. xvi. 21-28). Did our Lord mean to exclude Himself from the operation of the great principle here expressed—*self-renunciation the law of self-preservation; and its converse, self-preservation the law of self-destruction?* On the contrary, as He became Man to exemplify this fundamental law of the Kingdom of God in its most sublime form, so the very utterance of it on this occasion served to sustain His own spirit in the double prospect to which He had just alluded. **26. If any man serve me, let him follow me; and where I am, there shall also my servant be: If any man serve me, him will my Father honour.** Jesus, it will be observed, here claims the same absolute subjection to Himself, as the law of men's exaltation to honour, as He yielded to the Father.

man serve me, let him follow me; and [s]where I am, there shall also my
servant be: if any man serve me, him will *my* Father honour.
27 Now [t]is my soul troubled; and what shall I say? Father, save me
28 from this hour: [u]but for this cause came I unto this hour. Father,
glorify thy name. [v]Then came there a voice from heaven, *saying*, I
29 have both glorified *it*, and will glorify *it* again. The people therefore
that stood by, and heard *it*, said that it thundered: others said, An
30 angel spake to him. Jesus answered and said, [w]This voice came not
31 because of me, but for your sakes. Now is the judgment of this world:
32 now shall [x]the prince of this world be cast out. And I, if I be lifted up
33 from the earth, will draw [y]all *men* unto me. (This he said, signifying
what death he should die.)

A. D. 33.

s 1 Thes. 4. 17.
t Luke 12. 50. ch. 13. 21.
u Luke 22. 53.
v 2 Pet. 1. 17.
w ch. 11. 42.
x Luke 10. 18. ch. 14. 30. ch. 16. 11. Acts 26. 18. 2 Cor. 4. 4. Eph. 2. 2. Eph. 6. 12.
y Rom. 5. 18.

Mysterious Agitation of Christ's Spirit in prospect of His Death—His Prayer in consequence, and the Answer to it—Jesus Interprets that Answer (27-36). **27. Now is my soul troubled.** He means, at the prospect of His death, just alluded to. Strange view of the Cross this, immediately after representing it as the hour of His glory! (*v.* 23.) But the two views naturally meet, and blend into one. It was the Greeks, one might say, that troubled Him:—'Ah! they shall see Jesus, but *to Him* it shall be a costly sight.' **and what shall I say?** He is in a strait betwixt two. The death of the Cross was, and could not but be, appalling to His soul. But to shrink from absolute subjection to the Father, was worse still. In asking Himself, "What shall I say?" He seems as if thinking aloud, feeling His way between two dread alternatives, looking both of them sternly in the face, measuring, weighing them, in order that the choice actually made might be seen, *and even by Himself be the more vividly felt*, to be a profound, deliberate, spontaneous election. **Father, save me from this hour**—To take this as a question, 'Shall I say, Father, save Me', &c.—as some eminent editors and interpreters do, is unnatural and jejune. It is a real petition, like that in Gethsemane, "Let this cup pass from Me;" only whereas *there* He prefaces the prayer with an "If it be possible," *here* He follows it up with what is tantamount to that—**but for this cause came I unto this hour.** The sentiment conveyed, then, by the prayer, in both cases, is two-fold: First, that only one thing could reconcile Him to the death of the Cross—its being His Father's will that He should endure it—and, next, that in this view of it He yielded Himself freely to it. He recoils, not from subjection to His Father's will, but to show how tremendous a self-sacrifice that obedience involved, He first asks the Father to save Him from it, and then signifies how perfectly He knows that He is there for the very purpose of enduring it. Only by letting these mysterious words speak their full meaning do they become intelligible and consistent. As for those who see *no bitter elements in the death of Christ*—nothing beyond mere dying—what can they make of such a scene? and when they place it over against the feelings with which thousands of His adoring followers have welcomed death for His sake, how can they hold Him up to the admiration of men? **28. Father, glorify thy name**—by some present testimony. **Then came there a voice from heaven, saying, I have both glorified it**—referring specially to the voice from heaven at His *Baptism*, and again at His *Transfiguration*, **and will glorify it again**—that is, in the yet future scenes of His still deeper necessity; although even this very promise was a present and sublime testimony, which would irradiate the clouded spirit of the Son of Man. **29. The people**—'the multitude' [ὄχλος] **therefore that stood by, and heard it, said that it thundered: others said, An angel spake**—'hath spoken' [λελάληκεν] **to him**—some hearing only a sound; others an articulate, but to them unintelligible, voice. Our Lord now tells them for whom that voice from heaven had come, and then interprets, in a strain even more exalted than before, that "glorification of His name" which the voice announced was yet to take place. **30. Jesus answered, This voice came not because of me, but for your sakes**—[οὐ δι' ἐμὲ, ἀλλὰ δι' ὑμᾶς]—'not for My sake, but for your sakes:' probably to correct, in the first instance, the unfavourable impressions which His momentary agitation and mysterious prayer for deliverance may have produced on the beholders; and then to procure a more reverential ear for those sublime disclosures with which He was now to follow it up—disclosures which seem to have all at once dilated His own soul, for He utters them, it will be seen, in a kind of transport. **31. Now is the judgment of this world**—the world that "crucified the Lord of glory" (1 Cor. ii. 8), considered as a vast and complicated kingdom of Satan, breathing his spirit, doing his work, and involved in his doom, which Christ's death by its hands irrevocably sealed. **Now shall the prince of this world be cast out.** How differently is that fast-approaching "hour" regarded in the kingdoms of darkness and of light! 'The hour of relief from the dread Troubler of our peace—how near it is! Yet a little moment, and the day is ours!' So it was calculated and felt in the one region. "Now shall the prince of this world be cast out," is a somewhat different view of the same event. We know who was right. Though yet under a veil, He sees the triumphs of the Cross in unclouded and transporting light. **32. And I** [Κἀγὼ], **if I be lifted up from the earth, will draw all men unto me.** The "I" here is emphatic: I, in contrast with the world's ejected prince. "If lifted up," means not only *after that I have been lifted up*, but, *through the virtue of that Uplifting*. And does not the death of the Cross in all its significance, revealed in the light, and borne in upon the heart by the power, of the Holy Ghost, possess an attraction over the wide world—to civilized and savage, learned and illiterate alike—which breaks down all opposition, assimilates all to itself, and forms out of the most heterogeneous and discordant materials a kingdom of surpassing glory, whose uniting principle is adoring subjection "to Him that loved them"?—"Will draw all men 'UNTO ME,'" says He [πρὸς ἐμαυτὸν], or 'to Myself,' as it might more properly be rendered. What lips could presume to utter such a word but His, which "dropt as an honeycomb," whose manner of speaking was evermore in the same spirit of conscious equality with the Father? **33. (This he said, signifying what death** [ποίῳ θανάτῳ]—rather, 'what kind'

34 The people answered him, [z]We have heard out of the law that Christ
abideth for ever: and how sayest thou, The Son of man must be lifted up?
35 who is this Son of man? Then Jesus said unto them, Yet a little while
[a]is the light with you. [b]Walk while ye have the light, lest darkness
come upon you: for [c]he that walketh in darkness knoweth not whither
36 he goeth. While ye have light, believe in the light, that ye may be [d]the
children of light. These things spake Jesus, and departed, and did hide
himself from them.
37 But though he had done so many miracles before them, yet they
38 believed not on him: that the saying of Esaias the prophet might be
fulfilled, which he spake, [e]Lord, who hath believed our report? and to
39 whom hath the arm of the Lord been revealed? Therefore they could
40 not believe, because that Esaias said again, He [f]hath blinded their eyes,
and hardened their heart; that they should not see with *their* eyes, nor
understand with *their* heart, and be converted, and I should heal them.
41 These things said Esaias, when [g]he saw his glory, and spake of him.
42 Nevertheless among the chief rulers also many believed on him; but
because of the Pharisees they did not confess *him*, lest they should be
43 put out of the synagogue: for [h]they loved the praise of men more than
the praise of God.

A. D. 33.

[z] 2 Sam. 7. 13. Ps. 89. 36. Ps. 110. 4. Isa. 9. 7. Isa. 53. 8. Ezek. 37. 25. Dan. 2. 44. Mic. 4. 7.
[a] Isa. 42. 6. ch. 1. 9. ch. 8. 12. ch. 9. 5.
[b] Jer. 13. 16. Eph. 5. 8.
[c] ch. 11. 10. 1 John 2. 11.
[d] Luke 16. 8. Eph. 5. 8. 1 Thes. 5. 5.
[e] Isa. 53. 1. Rom. 10. 16.
[f] Isa. 6. 9. Matt. 13. 14.
[g] Isa. 6. 1.
[h] ch. 5. 44.

or 'manner of death' **he should die**)—that is, His being "lifted up from the earth" was meant to signify His being uplifted on the accursed tree (ch. iii. 14; viii. 28).

34. The people—'The multitude' [ὄχλος] **answered him, We have heard out of the law**—meaning the Scriptures of the Old Testament: referring, no doubt, to such places as Ps. lxxxix. 28, 29; cx. 4; Dan. ii. 44; vii. 13, 14, **that Christ**—'the Christ,' the promised Messiah, **abideth for ever: and how sayest thou, The Son of man must be lifted up? who is this Son of man?** How can that consist with this "uplifting?" They saw very well both that He was holding Himself up as *the Christ*, and *a Christ to die a violent death;* and as that ran counter to all their ideas of the Messianic prophecies, they were glad to get this seeming advantage to justify their unyielding attitude. **35. Then**—'Therefore' **Jesus said unto them, Yet a little while is the light with you. Walk while ye have the light, lest darkness come upon you: for**—rather, 'and' [καί] **he that walketh in darkness knoweth not whither he goeth. 36. While ye have** ('the') **light, believe in the light, that ye may be the children of light.** Instead of answering their question, He warns them, with mingled majesty and tenderness, against trifling with their last brief opportunity, and entreats them to let in the Light while they had it in the midst of them, that themselves might be "light in the Lord." In this case all the clouds which hung around His Person and Mission would speedily be dispelled, while if they continued to hate the light, bootless were all His answers to their merely speculative or captious questions. (See on Luke xiii. 23.) **These things spake Jesus, and departed, and did hide himself from them.** He who spake as never man spake, and immediately after words fraught with unspeakable dignity and love, had to "hide Himself" from His auditors! What, then, must *they* have been? He retired probably to Bethany. (See Matt. xxi. 17; Luke xxi. 37.)

General Result of Christ's Ministry (37-43). It is the manner of our Evangelist alone, as has been frequently remarked, to record his own reflections on the scenes he describes: but here, having arrived at what was virtually the close of our Lord's public ministry, he casts an affecting glance over the fruitlessness of His whole ministry on the bulk of the now doomed people. **37. But though he had done so many miracles** [σημεῖα] **before them**—which were all but so many glorious "signs" of a Divine Hand in the doing of them, **yet they believed not on him: 38. That the saying of Esaias the prophet might be fulfilled, which he spake** (Isa. liii. 1), **Lord, who hath believed our report? and to whom hath the arm of the Lord been revealed?**—*q. d.*, 'This unbelief did not at all set aside the purposes of God, but, on the contrary, fulfilled them.' **39. Therefore they could not believe, because that Esaias said again** (Isa. vi. 9, 10), **40. He hath blinded their eyes, and hardened their heart; that they should not see with their eyes, nor understand with their heart, and be converted, and I should heal them.** That this expresses *a positive divine act*, by which those who wilfully close their eyes and harden their hearts against the truth are judicially *shut up* in their unbelief and impenitence, is admitted by all candid critics—*Olshausen*, for example—though many of them think it necessary to contend that this is no way inconsistent with the liberty of the human will, which of course it is not. **41. These things said Esaias, when he saw his glory, and spake of him.** A key of immense importance to the opening of Isaiah's vision (Isa. vi.), and all similar Old Testament representations. 'THE SON,' says *Olshausen*, 'is "The King Jehovah" who rules in the Old Testament and appears to the elect, as in the New Testament THE SPIRIT, the invisible Minister of the Son, is the Director of the Church and the Revealer in the sanctuary of the heart.' **42. Nevertheless among the chief rulers also** [καὶ ἐκ τῶν ἀρχόντων]—rather, 'even of the rulers,' such as Nicodemus and Joseph, **many believed on him; but because of the Pharisees**—that is, the *leaders* of this sect; for they were of it themselves **they did not confess** [**him**]—or 'confess it' [οὐχ ὡμολόγουν], did not make an open confession of their faith in Jesus, **lest they should be put out of the synagogue.** (See on ch. ix. 22, 34.) **43. For they loved the praise of men more than the praise of God.** A severe remark, as *Webster and Wilkinson* justly observe, considering that several at least of these persons afterwards boldly confessed Christ. It indicates the displeasure with which God regarded their con-

44 Jesus cried and said, [i]He that believeth on me, believeth not on me,
45 but on him that sent me. And [j]he that seeth me seeth him that sent
46 me. I [k]am come a light into the world, that whosoever believeth on me
47 should not abide in darkness. And if any man hear my words, and
believe not, [l]I judge him not: for [m]I came not to judge the world, but
48 to save the world. He [n]that rejecteth me, and receiveth not my words,
hath one that judgeth him: the [o]word that I have spoken, the same shall
49 judge him in the last day. For [p]I have not spoken of myself; but the
Father which sent me, he gave me a commandment, what I should say,
50 and what I should speak. And I know that his commandment is life
everlasting: whatsoever I speak therefore, even as the Father said unto
me, so I speak.

A. D. 33.

[i] Mark 9. 37. 1 Pet. 1. 21.
[j] ch. 14. 9.
[k] ch. 3. 19. ch. 8. 12. ch. 9. 5, 39.
[l] ch. 5. 45. ch. 8. 15.
[m] ch. 3. 17.
[n] Luke 10.16.
[o] Deut. 18. 19. Mark 16.16.
[p] ch. 8. 38. ch. 14. 10.

duct at this time, and with which He continues to regard similar conduct.

Concluding Summary of our Lord's Public Teaching (44-50). **44. Jesus** ['I. δὲ]—rather, 'But Jesus' **cried**—expressive of the louder tone and peculiar solemnity with which He was wont to utter such great sayings as these (as ch. vii. 37). **and said.** This and the remaining verses of the chapter seem to be a supplementary record of some weighty proclamations, which, though recorded in substance already, had not been set down in so many words before; and they are introduced here as a sort of *summary and winding up* of His whole testimony. **He that believeth on me, believeth not on me, but on him that sent me. 45. And he that seeth me seeth him that sent me** [θεωρῶν—θεωρεῖ]—or 'beholdeth,' in the emphatic sense of ch. vi. 40. But what a saying is this! Even the Eleven, so late as at the Last Supper, were slow to apprehend the full reality of it (ch. xiv. 7-9). The glory of it they could but partially discern till Pentecostal light irradiated the Person and Mediation of Jesus in the eyes of His apostles. **46. I am come a light into the world, that whosoever believeth on me should not abide in darkness. 47. And if any man hear my words, and believe not** [πιστεύσῃ]. The true reading here, beyond doubt, is, 'and keep them not' [φυλάξῃ], **I judge him not: for I came not to judge the world, but to save the world.** See on ch. iii. 17. **48. He that rejecteth me, and receiveth not my words, hath one that judgeth him: the word that I have spoken, the same shall judge him in the last day.** This in substance will be found said repeatedly before. **49. For I have not spoken**—'spake not' [ἐλάλησα] **of** [ἐξ] **myself; but the Father which sent me, he gave me a commandment, what I should say, and what I should speak. 50. And I know that his commandment is life everlasting: whatsoever I speak therefore, even as the Father said**—or 'hath said' [εἴρηκε] **unto me, so I speak.** See on ch. viii. 28, 38, 47; and similar sayings, emphatically teaching what is here expressed in such terms of majestic dignity.

Remarks.—1. Once and again have we been led to consider what portion of this wonderful History most transcends the powers of human invention. And ever as we seem to have found it, some other portion rises to view and claims the preference. But certainly, of the present Section it may fearlessly be said that, to be *written*, it, at least, must of necessity first have been *real*. For who, sitting down to *frame* such a Life—or what is much the same in relation to powers of invention, to construct it out of a few fragments of fact—would have thought of meeting the desire of those Greeks to see Jesus with such an answer, taking no direct notice of it, but carrying His hearers into the future glorious issues of His death, yet couching even this in such enigmatic terms as to be scarcely half intelligible to the best instructed of His own disciples? Or, if we are to suppose this possible, who would think of interrupting this strain by a sudden inward agitation of the Speaker arising from no outward cause, but the pure result of what was passing in His own mind; and not only so, but of His *telling* His uninstructed and prejudiced audience that His soul was then agitated, and, amidst conflicting emotions, that He was at a loss what to say; uttering an audible prayer to be saved from His dread approaching "hour," but yet adding that to go through with that hour was just what He had come to it for? Who would have ever put so apparently damaging a thing down in a work which he expected to make way for itself by nothing but *its naked truth?* And then, after the prayer for glorification, with the immediate answer to it, and the explanation of that answer—as if relieved in proportion to the previous sinking—who could have thrown such gleams of exalted, sublime transport into the utterances that follow, and on which only the subsequent history of Christendom has set the seal of full truth? And let it be borne in mind, that if the truth of the History here is thus self-attested, it is the History precisely *as it stands;* not 'the substance' or 'spirit of it'—as some now talk—but this Evangelical Record, just as it here stands; for *entire* it must stand, or fall entire. 2. On the bearing of this agitation of the Redeemer's spirit in the prospect of His "hour," of His prayer for deliverance from it, and yet His submission to it, upon the *penal* character of His sufferings and death, we need but refer the reader to the remarks on that feature of His Agony in the Garden—of which this scene was a kind of momentary anticipation. See on Luke xxii. 39-46. 3. How affecting is the intimation that, just after the utterance of one of the most solemn and compassionate warnings—holding out, almost for the last time, in that spot at least, the sceptre of mercy, but at the same time the danger of closing their eyes upon the Light yet shining on them—He "departed, and did hide himself from them!" What must have been the exasperation of His audience to render that necessary. The Evangelist himself seems saddened at the thought of it, and can find relief under it for himself and his believing readers only in the judicial blindness and hardness which they had been long before taught by prophecy to expect. Nor are those who, in analogous circumstances, have to hold up in vain the glory of Christ, and all day long to stretch out their hands to a disobedient and gainsaying people, precluded from finding the same sad relief; but on the contrary, with their adorable Master, they may confidently say to them that believe not—when conscious that they are pure from the blood of all men, having not shunned

13 NOW before the feast of the passover, when Jesus knew that his hour
was come that he should depart out of this world unto the Father,
having loved his own which were in the world, he loved them unto the
2 end. And supper being ended, (the [a]devil having now put into the
3 heart of Judas Iscariot, Simon's *son*, to betray him,) Jesus knowing [b]that

A. D. 33.

CHAP. 13.
[a] Luke 22. 3.
[b] ch. 3. 35.
ch. 17. 2.
Acts 2. 36.

to declare unto them all the counsel of God—"But I said unto you that ye have even seen Him, and believe not: All that the Father giveth Him *shall* come to Him, and him that cometh to Him He will in no wise cast out." 4. Though a timid policy on the part of real believers is often overruled to the getting in of some faint dissent and some feeble protest against extreme measures on the part of those enemies of it to whose society they still adhere—as in the case of Nicodemus and Joseph of Arimathæa—that timid policy itself is highly offensive to God, and injurious to their own spiritual growth, springing as it does from a greater concern to stand well with men than with God. 5. The eternal condition of all who have heard the Gospel, whatever other elements may be found to affect it, will be found essentially to turn on the state of their minds and hearts towards Christ—in the way either of cordial subjection to Him or of disobedient rejection of Him. "He that is not with Me is against Me," will be the spirit of the decisions of "That Day" on all that have been brought within the pale of the Gospel.

CHAP. XIII. 1-38.—AT THE LAST SUPPER JESUS WASHES HIS DISCIPLES' FEET—THE DISCOURSE ARISING THEREUPON, IN THE MIDST OF WHICH THE TRAITOR, BEING INDICATED, LEAVES THE SUPPER-ROOM—THE DISCOURSE RESUMED—PETER'S SELF-CONFIDENCE—HIS FALL PREDICTED. The record of our Lord's public ministry has now been concluded—in the First Three Gospels by a solemn leave-taking of the *Temple*, until then "His Father's House" and the centre of all the Church's solemnities; in this Fourth Gospel by an equally solemn leave-taking of the *People*, in whom until then God's visible kingdom had stood represented. We are now in the Supper-room; the circumstances preparatory to which our Evangelist presumes his readers to be already familiar with through the other Gospels. What passed in this Supper-room, as recorded in this and the four following chapters, has been felt by the Church in every age to be stamped with a heavenly and divine impress, beyond all else even in this most divine Gospel, if one may so speak, and the glory of which no language can express.

Jesus, at the Supper-Table, Washes His Disciples' Feet (1-11). **1. Now before the feast of the passover.** This raises the question whether our Lord ate the passover with His disciples *at all* the night before He suffered; and if so, whether He did so *on the same day* with other Jews or *a day earlier*. To this question we adverted in the Remarks prefixed to the exposition of Luke xxii. 7-13, where we expressed it as our unhesitating conviction that He did eat it, and on the same day with others. That the First Three Evangelists expressly state this, admits of no reasonable doubt; and it is only because of certain expressions in the Fourth Gospel that some able critics think themselves bound to depart from that opinion. So *Greswell* and *Ellicott*, for example; while, among others, *Robinson*, *Wieseler*, and *Fairbairn* defend the opinion which we have expressed. Now, as this is the first of the passages in the Fourth Gospel which are thought to intimate that the "supper" which our Lord observed, if a passover at all, was "before the feast of the passover," as regularly observed, let us see how that is to be met. One way of meeting it is by understanding "the feast" here to mean, not the Paschal supper, but the seven days' "Feast of Unleavened Bread"—which began on the 15th Nisan, and was ushered in by the eating of the Passover on the 14th. (See Num. xxviii. 16, 17.) So *Robinson*. In this case the difficulty indeed vanishes. But there is no need to resort to that explanation, which seems somewhat unnatural. Understanding the Evangelist to refer to the Paschal supper itself, the meaning seems to be, not '*a day* before the passover,' but simply that '*ere* the feast began,' Jesus made solemn preparation for doing at it what is about to be recorded. We know from the other Gospels what precise directions Jesus gave to two of His disciples about getting ready the passover in the large upper room ere He and the other ten left Bethany. (See on Luke xxii. 7-13.) And what deep thoughts on the subject were passing in the mind of our Lord Himself in connection with these arrangements, we are here very sublimely told by our Evangelist (*vv.* 1, 2). See also on Luke xxii. 14-16. The meaning, then, we take it, is simply this, that Jesus, when He proceeded to wash His disciples' feet during the Paschal supper, did so not only with great deliberation, but in conformity with purposes and arrangements "before the feast." So substantially *Stier* and *Fairbairn*. **when Jesus knew that his hour was come that he should depart out of this world unto the Father.** On such beautiful euphemistic allusions to the Redeemer's death, see on Luke ix. 31, 51. **having loved his own which were in the world, he loved them unto the end.** That is, on the edge of His last sufferings—when it might have been supposed that His own awful prospects would absorb all His attention—He was so far from forgetting "His own," who were to be left struggling "in the world," after He had "departed out of it to the Father" (ch. xvii. 11), that in His care for them He seemed scarce to think of Himself save in connection with them. Herein is "love," not only enduring "to the end," but most affectingly manifested when, judging by a human standard, least to be expected. **2. And supper being ended** [γενομένου]. In this rendering our translators have followed *Luther* and *Beza*, but unfortunately, since from *v.* 26 it seems plain that the supper was not even then ended. The meaning either is, 'And supper being prepared,' or 'And supper going on.' So the same word is used, as *Alford* notices, in Matt. xxvi. 6, "While Jesus was in Bethany" [γενομένου], and in ch. xxi. 4, "when it was morning" [πρωΐας γενομένης]. [Of course, this must be the meaning if the reading γινομένου—in the present tense—be adopted, with *Tischendorf* and *Tregelles*. But the authority for it is scarcely so strong, we judge, as for the received reading, to which *Lachmann* adheres, and in which *Alford* concurs.] **(the devil having now** [ἤδη]—or rather 'already' **put into the heart of Judas Iscariot, Simon's son, to betray him)**—referring to the compact he had *already* made with the chief priests (see on Mark xiv. 10, 11). **3. Jesus knowing that the Father had given all things into his hands, and that he was come from God, and went to God** [ἐξῆλθεν—ὑπάγει]

the Father had given all things into his hands, and that he was come
4 from God, and went to God; he [c]riseth from supper, and laid aside his
5 garments; and took a towel, and girded himself. After that he poureth
water into a bason, and began to wash the disciples' feet, and to wipe
6 *them* with the towel wherewith he was girded. Then cometh he to Simon
Peter: and [1]Peter saith unto him, Lord, [d]dost thou wash my feet?
7 Jesus answered and said unto him, What I do thou knowest not now;
8 but thou shalt know hereafter. Peter saith unto him, Thou shalt never
wash my feet. Jesus answered him, [e]If I wash thee not, thou hast no
9 part with me. Simon Peter saith unto him, Lord, not my feet only, but
10 also *my* hands and *my* head. Jesus saith to him, [f]He that is washed
needeth not save to wash *his* feet, but is clean every whit: and [g]ye are
11 clean, but not all. For he knew who should betray him; therefore said
he, Ye are not all clean.

A. D. 33.

c Luke 22.27. Phil. 2. 7, 8.
1 he.
d Matt. 3. 14.
e Ezek. 36.25. ch. 3. 5. 1 Cor. 6. 11. Eph. 5. 26. Titus 3. 5. Heb. 10. 22.
f Eccl 7. 20. Eph. 4. 22-24. Eph. 5. 26, 27. 1 Thes. 5. 23.
g ch. 15. 3.

—or 'came forth from God, and was going to God.' This verse is very sublime, and as a preface to what follows, were we not familiar with it, would fill us with a delightful wonder. An unclouded perception of His essential relation to the Father, the commission He held from Him, and His approaching Return to Him, possessed His soul. **4. He riseth from supper, and laid**—rather, 'layeth' [τίθησι] **aside his garments**—which would have impeded the operation of washing, **and took a towel, and girded himself**—assuming a servant's dress. **5. After that he poureth water into a**—'the' **bason, and began**—or 'proceeded' **to wash the disciples' feet.** Three different words are used in Greek to express 'washing,' in three different senses; and all three are used in the New Testament. The *first* [νίπτω—a late form of νίζω] signifies to wash a part of the body,' as the *hands* (Mark vii. 3) and the *feet.* This accordingly is the word used here, and five other times in the verses following, of the washing of the feet. The *second* [λούω, λούεσθαι] signifies to 'wash the whole body,' as in a bath; to '*bathe.*' This accordingly is the word warily used in *v.* 10, of the washing of the entire person. The *third* [πλύνω] signifies to 'wash *clothes.*' This accordingly is used in Rev. vii. 14—"These are they that washed [ἔπλυναν] their robes;" and in ch. xxii. 14, according to what appears the true reading—"Blessed are they that wash their robes" [οἱ πλύνοντες τὰς στολὰς αὐτῶν], &c. The importance of distinguishing the first two will appear when we come to *v.* 10. **and to wipe them with the towel wherewith he was girded.** *Beyond all doubt the feet of Judas were washed*, as of all the rest. **6. Then cometh he to Simon Peter: and Peter saith unto him, Lord, dost thou wash my feet?** Our language cannot bring out the intensely vivid contrast between the "*Thou*" [σὺ] and the "*my*" [μου], which by bringing them together the original expresses. But every word of this question is emphatic. Thus far, and in the question itself, there was nothing but the most profound and beautiful astonishment at a condescension to him quite incomprehensible. Accordingly, though there can be no doubt that already Peter's heart rebelled against it as a thing not to be borne, Jesus ministers no rebuke as yet, but only bids him wait a little, and he should understand it all. **7. Jesus answered and said unto him, What I do thou knowest not now:**—*q. d.*, 'Such condescension *does* need explanation; it *is* fitted to astonish;' **but thou shalt know hereafter** [μετὰ ταῦτα]—lit., 'after these things,' meaning 'presently;' although viewed as a general maxim, applicable to all dark sayings in God's word, and dark doings in God's providence, these words are full of consolation. **8. Peter saith unto him, Thou shalt never wash**—more emphatically, 'Never shalt thou wash' **my feet:**—*q. d.*, 'That is an incongruity to which I can never submit.' How like the man! **Jesus answered him, If I wash thee not, thou hast no part with me.** What Peter could not submit to was, that the Master should serve His servant. But the whole saving work of Christ was one continued series of such services, only ending with and consummated by the most self-sacrificing and transcendent of all services: "THE SON OF MAN CAME not to be ministered unto, but TO MINISTER, AND TO GIVE HIS LIFE A RANSOM FOR MANY." (See on Mark x. 45.) If Peter, then, could not submit to let his Master go down so low as to wash his feet, *how should he suffer himself to be served*—and so saved—*by Him at all?* This is couched under the one pregnant word "wash," which though applicable to the *lower* operation which Peter resisted, is the familiar scriptural symbol of that *higher* cleansing, which Peter little thought he was at the same time virtually putting from him. It is not humility to refuse what the Lord deigns to do for us, or to deny what He has done, but it is self-willed presumption—not rare, however, in those inner circles of lofty religious profession and traditional spirituality, which are found wherever Christian truth has enjoyed long and undisturbed possession. The truest humility is to receive reverentially, and thankfully to own, the gifts of grace. **9. Simon Peter saith unto him, Lord, not my feet only, but also my hands and my head:**—*q. d.*, 'To be severed from Thee, Lord, is death to me: If that be the meaning of my speech, I tread upon it; and if to be washed of Thee have such significance, then not my feet only, but hands, head, and all, be washed!' This artless expression of clinging, life-and-death attachment to Jesus, and felt dependence upon Him for his whole spiritual well-being, compared with the similar saying in ch. vi. 68, 69 (on which see exposition), furnishes such evidence of *historic verity* as no thoroughly honest mind can resist. **10. Jesus saith to him, He that is washed** [λελουμένος]—not in the *partial* sense denoted by the word used for the washing of the *feet*, but in the complete sense denoted by the word here used, signifying to *wash the entire person;* as if we should render it, 'he that is bathed:' **needeth not**—to be *so* washed any more; needeth no *such* washing a second time. **save to wash** [νίψασθαι] **his feet**—that is, 'needeth to do no more than wash his feet;' the former word being now resumed. **but is clean every whit** [καθαρὸς ὅλος]—'clean as a whole,' or entirely clean. This

12 So after he had washed their feet, and had taken his garments, and was
set down again, he said unto them, Know ye what I have done to you?
13, Ye [h]call me Master and Lord: and ye say well; for *so* I am. If [i]I then,
14 *your* Lord and Master, have washed your feet, [j]ye also ought to wash
15 one another's feet. For [k]I have given you an example, that ye should
16 do as I have done to you. Verily, [l]verily, I say unto you, The servant
is not greater than his lord; neither he that is sent greater than he that
17 sent him. If [m]ye know these things, happy are ye if ye do them.
18 I speak not of you all: [n]I know whom I have chosen: but, that the
scripture may be fulfilled, [o]He that eateth bread with me hath lifted
19 up his heel against me. [2]Now I tell you before it come, that, when it
20 is come to pass, ye may believe that I am *he.* Verily, [p]verily, I say
unto you, He that receiveth whomsoever I send receiveth me; and
he that receiveth me receiveth him that sent me.
21 When [q]Jesus had thus said, [r]he was troubled in spirit, and testified,
and said, Verily, verily, I say unto you, That [s]one of you shall betray

A. D. 33.

h Luke 6. 46. 1 Cor. 8. 6. 1 Cor. 12. 3. Phil 2. 11.
i Luke 22.27.
j Rom. 12. 10. Gal. 6. 1. 1 Pet. 5. 5.
k Phil. 2. 5. 1 Pet. 2. 21.
l Luke 6. 40.
m Jas. 1. 25.
n 2 Tim. 2. 19.
o Ps. 41. 9.
2 henceforth.
p Luke 10.16.
q Luke 22.21.
r ch. 12. 27.
s Acts 1. 17.

sentence is singularly instructive. Of the *two cleansings*, the one points to that which takes place at the *commencement* of the Christian life, embracing *complete absolution from sin as a guilty state*, and *entire deliverance from it as a polluted life* (Rev. i. 5; 1 Cor. vi. 11)—or, in the language of theology, *Justification* and *Regeneration.* This cleansing is effected *once for all*, and is never repeated. The other cleansing, described as that of "the feet," is such, for example, as one walking from a bath quite cleansed still needs, in consequence of his contact with the earth. (Compare Exod. xxx. 18, 19.) It is the *daily* cleansing which we are taught to seek, when in the spirit of adoption we say, "Our Father which art in heaven—*forgive us our debts;*" and, when burdened with the sense of manifold shortcomings—as what tender heart of a Christian is not?—is it not a relief to be permitted thus to wash our feet after a day's contact with the earth? This is not to call in question the completeness of our past justification. Our Lord, while graciously insisting on washing Peter's feet, refuses to extend the cleansing farther, that the symbolical instruction intended to be conveyed might not be marred. **and ye are clean**—in the first and *whole* sense, **but not all** [ἀλλ' οὐχὶ πάντες]—'yet not all;' **11. For, &c.** A very important statement; as showing that Judas—instead of being at first as true-hearted a disciple as the rest, and merely *falling away* afterwards, as many represent it—*never experienced that cleansing at all which made the others what they were.*

Discourse Explanatory of this Washing (12-17). **12. So after he had washed their feet, and had taken his garments, and was set down again, he said unto them, Know ye what I have done to you?**—that is, 'Know ye the intent of it?' The question, however, was not intended to draw forth an answer, but, like many other of our Lord's questions, to summon their attention to His own answer. **13. Ye call me Master and Lord** [ὁ διδάσκαλος και ὁ Κύριος]—'Teacher and Lord;' *learning* of Him in the one capacity, *obeying* Him in the other: **and ye say well; for so I am.** The conscious dignity with which this claim is made is remarkable, following immediately on His laying aside the towel of service. Yet what is this whole history but a succession of such astonishing contrasts from first to last? **14. If I then, your Lord and Master, have washed your feet**—O ye *servants*, **ye also**—who are but fellow-servants, **ought to wash one another's feet**—not in the narrow sense of a literal washing, profanely caricatured by Popes and Emperors, but by the very humblest *real* services one to another. **15. For I have given you an example, that ye should do as I have done to you. 16. Verily, verily, I say unto you, The servant is not greater than his lord; neither he that is sent greater than he that sent him.** An oft-repeated saying (see on Matt. x. 24). **17. If ye know these things, happy are ye if ye do them.** A hint that even among real Christians the *doing* of such things would come lamentably short of the *knowing.*

The Traitor is now Indicated (18-27). **18. I speak not of you all**—the "happy *are* ye," of *v.* 17, being on no supposition applicable to Judas. **I know whom I have chosen**—in the *higher* sense: **but, that the scripture may be fulfilled:**—*q. d.*, 'Wonder not that one has been introduced into your number who is none of Mine: it is by no accident; there is no mistake; it is just that he might fulfil his predicted destiny.' **He that eateth bread with me**—"that did eat of *my bread*" (Ps. xli. 9), as one of My family; admitted to the nearest familiarity of discipleship and of social life, **hath lifted up his heel against me**—turned upon Me, adding *insult* to injury. (Compare Heb. x. 29.) In the Psalm the immediate reference is to Ahithophel's treachery against David (2 Sam. xvii.); one of those scenes in which the parallel of his story with that of his great Antitype is exceedingly striking. 'The eating bread,' says *Stier* (with whom, as with others who hold that Judas partook of the Lord's Supper, we agree), derives a fearful meaning from the participation in the sacramental Supper, a meaning which must be applied for ever to all unworthy communicants, as well as to all betrayers of Christ who eat the bread of His Church.' **19. Now** ['Απ' ἄρτι]—rather, 'From henceforth' **I tell you before it come**—consider yourselves as from this time forewarned, **that, when it is come to pass**—instead of being staggered, **ye may believe that I am he**—rather, confirmed in your faith: and indeed this did come to pass when they deeply needed such confirmation. **20. Verily, verily, I say unto you, He that receiveth whomsoever I send receiveth me; and he that receiveth me receiveth him that sent me.** See on Matt. x. 40. The connection here seems to be that despite the dishonour done to him by Judas, and similar treatment awaiting themselves, they were to be cheered by the assurance that their office, even as His own, was divine. **21. When Jesus had thus said, he was troubled in spirit, and testified, and said, Verily, verily, I say unto you, That one of you shall betray me.** The

22 me. Then the disciples looked one on another, doubting of whom he
23 spake. Now [t]there was leaning on Jesus' bosom one of his disciples,
24 whom Jesus loved. Simon Peter therefore beckoned to him, that he
25 should ask who it should be of whom he spake. He then lying on Jesus'
26 breast saith unto him, Lord, who is it? Jesus answered, He it is to
whom I shall give a [3]sop, when I have dipped *it*. And when he had
27 dipped the sop, he gave *it* to Judas Iscariot, *the son* of Simon. And
[u]after the sop Satan entered into him. Then said Jesus unto him, That
28 thou doest, do quickly. Now no man at the table knew for what intent
29 he spake this unto him. For some *of them* thought, [v]because Judas had
the bag, that Jesus had said unto him, Buy *those things* that we have
need of against the feast; or, that he should give something to the poor.

A. D. 33.

t 2 Sam. 12. 3. ch. 1. 18. ch. 19. 26. ch. 20. 2. ch. 21. 7.

3 Or, morsel. Ex. 12. 8.

u Ps. 109. 6. Mark 12. 45. Luke 22. 3. ch. 6. 70. Acts 5. 3.

v ch. 12. 6.

announcement of *v.* 18 seems not to have been plain enough to be quite apprehended, save by the traitor himself. He will therefore speak it out in terms not to be misunderstood. But how much it cost Him to do this, appears from the "trouble" that came over His "spirit"—visible emotion, no doubt—before He got it uttered. What wounded susceptibility does this disclose, and what exquisite delicacy in His social intercourse with the Twelve, to whom He cannot, without an effort, break the subject! **22. Then the disciples looked one on another, doubting**—or 'being in doubt' **of whom he spake.** Further intensely interesting particulars are given in the other Gospels. First, "They were exceeding sorrowful" (Matt. xxvi. 22). Second, "They began to enquire among themselves which of them it was that should do this thing" (Luke xxii. 23). Third, "They began to say unto Him one by one, Is it I? and another, Is it I?" (Mark xiv. 19). Generous, simple hearts! They abhorred the thought, but, instead of putting it on others, each was only anxious to purge *himself*, and know if *he* could be the wretch. Their putting it at once to Jesus Himself, as knowing doubtless who was to do it, was the best, as it certainly was the most spontaneous and artless, evidence of their own innocence. Fourth, Jesus—apparently while this questioning was going on—added, "The Son of Man goeth as it is written of Him: but woe unto that man by whom the Son of Man is betrayed! it had been good for that man if he had not been born" (Matt. xxvi. 24). Fifth, "Judas," *last of all*, "answered and said, *Lord, Is it I?*" evidently feeling that when all were saying this, if he were to hold his peace, that of itself would draw suspicion upon him. To prevent this the question is wrung out of him, but perhaps, amidst the stir and excitement at the table, in a half-suppressed tone—as we are inclined to think the answer also was—"Thou hast said" (Matt. xxvi. 25), or possibly by little more than a sign; for from *v.* 28, below, it is evident that till the moment when he went out he was not openly discovered. **23. Now there was leaning on Jesus' bosom** [ἀνακείμενος]—that is, next Him at the table, and so "on" or 'in His bosom' [ἐν τῷ κόλπῳ] **one of his disciples, whom Jesus loved.** As Jesus certainly loved all the Eleven, this must mean a peculiar, dear love which Jesus had for John. (Compare ch. xi. 3, 4, of Lazarus.) Once and again does our Evangelist thus denote himself. Doubtless it was on account of this love that Jesus placed him next to Himself—in His own bosom—at the table. But it is alluded to here to explain the facility which he had, from his position, of asking his Lord quietly whom He meant. **24. Simon Peter therefore beckoned**—'beckoneth' [νεύει] **to him, that he should ask who it should**—or 'might' **be of whom he spake.** Perhaps Peter reclined at the corresponding place on the other side of Jesus. **25. He then lying** [ἐπιπεσὼν]—'leaning over' or 'leaning back' **on Jesus' breast, saith unto him**—evidently *in a whisper*, **Lord, who is it? 26. Jesus answered**—'answereth,' clearly also *inaudibly;* the answer being conveyed probably from behind to Peter by John. **He it is to whom I shall give a sop** [τὸ ψωμίον]—rather, 'the sop' **when I have dipped it**—meaning a piece of the bread soaked in the wine or the sauce of the dish; one of the ancient ways of testifying peculiar regard. Compare *v.* 18, "*He that eateth bread with me.*" **And when he had dipped the sop, he gave**—or 'giveth' [δίδωσιν] **it to Judas Iscariot, the son of Simon.** Thus the sign of Judas' treachery was an affecting expression, and the last, of the Saviour's wounded love! **27. And after the sop Satan** [τότε]—'then' or 'straightway Satan' **entered into him.** Very solemn are these brief hints of the successive steps by which Judas reached the climax of his guilt. "The devil had already put it into his heart to betray his Lord." Yet who can tell what struggles he went through ere he brought himself to carry that suggestion into effect? Even after this, however, his compunctions were not at an end. With the thirty pieces of silver already in his possession, he seems still to have quailed—and can we wonder? When Jesus stooped to wash his feet, it may be the last struggle was reaching its crisis. But that word of the Psalm, about "one that did eat of His bread who would lift up his heel against Him," probably all but turned the dread scale, and the still more explicit announcement, that one of those sitting with Him at the table should betray Him, would beget the thought, 'I am detected; it is now too late to draw back.' At that moment the sop is given, by which offer of friendship was once more made—and how affectingly! But already "Satan has *entered into him*," and though the Saviour's act might seem enough to recall him even yet, hell is now in his bosom, and he says within himself, 'The die is cast; now let me go through with it; fear, begone!' See on Mark xiv. 1-11, Remark 8 at the close of that Section; also on Luke xi. 24-26.

The Traitor Leaves the Supper-Room (27-30).

27. Then said—'saith' [λέγει] **Jesus unto him, That thou doest, do quickly:**—*q. d.*, 'Why linger here? This is not the place for thee; thy presence here is a restraint to us and to thee alike; thy work stands still; thou hast already the wages of iniquity—go work for them.' **28. Now no man at the table knew for what intent he spake this unto him. 29. For some of them thought, because Judas had the bag, that Jesus had said unto him, Buy those things that we have need of against the feast; or, that he should give something to the poor.** A very important statement, showing how carefully Jesus had kept the secret, and Judas his hypocrisy, to the last. **30. He then having received the sop went immediately out**—

30 He then having received the sop went immediately out: and it was
night.
31 Therefore, when he was gone out, Jesus said, Now is the Son of man
32 glorified, and [w]God is glorified in him. If [x]God be glorified in him, God
shall also glorify him in himself, and shall straightway glorify him.
33 Little children, yet a little while I am with you. Ye shall seek me:
and as I said unto the Jews, Whither I go, ye cannot come; so now I
34 say to you. A [y]new commandment I give unto you, That ye love one
35 another; as I have loved you, that ye also love one another. By this
shall all *men* know that ye are my disciples, if ye have [z]love one to another.
36 Simon Peter said unto him, Lord, whither goest thou? Jesus answered
him, Whither I go, thou canst not follow me now; but [a]thou shalt
37 follow me afterwards. Peter said unto him, Lord, why cannot I follow

A. D. 33.

w ch. 14. 13. 1 Pet. 4. 11

x ch. 17. 1.

y Lev. 19. 18. Gal 6. 2. Eph. 5. 2. 1 Thes. 4. 9. Jas. 2. 8. 1 Pet. 1. 22. 1 John 2. 7. 1 John 3. 11. 1 John 4. 21. 2 John 5.

z Acts 2. 46.

a ch. 21. 18. 2 Pet. 1. 14.

thus, by his own act and deed, severing himself *for ever* from that holy society with which he never had any spiritual sympathy: **and it was night**—but far blacker night in the soul of Judas than in the sky over his head.

Relieved of the Traitor's Presence, the Discourse is Resumed (31-35). **31. Therefore, when he was gone out, Jesus said**—'saith' [λέγει], **Now is the Son of man glorified.** These remarkable words plainly imply that up to this moment our Lord had spoken *under a painful restraint;* the presence of a traitor within the little circle of His holiest fellowship on earth preventing the free and full outpouring of His heart. This is evident, indeed, from those oft-recurring clauses, "Ye are not all clean," "I speak not of you all," &c. "Now" the restraint is removed, and the embankment which kept in the mighty volume of living waters having broken down, they burst forth in a torrent which only ceases on His leaving the Supper-room and entering on the next stage of His great work—the scene in the Garden. But with what words is the silence first broken on the departure of Judas? By no reflections on the traitor, and, what is still more wonderful, by no reference to the dread character of His own approaching sufferings. He does not even name them, save by announcing, as with a burst of triumph, that the hour of His *glory* has arrived! And what is very remarkable, in five brief clauses He repeats this word "glorify" *five times*, as if to His view a coruscation of glories played at that moment about the Cross. (See on ch. xii. 23.) **and God is glorified in him**—the glory of each reaching its zenith in the death of the Cross! **32. If God be glorified in him, God shall also**—in return and reward of this highest of all services ever rendered to Him, or capable of being rendered, **glorify him in himself, and shall straightway glorify him**—referring now to the Son's Resurrection and Exaltation *after* this service was over, including all the honour and glory then put upon Him, and that will for ever encircle Him as Head of the new creation. **33. Little children** [Τεκνία]. From the height of His own glory He now descends, with sweet pity, to His "little children," *all now His own.* This term of endearment, nowhere else used in the Gospels, and once only employed by Paul (Gal. iv. 19), is appropriated by the beloved disciple himself, who no fewer than seven times employs it in his first Epistle. **yet a little while I am with you. Ye shall seek me**—shall feel the want of Me: **and as I said unto the Jews** (ch. vii. 34; viii. 21). A remarkable word this here—"the Jews." The Eleven were all themselves Jews. But now that He and they were on a higher footing, He leaves the name to those who were *Jews, and nothing but Jews.* **Whither I go, ye cannot come; so now I say to you.** But, O, in what a different sense! **34. A new commandment I give unto you, That ye love one another; as**—'even as' [καθὼς] **I have loved you, that ye also love one another.** This was the *new* feature of it. Christ's love to His people in giving His life a ransom for them was altogether new, and consequently as a Model and Standard for theirs to one another. It is not, however, something transcending the great moral law, which is "the *old* commandment" (1 John ii. 7; and see on Mark xii. 28-33), but that law *in a new and peculiar form.* Hence it is said to be both *new* and *old* (1 John ii. 7, 8). **35. By this shall all men know that ye are my disciples**—the disciples of Him who laid down His life for those He loved. **if ye have love one to another**—for My sake, and as one in Me; for to *such* love men outside the circle of believers know right well that they are entire strangers. Alas, how little of it there is even within this circle!

Peter, Protesting his Readiness to follow his Master, though it should be to Death, is Forewarned of his shameful Fall (36-38). **36. Simon Peter said**—'saith' [λέγει] **unto him**—seeing plainly, in these directions how to behave themselves, that He was indeed going from them, **Lord, whither goest thou?**—having hardly a glimmering of the real truth. **Jesus answered him, Whither I go, thou canst not follow me now; but thou shalt follow me afterwards.** How different this from what He said to the Jews, "Whither I go, *ye cannot come*" (ch. viii. 21). **37. Peter said**—'saith' **unto him, Why cannot I follow thee now? I will lay down my life for thy sake** [ὑπὲρ σοῦ]—'for Thee.' He seems now to see that it was *death* Christ referred to as what would sever Him from them, but is not staggered at following Him thither. Dear soul! It was thy heart's true and conscious affection for thy Master that prompted this speech, rash and presumptuous though it was. **38. Jesus answered him, Wilt thou lay down thy life for my sake?** [ὑπὲρ 'Εμοῦ]—'for Me?' In this repetition of Peter's words there is deep though affectionate irony; and this Peter himself would feel for many a day after his recovery, as he retraced the painful particulars. **Verily, verily, I say unto thee, The cock shall not crow, till thou hast denied me thrice.** See on Luke xxii. 31-34.

Remarks.—1. Among the unique features of this wonderful History, none is more remarkable than the union in the Lord Jesus of a perfect *foresight* of the future, entire preparedness for it, and a calm expectation of it, but yet a certain *freshness* of feeling which unforeseen events awaken in others. He comes into every scene, and holds intercourse with all classes, fully cognizant of every movement for and against Him, and with all hearts open to His gaze. And yet His own movements are so per-

38 thee now? I will [b]lay down my life for thy sake. Jesus answered him,
Wilt thou lay down thy life for my sake? Verily, verily, I say unto thee,
The cock shall not crow, till thou hast denied me thrice.

A. D. 33.

[b] Luke 22. 33. Pro. 16. 18.

fectly natural and manifestly human, that men have difficulty in believing the lofty things which He says of Himself, and all that is said and done in His presence awakens His sensibilities just as if it took Him as much by surprise as it would any other man. Look at this very chapter. With exalted Self-possession He rises from supper, girds Himself with the towel of service, pours water into a basin, and proceeds to wash His disciples' feet—all in the exercise of an eternal and unchanging love, and in furtherance of plans of action laid from the beginning. But see, on the other hand, how naturally each incident and saying at the Supper-table gives rise to another, and the whole susceptibilities of that tender Heart are awakened by the painful disclosures which had to be made, and become keener when the moment arrives for being quite plain. Peter's hesitation first, and then positive refusal, to be washed by his blessed Master had led to a hint how fatal that resolution would be to him in relation to the higher washing. Peter, who had never thought of that, is now all eagerness to be washed in every sense of the word; but he is told that he needs it not, having gotten that already, and so become "clean every whit"—as his fellows at the table with him also were. But the presence of the traitor stifled the word "all," and shaped it into "Ye are clean—but *not all.*" Still, as if loath to break it to them too abruptly, and as they evidently failed to catch the precise import of His hint, He proceeds to open up to them His design in washing their feet, holding this up as a high example of that self-denying humility and mutual service by which He expected them to be distinguished before the world. But this again brought up before His mind the dark shadow of the deed about to be done against Him, and the man that was to do it, sitting with Him at the table, and by his presence interrupting, beyond longer endurance, the free flow of His gracious speech during the brief space they were to be together. Now, therefore, He will come nearer to the point and hasten his exit. "I speak not of you all: I know whom I have chosen: but, that the scripture may be fulfilled, He that eateth bread with me hath lifted up his heel against me. Now I tell you before it come, that, when it is come to pass, ye may believe that I am He." And yet, even after He has come this length, He seems to pause; and, as if trying to throw off the unwelcome subject for a moment, He resumes what He had broken off—the lofty mission on which He was sending them forth —"Verily, verily, I say unto you, He that receiveth whomsoever I send receiveth Me; and he that receiveth Me receiveth Him that sent Me." So manifestly is this a resumption of the former subject, that if *vv.* 18, 19 were enclosed in a parenthesis, it would seem not to have been interrupted at all, save by a side hint. But the time for hints is past, and the moment for explicit disclosure has come. No doubt, the last hint—about one eating of His bread who was to lift up his heel against Him—was too plain not to pain the whole Eleven, and almost prevent them listening to anything else. Jesus, therefore, come to a point, will speak to them no more enigmatically. But mark the emotion which precedes the explicit announcement that there is a traitor at the table. "When Jesus had thus said, He was troubled in spirit, and testified, and said"—as if the utterance was almost choked, and the thing would hardly come out—"Verily, verily, I say unto you, One of you shall betray Me." What we wish to notice here is, that while all is manifestly naked and open beforehand to Him who calmly directed and lovingly presided at this Supper, His quick susceptibilities are kindled, and His heart's deepest emotions are stirred, when He has in naked terms to announce the deed of horror. In short, we have here Divine intelligence and warm Human feeling, so entirely in harmony in one and the same Person, and in every part of one and the same scene, as proclaim their own historic reality beyond all the powers of human invention to imitate. Nor is it the mere facts here presented to us, but the very form and pressure of them, that bear the stamp of manifest truth; so much so, that it is to us inconceivable how, even with the facts before him, they could have been so conveyed by the Evangelist as they are here, save on one explanation—"When the Comforter is come, He shall teach you all things, and bring all things to your remembrance, whatsoever I said unto you" (ch. xiv. 26). To continue this line of remark here were needless. But we cannot refrain from alluding to the *freedom* which Jesus seemed to breathe the moment that the traitor made his exit, and at the same time the sublime transport with which His all-embracing Eye saw in that movement His virtual elevation to glory through the Cross—"Now is the Son of Man glorified, and God is glorified in Him"! On every view of it but one this is inexplicable. That perfect combination of the Divine and the Human in the Subject of this History, which to have been written must have been real—that, and that alone, explains all. 2. How affecting is the contrast between the example here exhibited and the prevailing spirit of Christendom in almost every age of its history! At the most touching period of His intercourse with them—when He was with them for the last time—the Master descends to the position and the offices of a servant to His servants; doing for them the humblest of services: and this in order to exemplify in His own Person what He expected them to be and to do to one another in all succeeding time. To give this the more weight, He holds up the difference between Himself and them. Being themselves but servants, it was no great thing for *them* to serve one another. But if the Master voluntarily went down to that position, much more should they, in whose case to serve was no descent at all below their rightful dignity, but only making full proof of their proper calling. Alas, for the fruit! The pride of the clergy, how early did it blossom, and how proverbial has it become, and, as if to make this all the more noticeable, the language and the forms of humility and service have kept bitter pace with the palpable absence of the reality. How could such ministers teach and beget humility and lovingkindness in the Christian people? Some noble examples, both of ministers and people, are on record; and many, many, doubtless, there have been and are which will never be recorded. But the full and all-impressive manifestation of that humility which minds not high things, but condescends to men of low estate, and that love which lives for others, and thinks no service too mean which ministers to the comfort and well-being of the least of Christ's "brethren," is yet to come—when, "by this shall all men know that we are Christ's disciples, because we have love one to

14 LET not your heart be troubled: ye believe in God, believe also in me.
2 In [a]my Father's house are many mansions: if *it were* not *so,* I would
3 have told you. [b]I go to prepare a place for you. And if I go and prepare a place for you, I [c]will come again, and receive you unto myself;
that [d]where I am, *there* ye may be also.
4, 5 And whither I go ye know, and the way ye know. Thomas saith

A. D. 33.

CHAP. 14.
[a] 2 Cor. 5. 1. Rev. 3. 12, 21.
[b] ch. 13. 33.
[c] Acts 1. 11.
[d] 1 Thes. 4. 17.

another." The Lord hasten it in its time! 3. It is of immense consequence to the liberty and strength of Christians to be assured of their standing among the "washed" disciples of the Lord Jesus—the "clean every whit;" instead of having to be ever *trying* to get this length, ever settling that point, and thus all their lifetime subject to bondage. But the opposite error is equally to be eschewed, of supposing that when this point *is* settled, and that standing is attained, we have no more sin needing to be pardoned, no defilement to be washed away. This, we take it, is just what our Evangelist alludes to in his first Epistle, when he says, "If we say that we have no sin"—that is, as we understand it, If we say that being now clean every whit we have quite done with sinning—"we deceive ourselves, and the truth is not in us." On the difference between this statement and the similar one that follows—"If we say that we have not sinned, we make Him a liar, and His word is not in us"—see on 1 John i. 8, 10. On the warning here given to Peter, and the way in which he received it, see on Luke xxii. 31-34, Remark 3 at the end of that Section.

CHAP. XIV. 1-31.—DISCOURSE AT THE TABLE AFTER SUPPER. 'We now come,' says *Olshausen* admirably, 'to that portion of the Evangelical History which we may with propriety call its *Holy of Holies.* Our Evangelist, like a consecrated priest, alone opens up to us the view into this sanctuary. It is the record of the last moments spent by the Lord in the midst of His disciples before His passion, when words full of heavenly thought flowed from His sacred lips. All that His heart, glowing with love, had still to say to His friends, was compressed into this short season. At first the intercourse took the form of conversation; sitting at table, they talked familiarly together. But when the repast was finished, the language of Christ assumed a loftier strain; the disciples, assembled around their Master, listened to the words of life, and seldom spoke a word. At length, in the Redeemer's sublime intercessory prayer, His full soul was poured forth in express petitions to His heavenly Father on behalf of those who were His own. It is a peculiarity of these last chapters, that they treat almost exclusively of the most profound relations—as that of the Son to the Father, and of both to the Spirit; that of Christ to the Church, of the Church to the world, and so forth. Moreover, a considerable portion of these sublime communications surpassed the point of view to which the disciples had at that time attained: hence the Redeemer frequently repeats the same sentiments in order to impress them more deeply upon their minds, and, because of what they still did not understand, points them to the Holy Spirit, who would remind them of all His sayings, and lead them into all truth.'

The Confidence to be reposed in Christ during His Absence, and the loving Design of His Second Coming (1-3). **1. Let not your heart be troubled.** What myriads of souls have not these opening words cheered, in deepest gloom, since first they were uttered! **ye believe in God, believe also in me** [πιστεύετε εἰς τὸν Θεόν, καὶ εἰς ἐμὲ πιστεύετε]. This may with equal correctness be rendered four different ways. 1. As two imperatives —'Believe in God, and believe in Me.' (So *Chrysostom,* and several both Greek and Latin Fathers; *Lampe, Bengel, de Wette, Lücke, Tholuck, Meyer, Stier, Alford.*) But this, though the interpretation of so many, we must regard, with *Webster and Wilkinson,* as somewhat frigid. 2. As two indicatives—'Ye believe in God, and ye believe in Me.' So *Luther,* who gives it this turn—'If ye believe in God, then do ye also believe in Me.' But this is pointless. 3. The first imperative and the second indicative; but to make sense of this, we must give the second clause a future turn— 'Believe in God, and then ye will believe in Me.' To this *Olshausen* half inclines. But how unnatural this is, it is hardly necessary to say. 4. The first indicative and the second imperative, as in our version—'Ye believe in God, believe also in Me.' (So the *Vulgate, Maldonat, Erasmus, Calvin, Beza*—who, however, gives the first clause an interrogatory turn, 'Believe ye in God? Believe also in Me'—*Cranmer's* and the *Geneva* English versions, *Olshausen* prevailingly, *Webster and Wilkinson.*) This alone appears to us to bring out the natural and worthy sense—'Ye believe in God, as do all His true people, and the confidence ye repose in Him is the soul of all your religious exercises, actings and hopes: Well, *repose the same trust in Me.*' What a demand this to make, by one who was sitting familiarly with them at the same Supper-table! But it neither alienates our trust from its proper Object, nor divides it with a creature: it is but *the concentration of our trust in the Unseen and Impalpable One upon His Own Incarnate Son,* by which that trust, instead of the distant, unsteady and too often cold and scarce real thing it otherwise is, acquires a conscious reality, warmth, and power, which makes all things new. *This is Christianity in brief.* **2. In my Father's house are many mansions**—and so, room for all and a place for each: **if it were not so, I would have told you**—and not have deceived you all this time. **I go**—or, according to what is undoubtedly the true reading, 'because I go' **to prepare a place for you** [ὅτι before πορεύομαι has decisive authority, and is inserted by all critical editors.] The meaning is, 'Doubt not that there is for all of you a place in My Father's house, *for* I am going on purpose to prepare it.' In what sense? First, To establish their right to be there; Second, To take possession of it in their name; Third, To conduct them thither at last. **3. And if I go and prepare a place for you, I will come again**—*strictly,* at His Second Personal Appearing; but, in a secondary and comforting sense, to each individually, when he puts off this tabernacle, sleeping in Jesus, but his spirit "present with the Lord." **and receive you unto myself; that where I am, there ye may be also.** Mark here again the extent of the claim which Jesus makes—at His Second Coming to receive His people *to Himself* (see on Eph. v. 27; Col. i. 22; Jude 24), that where *He is,* there they may be also. He thinks it quite enough to re-assure them, to say that where He is, there they shall be.

Christ the Way to the Father, and Himself the Incarnate Revelation of the Father (4-12). **4. And whither I go ye know, and the way ye know.**

unto him, Lord, we know not whither thou goest; and how can we know
6 the way? Jesus saith unto him, I am [e]the way, and [f]the truth, and [g]the
7 life: [h]no man cometh unto the Father, but by me. If [i]ye had known me,
ye should have known my Father also: and from henceforth ye know him,
and have seen him.
8 Philip saith unto him, Lord, show us the Father, and it sufficeth us.
9 Jesus saith unto him, Have I been so long time with you, and yet hast
thou not known me, Philip? [j]he that hath seen me hath seen the
10 Father; and how sayest thou *then*, Show us the Father? Believest thou
not that [k]I am in the Father, and the Father in me? the words that I
speak unto you [l]I speak not of myself: but the Father, that dwelleth in
11 me, he doeth the works. Believe me that I *am* in the Father, and
12 the Father in me: or else believe me for the very works' sake. Verily,
verily, I say unto you, He that believeth on me, the works that I do
shall he do also; and greater *works* than these shall he do; because

A. D. 33.

e Matt. 11. 27. Rom. 5. 2. Heb. 9. 8.
f ch. 1. 17. ch. 8. 32.
g ch. 1. 4. ch. 6. 35.
h ch. 10. 9. Rom. 15. 16. 2 John 9. Rev. 5. 8, 9.
i ch. 8. 19.
j Col. 1. 15. Heb. 1. 3.
k ch. 10. 38. ch. 17. 21. 1 John 5. 7.
l ch. 5. 19.

5. Thomas saith unto him, Lord, we know not whither thou goest; and how can we know the way? [The reading of this last clause, according to *Lachmann* and *Tregelles*, 'how know we the way?' or with the "and" prefixed by *Tischendorf*—is hardly so well supported as the received text.] It seems strange that when Jesus said they knew both whither He went and the way, Philip should flatly say they did not. But doubtless the Lord meant thus rather to stimulate their enquiries, and then reply to them:—*q. d.*, 'Whither I go ye know—do ye not? and the way too?' Accordingly, verse **6. Jesus saith unto him, I AM THE WAY**—in what sense is explained in the last clause: but He had said it before in these words, "I am the door: *by Me* if any man enter in, he shall be saved" (ch. x. 9). **and THE TRUTH**—the *Incarnate Reality* of all we find in the Father, when through Christ we get to Him; for "in Him dwelleth all the fulness of the Godhead bodily" (Col. i. 19). **and THE LIFE**—the *vitality* of all that shall ever flow into us from the Godhead thus approached and thus manifested in Him: for "this is the true God, and eternal life" (1 John v. 20): **no man cometh unto the Father, but by me.** Of this three-fold statement of what He is, Jesus explains here only the first—His being "the Way;" not as if that were in itself more important than the other two, but because the *Intervention* or *Mediation* of Christ between God and men is the distinctive feature of Christianity. His being the *Truth* and the *Life* gives us what may be called *the Christian aspect of the Godhead*, as the Object of the soul's aspirations and the centre of its eternal bliss: but that God, even as thus viewed, is approachable and enjoyable by men only *through the mediation of Christ*, tells of that sinful separation of the soul from God, the knowledge and feeling of which constitute the necessary preparative to any and every saving approach to God, and to the believing reception and use of Christ as the Way to Him. Hence it is that our Lord comes back upon this, as in the first instance what needs most to be impressed upon us. **7. If ye had known me, ye should have known my Father also: and from henceforth** [ἀπ' ἄρτι]—'from now,' or from this time forth, that I have explained it to you, **ye know him, and have seen him.** Here also our Lord, by what He says, intends rather to gain their ear for further explanation, than to tell them how much they already knew.

8. Philip saith unto him, Lord, show us the Father, and it sufficeth us. Philip's grossness of conception gives occasion to something more than explanation; but O how winning is even the slight rebuke! **9. Jesus saith unto him, Have I been so long time with you, and yet hast thou not known me, Philip? he that hath seen me hath seen the Father**—hath seen all of the Father that can or ever will be seen; hath seen the Incarnate Manifestation of the Godhead; **and how sayest thou, Show us the Father?** To strain after expected but impossible discovery can only end in disappointment. Jesus, therefore, shuts up Philip—and with him all who waste their mental energies on such fruitless aims and expectations—to Himself, in whom dwelleth all the fulness of the Godhead bodily. **10. Believest thou not that I am in the Father, and the Father in me? the words that I speak unto you I speak not of**—or 'from' [ἀπὸ] **myself: but the Father, that dwelleth in me, he doeth the works.** Observe here how, in the expression of this *Mutual Inbeing* of the Father and the Son, our Lord passes insensibly, so to speak, from the *words* He spake to the *works* He did—as the Father's words uttered by His mouth and the Father's works done by His hand. What claim to essential equality with the Father could surpass this? **11. Believe me that I am in the Father, and the Father in me: or else believe me for the very works' sake:**—*q. d.*, 'By all your faith in Me, believe this on My simple *word:* but if so high a claim is more than your feeble faith can yet reach, let the *works* I have done tell their own tale, and it will need no more.' Can anything more clearly show that Christ claimed for His miracles a higher character than those of prophets or apostles? And yet this higher character lay not in the works themselves, but in His manner of doing them. (See on Mark vi. 30-56, Remark 1 at the close of that Section, page 163.) **12. Verily, verily, I say unto you, He that believeth on me, the works that I do shall he do also; and greater works than these shall he do; because I go unto my Father**—rather, 'the Father,' as the true reading appears to be. "The works that I do" and which "they should do also," were those miraculous credentials of their apostolic office which Christ empowered the Eleven to perform. But the "greater works than His" were not any more transcendent *miracles*—for there could be none such, and certainly they did none such—but such as He referred to in what He said to Nathanael (ch. i. 51)—that glorious ingathering of souls after His ascension—or "because He went to the Father"—which it was not His own Personal mission to the earth to accomplish. See on the promise, "From henceforth thou shalt catch men," Luke v. 10, and Remark 4 at the close of that Section. The substance, then, of these

13 I go unto my Father. And whatsoever ye shall ask in [m]my name,
14 that will I do, that the Father may be glorified in the Son. If ye
shall ask any thing in my name, I will do *it.*
15, If [n]ye love me, keep my commandments. And I will pray the Father,
16 and [o]he shall give you another Comforter, that he may abide with you
17 for ever; *even* [p]the Spirit of truth; [q]whom the world cannot receive,
because it seeth him not, neither knoweth him: but ye know him; for

A. D. 33.

m Jas. 1. 5. 1 John 3. 22.
n 1 John 5. 3.
o Rom. 8. 15.
p 1 John 2. 7. 1 John 4. 6.
q Rom. 8. 7. 1 Cor. 2. 14.

five rich verses (8-12) is this: that the Son is the ordained and perfect manifestation of the Father; that His own word for this ought, to His disciples, to be enough; that if any doubts remained His works ought to remove them; but yet that these works of His were designed merely to aid weak faith, and would be repeated, nay exceeded by His disciples, in virtue of the power He would confer on them after His departure. His miracles, accordingly, apostles wrought, though wholly in His name and by His power; while the "greater" works—not in degree but in kind—were the conversion of thousands in a day, by His Spirit accompanying them.

The Prevalency of Prayer in Christ's Name (13, 14). **13. And whatsoever ye shall ask in my name**—as Mediator, **that will I do**—as Head and Lord of the Kingdom of God. This comprehensive promise is repeated emphatically in the following verse. **14. If ye shall ask any thing in my name, I will do it.** Observe here, that while they are supposed to ask what they want, not of Him, but of the Father in His name, Jesus says it is He Himself that will "do it" for them. What a claim is this not only to be perfectly cognizant of all that is poured into the Father's ear by His loving disciples on earth, and of all the Father's counsels and plans as to the answers to be given to them, the precise nature and measure of the grace to be given them, and the proper time for it—but to be the authoritative Dispenser of all that these prayers draw down, and in that sense the *Hearer* of prayer! Let any one try to conceive of this statement apart from Christ's essential equality with the Father, and he will find it impossible. The emphatic repetition of this, that if they shall ask anything in His name, He will do it, speaks both the boundless *prevalency* of His name with the Father, and His *unlimited authority* to dispense the answer. But see further on ch. xv. 7.

First great Promise of the Comforter and the blessed Effects of this Gift (15-26). This portion of the Discourse is notable, as containing the first announcement of the Spirit, to supply the personal presence of the absent Saviour. **15. If ye love me, keep my commandments.** Christ's commandments are neither substituted in place of God's commandments in the moral law, nor are they something to be performed over and above that law. But they are that very law of God, laid on His disciples by the Lord Jesus, in the exercise of His proper authority, and to be obeyed as their proper service to Himself as their Lord and Master—from new motives and to new ends; for we are "*not without law to God, but under the law to Christ*" (1 Cor. ix. 21). This demand, on the principles of the two foregoing verses, is intelligible: on any other principles, it were monstrous. **16. And I will, &c.** The connection between this and what goes before is apt to escape observation. But it seems to be this, that as the proper temple for the indwelling Spirit of Jesus is a heart filled with an obediential love to Him—a love to Him which at once yields itself obediently to Him and lives actively for Him—so this was the fitting preparation for the promised gift, and He would accordingly get it for them. But how? **I will pray the Father.** It is perhaps a pity that the English word "pray" is ever used of Christ's askings of the Father. For of the two words used in the Gospels, that signifying to pray *as we do*—suppliantly, or as an inferior to a superior [αἰτεῖν]—is never used of Christ's askings of the Father, save once by Martha (ch. xi. 22), who knew no better. The word invariably used of Christ's askings by Himself [ἐρωτᾶν] signifies what one asks, not suppliantly, but familiarly, as equals do of each other. *Bengel* notes this, but the subject is fully and beautifully handled by *Trench* ('Synonyms of the New Testament'). **and he shall give you ANOTHER COMFORTER** [ἄλλον παράκλητον]. As this word is used in the New Testament exclusively by John—five times in this Discourse of the Holy Spirit (here; *v.* 26; xv. 26; xvi. 7), and once in his first Epistle, of Christ Himself (ii. 1)—it is important to fix the sense of it. Literally, the word signifies one 'called beside' or 'to,' another, to 'aid' him. In this most general sense the Holy Spirit is undoubtedly sent 'to our aid,' and every kind of aid coming within the proper sphere of His operations. But more particularly, the word denotes that kind of aid which an *Advocate* renders to one in a court of justice. So it was used by the Greeks; and so undoubtedly it is used in 1 John ii. 1, "If any man sin, we have an Advocate [παράκλητον] with the Father, Jesus Christ the righteous." But it also denotes that kind of aid which a *Comforter* affords to one who needs such. The question, then, is, Which of these is here intended—the general sense of a Helper; the more definite sense of an Advocate; or the other definite sense of a Comforter? Taking all the four passages in which the Spirit is thus spoken of in this Discourse, that of a Helper certainly lies at the foundation; but that of a *Comforter* seems to us to be the kind of help which suits best with the strain of the Discourse at this place. The comfort of Christ's personal presence with the Eleven had been such, that while they had it they seemed to want for nothing; and the loss of it would seem the loss of everything—utter desolation (*v.* 18). It is to meet this, as we think, that He says He will ask the Father to send them *another* Comforter; and in all these four passages, it is as an all-sufficient, all-satisfying *Substitute for Himself* that He holds forth this promised Gift. But this will open up more and more upon us as we advance in this Discourse. **that he may abide with you for ever**—never to go away from them, as in the body Jesus Himself was about to do. **17. Even the Spirit of truth**—so called for the reason mentioned in ch. xvi. 13; **whom the world cannot receive**—see on 1 Cor. ii. 14; **because it seeth**—or 'beholdeth' **him not** [θεωρεῖ], **neither knoweth him**—having no spiritual perception and apprehension: **but ye know him; for he dwelleth with you, and shall be in you.** [The reading—ἐστὶν—'is with you,' though adopted by *Lachmann* and *Tregelles*, and approved by *Tholuck*, *Stier*, and *Luthardt*, is insufficiently supported. *Tischendorf* abides by the received text, which is approved by *de Wette*, *Meyer*, and *Alford*. *Lücke* is doubtful.] Though the proper fulness of both these was yet future, our Lord, by speaking

18 he dwelleth with you, [r]and shall be in you. I will not leave you [1]com-
19 fortless: I will come to you. Yet a little while, and the world seeth me
20 no more; but [s]ye see me: [t]because I live, ye shall live also. At that day
ye shall know that [u]I *am* in my Father, and ye in me, and I in you.
21 He [v]that hath my commandments, and keepeth them, he it is that
loveth me: and he that loveth me shall be loved of my Father, and I
will love him, and will manifest myself to him.
22 Judas saith unto him, (not Iscariot,) Lord, how is it that thou wilt
23 manifest thyself unto us, and not unto the world? Jesus answered and
said unto him, If a man love me, he will keep my words: and my
Father will love him, [w]and we will come unto him, and make our abode
24 with him. He that loveth me not keepeth not my sayings: and [x]the
word which ye hear is not mine, but the Father's which sent me.
25 These things have I spoken unto you, being *yet* present with you.
26 But [y]the Comforter, *which is* the Holy Ghost, whom the Father will send

A. D. 33.

r Matt. 10. 20. Rom. 8. 10. 1 Cor. 14. 15. 1 John 2. 27.
1 Or, orphans.
s ch. 16. 16.
t 1 Cor. 15 20.
u ch. 10. 38. ch. 17. 21.
v 1 John 2. 5. 1 John 5. 3.
w Ps. 91. 1. 1 John 2. 24. 1 John 4. 16. Rev. 3. 20. Rev. 21. 3.
x ch. 7. 16.
y Luke 24. 49.

both of present and future time, seems plainly say that they *already* had the substance, though that only, of this great blessing.

18. I will not leave you comfortless [ὀρφανούς]—'orphans,' as in the margin; in a bereaved and desolate condition. **I will come to you** [ἔρχομαι]—rather, 'I am coming to you;' that is, by the Spirit, since it was His presence that was to make Christ's personal departure from them to be no bereavement. **19. Yet a little while, and the world seeth**—'beholdeth' **me no more; but ye see**—'behold' **me.** His bodily presence being all the sight of Him which the world was capable of, they were to behold Him no more on His departure to the Father: whereas by the coming of the Spirit the presence of Christ was not only continued to His spiritually enlightened disciples, but rendered far more efficacious and blissful than His bodily presence had been before. **because I live, ye shall live also.** He does not say, 'When I *shall* live, after My resurrection from the dead,' but "Because I do live;" for it is of that inextinguishable Divine life which He was even then living that He is speaking—in reference to which His approaching death and resurrection were but as momentary shadows passing over the sun's glorious disc. See Luke xxiv. 5; Rev. i. 18. And this grand saying Jesus uttered with death immediately in view. What a brightness does this throw over the next clause, **ye shall live also! 20. At**—or '**In**' [ἐν] **that day**—of the Spirit's coming, **ye shall know**—or have it made manifest to you **that I am in my Father, and ye in me, and I in you.** See on ch. xvii. 22, 23. **21. He that hath my commandments, and keepeth them, he it is that loveth me.** See on ch. xv. 16. **and he that loveth me shall be loved of my Father, and I will love him, and will manifest myself to him.** Mark the sharp line of distinction here, not only between the Divine Persons, but the actings of love in Each respectively, towards true disciples.

22. Judas saith unto him, (not Iscariot). Delightful parenthesis this! The traitor being no longer present, we needed not to be told that this question came not from *him;* nor even if he had been present would any that knew him have expected any such question from him. But the very name had got an ill savour in the Church ever since that black treason, and the Evangelist seems to take a pleasure in disconnecting from it all that was offensive in the association, when reporting the question of that dear disciple whose misfortune it was to have that name. He is the same with Lebbæus, whose surname was Thaddæus, in Matthew's catalogue of the Twelve. (See on Matt. x. 3.) **Lord, how is it that thou wilt manifest thyself unto us, and not unto the world?**—a question, as we think, most natural and pertinent, though interpreters (as *Lücke, Stier, Alford,* &c.) think it proceeded from a superficial, outside, Jewish misconception of Christ's kingdom. Surely the loving tone and precious nature of our Lord's reply ought to have suggested a better view of the question itself. **23. Jesus answered and said unto him, If a man love me, he will keep my words** [λόγον]—rather, '**My word:**' **and my Father will love him, and we will come unto him, and make our abode with him.** Astonishing disclosure! Observe the links in this golden chain. First, "If a man love Me." Such love is at first the *fruit* of love: "We love Him because He first loved us." Then this love to Christ makes His word dear to us. Accordingly, "If a man love Me, he will keep My word." Further, such is My Father's love to Me, that when any man loves Me, and My word is dear to him, My Father will love that man. Finally, such a man—with heart so prepared and so perfumed—shall become the permanent habitation of both My Father and Me—the seat not of occasional and distant discoveries, but of abiding and intimate manifestations of both My Father and Me, to his unspeakable satisfaction and joy. He shall not have to say with the weeping prophet, "O the Hope of Israel, the Saviour thereof in time of trouble, why shouldest Thou be as a *stranger* in the land, and as a wayfaring man that turneth aside to tarry *for a night?*" but from his own deep and joyous experience shall exclaim, "The Word was made flesh, and *dwelt* among us." He shall feel and know that the Father and the Son have come to make a permanent and eternal stay with him! **24. He that loveth me not keepeth not my sayings.** Hence it follows that all obedience *not* springing from love to Christ is in his eyes no obedience at all. **and the word which ye hear is not mine, but the Father's which sent me.** (See on Matt. x. 40.) It will be observed that when Christ refers back to His Father's authority, it is not in speaking of those who love Him and keep His sayings—in their case it were superfluous—but in speaking of those who love Him not and keep not His sayings, whom He holds up as chargeable with the double guilt of dishonouring the eternal Sender as well as the Sent.

25. These things have I spoken unto you, being yet present [μένων] **with you**—or 'while yet abiding with you.' **26. But the Comforter, which is the Holy Ghost, whom the Father will send in my name, he shall teach you all things**—see

in my name, [z]he shall teach you all things, and bring all things to your
27 remembrance, whatsoever I have said unto you. Peace [a]I leave with
you, my peace I give unto you: not as the world giveth, give I unto you.
28 Let not your heart be troubled, neither let it be afraid. Ye have heard
how I said unto you, I go away, and come *again* unto you. If ye loved
me, ye would rejoice, because I said, I go unto the Father: for [b]my

A. D. 33.

[z] 1 John 2. 27.
[a] Phil. 4. 7. Col. 3. 15.
[b] Isa. 9. 6. Isa. 42. 1. Isa. 49. 1-6. ch. 5. 18.

on *vv.* 16, 17; **and bring all things to your remembrance, whatsoever I have said unto you.** As the Son came in the Father's name, so the Father was to send the Spirit in the Son's name, with like divine authority and power—to do two great things. First, to "*teach* them all things," and second, to "*bring to remembrance* all things whatsoever Christ had said to them." So imperfectly did the apostles apprehend what Jesus said to them, that to have recalled it all to them merely as it fell on their ears from their Master's lips would have left them the same half-instructed and bewildered, weak and timid men, as before—all unfit to evangelize the world either by their preaching or their writings. But the Spirit was to *teach* as well as to *remind* them—to *reproduce the whole teaching of Christ*, not as they understood it, but *as He meant it to be understood.* But does not the promise of the Spirit to "teach them all things" mean something more than "to bring all things to their remembrance?" *This* promise at least does not; for the sense plainly is, "He shall teach you, and bring to your remembrance all things whatsoever I have said unto you"—the teaching and the recalling relating to the same things, namely, all that Christ had said to them. Thus have we here a double promise with reference to our Lord's actual teaching—that through the agency of the Holy Ghost it should stand up before their minds, when He was gone from them, in all its *entireness*, as at first *uttered*, and in all its vast *significance* as by Him *intended.* Before the close of this same Discourse, our Lord announces an extension even of this great office of the Spirit. They were not able to take in all that He had to tell them, and He had accordingly withheld some things from them. But when the Spirit should come, on His departure to the Father, He should "guide them into *all the truth*," filling up whatever was wanting to their *complete apprehension of the mind of Christ.* (See on ch. xvi. 12-15.) On these great promises rests the CREDIBILITY, in the highest sense of that term, OF THE GOSPEL HISTORY, and so, its DIVINE AUTHORITY.

Christ's Own Peace, His Legacy and Gift to His People (27). **27. Peace I leave with you, my peace I give unto you.** If the two preceding verses sounded like a note of preparation for departure, what would they take this to be but a farewell? But O how different from ordinary adieus! It *is* a parting word, but of richest import. It is the peace of a parting friend, sublimed in the sense of it, and made efficacious for all time by those Lips that "speak and it is done." As the Prince of peace (Isa. ix. 6) He brought it into flesh in His own Person; carried it up and down as His Own—"My peace," as He here calls it; died to make it ours, through the blood of His cross; left it as the heritage of His disciples here below; and from the right hand of the Majesty on high implants and maintains it by His Spirit in their hearts. Many a legacy is "left" that is never "given" to the legatee, many a gift destined that never reaches its proper object. But Christ is the Executor of His own Testament; the peace He "*leaves*" He "*gives.*" Thus all is secure. **not as the world giveth, give I unto you.** What hollowness is there in many of the world's givings: but Jesus gives *sincerely.* How superficial, even at their best, are the world's givings: but Jesus gives *substantially.* How temporary are all the world's givings: but what Jesus gives He gives *for ever!* Well, then, might He add, **Let not your heart be troubled, neither let it be afraid**—for the entrance of such words into any honest and good heart necessarily casteth out fear.

The Gain to Christ Himself of His Departure to the Father, and the Joy which this should inspire in His loving People (28). **28. Ye have heard how I said unto you, I go away, and come again unto you. If ye loved me, ye would rejoice, because I said, I go unto the Father: for my Father is greater than I.** This is one of the passages which have in all ages been most confidently appealed to by those who deny the supreme Divinity of Christ, in proof that our Lord claimed no proper equality with the Father: here, they say, He explicitly disclaims it. But let us see whether, on their principles, it would yield any intelligible sense at all. Were some holy *man* on his deathbed to say as he beheld his friends in tears at the prospect of losing him, 'Ye ought rather to rejoice than weep for me, and if ye loved me ye would'—the speech would be quite natural, and what many dying saints *have* said. But should these weeping bystanders ask *why* joy was more suitable than sorrow, and the dying man reply, "*Because my Father is greater than I,*" would they not start back with astonishment, if not with horror? Does not this strange speech, then, from Christ's lips presuppose such teaching on His part as would make it hard to believe that He could gain anything by departing to the Father, and render it needful to say expressly that there was a sense in which He *could* and *would* do so? Thus this startling saying, when closely looked at, seems *plainly intended to correct such misapprehensions* as might arise from the emphatic and reiterated teaching of *His proper equality with the Father*—as if joy at the prospect of heavenly bliss were inapplicable to *Him*—as if so Exalted a Person were incapable of any accession at all, by transition from this dismal scene to a cloudless heaven and the very bosom of the Father, and, by assuring them that it was just the reverse, to make them forget their own sorrow in His approaching joy. The Fathers of the Church, in repelling the false interpretation put upon this verse by the Arians, were little more satisfactory than their opponents; some of them saying it referred to the *Sonship* of Christ, in which respect He was inferior to the Father, others that it referred to His *Human Nature.* But the human nature of the Son of God is not less real in heaven than it was upon earth. Plainly, the inferiority of which Christ here speaks is not anything which would be the same whether He went or stayed, but something which would be removed by His going to the Father—on which account He says that if they loved Him they would rather rejoice on His account than sorrow at His departure. With this key to the sense of the words, they involve no real difficulty; and in this view of them all the most judicious interpreters, from Calvin downwards, substantially concur.

29 Father is greater than I. And now I have told you before it come to
pass, that, when it is come to pass, ye might believe.
30 Hereafter I will not talk much with you: [c]for the prince of this world
31 cometh, and [d]hath nothing in me. But that the world may know that
I love the Father; and [e]as the Father gave me commandment, even so
I do. Arise, let us go hence.

A. D. 33.

[c] ch. 12. 31.
[d] 2 Cor. 5. 21. Heb. 4. 15. 1 Pet. 1. 19. 1 John 3. 5.
[e] Phil. 2. 8. Heb. 5. 8.

Jesus about to Die, not because the Prince of this World had anything in Him, but out of Loving Obedience to His Father's Commandment (29-31).

29. And now I have told you before it come to pass—referring to His departure to the Father, and the gift of the Holy Ghost to follow thereon, **that, when it is come to pass, ye might believe**—or have your faith immoveably established.

30. Hereafter I will not talk much with you:—'I have a little more to say, but My work hastens apace, and the approach of the adversary will cut it short.' **for the prince of this world cometh** (see ch. xii. 31)—cometh with hostile intent, cometh for a last grand attack. Foiled in his first deadly assault, he had "departed"—but "till a season" only (see on Luke iv. 13). That season is now all but come, and his whole energies are to be once more put forth—with what effect the next words sublimely express. **and hath nothing in me**—*nothing of his own* in Me, *nothing of sin* on which to fasten as a righteous cause of condemnation: 'As the Prince of this world he wields his sceptre over willing subjects; but in Me he shall find no sympathy with his objects, no acknowledgment of his sovereignty, no subjection to his demands.' Glorious saying! The truth of it is the life of the world. (Heb. ix. 14; 1 John iii. 5; 2 Cor. v. 21.)

31. But that the world may know that I love the Father; and as the Father gave me commandment, even so I do. The sense must be completed thus: 'But though the Prince of this world, in plotting My death, hath nothing to fasten on, I am going to yield Myself up a willing Sacrifice, that the world may know that I love the Father, whose commandment it is that I give My life a ransom for many.' **Arise, let us go hence.** Did they then, at this stage of the Discourse, leave the Supper-room, as some able interpreters judge? If so, we cannot but think that our Evangelist would have mentioned it: on the contrary, in ch. xviii. 1, the Evangelist expressly says that not till the concluding prayer was offered did the meeting in the upper-room break up. But if Jesus did not "arise and go hence" when He summoned the Eleven to go with Him, how are we to understand His words? We think they were spoken in the spirit of that earlier saying, "I have a baptism to be baptized with, and how am I straitened till it be accomplished." It was a spontaneous and irrepressible expression of the deep eagerness of His spirit to get into the conflict. If it was responded to somewhat too literally by those who hung on His blessed lips, in the way of a movement to depart, a wave of His hand would be enough to show that He had not *quite* done. Or it may be that those loving disciples were themselves reluctant to move so soon, and signified their not unwelcome wish that He should prolong His Discourse. Be this as it may, that disciple whose pen was dipt in a love to his Master which made His least movement and slightest word during these last hours seem worthy of record, has reported this little hastening of the Lamb to the slaughter with such artless life-like simplicity, that we seem to be of the party ourselves, and to catch the words rather from the Lips that spake than the pen that recorded them.

Remark.—Referring the reader to the general observations, prefixed to this chapter, on the whole of this wonderful portion of the Fourth Gospel, let him recall for a moment the contents of the present chapter. It is complete within itself. For no sooner had the glorious Speaker uttered the last words of it than He proposed to "arise and go." All that follows, therefore, is supplementary. Everything essential is here, and here in what a form! The very fragrance of heaven is in these out-pourings of Incarnate Love. Of every verse of it we may say,

> 'O, it came o'er my ear like the sweet south,
> That breathes upon a bank of violets,
> Stealing and giving odour.'—SHAKSPERE.

Look at the varied lights in which Jesus holds forth *Himself* to the confidence and love and obedience of His disciples. To their fluttering hearts—ready to sink at the prospect of His sufferings, His departure from them, and their own desolation without Him, to say nothing of His cause when left in such incompetent hands—His opening words are, "Let not your heart be troubled: ye believe in God, believe also in Me." 'Though clouds and darkness are round about Him, and His judgments are a great deep, yet *ye believe in God.* What time, then, your heart is overwhelmed, *believe in Me*, and darkness shall become light before you, and crooked things straight.' What a claim is this on the part of Jesus—to be in the Kingdom of Grace precisely as God is in that of Nature and Providence, or rather to be the glorious Divine Administrator of all things whatsoever in the interests and for the purposes of Grace; in the shadow of Whose wings, therefore, all who believe in God are to put their implicit trust, for the purposes of salvation! For He is not sent merely to *show* men the way to the Father, no, nor merely to *prepare* that way; but Himself *is* the Way, and the Truth, and the Life. We go not *from* Him, but *in* Him, to the Father. For He is in the Father, and the Father in Him; the words that He spake are the Father's words, and the works that He did are the Father's works; and He that hath seen Him hath seen the Father, for He is the Incarnate manifestation of the Godhead. But there are other views of Himself, equally transcendent, in which Jesus holds Himself forth here. To what a cheerless distance did He seem to be going away, and when and where should His disciples ever find Him again! ''Tis but to My Father's home,' He replies, 'and in due time it is to be yours too.' In that home there will not only be room for all, but a mansion for each. But it is not ready yet, and He is going to prepare it for them. For them He is going thither; for them He is to live there; and, when the last preparations are made, for them He will at length return, to take them to that home of His Father and their Father, that *where He is, there they may be also.* The attraction of heaven to those who love Him is, it seems, to be His Own presence there, and the beatific consciousness that they are *where He is*—language intolerable in a *creature*, but in Him who is the Incarnate, manifested Godhead, supremely worthy, and to His believing people in every age unspeakably reassuring. But again, He had said that in heaven He was to occupy Himself in preparing a place

15, I AM the true vine, and my Father is the husbandman. Every
2 [a]branch in me that beareth not fruit he taketh away; and every *branch*
that beareth fruit he purgeth it, that it may bring forth more fruit.

A. D. 33.

[a] Matt. 15. 13. Heb. 6. 8.

for them; so, a little afterwards, He tells them one of the ways in which this was to be done. To "hear prayer" is the exclusive prerogative of Jehovah, and one of the brightest jewels in His crown. But, says Jesus here, "Whatsoever ye shall ask of the Father in My name, THAT WILL I DO"—not as interfering with, or robbing God of His glory, but on the contrary—"that the Father may be glorified in the Son: If ye shall ask anything in My name, I WILL DO IT." Further, He is the *Life* and the *Law* of His people. Much do we owe to Moses; much to Paul: but never did either say to those who looked up to them, "Because I live, ye shall live also; If ye love Me, keep My commandments; If a man love Me, he will keep My word, and My Father will love him, and WE will come unto him, and make OUR abode with him."

Such is Jesus, by His own account; and this is conveyed, not in formal theological statements, but in warm outpourings of the heart, in the immediate prospect of the hour and power of darkness, yet without a trace of that perturbation of spirit which he experienced afterwards in the Garden: as if while the Eleven were around Him at the Supper-table *their* interests had altogether absorbed Him. The tranquillity of heaven reigns throughout this Discourse. The bright splendour of a noon-tide sun is not here, and had been somewhat incongruous at that hour. But the serenity of a matchless sunset is what we find here, which leaves in the devout mind a sublime repose—as if the glorious Speaker had gone from us, saying, "Peace I *leave* with you, *My* peace I *give* unto you: not as the world giveth, give I unto you. Let not your heart be troubled, neither let it be afraid."

CHAP. XV. 1-27.—CONTINUATION OF THE DISCOURSE AT THE SUPPER-TABLE.

The Vine, the Branches, and the Fruit (1-8). By a figure familiar to Jewish ears (Isa. v. 1-7; Ezek. xv.; &c.) Jesus here beautifully sets forth the spiritual Oneness of Himself and His people, and His relation to them as the Source of all their spiritual life and fruitfulness. **1. I am the true vine**—of which the natural vine is no more than a shadow. **and my Father is the husbandman**—the great Proprietor of the Vineyard, the Lord of the spiritual Kingdom. **2. Every branch in me that beareth not fruit he taketh away** [αἴρει]; **and every branch that beareth fruit he purgeth it** [καθαίρει], **that it may bring forth more fruit.** There is a verbal play upon the two Greek words for "taketh away" and "purgeth" [*airein—kathairein*], which it is impossible to convey in English. But it explains why so uncommon a word as "purgeth," with reference to a fruit tree, was chosen—the one word no doubt suggesting the other. The sense of both is obvious enough, and the truths conveyed by the whole verse are deeply important. Two classes of Christians are here set forth—both of them *in Christ*, as truly as the branch is in the vine; but while the one class bear fruit, the other bear none. The natural husbandry will sufficiently explain the cause of this difference. A graft may be *mechanically attached* to a fruit tree, and yet take no vital hold of it, and have no *vital connection* with it. In that case, receiving none of the juices of the tree—no vegetable sap from the stem—it can bear no fruit. Such merely mechanical attachment to the True Vine is that of all who believe in the truths of Christianity, and are in visible membership with the Church of Christ, but, having no living faith in Jesus nor desire for His salvation, open not their souls to the spiritual life of which He is the Source, take no vital hold of Him, and have no living union to Him. All such are incapable of fruit-bearing. They have an external, mechanical connection with Christ, as members of His Church visible; and in that sense they are, not in name only but in reality, branches "in the true Vine." Mixing, as these sometimes do, with living Christians in their most sacred services and spiritual exercises, where Jesus Himself is, according to His promise, they may come into such close contact with Him as those did who "pressed upon Him" in the days of His flesh, when the woman with the issue of blood touched the hem of His garment. But just as the branch that opens not its pores to let in the vital juices of the vine to which it may be most firmly attached has no more vegetable *life*, and is no more capable of bearing *fruit*, than if it were in the fire; so such merely external Christians have no more spiritual life, and are no more capable of spiritual fruitfulness, than if they had never heard of Christ, or were already separated from Him. The reverse of this class are those "in Christ that bear fruit." Their union to Christ is a *vital*, not a mechanical one; they are *one spiritual life* with Him: only in Him it is a Fontal life; in them a derived life, even as the life of the branch is that of the vine with which it is vitally one. Of them Christ can say, "Because I live, ye shall live also:" of Him do they say, "Of His fulness have all we received, and grace for grace." Such are the two classes of Christians of which Jesus here speaks. Observe now the procedure of the great Husbandman towards each. Every fruitless branch He "taketh away." Compare what is said of the barren fig tree, "Cut it down" (see on Luke xiii. 1-9, Remark 5 at the close of that Section). The thing here intended is not the same as "casting it into the fire" (*v.* 6): that is a subsequent process. It is 'the severance of that tie which bound them to Christ' here; so that they shall no longer be fruitless branches *in* the true Vine, no longer unclothed guests at the marriage-feast. That condition of things shall not last always. "The ungodly shall not stand in the judgment, nor sinners in the congregation of the righteous" (Ps. i. 5). But "every branch that beareth fruit"—in virtue of such living connection with Christ and reception of spiritual life from Him as a fruitful branch has from the natural vine—"He purgeth it, that it may bring forth more fruit." Here also the processes of the natural husbandry may help us. Without the pruning knife a tree is apt to go all *to wood*, as the phrase is. This takes place when the sap of the tree goes exclusively to the formation and growth of fresh branches, and none of it to the production of fruit. To prevent this, the tree is *pruned;* that is to say, all superfluous shoots are lopped off, which would have drawn away, to no useful purpose, the sap of the tree, and thus the whole vegetable juices and strength of the tree go towards their proper use—the nourishment of the healthy branches and the production of fruit. But what, it may be asked, is that rankness and luxuriance in living Christians which requires the pruning knife of the great Husbandman? The words of another parable will sufficiently answer that question: "The cares of this world, and the deceitfulness of riches, and the lusts of other things

3 Now [b]ye are clean through the word which I have spoken unto you.
4 Abide [c]in me, and I in you. As the branch cannot bear fruit of itself,
except it abide in the vine; no more can ye, except ye abide in me.
5 I am the vine, ye *are* the branches: He that abideth in me, and I in
him, the same bringeth forth much [d]fruit: for [1]without me ye can do
6 nothing. If a [e]man abide not in me, he is cast forth as a branch, and
is withered; and men gather them, and cast *them* into the fire, and they
7 are burned. If ye abide in me, and my words abide in you, ye shall ask

A. D. 33.

[b] Eph. 5. 26. 1 Pet. 1. 22.
[c] Col. 1. 23. 1 John 2. 6.
[d] Hos. 14. 8. Phil. 4. 13.
[1] Or, severed from me.
[e] Heb 6. 4-6.

entering in, choke the word, and it becometh unfruitful" (see on Mark iv. 19). True, that is said of such hearers of the word as "bring no fruit to perfection" at all. But the very same causes operate to the *hindrance* of fruitfulness in the living branches of the true Vine, and the great Husbandman has to "purge" them of these, that they may bring forth more fruit; lopping off at one time their worldly prosperity, at another time the olive plants that grow around their table, and at yet another time their own health or peace of mind: a process painful enough, but no less needful and no less beneficial in the spiritual than in the natural husbandry. Not one nor all of these operations, it is true, will of themselves increase the fruitfulness of Christians. But He who afflicteth not willingly, but smites to heal—who purgeth the fruitful branches for no other end than that they may bring forth more fruit—makes these "chastenings afterward to yield the peaceable fruit of righteousness" in larger measures than before. **3. Now ye are clean through the word** [*"Ηδη ὑμεῖς καθαροί·ἐστε διὰ τὸν λόγον*]—'Already are ye clean by reason of the word' **which I have spoken unto you.** He had already said of the Eleven, using another figure, that they were "clean," and "needed only to wash their feet." Here He repeats this, reminding them of the means by which this was brought about—"the word which He had spoken to them." For "as many as received Him, to them gave He power to become the sons of God." He "purified their hearts by faith," and "sanctified them through His truth; His word was the truth." (See on ch. xvii. 17.) Such, then, being their state, what would He have them to do? **4. Abide in me, and I in you.** The latter clause may be taken as a *promise:* 'Abide in Me, and I will abide in you.' (So *Calvin, Beza, Meyer, Lücke, Luthardt* understand it.) But we rather take it as part of one *injunction:* 'See to it that ye abide in Me, and that I abide in you;' the twofold condition of spiritual fruitfulness. (So *Grotius, Bengel, Tholuck, Alford, Webster and Wilkinson* view it.) What follows seems to confirm this. **As the branch cannot bear fruit of itself, except it abide in the vine; no more can ye, except ye abide in me.** Should anything interrupt the free communication of a branch with the tree of which it is a part, so that the sap should not reach it, it could bear no fruit. In order to this it is absolutely necessary that the one abide in the other, in this vital sense of *reception* on the one hand, and *communication* on the other. So with Christ and His people. **5. I am the vine, ye are the branches: He that abideth in me, and I in him, the same bringeth forth much fruit.** This is just the positive form of what had been said negatively in the previous verse. But it is more. Without abiding in Christ we cannot bear any fruit at all; but he that abideth in Christ, and Christ in him, the same bringeth forth—not fruit merely, as we should expect, but—"much fruit:" meaning, that as Christ seeks only a *receptive* soul to be a *communicative* Saviour, so there is no limit to the communication from Him but in the power of reception in us. **for without me**—disconnected from Me, in the sense explained, **ye can do nothing**—nothing spiritually good, nothing which God will regard and accept as good. **6. If a man abide not in me, he is cast forth as a branch, and is withered.** This *withering*, it will be observed, comes before the *burning*, just as the withering is preceded by the *taking away* (*v.* 2). The thing intended seems to be the decay and disappearance of all that in religion (and in many cases this is not little) which even an external connection with Christ imparts to those who are destitute of vital religion. **and [men] gather them.** Compare what is said in the parable of the Tares: "The Son of Man shall send forth His angels, and they shall *gather* out of His kingdom all things that offend, and them which do iniquity" (Matt. xiii. 41). **and cast them into the fire, and they are burned.** The one proper use of the vine is to bear *fruit.* Failing this, it is useless, save for *fuel.* This is strikingly set forth in the form of a parable in Ezek. xv., to which there is here a manifest allusion: "Son of man, what is the vine tree more than any tree, or than a branch which is among the trees of the forest?"—Why is it planted in a vineyard, and dressed with such care and interest, more than any other tree save only for the *fruit* which it yields?—"Shall wood be taken thereof to do any work? or will a man take a pin of it to hang any vessel thereon?"—Does it admit of being turned to any of the purposes of woodwork, even the most insignificant?—"Behold, it is cast into the fire for fuel"—that is the one use of it, failing fruit;—"the fire devoureth both the ends of it, and the midst of it is burned"—not an inch of it is fit for aught else:—"Is it meet for any work?" **7. If ye abide in me, and my words abide in you.** Mark the change from the inhabitation of *Himself* to that of His *words.* But as we are clean through His word (*v.* 2), and sanctified through His word (ch. xvii. 17), so He dwells in us through "His words"—those words of His, the believing reception of which alone opens the heart to let Him come in to us. So in the preceding chapter (xiv. 23), "If a man love Me, he will keep My words: and My Father will love him, and we will come unto him, and make our abode with him." And so in the last of His epistles to the churches of Asia, "Behold, I stand at the door and knock: if any man *hear my voice*"—and so my words abide in him, "I will come in to him, and will sup with him, and he with Me" (Rev. iii. 20). **ye shall ask what ye will, and it shall be done unto you.** A startling latitude of asking this seems to be. Is it, then, to be understood with limitations? and if not, would not such boundless license seem to countenance all manner of fanatical extravagance? The one limitation expressly mentioned is all-sufficient to guide the askings so as to ensure the answering. If we but abide in Christ, and Christ's words abide in us, "every thought" is so "brought into captivity to the obedience of Christ," that no desires will rise and no petition be offered but such as are in harmony with the divine

8 what ye will, and it shall be done unto you. Herein [f]is my Father
glorified, that ye bear much fruit; so shall ye be my disciples.
9 As the Father hath loved me, so have I loved you: continue ye in my
10 love. If ye keep my commandments, ye shall abide in my love; even as
I have kept my Father's commandments, and abide in his love.
11 These things have I spoken unto you, that my joy might remain in you,
12 and [g]*that* your joy might be full. This [h]is my commandment, That ye
13 love one another, as I have loved you. Greater [i]love hath no man than
14 this, that a man lay down his life for his friends. Ye are my friends, if
15 ye do whatsoever I command you. Henceforth I call you not servants;
for the servant knoweth not what his lord doeth: but I have called you
friends; [j]for all things that I have heard of my Father I have made
16 known unto you. Ye [k]have not chosen me, but I have chosen you, and
[l]ordained you, that ye should go and bring forth fruit, and *that* your fruit

A. D. 33.

f Matt. 5. 16. Phil. 1. 11.
g ch 16. 24. 1 John 1. 4.
h 1 Thes. 4. 9. 1 Pet. 4. 8. 1 John 3. 11.
i Rom. 5. 7. Eph. 5. 2.
j Gen. 18. 17-19. Luke 10. 23, 24. Acts 20. 27.
k 1 John 4. 10.
l Mark 16. 15. Col. 1. 6.

will. The soul, yielding itself implicitly and wholly to Christ, and Christ's words penetrating and moulding it sweetly into conformity with the will of God, its very breathings are of God, and so cannot but meet with a divine response. **8. Herein is my Father glorified** [ἐδοξάσθη—on which peculiar use of the aorist, see on ch. x. 4], **that ye bear much fruit.** As His whole design in providing "the True Vine," and making men living branches in Him, was to obtain *fruit;* and as He purgeth every branch that beareth fruit, that it may bring forth *more fruit;* so herein is He glorified, that we bear *much fruit.* As the husbandman feels that his pains are richly rewarded when the fruit of his vineyard is abundant, so the eternal designs of Grace are seen to come to glorious effect when the vessels of mercy, the redeemed of the Lord, abound in the fruits of righteousness, which are by Jesus Christ unto the glory and praise of God, and then the Father of our Lord Jesus Christ "rests in His love and joys over them with singing." **so shall ye be** [γενήσεσθε]—or 'become' **my disciples**—that is, so shall ye manifest and evidence your discipleship.

How to Retain Christ's Love and our own Joy (9-11). **9. As the Father hath loved me, so have I loved you.** See on ch. xvii. 22, 26. **continue**—or 'abide' **ye in my love**—not, 'continue ye to love Me,' but 'abide ye in the possession and enjoyment of My love to you;' as is evident from what follows. **10. If ye keep my commandments, ye shall abide in my love**—the obedient spirit of true discipleship attracting and securing the continuance and increase of Christ's loving regard; **even as I have kept my Father's commandments, and abide in his love.** What a wonderful statement is this which Christ makes about Himself. In neither case, it will be observed, is obedience the original and proper ground of the love spoken of. As an earthly father does not *primarily* love his son for his obedience, but because of the filial relation which he bears to him, so the love which Christ's Father bears to Him is not primarily drawn forth by His obedience, but by the Filial relation which He sustains to Him. The Son's Incarnation neither added to nor diminished from this. But it provided a new form and manifestation of that love. As His own Son in our nature, the Father's affection went out to Him as the Son of Man; and just as a human father, on beholding the cordial and constant obedience of his own child, feels his own affection thereby irresistibly drawn out to him, so every beauty of the Son's Incarnate character, and every act of His Human obedience, rendered Him more lovely in the Father's eye, drew down new complacency upon Him, fresh love to Him. Thus, then, it was that by the keeping of His Father's commandments Jesus abode in the possession and enjoyment of His Father's love. And thus, says Jesus, shall it be between you and Me: If ye would retain My love to you, know that the whole secret of it lies in the keeping of My commandments: Never need ye be without the full sunshine of My love on your souls, if ye do but carry yourselves in the same obedient frame towards Me as I do towards My Father. **11. These things have I spoken unto you, that my joy might remain**—'abide' **in you, and that your joy might be full** [πληρωθῇ]—or 'be fulfilled.' We take "these things which Christ had spoken unto them" to mean, not all that Christ uttered on this occasion—as interpreters generally do—but more definitely, the things He had just before said about the true secret of His abiding in His Father's love and of their abiding in His love. In that case, the sense will be this: 'As it is My joy to have My Father's love resting on Me in the keeping of His commandments, so have I told how ye yourselves may have that very joy of Mine abiding in you and filling you full.'

The Love of the Brethren (12-17). **12. This is my commandment, That ye love one another, as I have loved you.** See on ch. xiii. 34, 35. **13. Greater love hath no man than this, that a man lay down his life for his friends.** The emphasis here lies, not on "friends," but on "*laying down his life*" for them:—*q. d.*, 'One can show no greater regard for those dear to him than to give his life for them, and this is the love ye shall find in Me.' **14. Ye are my friends, if ye do whatsoever I command you**—'if ye hold yourselves in absolute subjection to Me.' **15. Henceforth I call you not servants**—that is, in the restricted sense explained in the next words; for servants He still calls them (*v.* 20), and such they delight to call themselves, in the sense of being "under law to Christ" (1 Cor. ix. 21); **for the servant knoweth not what his lord doeth**—knows nothing of his master's *plans* and *reasons*, but simply receives and executes his orders: **but I have called you friends; for all things that I have heard of my Father I have made known unto you**—'I have admitted you to free, unrestrained fellowship, keeping back nothing from you which I have received to communicate.' (See Gen. xviii. 17; Ps. xxv. 14; Isa. l. 4). **16. Ye have not chosen me, but I have chosen you**—a wholesome memento after the lofty things He had just said about their mutual indwelling, and the unreservedness of the friendship to which He had admitted them. **and ordained** [ἔθηκα]—or 'appointed' **you, that ye should go and bring forth fruit**—that is, ye are to give yourselves to this as your proper business. The fruit intended, though embracing

should remain; that whatsoever ye shall ask of the Father in my name,
17 he may give it you. These things I command you, that ye love one
another.
18 If [m] the world hate you, ye know that it hated me before *it hated* you.
19 If [n] ye were of the world, the world would love his own: but [o] because ye
are not of the world, but I have chosen you out of the world, therefore
20 the world hateth you. Remember the word that I said unto you, The
servant is not greater than his lord. If they have persecuted me, they
will also persecute you; [p] if they have kept my saying, they will keep
21 yours also. But all these things will they do unto you for my name's
sake, because they know not him that sent me.
22 If [q] I had not come and spoken unto them, they had not had sin: [r] but
23 now they have no [2] cloak for their sin. He [s] that hateth me hateth my
24 Father also. If I had not done among them the works which none other
man did, they had not had sin: but now have they both seen and hated
25 both me and my Father. But *this cometh to pass*, that the word might be
fulfilled that is written in their law, [t] They hated me without a cause.

A. D. 33.

m Zec. 11. 8. Matt 5. 11. Mark 13.13. Luke 6. 22. 1 John 3. 1, 13.
n Luke 6. 32, 33. 1 John 4. 5.
o ch. 17. 14.
p 1 Sam. 8. 7. Isa. 53. 1, 3. Ezek. 3. 7.
q ch. 9. 41.
r Rom. 1. 20. Jas. 4. 17.
2 Or excuse.
s 1 John 2.23. 2 John 9.
t Ps. 35. 19. Ps. 69. 4. Ps. 109. 3.

all spiritual fruitfulness, is here specially that particular fruit of "loving one another," which *v.* 17 shows to be still the subject spoken of. **and that your fruit should remain**—showing itself to be an imperishable and ever-growing principle. (See Prov. iv. 18; 2 John 8.) **that whatsoever ye shall ask of the Father in my name, he may give it you.** See on *v.* 7. **17. These things I command you, that ye love one another.** Our Lord repeats here what He had said in *v.* 12, but He recurs to it here in order to give it fresh and affecting point. He is about to forewarn them of the certain hatred and persecution of the world, if they be His indeed. But before doing it, He enjoins on them anew the love of each other. It is as if He had said, 'And ye will have need of all the love ye can receive from one another, for outside your own pale ye have nothing to look for but enmity and opposition.' This, accordingly, is the subject of what follows.

How the World may be Expected to Regard and to Treat Christ's Genuine Disciples (18-21). The substance of these important verses has occurred more than once before. (See on Matt. x. 34-39, and Remark 2 at the close of that Section; and on Luke xii. 49-53, and Remark 4 at the end of that Section.) But the reader will do well to mark the peculiar light in which the subject is here presented. **18. If the world hate you, ye know that it hated me before it hated you. 19. If ye were of the world, the world would love his own: but because ye are not of the world, but I have chosen you out of the world** [ἐξελεξάμην], **therefore the world hateth you.** Here Jesus holds Himself forth as *the* Hated and Persecuted One; and this, not only as going before all His people in that respect, but as being the great Embodied Manifestation of that holiness which the world hates, and the Fountain of that hated state and character to all that believe in Him. From the treatment, therefore, which He met with they were not only to lay their account with the same, but be encouraged to submit to it, and cheered in the endurance of it, by the company they had and the cause in which it lighted upon them. Of course, this implies that if their separation from the world was to bring on them the world's enmity and opposition, then that enmity and opposition would be *just so great* as their separation from the world was, and no greater. Observe again that Christ here ascribes all that severance of His people from the world, which brings upon them its enmity and opposition, to His own 'choice of them out of it.' This cannot refer to the mere external separation of the Eleven to the apostleship, for Judas was so separated. Besides, this was spoken after Judas had voluntarily separated himself from the rest. It can refer only to such an inward operation upon them as made them entirely different in character and spirit from the world, and so objects of the world's hatred. **20. Remember the word that I said unto you, The servant is not greater than his lord. If they have persecuted me, they will also persecute you; if they have kept my saying, they will keep yours also.** See on Matt. x. 24, 25. **21. But all these things will they do unto you for my name's sake, because they know not him that sent me.** Here again are they cheered with the assurance that all the opposition they would experience from the world as His disciples would arise from its dislike to *Him*, and its estrangement in mind as well as heart from the Father that sent Him. But to impress this the more upon them, our Lord enlarges upon it in what follows.

The Inexcusableness of the World's Hatred of Christ (22-25). **22. If I had not come and spoken unto them, they had not had sin** [οὐκ εἶχον]—rather, 'would not have sin;' that is, of course, *comparatively:* all other sins being light compared with the rejection of the Son of God: **but now they have no cloak** [πρόφασιν]—or 'pretext' **for their sin. 23. He that hateth me hateth my Father also**—so brightly revealed in the incarnate Son that the hatred of the One was just naked enmity to the other. **24. If I had not done among them the works which none other man did** [ἐποίησεν is beyond doubt the true reading: the received text—πεποίηκεν, 'hath done'—has but inferior support]. **they had not had sin**—rather, as before, 'would not have sin,' *comparatively:* **but now have they both seen and hated both me and my Father:** they saw His Father revealed in Him, and in Him they hated both the Father and the Son. In *v.* 22 He places the peculiar aggravation of their guilt in His having "come and spoken to them;" here He makes it consist in their having seen Him do the works which none other man did. See on ch. xiv. 10, 11, where we have the same association of His *works* and His *words*, as either of them sufficient to show that the Father was in Him and He in the Father. **25. But [this cometh to pass], that the word might be fulfilled that is written in their law** (Ps. lxix. 4), **They hated me without a cause.** The New Testa-

26 But [u]when the Comforter is come, whom I will send unto you from the
Father, *even* the Spirit of truth, which proceedeth from the Father, [v]he
27 shall testify of me: And [w]ye also shall bear witness, because [x]ye have
been with me from the beginning.

A. D. 33.

[u] Acts 2. 33.
[v] 1 John 5. 6.
[w] Acts 1. 8.
[x] Luke 1. 2.

ment references to this Messianic psalm of suffering are numerous (see ch. ii. 17; Acts i. 20; Rom. xi. 9, 10; xv. 3), and this one, as here used, is very striking.

The Two-fold Witness which Christ was to receive from the Holy Ghost and from His chosen Apostles (26). **26. But when the Comforter is come, whom I will send unto you from the Father, even the Spirit of truth, which proceedeth from the Father.** How brightly are *Father, Son, and Holy Ghost*—in their distinct Personality, brought here before us! While the 'procession' of the Holy Ghost, as it is called, was by the whole ancient Church founded on this statement regarding Him, that He "proceedeth from the Father," the Greek Church inferred from it that, in the internal relations of the Godhead, the Spirit proceedeth *from* the Father only, *through* the Son; while the Latin Church insisted that He proceedeth from the Father *and the Son:* and one short word (*Filioque*), which the latter would exclude and the former insert in the Creed, was the cause of the great schism between the Eastern and the Western Churches. That the *internal* or *essential* procession of the Holy Ghost is the thing here intended, has been the prevailing opinion of the orthodox Churches of the Reformation, and is that of good critics even in our day. But though we seem warranted in affirming—in the technical language of divines—that the *economic* order follows the *essential* in the relations of the Divine Persons—in other words, that in the economy of Redemption the relations sustained by the Divine Persons do but reflect their essential relations—it is very doubtful whether more is expressed here than the *historical* aspect of this mission and procession of the Spirit from the Father by the Agency of the Son. **he shall testify of me**—referring to that glorious Pentecostal attestation of the Messiahship of the Lord Jesus which, in a few days, gave birth to a flourishing Christian Church in the murderous capital itself, and the speedy diffusion of it far and wide. **27. And ye also**—as the other witness required to the validity of testimony among men (Deut. xix. 15) **shall bear witness** [μαρτυρεῖτε]—or 'do bear witness' **because ye have been** [ἐστε]—or 'are' **with me from the beginning.** Our Lord here uses the present tense—"do testify" and "are with Me"—to express the opportunities which they had enjoyed for this office of witness-bearing, from their having been with Him from the outset of His ministry (see on Luke i. 2), and how this observation and experience of Him, being now all but completed, they were already virtually a company of chosen witnesses for His Name.

Remarks.—1. If the strain in which our Lord spoke of Himself in the foregoing chapter was such as befitted only Lips Divine, in no less exalted a tone does He speak throughout all this chapter. For any mere creature, however lofty, to represent himself as *the one Source of all spiritual vitality* in men, would be insufferable. But this our Lord here explicitly and emphatically does, and that at the most solemn hour of His earthly history—on the eve of His death. To abide in Him, he says, is to have spiritual life and fruitfulness; not to abide in Him is to be fit only for the fire—"whose end is to be burned." What prophet or apostle ever ventured to put forth for himself such a claim as this? Yet see how the Father's rights and honours are upheld. My Father, says Jesus, is the Husbandman of that great Vineyard whose whole spring of life and fruitfulness is in Me; and herein is My Father glorified, that all the branches in the True Vine do bear much fruit. Then, again, such power and prevalency with God does He attach to His people's abiding in Him, and His words abiding in them, that His Father will withhold nothing from such that they shall ask of Him. In a word, so perfect a manifestation of the Father does He declare Himself to be in our nature, that to see Him is to see Both at once, and to hate Him is to be guilty in one and the same act of deadly hostility to Both. 2. When our Lord said, "If ye abide in Me, and *My words* abide in you," He must have contemplated the *preservation of His words in a written Record*, and designed that, over and above the general truth conveyed by His teaching, the precise form in which He couched that truth should be carefully treasured up and cherished by His believing people. Hence the importance of that promise, that the Spirit should "bring all things to their remembrance, whatsoever He had said unto them." (See on ch. xiv. 26.) And hence the danger of those loose views of Inspiration which would abandon all faith even in the words of Christ, as reported in the Gospels, and abide by what is called the spirit or general import of them—as if even this could be depended upon when the form in which it was couched is regarded as uncertain. (See on ch. xvii. 17.) 3. If we would have *Christ Himself* abiding in us, it must be, we see, by "*His words* abiding in us" (*v.* 7). Let the word of Christ, then, dwell in you richly in all wisdom (Col. iii. 16). 4. How small is the confidence reposed in that promise of the Faithful and True Witness, "If ye abide in Me, and My words abide in you, ye shall ask what ye will, and it shall be done unto you"—if we may judge by the formal character and the languid and uncertain tone of the generality of Christian prayers! Surely, if we had full faith in such a promise, it would give to our prayers such a definite character and such a lively assured tone as, while themselves no small part of the true answer, to prepare the petitioner for the divine response to his suit. Such a manner of praying, indeed, is apt to be regarded as presumptuous by some even true Christians, who are too great strangers to the spirit of adoption. But if we abide in our living Head, and His words abide in us, our carriage in this exercise, as in every other, will commend itself. 5. Let Christians learn from their Master's teaching in this chapter whence proceeds much, if not most, of their darkness and uncertainty as to whether they be the gracious objects of God's saving love in Christ Jesus. "If ye keep My commandments," says Jesus, "ye shall abide in My love, even as I have kept My Father's commandments, and abide in His love." Habitual want of conscience as to any one of these will suffice to cloud the mind as to the love of Christ resting upon us. Take, for example, that one commandment which our Lord so emphatically reiterates in this chapter: "This is My commandment, That ye love one another, as I have loved you. These things I command you, that ye love one another." No ordinary love is this. "As I have loved you" is the sublime Model, as it is the only spring of this commanded love of the brethren. How much of this is there among

16 THESE things have I spoken unto you, that ye should not be offended.
2 They shall put you out of the synagogues: yea, the time cometh, [a]that
3 whosoever killeth you will think that he doeth God service. And [b]these
things will they do unto you, because they have not known the Father,
4 nor me. But these things have I told you, that, when the time shall
come, ye may remember that I told you of them. And these things I
5 said not unto you at the beginning, because I was with you. But now
I go my way to him that sent me; and none of you asketh me, Whither
6 goest thou? But because I have said these things unto you, sorrow
hath filled your heart.
7 Nevertheless I tell you the truth; It is expedient for you that I go
away: for if I go not away, the Comforter will not come unto you; but
8 [c]if I depart, I will send him unto you. And when he is come, he will [1]re-

A. D. 33.

CHAP. 16.
[a] Matt. 10. 28. Acts 5. 33. Acts 8. 1. Acts 9. 1. Acts 26. 9. Rom. 10. 2. Gal 1. 13.
[b] Rom. 10. 2. 1 Cor. 2. 8. 1 Tim. 1. 13.
[c] Acts 2. 33. Eph. 4. 8.
[1] Or, convince. 1 Cor. 14. 24.

Christians? To what extent is it characteristic of them—how far is it their notorious undeniable character? (See on ch. xvii. 21.) Alas! whether we look to churches or to individual Christians, the open manifestation of any such feeling is the exception rather than the rule. Or let us try how far the generality of Christians are like their Lord by the world's feeling towards them. We know how it felt towards Jesus Himself. It was what He was that the world hated: it was His fidelity in exposing its evil ways that the world could not endure. Had He been less holy than He was, or been contented to endure the unholiness that reigned around Him without witnessing against it, He had not met with the opposition that He did. "The world cannot hate you," said He to His brethren, "but Me it hateth, because I testify of it, that the works thereof are evil" (ch. vii. 7). And the same treatment, in principle, He here prepares His genuine disciples for, when He should leave them to represent Him in the world—"Remember the word that I said unto you, The servant is not greater than His lord. If ye were of the world, the world would love his own; but because ye are not of the world, but I have chosen you out of the world, therefore the world hateth you." Is it not, then, too much to be feared that the good terms which the generality of Christians are on with the world are owing, not to the near approach of the world to them, but to their so near approach to the world, that the essential and unchangeable difference between them is hardly seen? And if so, need we wonder that those words of Jesus seem too high to be reached at all—"If ye keep My commandments, ye shall abide in My love; even as I have kept My Father's commandments, and abide in His love"? When Christians cease from the vain attempt to serve two masters, and from receiving honour one of another, instead of seeking the honour that cometh from God only; when they count all things but loss, that they may win Christ, and the love of Christ constraineth them to live not unto themselves, but unto Him that died for them and rose again: then will they abide in Christ's love, even as He abode in His Father's love; His joy shall then abide in them; and their joy shall be full.

CHAP. XVI. 1-33.—CONCLUSION OF THE DISCOURSE AT THE SUPPER-TABLE.

Persecution, even unto Death, to be Expected (1-4). **1. These things have I spoken unto you, that ye should not be offended**—or 'scandalized;' referring back both to the warnings and the encouragements He had just given. **2. They shall put you out of the synagogues** [Ἀποσυναγώγους ποιήσουσιν ὑμᾶς]—(see on ch. ix. 22; see also xii. 42): **yea, the time cometh, that whosoever killeth you will think that he doeth God service** [λατρείαν προσφέρειν]—or 'that he is offering a [religious] service unto God;' as Saul of Tarsus did (Acts xxvi. 9, 10; Gal. i. 9, 10; Phil. iii. 6). **3. And these things will they do unto you, because they have not known the Father, nor me.** See on ch. xv. 21, of which this is nearly a verbal repetition. **4. But these things have I told you, that, when the time** [ὥρα]—or 'the hour' **shall come, ye may remember that I told you of them**—and so be confirmed in your faith and strengthened in courage. **And these things I said not unto you at the beginning, because I was with you.** He *had* said it pretty early (Luke vi. 22), but not so nakedly as in *v.* 2.

His approaching Departure to His Father again Announced, and the Necessity of it in order to the Mission of the Comforter (5-7). **5. But now I go my way to him that sent me.** While He was with them the world's hatred was directed chiefly against Himself; but His departure would bring it down upon them as His representatives. **and none of you asketh me, Whither goest thou?** They *had* done so in a sort, ch. xiii. 36; xiv. 5; but He wished more intelligent and eager enquiry on the subject. **6. But because I have said these things unto you, sorrow hath filled your heart.** And how, it may be asked, could it be otherwise? But this sorrow had too much paralyzed them, and He would rouse their energies. **7. Nevertheless I tell you the truth; It is expedient for you that I go away**—

'My Saviour, can it ever be
That I should gain by losing thee?'—KEBLE.

Yes, **for if I go not away, the Comforter will not come unto you; but if I depart, I will send him unto you.** See on ch. vii. 39, and Remark 3 at the end of that Section; and on ch. xiv. 16.

The Three-fold Office of the Comforter (8-11). This passage, says *Olshausen*, 'is one of the most pregnant with thought in the profound discourses of Christ. With a few great strokes He depicts all and every part of the ministry of the Divine Spirit in the world; His operation with reference to individuals as well as the mass, on believers and unbelievers alike.' It is laid out in three particulars, each of which is again taken up and explained in detail.

8. And when he is come, he will reprove the world of SIN, and of RIGHTEOUSNESS, and of JUDGMENT.

The word rendered 'reprove' [ἐλέγξει] means more than that. *Reproof* is indeed implied, and doubtless the work begins with it. But 'convict,' or, as in the margin, 'convince,' is the thing intended; and as the one word expresses the work of the Spirit on the *unbelieving* portion of man-

9 [1] prove the world of sin, and of righteousness, and of judgment: of [d] sin,
10 because they believe not on me; of [e] righteousness, because I go to my
11 Father, and ye see me no more; of [f] judgment, because [g] the prince of
this world is judged.

A. D. 33.

[d] Acts 2. 22.
[e] Acts 2. 32.
[f] Acts 26. 18.
[g] Luke 10.18.

kind, and the other on the *believing*, it is better not to restrict the term to either.

First, **9. Of SIN, because they believe not on me.** By this is not meant that He shall deal with men about *the sin of unbelief only;* nor yet about that sin as, in comparison with all other sins, *the greatest.* There is no comparison here between the sin of unbelief and other breaches of the moral law, in point of criminality. The key to this important statement will be found in such sayings of our Lord Himself as the following: "He that believeth is not condemned; but he that believeth not is condemned already, because he hath not believed in the name of the Only begotten Son of God: He that heareth My word, and believeth on Him that sent Me, hath everlasting life, and shall not come into condemnation, but is passed from death unto life: He that believeth not the Son shall not see life, but the wrath of God abideth on him" (ch. iii. 18, 36; v. 24). What the Spirit, then, does in the discharge of this first department of His work, is to bear in upon men's consciences the conviction that the one divinely provided way of deliverance from the guilt of *all sin* is believing on the Son of God; that *as soon* as they thus believe, there is no condemnation to them; but that *unless* and *until* they do so, they underlie the guilt of all their sins, with that of this crowning and all-condemning sin superadded. Thus does the Spirit, in fastening this truth upon the conscience, instead of extinguishing, only consummate and intensify the sense of all other sins; causing the convicted sinner to perceive that his complete absolution from guilt, or his remediless condemnation under the weight of all his sins, hangs upon his believing on the Son of God, or his deliberate rejection of Him.

But what, it may be asked, is the sinner to believe regarding Christ, in order to so vast a deliverance? The next department of the Spirit's work will answer that question.

Second, **10. Of RIGHTEOUSNESS, because I go to my Father, and ye see** [θεωρεῖτε]—or 'behold'—**me no more.** Beyond doubt, it is *Christ's personal righteousness* which the Spirit was to bring home to the sinner's heart. The evidence of this was to lie in the great *historical fact*, that He had "gone to His Father, and was no more visible to men:" for if His claim to be the Son of God, the Saviour of the world, had been a lie, how should the Father, who is "a jealous God," have raised such a blasphemer from the dead, and exalted him to His right hand? But if He was the "Faithful and True Witness," the Father's "Righteous Servant," "His Elect, in whom His soul delighted," then was His departure to the Father, and consequent disappearance from the view of men, but the fitting consummation, the august reward, of all that He did here below, the seal of His mission, the glorification of the testimony which He bore on earth, by the translation of its Bearer to the Father's bosom. This triumphant vindication of Christ's *rectitude* is to us divine evidence, bright as heaven, that He is indeed the Saviour of the world, God's Righteous Servant to justify many, because He bare their iniquities (Is. liii. 11). Thus the Spirit, in this second sphere of His work, is seen convincing men that there is in Christ perfect relief under the sense of *sin*, of which He had before convinced them; and so far from mourning over His absence from us, as an irreparable loss, we learn to glory in it, as the evidence of His perfect acceptance on our behalf, exclaiming with one who understood this point, "Who shall lay any thing to the charge of God's elect? It is God that justifieth; who is he that condemneth? It is Christ that died, *yea rather, that is risen again, who is even at the right hand of God,*" &c. (Rom. viii. 33, 34). 'But, alas!'—may some say, who have long been "sold under sin," who have too long been willing captives of the prince of this world—'Of what avail to me is deliverance from any amount of guilt, and investiture even in the righteousness which cannot be challenged, if I am to be left under the power of sin and Satan? for he that committeth sin is of the devil, and to be carnally minded is death.' But you are not to be so left. For there remains one more department of the Spirit's work, which exactly meets, and was intended to meet, your case.

Third, **11. Of JUDGMENT, because the prince of this world is**—or 'hath been' **judged.** By taking the word "judgment" to refer to the judgment of the great day—as is done even by good interpreters—the point of this glorious assurance is quite missed. Beyond all doubt, when it is said, "The prince of this world hath been *judged*" [κέκριται]—or, in our Lord's usual sense of that term, *condemned*—the meaning is the same as in a former chapter, where, speaking of His *death*, He says, "Now shall the prince of this world be *cast out* [ἐκβληθήσεται ἔξω]; and in both places the meaning clearly is, that the prince of this world is, by the death of Christ, *judicially overthrown*, or *condemned to lose his hold*, and so, "cast out" or *expelled from his usurped dominion* over men who, believing in the Son of God, are made the righteousness of God in Him: so that, looking to Him who spoiled principalities and powers, and made a show of them openly, triumphing over them in His cross, they need henceforth have no fear of his enslaving power. (See Col. ii. 15; Heb. ii. 14; 1 John iii. 8.)

Thus is this three-fold office of the Spirit entirely of one character. It is in all its departments *Evangelical* and *Saving:* bringing home to the conscience the sense of sin, as all consummated and fastened down upon the sinner who rejects Him that came to put away sin by the sacrifice of Himself; the sense of perfect relief in the *righteousness* of the Father's servant, now taken from the earth that spurned Him to that bosom where from everlasting He had dwelt; and the sense of emancipation from the fetters of Satan, whose *judgment* brings to men *liberty to be holy*, and transformation out of servants of the devil into sons and daughters of the Lord Almighty. To one class of men, however, all this will carry *conviction* only; they "will not come to Christ"—revealed though He be to them as the life-giving One—that they may have life. Such, abiding voluntarily under the dominion of the Prince of this world, are *judged in his judgment*, the visible consummation of which will be at the great day. But to another class this blessed teaching will have a different issue—translating them out of the kingdom of darkness into the kingdom of God's dear Son.

The Bearing of the Spirit's Work upon the Work of Christ (12-15). **12. I have yet many things to say unto you, but ye cannot bear them now.**

12 I have yet many things to say unto you, but ye cannot bear them
13 now. Howbeit when he, the Spirit of truth, is come, [h]he will guide you
into all truth: for he shall not speak of himself; but whatsoever he shall
14 hear, *that* shall he speak: and he will [i]show you things to come. He
shall glorify me; for he shall receive of mine, and shall show *it* unto you.
15 All [j]things that the Father hath are mine: therefore said I, that he
16 shall take of mine, and shall show *it* unto you. A little while, and ye
shall not see me: and again, a little while, and ye shall see me; because I go to the Father.
17 Then said *some* of his disciples among themselves, What is this that he
saith unto us, A little while, and ye shall not see me: and again, a little
18 while, and ye shall see me: and, Because I go to the Father? They said
therefore, What is this that he saith, A little while? we cannot tell what
19 he saith. Now Jesus knew that they were desirous to ask him, and said
unto them, Do ye enquire among yourselves of that I said, A little while,
and ye shall not see me: and again, a little while, and ye shall see me?
20 Verily, verily, I say unto you, That ye shall weep and lament, but the
world shall rejoice: and ye shall be sorrowful, but your sorrow shall be
21 turned into joy. A woman when she is in travail hath sorrow, because
her hour is come: but as soon as she is delivered of the child, she remembereth no more the anguish, for joy that a man is born into the
22 world. And ye now therefore have sorrow: but I will see you again, and

A. D. 33.

h ch. 14. 26. 1 Cor. 2, 10-13. Eph. 4. 7, 15. 1 John 2. 20, 27. Joel 2. 28. Acts 2. 17, 18. Acts 11. 28. Acts 20. 23. Acts 21. 9, 11. 2 Thes. 2. 3-12. 1 Tim. 4. 1. 2 Tim. 3. 1-5. 2 Pet. 2. 1. Rev. 1. 1,19.

j Matt. 11. 27. Matt. 28. 18. Luke 10. 22. ch. 3. 35. ch. 17. 10. Col 1. 19. Col. 2. 3, 9.

This refers not so much to truths not uttered by Himself at all, as to the full development and complete exposition of truths which at that stage could only be expressed generally or in their germs. **13. Howbeit when he, the Spirit of truth**—so called for the reason mentioned in the next clause, **is come, he will guide you into all truth** [πᾶσαν τὴν ἀλήθειαν]—rather, 'all the truth;' for the reference is not to 'truth in general,' but to 'that whole circle of truth whose burden is Christ and His redeeming work:' **for he shall not speak of himself** [ἀφ' ἑαυτοῦ]. The meaning is not, 'He shall not speak *concerning* Himself,' but 'He shall not speak *from* Himself;' in the sense immediately to be added. **but whatsoever he shall hear**—or receive to communicate, **that shall he speak: and he will show you things to come** [τὰ ἐρχόμενα]—'the things to come;' referring specially to those revelations which, in the Epistles partially, but most fully in the Apocalypse, open up a vista into the Future of the Kingdom of God, whose horizon is the everlasting hills. **14. He shall glorify me; for he shall receive of mine, and shall show it unto you.** Thus the whole design of the Spirit's office is to glorify Christ—not in His own Person, for this was done by the Father when He exalted Him to His own right hand—but in the view and estimation of men. For this purpose He was to "*receive of Christ*"—that is, all that related to His Person and Work—"and *show it unto them*," or make them, by His inward teaching, to discern it in its own light. The internal or *subjective* nature of the Spirit's teaching—how His office is to discover to the souls of men what Christ is outwardly or *objectively*—is here very clearly expressed; and, at the same time, the vanity of looking for revelations of the Spirit which shall do anything beyond throwing light in the soul upon what Christ Himself is, and taught, and did upon earth. **15. All things that the Father hath are mine: therefore said I, that he shall take** [λήμψεται, as in *v.* 14]—or, according to what appears the better supported reading, 'receiveth' [λαμβάνει], a lively way of saying 'He is just about to receive' **of mine, and shall show it unto you.** A plainer expression than this of *absolute community* with the Father in all things cannot be conceived, although the "all things" here have reference to the things of the Kingdom of Grace, which the Spirit was to receive that He might show them to us. We have here a wonderful glimpse into the *inner relations* of the Godhead. The design of this explanation seems to be to prevent any mistake as to the relations which He sustained to the Father.

Christ Soon to Go, but Soon to Return, and the Effect of these Movements on those who Loved and those who Hated Him (16-22). **16. A little while, and ye shall not see me** [θεωρεῖτε]—'and ye behold Me not:' **and again, a little while, and ye shall see me; because I go to the Father.** [The last clause—ὅτι ἐγὼ ὑπάγω πρὸς τὸν πατέρα—is omitted by *Tischendorf* and *Tregelles*, and bracketed by *Lachmann*. But the evidence in its favour is, in our judgment, preponderating; and the question of the disciples in *v.* 17 seems to presuppose it.] **17. Then said some of his disciples among themselves**—afraid, perhaps, to question the Lord Himself on the subject, or unwilling to interrupt Him, **What is this that he saith unto us, A little while, and ye shall not see me**—or, 'and ye behold Me not:' **and again, a little while, and ye shall see me: and, Because I go to the Father? 18. They said therefore, What is this that he saith, A little while?** [τὸ μικρόν]—rather, 'The,' or 'That little while?' **we cannot tell what he saith**—[οὐκ οἴδαμεν τί λαλεῖ]—'We know not what He speaketh of.' **19. Now Jesus knew that they were desirous to ask him**—showing with what tender minuteness He watched how far they apprehended His teaching, what impressions it produced upon them, and what steps it prompted to. **and said unto them, Do ye enquire among yourselves of that I said, A little while, &c. 20. Verily, verily, I say unto you, That ye shall weep and lament, but the world shall rejoice: and ye shall be sorrowful, but your sorrow shall be turned into joy. 21. A woman when she is in travail hath sorrow, &c. 22. And ye now therefore have sorrow: but I will see you again, and your heart shall rejoice, and your joy no man taketh from you.** The

23 [k]your heart shall rejoice, and your joy no man taketh from you. And
in that day ye shall ask me nothing. [l]Verily, verily, I say unto you,
Whatsoever ye shall ask the Father in my name, he will give *it* you.
24 Hitherto have ye asked nothing in my name: ask, and ye shall receive,
that your joy may be full.
25 These things have I spoken unto you in [2]proverbs: but the time
cometh, when I shall no more speak unto you in [3]proverbs, but I shall
26 show you plainly of the Father. At that day ye shall ask in my name:
27 and I say not unto you, that I will pray the Father for you; for [m]the
Father himself loveth you, because ye have loved me, and [n]have believed
28 that I came out from God. I [o]came forth from the Father, and am
come into the world: again, I leave the world, and go to the Father.
29 His disciples said unto him, Lo, now speakest thou plainly, and
30 speakest no [4]proverb. Now are we sure that [p]thou knowest all things,
and needest not that any man should ask thee: by this [q]we believe that
31 thou camest forth from God. Jesus answered them, Do ye now believe?

A. D. 33.

k Luke 24. 41. ch. 14. 1, 27. ch. 20. 20. Acts 2. 46. Acts 13. 52. 1 Pet. 1. 8.
l ch. 14. 13. ch. 15. 16.
2 Or, parables.
3 Or, parables.
m ch. 14. 21.
n ch. 3. 13. ch. 17. 8.
o ch. 13. 3.
4 Or, parable.
p ch. 21. 17.
q ch. 17. 8.

joy of the world at His disappearance seems to show that the thing meant was His removal from them by *death.* In that case, the joy of the disciples at seeing Him again must refer to their transport at His reappearance amongst them on His *resurrection*, when they could no longer doubt His identity. But the words go beyond this: for as His personal stay amongst them after His resurrection was brief, and His actual manifestations but occasional, while the language is that of permanence, we must view His return to them at His resurrection as virtually *uninterrupted by His ascension* to glory (according to His way of speaking in ch. xiv. 18-20). But the words carry us on even to the transport of the widowed Church when her Lord shall come again to receive her to Himself, that where He is, there she may be also.

The Relation of Believers to the absent Saviour and to the Father (23-27). **23. And in that day**—when He should return to them by resurrection, but be in glory, **ye shall ask**—or 'enquire of' **me nothing**—'ye shall not, as ye do now, bring all your enquiries to Me in Person, as one beside you.' **Verily, verily, I say unto you, Whatsoever ye shall ask the Father in my name, he will give it you.** See on ch. xiv. 13, 14; xv. 7. Thus would they be at no real loss for want of Him amongst them, in the way of earthly intercourse, but vastly the better. **24. Hitherto have ye asked nothing in my name.** Ordinary readers are apt to lay the emphasis of this statement on the word "nothing;" as if it meant, 'Hitherto your askings in My name have been next to nothing, but now be encouraged to enlarge your petitions.' Clearly the emphasis is on the words "in My Name," and the statement is absolute: 'hitherto your prayers to the Father have not been offered in My Name;' for, as *Olshausen* correctly says, prayer *in the name of Christ*, as well as prayer *to Christ*, presupposes His *glorification.* **ask**—'When I shall have gone to the Father, ye shall have but to ask in this new, all-prevailing form;' **and ye shall receive, that your joy may be full.** So that the new footing on which they would find themselves with Jesus—no longer beside them to be consulted in every difficulty, but with them, notwithstanding, as an all-prevalent Medium of communication with the Father—would be vastly preferable to the old.

25. These things have I spoken unto you in proverbs—or 'parables;' that is, in obscure language; as opposed to speaking "plainly" in the next clause: **but the time cometh**—'but there cometh an hour,' **when I shall no more speak unto you in proverbs, but I shall show**—or 'tell' you **plainly of the Father**—that is, by the Spirit's teaching. How "plain" that made all things, compared with anything they took up from Christ's own teaching, will be seen by comparing Peter's addresses after the day of Pentecost with his speeches while his Lord was going out and in with the Twelve. **26. At that day ye shall ask in my name.** He had before *bidden* them do so: here He intimates that this is to be the appropriate, characteristic exercise of the believing Church, in its intercourse with the Father. **and I say not, that I will pray the Father for you**—that is, as if the Father were of Himself *indisposed* to hear them, or as if His own solicitations were needed to incline an *unwilling* Ear. Christ *does* pray the Father for them, but certainly not for this reason. **27. For the Father himself loveth you, because ye have loved me, and have believed that I came out from God.** This love of theirs is that which is called forth by God's eternal love in the gift of his Son, *mirrored* in the hearts of those who believe, and resting on His dear Son.

The Disciples, Re-assured by the greater explicitness of their Master's Statements, are Warned how speedily they will Desert Him (28-32). **28. I came forth from the Father, and am come into the world: again, I leave the world, and go to the Father:**—'Ye have believed that I came out from God, and ye are right; for I came indeed forth from the Father, and am soon to return whence I came.' This echo of the truth alluded to in the preceding verse seems like *thinking aloud*, as if it were grateful to His own spirit on such a subject and at such an hour.

29. His disciples said unto him, Lo, now speakest thou plainly, and speakest no proverb. It was not much plainer than before—the time for perfect plainness was yet to come: but having caught a glimpse of His meaning—for it was little more—they eagerly express their satisfaction, as if glad to make anything of His words. How touchingly does this show both the simplicity of their hearts and the infantile character of their faith! **30. Now are we sure that thou knowest all things**—the very thought of their hearts, in this case, and how to meet it; **and needest not that any man should ask thee: by this we believe that thou camest forth from God.** There was more sincerity in this than enlightened knowledge of the meaning of their own words. But our Lord accepted it so far as it went. **31. Jesus answered them, Do ye now believe?**—'It is well ye do, for that faith is soon to be tested,

32 Behold, the hour cometh, yea, is now come, that ye shall be scattered,
every man to [5]his own, and shall leave me alone: and yet I am not
33 alone, because the Father is with me. These things I have spoken unto
you, that [r]in me ye might have peace. [s]In the world ye shall have
tribulation: but be of good cheer; [t]I have overcome the world.

A. D. 33.

[5] Or, his own home.
[r] Isa 9. 6.
[s] Acts 14. 22.
[t] Rom. 8. 37.

and in a way ye little expect.' **32. Behold, the hour cometh**—'there cometh an hour,' **that ye shall be scattered, every man to his own** [εἰς τὰ ἴδια]—'his own [home'], as in ch. xix. 27, what he formerly left for My sake, as *Bengel* explains it; **and shall leave me alone: and yet I am not alone.** A deep and awful sense of *wrong* experienced is certainly expressed here, but how lovingly! That He was not to be utterly deserted—that there was One who would not forsake Him—was to Him matter of ineffable support and consolation; but that He should be without all *human* countenance and cheer, who as Man was exquisitely sensitive to the law of sympathy, would fill themselves with as much *shame*, when they afterwards recurred to it, as the Redeemer's heart in His hour of need with pungent *sorrow*. "I looked for some to take pity, but there was none; and for comforters, but I found none" (Ps. lxix. 20.) **because the Father is with me**—how near, and with what sustaining power, who can express?

The Intent of this whole Discourse expressed in one comprehensive, closing word (33). **33. These things I have spoken unto you**—not the immediately preceding words, but this whole discourse, of which these were the very last words, and which He thus winds up; **that in me ye might have peace**—in the sublime sense before explained on ch. xiv. 27. **In the world ye shall have tribulation** [ἕξετε]—but this reading has very slender support: the true reading undoubtedly is, 'In the world ye have tribulation' [ἔχετε]; for being already "not of the world, but chosen out of the world," they were already beginning to experience its deadly opposition, and would soon know more of it. So that the "peace" promised was to be far from an unruffled one. **but be of good cheer; I have overcome the world**—not only *before* you, but *for* you, that ye may be not only encouraged, but enabled to do the same. (See 1 John v. 4, 5.) The last and crowning act of His victory, indeed, was yet to come. But it was all but come, and the result was as certain as if all had been already over—the consciousness of which, no doubt, was the chief source of that wonderful calm with which He went through the whole of this solemn scene in the upper room.

Remarks.—1. The language in which the blessed Spirit is spoken of throughout all this last Discourse of Our Lord is quite decisive of His DIVINE PERSONALITY. Nor does *Stier* express himself too strongly when he says that he who can regard all the *personal* expressions applied to the Spirit in these three chapters—"teaching," "reminding," "testifying," "coming," "convincing," "guiding," "speaking," "hearing," "prophesying," "taking"—as being no other than a long-drawn figure, deserves not to be recognized as an interpreter of intelligible words, much less an expositor of Holy Scripture. 2. As there is no subject in Christian Theology on which accurate thinking is of more importance than *the relation of the work of the Spirit to the work of Christ*, so there is no place in which that relation is more precisely defined and amply expressed than in this chapter. For, first, we are expressly told that the Spirit's teaching is limited to that which He receives to communicate (*v.* 13); that what He receives is "of that which is Christ's" [ἐκ τοῦ 'Εμοῦ]—or, in other words, that the Spirit's teaching relates wholly to Christ's Person and Errand into the world; and lest this should seem to narrow undesirably and disadvantageously the range of the Spirit's functions, we are told that Christ's things" embrace "all the Father's things" (*v.* 15)—that is to say, all that the Father contemplated and arranged from everlasting for the recovery of men in His Son Christ Jesus. Thus are the Spirit's functions not *narrow*, but only *definite:* they are as wide in their range as the work of Christ and the saving purposes of God in Him; but they are *no wider—no other*. Accordingly, when our Lord lays out in detail the subject-matter of the Spirit's teaching, He makes it all to centre in HIMSELF:—"He shall convince the world of sin, because they believe not on *Me;* of righteousness, because *I* go to My Father, and ye see Me no more; of judgment, because (by *My* "uplifting," ch. xii. 31, 32) the Prince of this world is judged." But secondly, this being so, it clearly follows that the whole design of the Spirit's work is to reveal to men's minds the true nature and glory of Christ's work in the flesh, as attested and crowned by His resurrection and glorification; to plant in men's souls the assurance of its truth; and to bring them to repose on it their whole confidence for acceptance with the Father and everlasting life. Thus, as Christ's work was *objective* and *for* men, the Spirit's work is *subjective* and *in* men. The one is what divines call the *purchase*, the other what they call the *application* of redemption. The one was done outwardly once for all, by Christ on earth; the other is done inwardly in each individual saved soul, by the Spirit from heaven. And thus have we here brought before us the FATHER, the SON, and the HOLY GHOST—one adorable Godhead, distinct in operation even as in Person, yet divinely harmonious and concurrent for the salvation of sinners. 3. How beautifully does Jesus here teach us to travel between the sense of His Personal *absence* and the sense of His spiritual *presence*. He would have us feel the desolating effect of His Personal absence, but not be paralyzed by it, inasmuch as His spiritual presence would be felt to be unspeakably real, sustaining, and consolatory. And by directing them to ask all things of the Father in His name, during the period of His departure, He would teach them to regard His absence for them in heaven to be vastly better for them than His presence with them as they then enjoyed it. At the same time, since even this would be a very inadequate compensation for His Personal Presence, He would have them to rest in nothing short of this, that He was coming again to receive them to Himself, that where He was, there they might be also. 4. In Christ's being "left alone" in His last sufferings, may there not be seen a divine arrangement for bringing out in manifest and affecting fulfilment that typical provision for the great day of atonement: "*And there shall be no man in the tabernacle of the congregation when he* (the high priest) *goeth in to make an atonement in the holy place, until he come out*"? (Lev. xvi. 17). 5. How sweet is the summation of this wonderful Discourse in its closing word—the last that Jesus was to utter to the whole Eleven before He suf-

17 THESE words spake Jesus, and lifted up his eyes to heaven, and said,
Father, the hour is come; glorify thy Son, that thy Son also may glorify
2 thee: as [a]thou hast given him power over all flesh, that he should give

A. D. 33.

CHAP. 17.

[a] Dan. 7. 14.

fered: "These things have I spoken unto you, that IN ME ye might have peace"—not untroubled peace, for "in the world they were to have tribulation;" but the assurance that "He had overcome the world" would make them too more than conquerors.

CHAP. XVII. 1-26. — THE INTERCESSORY PRAYER. For the general character of this portion of the Fourth Gospel, see the opening remarks on ch. xiv. As for this Prayer, had it not been recorded, what reverential reader would not have exclaimed, O to have been within hearing of such a prayer as that must have been, which wound up the whole of His past ministry and formed the point of transition to the dark scenes which immediately followed! But here it is, and with such signature of the Lips that uttered it that we seem rather to hear it from Himself than read it from the pen of His faithful reporter. Were it not almost profane even to advert to it, we might ask the reader to listen to the character given of this Prayer by the first critic, bearing a Christian name, who in modern times has questioned, though he afterwards admitted, the genuineness and authenticity of the Fourth Gospel (*Bretschneider*—with whom, as might be expected, *Strauss* agrees): he calls it 'frigid, dogmatic, metaphysical.' What a commentary on those apostolic words, "The natural man receiveth not the things of the Spirit of God; for they are foolishness unto him: neither can he know them, because they are spiritually discerned" (1 Cor. ii. 14). Happily, the universal instinct of Christendom recoils from such language, and feels itself, while standing within the precincts of this chapter, to be on holy ground, yea, in the very holy of holies. We may add, with *Bengel*, that this chapter is, in the words of it, the most simple, but in sense the most profound in all the Bible; or, as *Luther* said long before, that plain and simple as it sounds, it is so deep, rich, and broad, that no man can fathom it.

The Prayer naturally divides itself into three parts: *First*, What relates to the Son Himself, who offered the prayer (1-5); *secondly*, what had reference more immediately to those Eleven disciples in whose hearing the prayer was uttered (6-19); *thirdly*, what belongs to all who should believe on Him through their word, to the end of the world (20-24); with two concluding verses, simply breathing out His soul in a survey, at once dark and bright, of the whole past results of His mission.

We address ourselves to the exposition of this Prayer, with the warning to Moses sounding in our ears—and let it sound in thine, O reader!—"Put off thy shoes from off thy feet, for the place whereon thou standest is holy ground" (Exod. iii. 5); yet encouraged by the assurance of Him that uttered it, that the Comforter "shall glorify Him—receiving of His, and showing it unto us."

FIRST, *Jesus Prays for Himself* (1-5). **1. These words spake Jesus, and lifted up his eyes to heaven.** 'John,' says *Alford*, 'very seldom depicts the gestures or looks of our Lord, as here. But this was an occasion of which the impression was indelible, and the upward look could not be passed over.' **and said, Father.** Never does Jesus say in prayer, '*Our* Father,' though He directs His disciples to do it; but always "Father," and once, during His Agony, "My Father:" thus severing Himself as Man from all other men, as the "Separate from sinners," though "Bone of our bone, and Flesh of our flesh." **the hour is come.** But did not the Father, you will say, know that? O yes, and Jesus knew that He knew it. But He had not that narrow and distant and cold view of prayer which some even true Christians have, as if it was designed for nothing else but to express petitions for benefits needed, promised, expected. Prayer is the creature yearning after Him that gave it being, looking up into its Father's face, opening its bosom to the brightness and warmth of His felt presence, drinking in fresh assurances of safety under His wing, fresh inspirations of His love, fresh nobility from the consciousness of its nearness to Him. In prayer believers draw near to God, not merely when necessity drives them, but under the promptings of filial love, and just because "it is good for them to draw near to God." We like to breathe the air of His presence; we love to come to Him, though it were for nothing but to cry, in the spirit of adoption, "Abba, Father." "Walking in the light as He is in the light, we have fellowship One with the other—He with us and we with Him"—uplifting, invigorating, transfiguring fellowship. How much more, then, must Christ's prayers, and this one above all, have been of that character! Hear Him telling His Father here, with sublime simplicity and familiarity, that "the hour was come." What hour? The hour of hours; the hour with a view to which all the purposes of grace from everlasting were fixed; the hour with a view to which all the scaffolding of the ancient economy was erected; the hour with a view to which He had come into the world, and been set apart by Circumcision and Baptism and the Descent of the Spirit; the hour with a view to which He had lived and wrought and taught and prayed; the hour for which Heaven, for the ends of Grace, and Earth and Hell, to defeat those ends, were waiting alike with eager hope: *that* hour was now "come"—virtually come, all but come—'All things,' Father, 'are now ready.' **glorify thy Son**—'Put honour upon Thy Son, by openly *countenancing Him*, when all others desert Him; by *sustaining Him*, when the waters come in unto His soul and He sinks in deep mire where there is no standing; by *carrying Him through* the horrors of that hour, when it shall please the Lord to bruise Him, and make His soul an offering for sin.' **that thy Son [also] may glorify thee**—by a willing and absolute obedience unto death, even the death of the Cross, thus becoming a glorious Channel for the extension to a perishing world of Thine everlasting love. [The καί of the received text has insufficient authority, and is excluded by *Lachmann*, *Tischendorf*, and *Tregelles*.] **2. As thou hast given him** [Καθὼς ἔδωκας]—'According as thou gavest Him' **power over all flesh.** Compare ch. iii. 35, "The Father loveth the Son, and hath given all things into His hand;" Matt. xi. 27, "All things are delivered unto Me of My Father;" xxviii. 18, "All power is given unto Me in heaven and in earth." **that he should give eternal life to as many as thou hast given him.** The phraseology here is very peculiar: 'That *all that* which Thou hast given Him, He should give to *them* eternal life.' On the import of this language and of the whole sentiment expressed by it, see on ch. vi. 37-40, with the corresponding remarks at the close of that Section. **3. And this is life eternal** [ἡ αἰώνιος ζωή], **that they might know thee the**

3 eternal life to as many [b]as thou hast given him. And [c]this is life
eternal, that they might know thee [d]the only true God, and Jesus Christ,
4 whom thou hast sent. I have glorified thee on the earth: I have
5 finished the work which thou gavest me to do. And now, O Father,
glorify thou me with thine own self with the glory [e]which I had with
thee before the world was.
6 I [f]have manifested thy name unto the men which thou gavest me
out of the world: thine they were, and thou gavest them me; and they

A. D. 33.

[b] ch. 6. 37.
[c] Isa. 53. 11. Jer. 9. 24.
[d] 1 Cor. 8. 4. 1 Thes. 1. 9.
[e] ch. 1. 1. ch. 10. 30. ch. 14. 9.
[f] Ps. 22. 22.

only true God—the sole Personal, Living God, in glorious contrast with all forms of heathen *polytheism*, mystic *pantheism*, and philosophic *naturalism;* **and Jesus Christ, whom thou hast sent.** This is the only place where our Lord gives Himself the compound name "JESUS CHRIST," afterwards so current in apostolic preaching and writing. (See on Matt. i. 1.) Here all the words are employed in their strict signification: First, "JESUS," because He "*saves* His people from their sins;" Second, "CHRIST," as *anointed* with the measureless fulness of the Holy Ghost for the exercise of His saving offices (see on Matt. i. 16); Third, "WHOM THOU HAST SENT," in the plenitude of Divine Authority and Power, to save. 'The very juxtaposition here,' as *Alford* properly observes, 'of *Jesus Christ* with *the Father* is a proof, by implication, of our Lord's Godhead. The knowledge of *God and a creature* could not be eternal life, and such an association of the one with the other would be inconceivable.' Thus, then, "the life eternal" of which Jesus here speaks, and which He says it is His proper office to confer, is no merely conscious, unending existence, but a life whose most distinguishing characteristic is acquaintance with the Father of our Lord Jesus Christ, and with Jesus Himself as the Way to the Father, and the Truth and the Life (Job xxii. 21; Matt. xi. 27, &c.) **4. I have glorified thee on the earth: I have finished the work which thou gavest me to do**—or, keeping to the strict sense of the tenses here employed, 'I glorified Thee on the earth: I finished the work which Thou hast given Me to do' [ἐδόξασα-ἐτελείωσα-δέδωκας]. Observe here, first, the light in which Jesus presents Himself and His work before His Father's view. His whole life here below was, He says, a *glorification of the Father;* but in this He only did, He says, a *prescribed work*—a work "given Him to do." But observe, next, the *retrospective* light in which He speaks of this. He refers to the time when He was "*on the earth*," as a past time: His glorification of the Father was now completed; the "work given Him to do" was a "*finished*" work. Manifestly the work meant was not so much of His work merely as was over at the moment when He now spake; for the great consummating surrender of His life was yet to come. It is *His entire work in the flesh* of which He speaks as now finished. And in the sublime and erect consciousness that He was presenting before the Father's eye a glorification of Him in which He would see no flaw, a finished work in which would be found nothing lacking, He now asks the fitting return: **5. And now**—'the whole purpose I am here for being accomplished,' **O Father, glorify thou me with thine own self** [παρὰ Σεαυτῷ]—or 'beside Thine own Self (*apud Teipsum*, or *Temetipsum*, as the *Vulgate*, *Calvin*, and *Beza* render it). The nearest, strictest, Personal conjunction is beyond doubt meant, as in ch. i. 1, "The Word was *with* God" [πρὸς τὸν θεόν], and *v.* 18, The Only begotten Son who is *in*"—'on' or 'into'—"*the bosom* of the Father" [εἰς τὸν κόλπον τοῦ Πατρός]. Compare Zec. xiii. 7, "The Man that is My Fellow," or 'My Associate' [עֲמִיתִי]. **with the glory which I had with thee** [παρὰ Σοί]—or 'beside Thee,' **before the world was.** That the Son divested Himself of this glory *in some sense* by His incarnation, and continued divested of it during all the days of His flesh, is implied in the words. And that the restoration of this which He here asks was the restoration of what He laid aside—neither more nor less—is equally plain. But what that was is not easily conceived, though more easily conceived than expressed. Abstract theological discussions, as they do nothing whatever to clear this up, so on such a subject they are very unsavoury. But two things seem to meet the facts of the case, and pretty nearly to exhaust all that can safely be said upon the subject. First, In His ordinary intercourse with men here below, He *appeared not to be* what He was, and *appeared to be* what He was not. Instead of its being impossible for any person, at any moment, to doubt that He was the Everlasting Son of the Father in human flesh, it seemed hardly possible to believe it—so entirely like other men was He in His appearance and ordinary movements, and often even more helpless than many other men. Secondly, That this was a *shrouding of His proper glory*, and a continual and sublime exercise of *Self-restraint*, is evident not only from what we know of His proper glory and dignity and freedom, and what He once and again *said* of it, but from the occasional breakings forth of that glory and majesty of His—as if to let men see for a moment Whom they had in the midst of them, and what a carriage He might have assumed if it had been but fitting that His whole glorious Self should be habitually displayed before them. Well, He *submitted* during all the days of His flesh, for the high ends on which He came hither, thus to restrain Himself; and so "the world knew Him not" and "received Him not." But it could not be that He should be contented with this *abnormal* condition; it could not be but that He should desire its cessation and feel it to be such joy as He told His disciples, scarcely a brief half hour before this, they should rejoice in on His account (see on ch. xiv. 28). But the wonder of this restoration of the glory which He had with the Father before all time is, that it was to be *in our nature.* His Divine glory as the Only begotten of the Father was never lost, and could not be parted with; it was inalienable and essential. But during the days of His flesh it was shrouded from human view; it was not externally manifested; in respect of it, He restrained Himself. And what He now asks is, that this veil might be removed from Him as the *Incarnate* One, and that as the risen and ascended Representative of Humanity—the Second Adam—He might be invested and manifested in the glory which He had with the Father before the world was. Transporting thought!

Jesus Prays more immediately for the Eleven (6-19). **6. I have manifested** [Ἐφανέρωσα]—'I manifested' **thy name**—'Thy whole revealed character towards mankind,' **unto the men which**

7 have kept thy word. Now they have known that all things whatsoever
8 thou hast given me are of thee. For I have given unto them the
words which thou gavest me; and they have received *them*, and have
known surely that I came out from thee, and they have believed that
9 thou didst send me. I pray for them: [g]I pray not for the world, but
10 for them which thou hast given me; for they are thine. And [h]all
11 mine are thine, and thine are mine; and I am glorified in them. And
now I am no more in the world, but these are in the world, and I come
to thee. Holy Father, [i]keep through thine own name those whom thou
12 hast given me, that they may be one, [j]as we *are*. While I was with
them in the world, I [k]kept them in thy name: those that thou gavest
me I have kept, and [l]none of them is lost, [m]but the son of perdition;
13 [n]that the Scripture might be fulfilled. And now come I to thee; and
these things I speak in the world, that they might have my joy fulfilled
in themselves.

A. D. 33.

g 1 John 5. 19.
h ch. 10. 30. ch. 16. 14. Rom. 8. 30. 1 Cor. 3. 21. Col. 1. 15.
i 1 Pet. 1. 5.
j ch 10. 30.
k ch. 6. 39. ch. 10. 28. Heb. 2. 13.
l Luke 4. 26. ch. 18. 9. 1 John 2. 19.
m ch. 13. 18. 1 Thes. 2. 3.
n Ps. 109. 8. Acts 1. 20.

thou gavest [δέδωκας]—'hast given' **me out of the world.** He had said to them in the foregoing Discourse, "I have chosen you out of the world" (ch. xv. 19). Here He says the Father had first given them to Him out of the world; and it was in pursuance of that gift from everlasting that He in time made that *choice* of them. **thine they were**—as the sovereign Lord and Proprietor of all flesh (*v.* 2), **and thou gavest them me**—as the Incarnate Son and Saviour, to be themselves separated from the world and saved, in the first instance (according to the principles of ch. vi. 37-40), and then to be separated to the high office of gathering in others; **and they have kept thy word**—*retained* it (Luke viii. 15); not taking it up superficially, as multitudes did, only to abandon it when they saw whither it would lead them, but forsaking all for it. **7. Now they have known that all things whatsoever thou hast given me are of thee. 8. For I have given unto them the words which thou gavest**—'hast given' **me; and they have received them, and have known surely that I came out from thee, and they have believed that thou didst send me** [ἔλαβον—ἔγνωσαν—ἐπίστευσαν]—'they received them, and knew surely that I came out from Thee; and believed that Thou didst send Me;' referring doubtless to their own explicit declaration, but a little before, "Now are we sure"—'Now know we'—"that Thou knowest all things: by this we believe that Thou camest forth from God" (ch. xvi. 30). How benignant is this acknowledgment of the feeble faith of those infantile believers! Yet unless it had been genuine, and He had seen in it the germ of noblest faith afterwards to be displayed, He had not so spoken of it. **9. I pray for them**—not here as *apostles*, but as the following words show, as the representatives of those "chosen out of the world:" **I pray not for the world**—for the things sought for them were totally inapplicable to the world. Not that the *individuals* composing the world were shut out from Christ's compassions (see the last clause of *v.* 21), or ought to be shut out from ours; but they come within the sphere of this prayer only by "being chosen *out of the world.*" **but for them which thou hast given me; for they are thine.** He had just said that the Father "gave them to Him;" but here He says they were the Father's still, for the Father did not give them *out of His own hands* in committing them to the Son's. See on ch. x. 28-30. Accordingly He adds, **10. And all mine are thine, and thine are mine** [τὰ Ἐμὰ Σά ἐστιν, καὶ τὰ Σὰ Ἐμά]—'And all things that are Mine are Thine, and Thy things are Mine.' ABSOLUTE COMMUNITY OF PROPERTY BETWEEN THE FATHER AND THE SON is here expressed as nakedly as words could do it. **and I am glorified in them. 11. And** [now] **I am no more in the world, but these are in the world, and I come to thee.** 'Though My struggles are at an end, theirs are not: though I have gotten beyond the scene of strife, I cannot sever Myself in spirit from them, left behind, and only just entering on their great conflict.' **Holy Father**—an expression He nowhere else uses. "*Father*" is His wonted appellation, but "*holy*" is here prefixed, because His appeal was to that perfection of the Father's nature, to "keep" or preserve them from being tainted by the unholy atmosphere of "the world" they were still in. **keep through thine own name** [ἐν τῷ ὀνόματί σου]—rather, in 'Thy name;' in the exercise of that gracious and holy character which, as revealed, is the "name" by which God is known to men. **those whom thou hast given me.** The true reading clearly is 'what thou hast given me' [ᾧ, instead of οὓς]. So *Lachmann*, *Tischendorf*, and *Tregelles*, with whom the best critics concur. **that they may be one, as we are.** See on *v.* 21. **12. While I was with them in the world, I kept them in thy name**—'I preserved them from defection through the revelation to their souls of that "grace and truth" of Thine which, whenever they were staggered and ready to give way, held them fast.' **those that thou gavest me I have kept**—'Those whom Thou hast given Me I kept' or 'guarded' [δέδωκας—ἐφύλαξα], **and none**—'not one' **of them is lost, but the son of perdition.** If we take the expressions, "children of this world," "child of the devil," "the man of sin," "children of light," "children of Zion," to mean men who have in them the *nature* of the things mentioned as their proper character, then, "the son of perdition" must mean 'he who not only is *doomed* to, but has the materials of perdition already in his character.' So we are to understand the expression "children of wrath" (Eph. ii. 3). **that the Scripture might be fulfilled** (Ps. lxix. 25; cix. 8; Acts i. 16, 20). The phrase 'not one *but* (or 'but only') the son of perdition' [εἰ μὴ] is used in the same sense as in Luke iv. 26, 27 (on which see). 'It is not implied,' as *Webster and Wilkinson* correctly observe, 'that Judas was one of those whom the Father had given to the Son, but rather the contrary. See ch. xiii. 18.' **13. And now** [Νῦν δὲ]—'But now' **come I to thee.** He had just said this before; but He loves to say it again, the yearning of His whole soul after the Father thus finding natural relief. **and these things I speak in the world, that they might have my joy fulfilled in themselves**—'Such a strain befits rather the upper sanctuary

14 I have given them thy word; [o]and the world hath hated them,
15 because they are not of the world, even as I am not of the world. I
pray not that thou shouldest take them out of the world, but [p]that
16 thou shouldest keep them from the evil. They are not of the world,
17 even as I am not of the world. Sanctify [q]them through thy truth: thy
18 word is truth. As thou hast sent me into the world, even so have I
19 also sent them into the world. And [r]for their sakes I sanctify myself,
that they also might be [1]sanctified through the truth.

A. D. 33.

o 1 John 3. 13.
p Gal. 1. 4. 2 Thes. 3. 3. 1 John 5. 18.
q Acts 15. 9. Eph. 5. 26.
r 1 Cor. 1. 30.
1 Or, truly sanctified.

than the scene of conflict; but I speak so "*in the world,*" that My joy, the joy I experience in knowing that such intercessions are to be made for them by their absent Lord, may be tasted by those who now hear them, and by all who shall hereafter read the record of them.' See on ch. xv. 11; only here the *ground* of that joy seems more comprehensive than there.

14. I have given them thy word; and the world hath hated them [ἐμίσησεν]—'the world hated them,' **because they are not of the world, even as I am not of the world.** See on ch. xv. 18-21. **15. I pray not that thou shouldest take them out of the world**—for that, though it would secure their own safety, would leave the world unblessed by their testimony; **but that thou keep them from the evil** [ἐκ τοῦ πονηροῦ]—or 'from evil;' all evil in and of the world. The translation 'from the evil one' is to be rejected here, as not suiting the comprehensiveness of these petitions. See also, in the Lord's Prayer, on Matt. vi. 13. **16. They are not of the world, even as I am not of the world.** See on *vv.* 6-9; and on ch. xv. 18, 19. This is reiterated here to pave the way for the prayer which follows: **17. Sanctify them through** [ἐν]—or 'in' **thy truth: thy word is truth.** Principles of vast importance are here expressed. Observe, first, the connection between this petition and that of *v.* 15. As that was *negative*—"Keep them"—asking *protection* for them from the poisonous element which surrounded and pressed upon their renewed nature; so this prayer—"*Sanctify* them"—is positive, asking the *advancement and completion* of their begun sanctification. Observe, next, the *medium* or *element* of sanctification. All sanctification is represented as the fruit of *truth;* not truth in general, but what is called distinctively "God's truth," or 'Christ's Father's truth:' in other words, not only *religious* truth—as distinguished from all other truth, physical or metaphysical—but His *revealed truth.* Accordingly, as if to make this more clear—for the sake of those who listened to this prayer, and as many as should have it brought within their reach throughout all time—He defines what He means by "Thy truth," adding that important clause, "*Thy word* is truth." But what, it may be asked, is specifically meant by "Thy word?" This he had already explained in *v.* 14, "I have given them Thy word; and the world hath hated them, because they are not of the world, even as I am not of the world." And in a previous verse (8), "I have given unto them the words which Thou gavest Me, and they have received them," &c. *The whole of His own teaching,* then, as an express communication from the Father, through the Faithful and True Witness, was that "word of truth" through which He prays that they might be sanctified. It had fetched them in already (ch. xv. 3). But they had not done with it when it ceased to drop upon their ear from those Lips into which grace was poured. Nay, it was only when He "went unto His Father, and they saw Him no more," that it was, through the promised teaching of the Spirit, to take its full "sanctifying" effect upon them. For then only was it seen and felt to be but the fulness of all the Old Testament revelations, the perfection of all gracious communications from God to men, "spoken unto us in these last days by His own Son," and the substance of all that was to be unfolded in detail by His apostles in their preaching and by their writings for all time. (Eph. i. 13; Col. i. 5.) Accordingly, just before His ascension, He commissioned these same faithful Eleven, as the representatives of His ministering servants in every succeeding age, to teach the baptized disciples to "observe *all things whatsoever He had commanded them*"—not to the exclusion of all divine truth except that contained in the Gospels, but as comprehensive of all revealed, saving truth. (See on Matt. xxviii. 16-20, Remark 3 at the close of that Section.) But one other thing here must not be passed over. While our Lord holds prominently forth the ordained *medium* or *element* of sanctification—God's word of truth—He ascribes the sanctification which is thereby wrought entirely to God Himself, saying to His Father, "Sanctify *Thou* them." Great principles these in the divine economy of salvation, which cannot be too constantly and vividly present to the minds of believers, and especially of ministers. **18. As thou hast sent**—'sentest' **me into the world, even so have I also sent**—'sent I also' **them into the world.** As their mission was designed for no other end than to carry into effect the purpose of His own mission into the world, so He speaks of the *authority* by which He was sending them into the world as but an extension of the same authority by which Himself was sent of the Father. As He was the Father's Ambassador and Agent, so were they to be His. Nay, He represents them as already sent, just as He represents His own personal work on earth as already at an end; and what His soul is now filled with and looking forward to is the coming fruit of that work, the travail of His soul, and His satisfaction therein. **19. And for their sakes I sanctify myself, that they also might**—or 'may' **be sanctified through the truth** [ἐν ἀληθείᾳ]—'in the truth,' or 'in truth.' As the article is wanting in the original, we may translate, as in the margin, 'that they also may be *truly* sanctified,' in contrast with those *ritual* sanctifications with which as Jews they were so familiar. So *Chrysostom, Luther, Calvin, Beza, Bengel, Meyer.* But since, in 2 John 3, and 3 John 3, 4, the beloved disciple speaks of "walking *in* [the] *truth,*" without the article—meaning certainly not 'walking truly,' but 'walking in the truth of the Gospel'—it is much better to understand our Lord to refer here to that same truth of which he had spoken in *v.* 17 as the element or medium of all sanctification. So *Erasmus, Lücke, Tholuck, Alford, Lange.* 'The only difference,' says *Olshausen* excellently, 'between the application of the same term (sanctify) to Christ and the disciples is that, as applied to Christ, it means *only* to consecrate; whereas in application to the disciples, it means to consecrate with the *additional idea* of previous sanctification,

20 Neither pray I for these alone, but for them [s]also which shall believe
21 on me through their word; that [t]they all may be one; as [u]thou,
Father, *art* in me, and I in thee, that they also may be one in us: that

A. D. 33.

[s] Acts 2. 41.
[t] Rom. 12. 5.
[u] ch. 10. 38.

since nothing but what is holy can be presented as an offering. The whole self-sacrificing work of the disciples appears here as a mere *result* of the offering of Christ.' But it should be added, in further illustration of the vast difference between the sanctification of the Master and that of the servants, that He does not say, 'I sanctify Myself *through the truth*,' but simply, "I sanctify Myself," that is, 'set Myself apart by Self-consecration;' and while He says of His own sanctification that it was "*for their sakes*," He does not say that they were to be sanctified for others' sakes—though that, in a certain inferior and not unimportant sense, is true enough—but simply, "that they also might be sanctified through the truth." Thus, in language which brings His people into the nearest and most blessed conjunction with Himself—in a common sanctification—does Jesus, by sharpest lines of demarcation, distinguish between Himself and them in that sanctification.

Jesus Prays for all that should ever Believe on Him (20-24). **20. Neither pray I for these alone** [Οὐ περὶ τούτων δὲ ἐρωτῶ μόνον]—'Yet not for these alone do I pray,' **but for them also which shall believe on me.** The true reading here is one we should not have expected—'for them which believe on me' [πιστευόντων—not πιστευσόντων]. But the evidence in its favour is decisive, while the received reading has but feeble support. Of course, the sense is the same; but this reading exhibits the whole company of believers as already before the eye of Jesus in that character—a present multitude already brought in and filling His mighty soul with a Redeemer's "satisfaction." How striking is it, that while all future time is here viewed as *present*, the present is viewed as *past* and gone! **through their word.** The Eleven are now regarded as the carriers of the glad tidings of His salvation "to every creature;" but of course, only as the first of a race of preachers, whose sound was to go into all the earth, and their words unto the ends of the world; whose beautiful feet upon the mountains, as they carried the news of salvation from land to land, were hailed even by the evangelical prophet (Isa. lii. 7). **21. That they all may be one** [ἓν]—'one thing;' **as thou, Father, art in me, and I in thee, that they also may be one** [ἓν]—'one thing' **in us: that the world may believe that thou hast sent**—'sentest' **me.** No language which we at present have can adequately express the full import of these wonderful words, nor can any heart here below completely conceive it. But the three great unities here brought before us may be pointed out. First in order is the Unity of the Father and the Son—"as Thou, Father, art in Me, and I in Thee:" next, the assumption of all believers into that Unity, thus constituting a new Unity—"that they also may be one in Us:" Finally, and as the consequence of this, the Unity of all believers amongst themselves—"that they all may be one," that is, amongst themselves. Had our Lord been here speaking of the absolute or essential unity of the Father and the Son in the Godhead, He could not have prayed that believers might be taken into that Unity. But we have already seen (on ch. x. 30, where the very same remarkable expression is used), what He meant by the Father and Himself being "one thing" [ἓν]. They have *all in common*, They have *one interest*—in the Kingdom of Grace, the salvation of sinners, the recovery of Adam's family. *Oneness of essence* is the manifest basis of this *community of interest*, as only on that principle would the language be endurable from Human Lips. But the oneness here meant is 'oneness in thought, feeling, purpose, action, interest, property—in the things of salvation.' And it is into *this* Unity that Jesus prays that all believers may be taken up; so as to become one with the Father and the Son *spiritually*, yet really for all the purposes of salvation and glory. This explanation makes it easy to see what is meant by the first petition, that "all believers may be one." It is not *mere* unity—whether in a vast common external organization, or even in internal judgment and feeling about religious matters. It is oneness in the Unity of the Father and the Son—"that they also may be one IN Us"—in the matters of Grace and Salvation. Thus, it is a union *in spiritual life;* a union in *faith* on a common Saviour, in *love* to His blessed name, in *hope* of His glorious appearing: a union brought about by the teaching, quickening, and indwelling of the one Spirit of the Father and the Son in all alike; in virtue of which they have all one common character and interest—in freedom from the bondage of sin and Satan, in separation from this present evil world, in consecration to the service of Christ and the glory of God, in witnessing for truth and righteousness on the earth, in participation of all spiritual blessings in Christ Jesus. But one other thing remains to be noticed in this great prayer—"that the world may believe that Thou didst send Me." This shows clearly that the Unity of believers amongst themselves was meant to be such as would have an outstanding, visible manifestation—such as the vast outlying world might be able to recognize, and should be constrained to own as the work of God. Thus, the grand impression upon the world at large, that the mission of Christ is Divine, is to be produced by the manifested, undeniable *Unity of His disciples* in spiritual life, love, and holiness. It is not a merely formal, mechanical unity of ecclesiastical machinery. For as that may, and to a large extent does, exist in both the Western and Eastern Churches, with little of the Spirit of Christ, yea much, much with which the Spirit of Christ cannot dwell, so, instead of convincing the world *beyond its own pale* of the divinity of the Gospel, it generates infidelity to a large extent within its own bosom. But the Spirit of Christ, illuminating, transforming, and reigning in the hearts of the genuine disciples of Christ, drawing them to each other as members of one family, and prompting them to loving co-operation for the good of the world—this is what, when sufficiently glowing and extended, shall force conviction upon the world that Christianity is divine. Doubtless, the more that differences among Christians disappear—the more they can agree even in minor matters—the impression upon the world may be expected to be greater. But it is not altogether *dependent* upon this; for living and loving oneness in Christ is sometimes more touchingly seen even amidst and in spite of minor differences, than where no such differences exist to try the strength of their deeper unity. Yet till this living brotherhood in Christ shall show itself strong enough to destroy the sectarianism, selfishness, carnality, and apathy that eat out the heart of Christianity in all the visible sections of it, in vain shall we expect the world to be overawed by it. It is when "the Spirit shall be poured upon us from on high," as a Spirit of truth and love, and upon all parts of

22 the world may believe that thou hast sent me. And the glory which
thou gavest me I have given them; [v]that they may be one, even as we
23 are one: I in them, and thou in me, [w]that they may be made [x]perfect
in one; and that the world may know that thou hast sent me, and
hast loved them, as thou hast loved me.

A. D. 33.
[v] 1 John i. 3. 1 John 3. 24.
[w] Col. 3. 14.
[x] Heb. 12. 23.

the Christian territory alike, melting down differences and heart-burnings, kindling astonishment and shame at past unfruitfulness, drawing forth longings of catholic affection, and yearnings over a world lying in wickedness, embodying themselves in palpable forms and active measures—it is then that we may expect the effect here announced to be produced, and then it will be irresistible. **22. And the glory which thou gavest**—'hast given' **me I have given them; that they may be one, even as we are one.** This verse is to be viewed as the proper complement of the former one. Our Lord had prayed that those who believed on Him might be one, and one in the Unity of the Father and the Son. But what *grounds* were there for expecting such a thing, or rather, what *materials* existed for bringing it about? The answer to that question is what we have in the present verse. "In order," says Jesus, "that they *may* be one, even as We are one, I have given unto them the glory which Thou hast given unto Me." The glory, then, here meant is all that which Jesus received from the Father as the *Incarnate Redeemer and Head* of His people—the glory of a Perfect Acceptance as the Spotless Lamb—the glory of Free Access to the Father and Right to be Heard always—the glory of the Spirit's Indwelling and Sanctification—the glory of Divine Support and Victory over sin, death, and hell—the glory of finally inheriting all things. This glory, Jesus says not, 'I *will* give,' but "I *have* given them;" thus teaching us that this glory is the *present* heritage of all that believe, and the divine provision—the heaven-provided furniture—for their attaining even here to that exalted Unity amongst themselves which would stamp the mission of their Lord as Divine even in the eyes of the world. **23. I in them, and thou in me, that they may be made perfect in one** [εἰς ἓν]—'into one [thing];' **and that the world may know that thou hast sent**—'didst send' **me, and hast loved them, as thou hast loved me** [ἀπέστειλας—ἠγάπησας]—'and lovedst them even as Thou lovedst Me.' Everything in this verse, save the last clause, had been substantially said before. But while the reiteration adds weight to the wonderful sentiment, the variation in the way of putting it throws additional light on a subject on which all the light afforded us is unspeakably precious. Before, the oneness of believers was said to be simply 'in the Father and the Son.' Here, a certain arrangement of the steps, if we may so speak, is indicated. First in order is the Father's indwelling in the Son, by His Spirit—"Thou in Me;" next, the Son's indwelling in believers by the same Spirit—"I in them:" only "God giveth not His Spirit by measure unto the Son" (ch. iii. 34), but "anointeth Him with the oil of gladness above His fellows" (Ps. xlv. 7), because it is His of right, as the Son and the Righteous One in our nature. Thus is provision made for "their being made perfect into one," or wrought into a glorious Unity, only reflecting the Higher Divine Unity. We have said that the last clause of this verse is the only part of it which had not been expressed before; nor had such an astonishing word been ever uttered before by the Lord Jesus: "that the world may know that thou . . LOVEDST THEM EVEN AS THOU LOVEDST ME." In much that He had before said this was *implied;* but never till now was it actually expressed. Here, again, it is not the essential love of the Son by the Father, in their eternal Divine Personality, that Jesus here speaks of; for with that no creature may intermeddle. It is *the Father's love of His Incarnate Son*, as Head of His redeemed, that is meant—ravishing the Father's eye with the beauty of a divine character, a perfect righteousness, a glorious satisfaction for sin in our nature. This complacency of the Father in the Son passes over to and rests upon all that believe in the Son; or rather it descends from and penetrates through the Head to all the members of that living Unity which is made up of Him and them—"like the precious ointment upon the head, that ran down upon the beard, even Aaron's beard; that went down to the skirts of his garments; as the dew that descended upon the mountains of Zion: for there the Lord commanded the blessing, even life for evermore" (Ps. cxxxiii. 2, 3). But though we should suppose that of all things this was the most *invisible to the world*, yet it seems that even the conviction of this was in some sense to be impressed upon the world: "that the world may know that Thou hast loved them, as Thou hast loved Me." Of course this could only be by its *effects:* nor can even these be expected to convince the world that the Father's love to believers is the same as His love to His own Son, in any but a very general sense, so long as it remains "the world." But it would have a double effect: it would inspire the world, even as such, with a conviction, which they would be unable to resist and could ill conceal, that Christ and Christians are alike of God and owned of God; and that conviction, going deeper down into the hearts of some, would ripen into a surrender of themselves, as willing captives, to that love Divine which sent through the Son salvation to a lost world.

24. Father, I will [θέλω] **that they also whom thou hast given me.** [The reading ὃ here, instead of οὓς of the received text—'that that also which Thou hast given Me'—which *Tischendorf* and *Tregelles* have adopted, but not *Lachmann*—is insufficiently supported, as we judge, and to be rejected.] **be with me where I am; that they may behold my glory, which thou hast given me** [ἔδωκας]—'gavest Me;' but the true reading clearly is, 'which Thou hast given Me;' [δέδωκας]: **for thou lovedst me before the foundation of the world.** Here our Lord, having exhausted all His desires for His people which could be fulfilled here below, stretches them, in this *His last petition*, onwards to the eternal state. Let us attend, first, to the *style* of petition *here only* employed by our Lord: "I will." The majesty of this style of speaking is the first thing that strikes the reverential reader. Some good expositors, indeed (as *Beza*, who, instead of the *Volo* of the *Vulgate*, renders it *Velim*), conceive that nothing more is meant by this word than a simple wish, desire, request; and they refer us in proof of this to such passages as Mark x. 35; John xii. 21, (*Gr.*) But such a word from the mouth of a creature cannot determine its sense, when taken up into the lips of the Son of God. Thus, when He said to the leper (Matt. viii. 3), "I will [θέλω], be thou clean!" something more, surely, was meant than a mere

24 Father, [y]I will that they also whom thou hast given me be with me
where I am; that they may behold my glory, which thou hast given me:
25 for thou lovedst me before the foundation of the world. O righteous

A. D. 33.

y 1 Thes 4.17. Rev. 3. 21.

wish for his recovery. And such a *will*, we cannot doubt, was meant in this prayer of the Son to the Father, which breathes throughout the spirit of loftiest unity with the glorious Object addressed, and of highest claim to be heard, more particularly occurring as it does in the final petition, a petition manifestly designed to exhaust all that He had to ask in His people's behalf. 'In *vv.* 9, 15, 20,' says *Bengel*, 'He had said, "I pray" [ἐρωτῶ, *rogo*]; now the language rises, and the word is to be rendered "I will;" not by the weak "I desire." Jesus asks in the exercise of a right, and demands with confidence; as Son, not as servant (compare Ps. ii. 8).' To the same effect *de Wette*, *Meyer*, *Stier*, *Alford*, *Luthardt*, *Webster and Wilkinson*, *Lange*. But observe now the two things thus majestically asked. First, "that they also whom Thou hast given Me be with Me where I am." He had before assured His faithful Eleven, as representing all believers, that they should be so; using the same form of expression as here, "I will come again, and receive you unto Myself, that where I am [ὅπου εἰμὶ Ἐγώ], there ye may be also" (see on ch. xiv. 3). In now *asking* what He had before explicitly *promised*, the majestic authority of that "I will" is further revealed. But next, when they have arrived where I am, it is but in order "that they may behold My glory, which Thou hast given Me: for Thou lovedst Me before the foundation of the world." The glory here intended has been already explained. It is not His *essential* glory, the glory of His Divine Personality, but His glory as the Incarnate Head of His people, the Second Adam of a redeemed humanity, in which glory the Father beheld Him with ineffable complacency from everlasting. Jesus regards it as glory enough for us to be admitted to see and gaze for ever upon this *His* glory! This is 'the beatific vision;' but it shall be no mere vision—"we shall be like Him, for we shall see Him as He is" (1 John iii. 2).

Here end the petitions of this wonderful chapter. In the two concluding verses He just breathes forth His reflections into His Father's ear, but doubtless for the benefit of those mortal ears that were privileged to listen to Him, and of all who should read it in this priceless Gospel.

Concluding Breathings forth of the whole past Results of His Mission (25, 26). **25. O righteous Father, the world hath not known thee: but I have known thee, and these have known that thou hast sent me**—or, preserving the strict sense of the tenses, 'the world knew Thee not, but I knew Thee, and these knew that Thou didst send Me;' all this being regarded as *past*. 'The world knew Thee not.' Clearly this refers to its whole treatment of "Him whom He had sent." Accordingly, in a previous chapter, He says, "He that hateth Me hateth My Father also;" "Now have they both seen and hated both Me and My Father;" "All these things will they do unto you for My name's sake, because they know not Him that sent Me" (ch. xv. 23, 24, 21): for, "had they known it," says the apostle, "they would not have crucified the Lord of Glory" (1 Cor. ii. 8). Our Lord, it will be perceived, utters this with a certain tender mournfulness, which is rendered doubly affecting when He falls back, in the next words, upon the very different treatment which the Father had received from Himself—"The world knew Thee not, O righteous Father: *but I knew Thee!*" 'While the world was showing its disregard of Thee in its treatment of Him whom Thou hadst sent, from Me Thou gatest ever the glory due unto Thy name, O Lord, Thou knowest.' But Jesus has another source of consolation in the recognition of His Divine Mission by "THESE" Eleven that were in that upper room with Him, in whom doubtless His eye beheld a multitude that no man could number of kindred spirits to the end of time; just as in "the world" that knew Him not He must have seen the same blinded world in every age:—"I knew Thee, and these knew that Thou didst send Me." Once and again had He said the same thing in this prayer. But here He introduces it for the last time in bright and cheering contrast with the dark and dismal rejection of Him, and of the Father in Him, by the world. One other thing deserves notice in this verse. As before He had said "HOLY Father," when desiring the display of that perfection on His disciples (*v.* 11), so here He styles him "RIGHTEOUS Father," because He is appealing to his righteousness or justice, to make a distinction between those two diametrically opposite classes—"*the world*," on the one hand, which would not know the Father, though brought so nigh to it in the Son of His love, and, on the other, *Himself*, who recognized and owned Him, and along with Him *His disciples*, who owned His mission from the Father. **26. And I have declared** [ἐγνώρισα]—'I declared' or 'made known' **unto them thy name.** He had said this variously before (*vv.* 6, 8, 14, 22); but here He repeats it for the sake of adding what follows: **and will declare it**—or 'make it known' [ἐγνώρισα—γνωρίσω]. As this could not mean that He was to continue His own Personal ministry on earth, it can refer only to the ministry of His apostles after His ascension "with the Holy Ghost sent down from heaven," and of all who should succeed them, as ambassadors of Christ and ministers of reconciliation, to the end of time. This ministry—Jesus here tells His Father—would be but Himself continuing to make known His Father's name to men, or the *prolongation of His own ministry*. How consolatory a truth this to the faithful ministers of Jesus, and under what a responsibility does it lay all who from their lips hear the message of eternal life in Christ Jesus! **that the love wherewith thou hast loved** [ἠγάπησας]—'lovedst' **me may be in them, and I in them.** He had just expressed His desire "that the world may know that Thou lovedst them as Thou lovedst Me" (*v.* 23). Here it is the implantation and preservation of that love in His people's hearts that He speaks of; and the way by which this was to be done, He says, was "the making known to them of the Father's name;" that is, the revelation of it to their souls by the Spirit's efficacious sealing of the Gospel message—as He had explained in ch. xvi. 8-15. This eternal love of the Father, resting first on Christ, is by His Spirit imparted to and takes up its permanent abode in all that believe in Him; and "He abiding in them, and they in Him" (ch. xv. 5), they are "*one Spirit.*" 'With this lofty thought,' says *Olshausen*, 'the Redeemer concludes His prayer for His disciples, and in them for His Church through all ages. He has compressed into the last moments given Him for conversation with His own the most sublime and glorious sentiments ever uttered by mortal lips. But hardly has the sound of the last word died away, when He passes with the disciples over the

Father, [z]the world hath not known thee: but I have known thee, and
26 these have known that thou hast sent me. And I have declared unto

A. D. 33.

[z] 1 John 5.19.

brook Kedron to Gethsemane—and the bitter conflict draws on. The seed of the new world must be sown in Death, that thence Life may spring up.'

Remarks.—1. How strange is the spiritual obtuseness which can imagine it possible that such a Prayer should have been *penned* if it had not first been *prayed* by the glorious One of whom this Gospel is the historic Record! But it is not only the historic reality of this Prayer, in the Life of Jesus, which is self-evidencing. It throws a strong light upon the question of Inspiration also, which in this case at least must be held to attach to the *language* as well as to the *thoughts* which it conveys. In such a case, every intelligent reader must see that apart from the language of this Prayer, we can have no confidence that its thoughts are accurately conveyed to us. But who that has any spiritual discernment, and any of that spiritual taste and delicacy which constant dealing with Scripture in a devout and loving spirit begets, does not feel that the language of this Prayer is all-worthy of the thoughts which it conveys to us—worthy of the Lips that poured forth this Prayer: and what internal testimony to its inspiration could be stronger than this? We are not insensible to the difficulty of explaining all the facts of the Biblical language, considering it as inspired; but let not this despoil us of what is beyond reasonable dispute, as illustrated by the language of this Divine Prayer. Nor need we commit ourselves to the many rash and at least dubious theories, by which it has been sought to explain and reconcile acknowledged difficulties on this subject. Sitting loose to all these, let us nevertheless—planting our foot upon such a Prayer as this—rest perfectly assured that He of Whom the Lord Jesus promised that He should "bring all things to their remembrance, whatsoever He had spoken to them," has so guided the sacred penman in the reproduction of this Prayer that we have it not only in the substance and spirit of it, but in the *form* also in which it was poured forth in the upper room. 2. One feels it almost trifling to ask again whether such a Prayer as this could have been uttered by a creature? But it may not be amiss to call the reader's attention to *the studious care with which Jesus avoids mixing Himself up with His disciples as He associates Himself with the Father.* "THOU IN ME," He says, "and I IN THEE;" and again, "*I in them*, and *they in* Us." This, we think, is one of the most remarkable features in the phraseology of this chapter; and as it has a most important bearing on the subject of the foregoing Remark—the inspiration attaching to the *language*—so it is in singular harmony with our Lord's manner of speaking on other occasions (see on ch. iii. 7, and Remark 3 at the close of that Section; and on ch. xx. 17). 3. Has Christ, in order to give eternal life to as many as the Father hath given Him, obtained from the Father "power over all flesh"? With confidence, then, may we entrust to Him our eternal all, assured "that He is able to keep that which we have committed unto Him against that day" (see on 2 Tim. i. 12). For since His power is not limited to the objects of His saving operations, but extends to "all flesh," He can and assuredly will make "all things to work together for the good of them that love God, of them who are the called according to His purpose." 4. How fixed are the banks within which the waters of "eternal life" flow to men: "This is life eternal, to know Thee the only true God, and Jesus Christ whom Thou hast sent." Beyond this embankment the water of life may not be sought, and will not be found; and the spurious liberality which would break down this embankment is to be eschewed by all to whom the teaching of the Lord Jesus is sacred and dear. 5. Did Jesus yearn to "ascend up where He was before," and be "glorified beside the Father with the glory which He had along with Him before the world was"? What an affecting light does this throw upon His self-sacrificing love to His Father and to men, in coming hither and staying here during all the period of His work in the flesh—enduring the privations of life, the contradiction of sinners against Himself, the varied assaults of the great Enemy of souls, the slowness of His disciples' apprehension in spiritual things, not to speak of the sight of evil all around Him, and the sense of sin and the curse pressing upon His spirit all throughout, and bringing Him at length to the accursed tree! "Ye know the grace of the Lord Jesus, that though He was rich, yet for your sakes He became poor, that ye through His poverty might be rich." 6. Small indeed was the saving fruit of Christ's personal ministry—few the souls that were thoroughly won to Him; but those few—how dear were they to Him, as the representatives and pledges of a mighty harvest to come! and how does He yearn over those Eleven faithful ones, who represented those that were to gather His redeemed in all time! And will not His faithful servants learn from Him to value and cherish the first fruits of their labours in His service—however few and humble they may be—according to *His* valuation? 7. Hardly anything in this prayer is more remarkable than the *much* that Christ makes in it of the exceedingly small amount of light and faith to which His most advanced disciples had up to that time attained. But He looked doubtless rather to the frame of their hearts towards Him, and the degree of teachableness they had, than to the extent of their actual knowledge—to their *implicit* rather than their *explicit* belief in Him. The servants of Christ have much to learn from Him in this matter. While mere general goodness of heart is of no saving value, a guileless desire to be taught of God, and an honest willingness to follow that teaching wherever it may lead us—which distinguished the Eleven—is, in the sight of God and the estimation of Jesus, of great price. It was precisely this which Jesus commended in Nathanael, and in this respect they were in effect all Nathanaels. Is there not a tendency in some of the servants of Christ, jealous for soundness in the faith, to weigh all religious character in the scales of mere theological orthodoxy? to prefer rounded but cold accuracy of knowledge to the rudimental simplicity of a babe in Christ? to reject an implicit, if it be not an explicit faith? Of course, since the one of these advances surely into the other in the case of all divinely taught believers, even as the shining light shineth more and more unto the perfect day, so those who, under shelter of an implicit faith, advisedly, and after full opportunity, decline an explicit acknowledgment of the distinctive peculiarities of the Gospel, as they are opened up in the writings of the apostles under the full teaching of the Spirit, show clearly that they are void of that childlike faith in which they pretend to rest. But the tender and discerning eye of the true shepherd will look with as much benignity on

them thy name, and will declare *it;* that the love wherewith thou hast loved me may be in them, and [a]I in them.

A. D. 33.

[a] Eph. 3. 17.

the lambs of his flock as on the sheep of his pasture. 8. The whole treatment of believers by the Lord Jesus has three great divisions. The first is the drawing of them, and bringing them to commit their souls to Him for salvation; or in other words, their *conversion:* the second, the preserving of them in this state, and maturing them for heaven; or in other words, their *sanctification:* the third, the bringing of them at length to His Father's house; or in other words, their *glorification.* The first of these stages is, in this prayer, viewed as past. Those for whom He prays have received His word, and are His already. The second being that of which they now stood in need, and all depending upon that, the burden of this prayer is devoted to that sphere of His work: "*Keep* through Thine own name those whom Thou hast given Me;" "I pray not that Thou shouldest take them out of the world, but that Thou shouldest *keep* them from the evil;" "*Sanctify* them through Thy truth, Thy word is truth." One petition only, but that a majestic and all-comprehensive one, is devoted to the third department: "Father, I will that they also whom Thou hast given Me be with Me where I am; that they may behold My glory, which Thou hast given Me: for Thou lovedst me before the foundation of the world." 9. Does Jesus so emphatically pray here for His believing people, first, that His Father would "*keep* them through His own name" (*v.* 11); and then—dividing this keeping into its negative and positive elements—pray both negatively, that they may be "not taken out of the world, but *kept* from the evil" (*v.* 15), and positively, "that they may be sanctified through the truth"? (*v.* 17). What a tender and powerful call is this upon themselves, to keep praying *along with* and *under* their great Intercessor, to His Father and their Father, that He would do for them all that He here asks in their behalf! And is it not an interesting fact, that this "keeping" is the burden of some of the most precious *promises* of God to His ancient people, of many *of their* weightiest prayers, and of some of the chiefest passages of the New Testament; as if it had been designed to provide believers of every age with a Manual on this subject? Thus, "He will *keep* the feet of His saints" (1 Sam. ii. 9); "*Preserve* me, O God: for in Thee do I put my trust" (Ps. xvi. 1); "O that Thou wouldest bless me indeed, and that Thou wouldest *keep me from evil*, that it may not grieve me" (1 Chr. iv. 10); "He that scattered Israel will gather him, and *keep* him as a shepherd doth his flock" (Jer. xxxi. 10). "The Lord is faithful," says the apostle, "who shall stablish you, and *keep you from evil*" (2 Thess. iii. 3); "I know Whom I have believed, and am persuaded that He is able to *keep* that which I have committed unto Him against that day" (2 Tim. i. 12); "Now unto Him that is able to *keep* you from falling (this answers to the negative part of our Lord's petition here) and to *present you faultless* (this is the positive) before the presence of His glory with exceeding joy," &c. (Jude 24). But 10. In thus praying, we not only follow the example, and are encouraged by the model here presented to us, but we utter here below just what our great Intercessor within the veil is continually presenting in our behalf at the right hand of the Majesty on high. Indeed, as this Intercessory Prayer of Christ, though actually presented on earth and before His death, represents His work in the flesh in nearly every verse as already past—insomuch that He says, "Now I am no more in the world"—we are to regard it, and the Church has always so regarded it, as virtually a Prayer from within the veil, or a kind of specimen of the *things* He is now asking, and the *style* in which He now asks them, at the right hand of God. So that believers should never doubt that whensoever they pour out their hearts for what this Prayer teaches them to ask of the Father in Jesus' name a *double pleading* for the same things enters into the Father's ready ear—theirs on earth and Christ's in heaven; in their case the Spirit making intercession with groanings which often cannot be uttered (see on Rom. viii. 26), and so, as the Spirit who takes of the things of Christ and shows them unto us, making our cries to chime in with the mightier demands of Him who can say, "Father, I WILL." 11. Does Jesus so emphatically represent the Father's "*word*" as the *medium* through which He asks Him to sanctify them, and the very *element* of all true sanctification? How does this rebuke the rationalistic teaching of our day, which systematically depreciates the importance of Biblical truth to men's salvation! Between this view of God's truth, and that of our Lord here, there is all the difference that there is between utter and dismal uncertainty in eternal things, and solid footing and assured confidence founded on that which cannot lie. On the one we cannot live with comfort, nor die with any well-grounded hope; on the other we can rise above the ills of life and triumph over the terrors of death. On nothing less than, "*Thus saith the Lord,*" has the soul that repose which it irresistibly yearns for; but on this it enjoys unruffled peace, the peace of God which passeth all understanding. 12. Do believers realize the length and breadth of that saying of Jesus, "*The glory which Thou hast given Me I have given them,* that they may be one even as We are one"? The glory of a perfect *Righteousness;* the glory of a full *Acceptance;* the glory of a free and ready *Access;* the glory of an *indwelling Spirit* of life, and love, and liberty, and universal holiness; the glory of an assured and rightful and abundant *entrance into the everlasting kingdom*—and all this as a presently possessed, and to-be-presently realized glory? And lest this should seem an overstrained exposition of the mind of Christ in *v.* 22, the words which follow seem almost to go beyond it—"I in them, and thou in Me, that they may be made perfect in one; and that the world may know that Thou hast sent Me, and *hast loved them, as Thou hast loved Me:*" and the Prayer dies away with the expression of the means He had taken and should continue to take, in order "*that the love wherewith Thou hast loved Me* (says He) *may be in them, and I in them.*" It is too much to be feared that few believers rise to this. Yet "this," according to our Lord's intercessory Prayer, "is the heritage of the servants of the Lord, and their righteousness is of Me, saith the Lord" (Isa. liv. 17). A grovelling carnality, a false humility, and an erroneous style of teaching, growing out of both these, seem to be the main causes of the general indisposition to rise to the standing which the Lord here gives to all His believing people. But shall we not strive to shake these off, and "walk in the light as He is in the light"? Then shall we "have fellowship with each other"—He and we—"and the blood of Jesus Christ His Son shall cleanse us from all sin." And then may we sing,—

18 WHEN Jesus had spoken these words, he [a]went forth with his disciples
over the [b]brook Cedron, where was a garden, into the which he entered,
2 and his disciples. And Judas also, which betrayed him, knew the place;
3 [c]for Jesus ofttimes resorted thither with his disciples. Judas [d]then,
having received a band *of men* and officers from the chief priests and
Pharisees, cometh thither with lanterns and torches and weapons.
4 Jesus therefore, knowing all things that should come upon him, went

A. D. 33.

CHAP. 18.
[a] Luke 22. 39.
ch 14. 20.
Rom. 8. 10.
[b] 2 Sam. 15. 23.
[c] Luke 21. 37.
[d] Acts 1. 16.

'So nigh, so very nigh to God,
I cannot nearer be;
For in the Person of His Son
I am as near as He.

So dear, so very dear to God,
More dear I cannot be;
The love wherewith He loves the Son—
Such is His love to Me.'

CHAP. XVIII. 1-12.—BETRAYAL AND APPREHENSION OF JESUS. (= Matt. xxvi. 30, 36, 47-56; Mark xiv. 26, 32, 43-52; Luke xxii. 39, 47-54.) Here all the four Evangelists at length meet again; each of them recording the great historical facts at which we have now arrived—the departure from the upper room and out of the city, the entrance into Gethsemane, the treason of Judas, and the seizure of their Lord. But whereas all the first three Evangelists record the Agony in the Garden, John—holding this, no doubt, as already familiar to his readers—gives us, instead of it, some of the circumstances of the apprehension in more minute detail than had been before recorded.

The Betrayal (1-3). **1. When Jesus had spoken these words, he went forth with his disciples.** With this explicit statement before them, it is surprising that some good critics should hold that the departure took place when Jesus said, "Arise, let us go hence" (ch. xiv. 31), and that all which is recorded in ch. xv. and xvi., including the Prayer of ch. xvii., was uttered in the open air, and on the way to Gethsemane. As to how we are to view the *proposal* to depart so long before it actually took place, see on ch. xiv. 31. **over the brook Cedron** (Kedron)—a deep, dark ravine, to the north-east of Jerusalem, through which flowed this small 'storm-brook' or 'winter-torrent,' and which in summer is dried up. As it is in the *reflective* Gospel only that the circumstance of His crossing the brook Kedron is mentioned, we can hardly doubt that to the Evangelist's own mind there was present the strikingly *analogous* crossing of the same dark streamlet by the royal sufferer (2 Sam. xv. 23); possibly also certain other historical associations (see 2 Ki. xxiii. 12): 'Thus surrounded,' says *Stier*, by such memorials and typical allusions, the Lord descends into the dust of humiliation and anguish.' **where was a garden**—at the foot of the mount of Olives, "called Gethsemane" (Matt. xxvi. 30, 36) or 'oil-press' [גַּת שְׁמָנֵא], from the olives with which it was filled, **into the which he entered, and his disciples. 2. And Judas also, which betrayed him, knew the place; for Jesus ofttimes resorted thither with his disciples.** The baseness of this abuse of knowledge in Judas, derived from the privilege he enjoyed of admission to the closest privacies of His Master, is most touchingly conveyed here, though only in the form of simple narrative. Jesus, however, knowing that in this spot Judas would expect to find Him, instead of avoiding it, hies Him thither, as a Lamb to the slaughter. "No man taketh my life from me, but I lay it down of myself" (ch. x. 18). For other reasons why this spot was selected, see on the Agony in the garden (Luke xxii. 39-46), page 331, second column, third paragraph. **3. Judas then**—"He that was called Judas, one of the Twelve," says Luke (xxii. 47), in language which brands him with peculiar infamy, as *in* the sacred circle, though in no proper sense *of* it. **having received a band [of men] and officers from the chief priests and Pharisees** [τὴν σπεῖραν, καὶ εκ τῶν ἀρχιερέων καὶ Φαρισαίων ὑπηρέτας]—rather, 'the band (without the supplement, "of men") and officers' or 'servants of the chief priests and Pharisees.' Two bodies are here mentioned: "the band," meaning, as *Webster and Wilkinson* express it, the detachment of the Roman cohort on duty at the festival, for the purpose of maintaining order; and the officials of the ecclesiastical authorities—the captains of the temple and armed Levites. **cometh thither with lanterns and torches and weapons.** It was full moon, but in case He should have secreted Himself somewhere in the dark ravine, they bring the means of exploring its hiding-places—little knowing Whom they had to do with. The other Gospels tell us that the time when Judas drew near was "immediately, while Jesus yet spake," that is, while He was saying, after the Agony was over, to the three whom He had found sleeping for sorrow, "Rise, let us be going: behold, he is at hand that doth betray Me" (Matt. xxvi. 46, 47). The next step, as we take it, is the act of Betrayal—not recorded at all, but only alluded to, in our Fourth Gospel; the other Evangelists having given it fully, whom we shall now follow.

"Now he that betrayed Him gave," or had given "them a sign, saying, Whomsoever I shall kiss, that same is he: hold him fast" (Matt. xxvi. 48). The cold-bloodedness of this speech was only exceeded by the deed itself. "And Judas went before them (Luke xxii. 47), and said, Hail, Master! and kissed Him" (Matt. xxvi. 49: see, for illustration of the act, 1 Sam. xx. 41; and mark Prov. xxvii. 6.) The impudence of this atrocious deed shows how thoroughly he had by this time mastered all his scruples. If the dialogue between our Lord and His captors was *before* this, as some interpreters think it was, the kiss of Judas was purely gratuitous, and probably to make good his right to the money; our Lord having presented Himself unexpectedly before them, and rendered it unnecessary for any one to point him out. But a comparison of the narratives seems to show that our Lord's "coming forth" to the band was *subsequent* to the interview of Judas. "And Jesus said unto him, Friend" [Ἑταῖρε]. The difference between the term here studiously employed—which signifies rather 'companion' in mere social intercourse, and which is used on other occasions of remonstrance and rebuke (as Matt. xx. 13; xxii. 12)—and the endearing term properly rendered "friend" (in Luke xii. 4, and John xv. 13-15)—is very striking: "Wherefore art thou come?" (Matt. xxvi. 50). "Betrayest thou the Son of Man with a kiss?" (Luke xxii. 48)—imprinting on the foulest of all acts the mark of tenderest affection? What *wounded feeling* does this express! Of this Jesus showed Himself on various occasions keenly susceptible—as all generous and beautiful natures are. This brings us back to our own Gospel.

The Apprehension (4-12). **4. Jesus therefore,**

5 forth, and said unto them, Whom seek ye? They answered him, Jesus
of Nazareth. Jesus saith unto them, I am *he*. And Judas also, which
6 betrayed him, stood with them. As soon then as he had said unto
7 them, I am *he*, they went backward, and fell to the ground. Then asked
he them again, Whom seek ye? And they said, Jesus of Nazareth.
8 Jesus answered, I have told you that I am *he*. If therefore ye seek me,
9 [e]let these go their way: that the saying might be fulfilled which he
spake, [f]Of them which thou gavest me have I lost none.
10 Then [g]Simon Peter having a sword drew it, and smote the high
priest's servant, and cut off his right ear. The servant's name was
11 Malchus. Then said Jesus unto Peter, Put up thy sword into the sheath:
[h]the cup which my Father hath given me, shall I not drink it?

A. D. 33.

[e] Ps. 34. 15. Matt. 6. 25, 34. 1 Pet. 5. 7.
[f] ch. 6. 39. ch. 17. 12. 2 Tim. 4. 18. 1 Pet. 1. 5. Jude 1.
[g] Matt. 26. 51. Mark 14. 57. Luke 22. 49.
[h] Ps. 75. 8. Matt. 20. 22.

knowing all things that should come—or 'were coming' **upon him, went forth**—from the shade of the trees, probably, into open view, indicating His sublime preparedness to meet His captors, **and said unto them, Whom seek ye?**—partly to prevent a rush of the soldiery upon the disciples, as *Bengel* thinks (see Mark xiv. 51, 52, which may lend some countenance to this), but still more in the exercise of that courage and majesty which so overawed them:—He would not wait to be *taken*. **5. They answered him, Jesus of Nazareth**—just the sort of blunt, straightforward reply one expects from military men, simply acting on their instructions. **Jesus saith unto them, I am [he].** On this sublime expression, see on Mark vi. 50. **And Judas also, which betrayed him, stood with them.** No more is recorded here of *his* part of the scene, but we have found the gap painfully supplied by all the other Evangelists. **6. As soon then as he had said unto them, I am [he], they went backward**—recoiled, **and fell to the ground**—struck down by a power such as that which smote Saul of Tarsus and his companions to the earth (Acts xxvi. 14). It was the glorious effulgence of the majesty of Christ which overpowered them. 'This,' as *Meyer* well remarks, 'occurring before His surrender, would show His *power* over His enemies, and so the *freedom* with which He gave Himself up.' **7. Then asked he them again, Whom seek ye?**—giving them a door of escape from the guilt of a deed which *now* they were able in some measure to understand. **And they said, Jesus of Nazareth.** The stunning effect of His first answer wearing off, they think only of the necessity of executing their orders. **8. Jesus answered, I have told you that I am [he]. If therefore ye seek me, let these go their way**—Wonderful self-possession and consideration for others in such circumstances! **9. That the saying might be fulfilled which he spake, Of them which thou gavest**—'hast given' **me have I lost none.** The reference is to such sayings as ch. vi. 39; xvii. 12; showing how conscious the Evangelist was, that in reporting his Lord's former sayings, he was giving them not in *substance* merely, but in *form* also. (See on ch. xvii., Remark 1 at the close of that Section.) Observe, also, how the preservation of the disciples on this occasion is viewed as part of that *deeper preservation* undoubtedly intended in the saying quoted.

10. Then Simon Peter having a sword drew it, and smote the high priest's servant, and cut off his right ear. The servant's name was Malchus. None of the other Evangelists mention the name either of the ardent disciple or of his victim. But John being "known to the high priest" (*v.* 15), the mention of the servant's name by *him* is quite natural, and an interesting mark of truth in a small matter. As to the *right* ear, specified both here and in Luke, the man as *Webster and Wilkinson* remark, 'was likely foremost of those who advanced to seize Jesus, and presented himself in the attitude of a combatant; hence his right side would be exposed to attack. The blow of Peter was evidently aimed vertically at his head.' "And Jesus answered and said, Suffer ye thus far" (Luke xxii. 51). It seems unnatural to understand this as addressed to the captors, as if He had said, 'Suffer My disciples thus far to show their attachment to Me; excuse it to this extent; they shall do nothing more of this kind,' as *Webster and Wilkinson* put it, and *de Wette* and *van Osterzee* view it. Still less natural does *Alford's* view appear, which takes it as a request to those who were holding and binding Him, to permit Him to heal the wounded ear. It seems plainly to be addressed, as *Meyer* says, to the disciples, bidding them go no further in the way of defending Him; and so the majority of interpreters understand it. "And He touched his ear, and healed him." Luke only records this miracle, which in the apparently helpless circumstances in which our Lord stood, was most signal. But "The Son of Man came not to destroy men's lives, but to save them" (Luke ix. 56), and, even when they were destroying His, to save theirs. **11. Then said Jesus unto Peter, Put up thy sword into the sheath: the cup which my Father hath given me, shall I not drink it?** It is remarkable that though the Agony in the Garden is not here recorded, this question expresses with affecting clearness *both* the feelings which during that scene struggled in the breast of Jesus—'*aversion to the cup*, viewed in itself,' and, 'in the light of the Father's will, *perfect preparedness to drink it up*.' (See the exposition of that wonderful scene, on Luke xxii. 39-46.)

In the other Gospels we have some fuller particulars, Matt. xxvi. 52-56: "Put up thy sword into his place: for all they that take the sword shall perish by the sword." 'Those who take the sword must run all the risks of human warfare; but Mine is a warfare whose weapons, as they are not carnal, are attended with no such hazards, but carry certain victory.' "Thinkest thou that I cannot now"—even after things have proceeded so far, "pray to My Father, and He shall presently give Me"—rather, 'place at My disposal' [παραστήσει μοι] "more than twelve legions of angels;" with allusion, possibly, to the one angel who had, in His agony, "appeared to Him from Heaven strengthening Him" (Luke xxii. 43); and in the precise number, alluding to the *twelve* who needed the help, Himself and His eleven disciples. (The full complement of a legion of Roman soldiers was six thousand.) "But how then shall the Scripture be fulfilled that thus it must be?" He could not suffer, according to the Scripture, if He allowed Himself to be delivered from the predicted death.

12 Then the band and the captain and officers of the Jews took Jesus,
13 and bound him, and [i]led him away to [j]Annas first: for he was father-
14 in-law to Caiaphas, which was the high priest that same year.[1] Now
[k]Caiaphas was he which gave counsel to the Jews, that it was expedient
that one man should die for the people.
15 And Simon Peter followed Jesus, and *so did* another disciple. That
disciple was known unto the high priest, and went in with Jesus into
16 the palace of the high priest. But Peter stood at the door without.

A. D. 33.

i Matt. 26. 57.
j Luke 3. 2.
1 And Annas sent Christ bound unto Caiaphas, the high priest. ver. 24.
k ch. 11. 50.

12. Then the band and the captain and ('the') **officers of the Jews took Jesus, and bound him**—but not until He had made them feel that "no man took His life from Him, but that He laid it down of Himself" (ch. x. 18).

In the first three Gospels we have here the following additional particulars: Matt. xxvi. 55, "In that same hour," probably on the way to judgment, when the crowds were pressing upon Him, "said Jesus to the multitudes"—or as in Luke xxii. 52, "unto the chief priests, and captains of the temple, and the elders, which were come to Him"—"Are ye come out as against a thief with swords and staves for to take Me?" He thus keenly yet loftily expresses the indignity which He felt to be done to Him. "I sat daily with you teaching in the temple, and ye laid no hold on Me." "But this is your hour, and the power of darkness" (Luke xxii. 53.) Matthew continues (xxvi. 56) "But all this was done, that the Scriptures of the prophets might be fulfilled."

Here follows, in the first two Gospels, an affecting particular, the mention of which somewhere we should have expected from the sad announcement which Jesus had made at the Supper-table—"All ye shall be offended because of Me this night," &c. (Matt. xxvi. 31; Mark xiv. 27: see opening remarks on Luke xxii. 31-39). It is the same two Evangelists that report this warning who record the too speedy fulfilment.

Desertion and Flight of the Disciples (Matt. xxvi. 56; Mark xiv. 50). "Then all the disciples forsook Him, and fled."

A singular incident is here recorded by Mark alone (xiv. 51, 52): "And there followed Him a certain young man, having a linen cloth cast about his naked body"—they were wont, says *Grotius*, to sleep in linen, and in this condition this youth had started up from his bed: "and the young men laid hold on him"—the attendants of the chief priests, mentioned in John xviii. 3, or some of their junior assistants [but οἱ νεανίσκοι seems not to be genuine]: "And he left the linen cloth, and fled from them naked"—for, as *Bengel* says, in great danger fear conquers shame. The general object for which this was introduced is easily seen. The flight of all the apostles, recorded in the preceding verse, suggested the mention of this other flight, as one of the noticeable incidents of that memorable night, and as showing what terror the scene inspired in all who were attached to Jesus. By most interpreters it is passed over too slightly. One thing is stamped on the face of it—it is the narrative of an *eye-witness* of what is described. The mention of the fate of one individual, and him "a certain young man"—expressively put in the original [εἷς τις νεανίσκος]—of his single piece of dress, and that of "linen," of the precise parties who laid hold of him [though οἱ νεανίσκοι cannot be relied on], and how he managed to make a hair-breadth escape, even though it obliged him to part with all that covered his nakedness—this singular minuteness of detail suggests even more than the pen of an eye-witness. It irresistibly leads to a further question—Had the writer of this Gospel himself nothing to do with that scene?—'*To me*,' says *Olshausen*, '*it appears most probable that here Mark writes concerning himself.*' So also *Lange*.

Remarks.—1. But once only, from the time that the officers came to take Him till He expired on the cross, did Jesus think fit to show, by any overt act, how *voluntarily* He endured all that was inflicted on Him by the hands of men; and that was immediately before they proceeded to their first act of violence. One such manifestation of His glorious superiority to all the power of earth is what we should perhaps expect; and as it was put forth at the critical moment—when His disciples would be watching with breathless interest to see whether He would endure to be seized, and perhaps His captors were apprehensive of some difficulty in the matter—so it was of such a nature as rendered a second manifestation of it altogether superfluous. From this time forth it must have been seen, by any eye that could read what He had done, that all-unforced, He went as a Lamb to the slaughter. 2. How quickly, when men "sell themselves" to do evil, do their hearts become steeled against all feeling, and capable of whatever blackness of demon-like ingratitude and treachery may be required for the perpetration of the crimes they have resolved on! Think of Judas but a brief hour or two before this, sitting at the Supper-table as one of the apostles of the Lord Jesus, all unsuspected by the rest; think of him but six days before this at the house of Simon the leper, unsuspected in all likelihood even by himself, until his disappointment in the matter of the "three hundred pence" ripened into rage and suggested, apparently for the first time, the foul deed (see on Mark xiv. 1-11, Remark 8 at the close of that Section); and then think of the pitch of wickedness he had now reached. It may be thought that only the continual overawing presence of his Lord kept down the already matured wickedness of his heart. But it should rather be said, it kept the seeds of that wickedness, which undoubtedly were there from the first (ch. vi. 70), from coming to maturity and acquiring their full mastery before the time. Nay, the end which Judas made of himself seems clearly to show how far he was from being a long hardened wretch, what quick work Satan had made of his natural tendencies at the last, and how, when his full criminality stared him in the face, instead of being able to wipe his mouth, as those whose conscience is seared as with a hot iron, he felt it to be insupportable. We make these observations, not to lessen the execration with which the deed and the doer of it are instinctively regarded, but to show that there is nothing in this case of Judas but what may in substance have been done once and again since that time—nothing exceptional to the ordinary working of evil principles in the human heart and life. "Let him," then, "that thinketh he standeth take heed lest he fall!"

13-23. Jesus is Brought Privately before

Then went out that other disciple, which was known unto the high
priest, and spake unto her that kept the door, and brought in Peter.
17 Then saith the damsel that kept the door unto Peter, Art not thou
18 also *one* of this man's disciples? He saith, I am not. And the servants
and officers stood there, who had made a fire of coals; for it was cold:
and they warmed themselves: and Peter stood with them, and warmed
himself.
19 The high priest then asked Jesus of his disciples, and of his doctrine.
20 Jesus answered him, [l]I spake openly to the world; I ever taught in the
synagogue, and in the temple, whither the Jews always resort; and in
21 secret have I said nothing. Why askest thou me? ask them which
heard me, what I have said unto them: behold, they know what I said.
22 And when he had thus spoken, one of the officers which stood by
[m]struck Jesus [2]with the palm of his hand, saying, Answerest thou the
23 high priest so? Jesus answered him, [n]If I have spoken evil, bear witness
24 of the evil; but if well, why smitest thou me? Now Annas had sent
him bound unto Caiaphas the high priest.
25 And Simon Peter stood and warmed himself. [o]They said therefore
unto him, Art not thou also *one* of his disciples? He denied *it*, and
26 said, I am not. One of the servants of the high priest, being *his* kinsman whose ear Peter cut off, saith, Did not I see thee in the garden with
27 him? Peter then denied again: and [p]immediately the cock crew.
28 Then [q]led they Jesus from Caiaphas unto [3]the hall of judgment: and
it was early; and [r]they themselves went not into the judgment hall, lest

A. D. 33.
[l] Luke 4. 15. ch. 7. 14, 26, 28. ch. 8. 2.
[m] Isa. 50. 6. Jer. 20. 2. Mic. 5. 1. Acts 23. 2.
[2] Or, with a rod.
[n] Ps. 38. 12-14. Isa. 53. 7. Heb. 12. 3. 1 Pet. 2. 23.
[o] Matt. 26. 69, 71. Mark 14. 69. Luke 22. 58.
[p] Matt. 26. 74 Mark 14. 72. Luke 22. 60. ch. 13. 38.
[q] Matt. 27. 2. Mark 15. 1. Luke 23. 1. Acts 3. 13.
[3] Or, Pilate's house. Matt. 27. 27.
[r] Acts 10. 28. Acts 11. 3.

ANNAS FIRST—PETER OBTAINS ACCESS WITHIN THE QUADRANGLE OF THE HIGH PRIEST'S RESIDENCE, AND WARMS HIMSELF AT THE FIRE—THE LORD IS INTERROGATED BY ANNAS—HIS DIGNIFIED REPLY—HE IS TREATED WITH INDIGNITY BY ONE OF THE OFFICIALS—HIS MEEK REBUKE. For the exposition, see on Mark xiv. 53, &c., as far as page 204, second paragraph.

24-27.—JESUS IS LED FROM ANNAS TO CAIAPHAS TO BE JUDGED BY THE SANHEDRIM—THE FALL OF PETER. Our Evangelist, it would seem, had nothing to add to the ample details of the trial and condemnation of the Lord Jesus and the indignities with which He was thereafter treated, and next to nothing on the sad fall of Peter in the midst of these transactions. With all this he holds his readers already familiar, through the records of the three preceding Evangelists. In the first of these four verses, accordingly, he simply tells us that "Annas sent Him bound unto Caiaphas the high priest," without so much as mentioning what this was for, still less giving any particulars of the trial. And though he relates in the briefest terms two of Peter's denials, and the crowing of the cock, this is merely to supply one small but striking particular which had not been noticed in the preceding Gospels—how one of those who charged Peter with being a disciple of Jesus was able to identify him, by his own relationship to the man whose ear Peter had cut off in the garden, and who saw him do it (*v.* 26). For the exposition of all the Evangelical matter embraced by these four verses, see on Mark xiv. 53-72, page 203, second paragraph, and 204, second paragraph to page 211.

28—xix. 16.—JESUS BEFORE PILATE. (=Matt. xxvii. 1, 2, 11-31; Mark xv. 1-20; Luke xxiii. 1-7, 13-25.) As one of the most important details of this varied Section is omitted altogether by our Evangelist, while the rest are given very summarily, we must avail ourselves of the other Gospels in order to have the whole before us for exposition.

From the time of the deposition of Archelaus, and the reduction of Judea to the condition of a Roman province (see on Matt. ii. 22), the power of life and death was taken from the Jewish tribunals. No sentence of death, therefore, which they pronounced could be executed without the sanction of the Roman Governor. Accordingly, as soon as our Lord was condemned by the Sanhedrim to die, and the contemptuous treatment of Him which followed had time to spend itself—it being now early morn—they proceed to bring Him before Pilate that he might authorize His execution.

The Chief Priests, having brought Jesus to the Prætorium, Fail, in the first instance, in Persuading Pilate to Sanction His Execution (28-32). **28. Then led they** [Ἄγουσιν]—'Then lead they' **Jesus from Caiaphas unto the hall of judgment** [τὸ πραιτώριον]—rather, 'the *Prætorium*;' that is, the official residence of the Roman Governor. His usual place of residence was at Cæsarea; but during the Passover season it was his duty to be at Jerusalem, on account of the vast influx of strangers, to see that all things were conducted legally and peaceably. **and it was early.** We learn from Mark (xv. 1) that this step was the result of a special consultation: "And straightway in the morning the chief priests held a consultation with the elders and scribes and the whole council" [ὅλον τὸ συνέδριον]—no doubt to arrange their plans and frame their charge, "and bound Jesus, and carried Him away, and delivered Him to Pilate." **and they themselves went not into the judgment hall**—'the Prætorium,' **lest they should be defiled, but that they might eat the passover.** These words have occasioned immense research, and given rise to much controversy and not a few learned treatises. From these words chiefly it has been argued that the Jews had not eaten the Passover up to the time here referred to, and consequently, as our Lord and His apostles ate it the previous evening, they must have eaten it a day earlier than the proper statutory day. In that case

29 they should be defiled, but that they might eat [s]the passover. Pilate
then went out unto them, and said, What accusation bring ye against
30 this man? They answered and said unto him, If he were not a male-
31 factor, we would not have delivered him up unto thee. Then said Pilate
unto them, Take ye him, and judge him according to your law. The
Jews therefore said unto him, It [t]is not lawful for us to put any man to
32 death: That [u]the saying of Jesus might be fulfilled, which he spake,
signifying what death he should die.

A. D. 33.

[s] Deut. 16. 2. Matt 27. 23. Acts 23. 28.
[t] Gen 49. 10. Ezek. 21. 26, 27.
[u] Matt. 20. 19. ch. 12. 32, 33.

there is a manifest discrepancy between the first three Gospels and the fourth, and this on a point not only of considerable importance, but one on which it is difficult to conceive that there should on either side be any mistake. As to this particular passage, it is not easy to see how it helps the theory which it is supposed to establish. For supposing that the proper season for eating the Passover was not to be till *that evening after six o'clock*, and this party that brought Jesus to Pilate *in the morning* had ceremonially defiled themselves by going into the Prætorium, that defilement—as it would only have lasted, according to law, during the one day of twelve hours on which it was contracted—would have passed away of itself before the proper time for eating their Passover. Does not this show that the statement of our Evangelist here has no reference to *the regular time for eating the Passover?* Having already expressed our belief that all the four Gospels are at one on this subject, and that our Lord ate the Passover on the usual day—the 14th of the month Nisan (see opening remarks on the 'Preparation for the Passover,' on Luke xxii. 7-30; and on ch. xiii. 1)—it only remains that we here state what we take to be our Evangelist's meaning in the words before us. We cannot accept the explanation of some good critics—*Robinson*, for example—that by "eating the Passover" the Evangelist means, not the eating of the Paschal lamb, which was the first and principal part of the feast, but keeping the feast of unleavened bread. The passages which are thought to justify this way of speaking are insufficient; it is not, at least, according to the usual language of the Evangelists; and it has a forced appearance. But there is a simpler explanation of the words. If we suppose that the party who were bringing Jesus before the Governor had been so engrossed with the exciting circumstances of His capture and trial and condemnation the previous evening as not to have leisure to eat their Passover *at the proper time;* but that having only deferred it on the ground of unavoidable hindrances, and fully intending to eat it as early *that same day* as this urgent business would allow, they abstained from entering the Prætorium, because by doing so they would have been defiled, and so legally disqualified from eating it till the day was over—we have, in our judgment, a satisfactory explanation of our Evangelist's statement. Nor were similar postponements, and even omissions, of the most solemn observances of their ritual altogether unknown in the Jewish history, as may be seen in *Josephus*. (See an able Essay on this subject in *Fairbairn's* "Hermeneutical Manual.")

29. Pilate then went out unto them—since they would not come in to him, **and said, What accusation bring ye against this man?**—'State your charge.' **30. They answered and said unto him, If he were not a malefactor, we would not have delivered him up unto thee**—a very lame reply. But they were conscious they had *no case* of which Pilate could take cognizance and inferring death, or any punishment at all, according to the Roman law. They therefore simply insinuate that the case must have been bad enough before they would have come to him with it, and that having found him worthy of death by their own law, they merely wished him to sanction the execution. **31. Then said Pilate unto them, Take ye him** [λάβετε αὐτὸν ὑμεῖς]—'Take him yourselves,' **and judge him according to your law.** This was not an admission, as some view it, of their independence of him in matters of life and death: for they themselves say the contrary in the very next words, and Pilate surely did not need to learn what his powers were from these Jews. But by this general reply he would throw upon themselves the responsibility of all they should do against this Prisoner: for no doubt he had been informed to some extent of their proceedings. **The Jews therefore said unto him, It is not lawful for us to put any man to death.** See *Josephus* (Antt. xx. 9. 1), who tells us that the high priest was charged with acting illegally for assembling the Sanhedrim that condemned 'James the just' to die, without the consent of the Roman Governor. **32. That the saying of Jesus might be fulfilled, which he spake, signifying what death** [ποίῳ θανάτῳ]—'what kind' or 'manner of death' **he should die**—that is, the death of the *cross*, which Jesus had once and again predicted He should die (Matt. xx. 19; John iii. 14; viii. 28; xii. 32). Had it been left to the Jews to execute their own sentence, it would have been, as their law required in cases of blasphemy, by *stoning*. (Lev. xxiv. 16; 1 Ki. xxi. 10; Acts vi. 13, with vii. 58; and see on ch. x. 32, 33.) But as this would have defeated the divine arrangements, it was so ordered that they should not have this in their power; and the divinely fixed mode of *crucifixion*, being a Roman mode of execution, could only be carried into effect by order of the Roman Governor. Finding it now indispensable to success to get up a criminal charge against their Prisoner, they proceed with shameless audacity to say that they had found Him guilty of what on His trial they seem not so much as to have laid to His charge. This is recorded only in

Luke xxiii. 2: "And they began"—or 'proceeded' "to accuse Him, saying, We have found this [fellow] perverting the nation"—'our nation' the true reading probably is—"and forbidding to give tribute to Cesar, saying that He Himself is Christ a King." In two things this speech was peculiarly base. First, It was a lie that He had ever forbidden to give tribute to Cesar; nay, to some of themselves, not many days before this, in reply to their ensnaring question on this very subject, and with a Roman coin in His hands, He had said, "*Render to Cesar the things which be Cesar's*" (Luke xx. 25). Secondly, Their pretended jealousy for the rights and honours of Cesar was so far from being real, that their restless impatience under the Roman yoke was already creating uneasiness at Rome, and ultimately brought ruin on their whole commonwealth; nor can there be any doubt that if our Lord had given the least indication of a willingness to assume royal honours, in opposition to the Roman power, they would have

33 Then Pilate entered into the judgment hall again, and called Jesus,
34 and said unto him, Art thou the King of the Jews? Jesus answered him,
35 Sayest thou this thing of thyself, or did others tell it thee of me? Pilate
answered, Am I a Jew? Thine own nation and the chief priests have
36 delivered thee unto me: what hast thou done? Jesus [v]answered, [w]My
kingdom is not of this world. If my kingdom were of this world, then
would my servants fight, that I should not be delivered to the Jews: but

A. D. 33.
[v] 1 Tim. 6. 13. Rev. 1. 3.
[w] Isa. 9. 6. Dan. 2. 44. Dan. 7. 14. Luke 12. 14. ch. 6. 15. 2 Cor. 10. 4.

rallied around Him. But how does Pilate treat this charge against the blessed Jesus? It was at least a tangible charge, and whatever suspicion he might have as to the motives of His accusers, it was not to be trifled with. Perhaps rumours of our Lord's regal claims may have reached the Governor's ears; but instead of entering on the subject with the accusers, he resolves to interrogate the Accused Himself, and that alone, in the first instance.

Interview between Pilate and Jesus (33-38). **33. Then Pilate entered into the judgment hall**—'the Prætorium' **again, and called Jesus, and said unto him, Art thou the King of the Jews? 34. Jesus answered him, Sayest thou this thing of thyself, or did others tell it thee of me?**—'Is this question prompted by any evidence which has come to thine ears of treason on My part against the Roman government; or hast thou merely been *put up* to it by those who, having failed to convict Me of aught that is criminal, are yet urging thee to put Me to death?' **35. Pilate answered, Am I a Jew? Thine own nation and the chief priests have delivered thee unto me: what hast thou done?**—*q. d.*, 'Jewish questions I neither understand nor meddle with; but thou art here on a charge which, though it *seems* only Jewish, *may* yet involve treasonable matter. As *they* state it I cannot decide the point; tell me, then, what procedure of thine has brought thee into this position.' In modern phrase, Pilate's object in this question was merely to determine the *relevancy* of the charge, or whether the claims which he was accused of making were of a treasonable nature. If it should be found that they were, the *evidence* of His having actually advanced such claims would still remain to be sifted. **36. Jesus answered, My kingdom is not of this world** [Ἡ βασιλεία ἡ ἐμή]. The "My" here is emphatic:—*q. d.*, 'This kingdom of Mine.' He does not say it is not '*in*' or '*over*,' but it is not "*of* this world" [ἐκ τοῦ κόσμου τούτου], that is, in its *origin* and *nature;* and so, is no such kingdom as need give thee or thy master the least alarm. **If my kingdom were of this world, then would my servants fight, that I should not be delivered to the Jews**—'a very convincing argument,' as *Webster and Wilkinson* observe; 'for if His servants did not fight to prevent their king from being delivered up to His enemies, much less would they use force for the establishment of His kingdom:' **but now is**—'but the fact is' **my kingdom not from hence.** Our Lord only says whence His kingdom is *not*—first simply affirming it, next giving proof of it, then re-affirming it. This was all that Pilate had to do with. The *positive* nature of His kingdom He would not obtrude upon one who was as little able to comprehend it as entitled officially to information about it. It is worthy of notice that the "MY," which occurs *four* times in this one verse—*thrice* of His *kingdom* and *once* of His *servants*—is put in the emphatic form. **37. Pilate therefore said unto him, Art thou a king then?** There was no sarcasm or disdain in this question, as *Tholuck, Alford,* &c., allege, else our Lord's answer would have been different. Putting emphasis upon "*thou*," his question betrays a mixture of *surprise* and *uneasiness*, partly at the possibility of there being, after all, something dangerous under the claim, and partly from a certain awe which our Lord's demeanour probably struck into him. **Jesus answered, Thou sayest that I am a king** [Σὺ λέγεις ὅτι βασιλεύς εἰμι Ἐγώ]—or rather, 'Thou sayest [it], for a king I am.' **To this end was I**—'have I been' **born, and for this cause came I**—'to this end am I come' **into the world, that I should bear witness unto the truth.** His *birth* expresses His manhood; His *coming into the world*, His existence before assuming humanity: the truth, then, here affirmed, though Pilate would catch little of it, was, that 'His Incarnation was expressly in order to the assumption of Royalty in our nature.' Yet, instead of saying He came to be a king, which is His meaning, He says He came to *testify to the truth.* Why this? Because, in such circumstances, it required a noble courage not to flinch from His royal claims; and our Lord, *conscious that He was putting forth that courage,* gives a turn to His confession expressive of it. It is to this that Paul is commonly understood to allude, in those remarkable words to Timothy: "I charge thee before God, who quickeneth all things, and before Christ Jesus, who before Pontius Pilate witnessed *the good confession*" [τὴν καλὴν ὁμολογίαν] (1 Tim. vi. 13). But we have given our opinion (page 206, first column) that the reference is to the solemn confession which He witnessed before the supreme ecclesiastical council, that He was "THE CHRIST, THE SON OF THE BLESSED," which the apostle would hold up to Timothy as a sublime example of the fidelity and courage which he himself should display. These two confessions, however, are the complements of each other. For, in the beautiful words of *Olshausen*, 'As the Lord owned Himself *the Son of God* before the most exalted theocratic council, so He confessed His *regal dignity* in presence of the representative of the highest political authority on earth.' **Every one that is of the truth heareth my voice.** Our Lord here not only affirms that His word had in it a self-evidencing, self-recommending power, but gently insinuates the *true secret of the growth and grandeur of His kingdom:* it is a KINGDOM OF TRUTH, in its highest sense, into which all souls who have learnt to live and count all things but loss for the truth are, by a most heavenly attraction, drawn as into their proper element; whose KING Jesus is, fetching them in and ruling them by His captivating power over their hearts. **38. Pilate saith unto him, What is truth?**—*q. d.*, 'Thou stirrest the question of questions, which the thoughtful of every age have asked, but never man yet answered.' **And when he had said this**—as if, by putting such a question, he was getting into interminable and unseasonable enquiries, when this business demanded rather prompt action, **he went out again unto the Jews**—thus missing a noble opportunity for himself, and giving utterance to that consciousness of the want of all intellectual and moral certainty, which was the feel-

37 now is my kingdom not from hence. Pilate therefore said unto him, Art
thou a king then? Jesus answered, [x] Thou sayest that I am a king. To
this end was I born, and for this cause came I into the world, that I

A. D. 33.

[x] Luke 23. 3. 1 Tim. 6. 13.

ing of every thoughtful mind at that time. 'The only certainty,' says the elder *Pliny*, quoted by *Olshausen*, 'is that nothing is certain, nor more miserable than man, nor more proud.' 'The fearful laxity of morals,' adds the critic, 'at that time must doubtless be traced in a great degree to this scepticism. The revelation of the eternal truth alone was able to breathe new life into ruined human nature, and that in the apprehension of complete redemption.'

Pilate, again Going Forth to the Jews, Vainly Attempts to Obtain their Consent to the Release of Jesus (38). 38. . . **And when he had said this, he went out again unto the Jews, and saith unto them**—in the hearing of our Lord, who had been brought forth to them, **I find in him no fault** [**at all**]—that is, no ground of criminal charge, "touching those things whereof ye accuse him" (Luke xxiii. 14). This testimony is all the more important immediately after our Lord's explicit confession that He was a King, and speaking of "His kingdom." But how could Pilate with any truth say else than he did, after the explanation that His kingdom was not of a nature to come into collision at all with Cesar's? Indeed, it is clear that Pilate regarded our Lord as a high-minded Advocate of some mysterious religious principles, more or less connected with the Jewish Faith but at variance with the reigning ecclesiastical system—thoroughly sincere, at the least, but whether more than that he was unable to judge; yet cherishing no treasonable designs and meddling with no political affairs. This conclusion, candidly expressed, so exasperated "the chief priests and elders," who were panting for His death, that afraid of losing their Victim, they pour forth a volley of charges against Him, as if to overbear the Governor by their very vehemence. The precise succession of the incidents and speeches here, as reported by the different Evangelists, it is not quite easy to see, though the general course of them is plain enough.

Matt. xxvii. 12-14 (=Mark xv. 3-5):—"And when He was accused of the chief priests and elders, He answered nothing. Then said Pilate unto Him, Hearest thou not how many things they witness against thee? And He answered him to never a word"—Mark says, "Jesus yet answered nothing," or rather, 'answered nothing more' [οὐκέτι οὐδέν]; that is, nothing more than He *had* answered already to Pilate alone—"insomuch that the governor marvelled greatly." Pilate, fully persuaded of His innocence, seems to have been surprised that He did not refute nor even challenge their charges. But here a very important incident occurred—the transference of Jesus to Herod—which is recorded only in the third Gospel. It is thus introduced:—

Luke xxiii. 4, 5:—"Then said Pilate to the chief priests and to the people, I find no fault in him." (This appears to us clearly to be the same testimony as we found recorded in John, though *Robinson* in his 'Harmony' represents it as a second statement of the same thing.) "And they were the more fierce, saying, He stirreth up the people, teaching throughout all Jewry, beginning from Galilee to this place." They see no hope of getting Pilate's sanction to His death unless they can fasten upon Him some charge of conspiracy against the government; and as *Galilee* was noted for its turbulence (see Luke xiii. 1; Acts v. 37), and our Lord's ministry lay chiefly there, while Pilate might well be ignorant of much disaffection bred there, beyond his own jurisdiction, they artfully introduce this region as that in which the alleged treason had been hatched, and whence it had at length spread to Judea and the capital. In his perplexity, Pilate, hearing of Galilee, bethinks himself of sending the Prisoner to Herod, in the hope of thereby shaking off all further responsibility in the case. Accordingly we have in the sequel of this third Gospel the following remarkable incident:—

Jesus before Herod Antipas (Luke xxiii. 6-12). 6. "When Pilate heard of Galilee, he asked whether the man were a Galilean. 7. And as soon as he knew that He belonged unto Herod's jurisdiction, he sent Him to Herod, who also was at Jerusalem at that time"—hoping, as we have said, to escape the dilemma of an unjust condemnation or an unpopular release; possibly also in hope of some light being cast upon the case itself. Herod was then at Jerusalem, no doubt to keep the Passover. 8. "And when Herod saw Jesus, he was exceeding glad: for he was desirous to see him of a long season." (See Luke ix. 9.) This is not inconsistent with what is said in Luke xiii. 31; for Herod, though full of curiosity for a considerable time to see Jesus, might not care to have Him wandering about in his own dominions, and too near to the scene of the bloody deed done on his faithful reprover. "Because he had heard many things of Him, and he hoped to have seen some miracle done by him." Fine sport thou expectest, O coarse, crafty, cruel tyrant, as the Philistines with Samson (Jud. xvi. 25). But thou hast been baulked before (see on Luke xiii. 31-33), and shalt be again. 9. "Then he questioned with Him in many words; but He answered him nothing." (See Matt. vii. 6.) 10. "And the chief priests and scribes stood and vehemently accused Him"—no doubt both of *treason*, Herod being a *king*, and of *blasphemy*, for Herod, though of Idumean descent, was by religion a circumcised *Jew*. 11. "And Herod with his men of war" [τοῖς στρατεύμασιν]—or his body guard, "set Him at nought"—stung with disappointment at His refusal either to amuse him with miracles or to answer any of his questions. But a day is coming, O proud Herod, when He who now stands before thee, to outward appearance a helpless prisoner, shall from His great white throne "laugh at thy calamity, and *mock* when thy fear cometh"! —"and arrayed Him in a gorgeous (or 'bright') robe" [ἐσθῆτα λαμπρὰν]. If this mean, 'of shining white,' as sometimes, it may have been in derision of His claim to be "King of the Jews;" that being the royal colour among the Jews. But if so, he in reality honoured Him, as *Bengel* remarks, just as Pilate did by blazoning His true title on the Cross: "and sent Him again to Pilate" —instead of releasing Him as he ought, having established nothing against Him (*vv.* 14, 15). Thus, to use again the words of *Bengel*, did Herod implicate himself with Pilate in all the guilt of His condemnation; and accordingly he is classed with him in this deed in Acts iv. 27. 12. "And the same day Pilate and Herod were made friends together: for before they were at enmity between themselves"—perhaps about some point of disputed jurisdiction, which this exchange of the Prisoner might tend to heal.

Pilate, a second and a third time Failing to Obtain the Consent of the Jews to the Release of Jesus, even though Offering to Scourge Him, and Borne

should bear witness unto the truth. Every one that [y]is of the truth
38 heareth my voice. Pilate saith unto him, What is truth?
And when he had said this, he went out again unto the Jews, and

A. D. 33.

[y] ch. 8. 47. 1 John 3.19.

Down by Clamour, at length, in spite of a Divine Warning, Surrenders Him to their Will (39, 40.) The materials of this portion must be drawn chiefly from the other Gospels.

Luke xxiii. 13-16:—"And Pilate, when he had called together the chief priests and the rulers and the people, said unto them, Ye have brought this man unto me, as one that perverteth the people: and, behold, I, having examined him before you"—from the first three Gospels we should conclude that the whole examination hitherto had been in their presence, while John represents it as private; but in all likelihood the reference here is to what is related in *vv.* 3-5, though too briefly to enable us to see the precise form which the examination took throughout—"have found no fault in this man touching those things whereof ye accuse him: No, nor yet Herod: for I sent you to him; and, lo, nothing worthy of death is done unto Him" [αὐτῷ]—or rather, 'by Him,' as the phrase sometimes means classically, and here must be held to mean. "I will therefore chastise Him, and let Him go" [παιδεύσας—ἀπολύσω]—'When, therefore, I have corrected, I will dismiss Him.' Though the *kind* of correction which he proposed to inflict was not specified by Pilate on this occasion, there can be no doubt that scourging was what he meant, and the event soon proved it. It seems strange to our ideas of justice, that a Roman governor should propose to punish, however lightly, a prisoner whose innocence he had just proclaimed. But it was of the nature of a well meant yet indefensible offer, in hope of saving the prisoner's life.

At this moment, as would appear, two of those strange incidents occurred which throw such a lurid light on these awful transactions. We refer to the *choice of Barabbas* for release at the feast, *in preference to Jesus*, and *the dream of Pilate's wife.*

Matt. xxvii. 15-23:—15. "Now at that feast the governor was wont to release unto the people a prisoner, whom they would." 16. "And they had then a notable (or 'notorious') prisoner called Barabbas"—"which," says Mark (xv. 7), "lay bound with them that had made insurrection with him" [συστασιαστῶν], or 'with his fellow insurgents,' "who (that is, which insurgents) had committed murder in the insurrection." But in Luke (xxiii. 19) the murder is expressly ascribed to this Barabbas, who is also called "a robber." He was evidently the ringleader of this lawless gang; and there we learn that the "sedition" here referred to was "made in the city." "And the multitude," says Mark, "crying aloud, began to desire him to do as he had ever done unto them." This is peculiar to Mark, and enables us vividly to realize the rising of the popular excitement before which Pilate—reluctantly though it was—gave way. But this clamour for the exercise of his usual clemency at the feast suggested another expedient for saving his conscience—the selection of Jesus as the prisoner of his choice for this release; not doubting that between Jesus and such a villain as this Barabbas they would for very shame be forced to prefer the former. But he little knew his men, if he thought that. 17. "Therefore," continues Matthew, "when they were gathered together, Pilate saith unto them, Whom will ye that I release unto you? Barabbas, or Jesus which is called Christ?" 18. "For he knew that for envy they had delivered Him"—that is, out of jealousy at the popularity of Jesus, and fear of losing their own. This would seem to show that Pilate was not ignorant of the leading facts of this case.

At this stage of the proceedings, or rather just after they had formally begun, the strange message from his wife, recorded only by Matthew, seems to have deepened the anxiety of Pilate to save Jesus, and was probably what induced him to set up Barabbas as the only alternative he would give them for release, if they would not have Jesus. 19. "When he was set down on the judgment seat, his wife sent unto him"—it has been noticed as a striking confirmation of the historical accuracy of this Gospel, that (as *Tacitus* relates, in his Annals, iii. 33, 34) the Governors of provinces had not begun to take their wives with them till the time of Augustus—"saying, Have thou nothing to do with that just man" [μηδὲν σοὶ καὶ τῷ δικαίῳ ἐκείνῳ, see on John ii. 4]: "for I have suffered many things this day in a dream because of Him;" a testimony to the innocence of Jesus, and a warning to Pilate, from the unseen world, which, though finally ineffectual, made doubtless a deep impression upon his mind. 20. "But the chief priests and elders," continues Matthew, "persuaded the multitude that they should ask Barabbas, and destroy Jesus." Possibly they took advantage of the pause in the proceedings, occasioned by the delivering of the message from the Governor's wife. 21. "The governor answered and said unto them, Whether of the twain will ye that I release unto you? They said, Barabbas"—and said it with a vehemence which showed how successful the leaders had been in putting them up to this simultaneous way of clamouring. "And they cried out," says Luke, "all at once, saying, Away with this man, and release unto us Barabbas."

Pilate now makes a last feeble effort to induce them to acquiesce in the release of Jesus. "Pilate therefore," says Luke, "willing to release Jesus, spake again to them;" but what he said is recorded only by the first two Evangelists. 22. "Pilate," says Matthew, "said unto them, What shall I do then with Jesus which is called Christ?"—or, according to the keener form of the question in Mark, "Him whom ye call the King of the Jews?" This was just the thing they could not endure, and Pilate was sharp enough to see it. "But they all cried, Crucify Him, crucify Him" (Luke and Matthew). The shocking cry is redoubled. "And the governor said unto them the third time, Why, what evil hath he done? I have found no cause of death in Him: I will therefore chastise Him, and let Him go" (Luke). Why chastise Him, O Pilate, if thou hast found no fault in Him? But his remonstrances are waxing feebler; this offer of chastisement, already rejected as a compromise, is but another slight effort to stem the torrent, and presently he will give way. They see this, and hasten to bury his scruples in a storm of cries for His crucifixion. What a scene! 23. "But they cried out the more, saying, Let Him be crucified." Luke is more emphatic: "And they were instant with loud voices, requiring that He might be crucified, And the voices of them and of the chief priests prevailed."

A very striking incident is here again related in the first Gospel only.

Matt. xxvii. 24, 25:—24. "When Pilate saw that he could prevail nothing"—his humiliating helplessness was manifest to himself—"but that rather

KK

39 saith unto them, I [z]find in him no fault *at all*. But ye have a custom,
that I should release unto you one at the passover: will ye therefore that
40 I release unto you the King of the Jews? Then [a]cried they all again,
saying, Not this man, but Barabbas. [b]Now Barabbas was a robber.
19, THEN [a]Pilate therefore took Jesus, and scourged *him*. And the
2 soldiers platted a crown of thorns, and put *it* on his head, and they put
3 on him a purple robe, And said, Hail, King of the Jews! and they smote
him with their hands.
4 Pilate therefore went forth again, and saith unto them, Behold,
I bring him forth to you, [b]that ye may know that I find no fault
5 in him. Then came Jesus forth, wearing the crown of thorns, and
the purple robe. And *Pilate* saith unto them, Behold the man!
6 When [c]the chief priests therefore and officers saw him, they cried out,
saying, Crucify *him*, crucify *him*. Pilate saith unto them, Take ye him,

A. D. 33.

[z] Matt. 27. 18, 19, 24. Mark 15 14. Luke 23. 4, 14-16. ch. 19. 4, 6.
[a] Acts 3. 14.
[b] Luke 23. 19.

CHAP. 19.

[a] Isa 50. 6. Matt 20. 19. Matt. 27. 26. Mark 15. 15. Luke 18. 33.
[b] ch. 18. 38. 2 Cor. 5 21.
[c] Acts 3. 13.

a tumult was made, he took water, and washed his hands before the multitude" (compare, in illustration of this act, Deut. xxi. 6, 7; Ps. xxvi. 6), as a solemn and public protest against the deed, "saying, I am innocent of the blood of this [just] person:" [the words τοῦ δικαίου are omitted by *Tischendorf*, and bracketed by *Lachmann* and *Tregelles*. They appear to be of doubtful authority.] "see ye to it." 'Tis not so easy, O Pilate, to wash out sin, much less the innocent blood of the Holy One of God! But thy testimony to Him, and to the uneasiness of thy conscience in condemning Him, we accept with all thankfulness—to a Higher than thou. 25. "Then answered all the people, and said, His blood be on us, and on our children." O Jerusalem, Jerusalem, how heavy has that word been to thee! And the dregs of that cup of fury, voluntarily called down upon thine own head, are not all drunken yet. "But thou, O Lord, how long?" "And Pilate," says Luke, "gave sentence that it should be as they required. And he released unto them him that for sedition and murder was cast into prison, whom they desired; but he delivered Jesus to their will." There is a heavy reflection conveyed by these words, though they be but the studious repetition of the black facts of the case; for it is not the manner of the first three Evangelists to make reflections on the facts which they record, as the fourth does.

From the fulness of the matter embraced in the foregoing portions of the first three Gospels, it will at once be seen that the beloved disciple, in the two following verses, designed not so much to *record* as merely to *remind* his readers of facts already fully recorded and familiar to all Christians, in order to pave the way for the fuller details of what followed, which he was about to give: **39. But ye have a custom, that I should release unto you one at the passover: will ye therefore that I release unto you the King of the Jews? 40. Then cried they all again, saying, Not this man, but Barabbas. Now Barabbas was a robber.**

CHAP. XIX. 1-16.—*Jesus is Scourged by Pilate—After being Treated with other Severities and Insults, and Two more Efforts to Save Him Failing, He is Delivered Up and Led Away to be Crucified.*

The Scourging and Cruel Mockeries (1-3.) **1. Then Pilate therefore took Jesus, and scourged him.** As a compromise, he had offered before to commit this *less* injustice on the person of the prisoner, in hope of that contenting them. (See page 465, first column, second paragraph, and second column, third paragraph.) But this victim of conflicting emotions is now resigning himself to the fiendish clamours of a Jewish mob, set on by sacerdotal hypocrites. This scourging, says *Philo Judæus*, was what was inflicted on the worst criminals. The next step was the following, recorded in Matt. xxvii. 27; and Mark xv. 16: "Then the soldiers of the governor took Jesus into the common hall ('the Prætorium'), and gathered unto him the whole band (of soldiers)"—the body of the military cohort stationed there, to take part in the mock-coronation now to be enacted. **2. And the soldiers platted a crown of thorns, and put it on his head**—in mockery of a regal crown, **and they put on him a purple robe**—in mockery of the *imperial purple;* first "stripping Him" of His own outer garment (Matt. xxvii. 28). It is possible that this was the "gorgeous" robe in which Herod arrayed and sent Him back to Pilate (Luke xxiii. 11); but it may have been one of the military cloaks worn by the Roman officers. In Matthew (xxvii. 29) we have the following addition: "they put a reed in his right hand"—in mockery of the regal sceptre—"and they bowed the knee before Him, and mocked Him." **3. And said, Hail, King of the Jews!**—doing Him derisive homage in the form used on approaching the emperors (see also, on the same derisive epithet, page 472). **and they smote him with their hands.** Matthew says "they spit upon Him, and took the reed, and smote Him on the head" (see Mic. v. 1). The best comment on these affecting details is to *cover the face.*

Pilate Again Tries to save the Prisoner (4-13). **4. Pilate therefore went forth again, and saith unto them, Behold, I bring**—or 'am bringing' **him forth to you, that ye may know that I find no fault in him**—'and by scourging and allowing the soldiers to make sport of him, have gone as far to meet your exasperation as can be expected from a judge.' **5. Then came Jesus forth, wearing the crown of thorns, and the purple robe. And Pilate saith unto them, Behold the man!**—There is no reason to think that *contempt* dictated this memorable speech. There was clearly a struggle in the breast of this wretched man. Not only was he reluctant to surrender to mere clamour an innocent person, but a feeling of anxiety about His mysterious claims, as is plain from what follows, was beginning to rack his breast, and the object of his exclamation seems to have been to *move their pity.* But, be *his* meaning what it may, those three words have been eagerly appropriated by all Christendom, and enshrined for ever in its heart, as a sublime expression of its calm, rapt admiration of its suffering Lord. **6. When the chief priests therefore and officers saw him, they cried out, saying, Crucify him, crucify him.** (See page 465, second column, third paragraph.) **Pilate saith unto them, Take ye him, and crucify him: for I find no fault**

7 and crucify *him:* for I find no fault in him. The Jews answered him,
[d]We have a law, and by our law he ought to die, because he [e]made himself the Son of God.
8 When Pilate therefore heard that saying, he was the more afraid;
9 and went again into the judgment hall, and saith unto Jesus, Whence
10 art thou? But [f]Jesus gave him no answer. Then saith Pilate unto him,
Speakest thou not unto me? knowest thou not that I have power to
11 crucify thee, and have power to release thee? Jesus answered, [g]Thou
couldest have no power *at all* against me, except it were given thee from
above: therefore he that delivered me unto thee hath the greater sin.
12 And from thenceforth Pilate sought to release him: but the Jews cried
out, saying, [h]If thou let this man go, thou art not Cesar's friend: [i]who-
13 soever maketh himself a king speaketh against Cesar. When Pilate
therefore heard that saying, he brought Jesus forth, and sat down in the
judgment seat in a place that is called the Pavement, but in the Hebrew,
[1]Gabbatha.

A. D. 33.

d Lev. 24. 16.
e Matt. 26. 65. ch. 5. 18. ch. 10. 33.
f Isa. 53. 7. Matt. 27. 12, 14. Acts 8. 32.
g Gen. 45. 7, 8. Ps. 62. 11. Dan. 4. 17, 25. Matt. 6. 13. Luke 22. 53. ch. 7. 30. Acts 2. 23.
h Luke 23. 2.
i Acts 17. 7.
1 That is, elevated.

in him—as if that would relieve *him* of the responsibility, who, by surrendering him to an unrighteous death, incurred it all! **7. The Jews answered him, We have a law, and by our law he ought to die, because he made himself the Son of God.** Their criminal charges having come to nothing, they give that up, and as Pilate was throwing the whole responsibility upon them, they retreat into their own Jewish law, by which, as claiming equality with God (see on ch. v. 18, and viii. 58, 59), He ought to die; insinuating that it was Pilate's duty, even as civil governor, to protect their law from such insult.

8. When Pilate heard that saying, he was the more afraid—the name "SON OF GOD," the lofty sense evidently attached to it by His Jewish accusers, the dialogue he had already held with Him, and the dream of his wife (Matt. xxvii. 19), all working together in the breast of the unhappy man. **9. And went again into the judgment hall**—'the Prætorium,' **and saith unto Jesus, Whence art thou?**—a question relating, beyond all doubt, not to His *mission*, but to His *personal origin.* **But Jesus gave him no answer.** He had said enough; the time for answering such a question was past; the weak and wavering governor is already on the point of giving way. **10. Then saith Pilate unto him, Speakest thou not unto me?** The "me" is the emphatic word in the question. He falls back upon the *pride of office*, which doubtless tended to check the workings of his conscience. **knowest thou not that I have power to crucify thee, and have power to release thee?**—said to work upon the silent Prisoner at once by *fear* and by *hope.* **11. Jesus answered, Thou couldest** [οὐκ εἶχες]—rather, 'Thou shouldest' **have no power at all against me**—neither to crucify, nor to release, nor to do anything whatever against Me, as *Bengel* expresses it, **except it were**—'unless it had been' **given thee from above.**—*q. d.*, 'Thou thinkest too much of thy power, Pilate: against Me that power is none, save what is meted out to thee by special divine appointment, for a special end.' **therefore he that delivered me unto thee**—to wit, Caiaphas; but he only as representing the Jewish authorities as a body, **hath the greater sin**—as having better opportunities and more knowledge of such matters.

12. And from thenceforth—particularly this speech, which seems to have filled him with awe, and redoubled his anxiety, **Pilate sought to release him**—that is, to gain their *consent* to it; for he could have done it at once on his own authority: **but the Jews cried**—seeing their advantage, and not slow to profit by it, **If thou let this man go, thou art not Cesar's friend: whosoever maketh himself a king speaketh against Cesar.** 'This,' as *Webster and Wilkinson* observe, 'was equivalent to a threat of *impeachment*, which we know was much dreaded by such officers as the procurators, especially of the character of Pilate or Felix. It also consummates the treachery and disgrace of the Jewish rulers, who were willing, for the purpose of destroying Jesus, to affect a zeal for the supremacy of a foreign prince.' The reader will do well also to observe how they go backwards and forwards in their charges. Failing in obtaining a condemnation on the ground of *treason*, they had just before this fallen back in despair on the charge of *blasphemy*. But as they could not but see how weak that was as an argument with a mere civil governor, they avail themselves of Pilate's manifest embarrassment and vacillation to re-urge the charge of treason, but in the form of a threat against Pilate himself, if he should dismiss the Prisoner. **13. When Pilate heard that saying**—or, according to the preferable reading, 'these sayings,' **he brought Jesus forth, and sat down in**—'upon,' **the judgment seat**—that he might pronounce sentence against the Prisoner, on this charge, the more solemnly, **in a place that is called the Pavement** [λιθόστρωτον], **but in the Hebrew, Gabbatha** [גַּבְּתָא]—either from a word signifying to be 'high,' referring to the raised platform on which the judgment seat was placed; or from one signifying the 'back,' from its arched form. As the Greek word denotes, it was a tesselated pavement, much used by the Romans. There is a minute topographical accuracy in the use of this word which a learned defender of the authenticity of the Gospel History has not failed to notice. 'Jesus,' says *Hug*, 'is led out to receive His sentence, and Pilate sat in a place called the *Lithostrōton* to pass judgment (John xix. 13). The transaction is represeuted as if this place was in front of the Prætor's house, or at least at no great distance from it. And there is, in fact, such a place, which has been formerly overlooked, in the outworks of the Temple. Mention is made of it in an assault which the Romans made upon the Temple, on the side of the tower Antonia (*Joseph.* J. W. vi. 6 and 7). Here is the Lithostroton, and the house of the Prætor must have been opposite to this place. Now he lived, as appears from some incidental passages in *Philo* (compare *Leg. ad Caium* with *Joseph.* Antt. xviii. 4), in Herod's palace, which was certainly in this quarter and neighbourhood, north-west of the tower Antonia and the

14 And [j]it was the preparation of the passover, and about the sixth
15 hour: and he saith unto the Jews, Behold your King! But they
cried out, Away with *him,* away with *him,* crucify him. Pilate saith
unto them, Shall I crucify your King? The chief priests answered, [k]We
16 have no king but Cesar. Then [l]delivered he him therefore unto them to
be crucified.

A. D. 33.

[j] Matt. 27. 62.
[k] Gen. 49. 10. Ezek. 21. 26, 27.
[l] Matt. 27. 26, 31.

Temple: so that the proximity of the Lithostroton to the palace, which is implied in John's narrative, is strictly accurate.'

Pilate, After One More fruitless Effort to save Him, having finally Yielded the point, Jesus is Delivered Up and Led Away to be Crucified (14-16). **14. And**—or, 'Now' **it was the preparation of the passover.** This is another of the passages from which it has been concluded that the regular Passover had not up to that time been kept, and consequently that our Lord, in celebrating it with His disciples the previous evening, had anticipated the proper day for its observance. To this question we have adverted pretty fully—on Luke xxii. 7-30, page 324; on ch. xiii. 1; and on ch. xviii. 28. As to the present passage, there is no evidence that "the preparation of the Passover" means the preparation *for* it. The day before every sabbath was called "the preparation" (Mark xv. 42), from the preparations for its proper observance which were made on the previous day; insomuch that in enumerating the days of the week the Friday would be named 'Preparation' (day). But this was no ordinary 'preparation day.' It was 'the Passover preparation,' as the words of our Evangelist may be rendered; by which we understand that it was not only the Preparation Friday, but the Friday of the Paschal feast. Accordingly, it is called, in *v.* 31, "an high day." **and about the sixth hour.** As it cannot be conceived that our Evangelist meant to say here that it was already *noon,* according to Jewish reckoning—for Mark says (xv. 25), that the crucifixion itself took place at the third hour (nine o'clock, of our reckoning), and that is what we should naturally conclude from the progress of the events—two expedients have been resorted to for clearing up the difficulty, neither of which appears to us quite satisfactory. The one is to adopt the reading "third" instead of "sixth" hour, as *Bengel, Robinson, Webster and Wilkinson* do, and as *Alford* half inclines to do. But the evidence for this reading is so weak that it seems like a tampering with the sacred text to adopt it. The other way of solving the difficulty is to suppose that our Evangelist here adopts the *Roman* method of computation, and means that it was about six o'clock, according to our reckoning. So *Olshausen, Tholuck, Hug,* &c. But as there is no ground to suppose that in other cases our Evangelist adopts the Roman divisions of time, so the hour which that reckoning brings out here can hardly be the right one; for it must have been considerably *later* than six in the morning when that took place which is here related. It remains then to understand the Evangelist to refer to the two broad divisions of the day, so familiar to the Jews, the third and the sixth hours; and to suppose that as the event occurred between the two, the one Evangelist specified the *hither* terminus, while the other takes the *further* one. So *Ellicott* and others.

And he saith unto the Jews, Behold your King! Having now made up his mind to yield to them, he takes a sort of quiet revenge on them by this irony, which he knew would sting them. This only re-awakens their cry to despatch Him. **15. But they cried out, Away with him, away with him, crucify him. Pilate saith unto them, Shall I crucify your King? The chief priests answered, We have no king but Cesar.** Some of those who thus cried died miserably in rebellion against Cesar forty years afterwards, as *Alford* remarks. But it suited their present purpose. **16. Then delivered he him therefore unto them to be crucified**—against all justice, against his own conscience, against his solemnly and repeatedly pronounced judicial decision that He was innocent whom he now gave up. **And they took Jesus, and led him away.** And so, amidst the conflict of human passions and the advancing tide of crime, the Scripture was fulfilled which said, "He is led as a lamb to the slaughter."

Remarks.—1. If the complicated details of the *ecclesiastical* trial of our Lord bear such indubitable marks of truth as we have seen that they do (see on Mark xiv. 53-72, Remark 9 at the close of that Section, pages 210, 211), surely those of the *political* trial which followed are not less self-evidencing. Think first of the dark consistency with which His accusers held to their point of obtaining a condemnation from Pilate; the facility with which they oscillated between two kinds of charges—of treason against Cesar and treason against God—just as the chances of success by urging the one or the other of these charges seemed to preponderate for the moment; the ingenuity with which they set on the mob to shout for His crucifixion, and the fiendish violence with which, when Pilate wavered at the very last, they bore him down, and by insinuating the disloyalty of sparing the Prisoner, at length extorted compliance. Think, next, of that extraordinary conflict of emotions which agitated the breast of Pilate—such as we may safely say no literary ingenuity could have invented, and so artlessly managed as we have it told in the Evangelical Narratives. Think, finally, of the placid dignity of the Sufferer, in all these scenes—the dignity with which He *speaks,* when alone with Pilate, and what is even more remarkable, the dignity of His *silence* before the multitude and in the presence of Herod. Whether we look at each of these features of the political trial by itself, or at all of them as composing one whole—their originality, their consistency, their wonderful verisimilitude, must strike every intelligent and impartial reader. Can we be surprised that such a History makes way for itself throughout the world without the need of laboured books of evidence, and is rejected or suspected only by perverted ingenuity? Similar remarks are applicable even to the minor details of this Section, such as what is said of *Barabbas;* but the reader can follow this out for himself. 2. As the subjects of Christ's Kingdom are at the same time under the Civil Government of the country in which they reside, and may be helped or hindered by it in their Christian duties according to the procedure of that government towards them, it is plainly both the right and the duty of Christians to procure such civil arrangements as shall be most for the advantage of religion in the land. What these ought to be is a question on which Christians are not agreed, and on which they may reasonably differ; and, indeed, the varying conditions of civil society may render the policy which would be proper or warrantable in one case neither right nor

17 And they took Jesus, and led *him* away. And he bearing his cross
[m]went forth into a place called *the place* of a skull, which is called in

A. D. 33.

[m] Num. 15. 36.

practicable in another. But since Civil Government never will nor can nor ought to be altogether indifferent to Religion, it is the duty of Christians to endeavour that at least nothing injurious to Religion be enacted and enforced. But the Christian world has grievously erred on this subject. Since the days of Constantine, when the Roman Empire became externally Christian, the desire to turn civil government to the advantage of Christianity has led to the incorporation of such a multitude of civil elements with the government of the Church, that the lines of essential distinction between the political and the religious have been obliterated, not only under Romanism, but even in the constitution of Church and State in the countries of the Reformation; insomuch that the explicit declaration of our Lord to Pilate—"My Kingdom is not of this world"—would scarcely have satisfied the Roman Governor that His master's interests were unaffected by such a kingdom, if explained according to some modern principles of ecclesiastical government. Let Christians but interpret our Lord's explanation of the nature of His kingdom honestly and in all its latitude, and their differences on this subject, if they do not melt away, will become small and unimportant. 3. If in the sufferings and death of Christ we have the substitution of the Innocent for the guilty, we have a kind of visible exhibition of this in the choice of Barabbas, which was the escape of the guilty in virtue of the condemnation of the Innocent. 4. Often as we have had occasion to notice in this History the consistency of the divine determinations with the liberty of human actions, nowhere is it more conspicuous than in this Section. Observe how our Lord meets the threat of Pilate, when he asked Him if He knew not that the power of life and death was in his hands. 'No, Pilate, it is not in thine hands, but in Hands which thine only obey; *therefore* is the guilty man who delivered Me unto thee, the more guilty.' But "He taketh the wise in their own craftiness, and the counsel of the froward is carried headlong."

17-30.—CRUCIFIXION AND DEATH OF THE LORD JESUS. (= Matt. xxvii. 32-50; Mark xv. 21-37; Luke xxiii. 26-46.)

No sooner do those envenomed enemies of the Lord Jesus get Him again into their hands, than they renew their mockeries, as we learn from the first two Gospels.

Jesus is Again Subjected to Mockery (Matt. xxvii. 31; Mark xv. 20). "And after they had mocked Him, they took the (purple) robe off from Him, and put His own raiment on Him, and led Him away to be crucified."

The next two steps possess the deepest interest.

Jesus is first Made to Bear His Own Cross, but afterwards they Compel Simon the Cyrenian to Bear it for Him (17). **And he bearing his cross went forth**—that is, without the city; a most significant circumstance in relation to a provision of the Levitical law. "For," says the apostle, "the bodies of those beasts, whose blood is brought into the sanctuary by the high priest for sin, are burned *without the camp:* Wherefore Jesus also, that He might sanctify the people with His own blood, suffered *without the gate*" (Heb. xiii. 11, 12). None of the Evangelists but John mentions the important fact that Christ was made to bear His own cross; although we might have presumed as much, both from the practice of the Romans, which imposed upon criminals condemned to be crucified the burden of bearing their own cross, as *Plutarch* expressly states, and from our Lord's injunctions to his followers to bear their cross *after Him* (see on Matt. x. 38). But soon, it would appear, it became necessary to lay this burden upon some one else if He was not to sink under it. How this was done our Evangelist does not say, nor that it was done at all. But it had been related by all the three preceding Evangelists.

Matt. xxvii. 32; Mark xv. 21; Luke xxiii. 26:—"And as they came out," says Matthew, "they found a man of Cyrene," in Libya, on the north coast of Africa, "Simon by name," "who passed (or 'was passing') by," says Mark. He was not, then, one of the crowd that had come out of the city to witness the execution; and Mark adds that he was "coming out of the country," probably into the city, all ignorant, perhaps, of what was going on; and was "the father of Alexander and Rufus." This stranger, then, "they compelled to bear His cross." Jesus, it would appear, was *no longer able to bear it.* And when we think of the Agony through which He passed during the previous night, not to speak of other causes of exhaustion, under which the three disciples were unable to keep awake in the garden; if we think of the night He passed with Annas, and the early morn before the Sanhedrim, with all its indignities; of the subsequent scenes before Pilate first, then Herod, and then Pilate again; of the scourging, the crown of thorns, and the other cruelties before He was led forth to execution—can we wonder that it soon appeared necessary, if He was not to sink under this burden, that they should find another to bear it? For we must remember that "He was crucified through weakness" [ἐξ ἀσθενείας], 2 Cor. xiii. 4. (See on the "loud voice" which He emitted on the cross as He expired, page 474.)

It will be observed that this Simon the Cyrenian is said to be "the father of Alexander and Rufus" (Mark xv. 21). From this we naturally conclude that when Mark wrote his Gospel these two persons—Alexander and Rufus—were not only Christians, but well known as such among those by whom he expected his Gospel to be first read. Accordingly, when we turn to Romans xvi. 13, we find these words, "Salute *Rufus*, chosen in the Lord—that is, 'the choice one' or 'precious one in the Lord', and his mother and mine." That this is the same Rufus as Mark supposes his readers would at once recognize, there can hardly be a doubt. And when the apostle calls Rufus' mother 'his own mother,' in grateful acknowledgment of her motherly attentions to himself for the love she bore to his Master, does it not seem that Simon the Cyrenian's conversion dated from that memorable day when, 'passing casually by as he came from the country,' they "compelled him to bear" the Saviour's cross. Sweet compulsion, and noble pay for the enforced service to Jesus then rendered, if the spectacle which his eyes then beheld issued in his *voluntarily* taking up his own cross! Through him it is natural to suppose that his wife would be brought in, and that this believing couple, now "heirs together of the grace of life" (1 Pet. iii. 7), as they told their two sons, Alexander and Rufus, what honour had been put upon their father all unwittingly, at that hour of deepest and dearest interest to all Christians, might be blessed to the fetching in of both those sons. By the time that Paul wrote to the Romans, the elder of the two may have gone to reside in some other place, or de-

18 the Hebrew, Golgotha: where [n]they crucified him, and two others with him, on either side one, and Jesus in the midst.

A. D. 33.

[n] Isa. 53. 12.

parted to be with Christ, which was far better; and Rufus being left alone with his mother, they only were mentioned by the apostle.

The Spectacle of Christ's Sufferings Draws Tears from the Women that followed Him—His Remarkable Address to Them. For this we are indebted exclusively to the third Gospel.

Luke xxiii. 27-32:—27. "And there followed Him a great company (or 'multitude') of people, and of women, which also"—that is, the women [αἳ]—"bewailed and lamented Him." These women are not to be confounded with those precious Galilean women afterwards expressly mentioned. Our Lord's reply shows that they were merely a miscellaneous collection of females, whose sympathies for the Sufferer—of whom some would know more and some less—drew forth tears and lamentations. "But Jesus turning unto them said, Daughters of Jerusalem, weep not for Me, but weep for yourselves, and for your children." Noble spirit of compassion, rising above His own dread endurances in tender commiseration of sufferings yet in the distance and far lighter, but *without His supports and consolations!* "For, behold the days (or 'days') are coming, in the which they shall say, Blessed are the barren, and the wombs that never bare, and the paps which never gave suck. Then shall they begin to say to the mountains, Fall on us; and to the hills, Cover us." These words, taken from Hos. x. 8, are a lively way of expressing the feelings of persons flying hither and thither despairingly for shelter. The more immediate reference of them is to the sufferings which awaited them during the approaching siege of Jerusalem; but they are a premonition of cries of another and more awful kind (Rev. vi. 16, 17; and compare, for the language, Isa. ii. 10, 19, 21). "For if they do these things in a green tree"—that naturally resists the fire—"what shall be done in the dry," that attracts the flames, being their proper fuel. The proverb plainly means: 'If such sufferings alight upon the innocent One, the very Lamb of God, what must be in store for those who are provoking the flames?'

On Arriving at the Place of Execution, Jesus is Offered Vinegar to drink, but Having Tasted, He Refuses to drink it (17). Our Evangelist only brings us to Calvary. For the rest we are indebted to the first two Gospels. **17. he went forth into a place called the place of a skull**—or 'unto the place called Skull-place,' **which is called in the Hebrew, Golgotha** [גֻּלְגָּלְתָּא, softened into Γολγοθᾶ]. 'Roll-formed' or 'roll-shaped,' is the idea of the word. But whether this refer to the round shape of the *skulls* of criminals executed there, which has hitherto been the prevailing opinion, or to the shape of the ground—a round hill or knoll there—as others think, is not agreed. That a hill of that form lay to the north of the city seems true enough; but as this would place the spot outside the city, it is at least inconsistent with what is now shown as the place where our Lord suffered, which is within the city, and must have been so then, as *Dr. Robinson* contends—though *Mr. Williams*, who has examined the ground with equal care, endeavours to disprove his positions.

Matt. xxvii. 33, 34; Mark xv. 22, 23:—"And when they were come unto a place called Golgotha, that is to say, A place of a skull, they gave Him vinegar to drink mingled with gall;" using the words of the prophetic Psalm (lxix. 21), "They gave Me also gall for My meat; and in My thirst they gave Me vinegar to drink." But Mark, no doubt, gives the precise mixture: "They gave Him to drink wine mingled with myrrh." This potion was stupefying, and given to criminals just before execution, to deaden the sense of pain.

> 'Fill high the bowl, and spice it well, and pour
> The dews oblivious: for the Cross is sharp,
> The Cross is sharp, and He
> Is tenderer than a lamb.'

But *our Lord would die with every faculty clear, and in full sensibility to all His sufferings.*

> 'Thou wilt feel all, that thou may'st pity all;
> And rather would'st Thou wrestle with strong pain,
> Than overcloud Thy soul,
> So clear in agony,
> Or lose one glimpse of heaven before the time.
> O most entire and perfect sacrifice,
> Renewed in every pulse,' &c.—KEBLE.

The Act of Crucifixion between Two Malefactors (18). **18. Where they crucified him.** Four soldiers were employed in this operation, which was done by fastening the body—after being stripped of all clothing save a broad belt round the loins—by nails or bolts driven through the hands to the transverse part of the cross. The feet, though not *always* nailed, but simply bound, to the upright beam, were almost certainly so in this case (Ps. xxii. 16). The body was supported by a piece of wood passing between the legs. The excruciating agony of this kind of death is universally attested, and may easily be supposed. But the shame of it was equal to the torture. **and two others with him.** In Luke these are called by the general name of "malefactors," or 'evil-doers' [κακούργους]; in Matthew and Mark "thieves," or rather 'robbers' [λῃστάς]: **on either side one, and Jesus in the midst**—a hellish expedient to hold him up as the worst of the three. But in this, as in many other of their doings, "the Scripture was fulfilled which saith (Isa. liii. 12), *And He was numbered with the transgressors,*" as it is in Mark xv. 28—though the prophecy reaches deeper than that outside fulfilment. [This entire verse, however (Mark xv. 28), is of extremely doubtful genuineness. *Lachmann* inserts it, no doubt on the strength of the ancient versions; but the MS. evidence against it is very strong, and while *Tregelles* brackets it, *Tischendorf* excludes it altogether. It seems to have come in from Luke xxii. 37, where we have the same words from our Lord's own mouth.]

Jesus now Utters the First of His Seven Sayings on the Cross. Of these Seven *Sayings*—embalmed for ever in the hearts of believers—one is recorded by Matthew, three by Luke, and three by John. This first one is recorded in the third Gospel only.

Luke xxiii. 34: "Then said Jesus,"

First Saying: "FATHER, FORGIVE THEM; FOR THEY KNOW NOT WHAT THEY DO." [*Lachmann* unhappily brackets this most precious verse as of doubtful authority. But the evidence for it, external as well as internal, is most decisive; and both *Tischendorf* and *Tregelles* print it as it stands in the received text.]

The Evangelist seems to intimate that this was said as the executioners were doing, or just as they finished, their dread task. But we must not limit the prayer to them. Beyond doubt, it embraced all who had any hand, directly or indirectly, in the death of Him who offered that prayer—of all of whom, even the most enlightened, the apostle could with truth say, that, "had they known it, they would not have crucified the Lord of glory" (1 Cor. ii. 8: see also Acts iii. 17; xiii.

19 And Pilate wrote a title, and put *it* on the cross. And the writing
20 was, [o]JESUS OF NAZARETH THE KING OF THE JEWS. This
title then read many of the Jews; for the place where Jesus was crucified
was nigh to the city: and it was written [p]in Hebrew, *and* Greek, *and*
21 Latin. Then said the chief priests of the Jews to Pilate, Write not, The
22 King of the Jews; but that he said, I am King of the Jews. Pilate
answered, What I have written I have written.
23 Then the soldiers, when they had crucified Jesus, took his garments, and
made four parts, to every soldier a part; and also *his* coat: now the coat
24 was without seam, [2]woven from the top throughout. They said therefore among themselves, Let us not rend it, but cast lots for it, whose it
shall be: that the scripture might be fulfilled, which saith, [q]They parted
my raiment among them, and for my vesture they did cast lots. These
things therefore the soldiers did.

A. D. 33.

[o] ch. 1. 45, 46, 49. ch. 18. 33. ver. 3, 12. Acts 3. 6. Acts 26. 9.

[p] ch. 5. 2. ver. 13. Acts 21. 40. Acts 22. 2. Acts 26. 14. Rev. 16. 16.

[2] Or, wrought.

[q] Ps. 22. 18. Isa. 10. 7. Acts 13. 27.

27; and compare 1 Tim. i. 13). In a wider and deeper sense still, that prayer fulfilled the great Messianic prediction, "And He made intercession for the transgressors" (Isa. liii. 12)—extending to all whose sins He bore in His own body on the tree. In the Sermon on the Mount our Lord says, "Pray for them which despitefully use you and persecute you" (Matt. v. 44); and here, as in so many other cases, we find Him the first to fulfil His own precept—thus furnishing the right interpretation and the perfect model of the duty enjoined. And how quickly was it seen in "His martyr Stephen," that though He had left the earth in Person, His spirit remained behind, and Himself could, in some of His brightest lineaments, be reproduced in His disciples! (See on Acts vii. 60.) And what does the world in every age owe to these few words, spoken *where* and *as* they were spoken!

In the Title which Pilate Wrote and Put upon the Cross, he proclaims Jesus King of the Jews, and Refuses to Alter it (19-22). **19. And Pilate wrote a title, and put it on the cross. And the writing was, JESUS OF NAZARETH THE KING OF THE JEWS. 20. This title then read many of the Jews; for the place where Jesus was crucified was nigh to the city: and it was written in Hebrew**—that is, Syro-Chaldaic, the language of the country, **and Greek**—the current language, **and Latin**—the official language. These were then the chief languages of the earth, and this secured that all spectators should be able to read it. Stung by this, the Jewish ecclesiastics entreat that it may be so altered as to express, not His regal dignity, but His false claim to it. **21. Then said the chief priests of the Jews to Pilate, Write not, The King of the Jews; but that he said, I am King of the Jews.** But Pilate thought he had yielded quite enough to them; and having intended expressly to spite and insult them by this title, for having got him to act against his own sense of justice, he peremptorily refused them. **22. Pilate answered, What I have written I have written.** And thus, amidst the conflicting passions of men, was proclaimed, in the chief tongues of mankind, from the Cross itself, and in circumstances which threw upon it a lurid yet grand light, the truth which drew the Magi to His manger, and will yet be owned by all the world!

The Garments of Jesus are Parted among the soldiers, and For His Vesture They Cast Lots (23, 24). **23. Then the soldiers, when they had crucified Jesus, took his garments, and made four parts, to every soldier a part**—of the four soldiers who were the executioners, and whose perquisite they were. **and also his coat** [τὸν χιτῶνα]—the Roman tunic, or close-fitting vest: **now the coat was without seam, woven from the top throughout.** Perhaps, say *Webster and Wilkinson*, denoting considerable skill and labour, as necessary to produce such a garment—the work, probably, of one or more of the women who ministered in such things unto Him (Luke viii. 3). **24. They said therefore among themselves, Let us not rend it, but cast lots for it, whose it shall be: that the scripture might be fulfilled, which saith** (Ps. xxii. 18), **They parted my raiment among them, and for my vesture they did cast lots. These things therefore the soldiers did.** That a prediction so exceedingly specific—distinguishing one piece of dress from others, and announcing that while *those* should be parted amongst several, *that* should be given by lot to one person—that such a prediction should not only be fulfilled to the letter, but by a party of heathen military, without interference from either the friends or the enemies of the Crucified One, is surely eminently worthy to be ranked among the wonders of this all-wonderful scene. Now come the *mockeries*, which are passed by in silence by our Evangelist, as sufficiently recorded in the first three Gospels. These mockeries came from four distinct quarters.

Jesus is Mocked, first, by the Passers-by. For this particular we are indebted to the first two Gospels.

Matt. xxvii. 39, 40; Mark xv. 29, 30:—"And they that passed by reviled Him, wagging their heads"—in ridicule: see Ps. xxii. 7; cix. 25; and compare Job xvi. 4; Isa. xxxvii. 22; Jer. xviii. 16; Lam. ii. 15—"and saying," "Ah!" [Οὐά] an exclamation here of derision. "Thou that destroyest the temple, and buildest it in three days, save thyself"—"and come down from the cross." If one wonders that in seeking for evidence against our Lord at His trial, His enemies should be obliged to fall back upon a few words uttered by Him at the very outset of his ministry, and after having to distort even these, in order to give them even the appearance of indictable matter, that the charge should break down so completely that the high priest felt he had no pretext for condemning Him unless He could draw something worthy of death from Himself on the spot; much more may one wonder that the same distorted words which had failed at the most solemn moment should now be brought up afresh and cast in the teeth of the blessed One, as He hung upon the cross, even by the passers-by. (See on Mark xiv. 58, 59.) One thing it would seem to show, that the prosecutors in this case had had to send hither and thither for witnesses against our Lord, and collect from all quarters whatever might seem to tell against Him; that in this way the more

25 Now there stood by the cross of Jesus his mother, and his mother's
26 sister, Mary the *wife* of [3]Cleophas, and Mary Magdalene. When Jesus
therefore saw his mother, and [p]the disciple standing by whom he loved,
27 he saith unto his mother, [q]Woman, behold thy son! Then saith he to
the disciple, Behold thy mother! And from that hour that disciple took
her [r]unto his own *home*.

A. D. 33.

[3] Or, Clopas. Luke 24.18.
[p] ch. 13. 23. ch. 20. 2.
[q] ch. 2. 4.
[r] Gen. 47. 12. ch. 1. 11.

it came to be seen that the materials were few and trivial, the more stress would need to be laid upon the little they had to rest on; that thus it had come to be understood that if all failed, this speech at least would suffice to condemn Him; and as the ecclesiastical prosecutors were not likely to proclaim how signally they had failed in making out this charge, and too little time had elapsed between the Trial and the Execution for the proceedings of the Sanhedrim to get abroad, these "passers-by" had cast the saying in our Lord's teeth in their reckless simplicity, taking it for granted that He was now suffering for that speech as for other misdeeds. And yet that memorable speech *in its true sense* was now receiving the first part of its fulfilment —"Destroy *ye* this Temple;" as in His resurrection it was speedily to be fulfilled in the second part of it—"In three days *I* will raise it up." See John ii. 22.

Jesus is Mocked, secondly, by the Rulers. We have this in the first three Gospels, but most fully —as might be expected—in the first, the peculiarly *Jewish* Gospel.

Matt. xxvii. 41-43; Mark xv. 31, 32; Luke xxiii. 35:—"Likewise also the chief priests, mocking him, with the scribes and elders, said, He saved others; himself he cannot save." In this, as in other taunts (such as Luke xv. 2), there was a deep truth. Both things He could not do; for He had come to give *His* life a ransom for *many*. No doubt this added a sting to the reproach, unknown at that moment save to Himself. But the taunt of the rulers ends not here. "If He be the King of Israel (they add), let Him now come down from the cross, and we will believe Him." *No, they would not;* for those who resisted the evidence from the resurrection of Lazarus, and afterwards resisted the evidence of His own resurrection, were beyond the reach of any amount of merely *external* evidence. But they go on to say, "He trusted in God; let Him deliver Him now, if He will have Him [εἰ θέλει αὐτόν], answering to "seeing He delighted in Him" [חָפֵץ בּוֹ, ὅτι θέλει αὐτόν]. These are the words of the Messianic Psalm, xxii. 8. The last words of their taunt are, "for He said, I am the Son of God." We thank you, O ye chief priests, scribes, and elders, for this triple testimony, unconsciously borne by you, to our Christ: first to *His habitual trust in God*, as a feature in His character so marked and palpable that even ye found upon it your impotent taunt; next, *to His identity with the Sufferer of the 22nd Psalm*, whose very words ye unwittingly appropriate, thus *serving yourselves heirs* to the dark office and impotent malignity of Messiah's enemies; and again, to the true sense of that august title which He took to Himself, "THE SON OF GOD," which ye rightly interpreted at the very first (see on ch. v. 18), as a claim to that *oneness of nature* with Him, and *dearness* to Him, which a son has to his father.

Jesus is Mocked, thirdly, by the Soldiers. We have this in the third Gospel only.

Luke xxiii. 36, 37:—"And the soldiers also mocked Him, coming to Him, and offering Him vinegar, and saying, If thou be the King of the Jews, save thyself." They insultingly offer to share with Him their own vinegar, or sour wine, the usual drink of Roman soldiers, it being about the time of their mid-day meal. In the taunt of the soldiers we have one of those casual touches which so strikingly verify these historical records. While the ecclesiastics deride Him for calling Himself "the *Christ*, the *King of Israel*, the *Chosen*, the *Son of God*," the soldiers, to whom all such phraseology was mere Jewish jargon, make sport of Him as a pretender to *royalty*—"KING of the Jews"—an office and dignity which they would think it belonged to them to comprehend.

Jesus Mocked, fourthly, by One of His Fellow-Sufferers—Addresses to the Other, in answer to his penitent, believing Appeal, the Second of His Seven Sayings on the Cross. This is the only one of the four cases of mockery which is recorded by all the first three Evangelists; but the inestimable details are given only by Luke.

Matt. xxvii. 44; Mark xv. 32; Luke xxiii. 39-43:—"The thieves also, which were crucified with Him, cast the same in His teeth." So also Mark. But from Luke—the precision and fulness of whose narrative must rule the sense of the few brief words of the other two—we learn that the taunt came only from *one* of the thieves, whom the *other* in a wonderful style rebuked: "And one of the malefactors which were hanged railed on Him, saying, If thou be Christ, save thyself and us. But the other answering rebuked him, saying, Dost not thou fear God, seeing thou art in the same condemnation? And we indeed justly; for we receive the due reward of our deeds: but this man hath done nothing amiss. And he said unto Jesus, Lord, remember me when thou comest into thy kingdom. And Jesus said unto him"—this is His

Second Saying: "VERILY I SAY UNTO THEE, TO-DAY SHALT THOU BE WITH ME IN PARADISE."

For the exposition of this grand episode, see on Luke xxiii. 39-43, pages 337-339.

But we are now at length brought back to our Fourth Gospel.

Jesus, in the Third of His Seven Sayings on the Cross, Commits His Mother to the Beloved Disciple, Who takes Her to His own Home (25-27). **25. Now there stood** [Εἱστήκεισαν]—or 'were standing' **by the cross of Jesus his mother, and his mother's sister, Mary the wife of Cleophas.** This should be read, as in the margin, *Clopas;* the same person, as would seem, with "Alpheus": see on Matt. x. 3. The "Cleopas" of Luke xxiv. 18 was a different person. **and Mary Magdalene.** These dear women clustered around the cross; and where else should one expect them? The male disciples might be consulting for their own safety (though John was not); but those precious women would have died sooner than be absent from this scene. **26. When Jesus therefore saw his mother, and the disciple standing by whom he loved, he saith unto his mother,**

Third Saying: "WOMAN, BEHOLD THY SON!
27. Then saith he to the disciple,
"BEHOLD THY MOTHER!"

What forgetfulness of self, and what filial love, at such a moment! And what a parting word to both "mother and son"! **And from that hour that ('the') disciple took her to his own** [home]—that is, home with him; for his father, Zebedee,

28 After this, Jesus knowing that [s]all things were now accomplished, [t]that
29 the Scripture might be fulfilled, saith, I thirst. Now there was set a
vessel full of vinegar: and they filled a sponge with vinegar, and put *it*

A. D. 33.

[s] Gen. 3. 15.
[t] Ps. 69. 21.

and his mother, Salome, were both alive, and the latter was here present (Mark xv. 40).

A Supernatural Darkness Overspreads the Sky, about the extremity of which Jesus utters an Awful Cry, being the Fourth of His Seven Sayings on the Cross.

For this deeply significant stage of our Lord's Sufferings on the cross, we have the testimony of the first two Evangelists, and partially of the third. The beloved disciple accordingly passes it by, as sufficiently recorded.

Matt. xxvii. 45-49; Mark xv. 33-38; Luke xxiii. 44, 45:—"Now from the sixth hour"—the hour of noon—"there was darkness over all the land unto the ninth hour"—*the hour of the evening sacrifice.* No ordinary eclipse of the sun could have occurred at this time, it being then *full moon*, and this obscuration lasted about *twelve times* the length of any ordinary eclipse. (Compare Exod. x. 21-23.) Beyond doubt, the divine intention of the portent was to invest this darkest of all tragedies with a gloom expressive of its real character. "And about the ninth hour Jesus cried with a loud voice" (Ps. xxii. 1),

Fourth Saying: "ELI, ELI, LAMA SABACHTHANI? that is to say, MY GOD, MY GOD, WHY HAST THOU FORSAKEN ME?"

There is something deeply instructive in this cry being uttered, not in the tongue which our Lord, we believe, usually employed—the current Greek—but in that of the psalm from which it is quoted; and yet, not as it stands in the *Hebrew* original of that psalm [עֲזַבְתָּנִי], but in the native *Chaldee* [שְׁבַקְתַּנִי], or *Syriac* form ['Ελωΐ, the Syriac form of אֵלִי]—as if at that awful moment not only would no other words express His mind but those which had been prophetically prepared for that hour, but, as in the Agony in the Garden (see page 332, second column), that the mother-tongue came to Him spontaneously, as most natively and freely giving forth the deep cry. As the darkness commenced at the hour of noon, the second of the Jewish hours of prayer, and continued till the hour of the evening sacrifice, it probably *increased in depth*, and *reached its deepest gloom at the moment of this mysterious cry*—when the flame of the one great "Evening Sacrifice" was burning fiercest. The words, as we have said, were made ready to His hand, being the opening words of that psalm which is most full of the last "Sufferings of Christ and the glories which followed them" [τὰς μετὰ ταῦτα δόξας, 1 Pet. i. 11]. "FATHER," was the cry in the first prayer which He uttered on the cross; for matters had not then come to their worst; "FATHER" was the cry of His last prayer; for matters had then passed their worst. But at this crisis of His sufferings, "Father" does not issue from His lips, for the light of a Father's countenance was then mysteriously eclipsed. He falls back, however, on a title expressive of His *official* relation, which, though more distant in itself, yet when grasped in pure and naked faith, was mighty in its claims, and rich in psalmodic associations—"MY GOD." And what deep earnestness is conveyed by the redoubling of this title! But as for the cry itself, it will never be fully comprehended. An absolute desertion is not indeed to be thought of; but a total eclipse of the *felt* sense of God's presence it certainly expresses. It expresses *surprise*, as under the experience of something not only *never before known* but *inexplicable* on the footing which had till then subsisted between Him and God. *It is a question which the lost cannot utter.* They are forsaken, *but they know why.* Jesus is forsaken, but *does not know, and asks to know why.* It is thus *the cry of conscious innocence*, but of innocence unavailing to draw down at that moment the least token of approval from the unseen Judge —innocence whose only recognition at that moment lay in the thick surrounding gloom which but reflected the horror of great darkness that invested His own spirit. *There was indeed a cause for it,* and He knew it too — the "why" must not be pressed so far as to exclude this. *He must taste this bitterest of the wages of sin* "*Who did no sin.*" But that is not the point now. In Him there was no cause at all (ch. xiv. 30), and He takes refuge in the glorious fact. When no ray from above shines in upon Him, He strikes a light out of His own breast. If God will not own Him, He shall own Himself. On the rock of His unsullied allegiance to Heaven He will stand, till the light of Heaven return to His spirit. And it is near to come. Whilst He is yet speaking the fierceness of the flame is beginning to abate. One incident and insult more, and the experience of one other predicted element of suffering, and the victory is His. "Some of them that stood there, when they heard that"—the cry just mentioned—"said, This man calleth for Elias" (Matt. xxvii. 47). That in this they simply misunderstood the meaning of His cry—"Eli, Eli"—there can be no reasonable doubt; especially if, as is probable, this remark was made by Hellenistic spectators, or the Greek-speaking Jews from the provinces who had come up to worship at the feast.

Jesus Thirsting, Utters the Fifth of His Seven Sayings on the Cross, and Vinegar being Brought to Him, the Scripture is therein Fulfilled (28, 29).

28. After this, Jesus knowing that all things were now accomplished, that the Scripture might be fulfilled (Ps. lxix. 21), **saith—**

Fifth Saying: "I THIRST."

The meaning is, that perceiving that all prophetic Scripture regarding Him was accomplished, up to the very article of Death, save that one in Ps. lxix. 21, and that the moment had now arrived for the fulfilment of that final one, in consequence of the burning thirst which the fevered state of His frame occasioned (see Ps. xxii. 15)—He uttered this cry in order that of their own accord they might fulfil *their* prophetic destiny in fulfilling *His.* **29. Now there was set a vessel full of vinegar: and they filled a sponge with vinegar, and put it upon hyssop, and put it to his mouth.** The offer of the soldiers' vinegar, on His arriving at Golgotha, might seem to have sufficiently fulfilled the Scripture prediction on this subject already. But our Lord only regards this as properly done when done by "His own," who "received Him not." But in this case it is probable, as in the former, that "when He had tasted thereof, He would not drink it." Though a stalk of hyssop does not exceed eighteen inches in length, it would suffice, as the feet of crucified persons were not raised higher. At this time, some said, "Let alone" [῎Αφετε]—that is, probably, 'Stand off,' 'Stop that officious service'—"let us see whether Elias will come to take him down." This was the last cruelty which He was to suffer, and it was one of the most unfeeling.

30 upon hyssop, and put *it* to his mouth. When Jesus therefore had
received the vinegar, he said, [u]It is finished: and he bowed his head,
and [v]gave up the ghost.

A. D. 33.
[u] Isa 42. 21.
[v] 1 Thes.5.10.

Jesus Utters the Sixth of His Seven Sayings on the Cross. It is remarkable that while we have this glorious Saying only in the fourth Gospel, we have the *manner* in which it was uttered in the first three, and not in the fourth.

30. When Jesus therefore had received the vinegar, he said—or, as in all the first three Gospels, "He cried with a loud voice"—

Sixth Saying: "IT IS FINISHED" [Τετέλεσται].

In this one astonishing word believers will find the foundation of all their safety and bliss throughout eternal ages. The "loud voice" does not imply, as some able interpreters contend, that our Lord's strength was so far from being exhausted that He needed not to die then, and surrendered up His life sooner than nature required, merely because it was the appointed time. It was indeed the appointed time, but time that He should be crucified *through weakness* (2 Cor. xiii. 4), and nature was now reaching its utmost exhaustion. But just as even His own dying saints, particularly the martyrs of Jesus, have sometimes had such gleams of coming glory immediately before breathing their last as to impart to them a strength to utter their feelings which has amazed the by-standers, so this *mighty voice* of the expiring Redeemer was nothing else but the exultant spirit of the Dying Victor, perceiving the fruit of His travail just about to be embraced, and nerving the organs of utterance to an ecstatic expression of its sublime feelings in the one word, "*It is finished.*" What is finished? The Law is fulfilled as never before, and never since, in His obedience unto death, even the death of the cross. Messianic prophecy is accomplished; Redemption is completed: "He hath finished the transgression, and made an end of sin, and made reconciliation for iniquity, and brought in everlasting righteousness, and sealed up the vision and prophecy, and anointed a holy of holies." The scaffolding of the ancient economy is taken down: He has inaugurated the kingdom of God, and given birth to a new world.

Jesus, having Uttered the Last of His Seven Sayings on the Cross, Expires.

This Saying is given only by the third Evangelist.

Luke xxiii. 46:—"And when Jesus had cried with a loud voice, He said (Ps. xxxi. 5)—

Seventh Saying: "FATHER, INTO THY HANDS I COMMEND MY SPIRIT."

Yes, the darkness is past, and the true light now shineth. His soul has emerged from its mysterious horrors; "My God" is heard no more, but in unclouded light He yields sublime into His *Father's* hands the infinitely precious spirit—using here also, with His last breath, the words of those Psalms which were ever on His lips. **30. And**—"having said this" (Luke xxiii. 46), **he bowed his head, and gave up the ghost.**

Remarks.—1. When we read that Jesus "bearing His cross, went forth," and thus "suffered without the gate," can we wonder at the apostle's call to his fellow-believers of the house of Israel, "Let us go forth therefore unto Him without the camp"? (Heb. xiii. 13). For what was city, temple, or camp, after THE LORD of it had been judicially rejected, contemptuously led forth from it, and without the gate, as one accursed, put to the death of the cross? Behold, their house was left unto them desolate: the Glory was departed: and now, as never before, might be heard by those who still came to tread those once hallowed courts a Voice saying unto them, "Bring no more vain oblations; incense is an abomination unto me; the new moons and sabbaths, the calling of assemblies, I cannot away with; it is iniquity, even the solemn meeting. Your new moons and your appointed feasts my soul hateth: they are a trouble unto me; I am weary to bear them. And when ye spread forth your hands, I will hide mine eyes from you; yea, when ye make many prayers, I will not hear: your hands are full of blood" (Isa. i. 13-15). Judaism had virtually ceased to exist, and all the grace and glory which it contained—all that "Salvation" which "was of the Jews"—had taken up its abode with the handful of disciples from whom, as soon as the Holy Ghost should descend upon them at Pentecost, was to emerge the one living Church and Kingdom of God upon earth. Severe, doubtless, would be the wrench to many a Jew which severed him for ever from ecclesiastical connection with that fondly loved, time-honoured temple, and all its beautiful solemnities. One consideration only could reconcile him to it, but that one to the believer would be irresistible: his Lord was not there, and, what was worse, all that he saw there was associated with the dishonour and the death of his Lord; while in the assemblies of the disciples with whom he had now cast in his lot—all mean to the outward eye, and small in numbers, though they might be—Jesus Himself, now in glory, made His presence felt, Whom having not seen, all loved, in Whom, though now they saw Him not, yet believing, they rejoiced with joy unspeakable and full of glory, receiving the end of their faith, even the salvation of their souls. And has not the Lord been judicially cast out and "crucified" afresh "in the street of" another "great city" (Rev. xi. 8), regarding which the word is, "Come out of her, my people"? (Rev. xviii. 4). Trying to flesh and blood once was that wrench too, and others similar which the faithful witnesses for the truth have been called to suffer. But as where Jesus is not, the most gorgeous temples are but splendid desolation to the soul that lives and is ready to die for Him, so the rudest barns are beautiful temples when irradiated with the glory of His presence and perfumed with the incense of His grace. 2. The case of Simon the Cyrenian, won to Jesus by being "compelled" to bear His cross, has had its bright parallels in not a few who have been made to take part in the last sufferings of His martyrs. In one of the Homilies, for example, of the Greek Father, Basil the Great (A.D. 316-379), preached at the anniversary of the erection of the 'church of the Thirty Martyrs' at Cesarea, he tells us that when thirty of the noblest youths of the Roman army were to suffer for confessing Christ, by being condemned to freeze to death standing naked in a cold lake in the depth of winter, and one of them, after mortification had begun, had been tempted by the offer of hot baths to as many of them as would deny their Lord, and had plunged into a bath—only thereby to hasten his death—while the rest were mourning the breach in their number, one of the lictors, won by what he saw and heard from those servants of Jesus, gave away his badge of office, and exclaimed, "I am a Christian," stripped himself naked, and taking his place beside the rest, said, 'Now are your ranks filled up,' and nobly died with them for the name of Jesus. Analogous cases of various kinds will readily occur

31 The Jews therefore, [w]because it was the preparation, [x]that the bodies
should not remain upon the cross on the sabbath day, (for that sabbath
day was [y]an high day,) besought Pilate that their legs might be broken,
32 and *that* they might be taken away. Then came the soldiers, and brake
the legs of the first, and of the other which was crucified with him.
33 But when they came to Jesus, and saw that he was dead already, they

A. D. 33.
[w] Mark 15.42.
[x] Deut. 21. 23.
[y] Ex. 12. 18.
Lev. 23. 5-8.
Num. 28.17, 18.

to those to whom such victories of the cross are a study; nor is such a bearing in the followers of Christ as Simon the Cyrenian beheld in Him who went as a Lamb to the slaughter perhaps ever in vain. 3. Even natural sympathy, in those who are strangers to what is peculiarly Christian, is beautiful, and to the Christian sufferer grateful. The blessed One was touched by the tears of the daughters of Jerusalem. To the Redeemer's heart they were a grateful contrast to the savage cruelty of the rulers and the rudeness of the unfeeling crowd, and they drew from Him a tender though sad reply. Christians do wrong when they think so exclusively of the absence of grace in any as to overlook or depreciate in them those natural excellences which attracted the love even of the Lord Jesus. (See on Luke xviii. 21, and Remark 3 at the close of that Section.) 4. The *four quarters* whence proceeded the mockeries of Jesus, as He hung on the accursed tree, seem designed to represent the contempt of all the classes into which men can be divided with reference to religion. As the "passers-by" cover the whole region of religious indifference, so "the chief priests, the scribes, and the elders" fitly represent religious hypocrisy: and while in "the soldiers" we recognize the mere underlings of secular authority, whose religion lies all in slavish obedience to their superiors, the "malefactors" represent the notoriously wicked. From all these quarters, in quick succession, the Lord of glory experienced bitter revilings. But "when reviled, He reviled not again." When He did break silence, it was in blessing, and from His Lips salvation flowed. 5. There is something very striking, surely, in the fact that our Lord uttered on the cross precisely *Seven* Sayings—that number which all Scripture teaches us to regard as *sacred* and *complete;* and when we observe that of the Four Evangelists no one reports them all, while each gives some of them, we cannot but look upon them—with *Bengel*—as four voices which together make up one grand Symphony. 'The suffering Lord,' says *Stier* very beautifully, 'hanging upon the cross, broke the silence and opened His lips seven times: these words are to us as the bright lights of heaven shining at intervals through the darkness, or as the loud thunder-tones from above and from within, which *interpret* the cross, and *in which it receives*, so to speak, *another collective superscription.*' Observe now the varied notes of this grand seven-toned Symphony. The *first*, as a prayer for the forgiveness of those who were nailing Him to the tree, proclaims at the very outset the object of His whole mission, the essential character of His work: The *second* opens the kingdom of heaven even to the vilest true penitent that believes in Him: The *third* assures His desolate ones of all needful care and provision here below: The *fourth*, revealing to us the depths of penal darkness to which the Redeemer descended, assures us both that He was made a curse for us and that in our seasons of deepest spiritual darkness we have One who is experimentally acquainted with it, and is able to disperse it: The *fifth*, completing the circle of all previous fulfilments of Scripture in the intense sensation of thirst, and showing thereby that the fevered frame was almost at the extremity of its power of endurance, assures His acutely suffering people of the precious sympathy of Him

'Who not in vain
Experienced every human pain:'

The *sixth* is the briefest, brightest, richest proclamation of the glad tidings of great joy for all time, stretching into eternity itself: The *seventh* and last is an exalted Directory for dying believers of every age and in all circumstances—not only providing them with the language of serene assurance in the rendering up of the departing spirit into their Father's hands, but impregnating it with the strength and perfuming it with the odour of "the Firstborn among many brethren." Thus are we "complete in Him."

31-42.—Circumstances Following the Death of the Lord Jesus—The Burial. (=Matt. xxvii. 57-61; Mark xv. 42-47; Luke xxiii. 50-56.)

The Soldiers, Ordered to Put an End to the Life of the Sufferers, Break the Legs of the Malefactors, but, Perceiving that Jesus was Dead already, they Break Not His Legs, and thus unconsciously Fulfil the Scripture (31-33). These remarkable circumstances are recorded by our Evangelist alone. **31. The Jews therefore**—meaning, as usual in this Gospel, the *rulers* of the Jews, **because it was the preparation**—that is, "the day before the Sabbath" (Mark xv. 42), or our *Friday*, **that the bodies should not remain upon the cross on the sabbath day**—which, beginning at six in the evening, must have been close at hand. Indeed, Luke (xxiii. 54) says, "the Sabbath *drew on*" [ἐπέφωσκεν]—literally, 'was dawning,' like the morning. There was a remarkable command of the Mosaic law, which required that the body of one hanged on a tree for any sin worthy of death should not remain all night upon the tree, but should in any wise be buried that day; "(for he that is hanged is accursed of God;) that thy land be not defiled" (Deut. xxi. 22, 23). These punctilious rulers were afraid of the land being defiled by the body of the Holy One of God being allowed to remain over night upon the cross; but they had no sense of that deeper defilement which they had already contracted by having His blood upon themselves. **(for that sabbath day was an high day)** [μεγάλη]—or 'a great day;' as being the first Sabbath of the Feast of Unleavened Bread, the most sacred season of the whole Jewish ecclesiastical year. This made those hypocrites the more afraid lest the Sabbath hour should arrive ere the bodies were removed. **besought Pilate that their legs might be broken**—to hasten their death. It was usually done with clubs. **and that they might be taken away**—that is, taken down from the cross and removed. **32. Then came the soldiers, and brake the legs of the first, and of the other which was crucified with him.** Crucifixion being a very lingering death, the life of the malefactors was still in them, and was thus barbarously extinguished. **33. But when they came to Jesus, and saw that he was dead already**—for there were in His case elements of suffering unknown to the malefactors, which would naturally hasten His death, not to speak of His exhaustion from previous care and suffering, all the more telling on the frame now, from its having been en-

34 brake not his legs: but one of the soldiers with a spear pierced his side,
and forthwith [z]came thereout blood and water.
35 And [a]he that saw *it* bare record, and his record is true: and he knoweth
36 that he saith true, that ye might believe. For these things were done,
[b]that the scripture should be fulfilled, A bone of him shall not be broken.
37 And again another scripture saith, They [c]shall look on him whom they
pierced.
38 And [d]after this, Joseph of Arimathea, being a disciple of Jesus, but

A. D. 33.

z 1 John 5. 6, 8.
a ch. 17. 21, 23.
b Ex. 12. 46. Num. 9. 12.
c Ps. 22. 16, 17. Zec. 12. 10.
d Matt. 27. 57. Mark 15. 42.

dured in silence. **they brake not his legs**—a fact of vast importance, as showing that the *reality* of His death was visible to those whose business it was to see to it. The *other* divine purpose served by it will appear presently.

To Make Sure that Jesus was Dead, One of the Soldiers with a Spear Pierces His Side—What Flowed from this Wound, and How Another Scripture was thereby Fulfilled (34-37). **34. But one of the soldiers**—to make assurance of the fact doubly sure, **with a spear pierced his side**—making a wound deep and wide, as indeed is plain from ch. xx. 27-29. Had life still remained it must have fled now. **and forthwith came thereout blood and water.** 'It is now well known,' to use the words of *Webster and Wilkinson*, 'that the effect of long-continued and intense agony is frequently to produce a secretion of a colourless lymph within the pericardium (the membrane enveloping the heart), amounting in many cases to a very considerable quantity.'

35. And he that saw it bare—'hath borne' **record, and his record is true: and he knoweth that he saith true, that ye might believe**—'that ye also may believe,' is clearly the true reading [καὶ ὑμεῖς—so *Lachmann*, *Tischendorf*, and *Tregelles*]; that is, that all who read this Gospel may, along with the writer of it, believe. The use of the third person in this statement, instead of the first, gives solemnity to it, as *Alford* remarks. This solemn way of referring to his own testimony in this matter was at least intended to call attention both to the fulfilment of Scripture in these particulars, and to the undeniable evidence he was thus furnishing of the *reality* of Christ's death, and consequently of His resurrection; perhaps also to meet the growing tendency, in the Asiatic churches, to deny the reality of our Lord's body, or that "Jesus Christ is come in the flesh" (1 John iv. 1-3). But was this all? Some of the ablest critics think so. But if we give due weight to the words of this same beloved disciple in his First Epistle—"This is He that came by water and blood, even Jesus Christ; not by water only, but by water and blood" (1 John v. 6)—it is difficult to avoid thinking that he must have seen in the "blood and water" which flowed from that wounded side a symbolical exhibition of the "blood" of *atonement* and the "water" of *sanctification*, according to ceremonial language, which undoubtedly flow from the pierced Redeemer. Certainly the instincts of the Church have from age to age stamped this sense upon the fact recorded, and when the poet cries—

'Rock of Ages! cleft for me,
Let me hide myself in Thee:
Let the water and the blood
From Thy wounded side which flow'd
Be of sin the double cure;
Cleanse me from its guilt and power'—TOPLADY:

he does but nobly interpret our Evangelist's words to the heart of the living and dying Christian.

36. For these things were done, that the scripture should be fulfilled, A bone of him shall not be broken. The Scripture referred to can be no other than the stringent and remarkable ordinance regarding the Paschal Lamb, that *a bone of it should not be broken* (Exod. xii. 46; Num. ix. 12). And if so, we have this apostle, as well as Paul (1 Cor. v. 7), holding forth the Paschal Lamb as a typical foreshadowing of "the Lamb of God." There is indeed in the 34th Psalm a verse which some—regarding it as Messianic—have thought to be the passage referred to by the Evangelist: "He keepeth all his bones; not one of them is broken" (*v.* 20). But that is rather a definite way of expressing the minute care with which God watches over His people in the body; and the right view of its bearing on Christ is to mark how congruous it was that that should be *literally* realized in Him which was designed but *generally* to express the safety of all His saints. But we shall miss one of the most august designs of God in the sufferings of His Son if we rest here. Up to the moment of His death, every imaginable indignity had been permitted to be done to the sacred body of the Lord Jesus—as if, so long as the Sacrifice was incomplete, the Lord, who had laid upon Him the iniquity of us all, would not interpose. But no sooner has He "finished" the work given Him to do than an Unseen Hand is found to have provided against the clubs of the rude soldiers coming in contact with that Temple of the Godhead. Very different from such violence was that *spear-thrust*, for which not only doubting Thomas would thank the soldier, but intelligent believers in every age, to whom the certainty of their Lord's death and resurrection is the life of their whole Christianity. **37. And again another scripture saith** (Zec. xii. 10), **They shall look on him whom they pierced.** This quotation is not taken, as usual, from the Septuagint—the current Greek version—which here is all wrong, but direct from the Hebrew. And there is a remarkable nicety in the choice of the words employed both by the prophet and the evangelist for "piercing." The word in Zechariah [דָּקָרוּ] means to *thrust through* with spear, javelin, sword, or any such weapon. In that sense it is used in all the ten places, besides this, where it is found. How suitable this was to express the action of the Roman soldier is manifest; and our Evangelist uses the exactly corresponding word [ἐξεκέντησαν], while the word used by the LXX. [κατωρχήσαντο] signifies simply to 'insult' or 'triumph over.' There is a quite different word, which also signifies to 'pierce,' used in Ps. xxii. 16, "They *pierced* my hands and my feet" [כָּאֲרוּ, in קרי]. This word signifies to *bore* as with an awl or hammer—just as was done in fastening our Lord to the cross. How exceedingly striking are these small niceties and precisions!

The Burial (38-42). **38. And after this, Joseph of Arimathea**—a place which cannot now be identified. Matthew (xxvii. 57) says he was "a rich man"—thus fulfilling the prediction that Messiah should be "with the rich in His death" (Isa. liii. 9). Mark (xv. 43) says he was "an honourable counsellor" [εὐσχήμων βουλευτὴς]—or a member of the Sanhedrim and of superior position—"which

secretly [e]for fear of the Jews, besought Pilate that he might take away
the body of Jesus: and Pilate gave *him* leave. He came therefore, and
39 took the body of Jesus. And there came also [f]Nicodemus, (which at
the first came to Jesus by night,) and brought [g]a mixture of myrrh and
40 aloes, about an hundred pound *weight*. Then took they the body of
Jesus, and wound [h]it in linen clothes with the spices, as the manner of
41 the Jews is to bury. Now in the place where he was crucified there was
a garden; and in the garden a [i]new sepulchre, wherein was never man

A. D. 33.

e Pro. 29. 25. ch. 9. 22. ch. 12. 42.
f ch. 3. 1, 2. ch. 7. 50.
g 2 Chr. 16. 14. Luke 23. 56.
h Acts 5. 6.
i Luke 23. 53.

also waited for the kingdom of God," or was a devout expectant of Messiah's kingdom. Luke (xxiii. 50, 51) says further of him, "he was a good man and a just; the same had not consented to the counsel and deed of them"—or had not been a consenting party to the condemnation and death of Jesus. Perhaps, however, this does not mean that he openly dissented and protested against the decision and subsequent proceedings of the Council of which he was a member; but simply that he had avoided taking any active part in them, by absenting himself from their meetings. Finally, to complete our knowledge of this important person, for ever dear to the Christian Church for what is about to be related, our Evangelist adds, **being a disciple of Jesus, but secretly for fear of the Jews.** No wonder that he and Nicodemus are classed together. But if before, they were noted for *timid* discipleship, they are now signally one in *courageous* discipleship. Our Evangelist merely says, Joseph **besought Pilate that he might** [be permitted to] **take away the body of Jesus: and Pilate gave him leave.** But Mark, in the following passage, notices the *courage* which this required, and gives some other particulars of the deepest interest.

Mark xv. 43-45:—"Joseph . . . went in boldly" [τολμήσας εἰσῆλθεν]—or 'had the courage to go in,' "and craved the body of Jesus." That act would without doubt identify him *for the first time* with the disciples of Christ. Marvellous it certainly is, that one who while Jesus was yet alive merely refrained from condemning Him—not having the courage to espouse His cause by one positive act—should, now that He was dead, and His cause apparently dead with Him, summon up courage to go in personally to the Roman Governor and ask permission to take down and inter the body. But if this be the first instance, it is not the last, that a seemingly dead Christ has wakened a sympathy which a living one had failed to evoke. The heroism of faith is usually kindled by desperate circumstances, and is not seldom displayed by those who before were the most timid, and scarce known as disciples at all. "And Pilate marvelled if he were already dead" [εἰ ἤδη τέθνηκεν]—or rather, 'wondered that he was dead already'—"and calling the centurion, he asked him whether he had been any while (or 'long') dead." Pilate could hardly credit what Joseph had told him, that He had been dead 'some time,' and before giving up the body to His friends, would learn how the fact stood from the centurion, whose business it was to oversee the execution. "And when he knew it of the centurion," that it was as Joseph had said, "he gave" [ἐδωρήσατο]—or rather, 'made a gift of' "the body to Joseph;" struck, possibly, with the rank of the petitioner and the dignified boldness of the petition, in contrast with the spirit of the other party and the low rank to which he had been led to believe all the followers of Christ belonged. Nor would he be unwilling to show that he was not going to carry this scandalous proceeding any further. But whatever were Pilate's motives, two most blessed objects were thus secured: First, *The reality of our Lord's death was attested* by the party of all others most competent to decide on it, and certainly free from all bias—the officer in attendance—in full reliance on whose testimony Pilate surrendered the body. Second, The dead Redeemer, thus delivered out of the hands of His enemies, and committed by the supreme political authority to the care of His friends, was thereby protected from all further indignities; a thing most befitting indeed, now that His work was done, but not to have been expected if His enemies had been at liberty to do with Him as they pleased. How wonderful are even the minutest features of this matchless History! **He came therefore, and took the body of Jesus. 39. And there came also Nicodemus, (which at the first came to Jesus by night).** It is manifestly the Evangelist's design to direct his readers' attention to the *timidity* of both these friends of Jesus in their attachment to Him, when he says that the one was for fear of the Jews only a secret disciple, and reminds us that the visit of the other to Jesus at the outset of His ministry was made by night. **and brought a mixture of myrrh and aloes, about an hundred pound weight**—an immense quantity, betokening the greatness of their love, but part of it probably intended, as *Meyer* says, as a layer for the spot on which the body was to lie. (See 2 Chr. xvi. 14.) **40. Then took they the body of Jesus, and wound it in linen clothes with the spices, as the manner of the Jews is to bury**—the mixed and pulverized myrrh and aloes shaken into the folds, and the entire body, thus swathed, wrapt in an outer covering of "clean linen cloth" (Matt. xxvii. 59). Had the Lord's own friends had the least reason to think that the spark of life was still in Him, would *they* have done this? But even if one could conceive them mistaken, could any one have lain thus enveloped for the period during which He was in the grave, and life still remained? Impossible. When, therefore, He walked forth from the tomb, we can say with the most absolute certainty, "Now is Christ *risen from the dead*, and become the first-fruits of them that slept"! (1 Cor. xv. 20). No wonder that the learned and the barbarians alike were prepared to die for the name of the Lord Jesus; for such evidence was to the unprejudiced resistless. No mention is made of *anointing* in this operation. No doubt it was a hurried proceeding, for fear of interruption, and because it was close on the Sabbath. The women seem to have set the doing of this more perfectly as their proper task "as soon as the Sabbath should be past" (Mark xvi. 1). But as the Lord graciously held it as undesignedly anticipated by Mary at Bethany (Mark xiv. 8), so this was probably all the anointing, in the strict sense of it, which He received. **41. Now in the place where he was crucified there was a garden; and in the garden a new sepulchre, wherein was never man yet laid.** The choice of this tomb was, on *their* part, dictated by the double circumstance that it was so near at hand, and its belonging to a friend of the Lord; and as there was need of haste, even they would

42 yet laid. There [j]laid they Jesus therefore, because of the Jews' preparation *day;* for the sepulchre was nigh at hand.
20 THE [a]first *day* of the week cometh Mary Magdalene early, when it
was yet dark, unto the sepulchre, and seeth the stone taken away from
2 the sepulchre. Then she runneth, and cometh to Simon Peter, and
to the [b]other disciple whom Jesus loved, and saith unto them, They
have taken away the Lord out of the sepulchre, and we know not where
3 they have laid him. Peter [c]therefore went forth, and that other disciple,
4 and came to the sepulchre. So they ran both together: and the other
5 disciple did outrun Peter, and came first to the sepulchre. And he
stooping down, *and looking in,* saw [d]the linen clothes lying; yet went he
6 not in. Then cometh Simon Peter following him, and went into the
7 sepulchre, and seeth the linen clothes lie, and [e]the napkin, that was
about his head, not lying with the linen clothes, but wrapped together in
8 a place by itself. Then went in also that other disciple which came first
9 to the sepulchre, and he saw, and believed. For as yet they knew not
10 the [f]scripture, that he must rise again from the dead. Then the disciples
went away again unto their own home.

A. D. 33.

j Isa 53. 9.

CHAP. 20.
a Matt. 28. 1
Mark 16. 1
Luke 24. 1.
b ch. 13. 23.
ch. 19. 26.
ch. 21. 7, 20, 24.
c Luke 24.12.
d ch. 19. 40.
e ch. 11. 44.
f Ps. 16. 10.
Isa. 26. 19.
Isa. 53. 10-12.
Hos. 13. 14.
Matt. 16. 21.
Acts 2. 25-32.
Acts 13. 34.
1 Cor. 15. 4.

be struck with the providence which thus supplied it. **42. There laid they Jesus therefore, because of the Jews' preparation day; for the sepulchre was nigh at hand.** There was however one recommendation of it which probably would not strike them; but God had it in view. This was not its being "hewn out of a rock" (Mark xv. 46), accessible only at the entrance, though this doubtless would impress even themselves with its security and suitableness; but its being "a *new* sepulchre" (*v.* 41), "*wherein never man before was laid*" (Luke xxiii. 53); and in Matt. xxvii. 60 it is said that Joseph laid Him "in *his own new tomb*, which he had hewn out in the rock"—doubtless for his own use, and without any other design in it—but the Lord needed it. Thus, as he rode into Jerusalem on an ass "*whereon never man before had sat*," so now He shall lie in a tomb *wherein never man before had lain*, that from these specimens it might be seen that *in all things* He was "SEPARATE FROM SINNERS."

For remarks on the Burial of Christ, in connection with His Death and Resurrection, see on Matt. xxvii. 51-56, Remarks 4-8 at the close of that Section; and those on ch. xxviii. 1-15, at the close of that Section.

CHAP. XX. 1-31.—ON THE FIRST DAY OF THE WEEK MARY MAGDALENE VISITS THE SEPULCHRE AND RETURNS TO IT WITH PETER AND JOHN—HER RISEN LORD APPEARS TO HER—IN THE EVENING HE APPEARS TO THE ASSEMBLED DISCIPLES, AND AGAIN AFTER EIGHT DAYS—FIRST CLOSE OF THIS GOSPEL.

Mary first Visits the Sepulchre Alone (1). **1.** ['Now'] **The first day of the week cometh Mary Magdalene** (see on Luke viii. 2) **early, when it was yet dark** (see on Matt. xxviii. 1, and on Mark xvi. 2), **unto the sepulchre, and seeth the stone taken away from the sepulchre** (see on Mark xvi. 3, 4).

Mary, Returning to Peter and John, Reports to them that the Sepulchre had been Emptied—They Go to the Grave—The Result of that Visit (2-10). **2. Then she runneth**—her whole soul strung to its utmost tension with trepidation and anxiety, **and cometh to Simon Peter, and to the other disciple whom Jesus loved**—those two who were so soon to be associated in proclaiming the Saviour's resurrection, **and saith unto them, They have taken away the Lord out of the sepulchre, and we know not where they have laid him.** Dear disciple! Thy dead Lord is to thee "The Lord" still. **3. Peter therefore went forth, and that**—or 'the' **other disciple, and came to the sepulchre**—to see with their own eyes. **4. So they ran both together: and the other disciple**—being the younger of the two, **did outrun Peter**—but love, too, haply supplying swifter wings. How lively is the mention of this little particular, and at such a distance of time! Yet how could the very least particular of such a visit be ever forgotten? **5. And he stooping down,** [**and looking in**]. The supplement here should not be printed in Italics, as the one Greek word [παρακύψας] denotes both the *stooping* and the *looking*, as in *v.* 11, and in 1 Pet. i. 12 ('desire,' or 'stoop down, to look' into): **saw**—rather, 'seeth' [βλέπει] **the linen clothes lying; yet went he not in**—held back probably by a reverential fear. **6. Then cometh Simon Peter following him, and**—being of a bold, resolute character, he at once **went into the sepulchre**—and was rewarded with bright evidence of what had happened: **and seeth the linen clothes lie**—'lying.' **7. And the napkin, that was about his head, not lying with the linen clothes**—loosely, as if hastily thrown down, and indicative of a hurried and disorderly removal, **but wrapped**—or 'folded' **together in a place by itself**—showing with what grand tranquillity "the Living One" had walked forth from "the dead." (See on Luke xxiv. 5.) 'Doubtless,' says *Bengel*, 'the two attendant angels (*v.* 12) did this service for the Rising One; the one disposing of the linen clothes, the other of the napkin.' But perhaps they were the acts of the Risen One Himself, calmly laying aside, as of no further use, the garments of His mortality, and indicating the absence of all haste in issuing from the tomb. **8. Then went in also that**—or 'the' **other disciple which came first to the sepulchre.** The repetition of this, in connection with his not having gone in till after Peter, seems to show that at the moment of penning these words the advantage which each of these loving disciples had of the other was present to his mind. **and he saw and believed.** Probably he means, though he does not say, that He believed in his Lord's resurrection more immediately and certainly than Peter. **9. For as yet they knew**—*i. e.*, understood **not the scripture, that he must rise again from the dead.** In other words, they believed in His resurrection at first, not because they were prepared by Scripture to expect it; but *facts* carried resistless conviction of

11 But [g]Mary stood without at the sepulchre weeping: and as she wept,
12 she stooped down, *and looked* into the sepulchre, and seeth two angels
in white sitting, the one at the head, and the other at the feet, where the
13 body of Jesus had lain. And they say unto her, Woman, why weepest
thou? She saith unto them, Because they have taken away my Lord,
14 and I know not where they have laid him. And [h]when she had thus
said, she turned herself back, and saw Jesus standing, and [i]knew not
15 that it was Jesus. Jesus saith unto her, Woman, why weepest thou?
whom seekest thou? She, supposing him to be the gardener, saith unto
him, Sir, if thou have borne him hence, tell me where thou hast laid
16 him, and I will take him away. Jesus saith unto her, Mary! She
turned herself, and saith unto him, [j]Rabboni! which is to say, Master!
17 Jesus saith unto her, Touch me not; for I am not yet ascended to my
Father: but go to my [k]brethren, and say unto them, [l]I ascend unto my

A. D. 33.

g Mark 16. 5.
h Song 3. 3, 4. Matt. 28. 9. Mark 16. 9.
i Luke 24. 16, 31. ch. 21. 4.
j Song 2. 8 Matt. 23. 8-10. ch. 1. 38, 49.
k Ps. 22. 22. Matt. 28. 10. Rom. 8. 29. Heb. 2. 11.
l ch. 16. 28. 1 Pet 1. 3.

it in the first instance to their minds, and furnished afterwards a key to the Scripture predictions of it. **10. Then the disciples went away again unto their own home.**

Mary, Remaining at the Sepulchre Weeping, is Asked the cause of her tears by Two Angels in White sitting within the Sepulchre—Scarcely has she answered them when Her Risen Lord appears to her, but is not recognized—Transporting Disclosure and Sublime Address of Jesus to her—She goes and tells the tidings to the Disciples (11-18). **11. But Mary stood without at the sepulchre weeping.** Brief had been the stay of Peter and John. But Mary, who may have taken another way to the sepulchre after they left it, lingers at the spot, weeping for her missing Lord. **and as she wept, she stooped down, and looked**—through her tears, **into the sepulchre, 12. And seeth two angels.** There need be no difficulty in reconciling this with the accounts of the angelic appearances at the sepulchre in the other Gospels; since there can be no reasonable doubt, as *Olshausen* suggests, that angels can render themselves visible or invisible as the case may require, and so they may have been seen at one time and soon after unseen—seen also by one party and not by another, one seen by one set of visitants and two by another. 'What wonder,' asks *Alford* pertinently, 'if the heavenly hosts were variously and often visible on this great day, "when the morning stars sang together, and all the sons of God shouted for joy"?' **in white**—as from the world of light (see on Matt. xxviii. 3), **sitting**—as if their proper business had already been finished, but they had been left there to await the arrival of their Lord's friends, and reassure them—**the one at the head, and the other at the feet, where the body of Jesus had lain.** Why this peculiar posture? To proclaim silently, as *Luthardt, Alford,* &c., think, how *entirely* the body of the Lord Jesus was under the guardianship of the Father and his servants. But to us this is not a quite satisfactory explanation of the *posture.* What if it was designed to call mute attention to the narrow space within which the Lord of glory had contracted Himself?—as if they should say, Come, see within what limits, marked off by the space here between us two, THE LORD lay! But she is in tears, and these suit not the scene of so glorious an Exit. They are going to point out to her the incongruity. **13. And they say unto her, Woman, why weepest thou?**—You would think the vision too much for a lone woman. But absorbed in the one Object of her affection and pursuit, she speaks out her grief without fear. **She saith unto them, Because they have taken away my Lord, and I know not where they have laid him**—the very words she had used to Peter and John (*v.* 2) are here repeated to the bright visitants from the world of light:—*q. d.*, 'Can I choose but weep when thus bereft?' **14. And when she had thus said, she turned herself back, and saw Jesus standing, and knew not that it was Jesus. 15. Jesus saith unto her, Woman, why weepest thou? whom seekest thou?**—questions which, redoubled, so tenderly reveal the yearning desire to disclose Himself to that dear disciple. **She, supposing him to be the gardener.** Clad, therefore, in some such style He must have been. But if any ask, as too curious interpreters do, whence He got those habiliments, we answer, with *Olshausen* and *Luthardt*, where the two angels got theirs. The voice of His first words did not, it seems, reveal Him; for He would *try* her ere He would *tell* her. Accordingly, answering not the stranger's question, but coming straight to her point with him, she **saith unto him, Sir, if thou have borne him hence**—borne *whom?* She says not. She can think only of *One*, and thinks others must understand her. It reminds one of the question of the spouse, "Saw ye him whom my soul loveth?" (Song iii. 3.) **tell me where thou hast laid him, and I will take him away.** Wilt thou, dear fragile woman? But it is the language of sublime affection, that thinks itself fit for anything if once in possession of its Object. It is enough. Like Joseph, He can no longer restrain Himself (Gen. xlv. 1). **16. Jesus saith unto her, Mary!** It is not now the distant, though respectful "Woman." It is the oft-repeated name, uttered, no doubt, with all the wonted manner, and bringing a rush of unutterable and overpowering associations with it. **She turned herself, and saith unto him** [in the Hebrew tongue], **Rabboni! which is to say, Master!** [*Tischendorf* and *Tregelles* introduce into the text what we have placed in brackets—Ἑβραϊστί—on what appears to be preponderating evidence. *Lachmann* brackets it as we have done.] Mary uttered this word in the endeared mother-tongue, and the Evangelist, while perpetuating for all time the very term she used, gives his readers to whom that tongue was unknown the sense of it. But that single word of transported recognition was not enough for woman's full heart. Not knowing the change which had passed upon Him, she hastens to express by her actions what words failed to clothe: but she is checked. **17. Jesus saith unto her, Touch me not; for I am not yet ascended to my Father:**—'Old familiarities must now give place to new and more awful, yet sweeter approaches; but for these the time has not come yet.' This seems the spirit, at least, of these mysterious words, on which much difference of opinion has obtained, and not much that is satisfactory been said. **but go to my brethren.**

18 Father, and your Father; and *to* [m] my God, and your God. Mary
[n] Magdalene came and told the disciples that she had seen the Lord, and
that he had spoken these things unto her.
19 Then [o] the same day at evening, being the first *day* of the week, when
the doors were shut where the disciples were assembled for fear of the
Jews, came Jesus and stood in the midst, and saith unto them, Peace *be*
20 unto you. And when he had so said, he [p] showed unto them *his* hands
and his side. [q] Then were the disciples glad when they saw the Lord.
21 Then said Jesus to them again, Peace *be* unto you: [r] as *my* Father hath
22 sent me, even so send I you. And when he had said this, he breathed
23 on *them*, and saith unto them, Receive ye the Holy Ghost: whose
[s] soever sins ye remit, they are remitted unto them; *and* whose soever
sins ye retain, they are retained.
24 But Thomas, one of the twelve, [t] called Didymus, was not with them

A. D. 33.

m Eph. 1. 17.
n Matt. 28. 10. Luke 24. 10.
o Mark 16. 14. Luke 24. 36. 1 Cor. 15. 5.
p 1 John 1. 1.
q ch. 16. 22.
r Isa. 61. 1. Isa. 11. 2. Matt. 28. 18. ch 17. 18, 19. Heb. 3. 1. 2 Tim. 2. 2.
s Matt. 16. 19. Matt. 18. 18.
t ch. 11. 16.

(Compare Matt. xxviii. 10; Heb. ii. 11, 17.) That He had still our Humanity, and therefore "*is not ashamed to call us brethren*," is indeed grandly evidenced by these words. But it is worthy of most reverential notice, that *we nowhere read of any one who presumed to call Him Brother.* "My brethren?" exclaims devout *Bishop Hall*, 'Blessed Jesus, who are these? Were they not Thy followers? yea, Thy forsakers? . . . How dost Thou raise these titles with Thyself! At first they were Thy *servants;* then *disciples;* a little before Thy death, they were Thy *friends;* now, after Thy resurrection, they were Thy *brethren.* But O, mercy without measure! how wilt Thou, how canst Thou, call *them* brethren whom, in Thy last parting, Thou foundest fugitives? Did they not run from Thee? Did not one of them rather leave his inmost coat behind him than not be quit of Thee? And yet Thou sayest, "Go, tell My brethren!" It is not in the power of the sins of our infirmity to unbrother us.' **and say unto them, I ascend unto my Father, and your Father; and [to] my God, and your God**—words of incomparable glory! Jesus had called God habitually His *Father*, and on one occasion, in His darkest moments, His *God.* But both are here united, expressing that full-orbed relationship which embraces in its vast sweep at once Himself and His redeemed. Yet, note well, He says not, *Our* Father and *our* God. All the deepest of the Church Fathers were wont to call attention to this, as expressly designed to distinguish between what God is to Him and what He is to us—*His* Father essentially; *ours* not so: *our* God essentially; *His* not so: *His God* only in connection with us; *our Father* only in connection with Him. **18. Mary Magdalene came and told** [ἔρχεται ἀπαγγέλλουσα]—rather, 'cometh and telleth' **the disciples that she had seen the Lord, and that he had spoken these things unto her.** *To a woman was this honour given, to be the first that saw the risen Redeemer, and that woman was not his mother.*

On the Evening of this First Day of the Week Jesus Appears to the Assembled Disciples (19-23). **19. Then the same day at evening, being the first day of the week, when the doors were shut where the disciples were [assembled], for fear of the Jews.** [The word enclosed in brackets—συνηγμένοι—is probably not genuine.] **came Jesus and stood in the midst.** That this was not an entrance in the ordinary way is manifest not only from the very peculiar manner of expression, but from the corresponding language of Luke xxiv. 36. But there is no need to fancy any *penetrating through the doors*, as several of the Fathers did and some still do: far less reason is there to fear that by holding that He appeared amongst them without doing so we compromise the *reality* of His resurrection-body. The natural way of viewing it is to conclude that the *laws* of the resurrection-body are different from those of "flesh and blood," and that according to these the risen Saviour, without any miracle, but in the exercise of a power competent to the risen body, presented Himself amongst the assembled disciples. **and saith unto them, Peace be unto you**—not the mere *wish* that even His own exalted peace might be theirs (ch. xiv. 27); but conveying it into their hearts, even as He "opened their understandings to understand the Scriptures" (Luke xxiv. 45). **20. And when he had so said, he showed unto them his hands and his side**—not only as *ocular* and *tangible* evidence of the *reality* of His resurrection (see on Luke xxiv. 37-43), but as through "the *power* of that resurrection" dispensing all His peace to men. **21. Then said Jesus to them again**—now that they were not only calmed, but prepared to listen to Him in a new character. **Peace be unto you.** The reiteration of these precious words shows that this was what He designed to be not only the fundamental but ever-present, ever-conscious possession of His people. **as my Father**—rather, 'the Father' **hath sent me, even so send I you**—or rather, perhaps, 'even so am I sending you,' that is, just about to do it. (See on ch. xvii. 18.) **22. And when he had said this, he breathed on them**—a symbolical and expressive conveyance to them of the Spirit, which in Scripture is so often compared to *breath* (see on ch. iii. 8); **and saith unto them, Receive ye the Holy Ghost**—as an earnest and first-fruits of the more grand and copious Pentecostal effusion, without which it had been vain to send them at all. **23. Whose soever sins ye remit, they are remitted unto them; and whose soever sins ye retain, they are retained.** In any *literal* and *authoritative* sense *this power was never exercised by one of the apostles,* and plainly *was never understood by themselves as possessed by them or conveyed to them.* (See on Matt. xvi. 19.) The power to intrude upon the relation between men and God cannot have been given by Christ to His ministers in any but a *ministerial* or *declarative* sense—as the authorized interpreters of His word—while in the *actings* of His ministers, the real nature of the power committed to them is seen in the exercise of *church discipline.*

After Eight Days Jesus Again Appears to the Assembled Disciples, Giving to Doubting Thomas Affecting Evidence of the Reality of His Resurrection (24-29). **24. But Thomas, one of the twelve, called Didymus, was not with them when Jesus came**—that is, on the evening of the resurrection-day. Why he was absent we know not; but we cannot persuade ourselves, with *Stier*, *Alford*, and

25 when Jesus came. The other disciples therefore said unto him, We have
seen the Lord. But he said unto them, Except I shall see in his hands
the print of the nails, and put my finger into the print of the nails, and
thrust my hand into his side, I will not believe.
26 And after eight days, again his disciples were within, and Thomas with
them. *Then* came Jesus, the doors being shut, and stood in the midst,
27 and said, [u]Peace *be* unto you. Then saith he to Thomas, Reach hither
thy finger, and behold my hands; [v]and reach hither thy hand, and
28 thrust *it* into my side: and be not faithless, but believing. And Thomas
29 answered and said unto him, [w]My Lord and my God. Jesus saith unto
him, Thomas, because thou hast seen me, thou hast believed: blessed
[x]*are* they that have not seen, and *yet* have believed.
30 And [y]many other signs truly did Jesus in the presence of his disciples,
31 which are not written in this book: but [z]these are written, that ye might
believe that Jesus is the Christ, the Son of God; and [a]that believing ye
might have life through his name.

A. D. 33.

[u] Isa. 9. 7. Mic. 5. 5. Col. 1. 20.
[v] Ps. 103. 13, 14. 1 John 1. 1.
[w] Ps. 73. 25, 26. Ps. 91. 2. Ps. 118. 28. Luke 1. 46, 47. 1 Tim. 1. 17.
[x] 2 Cor. 5. 7. 1 Pet. 1. 8.
[y] ch. 21. 25.
[z] Luke 1. 4. Rom. 15. 4.
[a] ch. 3. 15, 16. ch. 5. 24. 1 Pet. 1. 9.

Luthardt, that it was intentional, from sullen obstinacy. Indeed, the mention here of the fact of his absence seems designed as a loving apology for his slowness of belief. **25. The other disciples therefore said unto him, We have seen the Lord.** This way of speaking of Jesus—as in *v.* 20, and ch. xxi. 7—so suited to His resurrection-state, was soon to become the prevailing style. **But he said unto them, Except I shall see in his hands the print of the nails, and put my finger into the print of the nails, and thrust my hand into his side, I will not believe.** The very form of this speech betokens the strength of his unbelief. For, as *Bengel* says, it is not, '*If I see*, I *will* believe,' but '*Unless I see*, I will *not* believe;' nor does he think he *will* see, though the rest had told him that they had. How Jesus Himself viewed this state of mind we know from Mark xvi. 14, "He upbraided them with their unbelief and hardness of heart, because they believed not them which had seen Him after He was risen." But whence springs this pertinacity of resistance in such minds? Not certainly from *reluctance* to believe, but as in Nathanael (see on ch. i. 46), from mere dread of mistake in so vital a matter.

26. And after eight days—that is, on the eighth or first day of the following week. They themselves probably met every day during the preceding week, but their Lord designedly reserved His second appearance amongst them till the recurrence of His resurrection-day, that He might thus inaugurate the delightful sanctities of THE LORD'S DAY (Rev. i. 10). **his disciples were within, and Thomas with them. Then came Jesus** [ἔρχεται ὁ Ἰησοῦς]—rather, 'Jesus cometh,' **the doors being shut** (see on *v.* 19), **and stood in the midst**—not 'sat;' for the manifestation was to be, as on the evening of the week preceding, merely to show Himself among them as their risen Lord. **27. Then saith he to Thomas, Reach hither thy finger, and behold my hands; and reach hither thy hand, and thrust it.** This is here rather too strong a word. Probably 'put it'—as the same word [βάλλω] is rendered in ch. x. 4—is the right English word here. **into my side: and be not faithless, but believing.** These words of Jesus, as *Luthardt* remarks, have something rhythmical in them. There are two parallel members, with an exhortation referring to both. And Jesus speaks purposely in the words of Thomas himself, that, as *Lampe* says, he might be covered with shame. But with what condescension and gentleness is this done! **28. [And].** This "And" is evidently no part of the genuine text. **Thomas answered and said unto him, My Lord and my God.** That Thomas did *not* do what Jesus invited him to do, and what he had made the condition of his believing, seems plain from *v.* 29—"Because thou hast *seen* Me thou hast believed." He is overpowered, and the glory of Christ now breaks upon him in a flood. His exclamation surpasses all that had been yet uttered, nor can it be surpassed by anything that ever will be uttered in earth or heaven. On the striking parallel in Nathanael, see on ch. i. 49. The Socinian evasion of the supreme Divinity of Christ here manifestly taught—as if it were a mere call upon God in a fit of astonishment—is beneath notice, save for the profanity which it charges upon this disciple, and the straits to which it shows themselves reduced. **29. Jesus saith unto him, [Thomas].** The word enclosed in brackets is almost totally destitute of authority. **because thou hast seen me, thou hast believed**—words of measured commendation, but of indirect, and doubtless painfully felt rebuke:—*q. d.*, Thou hast indeed believed; it is well; but it is only on the evidence of thy senses, and after peremptorily refusing all evidence short of that.' **blessed are they that have not seen, and yet have believed.** 'Wonderful indeed,' as *Alford* well says, 'and rich in blessing for us who have not seen Him, is this closing word of the Gospel.'

First Close of this Gospel (30, 31). **30. And many other signs**—or 'miracles' **truly did Jesus in the presence of his disciples, which are not written in this book: 31. But these are written**—as sufficient specimens, **that ye might believe that Jesus is the Christ, the Son of God; and that believing ye might have life**—in the sense of ch. vi. 27, &c., **through**—or rather, 'in' **his name.** Two things about Jesus the Evangelist says his Gospel was written to establish. First, That He was "THE CHRIST," or 'the Messiah,' the great Hope of all heaven-taught souls from the beginning; and next, that this Messiah was "THE SON OF GOD." The one of these titles was the *official* one with which all who were looking for the promised Deliverer were familiar; the other is intended to express His *Personal* dignity and relation to the Father—for claiming which the Jews once and again took up stones to stone Him, and at length put Him to death. Without the Sonship, the Messiahship would be of no avail to sinful men; nor would the Sonship have done aught for us without the Messiahship. But as the two together constitute that "all fulness" which "it hath pleased the Father

21 AFTER these things Jesus showed himself again to the disciples at
2 the sea of Tiberias: and on this wise showed he *himself*. There were
together Simon Peter, and Thomas called Didymus, and [a] Nathanael of

A. D. 33.

CHAP. 21.
[a] ch. 1. 45.

should dwell in Him" (Col. i. 19), so in the hallowed phrase, that "*Jesus is the Christ the Son of God*," we have that full Name which is as ointment poured forth to all that have ever tasted that the Lord is gracious.

Beautiful is the connection between these concluding verses and the last words of the preceding verse, about Thomas:—*q. d.*, 'And indeed, as the Lord pronounced them blessed who not having seen Him have yet believed, so for that one end have the whole contents of this Gospel been recorded, that all who read it may believe on Him, and believing, have life in that blessed Name.'

For Remarks on the Resurrection of Christ, see those on Matt. xxviii. 1-15, at the close of that Section, and on Luke xxiv. 13-53, Remarks 1 and 5 at the close of that Section. But on the distinctive features of the present Section we may add the following

Remarks.—1. Referring to the Remarks already made on Christian womanhood (on Luke viii. 1-3, at the close of that Section), one cannot but notice how exquisitely Woman's position in relation to Christ and His cause come out in this chapter. Indeed, were one internal evidence of the truth of the Bible, and of the divinity of the religion it discloses, to be demanded—one that should be at once decisive and level to ordinary capacity, perhaps *the position which it assigns to Woman* might as safely be fixed upon as any other; for whether we take her destination before the fall, her condition under the fall, or what the religion of the Bible has done to lift her out of it, the finger of God is alike clearly seen. But nowhere in the Bible—nowhere in Christianity—is her place more beautiful than here, in looking, ere others were astir, for the Saviour so dear to her, receiving from the lips that had fed so many His first word as the Risen One—a word, too, of such familiarity and love—and getting a commission from Him to carry the glad tidings to His disconsolate "brethren." O Woman! self-ruined but dearly ransomed, how much owest thou unto thy Lord! The Lord hath need of thee, not only for all thou hast in common with the other sex, but, over and above this, for all that sanctified Woman has to render to Him; and that is much. Some of the services of Woman to Christ are recorded in the New Testament for her encouragement in all time, (see on Mark xiv. 1-11, Remark 2 at the close of that Section; and on Rom. xvi.) But some of the most beautiful specimens of female Christianity will never be heard of till the resurrection-morn.

'Unseen, unfelt their earthly growth,
And self-accused of sin and sloth
They live and die: their names decay,
Their fragrance passes clean away;
Like violets in the freezing blast,
No vernal steam around they cast—
But they shall flourish from the tomb,
The breath of God shall wake them into od'rous bloom.'
KEBLE.

And this should be enough with male or female. 2. As "PEACE" was the *last* word which Jesus spoke to His assembled disciples before He suffered (ch. xvi. 33), so it was His *first* word to them as He presented Himself in the midst of them for the first time on the evening of His resurrection day (*v.* 19). As this was what His death emphatically *procured* (Eph. ii. 14, 15), so this is what His resurrection emphatically *sealed* (Heb. xiii. 20). Let the peace of God, then, rule in our hearts, to the which also we are called in one body (Col. iii. 15). 3. Did Jesus, when He was announcing to the Eleven His purpose to send them forth on a high mission into the world, even as His Father had sent Him, breathe on them and say, Receive ye the Holy Ghost? How impressively does this proclaim to all who go forth to preach the Gospel, that their speech and their preaching, if it is to be efficacious at all, must not be with enticing words of man's wisdom, but in demonstration of the Spirit and of power! (1 Cor. ii. 4). 4. Is not a Divine seal set upon the faithful exercise of church discipline in *v.* 23? (See on Matt. xviii. 18, and Remark 4 at the close of that Section.) 5. As our Lord, in very emphatic terms, exalts those who have not seen and yet have believed, over those who have believed only on the evidence of their senses, and as the miraculous *introduction* of the Gospel Economy has long ago given place to the noiseless *development* of it under the ordinary laws of the spiritual kingdom, so there is no reason to expect that this will ever on earth be superseded by the re-erection of a supernatural economy and the re-introduction of palpable intercourse between heaven and earth. "Blessed are they that have not seen, and yet have believed," is the fitting description of all who have been or ever shall be drawn to the Lord Jesus from the time of His departure till He come again and receive us to Himself, that where He is, we may be also. Even so, Come, Lord Jesus, come quickly!

CHAP. XXI. 1-25.—SUPPLEMENTARY PARTICULARS—MANIFESTATION OF THE RISEN SAVIOUR TO SEVEN OF THE APOSTLES AT THE SEA OF GALILEE—THE SEQUEL OF THIS—CONCLUSION. That this concluding chapter is an appendix by the Evangelist's own hand was never doubted by Christians till the days of *Grotius*. That *Neander* and *Lücke* should have expressed their opinion that it was written by another hand from *materials* left by John, and so is to be regarded as authentic history but not as the apostle's composition, is to be regretted rather than wondered at, considering their tendencies. We are sorry that *Wieseler* also should have given in to this opinion. But the vast majority of the ablest and most impartial critics are satisfied that there is no ground to doubt its being from the same beloved pen as the rest of this Gospel. It is in almost all the MSS. and Versions. As to the difference of style—of which *Alford*, while admitting it to be John's, makes fully too much—even *Credner*, the most searching investigator of the language of the New Testament, bears the following testimony, which, from him and in the present case, is certainly an impartial one:—'There is not a single external testimony against the 21st chapter; and regarded internally, this chapter displays almost all the peculiarities of John's style.' There is positively no other objection to it except that the Evangelist had already concluded his Gospel at the end of ch. xx. But neither in the Epistles of the New Testament nor in other good authors is it unusual to insert supplementary matter, and so have more than one conclusion.

Of the *ten* manifestations of the Risen Saviour recorded in Scripture, including that in 1 Cor. xv. 6, this in order is the *seventh*—or to His assembled disciples the *third*.

The Miraculous Draught of Fishes (1-12). **1. After these things Jesus showed**—or 'manifested' **himself again to the disciples at the sea of Tiberias: and on this wise showed he himself.**

Cana in Galilee, and [b]the *sons* of Zebedee, and two other of his disciples.
3 Simon Peter saith unto them, I go a fishing. They say unto him, We
also go with thee. They went forth, and entered into a ship immediately; and that night they caught nothing.
4 But when the morning was now come, Jesus stood on the shore: but
5 the disciples knew [c]not that it was Jesus. Then [d]Jesus saith unto them,
6 [1]Children, have ye any meat? They answered him, No. And he
said unto them, [e]Cast the net on the right side of the ship, and ye shall
find. They cast therefore; and now they were not able to draw it for
7 the multitude of fishes. Therefore [f]that disciple whom Jesus loved saith
unto Peter, It is the Lord. Now when Simon Peter heard that it was
the Lord, he girt *his* fisher's coat *unto him*, (for he was naked,) and [g]did
8 cast himself into the sea. And the other disciples came in a little ship;
(for they were not far from land, but as it were two hundred cubits,)
9 dragging the net with fishes. As soon then as they were come to land,
10 they saw [h]a fire of coals there, and fish laid thereon, and bread. Jesus
11 saith unto them, Bring of the fish which ye have now caught. Simon
Peter went up, and drew the net to land full of great fishes, an hundred
and fifty and three: and for all there were so many, yet was not the
net broken.

A. D. 33.

[b] Matt. 4. 21. Luke 24. 15, 16, 31.
[c] ch. 20. 14.
[d] Ps. 37. 3. Luke 24. 41. Phil. 4. 11-13, 19. Heb. 13. 5.
[1] Or, Sirs.
[e] Matt. 17. 27. Luke 5. 4, 6, 7.
[f] Ps. 118. 23. Mark 11. 3. Luke 2. 11. ch. 13. 23. ch. 19. 26. ch. 20. 2.
[g] Song 8. 7.
[h] 1 Ki. 19. 6. Matt. 4. 11. Mark 8. 3. Luke 12. 29-31.

This way of speaking shows that after His resurrection He appeared to them but occasionally, unexpectedly, and in a way quite unearthly, though yet really and corporeally. **2. There were together Simon Peter, and Thomas called Didymus, and Nathanael of**—or 'from' **Cana in Galilee**—as to whose identity with *Bartholomew* the apostle, see on Matt. x. 3; **and the sons of Zebedee.** Here only, as *Stier* observes, does John refer to himself in this manner. **and two other of his disciples**—that is, two other apostles: so there were *seven* in all present. **3. Simon Peter saith unto them, I go a fishing. They say unto him, We also go**—rather 'come' **with thee. They went forth, and entered into a ship immediately; and that night they caught nothing**—just as at the first miraculous draught; and no doubt it was so ordered that the miracle might strike them the more. The same principle is seen in operation throughout much of Christ's ministry, and is indeed a great law of God's spiritual procedure with His people. (See on Luke v. 1-11, Remark 1 at the close of that Section; and on ch. xi., Remark 4 at the close of that Section.)

4. But when the morning was now come, Jesus stood on the shore: but the disciples knew not that it was Jesus. Perhaps there had been some considerable interval since the last manifestation, and having agreed to betake themselves to their secular employment, they would be unprepared to expect Him. **5. Then Jesus saith unto them, Children.** This term would not necessarily identify Him, being not unusual from any superior; but when they did recognize Him, they would feel it sweetly like Himself. **have ye any meat?** [προσφάγιον]—'any food?' meaning, Have ye caught anything? **They answered him, No.** This was in His wonted style, making them *tell* their case, and so be better prepared for what was coming. **6. And he said unto them, Cast the net on the right side**—no doubt, by this very specific direction, intending to reveal to them His knowledge of the deep and power over it. **7. Therefore that disciple whom Jesus loved saith unto Peter, It is the Lord**—again having the advantage of his brother in quickness of recognition (see on ch. xx. 8), to be followed, however, in Peter by an alacrity *all his own.* **Now when Simon Peter heard that it was the Lord, he girt his fisher's coat** [unto]—or 'about' **him, (for he was naked)**—his vest only on, worn next the body, **and did cast himself into the sea**—the shallow part, not more than a hundred yards from the water's edge (*v.* 8); not meaning therefore to swim, but to get sooner to Jesus than in the full boat, which they could hardly draw to shore. **8. And**—or, 'But' **the other disciples came in a little ship** [τῷ πλοιαρίῳ]—rather, 'in the boat,' **(for they were not far from land, but as it were**—'but about' **two hundred cubits,) dragging the net with** ['the'] **fishes. 9. As soon then as they were come to land**—or 'had landed,' **they saw**—'see' **a fire of coals there, and fish laid thereon, and bread.** By comparing this with 1 Ki. xix. 6, and similar passages, the unseen agency by which Jesus made this provision will appear evident. **10. Jesus saith unto them, Bring of the fish which ye have now caught.** Observe the double supply thus provided—His and theirs. The meaning of this will appear presently. **11. Simon Peter went up**—went on board, **and drew the net to land full of great fishes, an hundred and fifty and three: and for all there were so many, yet was not the net broken.** The manifest reference here to the former miraculous draught (Luke v. 9) furnishes the key to this scene. There the draught was *symbolical* of the success of their future ministry: While "Peter and all that were with him were astonished at the draught of the fishes which they had taken, Jesus said unto him, Fear not, from henceforth thou shalt catch men." Nay, when first called, in the act of "casting their net into the sea, for they were fishers," the same *symbolic* reference was made to their secular occupation: "Follow me, and I will make you fishers of men" (Matt. iv. 18, 19). Here, then, if but the same symbolic reference be kept in view, the design of the whole scene will, we think, be clear. The *multitude* and the *size* of the fishes they caught symbolically foreshadowed the vast success of their now fast approaching ministry, and this only as a beginning of successive draughts, through the agency of a Christian ministry, till, "as the waters cover the sea, the earth should be full of the knowledge of the Lord." And whereas, at the first miraculous draught, the net "was breaking," through the weight of what it contained—expressive, perhaps, of the difficulty with which,

12 Jesus saith unto them, [i]Come *and* dine. And none of the disciples
13 durst ask him, Who art thou? knowing that it was the Lord. Jesus then
14 cometh, and taketh bread, and giveth them, and fish likewise. This is
now [j]the third time that Jesus showed himself to his disciples after
that he was risen from the dead.
15 So when they had dined, Jesus saith to Simon Peter, Simon, *son* of
Jonas, lovest thou me [k]more than these? He saith unto him, Yea,
Lord; [l]thou knowest that I love thee. He saith unto him, [m]Feed my
16 lambs. He saith to him again the second time, Simon, *son* of Jonas,
lovest thou me? He saith unto him, Yea, Lord; thou knowest that I
17 love thee. He [n]saith unto him, Feed my sheep. He saith unto him
[o]the third time, Simon, *son* of Jonas, lovest thou me? Peter was grieved
because he said unto him the third time, Lovest thou me? And he
said unto him, Lord, [p]thou knowest all things; thou knowest that I

A. D. 33.

i Acts 10. 41.
j ch. 20. 19, 26.
k Matt. 26. 33.
l 2 Ki. 20. 3.
m Acts 20. 28. Eph. 4. 11.
n Heb. 13. 20. 1 Pet. 2. 25. 1 Pet. 5. 2, 4.
o ch. 13. 38.
p Matt. 9. 4. Mark 2. 8. ch. 2. 24, 25. ch. 16. 30. Acts 1. 24. 1 Thes. 2. 4. Rev. 2. 23.

after they had "caught men," they would be able to retain, or keep them from escaping back into the world—while here, "for all they were so many, yet was not the net broken," are we not, as *Luthardt* hints, reminded of such sayings as these (ch. x. 28): "I give unto my sheep eternal life; and they shall never perish, neither shall any pluck them out of my hand"? But it is not through the agency of a Christian ministry that all true disciples are gathered. Jesus Himself, by unseen methods, gathers some, who afterwards are recognized by the constituted fishers of men, and mingle with the fruit of their labours. And are not these symbolized by that portion of our Galilean repast which the fishers found, in some unseen way, made ready to their hand?

The Repast, and the Re-establishment of Peter (12-17). **12. Jesus saith unto them, Come and dine** [Δεῦτε, ἀριστήσατε]—sweet familiarity, after such a manifestation of His command over the deep and its living contents! **And**—or, 'But' **none of the disciples durst ask him, Who art thou? knowing that it was the Lord**—implying that they *would* have liked Him just to say, "It is I;" but having such convincing *evidence*, they were afraid of being "upbraided for their unbelief and hardness of heart" if they ventured to put the question. **13. Jesus then cometh, and taketh** [the] **bread, and giveth them, and** [the] **fish likewise.** See on Luke xxiv. 30, 31. **14. This is now the third time that Jesus showed himself** [ἐφανερώθη]—rather, 'was manifested' **to his disciples**—that is, His *assembled* disciples; for if we reckon His appearances to individual disciples, they were certainly more; **after that he was risen from the dead.**

15. So when they had dined, Jesus saith to Simon Peter. Silence appears to have reigned during the meal; unbroken on *His* part, that by their mute observation of Him they might have their assurance of His identity the more confirmed; and on *theirs*, from reverential shrinking to speak till He did. **Simon, son of Jonas, lovest thou me more than these?**—referring lovingly to those sad words of Peter, shortly before denying his Lord, "Though *all men* shall be offended because of thee, *yet will I never* be offended" (Matt xxvi. 33), and intending by this allusion to bring the whole scene vividly before his mind and put him to shame. **He saith unto him, Yea, Lord; thou knowest that I love thee.** He adds not, "more than these," but prefixes a touching appeal to the Saviour's own omniscience for the truth of his protestation, which makes it a totally different kind of speech from his former. **Feed my lambs**—It is surely wrong to view this term, as some good critics do, as a mere diminutive of affection, and as meaning the same thing as "the sheep." It is much more according to usage to understand by the "lambs" *young and tender* disciples, whether in age or Christian standing (Isa. xl. 11; 1 John ii. 12, 13), and by the "sheep" the more *mature*. Shall we now say, with many, that Peter was here re-instated in office? Not exactly, since he was not actually excluded from it. But after such conduct as his, the deep wound which the honour of Christ had received, the stain brought on his office, and the damage done to his high standing among his brethren, nay even his own comfort, in prospect of the great work before him, required some such renewal of his call and re-establishment of his position as this. **16. He saith to him again the second time, Simon, son of Jonas, lovest thou me? He saith unto him, Yea, Lord; thou knowest that I love thee.** In this repetition of the question, though the wound was meant to be re-opened, the words, "*more than these*" are not repeated; for Christ is a *tender* as well as *skilful* Physician, and Peter's silence on that point was confession enough of his sin and folly. On Peter's repeating his protestation in the same words, our Lord rises higher in the manifestation of His restoring grace. **He saith unto him, Feed**—or 'Keep' **my sheep.** It has been observed, particularly by *Trench*, who has some beautiful remarks on this subject in his 'Synonyms of the New Testament,' that the word here is studiously changed from one signifying simply to 'feed' [βόσκω] to one signifying to 'tend' as a shepherd [ποιμαίνω], denoting the *abiding* exercise of the pastoral vocation and its highest functions. **17. He saith unto him the third time, Simon, son of Jonas, lovest thou me? Peter was grieved because he said unto him the third time, Lovest thou me? And he said unto him, Lord, thou knowest all things; thou knowest that I love thee.** This was the Physician's deepest incision into the wound, while the patient was yet smarting under the two former probings. Not till now would Peter discern the object of this succession of thrusts. The *third* time reveals it all, bringing up such a rush of dreadful recollections before his view, of his "*thrice* denying that he knew Him," that he feels it to the quick. It was fitting that he should; it was meant that he should. But this accomplished, the painful dialogue has a delightful conclusion. **Jesus saith unto him, Feed my sheep**—'My little sheep' [προβάτια] is the reading of *Tischendorf* and *Tregelles*, and approved by *Meyer* and *de Wette:* it has about equal support with that of the received text. If we so read it, we must not understand it to mean "My lambs," as in *v.* 15, but to be used as a varied form, and designed as a sweet diminutive, for "sheep;" just as He calls His disciples, "Little children." It is as if He should say, 'Now, Simon, the last speck of the cloud

18 love thee. Jesus saith unto him, Feed my sheep. Verily, [q] verily, I say
unto thee, When thou wast young, thou girdedst thyself, and walkedst
whither thou wouldest: but when thou shalt be old, thou shalt stretch
forth thy hands, and another shall gird thee, and carry *thee* whither
19 thou wouldest not. This spake he, signifying [r] by what death he should
glorify God. And when he had spoken this, he saith unto him, Follow
me.
20 Then Peter, turning about, seeth the disciple [s] whom Jesus loved following; which also leaned on his breast at supper, and said, Lord, which is
21 he that betrayeth thee? Peter seeing him saith to Jesus, Lord, and
22 [t] what *shall* this man *do?* Jesus saith unto him, If I will that he tarry
23 [u] till I come, what [v] *is that* to thee? Follow thou me. Then went this
saying abroad among the brethren, that that disciple should not die:
yet Jesus said not unto him, He shall not die; but, If I will that he
tarry till I come, what *is that* to thee?
24 This is the disciple which testifieth of these things, and wrote these
25 things: [w] and we know that his testimony is true. And there are also
many other things which Jesus did, the which, if they should be written

A. D. 33.
[q] ch. 13. 36. Acts 12. 3, 4.
[r] Phil. 1. 20. 1 Pet. 4. 11, 14. 2 Pet. 1. 14.
[s] ch. 13. 23, 25. ch. 20. 2.
[t] Matt. 24. 3, 4. Luke 13. 23. Acts 1. 6.
[u] Matt 16. 27. Matt. 24. 3. Matt. 25. 31. 1 Cor. 4. 5. 1 Cor. 11. 26. Rev. 2. 25. Rev. 3. 11.
[v] Deut. 29. 29.
[w] ch. 7. 17. ch. 19. 35. 3 John 12.

which overhung thee since that night of nights is dispelled: Henceforth thou art to Me and to My work as if no such scene had ever happened.'

Jesus Forewarns Peter of his Martyr-death, but Declines to Tell him how it should be with the Beloved Disciple—The Misunderstanding of this Corrected (18-23). **18. Verily, verily, I say unto thee, When thou wast young**—embracing the whole period of life to the verge of old age. **thou girdedst thyself, and walkedst whither thou wouldest**—in other words, 'thou wast thine own master:' **but when thou shalt be old**—or 'art grown old' [γηράσῃς], **thou shalt stretch forth thy hands**—to be bound for execution, though not necessarily meaning *on a cross.* There is no reason, however, to doubt the very early tradition, that Peter's death was by crucifixion. **19. This spake he, signifying by what**—'manner of' **death** [ποίῳ] **he should glorify God**—not, therefore, a mere prediction of the manner of his death, but of the *honour* to be conferred upon him by dying for his Master. And, indeed, beyond doubt, this prediction was intended to follow up his triple restoration:—'Yes, Simon, thou shalt not only feed My lambs, and feed My sheep, but after a long career of such service, shalt be counted worthy to die for the name of the Lord Jesus.' **And when he had spoken this, he saith unto him, Follow me.** By thus connecting the utterance of this prediction with the invitation to follow Him, the Evangelist would indicate the deeper sense in which the call was understood, not merely to go along with Him at that moment, but to come after Him, *taking up his cross.*

20. Then—or, 'But' **Peter, turning about**—showing that he followed immediately as directed. **seeth the disciple whom Jesus loved following; which also leaned on his breast at** [the] **supper, and said, Lord, which is he that betrayeth thee?** The Evangelist makes these allusions to the peculiar familiarity to which he had been admitted on the most memorable of all occasions, perhaps lovingly to account for Peter's somewhat forward question about him to Jesus; which is the rather probable as it was at Peter's suggestion that he had put the question about the traitor which he here recalls (ch. xiii. 24, 25). **Peter seeing him saith to Jesus, Lord, and what** [**shall**] **this man** [**do**]?—'What of this man?' or, 'How shall it fare with him?' **22. Jesus saith to him, If I will that he tarry till I come, what is that to thee? Follow thou me.** From the fact that John alone of the Twelve survived the destruction of Jerusalem, and so witnessed the commencement of that series of events which belong to "the last days," many good interpreters think that this is a virtual prediction of fact, and not a mere supposition. But this is very doubtful, and it seems more natural to consider our Lord as intending to give *no positive indication* of John's fate at all, but to signify that this was a matter which belonged to the Master of both, who would disclose or conceal it as He thought proper, and that Peter's part was to mind his own affairs. Accordingly, in "Follow thou me," the word "*thou*" is emphatic. Observe the absolute disposal of human life which Christ here claims: "IF I WILL that he tarry," &c. **23. Then went this saying abroad among the brethren, that that disciple should not die**—into which they the more easily fell, from the prevalent belief that Christ's Second Coming was then near at hand. **Yet Jesus said not unto him, He shall not die; but, If I will that he tarry till I come, what is that to thee?** The Evangelist is jealous for His Master's honour, which his death might be thought to compromise if such a misunderstanding should not be corrected.

Final Close of This Gospel (24, 25). **24. This is the disciple which testifieth of these things, and wrote these things**—thus identifying the author of the present Gospel, *including this supplementary chapter*, with all that it says of this disciple: **and we know that his testimony is true.** Compare ch. xix. 35. **25. And**—or, 'Moreover' **there are also many other things which Jesus did, the which, if they should be written every one, I suppose** [οἶμαι]—an expression used to show that what follows is not to be pressed too far. **that even the world itself could not contain the books that should be written.** This is to be taken as something more than a mere hyperbolical expression, which would hardly comport with the sublime simplicity of this writer. It is intended to let his reader know that, even now when he had done, he felt his materials so far from being exhausted, that he was still running over, and could multiply 'Gospels' to almost any extent within the strict limits of what "Jesus did." But in the *limitation* of these matchless Histories—in point of length and number alike—there is as much of that Divine wisdom which has presided over and pervades the living oracles, as in their *variety* and *fulness.*

every one, [x] I suppose that even the world itself could not contain the books that should be written. Amen.

A. D. 33.

[x] Amos 7. 10.

[**Amen.**] This "Amen" is excluded from the text by *Lachmann, Tischendorf,* and *Tregelles;* and as it seems insufficiently supported, it is probably rather the irresistible addition—shall we say?—of the transcribers, than from the pen of the Evangelist. See, on the same closing word of the Third Gospel, on Luke xxiv. 53.

Remark.—Thus end these peerless Histories—this Fourfold Gospel. And who that has walked with us through this Garden of the Lord, these "beds of spices," has not often said, with Peter on the mount of transfiguration, It is good to be here! Who that has reverentially and lovingly bent over the sacred text has not found himself in the presence of the Word made flesh—has not beheld the glory of the Only begotten of the Father, full of grace and truth—has not felt His warm, tender hand upon him, and heard that voice saying to himself, as so often to the disciples of old, "Fear not!" Well, dear reader, "Abide in Him," and let "*His words*"—as here recorded—"abide in thee." This Fourfold Gospel is the Sun of the Scripture, from which all the rest derives its light. It is, as observed in the Introduction, the serenest spot in the paradise of God; it is the four rivers of the water of life, the streams whereof make glad the City of God. Into it, as a Reservoir, all the foregoing revelations pour their full tide, and out of it, as a Fountain, flow all subsequent revelations. Till the day dawn, then, and the shadows flee away, I will get me to this mountain of myrrh, this hill of frankincense! (Song iv. 6.)

P.S.—In discussing the genuineness of the much disputed passage regarding *the woman taken in adultery*, John vii. 53--viii. 11 (pp. 400, 401), we came to the conclusion that it rested on evidence, external and internal, sufficient to satisfy the reasonable enquirer, and that its place—supposing its historical truth and canonical authority admitted—could be no other than that in which it stands in the received text. But there was one difficulty which we candidly acknowledged we were then unable to remove—as to Jesus having gone, on the evening before, to the mount of Olives (ch. viii. 1). The argument against the passage from this verse is, that 'nowhere else in this Gospel is "the mount of Olives" mentioned at all, nor does our Lord's passing the night there agree with this or any stage of His public life except the last.' Of this objection we said, at the close of the discussion, that it 'must be allowed to remain among the difficulties that we, at least, find it not easy to solve.' But since that paragraph was written, it has occurred to us that the following explanation sufficiently meets it. The first three Gospels record no visit of our Lord to Jerusalem except the last; nor should we have known for certain that He was there at all until He went thither to die, but for the fourth Gospel (see page 21, first column). It cannot then be proved, from the first three Gospels at least, that His retiring to the mount of Olives, instead of remaining in the city or going to Bethany, was inconsistent with any earlier stage of His life than the last. The utmost that could be fairly alleged would be, that the circumstances which led to His going to the mount of Olives at the time of His last visit had no parallel at any earlier stage. But the contrary of this may be plainly gathered from what is recorded immediately before the disputed passage. The Pharisees, having sent officers to apprehend Jesus, were galled at their returning not only without Him but with a confession of their impotence to lay hands on so incomparable a Teacher. Scarcely had they given vent to their rage, when one of themselves hinted at the illegality of condemning a man unheard. And though this division in their own camp had the effect of paralysing their efforts to arrest the Saviour at that time, it was so critical a juncture that He whose hour was not yet come might well decline to sleep that night in Jerusalem. In that case, whether He retired to the mount of Olives, only to spend some quiet hours alone, and then retired to sleep at Bethany, or whether He spent the whole night there—as at that season He could safely enough do—is of little moment. Enough that, either way, the only objection to the genuineness of this passage, from internal evidence, which has any plausibility, admits of sufficient explanation.